A Century of
Serial Publications
in Psychology
1850–1950
An International Bibliography

Bibliographies
in the
History of Psychology and Psychiatry
A Series

Robert H. Wozniak, General Editor

A Century of
Serial Publications
in Psychology
1850-1950
An International Bibliography

Donald V. Osier

AND

Robert H. Wozniak

KRAUS INTERNATIONAL PUBLICATIONS
Millwood, New York
A Division of Kraus-Thomson Organization Limited

First Printing 1984

Printed in the United States of America

Library of Congress Cataloging in Publication Data

Osier, Donald V.
    A century of serial publications in psychology,
1850-1950.

    (Bibliographies in the history of psychology and
psychiatry)
    Includes indexes.
    1. Psychology—Periodicals—Bibliography.
2. Psychology, Applied—Periodicals—Bibliography.
I. Wozniak, Robert H. II. Title. III. Series.
Z7203.08 1984 [BF121]   016.15′05   82-48989
ISBN 0-527-98196-6

To
Benjamin Rand, Carl Murchison, Chauncey Louttit,
Robert I. Watson, and all others who have preceded us
through the bibliographic maze that
is psychology

Contents

Preface

This project first began to take shape informally in 1972 when the second author, then on the faculty of the University of Minnesota, attempted to identify and locate a number of early and obscure psychology serials as source material for a contemplated historical research project. In the course of this search, he made the acquaintance of the first author who was then and still is the director of the Serials Exchange Program and gifts librarian at the University of Minnesota. The second author had also discovered, somewhat to his surprise and distress, that there were many more psychology serials than the standard references indicated, that these serials were bibliographically quite complex, and that systematic bibliographic treatment of this material was nonexistent.

In order to begin to bring this area under some measure of bibliographic control, the second author started to record the titles of psychology serials which he encountered, and he performed a preliminary and somewhat cursory search of the *Union List of Serials* for psychology material. At about the same time, he also became interested in problems of the social psychology of science; in addition, while examining social networks in psychology, he became aware that little or no historical research had focused on the influence of editorial networks on the direction of psychological publication. Together these suggested the possibility of a bibliography of serial publications in psychology which could serve as a guide to the various titles and their publishing histories and, at the same time, gather together available information on primary editors and editoral boards with the dates of their respective tenures.

When this idea was broached in conversation with the first author, it was warmly received, a collaboration was agreed upon, and work was begun in earnest. Starting with the preliminary list of titles, volumes were individually examined to extract publishing and editorial information and to compile entries. The majority of this difficult and time-consuming task was performed by the first author during a quarter leave from duties at the University of Minnesota.

During this period, the first author also engaged in a systematic search of the following sources: (1) Titus, Edna Brown, ed. *Union List of Serials in Libraries of the United States and Canada*. New York: H. W. Wilson, 1965 (3rd ed); (2) Stewart, James D., with Muriel E. Hammond and Erwin Saenger, eds. *British Union-Catalogue of Periodicals*. New York: Academic Press, and London: Butterworths Scientific Publications, 1955–1958; (3) *Bibliotheque Nationale, Paris. Departement des périodiques.*

Preface

Catalogue collectif des périodiques du début du XVIIe siècle à 1939. Paris: Bibliothèque Nationale, 1967–1977; (4) Smits, Rudolf, ed. *Half a Century of Soviet Serials, 1917–1968.* Washington, D.C.: Library of Congress, 1968; (5) *Harvard University. Library. Widener Library. Philosophy and Psychology.* Cambridge, Massachusetts: Harvard University Press, 1973; (6) *M.U.L.S. (Minnesota Union List of Serials).* Minneapolis: MINITEX, Wilson Library, University of Minnesota, 1981; (7) Bruhn, Peter, ed. *Gesamtverzeichnis russischer und sowjetischer Periodika und Serienwerke in Bibliotheken der Bundesrepublik Deutschland und West-Berlins.* Ed. by Werner Philipp. Wiesbaden: Harrassowitz, 1960–; (8) Hatin, Eugene, ed. *Bibliographie historique et critique de la presse périodique française.* Paris: Firmin-Didot, 1866 (repr. Hildesheim: Georg Olms Verlagsbuchhandlung, 1965); (9) *Chuan-kuo Chung-wen Chi-kan lien-ho mu-lu, 1833–1949* [Union List of Chinese Periodicals in China, 1833–1949]. Peking: Peking Library, 1961; and (10) *Gakujutsu Zasshi Sogo Mokuroku. Jimbun Kagaku Wabun Hen* [Union List of Scholarly Journals. Japanese Language Section. Humanities Part]. Tokyo: Association for Science Documents Information, 1973. This search yielded the bulk of additional titles. When these titles were not available for examination in the holdings of the University of Minnesota Library, necessary information was obtained through interlibrary loan.

As the major part of this information gathering was drawing to a close, the second author systematically examined: (1) Rand, Benjamin. *Bibliography of Philosophy, Psychology, and Cognate Subjects. Part II. In:* Baldwin, James Mark, ed. *Dictionary of Philosophy and Psychology.* Volume III, Part II. New York: Macmillan Co., 1905; (2) Murchison, Carl, ed. *Psychological Register.* Worcester: Clark University Press, 1932 (*see* entry 617); (3) the title lists of periodicals abstracted in *Psychological Abstracts* (*see* entry 568); and (4) the psychology serials holdings of Columbia University Libraries. This process yielded a number of additional main entries and all of the information on which the Appendix has been based. It also led to a final round of information gathering by the second author at the libraries of Yale University; the Universities of Pennsylvania, Ghent, Heidelberg, Wurzburg, and Geneva; the Library of Congress; the National Library of Medicine; and through interlibrary loan. The compilation of entries based on this information was then completed by the first author.

Although it is almost certain that a few titles have been missed, the process of search has been thorough. The authors hope that little of great significance has been overlooked. In a few cases, particularly for publications from the Soviet Union, other eastern European countries, and China, personal examination of material has been impossible. Information on these titles has been compiled from secondary sources. When this has been necessary, that fact is so noted within the appropriate entry. Finally, despite our best efforts, there are still a small number of entries which remain incomplete. These are also so noted. Users of our Bibliography who may have access to this information are encouraged to contact us.

November 1983   *D.V.O.*
                                                                                     R.H.W.

Acknowledgments

The list of people who have, in one way or another, assisted with the task of compiling this Bibliography is long indeed; the following people are among the most important. Paul Berrisford, Gary Shirk and Barbara Stelmasik helped to arrange the quarter leave during which the first author did much of the basic work of compilation. Marie Thayer, Sheila McManus and Robin Mano spent many hours locating and recording publication information from numerous sources. Malcolm Kottler, Horst Gundlach, and Marc De Mey provided assistance in obtaining material from the libraries of Harvard University and the Universities of Heidelberg and Ghent, respectively. Katherine Edstrom, Marijke Goossens, Ana Fernández, Ann Jensen, Tom Song, Richard Wang, Jacqueline Smith, Marie Gorranson, Anna Agell, Irene Levin, Graziella Pruiti and John Wozniak contributed invaluable help in proofreading entries in languages with which the authors wish they were more familiar. Michele Robins assisted with the process of index preparation and with the proofreading of galleys. Erika Linke and Jennifer Lewis at the library of the University of Minnesota; Daniel Bearss, Florence Goff, Andrew Patterson, Michael Rechel, and Robert Zaslavsky at the library of Bryn Mawr College; and interlibrary loan librarians around the world provided unflagging service without which this Bibliography would never have seen the light of day. Finally, the authors wish to extend special thanks to Marylea Osier, for her typing and patience, and to Robert Joel, John Keith and Lynn Wozniak, for their proofreading and patience; their remarkable contributions helped the authors see this project through to completion.

Introduction

The intent of this Bibliography is to provide general publishing and editorial information on serial titles in all languages which appeared before 1950 and which were substantially or regularly devoted to the publication of scientific psychology. Psychology is here broadly defined to include early mental philosophy, animal magnetism and hypnosis, medical psychology and psychotherapy, psychoanalysis, neuropsychology, criminal psychology, parapsychology (including scientific psychical research), child development, the psychology of mental deficiency and education (including experimental education), industrial and personnel psychology, characterology, and animal behavior, as well as the more usual experimental areas which typically characterize general psychology. Serials in astrology, theosophy, mental training (as in pelmanism or scientology), the occult, and mnemotechnics are specifically excluded as being outside the realm of scientific psychology, even though a few such serials have been given titles containing the term "psychology."

Structure of the Bibliography

The body of the Bibliography contains 1,107 main entries. Main entries are presented in chronological order, according to the inaugural year of publication. Titles that began publication in the same year are arranged in alphabetical order. An Appendix containing an additional 739 entries follows the main body of the bibliography. Appendix entries are grouped into 11 different subject matter classifications and are listed alphabetically within each classification. A Title Index and Name Index follow the Appendix.

Decisions concerning inclusion of a given title in the main body of the Bibliography or in the Appendix were based upon the relative quantity of psychological material in the title and the professional affiliation of the title's editors or contributors. Those serials primarily devoted to psychology, or for which editors or contributors were primarily psychologists, are included in the main entries. Those serials regularly carrying material relevant to psychology but which were primarily devoted to an allied field and written and edited largely by psychiatrists, philosophers, educators, anthropologists, sociologists, etc., are listed in the Appendix. All other titles have been excluded.

Although the focus of the Bibliography is on the period 1850 to 1950, the few serial publications in psychology that appeared before 1850 have been included to provide historical context for the body of the work. The first main entry, therefore, dates from 1783. Final main entries date from 1950. The year 1950 serves as a firm cutoff date for inclusion of information in the bibliography. Serials that initiated publication after 1950 are not included; and no information on serials that began before 1950 is provided for the period after 1950. The choice of this cutoff date was dictated by the geometrical rate of expansion in the number of serial titles in psychology after 1950 and by the authors' desire to focus on historical material.

Main Entries

Main entries for each serial include the title, sponsoring institution (if any), title variations, dates of publication, frequency, numbering variations, publisher, primary editors, associate editors or editorial board members (if any), and, in the case of monograph series, a list of the contents of the series. The various sections contain the following information presented according to the conventions described:

TITLES: Main entry titles include major subtitles and are generally provided in the format adopted by the *Union List of Serials*. In cases in which a serial is not contained in the *Union List* or in which the *Union List* is inconsistent, a comparable format has been employed. With the exception of place names (for which English language conventions have been uniformly adopted), all titles are given in the original language of publication. East Asian and Cyrillic titles are given in transliteration. For East Asian serials, an English translation of the title is provided in parentheses immediately following the transliterated title. Names of sponsoring institutions (if any), when not officially incorporated as part of a given title, are listed in brackets following the title.

TITLE VARIATIONS: Variant titles, minor subtitles, and title changes are described in this section. Frequent changes in minor subtitles are indicated by the phrase "Subtitle varies." If the main title changed but numbering was continuously maintained (e.g., Volume 1–3 was issued under one title, then Volume 4–7 issued under a changed title), the variant titles are given separate main entries in the Bibliography and a notation is provided that the serial "continues" or is "continued by" its retitled counterpart. If a main title changed and numbering was begun anew (e.g., Volume 1–3 was issued under one title, then the title was changed and numbering was begun again with Volume 1), the variant titles are given separate main entries and a notation is provided that the serial "supersedes" or is "superseded by" its retitled counterpart. The formation of titles through the merger of two previously independent titles is also indicated in this section.

DATES OF PUBLICATION: The numbers assigned to initial and final series, years, volumes, or issues; beginning and ending dates of publication; and periods of suspended publication (if any) are indicated in this section. Except for East Asian serials (for which English is used), numbering information is provided in the original language of publication. Continuation of a serial beyond 1950 is indicated by a plus sign (e.g., Volume 1–15+, 1936–1950+).

FREQUENCY: This section provides information on the frequency of appearance of years or volumes (when an entire year or volume was published simultaneously) or issues within years or volumes. If the frequency of publication was invariant over the life of the serial, only the respective designation is given (e.g., Quarterly, Monthly, etc.). If frequency of publication changed periodically but was constant within given periods, frequency designations are followed by the numbers and dates for which they are appropriate (e.g., **Quarterly,** Volume 1–6, 1935–1940; **Monthly,** Volume 7–10, 1941–1944). If frequency of publication was widely variable, the designation "Irregular" is employed. Finally, in those rare cases in which a serial ceased publication prior to the appearance of a single full volume, the indicated frequency, if known, is that which the publishers had projected for the initial volume or year.

NUMBERING VARIATIONS: Peculiarities of numbering (e.g., multinumber issues or omitted or duplicated numbers), parallel numbering (e.g., continuous whole numbering of issues also numbered by volume and part), and general facts of cross-numbering (e.g., numbering of individual articles, issues, or volumes in other series or subseries) are indicated in this section. Serials which are completely contained as subseries within other titles do not appear as separate main entries. Rather, they are listed in the main entry for the encompassing title with a cross-reference from the subseries title in the Title Index. Serials that are partially contained as subseries within one or more other serials do appear as separate main entries and the general fact of cross-numbering is indicated. When issues in nonmonographic serials bear specific titles (e.g., when an issue is a festschrift), this information is also provided.

PUBLISHER: This section presents the places of publication, names of publishers and dates for which publishers were responsible for the serial. Places of publication are always given in English (e.g., Munich rather than München and Vienna rather than Wien). The name of the publisher is given as it appears on the publication.

EDITORS: The names and dates of tenure of primary editors followed by the names and dates of tenure of associate editors or members of an editorial board are presented in the Editor sections. When editorship is under the control of an editorial board without designation of a chair or primary editor, all members of the editorial board are listed as primary editors. Editorial information is based solely on material provided on the serial masthead. Since some serials did not publish editorial information and this information is virtually irretrievable, editorial lists cannot be considered complete.

CONTENTS: Whole numbers, volume numbers (if any), authors and titles of each of the individual items of monograph serials are presented in this section. Dates of publication, page numbers, and specific information on cross-numbering of items within other serials follow each title. Undated or unpaginated publications are so designated. Lack of date or pagination should be taken to indicate that this information was unobtainable.

Appendix

Appendix entries include the serial title and dates of publication. In general, serial titles in this section are those employed for main entries by the *Union List of Serials*.

For names of sponsoring institutions (if any), title variations and continuations, numbering and numbering variations, consult relevant entries in the *Union List*.

Title Index

The Title Index contains references to entry numbers for all serial titles that appear in either the main body of the Bibliography or the Appendix. In addition, for main entries, all title variations, major and minor subtitles, and sponsoring agencies are cross-referenced to the main entry. All main entries accessed by placename can be reached through titles and/or subtitles which have been cross-referenced to the placename entry (e.g., *Washington, D.C. National Research Council. Committee on Child Development. Conference on Research in Child Development. Proceedings* can be reached by cross-reference from National Research Council, from Committee on Child Development of the National Research Council, or from Conference on Research in Child Development). Organizations, societies, laboratories, and institutions that publish Annals, Bulletins, Contributions, Journals, Transactions, etc., must be accessed through the name and/or place of the organization (e.g., the main entry for *Bulletin of the Analytical Psychology Club of New York* is *Analytical Psychology Club of New York. Bulletin*. This entry may also be reached by looking under New York. Analytical Psychology Club). East Asian serials, in addition to being accessible through the standard cross-references, can also be accessed by looking under the English translations for their titles.

Name Index

The Name Index contains references to entry numbers for all monograph authors, primary editors, and associate editors or editorial board members. Cross-references are provided for all hyphenated or double surnames (e.g., Ladd-Franklin, Christine can be reached from Franklin, Christine Ladd), for all known name changes (e.g., Dayhaw, Lawrence Toussaint can be reached from Chrysostome, Frère), and for common variant spellings of transliterated names (e.g., Bekhterev, Vladimir Mikhailovich can be reached from Bechterew, Wladimir von). Names are listed in two ways: either as monograph authors or as editors of the publication. A secondary designation is made as to whether the individual named is a primary editor of that entry or an associate editor.

A Brief History of
Serial Publication in Psychology

Robert H. Wozniak

In describing the evolution of psychology, intellectual historians frequently discuss the various effects which important books have had on the field. At the same time, however, the role played by serial publications is typically ignored.[1] Yet, as any psychologist knows, journal articles and monographs, not books, are psychology's most influential means of communication. Serial publications, therefore, provide a major source of information on the growth of psychology. Historians who fail to take that information into account do so at their own peril.

The history of serial publication in psychology is also worthy of study in its own right. Serial publications directly reflect the intellectual development of the field. As new areas of research interest spring up, new journals are created to communicate the results of that research. As interests shift away from one area (e.g., animal magnetism) and toward another (e.g., psychoanalysis), journals of one type disappear while journals of another multiply.

The evolution of serial publishing also provides a particularly sensitive barometer of the historical, economic, and social forces which have affected the discipline. Traces of the effects of World Wars I and II, the mid-1920s publishing boom, Stalinization in the Soviet Union, and the ascendancy of National Socialism in Germany can all be found in the rise and demise of serial publications. Similarly, changes in editorial networks can, at least to an extent, be read as indicating the rise and fall of "mainstream" or "minority" points of view.

Research of this type is, for the most part, yet to be done. In fact, the goal of this Bibliography is to provide a data base which will facilitate such research. Nonetheless, as a general preview of the information to be found in the body of the Bibliography and a preliminary indication of the direction which such research might take, a number of trends relating to the chronological evolution of psychology serials will be briefly described.

Chronology of Psychology Serials

A general chronological profile of serial publication in psychology, based on dates of first appearance,[2] is presented in Figure 1.

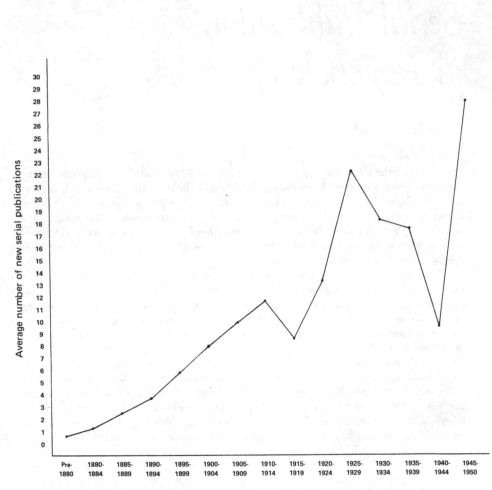

Figure 1. A chronological profile of serial publication in psychology, illustrating the average number of publications inaugurated per year during the time periods indicated.

As is evident from the figure, new serials were founded at an average rate which increased almost linearly from 1880 to the onset of World War I in 1914. During the First World War, the frequency of appearance of new serials dropped, although not drastically, from a yearly average of 11.8 to 8.6. After the war, the founding of new serials rebounded to a pre-World War II average high of 22.4 for the years 1925–1929. The peak of this activity was reached in 1925–1926, when an average of 29 new serials appeared each year. This was followed by a mild decline in the average to 18.4 during the depression and an abrupt drop during World War II. From 1940–1944, an average of only 9.6 new serials appeared each year, the lowest average for any five-year period following World War I. Finally, with the end of the second World War, the rate of appearance of new serials skyrocketed, jumping to a yearly average of 28 for the period 1945–1950.

Pre-1880

Psychology serials date from 1783. In that year, Karl Philipp Moritz (1757–1793) inaugurated the publication of *Gnothi Sauton. Magazin zur Erfahrungsseelenkunde als ein Lesebuch für Gelehrte und Ungelehrte.*[3] Explicitly committed to the value of empirical evidence, Moritz's *Magazin* was primarily concerned with the types and causes of psychic illness and the possibilities of "moral" cure. In addition, topics such as the nature and meaning of dreams, the possibility of unconsciously motivated action, and the psychology of religious mysticism were actively explored.

From 1783 to 1839, new serials appeared only sporadically (26 in 57 years). The majority of these early serials were German (54%) or French (31%), and the subject focus was animal magnetism (62%), general empirical psychology (27%), or psychological medicine (11%). One especially notable occurrence during this early period was the appearance in 1784 of the *Repertorium für Physiologie und Psychologie nach ihrem Umfange und ihrer Verbindung*, the first serial to use the word "psychology" in its title.

From 1840 to 1879, new journals were begun with greater regularity. The average for this period was almost exactly one new serial per year. Although the majority of these serials were still either German (24%) or French (27%), British (17%) and American (19%) publications began to appear with increased frequency. Subject focus, however, was still quite narrow. Animal magnetism (37%), psychological medicine (37%), and general empirical psychology (14%) accounted for the majority of titles.

A number of important events also marked this period. In France in 1842 and in Great Britain in 1853, journals were founded which were to act as major outlets for research and clinical description in psychological medicine throughout the nineteenth and twentieth centuries. The French journal, *Annales médico-psychologiques. Journal de l'aliénation mentale et de la médicine légale des aliénés* was founded by Jules Gabriel François Baillarger (1809–1890), in collaboration with Laurent Cerise (1809–1869) and François Achille Longet (1811–1871). Baillarger was a neurologist known for his work on hallucination and for his observation that aphasics who have lost the capacity for voluntary speech may still retain certain automatic expressions. He edited the journal in collaboration with others for a period of almost 50 years. During the 1930s and 1940s, the journal continued under René Charpentier, with an editorial board including such figures as René Semelaigne (1855–1934), Pierre Janet (1859–1947), and Henri Piéron (1881–1964). The British journal, the *Asylum Journal of Mental Science* (later titled *Journal of Mental Science* and eventually *British Journal of Psychiatry*), was founded by John Charles Bucknill (1817–1897) and later edited by, among others, Henry Maudsley (1834–1918) and Daniel Hack Tuke (1827–1895).

During this period, a number of serials also appeared which fostered the growth of empiricism in psychology. In 1851, Friedrich Eduard Beneke (1798–1854) founded the *Archiv für die pragmatische Psychologie; oder die Seelenlehre in der Anwendung auf das Leben*. Beneke was a strong proponent of an empirical and even experimental[4] approach to a psychology which he considered to be propadeutic to philosophy. These views, unfortunately, worked to Beneke's professional disadvantage in Hegelian Germany, and he never attained the level of academic recognition which should have been his due. Although this journal lasted only two years, it signaled the beginning of a return to a critical empiricism in Germany.

This empiricism is evident in the two years of the *Zentralblatt für Naturwissenschaften und Anthropologie*, inaugurated in 1853 by Gustav Theodor Fechner (1801–1887). In this important journal, Fechner published studies of sensory memory and of the relation between male and female strides; these studies exhibit his early attempts to develop statistical methods for the description of behavior.[5]

At about this same time, researchers in German philology began to investigate the psychological basis of language, myth, and culture. In 1859, Moritz Lazarus (1824–1903), a philosopher, and Heymann Steinthal (1823–1899), a philologist, founded the *Zeitschrift für Völkerpsychologie und Sprachwissenschaft* to provide a forum for empirical work on the psychological forms of social communities. The basic premise of the new "folk psychology" was that phenomena of human mental development such as speech, religion, and custom were originally created by and belonged to groups, not individuals. Although the methods of investigation employed in this work were primitive by modern standards, the journal provided an impetus to the study of questions of social psychology and the psychology of language which influenced a number of later figures, most notably Wilhelm Wundt (1832–1920).[6]

In 1867, William Torrey Harris (1835–1909), an American, founded the *Journal of Speculative Philosophy* as an outlet for his own work and that of the members of the St. Louis Philosophical Society.[7] That same year, Theodor Meynert (1833–1892) and Max Leidesdorf (1818–1889) issued the *Vierteljahrsschrift für Psychiatrie in ihren Beziehungen zur Morphologie und Pathologie des Central-Nervensystems, der physiologischen Psychologie, Statistik und gerichtlichen Medicin*. The *Vierteljahrsschrift* was the first journal explicitly including "physiological psychology" in its title; for the inaugural issue, the editors invited Wilhelm Wundt to contribute an article on recent advances in physiological psychology.[8] This article, Wundt's first published review of the new physiological psychology, can probably be viewed as marking the birth of scientific psychology in its modern sense.

Finally, in 1876, the British journal *Mind* was founded by Alexander Bain (1818–1903) under the editorship of George Croom Robertson (1842–1892).[9] This journal served as the primary English language journal for the "new psychology" until the *American Journal of Psychology* (founded 1887) and more especially the *Psychological Review* (founded 1894) were established.

1880–1889

In the 1880s, as psychology began to identify with science[10] and move away from philosophy, new serials began to appear at an average rate of almost two per year. With the exception of France, which inaugurated 6 journals during this period, the rate of appearance of new serials was fairly constant among the major psychological communities in Germany (2), the United States (3), Great Britain (2) and Russia (3). In addition, subject content remained quite focused. Of the 19 new journals which appeared, 89% dealt with general empirical psychology (8), psychological medicine (5), or "hypnotism" (4), the term by which animal magnetism was by then beginning to be known.

Although Wundt's *Grundzüge der physiologischen Psychologie*[11] was published in 1873–1874 and the first laboratory opened at Leipzig in 1879, the real growth of the "new psychology" began in the 1880s. That growth was reflected in the establishment of the first two periodicals devoted to this endeavor. In 1883, Wundt founded the *Philosophische Studien*[12] and, in 1887, G. Stanley Hall (1844–1924) founded the *American Journal of Psychology*.

Most of the experimental and theoretical work published in the *Philosophische Studien* came either from the Leipzig laboratory or from Wundt's students. Omitting theoretical or purely methodological papers, about one hundred articles representing the laboratory's first 20 years of experimental research were published in the journal.[13] The influence of these studies on later experimental psychology cannot be overestimated. An indication of their importance can be readily gleaned from the fact that Woodworth's 1938 *Experimental Psychology*,[14] published 35 years after the demise of the *Philosophische Studien*, still carried references to no fewer than 42 of the original group of studies.

Hall's *American Journal of Psychology*, although conceived as a journal of the "new psychology"—rigorously empirical and preferably experimental in method—was intended to be more general in content than the *Philosophische Studien*. In Hall's conception, one of the primary tasks of the *American Journal* was to define the field by gathering together "experimental investigations of the kind already common to the new psychology; 'inductive studies' in animal instinct, psychogenesis in children, and morbid and anthropological study; and, lastly, studies in nervous anatomy, physiology, and morphology."[15] Hall may initially have succeeded somewhat in this effort; but, in short order, his intransigence with respect to the exclusion of theoretical work from the journal—and his tendency to overrepresent his own work and that of his Clark colleagues and students—prompted James Mark Baldwin (1861–1934) and James McKeen Cattell (1860–1944) to found a competing journal, the *Psychological Review*, described in more detail below. Although the *American Journal* broadened somewhat under the later influence of Edward Bradford Titchener (1867–1927) and Karl M. Dallenbach (1889–1971) and continues to this day, it has never functioned as the mainstream journal it might have been, given its priority in the field.

Two other events of this period bear mention. The psychological congress held in Paris in 1889, titled *Congrès international de psychologie physiologique*, produced the first in the series of international congress proceedings and papers. In the same year, *Voprosy filosofii i psikhologii*, which carried many of the initial Russian contributions to the "new psychology," was founded by Nikolai Iakovlevich Grot (1852–1899) and

A. A. Abrikosov.[16] This journal flourished until the aftermath of the 1917 October Revolution.

1890–1899

In the 1890s, the rate at which new psychology serials appeared jumped to just under five per year. Although the number of new periodicals rose in Germany (8) and France (9), it remained constant in Russia (3) and declined in Great Britain (0). The overall increase was primarily a function of a huge jump in journals appearing in the United States (18) and of the spread of new serials over a much wider geographical area. Thus, during this period, five new journals were founded in Italy and one each in Australia, Canada, Belgium, and the Netherlands.[17] As geographical representation broadened, so too did serial content. While 75% of the new journals were still devoted to general psychology (22), psychological medicine (9), and hypnosis (5), a sizable number specialized in educational psychology (3), child/genetic psychology (3), abnormal psychology (3), and psychical research (3).

The need for broader, more general journals than the *Philosophische Studien* and *American Journal of Psychology* was felt in Germany and France, as well as in the United States. In 1890, Hermann Ebbinghaus (1850–1909) and Arthur König (1856–1901) founded the *Zeitschrift für Psychologie und Physiologie der Sinnesorgane*. Ebbinghaus enlisted the editorial assistance of Georg Elias Müller (1850–1934) and Carl Stumpf (1848–1936), whose laboratories at Göttingen and Berlin,[18] respectively, were the chief rivals to Wundt's at Leipzig. He also attracted a number of the most important German physiologists to the journal. These included Hermann Aubert (1826–1892), Sigmund Exner (1846–1926), Ewald Hering (1834–1918), Johannes von Kries (1853–1928), Wilhelm Preyer (1842–1897), and Hermann von Helmholtz (1821–1894). As Boring has aptly described it, "the *Zeitschrift* represented in a way a coalition of independents outside of the Wundtian school."[19]

In France, in 1894, Alfred Binet (1857–1911) initiated *L'Année psychologique*,[20] with the collaboration of Henri Beaunis (1830–1921) and the editorial assistance of Victor Henri (1872–1940) and later Jean Larguier des Bancels (1876–?) and Theodore Simon (1873–1961). *L'Année* contained original articles, topical reviews, and annotated bibliographies. Binet's commitment to breadth was such that he slated areas for review which included "anatomy, pathology, and physiology of the nervous system, aesthetics, linguistics, pedagogy, statistics of crime, mental retardation, philosophy, etc."[21] Binet himself published over 75 articles in *L'Année*, including the 1905, 1908, and 1911 versions of the intelligence scale.[22] In 1912, after Binet's death, editorial responsibility for the journal passed to Henri Piéron, with whom it remained for a period of over 50 years.

The year 1894, in the United States, also found Baldwin and Cattell collaborating on the founding of *Psychological Review*. In addition to the *Psychological Review* proper, which was first issued in 1894, the *Review* included the *Psychological Index*, the *Psychological Review. Monograph Supplements* (eventually titled *Psychological Monographs*), and the *Psychological Bulletin*. These appeared in 1894, 1895, and 1904, respectively. The events which led up to the founding of *Psychological Review* beautifully illustrate that blend of personal and professional factors which is influential in the growth of any field.[23]

Briefly, as indicated earlier, a group of younger American psychologists, without ties to Clark University or to G. Stanley Hall, were growing increasingly restless with Hall's hegemony over the only American outlet for publications devoted to the new psychology. In the spring and summer of 1893, under the leadership of Baldwin and Cattell, they drew up a set of proposals aimed at broadening editorial representation on the *American Journal* or encouraging Hall to sell the publication. The implication of the proposals was that Hall's failure to negotiate one or the other of these courses of action would leave them no option but the founding of a competitive journal. Negotiations broke down. The *Psychological Review* was born and has continued to date.

This time period also saw the establishment of the first journals specializing in genetic/child and educational psychology. In 1891, Hall founded the *Pedagogical Seminary. An International Record of Educational Literature, Institutions and Progress* (later titled *Pedagogical Seminary and Journal of Genetic Psychology*). Not wishing to "contaminate his university of pure science with the subject of pedagogy,"[24] Hall seems to have entered somewhat reluctantly into the *Pedagogical Seminary*. The first issue, in fact, carried nothing on child study and adopted instead a rather elitist posture with respect to the directive role that universities might play in educational reform. This posture began to change almost immediately, however. In 1891 and 1892, Hall travelled to the National Education Association meetings and attracted large audiences to informal discussions of child study.[25] The second number of the first volume (1891) and the final number of the second volume (1892) of the journal were devoted specifically to child study; by Volume 3 (1893), the entire journal was essentially given over to observations, questionnaire studies, and experiments with children and adolescents.

In 1897, the *Sammlung von Abhandlungen aus dem Gebiete der pädagogischen Psychologie und Physiologie* was founded under the editorship of Theodor Ziehen (1862–1950) and Herman Schiller (1839–1902). This appears to have been the first serial to include the term "educational psychology" in its title. It was followed two years later by the *Zeitschrift für pädagogische Psychologie*, edited by Ferdinand Kemsies.[26] This journal, under the later editorship of Otto Scheibner (1877–?), Ernst Meumann (1862–1915), and William Stern (1871–1938), became one of the preeminent serials in educational psychology. During the ascendancy of the Third Reich, editorial responsibilities were taken over by Erich Jaensch (1883–1940), Oswald Kroh (1887–1955), and Hans Volkelt (1886–?). In 1944, the journal ceased publication.

1900–1909

As the new century began, the rate at which serials appeared continued to climb. Over the ten-year period from 1900 to 1909, periodicals were inaugurated at an average rate of nine per year. Although 54% of these journals were still concentrated in Germany (25) and the United States (24), the remainder were spread among 11 other countries: France (9), Great Britain (8), Italy (5), Russia (4), Argentina, Austria, Belgium, the Netherlands, Spain, and Sweden (2 each) and Switzerland (1). Subject content similarly broadened. General psychology (39), psychological medicine (12), and hypnosis (4) now accounted for only 61% of the new serials. Journals devoted to applied psychology (5), abnormal psychology (7), social psychology (3), and animal psychology (1), psychology of religion (3), parapsychology (2), and psychoanalysis (3) added to those in educational psychology (6) and child/genetic (4) psychology as outlets for specialized publication.

In 1900 and 1906, respectively, two of the most influential monograph series of the first half of the century were established. In 1900, Leopold Loewenfeld (1847–1924) initiated a series of monographs dedicated to medical psychology, neurology, and the study of abnormal mental states. The *Grenzfragen des Nerven- und Seelenlebens* continued through 1927, eventually numbering 130 titles. Among the monographs were *Ueber den Traum,* by Sigmund Freud (1856–1939), a condensation of his *Die Traumdeutung,*[27] and works by Vladimir Mikhailovich Bekhterev (1857–1927), Christian von Ehrenfels (1859–1932), August Forel (1848–1931), Kurt Goldstein (1878–1965), Willy Hellpach (1877–1955), Theodor Lipps (1851–1914), and Albert Moll (1862–1939).

In 1906, Robert S. Woodworth (1869–1962) founded the *Archives of Psychology.* At that time, Columbia University required that doctoral dissertations be published prior to the granting of the degree. For 39 years, the *Archives* acted as the primary vehicle for the publication of dissertations written under the supervision of the Columbia psychology department. This series had great significance, because Columbia was then probably the leading center for psychology in the United States.[28] Over the life of the *Archives,* the dissertations of more than 200 students were published. These included, among others, many of whom were equally influential, Harry L. Hollingworth (1880–1956), Edward K. Strong (1884–1963), Albert T. Poffenberger (1885–1977), Arthur I. Gates (1890–1972), Harold E. Jones (1894–1960), David Wechsler (1896–1981), Samuel J. Beck (1896–1972), Gregory H. S. Razran (1901–1973), Rensis Likert (1903–1981), Solomon E. Asch (b. 1907), Anne Anastasi (b. 1908) and Robert I. Watson (1909–1980).

Also during this period, both Switzerland and Great Britain for the first time inaugurated periodicals devoted to the "new" scientific psychology. In 1901, in Geneva, Theodore Flournoy (1854–1920) and Éduard Claparède (1873–1940) founded the *Archives de psychologie.* Binet's *L'Année,* as the name implies, was an annual; Flournoy and Claparède wished to have a French-language journal that would provide more rapid dissemination of material.[29] In addition, they wanted to encourage the broadest possible definition of "psychology." This they indicated at the outset by including within the first volume articles on topics as diverse as the psychology of the English, mental pathology, somnambulism, classification of the association of ideas, the epistemological study of the law of correlation, spiritualism, and child study.

In 1904, James Ward (1843–1925) and W. H. R. Rivers (1864–1922) established the *British Journal of Psychology.* The academic establishment of Great Britain had been much slower than that of Germany, the United States, or France to recognize psychology as a field independent of philosophy.[30] This was clearly reflected in the apology for establishment of a journal which the editors apparently felt obliged to include in an editorial preface to the first issue. "Psychology . . . ," they insisted, "has now at length attained the position of a positive science . . . its inquiries are restricted entirely to 'facts'."[31] The time had come, in other words, to initiate an English journal excluding speculative philosophy and devoted specifically to psychology. With that, the *British Journal of Psychology* was inaugurated. It has continued to date under a series of eminent editors, including Charles S. Myers (1873–1946) and Frederic C. Bartlett (1886–1969).

Finally, as indicated above, this ten-year period also saw the first true proliferation of specialized journals. Serials appeared which were specifically devoted to animal psychology (*Annales de la psychologie zoologique,* founded 1901), the psychology of religion (*American Journal of Religious Psychology and Education,* founded 1904), the psychology of sex (*Bibliothek des Seelen- und Sexuallebens*, founded 1904), criminal psychology (*Monatsschrift für Kriminalpsychologie und Strafrechtsreform*, founded 1904), social psychology (*Gesellschaft: Sammlung sozialpsychologischer Monographien*, founded 1906, and *Revue de psychologie sociale*, founded 1907), abnormal psychology (*Journal of Abnormal Psychology*, founded 1906), clinical psychology (*Psychological Clinic. A Journal for the Study and Treatment of Retardation and Deviation*, founded 1907), psychoanalysis (*Schriften zur angewandten Seelenkunde*, founded 1907), and applied psychology (*Zeitschrift für angewandte Psychologie und psychologische Sammelforschung*, founded 1908).[32]

1910–1919

From 1910 to the start of World War I in 1914, the rate of initiation of new serials continued to increase. For this five-year period, an average of just under 12 new publications a year made their appearance. For the war and recovery years (1915–1919), this rate dropped to 8.6. The seemingly moderate decline in the face of the war, however, is a bit misleading. Of the 43 new serials begun between 1915 and 1919, well over half (24) were founded in the United States. If the figures for the United States are omitted from calculations, the average rates of appearance of new serials are 9.4 per year before and 3.8 during and just after the war. Clearly, for the countries most directly affected, the impact of the war on psychological publication was, as one would expect, quite significant.

As a result, the geographical distribution of new serials also changed. The past tendency for new publications to be concentrated in the United States and Germany grew even more extreme. Between 1910 and 1919, both the United States (36) and Germany (34) initiated a greater number of serials than all of the remaining countries taken together (32). While areas of subject content remained fairly constant, the concentration of new effort within those areas did not. Between the two decades, the number of new serials established to cover general psychology declined from 39 to 27. This is not particularly surprising, since most of the major psychological communities had, by that time, one or more well-established general psychology journals. Specialized journals, on the other hand, increased. The number of newly established applied psychology periodicals grew from 5 to 9. Inaugurations of new educational psychology serials increased from 6 to 13, of abnormal/clinical periodicals from 7 to 18, of animal psychology journals from 1 to 6, and of psychoanalytic serials from 3 to 10.

It is particularly instructive, in light of the geographical differences previously noted, to compare the journals begun in Great Britain, Germany, and France between 1910 and 1919 with those started in the United States. The growth of educational psychology and abnormal/clinical psychology appears to have been centered in the United States, while the increase in applied psychology seems to have occurred initially in Europe. Thus, 7 new applied journals were begun in Europe—in Germany (4), Great Britain (2), and France (1)—between 1910 and 1919, while only 1 was founded in the United States. By comparison, new educational psychology journals in the United States jumped from 1 to 9 and new abnormal/clinical journals increased from 3 to 12 during this period, while in Germany, France, and Britain taken together, only 3 new educational and 4 abnormal/clinical journals were begun.

Although new schools of thought such as behaviorism, psychoanalysis, and gestalt psychology were already beginning to emerge during 1900–1909,[33] the period 1910–1919 was the first in which these theoretical points of view exerted any great effect on the founding of new serials. As indicated above, these years were characterized by a trend away from the establishment of general journals and toward the founding of serials that were ever more narrowly defined either by content area or by the point of view which they represented.

Behaviorism, for example, had its journals even before it had its manifesto or its textbook.[34] In 1911, two years before his famous Columbia address, John B. Watson (1878–1958) started *Behavior Monographs*. In the same year, Robert M. Yerkes (1876–1956), equally committed to the study of behavior (though never a Watsonian), inaugurated the *Journal of Animal Behavior*. In 1916, Watson founded the *Journal of Experimental Psychology*, thus forging a link between behaviorism and experimentalism in the minds of psychologists which shaped the field for 40 years to follow. Finally, in 1917, Knight Dunlap (1875–1949), Watson's colleague at Johns Hopkins and also a strong advocate of behaviorism, inaugurated *Psychobiology*, a journal that merged in 1921 with the *Journal of Animal Behavior* to become the immensely influential *Journal of Comparative Psychology*.

Psychoanalysts also founded journals. In fact, two of the three[35] most influential psychoanalytic periodicals of the period preceding World War II were established during these years. In 1912, Freud, in collaboration with Otto Rank (1884–1932) and Hanns Sachs (1881–1947), founded *Imago; Zeitschrift für Anwendung der Psychoanalyse auf die Geisteswissenschaften*. A year later, Freud inaugurated the *Internationale Zeitschrift für ärztliche Psychoanalyse*, this time in collaboration with Rank, Sandor Ferenczi (1873–1933), and Ernest Jones (1879–1958). As might be expected, schisms within psychoanalysis were reflected in the new journals. Thus, for example, in 1912 and 1915, respectively, after Alfred Adler had broken with Freud,[36] he founded the *Verein für freie psychoanalytische Forschung. Schriften* and the *Zeitschrift für Individualpsychologie. Studien aus dem Gebiete der Psychotherapie, Psychologie und Pädagogik*.

Finally, gestalt psychologists also established journals that reflected their point of view. In 1913, Kurt Koffka (1886–1941) began a subseries within the *Zeitschrift für Psychologie und Physiologie des Sinnesorgane. Abteilung 1. Zeitschrift für Psychologie* devoted to the publication of studies motivated by the gestalt perspective. The subseries, entitled *Beiträge zur Psychologie der Gestalt- und Bewegungserlebnisse* continued within the *Zeitschrift* until it was transferred in 1922 to the newly founded *Psychologische Forschung; Zeitschrift für Psychologie und ihre Grenzwissenschaften*. Edited primarily by Koffka, Wolfgang Köhler (1887–1967), and Max Wertheimer (1880–1943), the *Psychologische Forschung* functioned as a primary publishing outlet for the gestalt movement.

1920–1929

From 1920 to 1929, as the recovery from World War I turned into an economic boom, the rate at which new psychology serials were established jumped from the war-time yearly average of 8.6 to 13.4 for 1920–1924 and a remarkable 22.4 for 1925–1929. In 1925 and 1926 alone, 58 new psychology periodicals appeared worldwide. Although the United States (44) and Germany (42) still accounted for greater numbers of new serials than any other countries, the overall geographical distribution had shifted markedly. Together, the United States and Germany now accounted for only 48% of the new publications. The Soviet Union, fresh from the revolution but also caught up in internal political turmoil (discussed below), initiated no fewer than 22 new serials during this period, over 7 times the number (3) begun in the previous decade. The remainder of the increase was spread over a large number of countries, including five (China, Hungary, India, Palestine, and Norway) that established psychology journals for the first time.

Subject content also changed. The percentage of new serials that specialized in child/genetic, educational, and applied psychology climbed from 25% during 1910–1919 to 41% during this period. This shift was due to three main factors: (1) the strength of the child development movement in the United States, (2) a strong tendency in smaller countries starting journals to focus their initial efforts on educational psychology, and (3) the development within applied psychology of specializations such as vocational guidance, personnel psychology, and the psychology of industrial skill and fatigue. Virtually all the other subject areas shrunk proportionately.

One of the most interesting developments during the 1920s was the sudden burst of the Soviet Union into prominence in the psychological community. Although new Russian serials had been appearing since the 1880s, this had always occurred in small numbers (only 13 for the entire 40-year period from 1880 to 1919). Suddenly, after the revolution, as the Communist government committed itself to creating the "new Soviet man",[37] the theoretical and educational possibilities inherent in psychology were seen as worthy of strong support.

As is true of the history of the country itself, the history of Soviet psychology during this period is exceedingly complicated.[38] The relations between Ivan Petrovich Pavlov's (1849–1936) physiologists, V. M. Bekhterev's reflexologists, and the psychologists,[39] under K. N. Kornilov (1879–1957) and others, were usually quite strained. The journals, as a result, typically reflected these divisions. Pavlov's journal, founded in 1925, was the *Akademiia nauk SSSR (Leningrad). Fiziologicheskii institut. Fiziologicheskii laboratorii akademika I. P. Pavlova. Trudy.* Bekhterev maintained several serials. Chief among them were *Voprosy psikhofiziologii, refleksologii i gigieny truda,* founded in 1923, and *Leningrad. Gosudarstvennyi refleksologicheskii institut po izucheniiu mozga. Novoe v refleksologii i fiziologii nervnoi sistemy,* founded in 1925.

Psychologists and pedologists (pedology was a kind of blend of genetic psychology, educational psychology, and mental testing) also maintained several journals. Perhaps the most important journal of this type for the period was *Zhurnal psikhologii, pedologii i psikhotekhniki,* founded in 1928. This journal was first issued in 3 series: *Seriia A. Psikhologiia, Seriia B. Pedologii,* and *Seriia V. Psikhofiziologiia truda i psikhotekhnika.* Then, in 1929, the journal was split into three separate periodicals based on the three series. The importance of the journal and its three descendants stemmed from two factors. First, the editors included Kornilov, Vladimir Maksimovich Borovskii,[40] Isaak Naftulievich Shpil'rein (1891–?) and Aaron Borisovich Zalkind (1888–?), the leaders of Soviet psychology. Second, the journal represented the three major foci of Soviet psychological research in the 1920s: general psychology, pedology, and applied psychology.

Paradoxically, Soviet psychology declined just as rapidly as it rose. Between 1924 and 1927, Joseph Stalin (1879–1953) solidified his power over the Soviet government. Part of the political struggle during this period revolved around control of scientific publishing, as well as the popular press. It is not a coincidence that over 14 new psychology serials were founded in the Soviet Union between 1925 and 1929, nor is it a coincidence that, with two exceptions,[41] the life of these serials was short (a slim 4.3 years on the average). Between 1932 and 1934, as Stalin began to question the value of psychology for Soviet society, virtually all of the psychology serials begun in the 1920s were abandoned.[42] In 1936, the Central Committee of the Communist Party of the Soviet Union issued "On Pedological Distortions in the Commissariats of Education,"[43] which sharply curtailed the role of psychology in education and other aspects of Soviet society; by this time, psychology journals in the Soviet Union were already effectively dead.

The other development of interest during this period was the growth of the child development movement in the United States. Following World War I, the "war to end all wars," children began to be seen as embodying humanity's hope for a peaceful future. Enthusiasm for the welfare of children ran high, but knowledge about children was woefully inadequate. In the mid-1920s, in the United States, the Laura Spelman Rockefeller Memorial stepped into the vacuum. Under the leadership of Beardsley Ruml (1894–1960) and Lawrence K. Frank (1890–1968), the Memorial set out: "(1) to develop child-study groups among mothers and parent training classes within the existing systems of public education; (2) to encourage the training of personnel to act as volunteer leaders of child-study groups and of professional workers to instruct parents within the state educational system; and (3) to develop centers of scientific research to study the problems of child care and development, thus providing information required for parent education and, also, the facilities for training personnel."[44]

It was this last aim which most directly affected research and serial publication in psychology. In 1924, child development research funds were made available to Teachers College, Columbia University, as part of an overall program aimed at training leaders for parent education. Work from this center eventually became the basis for the establishment, in 1929, of Columbia's *Child Development Monographs*. In 1925, Laura Spelman Rockefeller Memorial funds were employed to help establish a Committee on Child Development within the Division of Anthropology and Psychology of the National Research Council. Between 1925 and 1933, also with Rockefeller support, this Committee held four conferences on research in child development (for which there were published *Proceedings*), established the *Child Development Abstracts and Bibliography*, and founded the journal *Child Development*.

By 1927, Child Welfare Institutes had been established with Rockefeller funding at Minnesota, under John E. Anderson (1893–1966), and at Berkeley, California, under Harold E. Jones. The Rockefeller Memorial also was supporting child development research at the University of Iowa's Child Welfare Research Station, directed by Bird T. Baldwin (1875–1928), and at the University of Toronto's Institute of Child Study, directed by William E. Blatz (1895–1964). Among others, serials from these institutes such as the *Iowa. University. Studies in Child Welfare*, the *Minnesota. University. Institute of Child Welfare. Monograph Series*, the *California. University. Institute of Child Welfare. Bulletin*, and the *Toronto. University. Studies. Child Development Series* were all directly or indirectly supported by the Rockefeller Memorial.

1930–1939

From 1930 to 1939, the rate at which new psychology serials were founded declined slightly from the pre-war high of the previous five years (22.4). From 1930 to 1934 and 1935 to 1939, a yearly average of 18.4 and 17.6 new serials was maintained. A glance at the figures for geographical distribution, however, indicates that the overall statistics can be grossly misleading. The number of new serials inaugurated in the United States in this period (77) was almost double the number of the previous decade. In fact, 43% of all new psychology periodicals worldwide during the 1930s were founded in the United States. This huge increase is not accurately represented in total statistics for the period because it was accompanied by an almost symmetrical drop in new German and Russian serials. The German and Russian totals of 15 and 6, respectively, represented decreases of 66% and 73% from the previous decade's totals.

Subject matter concentration changed in only minor ways during the 1930s. General (47), applied (23), educational (21), abnormal/clinical, (20) and child/genetic (15) journals were, as they had been before, the most common new publications. The trend toward narrowly specialized serials also continued, particularly in the United States. For example, American serials were founded which focused on psychological tests and testing. These included the Psychological Corporation's *Test Service Bulletin;* Oscar K. Buros' (1905–1978) *Educational, Psychological, and Personality Tests* (which formed the basis for the later *Mental Measurements Yearbook); the Invitational Conference on Testing Problems. Proceedings,* sponsored by the American Council on Education and the Educational Testing Service; and the *Rorschach Research Exchange.* New serials in the United States also focused on psychology of music *(Iowa. University. Studies in the Psychology of Music),* statistical methodology *(Statistical Methodology Reviews),* student personnel psychology *(American Council on Education. Studies. Series VI: Student Personnel Work),* personnel administration *(Society for Personnel Administration. Pamphlet Series),* and psychological films *(Psychological Cinema Register).* Finally, in Germany (1934), the Netherlands (1935), and Roumania (1939), serials were founded which focused on psychology, war, and the military, as might have been expected given the events of the period.

Clearly, Adolf Hitler's (1889–1945) rise to power in 1932 was, as for the rest of the world, the one event of this period of greatest importance for psychology. Before the advent of the Third Reich, Germany had always been at the forefront of psychology. Between 1783 and 1929, 135 psychology serials were established in Germany, just a few more than in the United States (133) and far more than in any other country. Furthermore, psychology in Germany was intellectually vibrant, exerting an influence on the rest of the field not only through the quantity of its published work but through its quality.[45] Within a few short years of the triumph of National Socialism, however, German psychology was severely stunted if not moribund.[46]

Of the small number of new German psychology serials begun during this period, over one-half (8) were inaugurated before Hitler consolidated his power in 1933. Of those eight serials, all but one ceased by 1933. The one periodical that did continue was founded and edited by Erich Jaensch (1883–1940), whose political beliefs were well known to be sympathetic to those in power.[47] During the period of the Third Reich, 1933–1939, only seven new serials were initiated. With two interesting exceptions, the average length of publication for these serials was two years. The exceptions were an animal psychology journal, the *Zeitschrift für Tierpsychologie,* founded in 1937 and still in existence after the war, and *Soldatentum. Zeitschrift für Wehrpsychologie, Wehrerziehung, Menschenauslese,* published between 1934 and 1942 by the German War Ministry and edited by Max Simoneit (1896–?), among others. Apparently, either because of their content or their editorship, these serials were not perceived as a threat to the Nazis.

1940–1950

During the period 1940–1944, years in which the world was embroiled in war, the rate of appearance of new psychology serials plunged to a yearly average of 9.6, the lowest such average since the first World War. From 1945 to 1950, during the post-war recovery, new serials were founded at the extraordinary rate of 28 per year. As might be expected given the major role assumed by American psychology during the 1930s, both the plunge and resurgence may be attributed largely, if not entirely,[48] to changes in serial publication in the United States. Of the 85 new serials founded in the United States during this period (40% of the worldwide total), only 18 were published between 1940 and 1944. The remaining 67 were inaugurated during the six years following the war.

The only major shift in relative geographical distribution during this period came primarily after the war and consisted in the wide proliferation of psychology journals across countries which had never before had such publications. No fewer than 33 countries founded psychology serials between 1940 and 1950, including India, Turkey, Egypt, South Africa, New Zealand, Uruguay, Peru, Chile, Mexico, Brazil, Guatemala, and the Dominican Republic. With the exception of a mild increase in new social psychology periodicals and a slight decrease in new child/genetic journals, the distribution of new serials by subject matter remained about as it had been during the 1930s.

In addition, these years were rich with the sources of psychology's future trends. The rapid expansion of clinical psychology, the movement of social psychologists into attitude and opinion research, and the growth of the human performance movement all began during this period. Perhaps the most interesting development, however, and one not at all unrelated to the above trends, was the initiation of new journals and the use of older established serials to report the results of research carried out during the war.

Many of these new war-related serials deserve comment. The Foster Parents' Plan for War Children, established by Anna Freud (1895–1982) and Dorothy T. Burlingham (1891–1979), issued *Reports* throughout this period. In Great Britain, the Industrial Health Research Board issued its *(War) Emergency Reports* and, in the United States, psychologists in or just out of the military issued a series of research summaries. From 1942 to 1946, for example, the *Aviation Psychology Abstract Series* carried brief notices of over 190 pieces of war-related psychological research. From 1947 to 1948, the *United States. Army Air Forces. Aviation Psychology Program. Research Reports* summarized the achievements of that program. Especially noteworthy among these were the huge monograph by Arthur W. Melton (1906–1978), *Apparatus Tests*, which provided detailed descriptions of the many ingenious pieces of apparatus developed during the war to assess variables of human performance, and James J. Gibson's (1904–1979) *Motion Picture Testing and Research*, which exhibited the seeds of Gibson's later views on ecological optics. Finally, *Studies in Social Psychology in World War II*, published in 1949–1950 with the assistance of the Social Science Research Council, defined issues in the study of personality, mass communication, and measurement which were to concern social psychologists for years to come.

After 1950, the rate of increase in new psychology journals was geometric. For that reason, and because of this Bibliography's historical orientation, coverage of the later period is beyond the current scope. There is no doubt, however, that detailed analysis of serial publication during the years after 1950 would be worthwhile and should be pursued.

Notes

1. Exceptions to this, unfortunately, have been rare. In the first 19 volumes of the *Journal of the History of the Behavioral Sciences (JHBS)*, only 5 articles deal primarily with the analysis of periodical literature or the history of a particular journal. These are as follows: (a) Lissitz, R. W. "A Longitudinal Study of the Research Methodology in the *Journal of Abnormal and Social Psychology,* the *Journal of Nervous and Mental Disease,* and the *American Journal of Psychiatry.*" *JHBS,* 5(1969):248–255; (b) Evans, R. B. "The *Journal of American Psychology:* A Pioneering Psychological Journal." JHBS, 7(1971):283–284; (c) Eng, E. "Karl Philipp Moritz's *Magazin für Erfahrungsseelenkunde* (Magazine for Empirical Psychology) 1783–1793." *JHBS,* 9(1973):300–305; (d) Vande Kemp, H. "The Dream in Periodical Literature: 1860–1910." *JHBS,* 17(1981):88–113; and (e) Viney, W., Michaels, T., and Ganong, A. "A Note on the History of Psychology in Magazines." *JHBS,* 17(1981):270–272.

2. Dates of first appearance reflect only trends in the inauguration of new serials. Data on average length of time during which publication was sustained, total numbers of serials in print in given years, and dates of demise might be expected to reflect historical, economic, and social factors somewhat differently and should be explored.

3. See Eng., op. cit.

4. See Leary, D. E. "The Philosophical Development of the Conception of Psychology in Germany, 1780–1850." *Journal of the History of the Behavioral Sciences,* 14(1978):113–121.

5. Marilyn Marshall, personal communication.

6. A brief discussion of this influence is contained in: Diamond, S. "Wundt before Leipzig." In *Wilhelm Wundt and the Making of a Scientific Psychology.* Edited by R. W. Rieber. New York: Plenum Press, 1980, pp. 3–70.

7. See Leidecker, K. F. *Yankee Teacher. The Life of William Torrey Harris.* New York: Philosophical Library, 1946, pp. 324–327.

8. Wundt's article was entitled "Neuere Leistungen auf dem Gebiete der physiologischen Psychologie." For details, see Diamond, op. cit.

9. Bain describes the founding of *Mind* in a memoir of Robertson included in *Philosophical Remains of George Croom Robertson.* Edited by A. Bain and T. Whittaker. London and Edinburgh: Williams & Norgate, 1894.

10. For a case study of the conflict between science and philosophy felt by psychologists of this period, see Wozniak, R. H. "Metaphysics and Science, Reason and Reality: The Intellectual Origins of Genetic Epistemology." In *The Cognitive Developmental Psychology of James Mark Baldwin. Current Theory and Research in Genetic Epistemology.* Edited by J. Broughton and D. J. Freeman-Moir. Norwood, New Jersey: Ablex, pp. 13–45.

11. Wundt, Wilhelm. *Grundzüge der physiologischen Psychologie.* Leipzig: W. Engelmann, 1873–1874.

12. This date is incorrectly listed as 1881, in Boring, Edwin G. *A History of Experimental Psychology.* New York: Appleton-Century-Crofts, 1950, p. 324.

13. Boring, op. cit., p. 340.

14. Woodworth, Robert S. *Experimental Psychology.* New York: Henry Holt, 1938.

15. Ross, Dorothy. *G. Stanley Hall. The Psychologist as Prophet.* Chicago: University of Chicago, 1972, p. 171.

16. Dates unknown.

Serial
Publications

Pre-1850

1783

1. *Gnothi Sauton. Magazin zur Erfahrungsseelenkunde als ein Lesebuch für Gelehrte und Ungelehrte.*

TITLE VARIATIONS: None.

DATES OF PUBLICATION: Band 1–10, 1783–1793.

FREQUENCY: Triannual.

NUMBERING VARIATIONS: None.

PUBLISHER: **Berlin:** A. Mylius, 1783–1793.

PRIMARY EDITORS: **Karl P. Moritz**, 1783–1793; **Karl F. Pockels**, 1787–1788; **Salomon Maimon**, 1792–1793.

1784

2. *Repertorium für Physiologie und Psychologie nach ihrem Umfange und ihrer Verbindung.*

TITLE VARIATIONS: Also called *Repertorium der Psychologie und Physiologie nach ihrem Umfange und ihrer Verbindung.*

DATES OF PUBLICATION: Band 1–2, 1784–1786.

FREQUENCY: **Annual,** Band 1, 1784. **Biennial,** Band 2, Heft 1, 1785; Heft 2, 1786.

NUMBERING VARIATIONS: None.

PUBLISHER: **Hof, Germany:** Vierling, 1784–1786.

PRIMARY EDITOR: **Joh. Herm. Pfingslen,** 1784–1786.

1787

3. *Archiv für Magnetismus und Somnambulismus.*

TITLE VARIATIONS: None.

DATES OF PUBLICATION: Band 1–8, 1787–1788.

FREQUENCY: Quarterly.

NUMBERING VARIATIONS: None.

PUBLISHER: **Strasbourg:** Akademische Buchhandlung, 1787–1788. **Leipzig:** Hinrichs, 1787–1788.

PRIMARY EDITOR: **Joh. Lor. Bökmann**, 1787–1788.

4. *Magnetisches Magazin für Niederdeutschland.*

TITLE VARIATIONS: None.

DATES OF PUBLICATION: Stück 1–8, 1787–1788.

FREQUENCY: Irregular.

NUMBERING VARIATIONS: None.

PUBLISHER: **Bremen** [Rabenhorst im Leipzig]: 1787–1788.

PRIMARY EDITORS: None listed.

1792

5. *Allgemeines Repertorium für empirische Psychologie und verwandte Wissenschaften.*

TITLE VARIATIONS: Superseded by *Neues allgemeines Repertorium für empirische Psychologie und verwandte Wissenschaften* with Band 1, 1802.

DATES OF PUBLICATION: Band 1–6, 1792–1801.

FREQUENCY: **Irregular,** Band 1, 1792; Band 2, 1792; Band 3, 1793; Band 4, 1798; Band 5, 1799; and Band 6, 1801.

NUMBERING VARIATIONS: Band 5 and 6 also numbered as *Repertorium und Bibliothek für empirische Psychologie*, Band 1–2.

PUBLISHER: **Nuremberg:** Felsecker, 1792–1798. **Tübingen:** Heerbrand, 1799–1801.

PRIMARY EDITOR: **Immanuel D. Mauchart,** 1792–1801.

1795

6. *Auserlesene Abhandlungen für Ärzte, Naturforscher und Psychologen, aus den Schriften der literarisch–philosophischen Gesellschaft zu Manchester.*
   TITLE VARIATIONS: None.
   DATES OF PUBLICATION: Heft 1, 1795.
   FREQUENCY: Irregular.
   NUMBERING VARIATIONS: None.
   PUBLISHER: **Leipzig:** Cnobloch, 1795.
   PRIMARY EDITOR: **A. W. Schwenger**, 1795.
   NOTE: Translated and edited from *Manchester [England] Literary and Philosophical Society. Memoirs and Proceedings.*

1796

7. *Psychologisches Magazin.*
   TITLE VARIATIONS: None.
   DATES OF PUBLICATION: Stück 1–3, 1796–1797.
   FREQUENCY: Semiannual.
   NUMBERING VARIATIONS: None.
   PUBLISHER: **Jena:** Akademie Verhandlung, 1796–1797. **Altenburg:** Richter, 1796–1797.
   PRIMARY EDITOR: **F. G. Heynig**, 1796–1797.

1802

8. *Neues allgemeines Repertorium für empirische Psychologie und verwandte Wissenschaften.*
   TITLE VARIATIONS: Supersedes *Allgemeines Repertorium für empirische Psychologie und verwandte Wissenschaften.*
   DATES OF PUBLICATION: Band 1–2, 1802–1803.
   FREQUENCY: Annual.
   NUMBERING VARIATIONS: None.
   PUBLISHER: **Leipzig:** In der Sommerschen Buchhandlung, 1802–1803.
   PRIMARY EDITORS: **I. D. Mauchart**, 1802–1803; **H. G. Tzschirner**, 1802–1803.

1804

9. *Archiv für den thierischen Magnetismus.* [*1.*]
TITLE VARIATIONS: None.
DATES OF PUBLICATION: Stück 1–2, 1804–1808.
FREQUENCY: Irregular.
NUMBERING VARIATIONS: None.
PUBLISHER: **Jena:** Göpferdt, 1804–1808.
PRIMARY EDITOR: **August Wilhelm Nordhoff,** 1804–1808.

1805

10. *Magazin für die psychische Heilkunde.*
TITLE VARIATIONS: None.
DATES OF PUBLICATION: Band 1, Heft 1–4, 1805–1806.
FREQUENCY: Quarterly.
NUMBERING VARIATIONS: None.
PUBLISHER: **[Neimer]:** Verlag Lange, 1805–1806.
PRIMARY EDITORS: **J. C. Reil,** 1805–1806; ——— **Keyssler,** 1805–1806.

1814

11. *Annales du magnétisme animal.*
TITLE VARIATIONS: Superseded by *Bibliothèque du magnétisme animal* with Tome 1, 1817.
DATES OF PUBLICATION: Numéro 1–48, July 1814–1816.
FREQUENCY: **Semimonthly,** Numéro 1–12, July–December 1814. **Monthly,** Numéro 13–24, January–December 1815. **Semimonthly,** Numéro 25–48, January–December 1816.
NUMBERING VARIATIONS: None.
PUBLISHER: **Paris:** Au Bureau de Rédaction, rue Neuve-Saint-Martin, no. 29, 1814 (July–September). **Paris:** Au Bureau de Rédaction, rue des Cinq-Diamans, no. 27, 1814–1816.
PRIMARY EDITOR: **A. de Lausanne** (pseudonym for Alexandre André Victor Sarrazin de Montferrier), 1814–1816.

1815

12. *Journal för Animal Magnetism.*

TITLE VARIATIONS: None.

DATES OF PUBLICATION: Del 1–2, 1815–1821.

FREQUENCY: Irregular.

NUMBERING VARIATIONS: Issues also assigned whole numbers, Häft 1–6.

PUBLISHER: **Stockholm:** Carl Delén, 1815–1816. **Stockholm:** Hedmanska Tryckeriet, 1817. **Stockholm:** Joh. Imnelii Tryckeri, 1818–1821.

PRIMARY EDITOR: **P. G. Cederschiöld,** 1815–1821.

1816

13. *Magnetiser's Magazine, and Annals of Animal Magnetism.*

TITLE VARIATIONS: None.

DATES OF PUBLICATION: Number 1–2, July 1816–August 1816.

FREQUENCY: Monthly.

NUMBERING VARIATIONS: None.

PUBLISHER: **London:** Francis Corbaux (W. Welson, Printer), 1816.

PRIMARY EDITOR: **Francis Corbaux,** 1816.

1817

14. *Archiv für den thierischen Magnetismus.* [2.]

TITLE VARIATIONS: Superseded by *Sphinx: Neues Archiv für den thierischen Magnetismus* with Band 1, 1825.

DATES OF PUBLICATION: Band 1–12, 1817–1824.

FREQUENCY: **Annual,** Band 1, 1817. **Semiannual,** Band 2–11, 1818–1822. **Annual,** Band 12, 1824.

NUMBERING VARIATIONS: None

PUBLISHER: **Altenburg** and **Leipzig:** Brockhaus, 1817. **Halle:** Hemmerde & Schwetschke, 1818–1819. **Leipzig:** Herbing, 1820–1824.

PRIMARY EDITORS: **Carl August von Eschenmayer,** 1817–1824; **Dietrich Georg von Kieser,** 1817–1824.

15. *Bibliothèque du magnétisme animal.*

TITLE VARIATIONS: Supersedes *Annales du magnétisme animal.*

DATES OF PUBLICATION: Tome 1–8, July 1817–September 1819. Did not appear from July to September 1818. *See* Numbering Variations *below.*

FREQUENCY: Semimonthly.

NUMBERING VARIATIONS: Each issue is also assigned a whole number, Numéro 1–24. The July 1818 issue was replaced with a single, separately numbered issue of *Société du magnétisme animal. Journal.*

PUBLISHER: **Paris, Strasbourg,** and **London:** Poulet, 1817–1819.

PRIMARY EDITORS: None listed.

1818

16. *Société du magnétisme animal. Journal.*

TITLE VARIATIONS: None.

DATES OF PUBLICATION: Tome 1, Numéro 1, July 1818.

FREQUENCY: Quarterly.

NUMBERING VARIATIONS: This single issue replaced the July–September 1818 issue of *Bibliothèque du magnétisme animal.*

PUBLISHER: **Paris:** Barrois, 1818.

PRIMARY EDITORS: None listed.

1819

17. *Archiv för Animal Magnetism.*

TITLE VARIATIONS: None.

DATES OF PUBLICATION: Häft 1–3, March, May, August 1819.

FREQUENCY: Irregular.

NUMBERING VARIATIONS: None.

PUBLISHER: **Stockholm:** Z. Häggström, 1819.

PRIMARY EDITOR: **Charles Backman,** 1819.

1820

18. *Archives du magnétisme animal.*

TITLE VARIATIONS: None.

DATES OF PUBLICATION: Tome 1–8, May 1820–1823. Suspended publication during 1821.

FREQUENCY: Irregular.

NUMBERING VARIATIONS: Issues also assigned whole numbers, Numéro 1–24.

PUBLISHER: **Paris:** Imprimerie de P. Gueffier (publiées par le Baron d'Hénin de Cuvillers), 1820–1823.

PRIMARY EDITOR: **Baron d'Hénin de Cuvillers,** 1820–1823.

1824

19. *Archiv for Psychologie, Historie, Literatur og Kunst.*

TITLE VARIATIONS: None.

DATES OF PUBLICATION: Bind 1–13, 1824–1830.

FREQUENCY: Semiannual.

NUMBERING VARIATIONS: None.

PUBLISHER: **Copenhagen:** Trykt, Paa Udgiverens Bekostning i H. F. Popps Bogtrykkeri, 1824–1830.

PRIMARY EDITOR: **Niels Christian Oost,** 1824–1830.

1825

20. *Sphinx. Neues Archiv für den thierischen Magnetismus.*

TITLE VARIATIONS: Supersedes *Archiv für den thierischen Magnetismus.*

DATES OF PUBLICATION: Band 1, Heft 1–2, 1825–1826.

FREQUENCY: Irregular.

NUMBERING VARIATIONS: None.

PUBLISHER: **Leipzig:** Herbig, 1825–1826.

PRIMARY EDITOR: **D. G. Kieser,** 1825–1826.

1826

21. *Hermès. Journal du magnétisme animal.*

TITLE VARIATIONS: None.

DATES OF PUBLICATION: Tome 1–4, 1826–1829.

FREQUENCY: Irregular.

NUMBERING VARIATIONS: None.

PUBLISHER: **Paris:** Société de médecins de la faculté de Paris, Madame Levi, Libraire-éditeur, 1826–1829.

PRIMARY EDITOR: **V. Touchard,** 1826–1829.

1827

22. *Propagateur du magnétisme animal.*

TITLE VARIATIONS: None.

DATES OF PUBLICATION: Tome 1–2, 1827–1828.

FREQUENCY: Annual.

NUMBERING VARIATIONS: None.

PUBLISHER: **Paris:** Chapelain et Dupotet, 1827–1828.

PRIMARY EDITOR: **J. Dupotet,** 1827–1828.

1829

23. *Magazin für philosophische, medicinische und gerichtliche Seelenkunde.*

TITLE VARIATIONS: Continued by *Neues Magazin für philosophische, medicinische und gerichtliche Seelenkunde* with Heft 8, 1832.

DATES OF PUBLICATION: Heft 1–7, 1829–1831.

FREQUENCY: **Semiannual,** Heft 1, 1829; Heft 2, 1829; Heft 3, 1830; Heft 4, 1830; Heft 5, 1830; Heft 6, 1831; and Heft 7, 1831.

NUMBERING VARIATIONS: None.

PUBLISHER: **Würzburg:** Strecker, 1829–1831.

PRIMARY EDITOR: **J. B. Friedreich,** 1829–1831.

1832

24. *Neues Magazin für philosophische, medicinische und gerichtliche Seelenkunde.*

TITLE VARIATIONS: Continues *Magazin für philosophische, medicinische und gerichtliche Seelenkunde.* Superseded by *Archiv für Psychologie, für Aerzte und Juristen* with Heft 1, 1834.

DATES OF PUBLICATION: Heft 8–10, 1832–1833.

FREQUENCY: Semiannual. Heft 8, 1832; Heft 9, 1832; and Heft 10, 1833.

NUMBERING VARIATIONS: None.

PUBLISHER: **Würzburg:** Stahel, 1832–1833.

PRIMARY EDITOR: **J. B. Friedreich,** 1832–1833.

1834

25. *Archiv für Psychologie, für Aerzte und Juristen.*

TITLE VARIATIONS: Continues *Neues Magazin für philosophische, medicinische und gerichtliche Seelenkunde.* Superseded by *Blätter für Psychiatrie* with Heft 1, 1837.

DATES OF PUBLICATION: Heft 1–3, 1834.

FREQUENCY: Triannual/Quarterly, according to preface.

NUMBERING VARIATIONS: Also numbered as part of *Magazin für philosophische, medicinische und gerichtliche Seelenkunde,* Band 4, Heft 1–3, 1834.

PUBLISHER: **Heidelberg:** August Osswald's Universitäts Buchhandlung, 1834.

PRIMARY EDITORS: **J. B. Friedreich,** 1834; **C.J.A. Mittermaier,** 1834; **Fr. Groos,** 1834; **J. Chr. A. Grohmann,** 1834.

1837

26. *Blätter für Psychiatrie.*

TITLE VARIATIONS: Supersedes *Archiv für Psychologie, für Aerzte und Juristen.*

DATES OF PUBLICATION: Heft 1–3, 1837–1838.

FREQUENCY: Biannual.

NUMBERING VARIATIONS: None.

PUBLISHER: **Erlangen:** J. J. Palm und Ernst Enke, 1837–1838.

PRIMARY EDITORS: **Johann B. Friedreich,** 1837–1838; **G. Blumröder,** 1837.

27. *Révélateur. Journal de magnétisme animal.*

TITLE VARIATIONS: None.

DATES OF PUBLICATION: Année 1, Numéro 1–12, November 1837–September 1838.

FREQUENCY: Monthly.

NUMBERING VARIATIONS: None.

PUBLISHER: **Bordeaux:** Imprimerie de Suwerinck, 1837–1838.

PRIMARY EDITOR: **J.J.A. Ricard,** 1837–1838.

1839

28. *Journal du magnétisme animal.* [1].

TITLE VARIATIONS: Also as: *Journal de magnétisme animal.*

DATES OF PUBLICATION: Année 1–3, November 1839–March 1842.

FREQUENCY: Monthly.

NUMBERING VARIATIONS: None.

PUBLISHER: **Paris** and **Toulouse:** Bourgogne & Martinet, 1839–1842.

PRIMARY EDITOR: **J.J.A. Ricard,** 1839–1842.

1841

29. *Transactions du magnétisme animal.*

TITLE VARIATIONS: None.

DATES OF PUBLICATION: Année 1, Cahier 1–12, February 1841–January 1842.

FREQUENCY: Monthly.

NUMBERING VARIATIONS: None.

PUBLISHER: **Paris:** Imprimerie de P. Baudouin, chez J. B. Baillière, 1841–1842.

PRIMARY EDITOR: **Alphonse Teste,** 1841–1842.

1842

30. *Mesmeric Magazine; Or, Journal of Animal Magnetism.*

TITLE VARIATIONS: None.

DATES OF PUBLICATION: Volume 1, Number 1, July 1842.

FREQUENCY: Irregular.

NUMBERING VARIATIONS: None.

PUBLISHER: **Boston:** Saxton and Pierce, 1842.

PRIMARY EDITOR: **R. H. Collyer,** 1842.

1843

31. Albany Journal of Neurology; Devoted to Physiology, Phrenology, Medicine, and the Philosophy of Mesmerism.

TITLE VARIATIONS: None.

DATES OF PUBLICATION: Volume 1, Number 1, July 1843.

FREQUENCY: Monthly.

NUMBERING VARIATIONS: None.

PUBLISHER: **Albany, New York:** [Conducted by an Association of Physicians] from the Steam–Press of C. Van Benthuysen and Co., 1843.

PRIMARY EDITOR: **W. A. Hamilton,** 1843.

32. Annales médico–psychologiques. Journal de l'aliénation mentale et de la médicine légale des aliénés. [Official bulletin of the Société médico-psychologique, Paris.]

TITLE VARIATIONS: Subtitled *Revue psychiatrique*, 1931–1950+.

DATES OF PUBLICATIONS: Tome 1–108+, 1843–1950+.

FREQUENCY: **Bimonthly.** Série 1, 1843–1848. **Quarterly.** Série 2–3, 1849–1862. **Bimonthly.** Série 4–10, 1863–1920. **Monthly** except August–September, Série 11–15 and Tome 101–108+, 1921–1950+.

NUMBERING VARIATIONS: 1843–1848, called [Série 1,] Tome 1–12; 1849–1854, [Série 2,] Tome 1–6; 1855–1862, [Série 3,] Tome 1–8; 1863–1868, 4ᵉ Série, Tome 1–12; 1869–1878, 5ᵉ Série, Tome 1–20; 1879–1884, 6ᵉ Série, Tome 1–12; 1885–1894, 7ᵉ Série, Tome 1–20; 1895–1904, 8ᵉ Série, Tome 1–20; 1905–1911, 9ᵉ Série, Tome 1–14; 1912–1920, 10ᵉ Série, Tome 1–12; 1921, 11ᵉ Série, Tome 1–2; 1922–1930, 12ᵉ Série, 18 Tomes; 1931, 13ᵉ Série, 2 Tomes; 1932–1934, 14ᵉ Série, 6 Tomes; 1935–1942, 15ᵉ Série, 16 Tomes. Beginning in 1943 series note disappears from title page. Beginning with the 11ᵉ Série in 1921, the volume numbering within the series is discontinued. Each year is published in two volumes.

PUBLISHER: **Paris:** Bureau des annales médico–psychologiques, 1843. **Paris:** Chez Fortin, Masson et Cie, 1843–1846. **Paris:** Victor Masson, 1846–1848. **Paris:** Chez Victor Masson, Libraire, 1849–1854. **Paris:** La librairie de Victor Masson, 1854–1860. **Paris:** Victor Masson et fils, 1861–1871. **Paris:** Librairie de G. Masson, 1872–1873. **Paris:** G. Masson, éditeur, 1874–1896, 1898–1899. **Paris:** Masson et Cie, éditeurs, 1897, 1900–1940. **Cahors:** Imprimerie A. Coueslant, 1941–1950+.

PRIMARY EDITORS: **Jules Baillarger,** 1843–1891; **Laurent Cerise,** 1843–1869; **Achille Longet,** 1843–1848; **A. Brierre de Boismont,** 1850–1854; **J. Moreau,** 1855–1862; **L. Lunier,** 1867–1885; **Ach. Foville,** 1881–1888; **Ant. Ritti,** 1886–1920; **Henri Colin,** 1920–1930; **René Charpentier,** 1931–1950+.

33. *Annals of Mesmerism and Mesmero-Phrenology.*

TITLE VARIATION: None.

DATES OF PUBLICATION: Volume 1, Number 1–3, July 1843–September 1843.

FREQUENCY: Monthly.

NUMBERING VARIATIONS: None.

PUBLISHER: **London:** Henry Renshaw, 1843. **Edinburgh:** Maclachlan, Stewart and Co., 1843.

PRIMARY EDITOR: **Henry Renshaw,** 1843.

34. *Mesmerist; A Journal of Vital Magnetism.*

TITLE VARIATIONS: Also subtitled A *Weekly Journal of Vital Magnetism.*

DATES OF PUBLICATION: Number 1–20, May 13–September 23, 1843.

FREQUENCY: Weekly.

NUMBERING VARIATIONS: None.

PUBLISHER: **London:** W. Strange, 1843.

PRIMARY EDITOR: **W. Strange,** 1843.

35. ***Zoist; A Journal of Cerebral Physiology and Mesmerism, and Their Applications to Human Welfare.***

TITLE VARIATIONS: None.

DATES OF PUBLICATION: Volume 1–13, April 1843–January 1856.

FREQUENCY: Quarterly.

NUMBERING VARIATIONS: Each issue also assigned a whole number, Number 1–52.

PUBLISHER: **London:** Hippolyte Bailliere, Publisher, 1843–1855. **London:** Arthur Hall, Virtue and Co., Publishers, 1855–1856.

PRIMARY EDITORS: None listed.

1844

36. ***New-York Dissector; A Quarterly Journal of Medicine, Surgery, Magnetism, Mesmerism, and the Collateral Sciences.***

TITLE VARIATIONS: None.

DATES OF PUBLICATION: Volume 1–4, January 1844–December 1847.

FREQUENCY: Quarterly.

NUMBERING VARIATIONS: None.

PUBLISHER: **New York:** Published by the editor, 1844–1847.

PRIMARY EDITORS: **Henry Hall Sherwood,** 1844–1847.

37. ***Revue magnétique. Journal des faits et des cures magnétiques, des théories, etc.***

TITLE VARIATIONS: None.

DATES OF PUBLICATION: Tome 1–2, 1844–1846

FREQUENCY: Irregular.

NUMBERING VARIATIONS: None.

PUBLISHER: **Brussels** and **Paris:** Bureau de la "Revue magnétique," 1844–1846.

PRIMARY EDITOR: **Aubin Gauthier,** 1844–1846.

1845

38. *Journal du magnétisme.*
TITLE VARIATIONS: None.
DATES OF PUBLICATION: Tome 1–20, 1845–1861.
FREQUENCY: Monthly.
NUMBERING VARIATIONS: None.
PUBLISHER: **Paris:** Imprimerie de René, 1845–1861.
PRIMARY EDITOR: **J. Dupotet,** 1845–1861.

1846

39. *Almanach populaire du magnétiseur practicien.*
TITLE VARIATIONS: None.
DATES OF PUBLICATION: Année 1, 1846.
FREQUENCY: Annual.
NUMBERING VARIATIONS: None.
PUBLISHER: **Paris:** A.-L.-G.-F. Bréuté, 1846.
PRIMARY EDITOR: **J.J.A. Ricard,** 1846.

1848

40. *Journal of Psychological Medicine and Mental Pathology.*
TITLE VARIATIONS: Continued by *Medical Critic and Psychological Journal* with Volume 1, 1861.
DATES OF PUBLICATION: Volume 1–13, January 1848–October 1860.
FREQUENCY: Quarterly.
NUMBERING VARIATIONS: Volume 9–13, 1856–1860 called *New Series.* Volume 1–8, issues bear Whole Number 1–32; Volume 9–13, issues bear New Series Whole Number 1–20.
PUBLISHER: **London:** John Churchill, 1848–1860.
PRIMARY EDITOR: **Forbes Winslow,** 1848–1860.

1849

41. *Magnétiseur spiritualiste.*

TITLE VARIATIONS: None.

DATES OF PUBLICATION: Année 1–3, January 1849–October 1851.

FREQUENCY: **Quarterly,** Année 1, 1849. **Bimonthly,** Année 2, 1850. **Monthly,** Année 3, 1851.

NUMBERING VARIATIONS: Each issue is assigned a whole number, Numéro 1–20.

PUBLISHER: **Paris:** Société des magnétiseurs spiritualistes, Imprimerie de Picard, à Argenteuil, 1849–1851.

PRIMARY EDITORS: None listed.

1850-1859

42. *Journal des magnétiseurs et des phrénologistes spiritualistes.*

TITLE VARIATIONS: None.

DATES OF PUBLICATION: Année 1, Numéro 1, July 16, 1850.

FREQUENCY: Weekly.

NUMBERING VARIATIONS: None.

PUBLISHER: **Versailles:** Imprimerie de Beau jeune, 1850.

PRIMARY EDITORS: None listed.

1851

43. *Archiv für die pragmatische Psychologie; oder die Seelenlehre in der Anwendung auf das Leben.*

TITLE VARIATIONS: None.

DATES OF PUBLICATION: Band 1–3, 1851–1853.

FREQUENCY: Annual.

NUMBERING VARIATIONS: None.

PUBLISHER: **Berlin:** Verlag von E. G. Mittler und Sohn, 1851–1853.

PRIMARY EDITOR: **Eduard Beneke,** 1851–1853.

For serial publications that began before 1850 and were still being published during the decade 1850 to 1859, *see also* entries 32, 38, 40, 41.

1853

44. *American Psychological Journal. Devoted Chiefly to the Elucidation of Mental Pathology, and the Medical Jurisprudence of Insanity.*

TITLE VARIATIONS: None.

DATES OF PUBLICATION: Volume 1, Number 1–6, January–November 1853.

FREQUENCY: Bimonthly.

NUMBERING VARIATIONS: None.

PUBLISHER: **Cincinnati, Ohio:** Cincinnati Retreat, Printed at the Hygeia Press, 1853.

PRIMARY EDITOR: **Edward Mead,** 1853.

45. *Asylum Journal of Mental Science.* [Published by authority of the Association of Medical Officers of Asylums and Hospitals for the Insane.]

TITLE VARIATIONS: Continued by *Journal of Mental Science* with Volume 4, 1857.

DATES OF PUBLICATION: Volume 1–3, November 1853–July 1857.

FREQUENCY: **Irregular,** Volume 1, 1853–1855. **Quarterly,** Volume 2–3, October 1855–July 1857.

NUMBERING VARIATIONS: Each issue is also assigned a whole number: Volume 1 contains Number 1–14; Volume 2, Number 15–18; Volume 3, Number 19–22.

PUBLISHER: **London:** Samuel Highley, 1853–1855. **Exeter:** W. & H. Pollard, 1856. **London:** Longman, Brown, Green & Longman, 1856–1857. **London:** Longman, Brown, Green, Longman & Roberts, 1857.

PRIMARY EDITOR: **John Charles Bucknill,** 1853–1857.

46. *Zentralblatt für Naturwissenschaften und Anthropologie.*

TITLE VARIATIONS: None.

DATES OF PUBLICATION: Jahrgang 1–2, 1853–1854.

FREQUENCY: Weekly (Jahrgang 1, 52 issues; Jahrgang 2, 26 issues).

NUMBERING VARIATIONS: None.

PUBLISHER: **Leipzig:** Avenarius & Mendelssohn, 1853–1854.

PRIMARY EDITOR: **G. T. Fechner,** 1853–1854.

1854

47. Almanach magnétique.

TITLE VARIATIONS: Continued by *Nouvel almanach magnétique* with Tome 5, 1858.

DATES OF PUBLICATION: Tome 1–4, 1854–1857.

FREQUENCY: Annual.

NUMBERING VARIATIONS: None.

PUBLISHER: **Paris:** Delarue, 1854–1857.

PRIMARY EDITOR: **Dr. Fluidus** [pseud.], 1854–1857.

48. Deutsche Gesellschaft für Psychiatrie und gerichtliche Psychologie. Correspondenzblatt.

TITLE VARIATIONS: Jahrgang 16–17, 1869–1870 as *Deutsche Gesellschaft für Psychiatrie und gerichtliche Psychologie. Archiv verbunden mit Correspondenzblatt.* Superseded by *Zentralblatt für Nervenheilkunde. Psychiatrie und gerichtliche Psychopathologie* with Jahrgang 1, 1878.

DATES OF PUBLICATION: Jahrgang 1–23, 1854–1877.

FREQUENCY: **Semimonthly,** Jahrgang 1–11, July 1854–1864 (24 numbers). **Irregular,** Jahrgang 12–15, 1865–1868 (21 numbers). **Monthly,** Jahrgang 18–23, 1872–1877 (12 numbers).

NUMBERING VARIATIONS: None.

PUBLISHER: **Neuwied, Germany:** Heuser, 1854. **Berlin:** Th. Enslin, 1855. **Neuwied:** Heuser, 1856–1876. **Neuwied:** Heuser's Verlag, 1877.

PRIMARY EDITORS: —— **Bergmann,** 1854–1858; —— **Mansfeld,** 1854–1858; —— **Eulenberg,** 1854–1876; **A. Erlenmeyer,** 1854–1877; —— **Otto,** 1859–1876; —— **Kelp,** 1859–1876.

49. Deutsche Gesellschaft für Psychiatrie und gerichtliche Psychologie. Verhandlungen.

TITLE VARIATIONS: None.

DATES OF PUBLICATION: 1854–1856.

FREQUENCY: Biennial, 1854–1856.

NUMBERING VARIATIONS: Meetings are numbered only by date. *See* Contents *below.*

PUBLISHER: **Neuwied, Germany:** Heuser, 1854–1856.

PRIMARY EDITOR: **A. Erlenmeyer,** 1854–1856.

CONTENTS:
    1854. Göttingen vom 18–24 September.
    1856. Qien vom 16–22 September.

1857

50. *Journal of Mental Science.* [Published by authority of the Association of Medical Officers of Asylums and Hospitals for the Insane.]

TITLE VARIATIONS: Continues *Asylum Journal of Mental Science.* Continued by *British Journal of Psychiatry* in 1963. Association was renamed Medico-Psychological Association of Great Britain and Ireland in 1865.

DATES OF PUBLICATION: Volume 4–96 +, 1857–1950 +.

FREQUENCY: Quarterly.

NUMBERING VARIATIONS: Each issue is also assigned a whole number: Volume 4–96 contain Number 23–405. Number 37 + also numbered New Series, Number 1 +. Multinumber issues in Volume 89.

PUBLISHER: **London:** Longman, Brown, Green, Longman & Roberts, 1857–1859. **London:** Longman, Green, Longman & Roberts, 1859–1861. **London:** John Churchill, 1861–1862. **London:** John Churchill & Sons, 1863–1870. **London:** J. and A. Churchill, 1871–1950 +.

PRIMARY EDITORS: **John Charles Bucknill,** 1857–1862; **Charles A. Lockhart Robertson,** 1862–1870; **Henry Maudsley,** 1863–1879; **John Sibbald,** 1871–1872; **Thomas S. Clouston,** 1873–1881; **Daniel Hack Tuke,** 1881–1894; **George H. Savage,** 1881–1894; **Henry Rayner,** 1895–1911; **Conolly Norman,** 1895–1907; **A. Reid Urquhart,** 1895–1911; **Edwin Goodall,** 1895–1898; **James Chambers,** 1900–1914; **John R. Lord,** 1900–1931; **Lewis C. Bruce,** 1912–1916; **Thomas Drapes,** 1912–1919; **Henry Devine,** 1915–1926; **G. Douglas McRae,** 1915–1943; **William R. Dawson,** 1920–1921; **Thomas Beaton,** 1926–1930; **Alexander Walk,** 1928–1950 +; **Maurice Hamblin Smith,** 1931–1936; **Gerald William Thomas Hunter Fleming,** 1931–1950 +; **Lionel S. Penrose,** 1937–1938; **P. K. McCowan,** 1945–1950 +.

51. *Psyche. Zeitschrift für die Kenntniss des menschlichen Seelen- und Geisteslebens.*

TITLE VARIATIONS: Band 1 subtitled *Populär-wissenschaftliche Zeitschrift für die Kenntniss des menschlichen Seelen- und Geisteslebens.*

DATES OF PUBLICATION: Band 1–5, 1857–1862. Suspended publication 1858.

FREQUENCY: Bimonthly.

NUMBERING VARIATIONS: None.

PUBLISHER: **Leipzig:** D. Wigand, 1857–1862.

PRIMARY EDITOR: **Ludwig Noack,** 1857–1862.

1858

52. *Deutsche Gesellschaft für Psychiatrie und gerichtliche Psychologie. Archiv.*

TITLE VARIATIONS: United with *Deutsche Gesellschaft für Psychiatrie und gerichtliche Psychologie. Correspondenzblatt*, 1869–1870.

DATES OF PUBLICATION: Band 1–10, Heft 1, 1858–1872. Suspended publication 1867–1868, united with *Correspondenzblatt* 1869–1870, suspended publication 1871.

FREQUENCY: **Quarterly,** Band 1, 1858. **Semiannual,** Band 2–6, 1859–1863. **Annual,** Band 7–9, 1865–1867. **Irregular,** Band 10, Heft 1, 1872.

NUMBERING VARIATIONS: Band 10, Heft 1, is a monograph. *See* Contents *below.*

PUBLISHER: **Neuwied, Germany:** Heuser's Verlag, 1858–1872.

PRIMARY EDITOR: **A. A. Erlenmeyer,** 1858–1872.

CONTENTS:
 Band 10, Heft 1. Reich, E. Über Ursachen und Verhüten der Nervosität und Geistesstörung bei den Frauen. 1872. 132 pp.

53. *Nouvel almanach magnétique.*

TITLE VARIATIONS: Continues *Almanach magnétique.*

DATES OF PUBLICATION: Tome 5–22, 1858–1875.

FREQUENCY: Annual.

NUMBERING VARIATIONS: None.

PUBLISHER: **Paris:** Delarue, 1858–1875.

PRIMARY EDITOR: **Dr. Fluidus** [pseud.], 1858–1875.

1859

54. *Zeitschrift für Völkerpsychologie und Sprachwissenschaft.*

TITLE VARIATIONS: Continued as *Verein für Volkskunde. Zeitschrift. Neue Folge der Zeitschrift für Völkerpsychologie und Sprachwissenschaft* with Neue Folge, Band 1, 1891.

DATES OF PUBLICATION: Band 1–20, 1859–1890.

FREQUENCY: **Bimonthly,** Band 1, 1859–1860. **Quarterly,** Band 2–20, 1860–1890.

NUMBERING VARIATIONS: None.

PUBLISHER: **Berlin:** Dümmler's Verlagshandel, 1859–1885. **Leipzig:** W. Friedrich, 1887–1889. **Berlin:** Asher und Co., 1890.

PRIMARY EDITORS: **M. Lazarus,** 1859–1890; **H. Steinthal,** 1859–1890; **Ulrich Jahn,** 1890.

1860-1869

1861

55. *Journal de médecine mentale.*

TITLE VARIATIONS: None.

DATES OF PUBLICATION: Tome 1–10, 1861–1870.

FREQUENCY: Monthly.

NUMBERING VARIATIONS: Multinumber issues present.

PUBLISHER: **Paris:** Victor Masson et Fils, 1861–1870.

PRIMARY EDITOR: **Louis J. F. Delasiauve,** 1861–1870.

56. *Medical Critic and Psychological Journal.*

TITLE VARIATIONS: Continues *Journal of Psychological Medicine and Mental Pathology.* Continued by *Journal of Psychological Medicine and Mental Pathology* with New Series, Volume 1, 1875.

DATES OF PUBLICATION: Volume 1–3, 1861–1863. Suspended publication 1864–1874.

FREQUENCY: Quarterly.

NUMBERING VARIATIONS: Also called *Journal of Psychological Medicine and Mental Pathology, Series 2.* Each issue is also assigned a whole number, Number 1–12.

PUBLISHER: **London:** John W. Davies, 1861–1863.

PRIMARY EDITOR: **Forbes Winslow,** 1861–1863.

For serial publications that began before 1860 and were still being published during the decade 1860 to 1869, *see also* entries 32, 38, 40, 48, 50, 51, 52, 53, 54.

1862

57. Magnétisme. Journal des sciences magnétiques, hypnotiques et occultes.

TITLE VARIATIONS: Subtitle varies.

DATES OF PUBLICATION: Année 1, Numéro 1–19, February–September 1862.

FREQUENCY: Three times monthly. (Irregular).

NUMBERING VARIATIONS: None.

PUBLISHER: **Paris:** Imprimerie Cosson et Cie, 1862.

PRIMARY EDITORS: None listed.

1865

58. Cocodès, journal des imbéciles.

TITLE VARIATIONS: None.

DATES OF PUBLICATION: Numéro 1–4, August 17–September 7, 1865.

FREQUENCY: Weekly.

NUMBERING VARIATIONS: None.

PUBLISHER: **Lyon:** C. Joillet, 1865.

PRIMARY EDITORS: **J. Laguaite,** 1865; **B. Roux,** 1865.

1867

59. Journal of Speculative Philosophy.

TITLE VARIATIONS: None.

DATES OF PUBLICATION: Volume 1–22, 1867–1893.

FREQUENCY: Quarterly.

NUMBERING VARIATIONS: Volume 22, Number 1/2 is a double issue dated January/April 1888. Volume 22, Number 3–4 not dated. Title page for volume dated 1893.

PUBLISHER: **St. Louis, Missouri:** George Knapp, 1867–1869. **St. Louis:** R. P. Studley, 1870–1875. **St. Louis:** Gardiner S. Bouton, 1876–1877. **St. Louis:** G. I. Jones, 1878–1879. **New York:** D. Appleton and Co., 1880–1893.

PRIMARY EDITOR: **William T. Harris,** 1867–1893.

60. Quarterly Journal of Psychological Medicine and Medical Jurisprudence.

TITLE VARIATIONS: Continued by *Journal of Psychological Medicine; A Quarterly Review of Diseases of the Nervous System, Medical Jurisprudence, and Anthropology* with Volume 4, 1870.

DATES OF PUBLICATION: Volume 1–3, 1867–1869.

FREQUENCY: Quarterly.

NUMBERING VARIATIONS: Volume 1 has only two issues, July and October 1867. Volume 2 and 3 numbers are issued January, April, July and October 1868–1869.

PUBLISHER: **New York:** A. Simpson & Co., 1867. **New York:** D. Appleton & Co., 1868–1869.

PRIMARY EDITOR: **William A. Hammond,** 1867–1869.

61. Vierteljahrsschrift für Psychiatrie in ihren Beziehungen zur Morphologie und Pathologie des Central-Nervensystems, der physiologischen Psychologie, Statistik und gerichtlichen Medicin.

TITLE VARIATIONS: None.

DATES OF PUBLICATION: Jahrgang 1–2, 1867–1868.

FREQUENCY: Quarterly.

NUMBERING VARIATIONS: None.

PUBLISHER: **Neuwied, Germany:** Heuser's Verlag, 1867–1868.

PRIMARY EDITORS: **Max Leidesdorf,** 1867–1868; **Theodor Meynert,** 1867–1868.

1869

62. Revista espiritista. Periódico de estudios psicológicos.

TITLE VARIATIONS: None.

DATES OF PUBLICATION: Años 1–10, 1869–1878.

FREQUENCY: Monthly.

NUMBERING VARIATIONS: None.

PUBLISHER: **Barcelona:** Publisher unknown, 1869–1878.

PRIMARY EDITORS: None listed.

NOTE: Information on this title is from serials holdings of the National Library in Madrid.

1870-1879

63. *Journal of Psychological Medicine; A Quarterly Review of Diseases of the Nervous System, Medical Jurisprudence, and Anthropology.*

TITLE VARIATIONS: Continues *Quarterly Journal of Psychological Medicine and Medical Jurisprudence.* Continued by *Psychological and Medico-legal Journal* with New Series, Volume 1, July 1874.

DATES OF PUBLICATION: Volume 4–6, 1870–1872.

FREQUENCY: Quarterly.

NUMBERING VARIATIONS: None.

PUBLISHER: **New York:** D. Appleton & Co., 1870–1872.

PRIMARY EDITOR: **William A. Hammond,** 1870–1872.

1871

64. *Psychiatrisches Centralblatt.* [Organ of the Verein für Psychiatrie und forensische Psychologie in Wien.]

TITLE VARIATIONS: Superseded by *Jahrbücher für Psychiatrie und Neurologie* in 1879.

DATES OF PUBLICATION: Jahrgang 1–8, January 1871–1878.

FREQUENCY: Monthly.

NUMBERING VARIATIONS: Multinumber issues present.

PUBLISHER: **Vienna:** Wilhelm Braumüller, 1871–1878.

PRIMARY EDITORS: **H. Beer,** 1871–1876; **Max Gaustler,** 1871–1876; **M. Leidesdorf,** 1871–1876; **Theodor Meynert,** 1871–1878; **Mor. Gauster,** 1877–1878.

For serial publications that began before 1870 and were still being published during the decade 1870 to 1879, *see also* entries 32, 48, 50, 52, 53, 54, 55, 59, 62.

1873

65. Société de médecine mentale de Belgique. Bulletin.

TITLE VARIATIONS: Society also called Société de médecine mentale de Gand. Merges into *Journal de neurologie et de psychiatrie* which later becomes *Journal belge de neurologie et de psychiatrie.*

DATES OF PUBLICATION: Numero 1–194/195, 1873–October/December 1922. Suspended publication July 1914–July 1919.

FREQUENCY: **Biannual,** 1873–1878. **Triannual,** 1879. **Quarterly,** 1880–1902. **Bimonthly,** 1903–1922 (except 1904 and 1910 when only 5 issues appeared).

NUMBERING VARIATIONS: Multinumber issues present.

PUBLISHER: **Ghent:** L. Hebbelynck, imprimeur de la Société de médecine, 1873–1874. **Ghent** and **Leipzig:** Librairie Clemm, 1875–1890. **Ghent** and **Leipzig:** H. Engelcke, Libraire, 1890–1899. **Brussels:** H. Lamertin, 1900–1922(?).

PRIMARY EDITORS: None listed.

1874

66. Chicago Journal of Nervous and Mental Disease.

TITLE VARIATIONS: Continued by *Journal of Nervous and Mental Disease* with Volume 3, 1876.

DATES OF PUBLICATION: Volume 1–2, 1874–1875.

FREQUENCY: Quarterly.

NUMBERING VARIATIONS: None.

PUBLISHER: **Chicago:** 57 Washington Street (by the Editor), 1874–1875.

PRIMARY EDITORS: **J. S. Jewell,** 1874–1875; **H. M. Bannister,** 1874–1875.

67. Psychische Studien. Monatliche Zeitschrift vorzüglich der Untersuchung der wenig bekannten Phänomene des Seelenlebens gewidmet.

TITLE VARIATIONS: Continued by *Zeitschrift für Parapsychologie* with Jahrgang 53, 1926.

DATES OF PUBLICATION: Jahrgang 1–52, 1874–1925.

FREQUENCY: Monthly.

NUMBERING VARIATIONS: Jahrgang 26–52 also called Neue Folge, Jahrgang 1–27.

PUBLISHER: **Leipzig:** O. Mutze, 1874–1925.

PRIMARY EDITORS: **Alex. Aksakow,** 1874–1898; **Friedrich Maier,** 1899–1920; **Paul Sünner,** 1921–1925.

68. *Psychological and Medico-legal Journal.*

TITLE VARIATIONS: Continues *Journal of Psychological Medicine*. Continued by *American Psychological Journal (New York)* with Volume 3, November 1875.

DATES OF PUBLICATION: New Series, Volume 1–2, July 1874–June 1875.

FREQUENCY: Monthly.

NUMBERING VARIATIONS: None.

PUBLISHER: **New York:** F. W. Christern, July 1874–December 1874. **New York:** McDivitt, Campbell & Co., January 1875–June 1875.

PRIMARY EDITORS: **William A. Hammond,** 1874–1875; **T.M.B. Cross,** 1874–1875; **Allan McLane Hamilton,** 1875.

1875

69. *American Psychological Journal (New York).*

TITLE VARIATIONS: None. Continues *Psychological and Medico-legal Journal*.

DATES OF PUBLICATION: Volume 3, Number 1–3, November 1875–May 1876.

FREQUENCY: Quarterly.

NUMBERING VARIATIONS: None.

PUBLISHER: **New York:** McDivitt, Campbell and Co., 1875–1876.

PRIMARY EDITORS: **Allan McLane Hamilton,** 1875–1876; **Roberts Bartholow,** 1875–1876; **F. T. Miles,** 1875–1876; **Walter Hay,** 1875–1876; **E. G. Janeway,** 1875–1876; **J. K. Bauduy,** 1875–1876; **J.W.S. Arnold,** 1875–1876; **William B. Hazard,** 1875–1876; **Wharton Sinkler,** 1875–1876; **T. A. McBride,** 1875–1876; **A. E. MacDonald,** 1876; **E. Bierstadt,** 1876.

70. *Journal of Psychological Medicine and Mental Pathology. New Series.*

TITLE VARIATIONS: Continues *Medical Critic and Psychological Journal*.

DATES OF PUBLICATION: New Series, Volume 1–8, April 1875–October 1883.

FREQUENCY: Semiannual.

NUMBERING VARIATIONS: Also called *Journal of Psychological Medicine and Mental Pathology. Series 3*.

PUBLISHER: **London:** Smith, Elder, Co., 1875. **London:** Bailliere, Tindall & Cox, 1876–1883.

PRIMARY EDITOR: **Lyttleton S. Forbes Winslow,** 1875–1883.

71. *Psychological Society of Great Britain. Proceedings.*

TITLE VARIATIONS: None.

DATES OF PUBLICATION: 1st, 1875–1879.

FREQUENCY: Irregular. *See* Contents *below.*

NUMBERING VARIATIONS: None.

PUBLISHER: **London:** Privately printed, 1880.

PRIMARY EDITORS: None listed.

CONTENTS:
1st. PROCEEDINGS OF THE PSYCHOLOGICAL SOCIETY OF GREAT BRITAIN. 1875–1879. 1880. 296 pp.

1876

72. *Association of Medical Officers of American Institutions for Idiotic and Feeble-Minded Persons. Proceedings of the Annual Meetings.*

TITLE VARIATIONS: Continued by *American Association for the Study of the Feeble-Minded. Proceedings and Addresses* with Number 42, 1918.

DATES OF PUBLICATION: Number 1–41, 1876–1917.

FREQUENCY: Annual.

NUMBERING VARIATIONS: Number 20–41, 1896–1917 published in *Journal of Psycho-Asthenics.*

PUBLISHER: **Philadelphia:** J. B. Lippincott and Company, for the Association, 1876–1895.

PRIMARY EDITORS: Executive Committee of the Association acts as a publishing committee: **Hervey B. Wilbur,** 1876; **Edouard O. Seguin,** 1876; **Isaac N. Kerlin,** 1876; **Charles T. Wilbur,** 1878; **G. A. Doren,** 1878; **H. M. Knight,** 1879; **George Brown,** 1879; **J.Q.A. Stewart,** 1880; **George G. Tarbell,** 1880; **O. W. Archibald,** 1882; **J. C. Carson,** 1886; **George H. Knight,** 1886; **William B. Fish,** 1887; **A. C. Rogers,** 1888; **J. T. Armstrong,** 1889; **Walter E. Fernald,** 1890; **A. E. Osborne,** 1892; **Grace F. Barnes,** 1892; **S. Olin Garrison,** 1893; **A. W. Wilmarth,** 1894; **S. J. Fort,** 1894, **M. W. Barr,** 1895. *Note:* 18th Session, 1894, appointed first Official Reporter and Editor: **Isabel C. Barrows.** None listed, 1896–1917.

73. *Journal of Nervous and Mental Disease; An Educational Journal of Neuropsychiatry.* [Official Organ of the American Neurological Association.]

TITLE VARIATIONS: Subtitle varies. Continues *Chicago Journal of Nervous and Mental Disease.*

DATES OF PUBLICATION: Volume 3–112+, 1876–1950+.

FREQUENCY: **Quarterly,** Volume 3–12, 1876–1885. **Monthly,** Volume 13–112+, 1886–1950+.

NUMBERING VARIATIONS: Volume 3, 1876, also called New Series, Volume 1, 1876. Each issue is also assigned a whole number, Number 1–828.

PUBLISHER: **Chicago:** [The Editor,] 57 Washington Street, 1876. **Chicago:** [The Editor,] 70 Monroe Street; and Branch Office, **New York:** G. P. Putnam's Sons, 1877–1880. **New York:** G. P. Putnam's Sons, Journal of Nervous and Mental Disease, 1881–1889. **New York:** Journal of Nervous and Mental Disease, 25 West 45th Street [Editor's address], 1890–1900. **New York:** Journal of Nervous and Mental Disease, 48 Hamilton Terrace [Editor's address], 1901. **New York:** Journal of Nervous and Mental Disease, 231 West 71st Street [Editor's address], 1902. **New York:** Journal of Nervous and Mental Disease, Managing Editor and Publisher, Smith Ely Jelliffe, 64 West 56th Street, 1903–1918. **New York:** Journal of Nervous and Mental Disease, 64 West 56th Street, 1919–1945. **New York:** Coolidge Foundation, Publishers, 70 Pine Street, 1945–1950+.

PRIMARY EDITORS: **J. S. Jewell,** 1876–1885; **H. M. Bannister,** 1876–1885; **William A. Hammond,** 1876–1885; **S. Weir Mitchell,** 1876–1881; **E. H. Clarke,** 1876–1877; **Meredith Clymer,** 1878–1885; **William J. Morton,** 1882–1885; **Eduard O. Seguin,** 1882–1885; **Isaac Ott,** 1882–1885; **B. Sachs,** 1885–1889, 1897–1898; **J. G. Kiernan,** 1885; **Charles K. Mills,** 1885, 1897–1898; **Charles L. Dana,** 1897–1898; **Charles Henry Brown,** 1890–1901; **F. X. Dercum,** 1897–1898; **Philip Coombs Knapp,** 1897; **Jas. J. Putnam,** 1897–1898; **M. Allen Starr,** 1897–1898; **Philip Meirowitz,** 1897; **William G. Spiller,** 1897–1918; **Hugh T. Patrick,** 1898; **Smith Ely Jelliffe,** 1899–1944; **L. Pierce Clark,** 1902; **Stewart Paton,** 1903–1906; **E. W. Taylor,** 1906–1915; **W. P. Spratling,** 1907–1910; **E. E. Southard,** 1911–1915; **Nolan D. C. Lewis,** 1945–1950+.

EDITORIAL BOARD: Charles L. Dana, 1899–1918; F. X. Dercum, 1899–1915; Charles K. Mills, 1899–1918; Hugh T. Patrick, 1899–1918; Jas. J. Putnam, 1899–1918; B. Sachs, 1899–1915; M. Allen Starr, 1899–1918; William Osler, 1902–1918; Wharton Sinkler, 1902–1910; Frederick Peterson, 1902–1918; Adolf Meyer, 1904–1918; William A. White, 1904–1918; Lewellys E. Barker, 1911–1918; E. W. Taylor, 1916–1918; Pearce Bailey, 1916–1918; E. E. Southard, 1916–1918; Harvey Cushing, 1916–1918. None listed, 1919+.

74. *Mind. A Quarterly Review of Psychology and Philosophy.* [Issued by the Mind Association.]

TITLE VARIATIONS: None.

DATES OF PUBLICATION: Volume 1–16, 1876–1891; New Series, Volume 1–59+, 1892–1950+.

FREQUENCY: Quarterly.

NUMBERING VARIATIONS: Each issue in Volume 1–16 is also assigned a whole number, Number 1–64. Each issue in New Series, Volume 1–59+ is also assigned a whole number, Number 1–236+.

PUBLISHER: **London** and **Edinburgh:** Williams and Norgate, 1876–1891. **Wiesbaden:** Printed in Germany, Lessing-Druckerei, 1892–1898. **London** and **Edinburgh:** Williams and Norgate, 1899–1906. **London:** Macmillan & Co., Limited, 1907–1947. **Edinburgh:** T. Nelson & Sons Ltd., 1948–1950+.

1878

75. *Congrès international de médecine mentale. Comptes rendus.*

TITLE VARIATIONS: None.

DATES OF PUBLICATION: $1^{er} - 2^e$, 1878–1889.

FREQUENCY: Irregular.

NUMBERING VARIATIONS: None.

PUBLISHER: **Paris:** Imprimerie nationale, 1880. **Paris:** G. Masson, 1890.

PRIMARY EDITORS: *See* Contents *below.*

CONTENTS:

1er. COMPTES RENDUS STÉNOGRAPHIQUES; PUBLIÉS SOUS LES AUSPICES DU COMITÉ CENTRAL DES CONGRÈS ET CONFÉRENCES, ET LA DIRECTION DE CH. THIRION, SECRÉTAIRE DU COMITÉ. 1878. 344 pp.

2e. COMPTES RENDUS. Publiés par A. Ritti. 1889. 602 pp.

76. *Zentralblatt für Nervenheilkunde, Psychiatrie und gerichtliche Psychopathologie.*

TITLE VARIATIONS: Supersedes *Deutsche Gesellschaft für Psychiatrie und gerichtliche Psychologie. Correspondenzblatt.* Continued by *Zentralblatt für Nervenheilkunde und Psychiatrie. Internationale Monatsschrift für die gesamte Neurologie in Wissenschaft und Praxis mit besonderer Berücksichtigung der Degenerations-Anthropologie* with Jahrgang 13, April 1890.

DATES OF PUBLICATION: Jahrgang 1–12, 1878–1889. Suspended publication January–March 1890.

FREQUENCY: **Monthly** (12 Hefte), Jahrgang 1, 1878. **Biweekly** (26 Hefte), Jahrgang 2–5, 1879–1882. **Semimonthly** (24 Hefte), Jahrgang 6–12, 1883–1889.

NUMBERING VARIATIONS: None.

PUBLISHER: **Leipzig:** G. Böhme, 1878–1882. **Leipzig:** Thomas, 1883–1889.

PRIMARY EDITOR: **Albr. Erlenmeyer,** 1878–1889.

77. *Chaine magnétique.* [Organ of the Sociétés magnétiques de France et de l'étranger.]

TITLE VARIATIONS: None.

DATES OF PUBLICATION: Année 1–18, July 1879–October 1896.

FREQUENCY: Monthly.

NUMBERING VARIATIONS: Each issue is also assigned a whole number, Numéro 1–208.

PUBLISHER: **Paris:** G. Baillière, 1879–1896.

PRIMARY EDITOR: **J. Dupotet,** 1879–1881. None listed, 1882–1896.

1880-1889

1881

78. Encéphale; journal des maladies mentales et nerveuses.

TITLE VARIATIONS: Continued by *Encéphale; journal des maladies mentales et nerveuses et de physiologie cérébrale* with Année 9, 1889.

DATE OF PUBLICATION: Année 1–8, Numéro 6, March 1881–November 1888.

FREQUENCY: Bimonthly.

NUMBERING VARIATIONS: None.

PUBLISHER: **Paris:** G. Masson, éditeur, Libraire de l'Académie de médecine, 1881–1882. **Paris:** Librairie J. B. Bailliere et Fils, 1883–1888.

PRIMARY EDITORS: **B. Ball**, 1881–1888; **J. Luys**, 1881–1888.

1882

79. Society for Psychical Research. Proceedings.

TITLE VARIATIONS: None.

DATES OF PUBLICATION: Volume 1–48, 1882–July 1950+.

FREQUENCY: Irregular.

NUMBERING VARIATIONS: Each volume is made up of reports of committees of the Society. Each issue is also assigned a whole number, Part 1–178+. Number of parts per volume varies.

PUBLISHER: **London:** Trübner and Company, 1882–1889. **London:** Kegan Paul, Trench, Trübner and Co., 1889–1901. **London:** R. Brimley Johnson, 1901–1904. **Glasgow:** Robert Maclehose and Co., 1905–1909. **Glasgow:** Printed for the Society by Robert Maclehose and Co., University Press, 1909–1929. **London:** Society for Psychical Research, 1929–1950+.

For serial publications that began before 1880 and were still being published during the decade 1880 to 1890, *see also* entries 32, 50, 54, 59, 65, 67, 70, 72, 73, 74, 75, 76, 77.

PRIMARY EDITORS: No regular editor was appointed when the Society was founded. Editorial work was done by the Literary Committee. **Henry Sidgwick,** 1888–1897; **Richard Hodgson,** 1897–1899; **Alice Johnson,** 1899–1916; **R.A.H. Bickford-Smith,** 1907; **Helen de G.** Verrall-Salter, 1917–1946, 1949–1950+; **G.N.M. Tyrrell,** 1947; **D. J. West,** 1948.

1883

80. *American Psychological Journal (Philadelphia).* [Issued by the National Association for the Protection of the Insane and Prevention of Insanity.]

TITLE VARIATIONS: None.

DATES OF PUBLICATION: Volume 1–2, Number 3, April 1883–October 1884.

FREQUENCY: Quarterly.

NUMBERING VARIATIONS: None.

PUBLISHER: **Philadelphia:** P. Blakiston, Son & Company, 1883–1884.

PRIMARY EDITORS: **Joseph Parrish,** 1883–1884; **C. L. Dana,** 1883–1884; Alice **Bennett,** 1884; **H. M. Bannister,** 1883–1884; **J. C. Shaw,** 1883–1884; **A. A. Chevaillier,** 1883; **W. W. Godding,** 1883–1884.

81. *Arkhiv psikhiatrii, nevrologii i sudebnoi psikhopatologii.*

TITLE VARIATIONS: None.

DATES OF PUBLICATION: Tom 1–32, 1883–1898/1899.

FREQUENCY: **Quarterly,** 1883. **Bimonthly,** 1884–1899.

NUMBERING VARIATIONS: Each year contains two full volumes, except for the following: 1887, which contains Tom 9, 10, and 11, Vypusk 1; 1888, which contains Tom 11, Vypusk 2–3 and Tom 12; 1898, which contains Tom 31 and 32, Vypusk 1; and 1899, which contains Tom 32, Vypusk 2–3. Multinumber issues present.

PUBLISHER: **Kharkov:** Kontora redaktsii Ekaterinoslavskaia ul., No. 8, Moskovskaia ul., No. 7. Tipografiia gazety "Iuzhnyi krai", 1883. **Kharkov:** Kontora redaktsii Rybnaia ul., No. 27. Tipografiia M. Zil'berberga, 1883–1885. **Kharkov:** Kontora redaktsii Salovaia ul., No. 2. Tipografiia M. Zil'berberga, 1885–1887. **Kharkov:** Kontora redaktsii Mikhailovskaia ploshchad No. 18. Tipografiia M. Zil'berberga, 1887–1889. **Kharkov:** Kontora redaktsii Sumskaia ul. d. Dmitrieva. Tipografiia M. Zil'berberga, 1889–1890. **Kharkov:** Kontora redaktsii Novo-chernyshevskaia ul., No. 1 Tipografiia M. Zil'berberga, 1890. **Kharkov:** Kontora redaktsii Novo-chernyshevskaia ul., No. 1 Tipografiia I. M. Varshavchika, 1891–1892. **Kharkov:** Kontora redaktsii Novo-chernyshevskaia ul., No. 1. Tipografiia M. Zil'berberga, 1893. **Kharkov:** Kontora redaktsii Novo-chernyshevskaia ul., No. 1. Tipografiia Adol'fa Dappe, 1894–1895. **Warsaw:** Tipografiia varshavskago uchebnago okruga, 1895. **Warsaw:** Varshavskaia tipografiia i litografiia, 1895–1897. **St. Petersburg:** Tipografiia Kh. Braude, 1897. **St. Petersburg:** Tipografiia M. Akinfieva i I. Leont'eva, 1898–1898/1899.

PRIMARY EDITORS: **P. I. Kovalevskii,** 1883–1898/1899. **L. I. Popov,** 1896–1898/1899.

82. *Philosophische Studien.*

TITLE VARIATIONS: Superseded by *Archiv für die gesamte Psychologie* with Band 1, April 1903.

DATES OF PUBLICATION: Band 1–20, 1883–1903.

FREQUENCY: **Irregular.** Band 1, 1883; Band 2, 1885; Band 3, 1886; Band 4, 1888; Band 5, 1889; Band 6, 1891; Band 7, 1892; Band 8, 1893; Band 9, 1894; Band 10, 1894; Band 11, 1895; Band 12, 1896; Band 13, 1898; Band 14, 1898; Band 15, 1900; Band 16, 1900; Band 17, 1901; Band 18, 1903; Band 19, 1902; Band 20, 1902.

NUMBERING VARIATIONS: Band 19–20, issued before Band 18. Band 19 and 20 contain: FESTSCHRIFT. WILHELM WUNDT ZUM SIEBZIGSTEN GEBURTSTAGE ÜBERREICHT VON SEINEN SCHÜLERN. Teil I, 1902; Teil II, 1902.

PUBLISHER: **Leipzig:** Wilhelm Engelmann, 1883–1903.

PRIMARY EDITOR: **Wilhelm Wundt,** 1883–1903.

1884

83. *Buen deseo; Periódico mensual de estudios psicológicos.*

TITLE VARIATIONS: None.

DATES OF PUBLICATION: Tomo 1–2, Número 9, May 1884–January 15, 1886.

FREQUENCY: Monthly.

NUMBERING VARIATIONS: None.

PUBLISHER: **Matanzas, Cuba:** Centro Caridad, 1884–1886.

PRIMARY EDITORS: None listed (initials used in all issues are A. M. and G. G.).

84. *Society for Psychical Research. Journal.*

TITLE VARIATIONS: None.

DATES OF PUBLICATION: Volume 1–35 +, 1884/1885–1949/1950 +.

FREQUENCY: **Monthly,** Volume 1–2, 1884–1886. **Monthly,** except August–September, Volume 3–30, 1887–1939. **Bimonthly,** except July–August, Volume 31–33, 1939–1946. **Irregular,** except August, Volume 34, 1947–1948. **Bimonthly,** Volume 35 +, 1949/1950 +.

NUMBERING VARIATIONS: Each issue is also assigned a whole number, Number 1–661.

PUBLISHER: **London:** The Society's Rooms, 1884–1950+.

PRIMARY EDITORS: **William F. Barrett,** 1884–1885; **Henry Sidgwick,** 1885–1886, 1888–1897; **Edmund Gurney,** 1886–1888; **Eleanor Mildred Sidgwick,** 1888–1897; **Alice Johnson,** 1899–1907, 1908–1916; **Richard Hodgson,** 1897–1899; **R.A.H. Bickford-Smith,** 1907; **Theodore Besterman,** 1929–1934; **Helen de G. Verrall-(Salter),** 1917–1929; **Nea Walker,** 1934–1938; **Kenneth Richmond,** 1938–1945; **W. H. Salter,** 1945–1947; **T. Bosanquet,** 1947–1948; **Edward Osborn,** 1949–1950+.

1885

85. *Heath's Pedagogical Library.*

TITLE VARIATIONS: None.

DATES OF PUBLICATION: Number 1–34, 1885–1910.

FREQUENCY: Irregular. *See* Contents *below.*

NUMBERING VARIATIONS: This series was issued unnumbered before, between and after the above dates. The dates given below, therefore, are not neccessarily dates of first publication.

PUBLISHER: **Boston:** D. C. Heath and Company, 1885–1910.

PRIMARY EDITORS: None listed.

CONTENTS:

Number 1. Compayré, Gabriel. HISTORY OF PEDAGOGY. 1885. 598 pp.

Number 2. Compayré, Gabriel. LECTURES ON PEDAGOGY, THEORETICAL AND PRACTICAL. 1889. 491 pp.

Number 3. Compayré, Gabriel. PSYCHOLOGY APPLIED TO EDUCATION. 1896. 216 pp.

Number 4. Rousseau, Jean Jacques. EMILE; OR, CONCERNING EDUCATION. 1892. 157 pp.

Number 5. Peabody, Elizabeth Palmer. LECTURES IN THE TRAINING SCHOOLS FOR KINDERGARTNERS. 1906. 228 pp.

Number 6. Pestalozzi, Johann Heinrich. LEONARD AND GERTRUDE. 1901. 181 pp.

Number 7. Radestock, Paul. HABIT AND ITS IMPORTANCE IN EDUCATION. 1897. 117 pp.

Number 8. Rosmini-Serbati, Antonio. THE RULING PRINCIPLE OF METHOD APPLIED TO EDUCATION. 1903. 366 pp.

Number 9. Hall, G. Stanley. HINTS TOWARD A SELECT AND DESCRIPTIVE BIBLIOGRAPHY OF EDUCATION. 1893. 309 pp.

Number 10. Gill, John. SYSTEMS OF EDUCATION. 1903. 312 pp.

Number 11. De Garmo, Charles. ESSENTIALS OF METHOD. 1898. 136 pp.

Number 12. Malleson, W. I. NOTES ON THE EARLY TRAINING OF CHILDREN. 1898. 127 pp.

Number 13. White, A. D., W. F. Allen et al. METHODS OF TEACHING HISTORY. 1902. 391 pp.

Number 14. Newsholme, Arthur. SCHOOL HYGIENE. 1904. 143 pp.

Number 15. Lindner, Gustav Adolf. MANUAL OF EMPIRICAL PSYCHOLOGY AS AN INDUCTIVE SCIENCE. 1894. 274 pp.

Number 16. Lange, Karl. APPERCEPTION; A MONOGRAPH ON PSYCHOLOGY AND PEDAGOGY. 1898. 279 pp.

Number 17. Elliott, A. Marshall et al. METHODS OF TEACHING MODERN LANGUAGES. 1904. 217 pp.

Number 18. Felkin, Henry M. AN INTRODUCTION TO HERBART'S SCIENCE AND PRACTICE OF EDUCATION. 1900. 193 pp.

Number 19. Herbart, Johann Friedrich. SCIENCE OF EDUCATION: ITS GENERAL PRINCIPLES DEDUCED FROM ITS AIM AND THE AESTHETIC REVELATION OF THE WORLD. 1893. 268 pp.

Number 20. Froebel, Friedrich W. A. THE STUDENT'S FROEBEL; ADAPTED FROM DIE ERZIEHUNG DER MENSCHHEIT BY WILLIAM H. HERFORD. PART I. THEORY OF EDUCATION. 1896. 112 pp.

Number 21. Sanford, Edmund Clark. A LABORATORY COURSE IN PHYSIOLOGICAL PSYCHOLOGY. 1898. 449 pp.

Number 22. Tracy, Frederick. PSYCHOLOGY OF CHILDHOOD. 1901. 176 pp.

Number 23. Ufer, Christian. INTRODUCTION TO THE PEDAGOGY OF HERBART. 1894. 123 pp.

Number 24. Munroe, James Phinney. THE EDUCATIONAL IDEAL; AN OUTLINE OF ITS GROWTH IN MODERN TIMES. 1906. 262 pp.

Number 25. Lukens, Herman Tyson. THE CONNECTION BETWEEN THOUGHT AND MEMORY. 1896. 169 pp.

Number 26. Payne, William Morton (ed.) ENGLISH IN AMERICAN UNIVERSITIES. BY PROFESSORS IN THE ENGLISH DEPARTMENTS OF TWENTY REPRESENTATIVE INSTITUTIONS. 1895. 182 pp.

Number 27. Comenius, Johann Amos. COMENIUS' SCHOOL OF INFANCY. 1897. 99 pp.

Number 28. Russell, Elias Harlow. CHILD OBSERVATIONS. FIRST SERIES: IMITATION AND ALLIED ACTIVITIES. Compiled by Ellen M. Haskell. 1906. 267 pp.

Number 29. Lefevre, Arthur. NUMBER AND ITS ALGEBRA. 1896. 219 pp.

Number 30. Barnes, Mary Downing (Sheldon). STUDIES IN HISTORICAL METHOD. 1904. 144 pp.

Number 31. Adams, John. THE HERBARTIAN PSYCHOLOGY APPLIED TO EDUCATION. 1910. 284 pp.

Number 32. Ascham, Roger. THE SCHOOLMASTER. 1898. 317 pp.

Number 33. Thompson, D'Arcy Wentworth. DAY DREAMS OF A SCHOOLMASTER. 1906. 328 pp.

Number 34. Hollis, Andrew Phillip. THE CONTRIBUTION OF THE OSWEGO NORMAL SCHOOL TO EDUCATIONAL PROGRESS IN THE UNITED STATES. 1898. 128 pp.

86. *Société de psychologie physiologique. Bulletin.*

TITLE VARIATIONS: None.

DATES OF PUBLICATION. Tome 1–7, 1885–1891.

FREQUENCY; Annual.

NUMBERING VARIATIONS: None.

PUBLISHER: **Paris:** Ancienne librairie Germer Baillière et Cie, Félix Alcan, éditeur, 1886–1892.

PRIMARY EDITORS: None listed.

1886

87. *Archives de l'anthropologie criminelle et des sciences pénales.*

TITLE VARIATIONS: Continued by *Archives d'anthroplogie criminelle, de criminologie et de psychologie normale et pathologique* with Tome 8, 1893.

DATES OF PUBLICATION: Tome 1–7, 1886–1892.

FREQUENCY: Bimonthly.

NUMBERING VARIATIONS: None.

PUBLISHER: **Paris:** G. Masson, 1886–1892.

PRIMARY EDITORS: **Alexandre Lacassagne,** 1886–1892; **René Garraud,** 1886–1892; **Henry Coutagne,** 1886–1892; **Albert Bournet,** 1886–1892.

88. *Magnétisme. Revue générale des sciences physio-psychologiques.*

TITLE VARIATIONS: None.

DATES OF PUBLICATION: Numéro 1–18, February-October 1886.

FREQUENCY: Semimonthly.

NUMBERING VARIATIONS: None.

PUBLISHER: **Paris:** Imprimerie Schlaeber, 1886.

PRIMARY EDITOR: **A. [?] Donato,** 1886.

NOTE: Information on this entry is incomplete. The compilers were unable to examine this title.

89. *Revue de l'hypnotisme, expérimental & thérapeutique.*

TITLE VARIATIONS: Continued by *Revue de l'hypnotisme et de la psychologie physiologique* with Année 4, July 1889.

DATES OF PUBLICATION: Année 1–3, July 1886–June 1889.

FREQUENCY: Monthly.

NUMBERING VARIATIONS: None.

PUBLISHER: **Paris:** Bureau, 12 rue Vieille-du-Temple, 1886–1888. **Paris:** Émile Bouriot, 1888–1889.

PRIMARY EDITOR: **Edgar Bérillon,** 1886–1889.

1887

90. *American Journal of Psychology.*

TITLE VARIATIONS: None.

DATES OF PUBLICATION: Volume 1–63+, 1887–1950+.

FREQUENCY: Quarterly.

NUMBERING VARIATIONS: Irregular dates but all numbers present. Various articles also numbered in the following subseries: *Antioch College. Psychological Laboratory. Minor Studies;* or *Clark University. Psychological Laboratory. Minor Studies;* or *Cornell University. Psychological Laboratory. Minor Studies;* or *Harvard University. Psychological Laboratory. Minor Studies;* or *McGill University. Psychological Laboratory. Minor Studies;* or *Michigan. University. Psychological Laboratory. Studies;* or *Nebraska. University. Psychological Laboratory. Minor Studies;* or *Northwestern University. Psychological Laboratory. Minor Studies;* or *Pittsburgh. University. Psychological Laboratory. Minor Studies;* or *Princeton University. Psychological Laboratory. Minor Studies;* or *Stanford University. Psychological Laboratory. Minor Studies;* or *Vassar College. Psychological Laboratory. Studies;* or *Wellesley College. Psychological Laboratory. Minor Studies;* or *William Smith and Hobart Colleges. Psychological Laboratory. Minor Studies;* or *Wisconsin. University. Psychological Laboratory. Studies;* or *Yale University. Psychological Laboratory. Minor Studies.* Volume 14, Number 3–4, July-October, 1903 also titled: COMMEMORATIVE NUMBER ... TO GRANVILLE STANLEY HALL ... IN COMMEMORATION OF THE 25TH ANNIVERSARY OF HIS ATTAINMENT OF THE DOCTORATE IN PHILOSOPHY. Edited by E. C. Sanford and E. B. Titchener. Volume 39, Number 1–4, December, 1927 also titled: WASHBURN COMMEMORATIVE VOLUME. Edited by K. Dallenbach, M. Bentley and E. G. Boring. Volume 50, Number 1–4, November, 1937 also titled: GOLDEN JUBILEE VOLUME, 1887–1937. Edited by Karl M. Dallenbach. Volume 38, Number 1, dated January 1926 instead of 1927.

PUBLISHER: **Baltimore, Maryland:** N. Murray, 1887–1888. **Worcester, Massachusetts:** E. C. Sanford, 1888–1891. **Worcester:** J. H. Orpha, 1891–1895. **Worcester:** Clark University, J. H. Orpha, 1895–1898. **Worcester:** Clark University, Louis N. Wilson, Publisher, 1898–1904. **Worcester:** Clark University, Florence Chandler, Publisher, 1905–1911. **Albany, New York:** Florence Chandler, Publisher, 1912–1920. **Ithaca, New York:** Morrill Hall, Cornell University, 1921–1948. **Austin, Texas:** Sutton Hall, University of Texas, Sept. 1948–1950+.

PRIMARY EDITORS: **G. Stanley Hall,** 1887–1920; **Edmund Clark Sanford,**

1895–1920; **Edward Bradford Titchener,** 1895–1925. **John Wallace Baird,** 1911–1918; **Margaret F. Washburn,** 1926–1939; **Karl M. Dallenbach,** 1926–1950+; **Madison Bentley,** 1926–1950+; **Edwin G. Boring,** 1926–1946.

EDITORIAL BOARD: F. Angell, 1895–1925; H. Beaunis, 1895–1920; J. Delboeuf, 1895–1896; A. Kirschmann, 1895–1915; O. Külpe, 1895–1915; A. D. Waller, 1895–1920; H. K. Wolfe, 1895–1897; V. Henri, 1896–1902; C. F. Hodge, 1896–1920; G. Störring, 1896–1902; A. F. Chamberlain, 1897–1913; W. B. Pillsbury, 1897–1950; M. F. Washburn, 1903–1925; M. Bentley, 1903–1925; G. Stanley Hall, 1921–1924; Edmund C. Sanford, 1921–1924; Edwin G. Boring, 1921–1925, 1947–1950; H. P. Weld, 1921–1925; Karl M. Dallenbach, 1921–1925; E. S. Robinson, 1925–1937; J. P. Nafe, 1925–1939; L. B. Hoisington, 1925; C. A. Ruckmick, 1925–1938; Raymond Dodge, 1926–1938; S. W. Fernberger, 1926–1950; R. M. Ogden, 1926–1950; Joseph Peterson, 1926–1935; A. T. Poffenberger, 1926–1939; G. M. Stratton, 1926–1939; J. P. Guilford, 1940–1950; Harry Helson, 1940–1950; E. R. Hilgard, 1940–1950; W. S. Hunter, 1940–1950; J. G. Jenkins, 1940–1947; H. M. Johnson, 1940–1950; G. L. Kreezer, 1940–1950; D. G. Marquis, 1940–1950; J. A. McGeoch, 1940–1942.

91. *Revue des sciences hypnotiques.*

TITLE VARIATIONS: None.

DATES OF PUBLICATION: Volume 1, 1887–1888.

FREQUENCY: Monthly.

NUMBERING VARIATIONS: None.

PUBLISHER: **Paris:** Imprimerie Mersch, librairie Masson, 1887–1888.

PRIMARY EDITOR: **P. Robert,** 1887–1888.

1888

92. *Berlin. Gesellschaft für Experimental-Psychologie. Schriften.*

TITLE VARIATIONS: None.

DATES OF PUBLICATION: Stück 1–4, December 1888–1890.

FREQUENCY: *See* Contents *below.*

NUMBERING VARIATIONS: Stück 2/3 combined number. There are two issues numbered as Stück 1, one dated 1888, the other 1890.

PUBLISHER: **Leipzig:** Ernst Günthers Verlag, [1888]–1890.

PRIMARY EDITORS: None listed.

CONTENTS:
    Stück 1. Kiesewetter, Karl. ZUR GESCHICHTE DES MODERNEN OCCULTISMUS. December 1888. n.p.

Stück 1. Dessoir, Max. DAS DOPPEL-ICH. 1890. 42 pp.
Stück 2/3. Bastian, Adolf. ÜBER PSYCHISCHE BEOBACHTUNGEN BEI NATUR-VÖLKERN; and Hellwald, Friedrich von. DIE MAGIKER INDIENS. 1890. 32 pp.
Stück 4. Bentivegni, Adolf von. DIE HYPNOSE UND IHRE ZIVILRECHTLICHE BEDEUTUNG. 1890. 66 pp.

93. *Moscow. Universitet. Psikhologischeskoe obshchestvo. Trudy.*

TITLE VARIATIONS: Also called *Moskovskoe psikhologicheskoe obshchestvo. Trudy.*

DATES OF PUBLICATION: Vypusk 1–4, 1888–1890.

FREQUENCY: Irregular. *See* Contents *below.*

NUMBERING VARIATIONS: None.

PUBLISHER: **Moscow:** A. Gattsuka, 1888–1890.

PRIMARY EDITOR: **N. Ia. Grot,** 1888–1890.

CONTENTS:
Vypusk 1. Artur' Shopengauer'. OCHERKI EGO ZHIZNI I UCHENIIA. 1888. 240 pp.
Vypusk 2. Kant', Immanuil'. PROLEGOMENY KO VSIAKOI BUDUSHCHEI ME-TAFIZIKE MOGUSHCH EI VOZNIKNUT'V'SMYSLE NAUKI. Translated by Vladimir So-lov'ev. 1889. 367 pp.
Vypusk 3. O SVOBODE VOLI. OPYTY POSTANOVKI I RESHENIIA VOPROSA. 1889. 960 pp.
Vypusk 4. Leibnits, G. V. IZBRANNIIA FILOSOFSKIIA SOCHINENIIA. Trans-lated under editorship of V. P. Preobrazhenski. 1890. 363 pp.

1889

94. *Congrès international de l'hypnotisme expérimental et thérapeutique. Comptes rendus.*

TITLE VARIATIONS: None.

DATES OF PUBLICATION: 1ᵉ¹–2ᵉ, 1889–1900.

FREQUENCY: Irregular. *See* Contents *below.*

NUMBERING VARIATIONS: None.

PUBLISHER: **Paris:** O. Doin, 1889. **Paris:** Revue de l'hypnotisme, 1902.

PRIMARY EDITORS: *See* Contents *below.*

CONTENTS:
1ᵉʳ. Paris, 1889. COMPTES RENDUS. PUBLIÉS SOUS LA DIRECTION DE EDGAR BÉRILLON. 367 pp.
2ᵉ. Paris, 1900. COMPTES RENDUS. PUBLIÉS PAR LES SOINS DE EDGAR BÉRILLON ET DE PAUL FAREZ. 320 pp.

95. Encéphale; journal des maladies mentales et nerveuses et de physiologie cérébrale.

TITLE VARIATIONS: Continues *Encéphale; journal des maladies mentales et nerveuses.*

DATES OF PUBLICATION: Année 9, Numéro 1, January/February 1889.

FREQUENCY: Bimonthly.

NUMBERING VARIATIONS: None.

PUBLISHER: **Paris:** 130, Boulevard du Mont-Parnasse, 1889.

PRIMARY EDITORS. **B. Ball,** 1889; **J. Luys,** 1889; **Ch. Lerebours,** 1889.

96. International Congress of Psychology. Proceedings and Papers.

TITLE VARIATIONS: *See* Contents *below.*

DATES OF PUBLICATION: Number 1–12+, 1889–1948. Congresses not held 1910–1922 and 1938–1947.

FREQUENCY: Irregular. *See* Contents *below.*

NUMBERING VARIATIONS: None.

PUBLISHER: *See* Contents *below.*

PRIMARY EDITORS: *See* Contents *below.*

CONTENTS:

Number 1. CONGRÈS INTERNATIONAL DE PSYCHOLOGIE PHYSIOLOGIQUE. PREMIERE SESSION. Paris, 1889. Paris: Bureau des Revues, 1890. 159 pp.

Number 2. INTERNATIONAL CONGRESS OF EXPERIMENTAL PSYCHOLOGY. SECOND SESSION. London, 1892. London: Williams & Norgate, 1892. 186 pp.

Number 3. DRITTER INTERNATIONALER CONGRESS FÜR PSYCHOLOGIE IN MÜNCHEN VOM 4. BIS 7. August 1896. Munich: Verlag von J. F. Lehmann, 1897. 490 pp.

Number 4. IVᵉ CONGRÈS INTERNATIONAL DE PSYCHOLOGIE TENU À PARIS, DU 20 AU 26 AOÛT 1900 SOUS LA PRÉSIDENCE DE TH. RIBOT. COMPTE RENDU DES SÉANCES ET TEXTE DES MÉMOIRES. PUBLIÉS PAR LES SOIN DU PIERRE JANET. Paris: Félix Alcan, 1901. 814 pp.

Number 5. ATTI DEL V CONGRESSO INTERNAZIONALE DI PSICOLOGIA, TENUTO IN ROMA DAL 26 AL 30 APRILE 1905. PUBBLICATI DAL SANTE DE SANCTIS. Rome: Forzani E. C. Tipografi del Senato, 1905. 798 pp.

Number 6. VIᵐᵉ CONGRÈS INTERNATIONAL DE PSYCHOLOGIE, TENU À GÉNÈVE DU 2 AU 7 AOÛT 1909. SOUS LA PRÉSIDENCE DE TH. FLOURNOY. RAPPORTS ET COMPTES RENDUS PUBLIÉS PAR LES SOINS DE ÉD. CLAPARÈDE. Geneva: Librairie Kuendig, 1910. 877 pp.

Number 7. VIITH INTERNATIONAL CONGRESS OF PSYCHOLOGY. HELD AT OXFORD FROM JULY 26 TO AUGUST 2, 1923 UNDER THE PRESIDENCY OF CHARLES S. MYERS. PROCEEDINGS AND PAPERS EDITED BY THE PRESIDENT. Cambridge: At the University Press, 1924. 388 pp.

Number 8. VIIITH INTERNATIONAL CONGRESS OF PSYCHOLOGY. HELD AT GRONINGEN FROM 6 TO 11 SEPTEMBER 1926 UNDER THE PRESIDENCY OF G. HEYMANS. PROCEEDINGS AND PAPERS EDITED BY THE NATIONAL COMMITTEE. Groningen: P. Noordhoff, 1927. 452 pp.

Number 9. NINTH INTERNATIONAL CONGRESS OF PSYCHOLOGY. HELD AT YALE UNIVERSITY, NEW HAVEN, CONNECTICUT. SEPTEMBER 1ST TO 7TH, 1929, UNDER THE PRESIDENCY OF JAMES MCKEEN CATTELL. PROCEEDINGS AND PAPERS EDITED BY EDWIN G. BORING. Princeton, New Jersey: Psychological Review Company, 1930. 535 pp.

Number 10. PAPERS READ TO THE X. INTERNATIONAL CONGRESS OF PSYCHOLOGY AT COPENHAGEN, 1932. EDITED BY G. RÉVÉSZ. Hague: Martinus Nijhoff, 1935. 232 pp. (Also as *Acta Psychologica*, Volume 1, Number 1).

Number 11. ONZIÈME CONGRÈS INTERNATIONAL DE PSYCHOLOGIE. PARIS, 25–31 JUILLET 1937. RAPPORTS ET COMPTES RENDUS PUBLIÉS PAR LES SOINS DE H. PIÉRON ET I. MEYERSON. Paris: Librairie Félix Alcan, 1938. 571 pp.

Number 12. TWELFTH INTERNATIONAL CONGRESS OF PSYCHOLOGY. HELD AT THE UNIVERSITY OF EDINBURGH, JULY 23RD TO 29TH 1948, UNDER THE PRESIDENCY OF JAMES DREVER. PROCEEDINGS AND PAPERS EDITED BY MARY COLLINS. Edinburgh: Oliver and Boyd, Ltd., 1950. 152 pp.

97. *Revue de l'hypnotisme et de la psychologie physiologique.*

TITLE VARIATIONS: Continues *Revue de l'hypnotisme, expérimental & thérapeutique.* Continued by *Revue de psychothérapie et de psychologie appliquée* [1] with Série 2, Année 25, July 1910.

DATES OF PUBLICATION: Année 4–24, July 1889–June 1910.

FREQUENCY: Monthly.

NUMBERING VARIATIONS: None.

PUBLISHER: **Paris:** Émile Bouriot, 1889–1899. **Paris:** Ed. Bérillon, 1899–1908. **Paris:** J. Bérillon & Constant Laurent, 1908–1910.

PRIMARY EDITOR: **Edgar Bérillon,** 1889–1910.

98. *Voprosy filosofii i psikhologii.* [Published in collaboration with Moskovskoe psikhologicheskoe obshchestvo and S.-Peterburgskoe filosofskoe obshchestvo.]

TITLE VARIATIONS: None.

DATES OF PUBLICATION: Tom 1–29, November, 1889–1918.

FREQUENCY: 5 issues per year, bimonthly with no July/August issue.

NUMBERING VARIATIONS: Each issue is also assigned a whole number, Kniga 1–141/142. Kniga 132/133 and 139/140 published as joint issues.

PUBLISHER: **Moscow:** Tipo-litografia vysochaishe utverzhdennago T-va. I. N. Kushnerev i Ko., 1889–1898. **Moscow:** Tipo-litografia tovarishchestva I. N. Kushnerev i Ko., 1898–1917.

PRIMARY EDITORS: **N. Ia. Grot,** 1889–1895; **A. A. Abrikosov,** 1889–1893; **V. P. Preobrazhenskii,** 1896–1900; **L. M. Lopatin,** 1894–1897, 1900–1917; **S. N. Trubetskii,** 1900–1905.

ASSOCIATE EDITORS: V. A. Gol'tsev, 1898–1901; N. Ia. Grot, 1898; V. N. Ivanovskii, 1898–1901; N. A. Ivantsov, 1898–1901; S. S. Korsakov, 1898–1900; L. M. Lopatin, 1898–1900; V. S. Solov'ev, 1898–1900; A. A. Tokarskii, 1898–1901; S. N. Trubetskii, 1898–1900; N. A. Umov, 1898–1901. None listed, 1902–1918.

1890-1899

99. *Giornale del magnetismo ed ipnotismo.*

TITLE VARIATIONS: Continued by *Magnetismo ed ipnotismo* with Anno 2, 1891.

DATES OF PUBLICATION: Anno 1, January–December 1890.

FREQUENCY: Monthly.

NUMBERING VARIATIONS: None.

PUBLISHER: **Florence:** Tip. E. Bruscoli, 1890. **Florence:** Società medico-psicologica italiana, Tip. E. Bruscoli, 1890.

PRIMARY EDITOR: **Olinto Del Torto**, 1890.

100. *Paris. Clinique hypnotherapique de la charité. Bulletin mensuel.*

TITLE VARIATIONS: Supplement to *Revue d'hypnologie théorique et pratique,* 1890, and to *Annales de psychiatrie et d'hypnologie, dans leurs rapports avec la psychologie et la médecine legal,* 1891–1894.

DATES OF PUBLICATION: Année 1–4, Numéro 1, December 1890–January 1894.

FREQUENCY: Monthly.

NUMBERING VARIATIONS: Issues list month and date only.

PUBLISHER: **Paris:** Bureau des annales de psychiatrie et d'hypnologie, 1891–1894.

PRIMARY EDITOR: **J. Luys**, 1891–1894.

For serial publications that began before 1890 and were still being published during the decade 1890 to 1900, *see also* entries 32, 54, 59, 65, 67, 72, 73, 74, 77, 79, 81, 82, 84, 85, 86, 87, 90, 92, 93, 94, 96, 97, 98.

101. *Pennsylvania. University. Publications. Series in Philosophy.*

TITLE VARIATIONS: None.

DATES OF PUBLICATION: Number 1–4, April 1890–1900.

FREQUENCY: Irregular. *See* Contents *below.*

NUMBERING VARIATIONS: None.

PUBLISHER: **Philadelphia:** University of Pennsylvania Press, 1890–1900.

PRIMARY EDITORS: **George Stuart Fullerton,** 1890–1899; **James McKeen Cattell,** 1890–1892; **Edgar A. Singer, Jr.,** 1900.

CONTENTS:
> **Number 1.** Fullerton, G. S. ON SAMENESS AND IDENTITY. 1890. 156 pp.
> **Number 2.** [Cattell, James McKeen, and G. S. Fullerton.] ON THE PERCEPTION OF SMALL DIFFERENCES. 1892. 159 pp.
> **Number 3.** Fullerton, G. S. ON SPINOZISTIC IMMORTALITY. 1899. 154 pp.
> **Number 4.** Sugiura, Sadajiro. HINDU LOGIC AS PRESERVED IN CHINA AND JAPAN. 1900. 114 pp.

102. *Revue des sciences psychologiques illustrée.*

TITLE VARIATIONS: None.

DATES OF PUBLICATION: Tome 1–3, Numéro 2, March 1890–March 1892.

FREQUENCY: Bimonthly (November to April) and monthly (May to October).

NUMBERING VARIATIONS: None.

PUBLISHER: **Paris:** Imprimerie Noirot, 1890–1892.

PRIMARY EDITORS: None listed.

NOTE: Information on this entry is incomplete. The compilers were unable to examine this title.

103. *Revue d'hypnologie théorique et pratique.*

TITLE VARIATIONS: Continued by *Annales de psychiatrie et d'hypnologie dans leurs rapports avec la psychologie et la médecine légale* with Nouvelle Série, Année 1, January 1891.

DATES OF PUBLICATION: Année 1, Numéro 1–12, January–December 1890.

FREQUENCY: Monthly.

NUMBERING VARIATIONS: Supplement numbered as [*Paris.*] *Clinique hypnotherapique de la charité. Bulletin mensuel.*

PUBLISHER: **Paris:** Bureau des revue d'hypnologie théorique et pratique, 1890.

PRIMARY EDITORS: **J. Luys,** 1890; **Ch. Lefevre,** 1890.

104. *Zeitschrift für Psychologie und Physiologie der Sinnesorgane.*

TITLE VARIATIONS: Continued by *Zeitschrift für Psychologie und Physiologie der Sinnesorgane.* Abteilung I. *Zeitschrift für Psychologie* with Band 41, 1906, and *Zeitschrift für Psychologie und Physiologie der Sinnesorgane.* Abteilung II. *Zeitschrift für Sinnesphysiologie* with Band 41, 1907.

DATES OF PUBLICATION: Band 1–40, 1890–1906.

FREQUENCY: Monthly.

NUMBERING VARIATIONS: None.

PUBLISHER: **Hamburg** and **Leipzig:** Leopold Voss, 1890–1897. **Leipzig:** Johann Ambrosius Barth, 1897–1906.

PRIMARY EDITORS: **Hermann Ebbinghaus,** 1890–1906; **Arthur König,** 1890–1901; **W. A. Nagel,** 1902–1906.

EDITORIAL BOARD: Hermann Aubert, 1890–1892; Sigmund Exner, 1890–1906; Ewald Hering, 1890–1902; Johannes von Kries, 1890–1906; Theodor Lipps, 1890–1906; Georg Elias Müller, 1890–1906; Wilhelm Preyer, 1890–1897; Carl Stumpf, 1890–1906; Hermann von Helmholtz, 1891–1894; C. Pelman, 1893–1906; Theodor Ziehen, 1899–1906; Alexius Meinong, 1902–1906.

105. *Zentralblatt für Nervenheilkunde und Psychiatrie. Internationale Monatsschrift für die gesamte Neurologie in Wissenschaft und Praxis mit besonderer Berücksichtigung der Degenerations-Anthropologie.*

TITLE VARIATIONS: Subtitle varies. Continues *Zentralblatt für Nervenheilkunde, Psychiatrie und gerichtliche Psychopathologie.* Superseded by *Zeitschrift für die gesamte Neurologie und Psychiatrie* with Band 1, 1910.

DATES OF PUBLICATION: Jahrgang 13–33, April 1890–March 1910.

FREQUENCY: **Monthly,** Jahrgang 13–29 (Neue Folge, Band 1–17), April 1890–March 1907. **Semimonthly,** Jahrgang 30–32 (Neue Folge, Band 18–20), April 1907–March 1909. **Bimonthly,** Jahrgang 33 (Neue Folge, Band 21), April 1909–March 1910.

NUMBERING VARIATIONS. Also numbered Neue Folge, Band 1–21. Jahrgang 31 (Neue Folge, Band 19), 1908 contains 25 Hefte.

PUBLISHER: **Coblenz:** W. Groos, 1890–1901. **Berlin:** Vogel & Kreienbrink, 1902–1907. **Leipzig:** Johann Ambrosius Barth, 1907–1910.

PRIMARY EDITORS: **Robert Gaupp,** 1899–1910; **Albr. Erlenmeyer,** 1890–1901; **J.-M. Charcot,** 1890–1894; **Ch. M. van Deventer,** 1890–1901; **H. Kurella,** 1890–1901; **K. R. Sommer,** 1893–1894; **W. R. Gowers,** 1895–1901.

1891

106. Annales de psychiatrie et d'hypnologie dans leurs rapports avec la psychologie et la médecine légale.

TITLE VARIATIONS: Continues *Revue d'hypnologie théorique et pratique*. Continued by *Revue de psychiatrie de neurologie et d'hypnologie* with Nouvelle Série, Année 1, January/February 1896.

DATES OF PUBLICATION: Nouvelle Série, Année 1–5, January 1891–December 1895.

FREQUENCY: Monthly.

NUMBERING VARIATIONS: Supplement numbered as [*Paris.*] *Clinique hypnotherapique de la charité. Bulletin mensuel.*

PUBLISHER: **Paris:** Bureau des annales de psychiatrie et d'hypnologie, 1891–1895.

PRIMARY EDITORS: **J. Luys**, 1891; **Ch. Lefevre**, 1891; **René Semelaigne**, 1891–1893; **L. R. Régnier**, 1894–1895; **J. G. Natanson**, 1895.

107. Gesellschaft für psychologische Forschung. Schriften.

TITLE VARIATIONS: None.

DATES OF PUBLICATION: Heft 1–20, 1891–1916.

FREQUENCY: Irregular. *See* Contents *below*.

NUMBERING VARIATIONS: Also numbered Sammlung I–IV. I contains Heft 1–5; II, Heft 6–10; III, Heft 11–15; and IV, Heft 16–20. Hefte 3/4, 7/8, 9/10, 13/14, 18/20 multinumbered.

PUBLISHER: **Leipzig:** Verlag von A. Abel (Arthur Meiner), 1891–1893. **Leipzig:** Verlag von Johann Ambrosius Barth, 1893–1916.

PRIMARY EDITORS: None listed.

CONTENTS:

Heft 1. Schrenck-Notzing, A. von. DIE BEDEUTUNG NARCOTISCHER MITTEL FÜR DEN HYPNOTISMUS MIT BESONDERER BERÜCKSICHTIGUNG DES INDISCHEN HANFES; and, Forel, August. EIN GUTACHTEN ÜBER EINEN FALL VON SPONTANEM SOMNAMBULISMUS MIT ANGEBLICHER WAHRSAGEREI UND HELLSEHEREI. 1891. 90 pp.

Heft 2. Münsterberg, Hugo. ÜBER AUFGABEN UND METHODEN DER PSYCHOLOGIE. 1891. 182 pp.

Heft 3/4. Moll, Albert. DER RAPPORT IN DER HYPNOSE, UNTERSUCHUNGEN ÜBER DEN THIERISCHEN MAGNETISMUS. 1892. 242 pp.

Heft 5. Koeber, R. von. JEAN PAUL'S SEELENLEHRE. EIN BEITRAG ZUR GESCHICHTE DER PSYCHOLOGIE, and Offner, Max. DIE PHILOSOPHIE CHARLES BONNETS. EINE STUDIE ZUR GESCHICHTE DER PSYCHOLOGIE. 1893. 176 pp.

Heft 6. Bentivegni, A. von. ANTHROPOLOGISCHE FORMELN FÜR DAS VERBRECHERTUM. EINE KRITISCHE STUDIE. 1893. 45 pp.

Heft 7/8. Parish, Edmund. ÜBER DIE TRUGWAHRNEHMUNG (HALLUCINA-
TION UND ILLUSION). MIT BESONDERER BERÜCKSICHTIGUNG DER INTERNATION-
ALEN ENQUÊTE ÜBER WACHHALLUCINATION BEI GESUNDEN. 1894. 246 pp.

Heft 9/10. Lipps, Theodor. RAUMÄSTHETIK UND GEOMETRISCH-OPTISCHE
TÄUSCHUNGEN. 1897. 424 pp.

Heft 11. Wreschner, Arthur. METHODOLOGISCHE BEITRÄGE ZU PSYCHO-
PHYSISCHEN MESSUNGEN (AUF EXPERIMENTELLER GRUNDLAGE). 1898. 238 pp.

Heft 12. Stern, L. William. ÜBER PSYCHOLOGIE DER INDIVIDUELLEN DIF-
FERENZEN (IDEEN ZU EINER "DIFFERENTIELLEN PSYCHOLOGIE"). 1900. 146 pp.

Heft 13/14. Lipps, Theodor. VOM FÜHLEN, WOLLEN UND DENKEN. EINE
PSYCHOLOGISCHE SKIZZE. 1902. 196 pp. (2. Auflage, 1907, 275 pp.)

Heft 15. Baerwald, Richard. PSYCHOLOGISCHE FAKTOREN DES MODERNEN
ZEITGEISTES; and Möller, Paul. DIE BEDEUTUNG DES URTEILS FÜR DIE AUF-
FASSUNG. 1905. 110 pp.

Heft 16. Gallinger, August. DAS PROBLEM DER OBJECTIVEN MÖGLICHKEIT.
EINE BEDEUTUNGSANALYSE. 1912. 126 pp.

Heft 17. Hennig, R. DIE ENTWICKLUNG DES NATURGEFÜHLS. DAS
WESEN DER INSPIRATION. 1912. 160 pp.

Heft 18/20. Baerwald, Richard. ZUR PSYCHOLOGIE DER VORSTELLUNGS-
TYPEN MIT BESONDERER BERÜCKSICHTIGUNG DER MOTORISCHEN UND MUSIKAL-
ISCHEN ANLAGE. AUF GRUND EINER UMFRAGE DER PSYCHOLOGISCHEN GE-
SELLSCHAFT ZU BERLIN BEARBEITET. 1916. 444 pp.

108. *Journal of Comparative Neurology.* [*1.*]

TITLE VARIATIONS: Continued by *Journal of Comparative Neurology and Psychology* with Volume 14, 1904.

DATES OF PUBLICATION. Volume 1–13, 1891–1903.

FREQUENCY: Quarterly.

NUMBERING VARIATIONS: Double-number issues in Volume 5–9.

PUBLISHER: **Granville, Ohio:** By the Editor (Issue 1), 1891. **Cincinnati, Ohio:**
Robert Clarke & Co., 1891–1892. **Granville:** By the Editor, 1893, **Granville:**
By the Editors, 1894, 1896–1897. **Granville:** By the Editors, The University
Press, 1895. **Granville:** Published for the Editors by C. Judson Herrick,
1898–1899. **Granville:** By the Editors, Denison University, 1900–1903.

PRIMARY EDITORS: **C. L. Herrick,** 1891–1903; **C. Judson Herrick,** 1894–1903;
Oliver S. Strong, 1896–1903.

109. *Magnetismo ed ipnotismo.*

TITLE VARIATIONS: Continues *Giornale del magnetismo ed ipnotismo.* Continued by *Ipnotismo* with Anno 4, 1893.

DATES OF PUBLICATION: Anno 2–3, January 1891–December 1892.

FREQUENCY: Monthly.

NUMBERING VARIATIONS: None.

PUBLISHER: **Florence:** Società medico-psicologica italiana, Tip. E. Bruscoli, 1891–1892.

PRIMARY EDITOR: **Olinto Del Torto,** 1891–1892.

110. *Pedagogical Seminary. An International Record of Educational Literature, Institutions and Progress.*

TITLE VARIATIONS: Continued by *Pedagogical Seminary and Journal of Genetic Psychology* with Volume 32, 1925.

DATES OF PUBLICATION: Volume 1–31, 1891–1924.

FREQUENCY: **Triannual,** Volume 1–4, 1891–1897. **Quarterly,** Volume 5–31, 1897–1924 (December).

NUMBERING VARIATIONS: Volume 3, Number 1, dated October 1894. Volume 3, Number 2, dated October 1895. Volume 3, Number 3, dated June 1896.

PUBLISHER: **Worcester, Massachusetts:** J. H. Orpha, 1891–1899. **Worcester:** Louis N. Wilson, Publisher, 1900–1904. **Worcester:** Florence Chandler, Publisher, 1905–1921. **Worcester:** No publisher listed, Printed by Commonwealth Press, 1922–1924 (December).

PRIMARY EDITORS: **G. Stanley Hall,** 1891–1924; **William H. Burnham,** [1920]–1924.

111. *Verein für Volkskunde. Zeitschrift. Neue Folge der Zeitschrift für Völkerpsychologie und Sprachwissenschaft.*

TITLE VARIATIONS: Continues *Zeitschrift für Völkerpsychologie und Sprachwissenschaft.* Continued by *Zeitschrift für Volkskunde* with Band 39, 1929/1930.

DATES OF PUBLICATION: Neue Folge, Band 1–38, 1891–1928.

FREQUENCY: **Quarterly,** Band 1–24, 1891–1914. **Irregular,** Band 25–34, 1915–1923/1924. **Semiannual,** 4 Hefte in 2 years, Band 35/36–37/38, 1925/1926–1927/1928.

NUMBERING VARIATIONS: None.

PUBLISHER: **Berlin:** A. Asher & Co., 1891–1902. **Berlin:** Behrend & Co., 1903–1925. **Berlin:** Julius Springer, 1925–1928.

PRIMARY EDITORS: **Karl Weinhold,** 1891–1901; **Johannes Bolte,** 1902–1928; **Herman Michel,** 1911; **Fritz Böhm,** 1912–1928.

1892

112. *American Psychological Association. Proceedings.*

TITLE VARIATIONS: None.

DATES OF PUBLICATION: 1–59+, 1892–1950+.

FREQUENCY: Annual.

NUMBERING VARIATIONS: Number 1 was a Preliminary Meeting, Clark University, Worcester, Massachusetts, 1892. Number 2 was First Annual Meeting, University of Pennsylvania, Philadelphia, 1892. Number 3 was 2nd Annual Meeting, Columbia College, New York, 1893. Proceedings of annual meetings 3–11 were published in the *Psychological Review*, Volume 2–10, 1895–1903. Proceedings of annual meetings 12–58+ were published in the *Psychological Bulletin* beginning with Volume 1, 1904.

PUBLISHER: **New York** and **London:** Macmillan and Company, (1st–3rd), 1893.

PRIMARY EDITORS: See *Psychological Review*, 1895–1903 and *Psychological Bulletin*, 1904–1950+.

113. *Psychical Review. A Quarterly Journal of Psychical Science and Organ of the American Psychical Society.*

TITLE VARIATIONS: None.

DATES OF PUBLICATION: Volume 1–2, 1892–1894.

FREQUENCY: Quarterly.

NUMBERING VARIATIONS: Each issue is also assigned a whole number, Number 1–8. Volume 2, issue 6–7, November 1893–February 1894 issued as a double number.

PUBLISHER: **Grafton, Massachusetts:** American Psychical Society, 1892–1894.

PRIMARY EDITOR: **T. E. Allen,** 1892–1894.

114. *Yale University. Psychological Laboratory. Studies.*

TITLE VARIATIONS: Superseded by *Yale Psychological Studies. (See* entry no. 126.)

DATES OF PUBLICATION: Volume 1–10, 1892–1902.

FREQUENCY: Annual.

NUMBERING VARIATIONS: None.

PUBLISHER: **New Haven, Connecticut:** Yale University, 1892–1902.

PRIMARY EDITOR: **Edward W. Scripture,** 1892–1902.

115. *Zeitschrift für Hypnotismus, Suggestionstherapie, Suggestionslehre und verwandte psychologische Forschungen.*

TITLE VARIATIONS: Continued by *Zeitschrift für Hypnotismus, Psychotherapie sowie andere psychophysiologische und psychopathologische Forschungen* with Band 4, 1896.

DATES OF PUBLICATION: Band 1–3, October 1892–September 1895.

FREQUENCY: Monthly.

NUMBERING VARIATIONS: None.

PUBLISHER: **Berlin:** Verlag von Hermann Brieger, 1892–1895.

PRIMARY EDITOR: **J. Grossman,** 1892–1895.

1893

116. *Archives d'anthropologie criminelle, de criminologie et de psychologie normale et pathologique.*

TITLE VARIATIONS: Continues *Archives de l'anthropologie criminelle et des sciences pénales.* Continued by *Archives d'anthropologie criminelle, de médecine légale et de psychologie normale et pathologique* with Tome 24, 1908.

DATES OF PUBLICATION: Tome 8–23, 1893–1907.

FREQUENCY: **Bimonthly,** 1893–1901. **Monthly,** 1902–1907.

NUMBERING VARIATIONS: Tome 17–23 also numbered as Nouvelle Série, Tome 1–7, 1902–1907.

PUBLISHER: **Paris:** G. Masson, 1893–1898. **Paris:** Masson et Cie, 1899–1907.

PRIMARY EDITORS: **Alexandre Lacassagne,** 1893–1907; **Albert Bournet,** 1893–1895; **Gabriel Tarde,** 1893–1904; **Étienne Martin,** 1902–1907; **Paul Dubuisson,** 1905–1907.

117. *Ipnotismo.*

TITLE VARIATIONS: Continues *Magnetismo ed ipnotismo.*

DATES OF PUBLICATION: Anno 4–5, January 1893–December 1894.

FREQUENCY: Semimonthly.

NUMBERING VARIATIONS: Multinumber issues present.

PUBLISHER: **Florence:** Società medico-psicologica italiana, Tip. E. Bruscoli, 1893–1894.

PRIMARY EDITOR: **Olinto Del Torto,** 1893–1894.

118. *Paris. Sorbonne. Laboratoire de psychologie physiologique. Travaux.*

TITLE VARIATIONS: Laboratory later cited as [*Paris.*] *École pratique des hautes études. Laboratoire de psychologie physiologique.*

DATES OF PUBLICATION: Numéro 1–2, 1893–1894.

FREQUENCY: Annual.

NUMBERING VARIATIONS: 1893 publication contains publications of 1892. 1894 publication contains publications of 1893.

PUBLISHER: **Paris:** Ancienne Librairie Germer Baillière et Cie, Félix Alcan, éditeur, 1893–1894.

PRIMARY EDITORS: **Henri É. Beaunis,** 1893–1894; **A. Binet,** 1893–1894.

1894

119. *Année psychologique.* [Issued in connection with the Laboratoire de psychologie physiologique de la Sorbonne, 1894–1900.]

TITLE VARIATIONS: None.

DATES OF PUBLICATION: Année 1–51+, 1894–1949+.

FREQUENCY: Annual.

NUMBERING VARIATIONS: Année 20 contains 1914–1919; Année 22 contains 1920–1921; Année 41–42 contains 1940–1941; Année 43–44 contains 1942–1943; Année 45–46 contains 1944–1945; Année 47–48 contains 1946–1947; Année 50–51 contains 1949 but was published in 1951; Année 50 is Volume jubilaire offert en homage à Henri Piéron, 1949.

PUBLISHER: **Paris:** Ancienne Librairie Germer Baillière et Cie. Félix Alcan, éditeur, 1895–1896. **Paris:** Librairie C. Reinwald, Schleicher Frères, éditeurs, 1897–1903. **Paris:** Masson et Cie, éditeurs, 1904–1914, 1920. **Paris:** Librairie Félix Alcan, 1922–1938. **Paris:** Presses universitaires de France, 1940, 1942, 1945, 1947–1949+.

PRIMARY EDITORS: **H. Beaunis,** 1894–1906, 1910–1911; **Alfred Binet,** 1894–1912; **Th. Ribot,** 1894–1904; **Victor Henri,** 1894–1905; **J. Larguier des Bancels,** 1901–1912; **Henri Piéron,** 1913–1949+; **Marcel François,** 1924–1937; **Marguérite Lichtenberger,** 1924–1927; **Camille Nony,** 1938–1947; **Vincent Bloch,** 1948–1949+; **Alfred Fessard,** 1948–1949+; **Paul Fraisse,** 1948–1949+.

120. *Columbia University. Contributions to Philosophy, Psychology and Education.*

TITLE VARIATIONS: Continued by *Columbia University. Contributions to Philosophy and Psychology* with Volume 13, Number 3.

DATES OF PUBLICATION: Volume 1–13, Number 2, 1894–1905.

FREQUENCY: Irregular.

NUMBERING VARIATIONS: Various issues also numbered as *Psychological Review. Monograph Supplements* or as *Archives of Philosophy, Psychology and Scientific Methods.* Volume 11, Number 2 subtitled *Columbia University. Teachers College. Department of Educational Psychology. Studies. See* Contents *below.*

PUBLISHER: **New York:** Columbia College, 1894. **New York:** Macmillan and Co., 1895–1905.

PRIMARY EDITOR: Head of the Division of Philosophy, Psychology and Education, Columbia University, 1894–1905.

CONTENTS:
Volume 1, Number 1. Wilde, Norman. FRIEDRICH HEINRICH JACOBI; A STUDY IN THE ORIGIN OF GERMAN REALISM. 1894. 79 pp.

————, **Number 2.** Kant, Immanuel. IMMANUEL KANT'S INAUGURAL DISSERTATION OF 1770. Translated into English with an Introduction and Discussion by William J. Eckoff. 1894. 101 pp.

————, **Number 3.** Hertz, Joseph H. THE ETHICAL SYSTEM OF JAMES MARTINEAU. 1894. 85 pp.

————, **Number 4.** Brandt, Francis Burke. FRIEDRICH EDWARD BENEKE; THE MAN AND HIS PHILOSOPHY. AN INTRODUCTORY STUDY. 1895. 167 pp.

Volume 2, Number 1. Luqueer, Frederic Ludlow. HEGEL AS EDUCATOR. 1896. 185 pp.

————, **Number 2.** MacVannel, John Angus. HEGEL'S DOCTRINE OF THE WILL. 1896. 102 pp.

————, **Number 3.** Cole, Lawrence Thomas. THE BASIS OF EARLY CHRISTIAN THEISM. 1898. 60 pp.

————, **Number 4.** Jones, Adam Leroy. EARLY AMERICAN PHILOSOPHERS. 1898. 80 pp.

Volume 3, Number 1. Washington, William Morrow. THE FORMAL AND MATERIAL ELEMENTS OF KANT'S ETHICS. 1898. 67 pp.

————, **Number 2.** Hyslop, James H. SYLLABUS OF PSYCHOLOGY. 1899. 116 pp.

————, **Number 3/4.** Marvin, Walter T. A SYLLABUS OF AN INTRODUCTION TO PHILOSOPHY. 1899. 279 pp.

Volume 4, Number 1. Griffing, Harold. ON SENSATIONS FROM PRESSURE AND IMPACT, WITH SPECIAL REFERENCE TO THE INTENSITY, AREA AND TIME OF STIMULAION. 1895. 88 pp. (Also as *Psychological Review. Monograph Supplements*, Number 1.)

————, **Number 2.** Lay, Wilfrid. MENTAL IMAGERY EXPERIMENTALLY AND SUBJECTIVELY CONSIDERED. 1898. 59 pp. (Also as *Psychological Review. Monograph Supplements*, Number 7.)

————, **Number 3.** Thorndike, Edward L. ANIMAL INTELLIGENCE. AN EXPERIMENTAL STUDY OF THE ASSOCIATIVE PROCESSES IN ANIMALS. 1898. 109 pp. (Also as *Psychological Review. Monograph Supplements*, Number 8.)

————, **Number 4.** Dearborn, George Van Ness. THE EMOTION OF JOY. 1899. 70 pp. (Also as *Psychological Review. Monograph Supplements*, Number 9.)

Volume 5, Number 1. Dexter, Edwin G. CONDUCT AND THE WEATHER; AN INDUCTIVE STUDY OF THE MENTAL EFFECTS OF DEFINITE METEOROLOGICAL CONDITIONS. 1899. 103 pp. (Also as *Psychological Review. Monograph Supplements*, Number 10.)

————, **Number 2.** Franz, Shepherd Ivory. ON AFTER-IMAGES. 1899. 61 pp. (Also as *Psychological Review. Monograph Supplements*, Number 12.)

————, **Number 3.** Breese, Burtis Burr. ON INHIBITION. 1899. 65 pp. (Also as *Psychological Review. Monograph Supplements*, Number 11.)

————, **Number 4.** Woodworth, Robert Sessions. THE ACCURACY OF VOLUNTARY MOVEMENT. 1899. 114 pp. (Also as *Psychological Review. Monograph Supplements*, Number 13.)

Volume 6, Number 1–4. Parsons, Elsie Worthington (Clews). EDUCA-

TIONAL LEGISLATION AND ADMINISTRATION OF THE COLONIAL GOVERNMENTS. 1899. 524 pp.

Volume 7, Number 1. Spencer, Frank Clarence. EDUCATION OF THE PUEBLO CHILD; A STUDY IN ARRESTED DEVELOPMENT. 1899. 97 pp.

———, **Number 2.** Dyke, Charles Bartlett. THE ECONOMIC ASPECT OF TEACHERS' SALARIES. 1899. 84 pp.

———, **Number 3.** Chamberlain, William I. EDUCATION IN INDIA. 1899. 107 pp.

———, **Number 4.** Hubbell, George Allen. HORACE MANN IN OHIO. A STUDY OF THE APPLICATION OF HIS PUBLIC SCHOOL IDEALS TO COLLEGE ADMINISTRATION. 1900. 70 pp.

Volume 8, Number 1. Deahl, Jasper Newton. IMITATION IN EDUCATION; ITS NATURE, SCOPE AND SIGNIFICANCE. 1900. 103 pp.

———, **Number 2.** Reeder, Rudolph Rex. THE HISTORICAL DEVELOPMENT OF SCHOOL READERS AND OF METHODS IN TEACHING READING. 1900. 92 pp.

———, **Number 3/4.** Thorndike, Edward Lee. NOTES ON CHILD STUDY. 1901. 157 pp. (Also a second edition, 1903, 181 pp.)

Volume 9, Number 1. Thorndike, Edward Lee. THE MENTAL LIFE OF THE MONKEYS. 1901. 57 pp. (Also as *Psychological Review. Monograph Supplements*, Number 15.)

———, **Number 2.** Wissler, Clark. THE CORRELATION OF MENTAL AND PHYSICAL TESTS. 1901. 62 pp. (Also as *Psychological Review. Monograph Supplements*, Number 16.)

———, **Number 3.** Bair, Joseph Hershey. THE PRACTICE CURVE. A STUDY IN THE FORMATION OF HABITS. 1902. 70 pp. (Also as *Psychological Review. Monograph Supplements,* Number 19.)

———, **Number 4.** Miner, James Burt. MOTOR, VISUAL, AND APPLIED RHYTHMS. AN EXPERIMENTAL STUDY AND A REVISED EXPECTATION. 1903. 106 pp. (Also as *Psychological Review. Monograph Supplements,* Number 21.)

Volume 10, Number 1. Alexander, Hartley Burr. THE PROBLEM OF METAPHYSICS AND THE MEANING OF METAPHYSICAL EXPLANATION: AN ESSAY IN DEFINITIONS. 1902. 130 pp.

———, **Number 2.** Johnson, William Hallock. THE FREE-WILL PROBLEM IN MODERN THOUGHT. 1903. 94 pp.

———, **Number 3.** Hughes, Percy. THE CONCEPT ACTION IN HISTORY AND IN THE NATURAL SCIENCES. 1905. 108 pp.

———, **Number 4.** Bush, Wendell T. AVENARIUS AND THE STANDPOINT OF PURE EXPERIENCE. 1905. 79 pp. (Also as *Archives of Philosophy, Psychology and Scientific Methods,* Number 2.)

Volume 11, Number 1. Rollins, Frank. SCHOOL ADMINISTRATION IN MUNICIPAL GOVERNMENT. 1902. 106 pp.

———, **Number 2.** Thorndike, Edward Lee, ed. HEREDITY, CORRELATION AND SEX DIFFERENCES IN SCHOOL ABILITIES; STUDIES FROM THE DEPARTMENT OF EDUCATIONAL PSYCHOLOGY AT TEACHERS COLLEGE, COLUMBIA UNIVERSITY. 1903. 60 pp.

————, **Number 3/4.** Broome, Edwin Cornelius. A HISTORICAL AND CRITICAL DISCUSSION OF COLLEGE ADMISSION REQUIREMENTS. 1903. 157 pp.

Volume 12, Number 1–4. Luckey, George Washington Andrew. THE PROFESSIONAL TRAINING OF SECONDARY TEACHERS IN THE UNITED STATES. 1903. 391 pp.

Volume 13, Number 1. Messenger, James Franklin. THE PERCEPTION OF NUMBER. 1903. 44 pp. (Also as *Psychological Review. Monograph Supplements*, Number 22.)

————, **Number 2.** Henderson, Ernest Norton. A STUDY OF MEMORY FOR CONNECTED TRAINS OF THOUGHT. 1903. 94 pp. (Also as *Psychological Review. Monograph Supplements*, Number 23.)

121. *Psychological Index.*

TITLE VARIATIONS: Subtitled *A Bibliography of the Literature of Psychology and Cognate Subjects*. Subtitle varies slightly. Issued in connection with *Psychological Review*.

DATES OF PUBLICATION: Number 1–42, 1894–1935.

FREQUENCY: Annual.

NUMBERING VARIATIONS: Number 8–15, 1901–1908 also numbered as Bibliographical Supplement Number 1–8 to the *Dictionary of Philosophy and Psychology* edited by J. Mark Baldwin.

PUBLISHER: **New York** and **London:** Macmillan and Company, 1894–1896. **Lancaster, Pennsylvania, New York** and **London:** Macmillan Company, 1897–1899. **Lancaster** and **New York:** Macmillan Company, 1900–1905. **Lancaster** and **Baltimore:** Review Publishing Company, 1906–1911. **Lancaster** and **Princeton, New Jersey:** Psychological Review Company, 1912–1924. **Princeton:** For the American Psychological Association by the Psychological Review Company, 1925–1935.

PRIMARY EDITORS: **Howard C. Warren,** 1894–1914; **Livingstone Farrand,** 1894–1897; **Robert S. Woodworth,** 1898; **Madison Bentley,** 1906–1907, 1915–1924; **C. L. Vaughan,** 1907–1909; **Knight Dunlap,** 1908–1909; **Christian A. Ruckmick,** 1917–1918; **Coleman R. Griffith,** 1920–1924; **Walter S. Hunter,** 1925–1935; **Raymond R. Willoughby,** 1926–1935.

122. *Psychological Review.*

TITLE VARIATIONS: None.

DATES OF PUBLICATION: Volume 1–57+, 1894–1950+.

FREQUENCY: Bimonthly.

NUMBERING VARIATIONS: Volume 11, 1904 called New Series. Volume 11, Number 4/5 and Volume 12, Number 2/3 are joint issues.

PUBLISHER: **New York** and **London:** Macmillan and Company, 1894–1896. **Lancaster, Pennsylvania, New York** and **London:** Macmillan Company, 1897–1899. **Lancaster** and **New York:** Macmillan Company, 1900–1905. **Lancaster** and **Baltimore:** Review Publishing Company, 1906–1911. **Lancaster** and **Princeton, New Jersey:** Psychological Review Company, 1912–1924. **Lancaster** and **Princeton,** American Psychological Association by the Psychological Review Company, 1925–1937. **Lancaster** and **Columbus, Ohio:** American Psychological Association, Inc., 1938–1939. **Lancaster** and **Evanston, Illinois:** American Psychological Association, Inc., 1940–1945. **Lancaster** and **Washington, D.C.:** American Psychological Association, Inc., 1946–1950 +.

PRIMARY EDITORS: **J. Mark Baldwin,** 1894–1909; **J. McKeen Cattell,** 1894–1903; **Howard C. Warren,** 1904–1909, 1916–1934; **John B. Watson,** 1909–1915; **Herbert S. Langfeld,** 1934–1947; **Carroll C. Pratt,** 1948–1950 +.

ASSOCIATE EDITOR: Howard C. Warren, 1901–1903.

EDITORIAL BOARD: Alfred Binet, 1894–1909; John Dewey, 1894–1909; H. H. Donaldson, 1894–1903; G. S. Fullerton, 1894–1903; William James, 1894–1896; G. T. Ladd, 1894–1903; Hugo Münsterberg, 1894–1916; M. Allen Starr, 1894–1903; Carl Stumpf, 1894–1906; James Sully, 1894–1903; Joseph Jastrow, 1895–1929; G. H. Howison, 1898–1908; Pierre Janet, 1904–1909; A. C. Armstrong, 1904–1909; W. L. Bryan, 1904–1909; William Caldwell, 1904–1909; Mary W. Calkins, 1904–1929; J. R. Angell, 1904–1908; C. Ladd-Franklin, 1904–1909; H. N. Gardiner, 1904–1927; E. A. Pace, 1904–1909; G.T.W. Patrick, 1904–1908; Adolf Meyer, 1904–1929; C. Lloyd Morgan, 1904–1909; R. M. Wenley, 1904–1909; C. M. Bakewell, 1909; C. H. Judd, 1909–1929; G. M. Stratton, 1909–1929; R. P. Angier, 1910–1929; Raymond Dodge, 1910–1915; W. B. Pillsbury, 1910–1929; C. E. Seashore, 1910–1929; E. L. Thorndike, 1910–1915; Margaret F. Washburn, 1916–1929; R. S. Woodworth, 1925–1929; John B. Watson, 1927–1929. None listed, 1930 +.

123. *Sydney. University. Reprints of Papers Contributed to Scientific Journals.*

TITLE VARIATIONS: Superseded by [*Sydney. University.*] *University Reprints.* Series 12: *Social Science, Economics, Education, History, Philosophy and Psychology* with Number 1, 1924.

DATES OF PUBLICATION: 1894–1922.

FREQUENCY: Irregular.

NUMBERING VARIATIONS: *See* Note *below.*

PUBLISHER: Various. *See* Note *below.*

PRIMARY EDITORS: None listed.

NOTE: No original publications. Compilation of reprints of articles by members of the university staff.

1895

124. *Journal de neurologie & d'hypnologie. Neurologie, hypnologie, psychiatrie, psychologie.*

TITLE VARIATIONS: Continued by *Journal de neurologie. Neurologie, psychiatrie, psychologie, hypnologie* with Tome 3, 1898.

DATES OF PUBLICATION: Tome 1–2, December 1895–1897.

FREQUENCY: Semimonthly.

NUMBERING VARIATIONS: None.

PUBLISHER: **Brussels:** Rédaction, 1, rue du Parlement, 1895–1897.

PRIMARY EDITORS: **Xavier Francotte,** 1895–1897; **J. B. Crocq,** 1895–1897.

125. *Princeton University. Contributions to Psychology.*

TITLE VARIATIONS: Volume 1 subtitled *Reprinted from the Psychological Review and Other Journals.*

DATES OF PUBLICATION: Volume 1–4, 1895–1909.

FREQUENCY: Irregular.

NUMBERING VARIATIONS: None.

PUBLISHER: Various. *See* Note *below.*

PRIMARY EDITORS: **James Mark Baldwin,** 1895–1903; **Howard Crosby Warren,** 1904–1909.

NOTE: No original publications. Compilations of reprints of articles by members of the faculty of Princeton University primarily from *Psychological Review. Monograph Supplements,* but also from *American Naturalist; Carnegie Institution. Yearbook; Philosophische Studien; Psychological Bulletin;* and *Psychological Monographs.*

126. *Psychological Review. Monograph Supplements.*

TITLE VARIATIONS: Also cited as *Psychological Review. Psychological Monographs;* as *Psychological Review. Series of Monograph Supplements;* and as *Psychological Review. Psychological Monograph Supplements.* Continued by *Psychological Monographs* with Number 52, November 1910.

DATES OF PUBLICATION: Number 1–51, February 1895–April 1910.

FREQUENCY: Irregular. *See* Contents *below.*

NUMBERING VARIATIONS: Numbers often bound as Volume 1–12. *See* Contents *below.* Number 44 and 45 issued after Number 46 and 47. Various issues also numbered as *Columbia University. Contributions to Philosophy, Psychology and Education;* as *Harvard Psychological Studies;* as *Chicago. University. Contributions to Philosophy;* as *Iowa. University. Studies in Psychology;* as *Yale Psychological Studies;* as *Catholic University of America. Psychological Studies;*

as *Wesleyan University. Psychological Laboratory. Studies;* as *Johns Hopkins University. Studies in Philosophy and Psychology;* as *Johns Hopkins University. Psychological Laboratory. Studies;* as *Wellesley College. Studies in Psychology;* as *Illinois. University. Psychological Laboratory. Studies;* or as *Ohio. State University. Psychological Studies.* Number 36 issued in *Philosophical Monographs* with *Psychological Review. Monograph Supplement* numbering omitted.

PUBLISHER: **New York** and **London:** Macmillan and Company, 1895–1896. **Lancaster, Pennsylvania, New York** and **London:** Macmillan Company, 1897–1899. **Lancaster** and **New York:** Macmillan Company, 1900–1905. **Lancaster** and **Baltimore:** Review Publishing Company, 1906–1910.

PRIMARY EDITORS: **J. Mark Baldwin,** 1895–1903; **J. McKeen Cattell,** 1895–1903; **Charles H. Judd,** 1904–1909; **James R. Angell,** 1909–1910.

CONTENTS:

[**Volume 1**] **Number 1.** Griffing, Harold. ON SENSATIONS FROM PRESSURE AND IMPACT WITH SPECIAL REFERENCE TO THE INTENSITY, AREA AND TIME OF STIMULATION. February 1895. 89 pp. (Also as *Columbia University. Contributions to Philosophy, Psychology and Education,* Volume 4, Number 1.)

[————] **Number 2.** Calkins, Mary Whiton. ASSOCIATION. AN ESSAY ANALYTIC AND EXPERIMENTAL. February 1896. 56 pp.

[————] **Number 3.** Moore, Kathleen Carter. THE MENTAL DEVELOPMENT OF A CHILD. October 1896. 150 pp.

[————] **Number 4.** Buchner, Edward Franklin. A STUDY OF KANT'S PSYCHOLOGY WITH REFERENCE TO THE CRITICAL PHILOSOPHY. January 1897. 208 pp.

[**Volume 2**] **Number 5.** Quantz, J. O. PROBLEMS IN THE PSYCHOLOGY OF READING. December 1897. 51 pp.

[————] **Number 6.** Hylan, John Perham. THE FLUCTUATION OF ATTENTION. March 1898. 78 pp.

[————] **Number 7.** Lay, Wilfrid. MENTAL IMAGERY: EXPERIMENTALLY AND SUBJECTIVELY CONSIDERED. 1898. 59 pp. (Also as *Columbia University. Contributions to Philosophy, Psychology and Education,* Volume 4, Number 2.)

[————] **Number 8.** Thorndike, Edward L. ANIMAL INTELLIGENCE; AN EXPERIMENTAL STUDY OF THE ASSOCIATIVE PROCESS IN ANIMALS. June 1898. 109 pp. (Also as *Columbia University. Contributions to Philosophy, Psychology and Education,* Volume 4, Number 3.)

[————] **Number 9.** Dearborn, George Van Ness. THE EMOTION OF JOY. April 1899. 70 pp. (Also as *Columbia University. Contributions to Philosophy and Education,* Volume 4, Number 4.)

[————] **Number 10.** Dexter, Edwin Grant. CONDUCT AND THE WEATHER; AN INDUCTIVE STUDY OF THE MENTAL EFFECTS OF DEFINITE METEOROLOGICAL CONDITIONS. 1899. 103 pp. (Also as *Columbia University. Contributions to Philosophy, Psychology and Education,* Volume 5, Number 1.)

[**Volume 3**] **Number 11.** Breese, Burtis Burr. ON INHIBITION. 1899. 65 pp. (Also as *Columbia University. Contributions to Philosophy, Psychology and Education,* Volume 5, Number 3.)

[————] **Number 12.** Franz, Shepherd Ivory. ON AFTER-IMAGES. 1899. 61 pp. (Also as *Columbia University. Contributions to Philosophy, Psychology and Education*, Volume 5, Number 2.)

[————] **Number 13.** Woodworth, R. S. THE ACCURACY OF VOLUNTARY MOVEMENT. 1899. 114 pp. (Also as *Columbia University. Contributions to Philosophy, Psychology and Education*, Volume 5, Number 4.)

[————] **Number 14.** Bawden, H. Heath. A STUDY OF LAPSES. April 1900. 122 pp.

[————] **Number 15.** Thorndike, Edward L. THE MENTAL LIFE OF THE MONKEYS. May 1901. 57 pp. (Also as *Columbia University. Contributions to Philosophy, Psychology and Education*, Volume 9, Number 1.)

[————] **Number 16.** Wissler, Clark. THE CORRELATION OF MENTAL AND PHYSICAL TESTS. June 1901. 62 pp. (Also as *Columbia University. Contributions to Philosophy, Psychology and Education*, Volume 9, Number 2.)

[Volume 4] Number 17. Münsterberg, Hugo, ed. HARVARD PSYCHOLOGICAL STUDIES, VOLUME I: CONTAINING SIXTEEN EXPERIMENTAL INVESTIGATIONS FROM THE HARVARD PSYCHOLOGICAL LABORATORY. January 1903. 654 pp.

[Volume 5] Number 18. Jones, Joseph W. L. SOCIALITY AND SYMPATHY; AN INTRODUCTION TO THE ETHICS OF SYMPATHY. April 1903. 91 pp.

[————] **Number 19.** Bair, Joseph Hershey. THE PRACTICE CURVE; A STUDY IN THE FORMATION OF HABITS. November 1902. 70 pp. (Also as *Columbia University. Contributions to Philosophy, Psychology and Education*, Volume 9, Number 3.)

[————] **Number 20.** Hitchcock, Clara M. THE PSYCHOLOGY OF EXPECTATION. January 1903. 78 pp.

[————] **Number 21.** Miner, James Burt. MOTOR, VISUAL, AND APPLIED RHYTHMS; AN EXPERIMENTAL STUDY AND A REVISED EXPECTATION. June 1903. 106 pp. (Also as *Columbia University. Contributions to Philosophy, Psychology and Education*, Volume 9, Number 4.)

[————] **Number 22.** Messenger, James Franklin. THE PERCEPTION OF NUMBER. June 1903. 44 pp. (Also as *Columbia University. Contributions to Philosophy, Psychology and Education*, Volume 13, Number 1.)

[————] **Number 23.** Henderson, Ernest Norton. A STUDY OF MEMORY FOR CONNECTED TRAINS OF THOUGHT. December 1903. 94 pp. (Also as *Columbia University. Contributions to Philosophy, Psychology and Education*, Volume 13, Number 2.)

[Volume 6] Number 24. Moore, Thomas Verner. A STUDY IN REACTION TIME AND MOVEMENT. April 1904. 86 pp.

[————] **Number 25.** Tufts, James Hayden. THE INDIVIDUAL AND HIS RELATION TO SOCIETY AS REFLECTED IN THE BRITISH ETHICS OF THE EIGHTEENTH CENTURY. May 1904. 58 pp. (Also as *Chicago. University. Contributions to Philosophy*, Volume 1, Number 6.)

[————] **Number 26.** Boodin, John E. TIME AND REALITY. October 1904. 119 pp.

[————] **Number 27.** King, Irving. THE DIFFERENTIATION OF RELIGIOUS CONSCIOUSNESS. January 1905. 72 pp.

Year 1895

[————] **Number 28.** Seashore, Carl Emil, ed. UNIVERSITY OF IOWA STUDIES IN PSYCHOLOGY, No. IV. March 1905. 118 pp.

[Volume 7] Number 29. Judd, Charles H., ed. YALE PSYCHOLOGICAL STUDIES. New Series, Volume I, No. I. March 1905. 226 pp.

[————] **Number 30.** Dubray, Charles A. THE THEORY OF PSYCHICAL DISPOSITIONS. October 1905. 170 pp. (Also as *Catholic University of America. Psychological Studies,* [Number 1].)

[————] **Number 31.** Carr, Harvey. A VISUAL ILLUSION OF MOTION DURING EYE CLOSURE. August 1906. 127 pp.

[Volume 8] Number 32. Rowland, Eleanor H. THE PSYCHOLOGICAL EXPERIENCES CONNECTED WITH THE DIFFERENT PARTS OF SPEECH. January 1907. 42 pp.

[————] **Number 33.** Watson, John B. KINAESTHETIC AND ORGANIC SENSATIONS: THEIR ROLE IN THE REACTIONS OF THE WHITE RAT TO THE MAZE. May 1907. 100 pp.

[————] **Number 34.** Judd, Charles H., ed. YALE PSYCHOLOGICAL STUDIES. New Series, Volume I, Number II. June 1907. pp. 227–423.

[————] **Number 35.** Dodge, Raymond. AN EXPERIMENTAL STUDY OF VISUAL FIXATION. November 1907. 95 pp. (Also as *Wesleyan University. Psychological Laboratory. Studies,* Volume 1, Number 1.)

[————] **[Number 36].** Furry, William Davis. THE AESTHETIC EXPERIENCE. ITS NATURE AND FUNCTION IN EPISTEMOLOGY. 1908. 155 pp. (Also as *Philosophical Monographs,* Number 1 and as *Johns Hopkins University. Studies in Philosophy and Psychology,* Number 1.)

[Volume 9] Number 37. Downey, June E. CONTROL PROCESSES IN MODIFIED HAND-WRITING: AN EXPERIMENTAL STUDY. April 1908. 148 pp.

[————] **Number 38.** Seashore, Carl Emil, ed. UNIVERSITY OF IOWA STUDIES IN PSYCHOLOGY, Number V. June 1908. 148 pp.

[————] **Number 39.** Peterson, Joseph. COMBINATION TONES AND OTHER RELATED AUDITORY PHENOMENA. November 1908. 136 pp.

[Volume 10] Number 40. Stratton, George M., ed. STUDIES FROM THE JOHNS HOPKINS PSYCHOLOGICAL LABORATORY, [Number 1]. February 1909. 104 pp. (Also as *Johns Hopkins University. Studies in Philosophy and Psychology,* Number 2.)

[————] **Number 41.** Hayden, Edwin Andrew. THE SOCIAL WILL. April 1909. 93 pp.

[————] **Number 42.** Fernald, Grace Maxwell. THE EFFECT OF ACHROMATIC CONDITIONS ON THE COLOR PHENOMENA OF PERIPHERAL VISION. August 1909. 91 pp.

[————] **Number 43.** Gamble, Eleanor A. McC. A STUDY IN MEMORISING VARIOUS MATERIALS BY THE RECONSTRUCTION METHOD. September 1909. 210 pp. (Also as *Wellesley College. Studies in Psychology,* Number 1.)

[Volume 11] Number 44. Colvin, Stephen S., ed. STUDIES FROM THE PSYCHOLOGICAL LABORATORY OF THE UNIVERSITY OF ILLINOIS. Volume I, Number I, November 1909. 177 pp.

[————] **Number 45.** Haines, Thomas H., ed. OHIO STATE UNIVERSITY PSYCHOLOGICAL STUDIES, Volume I, Number 1. November 1909. 71 pp.

[————] **Number 46.** Yoakum, Clarence Stone. AN EXPERIMENTAL STUDY OF FATIGUE. August 1909. 131 pp.

[————] **Number 47.** Burrow, N. Trigant. THE DETERMINATION OF THE POSITION OF A MOMENTARY IMPRESSION IN THE TEMPORAL COURSE OF A MOVING VISUAL IMPRESSION. September 1909. 63 pp. (Also as *Johns Hopkins University. Psychological Laboratory. Studies,* Number 2 and *Johns Hopkins University. Studies in Philosophy and Psychology,* Number 3.)

[Volume 12] **Number 48.** Richardson, Florence. A STUDY OF SENSORY CONTROL IN THE RAT. October 1909. 124 pp.

[————] **Number 49.** Peterson, Harvey A. ON THE INFLUENCE OF COMPLEXITY AND DISSIMILARITY ON MEMORY. November 1909. 87 pp.

[————] **Number 50.** Bingham, W. Van Dyke. STUDIES IN MELODY. January 1910. 88 pp.

[————] **Number 51.** Seashore, Carl E., James R. Angell, Mary Whiton Calkins, Edmund C. Sanford, and Guy Montrose Whipple. (REPORT OF THE COMMITTEE OF THE AMERICAN PSYCHOLOGICAL ASSOCIATION ON THE TEACHING OF PSYCHOLOGY. PRESENTED TO THE ASSOCIATION DECEMBER 29, 1909.) April 1910. 93 pp.

127. *Psychologische Arbeiten.*

TITLE VARIATIONS: None.

DATES OF PUBLICATION: Band 1–9, Heft 3/4, 1895–Fall 1928. Suspended publication from December 1913–October 1920.

FREQUENCY: Quarterly.

NUMBERING VARIATIONS: Multinumber issues present.

PUBLISHER: **Leipzig:** Wilhelm Engelmann, 1895–1920. **Leipzig:** Buchhandlung von G. Fock, 1921. **Berlin:** Julius Springer, 1922–1928.

PRIMARY EDITOR: **Emil Kraeplin, 1895–1928.**

128. *Rivista di studi psichici; Periodico mensile dedicato alle ricerche sperimentali e critiche sui fenomeni di telepatia, telestesia, premonizione, medianità, ecc.*

TITLE VARIATIONS: Subtitle varies slightly. Continued by *Revue des études psychiques* with Série 2, Volume 1, 1901.

DATES OF PUBLICATION: Volume 1–6, 1895–1900.

FREQUENCY: Monthly.

NUMBERING VARIATIONS: Multinumber issues present in Volume 4–6. 12 numbers per year.

PUBLISHER: **Milan** and **Padua:** Redazione e amministrazione, 1895–1897. **Turin:** Direzione e amministrazione, 1898–1899. **Paris:** Direzione e amministrazione, 1899–1900.

PRIMARY EDITORS: **G. B. Ermacora, 1895–1897; Giorgio Finzi, 1895–1897; Cesare Baudi di Vesme, 1898–1900.**

1896

129. Archivio delle psicopatie sessuali. Rivista quindicinale di psicologia, psicopatologia umana e comparata, di medicina legale e di psichiatria forense ad uso dei medici, magistrati ed avvocati.

TITLE VARIATIONS: Superseded by *Rivista quindicinale di psicologia, psichiatria, neuropatologia ad uso del medici e del giuristi* with Volume 1, 1897.

DATES OF PUBLICATION: Fascicolo 1–22, 1/15 January 1896–15 November 1896.

FREQUENCY: Semimonthly.

NUMBERING VARIATIONS: Multinumber issues present. Supplement to Fascicolo 22 issued March 1897.

PUBLISHER: **Rome:** Fratelli Capaccini, 1896–1897.

PRIMARY EDITORS: **Pasquale Penta,** 1896–1897; **Raffaele Perrone-Capano,** 1896–1897; **Pompeo Nuccio,** 1896–1897.

130. Beiträge zur Psychologie und Philosophie.

TITLE VARIATIONS: None.

DATES OF PUBLICATION: Band 1, Heft 1–4, 1896–1905.

FREQUENCY: Irregular.

NUMBERING VARIATIONS: None.

PUBLISHER: **Leipzig:** Verlag von Wilhelm Engelmann, 1896–1905.

PRIMARY EDITOR: **Götz Martius,** 1896–1905.

131. Journal of Psycho-Asthenics; Devoted to the Care, Training and Treatment of the Feeble-Minded and of the Epileptic.

TITLE VARIATIONS: Subtitle added in 1900. Continued by *American Journal of Mental Deficiency* with Volume 45, July 1940.

DATES OF PUBLICATION: Volume 1–44, September 1896–1939.

FREQUENCY: **Quarterly,** Volume 1–22, 1896–June 1918. **Annual,** Volume 23–44, 1918–1939 (comprised of 4 issues published as one and containing annual proceedings. *See* Numbering Variations *below.*)

NUMBERING VARIATIONS: Combined issues in Volumes 6–15, 20–44. Volume 10, Number 1–2 is numbered Volume 9, Number 5–6; Volume 10, Number 3 is numbered Volume 9, Number 7. Volume 1–22 includes continuation of *Association of Medical Officers of American Institutions for Idiotic and Feeble-Minded Persons. Proceedings of the Annual Meetings,* Number 20–41, 1896–1917. Volume 23–37 includes *American Association for the Study of the Feeble-Minded. Annual Proceedings,* Number 42–56, 1918–1932. Volume

38–44 includes *American Association on Mental Deficiency. Proceedings and Addresses,* Number 57–63, 1933–1939.

PUBLISHER: **Faribault, Minnesota:** Association of Medical Officers of American Institutions for Idiotic and Feeble-Minded Persons, 1896–June 1902. **Faribault:** Association of Officers of American Institutions for the Feeble-Minded, September 1902–1905. **Faribault:** American Association for the Study of the Feeble-Minded, 1906–1917.

PRIMARY EDITORS: **A. C. Rogers,** 1896–1917; **Fred Kuhlmann,** 1912–1918; **Alexander Johnson,** 1896–1907; **F. M. Powell,** 1896–1903; **W. E. Fernald,** 1897–1918; **A. W. Wilmarth,** 1897–1908; **M. W. Barr,** 1897–1915; **George M. Mogridge,** 1904–1918; **A.R.T. Wylie,** 1904–1918; **E. R. Johnstone,** 1904–1908; **H. H. Bullard,** 1908–1909; **W. K. Weissbrodt,** 1908–1909; **H. H. Goddard,** 1909–1918; **H. G. Hardt,** 1909–1915; **C. S. Little,** 1909–1918; **Wm. Healy,** 1911–1918. None listed, 1919–1939.

132. *Moscow. Universitet. Psikhologicheskaia laboratoriia. Zapiski.*

TITLE VARIATIONS: Also called [*Moscow Université.*] *Laboratoire psychologique. Bulletin.*

DATES OF PUBLICATION: Number 1–5, 1896.

FREQUENCY: Bimonthly.

NUMBERING VARIATIONS: None.

PUBLISHER: **Moscow:** Tipografiia I. N. Kushnerev' i Ko. 1896.

PRIMARY EDITOR: **A. A. Tokarskii,** 1896.

133. *Obozrenie psikhiatrii, nevrologii i eksperimental'noi psikhologii.*

TITLE VARIATIONS: Continued by *Obozrenie psikhiatrii, nevrologii i refleksologii imeni V. M. Bekhtereva* with Tom 1, 1926.

DATES OF PUBLICATION: Tom 1–20, January 1896–1918. Suspended publication 1919–1925.

FREQUENCY: **Monthly,** Tom 1–18, January, 1896–December 1913. **Irregular,** Tom 19–20 (12 issues each), 1914/1915, 1916/1918.

NUMBERING VARIATIONS: None.

PUBLISHER: **Leningrad:** Gosudarstvennyi refleksologicheskii institut po izucheniiu mozga, 1896–1918.

PRIMARY EDITORS: Unknown.

NOTE: Information on this title was compiled from entries in *Half a Century of Soviet Serials.*

134. *Revue de psychiatrie de neurologie et d'hypnologie.*

TITLE VARIATIONS: Continues *Annales de psychiatrie et d'hypnologie dans leurs rapports avec la psychologie et la médecine légale.* Continued by *Revue de psychiatrie (médecine mentale, neurologie, psychologie)* with Nouvelle Série, Année 2, Numéro 6/7, June/July 1897.

DATES OF PUBLICATION: Nouvelle Série, Année 1–2, Numéro 5, January/ February 1896–May 1897.

FREQUENCY: Monthly.

NUMBERING VARIATIONS: Multinumber issues present.

PUBLISHER: **Paris:** Bureau de la revue de psychiatrie, January–November 1896. **Paris:** Maloine, Libraire-éditeur, December 1896–May 1897.

PRIMARY EDITORS: **A. Lutaud,** 1896; —— **Largueze,** 1896; **L. Jay,** 1897; **Eugène Daix,** 1897.

135. *Rivista di patologia nervosa e mentale.*

TITLE VARIATIONS: None.

DATES OF PUBLICATION: Volume 1–71 +, January 1896–1950 +.

FREQUENCY: **Monthly,** Volume 1–29, Numero 11/12, January 1896–November/ December 1924. **Bimonthly,** Volume 30–63, Numero 1/3, January/February 1925–January/June 1944. **Semiannual** (Irregular), Volume 64–70, 1945–1949. **Quarterly,** Volume 71 +, 1950 +.

NUMBERING VARIATIONS: Multinumber issues present.

PUBLISHER: **Florence:** Stabilimento tipografico Fiorentino, 1896–1897. **Florence:** Società tipografica Fiorentina, 1898–1906. **Florence:** Tipografia Galileiana, 1907–1917. **Florence:** Stabilimento tipografico Enrico Ariani, 1918–1921. **Siena:** Stabilimento tipografico S. Bernardino, 1922–1940. **Florence:** Tipografia Luigi Niccolai, 1941–1942. **Florence:** Ditta editrice Luigi Niccolai, 1943–1947. **Siena:** La Poligrafica, 1948–1950 +.

PRIMARY EDITORS: **E. Tanzi,** 1896–1933; **A. Tamburini,** 1896–1918; **E. Morselli,** 1896–1929; **E. Jugaro,** 1906–1940; **O. Rossi,** 1913–1936; **M. Zalla,** 1926–1950 +; **V. M. Buscaino,** 1927–1950 +; **A. Coppola,** 1933–1950 +; **G. C. Riquier,** 1937–1950 +; **C. Berlucchi,** 1938–1950 +; **D. Bolsi,** 1939–1950 +; **P. Ottonello,** 1950 +; **V. Longo,** 1950 +; **F. Cardona,** 1950 +; **V. Tronconi,** 1950 +.

136. *Voprosy nervno-psikhicheskoi meditsiny. Zhurnal posviashchennyi voprosam' psikhiatrii, nervnoi patologii, fiziologicheskoi psikhologii, nervno-psikhicheskoi gigieny i pr.*

TITLE VARIATIONS: With Tom 6, 1901, subtitle adds *vospitaniia* after *nervno-psikhicheskoi gigieny.*

DATES OF PUBLICATION: Tom 1–10, 1896–1905.

FREQUENCY: Quarterly.

NUMBERING VARIATIONS: Multinumber issues present.

PUBLISHER: **Kiev:** Tipografiia S. V. Kul'zhenko, 1896. **Kiev:** Tipografiia I. N. Kushnerev' i Ko., 1897–1905.

PRIMARY EDITOR: **Vladimir I. A. Sikorski,** 1896–1905.

137. *Zeitschrift für Hypnotismus, Psychotherapie sowie andere psychophysiologische und psychopathologische Forschungen.*

TITLE VARIATIONS: Continues *Zeitschrift für Hypnotismus, Suggestionstherapie, Suggestionslehre und verwandt psychologische Forschungen.* Superseded by *Journal für Psychologie und Neurologie* with Band 1, 1902.

DATES OF PUBLICATION: Band 4–10, 1896–1900.

FREQUENCY: Bimonthly.

NUMBERING VARIATIONS: None.

PUBLISHER: **Leipzig:** Johann Ambrosius Barth, 1896–1900.

PRIMARY EDITORS: **A. Forel,** 1896–1900; **O. Vogt,** 1896–1900.

1897

138. *American Psychological, Medical and Surgical Society. Journal.*

TITLE VARIATIONS: Continued by *Tubercle* with Volume 3, Number 1, January 1900.

DATES OF PUBLICATION: Volume 1–2, October 1897–September 1899.

FREQUENCY: Monthly.

NUMBERING VARIATIONS: None.

PUBLISHER: **Chicago:** Office Suite, 1207 Stewart Bldg. 92 State St., 1897–1899.

PRIMARY EDITOR: **Thomas Bassett Keyes,** 1897–1899.

139. *Congrès international de neurologie, de psychiatrie et de psychologie. Compte rendu.*

TITLE VARIATIONS: Also called *Congrès international de neurologie, de psychiatrie, d'électricité médicale et d'hypnologie.*

DATES OF PUBLICATION: 1er–5e, 1897–1924.

FREQUENCY: Irregular.

NUMBERING VARIATIONS: None.

PUBLISHER: Varies. *See* Contents *below.*

PRIMARY EDITORS: *See* Contents *below.*

CONTENTS:

1ᵉʳ. [Compte rendu,] Brussels, 1897. Rédigé par Jean Crocq. Paris: Bailliere, 1898. 3 Volumes in 1.

2ᵉ. [Compte rendu,] Vienna, 1908.

3ᵉ. [Compte rendu,] Ghent, 1913.

4ᵉ. [Compte rendu,] Paris, 1923.

5ᵉ. [Compte rendu,] Paris, 1924.

NOTE: Information on this entry is incomplete. The compilers have been unable to examine all numbers.

140. *Iowa. University. Studies in Psychology.*

TITLE VARIATIONS: None.

DATES OF PUBLICATION: Volume 1–24, 1897–1944.

FREQUENCY: Irregular.

NUMBERING VARIATIONS: Volumes 4–5 were issued as *Psychological Review. Monograph Supplements*, Number 28 and 38; and Volumes 6–24 were issued as *Psychological Monographs*, Number 69, 108, 140, 167, 168, 176, 178, 181, 187, 194, 198, 199, 200, 213, 214, 215, 217, 231 and 255. Volume 12 is SEASHORE COMMEMORATIVE NUMBER. Volume 18, 19 and 23 also numbered *Studies in the Psychology of Art*, Volume 1–3. Volume 14 and 20 also numbered *Studies in General Psychology*, Volume 1–2. Volume 21 also numbered *Studies in Psychology of Reading*, Volume 1. Volume 15, 16 and 22 also numbered *Studies in Clinical Psychology*, Volume 1–3. Volume 17 also called *Studies in Experimental and Theoretical Psychology*. Volume 24 also called *Studies in Language Behavior.*

PUBLISHER: **Iowa City, Iowa:** University of Iowa, Volume 1–3, 1897–1902. Various. See *Psychological Review. Monograph Supplements*, Volume 4–24, 1905–1944.

PRIMARY EDITORS: **George T. W. Patrick,** 1897–1902; **J. Allen Gilbert,** 1897; **Carl Emil Seashore,** 1905–1926; **Christian A. Ruckmick,** 1928–1937; **Walter R. Miles,** 1928; **Daniel Starch,** 1928; **Lee Edward Travis,** 1932–1937; **Norman Charles Meier,** 1933–1939; **Wendell Johnson,** 1944

141. *Kosmos. A Monthly Magazine Devoted to Cultural Ideals, the Psychology of Education, and the Educational Values of Citizenship.*

TITLE VARIATIONS: None.

DATES OF PUBLICATION: Volume 1–2, Number 6, August 1897–July 1898.

FREQUENCY: Monthly.

NUMBERING VARIATIONS: None.

PUBLISHER: **Vineland, New Jersey:** J. C. Parkinson, 1897–1898.

PRIMARY EDITOR: **Adolph Roeder,** 1897–1898.

142. *Psychologische bibliotheek (Amsterdam). [1].* [Issued by the Nederlandische psychologische vereniging.]

TITLE VARIATIONS: None.

DATES OF PUBLICATION: Number 1, 1897.

FREQUENCY: Irregular.

NUMBERING VARIATIONS: None.

PUBLISHER: **Amsterdam:** Fles & van Muijen, 1897.

PRIMARY EDITORS: None listed.

CONTENTS:

Nummer 1. Prel, Carl du. DE BETEEKENIS DER SUGGESTIE. Bewerkt door E.F.W. Croese. 1897.

143. *Revue de psychiatrie (médecine mentale, neurologie, psychologie).*

TITLE VARIATIONS: Continues *Revue de psychiatrie de neurologie et d'hypnologie.* Continued by *Revue de psychiatrie et de psychologie expérimentale* with Série 2, Année 5, Tome 5, January 1902.

DATES OF PUBLICATION: Nouvelle Série, Année 2, Numéro 6/7–Année 4, Tome 4, Numéro 12, June/July 1897–December 1901.

FREQUENCY: Monthly.

NUMBERING VARIATIONS: Issues for 1897–1898 do not carry a Tome number but constitute Année 2. Issues for 1899–1900 are numbered Tome 3 and constitute Année 3. Issues for 1901 are numbered Tome 4 and constitute Année 4.

PUBLISHER: **Paris:** A. Maloine, éditeur, 1897–1901.

PRIMARY EDITOR: **Édouard Toulouse,** 1897–1901.

EDITORIAL BOARD: N. Bajenoff, 1897–1901; G. Ballet, 1897–1901; A. Binet, 1897–1901; ——— Bogdam, 1897–1901; ——— Bouchereau, 1897–1901; H. Colin, 1897–1901; G. Dumas, 1897–1901; Maurice de Fleury, 1897–1901; A. Joffroy, 1897–1901; Alexandre Lacassagne, 1897–1901; M. Legrain, 1897–1901; V. Magnan, 1897–1901; Léona Manouvrier, 1897–1901; Maran-Don de Montyel, 1897–1901; J. Morel, 1897–1901; Enrico Morselli, 1897–1901; ——— Näcke, 1897–1901; C. F. Papillault, 1897–1901; Fulgence Raymond, 1897–1901; E. Régis, 1897–1901; Charles Richet, 1897–1901; Jules Séglas, 1897–1901; A. Vigouroux, 1897–1901; Pierre Janet, 1897–1901; M. Klippel, 1901; A. Marie, 1901; F. Pactet, 1901; Paul Sérieux, 1901.

144. *Revue de psychologie clinique et thérapeutique.*

TITLE VARIATIONS: None.

DATES OF PUBLICATION: Année 1–5, December 1897–December 1901.

FREQUENCY: Monthly.

NUMBERING VARIATIONS: Année 1 contains only one issue, dated December 1897.

PUBLISHER: **Paris:** Rédaction et administration, 1897–1901.

PRIMARY EDITORS: **P. Hartenberg,** 1897–1901; **P. Valentin,** 1897–1901.

145. *Rivista quindicinale di psicologia, psichiatria, neuropatologia ad uso dei medici e dei giuristi.*

TITLE VARIATIONS: Superseded by *Rivista mensile di neuropatologia e psichiatria* with Volume 1, July 1900.

DATES OF PUBLICATION: Volume 1–3, May 1897–April 1900.

FREQUENCY: 15 times per year.

NUMBERING VARIATIONS: None.

PUBLISHER: **Rome:** F. Capaccini, editori-tipografi, 1897–1900.

PRIMARY EDITORS: **Sante de Sanctis,** 1897–1900; **E. Sciamanna,** 1897–1900; **G. Sergi,** 1897–1900.

146. *Sammlung von Abhandlungen aus dem Gebiete der pädagogischen Psychologie und Physiologie.*

TITLE VARIATIONS: None.

DATES OF PUBLICATION: Band 1–8, Heft 7, 1897–1906.

FREQUENCY: Irregular. *See* Contents *below.*

NUMBERING VARIATIONS: Band 7, Heft 2/3, double number in 1904.

PUBLISHER: **Berlin:** Reuther & Reichard, 1897–1906.

PRIMARY EDITORS: **H. Schiller,** 1897–1902; **Theodor Ziehen,** 1897–1906; **Th. Ziegler,** 1902–1906.

CONTENTS:

Band 1, Heft 1. Schiller, H. DER STUDENPLAN. EIN KAPITEL AUS DER PÄDAGOGISCHEN PSYCHOLOGIE UND PHYSIOLOGIE. 1897. 69 pp.

————, **Heft 2.** Gutzmann, Herm. DIE PRAKTISCHE ANWENDUNG DER SPRACHPHYSIOLOGIE BEIM ERSTEN LESEUNTERRICHT. 1897. 52 pp.

————, **Heft 3.** Baumann, Jul. ÜBER WILLENS- UND CHARAKTERBILDUNG AUF PHYSIOLOGISCH-PSYCHOLOGISCHER GRUNDLAGE. 1897 86 pp.

————, **Heft 4.** Wagner, Ludwig. UNTERRICHT UND ERMÜDUNG. 1898. 134 pp.

————, **Heft 5.** Fauth, Fritz. DAS GEDÄCHTNIS. 1898. 88 pp.

————, **Heft 6.** Ziehen, Theodor. DIE IDEENASSOZIATION DES KINDES. 1898. 66 pp.

Band 2. Heft 1. Kemsies, Ferd. ARBEITSHYGIENE DER SCHULE AUF GRUND VON ERMÜDUNGSMESSUNGEN. 1898. 64 pp.

————, **Heft 2.** Cordes, G. PSYCHOLOGISCHE ANALYSE DER THATSACHE DER SELBSTERZIEHUNG. 1898. 54 pp.

————, **Heft 3.** Altenburg, Oskar. DIE KUNST DES PSYCHOLOGISCHEN BEOBACHTENS. 1898. 76 pp.

————, **Heft 4.** Fuchs, Heinrich, and August Haggenmüller. STUDIEN UND VERSUCHE ÜBER DIE ERLERNUNG DER ORTHOGRAPHIE. 1898. 63 pp.

————, **Heft 5.** Cramer, A. ÜBER DIE AUSSERHALB DER SCHULE LIEGENDEN URSACHEN DER NERVOSITÄT DER KINDER. 1899. 28 pp.

————, **Heft 6.** Huther, A. DIE PSYCHOLOGISCHE GRUNDLAGE DES UNTERRICHTS. 1899. 83 pp.

————, **Heft 7.** Ohlert, Arnold. DAS STUDIUM DER SPRACHEN UND DIE GEISTIGE BILDUNG. 1899. 50 pp.

————, **Heft 8.** Messer, August, DIE WIRKSAMKEIT DER APPERCEPTION IN DEN PERSÖNLICHEN BEZIEHUNGEN DES SCHULLEBENS. 1899. 69 pp.

Band 3, Heft 1. Schiller, Herm. DIE SCHULARZTFRAGE. 1899. 56 pp.

————, **Heft 2.** Monroe, William S. DIE ENTWICKELUNG DES SOZIALEN BEWUSSTSEINS DER KINDER. 1899. 88 pp.

————, **Heft 3.** Schmidt, Frz. ÜBER DEN REIZ DES UNTERRICHTENS. 1900. 36 pp.

————, **Heft 4.** Ziehen, Theodor. DIE IDEENASSOZIATION DES KINDES. 2 ABHANDLUNGEN. 1900. 59 pp.

————, **Heft 5.** Ziehen, Theodor. DAS VERHÄLTNIS DER HERBART'SCHEN PSYCHOLOGIE ZUR PHYSIOLOGISCH-EXPERIMENTELLEN PSYCHOLOGIE. 1900. 79 pp.

————, **Heft 6.** Messer, August. KRITISCHE UNTERSUCHUNGEN ÜBER DENKEN, SPRECHEN UND SPRACHUNTERRICHT. 1900. 51 pp.

————, **Heft 7.** Schneider, Georg. DIE ZAHL IM GRUNDLEGENDEN RECHENUNTERRICHT; ENTSTEHUNG, ENTWICKLUNG UND VERANSCHAULICHUNG DERSELBEN UNTER BEZUGNAHME AUF DIE PHYSIOLOGISCHE PSYCHOLOGIE. 1900. 87 pp.

Band 4, Heft 1. Schiller, H. DER AUFSATZ IN DER MUTTERSPRACHE. EINE PÄDAGOGISCH-PSYCHOLOGISCHE STUDIE. I. 1900. 68 pp.

————, **Heft 2.** Hornemann, F. DIE NEUESTE WENDUNG IM PREUSSICHEN SCHULSTREITE UND DAS GYMNASIUM. . . . I. DER KIELER ERLASS VOM 26. XI. 1900. 1901. 68 pp.

————, **Heft 3.** Liebmann, Alb. DIE SPRACHSTÖRUNGEN GEISTIG ZURÜCKGEBLIEBENER KINDER. 1901. 78 pp.

————, **Heft 4.** Ament, Wilhelm. DIE ENTWICKLUNG DER PFLANZENKENNTNIS BEIM KINDE UND BEI VÖLKERN. 1901. 59 pp.

————, **Heft 5.** Brauckmann, Karl. DIE PSYCHISCHE ENTWICKLUNG UND PÄDAGOGISCHE BEHANDLUNG SCHWERHÖRIGER KINDER. 1901. 96 pp.

————, **Heft 6.** Ganzmann, O. ÜBER SPRACH- UND SACHVORSTELLUNGEN. 1901. 80 pp.

Band 5, Heft 1. Ziehen, Theodor. DIE GEISTESKRANKHEITEN DES KINDESALTERS. 1. HEFT. 1902. 79 pp.

————, **Heft 2.** Leubuscher, G. STAATLICHE SCHULÄRZTE. 1902. 58 pp.

————, **Heft 3.** Schiller, H. DER AUFSATZ IN DER MUTTERSPRACHE. EINE PÄDAGOGISCH-PSYCHOLOGISCHE STUDIE. II. 1902. 61 pp.

————, **Heft 4.** Ament, Wilhelm. BEGRIFF UND BEGRIFFE DER BEGRIFFE DER KINDERSPRACHE. 1902. 85 pp.

———, **Heft 5.** Netschajeff, A. ÜBER MEMOIREN. 1902. 39 pp.

———, **Heft 6.** Zeissig, Emil. DIE RAUMPHANTASIE IM GEOMETRIEUN-TERRICHTE. 1902. 108 pp.

———, **Heft 7.** Lobsien, Marx. SCHWANKUNGEN DER PSYCHISCHEN KA-PAZITÄT. 1902. 110 pp.

Band 6, Heft 1. Scherer, H. DER WERKUNTERRICHT IN SEINER SOZIOLO-GISCHEN UND PHYSIOLOGISCH-PÄDAGOGISCHEN BEGRÜNDUNG. 1902. 50 pp.

———, **Heft 2.** Liebmann, Alb. STOTTERNDE KINDER. 1903. 96 pp.

———, **Heft 3.** Stilling, J. DIE KURZSICHTIGKEIT, IHRE ENTSTEHUNG UND BEDEUTUNG. 1903. 75 pp.

———, **Heft 4.** Orth, Johs. GEFÜHL UND BEWUSSTSEINSLAGE. 1903. 131 pp.

———, **Heft 5.** Stadelmann, Heinrich. SCHULEN FÜR NERVENKRANKE KINDER. 1903. 31 pp.

———, **Heft 6.** Mönkemöller, O. GEISTESSTÖRUNG UND VERBRECHEN IM KINDESALTER. 1903. 108 pp.

Band 7, Heft 1. Ziehen, Theodor. DIE GEISTESKRANKHEITEN DES KINDES-ALTERS MIT BESONDERER BERÜCKSICHTIGUNG DES SCHULPFLICHTIGEN ALTERS. 2. Heft. 1904. 94 pp.

———, **Heft 2/3.** Probst, M. GEHIRN UND SEELE DES KINDES. 1904. 148 pp.

———, **Heft 4.** Eggert, Bruno. DER PSYCHOLOGISCHE ZUSAMMENHANG IN DER DIDAKTIK DES NEUSPRACHLICHEN REFORMUNTERRICHTS. 1904. 74 pp.

———, **Heft 5.** Sallwürk, E. von. ÜBER DIE AUSFÜLLUNG DES GEMÜTS DURCH DEN ERZIEHENDEN UNTERRICHT. 1904. 47 pp.

———, **Heft 6.** Netschajeff, A. ÜBER AUFFASSUNG. 1904. 26 pp.

———, **Heft 7.** Nausester, Walt. DAS KIND UND DIE FORM DER SPRACHE. 1904. 51 pp.

Band 8, Heft 1. Lehmann, Rud. WEGE UND ZIELE DER PHILOSOPHISCHEN PROPÄDEUTIK. 1905. 59 pp.

———, **Heft 2.** Stern, William. HELEN KELLER. 1905. 76 pp.

———, **Heft 3.** Fauth, F. DER FREMDSPRACHLICHE UNTERRICHT AUF UN-SEREN HÖHEREN SCHULEN VOM STANDPUNKT DER PHYSIOLOGIE UND PSYCHO-LOGIE BELEUCHTET. 1905. 34 pp.

———, **Heft 4.** Kluge, O. ÜBER DAS WESEN UND DIE BEHANDLUNG DER GEISTIG ABNORMEN FÜRSORGEZÖGLINGE. 1905. 18 pp.

———, **Heft 5.** Binswanger, O. ÜBER DEN MORALISCHEN SCHWACHSINN. 1905. 36 pp.

———, **Heft 6.** Werner, Friedrich. PSYCHOLOGISCHE BEGRÜNDUNG DER DEUTSCHEN METHODE DES TAUBSTUMMEN-UNTERRICHTS. 1906. 50 pp.

———, **Heft 7.** Ziehen, Theodor. DIE GEISTESKRANKHEITEN DES KINDES-ALTERS. 3. Heft. 1906. 130 pp.

147. *Zeitschrift für Spiritismus und verwandte Gebiete.*

TITLE VARIATIONS: Continued by *Zeitschrift für Spiritismus, Somnambulis-mus, Magnetismus, Spiritualismus und verwandte Gebiete* with Jahrgang 3, 1899.

DATES OF PUBLICATION: Jahrgang 1–2, 1897–1898.

FREQUENCY: Weekly.

NUMBERING VARIATIONS: None.

PUBLISHER: **Leipzig:** D. Mutze, 1897–1898.

PRIMARY EDITOR: **Fritz Feilgenhauer,** 1897–1898.

1898

148. *Archives of Neurology and Psychopathology.*

TITLE VARIATIONS: Supersedes *State Hospitals Bulletin.* Superseded by *State Hospitals Bulletin,* later *Psychiatric Bulletin of the New York State Hospitals.*

DATES OF PUBLICATION: Volume 1–3, Number 3, December 1898–1901.

FREQUENCY: Quarterly.

NUMBERING VARIATIONS: None.

PUBLISHER: **Utica, New York:** State Hospitals Press, 1898–1901.

PRIMARY EDITORS: **George A. Blumer,** 1898–1901; **Ira Van Gleason,** 1898–1901.

149. *Bibliothèque de pédagogie et de psychologie.*

TITLE VARIATIONS: None.

DATES OF PUBLICATION: Volume 1–5, 1898–1903.

FREQUENCY: Irregular. *See* Contents *below.*

NUMBERING VARIATIONS: None.

PUBLISHER: **Paris:** Schleicher Frères, 1898–1902. **Paris:** Schleicher Frères & Cie, 1903.

PRIMARY EDITOR: **Alfred Binet,** 1898–1903.

CONTENTS:
 Volume 1. Binet, Alfred, and Victor Henri. LA FATIGUE INTELLECTUELLE. 1898. 338 pp.
 Volume 2. Sanford, Edmund C. COURS DE PSYCHOLOGIE EXPÉRIMENTALE. (SENSATIONS ET PERCEPTIONS). Traduit de l'anglais par Albert Schinz. 1900. 477 pp.
 Volume 3. Binet, Alfred. LA SUGGESTIBILITÉ. 1900. 391 pp.
 Volume 4. Bourdon, Benjamin. LA PERCEPTION VISUELLE DE L'ESPACE. 1902. 442 pp.
 Volume 5. Binet, Alfred. L'ÉTUDE EXPÉRIMENTALE DE L'INTELLIGENCE. 1903. 309 pp.

150. *Journal de neurologie. Neurologie, psychiatrie, psychologie, hypnologie.*

TITLE VARIATIONS: Continues *Journal de neurologie & d'hypnologie. Neurologie, hypnologie, psychiatrie, psychologie.* Continued by *Journal de neurologie. Neurologie, psychiatrie, psychologie* with Tome 13, 1907.

DATES OF PUBLICATION: Tome 3–12, 1898–1907.

FREQUENCY: Semimonthly.

NUMBERING VARIATIONS: None.

PUBLISHER: **Brussels:** Imprimerie maison Severeyns, 1898–1901. **Brussels:** Imprimerie scientifique maison Severeyns, 1902–1905. **Brussels:** Imprimerie scientifique L. Severeyns, 1906–1907. **Brussels:** Direction, J. Crocq, 62, rue Joseph II, 1907.

PRIMARY EDITORS: **Xavier Francotte,** 1898–1907; **J. Crocq,** 1898–1907; **A. Van Gehuchten,** 1898–1899; **F. Sano,** 1899–1906.

151. *Paris. Hospice de la Salpêtrière. Laboratoire de psychologie. Travaux.*

TITLE VARIATIONS: Variations in wording of series titles. Série 1–5, 1898–1911 titled *Travaux du laboratoire de psychologie de la clinique à la salpêtrière.* Série 6–10, 1919–1928 titled *Travaux du laboratoire de psychologie de la salpêtrière.*

DATES OF PUBLICATION: Série 1–10, 1898–1928.

FREQUENCY: Irregular. *See* Contents *below.*

NUMBERING VARIATIONS: None.

PUBLISHER: **Paris:** Félix Alcan, éditeur, 1898–1911. **Paris:** Librairie Félix Alcan, 1919–1928.

PRIMARY EDITORS: None listed.

CONTENTS:
Série 1/2. Janet, Pierre, and Fulgence Raymond. NÉVROSES ET IDÉES FIXES. 1898. 2 volumes.
Série 3/4. Janet, Pierre, and Fulgence Raymond. LES OBSESSIONS ET LA PSYCHASTHÉNIE. 1903. 2 volumes.
Série 5. Janet, Pierre. L'ÉTAT MENTAL DES HYSTÉRIQUES. LES STIGMATES MENTAUX DES HYSTÉRIQUES, LES ACCIDENTS MENTAUX DES HYSTÉRIQUES, ÉTUDES SUR DIVERS SYMPTOMES HYSTÉRIQUES, LE TRAITEMENT PSYCHOLOGIQUE DE L'HYSTÉRIE. 1911. 708 pp.
Série 6/8. Janet Pierrre. LES MÉDICATIONS PSYCHOLOGIQUES; ÉTUDES HISTORIQUES, PSYCHOLOGIQUES ET CLINIQUES SUR LES MÉTHODES DE LA PSYCHOTHÉRAPIE. 1919. 3 volumes.
Série 9/10. Janet, Pierre. DE L'ANGOISSE À L'EXTASE; ÉTUDES SUR LES CROYANCES ET LES SENTIMENTS. 1926–1928. 2 volumes.

152. *Princeton University. Contributions to Philosophy.*

TITLE VARIATIONS: None.

DATES OF PUBLICATION: Volume 1, Number 1–4; 1898–1905.

FREQUENCY: Irregular.

NUMBERING VARIATIONS: None.

PUBLISHER: **Princeton, New Jersey:** The University Press, 1898–1905.

PRIMARY EDITOR: **Alexander T. Ormond,** 1898–1905.

153. *Toronto. University. Studies. Psychology Series.*

TITLE VARIATIONS: Volume 1 as *Psychological Series.*

DATES OF PUBLICATION: Volume 1–5, Number 1, 1898–1940.

FREQUENCY: Irregular.

NUMBERING VARIATIONS: Volume 1 contains Number 1–4; Volume 2, Number 1–4; Volume 3, Number 1; Volume 4, Number 1–2; and Volume 5, Number 1. Volume 4 dated 1920, Volume 5 dated 1940.

PUBLISHER: **Toronto:** Librarian of the University of Toronto, 1898–1920. **Toronto:** University of Toronto Press, 1940.

PRIMARY EDITORS: **A. Kirschmann,** 1898–1907; **H. H. Langton,** 1908–1920; **Alison Ewart,** 1940.

1899

154. *New Jersey Association for the Study of Children and Youth. Proceedings.*

TITLE VARIATIONS: *See* Contents *below.*

DATES OF PUBLICATION: Number 1–3, 1899–1901.

FREQUENCY: Semiannual. *See* Note *below.*

NUMBERING VARIATIONS: None.

PUBLISHER: **Bloomfield, New Jersey:** Brotherhood Press for the New Jersey Association for the Study of Children and Youth, 1900–1901.

PRIMARY EDITOR: **William E. Chancellor,** 1899–1901.

CONTENTS:

    Number 1. ADDRESSES AND PAPERS. PROCEEDINGS OF THE NEW JERSEY ASSOCIATION FOR THE STUDY OF CHILDREN AND YOUTH AT THE FIRST SEMI-ANNUAL MEETING. NEWARK, NEW JERSEY, SATURDAY, MARCH 11TH, 1899. [1900.] 63 pp.

    Number 2. ADDRESSES AND PAPERS. PROCEEDINGS OF THE NEW JERSEY ASSOCIATION FOR THE STUDY OF CHILDREN AND YOUTH AT THE SECOND SEMI-ANNUAL MEETING, JERSEY CITY, NEW JERSEY, SATURDAY, JANUARY 20TH, 1900. 1900. 65 pp.

Number 3. REPORT OF THE PROCEEDINGS OF THE NEW JERSEY ASSOCIA-
TION FOR THE STUDY OF CHILDREN AND YOUTH, DECEMBER 7TH, 1901, NEW-
ARK, NEW JERSEY. 1901. 32 pp.

NOTE: Though called "semi-annual" meetings, meetings and proceedings appear to have been issued annually. *See* Contents *above.*

155. *Société libre pour l'étude psychologique de l'enfant. Bulletin.*

TITLE VARIATIONS: Also called *Bulletin mensuel.* Continued by [*Société Alfred Binet.*] *Psychologie de l'enfant et pédagogie expérimentale. Bulletin mensuel* with Numéro 118, October/November 1917.

DATES OF PUBLICATION: Année 1–17, Numéro 6, 1899–August/September 1917.

FREQUENCY: Monthly (during academic year).

NUMBERING VARIATIONS: Issues are also assigned whole numbers, Numéro 1–117. Each number can contain from one to three months.

PUBLISHER: **Paris:** Librairie Félix Alcan, 1899–1911 (January). **Paris:** Librairie F. Alcan, 1911–1917.

PRIMARY EDITORS: **M. F. Buisson** (Dir.), 1899–1917; [**M.**] **Roussel,** 1899–1911; **Mlle Giroud,** 1911–1913; [**M.**] **Dubus,** 1913–1914; **V. Vaney,** 1914–1917.

156. *Zeitschrift für pädgogische Psychologie.*

TITLE VARIATIONS: Continued by *Zeitschrift für pädagogische Psychologie und Pathologie* with Jahrgang 2, 1900.

DATES OF PUBLICATION: Jahrgang 1, 1899.

FREQUENCY: Bimonthly.

NUMBERING VARIATIONS: None.

PUBLISHER: **Berlin:** Verlag von Hermann Walther, 1899.

PRIMARY EDITOR: **Ferdinand Kemsies,** 1899.

157. *Zeitschrift für Spiritismus, Somnambulismus, Magnetismus, Spiritualismus und verwandte Gebiete.*

TITLE VARIATIONS: Continues *Zeitschrift für Spiritismus und verwandte Gebiete.* Continued by *Zeitschrift für Seelenleben, neuere Psychologie und verwandte Gebiete* with Jahrgang 21, 1918.

DATES OF PUBLICATION. Jahrgang 3–20, 1899–1917.

FREQUENCY: Weekly.

NUMBERING VARIATIONS: None.

PUBLISHER: **Leipzig:** D. Mutze, 1899–1917.

PRIMARY EDITORS: **Fritz Feilgenhauer,** 1899–1917; **Rud. Feilgenhauer,** 1911–1917.

1900-1909

158. Archivio di psicologia collectiva e scienze affini.

TITLE VARIATIONS: None.

DATES OF PUBLICATION: Anno 1, Fasicule 1, April 1900.

FREQUENCY: Irregular.

NUMBERING VARIATIONS: None.

PUBLISHER: **Cosenza:** Tip. N. Caputi e Figlio, 1900.

PRIMARY EDITOR: **P. Rossi,** 1900.

159. Breslau. Psychologische Gesellschaft. Vortrags-Cyklus über die Entwicklung der Psychologie und verwandter Gebiete des Wissens und des Lebens im neunzehnten Jahrhundert.

TITLE VARIATIONS: None.

DATES OF PUBLICATION: Heft 1/2–4, 6, 9 and 12, 1900–1903.

FREQUENCY: Irregular. *See* Contents *below.*

NUMBERING VARIATIONS: 14 Hefte were planned. Heft 5, 7, 8, 10, 11, 13 and 14 were never issued. All Hefte issued were published both as separates and as articles in the *Zeitschrift für pädagogische Psychologie und Pathologie* and *Zeitschrift für pädagogische Psychologie, Pathologie und Hygiene,* and collected as a Sammelband in 1904. *See* Contents *below.*

PUBLISHER: **Berlin:** Verlag von Hermann Walther, 1900–1903.

PRIMARY EDITOR: **L. William Stern,** 1900–1903.

For serial publications that began before 1900 and were still being published during the decade 1900 to 1909, *see also* entries 32, 50, 65, 67, 72, 73, 74, 79, 82, 84, 85, 90, 94, 96, 97, 98, 101, 104, 105, 107, 108, 110, 111, 112, 114, 116, 119, 120, 121, 122, 123, 125, 126, 127, 128, 130, 131, 133, 135, 136, 137, 139, 140, 143, 144, 145, 146, 148, 149, 150, 151, 152, 153, 154, 155, 157.

CONTENTS:

Heft 1/2. Stern, L. William. DIE PSYCHOLOGISCHE ARBEIT DES NEUNZEHN-TEN JAHRHUNDERTS INSBESONDERE IN DEUTSCHLAND. 1900. 48 pp. (Also as *Zeitschrift fur pädagogische Psychologie und Pathologie,* Jahrgang 2, Heft 5–6, 1900, pp. 329–352.)

Heft 3. Sachs, Heinrich. DIE ENTWICKLUNG DER GEHIRN-PHYSIOLOGIE IM XIX. JAHRHUNDERT. 1902. 29 pp. (Also as *Zeitschrift für pädagogische Psychologie und Pathologie,* Jahrgang 3, Heft 4, 1901, pp. 255–280.)

Heft 4. Gaupp, Robert. DIE ENTWICKLUNG DER PSYCHIATRIE IM 19. JAHRHUNDERT. 1900. 20 pp. (Also as *Zeitschrift für pädagogische Psychologie und Pathologie,* Jahrgang 2, Heft 3, 1900, pp. 209–226.)

Heft 6. Steinitz, Kurt. DER VERANTWORTLICHKEITSGEDANKE IM 19. JAHRHUNDERT. 1902. 32 pp. (Also as *Zeitschrift für pädagogische Psychologie und Pathologie,* Jahrgang 3, Heft 5, 1901, pp. 335–362.)

Heft 9. Hase, Karl von. DIE PSYCHOLOGISCHE BEGRÜNDUNG DER RELIGIÖSEN WELTANSCHAUUNG IM 19. JAHRHUNDERT. 1901. 26 pp. (Also as *Zeitschrift für pädagogische Psychologie und Pathologie,* Jahrgang 3, Heft 1, 1901, pp. 1–26.)

Heft 12. Kemsies, Ferdinand. DIE ENTWICKLUNG DER PÄDAGOGISCHEN PSYCHOLOGIE IM 19. JAHRHUNDERT. 1903. 42 pp. (Also as *Zeitschrift für pädagogische Psychologie, Pathologie und Hygiene,* Jahrgang 4, Heft 3–5/6, 1902, pp. 197–211, 342–355, 473–484.)

160. *Grenzfragen des Nerven- und Seelenlebens.*

TITLE VARIATIONS: None.

DATES OF PUBLICATION: Heft 1–128/130, 1900–1927. Suspended publication 1915–1916.

FREQUENCY: Irregular. *See* Contents *below.*

NUMBERING VARIATIONS: Multinumber issues are Heft 6/7, 128/130. Heft 55 published ahead of Heft 54. Heft 2 incorrectly paginated from p. 61. Heft 1–8 and 9–10 continuously paginated; all others individually paginated.

PUBLISHER: **Wiesbaden:** J. F. Bergmann, 1900–1920. **Munich** and **Wiesbaden:** J. F. Bergmann, 1920–1922. **Munich:** J. F. Bergmann, 1923–1927.

PRIMARY EDITORS: **Leopold Loewenfeld,** 1900–1922; **Hans Kurella,** 1900–1907, 1921; **Ernst Kretschmer,** 1923–1927.

CONTENTS:

Heft 1. Loewenfeld, Leopold. SOMNAMBULISMUS UND SPIRITISMUS. 1900. Pp.1–71.

Heft 2. Obersteiner, H. FUNKTIONELLE UND ORGANISCHE NERVENKRANKHEITEN. 1900. Pp. 61–92.

Heft 3. Möbius, P. J. ÜBER ENTARTUNG. 1900. Pp. 93–123.

Heft 4. Finzi, Jacopo. DIE NORMALEN SCHWANKUNGEN DER SEELENTÄTIGKEITEN. 1900. Pp. 125–158.

Heft 5. Koch, J.L.A. ABNORME CHARAKTERE. 1900. Pp. 159–200.

Heft 6/7. Friedmann, M. WAHNIDEEN IM VÖLKERLEBEN. 1901. Pp. 201–305.

Heft 8. Freud, Sigmund. ÜBER DEN TRAUM. 1901. Pp. (307)–344.

Heft 9. Lipps, Theodor. DAS SELBSTBEWUSSTSEIN; EMPFINDUNG UND GEFÜHL. 1901. Pp. 1–42.

Heft 10. Storch, E. MUSKELFUNKTION UND BEWUSSTSEIN. EINE STUDIE ZUM MECHANISMUS DER WAHRNEHMUNGEN. 1901. Pp. 43–86.

Heft 11. Adamkiewicz, Albert. DIE GROSSHIRNRINDE ALS ORGAN DER SEELE. 1902. 79 pp.

Heft 12. Sombart, Werner. WIRTSCHAFT UND MODE. 1902. 23 pp.

Heft 13. Schuppe, Wilhelm. DER ZUSAMMENHANG VON LEIB UND SEELE, DAS GRUNDPROBLEM DER PSYCHOLOGIE. 1902. 67 pp.

Heft 14. Hoche, A. DIE FREIHEIT DES WILLENS VOM STANDPUNKTE DER PSYCHOPATHOLOGIE. 1902. 40 pp.

Heft 15. Jentsch, Ernst. DIE LAUNE. EINE ÄRZTLICHPSYCHOLOGISCHE STUDIE. 1902. 60 pp.

Heft 16. Bechterew, W. von. DIE ENERGIE DES LEBENDEN. ORGANISMUS UND IHRE PSYCHO-BIOLOGISCHE BEDEUTUNG. 1902. (2te. auflage, retitled PSYCHE UND LEBEN, 1908. 209 pp.)

Heft 17. Möbius, Paul Julius. ÜBER DAS PATHOLOGISCHE BEI NIETZSCHE. 1902. 106 pp.

Heft 18. Naecke, P. ÜBER DIE SOGENANNTE "MORAL INSANITY." 1902. 65 pp.

Heft 19. Eulenburg, A. SADISMUS UND MASOCHISMUS. 1902. 89 pp. (2te Auflage, 1911. 106 pp.)

Heft 20. Lange, Karl. SINNESGENÜSSE UND KUNSTGENUSS. NACH SEINEM TODE HERAUSGEGEBEN VON HANS KURELLA. 1903. 100 pp.

Heft 21. Loewenfeld, Leopold. ÜBER DIE GENIALE GEISTESTÄTIGKEIT MIT BESONDERER BERÜCKSICHTIGUNG DES GENIES FÜR BILDENDE KUNST. 1903. 104 pp.

Heft 22. Wolff, Gustav. PSYCHIATRIE UND DICHTKUNST. 1903. 20 pp.

Heft 23. Oppenheimer, Z. "BEWUSSTSEIN—GEFÜHL." EINE PSYCHO-PHYSIOLOGISCHE UNTERSUCHUNG. 1903. 75 pp.

Heft 24. Kowalewski, Arnold. BEITRÄGE ZUR PSYCHOLOGIE DES PESSIMISMUS. 1904. 122 pp.

Heft 25. Hirt, Eduard. DER EINFLUSS DES ALKOHOLS AUF DAS NERVEN- UND SEELENLEBEN. 1904. 76 pp.

Heft 26. Hoffmann, Aug. BERUFSWAHL UND NERVENLEIDEN. 1904. 26 pp.

Heft 27. Tiling, Th. INDIVIDUELLE GEISTESENTARTUNG UND GEISTESSTÖRUNG. 1904. 59 pp.

Heft 28. Loewenfeld, Leopold. HYPNOSE UND KUNST. 1904. 24 pp.

Heft 29. Jentsch, Ernst. MUSIK UND NERVEN. I. NATURGESCHICHTE DES TONSINNES. 1904. 46 pp.

Heft 30. Meyer, Semi. ÜBUNG UND GEDÄCHTNIS. EINE PHYSIOLOGISCHE STUDIE. 1904. 64 pp.

Heft 31. Probst, Ferdinand. DER FALL OTTO WEININGER. EINE PSYCHIATRISCHE STUDIE. 1904. 40 pp.

Heft 32. Bäumer, Gertrud. DIE FRAU IN DER KULTURBEWEGUNG DER GEGENWART. MIT EINEM VORWORT VON L. LOEWENFELD. 1904. 49 pp.

Heft 33. Wanke, Georg. PSYCHIATRIE UND PÄDAGOGIK. 1905. 26 pp.

Heft 34. Laquer, B. TRUNKSUCHT UND TEMPERENZ IN DEN VEREINIGTEN STAATEN. STUDIEN UND EINDRÜCKE. 1905. 71 pp.

160. *(Continued)*

Heft 35. Kötscher, L. M. ÜBER DAS BEWUSSTSEIN, SEINE ANOMALIEN UND IHRE FORENSISCHE BEDEUTUNG. 1905. 190 pp.

Heft 36. Sachs, Heinrich. GEHIRN UND SPRACHE. 1905. 128 pp.

Heft 37. Obersteiner, H. ZUR VERGLEICHENDEN PSYCHOLOGIE DER VERSCHIEDENEN SINNESQUALITÄTEN. 1905. 55 pp.

Heft 38. Loewenfeld, L. ÜBER DIE GEISTIGE ARBEITSKRAFT UND IHRE HYGIENE. 1905. 69 pp.

Heft 39. Bechterew, E. von. DIE BEDEUTUNG DER SUGGESTION IM SOZIALEN LEBEN. 1905. 142 pp.

Heft 40. Hirt, Eduard. DIE TEMPERAMENTE, IHR WESEN, IHRE BEDEUTUNG FÜR DAS SEELISCHE ERLEBEN UND IHRE BESONDEREN GESTALTUNGEN. 1905. 54 pp.

Heft 41. Hellpach, Willy. NERVENLEBEN UND WELTANSCHAUUNG. IHRE WECHSELBEZIEHUNGEN IM DEUTSCHEN LEBEN VON HEUTE. 1906. 81 pp.

Heft 42. Hoppe, Hugo. ALKOHOL UND KRIMINALITÄT. IN ALLEN IHREN BEZIEHUNGEN. 1906. 208 pp.

Heft 43. Pflaum, Chr. D. DIE INDIVIDUELLE UND DIE SOZIALE SEITE DES SEELISCHEN LEBENS. 1906. 65 pp.

Heft 44. Buschan, Georg. GEHIRN UND KULTUR. 1906. 74 pp.

Heft 45. Bechterew, W. von. DIE PERSÖNLICHKEIT UND DIE BEDINGUNGEN IHRER ENTWICKLUNG UND GESUNDHEIT. 1906. 38 pp.

Heft 46. Lobedank, Emil. RECHTSSCHUTZ UND VERBRECHERBEHANDLUNG. ÄRZTLICH-NATURWISSENSCHAFTLICHE AUSBLICKE AUF DIE ZUKÜNFTIGE KRIMINALPOLITIK. 1906. 89 pp.

Heft 47. Meyer, Semi. DER SCHMERZ. EINE UUNTERSUCHUNG DER PSYCHOLOGISCHEN UND PHYSIOLOGISCHEN BEDINGUNGEN DES SCHMERZVORGANGES. 1906. 79 pp.

Heft 48. Dubois, P. DIE EINBILDUNG ALS KRANKHEITSURSACHE. 1907. 45 pp.

Heft 49. Lomer, Georg. LIEBE UND PSYCHOSE. 1907. 55 pp.

Heft 50. Weygandt, G. DIE ABNORMEN CHARAKTERE BEI IBSEN. 1907. 16 pp.

Heft 51. Kreuser, H. GEISTESKRANKHEIT UND VERBRECHEN. 1907. 73 pp.

Heft 52. Kötscher, L. M. DAS ERWACHEN DES GESCHLECHTSBEWUSSTSEINS UND SEINE ANOMALIEN. 1907. 82 pp.

Heft 53. Laquer, B. GOTENBURGER SYSTEM UND ALKOHOLISMUS. 1907. 73 pp.

Heft 54. Lessing, Theodor. DER LÄRM. EINE KAMPFSCHRIFT GEGEN DIE GERÄUSCHE UNSERES LEBENS. 1908. 94 pp.

Heft 55. Ehrenfels, Christian von. GRUNDBEGRIFFE DER ETHIK. 1907. 30 pp.

Heft 56. Ehrenfels, Christian von. SEXUALETHIK. 1907. 99 pp.

Heft 57. Loewenfeld, Leopold. HOMOSEXUALITÄT UND STRAFGESETZ. 1908. 35 pp.

Heft 58. Bumke, Oswald. LANDLÄUFIGE IRRTÜMER IN DER BEURTEILUNG VON GEISTESKRANKEN. 1908. 64 pp.

Heft 59. Sadger, J. KONRAD FERDINAND MEYER, EINE PATHOGRAPHISCH-PSYCHOLOGISCHE STUDIE. 1908. 64 pp.

Heft 60. Vorberg, Gaston. GUY DE MAUPASSANTS KRANKHEIT. 1908. 28 pp.

Heft 61. Kotik, Naum. DIE EMANATION DER PSYCHO-PHYSISCHEN ENERGIE. 1908. 130 pp.

Heft 62. Waldstein, Louis. DAS UNTERBEWUSSTE ICH UND SEIN VERHÄLTNIS ZU GESUNDHEIT UND ERZIEHUNG. 1908. 71 pp.

Heft 63. Pilcz, Alexander. DIE VERSTIMMUNGSZUSTÄNDE. 1909. 44 pp.

Heft 64. Birnbaum, Carl. ÜBER PSYCHOPATHISCHE PERSÖNLICHKEITEN. EINE PSYCHOPATHOLOGISCHE STUDIE. 1909. 88 pp.

Heft 65. Stekel, Wilhelm. DICHTUNG UND NEUROSE. BAUSTEINE ZUR PSYCHOLOGIE DES KÜNSTLERS UND DES KUNSTWERKES. 1909. 73 pp.

Heft 66. Freimark, Hans. TOLSTOJ ALS CHARAKTER. EINE STUDIE AUF GRUND SEINER SCHRIFTEN. 1909. 33 pp.

Heft 67. Stransky, Erwin. ÜBER DIE DEMENTIA PRAECOX. STREIFZÜGE DURCH KLINIK UND PSYCHOPATHOLOGIE. 1909. 46 pp.

Heft 68. Bumke, Oswald. ÜBER DIE KÖRPERLICHEN BEGLEITERSCHEINUNGEN PSYCHISCHER VORGÄNGE. 1909. 16 pp.

Heft 69. Hoffmann, Richard Adolf. KANT UND SWEDENBORG. 1909. 29 pp.

Heft 70. Sadger, J. HEINRICH VON KLEIST. EINE PATHOGRAPHISCH-PSYCHOLOGISCHE STUDIE. 1910. 63 pp.

Heft 71. Feis, Oswald. STUDIEN ÜBER DIE GENEALOGIE UND PSYCHOLOGIE DER MUSIKER. 1910. 97 pp.

Heft 72. Schultze, Ernst. DIE JUGENDLICHEN VERBRECHER IM GEGENWÄRTIGEN UND ZUKÜNFTIGEN STRAFRECHT. 1910. 74 pp.

Heft 73. Kurella, Hans. CESARE LOMBROSO ALS MENSCH UND FORSCHER. 1910. 90 pp.

Heft 74. Forel, A. ABSTINENZ ODER MÄSSIGKEIT? 1910. 21 pp.

Heft 75. Moll, Alb. BERÜHMTE HOMOSEXUELLE. 1910. 75 pp.

Heft 76. Sadée, Leop. VOM DEUTSCHEN PLUTARCH. EIN BEITRAG ZUR ENTWICKELUNGSGESCHICHTE DES DEUTSCHEN KLASSIZISMUS. 1911. 91 pp.

Heft 77. Bayerthal, Julius. ERBLICHKEIT UND ERZIEHUNG IN IHRER INDIVIDUELLEN BEDEUTUNG. 1911. 80 pp.

Heft 78. Jentsch, Ernst. MUSIK UND NERVEN. II. DAS MUSIKALISCHE GEFÜHL. 1911. 95 pp.

Heft 79. Birnbaum, Karl. DIE KRANKHAFTE WILLENSSCHWÄCHE UND IHRE ERSCHEINUNGSFORMEN. 1911. 75 pp.

Heft 80. Hinrichsen, O. ZUR PSYCHOLOGIE UND PSYCHOPATHOLOGIE DES DICHTERS. 1911. 95 pp.

Heft 81. Feis, Oswald. HECTOR BELIOZ. EINE PATHOGRAPHISCHE STUDIE. 1911. 28 pp.

Heft 82. Friedmann, Max. ÜBER DIE PSYCHOLOGIE DER EIFERSUCHT. 1911. 112 pp.

Heft 83. Strohmayer, W. PSYCHIATRISCH-GENEALOGISCHE UNTERSUCHUNG DER ABSTAMMUNG KÖNIG LUDWIGS II. UND OTTOS I. VON BAYERN. 1912. 68 pp.

Heft 84. Trömner, Ernst. DAS PROBLEM DES SCHLAFES. 1912. 89 pp.

Heft 85. Hinrichsen, O. SEXUALITÄT UND DICHTUNG. 1912. 81 pp.

160. *(Continued)*

Heft 86. Goldstein, Kurt. DIE HALLUZINATION, IHRE ENTSTEHUNG, IHRE URSACHEN UND IHRE REALITÄT. 1912. 72 pp.

Heft 87. Heilbronner, K. ÜBER GEWÖHNUNG AUF NORMALEM UND PATHO-LOGISCHEM GEBIETE. 1912. 51 pp.

Heft 88. Kurella, Hans. DIE INTELLEKTUELLEN UND DIE GESELLSCHAFT. EIN BEITRAG ZUR NATURGESCHICHTE BEGABTER FAMILIEN. 1913. 124 pp.

Heft 89. Loewenfeld, L. BEWUSSTSEIN UND PSYCHISCHES GESCHEHEN. DIE PHÄNOMENE DES UNTERBEWUSSTSEINS UND IHRE ROLLE IN UNSEREM GEISTES-LEBEN. 1913. 94 pp.

Heft 90. Jentsch, Ernst. DAS PATHOLOGISCHE BEI OTTO LUDWIG. 1913. 72 pp.

Heft 91. Freimark, Hans. ROBESPIERRE. EINE HISTORISCH-PSYCHOLOGISCHE STUDIE. 1913. 46 pp.

Heft 92. Franz, V. DER LEBENSPROZESS DER NERVENELEMENTE. 1913. 58 pp.

Heft 93. Rank, Otto, and Hanns Sachs. DIE BEDEUTUNG DER PSYCHOANA-LYSE FÜR DIE GEISTESWISSENSCHAFTEN. 1913. 111 pp.

Heft 94. Bechterew, W. von. DAS VERBRECHERTUM IM LICHTE DER OBJEK-TIVEN PSYCHOLOGIE. 1914. 53 pp.

Heft 95. Klieneberger, Otto. ÜBER PUBERTÄT UND PSYCHOPATHIE. 1914. 59 pp.

Heft 96. Berliner, Bernhard. DER EINFLUSS VON KLIMA, WETTER UND JAHR-ESZEIT AUF DAS NERVEN- UND SEELENLEBEN, AUF PHYSIOLOGISCHER GRUND-LAGE DARGESTELLT. 1914. 56 pp.

Heft 97. Laquer, Benno H. EUGENIK UND DYSGENIK, EIN VERSUCH. 1914. 62 pp.

Heft 98. Strohmayer, Wilhelm. DAS MANISCH-DEPRESSIVE IRRESEIN. 1914. 69 pp.

Heft 99. Stransky, Erwin. ÜBER KRANKHAFTE IDEEN, EINE KURZGEFASSTE ABHANDLUNG. 1914. 53 pp.

Heft 100. Loewenfeld, Leopold. ÜBER DEN NATIONAL-CHARAKTER DER FRANZOSEN UND DESSEN KRANKHAFTE AUSWÜCHSE (DIE PSYCHOPATHIA GALLICA) IN IHREN BEZIEHUNGEN ZUM WELTKRIEG. 1914. 42 pp.

Heft 101. Loewenfeld, Leopold. DIE SUGGESTION IN IHRER BEDEUTUNG FÜR DEN WELTKRIEG. 1917. 54 pp.

Heft 102. Stransky, Erwin. KRIEG UND GEISTESSTÖRUNG; FESTSTELLUNG UND ERWÄGUNGEN ZU DIESEM THEMA VOM STANDPUNKTE ANGEWANDTER PSY-CHIATRIE. 1918. 77 pp.

Heft 103. Birnbaum, Karl. PSYCHISCHE VERURSACHUNG SEELISCHER STÖRUNGEN UND DIE PSYCHISCH BEDINGTEN ABNORMEN SEELENVORGÄNGE. 1918. 77 pp.

Heft 104. Meyer, Semi. DIE ZUKUNFT DER MENSCHHEIT. 1918. 58 pp.

Heft 105. Friedmann, Max. ÜBER DIE NATUR DER ZWANGSVORSTELLUNGEN UND IHRE BEZIEHUNGEN ZUM WILLENSPROBLEM. 1920. 102 pp.

Heft 106. Tischner, Rudolf. ÜBER TELEPATHIE UND HELLSEHEN; EXPERI-MENTELLTHEORETISCHE UNTERSUCHUNGEN. 1921. 122 pp.

Heft 107. Freimark, Hans. DIE REVOLUTION ALS PSYCHISCHE MASSENER-
SCHEINUNG; HISTORISCH-PSYCHOLOGISCHE STUDIE. 1920. 110 pp.

Heft 108. Jacobi, Walter. DIE EKSTASE DER Alt-TESTAMENTLICHEN PROPHE-
TEN. 1920. 62 pp.

Heft 109. Tischner, Rudolf. EINFÜHRUNG IN DEN OKKULTISMUS UND SPIRI-
TISMUS. 1921. 142 pp.

Heft 110. Bohn, Wolfgang. DIE PSYCHOLOGIE UND ETHIK DES BUDDHISMUS.
1921. 76 pp.

Heft 111. Storch, Alfred. AUGUST STRINDBERG IM LICHTE SEINER SELBSTBIO-
GRAPHIE. EINE PSYCHOPATHOLOGISCHE PERSÖNLICHKEITSANALYSE. 1921.
75 pp.

Heft 112. Sichler, Albert. DIE THEOSOPHIE (ANTHROPOSOPHIE IN PSYCHO-
LOGISCHER BEURTEILUNG. 1921. 43 pp.

Heft 113. Meyer, Adolph F. MATERIALISATIONEN UND TELEPLASTIE. 1922.
62 pp.

Heft 114. Jacobi, Walter. DIE STIGMATISIERTEN. BEITRÄGE ZUR PSYCHOLO-
GIE DER MYSTIK. 1923. 57 pp.

Heft 115. Hoffmann, Hermann. ÜBER TEMPERAMENTS-VERERBUNG. 1923.
68 pp.

Heft 116. Birnbaum, Karl. GRUNDZÜGE DER KULTUR-PSYCHOPATHOLOGIE.
1924. 70 pp.

Heft 117. Heidenhain, Adolf. J. J. ROUSSEAU; PERSÖNLICHKEIT, PHILOSO-
PHIE UND PSYCHOSE. 1924. 84 pp.

Heft 118. Rust, Hans. DAS ZUNGENREDEN, EINE STUDIE ZUR KRITISCHEN
RELIGIONSPSYCHOLOGIE. 1924. 74 pp.

Heft 119. Henting, Hans von. ÜBER DEN CÄSARENWAHNSINN, DIE KRANK-
HEIT DES KAISERS TIBERIUS. 1924. 52 pp.

Heft 120. Tischner, Rudolf. FERNFÜHLEN UND MESMERISMUS (EXTERIORIS-
ATION DER SENSIBILITÄT). 1925. 42 pp.

Heft 121. Heyer, Gustav R. DAS KÖRPERLICH-SEELISCHE ZUSAMMENWIRKEN
IN DEN LEBENSVORGÄNGEN. AN HAND KLINISCHER UND EXPERIMENTELLER
TATSACHEN. 1925. 65 pp.

Heft 122. Strohmayer, Wilhelm. ÜBER DIE DARSTELLUNG PSYCHISCH AB-
NORMER UND GEISTESKRANKER CHARAKTERE AUF DER BÜHNE. 1925. 23 pp.

Heft 123. Zurukzoglu, Stavros. BIOLOGISCHE PROBLEME DER RASSENHY-
GIENE UND DIE KULTURVÖLKER. 1925. 184 pp.

Heft 124. Mezger, Edmund. PERSÖNLICHKEIT UND STRAFRECHTLICHE ZU-
RECHNUNG. 1926. 42 pp.

Heft 125. Riese, Walther. VINCENT VAN GOGH IN DER KRANKHEIT; EIN BEI-
TRAG ZUM PROBLEM DER BEZIEHUNG ZWISCHEN KUNSTWERK UND KRANKHEIT.
1926. 38 pp.

Heft 126. Stieve, Hermann. UNFRUCHTBARKEIT ALS FOLGE UNNATÜRLICHER
LEBENSWEISE; EIN VERSUCH DIE UNGEWOLLTE KINDERLOSIGKEIT DES MENSCHEN
AUF GRUND VON TIERVERSUCHEN UND ANATOMISCHEN UNTERSUCHUNGEN AUF
DIE FOLGEN DES KULTURLEBENS ZURÜCKZUFÜHREN. 1926. 52 pp.

Heft 127. Raecke, Julius. DIE QUERULANTENWAHN. EIN BEITRAG ZUR SOZI-
ALEN PSYCHIATRIE. 1926. 84 pp.

Heft 128/130. Leuba, James H. Die Psychologie der religiösen Mystik. 1927. 260 pp.

161. *Obschestvo eksperimental'noi psikhologii. Protokoly.*

TITLE VARIATIONS: None.

DATES OF PUBLICATION: 1900–1901.

FREQUENCY: Irregular.

NUMBERING VARIATIONS: None.

PUBLISHER: **St. Petersburg:** Unknown, 1900–1901.

PRIMARY EDITOR: Unknown.

NOTE: Information on this entry is incomplete. The compilers were unable to examine this title.

162. *Pädagogisch-psychologische Studien.*

TITLE VARIATIONS: Subtitle added in 1910.

DATES OF PUBLICATION: Jahrgang 1–23, 1900–1922.

FREQUENCY: Monthly.

NUMBERING VARIATIONS: Many multinumber issues. Jahrgang 23 has all 12 numbers in one issue.

PUBLISHER: **Leipzig:** Ernst Wunderlich, 1900–1922.

PRIMARY EDITORS: **Max Brahn,** 1900–1909; **Richard Seyfert,** 1910–1922; **Johannes Handrick,** 1920–1922.

163. *Paris. Institut général psychologique. Bulletin.*

TITLE VARIATIONS: Tome 1, 1900 titled *Bulletin de l'institut psychique international.* Tome 2, 1901–1902 titled *Bulletin de l'institut psychologique international.*

DATES OF PUBLICATION: Tome 1–33, Numéro 1/6, July 1900–1933.

FREQUENCY: **Irregular,** Tome 1, 1900. **Quarterly,** Tome 2, 1901–1902. **Bimonthly,** Tome 3–33, 1903–1933.

NUMBERING VARIATIONS: Many multiple-number issues. Title page and index for Tome 14 dated 1915 instead of 1914. Tome 33, Numéro 1/6 is special issue: Jubilé de M. d'Arsonval.

PUBLISHER: **Paris:** Félix Alcan, 1900. **Paris:** Au siege de la Société, 1901–1933.

PRIMARY EDITORS: **Pierre Janet,** 1900–1902; **Georges Dumas,** 1901–1902.

EDITORIAL BOARD: ———— d'Arsonval, 1903–1933; É. Duclaux, 1903–1904; L. Herbette, 1903–1919; Th. Ribot, 1903–1904; Émile Boutroux, 1903–1921; Paul Brouardel, 1903–1905; L. Liard, 1903–1917; Edmond Perrier, 1903–1921; Jules Courtier, 1903–1933; ————Bouchard, 1905–1915; A. Giard, 1907–[1910]; Henri Roujon, 1907–[1910]; Yves Delage, 1908–1919; Serge Yourievitch, 1911–1933; H. Poincaré, 1911–1912; F. Bordas, 1911–1933; G. Bigourdan,

1912–1930; A. Briand, 1912–1930; P. Richer, 1912–1919; F. Widal, 1919–1928;
P. Appell, 1920–1929; R. Bonaparte, 1920–1923; A. de Gramont, 1922–1923;
E. Leclainche, 1922–1933; J. Babinski, 1922–1930; L. Bouvier, 1922–1933; Paul
Léon, 1923–1933; Léona Manouvrier, 1923–1926.

164. *Psychological Studies.*

TITLE VARIATIONS: None.

DATES OF PUBLICATION: Number 1, July 1900.

FREQUENCY: Irregular.

NUMBERING VARIATIONS: None.

PUBLISHER: **Minneapolis, Minnesota:** Published by the author, 1900.

PRIMARY EDITOR: **Harlow Gale,** 1900.

165. *Rivista mensile di neuropatologia e psichiatria.*

TITLE VARIATIONS: Supersedes *Rivista quindicinale di psicologia, psichiatria, neuropatologia ad uso dei medici e dei giuristi.*

DATES OF PUBLICATION: Volume 1–2, July 1900–July 1901.

FREQUENCY: Monthly.

NUMBERING VARIATIONS: Multinumber issues present.

PUBLISHER: **Rome:** F. LLI Capaccini, editori-tipografi, 1900–1901.

PRIMARY EDITOR: **E. Sciamanna,** 1900–1901.

166. *Zeitschrift für pädagogische Psychologie und Pathologie.*

TITLE VARIATIONS: Continues *Zeitschrift für pädagogische Psychologie.* Continued by *Zeitschrift für pädagogische Psychologie, Pathologie und Hygiene* with Jahrgang 4, 1902.

DATES OF PUBLICATION: Jahrgang 2–3, 1900–1901.

FREQUENCY: Bimonthly.

NUMBERING VARIATIONS: None.

PUBLISHER: **Berlin:** Hermann Walther, 1900–1901.

PRIMARY EDITORS: **Ferdinand Kemsics,** 1900–1901; **Leo Hirschlaff,** 1901.

167. *Zeitschrift für Psychologie der Sinnesorgane. Ergänzungsband.*

TITLE VARIATIONS: Continued by *Zeitschrift für Psychologie und Physiologie der Sinnesorgane. Abteilung I. Zeitschrift für Psychologie. Ergänzungsband* with Heft 3, 1907/1909.

DATES OF PUBLICATION: Heft 1–2, 1900–1902.

FREQUENCY: *See* Contents *below.*

NUMBERING VARIATIONS: None.

PUBLISHER: **Leipzig:** Johann Ambrosius Barth, 1900–1902.

PRIMARY EDITOR: **Hermann Ebbinghaus,** 1900–1902; **Arthur König,** 1900.

CONTENTS:
Heft 1. Müller, Georg Elias, and A. Pilzecker. EXPERIMENTELLE BEITRÄGE ZUR LEHRE VOM GEDÄCHTNIS. 1900. 300 pp.
Heft 2. Meinong, A. ÜBER ANNAHMEN. 1902. 298 pp.

1901

168. *Annales de la psychologie zoologique.*

TITLE VARIATIONS: None.

DATES OF PUBLICATION: Année 1–2, 1901–1902.

FREQUENCY: Triannual.

NUMBERING VARIATIONS: Année 1, Numéro 1, published in October 1901. This is the only issue in Année 1. Année 2 has 3 issues.

PUBLISHER: **Paris:** L'institut de psychologie zoologique, 1901–1902. ·

PRIMARY EDITOR: **Pierre Hachet-Souplet,** 1901–1902.

169. *Archives de psychologie.*

TITLE VARIATIONS: Tome 1, Numéro 1–3, July 1901–1902 titled *Archives de psychologie de la suisse romande.*

DATES OF PUBLICATION: Tome 1–33, [Numéro 1]+, July 1901–July 1950+.

FREQUENCY: Irregular (four issues per volume).

NUMBERING VARIATIONS: Each volume is approximately 1 year but months of issue vary. Each issue from Tome 9, [Numéro 4]—Tome 33, [Numéro 1]+ is also assigned a whole number, Numéro 36–129+. Double numbers are present 1905, 1915, 1921, 1933, 1937, 1939, 1943, 1945, 1947.

PUBLISHER: **Geneva:** C. H. Eggimann et Cie, 1901–1902. **Geneva:** W. Kündig & fils, 1902–1906. **Geneva:** Librairie Kündig, 1906–1934. **Geneva:** Librairie Naville, 1935–1941. **Neuchâtel:** Delachaux & Niestlé, 1943–1950+.

PRIMARY EDITOR: **Theodore Flournoy,** 1901–1919; **Édouard Claparède,** 1901–1940; **Pierre Bovet,** 1913–1950+; **J. Larguier des Bancels,** 1913–1950+; **Jean Piaget,** 1921–1950+; **André Rey,** 1941–1950+; **Henri Flournoy,** 1943–1950+; **Georges de Morsier,** 1943–1950+; **Marc Lambercier,** 1946–1950+.

170. *Journal of Mental Pathology.*

TITLE VARIATIONS: None.

DATES OF PUBLICATION: Volume 1–8, Number 4, June 1901–December 1909.

FREQUENCY: **Monthly,** (Except in August and September), Volume 1–5, Number 4/5, June 1901–December/January 1903/1904. **Bimonthly,** (Except in August and September), Volume 6–8, Number 4, 1904–December/January 1908/1909.

NUMBERING VARIATIONS: Multinumber issues present.

PUBLISHER: **New York:** State Publishing Company, 1901–1902. **New York:** State Press, Publishers, 1903–1909.

PRIMARY EDITOR: **Louise G. Robinovitch,** 1901–1909.

EDITORIAL BOARD: V. Magnan, 1901–1909; A. Joffroy, 1901–1907; F. Raymond, 1901–1909; Chas. K. Mills, 1901–1909; Jul. Morel, 1901–1909; C. H. Hughes, 1901; F. Regis, 1901–1909; G. Cesare Ferrari, 1901–1905; G. Mingazzini, 1905–1909, Sante de Sanctis, 1905–1909; L. Luciani, 1905–1909.

171. *Psycho-therapeutic Journal. A Journal of the Proceedings of the London Psycho-therapeutic Society.*

TITLE VARIATIONS: Continued by *Health Record* with Number 62, January 1907.

DATES OF PUBLICATION: Number 1–61, October 1901–December 1906.

FREQUENCY: Monthly.

NUMBERING VARIATIONS: Also numbered Volume 1–5.

PUBLISHER: **London:** G. E. Hart for the London Psychotherapeutic Society, 1901–1906.

PRIMARY EDITOR: **G. E. Hart,** 1901–1906.

172. *Revue des études psychiques.*

TITLE VARIATIONS: Continues *Rivista di studi psichici.*

DATES OF PUBLICATION: Série 2, Année 1–4, January/February/March 1901–December 1904.

FREQUENCY: Monthly (Irregular).

NUMBERING VARIATIONS: Multinumber issues present.

PUBLISHER: **Paris:** Direction et administration à Paris, 23 Passage Saulnier, 1901–1904.

PRIMARY EDITOR: **Cesar di Vesme,** 1901–1904.

1902

173. *Berlin. Psychiatrische Klinik. Beiträge.*

TITLE VARIATIONS: None.

DATES OF PUBLICATION: Band 1, Heft 1–4, January 1902–June 1903.

FREQUENCY: Irregular.

NUMBERING VARIATIONS: None.

PUBLISHER: **Vienna:** Urban & Schwarzenberg, 1902–1903.

PRIMARY EDITOR: **Robert Sommer,** 1902–1903.

174. *Childhood Society for the Scientific Study of the Mental and Physical Conditions of Children. Transactions.*

TITLE VARIATIONS: None.

DATES OF PUBLICATION: Volume 1–4, 1902–1908.

FREQUENCY: Irregular.

NUMBERING VARIATIONS: Also numbered as *Proceedings of the Society* for the years 1901, 1902, 1903, 1904–1905, 1906–1907. Volume 2 published in 2 parts, 1902 and 1903.

PUBLISHER: **London:** Childhood Society for the Scientific Study of the Mental and Physical Conditions of Children, 1902–1908.

PRIMARY EDITOR: **W. J. Durrie Mulford** (Secretary), 1902–1908.

EDITORIAL COMMITTEE: G. E. Shuttleworth, 1902–1908; Fletcher Beach, 1902–1908; T. H. Jones, 1902–1904; H. R. Kenwood, 1902–1908; R. Langdon-Down, 1902–1906; J. W. Palmer, 1902–1908; E. White Wallis, 1902–1908; Francis Warner, 1902–1908; R. P. Cockburn, 1903–1906; M. Friedeberger, 1903–1908; A. B. Kingsford, 1903–1906; R. M. Hensley, 1905–1908; R. Denison Pedley, 1908; A. Ravenhill, 1908; Sidney Spokes, 1908.

175. *Colorado. University. Department of Psychology and Education. Investigations.*

TITLE VARIATIONS: None.

DATES OF PUBLICATION: Volume 1–3, Number 2, June 1902–April 1906.

FREQUENCY: Irregular. Volume 1, 4 issues; Volume 2, 3 issues; and, Volume 3, 2 issues.

NUMBERING VARIATIONS: None.

PUBLISHER: **Boulder, Colorado:** University of Colorado, 1902–1906.

PRIMARY EDITOR: **Arthur Allin,** 1902–1903. None listed, 1904–1906.

176. *Experimental Studies in Psychology and Pedagogy.*

TITLE VARIATIONS: Also titled *Psychological Monographs. A Series of Experimental Studies in Psychology and Pedagogy,* and [*Pennsylvania. University.*] *Publications. Experimental Studies in Psychology and Pedagogy.*

DATES OF PUBLICATION: Number 1–9, 1902–1922.

FREQUENCY: Irregular. *See* Contents *below.*

NUMBERING VARIATIONS: None.

PUBLISHER: **Boston:** Ginn & Company. The Athenaeum Press, 1902. **Philadelphia:** The Psychological Clinic Press, 1908–1922.

PRIMARY EDITOR: **Lightner Witmer,** 1902–1922.

CONTENTS:

Number 1. Cornman, Oliver P. SPELLING IN THE ELEMENTARY SCHOOLS: AN EXPERIMENTAL AND STATISTICAL INVESTIGATION. 1902. 98 pp.

Number 2. McKeag, Anna J. THE SENSATION OF PAIN AND THE THEORY OF THE SPECIFIC SENSE ENERGIES. 1902. 87 pp.

Number 3. Urban, F. M. THE APPLICATION OF STATISTICAL METHODS TO THE PROBLEMS OF PSYCHOPHYSICS. 1908. 221 pp.

Number 4. Town, Clara Harrison. TWO EXPERIMENTAL STUDIES OF THE INSANE. 1. THE TRAIN OF THOUGHT. 2. SOME PHYSIOLOGICAL CONDITIONS ACCOMPANYING STATES OF DEPRESSION. 1909. 84 pp.

Number 5. Heilman, Jacob Daniel. A CLINICAL STUDY OF ONE THOUSAND RETARDED CHILDREN IN THE PUBLIC SCHOOLS OF CAMDEN, NEW JERSEY. 1910. 106 pp.

Number 6. Snyder, Aaron Moyer. EXTENT AND CAUSES OF RETARDATION IN THE READING (PA.) PUBLIC SCHOOLS IN DECEMBER, 1910. A STATISTICAL STUDY. 1911. 72 pp.

Number 7. Humpstone, Henry J. SOME ASPECTS OF THE MEMORY SPAN TEST. A STUDY IN ASSOCIABILITY. 1917. 30 pp.

Number 8. Miller, Karl Greenwood. THE COMPETENCY OF FIFTY COLLEGE STUDENTS. 1922. 59 pp.

Number 9. Viteles, Morris S. JOB SPECIFICATIONS AND DIAGNOSTIC TESTS OF JOB COMPETENCY DESIGNED FOR THE AUDITING DIVISION OF A STREET RAILWAY COMPANY (A PSYCHOLOGICAL STUDY IN INDUSTRIAL GUIDANCE). 1922. 38 pp.

177. *Journal für Psychologie und Neurologie.* [Organ of the Kaiser Wilhelm Institut für Hirnforschung and of the Neuro-biologisches Institut der Universität Berlin.]

TITLE VARIATIONS: Absorbed *Zeitschrift für Hypnotismus, Psychotherapie sowie andere psychophysiologische und psychopathologische Forschungen.*

DATES OF PUBLICATION: Band 1–51, 1902–1942.

FREQUENCY: Bimonthly.

NUMBERING VARIATIONS: Volumes with Ergänzungshefte are as follows: Band 6, Ergänzungsheft 1, 1906; Band 8, Ergänzungsheft 1, 1907; Band 10, Ergänzungsheft 1, 1908; Band 12, Ergänzungsheft 1, 1909; Band 17, Ergänzungsheft 1, 1911; Band 18, Ergänzungsheft 1–5, 1911–1912; Band 19, Ergänzungsheft 1–2, 1912; Band 20, Ergänzungsheft 1–2, 1913; Band 21, Ergänzungsheft 1–2, 1915; Band 22, Ergänzungsheft 1–3, 1916–1917; Band 23, Ergänzungsheft 1, 1918; Band 25, Ergänzungsheft 1–3, 1919–1920. Ergänzungsheft to Band 17, 19 and 20 also numbered as *Internationale Gesellschaft für medizinische Psychologie und Psychotherapie. Verhandlungen,*

Heft 1–3, 1911–1913. All volumes have multinumber issues. Band 13 is FESTSCHRIFT ZU FORELS SECHZIGSTEM GEBURTSTAG. 1908. 435 pp.; Band 37, Heft 1–3 is GABRIEL ANTON SUM SIEBZIGSTEN GEBURTSTAG AM 28. AUGUST 1928. 1928. 467 pp.; Band 38, Heft 1 is AUGUST FOREL ZU SEINEM ACHTZIGJÄHRIGEN GEBURTSTAGE. 1929. 116 pp.; Band 38, Heft 2 is MAX BIELSCHOWSKY ZUM SECHZIGJÄHRIGEN GEBURTSTAGE. 1929. pp. 120–198; Band 39, Heft 4–6 is N. SEMASCHKO ZU ERINNERUNG AN SEINE ZEHNJÄHRIGE TÄTIGKEIT ALS VOLKSKOMISSAR DES GESUNDHEITSWESENS DER R.S.F.S.R. 1929. 504 pp.; Band 50, Heft 1–2 is ARTHUR MEINER ZU SEINEM 75. GEBURTSTAG UND SEINEM 50 JÄHRIGEN VERLAGSINHABER-JUBILÄUM. 1941. 160 pp.

PUBLISHER: **Leipzig:** Verlag von Johann Ambrosius Barth, 1902–1942.

PRIMARY EDITORS: **Korbinian Brodman,** 1902–1918; **August Forel,** 1902–1931; **Oskar Vogt,** 1902–1942; **Hugo Spatz,** 1938–1942; **Cecile Vogt,** 1922–1942; **E. Beck,** 1926–1927; **Maximilian Rose,** 1926–1929; **Marthe Vogt,** 1931–1937.

178. *Psychologische bibliotheek (Delft).*

TITLE VARIATIONS: None.

DATES OF PUBLICATION: Deel 1, 1902.

FREQUENCY: Irregular. *See* Contents *below.*

NUMBERING VARIATIONS: Deel 1 also issued in an expanded edition under a different title. *See* Contents *below.*

PUBLISHER: **Delft:** J. Vis, Jr.; and **Rotterdam:** D. Bolle, 1902.

PRIMARY EDITORS: None listed.

CONTENTS:
Deel 1. Ribot, Th. DE ZIEKTEN VAN HET GEHEUGEN. BEWERKT DOOR P. J. VAN MALSSEN, JR. MET EEN INLEIDING VAN J. GELUK. 1902. (Also issued in an expanded edition as *Zie bibliotheek van moderne philosophie,* Deel 4, 1904).

179. *Revue de psychiatrie et de psychologie expérimentale.*

TITLE VARIATIONS: Continues *Revue de psychiatrie (médecine mentale, neurologie, psychologie).*

DATES OF PUBLICATION: Série 2, Année 5, Tome 5-Série 8, Année 18, Tome 18, Numéro 6, January 1902–June 1914.

FREQUENCY: Monthly.

NUMBERING VARIATIONS: Numbering is irregular. The 12 issues for 1902 are numbered Série 2, Année 5, Tome 5–16. Année 6 is omitted in numbering. The first 11 issues for 1903 are numbered Série 3, Année 7, Tome 7–16 (Tome 7 is a double issue Numéro 1/2). Numéro 12 for 1903 adopts the previously used numbering Série 3, Année 7, Tome 7. Issues for 1904 are numbered Série 3, Année 8, Tome 8; for 1905, Série 4, Année 9, Tome 9; for 1906, Série 5, Année 10, Tome 10; for 1907, Série 5, Année 11, Tome 11; for 1908, Série 5, Année 12, Tome 12; for 1909, Série 5, Année 13, Tome 13; for 1910, Série 6, Année 14, Tome 14; for 1911, Série 7, Année 15, Tome 15; for 1912, Série 8,

Année 16, Tome 16; for 1913, Série 8, Année 17, Tome 17; for 1914, Série 8, Année 18, Tome 18. Supplements also numbered as *Bulletin bibliographique mensuel de psychiatrie et de psychologie expérimentale*, Tome 1–12.

PUBLISHER: **Paris:** A. Maloine, éditeur, 1902–1903. **Paris:** Octave Doin, éditeur, 1903–1908. **Paris:** Octave Doin & Fils, éditeurs, 1909–1914.

PRIMARY EDITOR: **Édouard Toulouse**, 1902–1914.

EDITORIAL BOARD: M. Klippel, 1902–1914; F. Pactet, 1902–1914; Henri Colin, 1902–1914; A. Marie, 1902–1914; ——— Blin, 1902–1914; Lucien Pique, 1902–1914; Paul Sérieux, 1902–1914; N. Vaschide, 1902–1906; L. Marchand, 1902–1914; A. Vigouroux, 1902–1914; Henri Piéron, 1902–1914; P. Juquelier, 1906–1914; M. Mignard, 1909–1914; J. Crinon, 1910–1914.

180. *Zeitschrift für pädagogishe Psychologie, Pathologie und Hygiene.*

TITLE VARIATIONS: Continues *Zeitschrift für pädagogische Psychologie und Pathologie.* Continued by *Zeitschrift für pädagogische Psychologie und experimentelle Pädagogik* with Jahrgang 12, 1911.

DATES OF PUBLICATION: Jahrgang 4–11, 1902–1910.

FREQUENCY: **Bimonthly**, Jahrgang 4–10, 1902–1909. **Monthly**, Jahrgang 11, 1910.

NUMBERING VARIATIONS: Double-number issues present. Supplements, 1907–1910, numbered in *Pädagogische Monographien.* Jahrgang 9, Heft 6 misnumbered Jahrgang 10, Heft 6. Various articles also numbered in subtitles *Beiträge zur Psychologie und Pädagogik der Kinderlügen und Kinderaussagen. Veröffentlichungen des Vereins für Kinderpsychologie zu Berlin* and *Sexuelle Aufklärung der Jugend. Veröffentlichungen des Vereins für Schulgesundheitspflege zu Berlin.*

PUBLISHER: **Berlin:** Hermann Walther, 1902–1909. **Leipzig:** Quelle & Meyer, 1909–1910.

PRIMARY EDITORS: **Ferdinand Kemsies**, 1902–1909; **Leo Hirschlaff**, 1902–1909; **M. Brahn**, 1910; **G. Deuchler**, 1910; **Otto Scheibner**, 1910.

1903

181. *Archiv für die gesamte Psychologie.*[Organ of the Gesellschaft für experimentelle Psychologie, 1925–1928 and of the Deutsche Gesellschaft für Psychologie, 1929+.]

TITLE VARIATIONS: Supersedes *Philosophische Studien.*

DATES OF PUBLICATION: Band 1–112, Heft 3/4, April 1903–October 1944. Suspended publication, 1944–1950+.

FREQUENCY: Irregular. Number of hefte per year varies from 2 (1941) to 28 (1929).

NUMBERING VARIATIONS: Each volume has four Hefte. Many are double issues. Band 46, 1924 contains FESTSCHRIFT ZU EHREN DES 70. GEBURTSTAGES VON PROF. DR. GÖTZ MARTIUS. 1. und 2. Teil. 416 pp. Band 47, 1924 contains Teil 3 (Schluss). Pp. 237–511. Band 77, 1930 contains STÖRRING-FESTSCHRIFT. 714 pp. Band 97, 1936 contains FESTSCHRIFT ZUM 60. GEBURTSTAG VON WILHELM WIRTH. 532 pp. Band 98, 1937 contains FESTSCHRIFT ZUM 65. GEBURTSTAG VON NARZISS Ach. Pp. 155–366. Numerous individual articles also numbered in *Sammlung von Abhandlungen zur psychologischen Pädagogik, aus dem Archiv für die gesamte Psychologie.*

PUBLISHER: **Leipzig:** Wilhelm Engelmann, 1903–1913 (May), 1914 (August)–1923 (December). **Leipzig** and **Berlin:** Wilhelm Engelmann, 1913 (July)–1914 (May). **Leipzig:** Akademische Verlagsgesellschaft, 1924–1940 (June). **Leipzig:** Akademische Verlagsgesellschaft Becker und Erler Kom.-Ges., 1940 (July)–1944 (October).

PRIMARY EDITORS: **Ernst Meumann,** 1903–1915; **Wilhelm Wirth,** 1905–1944; **Friedrich Sander,** 1938–1944.

182. *Archivos de terapéutica de las enfermedades nerviosas y mentales.*

TITLE VARIATIONS: None.

DATES OF PUBLICATION: Años 1–12, 1903–1914.

FREQUENCY: Bimonthly.

NUMBERING VARIATIONS: None.

PUBLISHER: **Barcelona:** Eco científico del "Manicomio de Reus," 1903–1914.

PRIMARY EDITOR: **A. Galceran Granes,** 1903–1914.

183. *Beiträge zur Psychologie der Aussage.*

TITLE VARIATIONS: Superseded by *Zeitschrift für angewandte Psychologie und psychologische Sammelforschung* with Band 1, 1908.

DATES OF PUBLICATION: Band 1–2, 1903–1906.

FREQUENCY: Semiannual. 4 issues per volume.

NUMBERING VARIATIONS: None.

PUBLISHER: **Leipzig:** Johann Ambrosius Barth, 1903–1906.

PRIMARY EDITOR: **L. William Stern,** 1903–1906.

184. *Harvard Psychological Studies.*

TITLE VARIATIONS: None.

DATES OF PUBLICATION: Volume 1–5, 1903–1922.

FREQUENCY: Irregular.

NUMBERING VARIATIONS: Volume 1 also numbered as *Psychological Review. Monograph Supplements*, Number 17, January 1903.

PUBLISHER: **Boston** and **New York:** Houghton Mifflin and Company (for the Harvard Psychological Laboratory), Volume 1–2, 1903–1906. **Cambridge:** Harvard University Press, Volume 3–5, 1913–1922.

PRIMARY EDITORS: **Hugo Münsterberg,** 1903–1915; **Herbert Sidney Langfeld,** 1916–1922.

NOTE: Volumes 1–2 contain original papers. Volumes 3–5 are bound collections of reprints of papers previously published elsewhere.

185. *Zhurnal psikho-grafologii.*

TITLE VARIATIONS: None.

DATES OF PUBLICATION: Tom 1–3, September 1903–1905.

FREQUENCY: Unknown.

NUMBERING VARIATIONS: None.

PUBLISHER: **St. Petersburg:** Unknown, 1903–1905.

PRIMARY EDITORS: Unknown.

NOTE: Above entry is based on partial information. The compilers were unable to examine this title.

1904

186. *American Journal of Religious Psychology and Education.*

TITLE VARIATIONS: Continued by *Journal of Religious Psychology, Including Its Anthropological and Sociological Aspects* with Volume 5, 1912.

DATES OF PUBLICATION: Volume 1–4, May 1904–July 1911.

FREQUENCY: Triannual.

NUMBERING VARIATIONS: Joint issues in Volumes 2, 4.

PUBLISHER: **Worcester, Massachusetts:** Louis N. Wilson, 1904–1911.

PRIMARY EDITOR: **G. Stanley Hall,** 1904–1911.

EDITORIAL BOARD: Jean du Buy, 1904–1911; George A. Coe, 1904–1907; Theodore Flournoy, 1904–1911; James H. Leuba, 1904–1911; Edwin D. Starbuck, 1904–1911; R. M. Wenley, 1904–1911.

187. *Bibliothek des Seelen- und Sexuallebens.*

TITLE VARIATIONS: None.

DATES OF PUBLICATION: Serie I, Heft 1–10, 1904.

FREQUENCY: Irregular. *See* Contents *below.*

NUMBERING VARIATIONS: Serie I apparently only series issued.

PUBLISHER: **Oranienburg:** Orania-Verlag, 1904.

PRIMARY EDITOR: **F. Koslowsky,** 1904.

CONTENTS:

Heft 1. Gerling, Reinhard. REFORM-EHE ODER EHE-REFORM? 1904. 26 pp.

Heft 2. Gerling, Reinhard. FREIE LIEBE ODER BÜRGERLICHE EHE? 1904. 30 pp.

Heft 3. Vierath, Willy. SINNLICHKEIT BEIM WEIBE. IST DAS WEIB SINN-LICHER ALS DER MANN? EINE PSYCHOLOGISCHER STUDIE. 1904. 28 pp.

Heft 4. Prager, F. DIE KRANKHEITEN DER EHELEBENS. 1904. 32 pp.

Heft 5. Wendel, G. DER KRANKHEITEN LETZTE URSACHE. 1904. 30 pp.

Heft 6. Vierath, Willy. FRAUEN-ELEND. EIN NEUES WORT ZUM ALTEN THEMA. 1904. 29 pp.

Heft 7. Gerling, Reinhard. IST SELBSTMORD KRANKHEIT ODER VER-BRECHEN? 1904. 28 pp.

Heft 8. Gerling, Reinhard. DAS VERSEHEN DER FRAUEN UND DIE VORGE-BURTLICHE ERZIEHUNG. 1904. 28 pp.

Heft 9. Linke, Heinz. WUNDER UND ABERGLAUBEN IN DER HEILKUNDE. KULTUR-GESCHICHTLICHE STUDIE ZUR CHARAKTERISIERUNG DER GEGENWART. 1904. 29 pp.

Heft 10. Rau, Hans. WOLLUST UND SCHMERZ. EINE PSYCHOLOGISCHE STUDIE. 1904. 26 pp.

188. *British Journal of Psychology.* [Issued by the British Psychological Society.]

TITLE VARIATIONS: Incorporates *British Psychological Society. Proceedings.* Continued by *British Journal of Psychology. General Section* with Volume 11, October 1920.

DATES OF PUBLICATION: Volume 1–10, 1904–July 1920.

FREQUENCY: Quarterly.

NUMBERING VARIATIONS: Double issues present.

PUBLISHER: **Cambridge:** University Press, 1904–1920.

PRIMARY EDITORS: **James Ward,** 1904–1910; **W.H.R. Rivers,** 1904–1913; **Charles Samuel Myers,** 1911–1920.

EDITORIAL BOARD: A. Kirschmann, 1904–1917; W. McDougall, 1904–1920; Charles Samuel Myers, 1904–1910; A. F. Shand, 1904–1920; C. S. Sherrington, 1904–1920; W. G. Smith, 1904–1919; Charles E. Spearman, 1909–1920; W. Brown, 1911–1920; G. Dawes Hicks, 1911–1920; Carveth Read, 1911–1920; James Ward, 1911–1920; H. J. Watt, 1911–1920; G. Udny Yule, 1911–1920; C. Burt, 1913–1920; T. H. Pear, 1913–1920; W.H.R. Rivers, 1913–1920; J. Drever, 1919–1920; B. Edgell, 1919–1920.

189. *Estudios de patología nerviosa y mental.*

TITLE VARIATIONS: None.

DATES OF PUBLICATION: Volumen 1, 1904.

FREQUENCY: Irregular. *See* Contents *below.*

NUMBERING VARIATIONS: None.

PUBLISHER: **Buenos Aires:** Librería de J. Menéndez, 1904.

PRIMARY EDITOR: **José Ingegnieros,** 1904.

CONTENTS:
> **Volumen 1.** Ingegnieros, José. LOS ACCIDENTES HISTÉRICOS Y LAS SUGESTIONES TERAPÉUTICAS. 1904. 371 pp. (2nd ed., 1907, titled HISTÉRIA Y SUGESTION.)

190. *Journal de psychologie normale et pathologique.*

TITLE VARIATIONS: None.

DATES OF PUBLICATION: Année 1–12, 17–43+, 1904–1950+. Année 13–16 never published. Suspended publication 1916–1919, 1942–1945.

FREQUENCY: **Bimonthly,** Année 1–12, 1904–1915. **Monthly,** Année 17–19, 1920–1922. **10 times yearly,** Année 20–25, 1923–1928. **5 double numbers,** Année 26–34, 1929–1937. **Quarterly,** Année 35–43+, 1938–1950+.

NUMBERING VARIATIONS: Double numbers in Année 20, 21, 23, 25, 30, 34–36. Année 36 is 8 numbers in 3 issues.

PUBLISHER: **Paris:** Félix Alcan, 1904–1915, 1920–1938. **Paris:** Presses universitaires de France, 1939–1941, 1946–1950+.

PRIMARY EDITORS: **Pierre Janet,** 1904–1937, (Honorary 1938–1941); **Georges Dumas,** 1904–1937, (Honorary 1938–1941); **G. Revault d'Allonnes,** 1907–1909; **Jean Dagnan-Bouveret,** 1910–1915; **I. Meyerson,** 1920–1939, 1946–1950+; **Ch. Blondel,** 1938; **P. Guillaume,** 1938–1941, 1946–1950+; **J. Delay,** 1940–1941.

191. *Journal of Comparative Neurology and Psychology.*

TITLE VARIATIONS: Continues *Journal of Comparative Neurology.* [*1.*] Continued by *Journal of Comparative Neurology.* [*2.*] with Volume 21, 1911.

DATES OF PUBLICATION: Volume 14–20, 1904–1910.

FREQUENCY: Bimonthly.

NUMBERING VARIATIONS: None.

PUBLISHER: **Granville, Ohio:** Denison University, 1904–1905. **Baltimore:** Waverly Press, 1906. **Baltimore:** Williams & Wilkins Company, 1907. **Philadelphia:** Wistar Institute of Anatomy and Biology, 1908–1910.

PRIMARY EDITORS: **C. L. Herrick,** 1904; **Charles Judson Herrick,** 1904–1907,

1910; **Robert M. Yerkes,** 1904–1907; **Oliver S. Strong,** 1904–1907; **Herbert S. Jennings,** 1904–1907.

EDITORIAL BOARD: Henry H. Donaldson, 1908–1910; Charles Judson Herrick, 1908–1910; Herbert S. Jennings, 1908–1910; J. B. Johnston, 1908–1910; Adolf Meyer, 1908–1910; Oliver S. Strong, 1908–1910; John B. Watson, 1908–1910; Robert M. Yerkes, 1908–1910.

192. *Journal of Philosophy, Psychology and Scientific Methods.*

TITLE VARIATIONS: Continued by *Journal of Philosophy* with Volume 18, 1921.

DATES OF PUBLICATION: Volume 1–17, 1904–1920.

FREQUENCY: Biweekly.

NUMBERING VARIATIONS: None.

PUBLISHER: **New York:** The Science Press, 1904–1916. **Lancaster, Pennsylvania:** Press of the New Era Printing Company, 1917–1920.

PRIMARY EDITOR: **Frederick J. E. Woodbridge,** 1904–1920; **Wendell T. Bush,** 1906–1920.

193. *Kongress für experimentelle Psychologie. Bericht.*

TITLE VARIATIONS: Continued by *Deutsche Gesellschaft für Psychologie. Kongress. Bericht* with Nummer 12, 1931.

DATES OF PUBLICATION: Nummer 1–11, 1904–1929. Suspended publication 1915–1920.

FREQUENCY: Biennial.

NUMBERING VARIATIONS: None.

PUBLISHER: **Leipzig:** Gesellschaft für experimentelle Psychologie, Verlag von Johann Ambrosius Barth, 1904–1914. **Jena:** Gesellschaft für experimentelle Psychologie, Verlag von Gustav Fischer, 1921–1927. **Jena:** Deutsche Gesellschaft für Psychologie, Verlag von Gustav Fischer, 1929.

PRIMARY EDITORS: **F. Schumann,** 1904–1914; **Karl Bühler,** 1921–1925; **Erich Becher,** 1927; **Hans Volkelt,** 1929.

194. *Monatsschrift für Kriminalpsychologie und Strafrechtsreform.*

TITLE VARIATIONS: Continued by *Monatsschrift für Kriminalbiologie und Strafrechtsreform* with Band 28, 1937.

DATES OF PUBLICATION: Band 1–27, April 1904–1936. Suspended publication February 1916–May 1917, July 1917–November 1921.

FREQUENCY: Monthly.

NUMBERING VARIATIONS: Multinumber issues present.

PUBLISHER: **Heidelberg:** C. Winter, Verlag, 1904–1935. **Munich:** J. F. Lehmanns Verlag, 1936.

PRIMARY EDITORS: **Alfred Kloss,** 1904–1930; **Karl von Lilienthal,** 1904–1927; **Franz von Liszt,** 1904–1919; **Gustav Aschaffenburg,** 1904–1936; **Hans von Hentig,** 1926–1930.

195. *Ohio. State University. Studies in Psychology.*

TITLE VARIATIONS: Continued by *Ohio. State University. Psychological Studies* with Number 5, 1909.

DATES OF PUBLICATION: Number 1–4, 1904–1905.

FREQUENCY: Irregular. *See* Contents *below.*

NUMBERING VARIATIONS: Number 1–4 also numbered as Volume 1, Number 1–4. Various issues also published as articles in *Psychological Review. See* Contents *below.*

PUBLISHER: **Lancaster, Pennsylvania** and **New York:** Macmillan Co., 1904–1905 (publisher of *Psychological Review*).

PRIMARY EDITORS: None listed.

CONTENTS:

Number 1. Haines, Thomas H., and Arthur Ernest Davies. THE PSYCHOLOGY OF AESTHETIC REACTION TO RECTANGULAR FORMS. (Also as *Psychological Review*, Volume 11, 1904. Pp. 249–281.)

Number 2. Haines, Thomas H., and John C. Williams. THE RELATION OF PERCEPTIVE AND REVIVED MENTAL MATERIAL AS SHOWN BY THE SUBJECTIVE CONTROL OF VISUAL AFTER-IMAGES. (Also as *Psychological Review*, Volume 12, 1905. Pp. 18–40).

Number 3. Davies, Arthur Ernest. AN ANALYSIS OF ELEMENTARY PSYCHIC PROCESS. Also as *Psychological Review*, Volume 12, 1905. Pp. 166–206.)

Number 4. Haines, Thomas H. THE SYNTHETIC FACTOR IN TACTUAL SPACE PERCEPTIONS. (Also as *Psychological Review*, Volume 12, 1905. Pp. 207–221.)

196. *Psychological Bulletin.*

TITLE VARIATIONS: Subtitle varies.

DATES OF PUBLICATION: Volume 1–47 +, January 1904–November 1950 +.

FREQUENCY: **Monthly,** Volume 1–26, 1904–1929. **Monthly,** except August and September, Volume 27–42, 1930–1945.

NUMBERING VARIATIONS: Volume 1 has 13 numbers, Number 7/8 dated June 15, 1904 is a double number.

PUBLISHER: **Lancaster, Pennsylvania** and **New York:** Macmillan Company, 1904–1905. **Lancaster** and **Baltimore:** Review Publishing Company, 1906–1910. **Lancaster** and **Baltimore:** Psychological Review Company, 1911–1912. **Lancaster** and **Princeton, New Jersey:** Psychological Review Company, 1913–1921. **Albany, New York** and **Princeton:** Psychological Review Company, 1922–1925. **Albany** and **Princeton:** For the American Psychological Association by the Psychological Review Company, 1926–1929. **Princeton:** The American Psychological Association by the Psychological Review Company, 1930–1936. **Columbus, Ohio:** The American Psychological Association by the Psychological Review

Company, 1937. **Columbus, Ohio:** American Psychological Association, Inc., 1938–1939. **Evanston, Illinois:** American Psychological Association, Inc., 1940–1945. **Washington, D.C.:** American Psychological Association, Inc., 1946–1950+.

PRIMARY EDITORS: **J. Mark Baldwin,** 1904–1909; **Howard C. Warren,** 1904–1909; **John B. Watson,** 1909; **Arthur H. Pierce,** 1910–1913; **Shepherd I. Franz,** 1914–1923; **Samuel W. Fernberger,** 1920–1930; **Edward S. Robinson,** June 1930–1934; **John A. McGeoch,** 1935–1942; **John E. Anderson,** 1942–1946; **Lyle H. Lanier,** 1947–1950+.

197. *Psychologische Studien (Berlin). Abteilung I. Beiträge zur Analyse der Gesichtswahrnehmungen.* [From the Psychologisches Institut der Universität Berlin.]

TITLE VARIATIONS: None

DATES OF PUBLICATION: Heft 1–7, 1904–1923.

FREQUENCY: Irregular.

NUMBERING VARIATIONS: Heft 5 never published.

PUBLISHER: **Leipzig:** J. A. Barth, 1904–1923.

PRIMARY EDITOR: **Friedrich Schumann,** 1904–1923.

198. *Psychologische Studien (Berlin). Abteilung II. Beiträge zur Psychologie der Zeitwahrnehmungen.* [From the Psychologisches Institut der Universität Berlin.]

DATES OF PUBLICATION: Heft 1, 1904.

FREQUENCY: Irregular.

NUMBERING VARIATIONS: None.

PUBLISHER: **Leipzig:** J. A. Barth, 1904.

PRIMARY EDITOR: **Friedrich Schumann,** 1904.

199. *Sammlung von Abhandlungen zur psychologischen Pädagogik, aus dem Archiv für die gesamte Psychologie.*

TITLE VARIATIONS: None.

DATES OF PUBLICATION: Band 1–4, Heft 1, 1904–1914.

FREQUENCY: Irregular. *See* Contents *below.*

NUMBERING VARIATIONS: All Hefte also numbered in *Archiv für die gesamte Psychologie. See* Contents *below.*

PUBLISHER: **Leipzig:** Wilhelm Engelmann, 1904–1914.

PRIMARY EDITOR: **Ernst Meumann,** 1904–1914.

Year 1904

CONTENTS:

Band 1, Heft 1. Messmer, Oskar. ZUR PSYCHOLOGIE DES LESENS BEI KINDERN UND ERWACHSENEN. 1904. 109 pp. (Also as *Archiv für die gesamte Psychologie,* Volume 2, 1903, pp. 190–298).

——— **Heft 2.** Ament, Wilhelm. FORTSCHRITTE DER KINDERSEELENKUNDE 1895–1903. 1904. 68 pp. 2te Auflage, 1906. 76 pp. (Also as *Archiv für die gesamte Psychologie,* Volume 2, 1904, pp. 69–136.)

———, **Heft 3.** Schmidt, Friedrich. EXPERIMENTELLE UNTERSUCHUNGEN ÜBER DIE HAUSAUFGABEN DES SCHULKINDES. 1904. 120 pp. (Also as *Archiv für die gesamte Psychologie,* Volume 3, 1904, pp. 33–152.)

———, **Heft 4.** Mayer, August. ÜBER EINZEL- UND GESAMTLEISTUNG DES SCHULKINDES. 1904. 136 pp. (Also as *Archiv für die gesamte Psychologie,* Volume 1, 1903, pp. 276–416.)

———, **Heft 5.** Ebert, E., and E. Meumann. ÜBER EINIGE GRUNDFRAGEN DER PSYCHOLOGIE DER ÜBUNGSPHÄNOMENE IM BEREICHE DES GEDÄCHTNISSES. 1904. 232 pp. (Also as *Archiv für die gesamte Psychologie,* Volume 4, 1904, pp. 1–232.)

Band 2, Heft 1. Pedersen, R. H. EXPERIMENTELLE UNTERSUCHUNGEN DER VISUELLEN UND AKUSTISCHEN ERINNERUNGSBILDER, ANGESTELLT AN SCHULKINDERN, and, Gheorgov, I. A. DIE ERSTEN ANFÄNGE DES SPRACHLICHEN AUSDRUCKS FÜR DAS SELBSTBEWUSSTSEIN BEI KINDERN. 1905. 96 pp. (Also as *Archiv für die gesamte Psychologie,* Volume 4, 1905, pp. 520–534; and Volume 5, 1905, pp. 329–405.)

———, **Heft 2.** Lehmann, Alfred, and R. H. Pedersen. DAS WETTER UND UNSERE ARBEIT. 1907. 106 pp. (Also as *Archiv für die gesamte Psychologie,* Volume 10, 1907, pp. 1–104.)

———, **Heft 3.** Gheorgov, I. A. EIN BEITRAG ZUR GRAMMATISCHEN ENTWICKLUNG DER KINDERSPRACHE. 1908. 191 pp. (Also as *Archiv für die gesamte Psychologie,* Volume 11, 1908, pp. 242–432.)

———, **Heft 4.** Huther, A. ÜBER DAS PROBLEM EINER PSYCHOLOGISCHEN UND PÄDAGOGISCHEN THEORIE DER INTELLEKTUELLEN BEGABUNG. 1910. 41 pp. (Also as *Archiv für die gesamte Psychologie,* Volume 18, 1910, pp. 193–233.)

———, **Heft 5.** Rakic, V. GEDANKEN ÜBER ERZIEHUNG DURCH SPIEL UND KUNST. 1912. 58 pp. (Also as *Archiv für die gesamte Psychologie,* Volume 21, 1911, pp. 521–579.)

Band 3, Heft 1. Kronfeld, Arthur. ÜBER DIE PSYCHOLOGISCHEN THEORIEN FREUDS UND VERWANDTE ANSCHAUUNGEN. 1912. 120 pp. (Also as *Archiv für die gesamte Psychologie,* Volume 22, 1911, pp. 130–248.

———, **Heft 2.** Josefovici, U. DIE PSYCHISCHE VEREBUNG. 1912. 155 pp. (Also as *Archiv für die gesamte Psychologie,* Volume 23, 1912, pp. 1–155.)

———, **Heft 3.** Anschütz, Georg. SPEKULATIVE, EXACTE UND ANGEWANDTE PSYCHOLOGIE. 1912. 88 pp. (Also as *Archiv für die gesamte Psychologie,* Volume 23, 1912, pp. 281–309; and Volume 24, 1912, Pp. 1–30, 111–140.)

———, **Heft 4.** Poppelreuter, Walther. ÜBER DIE ORDNUNG DES VORSTELLUNGSABLAUFES. 1. TEIL. 1913. 141 pp. (Also as *Archiv für die gesamte Psychologie,* Volume 25, 1912, pp. 208–349.)

————, **Heft 5.** Benussi, Vittorio. DIE ATMUNGSSYMPTOME DER LÜGE. 1914. 30 pp. (Also as *Archiv für die gesamte Psychologie,* Volume 31, 1914, pp. 244–273.)

Band 4, Heft 1. Schröbler, Erich. DIE ENTWICKLUNG DER AUFASSUNGSKATEGORIEN BEIM SCHULKINDE. 1914. 112 pp. (Also as *Archiv für die gesamte Psychologie,* Volume 30, 1913, pp. 1–112.)

200. *Training School.*

TITLE VARIATIONS: Continued by *Training School Bulletin* with Volume 10, Whole Number 103, March 1913.

DATES OF PUBLICATION: Volume 1–9, Number 10, March 1904–February 1913.

FREQUENCY: **Monthly,** Volume 1–6, Number 12, March 1904–February 1910. **Monthly** (except July and August), Volume 7–9, Number 10, March 1910–February 1913.

NUMBERING VARIATIONS: Each issue is also assigned a whole number, Number 1–102. Supplement 1–2 issued December 1907 and March 1908. Supplement 2 also numbered as *Training School,* Volume 5, Number 1.

PUBLISHER: **Vineland, New Jersey:** New Jersey Training School, 1904–1911. **Vineland:** Training School at Vineland, 1911–1912. **Vineland:** Training School, 1912–1913.

PRIMARY EDITORS: **E. R. Johnstone,** 1904–1913; **Henry H. Goddard,** 1904–1913; **Alice Morrison Nash,** 1904–1913.

201. *Vereinigung für gerichtliche Psychologie und Psychiatrie im Grossherzogtum Hessen. Berichte.*

TITLE VARIATIONS: None.

DATES OF PUBLICATION: Band 1–8, 1904–1910.

FREQUENCY: **Annual,** Band 1–5, 1904–1906/1907. **Biennial,** Band 6–8, 1907–1910.

NUMBERING VARIATIONS: Published as a subseries of *Juristisch-psychiatrische Grenzfragen:* Band 1, 1904 in *Juristisch-psychiatrische Grenzfragen,* Band 2, Heft 6, 1905; Band 2, 1905 in Band 3, Heft 8, 1906; Band 3, 1906 in Band 5, Heft 6, 1907; Band 4/5, 1906/1907 in Band 6, Heft 2 and 3, 1907; Band 6/7, 1907 in Band 6, Heft 7, 1908; and Band 8, 1910 in Band 7, Heft 4, 1910.

PUBLISHER: **Halle:** C. Marhold, 1904–1910.

PRIMARY EDITOR: **A. Dannemann,** 1904–1910.

202. *Vestnik psikhologii, kriminal'noi antropologii i gipnotizma.*

TITLE VARIATIONS: Continued by *Vestnik psikhologii, kriminal'noi antropologii i pedologii* with Tom 9, 1912.

DATES OF PUBLICATION: Tom 1–8, Vypusk 5, 1904–1911.

FREQUENCY: (10 issues per year), Tom 1–2, 1904–1905. (5 issues per year), Tom 3–8, Vypusk 5, 1906–1911.

NUMBERING VARIATIONS: None.

PUBLISHER: **St. Petersburg:** Psikhonevrologicheskii institut, 1904–1911.

PRIMARY EDITORS: Unknown.

NOTE: Information on this title was compiled from entries in *Half a Century of Soviet Serials.*

1905

203. *Archives of Philosophy, Psychology and Scientific Methods.*

TITLE VARIATIONS: Superseded by *Archives of Psychology* with Number 1, 1906 and *Archives of Philosophy* with Number 1, 1907.

DATES OF PUBLICATION: Number 1–8, September 1905–July 1906.

FREQUENCY: Irregular.

NUMBERING VARIATIONS: Also numbered as [*Columbia University.*] *Contributions to Philosophy and Psychology. See* Contents *below.*

PUBLISHER: **New York:** The Science Press, 1905–1906.

PRIMARY EDITORS: **J. McKeen Cattell,** 1905–1906; **Frederick J. E. Woodbridge,** 1905–1906.

CONTENTS:
    Number 1. Thorndike, Edward L. Measurements of Twins. 1905. 64 pp. (Also in [*Columbia University.*] *Contributions to Philosophy and Psychology,* Volume 13, Number 3.)
    Number 2. Bush, Wendell T. Avenarius and the Standpoint of Pure Experience. 1905. 79 pp. (Also in [*Columbia University.*] *Contributions to Philosophy and Psychology,* Volume 10, Number 4.)
    Number 3. Arnold, Felix. The Psychology of Association. 1906. 80 pp. (Also in [*Columbia University.*] *Contributions to Philosophy and Psychology,* Volume 13, Number 4.)
    Number 4. Dearborn, Walter Fenno. The Psychology of Reading. 1906. 134 pp. (Also in [*Columbia University.*] *Contributions to Philosophy and Psychology,* Volume 14, Number 1.)
    Number 5. Boas, Franz. The Measurement of Variable Quantities. 1906. 52 pp. (Also in [*Columbia University.*] *Contributions to Philosophy and Psychology,* Volume 14, Number 2.)
    Number 6. Wells, Frederic Lyman. Linguistic Lapses with Special Reference to the Perception of Linguistic Sounds. 1906. 110 pp. (Also in [*Columbia University.*] *Contributions to Philosophy and Psychology,* Volume 15, Number 1—incorrectly labeled Volume 14, Number 3.)

Number 7. Marsh, Howard Daniel. THE DIURNAL COURSE OF EFFICIENCY. 1906. 99 pp. (Also in [*Columbia University.*] *Contributions to Philosophy and Psychology,* Volume 14, Number 3.)

Number 8. Henmon, Vivian Allen Charles. THE TIME OF PERCEPTION AS A MEASURE OF DIFFERENCES IN SENSATIONS. 1906. 75 pp. (Also in [*Columbia University.*] *Contributions to Philosophy and Psychology,* Volume 14, Number 4.)

204. *Catholic University of America. Psychological Studies.*

TITLE VARIATIONS: None.

DATES OF PUBLICATION: Number 1–8, October 1905–1923.

FREQUENCY: Irregular. *See* Contents *below.*

NUMBERING VARIATIONS: Number 7 and 8 incorrectly numbered 6 and 7. Issues also numbered as *Psychological Review. Monograph Supplements* and as *Psychological Monographs. See* Contents *below.*

PUBLISHER: **Lancaster, Pennsylvania** and **New York:** The Macmillan Company, 1905. **Princeton, New Jersey** and **Lancaster:** Psychological Review Company, 1919–1922. **Princeton:** Psychological Review Company, 1923.

PRIMARY EDITOR: **Edward A. Pace.**

CONTENTS:

Number 1. Dubray, Charles A. THE THEORY OF PSYCHICAL DISPOSITIONS. October 1905. 170 pp. (Also as *Psychological Review. Monograph Supplements,* Number 30.)

Number 2. Hamel, Ignatius A. A STUDY AND ANALYSIS OF THE CONDITIONED REFLEX. 1919. 65 pp. (Also as *Psychological Monographs,* Number 118.)

Number 3. Moore, Thomas Verner. IMAGE AND MEANING IN MEMORY AND PERCEPTION. 1919. Pp. 67–296. (Also as *Psychological Monographs,* Number 119.)

Number 4. Moore, Thomas Verner. THE CORRELATION BETWEEN MEMORY AND PERCEPTION IN THE PRESENCE OF DIFFUSE CORTICAL DEGENERATION. 1919. Pp. 297–345. (Also as *Psychological Monographs,* Number 120.)

Number 5. CLINICAL AND PSYCHOANALYTIC STUDIES. i. Furfey, Paul Hanly. CONSCIOUS AND UNCONSCIOUS FACTORS IN SYMBOLISM; ii. Moore, Thomas Verner. HYPNOTIC ANALOGIES; iii. Loughran, Miriam E. CONCOMITANTS OF AMENTIA. 1919. Pp. 347–440. (Also as *Psychological Monographs,* Number 121.)

Number 6. McDonough, Agnes R. THE DEVELOPMENT OF MEANING. 1919. Pp. 441–515. (Also as *Psychological Monographs,* Number 122.)

Number 7. Moore, Thomas Verner. PERCY BYSSHE SHELLEY. AN INTRODUCTION TO THE STUDY OF CHARACTER. 1922. 62 pp. (Also as *Psychological Monographs,* Number 141.)

Number 8. McGrath, Marie Cecilia. A STUDY OF THE MORAL DEVELOPMENT OF CHILDREN. 1923. 190 pp. (Also as *Psychological Monographs,* Number 144.)

205. *Columbia University. Contributions to Philosophy and Psychology.*

TITLE VARIATIONS: Continues *Columbia University. Contributions to Philosophy, Psychology and Education.*

DATES OF PUBLICATION. Volume 13, Number 3–Volume 27, Number 4, 1905–1922.

FREQUENCY: Irregular. *See* Contents *below.*

NUMBERING VARIATIONS: Volume 15, Number 1 misnumbered Volume 14, Number 3. Volume 18, Number 1 repeated in numbering. Volume 23 omitted in numbering. Four unnumbered issues published in 1922. Some issues also published as *Archives of Philosophy, Psychology and Scientific Methods;* as *Archives of Philosophy;* or as *Archives of Psychology. See* Contents *below.*

PUBLISHER: **New York:** Science Press, 1905–1920. **New York:** No publisher listed, 1920–1922.

PRIMARY EDITORS: **J. McKeen Cattell** (for issues also published in *Archives of Philosophy, Psychology and Scientific Methods*), 1905–1906. **Frederick J. E. Woodbridge** (for issues also published in *Archives of Philosophy, Psychology and Scientific Methods* and in *Archives of Philosophy*), 1905–1915. **Robert S. Woodworth** (for issues also published in *Archives of Psychology*), 1906–1922.

CONTENTS:

Volume 13, Number 3. Thorndike, Edward Lee. MEASUREMENTS OF TWINS. 1905. 64 pp. (Also as *Archives of Philosophy, Psychology and Scientific Methods,* Number 1.)

————, **Number 4.** Arnold, Felix. THE PSYCHOLOGY OF ASSOCIATION. 1906. 80 pp. (Also as *Archives of Philosophy, Psychology and Scientific Methods,* Number 3.)

Volume 14, Number 1. Dearborn, Walter Fenno. THE PSYCHOLOGY OF READING; AN EXPERIMENTAL STUDY OF THE READING PAUSES AND THE MOVEMENTS OF THE EYE. 1906. 132 pp. (Also as *Archives of Philosophy, Psychology and Scientific Methods,* Number 4.)

————, **Number 2.** Boas, Franz. THE MEASUREMENT OF VARIABLE QUANTITIES. 1906. 52 pp. (Also as *Archives of Philosophy, Psychology and Scientific Methods,* Number 5.)

————, **Number 3.** Marsh, Howard Daniel. THE DIURNAL COURSE OF EFFICIENCY. 1906. 99 pp. (Also as *Archives of Philosophy, Psychology and Scientific Methods,* Number 7.)

————, **Number 4.** Henmon, Vivian Allen Charles. TIME OF PERCEPTION AS A MEASURE OF DIFFERENCES IN SENSATIONS. 1906. 75 pp. (Also as *Archives of Philosophy, Psychology and Scientific Methods,* Number 8.)

Volume 15, Number 1. Wells, Frederic Lyman. LINGUISTIC LAPSES WITH ESPECIAL REFERENCE TO THE PERCEPTION OF LINGUISTIC SOUNDS. 1906. 110 pp. (Also as *Archives of Philosophy, Psychology and Scientific Methods,* Number 6.)

————, **Number 2.** Norsworthy, Naomi. THE PSYCHOLOGY OF MENTALLY DEFICIENT CHILDREN. 1906. 111 pp. (Also as *Archives of Psychology,* Number 1.)

205. *(Continued)*

————, **Number 3.** Thorndike, Edward Lee. EMPIRICAL STUDIES IN THE THEORY OF MEASURMENT. 1907. 45 pp. (Also as *Archives of Psychology*, Number 3.)

————, **Number 4.** Lipsky, Abram. RHYTHM AS A DISTINGUISHING CHARACTERISTIC OF PROSE STYLE. 1907. 44 pp. (Also as *Archives of Psychology*, Number 4.)

Volume 16, Number 1. Ruediger, William Carl. THE FIELD OF DISTINCT VISION, WITH SPECIAL REFERENCE TO INDIVIDUAL DIFFERENCES AND THEIR CORRELATIONS. 1907. 67 pp. (Also as *Archives of Psychology*, Number 5.)

————, **Number 2.** Jones, Elmer Ellsworth. THE INFLUENCE OF BODILY POSTURE ON MENTAL ACTIVITIES. 1907. 60 pp. (Also as *Archives of Psychology*, Number 6.)

————, **Number 3.** Wells, Frederic Lyman. A STATISTICAL STUDY OF LITERARY MERIT, WITH REMARKS ON SOME NEW PHASES OF THE METHOD. 1907. 30 pp. (Also as *Archives of Psychology*, Number 7.)

————, **Number 4.** Froeberg, Sven. THE RELATION BETWEEN THE MAGNITUDE OF STIMULUS AND THE TIME OF REACTION. 1907. 38 pp. (Also as *Archives of Psychology*, Number 8.)

Volume 17, Number 1. Hamilton, Francis Marion. THE PERCEPTUAL FACTORS IN READING: A QUANTITATIVE STUDY OF THE PSYCHOLOGICAL PROCESSES INVOLVED IN WORD PERCEPTION. 1907. 56 pp. (Also as *Archives of Psychology*, Number 9.)

————, **Number 2.** Brown, Warner. TIME IN ENGLISH VERSE RHYTHM; AN EMPIRICAL STUDY OF TYPICAL VERSES BY THE GRAPHIC METHOD. 1908. 79 pp. (Also as *Archives of Psychology*, Number 10.)

————, **Number 3.** Bruner, Frank G. THE HEARING OF PRIMITIVE PEOPLES: AN EXPERIMENTAL STUDY OF THE AUDITORY ACUITY AND THE UPPER LIMIT OF HEARING OF WHITES, INDIANS, FILIPINOS, AINU AND AFRICAN PIGMIES. 1908. 113 pp. (Also as *Archives of Psychology*, Number 11.)

————, **Number 4.** Hollingworth, H. L. THE INACCURACY OF MOVEMENT WITH SPECIAL REFERENCE TO CONSTANT ERRORS. 1909. 87 pp. (Also as *Archives of Psychology*, Number 13.)

Volume 18, Number 1. Woodrow, Herbert. A QUANTITATIVE STUDY IN RHYTHM: THE EFFECT OF VARIATIONS IN INTENSITY, RATE AND DURATION. 1909. 66 pp. (Also as *Archives of Psychology*, Number 14.)

————, **Number 1.** Elkus, Savilla Alice. THE CONCEPT OF CONTROL. 1907. 40 pp. (Also as *Archives of Philosophy*, Number 1.)

————, **Number 2.** Cooley, William Forbes. THE INDIVIDUAL. A METAPHYSICAL INQUIRY. 1909. 95 pp. (Also as *Archives of Philosophy*, Number 3.)

————, **Number 3/4.** Sait, Una Bernard. THE ETHICAL IMPLICATIONS OF BERGSON'S PHILOSOPHY. 1914. 183 pp. (Also as *Archives of Philosophy*, Number 4.)

Volume 19, Number 1. Reisner, Edward Hartman. RELIGIOUS VALUES AND INTELLECTUAL CONSISTENCY. 1915. 59 pp. (Also as *Archives of Philosophy*, Number 5.)

————, **Number 2.** Ruger, Henry Alford. THE PSYCHOLOGY OF EFFICIENCY. AN EXPERIMENTAL STUDY OF THE PROCESSES INVOLVED IN THE SOLUTION OF MECHANICAL PUZZLES AND IN THE ACQUISITION OF SKILLS IN THEIR MANIPULATION. 1910. 88 pp. (Also as *Archives of Psychology*, Number 15.)

————, **Number 3.** Strong, Edward K. THE RELATIVE MERIT OF ADVERTISEMENTS: A PSYCHOLOGICAL AND STATISTICAL STUDY. 1911. 81 pp. (Also as *Archives of Psychology*, Number 17.)

————, **Number 4.** Breitwieser, Joseph Valentine. ATTENTION AND MOVEMENT IN REACTION TIME. 1911. 49 pp. (Also as *Archives of Psychology*, Number 18.)

Volume 20, Number 1. Whitley, Mary Theodora. AN EMPIRICAL STUDY OF CERTAIN TESTS FOR INDIVIDUAL DIFFERENCES. 1911. 146 pp. (Also as *Archives of Psychology*, Number 19.)

————, **Number 2.** Rice, David Edgar. VISUAL ACUITY WITH LIGHTS OF DIFFERENT COLORS AND INTENSITIES. 1912. 59 pp. (Also as *Archives of Psychology*, Number 20.)

————, **Number 3.** Bean, C. H. THE CURVE OF FORGETTING. 1912. 45 pp. (Also as *Archives of Psychology*, Number 21.)

————, **Number 4.** Hollingworth, H. L. THE INFLUENCE OF CAFFEIN ON MENTAL AND MOTOR EFFICIENCY. 1912. 166 pp. (Also as *Archives of Psychology*, Number 22.)

Volume 21, Number 1. Poffenberger, A. T. REACTION TIME TO RETINAL STIMULATION WITH SPECIAL REFERENCE TO THE TIME LOST IN CONDUCTION THROUGH NERVE CENTERS. 1912. 73 pp. (Also as *Archives of Psychology*, Number 23.)

————, **Number 2.** Culler, Arthur Jerome. INTERFERENCE AND ADAPTABILITY. AN EXPERIMENTAL STUDY OF THEIR RELATION WITH SPECIAL REFERENCE TO INDIVIDUAL DIFFERENCES. 1912. 80 pp. (Also as *Archives of Psychology*, Number 24.)

————, **Number 3.** Todd, John Welhoff. REACTION TO MULTIPLE STIMULI. 1912. 65 pp. (Also as *Archives of Psychology*, Number 25.)

————, **Number 4.** Myers, Garry C. A STUDY IN INCIDENTAL MEMORY. 1913. 108 pp. (Also as *Archives of Psychology*, Number 26.)

Volume 22, Number 1. Castle, Cora Sutton. A STATISTICAL STUDY OF EMINENT WOMEN. 1913. 90 pp. (Also as *Archives of Psychology*, Number 27.)

————, **Number 2.** Mayo, Marion J. THE MENTAL CAPACITY OF THE AMERICAN NEGRO. 1913. 70 pp. (Also as *Archives of Psychology*, Number 28.)

————, **Number 3.** Hollingworth, H. L. EXPERIMENTAL STUDIES IN JUDGMENT. 1913. 119 pp. (Also as *Archives of Psychology*, Number 29.)

————, **Number 4.** Henmon, V.A.C., Walter F. Dearborn, F. Lyman Wells, R. S. Woodworth,, H. L. Hollingworth and E. L. Thorndike. THE PSYCHOLOGICAL RESEARCHES OF JAMES MCKEEN CATTELL: A REVIEW BY SOME OF HIS PUPILS. 1914. 101 pp. (Also as *Archives of Psychology*, Number 30.)

Volume 24, Number 1. Martin, Melvin Albert. THE TRANSFER EFFECTS OF PRACTICE IN CANCELLATION TESTS. 1915. 68 pp. (Also as *Archives of Psychology*, Number 32.)

————, **Number 2.** Stenquist, John L., Edward Lee Thorndike and Marion R. Trabue. THE INTELLECTUAL STATUS OF CHILDREN WHO ARE PUBLIC CHARGES. 1915. 52 pp. (Also as *Archives of Psychology,* Number 33.)

————, **Number 3.** Lyon, Darwin Oliver. THE RELATION OF QUICKNESS OF LEARNING TO RETENTIVENESS. 1916. 60 pp. (Also as *Archives of Psychology,* Number 34.)

————, **Number 4.** Morgan, John J. B. THE OVERCOMING OF DISTRACTION AND OTHER RESISTANCES. 1916. 84 pp. (Also as *Archives of Psychology,* Number 35.)

Volume 25, Number 1. Ferguson, George Oscar. THE PSYCHOLOGY OF THE NEGRO. AN EXPERIMENTAL STUDY. 1916. 138 pp. (Also as *Archives of Psychology,* Number 36.)

————, **Number 2.** Evans, John E. THE EFFECT OF DISTRACTION ON REACTION TIME, WITH SPECIAL REFERENCE TO PRACTICE AND THE TRANSFER OF TRAINING. 1916. 106 pp. (Also as *Archives of Psychology,* Number 37.)

————, **Number 3.** Stecher, Lorle Ida. THE EFFECT OF HUMIDITY ON NERVOUSNESS AND ON GENERAL EFFICIENCY. 1916. 94 pp. (Also as *Archives of Psychology,* Number 38.)

————, **Number 4.** May, Mark A. THE MECHANISM OF CONTROLLED ASSOCIATION. 1917. 74 pp. (Also as *Archives of Psychology,* Number 39.)

Volume 26, Number 1. Gates, Arthur I. RECITATION AS A FACTOR IN MEMORIZING. 1917. 104 pp. (Also as *Archives of Psychology,* Number 40.)

————, **Number 2.** Garth, Thomas Russell. MENTAL FATIGUE DURING CONTINUOUS EXERCISE OF A SINGLE FUNCTION. 1918. 85 pp. (Also as *Archives of Psychology,* Number 41.)

————, **Number 3.** Paynter, Richard H., Jr. A PSYCHOLOGICAL STUDY OF TRADE-MARK INFRINGEMENT. 1920. 72 pp. (Also as *Archives of Psychology,* Number 42.)

————, **Number 4.** Bagg, Halsey J. INDIVIDUAL DIFFERENCES AND FAMILY RESEMBLANCES IN ANIMAL BEHAVIOR: A STUDY OF HABIT FORMATION IN VARIOUS STRAINS OF MICE. 1920. 58 pp. (Also as *Archives of Psychology,* Number 43.)

Volume 27, Number 1. Achilles, Edith Mulhall. EXPERIMENTAL STUDIES IN RECALL AND RECOGNITION. 1920. 80 pp. (Also as *Archives of Psychology,* Number 44.)

————, **Number 2.** Naccarati, Sante. THE MORPHOLOGIC ASPECT OF INTELLIGENCE. 1921. 44 pp. (Also as *Archives of Psychology,* Number 45.)

————, **Number 3.** Carothers, F. Edith. PSYCHOLOGICAL EXAMINATIONS OF COLLEGE STUDENTS. 1921. 82 pp. (Also as *Archives of Psychology,* Number 46.)

————, **Number 4.** Rogers, Herbert Wesley. SOME EMPIRICAL TESTS IN VOCATIONAL SELECTION. 1922. 47 pp. (Also as *Archives of Psychology,* Number 49.)

Unnumbered. Gough, Evelyn. THE EFFECTS OF PRACTICE ON JUDGMENTS OF ABSOLUTE PITCH. 1922. 94 pp. (Also as *Archives of Psychology.* Number 47.)

Unnumbered. Clark, Ruth S. AN EXPERIMENTAL STUDY OF SILENT THINKING. 1922. 102 pp. (Also as *Archives of Psychology,* Number 48.)

Unnumbered. Rogers, Margaret Cobb. ADENOIDS AND DISEASED TONSILS: THEIR EFFECT ON GENERAL INTELLIGENCE. 1922. 70 pp. (Also as *Archives of Psychology*, Number 50.)

Unnumbered. Burr, Emily. PSYCHOLOGICAL TESTS APPLIED TO FACTORY WORKERS. 1922. 93 pp. (Also as *Archives of Psychology*, Number 55.)

206. *Experimentelle Pädagogik.* [Organ of the Arbeitsgemeinschaft für experimentelle Pädagogik.]

TITLE VARIATIONS: Continued by *Zeitschrift für experimentelle Pädagogik, psychologische und pathologische Kinderforschung* with Band 5, 1907.

DATES OF PUBLICATION: Band 1–4, 1905–1907.

FREQUENCY: Quarterly.

NUMBERING VARIATIONS: None.

PUBLISHER: **Leipzig:** Otto Nemnich, 1905–1907.

PRIMARY EDITORS: **W. A. Lay,** 1905–1906; **Ernst Meumann,** 1905–1907.

207. *Florence. Università. Laboratorio di psicologia sperimentale. Ricerche di psicologia.*

TITLE VARIATIONS: Superseded by [*Florence. Università.*] *Istituto di psicologia. Studi e ricerche di psicologia* with Parte 1, 1938.

DATES OF PUBLICATION: Volume 1–3, 1905–1928.

FREQUENCY: **Biennial,** Volume 1–2, 1905–1907. **Annual,** Volume 3, 1928.

NUMBERING VARIATIONS: None.

PUBLISHER: **Florence:** Osvaldo Paggi & C., 1905. **Florence:** Tipografia Cooperative, 1907. **Florence:** F. Le Monnier, 1928.

PRIMARY EDITOR: **Francesco De Sarlo,** 1905–1928.

208. *Henderson Trust. Reports.*

TITLE VARIATIONS: Also called *William Ramsay Henderson Trust. Reports.* Superseded by *Henderson Trust. Lectures* with Number 1, 1924.

DATES OF PUBLICATION: Number 1–4, 1905–1924.

FREQUENCY: Irregular. *See* Contents *below.*

NUMBERING VARIATIONS: Number 2/3 published together and in connection with Number 4 below.

PUBLISHER: **Edinburgh:** Published for the William Ramsay Henderson Trust by Oliver and Boyd, 1924.

PRIMARY EDITORS: None listed.

CONTENTS:

Number 1. Tocher, J. F. AN ANTHROPOLOGICAL SURVEY OF THE INMATES OF LUNATIC ASYLUMS IN SCOTLAND. 1905. 139 pp.

Number 2/3. Tocher, J. F. THE ANTHROPOMETRIC CHARACTERISTICS OF THE NORMAL AND ASYLUM POPULATIONS OF THE NORTH-EAST OF SCOTLAND; and Tocher, J. F. A STUDY OF THE CHIEF PHYSICAL CHARACTERS OF SOLDIERS OF SCOTTISH NATIONALITY AND COMPARISON WITH THE PHYSICAL CHARACTERS OF THE INSANE POPULATION OF SCOTLAND. 1924. 172 pp.

Number 4. Brownlee, John. ORIGIN AND DISTRIBUTION OF RACIAL TYPES IN SCOTLAND. 1924. 29 pp.

209. *Louvain. Université catholique. Laboratoire de psychologie expérimentale. Travaux.* [Issued by the Bibliothèque de l'Institut supérieur de philosophie.]

TITLE VARIATIONS: None.

DATES OF PUBLICATION: Volume 1, Fasicule 1–2, 1905–1910.

FREQUENCY: Irregular. *See* Contents *below.*

NUMBERING VARIATIONS: None.

PUBLISHER: **Louvain** and **Paris:** Institut supérieur de philosophie; Félix Alcan, 1905. **Louvain** and **Geneva:** Institut supérieur de philosophie; Librairie Kuendig, 1910.

PRIMARY EDITORS: None listed.

CONTENTS:

Fasicule 1. Michotte, A. LES SIGNES RÉGIONAUX. 1905. 196 pp.

Fasicule 2. Michotte, A., and E. Prüm. ÉTUDE EXPÉRIMENTALE SUR LE CHOIX VOLONTAIRE ET SES ANTÉCÉDENTS IMMÉDIATS. 1910. 300 pp.

210. *Paris. Institut général psychologique. Mémoires.*

TITLE VARIATIONS: None.

DATES OF PUBLICATON: Numéro 1–7, 1905–1937.

FREQUENCY: Irregular. *See* Contents *below.*

NUMBERING VARIATIONS: There are five sections in the Institute: 1. Section de psychologie individuelle. 2. Section de psychologie moral et criminelle. 3. Section de psychologie artistique. 4. Section des recherches psychiques et physiologiques. 5. Section de psychologie zoologique. Each section publishes its own memoirs. These memoirs are then incorporated into the Mémoires of the Institut général psychologique. Numéro 5 was omitted and Numéro 6 was duplicated in numbering. *See* Contents *below.*

PUBLISHER: **Paris:** (Institut général psychologique), Au siège de la Société, 1905–1911. **Paris:** Librairie scientifique Hermann, 1934–1935.

PRIMARY EDITORS: None listed.

EDITORIAL BOARD: ——— d'Arsonval, 1905–1911; Edmond Perrier, 1905–1911; ——— Bouchard, 1905–1911; S. Yourievitch, 1905–1911; Émile Boutroux, 1905–1911; Jules Courtier, 1905–1911 (Sec.); Yves Delage, 1905–1911; Louis Herbette, 1905–1911; O. M. Lennelongue, 1905–1911; L. Liard, 1905–1911; Henri Poincaré, 1905–1911. None listed, 1912–1937.

Year 1905

CONTENTS:

Numéro 1. Bohn, Georges. ATTRACTIONS & OSCILLATIONS DES ANIMAUX MARINS SOUS L'INFLUENCE DE LA LUMIÈRE. 1905. 110 pp. (Also as *Section de psychologie zoologique*, Mémoire Numéro 1.)

Numéro 2. Cornetz, Victor. TRAJETS DE FOURMIS ET RETOURS AU NID; and ALBUM FAISANT SUITE AUX TRAJETS DE FOURMIS ET RETOURS AU NID. 1910. 167 pp. (Also as: *Section de psychologie zoologique*, Mémoire Numéro 2.)

Numéro 3. Henry, Charles. SENSATION ET ÉNERGIE. 1911. 296 pp. (Also as *Section de psychologie artistique*, Mémoire Numéro 1.)

Numéro 4. Henry, Charles. MÉMOIRE ET HABITUDE. 1911. 116 pp. (Also as *Section de psychologie artistique*, Mémoire Numéro 2.)

Numéro 6. Warrain, Francis. ESSAI SUR LES PRINCIPES DES ALGORITHMES PRIMITIFS. 1934. 151 pp. (Also as *Commission internationale de détermination mathématique*, Mémoire Numéro 1.)

Numéro 6. Warrain, Francis. ESPACE ET GÉOMÉTRIES. 1937. 197 pp.

Numéro 7. Warrain, Francis. EXAMEN PHILOSOPHIQUE DU TRANSFINI. 1935. 142 pp. (Also as *Commission internationale de détermination mathématique*, Mémoire Numéro 2.)

211. *Psychologische Untersuchungen.*

TITLE VARIATIONS: None.

DATE OF PUBLICATION: Band 1–2, Heft 3, 1905–1913.

FREQUENCY: Irregular. *See* Contents *below.*

NUMBERING VARIATIONS: Band 2, Heft 2/3 is double number.

PUBLISHER: **Leipzig:** Wilhelm Engelmann, 1905–1913.

PRIMARY EDITOR: Theodor Lipps, 1905–1913.

CONTENTS:

Band I, Heft 1. Lipps, Theodor. Bewusstsein und Gegenstände. 1905. Pp. 1–203.

———, **Heft 2.** Aster, E. von. UNTERSUCHUNGEN ÜBER DEN LOGISCHEN GEHALT DES KAUSALGESETZES. 1905. Pp. 205–323.

———, **Heft 3.** Geiger, Moritz. METHODOLOGISCHE UND EXPERIMEN- TELLE BEITRÄGE ZUR QUANTITÄTSLEHRE. 1907. Pp. 325–522.

———, **Heft 4.** Lipps, Theodor. DIE ERSCHEINUNGEN. 1907. Pp. 523–722.

Band II, Heft 1. Lipps, Theodor. ZUR "PSYCHOLOGIE" UND "PHILOSO- PHIE" WORTE. 1912. Pp. 1–110.

———, **Heft 2/3.** Lipps, Theodor. ZUR EINFÜHLUNG. 1913. Pp. 111–491.

212. *Rivista di psicologia applicata alla pedagogia ed alla psicopatologia.* [Organ of the Società italiana di psicologia and of the Istituti di psicologia sperimentale (Rome and Turin).]

TITLE VARIATIONS: Continued by *Rivista di psicologia applicata* with Volume 5, 1909.

DATES OF PUBLICATION: Volume 1–4, 1905–1908.

FREQUENCY: Bimonthly.

NUMBERING VARIATIONS: None.

PUBLISHER: **Bologna:** Stabilimento tipografico Zamorani e Albertazzi, 1905–1906. **Bologna:** Stabilimento poligrafico Emiliano, 1907–1908.

PRIMARY EDITORS: **Giulio Cesare Ferrari,** 1905–1908; **Edgardo Morpurgo,** 1905–1908.

213. *Yale Psychological Studies.*

TITLE VARIATIONS: Supersedes *Yale University. Psychological Laboratory. Studies.*

DATES OF PUBLICATION: New Series, Volume 1–2, March 1905–1917.

FREQUENCY: Irregular.

NUMBERING VARIATIONS: Each Volume contains 2 Numbers. Volume 1, Number 1–2 also numbered as *Psychological Review. Monograph Supplements,* Number 29 and 34. Volume 2, Number 1–2 also numbered as *Psychological Monographs,* Number 75 and 100.

PUBLISHER: **Lancaster, Pennsylvania** and **New York:** The Macmillan Company, 1905. **Lancaster** and **Baltimore:** Review Publishing Company, 1907. **Princeton, New Jersey** and **Lancaster:** Psychological Review Company, 1914–1917.

PRIMARY EDITORS: **Charles H. Judd,** 1905–1907; **Roswell P. Angier,** 1914–1917.

1906

214. *American Journal of Religious Psychology and Education. Monograph Supplement.*

TITLE VARIATIONS: None.

DATES OF PUBLICATION: Volume 1–2, September 1906 and November 1907.

FREQUENCY: Annual.

NUMBERING VARIATIONS: None.

PUBLISHER: **Worcester, Massachusetts:** Clark University Press, 1906–1907.

PRIMARY EDITOR: **G. Stanley Hall,** 1906–1907.

CONTENTS:

Volume 1. Morse, Josiah. PATHOLOGICAL ASPECTS OF RELIGIONS. 1906. 264 pp.

Volume 2. Morse, Josiah. THE PSYCHOLOGY AND NEUROLOGY OF FEAR. 1907. 106 pp.

215. *Archives of Psychology.*

TITLE VARIATIONS: Supersedes in part *Archives of Philosophy, Psychology and Scientific Methods.* Absorbed by *Psychological Monographs: General and Applied* with Number 288, 1948.

DATES OF PUBLICATION: Number 1–300, 1906–1945.

FREQUENCY: Irregular. *See* Contents *below.*

NUMBERING VARIATIONS: Number 92 incorrectly numbered 93. Various issues also numbered as [*Columbia University.*] *Contributions to Philosophy and Psychology,* or as [*Wisconsin University.*] *Contributions to Educational Psychology.* Issues also numbered in Volume 1–41. *See* Contents *below.*

PUBLISHER: **New York:** Science Press, 1906–1920. **New York:** No publisher listed, 1920–1945. From 1920–1925, G. E. Stechert and Company was listed as an agent. From 1927–1945, volume title pages but not individual monographs carried the imprint: New York. Columbia University. Archives of Psychology.

PRIMARY EDITOR: **Robert S. Woodworth,** 1906–1945.

CONTENTS:
[**Volume 1**] **Number 1.** Norsworthy, Naomi. THE PSYCHOLOGY OF MEN-TALLY DEFICIENT CHILDREN. 1906. 111 pp. (Also as [*Columbia University.*]. *Contributions to Philosophy and Psychology,* Volume 15, Number 2.)

[————] **Number 2.** Franz, Shepherd Ivory. ON THE FUNCTIONS OF THE CEREBRUM: THE FRONTAL LOBES. 1907. 64 pp.

[————] **Number 3.** Thorndike, Edward Lee. EMPIRICAL STUDIES IN THE THEORY OF MEASUREMENT. 1907. 45 pp. (Also as [*Columbia University.*] *Contributions to Philosophy and Psychology,* Volume 15, Number 3.)

[————] **Number 4.** Lipsky, Abram. RHYTHM AS A DISTINGUISHING CHAR-ACTERISTIC OF PROSE STYLE. 1907 44 pp. (Also as [*Columbia University.*] *Contributions to Philosophy and Psychology,* Volume 15, Number 4.)

[————] **Number 5.** Ruediger, William Carl. THE FIELD OF DISTINCT VISION, WITH SPECIAL REFERENCE TO INDIVIDUAL DIFFERENCES AND THEIR CORRELATIONS. 1907 67 pp. (Also as [*Columbia University.*] *Contributions to Philosophy and Psychology,* Volume 16, Number 1.)

[————] **Number 6.** Jones, Elmer Ellsworth. THE INFLUENCE OF BODILY POSTURE ON MENTAL ACTIVITIES. 1907. 60 pp. (Also as [*Columbia University.*] *Contributions to Philosophy and Psychology,* Volume 16, Number 2.)

[————] **Number 7.** Wells, Frederic Lyman. A STATISTICAL STUDY OF LITERARY MERIT, WITH REMARKS ON SOME PHASES OF THE METHOD. 1907. 30 pp. (Also as [*Columbia University.*] *Contributions to Philosophy and Psychology,* Volume 16, Number 3.)

[————] **Number 8.** Froeberg, Sven. THE RELATION BETWEEN THE MAG-NITUDE OF STIMULUS AND THE TIME OF REACTION. 1907. 38 pp. (Also as [*Columbia University.*] *Contributions to Philosophy and Psychology,* Volume 16, Number 4.)

[————] **Number 9.** Hamilton, Francis Marion. THE PERCEPTUAL FAC-TORS IN READING: A QUANTITATIVE STUDY OF THE PSYCHOLOGICAL PROCESSES INVOLVED IN WORD PERCEPTION. 1907. 56 pp. (Also as [*Columbia University.*] *Contributions to Philosophy and Psychology,* Volume 17, Number 1.)

215. *(Continued)*

[————] **Number 10.** Brown, Warner. TIME IN ENGLISH VERSE RHYTHM; AN EMPIRICAL STUDY OF TYPICAL VERSES BY THE GRAPHIC METHOD. 1908. 77 pp. (Also as [*Columbia University.*] *Contributions to Philosophy and Psychology,* Volume 17, Number 2.)

[**Volume 2**] **Number 11.** Bruner, Frank G. THE HEARING OF PRIMITIVE PEOPLES: AN EXPERIMENTAL STUDY OF THE AUDITORY ACUITY AND THE UPPER LIMIT OF HEARING OF WHITES, INDIANS, FILIPINOS, AINU AND AFRICAN PIGMIES. 1908. 113 pp. (Also as [*Columbia University.*] *Contributions to Philosophy and Psychology,* Volume 17, Number 3.)

[————] **Number 12.** Kirkpatrick, Edwin A., ed. STUDIES IN DEVELOPMENT AND LEARNING. CONTRIBUTIONS FROM THE DEPARTMENT OF PSYCHOLOGY AND CHILD STUDY IN THE FITCHBURG NORMAL SCHOOL, MADE BY THE ADVANCED CLASS OF 1907. 1909. 101 pp.

[————] **Number 13.** Hollingworth, H. L. THE INACCURACY OF MOVEMENT, WITH SPECIAL REFERENCE TO CONSTANT ERRORS. 1909. 87 pp. (Also as [*Columbia University.*] *Contributions to Philosophy and Psychology,* Volume 17, Number 4.)

[————] **Number 14.** Woodrow, Herbert. A QUANTITATIVE STUDY IN RHYTHM: THE EFFECT OF VARIATIONS IN INTENSITY, RATE AND DURATION. 1909. 66 pp. (Also as [*Columbia University.*] *Contributions to Philosophy and Psychology,* Volume 18, Number 1.)

[————] **Number 15.** Ruger, Henry Alford. THE PSYCHOLOGY OF EFFICIENCY. AN EXPERIMENTAL STUDY OF THE PROCESSES INVOLVED IN THE SOLUTION OF MECHANICAL PUZZLES AND IN THE ACQUISITION OF SKILLS IN THEIR MANIPULATION. 1910. 88 pp. (Also as [*Columbia University.*] *Contributions to Philosophy and Psychology,* Volume 19, Number 2.)

[————] **Number 16.** Wells, Frederic Lyman, and Alexander Forbes. ON CERTAIN ELECTRICAL PROCESSES IN THE HUMAN BODY AND THEIR RELATION TO EMOTIONAL REACTIONS. 1911. 39 pp.

[————] **Number 17.** Strong, Edward K. THE RELATIVE MERIT OF ADVERTISEMENTS: A PSYCHOLOGICAL AND STATISTICAL STUDY. 1911. 81 pp. (Also as [*Columbia University.*] *Contributions to Philosophy and Psychology,* Volume 19, Number 3.)

[————] **Number 18.** Breitwieser, Joseph Valentine. ATTENTION AND MOVEMENT IN REACTION TIME. 1911. 49 pp. (Also as [*Columbia University.*] *Contributions to Philosophy and Psychology,* Volume 19, Number 4.)

[**Volume 3**] **Number 19.** Whitley, Mary Theodora. AN EMPIRICAL STUDY OF CERTAIN TESTS FOR INDIVIDUAL DIFFERENCES. 1911. 146 pp. (Also as [*Columbia University.*] *Contributions to Philosophy and Psychology,* Volume 20, Number 1.)

[————] **Number 20.** Rice, David Edgar. VISUAL ACUITY WITH LIGHTS OF DIFFERENT COLORS AND INTENSITIES. 1912. 59 pp. (Also as [*Columbia University.*] *Contributions to Philosophy and Psychology,* Volume 20, Number 2.)

[————] **Number 21.** Bean, C. H. THE CURVE OF FORGETTING. 1912. 45

pp. (Also as [*Columbia University.*] *Contributions to Philosophy and Psychology*, Volume 20, Number 3.)

[————] **Number 22.** Hollingworth, H. L. THE INFLUENCE OF CAFFEIN ON MENTAL AND MOTOR EFFICIENCY. 1912. 166 pp. (Also as [*Columbia University.*] *Contributions to Philosophy and Psychology*, Volume 20, Number 4.)

[————] **Number 23.** Poffenberger, A. T. REACTION TIME TO RETINAL STIMULATION, WITH SPECIAL REFERENCE TO THE TIME LOST IN CONDUCTION THROUGH NERVE CENTERS. 1912. 73 pp. (Also as [*Columbia University.*] *Contributions to Philosophy and Psychology*, Volume 21, Number 1.)

[————] **Number 24.** Culler, Arthur Jerome. INTERFERENCE AND ADAPTABILITY: AN EXPERIMENTAL STUDY OF THEIR RELATION WITH SPECIAL REFERENCE TO INDIVIDUAL DIFFERENCES. 1912. 80 pp. (Also as [*Columbia University.*] *Contributions to Philosophy and Psychology*, Volume 21, Number 2.)

[————] **Number 25.** Todd, John Welhoff. REACTION TO MULTIPLE STIMULI. 1912. 65 pp. (Also as [*Columbia University.*] *Contributions to Philosophy and Psychology*, Volume 21, Number 3.)

[**Volume 4**] **Number 26.** Myers, Garry C. A STUDY IN INCIDENTAL MEMORY. 1913. 108 pp. (Also as [*Columbia University.*] *Contributions to Philosophy and Phychology.* Volume 21, Number 4.)

[————] **Number 27.** Castle, Cora Sutton. A STATISTICAL STUDY OF EMINENT WOMEN. 1913. 90 pp. (Also as [*Columbia University.*] *Contributions to Philosophy and Psychology.* Volume 22. Number 1.)

[————] **Number 28.** Mayo, Marion J. THE MENTAL CAPACITY OF THE AMERICAN NEGRO. 1913. 70 pp. (Also as [*Columbia University*] *Contributions to Philosophy and Psychology.* Volume 22, Number 2.

[————] **Number 29.** Hollingworth, H. L. EXPERIMENTAL STUDIES IN JUDGMENT. 1913. 119 pp. (Also as [*Columbia University.*] *Contributions to Philosophy and Psychology,* Volume 22, Number 3.)

[————] **Number 30.** Henmon, V.A.C., Walter F. Dearborn, F. Lyman Wells, R. S. Woodworth, H. L. Hollingworth, and E. L. Thorndike. THE PSYCHOLOGICAL RESEARCHES OF JAMES MCKEEN CATTELL: A REVIEW BY SOME OF HIS PUPILS. 1914. 101 pp. (Also as [*Columbia University.*] *Contributions to Philosophy and Psychology*, Volume 22, Number 4.)

[————] **Number 31.** Ash, Isaac Emery. FATIGUE AND ITS EFFECTS UPON CONTROL. 1914. 61 pp. (Also as [*Wisconsin. University.*] *Contributions to Educational Psychology*, Number 1.)

[————] **Number 32.** Martin, Melvin Albert. THE TRANSFER EFFECTS OF PRACTICE IN CANCELLATION TESTS. 1915. 68 pp. (Also as [*Columbia University.*] *Contributions to Philosophy and Psychology*, Volume 24, Number 1.)

[**Volume 5**] **Number 33.** Stenquist, J. L., E. L. Thorndike, and M. R. Trabue. THE INTELLECTUAL STATUS OF CHILDREN WHO ARE PUBLIC CHARGES. 1915. 52. pp. (Also as [*Columbia University.*] *Contributions to Philosophy and Psychology*, Volume 24, Number 2.)

[————] **Number 34.** Lyon, Darwin Oliver. THE RELATION OF QUICKNESS OF LEARNING TO RETENTIVENESS. 1916. 60 pp. (Also as [*Columbia University.*] *Contributions to Philosophy and Psychology*, Volume 24, Number 3.)

215. *(Continued)*

[————] **Number 35.** Morgan, John J. B. THE OVERCOMING OF DISTRAC-
TION AND OTHER RESISTANCES. 1916. 84 pp. (Also as [*Columbia University.*]
Contributions to Philosophy and Psychology, Volume 24, Number 4.)

[————] **Number 36.** Ferguson, George Oscar. THE PSYCHOLOGY OF THE
NEGRO. AN EXPERIMENTAL STUDY. 1916. 138 pp. (Also as [*Columbia University.*] *Contributions to Philosophy and Psychology,* Volume 25, Number 1.)

[————] **Number 37.** Evans, John E. THE EFFECT OF DISTRACTION ON
REACTION TIME, WITH SPECIAL REFERENCE TO PRACTICE AND THE TRANSFER OF
TRAINING. 1916. 106 pp. (Also as [*Columbia University.*] *Contributions to Phi-
losophy and Psychology,* Volume 25, Number 2.)

[————] **Number 38.** Stecher, Lorle Ida. THE EFFECT OF HUMIDITY ON
NERVOUSNESS AND ON GENERAL EFFICIENCY. 1916. 94 pp. (Also as [*Columbia
University.*] *Contributions to Philosophy and Psychology,* Volume 25, Number
3.)

[————] **Number 39.** May, Mark A. THE MECHANISM OF CONTROLLED
ASSOCIATION. 1917. 74 pp. (Also as [*Columbia University.*] *Contributions to
Philosophy and Psychology,* Volume 25, Number 4.)

[**Volume 6**] **Number 40.** Gates, Arthur I. RECITATION AS A FACTOR IN
MEMORIZING. 1917. 104 pp. (Also as [*Columbia University.*] *Contributions to
Philosophy and Psychology,* Volume 26, Number 1.)

[————] **Number 41.** Garth, Thomas Russell. MENTAL FATIGUE DURING
CONTINUOUS EXERCISE OF A SINGLE FUNCTION. 1918. (Also as [*Columbia
University.*] *Contributions to Philosophy and Psychology,* Volume 26, Num-
ber 2.)

[————] **Number 42.** Paynter, Richard H., Jr. A PSYCHOLOGICAL STUDY
OF TRADE-MARK INFRINGEMENT. 1920. 72 pp. (Also as [*Columbia University.*]
Contributions to Philosophy and Psychology, Volume 26, Number 3.)

[————] **Number 43.** Bagg, Halsy J. INDIVIDUAL DIFFERENCES AND FAM-
ILY RESEMBLANCES IN ANIMAL BEHAVIOR: A STUDY OF HABIT FORMATION IN
VARIOUS STRAINS OF MICE. 1920. 58 pp. (Also as [*Columbia University.*] *Con-
tributions to Philosophy and Psychology,* Volume 26, Number 4.)

[————] **Number 44.** Achilles, Edith Mulhall. EXPERIMENTAL STUDIES IN
RECALL AND RECOGNITION. 1920. 80 pp. (Also as [*Columbia University.*] *Contributions to Philosophy and Psychology,* Volume 27, Number 1.)

[————] **Number 45.** Naccarati, Sante. THE MORPHOLOGIC ASPECT OF
INTELLIGENCE. 1921. 44 pp. (Also as [*Columbia University.*] *Contributions to
Philosophy and Psychology,* Volume 27, Number 2.)

[————] **Number 46.** Carothers, F. Edith. PSYCHOLOGICAL EXAMINA-
TIONS OF COLLEGE STUDENTS. 1921. 82 pp. (Also as [*Columbia University.*]
Contributions to Philosophy and Psychology. Volume 27, Number 3.)

[**Volume 7**] **Number 47.** Gough, Evelyn. THE EFFECTS OF PRACTICE ON
JUDGMENTS OF ABSOLUTE PITCH. 1922. 94 pp. (Also as [*Columbia University.*]
Contributions to Philosophy and Psychology, Unnumbered.)

[————] **Number 48.** Clark, Ruth S. AN EXPERIMENTAL STUDY OF SILENT
THINKING. 1922. 10 pp. (Also as [*Columbia University.*] *Contributions to Philosophy and Psychology,* Unnumbered.)

[————] **Number 49.** Rogers, Herbert Wesley. SOME EMPIRICAL TESTS IN VOCATIONAL SELECTION. 1922. 47 pp. (Also as [*Columbia University.*] *Contributions to Philosophy and Psychology,* Volume 27, Number 4.)

[————] **Number 50.** Rogers, Margaret Cobb. ADENOIDS AND DISEASED TONSILS: THEIR EFFECT ON GENERAL INTELLIGENCE. 1922. 70 pp. (Also as [*Columbia University.*] *Contributions to Philosophy and Psychology.* Unnumbered.)

[————] **Number 51.** Martin, Alfred H. AN EXPERIMENTAL STUDY OF THE FACTORS AND TYPES OF VOLUNTARY CHOICE. 1922. 115 pp.

[————] **Number 52.** Morgenthau, Dorothy Ruth. SOME WELL-KNOWN MENTAL TESTS EVALUATED AND COMPARED. 1922. 54 pp.

[**Volume 8**] **Number 53.** Sullivan, Elizabeth T. MOOD IN RELATION TO PERFORMANCE. 1922. 71 pp.

[————] **Number 54.** Johanson, Albert M. THE INFLUENCE OF INCENTIVE AND PUNISHMENT UPON REACTION-TIME. 1922. 52 pp.

[————] **Number 55.** Burr, Emily. PSYCHOLOGICAL TESTS APPLIED TO FACTORY WORKERS. 1922. 93 pp. (Also as [*Columbia University.*] *Contributions to Philosophy and Psychology.* Unnumbered.

[————] **Number 56.** Garrett, Henry E. A STUDY OF THE RELATION OF ACCURACY TO SPEED. 1922. 104 pp.

[————] **Number 57.** Wada, Tomi. AN EXPERIMENTAL STUDY OF HUNGER IN ITS RELATION TO ACTIVITY. 1922. 65 pp.

[————] **Number 58.** Gates, Georgina Stickland. INDIVIDUAL DIFFERENCES AS AFFECTED BY PRACTICE. 1922. 74 pp.

[**Volume 9**] **Number 59.** Bregman, Elsie Oschrin. STUDIES IN INDUSTRIAL PSYCHOLOGY. 1922. 60 pp.

[————] **Number 60.** Tendler, Alexander D. THE MENTAL STATUS OF PSYCHONEUROTICS. 1923. 86 pp.

[————] **Number 61.** Newhall, Sidney M. EFFECTS OF ATTENTION ON THE INTENSITY OF CUTANEOUS PRESSURES AND ON VISUAL BRIGHTNESS. 1923. 75 pp.

[————] **Number 62.** Garfiel, Evelyn. THE MEASUREMENT OF MOTOR ABILITY. 1923. 47 pp.

[————] **Number 63.** Crane, Albert Loyal. RACE DIFFERENCES IN INHIBITION. BEING A PSYCHOLOGICAL STUDY OF THE COMPARATIVE CHARACTERISTICS OF THE NEGRO AND THE WHITE MAN AS MEASURED BY CERTAIN TESTS, WITH ESPECIAL REFERENCE TO THE PROBLEM OF VOLITION. 1923. 84 pp.

[**Volume 10**] **Number 64.** Shellow, Sadie Myers. INDIVIDUAL DIFFERENCES IN INCIDENTAL MEMORY. 1923. 77 pp.

[————] **Number 65.** Brown, William M. CHARACTER TRAITS AS FACTORS IN INTELLIGENCE TEST PERFORMANCE. 1923. 66 pp.

[————] **Number 66.** Davenport, Frances Isabel. ADOLESCENT INTERESTS; A STUDY OF THE SEXUAL INTERESTS AND KNOWLEDGE OF YOUNG WOMEN. 1923. 62 pp.

[————] **Number 67.** Trow, William Clark. THE PSYCHOLOGY OF CONFIDENCE—AN EXPERIMENTAL INQUIRY. 1923. 47 pp.

[————] **Number 68.** Jones, Harold E. EXPERIMENTAL STUDIES OF COLLEGE TEACHING: THE EFFECT OF EXAMINATION ON PERMANENCE OF LEARNING. 1923. 70 pp.

215. *(Continued)*

[**Volume 11**] **Number 69.** Paulsen, Alice E. THE INFLUENCE OF TREAT-MENT FOR INTESTINAL TOXEMIA ON MENTAL AND MOTOR EFFICIENCY. 1924. 45 pp.

[————] **Number 70.** Otis, Margaret. A STUDY OF SUGGESTIBILITY OF CHILDREN. 1924. 108 pp.

[————] **Number 71.** Hurlock, Elizabeth B. THE VALUE OF PRAISE AND REPROOF AS INCENTIVES FOR CHILDREN. 1924. 78 pp.

[————] **Number 72.** Nixon, Howard K. ATTENTION AND INTEREST IN AD-VERTISING. 1924. 67 pp.

[————] **Number 73.** Heidbreder, Edna. AN EXPERIMENTAL STUDY OF THINKING. 1924. 175 pp.

[**Volume 12**] **Number 74.** Axel, Robert. ESTIMATION OF TIME. 1924. 77 pp.

[————] **Number 75.** Sommerville, R. C. PHYSICAL, MOTOR AND SEN-SORY TRAITS. 1924. 108 pp.

[————] **Number 76.** Wechsler, David. THE MEASUREMENT OF EMO-TIONAL REACTIONS: RESEARCHES ON THE PSYCHOGALVANIC REFLEX. 1925. 181 pp.

[————] **Number 77.** Abel, Theodora Mead. TESTED MENTALITY AS RE-LATED TO SUCCESS IN SKILLED TRADE TRAINING. 1925. 82 pp.

[————] **Number 78.** Riddle, Ethel M. AGGRESSIVE BEHAVIOR IN A SMALL SOCIAL GROUP. BLUFFING, RISKING AND THE DESIRE TO BEAT, BEING STUDIED BY THE USE OF A POKER GAME AS AN EXPERIMENTAL TECHNIQUE. 1925. 196 pp.

[**Volume 13**] **Number 79.** Brandt, Edith R. THE MEMORY VALUE OF AD-VERTISEMENTS: WITH SPECIAL REFERENCE TO THE USE OF COLOR. 1925. 69 pp.

[————] **Number 80.** Anderson, Rose G. CRITICAL EXAMINATION OF TEST-SCORING METHODS. 1925. 50 pp.

[————] **Number 81.** Culler, Elmer A. K. THERMAL DISCRIMINATION AND WEBER'S LAW, WITH A THEORY ON THE NATURE AND FUNCTION OF SENSORY ADAPTATION. 1926. 134 pp.

[————] **Number 82.** Ackerson, Luton. A CORRELATIONAL ANALYSIS OF PROFICIENCY IN TYPING. WITH A CONTRIBUTION ON THE CORRELATION BETWEEN SPEED AND ACCURACY BY TRUMAN L. KELLEY. 1926. 73 pp.

[————] **Number 83.** Key, Cora Beale. RECALL AS A FUNCTION OF PER-CEIVED RELATIONS. 1926. 106 pp.

[————] **Number 84.** Dowd, Constance E. A STUDY OF THE CONSISTENCY OF RATE OF WORK. 1926. 33 pp.

[————] **Number 85.** Crawley, S. L. AN EXPERIMENTAL INVESTIGATION OF RECOVERY FROM WORK. 1926. 66 pp.

[**Volume 14**] **Number 86.** Jenkins, Thomas N. FACILITATION AND INHIBI-TION. 1926. 56 pp.

[————] **Number 87.** Weinland, James D. VARIABILITY OF PERFORMANCE IN THE CURVE OF WORK. 1927. 68 pp.

[————] **Number 88.** House, S. Daniel. A MENTAL HYGIENE INVENTORY: A CONTRIBUTION TO DYNAMIC PSYCHOLOGY. 1927. 114 pp.

[————] **Number 89.** Jersild, Arthur T. MENTAL SET AND SHIFT. 1927. 81 pp.

[————] **Number 90.** Manzer, Charles W. AN EXPERIMENTAL INVESTIGATION OF REST PAUSES. 1927. 84 pp.

[————] **Number 91.** Crafts, Leland W. ROUTINE AND VARYING PRACTICE AS PREPARATION FOR ADJUSTMENT TO A NEW SITUATION. 1927. 58 pp.

[Volume 15] Number 92. Warner, L. H., and C. J. Warden. THE DEVELOPMENT OF A STANDARDIZED ANIMAL MAZE. 1927. 35 pp. (Incorrectly numbered 93.)

[————] **Number 93.** Klineberg, Otto. AN EXPERIMENTAL STUDY OF SPEED AND OTHER FACTORS IN "RACIAL" DIFFERENCES. 1928. 111 pp.

[————] **Number 94.** Lemmon, Vernon W. THE RELATION OF REACTION TIME TO MEASURES OF INTELLIGENCE, MEMORY, AND LEARNING. 1927. 38 pp.

[————] **Number 95.** Rounds, George H. IS THE LATENT TIME IN THE ACHILLES TENDON REFLEX A CRITERION OF SPEED IN MENTAL REACTIONS? 1928. 91 pp.

[————] **Number 96.** Flemming, Edwin G. THE PREDICTIVE VALUE OF CERTAIN TESTS OF EMOTIONAL STABILITY AS APPLIED TO COLLEGE FRESHMAN. 1928. 61 pp.

[————] **Number 97.** Weeks, Angelina Louisa. A VOCABULARY INFORMATION TEST. 1928. 71 pp.

[————] **Number 98.** Cook, Sidney A. THE EFFECT OF VARIOUS TEMPORAL ARRANGEMENTS OF PRACTICE ON THE MASTERY OF AN ANIMAL MAZE OF MODERATE COMPLEXITY. 1928. 33 pp.

[Volume 16] Number 99. Seward, Georgene Hoffman. RECOGNITION TIME AS A MEASURE OF CONFIDENCE: AN EXPERIMENTAL STUDY OF REDINTEGRATION. 1928. 54 pp.

[————] **Number 100.** Harmann, George W. PRECISION AND ACCURACY. 1928. 42 pp.

[————] **Number 101.** Burdick, Edith Marie. A GROUP TEST OF HOME ENVIRONMENT. 1928. 115 pp.

[————] **Number 102.** Wilkins, Minna Cheeves. THE EFFECT OF CHANGED MATERIAL ON ABILITY TO DO FORMAL SYLLOGISTIC REASONING. 1928. 83 pp.

[————] **Number 103.** Hamilton, Hughbert C. THE EFFECT OF INCENTIVES ON ACCURACY OF DISCRIMINATION MEASURED ON THE GALTON BAR. 1929. 73 pp.

[————] **Number 104.** Shimberg, Myra E. AN INVESTIGATION INTO THE VALIDITY OF NORMS WITH SPECIAL REFERENCE TO URBAN AND RURAL GROUPS. 1929. 84 pp.

[Volume 17] Number 105. Chappell, Matthew N. BLOOD PRESSURE CHANGES IN DECEPTION. 1929. 39 pp.

[————] **Number 106.** Kellogg, W. N. AN EXPERIMENTAL COMPARISON OF PSYCHOPHYSICAL METHODS. 1929. 86 pp.

[————] **Number 107.** Schneck, Matthew M. R. THE MEASUREMENT OF VERBAL AND NUMERICAL ABILITIES. 1929. 49 pp.

[————] **Number 108.** Cushing, Hazel Morton. A PERSEVERATIVE TENDENCY IN PRE-SCHOOL CHILDREN: A STUDY IN PERSONALITY DIFFERENCES. 1929. 55 pp.

[————] **Number 109.** Anderson, L. Dewey. A PRELIMINARY STUDY OF

215. *(Continued)*

THE EFFECT OF TRAINING IN JUNIOR HIGH SCHOOL SHOP COURSES. 1929. 39 pp.

[————] Number 110. Adler, Mortimer Jerome. MUSIC APPRECIATION: AN EXPERIMENTAL APPROACH TO ITS MEASUREMENT. 1929. 102 pp.

[————] Number 111. Hurlock, Elizabeth B. MOTIVATION IN FASHION. 1929. 71 pp.

[————] Number 112. Kellogg, W. N. AN EXPERIMENTAL EVALUATION OF EQUALITY JUDGMENTS IN PSYCHOPHYSICS. 1930. 78 pp.

[Volume 18] Number 113. Israeli, Nathan. ILLUSIONS IN THE PERCEPTION OF SHORT TIME INTERVALS. 1930. 47 pp.

[————] Number 114. Skaggs, E. B., S. Grossman, Louise Krueger, and William C. F. Krueger. FURTHER STUDIES OF THE READING–RECITATION PROCESS OF LEARNING. 1930. 38 pp.

[————] Number 115. Davis, Roland C. FACTORS AFFECTING THE GALVANIC REFLEX. 1930. 64 pp.

[————] Number 116. Ripin, Rowena. A STUDY OF THE INFANT'S FEEDING REACTIONS DURING THE FIRST SIX MONTHS OF LIFE. 1930. 44 pp.

[————] Number 117. Babcock, Harriet. AN EXPERIMENT IN THE MEASUREMENT OF MENTAL DETERIORATION. 1930. 105 pp.

[————] Number 118. Selling, Lowell Sinn. AN EXPERIMENTAL INVESTIGATION OF THE PHENOMENON OF POSTURAL PERSISTENCE. 1930. 52 pp.

[————] Number 119. Bradshaw, Francis Foster. THE AMERICAN COUNCIL ON EDUCATION RATING SCALE: ITS RELIABILITY, VALIDITY, AND USE. 1930. 80 pp.

[————] Number 120. Anastasi, Anne. A GROUP FACTOR IN IMMEDIATE MEMORY. 1930. 61 pp.

[Volume 19] Number 121. Kambouropoulou, Polyxenie. INDIVIDUAL DIFFERENCES IN THE SENSE OF HUMOR AND THEIR RELATION TO TEMPERAMENTAL DIFFERENCES. 1930. 83 pp.

[————] Number 122. Williams, Griffith W. SUGGESTIBILITY IN THE NORMAL AND HYPNOTIC STATES. 1930. 83 pp.

[————] Number 123. Wendt, George Richard. AN ANALYTICAL STUDY OF THE CONDITIONED KNEE-JERK. 1930. 97 pp.

[————] Number 124. Dunlap, Jack W. RACE DIFFERENCES IN THE ORGANIZATION OF NUMERICAL AND VERBAL ABILITIES. 1931. 71 pp.

[————] Number 125. Cureton, Edward E. ERRORS OF MEASUREMENT AND CORRELATION. 1931. 60 pp.

[————] Number 126. Bird, Norma. RELATIONSHIPS BETWEEN EXPERIENCE FACTORS, TEST SCORES AND EFFICIENCY, AS SHOWN BY A STUDY OF FOUR SELECTED GROUPS OF WOMEN OFFICE WORKERS. 1931. 51 pp.

[————] Number 127. Allen, Chauncey Newell. INDIVIDUAL DIFFERENCES IN DELAYED REACTION OF INFANTS: A STUDY OF SEX DIFFERENCES IN EARLY RETENTIVENESS. 1931. 40 pp.

[Volume 20] Number 128. Peatman, John Gray. A STUDY OF FACTORS MEASURED BY THE THORNDIKE INTELLIGENCE EXAMINATION FOR HIGH SCHOOL GRADUATES. 1931. 56 pp.

[————] **Number 129.** Regensburg, Jeanette. STUDIES OF EDUCATIONAL SUCCESS AND FAILURE IN SUPERNORMAL CHILDREN. 1931. 150 pp.

[————] **Number 130.** Seward, John P., Jr. THE EFFECT OF PRACTICE ON THE VISUAL PERCEPTION OF FORM. 1931. 72 pp.

[————] **Number 131.** Harris, Daniel. THE RELATION TO COLLEGE GRADES OF SOME FACTORS OTHER THAN INTELLIGENCE. 1931. 55 pp.

[————] **Number 132.** Klineberg, Otto. A STUDY OF PSYCHOLOGICAL DIFFERENCES BETWEEN "RACIAL" AND NATIONAL GROUPS IN EUROPE. 1931. 58 pp.

[————] **Number 133.** Courthial, Andrée. EMOTIONAL DIFFERENCES OF DELINQUENT AND NON-DELIQUENT GIRLS OF NORMAL INTELLIGENCE. A STUDY OF TWO GROUPS PAIRED BY CHRONOLOGICAL AGE, INTELLIGENCE, AND ENVIRONMENT. 1931. 102 pp.

[Volume 21] **Number 134.** Cason, Hulsey. THE LEARNING AND RETENTION OF PLEASANT AND UNPLEASANT ACTIVITIES. 1932. 96 pp.

[————] **Number 135.** MacLeod, Robert Brodie. AN EXPERIMENTAL INVESTIGATION OF BRIGHTNESS CONSTANCY. 1932. 102 pp.

[————] **Number 136.** Beck, Samuel J. THE RORSCHACH TEST AS APPLIED TO A FEEBLE-MINDED GROUP. 1932. 84 pp.

[————] **Number 137.** Van Ormer, Edward B. RETENTION AFTER INTERVALS OF SLEEP AND OF WAKING. 1932. 49 pp.

[————] **Number 138.** Heiser, Florien. STIMULUS TEMPERATURE AND THERMAL SENSATION. 1932. 81 pp.

[————] **Number 139.** Schubert, Herman J. P. ENERGY COST MEASUREMENTS ON THE CURVE OF WORK: AN ANALYSIS OF THE ORGANISMIC RESPONSE IN TERMS OF OXYGEN METABOLISM, HEART RATE, AND BREATHING RATE. 1932. 62 pp.

[Volume 22] **Number 140.** Likert, Rensis. A TECHNIQUE FOR THE MEASUREMENT OF ATTITUDES. 1932. 55 pp.

[————] **Number 141.** DuBois, Philip Hunter. A SPEED FACTOR IN MENTAL TESTS. 1932. 38 pp.

[————] **Number 142.** Anastasi, Anne. FURTHER STUDIES ON THE MEMORY FACTOR. 1932. 60 pp.

[————] **Number 143.** Asch, Solomon E. AN EXPERIMENTAL STUDY OF VARIABILITY IN LEARNING. 1932. 55 pp.

[————] **Number 144.** Smith, Randolph B. THE DEVELOPMENT OF AN INVENTORY FOR THE MEASUREMENT OF INFERIORITY FEELINGS AT THE HIGH SCHOOL LEVEL. 1932. 118 pp.

[————] **Number 145.** McFarland, Ross A. THE PSYCHOLOGICAL EFFECTS OF OXYGEN DEPRIVATION (ANOXEMIA) ON HUMAN BEHAVIOR. 1932. 135 pp.

[————] **Number 146.** Simley, O. A. THE RELATION OF SUBLIMINAL TO SUPRALIMINAL LEARNING. 1933. 40 pp.

[Volume 23] **Number 147.** Harmon, Francis L. THE EFFECTS OF NOISE UPON CERTAIN PSYCHOLOGICAL AND PHYSIOLOGICAL PROCESSES. 1933. 81 pp.

[————] **Number 148.** Razran, Gregory H. S. CONDITIONED RESPONSES IN CHILDREN: A BEHAVIORAL AND QUANTITATIVE CRITICAL REVIEW OF EXPERIMENTAL STUDIES. 1933. 120 pp.

215. *(Continued)*

[————] **Number 149.** Outhit, Marion Currie. A STUDY OF THE RESEM-
BLANCE OF PARENTS AND CHILDREN IN GENERAL INTELLIGENCE. 1933. 60 pp.

[————] **Number 150.** Chen, William Keh-ching. THE INFLUENCE OF
ORAL PROPAGANDA MATERIAL UPON STUDENTS' ATTITUDES. 1933. 43 pp.

[————] **Number 151.** Pallister, Helen. THE NEGATIVE OR WITHDRAWAL
ATTITUDE: A STUDY IN PERSONALITY ORGANIZATION. 1933. 56 pp.

[————] **Number 152.** Bressler, Joseph. JUDGMENT IN ABSOLUTE UNITS
AS A PSYCHOPHYSICAL METHOD. 1933. 67 pp.

[————] **Number 153.** Winslow, Charles Nelson. VISUAL ILLUSIONS IN
THE CHICK. 1933. 83 pp.

[————] **Number 154.** Hartmann, George W. MEASURING TEACHING EF-
FICIENCY AMONG COLLEGE INSTRUCTORS. 1933. 45 pp.

[Volume 24] **Number 155.** Sears, Richard. PSYCHOGALVANIC RESPONSES
IN ARITHMETICAL WORK: EFFECTS OF EXPERIMENTAL CHANGES IN ADDITION.
1933. 62 pp.

[————] **Number 156.** Smith, George Milton, Jr. GROUP FACTORS IN
MENTAL TESTS SIMILAR IN MATERIAL OR IN STRUCTURE. 1933. 56 pp.

[————] **Number 157.** Wood, Austin Bigelow. A COMPARISON OF DE-
LAYED REWARD AND DELAYED PUNISHMENT IN THE FORMATION OF A BRIGHT-
NESS DISCRIMINATION HABIT IN THE CHICK. 1933. 40 pp.

[————] **Number 158.** Roe, Anne. A STUDY OF THE ACCURACY OF PER-
CEPTION OF VISUAL MUSICAL STIMULI. 1933. 61 pp.

[————] **Number 159.** Perl, Ruth Eastwood. THE EFFECT OF PRACTICE
UPON INDIVIDUAL DIFFERENCES. 1933. 54 pp.

[————] **Number 160.** Wilson, Douglas J. ANTAGONISTIC MUSCLE AC-
TION DURING THE INITIATORY STAGES OF VOLUNTARY EFFORTS. 1933. 48 pp.

[————] **Number 161.** Schiller, Belle. VERBAL, NUMERICAL AND SPATIAL
ABILITIES OF YOUNG CHILDREN. 1934. 69 pp.

[————] **Number 162.** Bryan, Alice I. ORGANIZATION OF MEMORY IN
YOUNG CHILDREN. 1934. 56 pp.

[Volume 25] **Number 163.** Kneeland, Natalie. SELF-ESTIMATES OF IM-
PROVEMENT IN REPEATED TASKS. 1934. 75 pp.

[————] **Number 164.** Goldstein, Hyman. A BIOCHEMICAL STUDY OF THE
METABOLISM OF MENTAL WORK. 1934. 57 pp.

[————] **Number 165.** Hall, O. Milton. ATTITUDES AND UNEMPLOYMENT:
A COMPARISON OF THE OPINIONS AND ATTITUDES OF EMPLOYED AND UNEM-
PLOYED MEN. 1934. 65 pp.

[————] **Number 166.** Rosenthal, Solomon P. CHANGE OF SOCIOECO-
NOMIC ATTITUDES UNDER RADICAL MOTION PICTURE PROPAGANDA. 1934.
46 pp.

[————] **Number 167.** Peatman, John Gray, and Norman M. Locke.
STUDIES IN THE METHODOLOGY OF THE DIGIT-SPAN TEST. 1934. 35 pp.

[————] **Number 168.** Seward, John P., and Georgene H. Seward. THE
EFFECT OF REPETITION ON REACTIONS TO ELECTRIC SHOCK: WITH SPECIAL
REFERENCE TO THE MENSTRUAL CYCLE. 1934. 103 pp.

[————] **Number 169.** Wilke, Walter H. AN EXPERIMENTAL COMPARISON OF THE SPEECH, THE RADIO, AND THE PRINTED PAGE AS PROPAGANDA DEVICES. 1934. 32 pp.

[————] **Number 170.** Thorne, Frederick C. THE PSYCHOLOGICAL MEASUREMENT OF THE TEMPORAL COURSE OF VISUAL SENSITIVITY. 1934. 66 pp.

[**Volume 26**] **Number 171.** Barr, Estelle DeYoung. A PSYCHOLOGICAL ANALYSIS OF FASHION MOTIVATION. 1934. 100 pp.

[————] **Number 172.** Steinberg, Janet. THE RELATION BETWEEN BASAL METABOLISM AND MENTAL SPEED. 1934. 39 pp.

[————] **Number 173.** Allport, Floyd H., Lynette Walker, and Eleanor Lathers. WRITTEN COMPOSITION AND CHARACTERISTICS OF PERSONALITY. 1934. 82 pp.

[————] **Number 174.** Guanella, Francis M. BLOCK BUILDING ACTIVITIES OF YOUNG CHILDREN. 1934. 92 pp.

[————] **Number 175.** Hinrichs, William Ernest. THE GOODENOUGH DRAWING IN RELATION TO DELINQUENCY AND PROBLEM BEHAVIOR. 1935. 82 pp.

[————] **Number 176.** Garrett, Henry E., Alice I. Bryan, and Ruth E. Perl. THE AGE FACTOR IN MENTAL ORGANIZATION. 1935. 31 pp.

[————] **Number 177.** Franzblau, Rose N. RACE DIFFERENCES IN MENTAL AND PHYSICAL TRAITS: STUDIES IN DIFFERENT ENVIRONMENTS. 1935. 44 pp.

[————] **Number 178.** Patrick, Catherine. CREATIVE THOUGHT IN POETS. 1935. 74 pp.

[**Volume 27**] **Number 179.** Henneman, Richard Hubbard. A PHOTOMETRIC STUDY OF THE PERCEPTION OF OBJECT COLOR. 1935. 88 pp.

[————] **Number 180.** Brandt, Hyman. THE SPREAD OF THE INFLUENCE OF REWARD TO BONDS REMOTE IN SEQUENCE AND TIME. 1935. 45 pp.

[————] **Number 181.** Eisenson, Jon. CONFIRMATION AND INFORMATION IN REWARDS AND PUNISHMENTS. 1935. 37 pp.

[————] **Number 182.** Bartlett, Marion R. THE AUDITORY THRESHOLD IN REVERIE: A STUDY OF NORMAL AND PSYCHOPATHIC INDIVIDUALS. 1935. 42 pp.

[————] **Number 183.** Henley, Eugene M. FACTORS RELATED TO MUSCULAR TENSION. 1935. 44 pp.

[————] **Number 184.** Foley, John Porter, Jr. THE EFFECT OF CONTEXT UPON PERCEPTUAL DIFFERENTIATION. 1935. 67 pp.

[————] **Number 185.** Stofflet, Elliott Holmes. A STUDY OF NATIONAL AND CULTURAL DIFFERENCES IN CRIMINAL TENDENCY. 1935. 60 pp.

[————] **Number 186.** Marks, Eli S. INDIVIDUAL DIFFERENCES IN WORK CURVES. 1935. 60 pp.

[————] **Number 187.** Sherif, Muzafer. A STUDY OF SOME SOCIAL FACTORS IN PERCEPTION. 1935. 60 pp.

[————] **Number 188.** Gilbert, Jeanne G. MENTAL EFFICIENCY IN SENESCENCE. 1935. 60 pp.

[**Volume 28**] **Number 189.** Hayward, Royal S. THE CHILD'S REPORT OF PSYCHOLOGICAL FACTORS IN THE FAMILY. 1935. 75 pp.

[————] **Number 190.** Benton, Arthur L. THE INTERPRETATION OF QUESTIONNAIRE ITEMS IN A PERSONALITY SCHEDULE. 1935. 38 pp.

215. *(Continued)*

[———] **Number 191.** Razran, Gregory H. S. CONDITIONED RESPONSES: AN EXPERIMENTAL STUDY AND A THEORETICAL ANALYSIS. 1935. 124 pp.

[———] **Number 192.** Page, James D. AN EXPERIMENTAL STUDY OF THE DAY AND NIGHT MOTILITY OF NORMAL AND PSYCHOTIC INDIVIDUALS. 1935. 40 pp.

[———] **Number 193.** Locke, Norman Malcolm. COLOR CONSTANCY IN THE RHESUS MONKEY AND IN MAN. 1935. 38 pp.

[———] **Number 194.** Horowitz, Eugene L. THE DEVELOPMENT OF ATTITUDE TOWARD THE NEGRO. 1936. 47 pp.

[———] **Number 195.** Asch, Solomon E. A STUDY OF CHANGE IN MENTAL ORGANIZATION. 1936. 30 pp.

[———] **Number 196.** Sanders, Jack H. THE EFFECT OF EXPERIENCE IN PERCEIVING VERBAL AND GEOMETRIC CONTEXTS. 1936. 58 pp.

[———] **Number 197.** Hertzman, Max. THE EFFECTS OF THE RELATIVE DIFFICULTY OF MENTAL TESTS ON PATTERNS OF MENTAL ORGANIZATION. 1936. 69 pp.

[———] **Number 198.** Gillette, Annette L. LEARNING AND RETENTION: A COMPARISON OF THREE EXPERIMENTAL PROCEDURES. 1936. 56 pp.

[Volume 29] **Number 199.** Elliott, Frank R. MEMORY FOR VISUAL, AUDITORY AND VISUAL-AUDITORY MATERIAL. 1936. 58 pp.

Number 200. Sells, Saul B. THE ATMOSPHERE EFFECT: AN EXPERIMENTAL STUDY OF REASONING. 1936. 72 pp.

[———] **Number 201.** Maxfield, Kathryn Erroll. THE SPOKEN LANGUAGE OF THE BLIND PRESCHOOL CHILD: A STUDY OF METHOD. 1936. 100 pp.

[———] **Number 202.** Block, Helen. THE INFLUENCE OF MUSCULAR EXERTION UPON MENTAL PERFORMANCE. 1936. 49 pp.

[———] **Number 203.** Diamond, Solomon. A STUDY OF THE INFLUENCE OF POLITICAL RADICALISM ON PERSONALITY DEVELOPMENT. 1936. 53 pp.

[———] **Number 204.** Dudycha, George. AN OBJECTIVE STUDY OF PUNCTUALITY IN RELATION TO PERSONALITY AND ACHIEVEMENT. 1936. 53 pp.

[———] **Number 205.** Abel, Lorraine B. THE EFFECTS OF SHIFT IN MOTIVATION UPON THE LEARNING OF A SENSORI-MOTOR TASK. 1936. 57 pp.

[———] **Number 206.** Seward, Georgene H., and John P. Seward. ALCOHOL AND TASK COMPLEXITY. 1936. 59 pp.

[———] **Number 207.** Hanks, Lucien Mason, Jr. PREDICTION FROM CASE MATERIAL TO PERSONALITY TEST DATA: A METHODOLOGICAL STUDY OF TYPES. 1936. 71 pp.

[Volume 30] **Number 208.** Waits, Johan Virgil. THE LAW OF EFFECT IN THE RETAINED SITUATION. 1937. 56 pp.

[———] **Number 209.** Long, Louis. A STUDY OF THE EFFECT OF PRECEDING STIMULI UPON THE JUDGMENT OF AUDITORY INTENSITIES. 1937. 57 pp.

[———] **Number 210.** Durkin, Helen E. TRIAL-AND-ERROR, GRADUAL ANALYSIS, AND SUDDEN REORGANIZATION: AN EXPERIMENTAL STUDY OF PROBLEM SOLVING. 1937. 85 pp.

[————] **Number 211.** Eisenberg, Philip. EXPRESSIVE MOVEMENTS RELATED TO FEELING OF DOMINANCE. 1937. 73 pp.

[————] **Number 212.** Boles, Mary Marjorie. THE BASIS OF PERTINENCE: A STUDY OF THE TEST PERFORMANCE OF AMENTS, DEMENTS AND NORMAL CHILDREN OF THE SAME MENTAL AGE. 1937. 51 pp.

[————] **Number 213.** Lawlor, Gerald W. EFFECT OF CHANGES IN BODILY SET ON ACCURACY OF PROPRIOCEPTIVE LOCALIZATION. 1937. 48 pp.

[————] **Number 214.** Morgan, Christine Margaret. THE ATTITUDES AND ADJUSTMENTS OF RECIPIENTS OF OLD AGE ASSISTANCE IN UPSTATE AND METROPOLITAN NEW YORK. 1937. 131 pp.

[————] **Number 215.** Ansbacher, Heinz. PERCEPTION OF NUMBER AS AFFECTED BY THE MONETARY VALUE OF THE OBJECTS. A CRITICAL STUDY OF THE METHOD USED IN THE EXTENDED CONSTANCY PHENOMENON. 1937. 88 pp.

[Volume 31] **Number 216.** Hanawalt, Nelson Gilbert. MEMORY TRACE FOR FIGURES IN RECALL AND RECOGNITION. 1937. 89 pp.

[————] **Number 217.** Rush, Grace Preyer. VISUAL GROUPING IN RELATION TO AGE. 1937. 95 pp.

[————] **Number 218.** Barmack, Joseph E. BOREDOM AND OTHER FACTORS IN THE PHYSIOLOGY OF MENTAL EFFORT: AN EXPLORATORY STUDY. 1937. 83 pp.

[————] **Number 219.** Foley, John P. Jr. AN EXPERIMENTAL STUDY OF THE EFFECT OF OCCUPATIONAL EXPERIENCE UPON MOTOR SPEED AND PREFERENTIAL TEMPO. 1937. 40 pp.

[————] **Number 220.** Rubin-Rabson, Grace. THE INFLUENCE OF ANALYTICAL PRE-STUDY IN MEMORIZING PIANO MUSIC. 1937. 53 pp.

[————] **Number 221.** Adams, Lois. FIVE METHODS OF SERIAL ROTE LEARNING: A COMPARATIVE STUDY. 1938. 67 pp.

[————] **Number 222.** Sheehan, Mary Rose. A STUDY OF INDIVIDUAL CONSISTENCY IN PHENOMENAL CONSTANCY. 1938. 95 pp.

[————] **Number 223.** Barrett, Dorothy Moss. MEMORY IN RELATION TO HEDONIC TONE. 1938. 61 pp.

[Volume 32] **Number 224.** Nadel, Aaron B. A QUALITATIVE ANALYSIS OF BEHAVIOR FOLLOWING CEREBRAL LESIONS: DIAGNOSED AS PRIMARILY AFFECTING THE FRONTAL LOBES. 1938. 60 pp.

[————] **Number 225.** Watson, Robert Irving. AN EXPERIMENTAL STUDY OF THE PERMANENCE OF COURSE MATERIAL IN INTRODUCTORY PSYCHOLOGY. 1938. 64 pp.

[————] **Number 226.** Breslaw, Bernard J. THE DEVELOPMENT OF A SOCIO-ECONOMIC ATTITUDE. 1938. 96 pp.

[————] **Number 227.** Gordon, Mary Agnes. GENERAL AND SPECIFIC FACTORS IN TRANSFER OF TRAINING WITHIN VERBAL TESTS. 1938. 41 pp.

[————] **Number 228.** Wendt, George Richard. METHODS OF RECORDING ACTION. 1938. 83 pp.

[————] **Number 229.** Halleran, Margaret M. THE EFFECT OF RICKETS ON THE MENTAL DEVELOPMENT OF YOUNG CHILDREN. 1938. 67 pp.

[————] **Number 230.** Gaudet, Frederick Joseph. INDIVIDUAL DIFFERENCES IN THE SENTENCING TENDENCIES OF JUDGES. 1938. 58 pp.

215. *(Continued)*

[Volume 33] **Number 231.** Thorndike, Edward L. STUDIES IN THE PSYCHOLOGY OF LANGUAGE. 1938. 67 pp.

[———] **Number 232.** Conkey, Ruth Clark. PSYCHOLOGICAL CHANGES ASSOCIATED WITH HEAD INJURIES. 1938. 62 pp.

[———] **Number 233.** Feinbloom, William. A QUANTITATIVE STUDY OF THE VISUAL AFTER-IMAGE. 1938. 46 pp.

[———] **Number 234.** Herrick, Colin J. AWARENESS IN THE INDUCTIVE SOLUTION OF PROBLEMS USING WORDS AS STIMULI. 1939. 87 pp.

[———] **Number 235.** Criswell, Joan Henning. A SOCIOMETRIC STUDY OF RACE CLEAVAGE IN THE CLASSROOM. 1939. 82 pp.

[———] **Number 236.** Gansl, Irene. VOCABULARY: ITS MEASUREMENT AND GROWTH. 1939. 52 pp.

[———] **Number 237.** Gilbert, G. M. DYNAMIC PSYCHOPHYSICS AND THE PHI PHENOMENON. 1939. 43 pp.

[———] **Number 238.** Sand, Margaret Cole. THE EFFECT OF LENGTH OF LIST UPON RETROACTIVE INHIBITION WHEN DEGREE OF LEARNING IS CONTROLLED. 1939. 49 pp.

[Volume 34] **Number 239.** Hollingworth, H. L. PSYCHO-DYNAMICS OF CHEWING. 1939. 90 pp.

[———] **Number 240.** Williams, Alexander Coxe. SOME PSYCHOLOGICAL CORRELATES OF THE ELECTROENCEPHALOGRAM. DEPRESSION AND FACILITATION OF THE ALPHA RHYTHM RESULTING FROM STIMULATION, ATTENTION, AND CHANGE IN GENERAL PSYCHOLOGICAL STATE. 1939. 48 pp.

[———] **Number 241.** Johnson, Donald M. CONFIDENCE AND SPEED IN THE TWO-CATEGORY JUDGMENT. 1939. 52 pp.

[———] **Number 242.** Capps, Harry Marcellus. VOCABULARY CHANGES IN MENTAL DETERIORATION. THE RELATIONSHIP OF VOCABULARY FUNCTIONING AS MEASURED BY A VARIETY OF WORD MEANING AND USAGE TESTS TO CLINICALLY ESTIMATED DEGREES OF MENTAL DETERIORATION IN "IDIOPATHIC" EPILEPSY. 1939. 81 pp.

[———] **Number 243.** Perry, Horace M. THE RELATIVE EFFICIENCY OF ACTUAL AND "IMAGINARY" PRACTICE IN FIVE SELECTED TASKS. 1939. 76 pp.

[———] **Number 244.** Gutteridge, Mary V. A STUDY OF MOTOR ACHIEVEMENTS OF YOUNG CHILDREN. 1939. 178 pp.

[Volume 35] **Number 245.** Tucker, Anthony Carter. SOME CORRELATES OF CERTAIN ATTITUDES OF THE UNEMPLOYED. 1940. 72 pp.

[———] **Number 246.** Orlansky, Jesse. THE EFFECT OF SIMILARITY AND DIFFERENCE IN FORM ON APPARENT VISUAL MOVEMENT. 1940. 85 pp.

[———] **Number 247.** Shaw, William A. THE RELATION OF MUSCULAR ACTION POTENTIALS TO IMAGINAL WEIGHT LIFTING. 1940. 50 pp.

[———] **Number 248.** Trawick, MacEldin. TRAIT–CONSISTENCY IN PERSONALITY: A DIFFERENTIAL INVESTIGATION. 1940. 45 pp.

[———] **Number 249.** Sargent, S. Stansfeld. THINKING PROCESSES AT VARIOUS LEVELS OF DIFFICULTY. A QUANTITATIVE AND QUALITATIVE STUDY OF INDIVIDUAL DIFFERENCES. 1940. 58 pp.

[————] **Number 250.** Rubenstein, Lawrence. PERSONAL ATTITUDES OF MALADJUSTED BOYS: A STUDY IN SELF-JUDGMENTS. 1940. 101 pp.

[————] **Number 251.** Granich, Louis. A QUALITATIVE ANALYSIS OF CONCEPTS IN MENTALLY DEFICIENT SCHOOLBOYS. 1940. 47 pp.

[**Volume 36**] **Number 252.** Bruce, Myrtle. FACTORS AFFECTING INTELLIGENCE TEST PERFORMANCE OF WHITES AND NEGROES IN THE RURAL SOUTH. 1940. 99 pp.

[————] **Number 253.** Clark, Kenneth B. SOME FACTORS INFLUENCING THE REMEMBERING OF PROSE MATERIAL. 1940. 73 pp.

[————] **Number 254.** Wegrocki, Henry J. GENERALIZING ABILITY IN SCHIZOPHRENIA: AN INQUIRY INTO THE DISORDERS OF PROBLEM THINKING IN SCHIZOPHRENIA. 1940. 76 pp.

[————] **Number 255.** Burgemeister, Bessie B. THE PERMANENCE OF INTERESTS OF WOMEN COLLEGE STUDENTS: A STUDY IN PERSONALITY DEVELOPMENT. 1940. 59 pp.

[————] **Number 256.** Scott, Winifred Starbuck. REACTION TIME OF YOUNG INTELLECTUAL DEVIATES. 1940. 64 pp.

[————] **Number 257.** Seitz, Clifford P. THE EFFECTS OF ANOXIA ON VISUAL FUNCTION: A STUDY OF CRITICAL FREQUENCY. 1940. 38 pp.

[————] **Number 258.** Seeleman, Virginia. THE INFLUENCE OF ATTITUDE UPON THE REMEMBERING OF PICTORIAL MATERIAL. 1940. 69 pp.

[**Volume 37**] **Number 259.** Long, Lillian Dick. AN INVESTIGATION OF THE ORIGINAL RESPONSE TO THE CONDITIONED STIMULUS. 1941. 43 pp.

[————] **Number 260.** Kennelly, Thomas W. THE ROLE OF SIMILARITY IN RETROACTIVE INHIBITION. 1941. 56 pp.

[————] **Number 261.** Rogers, Spaulding. THE ANCHORING OF ABSOLUTE JUDGMENTS. 1941. 42 pp.

[————] **Number 262.** Brown, M. Duane. VARIABILITY AS A FUNCTION OF ABILITY AND ITS RELATION TO PERSONALITY AND INTERESTS. 1941. 45 pp.

[————] **Number 263.** Arluck, Edward Wiltcher. A STUDY OF SOME PERSONALITY CHARACTERISTICS OF EPILEPTICS. 1941. 77 pp.

[————] **Number 264.** Thompson, Jane. DEVELOPMENT OF FACIAL EXPRESSION OF EMOTION IN BLIND AND SEEING CHILDREN. 1941. 47 pp.

[————] **Number 265.** Taves, Ernest Henry. TWO MECHANISMS FOR THE PERCEPTION OF VISUAL NUMEROUSNESS. 1941. 46 pp.

[————] **Number 266.** Travers, R.M.W. A STUDY IN JUDGING THE OPINIONS OF GROUPS. 1941. 73 pp.

[**Volume 38**] **Number 267.** Vinacke, William Edgar. THE DISCRIMINATION OF COLOR AND FORM AT LEVELS OF ILLUMINATION BELOW CONSCIOUS AWARENESS. 1942. 53 pp.

[————] **Number 268.** Madison, Thurber H. INTERVAL DISCRIMINATION AS A MEASURE OF MUSICAL APTITUDE. 1942. 99 pp.

[————] **Number 269.** Hyman, Herbert Hiram. THE PSYCHOLOGY OF STATUS. 1942. 94 pp.

[————] **Number 270.** Schoenfeld, Nathan. AN EXPERIMENTAL STUDY OF SOME PROBLEMS RELATING TO STEREOTYPES. 1942. 57 pp.

[————] **Number 271.** Margulies, Helen. RORSCHACH RESPONSES OF SUCCESSFUL AND UNSUCCESSFUL STUDENTS. 1942. 61 pp.

215. *(Continued)*

[————] **Number 272.** Fulcher, John Scott. "Voluntary" Facial Expression in Blind and Seeing Children. 1942. 49 pp.

[————] **Number 273.** Corbin, Horace Harlan. The Perception of Grouping and Apparent Movement in Visual Depth. 1942. 50 pp.

[**Volume 39**] **Number 274.** Jerome, Edward Alexander. Olfactory Thresholds Measured in Terms of Stimulus Pressure and Volume. 1942. 44 pp.

[————] **Number 275.** Klein, George Stuart. The Relation between Motion and Form-Acuity in Para-foveal and Peripheral Vision and Related Phenomena. 1942. 71 pp.

[————] **Number 276.** Chang, Chung-Yuan. A Study of the Relative Merits of the Vertical and Horizontal Lines in Reading Chinese Print. 1942. 64 pp.

[————] **Number 277.** Udow, Alfred B. The "Interviewer-Effect" in Public Opinion and Market Research Surveys. 1942. 36 pp.

[————] **Number 278.** Hamilton, Mildred Eckhardt. The Contribution of Practice Differences to Group Variability. 1943. 40 pp.

[————] **Number 279.** Lewis, Virginia W. Changing the Behavior of Adolescent Girls: A Description of Process. 1943. 87 pp.

[————] **Number 280.** Flynn, Bernard M. Pitch Discrimination: The Form of the Psychometric Function and Simple Reaction Time to Liminal Differences. 1943. 41 pp.

[————] **Number 281.** McGarvey, Hulda Rees. Anchoring Effects in the Absolute Judgment of Verbal Materials. 1943. 86 pp.

[**Volume 40**] **Number 282.** Levine, Kate Natalie. A Comparison of Graphic Productions with Scoring Categories of the Verbal Rorschach Record in Normal States, Organic Brain Disease, Neurotic and Psychotic Disorders. 1943. 63 pp.

[————] **Number 283.** Kay, Lillian Wald. The Relation of Personal Frames of Reference to Social Judgments. 1943. 53 pp.

[————] **Number 284.** Hsia, Yun. Whiteness Constancy as a Function of Difference in Illumination. 1943. 63 pp.

[————] **Number 285.** Thiesen, John Warren. Effects of Certain Forms of Emotion on the Normal Electroencephalogram. 1943. 85 pp.

[————] **Number 286.** Zucker, Herbert John. Affectional Identification and Delinquency. 1943. 60 pp.

[————] **Number 287.** Plotkin, Lawrence. Stimulus Generalization in Morse Code Learning. 1943. 39 pp.

[————] **Number 288.** Ross, Sherman. Motion Perception at Various Levels of Illumination in Monkeys and Children. 1943. 31 pp.

[————] **Number 289.** Chin, Robert. An Analysis of Conformity Behavior. 1943. 46 pp.

[**Volume 41**] **Number 290.** Shuey, Audrey M. Personality Traits of Jewish and Non-Jewish Students. 1944. 38 pp.

[———] **Number 291.** Clark, Mamie Phipps. CHANGES IN PRIMARY MENTAL ABILITIES WITH AGE. 1944. 30 pp.

[———] **Number 292.** Steinman, Alberta Ruth. REACTION TIME TO CHANGE COMPARED WITH OTHER PSYCHOPHYSICAL METHODS. 1944. 60 pp.

[———] **Number 293.** Hamlin, Roy M. AN ANALYSIS OF AGE-PROGRESS CURVES AS RELATED TO THE MENTAL GROWTH CURVE: A STUDY OF VOCABULARY. 1944. 37 pp.

[———] **Number 294.** DeCillis, Olga Elena. ABSOLUTE THRESHOLDS FOR THE PERCEPTION OF TACTUAL MOVEMENT. 1944. 52 pp.

[———] **Number 295.** Reichard, Suzanne. MENTAL ORGANIZATION AND AGE LEVEL. 1944. 30 pp.

[———] **Number 296.** Stavrianos, Bertha Kelso. THE RELATION OF SHAPE PERCEPTION TO EXPLICIT JUDGMENTS OF INCLINATION. 1945. 94 pp.

[———] **Number 297.** Koester, Theodore. THE TIME ERROR AND SENSITIVITY IN PITCH AND LOUDNESS DISCRIMINATION AS A FUNCTION OF TIME INTERVAL AND STIMULUS LEVEL. 1945. 69 pp.

[———] **Number 298.** Brown, Harold Chester. THE RELATION OF FLICKER TO STIMULUS AREA IN PERIPHERAL VISION. 1945. 61 pp.

[———] **Number 299.** Schonbar, Rosalea Ann. THE INTERACTION OF OBSERVER-PAIRS IN JUDGING VISUAL EXTENT AND MOVEMENT: THE FORMATION OF SOCIAL NORMS IN "STRUCTURED" SITUATIONS. 1945. 95 pp.

[———] **Number 300.** Fulton, Ruth Enterline. SPEED AND ACCURACY IN LEARNING MOVEMENTS. 1945. 53 pp.

216. *Encéphale; journal de psychiatrie.*

TITLE VARIATIONS: Continued by *Encéphale; journal mensuel de neurologie et de psychiatrie* with Année 2, 1907.

DATES OF PUBLICATION: Année 1, Numéro 1–6, January–November 1906.

FREQUENCY: Bimonthly.

NUMBERING VARIATIONS: None.

PUBLISHER: **Paris:** H. Delarue et Cie, Libraires-éditeurs, 1906.

PRIMARY EDITORS: **A. Antheaume,** 1906; **M. Klippel,** 1906.

217. *Gesellschaft; Sammlung sozialpsychologischer Monographien.*

TITLE VARIATIONS: None.

DATES OF PUBLICATION: Heft 1–40, 1906–1912.

FREQUENCY: Irregular. *See* Contents *below.*

NUMBERING VARIATIONS: Heft 14/15, 28/29, 35/36 and 37/38 issued as double numbers.

PUBLISHER: **Frankfurt:** Literarische Anstalt: Rütten & Loening, 1906–1912.

PRIMARY EDITORS: **Martin Buber,** 1906–1912.

CONTENTS:

218. *Informateur des aliénistes et des neurologistes. Journal d'information, d'intérêts professionnels et d'assistance.*

TITLE VARIATIONS: Subtitle varies. Supplement to *Encéphale.* Continued by *Hygiène mentale* with Année 20, Numéro 5, May 1925.

DATES OF PUBLICATION: Année 1–20, Numéro 4, March 1906–April 1925. Suspended publication August 1914–November 1919.

FREQUENCY: Monthly, Année 1–15, Numéro 5, March 1906–December 1920.

Monthly (except July/August and September/October), Année 16–20, Numéro 5, January 1921–May 1925.

NUMBERING VARIATIONS: 10 issues in Année 1.

PUBLISHER: **Paris:** H. Delarue et Cie, Libraires-éditeurs, 1906–1909. **Paris:** H. Delarue, Librairie-éditeur, 1910–1925.

PRIMARY EDITORS: **A. Antheaume,** 1906–1925; **Roger Mignot,** 1914–1925.

219. *Journal of Abnormal Psychology.* [Official Organ of the American Psychopathological Association and of the Psycho-Medical Society (England).]

TITLE VARIATIONS: Continued by *Journal of Abnormal and Social Psychology* with Volume 16, 1921.

DATES OF PUBLICATION: Volume 1–15, April 1906–December/March 1920/ 1921.

FREQUENCY: Bimonthly.

NUMBERING VARIATIONS: Volume 5–12 also reprinted in book form and numbered as *Studies in Abnormal Psychology,* Series 1–8. Volume 9–12 also reprinted in book form and numbered as *Contributions to Psychology,* Volume 9–12. Volume 15, Numbers 2/3 and 5/6 are double issues.

PUBLISHER: **Boston:** Richard G. Badger, the Gorham Press, 1906–1921.

PRIMARY EDITOR: **Morton Prince,** 1906–1921.

ASSISTANT EDITORS: John E. Donley, 1907–1912; Ernest Jones, 1910–1921; J. S. van Teslaar, 1912–1915.

ASSOCIATE EDITORS: Hugo Münsterberg, 1906–1916; James J. Putnam, 1906–1918; August Hoch, 1906–1919; Boris Sidis, 1906–1921; Charles L. Dana, 1906–1921; Adolf Meyer, 1906–1921; William McDougall, 1914–1921; E. E. Southard, 1918–1919; J. Ramsay Hunt, 1919–1921; John E. Donley, 1912–1914.

220. *London. National Association for the Feeble-Minded. Conference Report.*

TITLE VARIATIONS: None.

DATES OF PUBLICATION. 1906–1915.

FREQUENCY: Irregular. *See* Contents *below.*

NUMBERING VARIATIONS: Numbered only by date.

PUBLISHER: **London:** National Association for the Feeble-Minded, 1906–1915.

PRIMARY EDITOR: Secretary acted as editor.

CONTENTS:
    [1.] THE 1906 LONDON AFTER-CARE CONFERENCE REPORT.
    [2.] THE 1908 BRISTOL AFTER-CARE CONFERENCE REPORT.
    [3.] THE 1910 BRIGHTON AFTER-CARE CONFERENCE REPORT.
    [4.] THE 1912 LONDON AFTER-CARE CONFERENCE REPORT (ON LEGISLATION).

[5.] THE 1913 LONDON CONFERENCE REPORT.

[6.] THE 1915 LONDON CONFERENCE REPORT OF THE NATIONAL ASSOCIATION FOR THE FEEBLE-MINDED.

NOTE: Information on this entry is incomplete. The compilers were unable to examine this title.

221. *Psychologische Studien. Neue Folge der philosophischen Studien.*

TITLE VARIATIONS: None.

DATES OF PUBLICATION: Band 1–10, 1906–1918.

FREQUENCY: Irregular. Each Band contains 6 Hefte.

NUMBERING VARIATIONS: Band 7 issued with a supplement. *See* Contents *below.* Band 10 also numbered as *Königliche sächsische Forschungsinstitute zu Leipzig. Forschungsinstitut für Psychologie*, I–III. 1917–1918.

PUBLISHER: **Leipzig:** Wilhelm Engelmann, 1906–1912. **Leipzig** and **Berlin:** Wilhelm Engelmann, 1912–1914. **Leipzig:** Emmanuel Reinicke, 1917–1918.

PRIMARY EDITOR: **Wilhelm Wundt,** 1906–1918.

CONTENTS:
 Band 7, Beilage. Rehwoldt, Friedrich. ATLAS ÜBER RESPIRATORISCHE AFFEKTSYMPTOME. 1911. Pp. 141–195.

222. *Psyke. Tidskrift för psykologisk Forskning.*

TITLE VARIATIONS: United with *Svenskt Arkiv för Pedagogik* to form *Arkiv för Psykologi och Pedagogik* with Häfte 1, April 1922.

DATES OF PUBLICATION: Band 1–15, 1906–1920.

FREQUENCY: Irregular. Band 1, 2 Häfte. Band 2–15 have either 4 or 5 Häfte.

NUMBERING VARIATIONS: Multinumber issues in Band 3–15. Band 7 is special issue titled TILL PROFESSOR KARL REINHOLD GEIJER DEN 23 APRIL 1914. 198 pp.

PUBLISHER: **Stockholm:** Albert Bonniers Förlag, 1906–1907. **Uppsala & Stockholm:** Almqvist & Wiksells Boktryckeri, A.B., 1908–1920.

PRIMARY EDITORS: **Sydney Alrutz,** 1906–1920; **Harald Höffding,** 1906–1920; **Arvid Grotenfelt,** 1906–1920; **J. Mourly Vold,** 1906–1907; **Kristian Birch-Reichenwald Aars,** 1907–1917. **Anathon Aall,** 1918–1920.

223. *Zeitschrift für Psychologie und Physiologie der Sinnesorgane. Abteilung I. Zeitschrift für Psychologie.*

[Organ of the Gesellschaft für experimentelle Psychologie, 1925–1930 and of the Deutsche Gesellschaft für Psychologie, 1931–1940.]

TITLE VARIATIONS: Continues *Zeitschrift für Psychologie und Physiologie der Sinnesorgane.* Continued by *Zeitschrift für Psychologie* with Band 148, 1940.

DATES OF PUBLICATION: Band 41–147, 1906–May 1940.

FREQUENCY: Monthly (6 Hefte to a volume).

NUMBERING VARIATIONS: Multinumber issues present in most volumes. Portions of Band 67, 72, 73 and 82 also numbered as *Beiträge zur Psychologie der Gestalt- und Bewegungserlebnisse*. Portions of Band 146–147 also numbered as *Beiträge zur Geschichte der Psychologie*. Portion of Band 149 also numbered as *Beiträge zur Psychologie des gehaltserfüllten Lebens*. Band 85 also as *Festschrift zum 70. Geburtstag von Georg E. Müller;* Portion of Band 112 also as *Karl Marbe zu seinem 60. Geburtstag am 31. August 1929 überreicht;* Band 124 also as *Karl Groos zum 70. Geburtstag am 10. Dezember 1931 überreicht;* Band 127 also as *Theodor Ziehen zum 70. Geburtstag am 12. November 1932 überreicht.*

PUBLISHER: **Leipzig:** Johann Ambrosius Barth, 1906–1940.

PRIMARY EDITORS: **Hermann Ebbinghaus,** 1906–1909; **Friedrich Schumann,** 1909–1940; **David Katz,** 1931–1933; **Erich R. Jaensch,** 1933–1940; **Oswald Kroh,** 1933–1940.

EDITORIAL BOARD: Sigmund Exner, 1906–1926; Johannes von Kries, 1906–1929; Theodor Lipps, 1906–1914; Alexius Meinong, 1906–1921; Georg Elias Müller, 1906–1935; C. Pelman, 1906–1911; A. von Strümpell, 1906–1925; Carl Stumpf, 1906–1937; Armin von Tschermak, 1906–1939; Theodor Ziehen, 1906–1940; Friedrich Schumann, 1907–1909; Wilibald A. Nagel, 1909–1910; Narziss Ach, 1922–1940; Erich Becher, 1922–1929; Karl Bühler, 1922–1938; Joseph Fröbes, 1922–1940; Hans Henning, 1922–1938; Franz Hillebrand, 1922–1926; Erich R. Jaensch, 1922–1933; David Katz, 1922–1931; Felix Krueger, 1922–1940; Karl Marbe, 1922–1940; Wilhelm Peters, 1922–1933; Walther Poppelreuter, 1922–1939; Karl Groos, 1924–1940; Edgar Rubin, 1924–1935; Geza Révész, 1926–1936; Oswald Kroh, 1926–1933; Adhemar Gelb, 1929–1934; Kurt Schneider, 1931–1936; Heinz Werner, 1932–1933.

1907

224. *Congrès international de psychiatrie, de neurologie, de psychologie et de l'assistance des aliénés. Compte rendu.*

TITLE VARIATIONS: None.

DATES OF PUBLICATION: 1er, 1907.

FREQUENCY: Irregular.

NUMBERING VARIATIONS: None.

PUBLISHER: **Amsterdam:** Druk van J. H. de Bussy, 1907.

PRIMARY EDITORS: *See* Contents *below.*

CONTENTS:

1er. AMSTERDAM, 1907. COMPTE RENDU DES TRAVAUX DU 1er CONGRÈS IN-

TERNATIONAL DE PSYCHIATRIE, DE NEUROLOGIE, DE PSYCHOLOGIE ET DE L'ASSISTANCE DES ALIÉNÉS, TENU À AMSTERDAM DU 2 À 7 SEPTEMBRE 1907. Rédigé par G.A.M. van Wayenburg, secrétaire général du congrès. 1908. 934 pp.

225. Encéphale; journal mensuel de neurologie et de psychiatrie. [Official organ of the Société de psychiatrie, 1908–1915.]

TITLE VARIATIONS: Continues Encéphale; journal de psychiatrie. Continued by Encéphale; journal de neurologie et de psychiatrie with Année 16, 1921.

DATES OF PUBLICATION: Année 2–15, January 1907–December 1920. Suspended publication January 1916–November 1919.

FREQUENCY: Monthly.

NUMBERING VARIATIONS: Année 9, 14 issued irregularly. Année 10–13 omitted in numbering.

PUBLISHER: **Paris:** H. Delarue et Cie, Libraires-éditeurs, 1907–1909. **Paris:** H. Delarue Librairie-éditeur, 1910–1920.

PRIMARY EDITORS: **F. Raymond,** 1907–1910; **H. Claude,** 1907–1920; **A. Joffroy,** 1907–1908; **A. Antheaume,** 1907–1920; **Gilbert Ballet,** 1909–1919; **J. Dejerine,** 1911–1919.

EDITORIAL BOARD: G. Ballet, 1908; R. Cestan, 1908–1920; G. Deny, 1908–1920; E. Dupré, 1908–1920; G. Étienne, 1908–1920; [Pierre ?] Ingelrans, 1908; P. Keraval, 1908–1919; M. Klippel, 1908–1920; [M.?] Lannois, 1908; G. Rauzier, 1908–1919; E. Régis, 1908–1919; J. Séglas, 1908–1920; P. Sérieux, 1908–1920; Ch. Vallon, 1908–1920; H. Verger, 1908–1920; Mme. Dejerine, 1920; J. Dejerine, 1909–1910; J. Grasset, 1909–1919; ——— Pierret, 1909–1913; A. Pitres, 1909–1919; M. Laignel-Lavastine, 1911–1920; J. Lépine, 1913–1920; G. Raviart, 1913–1920; J. Abadie, 1920; J. Froment, 1920; J. Lhermitte, 1920; Rogues de Fursac, 1920; P. Sainton, 1920; J. Sicard, 1920; A. André-Thomas, 1920.

226. Health Record.

TITLE VARIATIONS: Continues Psycho-therapeutic Journal. A Journal of the Proceedings of the London Psycho-therapeutic Society.

DATES OF PUBLICATION: Number 62–Number 151, January 1907–June/September 1921.

FREQUENCY: **Monthly,** Number 62–Number 99, January 1907–May 1910. **Quarterly,** Number 100–151, June/September 1910–June/September 1921.

NUMBERING VARIATIONS: Number 62–123 also numbered as Volume 6–14. Multinumber issues present.

PUBLISHER: **London:** Office [of the] Health Record, 1907–1921.

PRIMARY EDITORS: None listed.

227. *Journal de neurologie. Neurologie, psychiatrie, psychologie.*

TITLE VARIATIONS: Continues *Journal de neurologie. Neurologie, psychiatrie, psychologie, hypnologie.* Continued by *Journal de neurologie et de psychiatrie.* [*1*] with Tome 23, 1923.

DATES OF PUBLICATION: Tome 13–22, 1907–1922. Suspended publication 1915–1919.

FREQUENCY: **Semimonthly,** Tome 13–19, 1907–1914. **Monthly,** Tome 20–22, 1920–1922.

NUMBERING VARIATIONS: None.

PUBLISHER: **Brussels:** Direction, J. Crocq, 62, rue Joseph II, 1907–1922.

PRIMARY EDITORS: **Xavier Francotte,** 1907–1922; **J. Crocq,** 1907–1922.

228. *Monographien über die seelische Entwicklung des Kindes.*

TITLE VARIATIONS: None.

DATES OF PUBLICATION: Band 1–2, 1907–1909.

FREQUENCY: Irregular. *See* Contents *below.*

NUMBERING VARIATIONS: None.

PUBLISHER: **Leipzig:** Johann Ambrosius Barth, 1907–1909.

PRIMARY EDITORS: **Clara Stern,** 1907–1909; **William Stern,** 1907–1909.

CONTENTS:

Band 1. Stern, Clara, and William Stern. DIE KINDERSPRACHE. EINE PSY-CHOLOGISCHE UND SPRACHTHEORETISCHE UNTERSUCHUNG. 1907. 394 pp. (2. Auflage, 1920).

Band 2. Stern, Clara, and William Stern. ERINNERUNG, AUSSAGE UND LÜGE IN DER ERSTEN KINDHEIT. 1909. 160 pp. (2. Auflage, 1920).

229. *Nervous and Mental Disease Monograph Series.*

TITLE VARIATIONS: Numbers 63 and 65+ titled *Nervous and Mental Disease Monographs.*

DATES OF PUBLICATION: Number 1–80+, 1907–1950+.

FREQUENCY: Irregular. *See* Contents *below.*

NUMBERING VARIATIONS: Number 9 and 41 also numbered as *New York Psychiatric Society. Studies in Psychiatry. See* Contents *below.*

PUBLISHER: **New York:** Journal of Nervous and Mental Disease Publishing Company, 1907–1916. **New York:** Nervous and Mental Disease Publishing Company, 1916–1918. **New York** and **Washington, D.C.:** Nervous and Mental Disease Publishing Company, 1919–1934. **New York:** Nervous and Mental Disease Monograph Series, 1935–1939. **New York:** Nervous and Mental Disease Monographs, 1940–1943. **New York:** Nervous and Mental Disease Monographs, Coolidge Foundation Publishers, 1946–1947. **New York:** Nervous and Mental Disease Monographs, 1948–1950+.

229. (*Continued*)

PRIMARY EDITORS: Smith Ely Jelliffe, 1907–1939; W. A. White, 1907–1939; none listed 1940 + .

CONTENTS:

Number 1. White, Wm. A. OUTLINES OF PSYCHIATRY. 1907. 232 pp.

Number 2. STUDIES IN PARANOIA. Gierlich, Nikolaus. PERIODIC PARANOIA AND THE ORIGIN OF PARANOID DELUSIONS; and Freidman, M. CONTRIBUTIONS TO THE STUDY OF PARANOIA. Trans. and ed. by Smith Ely Jelliffe. 1908. 78 pp.

Number 3. Jung, Carl G. PSYCHOLOGY OF DEMENTIA PRAECOX. Trans. by A. A. Brill. 1909. 153 pp.

Number 4. Freud, Sigmund. SELECTED PAPERS ON HYSTERIA AND OTHER PSYCHONEUROSES. 1912. 125 pp.

Number 5. Plaut, Felix. WASSERMAN SERO-DIAGNOSIS OF SYPHILIS IN ITS APPLICATION TO PSYCHIATRY. 1911. 188 pp.

Number 6. Sachs, B., Clark, L. Pierce et al. EPIDEMIC POLIOMYELITIS. REPORT ON NEW YORK EPIDEMIC OF 1907. 1910. 119 pp.

Number 7. Freud, S. THREE CONTRIBUTIONS TO THEORY OF SEX. 1910. 91 pp.

Number 8. White, Wm. A. MENTAL MECHANISMS. 1911. 151 pp.

Number 9. NEW YORK PSYCHIATRICAL SOCIETY. STUDIES IN PSYCHIATRY. VOLUME 1. 1912. 222 pp.

Number 10. Franz, S. I. HANDBOOK OF MENTAL EXAMINATION METHODS. 1912. 165 pp.

Number 11. Bleuler, E. THEORY OF SCHIZOPHRENIC NEGATIVISM. 1912. 279 pp.

Number 12. Andre-Thomas, A. CEREBELLAR FUNCTIONS. 1912. 223 pp.

Number 13. Nitsche, P., and K. Wilmanns. HISTORY OF THE PRISON PSYCHOSES. 1912. 84 pp.

Number 14. Kraepelin, E. GENERAL PARESIS. 1913. 200 pp.

Number 15. Abraham, Karl. DREAMS AND MYTHS. 1913. 74 pp.

Number 16. Wickman, I. ACUTE POLIOMYELITIS. 1913. 134 pp.

Number 17. Hitschmann, E. FREUD'S THEORIES OF THE NEUROSES. 1913. 154 pp.

Number 18. Rank, Otto. THE MYTH OF THE BIRTH OF THE HERO. 1914. 100 pp.

Number 19. Jung, Carl G. THEORY OF PSYCHOANALYSIS. 1915. 133 pp.

Number 20. Eppinger, H., and L. Hess. VAGOTONIA. 1915. 92 pp.

Number 21. Ricklin, F. WISHFULFILLMENT AND SYMBOLISM IN FAIRY TALES. 1915. 90 pp.

Number 22. Maeder, A. E. THE DREAM PROBLEM. 1916. 43 pp.

Number 23. Rank, Otto, and H. Sachs. THE SIGNIFICANCE OF PSYCHOANALYSIS FOR THE MENTAL SCIENCES. 1916. 127 pp.

Number 24. Adler, Alfred. A STUDY OF ORGAN INFERIORITY AND ITS PSYCHICAL COMPENSATION. 1917. 86 pp.

Number 25. Freud, S. HISTORY OF THE PSYCHOANALYTIC MOVEMENT. 1917. 57 pp.

Number 26. Jelliffe, S. E. TECHNIQUES OF PSYCHOANALYSIS. 1918. 163 pp.

Number 27. Higier, H. VEGETATIVE NEUROLOGY. 1919. 144 pp.

Number 28. Kempf, Edw. J. AUTONOMIC FUNCTIONS AND THE PERSONALITY. 1918. 156 pp.

Number 29. Hug-Hellmuth, H. STUDY OF THE MENTAL LIFE OF THE CHILD. 1919. 154 pp.

Number 30. Laignel-Lavastine, M. THE INTERNAL SECRETIONS AND THE NERVOUS SYSTEM. 1919. 59 pp.

Number 31. Sadger, J. SLEEP-WALKING AND MOON-WALKING. 1920. 140 pp.

Number 32. White, Wm. A. FOUNDATIONS OF PSYCHIATRY. 1921. 136 pp.

Number 33. Fay, Dudley W. A PSYCHOANALYTIC STUDY OF PSYCHOSES AND ENDOCRINOSES. 1922. 122 pp.

Number 34. Jelliffe, S. E., and Louise Brink. PSYCHOANALYSIS AND THE DRAMA. 1922. 162 pp.

Number 35. Lewis, Nolan D. C. CONSTITUTIONAL FACTORS IN DEMENTIA PRAECOX. 1923. 134 pp.

Number 36. Storch, A. PRIMITIVE ARCHAIC FORMS OF INNER EXPERIENCES AND THOUGHT IN SCHIZOPHRENIA. 1924. 111 pp.

Number 37. Brink, Louise. WOMEN CHARACTERS IN RICHARD WAGNER. 1924. 125 pp.

Number 38. White, Wm. A. AN INTRODUCTION TO THE STUDY OF THE MIND. 1924. 116 pp.

Number 39. Monakow, C. von. EMOTIONS, MORALITY AND THE BRAIN. 1925. 95 pp.

Number 40. Ferenczi, S., and O. Rank. DEVELOPMENT OF PSYCHO-ANALYSIS. 1925. 68 pp.

Number 41. NEW YORK PSYCHIATRIC SOCIETY. STUDIES IN PSYCHIATRY. Volume 2. 1925. 233 pp.

Number 42. Hollos, S., and S. Ferenczi. PSYCHOANALYSIS AND THE PSYCHIC DISORDERS OF GENERAL PARALYSIS. 1925. 48 pp.

Number 43. White, Wm. A. ESSAYS IN PSYCHOPATHOLOGY. 1925. 140 pp.

Number 44. Kretschmer, E. HYSTERIA. 1925. (120 pp.)

Number 45. Jelliffe, Smith Ely. POSTENCEPHALITIC RESPIRATORY DISORDERS. 1927. 135 pp.

Number 46. Schilder, Paul. HYPNOSIS. 1927. 118 pp.

Number 47. Coriat, Isador H. STAMMERING: A PSYCHOANALYTIC INTERPRETATION. 1928. 68 pp.

Number 48. Freud, Anna. INTRODUCTION TO THE TECHNIC OF CHILD ANALYSIS. 1928. 62 pp.

Number 49. Groddeck, Georg. THE BOOK OF THE IT. 1928. 244 pp.

Number 50. Schilder, Paul. INTRODUCTION TO A PSYCHOANALYTIC PSY-CHIATRY. 1928. 178 pp.

Number 51. White, Wm. A. LECTURES IN PSYCHIATRY. 1928. 168 pp.

Number 52. Alexander, Franz. PSYCHOANALYSIS OF THE TOTAL PERSON-ALITY. 1930. 176 pp.

Number 53. Schilder, Paul. BRAIN AND PERSONALITY. 1931. 136 pp.

Number 54. White, Wm. A. MEDICAL PSYCHOLOGY. 1931. 141 pp.

Number 55. Jelliffe, S. E. PSYCHOPATHOLOGY OF FORCED MOVEMENTS IN OCULOGYRIC CRISES. 1932. 219 pp.

Number 56. Chadwick, Mary. PSYCHOLOGICAL EFFECTS OF MENSTRUATION. 1932. 70 pp.

Number 57. White, Wm. A. FORTY YEARS OF PSYCHIATRY. 1933. 154 pp.

Number 58. Moreno, J. L. WHO SHALL SURVIVE? 1934. 435 pp.

Number 59. Karpman, Ben. THE INDIVIDUAL CRIMINAL. 1935. 317 pp.

Number 60. Hitschmann, Eduard, and Edmund Bergler. FRIGIDITY IN WOMEN: ITS CHARACTERISTICS AND TREATMENT. 1936. 76 pp.

Number 61. Breuer, J., and S. Freud. STUDIES IN HYSTERIA. Trans. by A. A. Brill. 1937. 241 pp.

Number 62. Sakel, Manfred. PHARMACOLOGICAL SHOCK TREATMENT OF SCHIZOPHRENIA. 1938. 136 pp.

Number 63. Beck, Samuel J. PERSONALITY STRUCTURE IN SCHIZOPHRENIA: A RORSCHACH INVESTIGATION IN 81 PATIENTS AND 64 CONTROLS. 1938. 88 pp.

Number 64. Terry, Gladys C., and Thomas A. C. Rennie. ANALYSIS OF PARERGASIA. 1938. 199 pp.

Number 65. Jelliffe, Smith Ely. SKETCHES IN PSYCHOSOMATIC MEDICINE. 1939. 155 pp.

Number 66. LaForgue, Rene. THE RELATIVITY OF REALITY. 1940. 92 pp.

Number 67. Hanfmann, Eugenia, and Jacob Kasanin. CONCEPTUAL THINKING IN SCHIZOPHRENIA. 1942. 115 pp.

Number 68. Sterba, Richard. INTRODUCTION TO THE PSYCHOANALYTIC THEORY OF THE LIBIDO. 1942. 81 pp.

Number 69. Roheim, Geza. ORIGIN AND FUNCTION OF CULTURE. 1943. 107 pp.

Number 70. Shakow, D. NATURE OF DETERIORATION IN SCHIZOPHRENIC CONDITIONS. 1946. 88 pp.

Number 71. Naumburg, Margaret. STUDIES OF THE "FREE" ART EXPRESSION OF BEHAVIOR PROBLEM CHILDREN AND ADOLESCENTS AS A MEANS OF DIAGNOSIS AND THERAPY. 1947. 225 pp.

Number 72. Cameron, Donald Ewen. REMEMBERING. 1947. 110 pp.

Number 73. Straus, Erwin W. M. ON OBSESSION. 1948. 92 pp.

Number 74. Nunberg, Herman. PRACTICE AND THEORY OF PSYCHOANALYSIS. (VOLUME 1). 1948. 218 pp.

Number 75. Eidelberg, L. STUDIES IN PSYCHOANALYSIS. 1948. 223 pp.

Number 76. Foxe, Arthur N. STUDIES IN CRIMINOLOGY. 1948. 162 pp.

Number 77. Alford, Leland B. CEREBRAL LOCALIZATION: OUTLINE OF A REVISION. 1948. 99 pp.

Number 78. Schneider, Daniel E. GROWTH CONCEPT OF NERVOUS INTEGRATION. 1949. 142 pp.

Number 79. Meerloo, Joost A. M. DELUSION AND MASS-DELUSION. 1949. 126 pp.

Number 80. Riese, Walther. PRINCIPLES OF NEUROLOGY IN THE LIGHT OF HISTORY AND THEIR PRESENT USE. 1950. 177 pp.

230. *Pädagogische Monographien.*

TITLE VARIATIONS: Supplement to *Zeitschrift für pädagogische Psychologie, Pathologie und Hygiene; Zeitschrift für pädagogische Psychologie und experi-*

mentelle Pädagogik; and *Zeitschrift für pädagogische Psychologie, experimentelle Pädagogik und jugendkundliche Forschung.*

DATES OF PUBLICATION: Band 1–24, 1907–1926.

FREQUENCY: Irregular. *See* Contents *below.*

NUMBERING VARIATIONS: None.

PUBLISHER: **Leipzig:** O. Nemnich, 1907–1920. **Leipzig** and **Munich:** O. Nemnich, 1922–1926.

PRIMARY EDITORS: **Ernst Meumann,** 1907–1918; **Gustav Deuchler,** 1919–1926; **Aloys Fischer,** 1919–1926.

CONTENTS:

Band 1. Radossawljewitsch, Paul R. DAS BEHALTEN UND VERGESSEN BEI KINDERN UND ERWACHSENEN NACH EXPERIMENTELLEN UNTERSUCHUNGEN. 1907. 197 pp.

Band 2. Pfeiffer, Ludwig. ÜBER VORSTELLUNGSTYPEN. 1907. 129 pp.

Band 3. Baade, Walt. EXPERIMENTELLE UND KRITISCHE BEITRÄGE ZUR FRAGE NACH DEN SEKUNDÄREN WIRKUNGEN DES UNTERRICHTS INSBESONDERE AUF DIE EMPFÄNGLICHKEIT DES SCHÜLERS. 1907. 124 pp.

Band 4. Neuert, Georg. ÜBER BEGABUNG UND GEHÖRSGRAD DER ZÖGLINGE DER BADISCHEN TAUBSTUMMENANSTALTEN GERLACHSHEIM UND MEERSBURG. 1907. 168 pp.

Band 5. Pfeiffer, Ludwig. EXPERIMENTELLE UNTERSUCHUNGEN ÜBER QUALITATIVE ARBEITSTYPEN. 1908. 281 pp.

Band 6. Lombroso, Paola. DAS LEBEN DER KINDER. 1909. 112 pp.

Band 7. Karrenberg, C. DER MENSCH ALS ZEICHENOBJEKT. 1910. 74 pp.

Band 8. Compayre, Gabriel. MORALISCHE ERZIEHUNG. 1910. 153 pp.

Band 9. Nagy, Ladislaw. PSYCHOLOGIE DES KINDLICHEN INTERESSES. 1912. 191 pp.

Band 10. Huther, A. GRUNDZÜGE DER ALLGEMEINEN CHARAKTEROLOGIE MIT BESONDERER BERÜCKSICHTIGUNG DES PÄDAGOGISCHEN. 1910. 95 pp.

Band 11. Schanoff, Botju. DIE VORGÄNGE DES RECHNENS. 1911. 120 pp.

Band 12. Schoeneberger, Hans. PSYCHOLOGIE UND PÄDAGOGIK DER GEDÄCHTNISSES. 1911. 148 pp.

Band 13. Pohlmann, Hans. BEITRAG ZUR PSYCHOLOGIE DES SCHULKINDES AUF GRUND SYSTEMATISCH-EMPIRISCHER UNTERSUCHUNGEN ÜBER DIE ENTWICKLUNG DES WORTVERSTÄNDNISSES UND DAMIT ZUSAMMENHÄNGERIDEM. SPRACHLICHE UND PSYCHOLOGISCHE PROBLEME BEI KINDERN IM ALTER VOM 5–14 JAHREN. 1912. 314 pp.

Band 14. Lasurski, Aleksandr Fedorovic. ÜBER DAS STUDIUM DER INDIVIDUALITÄT. 1912. 191 pp.

Band 15. Kappert, Hermann. PSYCHOLOGISCHE GRUNDLAGEN DES NEUSPRACHLICHEN UNTERRICHTS. 1915. 112 pp.

Band 16. Sallwürk, Ernst von. ERZIEHUNG DURCH DIE KUNST. 1918. 182 pp.

Band 17. Höfler, Alois. REIFWERDEN, REIFMACHEN UND REIFE-PRÜFEN. VOR- UND NACHKLÄNGE ZU DEN RUFEN VON KNILLING, WUNDT, EINSTEIN, KRAUS, MUNCKER, THOMAS MANN. 1919. 56 pp.

Band 18. Schmidkunz, Hans. LOGIK UND PÄDAGOGIK. 1920. 196 pp.

Band 19. Reiff, Paul. THEORIE UND PRAXIS DER RECHTSCHREIBMETHODEN UND GRUNDSÄTZE DES RECHTSCHREIBUNTERRICHTS IN EXPERIMENTELLPÄDAGOGISCHEN UNTERSUCHUNGEN. 1920. 78 pp.

Band 20. Kolb, Eduard. DIE SITTLICHE ENTWICKLUNG DES HERANWACHSENDEN. 1922. 131 pp.

Band 21. Ruland, Michael. DIE ENTWICKLUNG DES SITTLICHEN BEWUSSTSEINS IN DEN JUGENDJAHREN. 1923. 139 pp.

Band 22. Kesselring, Michael. INTELLIGENZPRÜFUNGEN UND IHR PÄDAGOGISCHER WERT. 1923. 199 pp.

Band 23. Wagner, Julius. PÄDAGOGISCHE WERTLEHRE. 1924. 177 pp.

Band 24. Weigel, Wenzel. VOM WERTEREICH DER JUGENDLICHEN, BAND 1. 1926. 214 pp.

231. *Psychological Clinic. A Journal for the Study and Treatment of Mental Retardation and Deviation.*

TITLE VARIATIONS: Continued by *Psychological Clinic. A Journal of Orthogenics for the Study and Treatment of Retardation and Deviation* with Volume 2, 1908.

DATES OF PUBLICATION: Volume 1, 1907–January 1908.

FREQUENCY: Monthly (except June–September).

NUMBERING VARIATIONS: None.

PUBLISHER: **Philadelphia:** Psychological Clinic Press, 1907–1908.

PRIMARY EDITOR: **Lightner Witmer,** 1907–1908.

232. *Revue de psychologie sociale.* [1].

TITLE VARIATIONS: Continued by *Revue de psychologie* with Tome 2, Numéro 2, February 1908.

DATES OF PUBLICATION: Volume 1–2, Numéro 1, June 1907–January 1908.

FREQUENCY: Monthly.

NUMBERING VARIATIONS: None.

PUBLISHER: **Paris:** Rédaction et administration, 1907–1908.

PRIMARY EDITORS: **A. Éspinas,** 1907–1908; **C. Gide,** 1907–1908; **E. Dupré,** 1907–1908.

233. *Schriften zur angewandten Seelenkunde.*

TITLE VARIATIONS: None.

DATES OF PUBLICATION: Heft 1–20, 1907–1925.

FREQUENCY: Irregular. *See* Contents *below.*

NUMBERING VARIATIONS: None.

PUBLISHER: **Vienna:** F. Deuticke, 1907–1920. **Leipzig** and **Vienna:** F. Deuticke, 1925. **Leipzig:** F. Deuticke, 1925.

Year 1907

PRIMARY EDITOR: **Sigmund Freud**, 1907–1925.

CONTENTS:

Heft 1. Freud, Sigmund. DER WAHN UND DIE TRÄUME IN W. JENSENS "GRADIVA". 1907. 81 pp.

Heft 2. Riklin, Frz. WUNSCHERFÜLLUNG UND SYMBOLIK IM MÄRCHEN. 1908. 96 pp.

Heft 3. Jung, Carl Gustaf. DER INHALT DER PSYCHOSE. AKADEMISCHER VORTRAG, GEHALTEN IM RATHAUSE DER STADT ZÜRICH AM 16. I. 1908. 1908. 26 pp.

Heft 4. Abraham, Karl. TRAUM UND MYTHUS. EINE STUDIE ZUR VÖLKERPSYCHOLOGIE. 1909. 74 pp.

Heft 5. Rank, Otto. DER MYTHUS VON DER GEBURT DES HELDEN. VERSUCH EINER PSYCHOLOGISCHEN MYTHENDEUTUNG. 1909. 93 pp.

Heft 6. Sadger, J. AUS DEM LIEBESLEBEN NICOLAUS LENAUS. 1909. 98 pp. 2nd ed. 1919.

Heft 7. Freud, Sigmund. EINE KINDHEITSERINNERUNG DES LEONARDO DA VINCI. 1910. 71 pp.

Heft 8. Pfister, Osk. DIE FRÖMMIGKEIT DES GRAFEN LUDWIG VON ZINZENDORF. EIN PSYCHOANALYTISCHER BEITRAG ZUR KENNTNIS DER RELIGIÖSEN SUBLIMIERUNGSPROZESSE UND ZUR ERKLÄRUNG DES PIETISMUS. 1910. 122 pp.

Heft 9. Graf, Max. RICHARD WAGNER IM "FLIEGENDEN HOLLÄNDER". EIN BEITRAG ZUR PSYCHOLOGIE KÜNSTLERISCHEN SCHAFFENS. 1911. 46 pp.

Heft 10. Jones, Ernest. DAS PROGRAMM DES HAMLET UND DER ODIPUS-KOMPLEX. ÜBERSETZT VON PAUL TAUSIG. 1911. 65 pp.

Heft 11. Abraham, Karl. GIOVANNI SEGANTINI. EIN PSYCHOANALYTISCHER VERSUCH. 1911. 65 pp.

Heft 12. Storfer, Adolf Josef. ZUR SONDERSTELLUNG DER VATERMORDES. EINE RECHTSGESCHICHTLICHE UND VÖLKERPSYCHOLOGISCHE STUDIE. 1911. 34 pp.

Heft 13. Rank, Otto. DIE LOHENGRINSAGE. EIN BEITRAG ZU IHRER MOTIVGESTALTUNG UND DEUTUNG. 1911. 181 pp.

Heft 14. Jones, Ernest. DER ALPTRAUM IN SEINER BEZIEHUNG ZU GEWISSEN FORMEN DES MITTELALTERLICHEN ABERGLAUBENS. Deutsch von E. H. Sachs. 1912. 149 pp.

Heft 15. Hug-Hellmuth, H. von. AUS DEM SEELENLEBEN DES KINDES. EINE PSYCHOANALYTISCHE STUDIE. 1913. 170 pp.

Heft 16. Sadger, Isidor. ÜBER NACHTWANDELN UND MONDSUCHT. EINE MEDIZINISCH-LITERARISCHE STUDIE. 1914. 171 pp.

Heft 17. Kielholz, Artur. JAKOB BOEHME: EIN PATHOGRAPHISCHER BEITRAG ZUR PSYCHOLOGIE DER MYSTIK. 1919. 95 pp.

Heft 18. Sadger, Isidor. FRIEDRICH HEBBEL. EIN PSYCHOANALYTISCHER VERSUCH. 1920. 374 pp.

Heft 19. Kaplan, Leo. SCHOPENHAUER UND DER ANIMISMUS. 1925. 197 pp.

Heft 20. Timerding, Heinrich. ROBERT MAYER UND DER ENTDECKUNG DER ENERGIEGESETZES. 1925. 120 pp.

234. Tijdschrift voor wijsbegeerte.

TITLE VARIATIONS: Continued by *Algemeen nederlands tijdschrift voor wijsbegeerte en psychologie* with Jaargang 27, 1934.

DATES OF PUBLICATION: Jaargang 1–26, 1907–1932.

FREQUENCY: **Bimonthly**, Jaargang 1–4, 1907–1910. **Quarterly**, Jaargang 5–26, 1911–1932.

NUMBERING VARIATIONS: None.

PUBLISHER: **Leiden:** E. J. Brill, 1907–1910. **Haarlem:** De Erven F. Bohn, 1911–1932.

PRIMARY EDITORS: **J. D. Bierens de Haan**, 1907–1925; **Julius de Boer**, 1907–1925; **L. H. Grondijs**, 1907–1925; **Ph. Kohnstamm**, 1907–1910; **W. Meijer**, 1907–1925; **K. J. Pen. Amst**, 1907–1910; **W. Versluys**, 1907–1910; **G. A. van den Bergh van Eysinga**, 1911–1925; **J. Clay**, 1911–1925; **G. Heymans**, 1911–1925; **J. A. der Mouw**, 1911–1919; **B.J.H. Ovink**, 1911–1925; **P. H. Ritter**, 1911–1912; **Ch. M. van Deventer**, 1920–1925; **C. J. Wijnaendts Francken**, 1911–1925; **R. Kranenburg**, 1916–1925. None listed 1926–1932.

235. Zeitschrift für experimentelle Pädagogik, psychologische und pathologische Kinderforschung.

TITLE VARIATIONS: Continues *Experimentelle Pädagogik*. United with *Zeitschrift für pädagogische Psychologie, Pathologie und Hygiene* to form *Zeitschrift für pädagogische Psychologie und experimentelle Pädagogik* with Band 12, 1911.

DATES OF PUBLICATION: Band 5–11, Heft 3, 1907–1910.

FREQUENCY: **Bimonthly**, Band 5–7, 1907–1908. **8 times per year**, Band 8–9, 1909. **Bimonthly**, Band 10–11, 1910.

NUMBERING VARIATIONS: Band 5–9 each contain 4 Hefte; Band 10–11 each contain 3 Hefte.

PUBLISHER: **Leipzig:** Otto Nemnich, 1907–1910.

PRIMARY EDITOR: **Ernst Meumann**, 1907–1910.

236. Zeitschrift für Psychologie und Physiologie der Sinnesorgane. Abteilung I. Zeitschrift für Psychologie. Ergänzungsband. [Organ of the Gesellschaft für experimentelle Psychologie, 1926–1930; and of the Deutsche Gesellschaft für Psychologie, 1931–1936.]

TITLE VARIATIONS: Continues *Zeitschrift für Psychologie der Sinnesorgane. Ergänzungsband*.

DATES OF PUBLICATION: Heft 3–25, 1907/1909–1936.

FREQUENCY: Irregular. *See* Contents *below*.

NUMBERING VARIATIONS: None.

PUBLISHER: **Leipzig:** Johann Ambrosius Barth, 1907–1936.

Year 1907

PRIMARY EDITORS: **Hermann Ebbinghaus**, 1907–1909; **Friedrich Schumann**, 1909–1936; **David Katz**, 1932; **Erich R. Jaensch**, 1934–1936; **Oswald Kroh**, 1934–1936.

CONTENTS:

Heft 3. Wreschner, Arthur. DIE REPRODUKTION UND ASSOZIATION VON VORSTELLUNGEN. 1907/1909. 599 pp.

Heft 4. Jaensch, Erich R. ZUR ANALYSE DER GESICHTSWAHRNEHMUNGEN. 1909. 388 pp.

Heft 5. Müller, Georg Elias. ZUR ANALYSE DER GEDÄCHTNISTÄTIGKEIT UND DES VORSTELLUNGSVERLAUFES. TEIL I. 1911. 403 pp.

Heft 6. Jaensch, Erich R. ÜBER DIE WAHRNEHMUNG DES RAUMES. 1911. 488 pp.

Heft 7. Katz, David. DIE ERSCHEINUNGSWEISEN DER FARBEN UND IHRE BEEINFLUSSUNG DURCH DIE INDIVIDUELLE ERFAHRUNG. 1911. 425 pp.

Heft 8. Müller, Georg Elias. ZUR ANALYSE DER GEDÄCHTNISTÄTIGKEIT UND DES VORSTELLUNGSVERLAUFES. TEIL III. 1913. 567 pp.

Heft 9. Müller, Georg Elias. ZUR ANALYSE DER GEDÄCHTNISTÄTIGKEIT UND DES VORSTELLUNGSVERLAUFES. TEIL II. 1917. 682 pp.

Heft 10. Werner, Heinz. GRUNDFRAGEN DER INTENSITÄTSPSYCHOLOGIE. 1922. 251 pp.

Heft 11. Katz, David. DER AUFBAU DER TASTWELT. 1925. 270 pp.

Heft 12. Ach, Narziss, Ernst Kuehle, and Ernst Passarge. BEITRÄGE ZUR LEHRE VON DER PERSEVERATION. 1926. 276 pp.

Heft 13. Hegge, Thorleif G. ZUR ANALYSE DES LERNENS MIT SINNVOLLER VERKNÜPFUNG. 1927. 187 pp.

Heft 14. Kroh, Oswald. EXPERIMENTELLE BEITRÄGE ZUR TYPENKUNDE. BAND I. 1929. 300 pp.

Heft 15. Pfahler, Gerhard. SYSTEM DER TYPENLEHRE. GRUNDLEGUNG EINER PÄDAGOGISCHEN TYPENLEHRE. 1929. 334 pp.

Heft 16. Jaensch, Erich R. ÜBER DEN AUFBAU DES BEWUSSTSEINS. TEIL I. 1930. 492 pp.

Heft 17. Müller, Georg Elias. ÜBER DIE FARBENEMPFINDUNGEN. PSYCHOPHYSISCHE UNTERSUCHUNGEN. BAND I. 1930. Pp. 1–434.

Heft 18. Müller, Georg Elias. ÜBER DIE FARBENEMPFINDUNGEN. PSYCHOPHYSISCHE UNTERSUCHUNGEN. BAND II. 1930. Pp. 435–648.

Heft 19. Ruppert, Hans. AUFBAU DER WELT DES JUGENDLICHEN. EIN BEITRAG ZUR FRAGE NACH DER BILDUNG UND ENTWICKLUNG DES WERTERLEBENS UND WERTBEWUSSTSEINS IN DER REIFEZEIT. 1931. 197 pp.

Heft 20. Düker, Heinrich. PSYCHOLOGISCHE UNTERSUCHUNGEN ÜBER FREIE UND ZWANGSLÄUFIGE ARBEIT. EXPERIMENTELLE BEITRÄGE ZUR WILLENS- UND ARBEITSPSYCHOLOGIE. 1931. 160 pp.

Heft 21. Rohracher, Hubert. THEORIE DES WILLENS AUF EXPERIMENTELLER GRUNDLAGE. 1932. 194 pp.

Heft 22. Kroh, Oswald. EXPERIMENTELLE BEITRÄGE ZUR TYPENKUNDE. BAND III. 1932. 356 pp.

Heft 23. Kardos, Ludwig. DING UND SCHATTEN. EINE EXPERIMENTELLE UNTERSUCHUNG ÜBER DIE GRUNDLAGEN DES FARBENSEHENS. 1934. 184 pp.

Heft 24. Kroh, Oswald. EXPERIMENTELLE BEITRÄGE ZUR TYPENKUNDE. BAND II. 1934. 233 pp.

Heft 25. Mall, Gerhart D. KONSTITUTION UND AFFEKT. 1936. 104 pp.

237. *Zeitschrift für Psychologie und Physiologie der Sinnesorgane. Abteilung II. Zeitschrift für Sinnesphysiologie.* [Organ of the Deutsche Gesellschaft für Psychologie, 1925–1940.]

TITLE VARIATIONS: Continues *Zeitschrift für Psychologie und Physiologie der Sinnesorgane.* Continued by *Zeitschrift für Sinnesphysiologie* with Band 69, 1940.

DATES OF PUBLICATION: Band 41–68, Heft 5/6, 1907–August 1940.

FREQUENCY: **Bimonthly** (6 Hefte to volume), Band 41–49, 1907–1916. **Irregular** (6 Hefte to volume), Band 50–51, 1919–1920. **Bimonthly** (6 Hefte to volume), Band 52–68, 1921–1940.

NUMBERING VARIATIONS: Many multinumber issues.

PUBLISHER: **Leipzig:** Johann Ambrosius Barth, 1907–1940.

PRIMARY EDITORS: **Wilibald A. Nagel,** 1907–1909. **Julius Richard Ewald,** 1910–1919; **Martin Gildemeister,** 1920–1940.

EDITORIAL BOARD: Sigmund Exner, 1907–1925; Johannes von Kries, 1907–1929; Theodor Lipps, 1907–1916; Alexius Meinong, 1907–1920; Georg Elias Müller, 1907–1934; Carl Stumpf, 1907–1936; Armin von Tschermak, 1907–1940; W. Uhthoff, 1907–1926; Theodor Ziehen, 1907–1940; Hendrik Zwaardemaker, 1907–1931; Wilibald A. Nagel, 1910; Julius Richard Ewald, 1920–1921; A. Kohlrausch, 1930–1940.

238. *Zeitschrift für Religionspsychologie. Grenzfragen der Theologie und Medizin.*

TITLE VARIATIONS: None.

DATES OF PUBLICATION: Band 1–6, April 1907–March 1913.

FREQUENCY: Monthly.

NUMBERING VARIATIONS: Band 2, Heft 11, pp. 425–432 never published.

PUBLISHER: **Halle:** Carl Marhold, 1907–March 1910. **Leipzig:** Johann Ambrosius Barth, 1910–1913.

PRIMARY EDITORS: **Joh. Bresler,** 1907–1913; **Georg Runze,** 1907–1913; **Otto Klemm,** 1910–1913.

1908

239. *Archives d'anthropologie criminelle, de médecine légale et de psychologie normale et pathologique.*

TITLE VARIATIONS: Continues *Archives d'anthropologie criminelle, de criminologie et de psychologie normale et pathologique.*

DATES OF PUBLICATION: Tome 24–29, 1908–1914.

FREQUENCY: Monthly.

NUMBERING VARIATIONS: None.

PUBLISHER: **Paris:** Masson et Cie, 1908–1914.

PRIMARY EDITORS: **Alexandre Lacassagne,** 1908–1914; **Étienne Martin,** 1908–1913; **Paul Dubuisson,** 1908; **A. Policard,** 1914.

240. *Bibliothèque de psychologie expérimentale et de métapsychie.*

TITLE VARIATIONS: Continued by *Collection de psychologie expérimentale et de métapsychie* with Tome 14, 1910.

DATES OF PUBLICATION: Tome 1–13, 1908–1909.

FREQUENCY: Irregular. *See* Contents *below.*

NUMBERING VARIATIONS: None.

PUBLISHER: **Paris:** Librairie Bloud & Cie, 1908–1909.

PRIMARY EDITOR: **Raymond Meunier,** 1908–1909.

CONTENTS:

Tome 1. Vaschide, N. LES HALLUCINATIONS TÉLÉPATHIQUES. 1908. 98 pp.

Tome 2. Viollet, Marcel. LE SPIRITISME DANS SES RAPPORTS AVEC LA FOLIE. 1908. 121 pp.

Tome 3. Marie, A. L'AUDITION MORBIDE. 1908. 147 pp.

Tome 4. Lubomirska, Princesse. LES PRÉJUGÉS SUR LA FOLIE. 1908. 89 pp.

Tome 5. Vaschide, N., and Raymond Meunier. LA PATHOLOGIE DE L'ATTENTION. 1908. 117 pp.

Tome 6. Loures, Henry. LES SYNESTHÉSIES. 1908. 99 pp.

Tome 7/8. Meunier, Raymond. LE HACHICH, ESSAÌ SUR LA PSYCHOLOGIE DES PARADIS EPHEMERES. 1909. 219 p.

Tome 9. Bouquet, Henri. L'ÉVOLUTION PSYCHOLOGIQUE DE L'ENFANT. 1909. 100 pp.

Tome 10. Marie, A, and R. Martial. TRAVAIL ET FOLIE. 1909. 110 pp.

Tome 11. Alber (Le Prestidigitateur). DE L'ILLUSION, SON MÉCANISME PSYCHO-SOCIAL. 1909. 119 pp.

Tome 12. Marie, A. LES DÉGÉNÉRESCENCES AUDITIVES. 1909. 110 pp.

Tome 13. Lavrand, H. RÉ-ÉDUCATION PHYSIQUE ET PSYCHIQUE. 1909. 123 pp.

241. *Child-Study. The Journal of the Child Study Society.*

TITLE VARIATIONS: Supersedes *Paidologist.*

DATES OF PUBLICATION: Volume 1–13, Number 2, April 1908–1920. Suspended publication 1918.

FREQUENCY: **Quarterly,** Volume 1–5, April 1908–January 1913. **Monthly,** (except January, July–September), Volume 6–9, 1913–1916. **Quarterly,** Volume 10, 1917. **Semiannual,** Volume 12–13, 1919–1920.

NUMBERING VARIATIONS: Volume 11, 1918, never issued.

PUBLISHER: **London:** E. Arnold, 1908–1917. **London & St. Albans:** E. Arnold; and Gibbs & Bamforth, 1919–1920.

PRIMARY EDITORS: **W.J.D. Mulford,** 1908–1910; **Henry Holman,** 1910–1916.

242. *International Psycho-Analytical Congress.*

TITLE VARIATIONS: Also called *Internationalen psychoanalytischen Kongress; Congresso psicoanalitico internazionale;* etc.

DATES OF PUBLICATION: 1st–16th+, 1908–1949+. Suspended publication 1940–1948.

FREQUENCY: Irregular. Varies between 1 and 4 years but predominantly 2.

NUMBERING VARIATIONS: None.

PUBLISHER: Varies with location of meeting.

PRIMARY EDITORS: None listed.

NOTE: Berichte; Proceedings; Acta etc. of the International Psycho-Analytical Congress have not been systematically published. Reports of individuals presenting papers and/or attending these congresses predominate. These are usually published in serials. Volume 5 of Alexander Grinstein's *Index of Psychoanalytic Writings* contains a section on reports that lists much of the material for these congresses.

243. *Johns Hopkins University. Studies in Philosophy and Psychology.*

TITLE VARIATIONS: None.

DATES OF PUBLICATION: Number 1–3, January 1908–1909.

FREQUENCY: Irregular. *See* Contents *below.*

NUMBERING VARIATIONS: Issues also numbered as *Philosophical Monographs;* as *Psychological Review. Monograph Supplements;* or as *Johns Hopkins University. Psychological Laboratory. Studies. See* Contents *below.*

PUBLISHER: **Baltimore:** Review Publishing Company, 1908. **Lancaster, Pennsylvania** and **Baltimore:** Review Publishing Company, 1909.

PRIMARY EDITORS: None listed.

CONTENTS:

    Number 1. Furry, William Davis. THE AESTHETIC EXPERIENCE: ITS NA-

TURE AND FUNCTION IN EPISTEMOLOGY. 1908. 155 pp. (Also as *Philosophical Monographs,* Number 1 and *Psychological Review. Monograph Supplements,* Number 36.)

Number 2. Stratton, George M, ed. STUDIES FROM THE JOHNS HOPKINS PSYCHOLOGICAL LABORATORY. 1909. 104 pp. (Also as *Psychological Review. Monograph Supplements,* Number 40.)

Number 3. Burrow, N. Trigant. THE DETERMINATION OF THE POSITION OF A MOMENTARY IMPRESSION IN THE TEMPORAL COURSE OF A MOVING VISUAL IMPRESSION. 1909. 63 pp. (Also as *Psychological Review. Monograph Supplements,* Number 47 and as *Johns Hopkins University. Psychological Laboratory. Studies,* Number 2.)

244. *Medical Society for the Study of Suggestive Therapeutics. Transactions.*

TITLE VARIATIONS: Continued by *Psycho-medical Society. Transactions* with Volume 2, Part 1, January 1910.

DATES OF PUBLICATION: Volume 1, Part 1–2, October 1908–January 1909.

FREQUENCY: Irregular. *See* Contents *below.*

NUMBERING VARIATIONS: None.

PUBLISHER: **North End, Croydon:** Printed at the Croydon Guardian Offices, 1908–1909.

PRIMARY EDITORS: None listed.

CONTENTS:
Volume 1, Part 1. Bramwell, Milne. OBSESSIONS AND THEIR TREATMENT BY SUGGESTION. October 1908.
———, Part 2. Taplin, A. Betts, METHODS IN THE TREATMENT BY HYPNOTIC SUGGESTION. January 1909.

245. *Montana. University. Publications in Psychology.*

TITLE VARIATIONS: Also called [*Montana. University.*] *Studies in Psychology;* and [*Montana. University.*] *Bulletin. Psychological Series.*

DATES OF PUBLICATION: Volume 1, 1908.

FREQUENCY: Irregular.

NUMBERING VARIATIONS: Also numbered as [*Montana. University.*] *Bulletin* 53, *Psychological Series,* Number 1.

PUBLISHER: **Missoula, Montana:** University (of Montana), 1908.

PRIMARY EDITOR: **William Frederick Book,** 1908.

CONTENTS:
Volume 1. Book, William Frederick. THE PSYCHOLOGY OF SKILL, WITH SPECIAL REFERENCE TO ITS ACQUISITION IN TYPEWRITING. December 1, 1908. 188 pp.

246. *Philosophical Monographs.*

TITLE VARIATIONS: Also called *Psychological Review. Philosophical Monographs.*

DATES OF PUBLICATION: Number 1–3, January 1908–March 1916.

FREQUENCY: Irregular. *See* Contents *below.*

NUMBERING VARIATIONS: One issue also numbered as *Psychological Review. Monograph Supplements* and as *Johns Hopkins University. Studies in Philosophy and Psychology. See* Contents *below.*

PUBLISHER: **Baltimore:** The Review Publishing Company, 1908–1910. **Princeton, New Jersey** and **Lancaster, Pennsylvania:** Psychological Review Company, 1916.

PRIMARY EDITORS: **J. Mark Baldwin,** 1908; **Howard C. Warren,** 1908–1916; **Charles H. Judd,** 1908; **John B. Watson,** 1910–1916; **James R. Angell,** 1910–1916; **Arthur H. Pierce,** 1910; **Shepherd I. Franz,** 1916; **Madison Bentley,** 1916.

CONTENTS:

Number 1. Furry, William Davis. THE AESTHETIC EXPERIENCE: ITS NATURE AND FUNCTION IN EPISTEMOLOGY. January 1908. 155 pp. (Also as *Psychological Review. Monograph Supplements,* [Number 36]; and *Johns Hopkins University. Studies in Philosophy and Psychology,* Number 1).

Number 2. MacKinnon, Flora Isabel. THE PHILOSOPHY OF JOHN NORRIS OF BEMERTON. October 1910. 104 pp.

Number 3. Dunham, James H. FREEDOM AND PURPOSE: AN INTERPRETATION OF THE PSYCHOLOGY OF SPINOZA. March 1916. 98 pp.

247. *Psychological Clinic. A Journal of Orthogenics for the Study and Treatment of Retardation and Deviation.*

TITLE VARIATIONS: Continues *Psychological Clinic. A Journal for the Study and Treatment of Mental Retardation and Deviation.* Continued by *Psychological Clinic. A Journal of Orthogenics for the Normal Development of Every Child* with Volume 8, 1914.

DATES OF PUBLICATION: Volume 2–7, 1908–1914.

FREQUENCY: Monthly (except July–September).

NUMBERING VARIATIONS: None.

PUBLISHER: **Philadelphia:** Psychological Clinic Press, 1908–1914.

PRIMARY EDITOR: **Lightner Witmer,** 1908–1914.

248. *Psychotherapy, A Course of Reading in Sound Psychology, Sound Medicine and Sound Religion.*

TITLE VARIATIONS: None.

DATES OF PUBLICATION: Volume 1–3, 1908–1909.

FREQUENCY: Irregular. Four numbers to a volume.

NUMBERING VARIATIONS: Each article in a volume is numbered. No dates are included except copyright 1908–1909.

PUBLISHER: **New York:** Centre Publishing Co., 1908–1909.

PRIMARY EDITORS: **W. B. Parker,** 1908–1909; **H. C. Judson,** 1909.

249. *Revue de psychologie.*

TITLE VARIATIONS: Continues *Revue de psychologie sociale.* Continued by *Vie contemporaine. Revue de psychologie sociale* with Volume 2, Numéro 3, March 1908.

DATES OF PUBLICATION: Volume 2, Numéro 2, February 1908.

FREQUENCY: Monthly.

NUMBERING VARIATIONS: None.

PUBLISHER: **Paris:** "Revue" rédaction et administration, 1908.

PRIMARY EDITORS: **A. Éspinas,** 1908; **C. Gide,** 1908; **E. Dupré,** 1908.

250. *Revue psychologique.*

TITLE VARIATIONS: None.

DATES OF PUBLICATION: Volume 1–7, Numéro 2, 1908–1914.

FREQUENCY: Quarterly.

NUMBERING VARIATIONS: None.

PUBLISHER: **Brussels:** Adressé de la direction et du secrétariat: 35 avenue Paul de Jaer, 1908–1910. **Brussels:** Misch & Thron, 1911–1914.

PRIMARY EDITORS: **I. Ioteyko,** 1908–1914; **V. Kipiani,** 1908–1914.

251. *Société clinique de médecine mentale (Paris). Bulletin.*

TITLE VARIATIONS: None.

DATES OF PUBLICATION: Tome 1–18, May 1908–November/December 1930. Suspended publication 1914–1917.

FREQUENCY: **Monthly,** (except August, September, October), Tome 1–12, May 1908–1917. **Irregular,** Tome 13–18, 1918–November/December 1930.

NUMBERING VARIATIONS: Tome 7, Numéro 8–Tome 12, Numéro 7, August 1914–1917 never published.

PUBLISHER: **Paris:** O. Doin et Fils, éditeurs, 1908–1930.

PRIMARY EDITORS: **Henri Colin,** 1908–1930; ——— **Trenel,** 1908–1910; **R.P.A. Leroy,** 1908–1910; **P. Juquelier,** 1908–1930; **J. Capgras,** 1911–1930; **Alfred Fillassier,** 1911–1930.

NOTE: Above entry based on partial information. The compilers were unable to examine this title.

252. *Training College Record.* [Organ of the Training College Association.]

TITLE VARIATIONS: Continued by *Journal of Experimental Pedagogy and Training College Record* with Volume 1, Number 6, March 1911.

DATES OF PUBLICATION: Volume 1, Number 1–5, March 1908–November 1910.

FREQUENCY: Irregular.

NUMBERING VARIATIONS: None.

PUBLISHER: **London:** Longmans, Green and Company, 1908–1910.

PRIMARY EDITOR: **J. A. Green,** 1908–1910.

253. *Vie contemporaine. Revue de psychologie sociale.*

TITLE VARIATIONS: Continues *Revue de psychologie.*

DATES OF PUBLICATION: Volume 2, Numéro 3–10, March–October 1908.

FREQUENCY: Monthly.

NUMBERING VARIATIONS: None.

PUBLISHER: **Paris:** Rédaction et administration, 1908.

PRIMARY EDITORS: **A. Éspinas,** 1908; **C. Gide,** 1908; **E. Dupré,** 1908.

254. *Zeitschrift für angewandte Psychologie und psychologische Sammelforschung.* [Organ of the Institut für angewandte Psychologie (Leipzig).]

TITLE VARIATIONS: Supersedes *Beiträge zur Psychologie der Aussage.* Continued by *Zeitschrift für angewandte Psychologie.* [1] with Band 11, 1916.

DATES OF PUBLICATION: Band 1–10, 1908–1915.

FREQUENCY: Irregular (6 Hefte per volume).

NUMBERING VARIATIONS: At least 2 double-number issues per volume. 3 double issues in Band 8.

PUBLISHER: **Leipzig:** Johann Ambrosius Barth, 1908–1915.

PRIMARY EDITORS: **William Stern,** 1908–1915; **Otto Lipmann,** 1908–1915.

1909

255. *Anales de psicología.*

TITLE VARIATIONS: None.

DATES OF PUBLICATION: Volumen 1, 1909.

FREQUENCY: Annual.

NUMBERING VARIATIONS: Volumen 1, 1909, was actually published 1910.

PUBLISHER: **Buenos Aires:** Sociedad de psicología de Buenos Aires, 1909/1910.

PRIMARY EDITORS: **José Ingegnieros,** 1909/1910; **Victor Mercante,** 1909/1910; **Clemente Onelli,** 1909/1910; **Horacio G.** Piñero, 1909/1910; **Carlos Rodriguez Etchart,** 1909/1910; **Nicolás Roveda,** 1909/1910; **Rodolfo Senet,** 1909/1910; **Francisco de Veyga,** 1909/1910.

256. *Jahrbuch für psychoanalytische und psychopathologische Forschungen.*

TITLE VARIATIONS: Continued by *Jahrbuch der Psychoanalyse* with Band 6, 1914.

DATES OF PUBLICATION: Band 1–5, 1909–1913.

FREQUENCY: Annual (each Band issued in 2 Häfte).

NUMBERING VARIATIONS: Häfte are continuously paginated.

PUBLISHER: **Vienna:** F. Deuticke, 1909–1913.

PRIMARY EDITORS: **E. Bleuler,** 1909–1913; **Sigmund Freud,** 1909–1913; **Carl Gustav Jung,** 1909–1913.

257. *Library of Genetic Science and Philosophy,*

TITLE VARIATIONS: None.

DATES OF PUBLICATION: Number 1–2, 1909.

FREQUENCY: Irregular.

NUMBERING VARIATIONS: None.

PUBLISHER: **Baltimore:** Review Publishing Co., 1909.

PRIMARY EDITOR: **James Mark Baldwin,** 1909.

CONTENTS:
    Number 1. Davies, Arthur Ernest. THE MORAL LIFE. A STUDY IN GE-NETIC ETHICS. 1909. 187 pp.
    Number 2. Baldwin, James Mark. DARWIN AND THE HUMANITIES. 1909. 118 pp.

258. *Maravilloso. Revista de psicología y dinamismo inexplicados.*

TITLE VARIATIONS: None.

DATES OF PUBLICATION: Años 1–2, 1909–1910.

FREQUENCY: 5 issues per year.

NUMBERING VARIATIONS: None.

PUBLISHER: **Madrid:** 1909–1910.

PRIMARY EDITORS: None listed.

NOTE: Information on this title is from serial holdings of the National Library in Madrid.

259. *Ohio. State University. Psychological Studies.*

TITLE VARIATIONS: Continues *Ohio. State University. Studies in Psychology.* Continued by *Ohio. State University. Contributions in Psychology* with Number 6, 1922.

DATES OF PUBLICATION: Number 5, 1909.

FREQUENCY: Irregular. *See* Contents *below.*

NUMBERING VARIATIONS: Number 5 also incorrectly numbered Volume 1, Number 1. Also numbered as *Psychological Review. Monograph Supplements. See* Contents *below.*

PUBLISHER: **Lancaster, Pennsylvania** and **Baltimore:** Review Publishing Co., 1909.

PRIMARY EDITORS: None listed.

CONTENTS:
 Number 5. Gatewood, L. C. AN EXPERIMENTAL STUDY OF DEMENTIA PRAECOX. 1909. 71 pp. (Also as *Psychological Review. Monograph Supplements,* Number 45.)

260. *Psychologie in Einzeldarstellungen.*

TITLE VARIATIONS: None.

DATES OF PUBLICATION: Band 1–6, 1909–1913.

FREQUENCY: Irregular. *See* Contents *below.*

NUMBERING VARIATIONS: None.

PUBLISHER: **Heidelberg:** Carl Winter, 1909–1913.

PRIMARY EDITORS: **Herm. Ebbinghaus,** 1909–1913; **Ernst Meumann,** 1909–1913.

CONTENTS:
 Band 1. Dürr, E. GRUNDZÜGE DER ETHIK. 1909. 383 pp.
 Band 2. Witasek, Steph. PSYCHOLOGIE DER RAUMWAHRNEHMUNG DES AUGES. 1910. 454 pp.
 Band 3. Heymans, G. DIE PSYCHOLOGIE DER FRAUEN. 1910 308 pp.
 Band 4. Dessoir, Max. ABRISS EINER GESCHICHTE DER PSYCHOLOGIE. 1911. 272 pp.
 Band 5. Becher, Erich. GEHIRN UND SEELE. 1911. 405 pp.
 Band 6. Benussi, Vittorio. PSYCHOLOGIE DER ZEITAUFFASSUNG. 1913. 581 pp.

261. *Psyke. Tidskrift. Tidskriften Psykes Monografiserie.*

TITLE VARIATIONS: None.

DATES OF PUBLICATION: Band 1–2. Häfte 1, 1909–1913.

FREQUENCY: Irregular. *See* Contents *below.*

NUMBERING VARIATIONS: None.

PUBLISHER: **Uppsala** and **Stockholm:** Almqvist & Wiksells Boktryckeri, A.B., 1909–1913.

PRIMARY EDITOR: **Sydney Alrutz,** 1909–1913.

CONTENTS
Band 1. Hammer, Bertil. "LAKLLAGELSEFÖRMÅGAN" INGÅR I PRENUMER-
ATIONEN FOR ÅR 1909. 1909. 94 pp.
Band 2 Häfte 1. Alrutz, Sydney. TILL NERVSYSTEMETS DYNAMIK; EXPER-
IMENTELLA UNDERSÖKNINGAR ÖFVER SENSIBILITETEN, MOTILITETEN, SUGGES-
TIBILITETEN OCH DEN NERVÖSA ENERGIEN I VAKET OCH HYPNOTISKT TILLSTÅND
I. 1913. 72 pp.

262. *Rivista di psicologia applicata.* [Organ of the Società italiana di psicologia and of the Istituti di psicologia sperimentale (Rome and Turin).]

TITLE VARIATIONS: Continues *Rivista di psicologia applicata alla pedagogia ed alla psicopatologie.* Continued by *Rivista di psicologia* [1] with Volume 8, 1913.

DATES OF PUBLICATION: Volume 5–7, 1909–1911.

FREQUENCY: Bimonthly.

NUMBERING VARIATIONS: None.

PUBLISHER: **Bologna:** Stabilimento poligrafico Emiliano, 1909–1911.

PRIMARY EDITORS: **Giulio Cesare Ferrari,** 1909–1911; **Luigi Baroncini,** 1909–1911.

263. *Rome. Università. Laboratorio di psicologia sperimentale. Contributi psicologici.*

TITLE VARIATIONS: Continued by [*Rome. Università.*] *Istituto di psicologia sperimentale. Contributi psicologici* with Volume 5, 1922.

DATES OF PUBLICATION: Volume 1–4, 1909–1917/1921.

FREQUENCY: Volume 1, 1909/1911; Volume 2, 1912/1913; Volume 3, 1914/1916; and, Volume 4, 1917/1921.

NUMBERING VARIATIONS: None.

PUBLISHER: **Rome:** Presso il laboratorio di psicologia sperimentale, 1910–1921.

PRIMARY EDITOR: **Sante de Sanctis,** 1910–1921.

NOTE: Volumes contain previously published material by members of the laboratory.

264. *Voprosy teorii i psikhologii tvorchestva.*

TITLE VARIATIONS: None.

DATES OF PUBLICATION: Tom 1–8, 1909–1923.

FREQUENCY: Irregular.

NUMBERING VARIATIONS: None.

PUBLISHER: **Kharkov:** Gubernskaia tipografiia (?), 1909–1923 (?).

PRIMARY EDITOR: **Boris Andreevich Lezin'**, 1909–1923.

265. *Wellesley College. Studies in Psychology.*

TITLE VARIATIONS: None.

DATES OF PUBLICATION: Number 1–2, September 1909–October 1916.

FREQUENCY: Irregular. *See* Contents *below.*

NUMBERING VARIATIONS: Issues also numbered as *Psychological Review. Monograph Supplements* and as *Psychological Monographs. See* Contents *below.*

PUBLISHER: **Lancaster, Pennsylvania** and **Baltimore:** The Review Publishing Company, 1909. **Princeton, New Jersey** and **Lancaster:** Psychological Review Company, 1916.

PRIMARY EDITOR: **Eleanor A. McC. Gamble,** 1909–1916.

CONTENTS:

Number 1. Gamble, Eleanor A. McC. A Study in Memorising Various Materials by the Reconstruction Method. September 1909. 210 pp. (Also as *Psychological Review. Monograph Supplements*, Number 43.)

Number 2. Gamble, Eleanor A. McC., ed. Wellesley College Studies in Psychology. No. 2. October 1916. 192 pp. (Also as *Psychological Monographs*, Number 96.)

266. *Zeitschrift für Psychotherapie und medizinische Psychologie.*

TITLE VARIATIONS: Subtitled *Mit Einschluss des Hypnotismus, der Suggestion und der Psychoanalyse, 1912 +*. Superseded by *Abhandlungen aus dem Gebiete der Psychotherapie und medizinischen Psychologie* with Heft 1, 1925, and, *Psychologie und Medizin* with Band 1, 1925.

DATES OF PUBLICATION: Band 1–8, 1909–December 1924.

FREQUENCY: Irregular (6 Hefte to a Band).

NUMBERING VARIATIONS: Many multinumber issues present.

PUBLISHER: **Stuttgart:** Verlag von Ferdinand Enke, 1909–1924.

PRIMARY EDITOR: **Albert Moll,** 1909–1924.

1910-1919

267. California. University. Publications in Psychology.

TITLE VARIATIONS: None.

DATES OF PUBLICATION: Volume 1–6, September 24, 1910–March 1950+.

FREQUENCY: Irregular. Volume 1, 6 numbers; Volume 2, 6 numbers; Volume 3, 8 numbers; Volume 4, 21 numbers; Volume 5, 10 numbers; Volume 6, 13 numbers.

NUMBERING VARIATIONS: Volume 5, Number 7–10 were published out of chronological order.

PUBLISHER: **Berkeley, California:** University of California Press, 1910–1947. **Berkeley and Los Angeles:** University of California Press, 1948–1950+.

PRIMARY EDITORS: **George Malcolm Stratton,** 1910–1928; **Warner Brown,** 1918–1950+; **Edward C. Tolman,** 1918–1950+; **Harold E. Jones,** 1928–1950+; **O. L. Bridgman,** 1932–1950+; **Egon Brunswik,** 1948–1950+; **C. W. Brown,** 1948–1950+; **R. M. Dorcus,** 1948–1950+; **Franklin Fearing,** 1948–1950+; **H. C. Gilhousen,** 1948–1950+; **R. C. Tryon,** 1948–1950+; **D. W. MacKinnon,** 1948–1950+.

CONTENTS:

Volume 1, Number 1. Brown, Warner. JUDGMENT OF DIFFERENCE, WITH SPECIAL REFERENCE TO THE DOCTRINE OF THE THRESHOLD, IN THE CASE OF LIFTED WEIGHTS. 1910. Pp. 1–71.

————, **Number 2.** Moore, Thomas Verner. THE PROCESS OF ABSTRACTION, AN EXPERIMENTAL STUDY. 1910. Pp. 73–197.

For serial publications that began before 1910 and were still being published in the decade 1910 to 1919, *see also* entries 32, 50, 65, 67, 72, 73, 74, 82, 84, 85, 90, 96, 97, 98, 101, 105, 107, 110, 111, 112, 119, 121, 122, 123, 126, 127, 131, 133, 135, 139, 140, 151, 153, 155, 157, 160, 162, 163, 169, 176, 177, 179, 180, 181, 182, 184, 186, 188, 190, 191, 192, 193, 194, 196, 197, 199, 200, 201, 202, 204, 205, 207, 208, 209, 210, 211, 213, 215, 217, 218, 219, 220, 221, 222, 223, 225, 226, 227, 229, 230, 233, 234, 235, 236, 237, 238, 239, 241, 242, 246, 247, 250, 251, 252, 254, 256, 258, 260, 261, 262, 263, 264, 265, 266.

267. *(Continued)*

————, **Number 3.** Brown, Warner. Judgment of Very Weak Sensory Stimuli, with Special Reference to the Absolute Threshold of Sensation for Common Salt. 1914. Pp. 199–268.

————, **Number 4.** Brown, Warner. Habit Interference in Sorting Cards. 1914. Pp. 269–321.

————, **Number 5.** Gates, Arthur I. Diurnal Variations in Memory and Association. 1916. Pp. 323–344.

————, **Number 6.** Gates, Arthur I. Correlations and Sex Differences in Memory and Substitution. 1916. Pp. 345–350.

Volume 2, Number 1. Gates, Arthur I. Variations in Efficiency during the Day, together with Practice Effects, Sex Differences, and Correlations. 1916. Pp. 1–156.

————, **Number 2.** Levy, J. M. Experiments on Attention and Memory, with Special Reference to the Psychology of Advertising. 1916. Pp. 157–197.

————, **Number 3.** Fuller, Justin K. Psychology and Physiology of Mirror-Writing. 1916. Pp. 199–265.

————, **Number 4.** Heller, Walter S., and Warner Brown. Memory and Association in the Case of Street-Car Advertising Cards. 1916. Pp. 267–275.

————, **Number 5.** Ito, Sangoro. A Comparison of the Japanese Folk-Song and the Occidental: A Study in the Psychology of Form. 1916. Pp. 277–290.

————, **Number 6.** Brown, Warner. Individual and Sex Differences in Suggestibility. 1916. Pp. 291–430.

Volume 3, Number 1. Bridgman, Olga. An Experimental Study of Abnormal Children, with Special Reference to the Problems of Dependency and Delinquency. 1918. Pp. 1–59.

————, **Number 2.** Heller, Walter S. Analysis of Package Labels. 1919. Pp. 61–72.

————, **Number 3.** Morrison, Beulah May. Study of the Major Emotions in Persons of Defective Intelligence. 1924. Pp. 73–145.

————, **Number 4.** Walker, Jean. Factors Contributing to the Delinquency of Defective Girls. 1925. Pp. 147–213.

————, **Number 5.** Truman, Stanley R. and E. G. Wever. The Judgment of Pitch as a Function of the Series. 1928. Pp. 215–223.

————, **Number 6.** Jones, Harold Ellis, assisted by Herbert Conrad and Aaron Horn. Psychological Studies of Motion Pictures, II. Observation and Recall as a Function of Age. 1928. Pp. 225–243.

————, **Number 7.** Conrad, Herbert S., and Harold Ellis Jones. Psychological Studies in Motion Pictures, III. Fidelity of Report as a Measure of Adult Intelligence. 1929. Pp. 245–276.

————, **Number 8.** Conrad, Herbert S., and Harold Ellis Jones. Psychological Studies of Motion Pictures, IV. Technique of Mental-Test Surveys among Adults. 1929. Pp. 277–284.

Volume 4, Number 1. Yoshioka, Joseph G. Preliminary Study in Discrimination of Maze Patterns by the Rat. 1928. Pp. 1–18.

————, **Number 2.** Elliott, Merle Hugh. EFFECT OF CHANGE OF REWARD ON THE MAZE PERFORMANCE OF RATS. 1928. Pp. 19–30.

————, **Number 3.** Williams, Katherine Adams. REWARD VALUE OF A CONDITIONED STIMULUS. 1929. Pp. 31–55.

————, **Number 4.** Hsiao, Hsiao Hung. EXPERIMENTAL STUDY OF THE RAT'S "INSIGHT" WITHIN A SPATIAL COMPLEX. 1929. Pp. 57–70.

————, **Number 5.** Tryon, Robert Choate. GENETICS OF LEARNING ABILITY IN RATS. PRELIMINARY REPORT. 1929. Pp. 71–89.

————, **Number 6.** Elliott, Merle Hugh. EFFECT OF APPROPRIATENESS OF REWARD AND OF COMPLEX INCENTIVES ON MAZE PERFORMANCE. 1929. Pp. 91–98.

————, **Number 7.** Tolman, E. C. et al. SELF-RECORDING MAZE WITH AN AUTOMATIC DELIVERY TABLE. 1929. Pp. 99–112.

————, **Number 8.** Blodgett, Hugh Carleton. EFFECT OF THE INTRODUCTION OF REWARD UPON THE MAZE PERFORMANCE OF RATS. 1929. Pp. 113–134.

————, **Number 9.** Yoshioka, Joseph G. FURTHER STUDY IN DISCRIMINATION OF MAZE PATTERNS BY THE RAT. 1929. Pp. 135–153.

————, **Number 10.** Yoshioka, Joseph G. WEBER'S LAW IN THE DISCRIMINATION OF MAZE DISTANCE BY THE WHITE RAT. 1929. Pp. 155–184.

————, **Number 11.** Elliott, Merle Hugh. EFFECT OF CHANGE OF "DRIVE" ON MAZE PERFORMANCE. 1929. Pp. 185–188.

————, **Number 12.** Tolman, E. C., C. H. Honzik, and E. W. Robinson. THE EFFECT OF DEGREES OF HUNGER UPON THE ORDER OF ELIMINATION OF LONG AND SHORT BLINDS. 1930. Pp. 189–202.

————, **Number 13.** Bruce, Robert Hall. EFFECT OF REMOVAL OF REWARD ON THE MAZE PERFORMANCE OF RATS. 1930. Pp. 203–214.

————, **Number 14.** Tolman, E. C., and C. H. Honzik. "INSIGHT" IN RATS. 1930. Pp. 215–232.

————, **Number 15.** Robinson, Esther W., and E. G. Wever. VISUAL DISTANCE PERCEPTION IN THE RAT. 1930. Pp. 233–239.

————, **Number 16.** Tolman, E. C., and C. H. Honzik. DEGREES OF HUNGER, REWARD AND NON-REWARD, AND MAZE LEARNING IN RATS. 1930. Pp. 241–256.

————, **Number 17.** Tolman, E. C., and C. H. Honzik. INTRODUCTION AND REMOVAL OF REWARD, AND MAZE PERFORMANCE IN RATS. 1930. Pp. 257–275.

————, **Number 18.** MacFarlane, D. A. ROLE OF KINESTHESIS IN MAZE LEARNING. 1930. Pp. 277–305.

————, **Number 19.** Honzik, C. H. DELAYED REACTION IN RATS. 1931. Pp. 307–318.

————, **Number 20.** Haney, George W. EFFECT OF FAMILIARITY ON MAZE PERFORMANCE OF ALBINO RATS. 1931. Pp. 319–333.

————, **Number 21.** Rose, Edward L. ESTABLISHMENT BY RATS OF TWO CONTRARY DISCRIMINATION HABITS. 1931. Pp. 335–345.

Volume 5, Number 1. Conrad, Herbert S., and Daniel Harris. THE FREE-ASSOCIATION METHOD AND THE MEASUREMENT OF ADULT INTELLIGENCE. 1931. Pp. 1–45.

————, **Number 2.** Jones, Harold Ellis. PATTERN OF ABILITIES AMONG ADULT AND JUVENILE DEFECTIVES. 1931. Pp. 47–61.

————, **Number 3.** Jones, H. E., H. S. Conrad, and M. B. Blanchard. ENVIRONMENTAL HANDICAP IN MENTAL TEST PERFORMANCE. 1932. Pp. 63–99.

————, **Number 4.** Sheldon, Muriel Inez. EFFECT ON LEARNING AND RETENTION OF AN INCREASE IN THE ACTIVITY OF PROPRIOCEPTIVE SENSE ORGANS. 1932. Pp. 101–114.

————, **Number 5.** Brown, Warner. AUDITORY AND VISUAL CUES IN MAZE LEARNING. 1932. Pp. 115–122.

————, **Number 6.** Brown, Warner. SPATIAL INTEGRATIONS IN A HUMAN MAZE. 1932. Pp. 123–134.

————, **Number 7.** Brown, Warner. REORIENTATION IN A MULTIPLE-PATH MAZE. 1937. Pp. 135–160.

————, **Number 8.** Wenger, M. A., Karl J. Holzinger, and Harry H. Harman. THE ESTIMATION OF PUPIL ABILITY BY THREE FACTORIAL SOLUTIONS. 1948. Pp. 161–252.

————, **Number 9.** Ghiselli, Edwin E. VALIDITY OF COMMONLY EMPLOYED OCCUPATIONAL TESTS. 1949. Pp. 253–288.

————, **Number 10.** Handlon, Joseph H. FACTORS IN DELAYED RESPONSE. 1950. Pp. 289–320.

Volume 6, Number 1. Hall, Calvin, and E. L. Ballachey. A STUDY OF THE RAT'S BEHAVIOR IN A FIELD. A CONTRIBUTION TO METHOD IN COMPARATIVE PSYCHOLOGY. 1932. Pp. 1–12.

————, **Number 2.** Krechevsky, I., and C. H. Honzik. FIXATION IN THE RAT. 1932. Pp. 13–26.

————, **Number 3/4.** Krechevsky, I. "HYPOTHESES" VERSUS "CHANCE" IN THE PRE-SOLUTION PERIOD IN SENSORY DISCRIMINATION-LEARNING; and Krechevsky, I. THE GENESIS OF "HYPOTHESES" IN RATS. 1932. Pp. 27–44, 45–64.

————, **Number 5/6.** Bruce, Robert Hall. EFFECT OF REMOVAL OF REWARD ON THE MAZE PERFORMANCE OF RATS. II AND III. 1932. Pp. 65–73, 75–82.

————, **Number 7.** Ballachey, E. L., and I. Krechevsky. "SPECIFIC" VS. "GENERAL" ORIENTATION FACTORS IN MAZE RUNNING. 1932. Pp. 83–97.

————, **Number 8.** Honzik, C. H. MAZE LEARNING IN RATS IN THE ABSENCE OF SPECIFIC INTRA- AND EXTRA-MAZE STIMULI. 1933. Pp. 99–144.

————, **Number 9.** Tolman, Edward C. BACKWARD ELIMINATION OF ERRORS IN TWO SUCCESSIVE DISCRIMINATION HABITS. 1934. Pp. 145–152.

————, **Number 10.** Batalla, Mariano B. LEARNING CURVE AND THE RELIABILITY OF LEARNING SCORES IN A BODY MAZE. 1936. Pp. 153–162.

————, **Number 11.** Harsh, Charles M. DISTURBANCE AND "INSIGHT" IN RATS. 1937. Pp. 163–168.

————, **Number 12.** Kuo, Zing Yang. FORCED MOVEMENT OR INSIGHT? 1937. Pp. 169–188.

————, **Number 13.** Rose, Edward L. SPATIAL AND TEMPORAL BASES FOR THE ESTABLISHMENT BY RATS OF CONTRARY DISCRIMINATION HABITS. 1939. Pp. 189–218.

268. *Collection de psychologie expérimentale et de métapsychie.*

TITLE VARIATIONS: Continues *Bibliothèque de psychologie expérimentale et de métapsychie.*

DATES OF PUBLICATION: Tome 14–22, 1910–1912.

FREQUENCY: Irregular.

NUMBERING VARIATIONS: Tome 15/16, 18/19, and 21/22 issued as combined numbers.

PUBLISHER: **Paris:** Bloud & Cie, 1910–1912.

PRIMARY EDITOR: **Raymond Meunier, 1910–1912.**

CONTENTS:

    Tome 14. Legrain, M. LES FOLIES À ÉCLIPSE. 1910. 120 pp.

    Tome 15/16. Meunier, Paul, and René Masselon. LES RÊVES ET LEUR INTERPRETATION. 1910. 213 pp.

    Tome 17. Bajenoff, N., and [Elizabeth] Ossipoff. LA SUGGESTION ET SES LIMITES. 1911. 119 pp.

    Tome 18/19. Vaschide, N., and Raymond Meunier. LA PSYCHOLOGIE DE L'ATTENTION. 1910. 198 pp.

    Tome 20. Abramowski, Édouard. L'ANALYSE PHYSIOLOGIQUE DE LA PERCEPTION. 1911. 121 pp.

    Tome 21/22. Meunier, Raymond. LES SCIENCES PSYCHOLOGIQUES, LEURS MÉTHODES ET LEURS APPLICATIONS. 1912. 180 pp.

269. *Congrès international de psychologie expérimentale. Compte rendu.*

TITLE VARIATIONS: None.

DATES OF PUBLICATION: 1er–3e, 1910–1923.

FREQUENCY: Irregular. *See* Contents *below.*

NUMBERING VARIATIONS: None.

PUBLISHER: **Paris:** H. Durville fils, 1910. **Paris:** H. et H. Durville, 1913. **Paris:** H. Durville, 1923.

PRIMARY EDITORS: *See* Contents *below.*

CONTENTS:

    1er. Paris, 1910. COMPTE-RENDU DES TRAVAUX, PAR HENRI DURVILLE FILS, SECRÉTAIRE GÉNÉRAL. 1910. 245 pp.

    2e. Paris, 1913. COMPTE RENDU DES TRAVAUX, PAR HENRI DURVILLE, SECRÉTAIRE GÉNÉRAL. 1913. 360 pp.

    3e. Paris, 1923. COMPTE RENDU DES TRAVAUX, PAR HENRI DURVILLE. 1923. 272 pp.

270. *Educational Psychology Monographs.*

TITLE VARIATIONS: Number 9 contains series subtitle *Including Experimental Pedagogy, Child Physiology and Hygiene and Educational Statistics.*

DATES OF PUBLICATION: Number 1–30, 1910–1932.

FREQUENCY: Irregular. *See* Contents *below.*

NUMBERING VARIATIONS: One unnumbered issue. Number 3 published after Number 4–6. *See* Contents *below.*

PUBLISHER: **Baltimore:** Warwick & York, 1910–1932.

PRIMARY EDITORS: No editor listed for Number 1–6, 24–30, 1910–1911, 1919–1932; **Guy Montrose Whipple,** Number 7–18, 20, 1912–1917; **J. Carleton Bell,** Number 19, 21, 1918; **James Rowland Angell,** Number 22, 1917; **Faculty of New York University,** Number 23, 1921.

CONTENTS:

Number 1. Dearborn, George V. N. MOTO-SENSORY DEVELOPMENT. OBSERVATIONS ON THE FIRST THREE YEARS OF A CHILD. 1910. 215 pp.

Number 2. Offner, Max. MENTAL FATIGUE. A COMPREHENSIVE EXPOSITION OF THE NATURE OF MENTAL FATIGUE, OF THE METHODS OF ITS MEASUREMENT AND OF THEIR RESULTS, WITH SPECIAL REFERENCE TO THE PROBLEMS OF INSTRUCTION. Translated by Guy Montrose Whipple. 1911. 133 pp.

Number 3. Huey, Edmund Burke. BACKWARD AND FEEBLEMINDED CHILDREN. CLINICAL STUDIES IN THE PSYCHOLOGY OF DEFECTIVES, WITH A SYLLABUS FOR THE CLINICAL EXAMINATION AND TESTING OF CHILDREN. 1912. 221 pp.

Number 4. Winch, W. H. WHEN SHOULD A CHILD BEGIN SCHOOL? AN INQUIRY INTO THE RELATION BETWEEN THE AGE OF ENTRY AND SCHOOL PROGRESS. 1911. 98 pp.

Number 5. Wallin, J. E. Wallace. SPELLING EFFICIENCY IN RELATION TO AGE, GRADE AND SEX, AND THE QUESTION OF TRANSFER. AN EXPERIMENTAL AND CRITICAL STUDY OF THE FUNCTION OF METHOD IN THE TEACHING OF SPELLING. 1911. 91 pp.

Number 6. Whipple, Guy Montrose. RELATIVE EFFICIENCY OF PHONETIC ALPHABETS. AN EXPERIMENTAL INVESTIGATION OF THE COMPARATIVE MERITS OF THE WEBSTER KEY ALPHABET AND THE PROPOSED KEY ALPHABET SUBMITTED TO THE NATIONAL EDUCATION ASSOCIATION. 1911. 52 pp.

Number 7. Wallin, J. E. Wallace. EXPERIMENTAL STUDIES OF MENTAL DEFECTIVES. A CRITIQUE OF THE BINET-SIMON TESTS AND A CONTRIBUTION TO THE PSYCHOLOGY OF EPILEPSY. 1912. 155 pp.

Number 8. Gray, Clarence Truman. VARIATIONS IN THE GRADES OF HIGH SCHOOL PUPILS. 1913. 120 pp.

Number 9. Noyes, Anna G. HOW I KEPT MY BABY WELL. 1913. 193 pp.

Number 10. Finkelstein, I. E. THE MARKETING SYSTEM IN THEORY AND PRACTICE. 1913. 88 pp.

Number 11. Winch, W. H. INDUCTIVE VERSUS DEDUCTIVE METHODS OF TEACHING. AN EXPERIMENTAL RESEARCH. 1913. 146 pp.

Number 12. Winch, W. H. CHILDREN'S PERCEPTIONS. AN EXPERIMENTAL STUDY OF OBSERVATION AND REPORT IN SCHOOL CHILDREN. 1914. 245 pp.

Number 13. Stern, William. THE PSYCHOLOGICAL METHODS OF TESTING INTELLIGENCE. Translated by Guy Montrose Whipple. 1914. 160 pp.

Number 14. Weidensall, Jean. THE MENTALITY OF THE CRIMINAL WOMAN. A COMPARATIVE STUDY OF THE CRIMINAL WOMAN, THE WORKING GIRL, AND THE EFFICIENT WORKING WOMAN IN A SERIES OF MENTAL AND PHYSICAL TESTS. 1916. 332 pp.

Number 15. Wang, Chang Ping. THE GENERAL VALUE OF VISUAL SENSE TRAINING IN CHILDREN. 1916. 85 pp.

Number 16. Hewins, Nellie P. THE DOCTRINE OF FORMAL DISCIPLINE IN THE LIGHT OF EXPERIMENTAL INVESTIGATION. 1916. 120 pp.

Number 17. Rugg, Harold Ordway. THE EXPERIMENTAL DETERMINATION OF MENTAL DISCIPLINE IN SCHOOL STUDIES. 1916. 132 pp.

Number 18. Terman, Lewis M., Grace Lyman, George Ordahl, Louise Ellison Ordahl, Neva Galbreath, and Wilford Talbert, assisted by Herbert E. Knollin, J. H. Williams, H. G. Childs, Helen Trost, Richard Zeidler, Charles Waddle, and Irene Cuneo. THE STANFORD REVISION AND EXTENSION OF THE BINET-SIMON SCALE FOR MEASURING INTELLIGENCE. 1917. 179 pp.

Number 19. Richardson, Roy Franklin. THE PSYCHOLOGY AND PEDAGOGY OF ANGER. 1918. 100 pp.

Number 20. Pintner, Rudolf, and Margaret M. Anderson. THE PICTURE COMPLETION TEST. 1917. 101 pp.

Number 21. Miner, James Burt. DEFICIENCY AND DELINQUENCY. AN INTERPRETATION OF MENTAL TESTING. 1918. 355 pp.

Number 22. Jones, Edward Safford. THE INFLUENCE OF AGE AND EXPERIENCE ON CORRELATIONS CONCERNED WITH MENTAL TESTS. 1917. 89 pp.

Number 23. Peaks, Archibald G. PERIODIC VARIATIONS IN EFFICIENCY AS SHOWN IN MENTAL AND PHYSICAL TESTS TOGETHER WITH SOME WEATHER EFFECTS. 1921. 95 pp.

Number 24. Downey, June E. GRAPHOLOGY AND THE PSYCHOLOGY OF HANDWRITING. 1919. 142 pp.

Number 25. Pyle, William Henry. NATURE AND DEVELOPMENT OF LEARNING CAPACITY. 1925. 122 pp.

Number 26. Laycock, Sam R. ADAPTABILITY TO NEW SITUATIONS. 1929. 170 pp.

Number 27. Edgerton, Harold Asahel. ACADEMIC PROGNOSIS IN THE UNIVERSITY. 1930. 83 pp.

Number 28. Filter, Raymond O., and Omar C. Held. THE GROWTH OF ABILITY. 1930. 174 pp.

Number 29. Overman, James Robert. AN EXPERIMENTAL STUDY OF CERTAIN FACTORS AFFECTING TRANSFER OF TRAINING IN ARITHMETIC. 1931. 235 pp.

Number 30. Hissong, Clyde. THE ACTIVITY MOVEMENT. 1932. 122 pp.

Unnumbered. Thompson, Mary Elizabeth. PSYCHOLOGY AND PEDAGOGY OF WRITING. A RESUMÉ OF THE RESEARCHES AND EXPERIMENTS BEARING ON THE HISTORY AND PEDAGOGY OF WRITING. 1911. 128 pp.

271. *Journal of Educational Psychology; Including Experimental Pedagogy, Child Physiology and Hygiene, and Educational Statistics.*

TITLE VARIATIONS: Continued by *Journal of Educational Psychology; Devoted Primarily to the Scientific Study of Problems of Learning and Teaching* with Volume 12, 1921.

DATES OF PUBLICATION: Volume 1–11, 1910–1920.

FREQUENCY: **Monthly** (except July and August), Volume 1–9, 1910–1918. **Monthly** (except June-August), Volume 10–11, 1919–1920.

NUMBERING VARIATIONS: Volume 10 includes double number, Number 5/6, 1919.

PUBLISHER: **Baltimore:** Warwick and York, Inc., 1910–1920.

PRIMARY EDITORS: **William Chandler Bagley,** 1910–1920; **Carl E. Seashore,** 1910–1920; **James Carleton Bell,** 1910–1920; **Guy Montrose Whipple,** 1910–1920.

272. *Leipzig. Institut für experimentelle Pädagogik und Psychologie des Leipziger Lehrervereins. Veröffentlichungen. Pädagogisch-psychologische Arbeiten.*

TITLE VARIATIONS: Continued by [*Leipzig.*] *Institut des Leipziger Lehrervereins. Pädagogisch-psychologische Arbeiten* with Volume 10, 1920.

DATES OF PUBLICATION: Band 1–9, 1910–1921.

FREQUENCY: **Annual,** Band 1–7, 1910–1916. **Irregular,** Band 8–9, 1918–1921.

NUMBERING VARIATIONS: Band 9 issued 1921. Band 10 issued 1920.

PUBLISHER: **Leipzig:** Alfred Hahns Verlag, 1910–1916. **Leipzig:** Verlag der Dürr'schen Buchhandlung, 1918–1921.

PRIMARY EDITOR: **Max Brahn,** 1910–1921.

273. *Psikhoterapiia. Obozrenie voprosov' psikhicheskago lecheniia i prikladnoi psikhologii.*

TITLE VARIATIONS: None.

DATES OF PUBLICATION: Tom 1–5, 1910–1914.

FREQUENCY: Bimonthly.

NUMBERING VARIATIONS: Multinumber issues present.

PUBLISHER: **Moscow:** Tipografiia shtaba moskovskago voennago okruga, 1910–1914.

PRIMARY EDITOR: **N. A. Vyrubov,** 1910–1914.

EDITORIAL BOARD: M. M. Asatian, 1910–1914; A. N. Bernshtein, 1910–1914; I. V. Kannabikh, 1910–1914; N. E. Osipov, 1910–1914; O. B. Fel'tsman, 1911–1914; V. N. Likhnitski, 1912–1914; Ch. Strasser, 1913–1914; A. Adler,

1913–1914; E. Wexberg, 1913–1914; O. Kaus, 1913–1914; —— Stein, 1913–1914; W. Stekel, 1913–1914; —— Frischauf, 1913–1914; F. M. Aznaurov', 1913–1914; I. A. Birshtein', 1913–1914; O. Hinrichsen, 1913; R. Assagioli, 1913–1914; Vera Eppelbaum, 1913–1914.

274. *Psycho-medical Society. Transactions.*

TITLE VARIATIONS: Continues *Medical Society for the Study of Suggestive Therapeutics. Transactions.*

DATES OF PUBLICATION: Volume 2–4, Part 2, January 1910–August 1913.

FREQUENCY: Irregular. *See* Contents *below.*

NUMBERING VARIATIONS: None.

PUBLISHER: **London:** Rebman Ltd., 1910. **Cockermouth:** Brash Bros., Ltd., 1911–1913.

PRIMARY EDITORS: None listed.

CONTENTS:
 Volume 2, Part 1. Renterghem, A. W. van. THE REHABILITATION OF THE FAMILY PHYSICIAN. January 1910.
 ——, **Part 2.** Cooper, Astley. THE ALCOHOL AND DRUG HABITS, THEIR TREATMENT BY PSYCHOTHERAPY AND OTHER MEANS. 1911.
 ——, **Part 3.** Mitchell, T. W. THE HYPNOIDAL STATE OF SIDIS. 1911.
 ——, **Part 4.** Wright, M. B. THE PSYCHICAL ASPECT OF NEURASTHENIA. 1911.
 Volume 3, Part 1. Bryan, Douglas. THE DEFINITIONS OF SUGGESTION, HYPNOSIS AND THE WAKING STATE. 1911.
 ——, **Part 2.** Hyslop, Theo. B. PSYCHOTHERAPY IN ITS RELATIONSHIP TO ALIENISM. 1912.
 ——, **Part 3.** Eder, M. D. FREUD'S THEORY OF DREAMS. 1912.
 ——, **Part 4.** Ferenczi, Sandor. THE PSYCHO-ANALYSIS OF SUGGESTION AND HYPNOSIS. 1912.
 Volume 4, Part 1. Ferenczi, S. A DISCUSSION ON THE PAPER "THE PSYCHO-ANALYSIS OF SUGGESTION AND HYPNOSIS." 1913.
 ——, **Part 2.** Jung, C. G. PSYCHO-ANALYSIS. August 1913.

275. *Psychological Monographs.*

TITLE VARIATIONS: Continues *Psychological Review. Monograph Supplements.* Continued by *Psychological Monographs: General and Applied* with Number 288, 1948.

DATES OF PUBLICATION: Number 52–287, November 1910–1947.

FREQUENCY: Irregular. *See* Contents *below.*

NUMBERING VARIATIONS: Number 69 (Volume 16, Number 3) incorrectly numbered Volume 17, Number 3; Number 98 incorrectly numbered 89. Issues also numbered in Volume 12–61. *See* Contents *below.* Various issues also numbered in the following series and subseries: *Yale University. Psychological Stud-*

275. *(Continued)*

ies; or *Wellesley College. Studies in Psychology;* or *Kansas. University. Studies in Psychology;* or *Catholic University of America. Psychological Studies;* or *Studies in the Psychology of the Deaf;* or *Iowa. University. Studies in Psychology;* and (as subseries of *Iowa. University. Studies in Psychology*) *Studies in the Psychology of Art;* or *Studies in Clinical Psychology;* or *Studies in General Psychology;* or *Studies in Psychology of Reading. See* Contents *below.*

PUBLISHER: **Lancaster, Pennsylvania** and **Baltimore:** Review Publishing Company, 1910–1911. **Princeton, New Jersey, Baltimore,** and **Lancaster:** Psychological Review Company, 1911–1912. **Princeton** and **Lancaster:** Psychological Review Company, 1912–1922. **Princeton:** Psychological Review Company, 1922–1925. **Princeton** and **Albany, New York:** Psychological Review Company, 1925. **Princeton** and **Albany:** Psychological Review Company for the American Psychological Association, 1925–1936. **Princeton:** Psychological Review Company for the American Psychological Association, 1937. **Columbus, Ohio:** Psychological Review Company [at] Ohio State University for the American Psychological Association, 1937–1938. **Columbus:** American Psychological Association [at] Ohio State University, 1938. Columbus: American Psychological Association [at] Publications Office, Ohio State University, 1939–1940. **Evanston, Illinois:** American Psychological Association, Inc. [at] Publications Office, Northwestern University, 1940–1945. **Washington, D.C.:** American Psychological Association, Inc. [at] Publications Office, 1945–1947.

PRIMARY EDITORS: **James Rowland Angell,** 1910–1925; **Shepherd Ivory Franz,** 1925–1927; **Raymond Dodge,** 1928–1931; **Herbert S. Langfeld,** 1931–1934; **Joseph Peterson,** 1934–1935; **John F. Dashiell,** 1936–1947.

CONTENTS:

[Volume 12] **Number 52.** Shepherd, William T. SOME MENTAL PROCESSES OF THE RHESUS MONKEY. November 1910. 61 pp.

[Volume 13] **Number 53.** Angell, James R. (Chairman), Charles Hubbard Judd, Walter B. Pillsbury, Carl E. Seashore, and Robert S. Woodworth. REPORT OF THE COMMITTEE OF THE AMERICAN PSYCHOLOGICAL ASSOCIATION ON THE STANDARDIZING OF PROCEDURE IN EXPERIMENTAL TESTS. December 1910. 108 pp.

[————] **Number 54.** Healy, William, and Grace Maxwell Fernald. TESTS FOR PRACTICAL MENTAL CLASSIFICATION. March 1911. 54 pp.

[————] **Number 55.** McComas, H. C., Jr. SOME TYPES OF ATTENTION. May 1911. 55 pp.

[————] **Number 56.** Franz, Shepherd Ivory, with the cooperation of Gonzalo R. Lafora. ON THE FUNCTIONS OF THE CEREBRUM: THE OCCIPITAL LOBES. September 1911. 118 pp.

[————] **Number 57.** Woodworth, R. S., and Frederic Lyman Wells. ASSOCIATION TESTS. BEING A PART OF THE REPORT OF THE COMMITTEE OF THE AMERICAN PSYCHOLOGICAL ASSOCIATION ON THE STANDARDIZATION OF PROCEDURE IN EXPERIMENTAL TESTS. December 1911. 85 pp.

[Volume 14] **Number 58.** Fernald, Mabel Ruth. THE DIAGNOSIS OF MENTAL IMAGERY. February 1912. 169 pp.

[————] **Number 59.** Adams, Henry Foster. AUTOKINETIC SENSATIONS. July 1912. 45 pp.

[————] **Number 60.** Hayes, Mary Holmes Stevens. A STUDY OF CUTANEOUS AFTER-SENSATIONS. September 1912. 89 pp.

[————] **Number 61.** Fernberger, Samuel W. ON THE RELATION OF THE METHODS OF JUST PERCEPTIBLE DIFFERENCES AND CONSTANT STIMULI. January 1913. 81 pp.

[Volume 15] Number 62. Rand, Gertrude. THE FACTORS THAT INFLUENCE THE SENSITIVITY OF THE RETINA TO COLOR: A QUANTITATIVE STUDY AND METHODS OF STANDARDIZING. March 1913. 166 pp.

[————] **Number 63.** Boring, Edwin G. LEARNING IN DEMENTIA PRECOX. Introduction by Shepherd Ivory Franz. June 1913. 101 pp.

[————] **Number 64.** Maxfield, Francis Norton. AN EXPERIMENT IN LINEAR SPACE PERCEPTION. July 1913. 56 pp.

[————] **Number 65.** Sylvester, Reuel Hull. THE FORM BOARD TEST. September 1913. 56 pp.

[————] **Number 66.** Wells, George R. THE INFLUENCE OF STIMULUS DURATION ON REACTION TIME. November 1913. 69 pp.

[Volume 16] Number 67. Rahn, Carl. THE RELATION OF SENSATION TO OTHER CATEGORIES IN CONTEMPORARY PSYCHOLOGY. A STUDY IN THE PSYCHOLOGY OF THINKING. December 1913. 131 pp.

[————] **Number 68.** Abbott, Edwina. THE EFFECT OF ADAPTATION ON THE TEMPERATURE DIFFERENCE LIMEN. March 1914. 36 pp.

[————] **Number 69.** Seashore, Carl E., ed. UNIVERSITY OF IOWA STUDIES IN PSYCHOLOGY, No. VI. June 1914. 177 pp.

[————] **Number 70.** Perrin, Fleming Allen Clay. AN EXPERIMENTAL AND INTROSPECTIVE STUDY OF THE HUMAN LEARNING PROCESS IN THE MAZE. July 1914. 97 pp.

[————] **Number 71.** Langfeld, Herbert Sidney. ON THE PSYCHOPHYSIOLOGY OF A PROLONGED FAST. July 1914. 62 pp.

[Volume 17] Number 72. Bridges, James Winfred. AN EXPERIMENTAL STUDY OF DECISION TYPES AND THEIR MENTAL CORRELATES. August 1914. 72 pp.

[————] **Number 73.** Moore, Henry Thomas. THE GENETIC ASPECT OF CONSONANCE AND DISSONANCE. September 1914. 68 pp.

[————] **Number 74.** Mitchell, David. THE INFLUENCE OF DISTRACTIONS ON THE FORMATION OF JUDGMENTS IN LIFTED WEIGHT EXPERIMENTS. October 1914. 58 pp.

[————] **Number 75.** Angier, Roswell P., ed. YALE PSYCHOLOGICAL STUDIES. New Series, Vol. II, No. I. December 1914. 155 pp.

[Volume 18] Number 76. Woodrow, Herbert. THE MEASUREMENT OF ATTENTION. December 1914. 158 pp.

[————] **Number 77.** Woolley, Helen Thompson, and Charlotte Rust Fischer. MENTAL AND PHYSICAL MEASUREMENTS OF WORKING CHILDREN. December 1914. 247 pp.

[————] **Number 78.** Feingold, Gustav A. RECOGNITION AND DISCRIMINATION. February 1915. 128 pp.

[————] **Number 79.** Kellogg, Chester Elijah. ALTERNATION AND INTERFERENCE OF FEELINGS. February 1915. 94 pp.

[————] **Number 80.** Crane, Harry W. A STUDY IN ASSOCIATION REAC-

275. *(Continued)*

TION AND REACTION TIME. WITH AN ATTEMPTED APPLICATION OF RESULTS IN DETERMINING THE PRESENCE OF GUILTY KNOWLEDGE. March 1915. 73 pp.

[Volume 19] Number 81. ON THE FUNCTIONS OF THE CEREBRUM: Franz, Shepherd Ivory. SYMPTOMATOLOGICAL DIFFERENCES ASSOCIATED WITH SIMILAR CEREBRAL LESIONS IN THE INSANE; and Franz, Shepherd Ivory, with the assistance of J. Duerson Scott. VARIATIONS IN DISTRIBUTION OF THE MOTOR CENTERS. April 1915. 162 pp.

[————] Number 82. Givler, Robert C. THE PSYCHOPHYSIOLOGICAL EFFECT OF THE ELEMENTS OF SPEECH IN RELATION TO POETRY. April 1915. 132 pp.

[————] Number 83. Schmitt, Clara. STANDARDIZATION OF TESTS FOR DEFECTIVE CHILDREN. July 1915. 181 pp.

[————] Number 84. DeCamp, J. Edgar. A STUDY OF RETROACTIVE INHIBITION. August 1915. 69 pp.

[Volume 20] Number 85. Hayes, Joseph Wanton. A HORIZONTAL–VERTICAL ILLUSION OF BRIGHTNESS IN FOVEAL VISION APPARENT IN ASTRONOMICAL OBSERVATIONS OF THE RELATIVE LUMINOSITY OF TWIN STARS. August 1915. 126 pp.

[————] Number 86. Owen, Roberts Bishop. RECOGNITION: A LOGICAL AND EXPERIMENTAL STUDY. October 1915. 154 pp.

[————] Number 87. Coover, John Edgar. FORMAL DISCIPLINE FROM THE STANDPOINT OF EXPERIMENTAL PSYCHOLOGY. January 1916. 307 pp.

[————] Number 88. Pintner, Rudolph, and Donald G. Paterson. LEARNING TESTS WITH DEAF CHILDREN. January 1916. 58 pp.

[Volume 21] Number 89. Haines, Thomas H. MENTAL MEASUREMENTS OF THE BLIND. A PROVISIONAL POINT SCALE AND DATA FOR A YEAR SCALE. April 1916. 86 pp.

[————] Number 90. Fisher, Sara Carolyn. THE PROCESS OF GENERALIZING ABSTRACTION; AND ITS PRODUCT, THE GENERAL CONCEPT. April 1916. 213 pp.

[————] Number 91. Batson, William Howard. ACQUISITION OF SKILL. July 1916. 92 pp.

[————] Number 92. Bentley, Madison, ed. STUDIES IN SOCIAL AND GENERAL PSYCHOLOGY FROM THE UNIVERSITY OF ILLINOIS. June 1916. 115 pp.

[Volume 22] Number 93. Barnes, Jasper Converse. VOLUNTARY ISOLATION OF CONTROL IN A NATURAL MUSCLE GROUP. August 1916. 50 pp.

[————] Number 94. Wallin, J. E. Wallace. PSYCHO-MOTOR NORMS FOR PRACTICAL DIAGNOSIS–A STUDY OF THE SEGUIN FROM BOARD, BASED ON THE RECORDS OF 4072 NORMAL AND ABNORMAL BOYS AND GIRLS, WITH YEARLY AND HALF-YEARLY NORMS. August 1916. 102 pp.

[————] Number 95. Weiss, A. P. APPARATUS AND EXPERIMENTS ON SOUND INTENSITY. October 1916. 59 pp.

[————] Number 96. Gamble, Eleanor A. McC., ed. WELLESLEY COLLEGE STUDIES IN PSYCHOLOGY. No. 2. October 1916. 192 pp.

[————] Number 97. Woodrow, Herbert, and Frances Lowell. CHILDREN'S ASSOCIATION FREQUENCY TABLES. 1916. 110 pp.

[Volume 23] Number 98. Kitson, Harry Dexter. THE SCIENTIFIC STUDY OF THE COLLEGE STUDENT. 1917. 81 pp.

[———] **Number 99.** Pechstein, Louis Augustus. WHOLE VS. PART METHODS IN MOTOR LEARNING. A COMPARATIVE STUDY. 1917. 80 pp.

[———] **Number 100.** Angier, Roswell P., ed. YALE PSYCHOLOGICAL STUDIES. NEW SERIES, VOLUME II, NO. 2. (1917). Pp. 159–331.

[———] **Number 101.** Ritter, Sarah Margaret. THE VERTICAL–HORIZONTAL ILLUSION. AN EXPERIMENTAL STUDY OF MERIDIONAL DISPARATIES IN THE VISUAL FIELD. 1917. 114 pp.

[Volume 24] **Number 102.** Brigham, Carl C. TWO STUDIES IN MENTAL TESTS. I. VARIABLE FACTORS IN THE BINET TESTS. II. THE DIAGNOSTIC VALUE OF SOME MENTAL TESTS. 1917. 254 pp.

[———] **Number 103.** Ferree, C. E., and Gertrude Rand. RADIOMETRIC APPARATUS FOR USE IN PSYCHOLOGICAL AND PHYSIOLOGICAL OPTICS. INCLUDING A DISCUSSION OF THE VARIOUS TYPES OF INSTRUMENTS THAT HAVE BEEN USED FOR MEASURING LIGHT INTENSITIES. (1917). 65 pp.

[———] **Number 104.** Webb, Louie Winfield. TRANSFER OF TRAINING AND RETROACTION. A COMPARATIVE STUDY. 1917. 90 pp.

[———] **Number 105.** Ruml, Beardsley. THE RELIABILITY OF MENTAL TESTS IN THE DIVISION OF AN ACADEMIC GROUP. 1917. 63 pp.

[———] **Number 106.** Rosenow, Curt. THE ANALYSIS OF MENTAL FUNCTIONS. (1917). 43 pp.

[Volume 25] **Number 107.** Tolman, Edward Chace. RETROACTIVE INHIBITION AS AFFECTED BY CONDITIONS OF LEARNING. (1917.) 50 pp.

[———] **Number 108.** Seashore, Carl E., ed. UNIVERSITY OF IOWA STUDIES IN PSYCHOLOGY, No. VII. 1918. 163 pp.

[———] **Number 109.** Rosanoff, A. J., Helen E. Martin and Isabel R. Rosanoff. A HIGHER SCALE OF MENTAL MEASUREMENT AND ITS APPLICATION TO CASES OF INSANITY. 1918. 113 pp.

[———] **Number 110.** Fukuya, Shoan Masuzo. AN EXPERIMENTAL STUDY OF ATTENTION FROM THE STANDPOINT OF MENTAL EFFICIENCY: A CONTRIBUTION TO EDUCATIONAL AND SOCIAL PROBLEMS. 1918. 42 pp.

[———] **Number 111.** Roback, Abraham A. THE INTERFERENCE OF WILL-IMPULSES. WITH APPLICATIONS TO PEDAGOGY, ETHICS AND PRACTICAL EFFICIENCY. 1918. 158 pp.

[Volume 26] **Number 112.** Dearborn, George Van Ness. THE PSYCHOLOGY OF CLOTHING. (1918.) 72 pp.

[———] **Number 113.** Shaw, Esther E. SOME IMAGINAL FACTORS INFLUENCING VERBAL EXPRESSION. A PRELIMINARY STUDY. 1918. 137 pp.

[———] **Number 114.** Thurstone, L. L. THE LEARNING CURVE EQUATION. 1919. 51 pp.

[———] **Number 115.** Arlitt, Ada Hart. THE EFFECT OF ALCOHOL ON THE INTELLIGENT BEHAVIOR OF THE WHITE RAT AND ITS PROGENY. 1919. 50 pp.

[———] **Number 116.** Kjerstad, Conrad L. THE FORM OF THE LEARNING CURVES FOR MEMORY. 1919. 89 pp.

[———] **Number 117.** Fernberger, Samuel W. AN INTROSPECTIVE ANALYSIS OF THE PROCESS OF COMPARING. 1919. 161 pp.

[Volume 27] **Number 118.** Hamel, Ignatius A. A STUDY AND ANALYSIS OF THE CONDITIONED REFLEX. 1919. 65 pp. (Also as *Catholic University of America. Psychological Studies*, Number 2.)

275. *(Continued)*

[————] **Number 119.** Moore, Thomas Verner. IMAGE AND MEANING IN MEMORY AND PERCEPTION. 1919. Pp. 67–296. (Also as *Catholic University of America. Psychological Studies,* Number 3.)

[————] **Number 120.** Moore, Thomas Verner. THE CORRELATION BETWEEN MEMORY AND PERCEPTION IN THE PRESENCE OF DIFFUSE CORTICAL DEGENERATION. 1919. Pp. 297–345. (Also as *Catholic University of America. Psychological Studies,* Number 4.)

[————] **Number 121.** CLINICAL AND PSYCHOANALYTIC STUDIES: Furfey, Paul Hanly. CONSCIOUS AND UNCONSCIOUS FACTORS IN SYMBOLISM; Moore, Thomas Verner. HYPNOTIC ANALOGIES; and Loughran, Miriam E. CONCOMITANTS OF AMENTIA. 1919. Pp. 347–440. (Also as *Catholic University of America. Psychological Studies.* Number 5.)

[————] **Number 122.** McDonough, Agnes R. THE DEVELOPMENT OF MEANING. 1919. Pp. 441–515. (Also as *Catholic University of America. Psychological Studies,* Number 6.)

[Volume 28] **Number 123.** Hull, Clark L. QUANTITATIVE ASPECTS OF THE EVOLUTION OF CONCEPTS. AN EXPERIMENTAL STUDY. 1920. 86 pp.

[————] **Number 124.** Snoddy, George S. AN EXPERIMENTAL ANALYSIS OF A CASE OF TRIAL AND ERROR LEARNING IN THE HUMAN SUBJECT. 1920. 78 pp.

[————] **Number 125.** Arps, George F. WORK WITH KNOWLEDGE OF RESULTS VERSUS WORK WITHOUT KNOWLEDGE OF RESULTS. AWARENESS AND PARTIAL AWARENESS AS FACTORS CONDITIONING EFFICIENCY. 1920. 41 pp.

[————] **Number 126.** Gatewood, Esther L. INDIVIDUAL DIFFERENCES IN FINGER REACTIONS. 1920. 43 pp.

[————] **Number 127.** Bills, Marion A. THE LAG OF VISUAL SENSATION IN ITS RELATION TO WAVE LENGTHS AND INTENSITY OF LIGHT. 1920. 101 pp.

[————] **Number 128.** Robinson, Edward Stevens. SOME FACTORS DETERMINING THE DEGREE OF RETROACTIVE INHIBITION. 1920. 57 pp.

[————] **Number 129.** Peterson, John C. THE HIGHER MENTAL PROCESSES IN LEARNING. 1920. 121 pp.

[Volume 29] **Number 130.** Crosland, Harold R. A QUALITATIVE ANALYSIS OF THE PROCESS OF FORGETTING. 1921. 159 pp.

[————] **Number 131.** Doll, Edgar A. THE GROWTH OF INTELLIGENCE. 1920. 130 pp.

[————] **Number 132.** Reamer, Jeanette Chase. MENTAL AND EDUCATIONAL MEASUREMENTS OF THE DEAF. 1921. 130 pp.

[————] **Number 133.** Root, William T. A SOCIO-PSYCHOLOGICAL STUDY OF FIFTY-THREE SUPERNORMAL CHILDREN. 1921. 134 pp.

[Volume 30] **Number 134.** Means, Mari Hackl. A TENTATIVE STANDARDIZATION OF A HARD OPPOSITES TEST. 1921. 65 pp.

[————] **Number 135.** Yarbrough, Joseph U. THE INFLUENCE OF THE TIME INTERVAL UPON THE RATE OF LEARNING IN THE WHITE RAT. 1921. 52 pp.

[————] **Number 136.** Bentley, Madison, ed. CRITICAL AND EXPERIMENTAL STUDIES IN PSYCHOLOGY FROM THE UNIVERSITY OF ILLINOIS. 1921. 94 pp.

[————] **Number 137.** Stockton, J. Leroy. THE DEFINITION OF INTELLI-

GENCE IN RELATION TO MODERN METHODS OF MENTAL MEASUREMENT. 1921. 118 pp.

[————] **Number 138.** Moore, Bruce V. PERSONNEL SELECTION OF GRADUATE ENGINEERS. THE DIFFERENTIATION OF APPRENTICE ENGINEERS FOR TRAINING AS SALESMEN, DESIGNERS, AND EXECUTIVES OF PRODUCTION. 1921. 85 pp.

[————] **Number 139.** Haught, B. F. THE INTERRELATION OF SOME HIGHER LEARNING PROCESSES. 1921. 71 pp.

[Volume 31] **Number 140.** Seashore, Carl E., ed. UNIVERSITY OF IOWA STUDIES IN PSYCHOLOGY, No. VIII. 1922. 382 pp.

[————] **Number 141.** Moore, Thomas Verner. PERCY BYSSHE SHELLEY. AN INTRODUCTION TO THE STUDY OF CHARACTER. 1922. 62 pp. (Also as *Catholic University of America. Psychological Studies*, Number 7, incorrectly numbered 6.)

[————] **Number 142.** Luh, C. W. THE CONDITIONS OF RETENTION. 1922. 87 pp.

[Volume 32] **Number 143.** Liljencrants, Johan. MEMORY DEFECTS IN THE ORGANIC PSYCHOSES. AN EXPERIMENTAL STUDY. 1922. 77 pp.

[————] **Number 144.** McGrath, Marie Cecelia. A STUDY OF THE MORAL DEVELOPMENT OF CHILDREN. 1923. 190 pp. (Also as *Catholic University of America. Psychological Studies*, Number 8, incorrectly numbered 7.)

[————] **Number 145.** Stetson, Raymond Herbert, ed. STUDIES FROM THE PSYCHOLOGICAL LABORATORY OF OBERLIN COLLEGE. 1923. 58 pp.

[————] **Number 146.** Wooster, Margaret. CERTAIN FACTORS IN THE DEVELOPMENT OF A NEW SPATIAL CO-ORDINATION. 1923. 96 pp.

[————] **Number 147.** Koch, Helen Lois. THE INFLUENCE OF MECHANICAL GUIDANCE UPON MAZE LEARNING. 1923. 113 pp.

[Volume 33] **Number 148.** Ludgate, Katherine Eva. THE EFFECT OF MANUAL GUIDANCE UPON MAZE LEARNING. 1923. 65 pp.

[————] **Number 149.** Stinchfield, Sarah Mae. THE FORMULATION AND STANDARDIZATION OF A SERIES OF GRADED SPEECH TESTS. 1923. 54 pp.

[————] **Number 150.** Hull, Clark L. THE INFLUENCE OF TOBACCO SMOKING ON MENTAL AND MOTOR EFFICIENCY. AN EXPERIMENTAL INVESTIGATION. 1924. 161 pp.

[————] **Number 151.** Freyd, Max. THE PERSONALITIES OF THE SOCIALLY AND THE MECHANICALLY INCLINED. A STUDY OF THE DIFFERENCES IN PERSONALITY BETWEEN MEN WHOSE PRIMARY INTEREST IS SOCIAL AND MEN WHOSE PRIMARY INTEREST IS IN MACHINES. 1924. 101 pp.

[————] **Number 152.** Merriman, Curtis. THE INTELLECTUAL RESEMBLANCE OF TWINS. 1924. 58 pp.

[————] **Number 153.** Kingsbury, Forest Alva. A GROUP INTELLIGENCE SCALE FOR PRIMARY GRADES. 1924. 60 pp.

[Volume 34] **Number 154.** Wang, Tsu Lien. THE INFLUENCE OF TUITION IN THE ACQUISITION OF SKILL. 1925. 51 pp.

[————] **Number 155.** Burnett, Charles T. SPLITTING THE MIND: AN EXPERIMENTAL STUDY OF NORMAL MEN. 1925. 132 pp.

[————] **Number 156.** Highsmith, J. A. RELATION OF THE RATE OF RESPONSE TO INTELLIGENCE. 1924. 33 pp.

275. *(Continued)*

[———] **Number 157.** Lee, Ang Lanfen. An Experimental Study of Retention and Its Relation to Intelligence. 1925. 45 pp.

[———] **Number 158.** Monroe, Margaret M. The Energy Value of the Minimum Visible Chromatic and Achromatic for Different Wave-Lengths of the Spectrum. 1924. 60 pp.

[———] **Number 159.** Raubenheimer, Albert Sydney. An Experimental Study of Some Behavior Traits of the Potentially Delinquent Boy. 1923. 107 pp.

[———] **Number 160.** Ruch, Giles Murrel. The Influence of the Factor of Intelligence on the Form of the Learning Curve. 1925. 64 pp.

[———] **Number 161.** Skaggs, Ernest Burton. Further Studies in Retroactive Inhibition. 1925. 60 pp.

[Volume 35] **Number 162.** Ortmann, Otto. On the Melodic Relativity of Tones. 1926. 47 pp.

[———] **Number 163.** Bentley, Madison, ed. Studies in Psychology from the University of Illinois. 1926. 151 pp.

[———] **Number 164.** Barton, J. W. Comprehensive Units in Learning Typewriting. (1926). 47 pp.

[———] **Number 165.** Amen, Elisabeth Wheeler. An Experimental Study of the Self in Psychology. (1926). 72 pp.

[———] **Number 166.** Koch, Helen Lois, and Rietta Simmons. A Study of the Test-Performance of American, Mexican, and Negro Children. (1926). 116 pp.

[Volume 36] **Number 167.** Seashore, Carl E., ed. University of Iowa Studies in Psychology, No. IX. 1926. 264 pp.

[———] **Number 168.** Seashore, Carl E., ed. University of Iowa Studies in Psychology, No. X. 1926. 114 pp.

[———] **Number 169.** Sullivan, Ellen B. Attitude in Relation to Learning. 1927. 149 pp.

[Volume 37] **Number 170.** Dillingham, Louise Bulkley. The Creative Imagination of Théophile Gautier: A Study in Literary Psychology. 1927. 355 pp.

[———] **Number 171.** Kenneth, J. H. An Experimental Study of Affects and Associations Due to Certain Odors. 1927. 64 pp.

[———] **Number 172.** Griffitts, Charles H. Individual Differences in Imagery. 1927. 91 pp.

[Volume 38] **Number 173.** Sloan, Louise L. The Effect of Intensity of Light, State of Adaptation of the Eye, and Size of Photometric Field on the Visibility Curve: A Study of the Purkinje Phenomenon. 1928. 87 pp.

[———] **Number 174.** Almack, Mary Ruth. A Quantitative Study of Chromatic Adaptation. 1928. 118 pp.

[———] **Number 175.** Travis, Roland C. and Raymond Dodge. Experi-

MENTAL ANALYSIS OF THE SENSORI-MOTOR CONSEQUENCES OF PASSIVE OSCIL-
LATION, ROTARY AND RECTILINEAR. 1928. 96 pp.

[————] **Number 176.** Ruckmick, Christian A., ed. UNIVERSITY OF IOWA
STUDIES IN PSYCHOLOGY, No. XI. 1928. 231 pp.

[Volume 39] Number 177. Cameron, Norman. CEREBRAL DESTRUCTION
IN ITS RELATION TO MAZE LEARNING. 1928. 68 pp.

[————] **Number 178.** Miles, Walter R., and Daniel Starch, eds. UNI-
VERSITY OF IOWA STUDIES IN PSYCHOLOGY, No. XII (Seashore Commemorative
Number.) 1928. 223 pp.

[————] **Number 179.** Griffith, Helen. TIME PATTERNS IN PROSE: A
STUDY IN PROSE RHYTHM BASED UPON VOICE RECORDS. 1929. 82 pp.

[————] **Number 180.** Wylie, Margaret. AN EXPERIMENTAL STUDY OF
RECOGNITION AND RECALL IN ABNORMAL MENTAL CASES. 1930. 81 pp.

[Volume 40] Number 181. Ruckmick, Christian A., ed. UNIVERSITY OF
IOWA STUDIES IN PSYCHOLOGY, No. XIII. 1930. 214 pp.

[————] **Number 182.** Cason, Hulsey. COMMON ANNOYANCES: A
PSYCHOLOGICAL STUDY OF EVERY-DAY AVERSIONS AND IRRITATIONS. 1930.
218 pp.

[————] **Number 183.** Wentworth, Hazel Austin. A QUANTITATIVE STUDY
OF ACHROMATIC AND CHROMATIC SENSITIVITY FROM CENTER TO PERIPHERY OF
THE VISUAL FIELD. 1930. 189 pp.

[Volume 41] Number 184. Hilgard, Ernest R. CONDITIONED EYELID RE-
ACTIONS TO A LIGHT STIMULUS BASED ON THE REFLEX WINK TO SOUND. 1931.
50 pp.

[————] **Number 185.** Reed, Homer B. THE INFLUENCE OF TRAINING ON
CHANGES IN VARIABILITY IN ACHIEVEMENT. 1931. 59 pp.

[————] **Number 186.** Kanner, Leo. JUDGING EMOTIONS FROM FACIAL
EXPRESSIONS. 1931. 91 pp.

[————] **Number 187.** Ruckmick, Christian A., ed. UNIVERSITY OF IOWA
STUDIES IN PSYCHOLOGY, No. XIV. 1931. 330 pp.

[Volume 42] Number 188. Peak, Helen. MODIFICATION OF THE LID-
REFLEX BY VOLUNTARILY INDUCED SETS. 1931. 68 pp.

[————] **Number 189.** Lumley, Frederick Hillis. AN INVESTIGATION OF
THE RESPONSES MADE IN LEARNING A MULTIPLE CHOICE MAZE. 1931. 61 pp.

[————] **Number 190.** Mibai, Sugi. AN EXPERIMENTAL STUDY OF APPAR-
ENT MOVEMENT. 1931. 91 pp.

[————] **Number 191.** Smoke, Kenneth L. AN OBJECTIVE STUDY OF CON-
CEPT FORMATION. 1932. 46 pp.

[————] **Number 192.** Cantril, Hadley. GENERAL AND SPECIFIC ATTI-
TUDES. 1932. 109 pp.

[————] **Number 193.** Petran, Laurence A. AN EXPERIMENTAL STUDY OF
PITCH RECOGNITION. 1932. 124 pp.

[Volume 43] Number 194. Ruckmick, Christian A., ed. with the cooperation of Lee Edward Travis. UNIVERSITY OF IOWA STUDIES IN PSYCHOLOGY, No.
XV. 1932. 303 pp.

275. *(Continued)*

[————] **Number 195.** Schanck, Richard Louis. A STUDY OF A COMMUNITY AND ITS GROUPS AND INSTITUTIONS CONCEIVED OF AS BEHAVIORS OF INDIVIDUALS. 1932. 133 pp.

[————] **Number 196.** Gilbert, Luther C. AN EXPERIMENTAL INVESTIGATION OF EYE MOVEMENTS IN LEARNING TO SPELL WORDS. 1932. 81 pp.

[Volume 44] Number 197. Wheeler, Raymond Holder, ed. UNIVERSITY OF KANSAS STUDIES IN PSYCHOLOGY, No. 1. 1933. 300 pp.

[————] **Number 198.** Ruckmick, Christian A., ed. UNIVERSITY OF IOWA STUDIES IN PSYCHOLOGY, No. XVI: STUDIES IN CLINICAL PSYCHOLOGY UNDER THE DIRECTION OF LEE EDWARD TRAVIS. 1933. 86 pp.

[————] **Number 199.** Ruckmick, Christian A., ed. UNIVERSITY OF IOWA STUDIES IN PSYCHOLOGY, No. XVII: STUDIES IN EXPERIMENTAL AND THEORETICAL PSYCHOLOGY. 1933. 121 pp.

[Volume 45] Number 200. Ruckmick, Christian A., ed. UNIVERSITY OF IOWA STUDIES IN PSYCHOLOGY, No. XVIII: STUDIES IN THE PSYCHOLOGY OF ART, [Volume I,] under the Direction of Norman C. Meier. 1933. 188 pp.

[————] **Number 201.** Bugg, Eugene Gower. AN EXPERIMENTAL STUDY OF FACTORS INFLUENCING CONSONANCE JUDGMENTS. 1933. 100 pp.

[————] **Number 202.** Cook, T. M. BINOCULAR AND MONOCULAR RELATIONS IN FOVEAL DARK ADAPTATION. 1934. 86 pp.

[————] **Number 203.** Gengerelli, J. A. BRAIN FIELDS AND THE LEARNING PROCESS. 1934. 115 pp.

[————] **Number 204.** Anastasi, Anne. PRACTICE AND VARIABILITY: A STUDY IN PSYCHOLOGICAL METHOD. 1934. 55 pp.

[Volume 46] Number 205. Lepley, William M. SERIAL REACTIONS CONSIDERED AS CONDITIONED REACTIONS. 1934. 56 pp.

[————] **Number 206.** Fritz, Martin F. A CLASSIFIED BIBLIOGRAPHY ON PSYCHODIETETICS. 1934. 53 pp.

[————] **Number 207.** Varon, Edith J. THE DEVELOPMENT OF ALFRED BINET'S PSYCHOLOGY. 1935. 129 pp.

[————] **Number 208.** Krout, Maurice H. AUTISTIC GESTURES: AN EXPERIMENTAL STUDY IN SYMBOLIC MOVEMENT. 1935. 126 pp.

[————] **Number 209.** Cason, Hulsey. THE NIGHTMARE DREAM. 1935. 51 pp.

[————] **Number 210.** Gibson, James J., ed. STUDIES IN PSYCHOLOGY FROM SMITH COLLEGE. 1935. 98 pp.

[Volume 47] Number 211. Allport, Gordon W., and Henry S. Odbert. TRAIT-NAMES: A PSYCHO-LEXICAL STUDY. 1936. 171 pp.

[————] **Number 212.** Miles, Walter R., ed. PSYCHOLOGICAL STUDIES OF HUMAN VARIABILITY (DODGE COMMEMORATIVE NUMBER). 1936. 415 pp.

[Volume 48] Number 213. Meier, Norman C., ed. STUDIES IN THE PSYCHOLOGY OF ART, Volume II. UNIVERSITY OF IOWA STUDIES IN PSYCHOLOGY, No. XIX, Edited by Christian A. Ruckmick. 1936. 175 pp.

[————] **Number 214.** Ruckmick, Christian A., ed. STUDIES IN GENERAL PSYCHOLOGY, Volume II. UNIVERSITY OF IOWA STUDIES IN PSYCHOLOGY, No. XX. 1936. 76 pp.

[———] **Number 215.** Tiffin, Joseph, ed. STUDIES IN PSYCHOLOGY OF READING, Volume I. UNIVERSITY OF IOWA STUDIES IN PSYCHOLOGY, No. XXI, edited by Christian A. Ruckmick. 1937. 149 pp.

[———] **Number 216.** Rosanoff, Aaron J., Leva M. Handy, and Isabel Rosanoff Plesset. THE ETIOLOGY OF MENTAL DEFICIENCY WITH SPECIAL REFERENCE TO ITS OCCURRENCE IN TWINS: A CHAPTER IN THE GENETIC HISTORY OF HUMAN INTELLIGENCE. 1937. 137 pp.

[Volume 49] Number 217. Travis, Lee Edward, ed. STUDIES IN CLINICAL PSYCHOLOGY, Volume III. UNIVERSITY OF IOWA STUDIES IN PSYCHOLOGY, No. XXII. 1937. 250 pp.

[———] **Number 218.** Werner, Heinz. DYNAMICS IN BINOCULAR DEPTH PERCEPTION. 1937. 127 pp.

[———] **Number 219.** Kao, Dji-Lih. PLATEAUS AND THE CURVE OF LEARNING IN MOTOR SKILL. 1937. 94 pp.

[———] **Number 220.** Ward, Lewis B. REMINISCENCE AND ROTE LEARNING. 1937. 64 pp.

[Volume 50] Number 221. Cameron, Norman. REASONING, REGRESSION AND COMMUNICATION IN SCHIZOPHRENICS. 1938. 34 pp.

[———] **Number 222.** Karwoski, Theodore F., and Henry S. Odbert. COLOR-MUSIC. 1938. 60 pp.

[———] **Number 223.** Baker, Lynn E. THE PUPILLARY RESPONSE CONDITIONED TO SUBLIMINAL AUDITORY STIMULI. 1938. 32 pp.

[———] **Number 224.** Nelson, Erland. RADICALISM–CONSERVATISM IN STUDENT ATTITUDES. 1938. 32 pp.

[———] **Number 225.** Lanier, Lyle H., ed. PEABODY STUDIES IN PSYCHOLOGY. (PETERSON MEMORIAL NUMBER.) 1938. 237 pp.

[———] **Number 226.** Bean, Kenneth L. AN EXPERIMENTAL APPROACH TO THE READING OF MUSIC. 1938. 80 pp.

[Volume 51] Number 227. Wolf, Ralph Robinson, Jr. DIFFERENTIAL FORECASTS OF ACHIEVEMENT AND THEIR USE IN EDUCATIONAL COUNSELING. 1939. 53 pp.

[———] **Number 228.** Arrington, Ruth E. TIME-SAMPLING STUDIES OF CHILD BEHAVIOR. 1939. 279 pp.

[———] **Number 229.** Thornton, George R. A FACTOR ANALYSIS OF TESTS DESIGNED TO MEASURE PERSISTENCE. 1939. 42 pp.

[———] **Number 230.** Mitrano, Anthony J. PRINCIPLES OF CONDITIONING IN HUMAN GOAL BEHAVIOR. 1939. 70 pp.

[———] **Number 231.** Meier, Norman C., ed. STUDIES IN THE PSYCHOLOGY OF ART, Volume III. UNIVERSITY OF IOWA STUDIES IN PSYCHOLOGY, No. XXIII. 1939. 158 pp.

[Volume 52] Number 232. STUDIES IN THE PSYCHOLOGY OF THE DEAF, No. 1. By Psychological Division, Clarence W. Barron Research Department, Clarke School for the Deaf. 1940. 153 pp.

[———] **Number 233.** Mowrer, O. H. PREPARATORY SET (EXPECTANCY)— SOME METHODS OF MEASUREMENT. 1940. 43 pp.

[———] **Number 234.** Woodrow, Herbert, ed. STUDIES IN QUANTITATIVE PSYCHOLOGY FROM THE University of Illinois. 1940. 71 pp.

275. *(Continued)*

[————] **Number 235.** Martin, John Rogers. REMINISCENCE AND GESTALT THEORY. 1940. 37 pp.

[————] **Number 236.** Collier, R. M. AN EXPERIMENTAL STUDY OF THE EFFECTS OF SUBLIMINAL STIMULI. 1940. 59 pp.

[————] **Number 237.** Anastasi, Anne, and John P. Foley, Jr. A SURVEY OF THE LITERATURE ON ARTISTIC BEHAVIOR IN THE ABNORMAL: III. SPONTANEOUS PRODUCTIONS. 1940. 71 pp.

[Volume 53] **Number 238.** Youtz, Adella Clark. AN EXPERIMENTAL EVALUATION OF JOST'S LAWS. 1941. 54 pp.

[————] **Number 239.** Goldstein, Kurt, and Martin Scheerer. ABSTRACT AND CONCRETE BEHAVIOR. AN EXPERIMENTAL STUDY WITH SPECIAL TESTS. 1941. 151 pp.

[————] **Number 240.** Schmidt, Hermann O. THE EFFECTS OF PRAISE AND BLAME AS INCENTIVES TO LEARNING. 1940. 56 pp.

[————] **Number 241.** Coffin, Thomas E. SOME CONDITIONS OF SUGGESTION AND SUGGESTIBILITY; A STUDY OF CERTAIN ATTITUDINAL AND SITUATIONAL FACTORS INFLUENCING THE PROCESS OF SUGGESTION. 1941. 125 pp.

[————] **Number 242.** Heider, Fritz, and Grace Moore Heider. STUDIES IN THE PSYCHOLOGY OF THE DEAF, No. 2. 1941. 158 pp.

[Volume 54] **Number 243.** Bell, Hugh M. REST PAUSES IN MOTOR LEARNING AS RELATED TO SNODDY'S HYPOTHESIS OF MENTAL GROWTH. 1942. 38 pp.

[————] **Number 244.** Watson, K. Brantley. THE NATURE AND MEASUREMENT OF MUSICAL MEANINGS. 1942. 43 pp.

[————] **Number 245.** Thomas, Lawrence G. MENTAL TESTS AS INSTRUMENTS OF SCIENCE. 1942. 87 pp.

[————] **Number 246.** Kleemeier, Robert Watson. FIXATION AND REGRESSION IN THE RAT. 1942. 34 pp.

[————] **Number 247.** Mowrer, O. H., and R. R. Lamoreaux. AVOIDANCE CONDITIONING AND SIGNAL DURATION—A STUDY OF SECONDARY MOTIVATION AND REWARD. 1942. 34 pp.

[————] **Number 248.** Luchins, Abraham S. MECHANIZATION IN PROBLEM SOLVING—THE EFFECT OF EINSTELLUNG. 1942. 95 pp.

[Volume 55] **Number 249.** Weaver, H. E., ed. STUDIES OF OCULAR BEHAVIOR IN MUSIC READING. 1943. 50 pp.

[————] **Number 250.** McHugh, Gelolo. CHANGES IN I.Q. AT THE PUBLIC SCHOOL KINDERGARTEN LEVEL. 1943. 34 pp.

[————] **Number 251.** Reese, Thomas Whelan. THE APPLICATION OF THE THEORY OF PHYSICAL MEASUREMENT TO THE MEASUREMENT OF PSYCHOLOGICAL MAGNITUDES, WITH THREE EXPERIMENTAL EXAMPLES. 1943. 89 pp.

[————] **Number 252.** Harrington, Wells. RECOMMENDATION QUALITY AND PLACEMENT SUCCESS. A STUDY OF THE RELATION BETWEEN AN ESTIMATE OF THE QUALITY OF WRITTEN RECOMMENDATIONS AND SUCCESS IN SECURING CERTAIN TYPES OF TEACHING POSITIONS. 1943. 62 pp.

[————] **Number 253.** Campbell, Albert A. ST. THOMAS NEGROES—A STUDY OF PERSONALITY AND CULTURE. 1943. 90 pp.

[**Volume 56**] **Number 254.** Brunswik, Egon. DISTAL FOCUSSING OF PERCEPTION: SIZE-CONSTANCY IN A REPRESENTATIVE SAMPLE OF SITUATIONS. 1944. 49 pp.

[————] **Number 255.** Johnson, Wendell, ed. STUDIES IN LANGUAGE BEHAVIOR. UNIVERSITY OF IOWA STUDIES IN PSYCHOLOGY, No. XXIV. 1944. 111 pp.

[————] **Number 256.** Zander, Alvin F. A STUDY OF EXPERIMENTAL FRUSTRATION. 1944. 38 pp.

[————] **Number 257.** Klee, James Butt. THE RELATION OF FRUSTRATION AND MOTIVATION TO THE PRODUCTION OF ABNORMAL FIXATIONS IN THE RAT. 1944. 45 pp.

[————] **Number 258.** Thompson, George G. THE SOCIAL AND EMOTIONAL DEVELOPMENT OF PRESCHOOL CHILDREN UNDER TWO TYPES OF EDUCATIONAL PROGRAM. 1944. 29 pp.

[————] **Number 259.** Lovell, Constance. THE EFFECT OF SPECIAL CONSTRUCTION OF TEST ITEMS ON THEIR FACTOR COMPOSITION. 1944. 26 pp.

[————] **Number 260.** Richardson, LaVange Hunt. THE PERSONALITY OF STUTTERERS. 1944. 41 pp.

[**Volume 57**] **Number 261.** Willmann, Rudolph R. AN EXPERIMENTAL INVESTIGATION OF THE CREATIVE PROCESS IN MUSIC: THE TRANSPOSABILITY OF VISUAL DESIGN STIMULI TO MUSICAL THEMES. 1944. 76 pp.

[————] **Number 262.** Wapner, Seymour. THE DIFFERENTIAL EFFECTS OF CORTICAL INJURY AND RETESTING ON EQUIVALENCE REACTIONS IN THE RAT. 1944. 59 pp.

[————] **Number 263.** Estes, William K. AN EXPERIMENTAL STUDY OF PUNISHMENT. 1944. 40 pp.

[————] **Number 264.** Hanfmann, Eugenia, Maria Rickers-Ovsiankina, and Kurt Goldstein. CASE LANUTI: EXTREME CONCRETIZATION OF BEHAVIOR DUE TO DAMAGE OF THE BRAIN CORTEX. 1944. 72 pp.

[————] **Number 265.** Sargent, Helen. AN EXPERIMENTAL APPLICATION OF PROJECTIVE PRINCIPLES TO A PAPER AND PENCIL PERSONALITY TEST. 1944. 57 pp.

[**Volume 58**] **Number 266.** Elkisch, Paula. CHILDREN'S DRAWINGS IN A PROJECTIVE TECHNIQUE. 1945. 31 pp.

[————] **Number 267.** Wyatt, Ruth F. IMPROVABILITY OF PITCH DISCRIMINATION. 1945. 58 pp.

[————] **Number 268.** Baldwin, Alfred L., Joan Kalhorn, and Fay Huffmann Breese. PATTERNS OF PARENT BEHAVIOR. 1945. 75 pp.

[————] **Number 269.** Scheerer, Martin, Eva Rothman, and Kurt Goldstein. A CASE OF "IDIOT SAVANT": AN EXPERIMENTAL STUDY OF PERSONALITY ORGANIZATION. 1945. 63 pp.

[————] **Number 270.** Duncker, Karl. ON PROBLEM-SOLVING. Translated by Lynn S. Lees. 1945. 113 pp.

[**Volume 59**] **Number 271.** Lantz, Beatrice. SOME DYNAMIC ASPECTS OF SUCCESS AND FAILURE. 1945. 40 pp.

[————] **Number 272.** Bach, George R. YOUNG CHILDREN'S PLAY FANTASIES. 1945. 69 pp.

275. *(Continued)*

[————] **Number 273.** Underwood, Benton J. THE EFFECT OF SUCCESSIVE INTERPOLATIONS ON RETROACTIVE AND PROACTIVE INHIBITION. 1945. 33 pp.

[————] **Number 274.** Meehl, Paul E. AN INVESTIGATION OF A GENERAL NORMALITY OR CONTROL FACTOR IN PERSONALITY TESTING. 1945. 62 pp.

[————] **Number 275.** Huxtable, Zelma Langdon, Miriam Harker White, and Marjorie Abernethy McCartor. A RE-PERFORMANCE AND RE-INTERPRETATION OF THE ARAI EXPERIMENT IN MENTAL FATIGUE WITH THREE SUBJECTS. 1946. 52 pp.

[————] **Number 276.** Peak, Helen. OBSERVATIONS ON THE CHARACTERISTICS AND DISTRIBUTION OF GERMAN NAZIS. 1945. 44 pp.

[Volume 60] **Number 277.** Armitage, Stewart G. AN ANALYSIS OF CERTAIN PSYCHOLOGICAL TESTS USED FOR THE EVALUATION OF BRAIN INJURY. 1946. 48 pp.

[————] **Number 278.** Wellman, Beth L., and Boyd R. McCandless. FACTORS ASSOCIATED WITH BINET IQ CHANGES OF PRESCHOOL CHILDREN. 1946. 29 pp.

[————] **Number 279.** Child, Irvin L., Elmer H. Potter, and Estelle M. Levine. CHILDREN'S TEXTBOOKS AND PERSONALITY DEVELOPMENT: AN EXPLORATION IN THE SOCIAL PSYCHOLOGY OF EDUCATION. 1946. 54 pp.

[————] **Number 280.** Child, Irvin L. CHILDREN'S PREFERENCE FOR GOALS EASY OR DIFFICULT TO OBTAIN. 1946. 31 pp.

[————] **Number 281.** Schmidt, Bernardine G. CHANGES IN PERSONAL, SOCIAL, AND INTELLECTUAL BEHAVIOR OF CHILDREN ORIGINALLY CLASSIFIED AS FEEBLEMINDED. 1946. 144 pp.

[Volume 61] **Number 282.** Rhinehart, Jesse B. SEX DIFFERENCES IN DISPERSION AT THE HIGH SCHOOL AND COLLEGE LEVELS. 1947. 37 pp.

[————] **Number 283.** Surgent, Louis Vincent. THE USE OF APTITUDE TESTS IN THE SELECTION OF RADIO TUBE MOUNTERS. 1947. 40 pp.

[————] **Number 284.** Ellis, Albert. A COMPARISON OF THE USE OF DIRECT AND INDIRECT PHRASING IN PERSONALITY QUESTIONNAIRES. 1947. 41 pp.

[————] **Number 285.** Loevinger, Jane. A SYSTEMATIC APPROACH TO THE CONSTRUCTION AND EVALUATION OF TESTS OF ABILITY. 1947. 49 pp.

[————] **Number 286.** STUDIES IN PILOT SELECTION: Lane, G. Gorham. THE PREDICTION OF SUCCESS IN LEARNING TO FLY LIGHT AIRCRAFT; Greene, Ronald R. THE ABILITY TO PERCEIVE AND REACT DIFFERENTIALLY TO CONFIGURATIONAL CHANGES AS RELATED TO THE PILOTING OF LIGHT AIRCRAFT. 1947. 28 pp.

[————] **Number 287.** Douglas, Anna Gertrude. A TACHISTOSCOPIC STUDY OF THE ORDER OF EMERGENCE IN THE PROCESS OF PERCEPTION. 1947. 133 pp.

276. *Revue de psychotherapie et de psychologie appliquée.* **[1.]**

TITLE VARIATIONS: Multiply subtitled *(Ancienne revue de l'hypnotisme)* and *Psychologie. Pédagogie. Médecine sociale. Maladies mentales et nerveuses.* Continues *Revue de l'hypnotisme et de la psychologie physiologique.* Continued by *Revue de psychologie appliquée* [1] with Série 4, Année 30, January 1920.

DATES OF PUBLICATION: Série 2, Année 25, July 1910–June 1911. Série 3, Année 26–29, July 1911–1915.

FREQUENCY: Monthly (Irregular)

NUMBERING VARIATIONS: None.

PUBLISHER: **Paris:** Redaction et administration, 4, rue Castellane, Société d'hypnologie et de psychologie, 1910–1915.

PRIMARY EDITORS: **Ed. Bérillon,** 1910–1915; **Paul Farez,** 1910–1915.

ASSOCIATE EDITORS: A. Pitres, 1910 ——— Raffegeau, 1910–1915; ——— Regnault, 1910–1915; ——— Pychlau, 1910–1915; Alb. Robin, 1910–1915; A. W. van Renterghem, 1910–1915; Fulgence Raymond, 1910–1912; H. Stadelman, 1910–1915; A. Tamburini, 1910–1915; Albert von Schrenck-Notzing, 1910–1915; ——— van Velsen, 1912–1915; J. Voisin, 1910–1915; ——— Vlavianos, 1910–1915, ——— Witry, 1910–1915; Joseph Babinski, 1910–1915; ——— Bahaddin-Bey, 1910–1915; ——— Bielitzky, 1913–1915; Marcel Briand, 1910–1915; J.M.A. Beni-Barde, 1910–1915; V. Bridou, 1910–1915; C. Binet-Sanglé, 1910–1915; ——— Coste de Lagrave, 1910–1915; L. Césari, 1910–1915; H. Crichton-Miller, 1913–1915; ——— Cruise, 1910–1912; J. Crocq, 1913–1915; ——— Dauriac, 1910–1915; ——— Damoglou, 1910–1915; A. Gine, 1913–1915; ——— Guimbeau, 1910–1915; Joseph Grasset, 1910–1915; ——— Huchard, 1910–1912; ——— Douglas Bryn, 1910–1915; V. Hernandez, 1910–1915; O. Jennings, 1910–1915; ——— Jauguaribe, 1910–1915; P. Joire, 1910–1915; Alexandre Lacassagne, 1910–1915; Paul Louis Ladame, 1910–1915; M. Legrain, 1910–1915; ——— Lemesle, 1910–1915; C. Lloyd Tuckey, 1910–1915; Léona Manouvrier, 1910–1915; A. Marie, 1913–1915; ——— Masoin, 1910–1915; J. Milne Bramwell, 1910–1915; Émile Magnin, 1910–1915; Enrico Morselli, 1910–1915; ——— de Packiewicz, 1910–1915; ——— Orlitzky, 1910–1915; ——— Preda, 1910–1915; ——— Pewnizky, 1910–1915; ——— Wiazemský, 1910–1915; Émile Boirac, 1910–1915; C. Stumpf, 1910–1915; ——— Julliot, 1910–1915; ——— Scié-tonfa, 1910–1915; ——— Podiapolsky, 1910–1915; ——— Swan, 1910–1915; ——— Ubeydoullah, 1910–1915; ——— Hamet, 1913–1915.

277. *Untersuchungen zur Psychologie und Philosophie.*

TITLE VARIATIONS: Continued by *Untersuchungen zur Psychologie, Philosophie und Pädagogik* with Band 4, 1924.

DATES OF PUBLICATION: Band 1–3, 1910–1921. Suspended publication 1914–1920.

FREQUENCY: Irregular. *See* Contents *below.*

NUMBERING VARIATIONS: Band 2, Heft 3 never published.

PUBLISHER: **Leipzig:** Quelle & Meyer, 1910–1913. **Bamberg:** C. C. Buchners Verlag, 1921.

PRIMARY EDITORS: **Narziss Ach,** 1910–1921.

CONTENTS:

Band 1, Heft 1. Ach, Narziss. ÜBER DEN WILLEN. 1910. 24 pp.

————, **Heft 2.** Hildebrandt, H. ÜBER DIE BEEINFLUSSUNG DER WILLENSKRAFT DURCH DEN ALKOHOL. 1910. 91 pp.

————, **Heft 3.** Meyer, Ernst. ÜBER DIE GESETZE DER SIMULTANEN ASSOZIATION UND DES WIEDERERKENNENS. 1910. 92 pp.

————, **Heft 4.** Ach, Narziss. ÜBER DEN WILLENSAKT. EINE REPLIK. 1911. 40 pp.

————, **Heft 5.** Ach, Narziss. I. EINE SERIENMETHODE FÜR REAKTIONSVERSUCHE. II. BEMERKUNG ZUR UNTERSUCHUNG DES WILLENS. 1912. 49 pp.

————, **Heft 6.** Hillgruber, Andr. FORTLAUFENDE ARBEIT UND WILLENSBETÄTIGUNG. 1912. 50 pp.

————, **Heft 7.** Glässner, Gustav. ÜBER WILLENSHEMMUNG UND WILLENSBAHNUNG. 1912. 143 pp.

————, **Heft 8.** Wiedenberg, Walter. DIE PERSEVERIEREND-DETERMINIERENDE HEMMUNG BEI FORTLAUFENDER TÄTIGKEIT. 1913. 109 pp.

Band 2, Heft 1. Rux, Curt. ÜBER DAS ASSOZIATIVE ÄQUIVALENT DER DETERMINATION. 1913. 149 pp.

————, **Heft 2.** Ach, Narziss. ÜBER DIE ERKENNTNIS A PRIORI INSBESONDERE IN DER ARITHMETIK. 1913. 70 pp.

————, **Heft 3.** Never published.

————, **Heft 4.** Friederici, Hugo. ÜBER DIE WIRKSAMKEIT DER SUKZESSIVEN ATTENTION. EIN BEITRAG ZUR LEHRE VOM WILLEN. 1913. 88 pp.

Band 3, Heft 1. Ach, Narziss. ÜBER DIE BEGRIFFSBILDUNG. EINE EXPERIMENTELLE UNTERSUCHUNG. 1921. 343 pp.

278. *Uppsala. Institutet för psykologisk Forskning. Meddelanden.*

TITLE VARIATIONS: None.

DATES OF PUBLICATION: Nummer 1-7, 1910–1916.

FREQUENCY: Annual. Irregular. Nummer 1, 1910; 2, 1911; 3, 1912; 4, 1912; 5, 1913; 6, 1915; 7, 1916.

NUMBERING VARIATIONS: Nummer 1, 2 and 5 were issued as *Psyke. Bilaga*, Nummer 1–3.

PUBLISHER: **Uppsala:** Almqvist & Wiksells Boktryckeri, 1910–1916.

PRIMARY EDITORS: **Sydney Alrutz,** 1910–1916; **Harald Höffding,** 1910–1916; **Arvid Grotenfelt,** 1910–1916; **Kristian Birch-Reichenwald Aars,** 1910–1916.

279. *Wiener psychoanalytischer Verein. Diskussionen.*

TITLE VARIATIONS: None.

DATES OF PUBLICATION: Heft 1–2, 1910–1912.

FREQUENCY: Irregular. *See* Contents *below.*

NUMBERING VARIATIONS: None.

PUBLISHER: **Wiesbaden:** J. F. Bergmann, 1910–1912.

PRIMARY EDITORS: None listed.

CONTENTS:
    Heft 1. ÜBER DEN SELBSTMORD. BEITRÄGE VON ALFRED ADLER, SIGMUND FREUD, J. K. KRIEDJUNG, KARL MOLITOR, R. REITLER, J. SADGER UND W. STEKEL. 1910. 60 pp.
    Heft 2. DIE ONANIE. 14 BEITRÄGE . . . VON B. DATTNER, PAUL FEDERN, S. FERENCZI, [S.] FREUD, JOS. K. KRIEDJUNG, E. HITSCHMANN, OTTO RANK, RUDOLPH REITLER, GASTON ROSENSTEIN, HANNS SACHS, J. SADGER, MAX STEINER, W. STEKEL UND VIKTOR TAUSK. 1912. 140 pp.

280. *Wyoming. University. Department of Psychology. Bulletin.*

TITLE VARIATIONS: None.

DATES OF PUBLICATION: Number 1–3, 1910–1919. Ceased publication.

FREQUENCY: Irregular. *See* Contents *below.*

NUMBERING VARIATIONS: Number 3 also numbered as [*Wyoming. University.*] *Bulletin. See* Contents *below.*

PUBLISHER: **Laramie, Wyoming:** Laramie Republican Company, Printer, 1910. **Laramie:** Laramie Republican Company, 1911. **Laramie:** University of Wyoming, 1919.

PRIMARY EDITORS: None listed.

CONTENTS:
    Number 1. Downey, June Etta. PRELIMINARY STUDY OF FAMILY RESEMBLANCE IN HANDWRITING. 1910. 51 pp.
    Number 2. Downey, June Etta. IMAGINAL REACTION TO POETRY: THE AFFECTIVE AND THE AESTHETIC JUDGMENT. 1911. 56 pp.
    Number 3. Downey, June Etta. THE WILL-PROFILE. A TENTATIVE SCALE FOR MEASUREMENT OF THE VOLITIONAL PATTERN. February 1919. 38 pp. (Also as [*Wyoming. University.*] *Bulletin.* Volume 15, Number 6A, February 1919. Second edition also as [*Wyoming. University.*] *Bulletin.* Volume 16, Number 46, November 1919.)

281. *Zeitschrift für die gesamte Neurologie und Psychiatrie.*

TITLE VARIATIONS: Supersedes in part *Zentralblatt für Nervenheilkunde und Psychiatrie.* United with *Archiv für Psychiatrie und Nervenheilkunde* which assumes its volume numbering with Band 179, October 1947.

DATES OF PUBLICATION: Band 1–178, Heft 2, 1910–March 8, 1945.

FREQUENCY: **Irregular** (annual volumes), Band 1–11. **Irregular,** Band 12–178.

NUMBERING VARIATIONS: Each Band may contain from 1 to 5 Hefte. Band 76, Heft 1/2, 1922 is FESTSCHRIFT FÜR ARNOLD PICK; Band 82, 1923 is FESTSCHRIFT FÜR EUGEN BLEULER; Band 94, Heft 2/3, 1924 is FESTSCHRIFT FÜR

ROBERT SOMMER; Band 94, Heft 4, 1924 is FESTSCHRIFT FÜR L. MINOR; Band 100, Heft 1, 1925 is FESTSCHRIFT FÜR W. BECHTEREW; Band 101, 1926 is FESTSCHRIFT FÜR EMIL KRAEPELIN; Band 110, Heft 2, 1927 is FESTSCHRIFT FÜR PAUL SCHUSTER; Band 127, Heft 4/5, 1930 is FESTSCHRIFT FÜR ROBERT GAUPP; Band 128, Heft 1/4, 1930 is FESTSCHRIFT FÜR WILHELM WEYGANDT; Band 131, Heft 1/3, 1931 is FESTSCHRIFT FÜR GUSTAV SPECHT.

PUBLISHER: **Berlin:** Julius Springer, 1910–1936. **Berlin:** Springer Verlag, 1936–1945.

PRIMARY EDITORS: **Alois Alzheimer,** 1910–1914; **Robert Gaupp,** 1910–1945; **Max Lewandowsky,** 1910–1914; **Karl Wilmanns,** 1910–1920; **Otfried Förster,** 1915–1945; **Hugo Liepmann,** 1915–1920; **F. Plaut,** 1915–1920; **Walther Spielmayer,** 1915–1930; **Oswald Bumke,** 1920–1925, 1931–1940; **Oskar Gagel,** 1941–1945.

282. *Zeitschrift für die gesamte Neurologie und Psychiatrie. Referate und Ergebnisse.*

TITLE VARIATIONS: Band 1–2 simply subtitled *Referate.* Continued by *Zentralblatt für die gesamte Neurologie und Psychiatrie. Referate und Ergebnisse* with Band 25, 1922.

DATES OF PUBLICATION: Band 1–24, 1910–1921.

FREQUENCY: Irregular. *See* Numbering Variations *below.*

NUMBERING VARIATIONS: Band 1–2 issued 1910; 3–4, 1911; 5–6, 1912; 7–8, 1913; 9–11, 1914; 12, 1915; 13, 1916; 14, 1917; 15–17, 1918; 18–19, 1919; 20–22, 1920; and 23–24, 1921.

PUBLISHER: **Berlin:** Julius Springer, 1910–1921.

PRIMARY EDITORS: **Alois Alzheimer,** 1910–1914; **Max Lewandowsky,** 1910–1918; **Walther Spielmeyer,** 1915–1921.

283. *Zentralblatt für Psychoanalyse. Medizinische Monatsschrift für Seelenkunde.* [Organ of the Internationale psychoanalytische Vereinigung.

TITLE VARIATIONS: Continued by *Zentralblatt für Psychoanalyse und Psychotherapie. Medizinische Monatsschrift für Seelenkunde* with Band 4, 1913.

DATES OF PUBLICATION: Band 1–3, January 1910–December 1912.

FREQUENCY: Monthly.

NUMBERING VARIATIONS: None.

PUBLISHER: **Wiesbaden:** J. F. Bergmann, 1910–1912.

PRIMARY EDITORS: **Sigmund Freud,** 1910–1912; **Alfred Adler,** 1910; **Wilhelm Stekel,** 1910–1912; **Karl Abraham,** 1910–1912; **A. A. Brill,** 1910; **S. Ferenczi,** 1910; **R. G. Assagioli,** 1911–1912; **Ludwig Binswanger,** 1911–1912.

1911

284. *Behavior Monographs.*

TITLE VARIATIONS: Susperseded by *Comparative Psychology Monographs* with Number 1, 1922.

DATES OF PUBLICATION: Number 1–21, 1911–1922.

FREQUENCY: Irregular. *See* Contents *below.*

NUMBERING VARIATIONS: Issues also numbered in volumes 1–4. *See* Contents *below.*

PUBLISHER: **Cambridge, Massachusetts:** Henry Holt & Company, 1911–1919. **Baltimore:** Williams & Wilkins Company, 1922.

PRIMARY EDITORS: **John B. Watson,** 1911–1919; **Walter S. Hunter,** 1922.

CONTENTS

[Volume 1] **Number 1.** Breed, Frederick S. THE DEVELOPMENT OF CERTAIN INSTINCTS AND HABITS IN CHICKS. 1911. 78 pp.

[————] **Number 2.** Yerkes, Robert M., and John B. Watson. METHODS OF STUDYING VISION IN ANIMALS. 1911. 90 pp.

[————] **Number 3.** Severin, Henry H. P., and Harry C. Severin. AN EXPERIMENTAL STUDY ON THE DEATH-FEIGNING OF BELOSTOMA (= ZAITHA AUCCT.) FLUMINEUM SAY AND NEPA APICULATA UHLER. 1911. 44 pp.

[————] **Number 4.** Dawson, Jean. THE BIOLOGY OF PHYSA. 1911. 120 pp.

[————] **Number 5.** Vincent, Stella Burnham. THE FUNCTION OF THE VIBRISSAE IN THE BEHAVIOR OF THE WHITE RAT. 1912. 81 pp.

[Volume 2] **Number 6.** Hunter, Walter S. THE DELAYED REACTION IN ANIMALS AND CHILDREN. 1913. 86 pp.

[————] **Number 7.** Sackett, Leroy Walter. THE CANADA PORCUPINE: A STUDY OF THE LEARNING PROCESS. 1913. 84 pp.

[————] **Number 8.** Johnson, Harry Miles. AUDITION AND HABIT FORMATION IN THE DOG. 1913. 78 pp.

[————] **Number 9.** Basset, Gardner Cheney. HABIT FORMATION IN A STRAIN OF ALBINO RATS OF LESS THAN NORMAL BRAIN WEIGHT. 1914. 46 pp.

[————] **Number 10.** Ulrich, John Linck. DISTRIBUTION OF EFFORT IN LEARNING IN THE WHITE RAT. 1915. 51 pp.

[————] **Number 11.** Hubbert, Helen B. THE EFFECT OF AGE ON HABIT FORMATION IN THE ALBINO RAT. 1915. 55 pp.

[Volume 3] **Number 12.** Yerkes, Robert M. THE MENTAL LIFE OF MONKEYS AND APES: A STUDY OF IDEATIONAL BEHAVIOR. 1916. 145 pp.

[————] **Number 13.** Hamilton, G. V. A STUDY OF PERSEVERANCE REACTIONS IN PRIMATES AND RODENTS. 1916. 65 pp.

[————] **Number 14.** Thompson, Elizabeth Lockwood. AN ANALYSIS OF THE LEARNING PROCESS IN THE SNAIL, *PHYSAGYRINA* SAY. 1917. 89 pp.

[————] **Number 15.** Peterson, Joseph. THE EFFECT OF LENGTH OF BLIND ALLEYS ON MAZE LEARNING: AN EXPERIMENT ON TWENTY-FOUR WHITE RATS. 1917. 53 pp.

[————] **Number 16.** Wylie, Harry H. AN EXPERIMENTAL STUDY OF TRANSFER OF RESPONSE IN THE WHITE RAT 1919. 65 pp.

[Volume 4] Number 17. Wiltbank, Rutledge T. TRANSFER OF TRAINING IN WHITE RATS UPON VARIOUS SERIES OF MAZES. 1919. 65 pp.

[————] **Number 18.** Brockbank, Thomas William. REDINTEGRATION IN THE ALBINO RAT. 1919. 65 pp.

[————] **Number 19.** Reeves, Cora D. DISCRIMINATION OF LIGHT OF DIFFERENT WAVE-LENGTHS BY FISH. 1919. 106 pp.

[————] **Number 20.** Bingham, Harold C. VISUAL PERCEPTION OF THE CHICK. 1922. 104 pp.

[————] **Number 21.** Coburn, Charles A. HEREDITY OF WILDNESS AND SAVAGENESS IN MICE. 1922. 71 pp.

285. *British Journal of Psychology. Monograph Supplements.*

TITLE VARIATIONS: None.

DATES OF PUBLICATION: Number 1–27+, 1911–1948+.

FREQUENCY: Irregular. *See* Contents *below.*

NUMBERING VARIATIONS: Issues also numbered in Volumes 1–8. *See* Contents *below.*

PUBLISHER: **Cambridge:** University Press, 1911–1948+.

PRIMARY EDITORS: None listed, 1911–1931; **James Drever,** 1932–1948+.

CONTENTS:

[Volume 1] Number 1. Wohlgemuth, A. ON THE EFFECTS OF SEEN MOVEMENTS. 1911. 117 pp.

[————] **Number 2.** Ballard, P. B. OBLIVISCENCE AND REMINISCENCE. 1913. 82 pp.

[————] **Number 3.** Webb, E. CHARACTER AND INTELLIGENCE. 1915. 99 pp.

[————] **Number 4.** Reaney, M. J. THE PSYCHOLOGY OF THE ORGANIZED GROUP GAME. 1916. 76 pp.

[Volume 2] Number 5. McQueen, E. Neil. THE DISTRIBUTION OF ATTENTION. 1917. 142 pp.

[————] **Number 6.** Wohlgemuth, A. PLEASURE–UNPLEASURE. 1919. 252 pp.

[Volume 3] Number 7. Bernstein, E. QUICKNESS AND INTELLIGENCE. 1924. 55 pp.

[————] **Number 8.** McFarlane, M. A STUDY OF PRACTICAL ABILITY. 1925. 75 pp.

[————] **Number 9.** Magson, E. H. HOW WE JUDGE INTELLIGENCE. 1926. 115 pp.

[————] **Number 10.** Hargreaves, H. L. THE "FACULTY" OF IMAGINATION. 1927. 74 pp.

[Volume 4] Number 11. Wells, H. M. THE PHENOMENOLOGY OF ACTS OF CHOICE: AN ANALYSIS OF VOLITIONAL CONSCIOUSNESS. 1927. 157 pp.

[————] Number 12. Stevanovic, B. P. AN EXPERIMENTAL STUDY OF THE MENTAL PROCESSES INVOLVED IN JUDGMENT. 1927. 138 pp.

[————] Number 13. Fluegel, J. C. PRACTICE, FATIGUE AND OSCILLATION. 1928. 92 pp.

[Volume 5] Number 14. Cattell, R. B. THE SUBJECTIVE CHARACTER OF COGNITION. 1930. 166 pp.

[————] Number 15. Line, W. THE GROWTH OF VISUAL PERCEPTION IN CHILDREN. 1931. 148 pp.

[————] Number 16. Lawrence, Evelyn M. AN INVESTIGATION INTO THE RELATION BETWEEN INTELLIGENCE AND INHERITANCE. 1931. 80 pp.

[Volume 6] Number 17. Philpott, S.J.F. FLUCTUATIONS IN HUMAN OUTPUT. 1932. 125 pp.

[————] Number 18. Richardson, C. A., and C. W. Stokes. THE GROWTH AND VARIABILITY OF INTELLIGENCE. 1933. 83 pp.

[————] Number 19. Alexander, W. P. INTELLIGENCE, CONCRETE AND ABSTRACT. 1935. 177 pp.

[Volume 7] Number 20. El Koussy, A.A.H. THE VISUAL PERCEPTION OF SPACE. 1935. 89 pp.

[————] Number 21. Philp, Howard L. AN EXPERIMENTAL STUDY OF THE FRUSTRATION OF WILL-ACTS AND CONATION. 1936. 103 pp.

[————] Number 22. Desai, M. M. SURPRISE, A HISTORICAL AND EXPERIMENTAL STUDY. 1939. 124 pp.

[————] Number 23. Richardson, Lewis F. GENERALIZED FOREIGN POLITICS. 1939. 89 pp.

[Volume 8] Number 24. Clarke, E. R. PREDICTABLE ACCURACY IN EXAMINATIONS. 1940. 48 pp.

[————] Number 25. Bowley, Agatha H. A STUDY OF THE FACTORS INFLUENCING THE GENERAL DEVELOPMENT OF THE CHILD DURING PRE-SCHOOL YEARS BY MEANS OF RECORD FORMS. 1942. 104 pp.

[————] Number 26. Pickford, R. W. THE PSYCHOLOGY OF CULTURAL CHANGE IN PAINTING. 1943. 62 pp.

[————] Number 27. Wing, Herbert. TESTS OF MUSICAL ABILITY AND APPRECIATION. 1948. 88 pp.

286. *Internationale Gesellschaft für medizinische Psychologie und Psychotherapie. Verhandlungen.*

TITLE VARIATIONS: Supplement to *Journal für Psychologie und Neurologie*, Band 17, 19, 20.

DATES OF PUBLICATION: Heft 1–3, 1911–1913.

FREQUENCY: Annual.

NUMBERING VARIATIONS: None.

PUBLISHER: **Leipzig:** Verlag von Johann Ambrosius Barth, 1910–1912.

PRIMARY EDITORS: Oskar Vogt, 1911–1913; **August Forel,** 1911–1913; **K. Brodmann,** 1911–1913.

CONTENTS:
Heft 1. JAHRESVERSAMMLUNG IN BRÜSSEL AM 7. UND 8. AUGUST 1910. 1911. Pp. 1–128.
Heft 2. JAHRESVERSAMMLUNG IN MÜNCHEN AM 25. UND 26. SEPTEMBER 1911. 1912. 142 pp.
Heft 3. JAHRESVERSAMMLUNG IN ZÜRICH AM 8. UND 9. SEPTEMBER 1912. 1913. Pp. 89–242.

287. *Journal of Animal Behavior.*

TITLE VARIATIONS: United with *Psychobiology* to form *Journal of Comparative Psychology* with Volume 1, 1921.

DATES OF PUBLICATION: Volume 1–7, 1911–1917.

FREQUENCY OF ISSUE: Bimonthly.

NUMBERING VARIATIONS: None.

PUBLISHER: **Albany, New York:** Henry Holt and Company of New York, 1911 [issue 1]. **Cambridge, Massachusetts:** Henry Holt and Company of New York, 1911 [issue 2]–1917.

PRIMARY EDITORS: **Robert M. Yerkes,** 1911–1917; **Harvey A. Carr,** 1916–1917.

EDITORIAL BOARD: Madison Bentley, 1911–1917; Harvey A. Carr, 1911–1917; Samuel, J. Holmes, 1911–1917; Herbert S. Jennings, 1911–1916; Edward L. Thorndike, 1911–1917; Margaret F. Washburn, 1911–1917; John B. Watson, 1911–1917; William M. Wheeler, 1911–1917; Robert M. Yerkes, 1911–1917; Gilbert V. Hamilton, 1914–1917; Walter S. Hunter, 1914–1917.

288. *Journal of Comparative Neurology.* [2.]

TITLE VARIATIONS: Continues *Journal of Comparative Neurology and Psychology.*

DATES OF PUBLICATION: Volume 21–93+, 1911–1950+.

FREQUENCY OF ISSUE: Bimonthly.

NUMBERING VARIATIONS: Number of issues per volume varies from 2–6. Volumes 56–57 also as CHARLES JUDSON HERRICK ANNIVERSARY VOLUMES, Part I–II. Volume 65 also as C. CARL HUBER MEMORIAL VOLUME.

PUBLISHER: **Philadelphia:** Wistar Institute of Anatomy and Biology, 1911–1950+.

PRIMARY EDITORS: **Charles Judson Herrick,** 1911–1927; **George E. Coghill,** 1927–1933; **Davenport Hooker,** 1933–1949; **Gerhardt von Bonin,** 1950+.

EDITORIAL BOARD: Henry H. Donaldson, 1911–1938; J. B. Johnston, 1911–1933; Adolf Meyer, 1911–1947; Oliver S. Strong, 1911–1941; Charles Judson Herrick, 1911–1947; Davenport Hooker, 1932–1950+; George E. Coghill,

1927–1941; Olof Larsell, 1937–1950+; Stephen Polyak, 1937–1947; Elizabeth C. Crosby, 1940–1950+; Donald H. Barron, 1948–1950+; Jan Jansen, 1948–1950+; Fred A. Mettler, 1948–1950+; Gerhardt von Bonin, 1948–1950+.

289. *Journal of Experimental Pedagogy and Training College Record.* [Organ of the Training College Association.]

TITLE VARIATIONS: Continues *Training College Record.* Continued by *Forum of Education* with New Series, Volume 1, February 1923.

DATES OF PUBLICATION: Volume 1, Number 6–Volume 6, Number 5/6, March 1911–June/December 1922.

FREQUENCY: Triannual (March, June, December).

NUMBERING VARIATIONS: Issues are double numbered.

PUBLISHER: **London:** Longmans, Green and Company, 1911–1922.

PRIMARY EDITORS: **J. A. Green,** 1911–1922.

290. *Società italiana di psicologia. Atti di Convegno.*

TITLE VARIATIONS: Also called *Convegno di psicologia sperimentale e psicotecnia.*

DATES OF PUBLICATION: 1°–8°, 1911–1931. Suspended publication, 1914–1921, 1932–50.

FREQUENCY: Irregular. 1°, 1911; 2°, 1913; 3°, 1922; 4°, 1926; 5°, 1927; 6°, 1928; 7°, 1929; 8°, 1931.

NUMBERING VARIATIONS: None.

PUBLISHER: **Bologna:** Stabilimento poligrafico Emiliano, 1911–1914. **Bologna:** Zanichelli, 1922–1931.

PRIMARY EDITORS: **Enzo Bonaventura,** 1931; **Mario F. Canella,** 1931.

291. *Zeitschrift für angewandte Psychologie und psychologische Sammelforschung. Beihefte.* [Organ of the Institut für angewandte Psychologie (Leipzig).]

TITLE VARIATIONS: Continued by *Zeitschrift für angewandte Psychologie. Beihefte* with Heft 13, 1916.

DATES OF PUBLICATION: Heft 1–12, 1911–1915.

FREQUENCY: Irregular. *See* Contents *below.*

NUMBERING VARIATIONS: None.

PUBLISHER: **Leipzig:** Johann Ambrosius Barth, 1911–1915.

PRIMARY EDITORS: **William Stern,** 1911–1915; **Otto Lipmann,** 1911–1915.

CONTENTS:

Heft 1. Lipmann, Otto. DIE SPUREN INTERESSEBETONTER ERLEBNISSE

UND IHRE SYMPTOME. THEORIE, METHODEN UND ERGEBNISSE DER "TATBESTANDSDIAGNOSTIK". 1911. 96 pp.

Heft 2. Cohn, J., and J. Dieffenbacher. UNTERSUCHUNGEN ÜBER GESCHLECHTS-, ALTERS- UND BEGABUNGS-UNTERSCHIEDE BEI SCHÜLERN. 1911. 213 pp.

Heft 3. Betz, W. ÜBER KORRELATION. 1911. 88 pp.

Heft 4. Margis, Paul. E.T.A. HOFFMAN. EINE PSYCHOGRAPHISCHE INDIVIDUAL-ANALYSE. 1911. 220 pp.

Heft 5. VORSCHLÄGE ZUR PSYCHOLOGISCHEN UNTERSUCHUNG PRIMITIVER MENSCHEN. GESAMMELT UND HERAUSGEGEBEN VOM INSTITUT FÜR ANGEWANDTE PSYCHOLOGIE UND PSYCHOLOGISCHE SAMMELFORSCHUNG. 1912. 124 pp.

Heft 6. Thurnwald, Richard. ETHNO-PSYCHOLOGISCHE STUDIEN AN SÜDSEEVÖLKERN AUF DEM BISMARCK-ARCHIPEL UND DEN SALOMO–INSELN. 1913. 163 pp.

Heft 7. Giese, Fritz. DAS FREIE LITERARISCHE SCHAFFEN BEI KINDERN UND JUGENDLICHEN. 1913. 242 pp.

Heft 8. Eng, Helga. ABSTRAKTE BEGRIFFE IM SPRECHEN UND DENKEN DES KINDES. 1914. 112 pp.

Heft 9. Damm, Hermann. KORRELATIVE BEZIEHUNGEN ZWISCHEN ELEMENTAREN VERGLEICHSLEISTUNGEN. EIN BEITRAG ZUR PSYCHOLOGISCHEN KORRELATIONSFORSCHUNG. 1914. 84 pp.

Heft 10. Brandell, Georg. DAS INTERESSE DER SCHULKINDER AN DEN UNTERRICHTSFÄCHERN. 1915. 168 pp.

Heft 11. Piorkowski, Curt. BEITRÄGE ZUR PSYCHOLOGISCHEN METHODOLOGIE DER WIRTSCHAFTLICHEN BERUFSEIGNUNG. 1915. 84 pp.

Heft 12. Stern, William, ed. JUGENDLICHES SEELENLEBEN UND KRIEG. MATERIALIEN UND BERICHTE. UNTER MITWIRKUNG DER BRESLAUER ORTSGRUPPE DES BUNDES FÜR SCHULREFORM. 1915. 181 pp.

292. *Zeitschrift für pädagogische Psychologie und experimentelle Pädagogik.*

TITLE VARIATIONS: Continues *Zeitschrift für pädagogische Psychologie, Pathologie und Hygiene.* Continued by *Zeitschrift für pädagogische Psychologie, experimentelle Pädagogik und jugendkundliche Forschung* with Jahrgang 26, 1925.

DATES OF PUBLICATION: Jahrgang 12–25, 1911–1924.

FREQUENCY: Monthly.

NUMBERING VARIATIONS: Multinumber issues present. Supplements, 1911–1924, numbered in *Pädagogische Monographien.*

PUBLISHER: **Leipzig:** Quelle & Meyer, 1911–1924.

PRIMARY EDITORS: **Ernst Meumann,** 1911–1915; **Otto Scheibner,** 1911–1924; **Aloys Fischer,** 1911–1924; **H. Gaudig,** 1911–1924; **William Stern,** 1916–1924.

293. *Zeitschrift für Pathopsychologie.*

TITLE VARIATIONS: None.

DATES OF PUBLICATION: Band 1–3, Heft 4, August 1911–1919.

FREQUENCY: Irregular.

NUMBERING VARIATIONS: Volume publishing dates are irregular: Band 1 was published 1911/1912; Band 2, 1912/1914; Band 3, 1914/1919.

PUBLISHER: **Leipzig:** Wilhelm Engelmann, 1911–1919.

PRIMARY EDITOR: **Wilhelm Specht,** 1911–1919.

EDITORIAL BOARD: Narziss Ach, 1911–1919; H. Bergson, 1911–1919; G. Heymans, 1911–1919.

1912

294. *Abhandlungen aus dem Gesamtgebiete der Kriminalpsychologie.*

TITLE VARIATIONS: Also called *Heidelberger Abhandlungen.*

DATES OF PUBLICATION: Heft 1–6, 1912–1929.

FREQUENCY: Irregular.

NUMBERING VARIATIONS: None.

PUBLISHER: **Berlin:** Julius Springer, 1912–1929.

PRIMARY EDITORS: **Karl von Lilienthal,** 1912–1921. **F. Nissl,** 1912. **S[igm.] Schott,** 1912–1929. **Karl Wilmanns,** 1912–1929. **Hans W. Gruhle,** 1929. **G. Radbruch,** 1929.

CONTENTS:

Heft 1. Gruhle, Hans W. DIE URSACHEN DER JUGENDLICHEN VERWAHRLOSUNG UND KRIMINALITÄT. 1912. 454 pp.

Heft 2. Homburger, August. LEBENSSCHICKSALE GEISTESKRANKER STRAFGEFANGENER. 1912. 207 pp.

Heft 3. Wetzel, Albrecht, ÜBER MASSENMÖRDER. 1920. 121 pp.

Heft 4. Schneider, Kurt. STUDIEN ÜBER PERSONLICHKEIT UND SCHICKSAL EINGESCHRIEBENER PROSTITUIERTER. 1921. 229 pp.

Heft 5. Dresel, E. G. DIE URSACHEN DER TRUNKSUCHT UND IHRE BEKÄMPFUNG DURCH DIE TRINKERFÜRSORGE IN HEIDELBERG. 1921. 125 pp.

Heft 6. Fuchs-Kamp, Adelheid. LEBENSSCHICKSAL UND PERSÖNLICHKEIT EHEMALIGER FÜRSORGEZÖGLINGE. 1929. 172 pp.

295. *Études de psychologie.*

TITLE VARIATIONS: None.

DATES OF PUBLICATION: Volume 1–6, 1912–1946.

FREQUENCY: Irregular. *See* Contents *below.*

NUMBERING VARIATIONS: Volume 5 appeared earlier than Volume 4. Some issues also numbered as *Contributions à l'étude de la morphologie des mouvements humains,* I–II. *See* Contents *below.* Volume 2 also numbered Volume 1, Fascicule 1.

PUBLISHER: **Louvain:** Librairie Universitaire, 1912–1925. **Louvain:** Institut de philosophie; and **Paris:** Librairie philosophique J. Vrin, 1928. **Louvain:** Éditions de l'institut supérieur de philosophie, 1934–1935. **Louvain:** Éditions de l'institut supérieur de philosophie; and **Paris:** Librairie philosophique J. Vrin, 1946.

PRIMARY EDITOR: **A. Michotte,** 1912–1946.

CONTENTS:

    Volume 1. Michotte, A. and C. Ransy. CONTRIBUTION À L'ÉTUDE DE LA MÉMOIRE LOGIQUE. Pp. 1–96; Michotte, A. NOUVELLES RECHERCHES SUR LA SIMULTANÉITÉ APPARENTE D'IMPRESSIONS DISPARATES PÉRIODIQUES (EXPÉRIENCE DE "COMPLICATION"). Pp. 97–192; Michotte, A. NOTE À PROPOS DE CONTRIBUTIONS RÉCENTES À LA PSYCHOLOGIE DE LA VOLONTÉ. Pp. 193–233; Michotte, A., and Th. Portych. DEUXIÈME ÉTUDE SUR LA MÉMOIRE LOGIQUE, LA REPRODUCTION APRÈS DES INTERVALLES TEMPORELS DE DIFFÉRENTES LONGUEURS. Pp. 237–364; and Michotte, A., and F. Fransen. NOTE SUR L'ANALYSE DES FACTEURS DE LA MÉMORISATION ET SUR L'INHIBITION ASSOCIATIVE. Pp. 365–413.

    Volume 2. Phelan, Gerald B. FEELING EXPERIENCE AND ITS MODALITIES. AN EXPERIMENTAL STUDY. 1925. 292 pp.

    Volume 3. Veldt, J. van der. L'APPRENTISSAGE DU MOUVEMENT ET L'AUTOMATISME. ÉTUDE EXPÉRIMENTALE. 1928. 350 pp.

    Volume 4. Montpellier, Gerard de. LES ALTÉRATIONS MORPHOLOGIQUES DES MOUVEMENTS RAPIDES. ÉTUDE EXPÉRIMENTALE. 1935. 251 pp. (Also as *Contributions à l'étude de la morphologie des mouvements humains, I.*)

    Volume 5. McNeill, Harry. MOTOR ADAPTATION AND ACCURACY; AN EXPERIMENTAL STUDY. 1934. 303 pp. (Also as *Contributions à l'étude de la morphologie des mouvements humains, II*).

    Volume 6. Michotte, A. LA PERCEPTION DE LA CAUSALITÉ. 1946. 296 pp.

296. *Fortschritte der Psychologie und ihrer Anwendungen.*

TITLE VARIATIONS: None.

DATES OF PUBLICATIONS: Band 1–5, June 1912–July 1922.

FREQUENCY: Irregular. Each Band consists of 6 Hefte.

NUMBERING VARIATIONS: Volume 1 published 1913; Volume 2, 1914; Volume 3, 1915; Volume 4, 1917; Volume 5, 1922.

PUBLISHER: **Leipzig** and **Berlin:** B. G. Teubner, 1913–1922.

PRIMARY EDITOR: **Karl Marbe,** 1912–1922.

297. *Imago; Zeitschrift für Anwendung der Psychoanalyse auf die Geisteswissenschaften.*

TITLE VARIATIONS: Continued by *Imago; Zeitschrift für Anwendung der Psychoanalyse auf die Natur- und Geisteswissenschaften* with Jahrgang 14, 1928.

DATES OF PUBLICATION: Jahrgang 1–13, 1912–1927.

FREQUENCY: **Bimonthly**, Jahrgang 1–5, March 1912–1919. **Quarterly**, Jahrgang 6–13, 1920–1927.

NUMBERING VARIATIONS: Jahrgang 1 contains only 5 Hefte. Jahrgang 4 contains 1915/1916; Jahrgang 5, 1917–1919. Jahrgang 12, Heft 2/3 is SIGM. FREUD ZUM SIEBZIGSTEN GEBURTSTAG, May 1926.

PUBLISHER: **Leipzig** and **Vienna:** Hugo Heller & Cie, 1912–1916. **Leipzig** and **Vienna:** Internationaler psychoanalytischer Verlag, 1917–1927.

PRIMARY EDITORS: **Sigmund Freud,** 1912; **Otto Rank,** 1912–1926; **Hanns Sachs,** 1912–1927; **A. J. Storfer,** 1924–1927; **Sandor Rado,** 1927.

298. *Journal of Psycho-Asthenics. Monograph Supplements.*

TITLE VARIATIONS: None.

DATES OF PUBLICATION: Volume 1, Number 1–3, September 1912–March 1917.

FREQUENCY: Irregular. *See* Contents *below.*

NUMBERING VARIATIONS: One issue also in *Journal of Delinquency. See* Contents *below.*

PUBLISHER: **Faribault, Minnesota:** Minnesota School for Feeble-Minded and Colony for Epileptics [for] American Association for the Study of the Feeble-Minded, 1912–1917.

PRIMARY EDITORS: **A. C. Rogers,** 1912–1917; **Fred Kuhlmann,** 1912–1917.

CONTENTS:

Volume 1, Number 1. Kuhlmann, F. A REVISION OF THE BINET–SIMON SYSTEM FOR MEASURING THE INTELLIGENCE OF CHILDREN. September 1912. 41 pp.

————, **Number 2.** Ordahl, Louise Ellison, and George Ordahl. QUALITATIVE DIFFERENCES BETWEEN LEVELS OF INTELLIGENCE IN FEEBLE-MINDED CHILDREN. June 1915. 50 pp.

————, **Number 3.** Crafts, L. W. BIBLIOGRAPHY OF FEEBLE-MINDEDNESS IN ITS SOCIAL ASPECTS. March 1917. (Also as *Journal of Delinquency,* Volume 1, Number 4, September 1916. Pp. 195–208.)

299. *Journal of Religious Psychology, Including Its Anthropological and Sociological Aspects.*

TITLE VARIATIONS: Continues *American Journal of Religious Psychology and Education.*

DATES OF PUBLICATION: Volume 5–7, 1912–December 1915.

FREQUENCY: **Quarterly,** Volume 5–6, 1912–1913. **Semiannual,** four issues to a Volume, Volume 7, January 1914–December 1915.

NUMBERING VARIATIONS: None.

PUBLISHER: **Worcester, Massachusetts:** Louis N. Wilson, Publisher, Clark University, 1912–1915.

PRIMARY EDITORS: **G. Stanley Hall,** 1912–1915; **Alexander F. Chamberlain,** 1912–1913.

300. *London. University. University College. Psychological Laboratory. Collected Papers.*

TITLE VARIATIONS: None.

DATES OF PUBLICATION: Volume 1–10, 1912–1928.

FREQUENCY: Irregular.

NUMBERING VARIATIONS: Volume 2–3 undated.

PUBLISHER: Various. *See* Note *below.*

PRIMARY EDITOR: **C. Spearman,** 1912–1928.

NOTE: No original publications. Compilation of reprints of articles by C. Spearman, J. C. Flugel, A. Wohlgemuth, C. Read, F. Aveling, and others.

301. *Psiche. Rivista di studi psicologici.*

TITLE VARIATIONS: None.

DATES OF PUBLICATION: Volume 1–4, January/February 1912–October/December 1915.

FREQUENCY: **Bimonthly,** Volume 1–2, 1912–1913. **Quarterly,** Volume 3–4, 1914–1915.

NUMBERING VARIATIONS: Volume 3–4, 1914–1915 contain ASSOCIAZIONE DI STUDI PSICOLOGICI. BOLLETINO, Volume 1–2; 1914–1915.

PUBLISHER: **Florence:** "Psiche" redazione ed amministrazione, 1912–1915.

PRIMARY EDITORS: **Enrico Morselli,** 1912–1915; **Sante de Sanctis,** 1912–1915; **Guido Villa,** 1912–1915; **Roberto Assagioli,** 1912–1915.

302. *Rivista di psicologia.* [*1.*][Organ of the Società italiana di psicologia and of the Istituti di psicologia sperimentale (Rome and Turin).]

TITLE VARIATIONS: Continues *Rivista di psicologia applicata.* Continued by *Rivista di psicologia e rassegna di studi pedagogici e filosofici* with Volume 17.

DATES OF PUBLICATION: Volume 8–16, 1912–1920.

FREQUENCY: **Bimonthly,** Volume 8–14, 1912–1918. **Quarterly,** Volume 15–16, 1919–1920.

NUMBERING VARIATIONS: Multinumber issues in Volume 12–16. Volume 15–16 also called Série II or Nuova Série.

PUBLISHER: **Bologna:** Stabilimento poligrafico Emiliano, 1912–1914. **Bologna:** Stabilimento poligrafico Riuniti, 1915–1918. **Bologna:** Nicola Zanichelli editore, 1919–1920.

PRIMARY EDITORS: **Giulio Cesare Ferrari,** 1912–1920. **Luigi Baroncini,** 1912–1918.

303. *Studies in Linguistic Psychology.*

TITLE VARIATIONS: Also called: [*James Millikin University.*] *Bulletin. Linguistic Psychology Series.*

DATES OF PUBLICATION: Volume 1, Number 1–2, 1912.

FREQUENCY: Quarterly (March, June, September and December).

NUMBERING VARIATIONS: None.

PUBLISHER: **Decatur, Illinois:** James Millikin University, 1912.

PRIMARY EDITOR: **Robert James Kellogg,** 1912.

304. *Verein für freie psychoanalytische Forschung. Schriften.*

TITLE VARIATIONS: Continued by *Verein für Individualpsychologie. Schriften* with Heft 5, 1914.

DATES OF PUBLICATION: Heft 1–4, 1912–1914.

FREQUENCY: Irregular. *See* Contents *below.*

NUMBERING VARIATIONS: None.

PUBLISHER: **Munich:** E. Reinhardt, 1912–1914.

PRIMARY EDITOR: **Alfred Adler,** 1912–1914.

CONTENTS:

Heft 1. Furtmüller, Carl. PSYCHOANALYSE UND ETHIK. EINE VORLÄUFIGE UNTERSUCHUNG. 1912. 34 pp.

Heft 2. Kaus, Otto. DER FALL GOGOL. 1912. 81 pp.

Heft 3. Schrecker, Paul. HENRI BERGSONS PHILOSOPHIE DER PERSÖNLICHKEIT. EIN ESSAY ÜBER ANALYTISCHE UND INTUITIVE PSYCHOLOGIE. 1912. 61 pp.

Heft 4. Asnaourow, Felix. SADISMUS, MASOCHISMUS IN KULTUR UND ERZIEHUNG. 1913. 40 pp.

305. *Vestnik psikhologii, kriminal'noi antropologii i pedologii.*

TITLE VARIATIONS: Continues *Vestnik psikhologii, kriminal'noi antropologii i gipnotizma.*

DATES OF PUBLICATION: Tom 9–14, 1912–1919. Suspended publication 1915 and 1918.

FREQUENCY: **5 issues per year,** Tom 9–11, 1912–1914. **Irregular,** Tom 12–14, 1916–1919.

NUMBERING VARIATIONS: None.

PUBLISHER: **St. Petersburg:** Psikhonevrologicheskii institut, 1912–1919.

PRIMARY EDITORS: Unknown.

NOTE: Information on this title was compiled from entries in *A Half Century of Soviet Serials.*

1913

306. *Beiträge zur Psychologie der Gestalt- und Bewegungserlebnisse.*

TITLE VARIATIONS: None.

DATES OF PUBLICATION: Heft 1–26, 1913–1937.

FREQUENCY: Irregular. *See* Contents *below.*

NUMBERING VARIATIONS: Some issues also numbered as part of *Zeitschrift für Psychologie und Physiologie der Sinnesorgane. Abteilung 1. Zeitschrift für Psychologie;* as part of *Psychologische Forschung;* or as part of *Smith College. William Allan Neilson Research Laboratory. Studies in Psychology. See* Contents *below.*

PUBLISHER: **Leipzig:** Johann Ambrosius Barth, 1913–1919. **Berlin:** Julius Springer, 1921–1937.

PRIMARY EDITOR: **Kurt Koffka,** 1913–1937.

CONTENTS:

Heft 1. Kenkel, Friedrich. UNTERSUCHUNGEN ÜBER DEN ZUSAMMENHANG ZWISCHEN ERSCHEINUNGSGRÖSSE UND ERSCHEINUNGSBEWEGUNG BEI EINIGEN SOGENANNTEN OPTISCHEN TÄUSCHUNGEN. (Also as *Zeitschrift für Psychologie und Physiologie der Sinnesorgane. Abteilung 1. Zeitschrift für Psychologie,* Band 67, 1913, pp. 353–449.)

Heft 2. Korte, Adolf. KINEMATOSKOPISCHE UNTERSUCHUNGEN. (Also as *Zeitschrift für Psychologie und Physiologie der Sinnesorgane. Abteilung 1. Zeitschrift für Psychologie,* Band 72, 1915, pp. 193–296.)

Heft 3. Koffka, Kurt. ZUR GRUNDLEGUNG DER WAHRNEHMUNGSPSYCHOLOGIE. EINE AUSEINANDERSETZUNG MIT V. BENUSSI. (Also as *Zeitschrift für Psychologie und Physiologie der Sinnesorgane. Abteilung 1. Zeitschrift für Psychologie,* Band 73, 1915, pp. 11–90.)

Heft 4. Koffka, Kurt. ZUR THEORIE EINFACHSTER GESEHENER BEWEGUNGEN. EIN PHYSIOLOGISCH-MATHEMATISCHER VERSUCH. (Also as *Zeitschrift für Psychologie und Physiologie der Sinnesorgane. Abteilung 1. Zeitschrift für Psychologie,* Band 82, 1919, pp. 257–292.)

Heft 5. Cermak, P., and K. Koffka. UNTERSUCHUNGEN ÜBER BEWEGUNGS- UND VERSCHMELZUNGSPHÄNOMENE. (Also as *Psychologische Forschung,* Band 1, 1922, pp. 66–129.)

Heft 6. Wulf, Friedrich. ÜBER DIE VERÄNDERUNG VON VORSTELLUNGEN (GEDÄCHTNIS UND GESTALT). (Also as *Psychologische Forschung,* Band 1, 1922, pp. 333–373.)

Heft 7. Lindemann, Erich. EXPERIMENTELLE UNTERSUCHUNGEN ÜBER DAS ENTSTEHEN UND VERGEHEN VON GESTALTEN. (Also as *Psychologische Forschung*, Band 2, 1922, pp. 5–60.)

Heft 8. Hartmann, Ludwig. NEUE VERSCHMELZUNGSPROBLEME. (Also as *Psychologische Forschung*, Band 3, 1923, pp. 319–396.)

Heft 9. Ackermann, Adolf. FARBSCHWELLE UND FELDSTRUKTUR. (Also as *Psychologische Forschung*, Band 5, 1924, pp. 44–84.)

Heft 10. Eberhardt, Margarete. UNTERSUCHUNGEN ÜBER FARBSCHWELLEN UND FARBENKONTRAST. (Also as *Psychologische Forschung*, Band 5, 1924, pp. 85–130.)

Heft 11. Stern, Annie. DIE WAHRNEHMUNGEN BEWEGUNGEN IN DER GEGEND DES BLINDEN FLECKS. (Also as *Psychologische Forschung*, Band 7, 1926, pp. 1–15.)

Heft 12. Feinberg, Nikolaus. EXPERIMENTELLE UNTERSUCHUNGEN ÜBER DIE WAHRNEHMUNG IM GEBIET DES BLINDEN FLECKS. (Also as *Psychologische Forschung*, Band 7, 1926, pp. 16–43.)

Heft 13. Noll, Adolf. VERSUCHE ÜBER NACHBILDER. (Also as *Psychologische Forschung*, Band 8, 1926, pp. 3–27.)

Heft 14. Hartgenbusch, Hanns Georg. ÜBER DIE MESSUNG VON WAHRNEHMUNGSBILDERN. (Also as *Psychologische Forschung*, Band 8, 1926, pp. 28–74.)

Heft 15. Kester, Paul. ÜBER LOKALISATIONS- UND BEWEGUNGSERSCHEINUNGEN BEI GERÄUSCHPAAREN. (Also as *Psychologische Forschung*, Band 8, 1926, pp. 75–113.)

Heft 16. Koffka, K., and Beatrix Tudor-Hart. STUDIES IN TRANSPARENCY, FORM AND COLOUR. (Also as *Psychologische Forschung*, Band 10, 1928, pp. 255–298.)

Heft 17. Koffka, K., and Alexander Mintz. ÜBER ÄQUIDISTANTE HELLIGKEITEN. (Also as *Psychologische Forschung*, Band 10, 1928, pp. 299–357.)

Heft 18. Harrower, M. R. SOME EXPERIMENTS ON THE NATURE OF γ-MOVEMENT. (Also as *Psychologische Forschung*, Band 13, 1930, pp. 55–63; and as *Smith College. William Allan Neilson Research Laboratory. Studies in Psychology*, Number 2, pp. 160–168.)

Heft 19. Koffka, K., and Alexander Mintz. ON THE INFLUENCE OF TRANSFORMATION AND CONTRAST ON COLOUR- AND BRIGHTNESS-THRESHOLDS. (Also as *Psychologische Forschung*, Band 14, 1931, pp. 183–198; and as *Smith College. William Allan Neilson Research Laboratory. Studies in Psychology*, Number 2, pp. 119–134.)

Heft 20. Sturm, Marthe. A STUDY OF THE DIRECTION IN THE MOVEMENT-AFTER-IMAGE. (Also as *Psychologische Forschung*, Band 14, 1931, pp. 269–293; and as *Smith College. William Allan Neilson Research Laboratory. Studies in Psychology*, Number 2, pp. 135–159.)

Heft 21. Koffka, K., and M. R. Harrower. COLOUR AND ORGANIZATION. Part I. (Also as *Psychologische Forschung*, Band 15, 1931, pp. 145–192; and as *Smith College. William Allan Neilson Research Laboratory. Studies in Psychology*, Number 3, pp. 177–220.)

Heft 22. Koffka, K., and M. R. Harrower. COLOUR AND ORGANIZATION. Part II. (Also as *Psychologische Forschung*, Band 15, 1931, pp. 193–275; and as *Smith College. William Allan Neilson Research Laboratory. Studies in Psychology*, Number 3, pp. 221–303.)

Heft 23. Koffka, K. SOME REMARKS ON THE THEORY OF COLOUR CONSTANCY. (Also as *Psychologische Forschung*, Band 16, 1932, pp. 329–354; also as *Smith College. William Allan Neilson Research Laboratory. Studies in Psychology*, Number 4, pp., 305–329.)

Heft 24. Heider, Grace Moore. NEW STUDIES IN TRANSPARENCY, FORM AND COLOR. (Also as *Psychologische Forschung*, Band 17, 1933, pp. 13–55; also as *Smith College. William Allan Neilson Research Laboratory. Studies in Psychology*, Number 4, pp. 330–371.)

Heft 25. Harrower, M. R. ORGANIZATION IN HIGHER MENTAL PROCESSES. (Also as *Psychologische Forschung*, Band 17, 1933, pp. 56–120; also as *Smith College. William Allan Neilson Research Laboratory. Studies in Psychology*, Number 4, pp. 381–444.)

Heft 26. Hanfmann, Eugenia. ON THE FACTORS UNDERLYING A PHENOMENON DISCOVERED BY HERING. (Also as *Psychologische Forschung*, Band 21, 1937, pp. 132–141.)

307. *Central Association for the Care of the Mentally Defective. Report.*

TITLE VARIATIONS: Also called *C.A.M.D. Report*. Continued by *Central Association for Mental Welfare. Report* with 8th Report, 1921/1922.

DATES OF PUBLICATION: 1st–7th, 1913/1915–1920/1921.

FREQUENCY: **Biennial,** 1st, 1913/1915. **Annual,** 2nd–7th, 1915/1916–1920/1921.

NUMBERING VARIATIONS: None.

PUBLISHER: **London:** Central Association for the Care of the Mentally Defective, 1915–1921.

PRIMARY EDITOR: Secretary acts as editor.

308. *Congrès international de psychologie et physiologie sportives. Compte rendu.*

TITLE VARIATIONS: None.

DATES OF PUBLICATION: 1er, 1913.

FREQUENCY: Irregular. *See* Contents *below.*

NUMBERING VARIATIONS: None.

PUBLISHER: **Lausanne:** E. Toso & Cie, 1913.

PRIMARY EDITORS: None listed.

CONTENTS:

1er. COMPTE RENDU . . . CONGRÈS INTERNATIONAL DE PSYCHOLOGIE ET PHYSIOLOGIE SPORTIVES SOUS LE HAUT PATRONAGE DU CONSEIL FÉDÉRAL DE LA CONFÉDÉRATION HELVÉTIQUE. Palais de l'université Lausanne 7–11 mai 1913. 241 pp.

309. *Gesellschaft für Tierpsychologie. Mitteilungen.*

TITLE VARIATIONS: None.

DATES OF PUBLICATION: Volume 1–4, Number 2, 1913–1916. New Series. Number 1–5, 1920–1924. Series 3, Number 1–3/4, 1927–1929. Series 4, Number 1–2, 1930–1934.

FREQUENCY: **Quarterly**, Volume 1–4, Number 2, 1913–1916. **Annual**, New Series, Number 1–5, 1920–1924. **Irregular**, Third Series, Number 1-3/4, 1927–1929. Fourth Series, Number 1–2, 1930–1934.

NUMBERING VARIATIONS: None.

PUBLISHER: **Stuttgart:** Gesellschaft für Tierpsychologie, 1913–1916, 1920–1924. **Stuttgart:** Gesellschaft für Tierpsychologie, Richard Jordan Verlag, 1927–1934.

PRIMARY EDITORS: **Heinrich Ernst Ziegler,** 1913–1924; **Karl Krall,** 1927–1929; **H. Krämer,** 1930–1934.

310. *Handbooks of Moral and Religious Education.*

TITLE VARIATIONS: None.

DATES OF PUBLICATION: Volume 1–10, 1913–1920.

FREQUENCY: Irregular. *See* Contents *below.*

NUMBERING VARIATIONS: Although 10 volumes were planned, only Volumes 2, 7, and 9 appear to have been issued.

PUBLISHER: **New York:** Macmillan Company, 1913–1920.

PRIMARY EDITOR: **E. Hershey Sneath,** 1913–1920.

CONTENTS:
Volume 2. Tracy, Frederick. PSYCHOLOGY OF ADOLESCENCE. 1920. 246 pp.
Volume 7. Sneath, E. Hershey, and George Hodges. MORAL TRAINING IN THE SCHOOL AND HOME; A MANUAL FOR TEACHERS AND PARENTS. 1913. 221 pp.
Volume 9. Sneath, E. Hershey, George Hodges, and Henry Hallam Tweedy. RELIGIOUS TRAINING IN THE SCHOOL AND HOME; A MANUAL FOR TEACHERS AND PARENTS. 1917. 341 pp.

311. *Internationale Zeitschrift für ärztliche Psychoanalyse.*
[Organ of the Internationale psychoanalytische Vereinigung.]

TITLE VARIATIONS: Supersedes *Zentralblatt für Psychoanalyse und Psychotherapie.* Continued by *Internationale Zeitschrift für Psychoanalyse* with Band 6, 1920.

DATES OF PUBLICATION: Band 1–5, 1913–1919.

FREQUENCY: **Bimonthly,** Band 1–4, 1913–1918. **Quarterly,** Band 5, 1919.

NUMBERING VARIATIONS: Band 4, 1918 contains *American Psychoanalytic Association. Report.*

PUBLISHER: **Leipzig** and **Vienna:** Hugo Heller & Cie, 1913–1918. **Leipzig** and **Vienna:** Internationaler psychoanalytischer Verlag, 1919.

PRIMARY EDITORS: **Sigmund Freud**, 1913–1919; **Sandor Ferenczi**, 1913–1919; **Otto Rank**, 1913–1919; **Ernest Jones**, 1913–1919; **Karl Abraham**, 1919; **Eduard Hitschmann**, 1919.

312. *Prace z psychologii doświadczalnej.*

TITLE VARIATIONS: Also called *L'année psychologique polonaise.*

DATES OF PUBLICATION: Tom 1, 1913.

FREQUENCY: Annual.

NUMBERING VARIATIONS: None.

PUBLISHER: **Warsaw:** Instytut psychologiczny w Warszawie (by) Skład główny w księgarni E. Wende i S-ka, 1913.

PRIMARY EDITOR: **Edward Abramowski**, 1913.

313. *Psychoanalytic Review. A Journal Devoted to an Understanding of Human Conduct.*

TITLE VARIATIONS: Continued by *Psychoanalytic Review. An American Journal of Psychoanalysis Devoted to an Understanding of Human Conduct* with Volume 19, 1932.

DATES OF PUBLICATION: Volume 1–18, 1913–1931.

FREQUENCY: Quarterly.

NUMBERING VARIATIONS: Each issue also assigned a whole number, Number 1–72.

PUBLISHER: **New York:** William A. White and Smith Ely Jelliffe, 1913–1916. **Lancaster, Pennsylvania** and **New York:** Nervous and Mental Disease Publishing Company, 1917. **Lancaster** and **Washington D.C.:** Nervous and Mental Disease Publishing Company, 1917–1931.

PRIMARY EDITORS: **William A. White**, 1913–1931. **Smith Ely Jelliffe**, 1913–1931.

314. *Revue des sciences psychologiques.*

TITLE VARIATIONS: None.

DATES OF PUBLICATION: Année 1, Numéro 1–4, January/March 1913–October/December 1913.

FREQUENCY: Quarterly.

NUMBERING VARIATIONS: None.

PUBLISHER: **Paris:** Marcel Rivière et Cie, éditeurs, 1913.

PRIMARY EDITORS: **J. Tastevin**, 1913; **P. L. Couchoud**, 1913.

315. *Sammlung zwangloser Abhandlungen zur Neuro- und Psychopathologie des Kindesalters.*

TITLE VARIATIONS: None.

DATES OF PUBLICATION: Band 1, Heft 1–7, 1913–1920.

FREQUENCY: Irregular. *See* Contents *below.*

NUMBERING VARIATIONS: Heft 1–3 is a single publication.

PUBLISHER: **Jena:** G. Fischer, 1913–1920.

PRIMARY EDITOR: **Ewald Stier,** 1913–1920.

EDITORIAL BOARD: Jusuff Ibrahim, 1913–1920; Ernst Trömner, 1913–1920; Franz Kramer, 1913–1920.

CONTENTS:

Heft 1–3. Stier, Ewald. WANDERTRIEB UND PATHOLOGISCHES FORTLAUFEN BEI KINDERN. 1913. 135 pp.

Heft 4. Ulrich, Martha. KLINISCHE BEITRÄGE ZUR LEHRE VON ANGEBORENEM KERNMANGEL. 1913. 74 pp.

Heft 5. Singer, Kurt. DIE SCHRECK-NEUROSE DES KINDESALTERS. 1918. 71 pp.

Heft 6. Stier, Ewald. ÜBER DIE RESPIRATORISCHEN AFFEKTKRÄMPFE DES FRÜHKINDLICHEN ALTERS. 1918. 105 pp.

Heft 7. Stier, Ewald. ÜBER OHNMACHTEN UND OHNMACHTSÄHNLICHE ANFÄLLE BEI KINDERN UND IHRE BEZIEHUNGEN ZUR HYSTERIE UND EPILEPSIE. 1920. 138 pp.

316. *Shinri Kenkyū.* [Psychological Research].

TITLE VARIATIONS: Superseded by *Shinrigaku Kenkyū. Shin Shirīzu.* [Psychological Research. New Series] with Volume 1, 1926.

DATES OF PUBLICATION: Volume 1–28, 1913–1926.

FREQUENCY: Unknown.

NUMBERING VARIATIONS: None.

PUBLISHER: **Tokyo:** Shinrigaku Kenkyūkai [Society for Psychological Research], 1913–1926.

PRIMARY EDITORS: None listed.

NOTE: Information for this entry was obtained from *Gakujutsu Zasshi Sōgō Mokuroku. Jimbun Kagaku Wabun Hen.* [Union List of Scholarly Journals. Japanese Language Section. Humanities Part]. Tokyo, 1973.

317. *Société lorraine de psychologie appliquée. Bulletin.*

TITLE VARIATIONS: None.

DATES OF PUBLICATION: Numéro 1–72, 1913–1939.

FREQUENCY: **Semiannual,** Numéro 1–32, 1913–1929. **Quarterly,** Numéro 33–72, 1930–1939.

NUMBERING VARIATIONS: None.

PUBLISHER: **Nancy:** Société lorraine de psychologie appliquée, siège social, 1913–1939.

PRIMARY EDITORS: **Émile Coué,** 1913–1926; None listed, 1927–1939.

318. *Svenskt Arkiv för Pedagogik.*

TITLE VARIATIONS: United with *Psyke* to form *Arkiv för Psykologi och Pedagogik* with Häfte 1, 1922.

DATES OF PUBLICATION: Band 1–9, 1913–1921.

FREQUENCY: Triannual, Band 1, 1913. Semiannual, published as combined issues Häfte 1/2, Häfte 3/4, Band 2–9, 1914–1921.

NUMBERING VARIATIONS: None.

PUBLISHER: **Stockholm:** P. A. Norstedt & Söner, 1913–1914. **Uppsala** and **Stockholm:** Almqvist & Wiksells Boktryckeri, 1915–1921.

PRIMARY EDITORS: **Bertil Hammer,** 1913–1921; **Georg Brandell,** 1921; **Walter Fevrell,** 1921; **David Lund,** 1921.

319. *Tierseele. Zeitschrift für vergleichende Seelenkunde.*

TITLE VARIATIONS: None.

DATES OF PUBLICATION: Band 1, Heft 1/2–4, 1913–1914.

FREQUENCY: Quarterly.

NUMBERING VARIATIONS: Heft 1/2 is a multinumber issue.

PUBLISHER: **Bonn:** Elberfeld (Hall 24), Oscar Stodt, 1913–1914.

PRIMARY EDITOR: **Karl Krall,** 1913–1914.

320. *Training School Bulletin.*

TITLE VARIATIONS: Continues *Training School.*

DATES OF PUBLICATION: Volume 10–47, Number 8+, March 1913–December 1950+.

FREQUENCY: Monthly (except July and August).

NUMBERING VARIATIONS: Each issue from Volume 10, Number 1 to Volume 20, Number 10, March 1913–February 1924 is also assigned a whole number, Number 103–211. Whole numbering apparently ceases with Number 211. Multinumber issues appear infrequently. Supplements to Volume 46, Number 3–4 and Volume 47 also numbered as *Training School Bulletin. Monograph Supplement Series,* Number 1–2.

PUBLISHER: **Vineland, New Jersey:** Training School, 1913–1950+

PRIMARY EDITORS: E. R. Johnstone, 1913–1927; Henry H. Goddard, 1913–1919; Alice Morrison Nash, 1913–1927, 1950+; Alexander Johnson, 1913–1919; Helen F. Hill, 1920–1949; S. D. Porteus, 1920–1927. Walter Jacob, 1950+; George W. Gens, 1950+; Marie Roberts, 1950+; Robert H. Cassel, 1950+; Yolande Pignatiello, 1950+;

321. *Wissenschaftliche Beiträge zur Pädagogik und Psychologie.*

TITLE VARIATIONS: None.

DATES OF PUBLICATION: Heft 1–5, 1913–1914.

FREQUENCY: Irregular. *See* Contents *below.*

NUMBERING VARIATIONS: None.

PUBLISHER: **Leipzig:** Verlag von Quelle & Meyer, 1913–1914.

PRIMARY EDITORS: **G. Deuchler,** 1913–1914; **David Katz,** 1913–1914.

CONTENTS:

Heft 1. Gassmann, E., and E. Schmidt. DER SPRACHLICHE AUFFASSUNGS-UMFANG DES SCHULKINDES. 1913. 133 pp.

Heft 2. Gassmann, E., and E. Schmidt. DIE FEHLERERSCHEINUNGEN BEIM NACHSPRECHEN VON SÄTZEN UND IHRE BEZIEHUNG ZUR SPRACHLICHEN ENTWICKLUNG DES SCHULKINDES. 1913. 289 pp.

Heft 3. Gassmann, E., and E. Schmidt. DAS NACHSPRECHEN VON SÄTZEN IN SEINE BEZIEHUNG ZUR BEGABUNG. EXPERIMENTELLE UNTERSUCHUNGEN ÜBER DEN SPRACHLICHEN AUFFASUNGSUMFANG DES SCHULKINDES. 1913. 101 pp.

Heft 4. Schäfer, Karl. BEITRÄGE ZUR KINDERFORSCHUNG INSBESONDERE DER ERFORSCHUNG DER KINDLICHEN SPRACHE; and Katz, David. STUDIEN ZUR KINDERPSYCHOLOGIE. 1913. 119 pp.

Heft 5. Schrenk, Johannes. ÜBER DAS VERSTÄNDNIS FÜR BILDLICHE DARSTELLUNG BEI SCHULKINDERN. 1914. 124 pp.

322. *Zentralblatt für Psychoanalyse und Psychotherapie. Medizinische Monatsschrift für Seelenkunde.* [Organ of the Internationale psychoanalytische Vereinigung.]

TITLE VARIATIONS: Continues *Zentralblatt für Psychoanalyse. Medizinische Monatsschrift für Seelenkunde.* Superseded by *Internationale Zeitschrift für ärztliche Psychoanalyse* with Band 1, 1913.

DATES OF PUBLICATION: Band 4, Heft 1–12, January–September 1913.

FREQUENCY: Monthly.

NUMBERING VARIATIONS: Multinumber issues present.

PUBLISHER: **Wiesbaden:** J. F. Bergmann, 1913.

PRIMARY EDITOR: **Wilhelm Stekel,** 1913.

1914

323. Aarskrift for psykisk Forskning. [Sponsored by the Seleskabet for psykisk Forskning.]

TITLE VARIATIONS: None.

DATES OF PUBLICATION: Bind 1–3, 1914–1916.

FREQUENCY: Annual.

NUMBERING VARIATIONS: None.

PUBLISHER: **Copenhagen:** Erslev & Hasselbalch, 1914. **Copenhagen:** Hasselbalch, 1915–1916.

PRIMARY EDITORS: None listed.

324. *Arbeiten zur Entwicklungs-Psychologie.*

TITLE VARIATIONS: None.

DATES OF PUBLICATION: Stück 1–21, 1914–1941.

FREQUENCY OF ISSUE: Irregular. *See* Contents *below.*

NUMBERING VARIATIONS: Stück 2 dated earlier than Stück 1. Also numbered as *Leipzig. Sächsische staatliche Forschungsinstitute. Forschungsinstitut für Psychologie. Abhandlungen. See* Contents *below.*

PUBLISHER: **Leipzig** and **Berlin:** Wilhelm Engelmann, 1914. **Leipzig:** Wilhelm Engelmann, 1915–1923. **Munich:** C. H. Beck'sche Verlagsbuchhandlung, 1926–1932, 1935–1941. **Munich** and **Berlin:** C. H. Beck'sche Verlagsbuchhandlung, 1934.

PRIMARY EDITOR: **Felix Krueger,** 1914–1941.

CONTENTS:

Stück 1. Krueger, Felix. ÜBER ENTWICKLUNGSPSYCHOLOGIE, IHRE SACHLICHE UND GESCHICHTLICHE NOTWENDIGKEIT. 1915. 232 pp.

Stück 2. Volkelt, Hans. ÜBER DIE VORSTELLUNGEN DER TIERE. 1914. 126 pp.

Stück 3. Werner, Heinz. DIE URSPRÜNGE DER METAPHER. 1919. 238 pp.

Stück 4. Golz, Bruno. WANDLUNGEN LITERARISCHER MOTIVE. I. HEBBELS AGNES BERNAUER. II. DIE LEGENDEN VON DEN ALTVÄTERN. 1920. 94 pp.

Stück 5. Freyer, Hans. DIE BEWERTUNG DER WIRTSHAFT IM PHILOSOPHISCHEN DENKEN DES 19. JAHRHUNDERTS. 1921 (2. auflage, 1939). 171 pp. (Also as *Leipzig. Sächsische staatliche Forschungsinstitute. Forschungsinstitut für Psychologie. Abhandlungen,* Stück 6.)

Stück 6. Gutmann, Bruno. AMULETTE UND TALISMANE BEI DEN DSCHAGGANEGERN AM KILIMANDSCHARO. 1923. 29 pp.

Stück 7. Gutmann, Bruno. DAS RECHT DER DSCHAGGA; and Krueger, Felix. ZUR ENTWICKLUNGSPSYCHOLOGIE DES RECHTS. NACHWORT. 1926. 778 pp. (Also as *Leipzig. Sächsische staatliche Forschungsinstitute. Forschungsinstitut für Psychologie. Abhandlungen,* Stück 7.)

Stück 8. Gantschewa, Sdrawka. KINDERPLASTIK DREI-BIS SECHSJÄHRIGER. EXPERIMENTALPSYCHOLOGISCH UNTERSUCHT. 1930. 132+32 pp. (Also as *Leipzig. Sächsische staatliche Forschungsinstitute. Forschungsinstitut für Psychologie. Abhandlungen,* Stück 37.)

Stück 9. Leitner, Hans. PSYCHOLOGIE JUGENDLICHER RELIGIOSITÄT INNERHALB DES DEUTSCHEN METHODISMUS. 1930. 142 pp. (Also as *Leipzig. Sächsische staatliche Forschungsinstitute. Forschungsinstitut für Psychologie. Abhandlungen,* Stück 38.)

Stück 10. Röttger, Fritz. PHONETISCHE GESTALTBILDUNG BEI JUNGEN KINDERN. 1931. 218 pp. (Also as *Leipzig. Sächsische staatliche Forschungsinstitute. Forschungsinstitut für Psychologie. Abhandlungen,* Stück 44.)

Stück 11. Vidor, Martha. WAS IST MUSIKALITÄT? EXPERIMENTELL-PSYCHOLOGISCHE VERSUCHE. 1931. 57 pp. (Also as *Leipzig. Sächsische staatliche Forschungsinstitute. Forschungsinstitut für Psychologie. Abhandlungen,* Stück 45.)

Stück 12. Gutmann, Bruno. DIE STAMMESLEHREN DER DSCHAGGA, I. BAND: DIE LEHREN VOR DER BESCHNEIDUNG. DER HAINGANG (LAGERGEMEINSCHAFT NACH DER BESCHNEIDUNG). 1932. 671 pp. (Also as *Leipzig. Sächsische staatliche Forschungsinstitute. Forschungsinstitut für Psychologie. Abhandlungen,* Stück 47.)

Stück 13. Obrig, Ilse. KINDER ERZÄHLEN ANGEFANGENE GESCHICHTEN WEITER. 1934. 70 pp. (Also as *Leipzig. Sächsische staatliche Forschungsinstitute. Forschungsinstitut für Psychologie. Abhandlungen,* Stück 55.)

Stück 14. Freiesleben, Gertraude, and Brigitte Freiesleben, in association with Hans Volkelt. EIN KINDERBRIEFWECHSEL. BRIEFE ZWEIER MÄDCHEN IM ALTER VON 10 BIS 16 JAHREN. 1934. 156 pp. (Also as *Leipzig. Sächsische staatliche Forschungsinstitute. Forschungsinstitut für Psychologie. Abhandlungen,* Stück 57.)

Stück 15. Bachmann, Armin. ZUR PSYCHOLOGISCHEN THEORIE DES SPRACHLICHEN BEDEUTUNGSWANDELS. 1935. 68 pp. (Also as *Leipzig. Sächsische staatliche Forschungsinstitute. Forschungsinstitut für Psychologie. Abhandlungen,* Stück 63.)

Stück 16. Gutmann, Bruno. DIE STAMMESLEHREN DER DSCHAGGA. II. BAND: DIE VORLEHREN. DIE LAGERLEHREN. 1935. 642 pp. (Also as *Leipzig. Sächsische staatliche Forschungsinstitute. Forschungsinstitut für Psychologie. Abhandlungen,* Stück 64.)

Stück 17. Feige, Johannes. DER ALTER FEIERABEND. 1936. 106 pp. (Also as *Leipzig. Sächsische staatliche Forschungsinstitute. Forschungsinstitut für Psychologie. Abhandlungen,* Stück 66.)

Stück 18. Leibold, Rudolf. AKUSTISCH-MOTORISCHER RHYTHMUS IN FRÜHER KINDHEIT. EINE STRUKTURPSYCHOLOGISCHE STUDIE. 1936. 62 pp. (Also as *Leipzig. Sächsische staatliche Forschungsinstitute. Forschungsinstitut für Psychologie. Abhandlungen,* Stück 67).

Stück 19. Gutmann, Bruno. DIE STAMMESLEHREN DER DSCHAGGA. III. (SCHLUSS-) BAND: DIE HOCHZEITSLEHREN. DIE LEHREN DER GROSSEN HOCHZEIT; and Krueger, Felix. SCHLUSSWORT DES HERAUSGEBERS. 1938. 662 pp.

Stück 20. Wellek, Albert. TYPOLOGIE DER MUSIKBEGABUNG IM DEUTSCHEN

VOLKE. GRUNDLEGUNG EINER PSYCHOLOGISCHEN THEORIE DER MUSIK UND MUSIKGESCHICHTE. MIT ALLGEMEINPSYCHOLOGISCHEN BEITRÄGEN ZUR "TONHÖHEN"-UNTERSCHIEDSEMPFINDLICHKEIT. 1939. 307 pp.
    Stück 21. Appel, Elsbeth. VOM FEHLEN DES GENETIV-S. 1941. 132 pp.

325. *Archiv für Religionspsychologie.* [Organ of the Gesellschaft für Religionspsychologie.]

TITLE VARIATIONS: Continued by *Archiv für Religionspsychologie und Seelenführung* with Band 4, 1929.

DATES OF PUBLICATION: Band 1–3, 1914–1921.

FREQUENCY: Irregular. Band 1, 1914; Band 2, 1921; Band 3, 1921.

NUMBERING VARIATIONS: Band 2–3 is a combined volume.

PUBLISHER: **Tübingen:** Gesellschaft für Religionspsychologie, 1914–1921.

PRIMARY EDITOR: **Wilhelm Stählin,** 1914–1921.

EDITORIAL BOARD: A. Dyroff, 1914–1921; Th. Flournoy, 1914–1921; K. Girgensohn, 1914–1921; H. Höffding, 1914–1921; O. Külpe, 1914–1921; A. Messer, 1914–1921; Fr. Rittelmeyer, 1914–1921; E. Troeltsch, 1914–1921; K. Koffka, 1914.

326. *British Society for the Study of Sex Psychology. Publications.*

TITLE VARIATIONS: None.

DATES OF PUBLICATION: Number 1–20, 1914–1924 + .

FREQUENCY: Irregular. *See* Contents *below.*

NUMBERING VARIATIONS: Publications issued without numbers were in some cases reissued in the numbered series.

PUBLISHER: **London:** C. W. Beaumont & Co., 1917 (Number 2); **London:** Printed for the Society by Battley Bros., 1917–1920 (Number 4–6); **London:** Printed for the Society by J. E. Francis, Athenaeum Press, 1920–1921 (Number 7–10); **London:** C. W. Beaumont & Co., 1924 (Number 13).

PRIMARY EDITORS: None listed.

CONTENTS:
    Number 1. British Society for the Study of Sex Psychology. POLICY AND PRINCIPLES. GENERAL AIMS. 1914. (Reissued in 1920.) 10 pp.
    Number 2. THE SOCIAL PROBLEM OF SEXUAL INVERSION. (An abridged translation from the German treatise entitled, "Was soll das Volk vom Dritten Geschlecht wissen?," published under the auspices of the Humanitarian-Science Committee [Wissenschaftlich-humanitären Komitee] of Leipzig and Berlin, in 1903.) Issued by the Society. [1917.] 19 pp.
    Number 3. Browne, F. W. Stella. SEXUAL VARIETY AND VARIABILITY AMONG WOMEN. (1917.) 14 pp.
    Number 4. Housman, L. THE RELATION OF FELLOW-FEELING TO SEX. (1917.) 15 pp.

Number 5. Ellis, Havelock. THE EROTIC RIGHTS OF WOMEN, AND THE OBJECTS OF MARRIAGE. TWO ESSAYS. 1918. 23 pp.

Number 6. Summers, Montague. THE MARQUIS DE SADE, A STUDY IN ALGOLAGNIA. 1920. 23 pp.

Number 7. Northcote, H. THE SOCIAL VALUE OF THE STUDY OF SEX PSYCHOLOGY. 1920. 19 pp.

Number 8. Westermarck, Edward. THE ORIGIN OF SEXUAL MODESTY. 1921. 20 pp.

Number 9. Ellis, Havelock. THE PLAY-FUNCTION OF SEX. 1921. 12 pp.

Number 10. Paul, Eden. THE SEXUAL LIFE OF THE CHILD. 1921. 20 pp.

Number 11/12. REJUVENATION: Paul, Eden. STEINACH'S REJUVENATION EXPERIMENTS; and Haire, Norman. RECENT DEVELOPMENTS OF STEINACH'S WORK. 1923. 35 pp.

Number 13. Carpenter, Edward. SOME FRIENDS OF WALT WHITMAN. 1924. 16 pp.

Number 14. Unknown.

NOTE: Information on this entry is incomplete. The compilers were unable to examine complete holdings of this title.

327. *Conference on Educational Measurements. Proceedings.*

TITLE VARIATIONS: None.

DATES OF PUBLICATION: 1st–29th, 1914–1942.

FREQUENCY: Annual.

NUMBERING VARIATIONS: Numbered as a subseries of [*Indiana. University.*] *Bulletin,* 1924–1942.

PUBLISHER: **Bloomington, Indiana:** Published by the Extension Division of Indiana University, 1914–1923. **Bloomington:** Published by the School of Education of Indiana University, 1924–1925. **Bloomington:** Bureau of Co-operative Research, 1926–1941. **Bloomington:** Bureau of Co-operative Research and Field Service, 1942.

PRIMARY EDITORS: None listed, 1914–1927; **Henry Lester Smith** (Director), 1928–1942; **Merrill T. Eaton,** 1940–1942.

328. *Internationale Zeitschrift für Psychoanalyse. Beihefte.*
[Organ of the Internationale psychoanalytische Vereinigung.]

TITLE VARIATIONS: Superseded by *Internationale Zeitschrift für Psychoanalyse und "Imago". Beihefte* with Stück, 1, 1934.

DATES OF PUBLICATION: Stück 1–5, 1914–1922.

FREQUENCY: Irregular. *See* Contents *below.*

NUMBERING VARIATIONS: None.

PUBLISHER: **Vienna:** Internationaler psychoanalytischer Verlag (durch F. Volckmar, Leipzig), 1914–1922.

PRIMARY EDITOR: **Sigmund Freud,** 1914–1922.

CONTENTS:
Stück 1. Jelgersma, G. UNBEWUSSTES GEISTESLEBEN. 1914. 32 pp.
Stück 2. Freud, Sigmund. JENSEITS DER LUSTPRINZIPS. 1920. 60 pp.
Stück 3. BERICHT ÜBER DIE FORTSCHRITTE DER PSYCHOANALYSE IN DEN JAHREN 1914–1919. 1921. 388 pp.
Stück 4. Stärcke, August. PSYCHOANALYSE UND PSYCHIATRIE. 1921. 64 pp.
Stück 5. Hollos, Stefan und Sandor Ferenczi. ZUR PSYCHOANALYSE DER PARALYTISCHEN GEISTESSTÖRUNG. 1922. 55 pp.

329. Jahrbuch der Psychoanalyse.

TITLE VARIATIONS: Continues *Jahrbuch für psychoanalytische und psychopathologische Forschungen*. Also called New Series of this title.

DATES OF PUBLICATION: Band 6, 1 Hälfte, 1914.

FREQUENCY: Annual.

NUMBERING VARIATIONS: None.

PUBLISHER: **Vienna:** F. Deuticke, 1914.

PRIMARY EDITORS: **Sigmund Freud,** 1914; **Karl Abraham,** 1914; **Edward Hitschmann,** 1914.

330. London. University. Bedford College for Women. Psychological Laboratory. Psychological Studies.

TITLE VARIATIONS: None.

DATES OF PUBLICATION: [Number 1], 1914.

FREQUENCY: Irregular. *See* Contents *and* Note *below.*

NUMBERING VARIATIONS: None.

PUBLISHER: **London:** University of London Press, 1914.

PRIMARY EDITOR: **Beatrice Edgell,** 1914.

CONTENTS:
[**Number 1**]. Macgregor, M., and J. Schinz. A STUDY OF LEARNING AND RELEARNING IN MICE AND RATS; Wilson E. H. A STUDY OF CONTROLLED ASSOCIATION; Fildes, L. C. AN EXPERIMENTAL INQUIRY INTO THE NATURE OF RECOGNITION; and Lunniss, B. A. A STUDY OF THOUGHT PROCESSES. 1914. 161 pp.

NOTE: Although titled as a serial, the only issue of this title was published unnumbered and it is not certain that additional issues were planned.

331. Moscow. Gosudarstvennyi Darvinskii muzei. Zoopsikhologicheskaia laboratoriia. Otchet.

TITLE VARIATIONS: None.

DATES OF PUBLICATION: Tom 1, 1914/1920.

FREQUENCY: Irregular.

NUMBERING VARIATIONS: None.

PUBLISHER: **Moscow:** Gosudarstvennyi Darvinskii muzei, Zoopsikhologiches-kaia laboratoriia, 1921.

PRIMARY EDITOR: **Nadezhda Nikolaevna Kots,** 1921.

332. *Münchener Studien zur Psychologie und Philosophie.*

TITLE VARIATIONS: None.

DATES OF PUBLICATION: Band 1, Heft 1–5, 1914–1920.

FREQUENCY: Irregular. *See* Contents *below.*

NUMBERING VARIATIONS: Pagination is continuous. *See* Contents *below.*

PUBLISHER: **Stuttgart:** Verlag von W. Spemann, 1914–1920.

PRIMARY EDITORS: **Oswald Külpe,** 1914–1920; **Karl Bühler,** 1914–1920.

CONTENTS:

Heft 1. Pauli, Richard. ÜBER EINE METHODE ZUR UNTERSUCHUNG UND DEMONSTRATION DER ENGE DES BEWUSSTSEINS SOWIE ZUR MESSUNG DER GE-SCHWINDIGKEIT DER AUFMERKSAMKEITSWANDERUNG. 1914. Pp. 1–36.

Heft 2. Rath, Carl. ÜBER DIE VERERBUNG VON DISPOSITIONEN ZUM VER-BRECHEN. 1914. Pp. 37–138.

Heft 3. Gerhards, Karl. MACHS ERKENNTNISTHEORIE UND DER REALIS-MUS. 1914. Pp. 139–296.

Heft 4. Segal, Jakob. ÜBER DAS VORSTELLEN VON OBJEKTEN UND SITUA-TIONEN. 1916. Pp. 297–495.

Heft 5. Mager, Alois. DIE ENGE DES BEWUSSTSEINS. 1920. Pp. 497–657.

333. *Psychological Clinic. A Journal of Orthogenics for the Normal Development of Every Child.*

TITLE VARIATIONS: Continues *Psychological Clinic. A Journal of Orthogenics for the Study and Treatment of Retardation and Deviation.*

DATES OF PUBLICATION: Volume 8–23, Number 1/2, 1914–January/June 1935.

FREQUENCY: **Monthly** (except July–September), Volume 8–20, 1914–1932. **Quarterly,** Volume 21–23, 1932–1935.

NUMBERING VARIATIONS: Volume 12–18 contain multinumber issues. Volume 23, Number 1/2, 1935, is *Report of Committee of Clinical Section of American Psychological Association.*

PUBLISHER: **Philadelphia:** Psychological Clinic Press, 1914–1931. **Lancaster, Pennsylvania** and **Philadelphia:** Psychological Clinic Press, 1931–1935.

PRIMARY EDITORS: **Lightner Witmer,** 1914–1935; **Miles Murphy,** 1928–1935; **Morris S. Viteles,** 1930–1934.

334. *Psychologische Abhandlungen.*

TITLE VARIATIONS: None.

DATES OF PUBLICATION: Band 1–7+, 1914–1950+.

FREQUENCY: Irregular. *See* Contents *below.*

NUMBERING VARIATIONS: None.

PUBLISHER: **Vienna:** F. Deuticke, 1914. **Zurich:** Rascher & Cie, 1928–1934. **Zurich:** Rascher Verlag, 1944–1950+.

PRIMARY EDITOR: **Carl Gustav Jung,** 1914–1950+.

CONTENTS:
>   **Band 1.** Jung, Carl Gustav. PSYCHOLOGISCHE ABHANDLUNGEN. 1914. 211 pp.
>   **Band 2.** Jung, Carl Gustav. ÜBER DIE ENERGETIK DER SEELE UND ANDERE PSYCHOLOGISCHE ABHANDLUNGEN. 1928. 224 pp.
>   **Band 3.** Jung, Carl Gustav. SEELENPROBLEME DER GEGENWART. 1931. 435 pp.
>   **Band 4.** Jung, Carl Gustav. WIRKLICHKEIT DER SEELE. 1934. 409 pp.
>   **Band 5.** Jung, Carl Gustav. PSYCHOLOGIE UND ALCHEMIE. 1944. 696 pp.
>   **Band 6.** Jung, Carl Gustav. SYMBOLIK DES GEISTES. 1948. 500 pp.
>   **Band 7.** Jung, Carl Gustav. GESTALTUNGEN DES UNBEWUSSTEN. 1950. 616 pp.

335. *Verein für Individualpsychologie. Schriften.*

TITLE VARIATIONS: Continues *Verein für freie psychoanalytische Forschung. Schriften.* Continued by *Schriften für angewandte Individualpsychologie* with Heft 7, 1917.

DATES OF PUBLICATION: Heft 5–6, 1914.

FREQUENCY: Irregular. *See* Contents *below.*

NUMBERING VARIATIONS: None.

PUBLISHER: **Munich:** E. Reinhardt, 1914.

PRIMARY EDITOR: **Alfred Adler,** 1914.

CONTENTS:
>   **Heft 5.** Strasser-Eppelbaum, Vera. ZUR PSYCHOLOGIE DES ALKOHOLISMUS. ERGEBNISSE EXPERIMENTELLER UND INDIVIDUALPSYCHOLOGISCHER UNTERSUCHUNGEN. 1914. 52 pp.
>   **Heft 6.** Schulhof, Hedwig. INDIVIDUALPSYCHOLOGIE UND FRAUENFRAGE. 1914. 31 pp.

336. *Vineland, New Jersey. Training School. Department of Research. Publications.*

TITLE VARIATIONS: None.

DATES OF PUBLICATION: Number 1–25, 1914–1924. Later publications issued unnumbered.

FREQUENCY: Irregular. *See* Contents *below.*

NUMBERING VARIATIONS: Some issues also numbered as *Training School Bulletin* and in *School and Society. See* Contents *below.*

PUBLISHER: **Vineland, New Jersey:** Training School, Department of Research, Number 1–10, 13–23, 1914–1920. **Baltimore:** Williams and Wilkins, Number 11–12, 1916. **Vineland:** Smith Printing House, Number 24–25, 1923–1924.

PRIMARY EDITORS: None listed.

CONTENTS:

Number 1. Goddard, Henry H. THE RESEARCH DEPARTMENT: WHAT IT IS, WHAT IT IS DOING, WHAT IT HOPES TO DO. May 1914. 30 pp.

Number 2. Unknown.

Number 3. Petersen, Anna M., and Edgar A. Doll. SENSORY DISCRIMINATION IN NORMAL AND FEEBLE-MINDED CHILDREN. December 1914. 18 pp. (Also as *Training School Bulletin*, Volume 11, 1914, pp. 110–118, 135–144.)

Number 4. Goddard, Henry H. THE ADAPTATION BOARD AS A MEASURE OF INTELLIGENCE. February 1915. 7 pp. (also as *Training School Bulletin*, Volume 11, 1915, pp. 182–188.)

Number 5. Unknown.

Number 6. Doll, Edgar A. WOOLEY AND FISCHER'S "MENTAL AND PHYSICAL MEASUREMENTS OF WORKING CHILDREN." A CRITICAL REVIEW. January 1916. 20 pp.

Number 7. Doll, Edgar A. NOTE ON THE "INTELLIGENCE QUOTIENT." January 1916. 6 pp. (Also as *Training School Bulletin*, Volume 13, 1916, pp. 36–41.)

Number 8. Doll, Edgar A. ANTHROPOMETRY AS AN AID TO MENTAL DIAGNOSIS; A SIMPLE METHOD FOR THE EXAMINATION OF SUB-NORMALS. February 1916. 91 pp.

Number 9. Godin, Paul. RECORD OF INDIVIDUAL GROWTH. A GUIDE TO PARENTS, PHYSICIANS AND TEACHERS. Translated by Carroll T. Jones. March 1916. 39 pp.

Number 10. Goddard, Henry H. A COURSE OF STUDY FOR TEACHERS OF MENTAL DEFECTIVES. April 1916. 16 pp. (Also as *School and Society*, Volume 3, 1916, pp. 497–502.)

Number 11. Binet, Alfred, and Th. Simon. THE DEVELOPMENT OF INTELLIGENCE IN CHILDREN. Translated by Elizabeth S. Kite. May 1916. 336 pp.

Number 12. Binet, Alfred, and Th. Simon. THE INTELLIGENCE OF THE FEEBLE-MINDED. Translated by Elizabeth S. Kite. June 1916. 328 pp.

Number 13. Doll, Edgar A. PRELIMINARY NOTE ON THE DIAGNOSIS OF POTENTIAL FEEBLE-MINDEDNESS. June 1916. 8 pp. (Also as *Training School Bulletin*, Volume 13, 1916, pp. 54–61.)

Number 14. Martin, Anna Leila. A CONTRIBUTION TO THE STANDARDIZATION OF THE DESANCTIS TESTS. September 1916. 18 pp. (Also as *Training School Bulletin*, Volume 13, 1916, pp. 93–110.)

Number 15. Porteus, S. D. CEPHALOMETRY OF FEEBLE-MINDED. June 1919. 24 pp. (Also as *Training School Bulletin*, Volume 16, 1919, pp. 49–72.)

Number 16. Porteus, S. D. PORTEUS TESTS—THE VINELAND REVISION. September 1919. 44 pp.

Number 17. Porteus, S. D. A STANDARDIZED INFORMATION RECORD. October 1919. 8 pp. (Also as *Training School Bulletin*, Volume 16, 1919, pp. 103–111.)

Number 18. Nash, Alice M., and S. D. Porteus. EDUCATIONAL TREATMENT OF DEFECTIVES. November 1919. 19 pp. (Also as *Training School Bulletin*, Volume 16, 1919, pp. 113–131.)

Number 19. A CONDENSED GUIDE TO THE BINET TESTS: Part I. Porteus, S. D. BINET TESTS AND DIAGNOSIS; and Part II. Porteus, S. D., and Helen F. Hill. TEST AND TEST PROCEDURE. March/April 1920. 39 pp. (Also as *Training School Bulletin*, Volume 17, 1920, pp. 1–39.)

Number 20. Jones, C. Thompson. VERY BRIGHT AND FEEBLE-MINDED CHILDREN: A STUDY OF QUALITATIVE DIFFERENCES. 1920. 28 pp. (Also as *Training School Bulletin*, Volume 16, 1920, pp. 137–141, 153–164, 169–180.)

Number 21. Berry, Richard A., and S. D. Porteus. INTELLIGENCE AND SOCIAL VALUATION. A PRACTICAL METHOD FOR THE DIAGNOSIS OF MENTAL DEFICIENCY AND OTHER FORMS OF SOCIAL INEFFICIENCY. May 1920. 100 pp.

Number 22. Bassett, Dorothy M., and S. D. Porteus. SEX DIFFERENCES IN PORTEUS MAZE TEST PERFORMANCE. November 1920. 15 pp. (Also as *Training School Bulletin*, Volume 17, 1920, pp. 105–120.)

Number 23. Porteus, S. D. A STUDY OF PERSONALITY OF DEFECTIVES WITH A SOCIAL RATING SCALE. December 1920. 22 pp.

Number 24. Porteus, S. D. STUDIES IN MENTAL DEVIATIONS. 1923. 276 pp.

Number 25. Porteus, S. D. GUIDE TO THE PORTEUS MAZE TESTS. 1924. 48 pp.

337. *Zeitschrift für Individualpsychologie. Studien aus dem Gebiete der Psychotherapie, Psychologie und Pädagogik.*

TITLE VARIATIONS: Continued by *Internationale Zeitschrift für Individualpsychologie. Arbeiten aus dem Gebiete der Psychotherapie, Psychologie und Pädagogik* with Band 2, 1923.

DATES OF PUBLICATION: Band 1, Heft 1–9, April 1914–September 1916. Suspended publication October 1916–August 1923.

FREQUENCY: Irregular. Band 1, Heft 1, April 1914; Heft 2, May 1914; Heft 3, June 1914; Heft 4/5, July/August 1914; Heft 6/9, September 1916.

NUMBERING VARIATIONS: None.

PUBLISHER: **Munich:** Ernst Reinhardt, 1914–1916.

PRIMARY EDITORS: **Alfred Adler,** 1914–1916; **Carl Furtmüller,** 1914–1916; **Charlot Strasser,** July 1914–1916.

338. *Zeitschrift für Pathopsychologie. Ergänzungsband.*

TITLE VARIATIONS: None.

DATES OF PUBLICATION: Heft 1, 1914.

FREQUENCY: Irregular. *See* Contents *below.*

NUMBERING VARIATIONS: None.

PUBLISHER: **Leipzig:** Wilhelm Engelmann, 1914.

PRIMARY EDITOR: **Wilhelm Specht,** 1914.

CONTENTS:

Heft 1. OFFIZIELLER BERICHT DER VERHANDLUNGEN DES INTERNATION-
ALEN VEREINS FÜR MEDIZIN, PSYCHOLOGIE UND PSYCHOTHERAPIE IN WIEN VOM
19.–20. IX. 1913. Unter dem Vorsitze von Eugen Bleuler. 1914. 226 pp.

339. *Zeitschrift für Sexualwissenschaft. Internationales
Zentralblatt für die Biologie, Psychologie, Pathologie und
Soziologie der Sexuallebens.* [Organ of the Ärztliche
Gesellschaft für Sexualwissenschaft und Eugenik (Berlin).]

TITLE VARIATIONS: Subtitle omitted, Band 6–12, 1919–1926. Continued by
Zeitschrift für Sexualwissenschaft und Sexualpolitik with Band 13, 1926.

DATES OF PUBLICATION: Band 1–12, April 1914–March 1926.

FREQUENCY: Monthly.

NUMBERING VARIATIONS: None.

PUBLISHER: **Bonn:** A. Marcus & E. Weber, 1914–1924. **Bonn** and **Berlin:** A.
Marcus & E. Weber's Verlag, 1925–1926.

PRIMARY EDITORS: **Albert Eulenburg,** 1914–1915; **Iwan Bloch,** 1914–1915;
Max Marcuse, 1915–1926.

340. *Zentralblatt für Psychologie und psychologische
Pädagogik.*

TITLE VARIATIONS: None.

DATES OF PUBLICATION: Band 1–2, April 1914–July 1915.

FREQUENCY: Monthly (10 Hefte per Band).

NUMBERING VARIATIONS: Multinumber Hefte present.

PUBLISHER: **Würzburg:** C. Kabitzsch, 1914–1915. **Würzburg** and **Leipzig:** C.
Kabitzsch, 1915.

PRIMARY EDITORS: **Wilhelm Peters,** 1914–1915; **J. Carleton Bell,** 1914–1915;
Karl Bühler, 1914–1915; **M. Isserlin,** 1914; **Sidney Alrutz,** 1915.

1915

341. *Chicago. House of Correction. Research Department.
Bulletin.*

TITLE VARIATIONS: Also called [*Chicago.*] *House of Correction. Bulletin;* [*Chicago.*] *House of Correction. Psychopathic Department Series;* and [*Chicago.*]
House of Correction. Medical Department Series.

DATES OF PUBLICATION: Number 1–3, July-November 1915.

FREQUENCY: Bimonthly.

NUMBERING VARIATIONS: Issues also numbered as [*Chicago.*] *House of Correction. Psychopathic Department Series* and [*Chicago.*] *House of Correction. Medical Department Series. See* Contents *below.*

PUBLISHER: **Chicago:** House of Correction Press, 1915.

PRIMARY EDITOR: **Samuel C. Kohs,** 1915.

CONTENTS:

    Number 1. Kohs, Samuel C. A NEW DEPARTURE IN THE TREATMENT OF INMATES OF PENAL INSTITUTIONS. July 1915. 14 pp. (Also as [*Chicago.*] *House of Correction. Psychopathic Department Series,* Number 1).

    Number 2. Sceleth, Charles E., and Arthur F. Beifeld. (CEREBRAL EDEMA (WET BRAIN) IN CHRONIC ALCOHOLISM.) September 1915. 9 pp. (Also as [*Chicago.*] *House of Correction. Medical Department Series,* Number 1).

    Number 3. Kohs, Samuel C. THE PRACTICABILITY OF THE BINET SCALE AND THE QUESTION OF THE BORDERLINE CASE. November 1915. 23 pp. (Also as [*Chicago.*] *House of Correction. Psychopathic Department Series,* Number 2).

342. *Committee on Provision for the Feeble-Minded. Bulletin.*

TITLE VARIATIONS: None.

DATES OF PUBLICATION: Number 1–4, 1915–1917.

FREQUENCY: Irregular. *See* Contents *below.*

NUMBERING VARIATIONS: None.

PUBLISHER: **Philadelphia:** Committee on Provision for the Feeble-Minded, 1915–1917.

PRIMARY EDITORS: **Joseph P. Byers,** 1915–1917; **Alexander Johnson,** 1915–1917.

CONTENTS:

    Number 1. Kite, E. S. THE BINET–SIMON MEASURING SCALE OF INTELLIGENCE. WHAT IT IS; WHAT IT DOES; HOW IT DOES IT; WITH A BRIEF BIOGRAPHY OF ITS AUTHORS, ALFRED BINET AND DR. THOMAS [sic] SIMON. (1915.) 29 pp.

    Number 2. STIMULATING PUBLIC INTEREST IN THE FEEBLE-MINDED. HOW IT WAS DONE IN NEW JERSEY. (1916.) 10 pp.

    Number 3. COLONY CARE FOR THE FEEBLE-MINDED. 1916. 19 pp.

    Number 4. SPECIAL CLASSES IN THE PUBLIC SCHOOLS. 1917. 8 pp.

343. *Committee on Provision for the Feeble-Minded. Report of the Year's Work.*

TITLE VARIATIONS: None.

DATES OF PUBLICATION: 1st–2nd, 1915/1916 and 1916/1917.

FREQUENCY: Annual.

NUMBERING VARIATIONS: None.

PUBLISHER: **Philadelphia:** Committee on Provision for the Feeble-Minded, 1915–1917.

PRIMARY EDITORS: **Joseph P. Byers,** 1915–1917; **Alexander Johnson,** 1915–1917.

344. *Criminal Science Monographs.* [Published under the auspices of the American Institute of Criminal Law and Criminology.]

TITLE VARIATIONS: Series is a supplement to the *Journal of Criminal Law and Criminology.*

DATES OF PUBLICATION: Number 1–4, 1915–1923.

FREQUENCY: Irregular. *See* Contents *below.*

NUMBERING VARIATIONS: None.

PUBLISHER: **Boston:** Little, Brown, and Company, 1915–1923.

PRIMARY EDITOR: **Robert H. Gault,** 1915–1923.

CONTENTS:

Number 1. Healy, William, and Mary Jenney Healy. PATHOLOGICAL LYING, ACCUSATION, AND SWINDLING. A STUDY IN FORENSIC PSYCHOLOGY. 1915. 286 pp.

Number 2. Glueck, Bernard. STUDIES IN FORENSIC PSYCHIATRY. 1916. 269 pp.

Number 3. Kammerer, Percy Gamble. THE UNMARRIED MOTHER. A STUDY OF FIVE HUNDRED CASES. 1918. 342 pp.

Number 4. Thomas, William Isaac. THE UNADJUSTED GIRL. 1923. 261 pp.

345. *Massachusetts. State Hospital (Boston). Psychopathic Department. Monographs.*

TITLE VARIATIONS: Also called [*Boston.*] *Psychopathic Hospital. Monograph(s).*

DATES OF PUBLICATION: Number 1–3, 1915–1919. Suspended publication 1920–1967.

FREQUENCY: Biennial.

NUMBERING VARIATIONS: None.

PUBLISHER: **Baltimore:** Warwick & York, Inc., 1915. **Boston:** W. M. Leonard, 1917–1919.

PRIMARY EDITORS: None listed.

CONTENTS:

Number 1. Yerkes, Robert M., James W. Bridges, and Rose S. Hardwick. A POINT SCALE FOR MEASURING MENTAL ABILITY. 1915. 218 pp.

Number 2. Southard, E. E., and H. C. Solomon. NEUROSYPHILIS. MODERN SYSTEMATIC DIAGNOSIS AND TREATMENT. PRESENTED IN ONE HUNDRED AND THIRTY-SEVEN CASE HISTORIES. 1917. 406 pp.

Number 3. Southard, E. E. SHELL-SHOCK AND OTHER NEURO-PSYCHIATRIC PROBLEMS. 1919. 982 pp.

1916

346. *American Psychological Association. Yearbook.*

TITLE VARIATIONS: Titled *Constitution and List of Officers and Members,* 1916–1918 and *By-laws and List of Officers and Members,* 1919–1936. Continued by *American Psychological Association. Directory* in 1948.

DATES OF PUBLICATION: 1916–1947.

FREQUENCY: Annual.

NUMBERING VARIATIONS: Numbered by date only. 1946/1947 is a double issue.

PUBLISHER: N.p.: American Psychological Association, 1916–1924. (Secretary and Council determine where Yearbook is printed.) **Washington, D.C.:** American Psychological Association, Inc., 1925–1946/1947.

PRIMARY EDITORS: Secretary acted as compiler-editor for *Yearbook.* **Robert M. Ogden,** 1916; **Herbert S. Langfeld,** 1917–1919; **Edwin G. Boring,** 1920–1922; **John Edward Anderson,** 1923–1925; **Samuel W. Fernberger,** 1926–1928; **Carl C. Brigham,** 1929–1931; **Donald G. Paterson,** 1931–1937; **Willard C. Olson,** 1938–1945; **Dael Wolfle,** 1946/1947.

347. *Bryn Mawr College. Monographs. Reprint Series. Contributions from the Psychological Laboratory.*

TITLE VARIATIONS: None.

DATES OF PUBLICATION: Volume 11–12, 14, 1916–1925.

FREQUENCY: Irregular.

NUMBERING VARIATIONS: Volume 1–10, 13, 15+ of *Bryn Mawr College. Monographs. Reprint Series* did not contain *Contributions from the Psychological Laboratory.* Each article issued by one of numerous scientific journals. *See* Note *below.*

PUBLISHER: Various. *See* Note *below.*

PRIMARY EDITORS: None listed.

NOTE: No original publications. Compilation of reprints of articles by Clarence E. Ferree, Gertrude Rand and collaborators.

348. *Deutsche Psychologie. Zeitschrift für reine und angewandte Seelenkunde.*

TITLE VARIATIONS: Continued by *Deutsche Psychologie. Arbeitenreihe* with Band 3, 1920.

DATES OF PUBLICATION: Band 1–2, February 1916–May 1919.

FREQUENCY: Irregular. Band 1, Heft 1–6 issued between February 1916–February 1918. Band 2, Heft 1–6 issued between July 1918–May 1919.

NUMBERING VARIATIONS: None.

PUBLISHER: **Langensalza, Germany:** Druck und Verlag von Wendt & Klauwell, 1916–1919.

PRIMARY EDITOR: **Fritz Giese,** 1916–1919.

349. *Journal of Delinquency.*

TITLE VARIATIONS: Continued by *Journal of Juvenile Research* with Volume 12, Number 2, 1928.

DATES OF PUBLICATION: Volume 1–12, Number 2, March 1916–June 1928.

FREQUENCY: **Bimonthly,** Volume 1–10, March 1916–November 1926. **Quarterly,** Volume 11–12, March 1927–June 1928.

NUMBERING VARIATIONS: Only 5 issues in Volume 1. Multinumber issues present.

PUBLISHER: **Whittier, California:** Whittier State School, Department of Research, 1916–1920. **Whittier:** California Bureau of Juvenile Research, Whittier State School, 1921–1922, 1928. **Whittier:** Department of Research, California Bureau of Juvenile Research, Whittier State School, 1923–1925. **Whittier:** Whittier State School, Department of Research, 1926–1927.

PRIMARY EDITORS: **J. Harold Williams,** 1916–1923; **Arnold L. Gesell,** 1916–1928; **Ellen B. Sullivan,** 1925–1928; **H. H. Goddard,** 1916–1928; **Thomas H. Haines,** 1916–1928; **William Healy,** 1916–1928; **Lewis M. Terman,** 1916–1928; **Maud A. Merrill,** 1923; **Catharine M. Cox,** 1925.

350. *Journal of Experimental Psychology.*

TITLE VARIATIONS: None.

DATES OF PUBLICATION: Volume 1–40+, 1916–1950+. Suspended publication, 1918–1919.

FREQUENCY: **Bimonthly,** Volume 1–19, 1916–1936. **Monthly** (2 Volumes per year), Volume 20–33, 1937–1943. **Bimonthly,** Volume 34–40, 1944–1950+.

NUMBERING VARIATIONS: None.

PUBLISHER: **Princeton, New Jersey:** Psychological Review Company, 1916–1926. **Lancaster, Pennsylvania** and **Princeton:** Psychological Review Company for the American Psychological Association, 1927–1938. **Lancaster** and **Columbus, Ohio:** By the American Psychological Association, Inc.,

1939–1940. **Lancaster** and **Evanston, Illinois:** By The American Psychological Association, Inc., 1940–1945. **Lancaster** and **Washington, D.C.:** By the American Psychological Association, Inc., 1946–1950+.

PRIMARY EDITORS: **John B. Watson,** 1916–1925; **Madison Bentley,** 1926–1929; **Samuel W. Fernberger,** 1930–1941; **Francis W. Irwin,** 1942–1950+.

351. *Kinderstudie. Paedologische bladen.*

TITLE VARIATIONS: Continued by *Kinderstudie. Paedologische en psychologische bladen* with Deel 6, 1924.

DATES OF PUBLICATION: Deel 1–5, 1916–1922/1923.

FREQUENCY: **Annual,** Deel 1–3, 1916–1919. **Biennial,** Deel 4–5, 1920/1921–1922/1923.

NUMBERING VARIATIONS: None.

PUBLISHER: **Zwolle, Netherlands:** J. Ploegsma, 1916. **Zeist:** J. Ploegsma, 1917–1923.

PRIMARY EDITORS: **G.A.M. van Wayenburg,** 1916–1923; **J. H. Gunning,** 1916–1923; **C. M. Soeters,** 1916–1923; **W. H. ten Seldam,** 1916–1923; **K. Herman Bouman,** 1916–1923; **F. J. van der Molen,** 1916–1923.

352. *Leipzig. Sächsische staatliche Forschungsinstitute. Forschungsinstitut für Psychologie. Veröffentlichungen.*

TITLE VARIATIONS: Numero 1/3 titled *Königliche sächsische Forschungsinstitute zu Leipzig. Forschungsinstitut für Psychologie. Veröffentlichungen.* Continued by *Leipzig. Sächsische staatliche Forschungsinstitute. Forschungsinstitut für Psychologie. Abhandlungen* with Stück 6, 1921.

DATES OF PUBLICATION: Numero 1–5, 1916–1920.

FREQUENCY: Irregular. *See* Contents *below.*

NUMBERING VARIATIONS: Multinumber issue present. Also numbered as *Psychologische Studien* and as *Arbeiten zur Entwicklungs-Psychologie*. *See* Contents *below.*

PUBLISHER: **Leipzig:** Verlag von Emmanuel Reinicke, 1916–1918. **Leipzig:** Wilhelm Engelmann, 1919–1920.

PRIMARY EDITORS: **Wilhelm Wundt,** 1916–1918; **Felix Krueger,** 1919–1920.

CONTENTS:
Numero 1/3. Wundt, Wilhelm, ed. PSYCHOLOGISCHE STUDIEN. NEUE FOLGE DER PHILOSOPHISCHEN. Band 10. 1916–1918. 575 pp.
Numero 4. Werner, Heinz. DIE URSPRÜNGE DER METAPHER. 1919. 238 pp. (Also as *Arbeiten zur Entwicklungs-Psychologie*, Stück 3.)
Numero 5. Golz, Bruno. WANDLUNGEN LITERARISCHER MOTIVE. 1920. 94 pp. (Also as *Arbeiten zur Entwicklungs-Psychologie*, Stück 4.

353. Munich. Universität. Psychologisches Institut. Arbeiten.

TITLE VARIATIONS: None.

DATES OF PUBLICATION: [Serie 1.] Band 1–10, 1916–1929. [Serie 2] Band 1–9, 1930–1938.

FREQUENCY: Irregular. [Serie 1:] Band 1, 5 Hefte (1916); Band 2, 6 Hefte (1917), 6 Hefte (1918), 8 Hefte (1919); Band 3, 7 Hefte (1920); Band 4, 7 Hefte (1921), 5 Hefte (1922); Band 5, 8 Hefte (1923); Band 6, 10 Hefte (1924), 8 Hefte (1925); Band 7, 12 Hefte (1926); Band 8, 13 Hefte (1927); Band 9, 9 Hefte (1928); Band 10, 7 Hefte (1929). [Serie 2:] Band 1, 10 Hefte (1930); Band 2, 10 Hefte (1931); Band 3, 9 Hefte (1932); Band 4, 12 Hefte (1933); Band 5, 13 Hefte (1934); Band 6, 15 Hefte (1935); Band 7, 10 Hefte (1936); Band 8, 8 Hefte (1937); Band 9, 13 Hefte (1938).

NUMBERING VARIATIONS: None.

PUBLISHER: **Munich:** Psychologisches Institut der Universität München, 1916–1938.

PRIMARY EDITORS: **Erich Becher,** 1916–1929; **Joseph Geyser,** 1916–1929.

NOTE: No original publications. Compilation of previously published books and articles reprinted from other serials.

354. Washington, D.C. National Research Council. Activities of Divisions and Divisional Committees. Reports.

TITLE VARIATIONS: Included in above publication are: *National Research Council. Division of Anthropology and Psychology. Report; National Research Council. Division of Anthropology and Psychology. Committee on Selection and Training of Aircraft Pilots. Annual Meeting;* and *National Research Council. Committee on Aviation Psychology. Annual Meeting.*

DATES OF PUBLICATION: 1st–[35th]+, 1916–1950/1951+.

FREQUENCY: Annual (calendar year 1916–1923; fiscal year 1923/1924–1950/1951+).

NUMBERING VARIATIONS: None.

PUBLISHER: **Washington, D.C.:** Government Printing Office, 1916–1950/1951+.

PRIMARY EDITORS: None listed.

355. Zeitschrift für angewandte Psychologie. [1.] [Organ of the Institut für angewandte Psychologie (Leipzig).]

TITLE VARIATIONS: Continues *Zeitschrift für angewandte Psychologie und psychologische Sammelforschung.* Continued by *Zeitschrift für angewandte Psychologie und Charakterkunde* with Band 48, 1935.

DATES OF PUBLICATION: Band 11–47, 1916–1934.

FREQUENCY: **Irregular,** Band 11–43, 1916–1932. **Bimonthly,** Band 44–47, 1933–1934.

NUMBERING VARIATIONS: Most are double or triple numbers. 1 or 2 volumes issued per year, 6 Hefte to a volume.

PUBLISHER: **Leipzig: Johann Ambrosius Barth**, 1916–1934.

PRIMARY EDITORS: **William Stern**, 1916–1933; **Otto Lipmann**, 1916–1933; **Otto Klemm**, 1934; **Philipp Lersch**, 1934.

356. *Zeitschrift für angewandte Psychologie. Beihefte.* [Organ of the Institut für angewandte Psychologie (Leipzig).]

TITLE VARIATIONS: Continues *Zeitschrift für angewandte Psychologie und psychologische Sammelforschung. Beihefte.* Continued by *Zeitschrift für angewandte Psychologie und Charakterkunde. Beihefte* with Heft 70, 1935.

DATES OF PUBLICATION: Heft 13–69, 1916–1934.

FREQUENCY: Irregular. *See* Contents *below.*

NUMBERING VARIATIONS: Heft 14 issued in two parts, 14a and 14b. Various issues also numbered as *Hamburger Arbeiten zur Begabungsforschung;* or as *Beiträge zur Jugendpsychologie;* or as *Hamburger Untersuchungen zur Jugend- und Sozialpsychologie. See* Contents *below.*

PUBLISHER: **Leipzig: Johann Ambrosius Barth**, 1916–1934.

PRIMARY EDITORS: **William Stern**, 1916–1934; **Otto Lipmann**, 1916–1933; **Otto Klemm**, 1934; **Philipp Lersch**, 1934; **Oswald Kroh**, 1929–1930 (for *Beiträge zur Jugendpsychologie*).

CONTENTS:

Heft 13. Valentiner, Th. DIE PHANTASIE IM FREIEN AUFSATZE DER KINDER UND JUGENDLICHEN. 1916. 168 pp.

Heft 14. Lipmann, Otto. PSYCHISCHE GESCHLECTSUNTERSCHIEDE. ERGEBNISSE DER DIFFERENTIELLEN PSYCHOLOGIE. 1917. 2 Teile, Teil 1: 108 pp.; Teil 2: 172 pp.

Heft 15. Baumgarten, Franziska. DIE LÜGE BEI KINDERN UND JUGENDLICHEN. EINE UMFRAGE IN DEN POLNISCHEN SCHULEN VON LODZ. 1917. 111 pp.

Heft 16. Bürklen, Karl. DAS TASTLESEN DER BLINDENPUNKTSCHRIFT. NEBST KLEINEN BEITRÄGEN ZUR BLINDENPSYCHOLOGIE VON P. GRASEMANN, L. COHN UND W. STEINBERG. 1917. 93 pp.

Heft 17. Bühler, Charlotte. DAS MÄRCHEN UND DIE PHANTASIE DES KINDES. 1918. 82 pp.

Heft 18. Peter, Rudolf, and William Stern. DIE AUSLESE BEFÄHIGTER VOLKSSCHÜLER IN HAMBURG. BERICHT ÜBER DAS PSYCHOLOGISCHE VERFAHREN. In Gemeinschaft mit Otto Bobertag, Lenore Heitsch, H. Meins, Martha Muchow, Anton Penkert, H. P. Roloff, Gustav Schober, Heinz Werner, und Otto Wiegmann. 1919. 157 pp. (Also as *Hamburger Arbeiten zur Begabungsforschung,* Heft 1.)

Heft 19. Minkus, W., W. Stern, H. P. Roloff, G. Schober, A. Schober and A. Penkert. UNTERSUCHUNGEN ÜBER DIE INTELLIGENZ VON KINDERN UND JUGENDLICHEN. 1919. 167 pp. (Also as *Hamburger Arbeiten zur Begabungsforschung,* Heft 2.)

Heft 20. Wiegmann, Otto, and William Stern. METHODENSAMMLUNG ZUR INTELLIGENZPRÜFUNG VON KINDERN UND JUGENDLICHEN. 1920. 256 pp. (Also as *Hamburger Arbeiten zur Begabungsforschung*, Heft 3.) (2. Auflage, 1922.)

Heft 21. BEITRÄGE ZUR PSYCHOLOGIE DES KRIEGES: Plaut, Paul. PSYCHOGRAPHIE DES KRIEGERS; and Ludwig, Walter. BEITRÄGE ZUR PSYCHOLOGIE DER FURCHT IM KRIEGE; and Schiche, E. ZUR PSYCHOLOGIE DER TODESAHNUNGEN. 1920. 180 pp.

Heft 22. Herwagen, Karl. DER SIEBENJÄHRIGE. VERSUCH EINER GEFÜHLS- UND VORSTELLUNGSTYPIK UND IHRE ANWENDUNG AUF DEN GESINNUNGSUNTERRICHT. 1920. 92 pp.

Heft 23. Gellhorn, Ernst. ÜBUNGSFÄHIGKEIT UND ÜBUNGSFESTIGKEIT BEI GEISTIGER ARBEIT. 1920. 76 pp.

Heft 24. Jacobsohn-Lask, L. ÜBER DIE FERNALD'SCHE METHODE ZUR PRÜFUNG DES SITTLICHEN FÜHLENS UND ÜBER IHRE WEITERE AUSGESTALTUNG. 1920. 84 pp.

Heft 25. Katz, David. ZUR PSYCHOLOGIE DES AMPUTIERTEN UND SEINER PROTHESE. 1921. 118 pp.

Heft 26. Stern, Erich. DIE FESTELLUNG DER PSYCHISCHEN BERUFSEIGNUNG UND DIE SCHULE. 1921. 153 pp. (Also as *Hamburger Arbeiten zur Begabungsforschung*, Heft 4.)

Heft 27. Roloff, Hans Paul. VERGLEICHEND-PSYCHOLOGISCHE UNTERSUCHUNGEN ÜBER KINDLICHE DEFINITIONSLEISTUNGEN. 1922. 164 pp. (Also as *Hamburger Arbeiten zur Begabungsforschung*, Heft 5.)

Heft 28. Valentiner, Th. ZUR AUSLESE FÜR DIE HÖHEREN SCHULEN. EIN BEITRAG ZUR DIFFERENTIELLEN PSYCHOLOGIE UND BEGABUNGSFORSCHUNG. 1921. 102 pp.

Heft 29. Lipmann, Otto and William Stern, eds. VORTRÄGE ÜBER ANGEWANDTE PSYCHOLOGIE, GEHALTEN BEIM 7. KONGRESS FÜR EXPERIMENTELLE PSYCHOLOGIE. (Marburg, 20–23. April 1921.)

Heft 30. Eng, Helga. EXPERIMENTELLE UNTERSUCHUNGEN ÜBER DAS GEFÜHLSLEBEN DES KINDES IM VERGLEICH MIT DEM DES ERWACHSENEN. 1922. 258 pp.

Heft 31. Gregor, A. and E. Voigtländer. CHARAKTERSTRUKTUR VERWAHRLOSTER KINDER UND JUGENDLICHER. 1922. 72 pp.

Heft 32. Busse, Hans Heinrich. DAS LITERARISCHE VERSTÄNDNIS DER WERKTÄTIGEN JUGEND ZWISCHEN 14 UND 18. EINE ENTWICKLUNGS- UND SOZIALPSYCHOLOGISCHE STUDIE. 1923. 289 pp.

Heft 33. Kaine, Friedrich. DAS STEIGERUNGSPHÄNOMEN ALS KÜNSTLERISCHES GESTALTUNGSPRINZIP. EINE LITERARPSYCHOLOGISCHE UNTERSUCHUNG. 1924. 145 pp.

Heft 34. Stern, William. NEUE BEITRÄGE ZUR THEORIE UND PRAXIS DER INTELLIGENZPRÜFUNG. 1925. 193 pp. (Also as *Hamburger Arbeiten zur Begabungsforschung*, Heft 6.)

Heft 35. Eliasberg, W. PSYCHOLOGIE UND PATHOLOGIE DER ABSTRAKTION. 1925. 188 pp.

Heft 36. Brehmer, Fritz. MELODIEAUFFASSUNG UND MELODISCHE BEGABUNG DES KINDES. 1925. 180 pp. (Also as *Hamburger Arbeiten zur Begabungsforschung*, Heft 7.)

356. *(Continued)*

Heft 37. Sassenhagen, Robert. ÜBER GEISTIGE LEISTUNGEN DES LAND-KINDES UND DES STADTKINDES. VERGLEICHEND-PSYCHOLOGISCHE UNTER-SUCHUNGEN. 1926. 198 pp. (Also as *Hamburger Arbeiten zur Begabungsforschung*, Heft 8.)

Heft 38. Tobie, Hans, DIE ENTWICKLUNG DER TEILINHALTLICHEN BEACH-TUNG VON FARBE UND FORM IM VORSCHULPFLICHTIGEN KINDESALTER. 1927. 104 pp.

Heft 39. Eng, Helga. KINDERZEICHNEN. VOM ERSTEN STRICH BIS ZU DEN FARBENZEICHNUNGEN DES ACHTJÄHRIGEN. 1927. 198 pp.

Heft 40. Lämmermann, Hans. DAS MANNHEIMER KOMBINIERTE VERFAHR-EN DER BEGABTEN-AUSLESE. EINE STATISTISCHE UNTERSUCHUNG ÜBER DIE BE-WAHRUNG AN HÖHEREN SCHULEN. 1927. 197 pp.

Heft 41. Roloff, Hans Paul. ÜBER EIGNUNG UND BEWÄHRUNG. FOR-SCHUNGEN ZUR INDUSTRIELLEN PSYCHOTECHNIK. 1928. 148 pp. (Also as *Hamburger Arbeiten zur Begabungsforschung*, Heft 9.)

Heft 42. Kelchner, Mathilde, and Ernst Lau. DIE BERLINER JUGEND UND DIE KRIMINALLITERATUR. EINE UNTERSUCHUNG AUF GRUND VON AUFSÄTZEN JU-GENDLICHER. 1928. 110 pp.

Heft 43. Bonte, Theodor, E. Liefmann, and Fritz Rössler. UNTERSUCH-UNGEN ÜBER DIE EIDETISCHE VERANLAGUNG VON KINDERN UND JUGENDLICHEN. 1928. 371 pp.

Heft 44. Giese, Fritz. DIE ÖFFENTLICHE PERSÖNLICHKEIT. STATISTISCHE UNTERSUCHUNGEN AN GEISTIGEN FÜHRERN DER GEGENWART. 1928. 249 pp.

Heft 45. Kühn, Hanna, PSYCHOLOGISCHE UNTERSUCHUNGEN ÜBER DAS STIEFMUTTERPROBLEM. DIE KONFLIKTMÖGLICHKEITEN IN DER STIEFMUTTER-FAMILIE UND IHRE BEDEUTUNG FÜR DIE VERWAHRLOSUNG DES STIEFKINDES. 1929. 162 pp. (Also as *Hamburger Untersuchungen zur Jugend- und Sozialpsychologie* 1.)

Heft 46. Herrmann, Gertrud. FORMEN DES GEMEINSCHAFTSLEBENS JU-GENDLICHER MÄDCHEN. SOZIALPSYCHOLOGISCHE UNTERSUCHUNGEN IN EINEM FÜRSORGEERZIEHUNGSHEIM. 1929. 160 pp. (Also as *Hamburger Untersuchungen zur Jugend- und Sozialpsychologie* 2.)

Heft 47. Zeininger, Karl. MAGISCHE GEISTESHALTUNG IM KINDESALTER UND IHRE BEDEUTUNG FÜR DIE RELIGIÖSE ENTWICKLUNG. 1929. 155 pp. (Also as *Beiträge zur Jugendpsychologie* 1.)

Heft 48. Krauss, Reinh. ÜBER GRAPHISCHEN AUSDRUCK. EINE EXPERIMEN-TELLE UNTERSUCHUNG ÜBER DAS ERZEUGEN UND AUSDEUTEN VON GEGEN-STANDSFREIEN LINIEN. 1930. 141 pp.

Heft 49. Meistring, Walter. BEITRÄGE ZUR PRÜFUNG DER KOORDI-NATIONSFÄHIGKEIT. 1930. 154 pp.

Heft 50. Krautter, Otto. DIE ENTWICKLUNG DES PLASTISCHEN GESTALT-ENS BEIM VORSCHULPFLICHTIGEN KINDE. EIN BEITRAG ZUR PSYCHOGENESE DER GESTALTUNG. 1930. 99 pp. (Also as *Beiträge zur Jugendpsychologie* 2.)

Heft 51. Jaehner, Doris, ZWEI TAGE AUS DEM LEBEN DREIER GESCHWI-STER. 1930. 176 pp.

Heft 52. Nestele, Albert. Die musikalische Produktion im Kindesalter. Eine experimentele Untersuchung der kindlichen Melodik.
1930. 198 pp. (Also as *Beiträge zur Jugendpsychologie* 3.)

Heft 53. Fuxloch, Karl. Das soziologische im Spiel des Kindes. 1930.
96 pp. (Also as *Beiträge zur Jugendpsychologie*, Heft 4.)

Heft 54. Bernfeld, Siegfried. Trieb und Tradition im Jugendalter.
Kulturpsychologische Studien in Tagebüchern. 1931. 181 pp.

Heft 55. Hermsmeier, Friedreich. Experimentellpsychologische Untersuchungen zur Charakterforschung. (Vergleichende Prüfung der
Methoden zur Untersuchung der ethischen Begriffe und Gefühle.)
1931. 230 pp.

Heft 56. Tripp, Erich. Untersuchungen zur Rechtspsychologie des
Individuums mit besonderer Berücksichtigung des Problems der Er-
folgshaftung. 1931. 142 pp.

Heft 57. Oseretzky, N. Psychomotorik. Methoden zur Untersuchung der Motorik. 1931. 162 pp.

Heft 58. Bogen, H. and O. Lipmann. Gang und Charakter. Ergebnisse eines Preisausschreibens. 1931. 122 pp.

Heft 59. Festschrift William Stern zum 60. Geburtstag am 29. April
1931. Herausgegeben von seinen Mitarbeitern am Psychologischen Institut
Hamburg. 1931. 264 pp.

Heft 60. Kahle, Margarete. Beziehungen Weiblicher Fürsorgezöglinge zur Familie. 1931. 188 pp. (Also as *Hamburger Untersuchungen zur
Jugend- und Sozialpsychologie*, Heft 3.)

Heft 61. Lottig, Heinrich. Hamburger Zwillings-studien. Anthropologische und Charakterologische Untersuchungen an ein- und zwei-
eiigen Zwillingen. 1931. 122 pp.

Heft 62. Sarris, Emanuel Georg. Sind wir berechtigt, vom Wortver-
ständnis des Hundes zu sprechen? 1931. 140 pp.

Heft 63. Kelchner, Mathilde. Schuld und Sühne im Urteil jugendlicher Arbeiter und Arbeiterinnen. 1932. 147 pp.

Heft 64. Brunswik, Egon. Untersuchungen zur Entwicklung des
Gedächtnisses. 1932. 158 pp.

Heft 65. Plaut, Paul. Psychologische Gutachten in Strafprozessen.
1932. 160 pp.

Heft 66. Kipp, Hildegard. Die Unehelichkeit; Ihre psychologische
Situation und Problematik. 1933. 180 pp. (Also as *Hamburger Untersuchungen zur Jugend- und Sozialpsychologie*, Heft 4.)

Heft 67. Kunert, Sophie, Straffälligkeit bei Frauen, ihre Entstehung und Beschaffenheit. 1933. 200 pp. (Also as *Hamburger Untersuchungen zur Jugend- und Sozialpsychologie*, Heft 5.)

Heft 68. Gottschaldt, Kurt, Der Aufbau des kindlichen Handelns.
1933. 228 pp.

Heft 69. Feige, Karl. Präzisionsleistungen menschlicher Motorik.
1934. 88 pp.

1917

357. *Abhandlungen aus der Neurologie, Psychiatrie, Psychologie und ihren Grenzgebieten.*

TITLE VARIATIONS: Also as *Monatsschrift für Psychiatrie und Neurologie. Beihefte.* Continued by *Bibliotheca Psychiatrica et Neurologica* with Heft 88, 1948.

DATES OF PUBLICATION: Heft 1–87, 1917–1939.

FREQUENCY: Irregular. *See* Contents *below.*

NUMBERING VARIATIONS: One issue also numbered as *Internationale Tagung für angewandte Psychopathologie und Psychologie. Referate und Vorträge,* I. *See* Contents *below.*

PUBLISHER: **Berlin:** S. Karger, 1917–1937. **Basel:** S. Karger, 1937. **Basel** and **Leipzig:** S. Karger, 1937–1938. **Basel:** S. Karger, 1939.

PRIMARY EDITOR: **Karl Bonhöffer,** 1917–1939.

CONTENTS:

Heft 1. Stertz, Georg. TYPHUS UND NERVENSYSTEM. 1917. 104 pp.

Heft 2. Pernet, Jean. ÜBER DIE BEDEUTUNG VON ERBLICHKEIT UND VORGESCHICHTE FÜR DAS KLINISCHE BILD DER PROGRESSIVEN PARALYSE. 1917. 126 pp.

Heft 3. Fröschels, Emil. KINDERSPRACHE UND APHASIE. 1918. 165 pp.

Heft 4. Vorkastner, W. EPILEPSIE UND DEMENTIA PRAECOX. 1918. 112 pp.

Heft 5. Schmidt, Wilhelm, FORENSISCH-PSYCHIATRISCHE ERFAHRUNGEN IM KRIEGE. 1918. 219 pp.

Heft 6. Seelert, Hans. VERBINDUNG ENDOGENER UND EXOGENER FAKTOREN IN DEM SYMPTOMENBILDE UND DER PATHOGENESE VON PSYCHOSEN. 1919. 88 pp.

Heft 7. Pötzl, Otto. ZUR KLINIK UND ANATOMIE DER REINEN WORTTAUBHEIT. 1919. 82 pp.

Heft 8. Schröder, Paul. DIE SPIELBREITE DER SYMPTOME BEIM MANISCH-DEPRESSIVEN IRRESEIN UND BEI DEN DEGENERSTIONSPSYCHOSEN. 1920. 59 pp.

Heft 9. Krisch, Hans, DIE SYMPTOMATISCHEN PSYCHOSEN UND IHRE DIFFERENTIALDIAGNOSE. 1920. 70 pp.

Heft 10. Ewald, Gottfried. DIE ABDERHALDENSCHE REAKTION MIT BESONDERER BERÜCKSICHTIGUNG IHRER ERGEBNISSE IN DER PSYCHIATRIE. 1920. 210 pp.

Heft 11. Stertz, G. DER EXTRAPYRAMIDALE SYMPTOMENKOMPLEX (DAS DYSTONISCHE SYNDROM) UND SEINE BEDEUTUNG IN DER NEUROLOGIE. 1921. 96 pp.

Heft 12. Albrecht, Othmar. DER ANETHISCHE SYMPTOMENKOMPLEX. 1921. 108 pp.

Heft 13. Pick, Arnold. DIE NEUROLOGISCHE FORSCHUNGSRICHTUNG IN DER PSYCHOPATHOLOGIE. 1921. 247 pp.

Heft 14. Benedek, Ladislaus and Franz Oskar Porsche. ÜBER DIE ENTSTEHUNG DER NEGRISCHEN KÖRPERCHEN. 1921. 86 pp.

Heft 15. Kläsi, Jakob. ÜBER DIE BEDEUTUNG UND ENTSTEHUNG DER STEREOTYPIEN. 1922. 111 pp.

Heft 16. Allers, Rudolf. ÜBER PSYCHOANALYSE. EINLEITENDER VORTRAG. Edited by Erwin Stransky and Bernhard Dattner. 1922. 119 pp.

Heft 17. Monchy, S.J.R. de. DIE ZERGLIEDERUNG DES PSYCHISCHEN KRANKHEITSBILDES BEI ARTERIOSKLEROSISCEREBRI. 1922. 84 pp.

Heft 18. Krisch, Hans. EPILEPSIE UND MANISCH-DEPRESSIVES IRRESEIN. 1922. 108 pp.

Heft 19. Försterling, Wilhelm. ÜBER DIE PARANOIDEN REAKTIONEN IN DER HAFT. 1923. 106 pp.

Heft 20. Löwy, Max. DEMENTIA PRAECOX, INTERMEDIÄRE PSYCHISCHE SCHICHT. 1923. 120 pp.

Heft 21. Bychowski, Gustav. METAPHYSIK UND SCHIZOPHRENIE. 1923. 160 pp.

Heft 22. Weichbrodt, Raphael. DER SELBSTMORD. 1923. 44 pp.

Heft 23. Ahlenstiel, Heinz. ÜBER DIE STELLUNG DER PSYCHOLOGIE IM STAMMBAUM DER WISSENSCHAFTEN UND DIE DIMENSION IHRER GRUNDBEGRIFFE. 1923. 56 pp.

Heft 24. Fabritius, Harald. ZUR KLINIK DER NICHTPARALYTISCHEN LUES-PSYCHOSEN. 1924. 103 pp.

Heft 25. Leyser, E. HERZKRANKHEITEN UND PSYCHOSEN. 1924. 84 pp.

Heft 26. Jacobsohn-Lask, Louis. DIE KREUZUNG DER NERVENBAHNEN UND DIE BILATERALE SYMMETRIE DES TIERISCHEN KÖRPERS. 1924. 125 pp.

Heft 27. Niessl von Mayendorf, Erwin. KRITISCHE STUDIEN ZUR METHODIK DER APHASIELEHRE. 1925. 108 pp.

Heft 28. Straus, Erwin. WESEN UND VORGANG DER SUGGESTION. 1925. 86 pp.

Heft 29. Pohlisch, Kurt. DER HYPERKINETISCHE SYMPTOMENKOMPLEX UND SEINE NOSOLOGISCHE STELLUNG. 1925. 92 pp.

Heft 30. Pophal, Rudolph. DER KRANKHEITSBEGRIFF IN DER KÖRPERMEDIZIN UND PSYCHIATRIE. 1925. 111 pp.

Heft 31. Bolten, Gerard Christian. ÜBER GENESE UND BEHANDLUNG DER EXSUDATIVEN PAROXYSMEN. 1925. 110 pp.

Heft 32. Hoffman, Hermann FAMILIENPSYCHOSEN IM SCHIZOPHRENEN ERBKREIS. 1926. 120 pp.

Heft 33. Szymanski, J. S. GEFÜHL UND ERKENNEN. 1926. 204 pp.

Heft 34. Benedek, Ladislaus. DER HEUTIGE STAND DER BEHANDLUNG DER PROGRESSIVEN PARALYSE. 1926. 219 pp.

Heft 35. Herrmann, Georg, and Otto Pötzl. ÜBER DIE AGRAPHIE UND IHRE LOKALDIAGNOSTISCHEN BEZIEHUNGEN. 1926. 380 pp.

Heft 36. Thiele, Rudolf. ZUR KENNTNIS DER PSYCHISCHEN RESIDUÄRZUSTÄNDE. . . . 1926. 100 pp.

Heft 37. Runge, Werner, and Otto Rehm, ÜBER DIE VERWAHRLOSUNG DER JUGENDLICHEN. 1926. 156 pp.

Heft 38. Hildebrandt, Kurt. GESUNDHEIT UND KRANKHEIT IN NIETZSCHES LEBEN UND WERK. 1926. 160 pp.

Heft 39. Hartmann, Karl Julius. DAS WESEN DER AFFEKTFREIEN QUALITATIVEN BEDEUTUNGSGEFÜHLE. 1926. 120 pp.

357. *(Continued)*

Heft 40. Bachmann, Fritz. ÜBER CONGENITALE WORTBLINDHEIT. 1927. 72 pp.

Heft 41. Scheer, W. M. BEITRÄGE ZUR KENNTNIS DER MONGOLOIDEN MISSBILDUNG. 1927. 162 pp.

Heft 42. Schindler, Rudolf. NERVENSYSTEM UND SPONTANE BLUTUNGEN. 1927. 68 pp.

Heft 43. Wilder, Josef, and J. Silbermann. BEITRÄGE ZUM TICPROBLEM. 1927. 100 pp.

Heft 44. Kauders, Otto. KEIMDRÜSE, SEXUALITÄT UND ZENTRAL-NERVENSYSTEM. 1928. 194 pp.

Heft 45. Nachmansohn, M. DIE WISSENSCHAFTLICHEN GRUNDLAGEN DER PSYCHOANALYSE FREUDS. 1928. 106 pp.

Heft 46. Janota, Otakar, and Klement Weber. DIE PAROXYSMALE LÄHMUNG. 1928. 118 pp.

Heft 47. Herrmann, Georg, and Otto Pötzl. DIE OPTISCHE ALLÄSTHESIE. 1928. 302 pp.

Heft 48. Neustadt, Rudolf. DIE PSYCHOSEN DER SCHWACHSINNIGEN. 1928. 188 pp.

Heft 49. Stockert, F. G. ÜBER UMBAU UND ABBAU DER SPRACHE BEI GEISTESSTÖRUNG. 1929. 82 pp.

Heft 50. Marcuse, Harry. DIE PSYCHISCHEN REAKTIONSFORMEN. 1929. 262 pp.

Heft 51. Jacobi, Walter. PSYCHIATRIE UND WELTANSCHAUUNG. 1929. 91 pp.

Heft 52. Speranski, W. N. INNERE SEKRETION UND PSYCHISCHE PROZESSE. 1929. 150 pp.

Heft 53. Börnstein, Walter. DER AUFBAU DER FUNKTIONEN IN DER HÖRSPHÄRE. 1930. 126 pp.

Heft 54. Hoff, Hans. DIE ZENTRALE ABSTIMMUNG DER SEHSPHÄRE. 1930. 96 pp.

Heft 55. Herzberg, Alexander. ANALYSE DER SUGGESTIONSPHÄNOMENE UND THEORIE DER SUGGESTION. 1930. 128 pp.

Heft 56. Goldflam, Samuel. DIE DIAGNOSTISCHE BEDEUTUNG DES ROSSOLIMOSCHEN REFLEXES. 1930. 274 pp.

Heft 57. Müller, Max. ÜBER HEILUNGSMECHANISMEN IN DER SCHIZOPHRENIE. 1930. 143 pp.

Heft 58. Schilder, Paul. STUDIEN ZUR PSYCHOLOGIE UND SYMPTOMATOLOGIE DER PROGRESSIVEN PARALYSE. 1930. 176 pp.

Heft 59. Panse, Friedrich. DIE SCHÄDIGUNGEN DES NERVENSYSTEMS DURCH TECHNISCHE ELEKTRIZITÄT. 1930. 155 pp.

Heft 60. Krisch, Hans. DIE ORGANISCHEN EINSCHLIESSLICH DER EXOGENEN REAKTIONTYPEN. 1930. 146 pp.

Heft 61. REFERATE UND VORTRÄGE DER 1. INTERNATIONALEN TAGUNG FÜR ANGEWANDTE PSYCHOPATHOLOGIE UND PSYCHOLOGIE, WIEN, 5.–7. JUNI 1930. 1931. 241 pp.

Heft 62. Meyer, Fr. DAS RETIKULO-ENDOTHELIALE SYSTEM DER SCHIZOPHRENEN. 1931. 124 pp.

Heft 63. Sittig, Otto. Über Apraxie. 1931. 248 pp.

Heft 64. Kauders, Otto. Zur Klinik und Analyse der psychomotorischen Störung. 1931. 132 pp.

Heft 65. Bonhöffer, K. and P. Jossmann, eds. Ergebnisse der Reiztherapie bei progressiver Paralyse. 1932. 154 pp.

Heft 66. Hirschberg, Nikolai. Fleckfieber und Nervensystem. 1932. 124 pp.

Heft 67. Benedek, Ladislaus. Über die Schädelperkussion. 1932. 112 pp.

Heft 68. Ewald, Gottfried. Temperament und Charakter, Teil II. 1932. 138 pp.

Heft 69. Thiele, Rudolf, and Hermann Bernhardt. Beiträge zur Kenntnis der Narkolepsie. 1933. 187 pp.

Heft 70. Löwenstein, Otto, and Alexander Westphal. Experimentelle und klinische Studien zur Physiologie und Pathologie der Pupillenbeweggen. 1933. 181 pp.

Heft 71. Crinis, Max de. Aufbau und Abbau der Grosshirnleistungen und ihre anatomischen Grundlagen. 1934. 95 pp.

Heft 72. Störring, Gust. E. Zur Psychopathologie und Klinik der Angstzustände. 1934. 117 pp.

Heft 73. Betzendahl, Walter. Ausdrucksformen des Wahnsinns. 1935. 112 pp.

Heft 74. Menninger-Lerchenthal, E. Truggebilde der eigenen Gestalt. 1935. 196 pp.

Heft 75. Kinnier-Wilson, S. A. Die zentralen Beweggsstörungen. Die akuten und chronischen choreatischen Erkrankungen und die Myoklonien von Karl Bonhöffer. 1936. 136 pp.

Heft 76. Grünthal, E. Über die Erkennung der traumatischen Hirnverletzung. 1936. 116 pp.

Heft 77. Fünfgeld, Ernst. Motilitätspsychosen und Verwirrtheiten. 1936. 92 pp.

Heft 78. Binder, Hans, Psychologie der Zwangsvorgänge. 1936. 96 pp.

Heft 79. Fernandes, Barahona. Klinische Untersuchungen über motorische Erscheinungen bei Psychosen und organischen Hirnkrankheiten. 1937. 112 pp.

Heft 80. Hoesch, Kurt. Nebenschilddrusen-Epilepsie. 1937. 135 pp.

Heft 81. Anastasopoulos, Georg. Klinische Untersuchungen an Hirntumoren zur Frage der Entstehung der Stauungspapille. 1937. 115 pp.

Heft 82. Wyrsch, Jakob. Über akute schizophrene Zustände, ihren psychopathologischen Aufbau und ihre praktische Bedeutung. 1937. 80 pp.

Heft 83. Wyss, Walter H. von. Grundformen der Affektivität. 1938. 104 pp.

Heft 84. Weber, Arnold. Über nihilistischen Wahn und Depersonalisation. 1938. 137 pp.

Heft 85. Kehrer, Ferdinand. Die Verbindung von chorea- und ticförmigen Bewegungen mit Zwangsvorstellungen und ihre

BEZIEHUNGEN ZU DEN ZWANGSVORGÄNGEN BEI ZWANGSNEUROSE UND ENCEPH-
ALITIS EPIDEMICA. 1938. 88 pp.

Heft 86. Störring, Ernst. DIE STÖRUNGEN DES PERSÖNLICHKEITS-
BEWUSSTSEINS BEI MANISCH-DEPRESSIVEN ERKRANKUNGEN. 1938. 60 pp.

Heft 87. Binswanger, Herbert. FAMILIENPFLEGE IM KANTON ZURICH
1909–1936. 1939. 128 pp.

358. Colorado College. Department of Psychology and Education. Studies in Education and Psychology.

TITLE VARIATIONS: None.

DATES OF PUBLICATION: Number 1–2, 1917–1918.

FREQUENCY: Irregular.

NUMBERING VARIATIONS: None.

PUBLISHER: **Colorado Springs, Colorado:** Colorado College. Department of
Psychology and Education, 1917–1918.

PRIMARY EDITOR: **Joseph Valentine Breitwieser,** 1917–1918.

CONTENTS:

Number 1. Gerlach, Frederick Matthew. VOCABULARY STUDIES. 1917.
123 pp.

Number 2. Breitwieser, Joseph Valentine. PSYCHOLOGICAL EFFECTS OF
ALTITUDE. 1918. 44 pp.

359. Journal of Applied Psychology.

TITLE VARIATIONS: None.

DATES OF PUBLICATION: Volume 1–34+, 1917–1950+.

FREQUENCY: **Quarterly,** Volume 1–10, 1917–1926. **Bimonthly,** Volume
11–34+, 1927–1950+.

NUMBERING VARIATIONS: None.

PUBLISHER: **Worcester, Massachusetts:** Florence Chandler, Publisher,
1917–1921. **Bloomington, Indiana:** Published by the Editors, Indiana University Press, 1922–1923. **Baltimore:** Published by the Editors, Williams and Wilkins Company, 1924–1928. **Baltimore:** Published by the Editors, Waverly
Press, Inc., 1929–1931. **Lancaster, Pennsylvania:** Published by the Editor,
Science Press Printing Company, 1931, 1935–1942. **Indianapolis, Indiana:** By
the Editors, C. E. Pauley and Co., 1932–1934. **Lancaster:** American Psychological Association, Inc. with the cooperation of the American Association for
Applied Psychology, 1943–1945. **Washington, D.C.:** American Psychological
Association, Inc., 1946–1950+.

PRIMARY EDITORS: **G. Stanley Hall,** 1917–1919; **John Wallace Baird,**
1917–1918; **L. R. Geissler,** 1917–1919; **James P. Porter,** 1920–1942; **William
F. Book,** 1920–1927; **Paul S. Achilles,** 1940–1942; **Henry C. Link,** 1940–1942;
Donald G. Paterson, 1943–1950+.

360. *Los Angeles City School District. Division of Educational Research. Yearbook.*

TITLE VARIATIONS: Continued by *Los Angeles City School District. Department of Psychology and Educational Research. Yearbook* with 3rd, 1927–1929.

DATES OF PUBLICATION: 1st–2nd, 1917/1918–1918/1927.

FREQUENCY: **Annual,** 1st, 1917/1918. **Irregular,** 2nd, 1918/1927.

NUMBERING VARIATIONS: 1st yearbook also issued as *Los Angeles City School District. Publication,* Number 21.

PUBLISHER: **Los Angeles:** Los Angeles City School District, 1918–1927.

PRIMARY EDITORS: None listed.

361. *Mental Hygiene.*

TITLE VARIATIONS: None.

DATES OF PUBLICATION. Volume 1–34 + , January 1917–October 1950 + .

FREQUENCY: Quarterly.

NUMBERING VARIATIONS: Book Review Supplement to Volume 8, Number 1 issued January 1924.

PUBLISHER: **New York:** National Committee for Mental Hygiene, Inc., 1917–July 1950. **New York:** National Association for Mental Health, October 1950 + .

PRIMARY EDITORS: **Frankwood E. Williams,** 1922–1931; **Clarance M. Hincks,** 1931–1939; **Margaret H. Wagenhals,** 1932–1950 + ; **George S. Stevenson,** 1940–1950 + .

EDITORIAL BOARD: Thomas W. Salmon, 1917–1926; Frankwood E. Williams, 1917–1921; George Blumer, 1917–1920; C. Macfie Campbell, 1917–1931; Stephen P. Duggan, 1917–1922; Walter E. Fernald, 1917–1924; August Hoch, 1917–1919; Stewart Paton, 1917–1930; Howard W. Potter, 1931–1950 + ; Bernard Glueck, 1931; William A. White, 1931; Margaret H. Wagenhals, 1931; Horatio M. Pollock, 1932–1949; Edward A. Strecker, 1932–1950 + ; Sheldon Glueck, 1932–1950 + .

362. *Neudrucke zur Psychologie.*

TITLE VARIATIONS: None.

DATES OF PUBLICATION: Band 1–3, Heft 1, 1917–1918.

FREQUENCY: Irregular. *See* Contents *below.*

NUMBERING VARIATIONS: None.

PUBLISHER: **Langensalza, Germany:** Wendt & Klauwell, 1917–1918.

PRIMARY EDITORS: Fritz Giese, 1917–1918.

CONTENTS:

    Band 1. Humboldt, Wilhelm von. ÜBER DEN GESCHLECHSUNTERSCHIED. ÜBER DIE MÄNNLICHE UND WEIBLICHE FORM. 1917. 231 pp.

Band 2. Gerhardt, Ferdinand von. MATERIALIEN ZUR BLINDENPSYCHO-
LOGIE. 1917. 283 pp.

Band 3, Heft 1. Giese, Fritz, ed. DER KRIEG UND DIE KOMPLEMENTÄRE
KULTURPSYCHOLOGIE. Heft 1: Wittig, Kurt. DER ETHISCHE MINDERWERT. JU-
GENBLICHE UND DER KRIEG. 1918. 70 pp.

363. *Psikho-nevrologicheskii vestnik'; Zhurnal' psikhiatrii, nevrologii, eksperimentalnoi psikhologii, obshchestvennoi i kriminalnoi psikhopatologii.*

TITLE VARIATIONS: None.

DATES OF PUBLICATION: Vypusk 1–2/4, 1917.

FREQUENCY: Irregular.

NUMBERING VARIATIONS: Multinumber issue present.

PUBLISHER: **Moscow:** Psikhiatricheskaia klinika Moskovskago Universiteta,
1917.

PRIMARY EDITORS: **Ia. A. Anfimov,** 1917; **L. O. Darkshevich,** 1917; **A. A.
Kornilov,** 1917; **A. M. Levkovsky,** 1917; **Th. E. Rybakov,** 1917.

364. *Psychobiology.*

TITLE VARIATIONS: Merged with the *Journal of Animal Behavior* and continued under the title *Journal of Comparative Psychology* with Volume 1, 1921.

DATES OF PUBLICATION: Volume 1–2, July 1917–December 1920. Suspended
publication June 1918–December 1919.

FREQUENCY: **Bimonthly,** Volume 1, July 1917–May 1918. **Bimonthly,** Volume
2, February 1920–December 1920.

NUMBERING VARIATIONS: None.

PUBLISHER: **Baltimore:** Williams and Wilkins, 1917–1920.

PRIMARY EDITOR: **Knight Dunlap,** 1917–1920.

365. *Schriften für angewandte Individualpsychologie.*

TITLE VARIATIONS: Continues *Verein für Individualpsychologie. Schriften.*

DATES OF PUBLICATION: Heft 7, 1917.

FREQUENCY: Irregular. *See* Contents *below.*

NUMBERING VARIATIONS: None.

PUBLISHER: **Munich:** E. Reinhardt, 1917.

PRIMARY EDITOR: **Alfred Adler,** 1917.

CONTENTS:

Heft 7. Adler, Alfred. DAS PROBLEM DER HOMOSEXUALITÄT. 1917. 52 pp.

366. *Société Alfred Binet. Psychologie de l'enfant et pédogogie expérimentale. Bulletin.*

TITLE VARIATIONS: Subtitles *Bulletin* and *Bulletin mensuel* both used. Continues *Société libre pour l'étude psychologique de l'enfant. Bulletin.*

DATES OF PUBLICATION: Numéro 118–397+, October/November 1917 –November/December 1950+.

FREQUENCY: Monthly (academic year).

NUMBERING VARIATIONS: Multinumber issues present.

PUBLISHER: **Paris:** Librairie F. Alcan, 1917–1920. **Cahors (Lot), France:** Imprimerie Coueslant, 1920–1945. **Cahors (Lot):** Imprimerie A. Coueslant, 1946–1950+.

PRIMARY EDITORS: **V. Vaney,** 1917–1923; **Th. Simon,** 1923–1929; **Mad. Rémy,** 1930–1950+.

367. *Stanford University. Publications. Psychical Research Monographs.*

TITLE VARIATIONS: Also called *Leland Stanford Junior University. Publications. Psychical Research Monographs.*

DATES OF PUBLICATION: Number 1, 1917.

FREQUENCY: Irregular. *See* Contents *below.*

NUMBERING VARIATIONS: None.

PUBLISHER: **Stanford University, California:** Published by the University, 1917.

PRIMARY EDITORS: None listed.

CONTENTS:

   Number 1. Coover, John Edgar, EXPERIMENTS IN PSYCHICAL RESEARCH AT LELAND STANFORD JUNIOR UNIVERSITY. 1917. 641 pp.

368. *Supplementary Educational Monographs*

TITLE VARIATIONS: Also called [*Chicago. University.*] *Supplementary Educational Monographs.* Published in conjunction with the *School Review* and the *Elementary School Journal.*

DATES OF PUBLICATION: Number 1–73+, 1917–1950+.

FREQUENCY: Irregular. *See* Contents *below.*

NUMBERING VARIATIONS: Number 1–16 also irregularly numbered as Volume 1–3; volume numbering ceased with Volume 3. Number 28 includes supplements: 1924/1925, 1925/1926 and 1926/1927. Various issues also numbered as [*Chicago. University.*] *University High School. Studies in Secondary Education;* as [*Chicago. University.*] *Conference on Reading;* as [*Chicago. University.*] *Annual Conference on Arithmetic. Papers;* or as [*Chicago. University.*] *Reading Clinic Staff. Clinical Studies in Reading. See* Contents *below.*

368. *(Continued)*

PUBLISHER: **Chicago:** University of Chicago Press, 1917–1950+.

PRIMARY EDITORS: Editorial Committee of the Faculty of the School of Education, University of Chicago, 1917–1929. Members include: **Franklin Bobbitt, Guy Thomas Buswell, Isaac Newton Edwards, Frank Nugent Freeman, Harry Orrin Gillet, William Scott Gray, Karl John Holzinger, Charles Hubbard Judd, Rollo LaVerne Lyman, Henry Clinton Morrison, William Clause Reavis, Rolla Milton Tryon.** Faculty of the School of Education, University of Chicago, 1931–1937. Faculty of the Department of Education, University of Chicago, 1937–1950+.

CONTENTS:

[Volume 1] **Number 1.** Gray, William Scott. STUDIES OF ELEMENTARY-SCHOOL READING THROUGH STANDARDIZED TESTS. 1917. 157 pp.

[————] **Number 2.** Schmidt, William Anton. AN EXPERIMENTAL STUDY IN THE PSYCHOLOGY OF READING. 1917. 126 pp.

[————] **Number 3.** Koos, Leonard V. THE ADMINISTRATION OF SECONDARY-SCHOOL UNITS. 1917. 194 pp.

[————] **Number 4.** Counts, George Sylvester. ARITHMETIC TESTS AND STUDIES IN THE PSYCHOLOGY OF ARITHMETIC. 1917. 127 pp.

[————] **Number 5.** Gray, Clarence Truman. TYPES OF READING ABILITY AS EXHIBITED THROUGH TESTS AND LABORATORY EXPERIMENTS. AN INVESTIGATION SUBSIDIZED BY THE GENERAL EDUCATION BOARD. 1917. 196 pp.

[————] **Number 6.** Temple, Alice. SURVEY OF THE KINDERGARTENS OF RICHMOND. INDIANA. 1917. 58 pp.

[Volume 2] **Number 7.** Rugg, Harold Ordway, and John Roscoe Clark. SCIENTIFIC METHOD IN THE RECONSTRUCTION OF NINTH-GRADE MATHEMATICS. A COMPLETE REPORT OF THE INVESTIGATION OF THE ILLINOIS COMMITTEE ON STANDARDIZATION OF NINTH-GRADE MATHEMATICS, 1913–1918. 1918. 189 pp.

[————] **Number 8.** Beeley, Arthur L. AN EXPERIMENTAL STUDY IN LEFT-HANDEDNESS WITH PRACTICAL SUGGESTIONS FOR SCHOOLROOM TESTS. 1918. 74 pp.

[————] **Number 9.** Freeman, Frank N., with the assistance of H. W. Nutt, Mary L. Dougherty, C. F. Dunn, and P. V. West. THE HANDWRITING MOVEMENT; A STUDY OF THE MOTOR FACTORS OF EXCELLENCE IN PENMANSHIP. AN INVESTIGATION CARRIED ON WITH THE AID OF A SUBSIDY BY THE GENERAL EDUCATION BOARD. 1918. 169 pp.

[————] **Number 10.** Judd, Charles Hubbard, with the cooperation of William Scott Gray, Katherine McLaughlin, Clarence Truman Gray, Clara Schmitt, and Adam Raymond Gilliland. READING: ITS NATURE AND DEVELOPMENT. 1918. 192 pp.

[Volume 3] **Number 11.** Hobson, Elsie Garland. EDUCATIONAL LEGISLATION AND ADMINISTRATION IN THE STATE OF NEW YORK FROM 1777 TO 1850. 1918. 267 pp.

[Volume 2] **Number 12.** Lyon, Leverett. A SURVEY OF COMMERCIAL EDUCATION IN THE PUBLIC HIGH SCHOOLS OF THE UNITED STATES. 1919. 59 pp.

[Volume 3] **Number 13.** Miller, Edward Alanson. THE HISTORY OF EDU-

CATIONAL LEGISLATION IN OHIO FROM 1803 TO 1850. 1920. 248 pp. (Also in *Ohio Archaeological and Historical Quarterly*, Volume 27, Numbers 1 and 2.)

[Volume 2] Number 14. Trilling, Mabel Barbara, Ethel Wyn Miller, Leona Florence Bowman, Florence Williams, Clara Blanche Knapp, Viola Maria Bell, Bertha Miller Rugg, with the collaboration of Harold Ordway Rugg. HOME ECONOMICS IN AMERICAN SCHOOLS. 1920. 122 pp.

[Volume 3] Number 15. Stout, John Elbert, THE DEVELOPMENT OF HIGH-SCHOOL CURRICULA IN THE NORTH CENTRAL STATES FROM 1860 TO 1918. 1921. 322 pp.

[Volume 3] Number 16. Weathersby, William Henington. A HISTORY OF EDUCATIONAL LEGISLATION IN MISSISSIPPI FROM 1798 TO 1860. 1921. 204 pp.

Number 17. Buswell, Guy Thomas. AN EXPERIMENTAL STUDY OF THE EYE-VOICE SPAN IN READING. 1920. 105 pp.

Number 18. Terry, Paul Washington. HOW NUMERALS ARE READ. AN EXPERIMENTAL STUDY OF THE READING OF ISOLATED NUMERALS AND NUMERALS IN ARITHMETIC PROBLEMS. 1922. 109 pp.

Number 19. Counts, George Sylvester. THE SELECTIVE CHARACTER OF AMERICAN SECONDARY EDUCATION. 1922. 162 pp.

Number 20. Bobbitt, Franklin. CURRICULUM-MAKING IN LOS ANGELES. 1922. 106 pp.

Number 21. Buswell, Guy Thomas. FUNDAMENTAL READING HABITS: A STUDY OF THEIR DEVELOPMENT. 1922. 150 pp.

Number 22. Gray, William Scott, with the cooperation of Delia Kibbe, Laura Lucas, and Lawrence William Miller. REMEDIAL CASES IN READING: THEIR DIAGNOSIS AND TREATMENT. 1922. 208 pp.

Number 23. Judd, Charles Hubbard, and Guy Thomas Buswell. SILENT READING: A STUDY OF THE VARIOUS TYPES. 1922. 160 pp.

Number 24. Chicago. University UNIVERSITY HIGH SCHOOL. STUDIES IN SECONDARY EDUCATION. VOLUME 1. 1923. 150 pp.

Number 25. Glass, James M. CURRICULUM PRACTICES IN THE JUNIOR HIGH SCHOOL AND GRADES 5 AND 6. 1924. 181 pp.

Number 26. Chicago. University. UNIVERSITY HIGH SCHOOL. STUDIES IN SECONDARY EDUCATION. VOLUME 2. 1925. 202 pp.

Number 27. Buswell, Guy Thomas, and Charles Hubbard Judd. SUMMARY OF EDUCATIONAL INVESTIGATIONS RELATING TO ARITHMETIC. 1925. 212 pp.

Number 28. William Scott. SUMMARY OF INVESTIGATIONS RELATING TO READING. 1925. 275 pp.

Number 29. Counts, George S. THE SENIOR HIGH SCHOOL CURRICULUM. 1926. 160 pp.

Number 30. Buswell, Guy T. with the cooperation of Lenore John. DIAGNOSTIC STUDIES IN ARITHMETIC. 1926. 212 pp.

Number 31. Bobbitt, Franklin, with the cooperation of Paul L. Palmer, John A. Nietz, Irl H. Dulebohn, Genevieve K. Bixler, Clara H. Lorenzen, Sarah A. Bobbitt, Robert C. Scarf, Harvey C. Lehman, Clara A. Dyer, Harriet M. Mott, and Harold H. Postel. CURRICULUM INVESTIGATIONS. 1926. 204 pp.

Number 32. Judd, Charles Hubbard. PSYCHOLOGICAL ANALYSIS OF THE FUNDAMENTALS OF ARITHMETIC. 1927. 121 pp.

Number 33. Counts, George S. THE SOCIAL COMPOSITION OF BOARDS OF

368. *(Continued)*

EDUCATION. A STUDY IN THE SOCIAL CONTROL OF PUBLIC EDUCATION. 1927. 100 pp.

Number 34. Brooks, Eugene C., Samuel P. Capen, Edward S. Evenden, Thomas H. Harris, Charles H. Judd, George Melcher, Clarence L. Phelps, Peter Sandiford, Payson Smith, and Henry Suzzallo. REPORT OF THE COMMISSION ON LENGTH OF ELEMENTARY EDUCATION. 1927. 167 pp.

Number 35. Brownell, William A. THE DEVELOPMENT OF CHILDREN'S NUMBER IDEAS IN THE PRIMARY GRADES. 1928. 241 pp.

Number 36. Lyman, R. L. SUMMARY OF INVESTIGATIONS RELATING TO GRAMMAR, LANGUAGE, AND COMPOSITION. 1929. 302 pp.

Number 37. Wood, Ernest Richard. A GRAPHIC METHOD OF OBTAINING THE PARTIAL-CORRELATION COEFFICIENTS AND THE PARTIAL-REGRESSION COEFFICIENTS OF THREE OR MORE VARIABLES. 1931. 72 pp.

Number 38. Buswell, Guy T., and Lenore John. THE VOCABULARY OF ARITHMETIC. 1931. 146 pp.

Number 39. Lyman, R. L. THE ENRICHMENT OF THE ENGLISH CURRICULUM. 1932. 251 pp.

Number 40. Gray, Williams S. with the Assistance of Gertrude Whipple. IMPROVING INSTRUCTION IN READING. AN EXPERIMENTAL STUDY. 1933. 226 pp.

Number 41. SELECTED REFERENCES IN EDUCATION, REPRINTED FROM THE *SCHOOL REVIEW* AND THE *ELEMENTARY SCHOOL JOURNAL* FROM JANUARY TO DECEMBER, 1933. 1934. 190 pp.

Number 42. SELECTED REFERENCES IN EDUCATION, REPRINTED FROM THE *SCHOOL REVIEW* AND THE *ELEMENTARY SCHOOL JOURNAL* FROM JANUARY TO DECEMBER, 1934. 1935. 189 pp.

Number 43. SELECTED REFERENCES IN EDUCATION, REPRINTED FROM THE *SCHOOL REVIEW* AND THE *ELEMENTARY SCHOOL JOURNAL* FROM JANUARY TO DECEMBER, 1935. 1936. 198 pp.

Number 44. SELECTED REFERENCES IN EDUCATION, REPRINTED FROM THE *SCHOOL REVIEW* AND THE *ELEMENTARY SCHOOL JOURNAL* FROM JANUARY TO DECEMBER, 1936. 1937. 215 pp.

Number 45. Buswell, Guy T. HOW ADULTS READ. 1937. 154 pp.

Number 46. SELECTED REFERENCES IN EDUCATION, REPRINTED FROM THE *SCHOOL REVIEW* AND THE *ELEMENTARY SCHOOL JOURNAL* FROM JANUARY TO DECEMBER, 1937. 1938. 224 pp.

Number 47. SELECTED REFERENCES IN EDUCATION, REPRINTED FROM THE *SCHOOL REVIEW* AND THE *ELEMENTARY SCHOOL JOURNAL* FROM JANUARY TO DECEMBER, 1938. 1939. 221 pp.

Number 48. Holzinger, Karl, and Frances Swineford. A STUDY IN FACTOR ANALYSIS: THE STABILITY OF A BI-FACTOR SOLUTION. 1939. 91 pp.

Number 49. Gray, William S., ed. RECENT TRENDS IN READING. PROCEEDINGS OF THE CONFERENCE ON READING HELD AT THE UNIVERSITY OF CHICAGO, VOLUME I. 1939. 366 pp.

Number 50. Buswell, Guy T. REMEDIAL READING AT THE COLLEGE AND ADULT LEVELS. AN EXPERIMENTAL STUDY. 1939. 72 pp.

Number 51. Gray, William S., ed. READING AND PUPIL DEVELOPMENT. PROCEEDINGS OF THE CONFERENCE ON READING HELD AT THE UNIVERSITY OF CHICAGO, VOLUME II. 1940. 355 pp.

Number 52. Gray, William S., ed. ADJUSTING READING PROGRAMS TO INDIVIDUALS. PROCEEDINGS OF THE CONFERENCE ON READING HELD AT THE UNIVERSITY OF CHICAGO, VOLUME III. 1941. 344 pp.

Number 53. Swineford, Frances, and Karl J. Holzinger. A STUDY IN FACTOR ANALYSIS. THE RELIABILITY OF BI-FACTORS AND THEIR RELATION TO OTHER MEASURES. 1942. 88 pp.

Number 54. Burgess, Ernest W., W. Lloyd Warner, Franz Alexander, and Margaret Mead. ENVIRONMENT AND EDUCATION, A SYMPOSIUM HELD IN CONNECTION WITH THE FIFTIETH ANNIVERSARY CELEBRATION OF THE UNIVERSITY OF CHICAGO. 1942. 66 pp.

Number 55. McConnell, T. R., Douglas E. Scates, and Frank N. Freeman. THE CONCEPTUAL STRUCTURE OF EDUCATIONAL RESEARCH. A SYMPOSIUM HELD IN CONNECTION WITH THE FIFTIETH ANNIVERSARY CELEBRATION OF THE UNIVERSITY OF CHICAGO. 1942. 47 pp.

Number 56. Gray, William S., ed. CO-OPERATIVE EFFORT IN SCHOOLS TO IMPROVE READING. PROCEEDINGS OF THE CONFERENCE ON READING HELD AT THE UNIVERSITY OF CHICAGO, VOLUME IV. 1942. 338 pp.

Number 57. Gray, William S., ed. ADAPTING READING PROGRAMS TO WARTIME NEEDS. PROCEEDINGS OF THE CONFERENCE ON READING HELD AT THE UNIVERSITY OF CHICAGO, VOLUME V. 1943. 283 pp.

Number 58. Gray, William S., ed. READING IN RELATION TO EXPERIENCE AND LANGUAGE. PROCEEDINGS OF THE CONFERENCE ON READING HELD AT THE UNIVERSITY OF CHICAGO, VOLUME VI. 1944. 226 pp.

Number 59. Reavis, William C., and Dan H. Cooper. EVALUATION OF TEACHER MERIT IN CITY SCHOOL SYSTEMS. 1945. 138 pp.

Number 60. Buswell, Guy T. NON-ORAL READING: A STUDY OF ITS USE IN THE CHICAGO PUBLIC SCHOOLS. 1945. 56 pp.

Number 61. Gray, William S., ed. THE APPRAISAL OF CURRENT PRACTICES IN READING. PROCEEDINGS OF THE ANNUAL CONFERENCE ON READING HELD AT THE UNIVERSITY OF CHICAGO, VOLUME VII. 1945. 255 pp.

Number 62. Gray, William S., ed. IMPROVING READING IN CONTENT FIELDS. PROCEEDINGS OF THE ANNUAL CONFERENCE ON READING HELD AT THE UNIVERSITY OF CHICAGO, 1946, VOLUME VIII. 1947. 240 pp.

Number 63. Buswell, Guy T., ed. "ARITHMETIC IN 1947." PAPERS PRESENTED AT THE SECOND ANNUAL CONFERENCE ON ARITHMETIC HELD AT THE UNIVERSITY OF CHICAGO, JUNE 30, JULY 1 AND 2, 1947. 1947. 73 pp.

Number 64. Gray, William S., ed. PROMOTING PERSONAL AND SOCIAL DEVELOPMENT THROUGH READING. PROCEEDINGS OF THE ANNUAL CONFERENCE ON READING HELD AT THE UNIVERSITY OF CHICAGO, 1947, VOLUME IX. 1947. 236 pp.

Number 65. Gray, William S., ed. BASIC INSTRUCTION IN READING IN ELEMENTARY AND HIGH SCHOOLS. PROCEEDINGS OF THE ANNUAL CONFERENCE ON READING HELD AT THE UNIVERSITY OF CHICAGO, 1948, VOLUME X. 1948. 237 pp.

368. *(Continued)*

Number 66. Buswell, Guy T., ed. "ARITHMETIC 1948." PAPERS PRESENTED AT THE THIRD ANNUAL CONFERENCE ON ARITHMETIC HELD AT THE UNIVERSITY OF CHICAGO, JULY 7, 8, AND 9, 1948. 1948. 90 pp.

Number 67. Swineford, Frances. A STUDY IN FACTOR ANALYSIS: THE NATURE OF THE GENERAL, VERBAL, AND SPATIAL BI-FACTORS. 1948. 71 pp.

Number 68. Chicago. University. Reading Clinic Staff. CLINICAL STUDIES IN READING I. 1949. 173 pp.

Number 69. Gray, William S., ed. CLASSROOM TECHNIQUES IN IMPROVING READING. PROCEEDINGS OF THE ANNUAL CONFERENCE ON READING HELD AT THE UNIVERSITY OF CHICAGO, 1949, VOLUME XI. 1949. 246 pp.

Number 70. Buswell, Guy T., and Maurice L. Hartung, eds. "ARITHMETIC 1949." PAPERS PRESENTED AT THE FOURTH ANNUAL CONFERENCE ON ARITHMETIC HELD AT THE UNIVERSITY OF CHICAGO, JULY 6, 7, AND 8, 1949. 1949. 100 pp.

Number 71. Herrick, Virgil E., and Ralph W. Tyler, eds. TOWARD IMPROVED CURRICULUM THEORY. PAPERS PRESENTED AT THE CONFERENCE ON CURRICULUM THEORY HELD AT THE UNIVERSITY OF CHICAGO, OCTOBER 16 AND 17, 1947. 1950. 124 pp.

Number 72. Gray, William S., ed. KEEPING READING PROGRAMS ABREAST OF THE TIMES. PROCEEDINGS OF THE ANNUAL CONFERENCE ON READING HELD AT THE UNIVERSITY OF CHICAGO, 1950, VOLUME XII. 1950. 247 pp.

Number 73. Bloom, Benjamin S., and Lois J. Broder. PROEBLM-SOLVING PROCESSES OF COLLEGE STUDENTS. AN EXPLORATORY INVESTIGATION. 1950. 109 pp.

1918

369. *Abhandlungen aus dem Gebiete der Sexualforschung.*
[Sponsored by the Internationale Gesellschaft für Sexualforschung.]

TITLE VARIATIONS: None.

DATES OF PUBLICATION: Band 1–6, Heft 2, 1918–1931.

FREQUENCY: Irregular. *See* Contents *below.*

NUMBERING VARIATIONS: None.

PUBLISHER: **Bonn:** A. Marcus & E. Weber, 1918–1925. **Bonn** and **Berlin:** A. Marcus & E. Weber, 1926–1930. **Berlin:** Marcus & Weber, 1931.

PRIMARY EDITOR: **Max Marcuse,** 1918–1931.

CONTENTS:

Band 1, Heft 1. Marcuse, Max. WANDLUNGEN DES FORTPFLANZUNGS-GEDANKENS UND -WILLENS. 1918. 73 pp.

————, **Heft 2.** Schultze, Ernst. DIE PROSTITUTION BEI DER GELBEN VÖLKERN. 1918. 46 pp.

————, **Heft 3.** Winge, Paul. DER MENSCHLICHE GONOCHERISMUS UND DIE HISTORISCHE WISSENSCHAFT. 1918. 38 pp.

————, **Heft 4.** May, Raphael Ernst. DER FRAUENÜBERSCHUSS NACH KONFESSIONEN; and Kickh, Adolf. BEITRÄGE ZUR ZAHLENVERHÄLTNISSE DER GESCHLECHTER. 1919. 38 pp.

————, **Heft 5.** Gerson, Adolf. DIE SCHAM. BEITRÄGE ZUR PHYSIOLOGIE, ZUR PSYCHOLOGIE UND ZUR SOZIOLOGIE DER SCHAMGEFÜHLS. 1919. 68 pp.

————, **Heft 6.** Schneickert, Hans. DAS WEIB ALS ERPRESSERIN UND AN-STIFTERIN. KRIMINALPSYCHOLOGISCHE STUDIEN. 1919. 39 pp.

Band 2, Heft 1. Mittermaier, Wolfgang. DER EHEBRUCH. 1919. 27 pp.

————, **Heft 2.** Hurwicz, Elias. DER LIEBES-DOPPELSELBSTMORD. EINE PSYCHOLOGISCHE STUDIE. 1920. 34 pp.

————, **Heft 3.** Gross, Otto. 3 AUFSÄTZE ÜBER DEN INNEREN KONFLIKT. 1920. 39 pp.

————, **Heft 4.** Marcuse, Max. ÜBER DIE FRUCHTBARKEIT DER CHRIST-LICH-JUDISCHEN MISCHEHE. 1920. 20 pp.

————, **Heft 5.** Kickh, Adolf. SEXUELLE UND ALKOHOL-FRAGEN. 1920. 68 pp.

————, **Heft 6.** Praetorius, Muma. DAS LIEBESLEBEN LUDWIGS XIII VON FRANKREICH. 1920. 62 pp.

Band 3, Heft 1. Scheuer, Oskar F. DAS LIEBESLEBEN DER DEUTSCHEN STUDENTEN IM WANDEL DER ZEITEN. 1920. 74 pp.

————, **Heft 2.** Marx, Otto. DAS SELBSTBESTIMMUNGSRECHT IN EHE UND LIEBE. ZUR REFORM DER EHESCHEIDUNG. 1920. 32 pp.

————, **Heft 3.** Licht, Hans. DIE HOMOEROTIK IN DER GRIECHISCHEN LIT-ERATUR. LUKANIOS VON SAMOSATA. 1921. 78 pp.

————, **Heft 4.** Fehlinger, H. DIE FORTPFLANZUNG DER NATUR- UND KULTURVÖLKER. 1921. 55 pp.

————, **Heft 5.** Moll, Albert. BEHANDLUNG DER HOMOSEXUALITÄT. 1921. 71 pp.

————, **Heft 6.** Vorberg, Gaston. DER KLATSCH ÜBER DAS GESCHLECHTS-LEBEN FRIEDRICHS II. DER FALL JEAN JACQUES ROUSSEAU. 1921. 30 pp.

Band 4, Heft 1. Vaerting, M. PHYSIOLOGISCHE URSACHEN GEISTIGER HÖCHSTLEISTUNGEN BEI MANN UND WEIB. 1922. 23 pp.

————, **Heft 2.** Strassmann, Fritz. DER MENSCHLICHE SAMEN IN DER GE-RICHTLICHEN MEDIZIN. 1922. 37 pp.

————, **Heft 3.** Senf, Max Rudolf. HOMOSEXUALISIERUNG. 1924. 74 pp.

————, **Heft 4.** Timerding, Heinrich Emil. DAS PROBLEM DER LEDIGEN FRAU. 1925. 44 pp.

————, **Heft 5.** Zucker, Ralph. DIE AUSBILDUNG DER GESCHLECHTS-CHARAKTERE UND IHRE BEZIEHUNG ZU DEN KEIMDRÜSEN. ·1925. 84 pp.

————, **Heft 6.** Fehlinger, Hans. GESCHLECHTSLEBEN UND FORTPFLAN-ZUNG DER ESKIMO. 1926. 36 pp.

Band 5, Heft 1. Haustein, Hans. ZUR SEXUELLEN HYGIENE IN SOWJET-RUSSLAND. 1926. 41 pp.

————, **Heft 2.** Weissenberg, S. Beiträge zur Frauenbiologie. 1927. 29 pp.

————, **Heft 3.** Klimowsky, Ernst. Sexualtyp und Kultur. 1928. 80 pp.

————, **Heft 4.** Galant, Johann Susmann. Die eingebildete Schwangerschaft. 1928. 68 pp.

————, **Heft 5.** Gosney, E. S. and Paul Popenoe. Sterilisierung zum Zwecke des Aufbesserung der Menschengeschlechts. 1930. 78 pp.

Band 6, Heft 1. Kauschansky, David Moiseewitsch. Evolution des sowjetrussischen Eherechts. 1931. 47 pp.

————, **Heft 2.** Kauschansky, David Moiseewitsch. Evolution der sowjetrussischen Familienrechts. 1931. 36 pp.

370. *American Association for the Study of the Feeble-Minded. Proceedings and Addresses.*

TITLE VARIATIONS: Continues *Association of Medical Officers of American Institutions for Idiotic and Feeble-Minded Persons. Proceedings of the Annual Meetings.* Continued by *American Association on Mental Deficiency. Proceedings and Addresses* with Volume 38, 1933.

DATES OF PUBLICATION: Number 42–56, 1918–1932.

FREQUENCY: Annual. (Comprised of four issues published as one volume and containing Annual Proceedings only.)

NUMBERING VARIATIONS: Number 42–56 published in *Journal of Psycho-Asthenics,* Volume 23–37, 1918–1932.

PUBLISHER: **Faribault, Minnesota:** By the Association, 1918–1920. [**St. Paul, Minnesota:**] By the Association, 1920–1921. [**Manchester, New Hampshire:**] By the Association, 1921–1924. N.p.: By the Association, 1924–1932.

PRIMARY EDITORS: **Fred Kuhlmann,** 1918–1921; **J. M. Murdock,** 1918–1920, **Benjamin W. Baker,** 1920–1924; **Howard W. Potter,** 1924–1930; **Groves Blake Smith,** 1930–1932.

371. *California Society for Mental Hygiene. Publications.*

TITLE VARIATIONS: None.

DATES OF PUBLICATION: Number 1–5, 1918–1921.

FREQUENCY: Irregular. *See* Contents *below.*

NUMBERING VARIATIONS: Number 3 was issued without the designation *California Society for Mental Hygiene* and is also numbered as *California Council of National Defense. Women's Committee. Children's Year Bulletin. See* Contents *below.*

PUBLISHER: **San Francisco:** California Society for Mental Hygiene, Number 1–2, 4–5, 1918–1921. **Sacramento:** California State Printing Office, Number 3, undated.

PRIMARY EDITOR: **Lillien J. Martin,** 1918–1921.

CONTENTS:
Number 1. CALIFORNIA SOCIETY FOR MENTAL HYGIENE. PURPOSES, WORK AND OFFICERS. August 1918. 4 pp.
Number 2. Krafft, Elsie. THE MENTAL HYGIENE CLINIC. August 1918. 7 pp.
Number 3. Bridgman, Olga. MENTAL TRAINING OF THE YOUNG CHILD. Undated. 7 pp. (Also as *California Council of National Defense. Women's Committee. Children's Year Bulletin*, Number 1.)
Number 4. Martin, Lillien J. THE TRAINING OF THE EMOTIONS. August 1918. 7 pp.
Number 5. Martin, Lillien J. THE WORK OF A MENTAL HYGIENE CLINIC FOR PRE-SCHOOL AGE CHILDREN. July 1921. 4 pp.

372. *Great Britain. Industrial Fatigue Research Board. Annual Report.*

TITLE VARIATIONS: Continued by [*Great Britain.*] *Industrial Health Research Board. Annual Report* with Number 9, 1928.

DATES OF PUBLICATION: Number 1–8, 1918/1920–1927.

FREQUENCY: Annual (Reporting year is irregular).

NUMBERING VARIATIONS: None.

PUBLISHER: London: Printed and Published by His Majesty's Stationery Office, 1920–1927.

PRIMARY EDITOR: D. R. Wilson (Secretary), 1920–1928.

373. *Illinois. University. Bureau of Educational Research. Bulletin.*

TITLE VARIATIONS: None.

DATES OF PUBLICATION: Number 1–63, September 1918–1947. Suspended publication 1933–1945.

FREQUENCY: Irregular. *See* Contents *below*.

NUMBERING VARIATIONS: Issues also numbered as *University of Illinois. Bulletin*.

PUBLISHER: Urbana, Illinois: University of Illinois, 1918–1931. Urbana: College of Education, University of Illinois, 1932–1947.

PRIMARY EDITORS: B. R. Buckingham, 1918–1920; Walter S. Monroe, 1921–1947.

CONTENTS:
Number 1. Buckingham, B. R. BUREAU OF EDUCATIONAL RESEARCH, ANNOUNCEMENT, 1918–19. September 30, 1918. 24 pp.
Number 2. FIRST ANNUAL REPORT. October 1919. 78 pp.
Number 3. Bamesberger, Velda C. STANDARD REQUIREMENTS FOR MEMORIZING LITERARY MATERIAL. 1920. 93 pp.

373. *(Continued)*

Number 4. Holley, Charles E. MENTAL TESTS FOR SCHOOL USE. 1920. 91 pp.

Number 5. Monroe, Walter S. REPORT OF DIVISION OF EDUCATIONAL TESTS FOR 1919–20. 1921. 64 pp.

Number 6. Monroe, Walter S. THE ILLINOIS EXAMINATION. (1921). 70 pp.

Number 7. Monroe, Walter S. TYPES OF LEARNING REQUIRED OF PUPILS IN THE SEVENTH AND EIGHTH GRADES AND IN THE HIGH SCHOOL. 1921. 16 pp.

Number 8. Monroe, Walter S. A CRITICAL STUDY OF CERTAIN SILENT READING TESTS. 1922. 52 pp.

Number 9. Monroe, Walter S. WRITTEN EXAMINATIONS AND THEIR IMPROVEMENT. 1922. 71 pp.

Number 10. Bureau of Educational Research. RELATION OF SIZE OF CLASS TO SCHOOL EFFICIENCY. 1922. 39 pp.

Number 11. Monroe, Walter S. RELATION OF SECTIONING A CLASS TO THE EFFECTIVENESS OF INSTRUCTION. 1922. 18 pp.

Number 12. Odell, Charles W. THE USE OF INTELLIGENCE TESTS AS A BASIS OF SCHOOL ORGANIZATION AND INSTRUCTION. 1922. 78 pp.

Number 13. Monroe, Walter S., and I. O. Foster. THE STATUS OF THE SOCIAL SCIENCES IN THE HIGH SCHOOLS OF THE NORTH CENTRAL ASSOCIATION. 1922. 38 pp.

Number 14. Monroe, Walter S., and Ralph E. Carter. THE USE OF DIFFERENT TYPES OF THOUGHT QUESTIONS IN SECONDARY SCHOOLS AND THEIR RELATIVE DIFFICULTY FOR STUDENTS. 1923. 26 pp.

Number 15. Monroe, Walter S. THE CONSTANT AND VARIABLE ERRORS OF EDUCATIONAL MEASUREMENTS. 1923. 30 pp.

Number 16. Odell, Charles W. AN ANNOTATED BIBLIOGRAPHY DEALING WITH THE CLASSIFICATION AND INSTRUCTION OF PUPILS TO PROVIDE FOR INDIVIDUAL DIFFERENCES. 1923. 50 pp.

Number 17. Monroe, Walter S., and Lloyd B. Souders. PRESENT STATUS OF WRITTEN EXAMINATIONS AND SUGGESTIONS FOR THEIR IMPROVEMENT. 1923. 77 pp.

Number 18. Streitz, Ruth. TEACHERS' DIFFICULTIES IN ARITHMETIC AND THEIR CORRECTIVES. 1924. 34 pp.

Number 19. Odell, Charles W. THE PROGRESS AND ELIMINATION OF SCHOOL CHILDREN IN ILLINOIS. 1924. 76 pp.

Number 20. Monroe, Walter S., and Dora Keen Mohlman. TRAINING IN THE TECHNIQUE OF STUDY. 1924. 66 pp.

Number 21. Monroe, Walter S. A SURVEY OF THE CITY SCHOOLS OF MARION, ILLINOIS. 1924. 60 pp.

Number 22. Odell, Charles W. CONSERVATION OF INTELLIGENCE IN ILLINOIS HIGH SCHOOLS. 1925. 55 pp.

Number 23. Streitz, Ruth. TEACHERS' DIFFICULTIES IN READING AND THEIR CORRECTIVES. 1925. 35 pp.

Number 24. Seybolt, Robert Francis. THE EVENING SCHOOL IN COLONIAL AMERICA. 1925. 68 pp.

Number 25. Monroe, Walter S., and Nell Bomar Johnston. REPORTING EDUCATIONAL RESEARCH. 1925. 63 pp.

Number 26. Brownell, William Arthur. A STUDY OF SUPERVISED STUDY. 1925. 48 pp.

Number 27. Glick, H. N. EFFECT OF PRACTICE ON INTELLIGENCE TESTS. 1925. 23 pp.

Number 28. Seybolt, Robert Francis. SOURCE STUDIES IN AMERICAN COLONIAL EDUCATION—THE PRIVATE SCHOOL. 1925. 109 pp.

Number 29. Odell, Charles W., assisted by John H. Blough. AN ANNOTATED BIBLIOGRAPHY DEALING WITH EXTRACURRICULAR ACTIVITIES IN ELEMENTARY AND HIGH SCHOOLS. 1926. 40 pp.

Number 30. Monroe, Walter S. THE DUTIES OF MEN ENGAGED AS PHYSICAL DIRECTORS OR ATHLETIC COACHES IN HIGH SCHOOLS. 1926. 22 pp.

Number 31. Monroe, Walter S., assisted by John A. Clark. THE TEACHER'S RESPONSIBILITY FOR DEVISING LEARNING EXERCISES IN ARITHMETIC. 1926. 92 pp.

Number 32. Odell, Charles W. THE INTERPRETATON OF THE PROBABLE ERROR AND THE COEFFICIENT OF CORRELATION. 1926. 49 pp.

Number 33. Monroe, Walter S., and M. E. Herriott. OBJECTIVES OF UNITED STATES HISTORY IN GRADES SEVEN AND EIGHT. 1926. 68 pp.

Number 34. Odell, Charles W. ARE COLLEGE STUDENTS A SELECT GROUP? 1927. 45 pp.

Number 35. Ojemann, R. H. THE CONSTANT AND VARIABLE OCCUPATIONS OF THE UNITED STATES IN 1920. 1927. 47 pp.

Number 36. Monroe, Walter S., and Ollie Asher. A BIBLIOGRAPHY OF BIBLIOGRAPHIES. 1927. 60 pp.

Number 37. Odell, Charles W. PREDICTING THE SCHOLASTIC SUCCESS OF COLLEGE FRESHMEN. 1927. 54 pp.

Number 38. Monroe, Walter S., and Max D. Engelhart. THE TECHNIQUES OF EDUCATIONAL RESEARCH. 1928. 84 pp.

Number 39. Monroe, Walter S., Darwin A. Hindman, and Roy S. Lundin. TWO ILLUSTRATIONS OF CURRICULUM CONSTRUCTION 1928. 53 pp.

Number 40. Odell, Charles W. A GLOSSARY OF THREE HUNDRED TERMS USED IN EDUCATIONAL MEASUREMENT AND RESEARCH. 1928. 68 pp.

Number 41. Monroe, Walter S., and M. E. Herriott. REORGANIZATION OF THE SECONDARY SCHOOL CURRICULUM: ITS MEANING AND TRENDS. 1928. 120 pp.

Number 42. Monroe, Walter S., Charles W. Odell, M. E. Herriott, Max D. Engelhart, and Mabel R. Hull. TEN YEARS OF EDUCATIONAL RESEARCH, 1918–1927. 1928. 367 pp.

Number 43. Odell, Charles W. A SELECTED ANNOTATED BIBLIOGRAPHY DEALING WITH EXAMINATIONS AND SCHOOL MARKS. 1929. 42 pp.

Number 44. Monroe, Walter S. HOW PUPILS SOLVE PROBLEMS IN ARITHMETIC. 1929. 31 pp.

Number 45. Odell, Charles W. A CRITICAL STUDY OF MEASURES OF ACHIEVEMENT RELATIVE TO CAPACITY. 1929. 58 pp.

Number 46. Odell, Charles W. THE USE OF SCALES FOR RATING PUPILS' ANSWERS TO THOUGHT QUESTIONS. 1929. 34 pp.

Number 47. Herriott, M. E. ATTITUDES AS FACTORS OF SCHOLASTIC SUCCESS. 1929. 72 pp.

Number 48. Monroe, Walter S., and Max D. Engelhart. EXPERIMENTAL RESEARCH IN EDUCATION. 1930. 105 pp.

Number 49. Odell, Charles W. SUMMER WORK IN PUBLIC SCHOOLS. 1930. 42 pp.

Number 50. Monroe, Walter S., Thomas T. Hamilton, Jr., and V. T. Smith. LOCATING EDUCATIONAL INFORMATION IN PUBLISHED SOURCES. 1930. 142 pp.

Number 51. Monroe, Walter S., and Max D. Engelhart. STIMULATING LEARNING ACTIVITY. 1930. 58 pp.

Number 52. Odell, Charles W. PREDICTING THE SCHOLASTIC SUCCESS OF COLLEGE STUDENTS. 1930. 43 pp.

Number 53. A PROJECT IN FOURTH-YEAR ENGLISH COMPOSITION. A DESCRIPTION OF THE UNIVERSITY HIGH SCHOOL. 1930. 36 pp.

Number 54. PROCEEDINGS OF THE ANNUAL CONFERENCE OF THE FACULTY OF THE COLLEGE OF EDUCATION, UNIVERSITY OF ILLINOIS, WITH THE SUPERINTENDENTS OF SCHOOLS OF ILLINOIS. URBANA, ILLINOIS, NOVEMBER 20, 1930. 1931. 36 pp.

Number 55. Gregg, Russell T., and Thomas T. Hamilton, Jr. ANNOTATED BIBLIOGRAPHY OF GRADUATE THESES IN EDUCATION AT THE UNIVERSITY OF ILLINOIS. 1931. 80 pp.

Number 56. Hendrix, S. Gertrude. TEACHING DEVICES ON THE HIGH-SCHOOL LEVEL. 1931. 42 pp.

Number 57. Clevenger, Arthur W., and Charles W. Odell. HIGH-SCHOOL LIBRARIES IN ILLINOIS. 1931. 41 pp.

Number 58. Monroe, Walter S., and Max D. Engelhart. A CRITICAL SUMMARY OF RESEARCH RELATING TO THE TEACHING OF ARITHMETIC. 1931. 115 pp.

Number 59. Odell, Charles W. PROVISIONS FOR MENTALLY ATYPICAL PUPIL. 1931. 73 pp.

Number 60. Astell, Louis A., and Charles W. Odell. HIGH SCHOOL SCIENCE CLUBS. 1932. 77 pp.

Number 61. Clement, John Addison, and Vivian Thomas Smith. PUBLIC JUNIOR COLLEGE LEGISLATION IN THE UNITED STATES. 1932. 61 pp.

Number 62. Mays, Arthur B. CONCEPT OF VOCATIONAL EDUCATION IN THE THINKING OF THE GENERAL EDUCATION, 1845–1945. 1946. 107 pp.

Number 63. Hamlin, Herbert M. USING ADVISORY COUNCILS IN AGRICULTURAL EDUCATION. 1947. 74 pp.

374. *Martin Mental Hygiene Publications.*

TITLE VARIATIONS: None.

DATES OF PUBLICATION: Number 1–[9], 1918–1930.

FREQUENCY: Irregular. *See* Contents *below.*

NUMBERING VARIATIONS: Numbering is sporadic and inconsistent. Number 6–9 typically unnumbered. Numbers assigned here follow chronological order of publication. Number 3 also as *California Society for Mental Hygiene. Publication. See* Contents *below.*

PUBLISHER: **Baltimore:** Warwick & York, Inc. Number 1, 1920. **San Francisco:** California Society for Mental Hygiene, Number 2–5, 1918–1921. **San Francisco:** Harr Wagner Publishing Co., Number 6–7, 1923–1927. **San Francisco:** J. W. Stacey, Inc., Number 8, 1927. **New York:** Macmillan Company, Number 9, 1930.

PRIMARY EDITOR: **Lillien J. Martin,** 1918–1930.

CONTENTS:

Number 1. Martin, Lillien J. MENTAL HYGIENE. TWO YEARS' EXPERIENCE AS A CLINICAL PSYCHOLOGIST. 1920. 89 pp.

Number 2. Krafft, E. A MENTAL HYGIENE CLINIC. 1918. 7 pp.

Number 3. Martin, Lillien J. THE TRAINING OF THE EMOTIONS. 1918. 7 pp. (Also as *California Society for Mental Hygiene. Publications*, Number 4.)

Number 4. Martin, Lillien J. THE WORK OF A MENTAL HYGIENE CLINIC FOR PRESCHOOL AGE CHILDREN. 1921.

Number 5. Martin, Lillien J. PEDAGOGICAL HINTS FROM THE RESULTS OF A SURVEY OF A SAN FRANCISCO PUBLIC SCHOOL FOR DELINQUENT BOYS. 1921. 18 pp.

[Number 6.] Martin. Lillien J., and Clare de Gruchy. MENTAL TRAINING FOR THE PRESCHOOL AGE CHILD. 1923. 108 pp.

[Number 7.] Martin, Lillien J., and Clare de Gruchy. GROUP TESTS MADE TO YIELD INDIVIDUAL DIAGNOSIS. 1927. 31 pp.

[Number 8.] Martin, Lillien J. ROUND THE WORLD WITH A PSYCHOLOGIST. 1927. 122 pp.

[Number 9.] Martin, Lillien J., and Clare de Gruchy. SALVAGING OLD AGE. 1930. 175 pp.

375. *Munich. Universität. Psychologisches Institut. Arbeiten. Ergänzungsband.*

TITLE VARIATIONS: None.

DATES OF PUBLICATION: Heft 1–9, 1918–1927; Reihe 2, Heft 1–4, 1930–1939.

FREQUENCY: Irregular. *See* Contents *below.*

NUMBERING VARIATIONS: Heft 8 also in Kafka, Gustav, ed. *Handbuch der vergleichenden Psychologie.* Some Hefte also numbered in *Wissenschaft und Bildung* and *Zeitschrift für ungewandte Psychologie und Charakterkunde. Beiheft. See* Contents *below.*

PUBLISHER: Various. *See* Contents *below.*

PRIMARY EDITORS: **Erich Becher,** 1918–1927; **Joseph Geyser,** 1918–1927. None listed, 1930–1939.

CONTENTS:

Heft 1. Bühler, Karl. DIE GEISTIGE ENTWICKLUNG DES KINDES. Jena: Gustav Fischer, 1918. 378 pp.

Heft 2. Pauli, W. E., and R. Pauli. PHYSIOLOGISCHE OPTIK, DARGESTELLT FÜR NATURWISSENSCHAFTLER. Jena: Gustav Fischer, 1919. 111 pp.

Heft 3. Ebbinghaus, Hermann. ABRISS DER PSYCHOLOGIE. (6. auflage, durchgesehen von Karl Bühler). Leipzig: Veit & Comp., 1919. 206 pp.

Heft 4. Ebbinghaus, Hermann. GRUNDZÜGE DER PSYCHOLOGIE. Band 1. (4th ed., revised by Karl Bühler.) Leipzig: J. A. Barth, 1919. 208 pp.

Heft 5. Lindworksy, Johannes. DER WILLE, SEINE ERSCHEINUNG UND SEINE BEHERRSCHUNG NACH DEN ERGEBNISSEN DER EXPERIMENTELLEN FORSCHUNG. Leipzig: J. A. Barth, 1919. 208 pp.

Heft 6. Pauli, R. PSYCHOLOGISCHES PRAKTIKUM. LEITFADEN FÜR EXPERIMENTELLPSYCHOLOGISCHE ÜBUNGEN. Jena: Gustav Fischer, 1919. 223 pp. (2nd ed., 1920. 236 pp.; 3rd ed., 1923. 247 pp.)

Heft 7. Külpe, Oswald. VORLESUNGEN ÜBER PSYCHOLOGIE. HERAUSGEGEBEN VON KARL BÜHLER. Leipzig: S. Hirzel, 1920. 304 pp.

Heft 8. Kafka, Gustav. TIERPSYCHOLOGIE. Munich: E. Reinhardt, 1922. 144 pp. (Also as Kafka, Gustav, ed. *Handbuch der vergleichenden Psychologie*, Band 1, Abteilung 1.)

Heft 9. Pauli, R. EINFÜHRUNG IN DIE EXPERIMENTELLE PSYCHOLOGIE. Leipzig: Verlag von Quelle & Meyer, 1927. 144 pp. (Also as *Wissenschaft und Bildung*, Heft 229.)

Reihe 2, Heft 1. Pauli, R. PSYCHOLOGISCHES PRAKTIKUM. LEITFADEN FÜR EXPERIMENTELL-PSYCHOLOGISCHE ÜBUNGEN. Jena: Verlag von Gustav Fischer, 1930 (4th ed.). 244 pp.

————, **Heft 2.** Pfänder, Alexander. DIE SEELE DES MENSCHEN. VERSUCH EINER VERSTEHENDEN PSYCHOLOGIE. Halle: Max Niemeyer, 1933. 416 pp.

————, **Heft 3.** Grassl, Erich. DIE WILLENSSCHWÄCHE. GLEICHZEITIG EIN BEITRAG ZUR THEORIE DES WILLENS DER WILLENSENTWICKLUNG UND WILLENSERZIEHUNG. Leipzig: Johann Ambrosius Barth, 1937. 254 pp. (Also as *Zeitschrift für angewandte Psychologie und Charakterkunde*. Beiheft 77.)

————, **Heft 4.** Greither, Aloys. SELBSTMORD UND ERZIEHUNG. EINE KULTURPHILOSOPHISCHE, PSYCHOLOGISCHE UND PÄDAGOGISCHE STUDIE. Leipzig: Felix Meiner Verlag, 1939. 212 pp.

376. *Psychologische Analysen hirnpathologischer Fälle.*

TITLE VARIATIONS: Some individual numbers bear the more complete title: *Psychologische Analysen hirnpathologischer Fälle auf Grund von Untersuchungen Hirnverletzer. (Abhandlung).*

DATES OF PUBLICATION: Heft 1–14, 1918–1932.

FREQUENCY: Irregular. *See* Contents *below.*

NUMBERING VARIATIONS: Heft 1–6 were also collected and numbered as Band 1. A second volume was apparently projected but did not appear. Heft 7–14 appeared in various journals under the general series title. Various issues also numbered as *Zeitschrift für die gesamte Neurologie und Psychiatrie;* as *Neurologisches Centralblatt;* as *Zeitschrift für Psychologie und Physiologie der Sinnesorgane. 1 Abteilung. Zeitschrift für Psychologie;* as *Graefes Archiv für Ophthalmologie;* or as *Psychologische Forschung. See* Contents *below.*

PUBLISHER: **Leipzig:** Johann Ambrosius Barth, 1920 (Band 1). Various, 1918–1932 (for individual Hefte). *See* Numbering Variations *above*.

PRIMARY EDITORS: **Adhemar Gelb,** 1918–1932; **Kurt Goldstein,** 1918–1932.

CONTENTS:

Band 1, Heft 1. Gelb, A., and K. Goldstein. Zur Psychologie des optischen Wahrnehmungs- und Erkennungsvorganges. 1920. Pp. 1–142. (Also in *Zeitschrift für die gesamte Neurologie und Psychiatrie,* Band 41, 1918, pp. 1–142.)

————, **Heft 2.** Gelb, A., and K. Goldstein. Das "röhrenförmige Gesichtsfeld" nebst einer Vorrichtung für perimetrische Gesichtsfelduntersuchungen in verschiedenen Entfernungen (vorläufige Mitteilung). 1920. Pp. 143–156. (Also as *Neurologisches Centralblatt,* Band 37, 1918, pp. 738–748.)

————, **Heft 3.** Gelb, A., and K. Goldstein. Über den Einfluss des vollständigen Verlustes des optischen Vorstellungsvermögens auf das taktile Erkennen. 1920. Pp. 157–250. (Also as *Zeitschrift für Psychologie und Physiologie der Sinnesorgane. 1. Abteilung. Zeitschrift für Psychologie,* Band 83, 1920, pp. 1–94.)

————, **Heft 4.** Fuchs, W. Untersuchungen über das Sehen der Hemianopiker und Hemiamblyopiker. I. Teil: Verlagerungserscheinungen. 1920. Pp. 251–353. (Also as *Zeitschrift für Psychologie und Physiologie der Sinnesorgane. 1. Abteilung. Zeitschrift für Psychologie.* Band 84, 1920, pp. 67–169.)

————, **Heft 5.** Gelb, A. Über den Wegfall der Wahrnehmung von "Oberflächenfarben." 1920. Pp. 354–418. (Also as *Zeitschrift für Psychologie und Physiologie der Sinnesorgane. 1. Abteilung. Zeitschrift für Psychologie.* Band 84, 1920, pp. 193–257.)

————, **Heft 6.** Fuchs, W. Untersuchungen über das Sehen der Hemianopiker und Hemiamblyopiker. II. Teil: Die totalisierende Gestaltauffasung. 1920. Pp. 419–561. (Also as *Zeitschrift für Psychologie und Physiologie der Sinnesorgane. 1. Abteilung. Zeitschrift für Psychologie,* Band 86, 1921, pp. 1–143.)

Heft 7. Gelb, A., and K. Goldstein. Über Gesichtsfeldbefunde bei abnormer "Ermüdbarkeit" des Auges (sogenannte "Ringskotome"). (Also as *Graefes Archiv für Ophthalmologie,* Band 109, 1922, pp. 387–403.)

Heft 8. Benary, W. Studien zur Untersuchung der Intelligenz bei einem Fall von Seelenblindheit. (Also as *Psychologische Forschung,* Band 2, 1922, pp. 209–297.)

Heft 9. Gelb, A. Über eine eigenartige Sehstörung ("Dysmorphopsie") infolge von Gesichtsfeldeinengung. Ein Beitrag zur Lehre von den Beziehungen zwischen "Gesichtsfeld" und "Sehen". (Also as *Psychologische Forschung,* Band 4, 1923, pp. 42–63).

Heft 10. Gelb, A., and K. Goldstein. Über Farbennamenamnesie, nebst Bemerkungen über das Wesen der amnestischen Aphasie überhaupt und die Beziehung zwischen Sprache und Verhalten zur Umwelt. (Also as *Psychologische Forschung,* Band 6, 1925, pp. 127–168).

Heft 11. Gelb, A., and K. Goldstein. ZUR FRAGE NACH DER GEGENSEITIGEN FUNKTIONELLEN BEZIEHUNG DER GESCHÄDIGTEN UND DER UNGESCHÄDIGTEN SEHSPHÄRE BEI HEMIANOPSIE. (MIKROPSIE INFOLGE DER VORHERRSCHAFT DER VORGÄNGE IN DER GESCHÄDIGTEN SEHSPHÄRE.) (Also as *Psychologische Forschung,* Band 6, 1925, pp. 187–189).

Heft 12. Mäki, N. NATÜRLICHE BEWEGUNGSTENDENZEN DER RECHTEN UND DER LINKEN HAND UND IHR EINFLUSS AUF DAS ZEICHNEN UND DEN ERKENNUNGSVORGANG. (Also as *Psychologische Forschung,* Band 10, 1928, pp. 1–19.)

Heft 13. Hochheimer, W. ANALYSE EINES "SEELENBLINDEN" VON DER SPRACHE AUS. EIN BEITRAG ZUR FRAGE NACH DER BEDEUTUNG DER SPRACHE FÜR DAS VERHALTEN ZUR UMWELT. (Also as *Psychologische Forschung,* Band 16, 1932, pp. 1–69).

Heft 14. Siekmann, W. PSYCHOLOGISCHE ANALYSE DES FALLES RAT . . . (EIN FALL VON SOGENANNTER MOTORISCHER APHASIE). (Also as *Psychologische Forschung,* Band 16, 1932, pp. 201–250).

377. *Schriften zur Psychologie der Berufseignung und des Wirtschaftslebens.*

TITLE VARIATIONS: Continued by Schriften zur Wirtschaftspsychologie und zur Arbeitswissenschaft with Heft 45, 1933.

DATES OF PUBLICATION: Heft 1–44, 1918–1932.

FREQUENCY: Irregular. *See* Contents *below.*

NUMBERING VARIATIONS: Various issues reprinted from the *Zeitschrift für angewandte Psychologie.*

PUBLISHER: **Leipzig:** Johann Ambrosius Barth, 1918–1932.

PRIMARY EDITORS: **Max Brahn,** 1918–1920; **Otto Lipmann,** 1918–1932; **William Stern,** 1918–1932.

CONTENTS:

Heft 1. Lipmann, Otto. WIRTSCHAFTSPSYCHOLOGIE UND PSYCHOLOGISCHE BERUFSBERATUNG. 1918. 26 pp. (2nd ed., 1921.)

Heft 2. Stern, William. ÜBER EINE PSYCHOLOGISCHE EIGNUNGSPRÜFUNG FUR STRASSENBAHNFAHRERINNEN. 1918. 16 pp.

Heft 3. Lipmann, Otto. DIE BERUFSEIGNUNG DER SCHRIFTSETZER; and Krais, Dora. EIGNUNGSPRÜFUNGEN BEI DER EINFÜHRUNG VON WEIBLICHEN ERSATZKRÄFTEN IN DEM STUTTGARTER BUCHDRUCKGEWERBE. 1918. 37 pp.

Heft 4. Heinitz, Wilhelm. VORSTUDIEN ÜBER DIE PSYCHOLOGISCHEN ARBEITSBEDINGUNGEN DES MASCHINENSCHREIBENS. 1918. 56 pp.

Heft 5. Ulrich, Martha. DIE PSYCHOLOGISCHE ANALYSE DER HÖHEREN BERUFE ALS GRUNDLAGE EINER KÜNFTIGEN BERUFSBERATUNG. 1918. 38 pp.

Heft 6. Dück, Johs. DIE BERUFSEIGNUNG DER KANZLEIANGESTELLTEN. 1919. 24 pp.

Heft 7. Braunshausen, N. PSYCHOLOGISCHE PERSONALBOGEN ALS HILFSMITTEL FÜR PÄDAGOGIK UND BERUFSBERATUNG. 1919. 34 pp.

Heft 8. Benary, W., A. Kronfeld, E. Stern, and O. Selz. UNTERSUCHUNGEN ÜBER DIE PSYCHISCHE EIGNUNG ZUM FLUGDIENST. 1919. 142 pp.

Heft 9. Lipmann, Otto Die psychische Eignung der Funkentele-graphisten. 1919. 40 pp.

Heft 10. Martens, Hans A. Psychologie und Verkehrswesen. 1919. 14 pp.

Heft 11. Lipmann, Otto, and Otto Stolzenberg. Methoden zur Auslese hochwertiger Facharbeiter der Metallindustrie. 1920. 79 pp.

Heft 12. Benary, Wilhelm. Kurzer Bericht über Arbeiten zu Eignungsprüfungen für Flieger-Beobachter. 1920. 61 pp.

Heft 13. Wirtschaftsleben und Berufseignung in Überseeländern. Steinmetz, S. Rudolf. Fragen zur Erforschung des Wirtschaftslebens der Naturvölker; and Henning, Hans. Die Wirtschaftspsychologie und Berufseignung in Überseeländern. 1920. 52 pp.

Heft 14. Sachs, Hildegard. Zur Organisation der Eignungspsycholo-gie. 1920. 16 pp.

Heft 15. Sachs, Hildegard. Methode zur Prüfung der Aufmerk-samkeit und Reaktionsweise. 1920. 27 pp.

Heft 16. Heinitz, Wilhelm. Untersuchungen über die Fehlleistun-gen beim Maschinenschreiben. 1921. 17 pp.

Heft 17. Schulte, Robert Werner. Die Berufseignung des Damenfri-seurs. 1921. 77 pp.

Heft 18. Streller, Justus. Die Berufseignung des mittleren kauf-männischen Bureaubeamten im Buchhandel. 1921. 61 pp.

Heft 19. Winkler, Herbert. Die Monotonie der Arbeit. 1922. 45 pp.

Heft 20. Baumgarten, Franziska, and Otto Lipmann. Bibliographie zur psychologischen Berufsberatung, Berufseignungsforschung und Be-rufskunde. 1922. 60 pp.

Heft 21. Huth, Albert. Die Münchner Eignungsprüfung für Buch-drucker und Schriftsetzer. 1922. 28 pp.

Heft 22. Wisse, Annie. Die Fakultätsdifferenzen als psycholo-gische Gruppenunterschiede bei den Universitätsstudenten. 1922. 83 pp.

Heft 23. Doevenspeck, Heinrich. Taylorsystem und schwere Muskel-arbeit. 1923. 38 pp.

Heft 24. Giese, Fritz. Berufspsychologische Beobachtungen im Reichstelegraphendienst. 1923. 74 pp.

Heft 25. Sachs, Hildegard. Die Träger der exerimentellen Eignungs-psychologie. 1923. 34 pp.

Heft 26. Klemm, Otto, and Friedrich Sander. Arbeitspsychologische Untersuchungen an der Häckselmaschine. 1924. 20 pp.

Heft 27. Baumgarten, Franziska. Zur Psychologie und Psychotechnik des Versicherungsagenten. (Beiträge zur Berufskunde des Versiche-rungswesens. I.) 1925. 62 pp.

Heft 28. Eliasberg, Wladimir. Grundriss einer allgemeinen Arbeits-pathologie. 1924. 41 pp.

Heft 29. Baumgarten, Franziska. Zur Psychotechnik und Charakter-ologie des Regulierungsbeamten. (Beiträge zur Berufskunde des Ver-sicherungswesens. II.) 1925. 64 pp.

Heft 30. Arnold, Richard, BEITRÄGE ZUR EIGNUNGSPRÜFUNG FÜR DAS TISCHLERGEWERBE. 1925. 31 pp.

Heft 31. Wunderlich, Herbert. DIE EINWIRKUNG EINFÖRMIGER, ZWANG-LÄUFIGER ARBEIT AUF DIE PERSÖNLICHKEITSSTRUKTUR. 1925. 53 pp.

Heft 32. Bramesfeld, Erwin. DER INGENIEURBERUF. 1925. 94 pp.

Heft 33. Grünbaum-Sachs, Hildegard. TIEFENPSYCHOLOGIE UND BERUFS-BERATUNG. 1926. 49 pp.

Heft 34. Roloff, Hans Paul. EXPERIMENTELLE UNTERSUCHUNG DER WER-BEWIRKUNG VON PLAKATENTWÜRFEN. 1927. 44 pp.

Heft 35. Joseph-Lussheimer, Emmy. ZUR THEORIE DER BERUFSWAHL UN-TER BENUTZUNG DER BERUFSWAHLTATSACHEN DER ABITURIENTEN EINER GROSSSTADT. 1928. 80 pp.

Heft 36. Stäbler, Ferdinand. BEGABTENFÖRDERUNG UND BERUFSSCHICK-SAL. 1930. 74 pp.

Heft 37. Feick, Paul. ZUR ANALYSE DES BANKBERUFS. 1930. 48 pp.

Heft 38. Knoblauch, Elisabeth. ZUR PSYCHOLOGIE DER STUDIERENDEN FRAU. 1930. 88 pp.

Heft 39. Bruker, Emil. PSYCHOTECHNISCHE UNTERSUCHUNGEN ZUR BANDARBEIT. 1931. 50 pp.

Heft 40. Dieck, Herman. ZUR EIGNUNGSPRÜFUNG FÜR DEN VER-MESSUNGSTECHNIKERBERUF. 1931. 81 pp.

Heft 41. Rüssel, Arnulf. BERUFSPSYCHOLOGISCHE STUDIEN IN DER EDEL-METALL-INDUSTRIE. 1932. 68 pp.

Heft 42. Eliasberg, Wladimir. VON DER VERNUNFT BIS ZUR RATIONALISIE-RUNG. 1932. 96 pp.

Heft 43. Katzenstein, Betti, DIE EIGNUNGSPSYCHOLOGISCHE ERFASSUNG DES ARBEITSCHARAKTERS. 1932. 71 pp.

Heft 44. Jaensch, Erich, and Edm. Schneider. DER BERUFSTYPUS DES SCHAUSPIELERS IM ZUSAMMENHANG MIT DEN ALLGEMEINEN KUNST- UND KUL-TURFRAGEN DER GEGENWART. 1932. 132 pp.

378. *Waverly Researches in the Pathology of the Feeble-minded. Research Series.*

TITLE VARIATIONS: None.

DATES OF PUBLICATION: Series 1–5, 1918–1940.

FREQUENCY: Irregular. *See* Contents *below.*

NUMBERING VARIATIONS: Pagination is continuous. Contents of Series 1–5 also numbered as Cases 1–50. Some Series also numbered as *American Academy of Arts and Sciences. Memoirs. See* Contents *below.*

PUBLISHER: **Waverly, Massachusetts:** Massachusetts School for the Feeble-minded, 1918–1921. **Boston, Massachusetts:** Massachusetts Department of Mental Health, 1938–1940.

PRIMARY EDITORS: **W. E. Fernald,** 1918–1921; **E. E. Southard,** 1918–1921; **Annie E. Taft,** 1918–1939; **Myrtle M. Canavan,** 1921–1940; **O. J. Raeder,** 1921; **Louise Eisenhardt,** 1940.

CONTENTS:
> **Series 1.** Cases 1–10, 1918 (Also as *American Academy of Arts and Sciences. Memoirs*, Volume 14, Number 2, May 1918.)
> **Series 2.** Cases 11–20, 1921. (Also as *American Academy of Arts and Sciences. Memoirs*, Volume 14, Number 3, December 1921.)
> **Series 3.** Cases 21–30, 1938.
> **Series 4.** Cases 31–40, 1939.
> **Series 5.** Cases 41–50, 1940.

379. *Zeitschrift für Seelenleben, neuere Psychologie und verwandte Gebiete.*

TITLE VARIATIONS: Continues *Zeitschrift für Spiritismus, Somnambulismus, Magnetismus, Spiritualismus und verwandte Gebiete.* Continued by *Zeitschrift für Seelenleben* with Jahrgang 27, 1923.

DATES OF PUBLICATION: Jahrgang 21–26, 1918–1922.

FREQUENCY: Weekly.

NUMBERING VARIATIONS: None.

PUBLISHER: **Leipzig:** D. Mutze, 1918–1922.

PRIMARY EDITORS: **Rud. Feilgenhauer**, 1918–1922; **Fritz Feilgenhauer**, 1918–1922.

1919

380. *Archivos de neurobiología, psicología, fisiología, histología, neurología y psiquiatría.*

TITLE VARIATIONS: Title varies slightly.

DATES OF PUBLICATION: Tomo 1–15, Número 4, 1919–1935. Suspended publication 1925 and 1930.

FREQUENCY: **Quarterly,** Tomo 1–9, Número 4, 1919–October/December 1929. **Bimonthly,** Tomo 10–15, Número 4, January/February 1930–July/August 1935.

NUMBERING VARIATIONS: Multinumber issues present.

PUBLISHER: **Madrid:** Ruiz Hermanos, Editores, 1919–1924. **Madrid:** Editorial Paracelso, 1926–1928. **Madrid:** Redactor Jefe: J. Germain, 1929. **Madrid:** Ruiz Hermanos, Editores, 1931–1935.

PRIMARY EDITORS: **J. Ortega Gasset,** 1919–1927; **G. R. Lafora,** 1919–1927; **J. M. Sacristan,** 1919–1927; **J. Sanchiz Banus,** 1926; **M. Prados,** 1926; **E. Mira,** 1926; **W. Lopez Albo,** 1926; **J. Germain,** 1927–1935.

EDITORIAL BOARD: None listed, 1919–1926; D. Santiago Ramon y Cajal, 1927–1935; J. Germain, 1927–1935; G. R. Lafora, 1927–1935; W. Lopez Albo, 1927–1935; E. Mira Lopez, 1927–1935; M. Prados Such, 1927–1935; B. Rodriguez Arias, 1927–1935; J. M. Sacristan, 1927–1935; J. Sanchiz Banus, 1927–1932.

381. *Canadian Journal of Mental Hygiene.*

TITLE VARIATIONS: None.

DATES OF PUBLICATION: Volume 1–3, April 1919–January 1922.

FREQUENCY: Quarterly.

NUMBERING VARIATIONS: None.

PUBLISHER: **Toronto:** Published by the Canadian National Committee for Mental Hygiene, 1919. **Montreal:** Published by the Canadian National Committee for Mental Hygiene, 1920–1922.

PRIMARY EDITORS: None listed.

382. *Colorado College. Publications. Education and Psychology Series.*

TITLE VARIATIONS: None.

DATES OF PUBLICATION: Volume 1, Number 1, September 1919.

FREQUENCY: Was to have been published at 6 week intervals during the academic year.

NUMBERING VARIATIONS: Issue listed below also numbered as *Colorado College. General Series*, Number 103.

PUBLISHER: **Colorado Springs, Colorado:** Published by Authority of the Board of Trustees of Colorado College, 1919.

PRIMARY EDITOR: **J. V. Breitwieser**, 1919.

CONTENTS:

Volume 1, Number 1. McGeoch, John A. THE PRESENT STATUS OF PSYCHOLOGY. 1919. 100 pp.

383. *Great Britain. Industrial Health Research Board. Reports.*

TITLE VARIATIONS: Number 1–4 subheaded *Medical Research Committee and Department of Scientific and Industrial Research;* Number 5–11 subheaded *Medical Research Council and Department of Scientific and Industrial Research;* Number 12+ subheaded *Medical Research Council.* Industrial Health Research Board initially called Industrial Fatigue Research Board.

DATES OF PUBLICATION: Number 1–90, 1919–1947.

FREQUENCY: Irregular. *See* Contents *below.*

NUMBERING VARIATIONS: Number 1–23 also numbered in the following subseries: *General Series; Metal Trades Series; Textile Series; Boot and Shoe Series; Potteries Series;* and *Laundry Series.* Number 1–2 of *General Series* and Number 1–3 of the *Metal Trades Series* were issued without subseries note. Number

3 of the *General Series* incorrectly numbered 4. Number 5 of the *Metal Trades Series* simply listed as *Metal Series* Number 5. *See* Contents *below.*

PUBLISHER: **London:** H. M. Stationary Office, 1919–1947.

PRIMARY EDITORS: None listed.

CONTENTS:

Number 1. Vernon, H. M. THE INFLUENCE OF HOURS OF WORK AND OF VENTILATION ON OUTPUT IN TINPLATE MANUFACTURE. 1919. 29 pp. (Also as *Metal Trade Series,* Number 1.)

Number 2. Osborne, Ethel E. THE OUTPUT OF WOMEN WORKERS IN RELATION TO HOURS OF WORK IN SHELL-MAKING. 1919. 23 pp. (Also as *Metal Trades Series,* Number 2.)

Number 3. Myers, C. S. A STUDY OF IMPROVED METHODS IN AN IRON FOUNDRY. 1919. 8 pp. (Also as *Metal Trades Series,* Number 3.)

Number 4. Greenwood, Major, and Hilda M. Woods. THE INCIDENCE OF INDUSTRIAL ACCIDENTS UPON INDIVIDUALS, WITH SPECIAL REFERENCE TO MULTIPLE ACCIDENTS. 1919. 28 pp. (Also as *General Series,* Number 1.)

Number 5. Vernon, H. M. FATIGUE AND EFFICIENCY IN THE IRON AND STEEL INDUSTRY. 1920. 99 pp. (Also as *Metal Trades Series,* Number 4.)

Number 6. Vernon, H. M. THE SPEED OF ADAPTATION OF OUTPUT TO ALTERED HOURS OF WORK. 1920. 33 pp. (Also as *General Series,* Number 2.)

Number 7. Wyatt, S. INDIVIDUAL DIFFERENCES IN OUTPUT IN THE COTTON INDUSTRY. 1920. 13 pp. (Also as *Textile Series,* Number 1.)

Number 8. Wyatt, S., and H. C. Weston. SOME OBSERVATIONS ON BOBBIN-WINDING. 1920. 40 pp. (Also as *Textile Series,* Number 2.)

Number 9. Elton, P. M. A STUDY OF OUTPUT IN SILK WEAVING DURING THE WINTER MONTHS. 1920. 69 pp. (Also as *Textile Series,* Number 3.)

Number 10. PRELIMINARY NOTES ON THE BOOT AND SHOE INDUSTRY: Loveday, J. HISTORICAL SKETCH; Loveday, J., and S. H. Munro. DESCRIPTION OF PROCESSES; Loveday, J., and S. H. Munro. DAILY RECORDS OF OUTPUT; and Loveday, J. AN EXPERIMENT WITH REST PAUSES. 1920. 32 pp. (Also as *Boot and Shoe Series,* Number 1.)

Number 11. Hambly, W. D., and T. Bedford. PRELIMINARY NOTES ON ATMOSPHERIC CONDITIONS IN BOOT AND SHOE FACTORIES. 1921. 69 pp. (Also as *Boot and Shoe Series,* Number 2.)

Number 12. Muscio, B. VOCATIONAL GUIDANCE. (A Review of the Literature). 1921. 57 pp. (Also as *General Series,* Number 3.)

Number 13. Broughton, Gladys M., Ethel M. Newbold, and Edith C. Allen. A STATISTICAL STUDY OF LABOUR TURNOVER IN MUNITION AND OTHER FACTORIES. 1921. 92 pp. (Also as *General Series,* Number 4.)

Number 14. Farmer, E. TIME AND MOTION STUDY. 1921. 63 pp. (Also as *General Series,* Number 5.)

Number 15. Farmer, E., assisted by R. S. Brooke. MOTION STUDY IN METAL POLISHING. 1921. 65 pp. (Also as *Metal Trades Series,* Number 5.)

Number 16. THREE STUDIES IN VOCATIONAL SELECTION: Muscio, B. THE PSYCHO-PHYSIOLOGICAL CAPACITIES REQUIRED BY THE HAND COMPOSITOR; Muscio, B., assisted by A.B.B. Eyre. THE MEASUREMENT OF PHYSICAL

383. *(Continued)*

STRENGTH WITH REFERENCE TO VOCATIONAL GUIDANCE; and, Farmer, Eric. PHYSICAL MEASUREMENTS IN A SWEET FACTORY. 1922. 86 pp. (Also as *General Series*, Number 6.)

Number 17. Elton, P. M. AN ANALYSIS OF THE INDIVIDUAL DIFFERENCES IN THE OUTPUT OF SILK-WEAVERS. 1922. 38 pp. (Also as *Textile Series*, Number 4.)

Number 18. Vernon, H. M., assisted by T. Bedford. TWO INVESTIGATIONS IN POTTERS' SHOPS. 1922. 74 pp. (Also as *Potteries Series*, Number 1.)

Number 19. TWO CONTRIBUTIONS TO THE STUDY OF ACCIDENT CAUSATION: Osborne, Ethel E., and H. M. Vernon. THE INFLUENCE OF TEMPERATURE AND OTHER CONDITIONS ON THE FREQUENCY OF INDUSTRIAL ACCIDENTS; and Muscio, B. ON THE RELATION OF FATIGUE AND ACCURACY TO SPEED AND DURATION OF WORK. 1922. 36 pp. (Also as *General Series*, Number 7.)

Number 20. Weston, H. C. A STUDY OF EFFICIENCY IN FINE LINEN WEAVING. 1922. 28 pp. (Also as *Textile Series*, Number 5.)

Number 21. Wyatt, S. ATMOSPHERIC CONDITIONS IN COTTEN WEAVING. 1923. 36 pp. (Also as *Textile Series*, Number 6.)

Number 22. Smith, May. SOME STUDIES IN THE LAUNDRY TRADE. 1922. 57 pp. (Also as *Laundry Series*, Number 1.)

Number 23. Wyatt, S. VARIATIONS IN EFFICIENCY IN COTTON WEAVING. 1923 60 pp. (Also as *Textile Series*, Number 7.)

Number 24. Farmer, E., assisted by R. S. Brooke and E. G. Chambers. A COMPARISON OF DIFFERENT SHIFT SYSTEMS IN THE GLASS TRADE. 1923. 24 pp.

Number 25. TWO STUDIES ON REST PAUSES IN INDUSTRY: Vernon, H. M., and T. Bedford, assisted by C. G. Warner. THE INFLUENCE OF REST PAUSES ON LIGHT INDUSTRIAL WORK; and Wyatt, S., assisted by A. D. Ogden. NOTES ON AN EXPERIMENT ON REST PAUSES. 1924. 34 pp.

Number 26. ON THE EXTENT AND EFFECTS OF VARIETY IN REPETITIVE WORK: Vernon, H. M. THE DEGREE OF VARIETY IN REPETITIVE INDUSTRIAL WORK; and Wyatt, S., assisted by A. D. Ogden. THE EFFECT OF CHANGES IN ACTIVITY. 1924. 38 pp.

Number 27. RESULTS OF INVESTIGATION IN CERTAIN INDUSTRIES. 1924. 17 pp.

Number 28. Yule, G. Udny. THE FUNCTION OF STATISTICAL METHOD IN SCIENTIFIC INVESTIGATION. 1924. 14 pp.

Number 29. THE EFFECTS OF POSTURE AND REST IN MUSCULAR WORK: Bedale, E. M. A COMPARISON OF THE ENERGY EXPENDITURE OF A WOMAN CARRYING LOADS IN EIGHT DIFFERENT POSITIONS; and Vernon, H. M. THE INFLUENCE OF REST-PAUSES AND CHANGES OF POSTURE ON THE CAPACITY FOR MUSCULAR WORK. 1924. 55 pp.

Number 30. Burnett, Isabel. AN EXPERIMENTAL INVESTIGATION INTO REPETITIVE WORK. 1925. 26 pp.

Number 31. Gaw, Frances. PERFORMANCE TESTS OF INTELLIGENCE. 1925. 45 pp.

Number 32. Wyatt, S., assisted by J. A. Fraser. STUDIES IN REPETITIVE WORK WITH SPECIAL REFERENCE TO REST PAUSES. 1925. 43 pp.

Number 33. Gaw, Frances, Lettice Ramsey, May Smith, and Winifred Spielman, under the general direction of Cyril Burt. A STUDY OF VOCATIONAL GUIDANCE CARRIED OUT BY THE INDUSTRIAL FATIGUE RESEARCH BOARD AND THE NATIONAL INSTITUTE OF INDUSTRIAL PSYCHOLOGY. 1926. 106 pp.

Number 34. Newbold, E. M. A CONTRIBUTION TO THE STUDY OF THE HUMAN FACTOR IN THE CAUSATION OF ACCIDENTS. 1926. 74 pp.

Number 35. Vernon, H. M., and T. Bedford, assisted by C. G. Warner. A PHYSIOLOGICAL STUDY OF THE VENTILATION AND HEATING IN CERTAIN FACTORIES. 1926. 84 pp.

Number 36. Legros, L. A., and H. C. Weston. ON THE DESIGN OF MACHINERY IN RELATION TO THE OPERATOR. 1926. 34 pp.

Number 37. Wyatt, S., assisted by J. A. Fraser and F.G.L. Stock. FAN VENTILATION IN A HUMID WEAVING SHED. AN EXPERIMENT MADE FOR THE DEPARTMENTAL COMMITTEE ON HUMIDITY IN COTTON WEAVING. 1926. 33 pp.

Number 38. Farmer, E., and E. G. Chambers. A PSYCHOLOGICAL STUDY OF INDIVIDUAL DIFFERENCES IN ACCIDENT RATES. 1926. 46 pp.

Number 39. Vernon, H. M., and T. Bedford, assisted by C. G. Warner. THE RELATION OF ATMOSPHERIC CONDITIONS TO THE WORKING CAPACITY AND THE ACCIDENT RATE OF COAL MINERS. 1927. 34 pp.

Number 40. Weston, H. C., and S. Adams. THE EFFECT OF EYESTRAIN ON THE OUTPUT OF LINKERS IN THE HOSIERY INDUSTRY. 1927. 20 pp.

Number 41. Vernon, H. M., and T. Bedford, assisted by C. G. Warner. REST PAUSES IN HEAVY AND MODERATELY HEAVY INDUSTRIAL WORK. 1927. 24 pp.

Number 42. Wyatt, S. REST PAUSES IN INDUSTRY (A REVIEW OF THE RESULTS OBTAINED). 1927. 24 pp.

Number 43. Smith, May, Millais Culpin, and Eric Farmer. A STUDY OF TELEGRAPHISTS' CRAMP. 1927. 46 pp.

Number 44. Cathcart, E. P., E. M. Bedale, C. Blair, K. Macleod, and E. Weatherhead, with a special section by Sybil G. Overton. THE PHYSIQUE OF WOMEN IN INDUSTRY. A CONTRIBUTION TOWARDS THE DETERMINATION OF THE OPTIMUM LOAD. 1927. 142 pp.

Number 45. TWO CONTRIBUTIONS TO THE EXPERIMENTAL STUDY OF THE MENSTRUAL CYCLE: Sowton, S.C.M., and C. S. Myers. ITS INFLUENCE ON MENTAL AND MUSCULAR EFFICIENCY; and Bedale, E. M. ITS RELATION TO GENERAL FUNCTIONAL ACTIVITY. 1928. 72 pp.

Number 46. Vernon, H. M., and M. D. Vernon, assisted by Isabel Lorrain-Smith. A PHYSIOLOGICAL INVESTIGATION OF THE RADIANT HEATING IN VARIOUS BUILDINGS. 1928. 61 pp.

Number 47. TWO STUDIES ON HOURS OF WORK: Vernon, H. M., and M. D. Vernon, assisted by I. Lorrain-Smith FIVE-HOUR SPELLS FOR WOMEN, WITH REFERENCE TO REST PAUSES; and Smith, May, and M. D. Vernon. THE TWO-SHIFT SYSTEM IN CERTAIN FACTORIES. 1928. 35 pp.

Number 48. Hill, A. Bradford. ARTIFICIAL HUMIDIFICATION IN THE COTTON WEAVING INDUSTRY: ITS EFFECT UPON THE SICKNESS RATES OF WEAVING OPERATIVES. 1927. 78 pp.

Number 49. Weston, H. C., and S. Adams. ON THE RELIEF OF EYESTRAIN AMONG PERSONS PERFORMING VERY FINE WORK. 1928. 30 pp.

383. *(Continued)*

Number 50. Crowden, G. P. THE PHYSIOLOGICAL COST OF THE MUSCULAR MOVEMENTS INVOLVED IN BARROW WORK. 1928. 22 pp.

Number 51. Vernon, H. M., and T. Bedford, assisted by C. G. Warner. A STUDY OF ABSENTEEISM IN A GROUP OF TEN COLLIERIES. 1928. 68 pp.

Number 52. Wyatt, S., and J. A. Fraser, assisted by F.G.L. Stock. THE COMPARATIVE EFFECTS OF VARIETY AND UNIFORMITY IN WORK. 1928. 36 pp.

Number 53. Earle, F. M., M. Milner et al. THE USE OF PERFORMANCE TESTS OF INTELLIGENCE IN VOCATIONAL GUIDANCE. AN INVESTIGATION CONDUCTED FOR THE NATIONAL INSTITUTE OF INDUSTRIAL PSYCHOLOGY. 1929. 76 pp.

Number 54. Hill, A. Bradford. AN INVESTIGATION INTO THE SICKNESS EXPERIENCE OF PRINTERS (WITH SPECIAL REFERENCE TO THE INCIDENCE OF TUBERCULOSIS). 1929. 114 pp.

Number 55. Farmer, Eric, and E. G. Chambers. A STUDY OF PERSONAL QUALITIES IN ACCIDENT PRONENESS AND PROFICIENCY. 1929. 84 pp.

Number 56. Wyatt, S., and J. A. Fraser, assisted by F.G.L. Stock. THE EFFECTS OF MONOTONY IN WORK: A PRELIMINARY INQUIRY. 1929. 53 pp.

Number 57. Weston, H. C., and S. Adams. FURTHER EXPERIMENTS ON THE USE OF SPECIAL SPECTACLES IN VERY FINE PROCESSES. 1929. 34 pp.

Number 58. Vernon, H. M., and T. Bedford, assisted by C. G. Warner. A STUDY OF HEATING AND VENTILATION IN SCHOOLS. 1930. 72 pp.

Number 59. Hill, A. Bradford. SICKNESS AMONGST OPERATIVES IN LANCASHIRE COTTON SPINNING MILLS (WITH SPECIAL REFERENCE TO THE CARDROOM). 1930. 91 pp.

Number 60. Vernon H. M., and T. Bedford, assisted by C. G. Warner. THE ATMOSPHERIC CONDITIONS IN PITHEAD BATHS. 1930. 39 pp.

Number 61. Culpin, Millais, and May Smith. THE NERVOUS TEMPERAMENT. 1930. 52 pp.

Number 62. TWO STUDIES OF ABSENTEEISM IN COAL MINES: Vernon, H. M., and T. Bedford, assisted by C. G. Warner. THE ABSENTEEISM OF MINERS IN RELATION TO SHORT TIME AND OTHER CONDITIONS; and Bedford, T., and C. G. Warner. A STUDY OF ABSENTEEISM AT CERTAIN SCOTTISH COLLIERIES. With Appendix by E. P. Cathcart and James Taylor. 1931. 59 pp.

Number 63. Wyatt, S., and J. N. Langdon. INSPECTION PROCESSES IN INDUSTRY. (A PRELIMINARY REPORT). 1932. 60 pp.

Number 64. Long, Amalie E. Weiss, and T. H. Pear. A CLASSIFICATION OF VOCATIONAL TESTS OF DEXTERITY. 1932. 71 pp.

Number 65. TWO STUDIES IN THE PSYCHOLOGICAL EFFECTS OF NOISE: Pollock, K. G., and F. C. Bartlett. PSYCHOLOGICAL EXPERIMENTS ON THE EFFECTS OF NOISE; and Weston, H. C., and S. Adams. THE EFFECTS OF NOISE ON THE PERFORMANCE OF WEAVERS. 1932. 70 pp.

Number 66. Langdon, J. N. AN EXPERIMENTAL STUDY OF CERTAIN FORMS OF MANUAL DEXTERITY. 1932. 64 pp.

Number 67. MANUAL DEXTERITY; EFFECTS OF TRAINING: Henshaw, E. M., P. Holman, and J. N. Langdon. TRANSFER OF TRAINING IN MANUAL DEX-

TERITY AND VISUAL DISCRIMINATION; and Henshaw, E. M., and P. Holman. DISTRIBUTION OF PRACTICE IN MANUAL DEXTERITY. 1933. 45 pp.

Number 68. Farmer, E., E. G. Chambers, and F. J. Kirk. TESTS FOR ACCIDENT PRONENESS. 1933. 44 pp.

Number 69. Wyatt, S., assisted by L. Frost and F.G.L. Stock. INCENTIVES IN REPETITIVE WORK; A PRACTICAL EXPERIMENT IN A FACTORY. 1934. 67 pp.

Number 70. Weston, H. C., and S. Adams. THE PERFORMANCE OF WEAVERS UNDER VARYING CONDITIONS OF NOISE. 1935. 24 pp.

Number 71. Cathcart, E. P., D.E.R. Hughes, and J. G. Chalmers. THE PHYSIQUE OF MAN IN INDUSTRY. 1935. 52 pp.

Number 72. Mace, C. A. INCENTIVES; SOME EXPERIMENTAL STUDIES. 1935. 69 pp.

Number 73. Blackburn, J. M. THE ACQUISITION OF SKILL: AN ANALYSIS OF LEARNING CURVES. 1936. 92 pp.

Number 74. Farmer, E., and E. G. Chambers. THE PROGNOSTIC VALUE OF SOME PSYCHOLOGICAL TESTS. 1936. 50 pp.

Number 75. SICKNESS ABSENCE AND LABOUR WASTAGE: Smith, May, and Margaret A. Leiper, with the cooperation of Millais Culpin. SICKNESS ABSENCE: ITS MEASUREMENT AND INCIDENCE IN CLERICAL WORK AND LIGHT OCCUPATIONS; and Greenwood, Major, and May Smith. LABOUR WASTAGE. 1936. 70 pp.

Number 76. Bedford, T. THE WARMTH FACTOR IN COMFORT AT WORK; A PHYSIOLOGICAL STUDY OF HEATING AND VENTILATION. 1936. 110 pp.

Number 77. Wyatt, S., and J. N. Langdon, assisted by F.G.L. Stock. FATIGUE AND BOREDOM IN REPETITIVE WORK. 1937. 86 pp.

Number 78. Rodger, Alec. A BORSTAL EXPERIMENT IN VOCATIONAL GUIDANCE. 1937. 50 pp.

Number 79. Hill, A. Bradford. AN INVESTIGATION INTO THE SICKNESS EXPERIENCE OF LONDON TRANSPORT WORKERS, WITH SPECIAL REFERENCE TO DIGESTIVE DISTURBANCES. 1937. 33 pp.

Number 80. Browning, Ethel, under the direction of the Committee on the Toxicity of Industrial Solvents. TOXICITY OF INDUSTRIAL ORGANIC SOLVENTS: SUMMARIES OF PUBLISHED WORK. 1937. 396 pp.

Number 81. Weston, H. C. THE EFFECTS OF CONDITIONS OF ARTIFICAL LIGHTING ON THE PERFORMANCE OF WORSTED WEAVERS. 1938. 38 pp.

Number 82. Wyatt, S., and J. N. Langdon, assisted by F.G.L. Stock. THE MACHINE AND THE WORKER: A STUDY OF MACHINE-FEEDING PROCESSES. 1938. 54 pp.

Number 83. Vernon, P. E. THE ASSESSMENT OF PSYCHOLOGICAL QUALITIES BY VERBAL METHODS; A SURVEY OF ATTITUDE TESTS, RATING SCALES AND PERSONALITY QUESTIONNAIRES. 1938. 132 pp.

Number 84. Farmer, E. and E. G. Chambers. A STUDY OF ACCIDENT PRONENESS AMONG MOTOR DRIVERS. 1939. 56 pp.

Number 85. THE RECORDING OF SICKNESS ABSENCE IN INDUSTRY. (A PRELIMINARY REPORT). By a Sub-Committee of the Industrial Health Research Board. 1944. 17 pp.

Number 86. Wyatt, S., assisted by R. Marriott, W. M. Dawson, Norah

M. Davis, D.E.R. Hughes, and F.G.L. Stock. A STUDY OF CERTIFIED SICKNESS ABSENCE AMONG WOMEN IN INDUSTRY. 1945. 34 pp.

Number 87. Weston, H. C. THE RELATION BETWEEN ILLUMINATION AND VISUAL EFFICIENCY, THE EFFECT OF BRIGHTNESS CONTRAST. 1945. 35 pp.

Number 88. Wyatt, S., assisted by R. Marriott, W. M. Dawson, Norah M. Davis, D.E.R. Hughes, and F.G.L. Stock. A STUDY OF WOMEN ON WAR WORK IN FOUR FACTORIES. 1945. 44 pp.

Number 89. Colebrook, Dora. ARTIFICIAL SUNLIGHT TREATMENT IN INDUSTRY. A REPORT ON THE RESULTS OF THREE TRIALS—IN AN OFFICE, A FACTORY AND A COAL MINE. 1946. 64 pp.

Number 90. Fraser, Russell, with the collaboration of Elizabeth Bunbury, Barbara Danniell, M. Elizabeth Barling, F. Estelle Waldron, P. Mary Kemp, and Imogen Lee. THE INCIDENCE OF NEUROSIS AMONG FACTORY WORKERS. 1947. 66 pp.

384. *Internationale psychoanalytische Bibliothek.*

TITLE VARIATIONS: None.

DATES OF PUBLICATION: Number 1–22, 1919–1927.

FREQUENCY: Irregular. *See* Contents *below.*

NUMBERING VARIATIONS: None.

PUBLISHER: **Leipzig** and **Vienna:** Internationaler psychoanalytischer Verlag, 1919. **Leipzig, Vienna, Zurich, London, New York:** Internationaler psychoanalytischer Verlag, 1919–1920. **Leipzig, Vienna, Zurich:** Internationaler psychoanalytischer Verlag, 1921–1927.

PRIMARY EDITORS: None listed.

CONTENTS:

Number 1. ZUR PSYCHOANALYSE DER KRIEGSNEUROSEN. 1919. 83 pp.

Number 2. Ferenczi, Sandor. HYSTERIE UND PATHONEUROSEN. 1919. 79 pp.

Number 3. Freud, Sigmund. ZUR PSYCHOPATHOLOGIE DES ALLTAGSLEBENS. 1919. 312 pp.

Number 4. Rank, Otto. PSYCHOANALYTISCHE BEITRÄGE ZUR MYTHENFORSCHUNG. 1919. 420 pp.

Number 5. Reik, Theodor. PROBLEME DER RELIGIONSPSYCHOLOGIE. 1919. 311 pp.

Number 6. Roheim, Geza. SPIEGELZAUBER. 1919. 263 pp.

Number 7. Hitschmann, Eduard, GOTTFRIED KELLER, PSYCHOANALYSE DES DICHTERS, SEINER GESTALTEN UND MOTIVE. 1919. 125 pp.

Number 8. Pfister, Oskar. ZUM KAMPF UM DIE PSYCHOANALYSE. 1920. 463 pp.

Number 9. Kolnai, Aurel. PSYCHOANALYSE UND SOZIOLOGIE. ZUR PSYCHOLOGIE VON MASSE UND GESELLSCHAFT. 1920. 152 pp.

Number 10. Abraham, Karl. KLINISCHE BEITRÄGE ZUR PSYCHOANALYSE AUS DEN JAHREN 1907–1920. 1921. 303 pp.

Number 11. Jones, Ernest. THERAPIE DER NEUROSEN. 1921. 175 pp.

Number 12. Varendonck, Julien. ÜBER DAS VORBEWUSSTE PHANTASI-ERENDE DENKEN. 1922. 172 pp.

Number 13. Ferenczi, Sandor. POPULÄRE VORTRÄGE ÜBER PSYCHOANA-LYSE. 1922. 189 pp.

Number 14. Rank, Otto. DAS TRAUMA DER GEBURT UND SEINE BEDEU-TUNG FÜR DIE PSYCHOANALYSE. 1924. 207 pp.

Number 15. Ferenczi, Sandor. VERSUCH EINER GENITALTHEORIE. 1924. 128 pp.

Number 16. Abraham, Karl. PSYCHOANALYTISCHE STUDIEN ZUR CHARAK-TERBILDUNG. 1925. 64 pp.

Number 17. Schilder, Paul. ENTWURF ZU EINER PSYCHIATRIE AUF PSY-CHOANALYTISCHER GRUNDLAGE. 1925. 208 pp.

Number 18. Reik, Theodor. GESTÄNDNISZWANG UND STRAFBEDÜRFNIS. 1925. 238 pp.

Number 19. Aichhorn, August. VERWAHRLOSTE JUGEND. 1925. 291 pp.

Number 20. Levine, Israel. DAS UNBEWUSSTE. 1926. 215 pp.

Number 21. Rank, Otto. SEXUALITÄT UND SCHULDGEFÜHL. 1926. 160 pp.

Number 22. Alexander, Franz. PSYCHOANALYSE DER GESAMTPERSÖN-LICHKEIT. 1927. 240 pp.

385. *Journal of Delinquency. Monograph.*

TITLE VARIATIONS: None.

DATES OF PUBLICATION: Number 1–2, January, 1919–April, 1923.

FREQUENCY: Irregular *See* Contents *below.*

NUMBERING VARIATIONS: None.

PUBLISHER: **Whittier, California:** Whittier State School, Department of Research, January, 1919–April, 1923.

PRIMARY EDITORS: **Fred. C. Nelles,** 1919–1923.

CONTENTS:

Number 1. Williams, J. Harold. THE INTELLIGENCE OF THE DELINQUENT BOY. January, 1919. 198 pp.

Number 2. Cady, Vernon M. THE ESTIMATION OF JUVENILE INCORRIGI-BILITY. A REPORT OF EXPERIMENTS IN THE MEASUREMENT OF JUVENILE INCOR-RIGIBILITY BY MEANS OF CERTAIN NON-INTELLECTUAL TESTS. Foreword by Lewis M. Terman. April, 1923. 140 pp.

386. *Oregon. University. Publications.*

TITLE VARIATIONS: None.

DATES OF PUBLICATION: Volume 1–2, Number 10, November 1919–April 1926.

FREQUENCY: Irregular. *See* Contents *below.*

NUMBERING VARIATIONS: Many psychology titles were included in this series; only such titles are listed in the Contents section below.

PUBLISHER: **Eugene, Oregon:** University of Oregon, 1919–1926.

PRIMARY EDITORS: None listed.

CONTENTS:

Volume 1, Number 2. Wheeler, Raymond H. AN EXPERIMENTAL INVESTIGATION OF THE PROCESS OF CHOOSING. January 1920. 59 pp.

———, **Number 4.** Conklin, Edmund S. THE FOSTER-CHILD FANTASY. March 1920. 20 pp.

———, **Number 5.** Wheeler, Raymond H. THE SYNAESTHESIA OF A BLIND SUBJECT. May 1920. 61 pp.

———, **Number 7.** Ruch, Giles Murrel. A STUDY OF THE MENTAL, PEDAGOGICAL AND PHYSICAL DEVELOPMENT OF THE PUPILS OF THE JUNIOR DIVISION OF THE UNIVERSITY HIGH SCHOOL, EUGENE, OREGON. September 1920. 48 pp.

———, **Number 10.** Wheeler, Raymond H. and Thomas D. Cutsforth. THE SYNAESTHESIA OF A BLIND SUBJECT WITH COMPARATIVE DATA FROM AN ASYNAESTHETIC BLIND SUBJECT. June 1922. 104 pp.

———, **Number 11.** Young, Kimball. MENTAL DIFFERENCES IN CERTAIN IMMIGRANT GROUPS, PSYCHOLOGICAL TESTS OF SOUTH EUROPEANS IN TYPICAL CALIFORNIA SCHOOLS WITH BEARING ON THE EDUCATIONAL POLICY AND ON THE PROBLEMS OF RACIAL CONTACTS IN THIS COUNTRY. July 1922. 103 pp.

Volume 2, Number 1. Conklin, Edmund S. THE SCALE OF VALUES METHODS FOR STUDIES IN GENETIC PSYCHOLOGY. May 1923. 36 pp.

———, **Number 6.** Crosland, Harold R. AN INVESTIGATION OF PROOFREADER'S ILLUSIONS. October 1924. 168 pp.

387. *Praktische Psychologie. Monatsschrift für die gesamte angewandte Psychologie, für Berufsberatung und industrielle Psychotechnik.*

TITLE VARIATIONS: None.

DATES OF PUBLICATION: Jahrgang 1–4, October 1919–December 1923.

FREQUENCY: Monthly.

NUMBERING VARIATIONS: None.

PUBLISHER: **Leipzig:** S. Hirzel, 1919–1923.

PRIMARY EDITORS: **Walther Moede,** 1919–1923; **Curt Piorkowski,** 1919–1923.

388. *Quellenschriften zur seelischen Entwicklung.*

TITLE VARIATIONS: None.

DATES OF PUBLICATION: Band 1–3, 1919–1924.

FREQUENCY: Irregular. *See* Contents *below.*

NUMBERING VARIATIONS: None.

PUBLISHER: **Vienna:** Internationaler psychoanalytischer Verlag, 1919–1924.

PRIMARY EDITORS: None listed.

CONTENTS:

Band 1. Hug-Hellmuth, Hermine, ed. TAGEBUCH EINES HALBWÜCHSIGEN MÄDCHENS (VON 11–14½ JAHREN). 1919. 190 pp.

Band 2. Bernfeld, Siegfried, ed. VOM GEMEINSCHAFTSLEBEN DER JUGEND. BEITRÄGE ZUR JUGENDFORSCHUNG. 1922. 271 pp.

Band 3. Bernfeld, Siegfried. VOM DICHTERISCHEN SCHAFFEN DER JUGEND. NEUE BEITRÄGE ZUR JUGENDFORSCHUNG. 1924. 286 pp.

389. *Société de neurologie, psychiatrie et psychologie de Jassy. Bulletin.*

TITLE VARIATIONS: Also called *Societatea română de neurologie, psichiatrie, psichologie si endocrinologie. Bulletin.* Continued by *Association des psychiatres roumaines. Bulletin* with Tome 4, 1922.

DATES OF PUBLICATION: Tome 1–3, February 1919–January 1922.

FREQUENCY: Monthly.

NUMBERING VARIATIONS: None.

PUBLISHER: **Bucharest:** Société de neurologie, psychiatrie et psychologie, 1912–1922.

PRIMARY EDITORS: None listed.

1920-1929

390. *Arbeiten zur Psychologie und Philosophie.*

TITLE VARIATIONS: None.

DATES OF PUBLICATION: Heft 1, 1920.

FREQUENCY: Irregular. *See* Contents *below.*

NUMBERING VARIATIONS: None.

PUBLISHER: Leipzig: Verlag von Johann Ambrosius Barth, 1920.

PRIMARY EDITOR: **E. R. Jaensch,** 1920.

CONTENTS:

Heft 1. Jaensch, E. R. EINIGE ALLGEMEINERE FRAGEN DER PSYCHOLOGIE UND BIOLOGIE DES DENKENS, ERLÄUTERT AN DER LEHRE VOM VERGLEICH. 1920. 31 pp.

391. *Archivio generale di neurologia e psichiatria.*

TITLE VARIATIONS: Continued by *Archivio generale di neurologia, psichiatria e psicoanalisi* with Volume 2, 1921.

DATES OF PUBLICATION: Volume 1, Fascicolo 1–2, March 1920–July 1920.

FREQUENCY: Irregular.

NUMBERING VARIATIONS: None.

For serial publications that began before 1920 and were still being published during the decade 1920 to 1929, *see also* entries 32, 50, 65, 67, 73, 74, 79, 84, 90, 96, 110, 111, 112, 119, 121, 122, 123, 127, 131, 135, 139, 140, 151, 153, 160, 162, 163, 169, 176, 177, 181, 184, 188, 190, 192, 193, 196, 197, 204, 205, 207, 208, 210, 215, 218, 219, 222, 223, 225, 226, 227, 229, 230, 233, 234, 236, 237, 241, 242, 263, 264, 266, 267, 269, 270, 271, 272, 275, 277, 281, 282, 284, 285, 288, 289, 290, 292, 294, 295, 296, 297, 300, 302, 306, 307, 309, 310, 313, 315, 316, 317, 318, 320, 324, 325, 326, 327, 328, 331, 332, 333, 334, 336, 339, 344, 346, 347, 349, 350, 351, 352, 353, 354, 355, 356, 357, 359, 360, 361, 364, 366, 368, 369, 370, 371, 372, 373, 374, 375, 376, 377, 378, 379, 380, 381, 383, 384, 385, 386, 387, 388, 389.

PUBLISHER: **Naples:** R. stabilimento tipografico Francesco Giannini & Figli, 1920.

PRIMARY EDITOR: **M. Levi Bianchini,** 1920.

EDITORIAL BOARD: G. Antonini, 1920; C. Colucci, 1920; S. de Sanctis, 1920; E. La Pegna, 1920; E. Medea, 1920; G. Mingazzini, 1920; G. Modena, 1920; D. Ventra, 1920; L. Zanon del Bo, 1920.

392. *Archivio italiano di psicologia.*

TITLE VARIATIONS: Subtitle added *Generale del lavoro,* 1937–1938.

DATES OF PUBLICATION: Volume 1–16, 1920–1938.

FREQUENCY: **Biannual,** Volume 1–4, 1920–1926. **Annual,** Volume 5–16, 1927–1938.

NUMBERING VARIATIONS: None.

PUBLISHER: **Turin:** Istituto di psicologia sperimentale della R. Università di Torino, 1920–1938.

PRIMARY EDITORS: **Federico Kiesow,** 1920–1938; **A. Gemelli,** 1920–1921.

393. *Bibliographie der Philosophie und Psychologie.*

TITLE VARIATIONS: None.

DATES OF PUBLICATION: Heft 1–19, 1920–1938.

FREQUENCY: Annual.

NUMBERING VARIATIONS: None.

PUBLISHER: **Leipzig:** Wilhelm Heims, 1920–1938.

PRIMARY EDITOR: **Rudolf A. Dimpfel,** 1920–1938.

394. *British Journal of Psychology. General Section.* [Issued by the British Psychological Society.]

TITLE VARIATIONS: Incorporates *British Psychological Society. Proceedings,* 1920–1947. Continues *British Journal of Psychology.*

DATES OF PUBLICATION: Volume 11–41+, October 1920–1950+.

FREQUENCY: **Quarterly,** Volume 11–33, 38–41+, 1920–1943, 1947–1950+. **Triannual,** Volume 34–37, 1943–1947.

NUMBERING VARIATIONS: Double issues present.

PUBLISHER: **Cambridge:** University Press, 1920–1950+.

PRIMARY EDITORS: **Charles Samuel Myers,** 1920–1924; **F. C. Bartlett,** 1924–1949; **D. W. Harding,** 1949–1950+.

ASSISTANT EDITORS: F. C. Bartlett, 1920–1924; S. S. (Brierley) Isaacs, 1920–1949; C. Burt, 1920–1950+; J. Drever, 1924–1950; J. W. Reeves, 1950+.

EDITORIAL BOARD: W. McDougall, 1920–1938; Charles Samuel Myers, 1924–1946; A. F. Shand, 1920–1936; C. S. Sherrington, 1920–1950+; Charles

E. Spearman, 1920–1945; W. Brown, 1920–1950+; G. Dawes Hicks, 1920–1941; Carveth Read, 1920–1933; James Ward, 1920–1924; H. J. Watt, 1920–1927; G. Udny Yule, 1920–1950+; T. H. Pear, 1920–1950+; W.H.R. Rivers, 1920–1924; J. Drever, 1920–1924; B. Edgell, 1920–1948; F. Aveling, 1920–1941; E. A. Bott, 1924–1950+; J. T. MacCurdy, 1927–1947; E. Bullough, 1928–1935; R. H. Thouless, 1943–1950+; F. C. Bartlett, 1949–1950+; W.J.H. Sprott, 1949–1950+.

395. *British Journal of Psychology. Medical Section.*

TITLE VARIATIONS: Continued by *British Journal of Medical Psychology* with Volume 3, 1923.

DATES OF PUBLICATION: Volume 1–2, 1920/1921–1921/1922.

FREQUENCY: Quarterly.

NUMBERING VARIATIONS: Multinumber issues present in Volume 1.

PUBLISHER: **London:** Cambridge University Press, 1920–1922.

PRIMARY EDITORS: **T. W. Mitchell,** 1920–1922; **William Brown,** 1920–1922; **Ernest Jones,** 1920–1922; **Constance Long,** 1920–1922; **George Riddoch,** 1920–1922; **W.H.R. Rivers,** 1920–1922.

396. *Deutsche Psychologie. Arbeitenreihe.*

TITLE VARIATIONS: Continues *Deutsche Psychologie. Zeitschrift für reine und angewandte Seelenkunde.* Continued by *Deutsche Psychologie. Arbeitenreihe zur Kulturpsychologie und Psychologie der Praxis. Psychotechnik* with Band 5, Heft 2, 1928.

DATES OF PUBLICATION: Band 3–5, Heft 1, 1920–1926.

FREQUENCY: Irregular. *See* Contents *below.*

NUMBERING VARIATIONS: Band 4, Heft 1 also numbered as *Psychotechnische Forschungen zur Berufsberatung. See* Contents *below.*

PUBLISHER: **Langensalza, Germany:** Verlag von Wendt & Klauwell, 1920–1921. **Halle:** Carl Marhold Verlagsbuchhandlung, 1925–1926.

PRIMARY EDITOR: **Fritz Giese,** 1920–1926.

CONTENTS:
   Band 3, Heft 1. Ostwald, W. FARBENPSYCHOLOGIE; and Meyer, S. ENT-WICKLUNG DER SINNESORGANE UND DER EMPFINDUNG. 1920. Pp. 1–58.
   ———, **Heft 2.** Giese, Fritz. PSYCHISCHE NORMEN FÜR GRUNDSCHULE UND BERUFSBERATUNG. 1920. Pp. 59–147.
   ———, **Heft 3.** ZUR MASSENPSYCHOLOGIE: Hösch-Ernst, Lucy. BEITRAG ZUR PSYCHOLOGIE DER SCHULKINDER BEIM BETRACHTEN VON BIDERN; Kollarits, Jeno. KANN DIE VOLKSSEELE AUS DER GESCHICHTE LERNEN?; and Voigtländer, Else. ZUR PSYCHOLOGIE DER POLITISCHEN STELLUNGNAHME. 1920. Pp. 149–206.
   ———, **Heft 4.** ZUR PATHOPSYCHOLOGIE. 1921. Pp. 207–289.
   ———, **Heft 5/6.** ZUR WIRTSCHAFTSPSYCHOLOGIE. 1921. Pp. 291–354.
   Band 4, Heft 1. Lang, Emmy. PSYCHOLOGISCHE MASSENPRÜFUNGEN FÜR

ZWECKE DER BERUFSBERATUNG; and Rüssel, Arnulf. DIE EIGNUNGSPRÜFUNG ALS ERLEBNIS DER JUGENDLICHEN. 1925. 68 pp. (Also as *Psychotechnische Forschungen zur Berufsberatung,* Heft 1.)

————, **Heft 2.** Lessing, Theodor. PRINZIPIEN DER CHARAKTEROLOGIE. 1926. 50 pp.

————, **Heft 3.** Rossolimo, Grigorii Ivanovich. DAS PSYCHOLOGISCHE PROFIL UND ANDERE EXPERIMENTELL-PSYCHOLOGISCHE, INDIVIDUALE UND KOLLEKTIVE METHODEN ZUR PRÜFUNG DER PSYCHOMECHANIK BEI ERWACHSENEN UND KINDERN. 1926. 139 pp.

————, **Heft 4.** Hische, Wilhelm. DAS EIGNUNGSPRINZIP. 1926. 44 pp.

————, **Heft 5.** Kinast, Erich. IMMANUEL KANT. ANTON BRUCKNER. 1926. 72 pp.

————, **Heft 6.** Müller-Freienfels, Richard. ZUR PSYCHOLOGIE UND SOZIOLOGIE DER MODERNEN KUNST. 1926. 56 pp.

Band 5, Heft 1. Seeling, Otto. DER COUÉISMUS IN SEINER PSYCHOLOGISCHEN UND PÄDAGOGISCHEN BEDEUTUNG. 1926. 70 pp.

397. *International Journal of Psycho-Analysis.* [Organ of the International Psycho-analytical Association.]

TITLE VARIATIONS: None.

DATES OF PUBLICATION: Volume 1–31+, 1920–1950+.

FREQUENCY: Quarterly.

NUMBERING VARIATIONS: Double-numbered issues present. Volume 19 (April 1938), Part 2 lacking.

PUBLISHER: **London:** International Psycho-Analytical Press, 1920–1924. **London:** Published for the Institute of Psycho-Analysis by Bailliere, Tindall & Cox, 1925–1950+.

PRIMARY EDITORS: **Ernest Jones,** 1920–1939; **James Strachey,** 1940–1945; **Marjorie Brierley,** 1940–1946; **Sylvia Payne,** 1940–1946; **C. P. Oberndorf,** 1940–1950+; **John Rickman,** 1940–1950+; **Adrian Stephen,** 1946; **W. Clifford M. Scott,** 1947–1950+; **W. Hoffer,** 1947–1950+.

EDITORIAL BOARD: Douglas Bryan, 1921–1939; A. A. Brill, 1921–1935, 1937–1947; J. C. Flugel, 1921–1939; H. W. Frink, 1921–1924; C. P. Oberndorf, 1921–1931, 1933–1939; Karl Abraham, 1922–1925; J.E.G. van Emden, 1922–1931, 1934–1937; G. Bose, 1922–1950+; Sandor Ferenczi, 1922–1933; E. Oberholzer, 1922–1928; Otto Rank, 1922–1924; M. Wulff, 1925–1928; Adolf Stern, 1927–1929, 1940–1941, 1947; Ernst Simmel, 1927–1929, 1943, 1946; Philipp Sarasin, 1929–1950+; J. W. Kannabich, 1929–1943, 1945–1948; Max Eitingon, 1930–1942; W. A. White, 1930–1932; N. L. Blitzsten, 1932–1934; J.H.W. van Ophuijsen, 1932–1933; Lucile Dooley, 1933–1935, 1938–1939; Y. K. Yabe, 1933–1941; Istvan Hollos, 1934–1940, 1946–1948; S.J.R. De-Monchy, 1934–1940; F. Boehm, 1934–1938; A. Borel, 1934; K. Marui, 1934–1941; E. Pichon, 1935–1937; Karl A. Menninger, 1935, 1944–1945; Martin Peck, 1935–1937; Thomas M. French, 1936–1937; L. B. Hill, 1936–1937; B. D. Lewin, 1936–1939; Edoardo Weiss, 1937–1938; M. Ralph Kaufman, 1937–1939;

F. Alexander, 1938–1939; H. K. Schjelderup, 1938–1940; Charles L. Odier, 1938–1940; Alfild Tamm, 1938–1948; Helen V. McLean, 1938–1939; S. G. Biddle, 1940–1941; Helene Deutsch, 1940; Robert P. Knight, 1940–1942; George J. Mohr, 1940–1941; Ernest Jones, 1940–1950+; David M. Levy, 1940–1941, 1948–1950+; Isador H. Coriat, 1937, 1941; Frieda Fromm-Reichmann, 1940–1946; Leo H. Bartemeier, 1941–1945, 1950+; John M. Murray, 1942–1943; Leonard Blumgart, 1942–1944; Dexter Bullard, 1942–1943; O. Spurgeon English, 1942–1943; Edwin R. Eisler, 1942–1943; Ernst Lewy, 1942–1943; Erich Lindemann, 1944–1945; Gerald H. J. Pearson, 1944–1945; Edith Weigert, 1944–1945; Margaret W. Gerard, 1944–1945; Emanuel Windholz, 1944–1945; Sylvia Payne, 1944; M. (Wulff) Woolf, 1944–1950+; Sara A. Bonnett, 1945; A. Aichhorn, 1946–1949; Ives Hendrick, 1946–1947; Durval Marcondes, 1946–1950+; H. van der Waals, 1946–1948; William C. Barrett, 1946–1947; P. G. Dane, 1946–1950+; Philip R. Lehrman, 1946–1947; L. Rascovsky, 1946–1948; Richard F. Sterba, 1946–1947; 1949–1950+; Sandor Lorand, 1947; Benjamin I. Weininger, 1946–1947; G. Leonard Harrington, 1946–1947; LeRoy M. A. Maeder, 1946–1947; George W. Wilson, 1946–1947; George E. Daniels, 1947; Edward Bibring, 1948–1949; Harry B. Lee, 1948–1950+; Robert T. Morse, 1948–1949; A. Russell Anderson, 1948–1950+; Alfred Gross, 1948–1949; Charles W. Tidd, 1948–1950+; Bernhard Berliner, 1948–1950+; Henry A. Bunker, Jr., 1948–1950+; G. Henry Katz, 1948–1950+; Nicola Perotti, 1949–1950+; M. Maurice Dugautiez, 1949–1950+; P. J. van der Leeuw, 1949–1950+; Angel Garma, 1949–1950+; Fernando Allende Navarro, 1949–1950+; John Leuba, 1949; William C. Menninger, 1949–1950+; Gunnar Nycander, 1949–1950+; Sacha Nacht, 1950+; Rex E. Buxton, 1950+; Alfred Fr. von Winterstein, 1950+; M. Ralph Kaufman, 1950+; John M. Murray, 1950+.

398. *Internationale Zeitschrift für Psychoanalyse.* [Organ of the Internationale psychoanalytische Vereinigung.]

TITLE VARIATIONS: Continues: *Internationale Zeitschrift für ärztliche Psychoanalyse.* Continued by *Internationale Zeitschrift für Psychoanalyse und "Imago"* with Band 24, 1939.

DATES OF PUBLICATION: Band 6–23, 1920–1937.

FREQUENCY: Quarterly.

NUMBERING VARIATIONS: Band 6, 1920 contains *American Psychoanalytic Association. Report;* Band 13, 1927, Band 14, 1928 and Band 16, 1930 contain *Russian Psychoanalytic Society. Report;* Band 14, 1928 and Band 16, 1930 contain *Indian Psychoanalytic Society. Report.*

PUBLISHER: **Leipzig** and **Vienna:** Internationaler psychoanalytischer Verlag, 1920–1923. **Leipzig, Zurich,** and **Vienna:** Internationaler psychoanalytischer Verlag, 1924–1930. **Vienna:** Internationaler psychoanalytischer Verlag, 1931–1937.

PRIMARY EDITORS: **Otto Rank,** 1920–1924; **Sandor Ferenczi,** 1924–1932; **Sandor Rado,** 1925–1936; **M. Eitingon,** 1925–1932; **Paul Federn,** 1933–1935; **Heinz Hartmann,** 1933–1937; **Edward Bibring,** 1936–1937.

399. *Iowa. University. Studies in Child Welfare.*

TITLE VARIATIONS: None.

DATES OF PUBLICATION: Volume 1–20, 1920–1944.

FREQUENCY: Irregular. *See* Contents *below.*

NUMBERING VARIATIONS: Also numbered as [*Iowa. University.*] *Studies. First Series* and as [*Iowa. University.*] *Studies. New Series.* Various volumes and issues also numbered in the subseries *Measurement of Musical Development; Researches in Parent Education; Studies in Emotional Adjustment; Studies in Infant Behavior; Studies in Preschool Education;* and *Studies in Topological and Vector Psychology. See* Contents *below.*

PUBLISHER: **Iowa City, Iowa:** University of Iowa. Iowa Child Welfare Research Station, 1922–1944.

PRIMARY EDITORS: **Bird T. Baldwin,** 1920–1926; **George Dinsmore Stoddard,** 1929–1941; **Robert R. Sears,** 1943–1944.

CONTENTS:
Volume 1, Number 1. Baldwin, Bird T. THE PHYSICAL GROWTH OF CHILDREN FROM BIRTH TO MATURITY. 1921. 411 pp. (Also as [*Iowa. University.*] *Studies. First Series*, Number 50.)

————, **Number 2.** Seashore, Carl E. A SURVEY OF MUSICAL TALENT IN THE PUBLIC SCHOOLS. 1920. 36 pp. (Also as [*Iowa. University.*] *Studies. First Series*, Number 37.)

————, **Number 3.** Stinchfield, Sara M. A PRELIMINARY STUDY IN CORRECTIVE SPEECH. 1920. 36 pp. (Also as [*Iowa. University.*] *Studies. First Series*, Number 39.)

————, **Number 4.** Town, Clara H. ANALYTIC STUDY OF A GROUP OF FIVE- AND SIX-YEAR-OLD CHILDREN. 1921. 87 pp. (Also as [*Iowa. University.*] *Studies. First Series*, Number 48.)

————, **Number 5.** Daniels, Amy L., Albert H. Byfield, and Rosemary Loughlin. INVESTIGATIONS IN THE ARTIFICIAL FEEDING OF CHILDREN (RE-

PRINTS). 1921. 36 pp. (Also as [*Iowa. University.*] *Studies. First Series*, Number 44.)

————, **Number 6.** Horack, Frank E. CHILD LEGISLATION IN IOWA. 1921. 36 pp. (Also as [*Iowa. University.*] *Studies. First Series*, Number 42.)

————, **Number 7.** Hart, Hornell Norris. SELECTIVE MIGRATION AS A FACTOR IN CHILD WELFARE IN THE UNITED STATES, WITH SPECIAL REFERENCE TO IOWA. 1921. 137 pp. (Also as [*Iowa. University.*] *Studies. First Series*, Number 53.)

Volume 2, Number 1. Baldwin, Bird T., and Lorle I. Stecher. MENTAL GROWTH CURVE OF NORMAL AND SUPERIOR CHILDREN, STUDIED BY MEANS OF CONSECUTIVE INTELLIGENCE EXAMINATIONS. 1922. 61 pp. (Also as [*Iowa. University.*] *Studies. First Series*, Number 56.)

————, **Number 2.** Hart, Hornell Norris. DIFFERENTIAL FECUNDITY IN IOWA. 1922. 39 pp. (Also as [*Iowa. University.*] *Studies. First Series*, Number 62.)

————, **Number 3.** Bliss, A. Ione. IOWA CHILD WELFARE LEGISLATION MEASURED BY FEDERAL CHILDREN'S BUREAU STANDARDS. 1922. 52 pp. (Also as [*Iowa. University.*] *Studies. First Series*, Number 65.)

————, **Number 4.** Hart, Hornell Norris. A TEST OF SOCIAL ATTITUDES AND INTERESTS. 1923. 40 pp. (Also as [*Iowa. University.*] *Studies. First Series*, Number 69.)

Volume 3, Number 1. Whiting, P. W. A STUDY OF HEREDITARY AND ENVIRONMENTAL FACTORS DETERMINING A VARIABLE CHARACTER: DEFECTIVE AND FREAK VENATION IN THE PARASITIC WASP HABROBRACON JUGLANDIS (ASHM.). 1924. 80 pp. (Also as [*Iowa. University.*] *Studies. First Series*, Number 73.)

————, **Number 2.** Wagoner, Lovisa C. THE CONSTRUCTIVE ABILITY OF YOUNG CHILDREN. 1925. 55 pp. (Also as [*Iowa. University.*] *Studies. First Series*, Number 94.)

————, **Number 3.** Marston, Leslie R. THE EMOTIONS OF YOUNG CHILDREN: AN EXPERIMENTAL STUDY IN INTROVERSION AND EXTROVERSION. 1925. 99 pp. (Also as [*Iowa. University.*] *Studies. First Series*, Number 95.)

————, **Number 4.** Wellman, Beth. THE DEVELOPMENT OF MOTOR COORDINATION IN YOUNG CHILDREN: AN EXPERIMENTAL STUDY IN THE CONTROL OF HAND AND ARM MOVEMENTS. 1926. 93 pp. (Also as [*Iowa. University.*] *Studies. First Series*, Number 108.)

————, **Number 5.** Smith, Madorah E. AN INVESTIGATION OF THE DEVELOPMENT OF THE SENTENCE AND THE EXTENT OF VOCABULARY IN YOUNG CHILDREN. 1926. 92 pp. (Also as [*Iowa. University.*] *Studies. First Series*, Number 109.)

————, **Number 6.** Kirkwood, Julia A. THE LEARNING PROCESS IN YOUNG CHILDREN: AN EXPERIMENTAL STUDY IN ASSOCIATION. 1926. 107 pp. (Also as [*Iowa. University.*] *Studies. First Series*, Number 110.)

Volume 4, Number 1. Baldwin, Bird T., Laura M. Busby, and Helen V. Garside. ANATOMIC GROWTH OF CHILDREN. 1929. 88 pp. (Also as [*Iowa. University.*] *Studies. First Series*, Number 164.)

————, **Number 2.** Berne, Esther van Cleave. AN INVESTIGATION OF THE WANTS OF SEVEN CHILDREN. 1929. 61 pp. (Also as [*Iowa. University.*] *Studies. First Series*, Number 171.)

399. *(Continued)*

————, **Number 3.** Berne, Esther van Cleave. AN EXPERIMENTAL INVESTIGATION OF SOCIAL BEHAVIOR PATTERNS IN YOUNG CHILDREN. 1930. 93 pp. (Also as [*Iowa. University.*] *Studies. First Series,* Number 175.)

————, **Number 4.** Updegraff, Ruth. THE VISUAL PERCEPTION OF DISTANCE IN YOUNG CHILDREN AND ADULTS: A COMPARATIVE STUDY. 1930. 102 pp. (Also as [*Iowa. University.*] *Studies. New Series,* Number 190.)

————, **Number 5.** Hicks, James Allan. THE ACQUISITION OF MOTOR SKILL IN YOUNG CHILDREN. 1931. 80 pp. (Also as [*Iowa. University.*] *Studies. New Series,* Number 204.)

————, **Number 6.** Moore, Elizabeth Skelding. THE DEVELOPMENT OF MENTAL HEALTH IN A GROUP OF YOUNG CHILDREN. 1931. 128 pp. (Also as [*Iowa. University.*] *Studies. New Series,* Number 207.)

Volume 5, Number 1. Wallis, Ruth Sawtell. HOW CHILDREN GROW. 1931. 137 pp. (Also as [*Iowa. University.*] *Studies. New Series,* Number 208.)

————, **Number 2.** Wellman, Beth L., Ida Mae Case, Ida Gaarder Mengert, and Dorothy E. Bradbury. SPEECH SOUNDS OF YOUNG CHILDREN. 1931. 82 pp. (Also as [*Iowa. University.*] *Studies. New Series,* Number 212.)

————, **Number 3.** Chase, Lucile. MOTIVATION OF YOUNG CHILDREN. 1932. 119 pp. (Also as [*Iowa. University.*] *Studies. First Series,* Number 223.)

————, **Number 4.** Scoe, Hjalmar Fletcher. BLADDER CONTROL IN INFANCY AND EARLY CHILDHOOD. 1933. 83 pp. (Also as [*Iowa. University.*] *Studies. New Series,* Number 253.)

————, **Number 5.** Johnson, Wendell. THE INFLUENCE OF STUTTERING ON THE PERSONALITY. 1932. 140 pp. (Also as [*Iowa. University.*] *Studies. First Series,* Number 224.)

Volume 6. Hattendorf. Katharine Wood, Ralph H. Ojemann, Hazel Spencer Schaus, Lois M. Jack, Gertrude Hill Nystrom, and Laura L. Remer. RESEARCHES IN PARENT EDUCATION. I. 1932. 288 pp. (Also as [*Iowa. University.*] *Studies. New Series,* Number 241.)

Volume 7, Number 1. Williams, Harold M., Clement H. Sievers, and Melvin S. Hattwick. THE MEASUREMENT OF MUSICAL DEVELOPMENT. 1932 and January 15, 1933 (both dates on publication). 191 pp. (Also as [*Iowa. University.*] *Studies. New Series,* Number 243.)

————, **Number 2.** Skeels, Harold Manville. A STUDY OF SOME FACTORS IN FORM BOARD ACCOMPLISHMENTS OF PRESCHOOL CHILDREN. 1933. 148 pp. (Also as [*Iowa. University.*] *Studies. New Series,* Number 249.)

————, **Number 3.** Roberts, Katherine Elliott. LEARNING IN PRESCHOOL AND ORPHANAGE CHILDREN. 1933. 94 pp. (Also as [*Iowa. University.*] *Studies. New Series,* Number 251.)

————, **Number 4.** Hagman, Elizabeth Pleger. THE COMPANIONSHIPS OF PRESCHOOL CHILDREN. 1933. 69 pp. (Also as [*Iowa. University.*] *Studies. New Series,* Number 255.)

————, **Number 5.** Kelly, Helen Garside. A STUDY OF INDIVIDUAL DIFFERENCES IN BREATHING CAPACITY IN RELATION TO SOME PHYSICAL CHARACTERISTICS. 1933. 59 pp. (Also as [*Iowa. University.*] *Studies. New Series,* Number 264.)

Volume 8. Ojemann, Ralph H., Mary Price Roberts, David P. Phillips, Eva A. Fillmore, Josephine Pollock, and Rose L. Hanson. RESEARCHES IN PARENT EDUCATION. II. 1934. 334 pp. (Also as [*Iowa. University.*] *Studies. New Series*, Number 270.)

Volume 9, Number 1. Horack, Frank E. LEGISLATION PERTAINING TO WOMEN AND CHILDREN IN IOWA. 1934. 67 pp. (Also as [*Iowa. University.*] *Studies. New Series*, Number 273.)

————, Number 2. Francis, Kenneth V., and Eva A. Fillmore. THE INFLUENCE OF ENVIRONMENT UPON THE PERSONALITY OF CHILDREN. 1934. 71 pp. (Also as [*Iowa. University.*] *Studies. New Series*, Number 274.)

————, Number 3. Jack, Lois M., Elizabeth Moore Manwell, Ida Gaarder Mengert, Esther van Cleave Berne, Helen Garside Kelly, Laberta A. Weiss, and Agnes Fairlie Ricketts. BEHAVIOR OF THE PRESCHOOL CHILD. 1934. 171 pp. (Also as [*Iowa. University.*] *Studies. New Series*, Number 275.)

————, Number 4. Irwin, Orvis C., LaBerta A. Weiss, and Esther M. Stubbs. STUDIES IN INFANT BEHAVIOR. I. 1934. 175 pp. (Also as [*Iowa. University.*] *Studies. New Series*, Number 281.)

Volume 10. Ojemann, Ralph H., Lois Alberta Ackerly, Evelyn Ini Butler, and Blanche E. Hedrick. RESEARCHES IN PARENT EDUCATION. III. 1935. 391 pp. (Also as [*Iowa. University.*] *Studies. New Series*, Number 285.)

Volume 11, Number 1. Richards, T. W., and Orvis C. Irwin. STUDIES IN INFANT BEHAVIOR. II. 1935. 146 pp. (Also as [*Iowa. University.*] *Studies. New Series*, Number 287.)

————, Number 2. Hattwick, Melvin S., and Harold M. Williams. THE MEASUREMENT OF MUSICAL DEVELOPMENT. II. 1935. 100 pp. (Also as [*Iowa. University.*] *Studies. New Series*, Number 290.)

————, Number 3. Meredith, Howard V. THE RHYTHM OF PHYSICAL GROWTH. 1935. 128 pp. (Also as [*Iowa. University.*] *Studies. New Series*, Number 292.)

————, Number 4. Fillmore, Eva A. IOWA TESTS FOR YOUNG CHILDREN. 1936. 58 pp. (Also as [*Iowa. University.*] *Studies. New Series*, Number 315.)

Volume 12, Number 1. Wenger, M. A., Josephine M. Smith, Charles Hazard, and Orris C. Irwin. STUDIES IN INFANT BEHAVIOR. III. 1936. 207 pp. (Also as [*Iowa. University.*] *Studies. New Series*, Number 325.)

————, Number 2. McCloy, Charles H. APPRAISING PHYSICAL STATUS: THE SELECTION OF MEASUREMENTS. 1936. 126 pp. (Also as [*Iowa. University.*] *Studies. New Series*, Number 356.)

————, Number 3. Page, Marjorie Lou. THE MODIFICATION OF ASCENDANT BEHAVIOR IN PRESCHOOL CHILDREN. 1936. 69 pp. (Also as [*Iowa. University.*] *Studies. New Series*, Number 324.)

————, Number 4. Boynton, Bernice. THE PHYSICAL GROWTH OF GIRLS. 1936. 105 pp. (Also as [*Iowa. University.*] *Studies. New Series*, Number 325.)

————, Number 5. Kelby, Harriet J. ANATOMIC AGE AND ITS RELATION TO STATURE. 1937. 38 pp. (Also as [*Iowa. University.*] *Studies. New Series*, Number 329.)

Volume 13, Number 1. Crissey, Orlo L. MENTAL DEVELOPMENT AS RELATED TO INSTITUTIONAL RESIDENCE AND EDUCATIONAL ACHIEVEMENT. 1937. 81 pp. (Also as [*Iowa. University.*] *Studies. New Series*, Number 332.)

————, **Number 2.** Williams, Harold M., Mary L. McFarland, and Marguerite F. Little. DEVELOPMENT OF LANGUAGE AND VOCABULARY IN YOUNG CHILDREN. 1937. 94 pp. (Also as [*Iowa. University.*] *Studies. New Series,* Number 336.)

————, **Number 3.** Kantrow, Ruth Wildenberg. STUDIES IN INFANT BEHAVIOR. IV. 1937. 64 pp. (Also as [*Iowa. University.*] *Studies. New Series.* Number 338.)

————, **Number 4.** Brandt, Hyman, Harold M. Williams, and Harold S. Carlson. STUDIES IN EMOTIONAL ADJUSTMENT. 1937. 102 pp. (Also as [*Iowa. University.*] *Studies. New Series,* Number 340.)

Volume 14. Updegraff, Ruth, Mary Elizabeth Keister, Louise Heiliger, Janet Learned, Marjorie Mantor, Eleanor A. Lack, and Theresa J. Peterson. STUDIES IN PRESCHOOL EDUCATION. I. 1937. 283 pp. (Also as [*Iowa. University.*] *Studies. New Series,* Number 346.)

Volume 15, Number 1. Houtchens, H. Max, Newell C. Kephart, and Delia Larson Sharp. STUDIES IN EMOTIONAL ADJUSTMENT. II. 1937 and January 15, 1938 (both dates on publication). 196 pp. (Also as [*Iowa. University.*] *Studies. New Series,* Number 347.)

————, **Number 2.** McCloy, C. H. APPRAISING PHYSICAL STATUS: METHODS AND NORMS. 1938. 260 pp. (Also as [*Iowa. University.*] *Studies. New Series,* Number 356.)

————, **Number 3.** Wellman, Beth L. THE INTELLIGENCE OF PRESCHOOL CHILDREN AS MEASURED BY THE MERRILL–PALMER SCALE OF PERFORMANCE TESTS. 1938. 150 pp. (Also as [*Iowa. University.*] *Studies. New Series,* Number 361.)

————, **Number 4.** Skeels, Harold M., Ruth Updegraff, Beth L. Wellman, and Harold M. Williams. A STUDY OF ENVIRONMENTAL STIMULATION. 1938. 191 pp. (Also as [*Iowa. University.*] *Studies. New Series,* Number 363.)

Volume 16, Number 1. Skodak, Marie. CHILDREN IN FOSTER HOMES: A STUDY OF MENTAL DEVELOPMENT. 1939. 156 pp. (Also as [*Iowa. University.*] *Studies. New Series,* Number 364.)

————, **Number 2.** Lederer, Ruth Klein, and Janet Redfield. STUDIES IN INFANT BEHAVIOR. V. 1939. 157 pp. (Also as [*Iowa. University.*] *Studies. New Series,* Number 376.)

————, **Number 3.** Lewin, Kurt, Ronald Lippitt, and Sibylle Korsch Escalona. STUDIES IN TOPOLOGICAL AND VECTOR PSYCHOLOGY. I. 1940. 307 pp. (Also as [*Iowa. University.*] *Studies. New Series,* Number 380.)

Volume 17. Ojemann, Ralph H., Vera H. Brandon, Eva I. Grant, Ruth Musgrove, Anne Gabriel, and Louise C. Coast. RESEARCHES IN PARENT EDUCATION. IV. 1939. 181 pp. (Also as [*Iowa. University.*] *Studies. New Series,* Number 381.)

Volume 18, Number 1. Barker, Roger, Tamara Dembo, and Kurt Lewin. FRUSTRATION AND REGRESSION: AN EXPERIMENT WITH YOUNG CHILDREN. STUDIES IN TOPOLOGICAL AND VECTOR PSYCHOLOGY. II. 1941. 314 pp. (Also as [*Iowa. University.*] *Studies. New Series,* Number 386.)

————, **Number 2.** Methany, Eleanor. BREATHING CAPACITY AND GRIP STRENGTH OF PRESCHOOL CHILDREN. 1940. 207 pp. (Also as [*Iowa. University.*] *Studies. New Series,* Number 390.)

————, **Number 3.** Knott, Virginia Bergstresser. PHYSICAL MEASURE-MENT OF YOUNG CHILDREN: A STUDY OF ANTHROPOMETRIC RELIABILITIES FOR CHILDREN THREE TO SIX YEARS OF AGE. 1941. 99 pp. (Also as [*Iowa. University.*] *Studies. New Series,* Number 394.)

Volume 19. Meredith, Howard V. PHYSICAL GROWTH FROM BIRTH TO TWO YEARS: I. STATURE. 1943. 255 + 79 pp. (Also as [*Iowa. University.*] *Studies. New Series,* Number 407.)

Volume 20. Lewin, Kurt, Charles E. Meyers, Joan Kalhorn, Maurice L. Farber, and John R. P. French. AUTHORITY AND FRUSTRATION. STUDIES IN TO-POLOGICAL AND VECTOR PSYCHOLOGY. III. 1944. 307 pp. (Also as [*Iowa. University.*] *Studies. New Series,* Number 409.)

400. *Journal of Educational Research.* [Organ of the National Association of Directors of Educational Research, 1920–1928.]

TITLE VARIATIONS: Association was renamed the Educational Research Association in 1922 and the American Educational Research Association in 1928.

DATES OF PUBLICATION: Volume 1–43+, January 1920–May 1950+. Suspended publication June–August 1932.

FREQUENCY: **Monthly,** Volume 1–25, January 1920–April/May 1932. **Monthly** (September–May), Volume 26–43+, September 1932–May 1950+.

NUMBERING VARIATIONS: Multinumber issue April/May 1932.

PUBLISHER: **Bloomington, Illinois:** Published for the Bureau of Educational Research, University of Illinois by the Public School Publishing Company, 1920. **Bloomington:** Published for the College of Education, Bureau of Educational Research, University of Illinois by the Public School Publishing Company, 1921. **Bloomington:** Public School Publishing Company, 1922–1941. **Madison, Wisconsin:** A. S. Barr, 1941–1945. **Madison:** Dembar Publications, Inc., 1945–1950+.

PRIMARY EDITORS: **B. R. Buckingham,** 1920–1928; **E. J. Ashbaugh,** 1920–1921, 1928–1950+; **L. P. Ayres,** 1920; **W. W. Charters,** 1920–1921; **S. A. Courtis,** 1920–1921; **Walter S. Monroe,** 1920–1921; **George D. Strayer,** 1920–1921; **Lewis M. Terman,** 1920–1921; **G. M. Whipple,** 1921; **A. S. Barr,** 1928–1950+; **Earl Hudelson,** 1928–1929; **V. T. Thayer,** 1929–1931; **Carter V. Good,** 1931–1945; **Harry J. Baker,** 1932–1941; **Leo J. Brueckner,** 1932–1950+; **Ernest Horn,** 1932–1934; **Kai Jensen,** 1932–1945; **Charles W. Knudsen,** 1932–1939; **Clifford Woody,** 1932–1950+; **A. K. Loomis,** 1934–1950+; **Douglas E. Scates,** 1939–1950+; **Percival M. Symonds,** 1939–1950+; **Harl R. Douglass,** 1941–1950+; **Willard C. Olson,** 1945–1950+.

401. *Journal of Neurology and Psychopathology.*

TITLE VARIATIONS: Continued by *Journal of Neurology and Psychiatry* with New Series, Volume 1, 1938.

DATES OF PUBLICATION: Volume 1–17, May 1920–April 1937.

FREQUENCY: Quarterly.

NUMBERING VARIATIONS: Issues also assigned whole numbers, Number 1–68.

PUBLISHER: **Bristol:** John Wright and Sons Ltd., 1920–1923. **London:** William Heinemann (Medical Books) Ltd., 1923–1926. **London:** British Medical Association, 1926–1937.

PRIMARY EDITOR: **S. A. Kinnier Wilson,** 1923–1937.

EDITORIAL BOARD: S. A. Kinnier Wilson, 1920–1923; T. Graham Brown, 1920–1937; R. M. Stewart, 1920–1937; C. P. Symonds, 1920–1926; Carey F. Coombs, 1920–1926; Bernard Hart, 1920–1937; Henry Devine, 1920–1937; Maurice Nicoll, 1920–1923; Charles Stanford Read, 1920–1937; R. Foster Kennedy, 1922–1937; R. G. Gordon, 1922–1937; C. Macfie Campbell, 1922–1937; Edwin Bramwell, 1926–1937; A. Feiling, 1926–1937; J. G. Greenfield, 1926–1937; C. C. Worster-Drought, 1926–1937; H. G. Baynes, 1926–1937; William Brown, 1926–1937; R. D. Gillespie, 1926–1937.

402. *Leipzig. Institut des Leipziger Lehrervereins. Pädagogisch-psychologische Arbeiten.*

TITLE VARIATIONS: Continues *Leipzig. Institut für experimentelle Pädagogik und Psychologie des Leipziger Lehrervereins. Veröffentlichungen. Pädagogisch-psychologische Arbeiten.*

DATES OF PUBLICATION: Band 10–20, 1920–1933.

FREQUENCY: Annual (Irregular).

NUMBERING VARIATIONS: Band 19, 20 issued in two parts.

PUBLISHER: **Leipzig:** Verlag der Dürr'schen Buchhandlung, 1920–1933.

PRIMARY EDITORS: **Rudolf Schulze,** 1920–1922; **Max Döring,** 1924–1929; **Felix Schlotte,** 1930–1932; **Johannes Schlag,** 1933.

403. *Nihon Shinrigaku Zasshi.* [Japanese Journal of Psychology.] [*1.*]

TITLE VARIATIONS: Superseded by: Nihon Shinrigaku Zasshi [Japanese Journal of Psychology.] [2.] with Volume 1, 1924.

DATES OF PUBLICATION: Volume 1–3, 1920–1924.

FREQUENCY: Unknown.

NUMBERING VARIATIONS: None.

PUBLISHER: **Kyoto:** Hoshiao Shoten [Hoshiao Bookstore], 1920–1924.

PRIMARY EDITORS: None listed.

NOTE: Information for this entry was obtained from *Gakujutsu Zasshi Sōgō Mokuroku. Jimbun Kagaku Wabun Hen* [Union List of Scholarly Journals. Japanese Language Section. Humanities Part], Tokyo, 1973.

404. *Nordiske Race. Tidsskrift for Racebiologi, Racepsykologi og Racehygiene.*

TITLE VARIATIONS: Subtitle varies slightly.

DATES OF PUBLICATION: Volume 1–10, 1920–1929.

FREQUENCY: **Semiannual,** Volume 1–7, 1920–1926. **Annual,** Volume 8–10, 1927–1929.

NUMBERING VARIATIONS: None.

PUBLISHER: **Oslo, Norway:** Vinderen Laboratorium, 1920–1929.

PRIMARY EDITORS: **Jon Alfred Mjøen,** 1920–1928; **Karl Larsen,** 1920; **Clara Mjøen,** 1929. **Heljar Mjøen,** 1929; **Arvid Brodersen,** 1929.

405. *Psyche and Eros. An International Bi-monthly Journal of Psychoanalysis, Applied Psychology and Psychotherapeutics.*

TITLE VARIATIONS: Subtitle varies. Merged into *Journal of Sexology and Psychoanalysis* with Volume 1, January 1923.

DATES OF PUBLICATION: Volume 1–3, July 1920–May/June 1922.

FREQUENCY: Bimonthly.

NUMBERING VARIATIONS: None.

PUBLISHER: **New York:** Psyche and Eros Publishing Company, 1920–1922.

PRIMARY EDITORS: **Samuel A. Tannenbaum,** 1920–1922; **Charles Baudouin,** 1920–1922; **Ferd. Morel,** 1920; **Éd. Claparède,** 1920; **Herbert Silberer,** 1920–1922; **Wilhelm Stekel,** 1920–1922.

406. *Psychic Research Quarterly.*

TITLE VARIATIONS: Continued by *Psyche. A Quarterly Review of Psychology* with Volume 2, 1921.

DATES OF PUBLICATION: Volume 1, Number 1–4, July 1920–April 1921.

FREQUENCY: Quarterly.

NUMBERING VARIATIONS: None.

PUBLISHER: **London:** Kegan Paul, Trench, Trubner & Co., Ltd., 1920–1921.

PRIMARY EDITORS: None listed.

407. *Psychologie appliquée.*

TITLE VARIATIONS: None.

DATES OF PUBLICATION: Année 1–2, January 1920–December 1921.

FREQUENCY: Monthly.

NUMBERING VARIATIONS: Issues also assigned whole numbers, Numéro 1–12.

PUBLISHER: **Paris:** Rédaction et administration, 4, rue de Castellane, 1920–1921.

PRIMARY EDITORS: **Edgar Bérillon,** 1920–1921; **Paul Farez,** 1920–1921.

408. *Revue de psychologie appliquée. [1.]*

TITLE VARIATIONS: Continues *Revue de psychothérapie et de psychologie ap-*

pliquée. [1]. Continued by *Revue de psychothérapie et de psychologie appliquée* [2] with Série 4, Année 38, January 1929.

DATES OF PUBLICATION: Série 4, Année 30–37, January 1920–December 1928.

FREQUENCY: Monthly.

NUMBERING VARIATIONS: None.

PUBLISHER: **Paris:** Revue de psychologie appliquée, rédaction et administration, 4, rue de Castellane, 1920–1928.

PRIMARY EDITORS: **E. Bérillon,** 1920–1928; **Paul Farez,** 1915–1928.

409. *Studies in Mental Inefficiency.*

TITLE VARIATIONS: Continued by *Mental Welfare* with Volume 6, 1925.

DATES OF PUBLICATION: Volume 1–5, 1920–1924.

FREQUENCY: Quarterly.

NUMBERING VARIATIONS: None.

PUBLISHER: **London:** Central Association for the Care of the Mentally Defective, 1920–1921. **London:** Central Association for Mental Welfare, 1922–1924.

PRIMARY EDITORS: **S. Luce,** 1920–1921; ———— **Welfare,** 1920–1924; **A. L. Hargrove,** 1921–1924; **D. Leburn,** 1923.

410. *Voprosy izucheniia i vospitaniia lichnosti; Pedologiia i defektologiia.*

TITLE VARIATIONS: None.

DATES OF PUBLICATION: Tom 1–10, 1920–1932. Suspended publication 1923–1925.

FREQUENCY: **Irregular,** (5 issues), Tom 1–3, 1920/1922. **Triannual,** Tom 4, Vypusk 1–2/3, 1926. **Quarterly,** Tom 5–6, Vypusk 3/4. 1927–1928. **Bimonthly,** Tom 7, Vypusk 1/2–5/6, 1929. **Irregular,** (4 issues), Tom 8–10, 1930/1932.

NUMBERING VARIATIONS: Volumes are not numbered on title pages. Many multinumber issues.

PUBLISHER: **Leningrad:** Institut po izucheniiu mozga i psikhicheskoi deiatelnosti, 1920–1922. **Leningrad:** Gosudarstvennaia psikho-nevrologicheskaia akademiia, Gosudarstvennyi refleksologicheskii institut po izucheniiu mozga, 1926–1932.

PRIMARY EDITORS: **V. M. Bekhterev,** 1920–1927; **A. S. Griboedov,** 1928–1932; **V. N. Osipova,** 1928–1932.

NOTE: Information on this title was compiled from entries in *Half a Century of Soviet Serials.*

411. *Zurich. Universität. Psychologisches Institut. Veröffentlichungen.*

TITLE VARIATIONS: None.

DATES OF PUBLICATION: Heft 1–11, 1920–1931.

FREQUENCY: Irregular. *See* Contents *below*.

NUMBERING VARIATIONS: None.

PUBLISHER: **Zurich:** Leemann, 1920–1931.

PRIMARY EDITOR: **Gottlob Friedrich Lipps,** 1920–1931.

CONTENTS:

Heft 1. Guyer, Walter. DAS TONERLEBNIS. 1920. 54 pp.

Heft 2. Sidler, Martha. DIE AUFFASSUNG VON BEZIEHUNGEN ZWISCHEN GEGENSTÄNDEN. 1924. 79 pp.

Heft 3. Schweizer, August. DIE MITTENEMPFINDUNG. EINE EXPERIMEN-TELL-PSYCHOLOGISCHE UNTERSUCHUNG. 1926. 47 pp.

Heft 4. Brunner, Sophie. ÜBER DAS VORSTELLUNGSLEBEN DES SCHUL-KINDES. 1926. 74 pp.

Heft 5. Kuhn, Franz. DER SPEZIALKLASSENSCHÜLER. EINE UNTER-SUCHUNG ÜBER DIE GEISTIGE ENTWICKLUNG SCHWACHBEGABTER KINDER. 1927. 87 pp.

Heft 6. Peter, Fritz. ÜBER MODERNE ERZIEHUNGSPRINZIPIEN. 1927. 69 pp.

Heft 7. Farner, Gustav Adolf. DAS ERFASSEN DER WIRKLICHKEIT. EINE EXPERIMENTELL-PSYCHOLOGISCHE UNTERSUCHUNG AUF GRUND VON BIBEL-BETRACHTUNGEN. 1927. 111 pp.

Heft 8. Honegger, Robert. DER BILDUNGSWERT DER MANUELLEN BETÄTIGUNG. 1929. 134 pp.

Heft 9. Scheller, Heinrich. EIN BEITRAG ZUR ERFASSUNG DER PER-SÖNLICHKEIT SCHWERERZIEHBARER KNABEN. 1929. 58 pp.

Heft 10. Surber, Paul. REAKTIONEN AUF SCHALLREIZE. 1930. 49 pp.

Heft 11. Bieri, Ernst. EIN BEITRAG ZUR KENNTNIS DER GEISTIGEN ENT-WICKLUNG DES TAUBSTUMMEN SCHULKINDES (VERGLEICHENDE UNTERSUCHUN-GEN ÜBER DIE ENTWICKLUNG DES VORSTELLUNGLEBENS, DER RAUM-, ZAHL-UND GEGENSTANDSAUFFASUNG BEI TAUBSTUMMEN, PRIMÄR- UND SEKUND-ARSCHÜLERN). 1931. 86 pp.

1921

412. *Archivio generale di neurologia, psichiatria e psicoanalisi.*

TITLE VARIATIONS: Continues *Archivio generale di neurologia e psichiatria.* Superseded by *Archivio di psicologia, neurologia, psichiatria e psicoterapia* with Anno 1, 1939.

DATES OF PUBLICATION: Volume 2–20, June 1921–1938.

FREQUENCY: **Semiannual,** Volume 2, Fascicolo 1–2, June & December 1921. **Annual,** Volume 3–6, 1922–1925. **Quarterly,** Volume 7–19, March 1926–1938. **Irregular,** Volume 20, 1938.

NUMBERING VARIATIONS: None.

PUBLISHER: **Naples:** R. stabilimento tipografico Francesco Giannini & Figli,

1921–1925. **Teramo** (**Abruzzi**): Società anonima tipografica "La Fiorita", 1926–1929. **Naples:** Francesco Giannini & Figli, 1930–1934. **Naples:** Industrie tipografiche editoriali Affini, 1934–1937. **Naples:** Industrie tipografiche editoriali Assimilate, 1938.

PRIMARY EDITOR: **Marco Levi-Bianchini,** 1921–1938.

EDITORIAL BOARD: G. Antonini, 1921–1922; C. Colucci, 1921; S. de Sanctis, 1921–1935; E. La Pegna, 1921; E. Medea, 1921; G. Mingazzini, 1921–1929; G. Modena, 1921–1922; G. Volpi Ghirardini, 1921–1922; D. Ventra, 1921; L. Zanon Del Bo, 1921–1922; C. Frank, 1922; L. De Lisi, 1930–1938; O. Rossi, 1936; U. Cerletti, 1937–1938.

413. *Beiträge zur Pädagogik und Psychologie.*

TITLE VARIATIONS: None.

DATES OF PUBLICATION: Heft 1–12, 1921–1931.

FREQUENCY: Irregular. *See* Contents *below.*

NUMBERING VARIATIONS: Also numbered as *Friedrich Manns pädagogisches Magazin. See* Contents *below.*

PUBLISHER: **Langensalza, Germany:** Hermann Beyer & Söhne (Beyer & Mann), 1921–1931.

PRIMARY EDITOR: **G. F. Lipps,** 1921–1931.

CONTENTS:

Heft 1. Mladenowitsch, Woj. R. ÜBER DIE GRUNDLAGE DER ERZIEHUNGS-LEHRE. 1921. 104 pp. (Also as *Friedrich Manns pädagogisches Magazin,* Heft 846.)

Heft 2. Beyme, Marie. DIE STROBOSKOPISCHEN ERSCHEINUNGEN. 1922. 78 pp. (Also as *Friedrich Manns pädagogisches Magazin,* Heft 855.)

Heft 3. Lee, Kwanyong. DAS WOLLEN, ALS GRUNDTATSACHE DES BEWUSSTSEINS. 1922. (89) pp. (Also as *Friedrich Manns pädagogisches Magazin,* Heft 869.)

Heft 4. Simmen, Martin. VOLKSSCHULE UND HANDARBEIT. 1922. 83 pp. (Also as *Friedrich Manns Pädagogisches Magazin,* Heft 883.)

Heft 5. Witzig, Jean. MASS UND ZAHL IM BEREICHE DER LEBENSERSCHEI-NUNGEN. 1924. 118 pp. (Also as *Friedrich Manns pädagogisches Magazin,* Heft 936.)

Heft 6. Leemann, Lydia. DIE SITTLICHE ENTWICKLUNG DES SCHUL-KINDES. 1923. 124 pp. (Also as *Friedrich Manns pädagogisches Magazin,* Heft 937.)

Heft 7. Schälchlin, Hans. ÜBER DIE BEWUSSTSEINSTÄTIGKEIT BEI DER AUF-FASUNG VOM NATURVORGÄNGEN. 1923. 83 pp. (Also as *Friedrich Manns pädagogisches Magazin,* Heft 943.)

Heft 8. Bell, Emil. BEITRÄGE ZUR THEORIE DER KOLLEKTIVGEGENSTÄNDE. 1923. 67 pp. (Also as *Friedrich Manns pädagogisches Magazin,* Heft 961.)

Heft 9. Camenzind, Clara. DIE ANTIKE UND MODERNE AUFFASUNG VOM NATURGESCHEHEN. 1926. 83 pp. (Also as *Friedrich Manns pädagogisches Magazin,* Heft 1067.)

Heft 10. Göpfert, Christian. Üeber Binet-Simon-Teste. 1927. 88 pp. (Also as *Friedrich Manns pädagogisches Magazin,* Heft 1116.)

Heft 11. Witzig, Jean. Der Entwicklungsgedanke bei Pestalossi. 1929. 134 pp. (Also numbered as *Friedrich Manns pädagogisches Magazin,* Heft 1236.)

Heft 12. Dorosz, Hedwig. Grundlegung der Ästhetik. 1931. 74 pp. (Also as *Friedrich Manns pädagogisches Magazin,* Heft 1348.)

414. *Central Association for Mental Welfare. Report.*

TITLE VARIATIONS: Continues *Central Association for the Care of the Mentally Defective. Report.*

DATES OF PUBLICATION: 8th–22nd, 1921/1922–1935/1936.

FREQUENCY: Annual.

NUMBERING VARIATIONS: None.

PUBLISHER: **London:** Central Association for Mental Welfare, 1922–1936.

PRIMARY EDITOR: Secretary acted as editor.

415. *Encéphale; journal de neurologie et de psychiatrie.* [*1.*]

TITLE VARIATIONS: Continues *Encéphale; journal mensuel de neurologie et de psychiatrie.* Continued by *Encéphale; journal de neurologie, de psychiatrie, de biologie et de physiologie pathologique du système nerveux* with Année 20, 1925.

DATES OF PUBLICATION: Année 16–19, 1921–1924.

FREQUENCY: Monthly (except July/August and September/October).

NUMBERING VARIATIONS: None.

PUBLISHER: **Paris:** H. Delarue, Libraire-éditeur, 1921–1924.

PRIMARY EDITORS: **A. Antheaume,** 1921–1924; **Henri Claude,** 1921–1924.

EDITORIAL BOARD: J. Abadie, 1921–1924; R. Cestan, 1921–1924; Mme. Dejerine, 1921–1924; G. Deny, 1921–1922; E. Dupré, 1921–1922; G. Étienne, 1921–1924; J. Froment, 1921–1924; M. Klippel, 1921–1924; M. Laignel-Lavastine, 1921–1924; J. Lépine, 1921–1924; J. Lhermitte, 1921–1924; G. Raviart, 1921–1924; Rogues de Fursac, 1921–1924; P. Sainton, 1921–1924; J. Séglas, 1921–1924; P. Sérieux, 1921–1924; J Sicard, 1921–1924; A. André-Thomas, 1921–1924; Ch. Vallon, 1921–1924; H. Verger, 1921–1924; J. Euzière, 1922–1924; A. Hesnard, 1922–1924; R. Mignot, 1922–1924; E. Toulouse, 1922–1924; L. Bour, 1922–1923; H. Roger, 1923–1924; J. Roubinovitch, 1923–1924; G. Guillain, 1924; J. Lévi-Valensi, 1924.

416. *International Association of Applied Psychology. Congress. Proceedings.*

TITLE VARIATIONS: Variations are by language of publication.

DATES OF PUBLICATION: 2nd–9th +, 1921–1950 +.

FREQUENCY: Irregular. *See* Contents *below.*

NUMBERING VARIATIONS: None.

PUBLISHER: Varies: *See* Contents *below.*

PRIMARY EDITORS: Varies. Usually none listed. *See* Contents *below.*

CONTENTS:

2nd. BARCELONA, 1921. SEGONA CONFERÈNCIA INTERNACIONAL DE PSI-COTÈCNICA APLICADA A L'ORIENTACIÓ PROFESSIONAL I A L'ORGANITZACIÓ CIENTÍFICA DEL TREBALL. Barcelona: Institut d'Orientació Professional, 1922. 419 pp.

3rd. MILAN, 1922. ATTI DELLA III CONFERENZA INTERNAZIONALE DI PSI-COTECNICA APPLICATA ALL'ORIENTAMENTO PROFESSIONALE, MILANO, 2–3–4 OT-TOBRE 1922. Milano: Societa umanitaria, 1923. 255 pp.

4th. PARIS, 1927. COMPTES RENDUS DE LA IVme CONFÉRENCE INTERNA-TIONALE DE PSYCHOTECHNIQUE, PARIS, INSTITUT INTERNATIONAL DE COOPÉRATION INTELLECTUELLE, 10–14 OCTOBRE 1927. Paris: Felix Alcan, 1929. 686 pp.

5th. UTRECHT, 1928. COMPTES RENDUS DE LA CINQUIÈME CONFÉRENCE INTERNATIONALE DE PSYCHOTECHNIQUE TENU À UTRECHT DU 10 AU 14 SEP-TEMBRE 1928, SOUS LA PRÉSIDENCE DE F. ROELS. Publiés par le comité national. Utrecht-Nijmegen: N. V. Dekker & v.d. Vegt & J. W. van Leeuwen, n.d. 318 pp.

6th. BARCELONA, 1930. VIA CONFERÈNCIA INTERNACIONAL DE PSICOTÈCNICA (RECULL DELS TREBALLS PRESENTATS), 26–30 ABRIL 1930. Barcelona: Escola del treball, n.d. 362 pp.

7th. MOSCOW, 1931. 7-ÈME CONFÉRENCE INTERNATIONALE DE PSYCHO-TECHNIQUE, MOSCOU, LE 8–13 SEPTEMBRE 1931. Résumés des rapports. Mos-cow: Édition d'état de littérature économique-sociale, 1931. n.p.

8th. PRAGUE, 1934. VIIIe CONFÉRENCE INTERNATIONALE DE PSYCHO-TECHNIQUE. COMPTES RENDUS. Publiés par le comité national d'organisation. Prague: Librairie dépositaire "Orbis," 1935. 863 pp.

9th. BERN, 1949. LA PSYCHOTECHNIQUE DANS LE MONDE MODERNE. COMPTE RENDU DU IXe CONGRES INTERNATIONALE DE PSYCHOTECHNIQUE, BERNE, 12–17 SEPTEMBRE 1949. Edited by Franziska Baumgarten. Paris: Presses universitaires de France, 1952. 630 pp.

417. *International Psycho-Analytical Library.*

TITLE VARIATIONS: None.

DATES OF PUBLICATION: Number 1–37+, 1921–1950+.

FREQUENCY: Irregular. *See* Contents *below.*

NUMBERING VARIATIONS: None.

PUBLISHER: **London:** Hogarth Press for the Institute of Psycho-Analysis, 1921–1950+.

PRIMARY EDITOR: **Ernest Jones,** 1921–1950+

CONTENTS:

Number 1. Putnam, J. J. ADDRESSES ON PSYCHO-ANALYSIS. 1921. 470 pp.

Number 2. Ferenczi, Sandor et al. PSYCHO-ANALYSIS AND THE WAR NEUROSES. 1921. 59 pp.

Number 3. Flugel, J. C. THE PSYCHO-ANALYTIC STUDY OF THE FAMILY. 1921. 259 pp.

Number 4. Freud, Sigmund. BEYOND THE PLEASURE PRINCIPLE. 1922. 90 pp.

Number 5. Jones, Ernest. ESSAYS IN APPLIED PSYCHO-ANALYSIS. 1923. 454 pp.

Number 6. Freud, Sigmund. GROUP PSYCHOLOGY AND THE ANALYSIS OF THE EGO. 1922. 134 pp.

Number 7. Freud, Sigmund. COLLECTED PAPERS. VOLUME I. 1924. 359 pp.

Number 8. Freud, Sigmund. COLLECTED PAPERS. VOLUME II. 1924. 404 pp.

Number 9. Freud, Sigmund. COLLECTED PAPERS. VOLUME III. 1925. 607 pp.

Number 10. Freud, Sigmund. COLLECTED PAPERS. VOLUME IV. 1924. 508 pp.

Number 11. Ferenczi, Sandor. FURTHER CONTRIBUTIONS TO THE THEORY AND TECHNIQUE OF PSYCHO-ANALYSIS. 1927. 473 pp.

Number 12. Freud, Sigmund. THE EGO AND THE ID. 1927. 88 pp.

Number 13. Abraham, Karl. SELECTED PAPERS. 1927. 527 pp.

Number 14. Rickman, John. INDEX PSYCHO-ANALYTICUS, 1893–1926. 1928. 276 pp.

Number 15. Freud, Sigmund. THE FUTURE OF AN ILLUSION. 1928. 98 pp.

Number 16. Money-Kyrle, R. THE MEANING OF SACRIFICE. 1930. 273 pp.

Number 17. Freud, Sigmund. CIVILIZATION AND ITS DISCONTENTS. 1930. 114 pp.

Number 18. Flugel, J. C. THE PSYCHOLOGY OF CLOTHES. 1930. 256 pp.

Number 19. Reik, Theodor. RITUAL. Preface by Sigmund Freud. 1931. 367 pp.

Number 20. Jones, Ernest. ON THE NIGHTMARE. 1931. 374 pp.

Number 21. Laforgue, Rene. THE DEFEAT OF BAUDELAIRE. 1932. 192 pp.

Number 22. Klein, Melanie. THE PSYCHO-ANALYSIS OF CHILDREN. 1932. 393 pp.

Number 23. Deutsch, Helene. THE PSYCHO-ANALYSIS OF THE NEUROSES. 1932. 239 pp.

Number 24. Freud, Sigmund. NEW INTRODUCTORY LECTURES ON PSYCHO-ANALYSIS. 1933. 240 pp.

Number 25. Roheim, Geza. THE RIDDLE OF THE SPHINX. 1934. 302 pp.

Number 26. Freud, Sigmund. AN AUTOBIOGRAPHICAL STUDY. 1935. 153 pp.

Number 27. Reik, Theodor. THE UNKNOWN MURDERER. 1936. 260 pp.

Number 28. Freud, Sigmund. INHIBITIONS, SYMPTOMS, AND ANXIETY. 1936. 179 pp.

Number 29. Sharpe, Ella. DREAM ANALYSIS. 1938. 211 pp.

Number 30. Freud, Anna. THE EGO AND THE MECHANISMS OF DEFENCE. 1937. 196 pp.

Number 31. Laforgue, Rene. CLINICAL ASPECTS OF PSYCHO-ANALYSIS. 1938. 300 pp.

Number 32. Reik, Theodor. FROM THIRTY YEARS WITH FREUD. 1940. 241 pp.

Number 33. Freud, Sigmund. MOSES AND MONOTHEISM. 1939. 218 pp.

Number 34. Klein, Melanie. CONTRIBUTIONS TO PSYCHO-ANALYSIS, 1921–1945. 1948. 416 pp.

Number 35. Freud, Sigmund. OUTLINE OF PSYCHO-ANALYSIS. 1949. 127 pp.

Number 36. Sharpe, E.la Freeman. COLLECTED PAPERS IN PSYCHO-ANALYSIS. 1950. 280 pp.

Number 37. Freud, Sigmund. COLLECTED PAPERS. Volume V. 1950. 396 pp.

418. *Journal of Abnormal Psychology and Social Psychology.*

TITLE VARIATIONS: Continues *Journal of Abnormal Psychology.* Continued by *Journal of Abnormal and Social Psychology* with Volume 20, 1925.

DATES OF PUBLICATION: Volume 16–19, 1921–1925.

FREQUENCY: **Bimonthly,** Volume 16, April 1921–December/March 1921/1922. **Quarterly,** Volume 17–19, April 1922–January/March 1925.

NUMBERING VARIATIONS: Volume 16, Number 2/3, 5/6, 1921 are double numbers.

PUBLISHER: **Boston:** Richard G. Badger, The Gorham Press, 1921–1922. **Albany, New York:** Boyd Printing Company, Inc., 1922–1925.

PRIMARY EDITORS: **Morton Prince,** 1921–1925; **Floyd H. Allport,** 1921–1925; **Adolf Meyer,** 1921–1925; **Boris Sidis,** 1921–1923; **William McDougall,** 1921–1925; **Charles L. Dana,** 1921–1925; **J. Ramsay Hunt,** 1921–1925.

419. *Journal of Comparative Psychology.*

TITLE VARIATIONS: Formed by the union of *Psychobiology* and *Journal of Animal Behavior.* Continued by *Journal of Comparative and Physiological Psychology* with Volume 40, 1947.

DATES OF PUBLICATION: Volume 1–39, 1921–1946.

FREQUENCY: Bimonthly.

NUMBERING VARIATIONS: Double number in Volume 4. Volume 8 has issues 1–5. Published in 3 volumes of 4 issues each per 2-year period, 1930–1931, and 2 volumes of 3 issues each per year, 1932–1943.

PUBLISHER: **Baltimore:** Williams and Wilkins Company, 1921–1946.

PRIMARY EDITORS: **Knight Dunlap,** 1921–1943; **Robert M. Yerkes,** 1921–1943; **Roy M. Dorcus,** 1936–1946.

420. *Journal of Educational Psychology; Devoted Primarily to the Scientific Study of Problems of Learning and Teaching.*

TITLE VARIATIONS: Continues *Journal of Educational Psychology; Including*

Experimental Pedagogy, Child Physiology and Hygiene, and Educational Statistics.

DATES OF PUBLICATION: Volume 12–41+, 1921–1950+.

FREQUENCY: Monthly (except June-August).

NUMBERING VARIATIONS: None.

PUBLISHER: **York, Pennsylvania** and **Baltimore:** Warwick and York, Inc., 1921–1928. **Baltimore:** Warwick and York, Inc., 1929–1950+.

PRIMARY EDITORS: **Harold Ordway Rugg,** 1921–1932; **Jack W. Dunlap,** 1933–1945; **Harold E. Jones, 1933–1939; Percival M. Symonds,** 1933–1939; none listed, 1946–1950+. *See* Note *below.*

EDITORIAL BOARD: James Carleton Bell, 1921–1933; Frank Nugent Freeman, 1921–1933; Arthur Irving Gates, 1921–1933; Vivian Allen Charles Henmon, 1921–1933; Rudolf Pintner, 1921–1933; Beardsley Ruml, 1921–1932; Lewis Madison Terman, 1921–1933; Edward Lee Thorndike, 1921–1933; Harold Ordway Rugg, 1933; Laura Zirbes (Assistant Editor), 1921–1924; H. E. Buchholz (Managing Editor), 1933–1950+; Goodwin B. Watson, 1933; Stephen M. Corey, 1940–1950+; John G. Darley, 1940–1948; Jack W. Dunlap, 1946–1950+; Bertha Peterson Harper, 1943–1948; Harold E. Jones, 1940–1950+; H. H. Remmers, 1940–1950+; Percival M. Symonds, 1940–1950+; Paul A. Witty, 1940–1950+; Karl J. Holzinger, 1949–1950+; Robert T. Rock, Jr., 1949; Miles A. Tinker, 1949–1950+; Alexander G. Wesman, 1949–1950+; J. B. Stroud, 1950+.

NOTE: From 1946–1950+, editorial direction was provided by the editorial board. No member of the board is listed as chairman for this period.

421. *Journal of Educational Research. Monographs.*

TITLE VARIATIONS: Continued by *Educational Research Monographs* with Number 9, 1927.

DATES OF PUBLICATION: Number 1–8, 1921–1925.

FREQUENCY: Irregular. *See* Contents *below.*

NUMBERING VARIATIONS: None.

PUBLISHER: **Bloomington, Illinois:** Public School Publishing Company, 1921–1925.

PRIMARY EDITOR: **B. R. Buckingham,** 1921–1925.

CONTENTS:

Number 1. Proctor, William Martin. THE USE OF PSYCHOLOGICAL TESTS IN THE EDUCATIONAL AND VOCATIONAL GUIDANCE OF HIGH SCHOOL PUPILS. June, 1921. 70 pp.

Number 2. Yates, Dorothy Hazeltine. A STUDY OF SOME HIGH SCHOOL SENIORS OF SUPERIOR INTELLIGENCE. June, 1922. 75 pp.

Number 3. Ashbaugh, Ernest J. THE IOWA SPELLING SCALES. THEIR DERIVATION, USES, AND LIMITATIONS. June, 1922. 144 pp.

Number 4. Stevenson, P. R. SMALLER CLASSES OR LARGER. A STUDY OF
THE RELATION OF CLASS-SIZE TO THE EFFICIENCY OF TEACHING. 1923. 127 pp.

Number 5. Hansen, Allen Oscar. EARLY EDUCATIONAL LEADERSHIP IN
THE OHIO VALLEY. A STUDY OF EDUCATIONAL RECONSTRUCTION THROUGH THE
WESTERN LITERARY INSTITUTE AND COLLEGE OF PROFESSIONAL TEACHERS,
1829–1841. 1923. 120 pp.

Number 6. Whitney, Frederick Lamson. THE PREDICTION OF TEACHING
SUCCESS. 1924. 85 pp.

Number 7. Coxe, Warren W. THE INFLUENCE OF LATIN ON THE SPELLING
OF ENGLISH WORDS. 1924. 122 pp.

Number 8. Winch, W. H. TEACHING BEGINNERS TO READ IN ENGLAND:
ITS METHODS, RESULTS, AND PSYCHOLOGICAL BASES. 1925. 185 pp.

422. *Journal of Philosophy.*

TITLE VARIATIONS: Continues *Journal of Philosophy, Psychology and Scientific Methods.*

DATES OF PUBLICATION: Volume 18–47+, 1921–1950+.

FREQUENCY: Biweekly.

NUMBERING VARIATIONS: Volume 31–33, Numbers 17–18, are joint issues
containing a Bibliography of Philosophy, 1933–1935. Volume 34, Number
16–17, contains Bibliography of Philosophy, 1936.

PUBLISHER: **Lancaster, Pennsylvania:** Press of the New Era Printing Company for the Journal of Philosophy, Inc., New York, 1921–1950+.

PRIMARY EDITORS: **Frederick J. E. Woodbridge,** 1921–1940; **Wendell T.
Bush,** 1921–1941; **Herbert W. Schneider,** 1925–1950+; **John H. Randall, Jr.,**
1938–1950+; **Ernest Nagel,** 1940–1950+.

423. *Leipzig. Sächsische staatliche Forschungsinstitute. Forschungsinstitut für Psychologie. Abhandlungen.*

TITLE VARIATIONS: Continues: *Leipzig. Sächsische staatliche Forschungsinstitute. Forschungsinstitut für Psychologie. Veröffentlichungen.*

DATES OF PUBLICATION: Stück 6–67, 1921–1936.

FREQUENCY: Irregular. *See* Contents *below.*

NUMBERING VARIATIONS: Also numbered as *Arbeiten zur Entwicklungs-Psychologie;* and as *Neue psychologische Studien. See* Contents *below.* Issues crossnumbered in *Neue psychologische Studien* are gathered in volumes with volume
editors. [See entry number 538.] Stück 55 and 65 incorrectly repeated in numbering.

PUBLISHER: **Leipzig:** Wilhelm Engelmann, 1921. **Munich:** C. H. Beck'sche
Verlagsbuchhandlung, 1926–1936.

PRIMARY EDITOR: **Felix Krueger,** 1921–1936.

CONTENTS:
Stück 6. Freyer, Hans. DIE BEWERTUNG DER WIRTSCHAFT IM PHILO-

SOPHISCHEN DENKEN DES 19. JAHRHUNDERTS. 1921. 171 pp. (Also as *Arbeiten zur Entwicklungs-Psychologie*, Stück 5, 1921, 171 pp.)

Stück 7. Gutmann, Bruno. DAS RECHT DER DSCHAGGA; and, Krueger, Felix. ZUR ENTWICKLUNGSPSYCHOLOGIE DES RECHTS. NACHWORT. 1926. 778 pp. (Also as *Arbeiten zur Entwicklungs-Psychologie*, Stück 7, 1926, 778 pp.)

Stück 8. Krueger, Felix. ZUR EINFÜHRUNG. ÜBER PSYCHISCHE GANZHEIT. 1926. 122 pp. (Also as *Neue psychologische Studien*, Band 1, Heft 1, 1926, pp. 1–122.)

Stück 9. Sander, Friedrich. ÜBER RÄUMLICHE RHYTHMIK. EXPERIMENTELLE UNTERSUCHUNGEN ÜBER RHYTHMUSARTIGE REIHEN- UND GRUPPENBILDUNGEN BEI SIMULTANEN GESICHTSEINDRÜCKEN. 1926. 36 pp. (Also as *Neue psychologische Studien*, Band 1, Heft 2, 1926, pp. 123–158.)

Stück 10. Sander, Friedrich. OPTISCHE TÄUSCHUNGEN UND PSYCHOLOGIE. 1926. 8 pp. (Also as *Neue psychologische Studien*, Band 1, Heft 2, 1926, pp. 159–166.)

Stück 11. Ipsen, Gunther. ÜBER GESTALTAUFFASSUNG. ERÖRTERUNG DES SANDERSCHEN PARALLELOGRAMMS. 1926. 112 pp. (Also as *Neue psychologische Studien*, Band 1, Heft 2, 1926, pp. 167–278.)

Stück 12. Ipsen, Gunther. ZUR THEORIE DES ERKENNENS. UNTERSUCHUNGEN ÜBER GESTALT UND SINN SINNLOSER WÖRTER. 1926. 14 pp. (Also as *Neue psychologische Studien*, Band 1, Heft 3, 1926, pp. 279–292.)

Stück 13. Herrmann, Johannes. GESAMTERLEBNISSE BEI GERÜCHEN. 1926. 34 pp. (Also as *Neue psychologische Studien*, Band 1, Heft 4, 1926, pp. 473–506.)

Stück 14. Würdemann, Wilhelm. ÜBER DIE BEDEUTUNG DES GEFÜHLS FÜR DAS BEHALTEN UND ERINNERN. 1926. 66 pp. (Also as *Neue psychologische Studien*, Band 1, Heft 4, 1926, pp. 507–572.)

Stück 15. Lenk, Erhard. ÜBER DIE OPTISCHE AUFFASSUNG GEOMETRISCH-REGELMÄSSIGER GESTALTEN. 1926. 40 pp. (Also as *Neue psychologische Studien*, Band 1, Heft 4, 1926, pp. 573–612.)

Stück 16. Rudert, Johannes. KASUISTISCHER BEITRAG ZUR LEHRE VON DER FUNKTIONELLEN ASYMMETRIE DER GROSSHIRNHEMISPHÄREN. 1926. 80 pp. (Also as *Neue psychologische Studien*, Band 1, Heft 4, 1926, pp. 613–692.)

Stück 17. Bergfeld, Emil. DIE STRECKENEINTEILUNG UND DIE GEBRÄUCHLICHSTEN ZAHLENSYSTEME. NEUE VERSUCHE ZUR DEZIMALGLEICHUNG. 1926. 46 pp. (Also as *Neue psychologische Studien*, Band 2, Heft 1, 1926, pp. 15–60.)

Stück 18. Schjelderup-Ebbe, Thorleif. DER KONTRAST AUF DEM GEBIETE DES LICHT- UND FARBENSINNS. I. TEIL. 1926. 65 pp. (Also as *Neue psychologische Studien*, Band 2, Heft 1, 1926, pp. 61–126.)

Stück 19. Kirschmann, August. FARBENTERMINOLOGIE. 1926. 12 pp. (Also as *Neue psychologische Studien*, Band 2, Heft 2, 1926, pp. 127–138.)

Stück 20. Donath, Friedrich. DIE FUNKTIONALE ABHÄNGIGKEIT ZWISCHEN REIZ UND EMPFINDUNG BEI DER FARBENSÄTTIGUNG. 1926. 70 pp. (Also as *Neue psychologische Studien*, Band 2, Heft 2, 1926, pp. 139–208.)

Stück 21. Ehrler, Fritz. ÜBER DAS FARBENGEDÄCHTNIS UND SEINE BEZIEHUNGEN ZUR ATELIER- UND FREILICHTMALEREI. 1926. 10 pp. (Also as *Neue psychologische Studien*, Band 2, Heft 2, 1926, pp. 209–308.)

423. *(Continued)*

Stück 22. Weissenborn, Friedrich. DIE LAGE DER QUALITÄTEN IM FAR-
BENKREIS UND IHRE KOMPLEMENTÄRVERHÄLTNISSE, NACH DER SCHWELLEN-
METHODE UNTERSUCHT. 1926. 34 pp. (Also as *Neue psychologische Studien*,
Band 2, Heft 3, 1926, pp. 309–342.)

Stück 23. Fiedler, Kurt. DAS SCHWARZ-WEISS-PROBLEM. 1926. 68 pp.
(Also as *Neue psychologische Studien*, Band 2, Heft 3, 1926, pp. 343–410.)

Stück 24. Kirschmann, August. DAS UMGEKEHRTE SPEKTRUM UND SEINE
FARBEN SOWIE SEINE BEDEUTUNG FÜR DIE OPTISCHE WISSENSCHAFT. 1926. 32
pp. (Also as *Neue psychologische Studien*, Band 2, Heft 3, 1926, pp. 411–442.)

Stück 25. Buchholz, Heinrich. DAS PROBLEM DER KONTINUITÄT. 1927. 110
pp. (Also as *Neue psychologische Studien*, Band 3, Heft 1, 1927, pp. 1–110.)

Stück 26. Buchholz, Heinrich. DIE UNMÖGLICHKEIT ABSOLUTER ME-
TRISCHER PRÄZISION UND DIE ERKENNTNISTHEORETISCHEN KONSEQUENZEN
DIESER UNMÖGLICHKEIT. 1927. 23 pp. (Also as *Neue psychologische Studien*,
Band 3, Heft 1, 1927, pp. 111–133.)

Stück 27. Bergfeld, Emil. DIE AXIOME DER EUKLIDISCHEN GEOMETRIE
PSYCHOLOGISCH UND ERKENNTNISTHEORETISCH UNTERSUCHT. 1927. 84 pp. (Also
as *Neue psychologische Studien*, Band 3, Heft 2, 1927, pp. 135–218.)

Stück 28. Wundt, Eleonore. WILHELM WUNDTS WERKE. 1927. 77 pp.

Stück 29. Fischer, Hugo. HEGELS METHODE IN IHRER IDEENGESCHICHT-
LICHEN NOTWENDIGKEIT. 1928. 335 pp.

Stück 30. Lippert, Elisabeth. UNTERSCHIEDSEMPFINDLICHKEIT BEI MO-
TORISCHEN GESTALTBILDUNGEN DES ARMES. 1928. 84 pp. (Also as *Neue psychologische Studien*, Band 4, Heft 1, 1928, pp. 1–84.)

Stück 31. Schneider, Carl. UNTERSUCHUNGEN ÜBER DIE UNTERSCHIEDS-
EMPFINDLICHKEIT VERSCHIEDEN GEGLIEDERTER OPTISCHER GESTALTEN. 1928.
75 pp. (Also as *Neue psychologische Studien*, Band 4, Heft 1, 1928, pp. 85–159.)

Stück 32. Fischer, Hugo. ERLEBNIS UND METAPHYSIK. ZUR PSYCHOLOGIE
DES METAPHYSISCHEN SCHAFFENS. 1928. 222 pp. (Also as *Neue psychologische
Studien*, Band 3, Heft 3, 1928, pp. 219–440.)

Stück 33. Weidauer, Friedrich. ZUR SYLLOGISTIK. 1928. 204 pp. (Also as
Neue psychologische Studien, Band 3, Heft 4, 1928, pp. 441–644.)

Stück 34. Klemm, Otto. ERFAHRUNGEN BEI EINER EIGNUNGSPRÜFUNG AN
KRIMINALBEAMTEN; Klemm, Otto. ZUFALL ODER GESCHICKLICHKEIT?;
Benscher, Ilse. ZUR PSYCHOLOGIE DES GEDANKENLESENS; Klemm, Otto. ÜBER
DIE ATMUNGSSYMPTOMATIK BEI UNTERSUCHUNGSGEFANGENEN; and Klemm,
Otto. DUNKLES BEIM HELLSEHEN. 1929. 142 pp. (Also as *Neue psychologische
Studien*, Band 5, Heft 1, 1929, pp. 1–142.)

Stück 35. Klemm, Otto. GEDANKEN ÜBER LEIBESÜBUNGEN; Benscher,
Ilse, and Otto Klemm. KORRELATIONSTHEORETISCHES ZUR GANZHEIT; Tauscher,
Erwin. ÜBER DIE KORRELATION ZWISCHEN HANDGESCHICKLICHKEIT UND
INTELLIGENZ; Ulbricht, Oswald. ÜBER DIE OPTIMALEN BEDINGUNGEN BEI DER
ARBEIT AN DREHKURBELN; Doležal, Jan. ÜBER DIE BEWEGUNGSFORM BEI DER
ARBEIT AN DREHKURBELN; and Wilsdorf, Otto-Hermann. GRIFFSTUDIEN AN DER
SPULMASCHINE. 1930. 326 pp. (Also as *Neue psychologische Studien*, Band 5,
Heft 2, 1930, pp. 145–470.)

Stück 36. Biemüller, Wilhelm. Wiedergabe der Gliederanzahl und Gliederungsform optischer Komplexe; and Heiss, Alfred. Zum Problem der isolierenden Abstraktion. Genetisch vergleichende Studien. 1930. 157 pp. (Also as *Neue psychologische Studien*, Band 4, Heft 2, 1930, pp. 161–318.)

Stück 37. Gantschewa, Sdrawka. Kinderplastik drei-bis sechsjähriger. Experimentalpsychologisch untersucht. 1930. 132 pp. (Also as *Arbeiten zur Entwicklungs-Psychologie*, Stück 8, 1930.)

Stück 38. Leitner, Hans. Psychologie jugendlicher Religiosität innerhalb des deutschen Methodismus. 1930. 142 pp. (Also as *Arbeiten zur Entwicklungs-Psychologie*, Stück 9, 1930.)

Stück 39. Podestà, Hans. Beiträge zur Systematik der Farbenempfindungen; Gebhardt, Martin. Goethe und das umgekehrte Spektrum; Weissenborn, Fritz. August Kirschmanns schiefer Farbenkegel, verglichen mit einigen vorher und nachher entstandenen Farbensystemen; and, Kiesow, Friedrich. Über die Entstehung der Braunempfindung. 1930. 130 pp. (Also as *Neue psychologische Studien*, Band 6, Heft 1, 1930, pp. 1–130.)

Stück 40. Schwarz, Georg. Über konzentrische Gesichtsfeldeinengung bei psychisch Normalen. 1930. 122 pp. (Also as *Neue psychologische Studien*, Band 6, Heft 2, 1930, pp. 131–252.)

Stück 41. Heuss, Eugen. Zur Metaphysik des Lichtes; Wirth, Wilhelm. Die Konstanz des üblichen Masses für den simultanen Helligkeitskontrast; Rüssel, Arnulf. Über Helligkeitskonstanz der Sehdinge; Angyal, Andreas. Die Lagebeharrung der optisch vorgestellten räumlichen Umgebung; Grund, Erich. Das Lesen des Wortanfanges bei Volksschulkindern verschiedener Altersstufen. Tachistoskopisch untersucht; Schneider, Karl Max. Beobachtungen über die Pupillengestalt bei einigen lebenden Säugetieren. 1930. 104 pp. (Also as *Neue psychologische Studien*, Band 6, Heft 3, 1930, pp. 253–356.)

Stück 42. Du Preez, Nicolaas. Beiträge zur Eignungsprüfung für den Lenkerberuf; Ehrhardt, Adolf. Das Ranschburgsche Phänomen bei Reaktionsbewegungen; and Herrmann, Johannes. Die Bedeutung der persönlichen Gleichung für die Lenkertätigkeit. Mit einem Beitrag zur Theorie der Zeitverschiebungen. 1931. 124 pp. (Also as *Neue psychologische Studien*, Band 5, Heft 3, 1931, pp. 347–470.)

Stück 43. Rüssel, Arnulf. Über Formauffassung zwei- bis fünfjähriger Kinder. 1931. 108 pp. (Also as *Neue psychologische Studien*, Band 7, Heft 1, 1931, pp. 1–108.)

Stück 44. Röttger, Fritz. Phonetische Gestaltbildung bei jungen Kindern. 1931. 218 pp. (Also as *Arbeiten zur Entwicklungs-Psychologie*, Stück 10, 1931.)

Stück 45. Vidor, Martha. Was ist Musikalität? Experimentell-psychologische Versuche. 1931. 57 pp. (Also as *Arbeiten zur Entwicklungs-Psychologie*, Stück 11, 1931.)

Stück 46. Klemm, Otto. Die binokulare Zeitparallaxe; Durckheim, Graf Karlfried von. Untersuchungen zum gelebten Raum (Erlebniswirklichkeit und ihr Verständnis. Systematische Untersuchungen II); and

423. *(Continued)*

Krueger, Felix. August Kirschmann. 1932. 157 pp. (Also as *Neue psychologische Studien*, Band 6, Heft 4, 1932, pp. 357–513.)

Stück 47. Gutmann, Bruno. Die Stammeslehren der Dschagga, I. Band: Die Lehren vor der Beschneidung. Der Haingang (Lagergemeinschaft nach der Beschneidung). 1932. 671 pp. (Also as *Arbeiten zur Entwicklungs-Psychologie*, Stück 12, 1932.)

Stück 48. Sander, Friedrich. Gestaltpsychologie und Kunsttheorie. Ein Beitrag zur Psychologie architektonischer Gestalten; and Wohlfahrt, Erich. Der Auffassungsvorgang an kleinen Gestalten. Ein Beitrag zur Psychologie des Vorgestalterlebnisses. 1932. 96 pp. (Also as *Neue psychologische Studien*, Band 4, Heft 3, 1932, pp. 319–414.)

Stück 49. Voigt, Erich. Über den Aufbau von Bewegungsgestalten; and Haferkorn, Walter. Über die zeitliche Eingliederung von Willkürbewegungen. 1933. 63 pp. (Also as *Neue psychologische Studien*, Band 9, Heft 1, 1933, pp. 1–63.)

Stück 50. Müssler, Marianne. Das Bauen des Kindes mit zweifarbigem Material. 1933. 124 pp. (Also as *Neue psychologische Studien*, Band 8, Heft 1, 1933, pp. 1–124.)

Stück 51. Kern, Gerhard. Motorische Umreissung optischer Gestalten; Stimpel, Edmund. Der Wurf; and Drill, Rudolf. Der Hammerschlag. 1933. 144 pp. (Also as *Neue psychologische Studien*, Band 9, Heft 2, 1933, pp. 65–208.)

Stück 52. Riedel, Gerhard. Über die Abhängigkeit optischer Kontraste von Gestaltbedingungen; Kunz-Henriquez, Guillermina. Über die Änderungsempfindlichkeit für optische Gestalten; and Viergutz, Felix. Das Beschreiben. Experimentelle Untersuchung des Beschreibens von Gegenständen. 1933. 194 pp. (Also as *Neue psychologische Studien*, Band 10, Heft 1 & 2, 1933, 102 pp., 92 pp.)

Stück 53. Haubold, Marianne. Bildbetrachtung durch Kinder und Jugendliche. (Versuche über das Unterschieden von Bildern verschiedenen Stiles). 1933. 108 pp. (Also as *Neue psychologische Studien*, Band 7, Heft 2, 1933.)

Stück 54. Burkhardt, Heinz. Über Verlagerung räumlicher Gestalten. 1934. 158 pp. (Also as *Neue psychologische Studien*, Band 7, Heft 3, 1934.)

Stück 55. Meyer, Edith. Ordnen und Ordnung bei drei- bis sechsjährigen Kindern. 1934. 100 pp. (Also as *Neue psychologische Studien*, Band 10, Heft 3, 1934.)

Stück 55. Obrig, Ilse. Kinder erzählen angefangene Geschichten weiter. 1934. 70 pp. (Also as *Arbeiten zur Entwicklungs-Psychologie*, Stück 13, 1934.)

Stück 56. Tittel, Käthe. Untersuchungen über Schreibgeschwindigkeit. Ein Beitrag zur experimentellen Graphologie. 1934. 58 pp. (Also as *Neue psychologische Studien*, Band 11, Heft 1, 1934.)

Stück 57. Freiesleben, Gertraude, and Brigitte Freiesleben, in association with Hans Volkelt. Ein Kinderbriefwechsel. Briefe zweier Mädchen im

ALTER VON 10 bis 16 JAHREN. 1934. 156 pp. (Also as *Arbeiten zur Entwicklungs-Psychologie,* Stück 14, 1934.)

Stück 58. Schadeberg, Walter. ÜBER DEN EINSTELLUNGSCHARAKTER KOMPLEXER ERLEBNISSE. 1934. 69 pp. (Also as *Neue psychologische Studien,* Band 10, Heft 4, 1934.)

Stück 59. Hippius, Rudolf. ERKENNENDES TASTEN ALS WAHRNEHMUNG UND ALS ERKENNTNISVORGANG. 1934. 163 pp. (Also as *Neue psychologische Studien,* Band 10, Heft, 5, 1934.)

Stück 60. Klemm, Otto, Hans Volkelt, and Karlfried Graf von Durckheim-Montmartin, eds. GANZHEIT UND STRUKTUR. FESTSCHRIFT ZUM 60. GEBURTSTAG FELIX KRUEGERS. HEFT 1. WEGE ZUR GANZHEITSPSYCHOLOGIE. 1934. 214 pp. (Also as *Neue psychologische Studien,* Band 12, Heft 1, 1934.)

Stück 61. Klemm, Otto, Hans Volkelt, and Karlfried Graf von Durckheim-Montmartin, eds. GANZHEIT UND STRUKTUR. FESTSCHRIFT ZUM 60. GEBURTSTAG FELIX KRUEGERS. HEFT 2. SEELISCHE STRUKTUREN. 1934. 134 pp. (Also as *Neue psychologische Studien,* Band 12, Heft 2, 1934.)

Stück 62. Klemm, Otto, Hans Volkelt, and Karlfried Graf von Durckheim-Montmartin, eds. GANZHEIT UND STRUKTUR. FESTSCHRIFT ZUM 60. GEBURTSTAG FELIX KRUEGERS. HEFT 3. GEISTIGE STRUKTUREN. 1934. 134 pp. (Also as *Neue psychologische Studien,* Band 12, Heft 3, 1934.)

Stück 63. Bachmann, Armin. ZUR PSYCHOLOGISCHEN THEORIE DES SPRACHLICHEN BEDEUTUNGSWANDELS. 1935. 68 pp. (Also as *Arbeiten zur Entwicklungs-Psychologie,* Stück 15, 1935.)

Stück 64. Gutmann, Bruno. DIE STAMMESLEHREN DER DSCHAGGA. II. BAND: DIE VORLEHREN. DIE LAGERLEHREN. 1935. 642 pp. (Also as *Arbeiten zur Entwicklungs-Psychologie,* Stück 16, 1935.)

Stück 65. Rüssel, Arnulf. ZUR PSYCHOLOGIE DER OPTISCHEN AGNOSIEN. 1936. 92 pp. (Also as *Neue psychologische Studien,* Band 13, Heft 1, 1936.)

Stück 65. Mantell, Ursula. AKTUALGENETISCHE UNTERSUCHUNGEN AN SITUATIONSDARSTELLUNGEN (UNTER BERÜCKSICHTIGUNG DER KÜNSTLERISCHEN FORMUNG). 1936. 96 pp. (Also as *Neue psychologische Studien,* Band 13, Heft 2, 1936.)

Stück 66. Feige, Johannes. DER ALTE FEIERABEND. 1936. 106 pp. (Also as *Arbeiten zur Entwicklungs-Psychologie,* Stück 17, 1936.)

Stück 67. Leibold, Rudolf. AKUSTISCH-MOTORISCHER RHYTHMUS IN FRÜHER KINDHEIT. EINE STRUKTURPSYCHOLOGISCHE STUDIE. 1936. 62 pp. (Also as *Arbeiten zur Entwicklungs-Psychologie,* Stück 18, 1936.)

424. *National Vocational Guidance Association. Bulletin.*

TITLE VARIATIONS: Continued by *Vocational Guidance Magazine* with Volume 2, Number 6, March 1924.

DATES OF PUBLICATION: Volume 1–2, Number 5, August 1921–February 1924.

FREQUENCY: **Irregular,** Volume 1, Number 1–10, August 1921–May 1923. **Monthly,** Volume 2, Number 1–5, October 1923–February 1924.

NUMBERING VARIATIONS: None.

PUBLISHER: **Chicago:** National Vocational Guidance Association, 1921–1922. **Cambridge, Massachusetts:** Published for the Association by the Bureau of Vocational Guidance, Graduate School of Education, Harvard University with the co-operation of the New England Vocational Guidance Association, 1922–1924.

PRIMARY EDITORS: **Ann S. Davis,** 1921–1922; **Frederick J. Allen,** 1923–1924.

425. *Philosophische und psychologische Arbeiten.*

TITLE VARIATIONS: None.

DATES OF PUBLICATION: Heft 1–15, 1921–1932.

FREQUENCY: Irregular. *See* Contents *below.*

NUMBERING VARIATIONS: Also numbered as *Friedrich Manns pädagogisches Magazin. See* Contents *below.*

PUBLISHER: **Langensalza, Germany:** H. Beyer & Söhne, 1921–1932.

PRIMARY EDITOR: **Theodor Ziehen,** 1921–1932.

CONTENTS:

Heft 1. Ziehen, Theodor. Über das Wesen der Beanlagung und ihre methodische Erforschung. 1921. 59 pp. (Also as *Friedrich Manns pädagogisches Magazin,* Heft 683.)

Heft 2. Martin, Anna. Die Gefühlsbetonung von Farben und Farbenkombinationen bei Kindern. 1921. 44 pp. (Also as *Friedrich Manns pädagogisches Magazin,* Heft 831.)

Heft 3. Asmus, Karl. Ein Beitrag zur Lehre von der Entwicklung der optischen Raumauffassung und des optischen Raumgedächtnisses bei Schulkindern. 1922. 61 pp. (Also as *Friedrich Manns pädagogisches Magazin,* Heft 881.)

Heft 4. Schulze, Kurt. Gestaltswahrnehmung von drei und mehr Punkten auf dem Gebiete des Hautsinns. 1922. 57 pp. (Also as *Friedrich Manns pädagogisches Magazin,* Heft 882.)

Heft 5. Danzfuss, Karl. Die Gefühlsbetonung einiger unanalysierter Zweiklänge. 1923. 87 pp. (Also as *Friedrich Manns pädagogisches Magazin,* Heft 915.)

Heft 6. Ziehen, Theodor. Das Seelenleben der Jugendlichen. 1923. 90 pp. (Also as *Friedrich Manns pädagogisches Magazin,* Heft 916.)

Heft 7. Scherke, Felix. Über das Verhalten der Primitiven zum Tode. 1923. 232 pp. (Also as *Friedrich Manns pädagogisches Magazin,* Heft 938.)

Heft 8. Fabian, Gerd. Beitrag zur Geschichte des Leib-Seele-Problems. 1925. 240 pp. (Also as *Friedrich Manns pädagogisches Magazin,* Heft 1012.)

Heft 9. Nowack, Walter. Zur Lehre von den Gesetzen der Ideenassoziation seit Herbart bis 1880. 1925. 136 pp. (Also as *Friedrich Manns pädagogisches Magazin,* Heft 1018.)

Heft 10. Japha, Käthe. Über die Reaktionzeit von Kindern und ihre

KORRELATION ZUR INTELLIGENZ. 1926. 30 pp. (Also as *Friedrich Manns pädagogisches Magazin,* Heft 1084.)

Heft 11. Sander, Julie. UNTERSUCHUNGEN ÜBER DIE SINNLICHE LEBHAF-TIGKEIT VON VORSTELLUNGEN. 1927. 140 pp. (Also as *Friedrich Manns pädagogisches Magazin,* Heft 1156.)

Heft 12. Scheringer, Erika. EXPERIMENTELLE UNTERSUCHUNGEN ÜBER DIE ANSCHAULICH-MOTORISCHE KOMBINATION (PRAKTISCHE INTELLIGENZ). 1928. 112 pp. (Also as *Friedrich Manns pädagogisches Magazin,* Heft 1195.)

Heft 13. Frässdorf, Walter. DIE PSYCHOLOGISCHEN ANSCHAUUNGEN J. J. ROUSSEAUS. 1929. 248 pp. (Also as *Friedrich Manns pädagogisches Magazine,* Heft 1214.)

Heft 14. Ziehen, Theodor. DIE GRUNDLAGEN DER CHARAKTEROLOGIE. 1930. 372 pp. (Also as *Friedrich Manns pädagogisches Magazine,* Heft 1300.)

Heft 15. Odenbach, Karl. NEUE VERSUCHE ÜBER DENKTYPEN AN MEHR ALS 2000 SCHULKINDERN. 1932. 84 pp. (Also as *Friedrich Manns pädagogisches Magazin,* Heft 1363.)

426. *Poznan. Poznańskie towarzystwo przyjaciol nauk. Komisja filozoficzna. Prace.*

TITLE VARIATIONS: None.

DATES OF PUBLICATION: Tom 1–7+, 1921–1949+. Suspended publication 1950–1954.

FREQUENCY: Irregular. *See* Contents *below.*

NUMBERING VARIATIONS: None.

PUBLISHER: **Poznan:** Poznańskie towarzystwo przyjaciol nauk, 1921–1948+.

PRIMARY EDITORS: None listed.

CONTENTS:

Tom 1, Zeszyt 1. Błachowski, Stefan. O NIEKTÓRYCH ZWIĄZKACH ZA-CHODZĄCYCH MIĘDZY TYPAMI PAMIĘCIOWYMI. 1921. 30 pp.

————, **Zeszyt 2.** Błachowski, Stefan. STRUKTURA TYPÓW WYOBRAŻENIO-WYCH I PAMIĘĆ LICZB W ŚWIETLE ANALIZY PRZYPADKU WYBITNYCH ZDOLNOŚCI RA-CHUNKOWYCH. 1924. 109 pp.

————, **Zeszyt 3.** Dobrzyńska-Rybicka, Ludwika. ZE STUDJÓW NAD AU-TOMATYZMEM GRAFICZNYM. 1925. 48 pp.

————, **Zeszyt 4.** Dryjski, Albert. BADANIA EKSPERYMENTALNE NAD AU-TOMATYZMEM GRAFICZNYM. 1925. 140 pp.

————, **Zeszyt 5.** Wiegner, Adam. ZAGADNIENIE POZNAWCZE W OŚWIET-LENIU L. NELSONA. 1925. 70 pp.

Tom 2. Zołtowski, Adam. FILOZOFJA KANTA, JEJ DOGMATY, ZŁUDZENIA I ZDOBYCZE. 1923. 522 pp.

Tom 3. Szuman, Stefan. BADANIA NAD ROZWOJEM APERCEPCJI I REPRO-DUKCJI PROSTYCH KSZTAŁTOW U DZIECI; Rymarkiewicz, Maria. POJECIE BOGA W FILOZOFJI LIBELTA; Dziembowska, Anna. ZAGADNIENIE ZŁA U SŁOWACKIEGO NA TLE HISTORYCZNEGO ZARYSU PROBLEMU; Gruszecka, Anna. ZAFAŁSZOWANIA ASY-

MILACYJNE U DZIECI W WIEKU PRZEDSZKOLNYM; and Wiegner, Adam. W SPRA-
WIE ZASADY ODWROTNOŚCI MIĘDZY TREŚCIA A ZAKRESEM POJĘĆ. 1930. 306 pp.

Tom 4. Rymarkiewicz, Maria. FILOZOFJA LIBELTA; Wiegner, Adam. O IS-
TOCIE ZJAWISK PSYCHICZNYCH; and Zawirski, Zygmunt. STOSUNEK LOGIKI WIE-
LOWARTOŚCIOWEJ DO RACHUNKU PRAWDOPODOBIEŃSTWA. 1934. 240 pp.

Tom 5. Zołtowski, Adam. DESCARTES. 1937. 266 pp.

Tom 6. Jordan, Zbigniew. O MATEMATYCZNYCH PODSTAWACH SYSTEMU
PLATONA. 1937. 328 pp.

Tom 7. Zeszyt 1. Dybowski, Mieczysław. WPŁYW WOLI I TYPU ANTROPOL-
OGICZNEGO NA OTAMOWANIE STRACHU. 1947. 36 pp.

————, Zeszyt 2. Miełczarska, Wladyslawa. PRZEZYCIE OPORU I JEGO STO-
SUNEK DO WOLI. 1948. 101 pp.

————, Zeszyt 3. Duszyńska, Bolesława. ZASADA SOMATOLOGII STOICKIEJ.
1948. 64 pp.

————, Zeszyt 4. Reutt, Józef. BADANIA PSYCHOLOGICZNE NAD WAHAN-
IEM. 1949. 166 pp.

————, Zeszyt 5. Suszkco, Roman. O ANALITCZNYCH AKSJOMATACH I LOG-
ICZNYCH REGUŁACH WNIOSKOWANIE. Z TEORII DEFINICJI. 1949. 59 pp.

427. Psyche. A Quarterly Review of Psychology. [Published in
connection with the Orthological Institute, Cambridge.]

TITLE VARIATIONS: Subtitle varies. Continues *Psychic Research Quarterly.*
Continued by *Psyche. An Annual of General and Linguistic Psychology* with
Volume 13, 1933.

DATES OF PUBLICATION: Volume 2–12, 1921–1932.

FREQUENCY: Quarterly.

NUMBERING VARIATIONS: Published in conjunction with *Psyche Miniatures;
General Series* and *Psyche Miniatures; Medical Series.* Volume 10, Number 1
incorrectly numbered Volume 9, Number 5.

PUBLISHER: **London:** Kegan Paul, Trench, Trubner and Co., Ltd., 1921–1932.

PRIMARY EDITORS: **C. K. Ogden,** 1921–1932; **Warren J. Vinton,** 1925–1926;
N. Mallinson, 1928–1929.

**428. Psychologische Forschung; Zeitschrift für Psychologie und
ihre Grenzwissenschaften.**

TITLE VARIATIONS: None.

DATES OF PUBLICATION: Band 1–23+, 1921–1950+. Suspended publication
1939–1948.

FREQUENCY: Quarterly.

NUMBERING VARIATIONS: Multinumber issues present. Band 3, Heft 3/4 is
FESTGABE FÜR JOHANNES VON KRIES ZUM 70. GEBURTSTAG AM 6 OKTOBER 1923;
Band 4, Heft 1–4 is FESTSCHRIFT FÜR CARL STUMPF ZUM 75. GEBURTSTAG, 1924.
Various articles also numbered in the subseries *Psychologische Analysen hirn-*

pathologischer Fälle; Untersuchungen zur Handlungs- und Affekt-Psychologie; and *Untersuchungen zur Lehre von der Gestalt.*

PUBLISHER: **Berlin:** Julius Springer, 1921–1938. **Berlin, Göttingen, and Heidelberg:** Springer Verlag, 1949–1950+.

PRIMARY EDITORS: **K. Koffka,** 1921–1935; **Wolfgang Köhler,** 1921–1938; **Max Wertheimer,** 1921–1935; **Kurt Goldstein,** 1921–1933; **H. Gruhle,** 1921–1935, 1949–1950+; **A. Gelb,** 1930–1935; **J. von Allesch,** 1949–1950+.

429. *Rivista di psicologia e rassegna di studi pedagogici e filosofici.* [Organ of the Società italiana di psicologia and of the Istituti di psicologia sperimentale (Rome and Turin).]

TITLE VARIATIONS: Continues *Rivista di psicologia.* [1]. Continued by *Rivista di psicologia.* [2] with Volume 18, 1922.

DATES OF PUBLICATION: Volume 17, 1921.

FREQUENCY: Quarterly.

NUMBERING VARIATIONS: None.

PUBLISHER: **Bologna:** Nicola Zanichelli editore, 1921.

PRIMARY EDITORS: **Giulio Cesare Ferrari,** 1921; **Giuseppe Tarozzi,** 1921.

430. *Schriften zur Seelenkunde und Erziehungskunst.*

TITLE VARIATIONS: None.

DATES OF PUBLICATION: Heft 1–9, 1921–1923.

FREQUENCY: Irregular. *See* Contents *below.*

NUMBERING VARIATIONS: None.

PUBLISHER: **Bern:** Verlag E. Bircher, 1921–1923. **Bern:** Hans Huber, 1923.

PRIMARY EDITOR: **Oskar Pfister,** 1921–1923.

CONTENTS:
Heft 1. Pfister, Oskar. DIE BEHANDLUNG SCHWER ERZIEHBARER UND ABNORMER KINDER. (1921). 129 pp.
Heft 2. Frost, Marie. ERZIEHERLIEBE ALS HEILMITTEL. 1921. 42 pp.
Heft 3. Silberer, Herbert. DER ZUFALL UND DIE KOBOLDSTREICHE DES UNBEWUSSTEN. 1921. 72 pp.
Heft 4. Pfister, Oskar. VERMEINTLICHE NULLEN UND ANGEBLICHE MUSTERKINDER. (1921.) 35 pp.
Heft 5. Zulliger, Hans. PSYCHOANALYTISCHE ERFAHRUNGEN AUS DER VOLKSSCHULPRAXIS. 1921. 146 pp.
Heft 6. Pfister, Oskar. ZUR PSYCHOLOGIE DES PHILOSOPHISCHEN DENKENS. 1923. 86 pp.
Heft 7. Pfister, Oskar. DER SEELISCHE AUFBAU DES KLASSISCHEN KAPITALISMUS UND DER GELDGEISTER. 1923. 85 pp.
Heft 8. Silberer, Herbert. DER ABERGLAUBE. 1923. 55 pp.
Heft 9. Zulliger, Hans. AUS DEM UNBEWUSSTEN SEELENLEBEN UNSERER SCHULJUGEND. 1923. 110 pp.

431. *Sozialpsychologische Forschungen.* [*1.*]

TITLE VARIATIONS: None.

DATES OF PUBLICATION: Band 1, 1921.

FREQUENCY: Irregular. *See* Contents *below.*

NUMBERING VARIATIONS: None.

PUBLISHER: **Vienna:** M. Perles, 1921.

PRIMARY EDITOR: **Peter Nemeth,** 1921.

CONTENTS:

Band 1. Szirtes, Artur. Zur Psychologie der öffentlichen Meinung. 1921. 100 pp.

432. *Zentralblatt für die gesamte Neurologie und Psychiatrie. Referatenteil.*

TITLE VARIATIONS: Continues *Zeitschrift für die gesamte Neurologie und Psychiatrie. Referate und Ergebnisse.* Supplement to *Zeitschrift für die gesamte Neurologie und Psychiatrie, 1921–1943.* Absorbed *Neurologische Centralblatt* in 1921.

DATES OF PUBLICATION: Band 25–111 +, 1921–1950 +. Suspended publication December 1943–July 1948.

FREQUENCY: Irregular (8–18 Hefte per volume; 2–6 Bände per year).

NUMBERING VARIATIONS: None.

PUBLISHER: **Berlin:** Julius Springer, 1921–1936. **Berlin:** Springer Verlag, 1936–1940. **Berlin, Göttingen, Heidelberg:** Springer-Verlag, 1941–1950 +.

PRIMARY EDITORS: **Kurt Mendel,** 1921–1931; **Walter Spielmeyer,** 1921–1931; **Robert Hirschfeld,** 1921–1931; **E. Mendel,** 1931–1941; **Karl Bonhöffer,** 1931–1950 +; **Kurt Schneider,** 1948–1950 +.

1922

433. *Abhandlungen zur Philosophie und Psychologie der Religion.*

TITLE VARIATIONS: Continued by *Abhandlungen zur Philosophie, Psychologie und Soziologie der Religion* with Heft 2/3, 1951 +.

DATES OF PUBLICATION: Heft 1–52/53, 1922–1941. Neue Folge, Heft 1 +, 1948 +. Suspended publication 1942–1947.

FREQUENCY: Irregular. *See* Contents *below.*

NUMBERING VARIATIONS: *See* Contents *below.*

PUBLISHER: **Würzburg:** C. J. Becker, 1922–1941. **Würzburg:** F. Schöningh, 1948.

Year 1922

PRIMARY EDITOR: Georg Wunderle, 1922–1948 + .

CONTENTS:

Heft 1. Schuck, Johannes. DAS RELIGIÖSE ERLEBNIS BEIM HEILIGEN BERNHARD VON CLAIRVAUX. 1922. 111 pp.

Heft 2. Faulhaber, Ludwig, WISSENSCHAFTLICHE GOTTESERKENNTNIS UND KAUSALITÄT. 1922. 122 pp.

Heft 3. Lenz, Joseph. DIE DOCTA IGNORANTIA; ODER DIE MYSTISCHE GOTTESERKENNTNIS DES NIKOLAUS CUSANUS IN IHREN PHILOSOPHISCHEN GRUNDLAGEN. 1923. 132 pp.

Heft 4. Wunderle, Georg. FRÜNKINDLICHE RELIGIÖSE ERLEBNISSE IM LICHTE SPÄTERER ERINNERUNG. 1923. 61 pp.

Heft 5. Faulhaber, Ludwig. DIE "DREI WEGE" DER GOTTESERKENNTNIS UND DER WISSENSCHAFTLICHE GOTTESBEGRIFF. 1924. 83 pp.

Heft 6/7. Fröhlich, Karl. STUDIEN ZUR FRAGE NACH DER REALITÄT DES GÖTTLICHEN IN DER NEUESTEN DEUTSCHEN RELIGIONSPHILOSOPHIE. 1925. 196 pp.

Heft 8/9. Stamer, Ludwig. DAS ÜBERNATÜRLICHE BEI SCHLEIERMACHER. 1925. 150 pp.

Heft 10. Meerpohl, Franz. MEISTER ECKHARTS LEHRE VOM SEELENFÜNKLEIN. 1926. 114 pp.

Heft 11. Haehling von Lanzenauer, Reiner. DIE GRUNDLAGEN DER RELIGIÖSEN ERFAHRUNG BEI KARL BARTH. 1927. 75 pp.

Heft 12/13. Hasenfuss, Josef. DIE GRUNDLAGEN DER RELIGION BEI KANT. 1927. 183 pp.

Heft 14/15. Wanninger, Joseph. DAS HEILIGE IN DER RELIGION DER AUSTRALIER. 1927. 137 pp.

Heft 16/17. Newe, Heinrich. DIE RELIGIÖSE GOTTESERKENNTNIS UND IHR VERHÄLTNIS ZUR METAPHYSICHEN BEI MAX SCHELER. 1928. 154 pp.

Heft 18. Pascher, Joseph. DIE PLASTISCHE KRAFT IM RELIGIÖSEN GESTALTUNGSVORGANG NACH JOSEPH VON GÖRRES. 1928. 76 pp.

Heft 19. Karrer, Otto. DAS GÖTTLICHE IN DER SEELE BEI MEISTER ECKHART. 1928. 126 pp.

Heft 20/21. Tuebben, Herbert. DIE FREIHEITSPROBLEMATIK BAADERS UND DEUTINGERS UND DER DEUTSCHE IDEALISMUS. 1929. 152 pp.

Heft 22. Barion, Jakob. DIE INTELLEKTUELLE ANSCHAUUNG BEI J. G. FICHTE UND SCHELLING UND IHRE RELIGIONSPHILOSOPHISCHE BEDEUTUNG. 1929. 115 pp.

Heft 23. Pascher, Joseph. DER SEELENBEGRIFF IM ANIMISMUS EDWARD BURNETT TYLORS. 1929. 110 pp.

Heft 24. Back Andreas. DAS MYSTISCHE ERLEBNIS DER GOTTESNÄHE BEI DER HEILIGEN THERESIA VON JESUS. 1930. 112 pp.

Heft 25. Schäfer, Peter. DAS SCHULDBEWUSSTSEIN IN DEN CONFESSIONES DES HEILIGEN AUGUSTINUS. 1930. 144 pp.

Heft 26. Wunderle, Georg. UM KONNERSREUTH. 1931. 65 pp.

Heft 27/28. Schilling, Jakob. DIE AUFFASSUNGEN KANTS UND DES HEILIGEN THOMAS VON AQUIN VON DER RELIGION. 1932. 240 pp.

Heft 29. Mahr, Franz. RELIGION UND KULTUR. 1932. 132 pp.

Heft 30. Meerpohl, Bernhard. VERZWEIFLUNG ALS METAPHYSISCHES PHÄNOMEN IN DER PHILOSOPHIE SÖREN KIERKEGAARDS. 1934. 131 pp.

Heft 31/32. Rintelen, Frederick Maria. WEGE ZU GOTT. 1934. 100 pp.

Heft 33/34. Hasenfuss, Josef. RELIGIONSPHILOSOPHIE BEI JAKOB FRIEDRICH FRIES. 1935. 315 pp.

Heft 35/36. Hohmann, Firmin. BONAVENTURA UND DAS EXISTENZIELLE SEIN DES MENSCHEN. 1935. 239 pp.

Heft 37. Jaspers, Ludger, DER BEGRIFF DER MENSCHLICHEN SITUATION IN DER EXISTENZPHILOSOPHIE VON KARL JASPERS. 1936. 93 pp.

Heft 38/39. Delahaye, Karl. DIE "MEMORIA INTERIOR"—LEHRE DES HEILIGEN AUGUSTINUS UND DER BEGRIFF DER "TRANSZENDENTALEN APPERZEPTION" KANTS. 1936. 166 pp.

Heft 40. Wunderle, Georg. DIE GESTALTENDE KRAFT DER RELIGION IM SEELENLEBEN DES MENSCHEN. 1936. 36 pp.

Heft 41. Hämel-Stier, Angela. DAS SEELENLEBEN DER HEILIGEN JOHANNA FRANZISKA VON CHANTAL. 1937. 68 pp.

Heft 42. Anwander, Anton. DAS PRINZIP DER GEGENSATZES IN DEN RELIGIONEN. 1937. 95 pp.

Heft 43/44. Spreckelmeyer, Hermann. DIE PHILOSOPHISCHE DEUTUNG DES SÜNDENFALLS BEI FRANZ BAADER. 1938. 312 pp.

Heft 45. Kümmet, Heribert. DIE GOTTESERFAHRUNG IN DER "SUMMA THEOLOGIAE MYSTICAE" DES KARMELITEN PHILIPPUS A. SS. TRINITATE. 1938. 123 pp.

Heft 46. Borgolte, P, A. ZUR GRUNDLEGUNG DER LEHRE VON DER BEZIEHUNG DES SITTLICHEN ZUM RELIGIÖSEN IM·ANSCHLUSS AND DIE ETHIK NIC. HARTMANNS. 1938. 172 pp.

Heft 47/48. Volk, Hermann. KREATURAUFFASSUNG BEI KARL BARTH. 1938. 332 pp.

Heft 49. Kuhaupt, Hermann. DAS PROBLEM DES ERKENNTNISTHEORETISCHEN REALISMUS IN NICOLAI HARTMANNS METAPHYSIK DER ERKENNTNIS. 1938. 108 pp.

Heft 50. Englhauser, Johann. METAPHYSISCHE TENDENZEN IN DER PSYCHOLOGIE DILTHEYS. 1938. 94 pp.

Heft 51. Hammer, Alfons. VOM PROBLEM DES RELIGIÖSEN ERLEBNISSES. 1939. 104 pp.

Heft 52/53. Anwander, Anton. GLORIA DEI. 1941. 212 pp.

Neue Folge, Heft 1. Wunderle, Georg. DER RELIGIÖSE AKT ALS SEELISCHES PROBLEM. 1948. 36 pp.

434. *Arkiv för Psykologi och Pedagogik.*

TITLE VARIATIONS: Formed by the union of *Psyke* and *Svenskt Arkiv för Pedagogik.*

DATES OF PUBLICATION: Häfte 1–8, 1922–1929.

FREQUENCY: Quarterly.

NUMBERING VARIATIONS: Two double-number issues per year.

PUBLISHER: **Uppsala** and **Stockholm:** Almquist & Wiksells, 1922–1929.

PRIMARY EDITORS: **Sydney Alrutz,** 1922–1925; **Bertil Hammer,** 1922–1929; **Axel Herrlin,** 1922–1929.

435. *Association des psychiatres roumaines. Bulletin.*

TITLE VARIATIONS: Also called *Societatea română de neurologie, psichiatrie, psichologie și endocrinologie. Bulletin.* Continues *Société de neurologie, psychiatrie et psychologie de Jassy. Bulletin.* Continued by *Société roumaine de neurologie, psychiatrie, psychologie et endocrinologie. Bulletin* with [Nouvelle Série], Tome 1, October 1924.

DATES OF PUBLICATION: Tome 4–5, February 1922–January 1924.

FREQUENCY: Monthly.

NUMBERING VARIATIONS: None.

PUBLISHER: **Bucharest:** Association des psychiatres roumaines, 1922–1924.

PRIMARY EDITORS: None listed.

436. *Australasian Association of Psychology and Philosophy. Monograph Series.*

TITLE VARIATIONS: None.

DATES OF PUBLICATION: Number 1–4, 1922–1926.

FREQUENCY: Irregular. *See* Contents *below.*

NUMBERING VARIATIONS: None.

PUBLISHER: **Sydney:** Australasian Association of Psychology and Philosophy, 1922–1926.

PRIMARY EDITORS: None listed.

CONTENTS:
>   **Number 1.** Anderson, Francis. LIBERTY, FRATERNITY, EQUALITY. 1922. 24 pp.
>> **Number 2.** Lovell, Henry Tasman. DREAMS. 1923. 73 pp.
>> **Number 3.** Miller, Edmund Morris. THE BASIS OF FREEDOM. 1924. 84 pp.
>> **Number 4.** Miller, Edmund Morris. BRAIN CAPACITY AND INTELLIGENCE. 1926. 79 pp.

437. *California. University. School of Education. Bureau of Research in Education. Studies. (Sub-Series). Applications of Psychology to Education.*

TITLE VARIATIONS: None.

DATES OF PUBLICATION: Study 4–7, 1922.

FREQUENCY: Irregular. *See* Contents *below.*

NUMBERING VARIATIONS: Total series of *Bureau of Research in Education. Studies* are numbered 1–13, 1921–1923. Only Study 4–7 exist in this Subseries.

PUBLISHER: **Berkeley, California:** University of California, School of Education. Bureau of Research in Education, 1922.

PRIMARY EDITOR: **Joseph Valentine Breitwieser,** 1922.

CONTENTS:

Study 4. Adams, Frederick J. MODOC COUNTY MENTAL SURVEY. 1922.

Study 5. Bischoff, Adele. FALSE DEFINITION TEST IN THE SEVENTH AND EIGHT GRADES. 1922.

Study 6. Breitwieser, J. V. TRAINING FOR RAPID READING. 1922.

Study 7. Martens, Elise H. A STUDY OF INDIVIDUAL RETESTS. 1922.

NOTE: Total pagination for these four Studies is 28 pp.

438. *Comparative Psychology Monographs.*

TITLE VARIATIONS: Supersedes *Behavior Monographs.*

DATES OF PUBLICATION: Number 1–104+, 1922–1950+. (Ceased publication 1951.)

FREQUENCY: Irregular. *See* Contents *below.*

NUMBERING VARIATIONS: Issues also numbered in Volume 1–20+. *See* Contents *below.*

PUBLISHER: **Baltimore:** Williams and Wilkins, 1922–1927. **Baltimore:** Johns Hopkins Press, 1928–1940. **Baltimore:** Williams and Wilkins, 1941–1946. **Berkeley** and **Los Angeles:** University of California Press, 1948–1950+.

PRIMARY EDITORS: **Walter S. Hunter,** 1922–1927; **Knight Dunlap,** 1928–1936; **Roy M. Dorcus,** 1936–1946; **Franklin Fearing,** 1948–1950+.

ASSISTANT EDITOR: Roy M. Dorcus, 1934–1936.

EDITORIAL BOARD: John E. Anderson, 1928–1950+; Harvey A. Carr, 1922–1946; Roy M. Dorcus, 1948–1950+; Knight Dunlap, 1936–1946; Ward C. Halstead, 1948–1950+; S. J. Holmes, 1922–1927; Walter S. Hunter, 1928–1946; W. N. Kellogg, 1948–1950+; Alfred V. Kidder, 1928–1946; Clyde Kluckhohn, 1948–1950+; K. S. Lashley, 1922–1927; N.R.F. Maier, 1948–1950+; Samuel O. Mast, 1928–1946; T. C. Schneirla, 1948–1950+; R. C. Tryon, 1948–1950+; P. T. Young, 1948–1950+; R. M. Yerkes, 1922–1946.

CONTENTS:

[Volume 1] **Number 1.** Heron, William T. and Walter S. Hunter. STUDIES OF THE RELIABILITY OF THE PROBLEM BOX AND THE MAZE WITH HUMAN AND ANIMAL SUBJECTS. July 1922. 56 pp.

[———] **Number 2.** Richter, Curt P. A BEHAVIORISTIC STUDY OF THE ACTIVITY OF THE RAT. September 1922. 55 pp.

[———] **Number 3.** Warden, Carl John. THE DISTRIBUTION OF PRACTICE IN ANIMAL LEARNING. January 1923. 64 pp.

[———] **Number 4.** Anderson, Lewis O. STUTTERING AND ALLIED DISORDERS. AN EXPERIMENTAL INVESTIGATION OF UNDERLYING FACTORS. March 1923. 78 pp.

[———] **Number 5.** Peterson, Joseph, THE COMPARATIVE ABILITIES OF WHITE AND NEGRO CHILDREN. July 1923. 141 pp.

[**Volume 2**] **Number 6.** Wang, G. H. The Relation between "Spontaneous" Activity and Oestrous Cycle in the White Rat. September 1923. 27 pp.

[———] **Number 7.** Simmons, Rietta. The Relative Effectiveness of Certain Incentives in Animal Learning. January 1924. 79 pp.

[———] **Number 8.** Heron, William T. Individual Differences in Ability versus Chance in the Learning of the Stylus Maze. April 1924. 60 pp.

[———] **Number 9.** Sherman, Irene Case. The Suggestibility of Normal and Mentally Defective Children. August 1924. 34 pp.

[———] **Number 10.** Merrill, Maud A. On the Relation of Intelligence to Achievement in the Case of Mentally Retarded Children. September 1924. 100 pp.

[———] **Number 11.** Tsai, Chiao. A Comparative Study of Retention Curves for Motor Habits. October 1924. 29 pp.

[———] **Number 12.** Rickey, Edna. The Thyroid Influence on the Behavior of the White Rat. May 1925. 76 pp.

[**Volume 3**] **Number 13.** Totten, Edith. Oxygen Consumption during Emotional Stimulation. June 1925. 79 pp.

[———] **Number 14.** Paschal, Franklin C., and Louis R. Sullivan. Racial Influences in the Mental and Physical Development of Mexican Children. October 1925. 76 pp.

[———] **Number 15.** Darsie, Marvin L. The Mental Capacity of American-Born Japanese Children. January 1926. 89 pp.

[———] **Number 16.** Kuroda, Ryo, Experimental Researches upon the Sense of Hearing in Lower Vertebrates, including Reptiles, Amphibians, and Fishes. May 1926. 50 pp.

[———] **Number 17.** Holden, Frances. A Study of the Effect of Starvation upon Behavior by Means of the Obstruction Method. October 1926. 45 pp.

[**Volume 4**] **Number 18.** Williams, Joseph A. Experiments with Form Perception and Learning in Dogs. November 1926. 70 pp.

[———] **Number 19.** Fisher, Vivian Ezra. An Experimental Study of the Effects of Tobacco Smoking on Certain Psycho-physical Functions. February 1927. 50 pp.

[———] **Number 20.** Eagleson, Helen E. Periodic Changes in Blood Pressure, Muscular Coordination, and Mental Efficiency in Women. March 1927. 65 pp.

[———] **Number 21.** Perkins, Nellie Louise. Human Reactions in a Maze of Fixed Orientation. May 1927. 92 pp.

[———] **Number 22.** Warner, L. H. A Study of Sex Behavior in the White Rat by Means of the Obstruction Method. July 1927. 68 pp.

[**Volume 5**] **Number 23.** Bingham, Harold C. Sex Development in Apes. May 1928. 165 pp.

[———] **Number 24.** Yerkes, Robert M. The Mind of a Gorilla. Part III. Memory. December 1928. 92 pp.

[———] **Number 25.** Bingham, Harold C. Chimpanzee Translocation by Means of Boxes. February 1929. 91 pp.

438. *(Continued)*

[———] **Number 26.** Bingham, Harold C. SELECTIVE TRANSPORTATION BY CHIMPANZEES. May 1929. 45 pp.

[**Volume 6**] **Number 27.** Adams, Donald Keith. EXPERIMENTAL STUDIES OF ADAPTIVE BEHAVIOR IN CATS. May 1929. 168 pp.

[———] **Number 28.** Ligon, Ernest Mayfield. A COMPARATIVE STUDY OF CERTAIN INCENTIVES IN THE LEARNING OF THE WHITE RAT. June 1929. 95 pp.

[———] **Number 29.** Maier, Norman R. F. REASONING IN WHITE RATS. July 1929. 93 pp.

[———] **Number 30.** Schneirla, T. C. LEARNING AND ORIENTATION IN ANTS. July 1929. 143 pp.

[**Volume 7**] **Number 31.** Perkins, F. Theodore, and Raymond Holder Wheeler. CONFIGURATIONAL LEARNING IN THE GOLDFISH. March 1930. 50 pp.

[———] **Number 32.** Dashiell, J. F. DIRECTION ORIENTATION IN MAZE RUNNING BY THE WHITE RAT. April 1930. 72 pp.

[———] **Number 33.** Heinlein, Julia Heil. PREFERENTIAL MANIPULATION IN CHILDREN. May 1930. 121 pp.

[———] **Number 34.** Skalet, Magda. THE SIGNIFICANCE OF DELAYED RE-ACTIONS IN YOUNG CHILDREN. February 1931. 82 pp.

[———] **Number 35.** Hanawalt, Ella May. WHOLE AND PART METHODS IN TRIAL AND ERROR LEARNING. May 1931. 65 pp.

[**Volume 8**] **Number 36.** Nissen, Henry W. A FIELD STUDY OF THE CHIM-PANZEE. OBSERVATIONS OF CHIMPANZEE BEHAVIOR AND ENVIRONMENT IN WEST-ERN FRENCH GUINEA. Foreword by Robert M. Yerkes. December 1931. 122 pp.

[———] **Number 37.** McAllister, Walter G. A FURTHER STUDY OF THE DELAYED REACTION IN THE ALBINO RAT. January 1932. 103 pp.

[———] **Number 38.** Yerkes, Robert M. YALE LABORATORIES OF COMPAR-ATIVE PSYCHOBIOLOGY. February 1932. 33 pp.

[———] **Number 39.** Thorndike, Edward L. REWARD AND PUNISHMENT IN ANIMAL LEARNING. March 1932. 65 pp.

[———] **Number 40.** Spence, Kenneth W. THE RELIABILITY OF THE MAZE AND METHODS OF ITS DETERMINATION. May 1932. 45 pp.

[**Volume 9**] **Number 41.** Jacobsen, Carlyle F., Marion M. Jacobsen and Joseph G. Yoshioka. DEVELOPMENT OF AN INFANT CHIMPANZEE DURING HER FIRST YEAR. September 1942. 94 pp.

[———] **Number 42.** Fields, Paul E. STUDIES IN CONCEPT FORMATION. December 1932. 70 pp.

[———] **Number 43.** Newall, Sidney M., and Robert R. Sears. CONDI-TIONING FINGER RETRACTION TO VISUAL STIMULI NEAR THE ABSOLUTE THRESH-OLD. January 1933. 25 pp.

[———] **Number 44.** Dunlap, Jack W. THE ORGANIZATION OF LEARNING AND OTHER TRAITS IN CHICKENS. May 1933. 55 pp.

[———] **Number 45.** Mowrer, O. H. THE MODIFICATION OF VESTIBULAR NYSTAGMUS BY MEANS OF REPEATED ELICITATION. February 1934. 48 pp.

[———] **Number 46.** Peterson, Geo. M. MECHANISMS OF HANDEDNESS IN THE RAT. April 1934. 67 pp.

[**Volume 10**] **Number 47.** Yerkes, Robert M. MODES OF BEHAVIORAL AD-APTATION IN CHIMPANZEE TO MULTIPLE-CHOICE PROBLEMS. May 1934. 108 pp.

[————] **Number 48.** Carpenter, C. R. A FIELD STUDY OF THE BEHAVIOR AND SOCIAL RELATIONS OF HOWLING MONKEYS. May 1934. 168 pp.

[————] **Number 49.** Wendt, G. R. AUDITORY ACUITY OF MONKEYS. November 1934. 51 pp.

[————] **Number 50.** Tsang, Yü-Chüan. THE FUNCTIONS OF THE VISUAL AREAS OF THE CEREBRAL CORTEX OF THE RAT IN THE LEARNING AND RETENTION OF THE MAZE. I. December 1934. 56 pp.

[Volume 11] Number 51. Liddell, H. S., W. T. James, and O. D. Anderson. THE COMPARATIVE PHYSIOLOGY OF THE CONDITIONED MOTOR REFLEX. BASED ON EXPERIMENTS WITH THE PIG, DOG, SHEEP, GOAT, AND RABBIT. December 1934. 89 pp.

[————] **Number 52.** Lashley, K. S. STUDIES OF CEREBRAL FUNCTION IN LEARNING: XI. THE BEHAVIOR OF THE RAT IN LATCH BOX SITUATIONS. THE MECHANISM OF VISION; XII. NERVOUS STRUCTURES CONCERNED IN THE ACQUISITION AND RETENTION OF HABITS BASED ON REACTIONS TO LIGHT. February 1934. 79 pp.

[————] **Number 53.** Totten, Edith. EYE-MOVEMENT DURING VISUAL IMAGERY. March 1935. 46 pp.

[————] **Number 54.** Boder, David P. THE INFLUENCE OF CONCOMITANT ACTIVITY AND FATIGUE UPON CERTAIN FORMS OF RECIPROCAL HAND MOVEMENT AND ITS FUNDAMENTAL COMPONENTS. June 1935. 121 pp.

[————] **Number 55.** Kirk, Samuel A. HEMISPHERIC CEREBRAL DOMINANCE AND HEMISPHERIC EQUIPOTENTIALITY. November 1935. 41 pp.

[Volume 12] Number 56. Halstead, Ward. THE EFFECTS OF CEREBELLAR LESIONS UPON THE HABITUATION OF POST-ROTATIONAL NYSTAGMUS. December 1935. 130 pp.

[————] **Number 57.** Tsang, Yü-Chüan. THE FUNCTIONS OF THE VISUAL AREAS OF THE CEREBRAL CORTEX OF THE RAT IN THE LEARNING AND RETENTION OF THE MAZE. II. January 1936. 41 pp.

[————] **Number 58.** Layman, John D. THE AVIAN VISUAL SYSTEM. I. CEREBRAL FUNCTION OF THE DOMESTIC FOWL IN PATTERN VISION. January 1936. 36 pp.

[————] **Number 59.** Sherman, Mandel, Irene Sherman, and Charles D. Flory. INFANT BEHAVIOR. April 1936. 107 pp.

[————] **Number 60.** Wolfe, John B. EFFECTIVENESS OF TOKEN-REWARDS FOR CHIMPANZEES. May 1936. 72 pp.

[Volume 13] Number 61. Burchard, Edward M. L. PHYSIQUE AND PSYCHOSIS. AN ANALYSIS OF THE POSTULATED RELATIONSHIP BETWEEN BODILY CONSTITUTION AND MENTAL DISEASE SYNDROME. June 1936. 73 pp.

[————] **Number 62.** Spragg, S.D.S. ANTICIPATORY RESPONSES IN SERIAL LEARNING BY CHIMPANZEE. July 1936. 72 pp.

[————] **Number 63.** Jacobsen, C. F., with the cooperation of J. H. Elder and G. M. Haslerud. STUDIES OF CEREBRAL FUNCTION IN PRIMATES. August 1936. 68 pp.

[————] **Number 64.** Honzik, C. H. THE SENSORY BASIS OF MAZE LEARNING IN RATS. September 1936. 113 pp.

[————] **Number 65.** Yerkes, Robert M. and James H. Elder. OESTRUS, RECEPTIVITY, AND MATING IN CHIMPANZEE. October 1936. 39 pp.

438. *(Continued)*

[————] **Number 66.** Morsh, Joseph Eugene. MOTOR PERFORMANCE OF THE DEAF. November 1936. 51 pp.

[Volume 14] **Number 67.** Ball, Josephine. A TEST FOR MEASURING SEXUAL EXCITABILITY IN THE FEMALE RAT. January 1937. 37 pp.

[————] **Number 68.** Crawford, Meredith P. THE COOPERATIVE SOLVING OF PROBLEMS BY YOUNG CHIMPANZEES. June 1937. 88 pp.

[————] **Number 69.** Vaughn, Charles L. FACTORS IN RAT LEARNING: AN ANALYSIS OF THE INTERCORRELATIONS BETWEEN 34 VARIABLES. July 1937. 41 pp.

[————] **Number 70.** Dunlap, Sarah C. THE EFFECT OF VOLUNTARY ACTIVITY ON THE KNEE-JERK. August 1937. 62 pp.

[————] **Number 71.** Cowles, John T. FOOD-TOKENS AS INCENTIVES FOR LEARNING BY CHIMPANZEES. September 1937. 96 pp.

[————] **Number 72.** Anderson, E. E. THE INTERRELATIONSHIP OF DRIVES IN THE MALE ALBINO RAT. II. INTERCORRELATIONS BETWEEN 47 MEASURES OF DRIVES AND OF LEARNING. February 1938. 119 pp.

[Volume 15] **Number 73.** Maier, Norman R. F. A FURTHER ANALYSIS OF REASONING IN RATS: II THE INTEGRATION OF FOUR SEPARATE EXPERIENCES IN PROBLEM SOLVING. III. THE INFLUENCE OF CORTICAL INJURIES ON THE PROCESS OF "DIRECTION." April 1938. 85 pp.

[————] **Number 74.** Biel, William C. THE EFFECT OF EARLY INANITION UPON MAZE LEARNING IN THE ALBINO RAT. May 1938. 33 pp.

[————] **Number 75.** Spence, Kenneth W. THE SOLUTION OF MULTIPLE CHOICE PROBLEMS BY CHIMPANZEES. April 1939. 54 pp.

[————] **Number 76.** Grether, Walter F. COLOR VSION AND COLOR BLINDNESS IN MONKEYS. June 1939. 38 pp.

[————] **Number 77.** Riesen, Austin H. DELAYED REWARD IN DISCRIMINATION LEARNING BY CHIMPANZEES. February 1940. 54 pp.

[————] **Number 78.** Winslow, Charles Nelson. A STUDY OF EXPERIMENTALLY INDUCED COMPETITIVE BEHAVIOR IN THE WHITE RAT. March 1940. 35 pp.

[————] **Number 79.** Spragg, S. D. S. MORPHINE ADDICTION IN CHIMPANZEES. April 1940. 132 pp.

[Volume 16] **Number 80.** Maier, Norman R. F., and Nathan M. Glaser. STUDIES OF ABNORMAL BEHAVIOR IN THE RAT. II. A COMPARISON OF SOME CONVULSION-PRODUCING SITUATIONS. May 1940. 30 pp.

[————] **Number 81.** Spirer, Jess. NEGRO CRIME. June 1940. 64 pp.

[————] **Number 82.** Fletcher, Frank Milford. EFFECTS OF QUANTITATIVE VARIATION OF FOOD-INCENTIVE ON THE PERFORMANCE OF PHYSICAL WORK BY CHIMPANZEES. June 1940. 46 pp.

[————] **Number 83.** Margolin, S. E., and M. E. Bunch THE RELATIONSHIP BETWEEN AGE AND THE STRENGTH OF HUNGER MOTIVATION. October 1940. 34 pp.

[————] **Number 84.** Carpenter, C. R. A FIELD STUDY IN SIAM OF THE BEHAVIOR AND SOCIAL RELATIONS OF THE GIBBON (HYLOBATES LAR). December 1940. 212 pp.

[**Volume 17**] **Number 85.** Nowlis, Vincent. COMPANIONSHIP PREFERENCE AND DOMINANCE IN THE SOCIAL INTERACTION OF YOUNG CHIMPANZEES. March 1941. 57 pp.

[———] **Number 86.** Ling, Bing-Chung. FORM DISCRIMINATION AS A LEARNING CUE IN INFANTS. April 1941. 66 pp.

[———] **Number 87.** Geier, Frederic M., Max Levin, and Edward C. Tolman. INDIVIDUAL DIFFERENCES IN EMOTIONALITY, HYPOTHESIS FORMATION, VICARIOUS TRIAL AND ERROR, AND VISUAL DISCRIMINATION LEARNING IN RATS. May 1941. 20 pp.

[———] **Number 88.** Weiss, Paul. SELF-DIFFERENTIATION OF THE BASIC PATTERNS OF COORDINATION. September, 1941. 96 pp.

[———] **Number 89.** Brody, Elizabeth Graves. GENETIC BASIS OF SPONTANEOUS ACTIVITY IN THE ALBINO RAT. August 1942. 24 pp.

[———] **Number 90.** Loken, Robert D. THE NELA TEST OF COLOR VISION. September 1942. 37 pp.

[———] **Number 91.** Cooper, Joseph B. AN EXPLORATORY STUDY ON AFRICAN LIONS. October 1942. 48 pp.

[———] **Number 92.** Griffiths, William J., Jr. THE PRODUCTION OF CONVULSIONS IN THE WHITE RAT. November 1942. 29 pp.

[**Volume 18**] **Number 93.** Harris, J. Donald. STUDIES IN NONASSOCIATIVE FACTORS INHERENT IN CONDITIONING. March 1943. 74 pp.

[———] **Number 94.** Marx, Melvin H. THE EFFECTS OF CUMULATIVE TRAINING UPON RETROACTIVE INHIBITION AND TRANSFER. March 1944. 62 pp.

[———] **Number 95.** Young, Paul Thomas, and James P. Chaplin. STUDIES OF FOOD PREFERENCE, APPETITE AND DIETARY HABIT. III. PALATABILITY AND APPETITE IN RELATION TO BODILY NEED. January 1945. 45 pp.

[———] **Number 96.** Scott, J. P. SOCIAL BEHAVIOR, ORGANIZATION AND LEADERSHIP IN A SMALL FLOCK OF DOMESTIC SHEEP. February 1945. 29 pp.

[———] **Number 97.** Jones, F. Nowell, and Marion Graves Arrington. THE EXPLANATIONS OF PHYSICAL PHENOMENA GIVEN BY WHITE AND NEGRO CHILDREN. May 1945. 43 pp.

[**Volume 19**] **Number 98.** Young, Paul Thomas. STUDIES OF FOOD PREFERENCE, APPETITE AND DIETARY HABIT. V. TECHNIQUES FOR TESTING FOOD PREFERENCE AND THE SIGNIFICANCE OF RESULTS OBTAINED WITH DIFFERENT METHODS. May 1945. 58 pp.

[———] **Number 99.** Yacorzynski, G. K. DIFFERENTIAL MODIFICATION OF POST-ROTATIONAL NYSTAGMUS OF PIGEONS WITH CEREBRAL LESIONS. August 1946. 38 pp.

[———] **Number 100.** Andrew, Gwen, and H. F. Harlow. PERFORMANCE OF MACAQUE MONKEYS ON A TEST OF THE CONCEPT OF GENERALIZED TRIANGULARITY. March 1948. 20 pp.

[———] **Number 101.** Wenger, M. A. STUDIES OF AUTONOMIC BALANCE IN ARMY AIR FORCES PERSONNEL. June 1948. 111 pp.

[———] **Number 102.** Young, Paul Thomas. STUDIES OF FOOD PREFERENCE, APPETITE, AND DIETARY HABIT: IX. PALATABILITY VERSUS APPETITE AS DETERMINANTS OF THE CRITICAL CONCENTRATIONS OF SUCROSE AND SODIUM CHLORIDE; and Young, Paul Thomas and James P. X. Chaplin. PREFERENCES

OF ADRENOLECTOMIZED RATS FOR SALT SOLUTIONS OF DIFFERENT CONCENTRA-
TIONS. February 1949. 74 pp.

[Volume 20] Number 103. Halstead, Ward C. ed. BRAIN AND BEHAVIOR:
A SYMPOSIUM. January 1950. Pp. 1–94.

[———] Number 104. Worchel, Philip, and George Gentry. STUDIES IN
ELECTROCONVULSIVE SHOCK. ELECTROCONVULSIVE SHOCK AND MEMORY: THE
EFFECT OF SHOCKS ADMINISTERED IN RAPID SUCCESSION; and Lockwood, Wal-
lace. SOME RELATIONS BETWEEN RESPONSE TO FRUSTRATION (PUNISHMENT) AND
OUTCOME OF ELECTRIC CONVULSIVE THERAPY: AN EXPERIMENTAL STUDY IN PSY-
CHIATRIC THEORY. October 1950. Pp. 95–186.

439. *Harvard Monographs in Education. Studies in Educational Psychology and Educational Measurement.*

TITLE VARIATIONS: Titled *Harvard Monographs in Education, Series I. Studies in Educational Psychology and Educational Measurement, Number 1–7,
1922–1926.*

DATES OF PUBLICATION: Number 1–12, 1922–1933.

FREQUENCY: Irregular. *See* Contents *below.*

NUMBERING VARIATIONS: Early issues also numbered in Volume 1–2. Volume numbering ceased with Volume 2. *See* Contents *below.*

PUBLISHER: **Cambridge, Massachusetts:** Harvard University. Graduate
School of Education, 1922–1925. **Cambridge:** Harvard University Press,
1926–1933.

PRIMARY EDITORS: **Walter F. Dearborn,** 1922–1926. No editor listed,
1927–1933.

CONTENTS:

[Volume 1] Number 1. Shaw, Edwin A., and Edward A. Lincoln. A COM-
PARISON OF THE INTELLIGENCE AND TRAINING OF SCHOOL CHILDREN IN A MAS-
SACHUSETTS TOWN. 1922. 49 pp.

[———] Number 2. Hopkins, L. Thomas. THE MARKING SYSTEM OF THE
COLLEGE ENTRANCE EXAMINATION BOARD. 1921. 15 pp.

[———] Number 3. Dearborn, Walter F., Edward A. Lincoln, and Edwin A. Shaw. STANDARD EDUCATIONAL TESTS IN THE ELEMENTARY TRAINING
SCHOOLS OF MISSOURI. 1922. 89 pp.

[———] Number 4. Dearborn, Walter F., Edwin A. Shaw, and Edward
A. Lincoln. A SERIES OF FORM BOARD AND PERFORMANCE TESTS OF INTELLI-
GENCE. 1923. 63 pp.

[———] Number 5. Prescott, Daniel Alfred. THE DETERMINATION OF AN-
ATOMICAL AGE IN SCHOOL CHILDREN AND ITS RELATION TO MENTAL DEVELOP-
MENT. 1923. 59 pp.

[Volume 2] Number 6. Lord, Elizabeth E., Leonard Carmichael, and
Walter F. Dearborn. SPECIAL DISABILITIES IN LEARNING TO READ AND WRITE.
1925. 76 pp.

[———] Number 7. Hincks, Elizabeth M. DISABILITY IN READING AND ITS
RELATION TO PERSONALITY. 1926. 92 pp. [End of Volume numbering.]

Number 8. Stoke, Stuart M. Occupational Groups and Child Development. A Study of the Mental and Physical Growth of Children in Relation to Occupational Grouping of Parent. 1927. 92 pp.

Number 9. Cattell, Psyche. Dentition as a Measure of Maturity. 1928. 91 pp.

Number 10. Payne, Cassie Spencer. The Derivation of Tentative Norms for Short Exposures in Reading. 1930. 84 pp.

Number 11. Bird, Milton H. A Study in Aesthetics. 1932. 117 pp.

Number 12. Selzer, Charles A. Lateral Dominance and Visual Fusion. Their Application to Difficulties in Reading, Writing, Spelling, and Speech. 1933. 119 pp.

440. *Hsin li.* [Psychology.]

TITLE VARIATIONS: Also cited in English as *Chinese Journal of Psychology.*

DATES OF PUBLICATION: Volume 1–4, Number 2, January 1922–January 1927.

FREQUENCY: Quarterly (Irregular).

NUMBERING VARIATIONS: None.

PUBLISHER: **Peking:** Kuo li Shih-fan ta hsüeh, Chung-hua hsin li hsüeh hui [National Normal University, Chinese Psychological Society], 1922–1927.

PRIMARY EDITOR: **Y. C. Chang,** 1922–1927.

NOTE: Above publishing information appears in English on issues in Volume 3–4. However, *Chuan-kuo Chung-wen Chi-kan lien-ho mu-lu, 1833–1949* [Union List of Chinese Periodicals in China, 1833–1949] lists publisher as: Shanghai: Chung-hua hsin li hsüeh hui [Chinese Psychological Society].

441. *Illinois. University. Bureau of Educational Research. Educational Research Circular.*

TITLE VARIATIONS: None.

DATES OF PUBLICATION: Number 12–60, 1922–September 1947. Suspended publication 1933–1945.

FREQUENCY: Irregular. *See* Contents *below.*

NUMBERING VARIATIONS: Number 1–11 issued only informally. Regular numbering began with Number 12. Number 27 mismarked Number 26. Also numbered as *Illinois. University. Bulletin. See* Contents *below.*

PUBLISHER: **Urbana, Illinois:** University of Illinois, 1922–1947.

PRIMARY EDITOR: **Walter S. Monroe,** 1922–1947.

CONTENTS:

Number 12. Monroe, Walter S. Announcements of the Bureau of Educational Research for 1922–23. 1922. (Also as *Illinois. University. Bulletin,* Volume 20, Number 2.)

441. *(Continued)*

Number 13. Monroe, Walter S. DEFINITIONS OF THE TERMINOLOGY OF EDUCATIONAL MEASUREMENTS. 1922. 17 pp. (Also as *Illinois. University. Bulletin*, Volume 20, Number 6.)

Number 14. Streitz, Ruth. GIFTED CHILDREN AND PROVISIONS FOR THEM IN OUR SCHOOLS. 1922. 12 pp. (Also as *Illinois. University. Bulletin*, Volume 20, Number 13.)

Number 15. Monroe, Walter S. EDUCATIONAL TESTS FOR USE IN ELEMENTARY SCHOOLS. 1922. 22 pp. (Also as *Illinois. University. Bulletin*, Volume 20, Number 16.)

Number 16. Odell, Charles W. THE EFFECT OF ATTENDANCE UPON SCHOOL ACHIEVEMENT. 1923. 8 pp. (Also as *Illinois. University. Bulletin*, Volume 20, Number 31.)

Number 17. Mohlman, Dora Keen. THE ELEMENTARY SCHOOL PRINCIPALSHIP. 1923. 14 pp. (Also as *Illinois. University. Bulletin*, Volume 20, Number 36.)

Number 18. Monroe, Walter S. EDUCATIONAL TESTS FOR USE IN HIGH SCHOOLS. 1923. 18 pp. (Also as *Illinois. University. Bulletin*, Volume 20, Number 38.)

Number 19. Streitz, Ruth. PROVISIONS FOR EXCEPTIONAL CHILDREN IN 191 ILLINOIS CITIES. 1923. 13 pp. (Also as *Illinois. University. Bulletin*, Volume 20, Number 40.)

Number 20. McClusky, Frederick Dean. PLACE OF MOVING PICTURES IN VISUAL EDUCATION. 1923. 11 pp. (Also as *Illinois. University. Bulletin*, Volume 20, Number 46.)

Number 21. Monroe, Walter S. ANNOUNCEMENT OF THE BUREAU OF EDUCATIONAL RESEARCH FOR 1923–24. 1923. 8 pp. (Also as *Illinois. University. Bulletin*, Volume 21, Number 3.)

Number 22. Odell, Charles W. PROVISIONS FOR THE INDIVIDUAL DIFFERENCES OF HIGH SCHOOL PUPILS. 1923. 15 pp. (Also as *Illinois. University. Bulletin*, Volume 21, Number 4.)

Number 23. Monroe, Walter S. EDUCATIONAL GUIDANCE IN HIGH SCHOOLS. 1923. 14 pp. (Also as *Illinois. University. Bulletin*, Volume 21, Number 15.)

Number 24. Nolan, Aretas W. THE PROJECT IN EDUCATION WITH SPECIAL REFERENCE TO TEACHING AGRICULTURE. 1923. 16 pp. (Also as *Illinois. University. Bulletin*, Volume 21, Number 16.)

Number 25. Monroe, Walter S., and John A. Clark. MEASURING TEACHING EFFICIENCY. 1924. 26 pp. (Also as *Illinois. University. Bulletin*, Volume 21, Number 22.)

Number 26. Barton, H. J., E. L. Clark, Helen Pence, and Others. NOTES ON THE TEACHING OF LATIN IN HIGH SCHOOLS. 1924. 25 pp. (Also as *Illinois. University. Bulletin*, Volume 21, Number 28.)

Number 27. Streitz, Ruth. EDUCATIONAL DIAGNOSIS. 1924. 16 pp. (Also as *Illinois. University. Bulletin*, Volume 21, Number 41.)

Number 28. Staley, Seward C. THE PROGRAM OF SPORTSMANSHIP EDU-

CATION. 1924. 27 pp. (Also as *Illinois. University. Bulletin*, Volume 21, Number 49.)

Number 29. Odell, Charles W. THE USE OF THE QUESTION IN CLASSROOM INSTRUCTION. 1924. 18 pp. (Also as *Illinois. University. Bulletin*, Volume 22. Number 5.)

Number 30. Odell, Charles W. THE EVALUATION AND IMPROVEMENT OF SCHOOL BUILDINGS, GROUNDS AND EQUIPMENT. 1924. 18 pp. (Also as *Illinois. University. Bulletin*, Volume 22, Number 6.)

Number 31. Monroe, Walter S. THE PLANNING OF TEACHING. 1924. 41 pp. (Also as *Illinois. University. Bulletin*, Volume 22, Number 7.)

Number 32. Miller, F. J., Roy C. Flickinger, Rachel L. Sargent, Ethel J. Luke, Glenna D. Thompson et al. LATIN IN HIGH SCHOOLS. 1924. 28 pp. (Also as *Illinois. University. Bulletin*, Volume 22, Number 12.)

Number 33. Odell, Charles W. EDUCATIONAL TESTS FOR USE IN ELEMENTARY SCHOOLS, REVISED. 1924. 22 pp. (Also as *Illinois. University. Bulletin*, Volume 22, Number 16.)

Number 34. Odell, Charles W. EDUCATIONAL TESTS FOR USE IN HIGH SCHOOLS, REVISED. 1925. 19 pp. (Also as *Illinois. University. Bulletin*, Volume 22, Number 37.)

Number 35. Monroe, Walter S. THE MAKING OF A COURSE OF STUDY. 1925. 35 pp. (Also as *Illinois. University. Bulletin*, Volume 23, Number 2.)

Number 36. Reagan, George W. PRINCIPLES RELATING TO THE ENGINEERING OF SPECIFIC HABITS. 1925. 23 pp. (Also as *Illinois. University. Bulletin*, Volume 23, Number 5.)

Number 37. Herriott, M. E. HOW TO MAKE A COURSE OF STUDY IN ARITHMETIC. 1925. 50 pp. (Also as *Illinois. University. Bulletin*, Volume 23, Number 6.)

Number 38. Odell, Charles W. THE ASSIGNMENT OF LESSONS. 1925. 20 pp. (Also as *Illinois. University. Bulletin*, Volume 23, Number 7.)

Number 39. Prescott, Henry W., Roy C. Flickinger, Laura B. Woodruff, Irene G. Whaley, et al. APPRECIATION OF LATIN. 1925. 35 pp. (Also as *Illinois. University. Bulletin*, Volume 23, Number 15.)

Number 40. Orata, Pedro T. ADAPTATION OF SUBJECT-MATTER AND INSTRUCTION TO INDIVIDUAL DIFFERENCES IN THE ELEMENTARY SCHOOL. 1926. 19 pp. (Also as *Illinois. University. Bulletin,* Volume 23 [mismarked as Volume 13], Number 20.)

Number 41. Herriott, M. E. MODIFYING TECHNIQUE OF INSTRUCTION FOR GIFTED CHILDREN. 1926. 17 pp. (Also as *Illinois. University. Bulletin*, Volume 23, Number 18.)

Number 42. Herriott, M. E. HOW TO MAKE A COURSE OF STUDY IN READING. 1926. 37 pp. (Also as *Illinois. University. Bulletin*, Volume 23, Number 18.)

Number 43. Monroe, Walter S. PROJECTS AND THE PROJECT METHOD. 1926. 20 pp. (Also as *Illinois. University. Bulletin*, Volume 23, Number 30.)

Number 44. Odell, Charles W. OBJECTIVE MEASUREMENT OF INFORMATION. 1926. 27 pp. (Also as *Illinois. University. Bulletin*, Volume 23, Number 36.)

Number 45. Monroe, Walter S. TEACHERS' OBJECTIVES. 1926. 24 pp. (Also as *Illinois. University. Bulletin,* Volume 23, Number 39.)

Number 46. Herriott, M. E. HOW TO MAKE COURSES OF STUDY IN THE SOCIAL STUDIES. 1926. 52 pp. (Also as *Illinois. University. Bulletin,* Volume 24, Number 5.)

Number 47. Alter, Donald R., Genevieve Duguid, Walter R. Kukets, Liesette J. McHarry, S. Helen Taylor, and Anne Thomsen. INSTRUCTIONAL ACTIVITIES IN THE UNIVERSITY HIGH SCHOOL. 1926. 28 pp. (Also as *Illinois. University. Bulletin,* Volume 24, Number 13.)

Number 48. Odell, Charles W. EDUCATIONAL TESTS FOR USE IN HIGH SCHOOLS, SECOND REVISION. 1927. 43 pp. (Also as *Illinois. University. Bulletin,* Volume 24, Number 33.)

Number 49. Odell, Charles W. EDUCATIONAL TESTS FOR USE IN ELEMENTARY SCHOOLS, SECOND REVISION. 1927. 44 pp.

Number 50. Williams, Lewis W. SUPPLY AND DEMAND AS APPLIED TO HIGH-SCHOOL TEACHERS. 1929. 11 pp. (Also as *Illinois. University. Bulletin,* Volume 26, Number 26.)

Number 51. Odell, C. W. THE COMPARISON OF PUPIL'S ACHIEVEMENT WITH THEIR CAPACITY. 1929. 2 pp. (Also as *Illinois. University. Bulletin,* Volume 26, Number 28.)

Number 52. Nolan, Aretas W. TECHNIQUES USED IN DEALING WITH CERTAIN PROBLEMS OF COLLEGE TRAINING. 1929. 25 pp. (Also as *Illinois. University. Bulletin,* Volume 26, Number 40.)

Number 53. Odell, C. W. EDUCATIONAL TESTS FOR USE IN HIGH SCHOOLS, THIRD REVISION. 1929. 50 pp. (Also as *Illinois. University. Bulletin,* Volume 27, Number 3.)

Number 54. Bottenfield, E. O. A PROGRAM OF EDUCATIONAL GUIDANCE FOR HIGH SCHOOLS. 1929. 30 pp. (Also as *Illinois. University. Bulletin,* Volume 27, Number 5.)

Number 55. Kinder, J. S., and C. W. Odell. EDUCATIONAL TESTS FOR USE IN INSTITUTIONS OF HIGHER LEARNING. 1930. 95 pp. (Also as *Illinois. University. Bulletin,* Volume 27, Number 49.)

Number 56. Odell, Charles W. SPECIAL SCHOOL FEATURES REPORTED BY ILLINOIS SUPERINTENDENTS AND PRINCIPALS. 1932. 11 pp. (Also as *Illinois. University. Bulletin,* Volume 29, Number 37.)

Number 57. Hand, Harold C., ed. LIVING IN THE ATOMIC AGE. 1946. 59 pp. (Also as *Illinois. University. Bulletin,* Volume 44, Number 23.)

Number 58. THE ROLE OF THE PUBLIC JUNIOR COLLEGE IN ILLINOIS. Prepared by the Junior-College Committee of the Curriculum Committee of the Illinois Secondary School Principals' Association. 1947. 43 pp. (Also as *Illinois. University. Bulletin,* Volume 44, Number 43.)

Number 59. Sumption, Merle R., and Harlan D. Beem. A GUIDE TO SCHOOL REORGANIZATION IN ILLINOIS. 1947. 52 pp. (Also as *Illinois. University. Bulletin,* Volume 44, Number 60.)

Number 60. Reeder, Edwin Hewett, A GUIDE TO SUPERVISION IN THE ELEMENTARY SCHOOLS. 1947. 71 pp. (Also as *Illinois. University. Bulletin,* Volume 45, Number 7.)

442. Journal of Personnel Research.

TITLE VARIATIONS: Continued by *Personnel Journal* with Volume 6, 1927/1928.

DATES OF PUBLICATION: Volume 1–5, May 1922–April 1927.

FREQUENCY: Monthly.

NUMBERING VARIATIONS: None.

PUBLISHER: **Baltimore:** Williams and Wilkins Company, 1922–1927.

PRIMARY EDITORS: **Leonard Outhwaite,** 1922–1923; **Clarence S. Yoakum,** 1922–1927; **Walter V. Bingham,** 1923–1927; **Louis L. Thurstone,** 1923–1926; **Max Freyd,** 1926–1927.

EDITORIAL BOARD: Leonard Outhwaite, 1922–1927; Clarence S. Yoakum, 1922–1927; Alfred D. Flinn, 1922–1927; Alice Hamilton, 1922–1926; Richard W. Husband, 1922–1925; Wesley C. Mitchell, 1922–1927; Lewis M. Terman, 1922–1927; Mary Van Kleek, 1922–1927; Joseph H. Willits, 1922–1927; Frankwood E. Williams, 1922–1927; Matthew Woll, 1922–1927; Louis L. Thurstone, 1926–1927.

443. Karlsruhe. Technische Hochschule. Institut für Sozialpsychologie. Sozialpsychologische Forschungen.

TITLE VARIATIONS: None.

DATES OF PUBLICATION: Band 1–2, 1922.

FREQUENCY: Irregular. *See* Contents *below.*

NUMBERING VARIATIONS: None.

PUBLISHER: **Berlin:** Julius Springer, 1922.

PRIMARY EDITOR: **Willy Hellpach,** 1922.

CONTENTS:
Band 1. Lang, Richard, and Willy Hellpach. GRUPPENFABRIKATION. 1922. 186 pp.
Band 2. Rosenstock, Eugen. WERKSTATTAUSSIEDLUNG. 1922. 286 pp.

444. Kleine Schriften zur Seelenforschung.

TITLE VARIATIONS: Continued by *Schriften zur Seelenforschung* with Band 19, 1928.

DATES OF PUBLICATION: Band 1–17, 1922–1927.

FREQUENCY: Irregular. *See* Contents *below.*

NUMBERING VARIATIONS: Band 18 omitted in numbering.

PUBLISHER: **Stuttgart:** J. Püttmann, 1922–1927.

PRIMARY EDITOR: **Arthur Kronfeld,** 1922–1927.

CONTENTS:
Band 1. Friedrichs, Theodor, ZUR PSYCHOLOGIE DER HYPNOSE UND DER SUGGESTION. 1922. 32 pp.
Band 2. Kronfeld, Arthur. ÜBER GLEICHGESCHLECHTIGKEIT. 1922. 43 pp.

Band 3. Haas, Wilhelm. DAS PROBLEM DER MEDIUMISMUS. 1923. 48 pp.

Band 4. Lurje, Walter. MYSTISCHES DENKEN, GEISTESKRANKHEIT UND MODERNE KUNST. 1923. 24 pp.

Band 5. Roffenstein, Gaston. DAS PROBLEM DES UNBEWUSSTEN. 1923. 51 pp.

Band 6. Kronfeld, Arthur. DAS SEELISCH ABNORME UND DIE GEMEIN-SCHAFT. 1923. 21 pp.

Band 7. Singer, Kurt. VOM WESEN DER MUSIK. 1924. 45 pp.

Band 8. Plaut, Paul DER PSYCHOLOGISCHE RAUM. 1924. 33 pp.

Band 9. Alrutz, Sydney. NEUE STRAHLEN DES MENSCHLICHEN ORGANIS-MUS. 1924. 32. pp.

Band 10. Hildebrandt, Kurt. GEDANKEN ZUR RASSENPSYCHOLOGIE. 1924. 20 pp.

Band 11. Bruck, Karl. EXPERIMENTELLE TELEPATHIE. 1925. 80 pp.

Band 12. Scherk, Gerhard. ZUR PSYCHOLOGIE DER EUNUCHOIDEN. 1924. 24 pp.

Band 13. Brandess, Theo. ÜBER SEELISCH BEDINGTE STÖRUNGEN DER MENSTRUATION. 1925. 32 pp.

Band 14. Decsi, Emerich. ÜBER AUTOSUGGESTIONSBEHANDLUNG INSBE-SONDERE DIE LEHREN VON CONE. 1925. 41 pp.

Band 15. Roffenstein, Gaston. DAS PROBLEM DES PSYCHOLOGISCHEN VER-STEHENS. 1926. 160 pp.

Band 16. Singer, Kurt. HEILWIRKUNG DER MUSIK. 1927. 33 pp.

Band 17. Arco, Graf George von, and Alexander Herzberg. DIE BIS-SKYSCHE DIAGNOSKOPIE. 1927. 32 pp.

445. *London. National Institute of Industrial Psychology. Journal.*

TITLE VARIATIONS: Continued by *Human Factor* with Volume 6, 1932.

DATES OF PUBLICATION: Volume 1–5, January 1922–October 1931.

FREQUENCY: Quarterly (each volume contains 8 numbers issued over 2 years).

NUMBERING VARIATIONS: None.

PUBLISHER: **London:** National Institute of Industrial Psychology, 1922–1931.

PRIMARY EDITORS: **Charles S. Myers,** 1922–1931; **George H. Miles,** 1922–1927; **Margaret Horsey,** 1928–1931.

446. *North Dakota. University. Departmental Bulletins. Art Psychology Bulletin.*

TITLE VARIATIONS: Titled *Art Bulletin,* Number 1–2, 1922–1924. Also called [*North Dakota. University.*] *Department of Art. Art Psychology Bulletin.*

DATES OF PUBLICATION: Number 1–4, November 1922–November 1926.

FREQUENCY: Irregular. *See* Contents *below.*

NUMBERING VARIATIONS: Also numbered as *Departmental Bulletin. See* Contents *below.*

PUBLISHER: **Grand Forks, North Dakota:** University of North Dakota, Art Department, 1922–1924. **Grand Forks:** University of North Dakota, 1925–1926.

PRIMARY EDITORS: **Erwin O. Christensen,** 1922–1926; **Theodore Karwoski,** 1925–1926.

CONTENTS:

Number 1. Christensen, Erwin O. WALLS AND PICTURES. November 1922. 24 pp. (Also as *Departmental Bulletin,* Volume 6, Number 5, 1922.)

Number 2. Christensen, Erwin O. APPRECIATION OF ART: PAINTING. January 1924. 32 pp. (Also as *Departmental Bulletin,* Volume 8, Number 1, 1924.)

Number 3. Christensen, Erwin O. and Theodore Karwoski. A TEST IN ART APPRECIATION: A PRELIMINARY REPORT. January 1925. 77 pp. (Also as *Departmental Bulletin,* Volume 9, Number 1, 1925.)

Number 4. Christensen, Erwin O. and Theodore Karwoski. A TEST IN ART APPRECIATION: SECOND REPORT. November 1926. 76 pp. (Also as *Departmental Bulletin,* Volume 10, Number 7, 1926.)

447. *Ohio. State University. Contributions in Psychology.*

TITLE VARIATIONS: Continues *Ohio. State University. Psychological Studies.*

DATES OF PUBLICATION: Number 6–12, 1922–1934.

FREQUENCY: Irregular. *See* Contents *below.*

NUMBERING VARIATIONS: Number 6 incorrectly numbered 1. Number 6 and 7 also numbered as *Ohio. State University. Bulletin* and *Ohio. State University. Studies* respectively. *See* Contents *below.* Number 8 bears the additional unnumbered designation *Ohio. State University. Studies.* Number 9–12 bear the additional unnumbered designation *Ohio. State University. Studies. Graduate School Series.*

PUBLISHER: **Columbus, Ohio:** The Ohio State University Press, 1922–1934.

PRIMARY EDITORS: None listed.

CONTENTS:

Number 6. THE UNIVERSITY INTELLIGENCE TESTS, 1919–1922. Under the direction of the Department of Psychology. 1922. 36 pp (Also as *Ohio. State University. Bulletin,* Volume 27, Number 5, November 30, 1922.)

Number 7. Leatherman, Zoe Emily, and Edgar A. Doll. A STUDY OF A MALADJUSTED COLLEGE STUDENT. 1925. 56 pp. (Also as *Ohio. State University. Studies,* Volume 2, Number 2, July 30, 1925.)

Number 8. Cohen, Irma Loeb. THE INTELLIGENCE OF JEWS AS COMPARED WITH NON-JEWS. 1927. 43 pp.

Number 9. Koch, Berthe Couch. THE APPARENT WEIGHT OF COLORS. 1928. 27 pp.

Number 10. Pratt, Karl Chapman, Amalie Kraushaar Nelson, and Kuo Hua Sun, supervised by Albert Paul Weiss and Andrews Rogers. THE BEHAVIOR OF THE NEWBORN INFANT. 1930. 237 pp.

Number 11. Weiss, Albert P., and Alvhh R. Lauer, under the auspices of the National Research Council, 1927–1929. PSYCHOLOGICAL PRINCIPLES IN AUTOMOTIVE DRIVING. 1930. 165 pp.

Number 12. Dockeray, F. C., ed. STUDIES IN INFANT BEHAVIOR: Disher, Dorothy Rose. THE REACTIONS OF NEWBORN INFANTS TO CHEMICAL STIMULI ADMINISTERED NASALLY; Valentine, W. L., and Isabelle Wagner. RELATIVE ARM MOTILITY IN THE NEWBORN INFANT; Taylor, James H. INNATE EMOTIONAL RESPONSES IN INFANTS; and Dockeray, F. C., and Charlotte Rice. RESPONSES OF NEWBORN INFANTS TO PAIN STIMULATION. 1934. 93 pp.

448. *Psikhiatriia, nevrologiia i eksperimental'naia psikhologiia.*
[Organ of the Obshchestvo psikhiatrov i nevropatologov v Petrograde.]

TITLE VARIATIONS: None.

DATES OF PUBLICATION: Tom 1–3, 1922–1923.

FREQUENCY: Semiannual.

NUMBERING VARIATIONS: None.

PUBLISHER: **St. Petersburg:** Gosudarstvennoe izdatel'stvo, 1922–1923.

PRIMARY EDITORS: Unknown.

449. *Psychology Classics; A Series of Reprints and Translations.*

TITLE VARIATIONS: None.

DATES OF PUBLICATION: Number 1–3, 1922–1930.

FREQUENCY: Irregular. *See* Contents *below.*

NUMBERING VARIATIONS: None.

PUBLISHER: **Baltimore:** Williams & Wilkins Company, 1922–1930.

PRIMARY EDITOR: **Knight Dunlap,** 1922–1930.

CONTENTS:
 Number 1. Lange, Carl Georg, and William James. THE EMOTIONS. 1922. 135 pp.
 Number 2. Lipps, Theodor. PSYCHOLOGICAL STUDIES. Translated by Herbert C. Sanborn from 2nd revised and enlarged edition. 1926. 333 pp.
 Number 3. Maine de Biran. THE INFLUENCE OF HABIT ON THE FACULTY OF THINKING. Translated by Margaret Donaldson Boehm. Introduction by George Boas. December 1929. 227 pp.

450. *Rivista di psicologia.* [2.] [Organ of the Società italiana di psicologia and of the Istituti di psicologia sperimentale (Rome and Turin).]

TITLE VARIATIONS: Continues *Rivista di psicologia e rassegna di studi pedagogici e filosofici.* Continued by *Rivista di psicologia normale e patologica* with Volume 29, 1933.

DATES OF PUBLICATION: Volume 18–28, 1922–1932.

FREQUENCY: Quarterly.

NUMBERING VARIATIONS: Multinumber issues in Volume 18–19. Volume 18–28 also called Série II or Nuova Série.

PUBLISHER: **Bologna:** Nicola Zanichelli editore, 1922–1932.

PRIMARY EDITORS: **Guilio Cesare Ferrari,** 1922–1932; **Mario F. Canella,** 1927–1932.

451. *Rome. Università. Istituto di psicologia sperimentale. Contributi psicologici.*

TITLE VARIATIONS: Continues [*Rome. Università.*] *Laboratorio di psicologia sperimentale. Contributi psicologici.*

DATES OF PUBLICATION: Volume 5–6, 1922/1928–1929/1933.

FREQUENCY: Volume 5, 1922/1928; and Volume 6, 1929/1933.

NUMBERING VARIATIONS: None.

PUBLISHER: **Rome:** Presso l'Istituto di psicologia sperimentale, 1928–1933.

PRIMARY EDITOR: **Sante De Sanctis,** 1928–1933.

NOTE: Volumes contain previously published material by members of the Istituto.

452. *Scandinavian Scientific Review; Contributions to Philosophy, Psychology and the Science of Education by Northern Scientists.*

TITLE VARIATIONS: None.

DATES OF PUBLICATION: Volume 1–3, September 1922–September/December, 1924.

FREQUENCY: Quarterly.

NUMBERING VARIATIONS: Volume 1 complete with issue Number 1. Multinumber issues in Volumes 2 and 3.

PUBLISHER: **Oslo, Norway:** With & Co.s Forlag, 1922–1923. **Oslo:** Scandinavian Scientific Press, 1923–1924.

PRIMARY EDITORS: **Martin L. Reymert,** 1922–1924; **Anne Ross Reymert,** 1923–1924.

NATIONAL ADVISORS: Anathon Aall, 1922–1924; A. Bjarnason, 1922–1924; A. Grotenfelt, 1922–1924; G. A. Jaederholm, 1922–1924; Victor Kuhr, 1922–1924.

453. *Warsaw. Komisja pedagogiczna. Wydawnictwa.*

TITLE VARIATIONS: Also called *Varsovie. Commission pédagogique du ministere des cultes et de l'instruction publique. Section de psychologie pédagogique;* and *Ministerstwo wyznań religijnych i oświęcenia publicznego. Komisja pedagogiczna.*

DATES OF PUBLICATION: Książka 1, 3, 4, 6, 10, 11; 1922–1928.

FREQUENCY: Irregular. *See* Contents *below.*

NUMBERING VARIATIONS: Other numbers may exist. *See* Note *below.* One issue also numbered as *Prace psychologiczne, 2.*

PUBLISHER: **Warsaw:** W Książnicy polskiej towarzystwa nauczycieli szkoł wyższych, 1922–1928.

PRIMARY EDITORS: None listed.

CONTENTS:

    Książka 1. Materjaly i opracowania z zakresu pedagogik. 1922.

    Książka 3. Nawroczyński, Bogdan. Uczeń i klasa. 1923. 326 pp.

    Książka 4. Bykowski, L. J. Badania eksperymentalne nad znaczeniem współzawodnictwa. 1923. 79 pp. (Also as *Prace psychologiczne, 2.*)

    Książka 6. Falski, M. Materjały do projektu sieci szkoł powszechnych. 1925.

    Książka 10. Szuman, S. Sztuka dziecka. Psychologja twórczości rysunkowej dziecka. 1927. 224 pp.

    Książka 11. Znaniecki, F. Socjologja wychowania, Tom 1, 1928. [Tom 2 issued 1930 but not as part of this series.]

NOTE: Numbers listed above are only numbers listed in the *National Union Catalogue of Pre-1956 Imprints* and the *British Museum Catalogue of Books.* Other numbers may exist.

454. *Zhurnal psikhologii, nevrologii i psikhiatrii.*

TITLE VARIATIONS: None.

DATES OF PUBLICATION: Vypusk 1–5, 1922–1924.

FREQUENCY: Irregular.

NUMBERING VARIATIONS: None.

PUBLISHER: **Moscow:** Glavnyi upravlenie nauchnymi uchrezhdeniiami, 1922–1924.

PRIMARY EDITORS: Unknown.

NOTE: Information on this title was compiled from entries in *A Half Century of Soviet Serials.*

1923

455. *Australasian Journal of Psychology and Philosophy.*

TITLE VARIATIONS: Continued by *Australasian Journal of Philosophy* with Volume 25, 1947.

DATES OF PUBLICATION: Volume 1–24, March 1923–December 1946.

FREQUENCY: **Quarterly,** Volume 1–15, March 1923–December 1937. **Triannual,** Volume 16–24, April 1938–December 1946.

NUMBERING VARIATIONS: Volume 21, Number 2/3, December 1943, Volume 22, Number 1/2, September 1944, and Volume 24, Number 1/2, September 1946 are double issues. Volume 23, Number 1–3, December 1945 is a triple issue.

PUBLISHER: **Sydney:** Australasian Association of Psychology and Philosophy, 1923–1936. **Glebe, New South Wales:** Australasian Association of Psychology and Philosophy, 1937–1946.

PRIMARY EDITORS: **Francis Anderson,** 1923–1926; **H. Tasman Lovell,** 1927–1934; **John Anderson,** 1935–1946; **J. A. Passmore,** 1947.

456. *British Journal of Medical Psychology; Being the Medical Section of the British Journal of Psychology.*

TITLE VARIATIONS: Continues *British Journal of Psychology. Medical Section.*

DATES OF PUBLICATION: Volume 3–23+, January 1923–1950+.

FREQUENCY: Quarterly (Irregular).

NUMBERING VARIATIONS: Multinumber issues present.

PUBLISHER: **London:** Cambridge University Press, 1923–1950+.

PRIMARY EDITORS: **Thomas W. Mitchell,** 1923–1944; **H. G. Baynes,** 1923–1946; **William Brown,** 1923–1950+; **Ernest Jones,** 1923–1950+; **George Riddoch,** 1923–1934; **John Rickman,** 1925–1950+; **Major Greenwood,** 1936–1950+; **Susan Isaacs,** 1936–1948; **O. Zangwill,** 1949–1950+; **C. S. Myers,** 1936–1946; **Lionel S. Penrose,** 1936–1950+; **C. G. Seligman,** 1936–1946; **F. R. Winton,** 1936–1950+; **W. Clifford M. Scott,** 1941–1949; **John D. Sutherland,** 1947–1950+; **M.S.M. Fordham,** 1949–1950+; **T. F. Main,** 1949–1950+; **T. F. Roger,** 1949–1950+.

457. *Clínica psicopedagógica. Revista de neuropsiquiatría infantil.*

TITLE VARIATIONS: None.

DATES OF PUBLICATION: Año 1–3, Número 1, August 1923–January/February/March 1925.

FREQUENCY: Quarterly.

NUMBERING VARIATIONS: None.

PUBLISHER: **Buenos Aires:** Instituto psicopedagógico para niños nerviosos, 1923–1925.

PRIMARY EDITORS: None listed.

458. *Educational Problem Series.*

TITLE VARIATIONS: None.

DATES OF PUBLICATION: Number 1–15, 1923–1932.

FREQUENCY: Irregular. *See* Contents *below.*

NUMBERING VARIATIONS: None.

PUBLISHER: **Bloomington, Illinois:** Public School Publishing Company, 1923–1932.

PRIMARY EDITOR: **Guy M. Whipple,** 1923–1932.

CONTENTS:

Number 1. Whipple, Guy Montrose. PROBLEMS IN EDUCATIONAL PSYCHOLOGY. 1923. 86 pp.

Number 2. Edmonson, James B. PROBLEMS IN SECONDARY EDUCATION. 1923. 83 pp.

Number 3. Woody, Clifford. PROBLEMS IN ELEMENTARY SCHOOL INSTRUCTION. 1923. 65 pp.

Number 4. Edmonson, J. B., and E. E. Lewis. PROBLEMS IN THE ADMINISTRATION OF A SCHOOL SYSTEM. 1924. 94 pp.

Number 5. Edmonson, J. B., and Raleigh Schorling. PROBLEMS OF THE HIGH SCHOOL TEACHER. 1924. 78 pp.

Number 6. Pittman, Marvin S. PROBLEMS OF THE RURAL TEACHER. 1924. 77 pp.

Number 7. Whipple, Guy M., and J. B. Edmonson. PROBLEMS OF A HIGH SCHOOL TEACHING STAFF. 1924. 67 pp.

Number 8. Davis, Calvin O., and E. E. Lewis. PROBLEMS OF THE JUNIOR HIGH SCHOOL. 1925. 76 pp.

Number 9. Whipple, Guy M., and Helen Davis. PROBLEMS IN MENTAL TESTING. 1925. 67 pp.

Number 10. Edmonson, James B. NEW PROBLEMS IN SECONDARY EDUCATION. 1926. 83 pp.

Number 11. Payne, Wilfred. PROBLEMS IN LOGIC. 1926. 54 pp.

Number 12. Bennett, Guy V. PROBLEMS OF THE ELEMENTARY SCHOOL PRINCIPAL. 1928. 88 pp.

Number 13. Payne, Wilfred. NEW PROBLEMS IN LOGIC. 1929. 86 pp.

Number 14. Lewis, Ervin E., and J. B. Edmonson. PROBLEMS IN THE ADMINISTRATION OF A SMALL SCHOOL SYSTEM. 1929. 84 pp.

Number 15. Woody, C. NEW PROBLEMS IN ELEMENTARY SCHOOL INSTRUCTION. 1932. 67 pp.

459. *Forum of Education.*

TITLE VARIATIONS: Subtitled *A Journal of Enquiry and Research in the Psychology, Philosophy and Method of Education,* Volume 7–8, 1929–1930. Continues *Journal of Experimental Pedagogy and Training College Record.* Incorporated into *British Journal of Educational Psychology* with Volume 1, 1931.

DATES OF PUBLICATION: New Series, Volume 1–8, February 1923–November 1930.

FREQUENCY: Triannual.

NUMBERING VARIATIONS: None.

PUBLISHER: **London:** Training College Association, Longmans, Green and Company, 1923–1930.

PRIMARY EDITOR: **C. W. Valentine,** 1923–1930.

EDITORIAL BOARD: John Adams, 1923–1930; R. L. Archer, 1923–1930; Graham Balfour, 1923–1929; Cyril Burt, 1923–1930; Winifred Mercier, 1923–1930; H. Crichton-Miller, 1923–1930; W. H. Moberly, 1923–1930; T. Percy Nunn, 1923–1930; H. Bompas Smith, 1923–1930; John Strong, 1923–1930; Godfrey H. Thomson, 1923–1930; Helen M. Wodehouse, 1923–1930; C. E. Spearman, 1925–1930.

460. *Internationale Zeitschrift für Individualpsychologie. Arbeiten aus dem Gebiete der Psychotherapie, Psychologie und Pädagogik.*

TITLE VARIATIONS: Continues *Zeitschrift für Individualpsychologie. Studien aus dem Gebiete der Psychotherapie, Psychologie und Pädagogik.*

DATES OF PUBLICATION: Band 2–19+, 1923–1950+. Suspended publication July/December 1937–January/March 1947.

FREQUENCY: **Bimonthly,** Band 2–11, September 1923–1933. **Quarterly,** Band 12–19+, 1934–1950+.

NUMBERING VARIATIONS: Multinumber issues present. Band 8, Heft 1, 1930 is SELBSTERZIEHUNG DES CHARAKTERS. ALFRED ADLER ZUM 60. GEBURTSTAGE . . .

PUBLISHER: **Vienna:** Verlag Individualpsychologie, 1923–1926. **Leipzig:** Verlag S. Hirzel, 1927–1933. **Vienna:** Perles, 1934–1937. **Vienna:** Springer-Verlag, 1947–1950+.

PRIMARY EDITORS: **Alfred Adler,** 1923–1935; **Leonhard Seif,** 1925–1935; **Fritz Künkel,** 1925–1931; **Hermann Weiskopf,** 1925; **Alice Rühle-Gerstel,** 1925; **Wilhelm Fürnrohr,** 1925–1935; **M. Stam,** 1926–1931; **Ladislaus Zilahi,** 1927–1937; **Alexandra Adler,** 1947; **Ferdinand Birnbaum,** 1947; **Maria Birnbaum,** 1948–1950+; **Karl Mowotny,** 1948–1950+; **O. Spiel,** 1948–1950+.

461. *Journal de neurologie et de psychiatrie.* [*1.*] [Official organ of the Société de médecine mentale de belgique; the Société belge de neurologie; the Groupément belge d'études oto-neuro-ophtalmologiques et neuro-chirurgicales; and official bulletin of the Congrès belge de neurologie et de psychiatrie, 1932].

TITLE VARIATIONS: Continues *Journal de neurologie. Neurologie, psychiatrie, psychologie.* Continued by *Journal belge de neurologie et de psychiatrie* with Tome 33, 1933.

DATES OF PUBLICATION: Tome 23–32, 1923–1932.

FREQUENCY: Monthly.

NUMBERING VARIATIONS: None.

PUBLISHER: **Brussels:** Direction, J. Crocq, 62, rue Joseph II, 1923–1924. **Brussels:** Imprimerie J. Vromans & cie, 1925–1929. **Brussels:** Des Presses de J. Vromans, 1930–1932.

PRIMARY EDITOR: **J. Crocq,** 1923–1924; **H. Hoven,** 1925–1928; **Rodolphe Ley,** 1925–1932; **L. Van Bogaert,** 1925–1932; **A. Leroy,** 1929–1932.

462. *Journal of Sexology and Psychoanalysis.*

TITLE VARIATIONS: Supersedes *American Journal of Urology and Sexology;* and *Psyche and Eros.*

DATES OF PUBLICATION: Volume 1–2, Number 6, January 1923–November/ December 1924.

FREQUENCY: Bimonthly.

NUMBERING VARIATIONS: None.

PUBLISHER: **New York:** The American Sexanalytic Press, 1923–1924.

PRIMARY EDITORS: **William J. Robinson,** 1923–1924; **S. A. Tannenbaum,** 1923–1924.

463. *Mental Hygiene Bulletin.*

TITLE VARIATIONS: None.

DATES OF PUBLICATION: Volume 1–10, Number 9/10, January 1923–November/ December 1932.

FREQUENCY: Monthly (except July and August).

NUMBERING VARIATIONS: Multinumber issues present.

PUBLISHER: **New York:** National Committee for Mental Hygiene, 1923. **Albany, New York:** National Committee for Mental Hygiene, 1923–1932.

PRIMARY EDITORS: **Frankwood E. Williams,** 1923–1930; **Edith M. Furbush,** 1923–1927; **Paul O. Komora,** 1927–1932.

464. *Moscow. Akademiia sotsial'nogo vospitaniia. Psikhologicheskaia laboratoriia. Zapiski.*

TITLE VARIATIONS: None.

DATES OF PUBLICATION: Tome 1, 1923.

FREQUENCY: Irregular.

NUMBERING VARIATIONS: None.

PUBLISHER: **Moscow:** Akademiia sotsial'nogo vospitaniia, Psikhologicheskaia laboratoriia, 1923.

PRIMARY EDITORS: Unknown.

NOTE: Information on this title was compiled from entries in *Half a Century of Soviet Serials.*

465. Moscow. Gosudarstvennyi Darvinskii muzei. Zoopsikhologicheskaia laboratoriia. Trudy.

TITLE VARIATIONS: None.

DATES OF PUBLICATION: Tom 1–3, 1923–1935.

FREQUENCY: Irregular. *See* Contents *below.*

NUMBERING VARIATIONS: Tom 1 and 2 not numbered.

PUBLISHER: **Moscow:** Gosudarstvennyi Darvinskii muzei. Zoopsikhologiches-kaia laboratoriia, 1923–1935.

PRIMARY EDITOR: **Nadezhda Nikolaevna Kots,** 1923–1935.

CONTENTS:
Tom 1. Kots, Nadezhda Nikolaevna. ISSLEDOVANIE POSNAVATEL'NYKH SPO-SOBNOSTEL SHIMPANSE. 1923. 406 pp.
Tom 2. Kots, Nadezhda Nikolaevna. PRISPOSOBITEL'NYE MOTORNYE NA-VYKI MAKAKA V USLOVIIAKH EKSPERIMENTA. 1928. 308 pp.
Tom 3. Kots, Nadezhda Nikolaevna. DITIA SHIMPANZE I DITIA CHELOVEKA V IKH INSTINKLAKH, EMOTSIAKH, IGRAKH, PRIVYCHKAKH I VYRAZITEL'NYKH DVI-ZHENIAKH. 1935. 595 pp.

466. Public Personnel Studies.

TITLE VARIATIONS: Continued by *New Public Personnel Studies* with Volume 10, Number 1, June 1941.

DATES OF PUBLICATION: Volume 1–9, Number 1, October 15, 1923–January/February 1931.

FREQUENCY: **Semimonthly,** Volume 1, Number 1–6, October 15, 1923–December 31, 1923. **Bimonthly,** Volume 2, Number 1–3, January/February 1924–May/June 1924. **Monthly,** Volume 2, Number 4–9, July 1924–December 1924. **Monthly,** Volume 3–9, Number 1, January 1925–January/February 1931.

NUMBERING VARIATIONS: Issues also assigned whole numbers, Number 1–89. Only 10 issues, Volume 8, 1930.

PUBLISHER: **Washington, D.C.:** Bureau of Public Personnel Administration, Institute for Government Research, 1923. **Washington, D.C.:** Editorial Office. Bureau of Public Personnel Administration. Institute for Government Research. Office of Publication: and **Baltimore:** Johns Hopkins University Press, 1924. **Washington, D.C.:** Bureau of Public Personnel Administration, Institute of Government Research, 1924–1926. **Washington, D.C.:** Bureau of Public Personnel Administration, 1926–1931.

PRIMARY EDITORS: **W. F. Willoughby,** 1923–1926; **Fred Telford,** 1926–1931.

EDITORIAL BOARD: Fred Telford, 1923–1926; L. L. Thurstone, 1923–1924; Lewis Meriam, 1923–1924; Thelma Gwinn, 1923–1924; L. J. O'Rourke, 1923–1924; F. A. Moss, 1924–1925; J. E. Bathurst, 1928–1931; I. A. Haupt, 1928–1931; G. A. Churchill, 1928–1929; J. B. Probst, 1929–1931; O. C. Short, 1929–1931.

CONTENTS:
Volume 1, Number 1. Thurstone, L. L. INTELLIGENCE TESTS IN THE CIVIL SERVICE. October 15, 1923. 24 pp.
————, Number 2. Thurstone, L. L. COMPARATIVE STUDY OF CLERICAL TESTS. PART 1, ARITHMETIC AND SPELLING. November 1, 1923. 28 pp.
————, Number 3. Thurstone, L. L. COMPARATIVE STUDY OF CLERICAL TESTS. PART 2, CLASSIFYING AND TABULATING. November 15, 1923. 25 pp.
————, Number 4. Thurstone, L. L. COMPARATIVE STUDY OF CLERICAL TESTS. PART 3, TESTS OF BUSINESS INFORMATION. December 1, 1923. 22 pp.
————, Number 5. Thurstone, L. L. COMPARATIVE STUDY OF CLERICAL TESTS. PART 4, GRAMMAR, READING, LETTER WRITING, ORAL ENGLISH. December 15, 1923. 44 pp.
————, Number 6. Thurstone, L. L. COMPARATIVE STUDY OF CLERICAL TESTS. PART 5, PROOF READING, ALPHABETIZING, FILING. December 31, 1923. 27 pp.
Volume 2, Number 1. Thurstone, L. L. THE CIVIL SERVICE TESTS FOR PATROLMEN IN PHILADELPHIA; and, Telford, Fred. CLASSIFICATION OF LABOR POSITIONS AND THE TESTING OF LABOR APPLICANTS IN THE PUBLIC SERVICE. January/February 1924. Pp. 1–11.
————, Number 2. METHODS OF SELECTING EMPLOYEES TO FILL HIGH GRADE POSITIONS IN THE PUBLIC SERVICE. March/April 1924. Pp. 12–59.
————, Number 3. SUGGESTED TESTS FOR PRISON GUARDS. TYPICAL QUESTIONS AND ANSWERS. May/June 1924. Pp. 60–101.

NOTE: The first nine issues of this title were monographic in nature. Only these are listed here.

467. *Shinrigaku Kenkyū.* [Psychological Research.]

TITLE VARIATIONS: Also cited in English as *Japanese Journal of Psychology.* Superseded by *Shinrigaku Kenkyū. Shin Shirīzu [Psychological Research. New Series] with Volume 1, 1926.*

DATES OF PUBLICATION: Volume 1–3, January 1923–December 1925.

FREQUENCY: Quarterly.

NUMBERING VARIATIONS: None.

PUBLISHER: **Tokyo:** Tōkyō Teikoku Daigaku [Tokyo Imperial University], 1923–1925.

PRIMARY EDITORS: **Matataro Matsumoto,** 1923–1925; **Hiroshi Hayami,** 1923–1925; **Koreshige Masuda,** 1923–1925.

468. *Voprosy psikhofiziologii, refleksologii i gigieny truda.*
[Organ of the TNKT Kazanskii institut nauchnoi organizatsii truda and the NKP Petrogradskii institut po izucheniiu mozga i psikhicheskoi deiatel'nosti. Gosudarstvennaia laboratoriia truda.]

DATES OF PUBLICATION: Tom 1–3, 1923–1928.

FREQUENCY: Irregular (Tom 1, 1923; Tom 2, 1926; Tom 3, 1928).

NUMBERING VARIATIONS: None.

PUBLISHER: **Kazan:** Kazanskii institut nauchnoi organizatsii truda, 1923–1928.

PRIMARY EDITORS: **V. M. Bekhterev,** 1923–1928; **N. A. Mislavskii,** 1923–1928.

NOTE: Information on this title was compiled from entries in *A Half Century of Soviet Serials.*

469. *Zeitschrift für Seelenleben.*

TITLE VARIATIONS: Continues *Zeitschrift für Seelenleben, neuere Psychologie und verwandte Gebiete.* Continued by *Zeitschrift für Selenleben und neuere Psychologie und verwandte Gebiete* with Jahrgang 30, 1926.

DATES OF PUBLICATION: Jahrgang 27–29, Heft 26, 1923–1925.

FREQUENCY: Biweekly.

NUMBERING VARIATIONS: None.

PUBLISHER: **Leipzig:** D. Mutze, 1923–1925.

PRIMARY EDITOR: **H. B. Fischer,** 1923–1925.

1924

470. *Berlin. Universität. Sexualpsychologisches Seminar. Arbeiten.*

TITLE VARIATIONS: None.

DATES OF PUBLICATION: Band 1, Heft 1–3, 1924–1926.

FREQUENCY: Annual.

NUMBERING VARIATIONS: None.

PUBLISHER: **Bonn:** A. Marcus und E. Weber's Verlag, 1924–1926.

PRIMARY EDITORS: **Wilhelm Liepmann,** 1924–1926; **Walter von Hauff,** 1924–1926.

CONTENTS:

Band 1, Heft 1. Hauff, Walter von. SEXUALPSYCHOLOGISCHES IM ALTEN TESTAMENT. 1924. 60 pp.

————, **Heft 2.** Hartoch, Werner. SEXUALPSYCHOLOGISCHE STUDIE ZUR HOMOSEXUALITÄT; and Brann, Hellmut Walter. DAS WEIB IN WEININGERS GESCHLECHTSCHARAKTEROLOGIE. 1924. 39 pp.

————, **Heft 3.** Eichler, Oskar. DIE WURZELN DES FRAUENHASSES BEI ARTHUR SCHOPENHAUER. 1926. 65 pp.

471. *Bio-Psychology.*

TITLE VARIATIONS: Although *Bio-Psychology* is the serial title, each issue has a distinctive variant title: *Bulletin of Bio-Psychology,* 1924; and *Bulletin of the Cartesian Research Society Devoted to Scientific Statements Concerning Biological Psychology or Bio-Psychology,* 1925/1926.

DATES OF PUBLICATION: Number 1–2, 1924–1926.

FREQUENCY: **Annual,** Number 1, 1924. **Biennial,** Number 2, 1925/1926.

NUMBERING VARIATIONS: None.

PUBLISHER: **Philadelphia:** Cartesian Research Society, 1924–1926.

PRIMARY EDITORS: None listed.

472. *Henderson Trust. Lectures.*

TITLE VARIATIONS: Also called *William Ramsay Henderson Trust. Lectures.* Supersedes *Henderson Trust. Reports.*

DATES OF PUBLICATION: Number 1–13/16, 1924–1938. Suspended publication 1939–1953.

FREQUENCY: Irregular. *See* Contents *below.*

NUMBERING VARIATIONS: Multinumber publication present.

PUBLISHER: **Edinburgh:** Oliver and Boyd, 1924. **Edinburgh** and **London:** Oliver and Boyd, 1924–1938.

PRIMARY EDITOR: The Chairman of the Henderson Trust acted as editor for the series.

CONTENTS:

Number 1. Smith, G. Elliot. OLD AND THE NEW PHRENOLOGY. 1924. 15 pp.

Number 2. Crichton-Browne, James. THE STORY OF THE BRAIN. 1924. 28 pp.

Number 3. Keith, Arthur. PHRENOLOGICAL STUDIES OF THE SKULL AND ENDOCRANIAL CAST OF SIR THOMAS BROWNE OF NORWICH. 1924. 30 pp.

Number 4. Graves, William Washington. RELATIONS OF SHOULDER BLADE TYPES TO PROBLEMS OF MENTAL AND PHYSICAL ADAPTABILITY. 1925. 35 pp.

Number 5. Pearson, Karl. ON THE SKULL AND PORTRAITS OF GEORGE BUCHANAN. 1926. 28 pp.

Number 6. Clarkson, Robert D. SOME TYPES OF MENTAL DEFECTIVES. 1926.

Number 7. Burt, Cyril. THE MEASUREMENT OF MENTAL CAPACITIES. 1927. 52 pp.

Number 8. East, W. Norwood. THE RELATION OF THE SKULL AND BRAIN TO CRIME. 1928. 28 pp.

Number 9. Armstrong-Jones, Robert. THE GROWTH OF THE MIND. 1929. 29 pp.

Number 10. Smith, Sydney. ALCOHOL AND BEHAVIOUR. 1930. 37 pp.

Number 11. Smith, G. Elliot. THE SIGNIFICANCE OF THE PEKING MAN. 1931. 20 pp.

Number 12. Bolton, J. Shaw. THE CORTICAL LOCALISATION OF CEREBRAL FUNCTION. 1933. 23 pp.

Number 13/16. Clark, Wilfrid Edward Le Gros. HYPOTHALAMUS, MORPHOLOGICAL, FUNCTIONAL, CHEMICAL AND SURGICAL ASPECTS. FOUR LECTURES ON THE HYPOTHALAMUS. (Edited by James C. Brash.) 1938. 211 pp.

473. *Industrielle Psychotechnik; Angewandte Psychologie in Industrie. Handel. Verkehr. Verwaltung.*

TITLE VARIATIONS: Continued by *Industrielle Psychotechnik; Der Mensch, Eignung, Leistung, Charakter, Verhalten* with Jahrgang 11, 1934.

DATES OF PUBLICATION: Jahrgang 1–10, Number 12, May/June 1924–December 1933.

FREQUENCY: Monthly.

NUMBERING VARIATIONS: Jahrgang 1 has 9 Hefte, 3 are combined issues 1/2, 5/6 and 7/8, May/June 1924–December 1924. Combined issues are also in Jahrgang 2, 4–7, and 9.

PUBLISHER: **Berlin:** Verlag von Julius Springer, 1924–1928. **Berlin:** Buchholz und Weisswange, 1929–1933.

PRIMARY EDITOR: **Walther Moede,** 1924–1933.

474. *Jahrbuch der Charakterologie.*

TITLE VARIATIONS: None.

DATES OF PUBLICATION: Band 1–6, 1924–1929.

FREQUENCY: **Annual,** Band 1, 1924. **Biennial,** Band 2/3, 1925/1926. **Annual,** Band 4–6, 1927–1929.

NUMBERING VARIATIONS: Band 2/3 joint publication for 1925/1926.

PUBLISHER: **Berlin:** Pan Verlag R. Heise, 1924. **Berlin and Leipzig:** Pan Verlag K. Metzner, 1925–1929.

PRIMARY EDITOR: **Emil Utitz,** 1924–1929.

475. *Kinderstudie. Paedologische en psychologische bladen.*

TITLE VARIATIONS: Continues *Kinderstudie. Paedologische bladen.*

DATES OF PUBLICATION: Deel 6–7, 1924–1925.

FREQUENCY: Annual.

NUMBERING VARIATIONS: None.

PUBLISHER: **Zeist, Netherlands:** J. Ploegsma, 1924–1925.

PRIMARY EDITORS: **G.A.M. van Wayenburg,** 1924–1925; **J. H. Gunning,** 1924; **W. H. ten Seldam,** 1924–1925; **K. Herman Bouman,** 1924–1925; **F. J. van der Molen,** 1924–1925; **D. Herderschee,** 1924–1925; **H.J.F.W. Brugmans,** 1925; **H. van der Hoeven,** 1925; **H. Postma,** 1925.

476. *Neue Arbeiten zur ärztlichen Psychoanalyse.*

TITLE VARIATIONS: None.

DATES OF PUBLICATION: Heft 1–6, 1924–1927.

FREQUENCY: Irregular. *See* Contents *below.*

NUMBERING VARIATIONS: None.

PUBLISHER: **Vienna:** Internationaler psychoanalytischer Verlag, 1924–1927.

PRIMARY EDITOR: **Sigmund Freud,** 1924–1927.

CONTENTS:

Heft 1. Ferenczi, Sandor, and Otto Rank. ENTWICKLUNGSZIELE DER PSYCHOANALYSE. 1924. 68 pp.

Heft 2. Abraham, Karl. VERSUCH EINER ENTWICKLUNGSGESCHICHTE DES LIBIDO. 1924. 97 pp.

Heft 3. Rank, Otto. EINE NEUROSENANALYSE IN TRÄUMEN. 1924. 231 pp.

Heft 4. Reich, Wilhelm. DER TRIEBHAFTE CHARAKTER. 1925. 132 pp.

Heft 5. Deutsch, Helene. PSYCHOANALYSE DER WEIBLICHEN SEXUALFUNKTIONEN. 1925. 111 pp.

Heft 6. Reich, Wilhelm. DIE FUNKTION DES ORGASMUS. 1927. 206 pp.

477. *Nihon Shinrigaku Zasshi.* [Japanese Journal of Psychology.] [2.]

TITLE VARIATIONS: Supersedes *Nihon Shinrigaku Zasshi* [Japanese Journal of Psychology]. [1]. Superseded by *Shinrigaku Kenkyū. Shin Shirīzu* [Psychological Research. New Series] with Volume 1, 1926.

DATES OF PUBLICATION: Volume 1–3, 1924–1925.

FREQUENCY: Unknown.

NUMBERING VARIATIONS: None.

PUBLISHER: **Kyoto:** Nihon Shinrigaku Zasshi, henshubu [Japanese Journal of Psychology, Editorial Department], 1924–1925.

PRIMARY EDITORS: None listed.

NOTE: Information for this entry was obtained from *Gakujutsu Zasshi Sōgō Mokuroku. Jimbun Kagaku Wabun Hen.* [*Union List of Scholarly Journals. Japanese Language Section. Humanities Part*]. Tokyo, 1973.

478. *Practical Psychology. The Magazine of Health, Success, Happiness.*

TITLE VARIATIONS: None.

DATES OF PUBLICATION: October 1924–November 1925.

FREQUENCY: Monthly.

NUMBERING VARIATIONS: Issues numbered by date only.

PUBLISHER: **Blackpool,** England: [Blackpool *Herald*?], 1924–1925.

PRIMARY EDITORS: None listed.

479. *Société roumaine de neurologie, psychiatrie, psychologie et endocrinologie. Bulletin.*

TITLE VARIATIONS: Also called *Societatea română de neurologie, psichiatrie, psichologie şi endocrinologie. Bulletin.* Continues *Association des psychiatres roumaines. Bulletin.*

DATES OF PUBLICATION: [Nouvelle Série], Tome 1–18, October 1924–September 1941.

FREQUENCY: Monthly.

NUMBERING VARIATIONS: [Nouvelle Série] Tome 5, Numéro 3 and 6 and Tome 6–9 never published.

PUBLISHER: **Bucharest:** Société roumaine de neurologie, psychiatrie, psychologie et endocrinologie, 1924–1941.

PRIMARY EDITORS: None listed.

480. *Sydney. University. University Reprints. Series 12. Social Science, Economics, Education, History, Philosophy and Psychology.*

TITLE VARIATIONS: Supersedes [*Sydney. University.*] *Reprints of Papers Contributed to Scientific Journals.*

DATES OF PUBLICATION: Number 1–[?], 1924–[?].

FREQUENCY: Irregular.

NUMBERING VARIATIONS: *See* Note *below.*

PUBLISHER: Various. *See* Note *below.*

PRIMARY EDITORS: None listed.

NOTE: No original publications. Compilation of reprints of articles by members of the university staff. Information on this entry is incomplete. The compilers were unable to examine a complete run of this title.

481. *Untersuchungen zur Psychologie, Philosophie und Pädagogik.*

TITLE VARIATIONS: Continues *Untersuchungen zur Psychologie und Philosophie.*

DATES OF PUBLICATION: Band 4–6, 1924–1927. Neue Folge, Band 7–14, Heft 4, 1928–1939.

FREQUENCY: Irregular. *See* Contents *below.*

NUMBERING VARIATIONS: Band 4–7 each consist of 4 Hefte; Band 8–13 each consist of 5 Hefte; Band 14 consists of 4 Hefte. Band 6, Heft 3/4 never published. Multinumbered issues present. Two issues also numbered as *Intelligenz und Artbeitsschule,* Stück 3–4 (Stück 1–2 never published.) *See* Contents *below.*

PUBLISHER: **Göttingen:** Akademische Buchhandlung G. Calvör Nachfolger. A. Reber, 1924–1936. **Bamberg:** C. C. Buchners Verlag, 1936–1939.

PRIMARY EDITOR: **Narziss Ach,** 1924–1939.

481. *(Continued)*

CONTENTS:

Band 4, Heft 1/2. Heinrich, Richard. Über Komplexbildung und Assoziation; and Peiser, Artur. Untersuchungen zur Psychologie der Blinden. 1924. Pp. 1–75, 76–154.

——, Heft 3/4. Sareyko, Max. Apperzeption und sukzessive Attention als Grundbegriffe der Arbeitsschul-Didaktik. Eine psychologisch-pädagogische Untersuchung an Hand der Suchmethode; and Bacher, Georg. Die Ach'sche Suchmethode in ihrer Verwendung zur Intelligenzprüfung. Ein Beitrag zur Psychologie der Schwachsinns. 1925. Pp. 155–208, 209–330.

Band 5, Heft 1. Kirek, Hermann. Über die Bedeutung der sensoriellen Veranlagung für die Bildung von Objektvorstellungen, insbesondere auch bei Eidetikern. 1925. 96 pp.

——, Heft 2. Düker, Heinrich. Über das Gesetz der speziellen Determination. Ein experimenteller Beitrag zur Lehre vom Willen. 1925. Pp. 97–174.

——, Heft 3/4. Rimat, Franz. Intelligenzuntersuchungen anschliessend an die Ach'sche Suchmethode. 1925. 116 pp. (Also as *Intelligenz und Arbeitsschule*, Stück 3.)

Band 6, Heft 1. Sterzinger, Othmar. Rechts- und Linkshändigkeit bei Amputierten. Eine psychologische Untersuchung. 1927. 140 pp.

——, Heft 2. Brinkmann, Matthias. Über die Schulung der Beobachtung und ihre Bedeutung insbesondere für die Arbeitsschule. 1927. 228 pp. (Also as *Intelligenz und Arbeitsschule*, Stück 4.)

——, Heft 3/4. Never published.

Band 7, Heft 1. Fischer, Heinrich. Über den Einfluss von Hemmungen auf den Ablauf willkürlicher Bewegungen. Ein experimenteller Beitrag zur Lehre vom Willen. 1928. 107 pp.

——, Heft 2. Lüderitz, Heinrich. Beitrag zur experimentellen Untersuchung des Wahlvorganges. 1929. 94 pp.

——, Heft 3. Schulze, Heinrich. Kritische Untersuchungen zum Problem der Enge des Bewusstseins. 1929. 65 pp.

——, Heft 4. Neuhaus, Wilhelm. Mikropsie bei Einengung des Gesichtsfeldes. 1929. 31 pp.

Band 8, Heft 1. Firgau, Hans Joachim. Experimentelle Untersuchungen über die Flimmergrenze. 1934. 57 pp.

——, Heft 2. Schulz, Oskar. Experimentelle Untersuchungen über Lüge und Charakter. 1934. 60 pp.

——, Heft 3. Gérard, Walt. Stereophänomene in vergleichender Darstellung. 1934. 107 pp.

——, Heft 4. Kirsch, Eberhard. Aufmerksamkeit und Objektionsfähigkeit. Ein Beitrag zur Typenlehre. 1934. 70 pp.

——, Heft 5. Voss, Wilhelm. Die geistige Schulung durch die Suchmethode. 1934. 174 pp.

Band 9, Heft 1. Niemeyer, Otto. Über die Entstehung des Satzbewusstseins. Ein experimenteller Beitrag zur Sprachpsychologie. 1935. 92 pp.

————, **Heft 2.** Hess, Franziska. Umstellungsfähigkeit und Perseveration. 1935. 55 pp.

————, **Heft 3.** Lindstaedt, Willi. Experimentelle Untersuchungen über das Küchenmeister-Phänomen. 1935. 61 pp.

————, **Heft 4.** Schwegmann, Rud. Experimentelle Untersuchung zur Lesbarkeit von Fraktur und Antiqua und von Gross- und Kleinschreibung. 1935. 47 pp.

————, **Heft 5.** Haier, Hildegard. Über die Abstraktion als geistiges Mittel zur Lösung von Aufgaben und ihre Beziehung zur Typologie. 1935. 61 pp.

Band 10, Heft 1. Madlung, Heinz. Über den Einfluss der typologischen Veranlagung auf die Flimmergrenzen. 1935. 70 pp.

————, **Heft 2.** Sondergeld, Walt. Affektive Erregbarkeit und Objektionsfähigkeit. 1935. 66 pp.

————, **Heft 3.** Hartmann, Annelisse. Über den Einfluss des Rhythmus auf die Flimmergrenze und ihre Beziehung zum Typus der Persönlichkeit. 1935. 34 pp.

————, **Heft 4.** Nolte, Erwin. Über den Schwierigkeitsgrad von Tätigkeiten und der Rangreihenprobleme. 1935. 99 pp.

————, **Heft 5.** Volkenborn, Hans. Experimentelle Beiträge zur Lehre vom Beweis, unter besonderer Berücksichtigung der Typen. 1935. 42 pp.

Band 11, Heft 1. Knöpfel, Walt. Untersuchungen zur Schall-Lokalisation und ihre Beziehungen zum Persönlichkeitstypus. 1936. 40 pp.

————, **Heft 2.** Buck, Heinrich. Ein Beitrag zur Lehre vom Drehschwindel und den Konstitutionstypen. 1936. 58 pp.

————, **Heft 3.** Pohl, Ursula. Experimentelle Untersuchungen zur Typologie graphologischer Beurteilung. 1936. 46 pp.

————, **Heft 4.** Stoller, Wern. Wahlentscheidung und nicht realisierte Determination. 1936. 102 pp.

————, **Heft 5.** Bartels, Erich. Experimentelle Untersuchungen über die Materialtäuschung, unter besonderer Berücksichtigung der Persönlichkeitsforschung. 1937. 37 pp.

Band 12, Heft 1. Fürstenberg, Hans-Egon. Experimentelle Untersuchungen über die Zusammenhänge des binokularen Tiefensehens mit dem Persönlichkeitstypus. 1937. 45 pp.

————, **Heft 2.** Flechtner, Gerhard. Über die Monotonie. Zugleich ein Beitrag zu Persönlichkeitsforschungen. 1937. 81 pp.

————, **Heft 3.** Spilker, Gustav. Fusionierende Aufmerksamkeit und Konstitutionstypen. 1937. 71 pp.

————, **Heft 4.** Schnorr, Friedrich. Die stroboskopische Erscheinung und ihre Beziehung zum Persönlichkeitstypus. 1937. 54 pp.

————, **Heft 5.** Schade, Karl-Heinz. Über die motorische Perseveration unter Berücksichtigung der Persönlichkeitsforschung. 1937. 64 pp.

Band 13, Heft 1. Stisser, Ludwig. Über Affekte, emotionale Objektion, Ganzheitsauffassung und Persönlichkeitsveranlagung. 1937. 91 pp.

————, **Heft 2.** Bourwieg, Hans. EXPERIMENTELLE UNTERSUCHUNG DER SEJUNKTION. 1937. 54 pp.

————, **Heft 3.** Niemann, Ewald. DIE ORIENTIERUNG BEI ZWANGSWEISER VERLAGERUNG DER RÄUMLICHEN UMGEBUNG. 1938. 42 pp.

————, **Heft 4.** Behrens, Helmut. VERSUCHE ÜBER DIE HÖRBARKEIT VON EINFACHEN UND MODULIERTEN TÖNEN UNTER BERÜCKSICHTIGUNG DES PERSÖNLICHKEITSTYPUS. 1938. 41 pp.

————, **Heft 5.** Philipps, Gerhard. DIE VERSCHMELZUNG VON MODULIERTEN TÖNEN UND IHRE BEZIEHUNG ZUM PERSÖNLICHKEITSTYPUS. 1938. 60 pp.

Band 14, Heft 1. Textor, Heinrich. WAHRNEHMUNG UND KONSTITUTIONELL-TYPOLOGISCHE VERANLAGUNG. 1938. 45 pp.

————, **Heft 2.** Nancken, Karl. BEITRAG ZUR PERSÖNLICHKEITSFORSCHUNG AUF GRUND EINER FEINMOTORISCHEN TÄTIGKEIT. 1938. 39 pp.

————, **Heft 3.** Grüttner, Reinhold. UBER GEWÖHNUNG UND UNGEWÖHNUNG BEI FORTLAUFENDEN WILLENSHANDLUNGEN. 1938. 41 pp.

————, **Heft 4.** Frühauf, Werner. DIE SUCHMETHODE UND IHRE ANWENDUNG. 1939. 86 pp.

482. *Utrecht. Rijksuniversiteit. Psychologisch laboratorium. Mededeelingen.*

TITLE VARIATIONS: None.

DATES OF PUBLICATION: Deel 1–7, 1924–1933.

FREQUENCY: **Biennial,** Deel 1–4, 1924–1930. **Annual,** Deel 5–7, 1931–1933.

NUMBERING VARIATIONS: None.

PUBLISHER: **Utrecht:** Psychologisch laboratorium der rijksuniversiteit, 1925–1933.

PRIMARY EDITORS: None listed.

NOTE: This title may continue beyond 1933. The compilers have been unable to locate any later issues.

483. *Vocational Guidance Magazine.* [Organ of the National Vocational Guidance Association.]

TITLE VARIATIONS: Continues *National Vocational Guidance Association. Bulletin.* Continued by *Occupations; The Vocational Guidance Journal* with Volume 12, June 1933.

DATES OF PUBLICATION: Volume 2, Number 6–Volume 11, March 1924–May 1933.

FREQUENCY: 8 times yearly (October–May).

NUMBERING VARIATIONS: None.

PUBLISHER: **Cambridge, Massachusetts:** For the National Vocational Guidance Association by the Bureau of Vocational Guidance, Graduate School of

Education, Harvard University, with the Co-operation of the New England Vocational Guidance Association, 1924–April 1925. **Cambridge:** Published for the National Vocational Guidance Association by the Bureau of Vocational Guidance, Graduate School of Education, Harvard University, May 1925–1933.

PRIMARY EDITORS: **Frederick J. Allen,** 1924–1927; **Fred C. Smith,** 1927–1933.

484. *Wiener Arbeiten zur pädagogischen Psychologie.*

TITLE VARIATIONS: Continued by *Schulreifetest* with Heft 8, 1931.

DATES OF PUBLICATION: Heft 1–7, 1924–1929.

FREQUENCY: Irregular. *See* Contents *below.*

NUMBERING VARIATIONS: None.

PUBLISHER: **Vienna:** Deutscher Verlag für Jugend und Volk, 1924–1929.

PRIMARY EDITORS: **Charlotte Bühler,** 1924–1929; **Viktor Fadrus,** 1924–1929.

CONTENTS:

Heft 1. Bühler, Charlotte, and Johanna Haas. GIBT ES FÄLLE, IN DENEN MAN LÜGEN MUSS? EINE PÄDAGOGISCH-PSYCHOLOGISCHE UNTERSUCHUNG ÜBER DIE KINDERLÜGE AUF GRUND EINER ERHEBUNG. 1924. 49 pp.

Heft 2. Reininger, Karl. ÜBER SOZIALE VERHALTUNGSWEISEN IN DER VORPUBERTÄT. 1925. 111 pp.

Heft 3. Hetzer, Hildegard. DIE SYMBOLISCHE DARTSTELLUNG IN DER FRÜHEN KINDHEIT. I. BEITRAG ZUR PSYCHOLOGISCHEN BESTIMMUNG DER SCHULREIFE. 1926. 92 pp.

Heft 4. Ormian, Heinrich. DAS SCHLUSSFOLGERNDE DENKEN DES KINDES. EINE PSYCHOGENETISCHE UNTERSUCHUNG AUF EXPERIMENTELLER GRUNDLAGE. 1926. 124 pp.

Heft 5. Zweigel, Chaim J. ÜBER DIE WIRKSAMKEIT VON AUFGABEN IN DER FRÜHEN KINDHEIT. EIN BEITRAG ZUR PSYCHOLOGISCHEN BESTIMMUNG DER SCHULREIFE. 1929. 71 pp.

Heft 6. Hetzer, Hildegard. DAS VOLKSTÜMLICHE KINDERSPIEL. 1927. 84 pp.

Heft 7. Reininger, Karl. DAS SOZIALE VERHALTEN VON SCHULNEULINGEN. WIENER LEHRERGRUPPENARBEIT. NACH 30 BEOBACHTUNGSBERICHTEN VON LEHRERN. Introduction by C. Bühler. 1929. 84 pp.

1925

485. *Abhandlungen aus dem Gebiete der Psychologie, Jugendkunde und Pädagogik.*

TITLE VARIATIONS: None.

DATES OF PUBLICATION: Heft 1–[3], 1925–1926.

FREQUENCY: Irregular. *See* Contents *below.*

NUMBERING VARIATIONS: Heft 3 is not numbered on the publication.

PUBLISHER: **Vienna:** Österreicher Bundesverlag, 1925–1926.

PRIMARY EDITORS: **Othmar Sterzinger,** 1925–1926; **Otto Tumlirz,** 1925–1926.

CONTENTS:

Heft 1. Tumlirz, Otto. PROBLEME UND ZUKUNFTSAUFGABEN DER JUGEND-KUNDE. 1925. 48 pp.

Heft 2. PÄDAGOGISCH-PSYCHOLOGISCHE UNTERSUCHUNGEN DER GEDÄCHT-NISLEHRE. 1925. 66 pp.

[Heft 3.] Mayer, Theodora, and Othmar Sterzinger. DIE BERUFSEIGNUNG DER SCHUSTERS. 1926. 52 pp.

486. *Abhandlungen aus dem Gebiete der Psychotherapie und medizinischen Psychologie.*

TITLE VARIATIONS: Supersedes *Zeitschrift für Psychotherapie und medizinische Psychologie.*

DATES OF PUBLICATION: Heft 1–15, 1925–1931.

FREQUENCY: Irregular.

NUMBERING VARIATIONS: None.

PUBLISHER: **Stuttgart:** F. Enke, 1925–1931.

PRIMARY EDITORS: **Albert Moll,** 1925–1931. **Paul Plaut,** 1930–1931.

CONTENTS:

Heft 1. Schultz, Johannes Heinrich. DIE SCHICKSALSSTUNDE DER PSY-CHOTHERAPIE. 1925. 56 pp.

Heft 2. Kern Benno, and Fritz Schoene. SONDERSTELLUNG GEWISSER FARBTÖNE UND HEILBEHANDLUNG VON FARBENSCHWÄCHE. 1925. 163 pp.

Heft 3. Levy-Suhl, Max. NEUE WEGE IN DER PSYCHIATRIE. 1925. 72 pp.

Heft 4. Zeehandelaar, Israel. AFFEKTE, PSYCHOTONIE UND AUTONOMES NERVENSYSTEM IN DER PSYCHOTHERAPIE. 1926. 55 pp.

Heft 5. Cohn, Max. GRENZEN UND MYSTIZISMUS DER PSYCHO-ANALYSE. 1926. 55 pp.

Heft 6. Alfven, Johannes. DAS PROBLEM DER ERMÜDUNG. 1927. 78 pp.

Heft 7. Flatau, Georg. NEUE ANSCHAUUNGEN ÜBER DIE NEUROSEN. 1928. 32 pp.

Heft 8. Plaut, Paul. DIE ZEUGENAUSSAGEN JUGENDLICHER PSYCHO-PATHEN. 1928. 86 pp.

Heft 9. Gumpertz, Karl. PSYCHOTHERAPIE UND RELIGIÖSE KULTHANDLUN-GEN. 1929. 58 pp.

Heft 10. Steyerthal, Armin. PATHOLOGIE DES UNBEWUSSTEN. 1929. 47 pp.

Heft 11. Moll, Albert. PSYCHOLOGIE UND CHARAKTEROLOGIE DER OKKUL-TISTEN. 1929. 130 pp.

Heft 12. Lifschitz, Samuel. HYPNOANALYSE. 1930. 122 pp.

Heft 13. Bien, Elias. DIE ANGST VOR DEM ERRÖTEN. 1930. 99 pp.

Heft 14. Peschke, Kurt, and Paul Plaut. NOTZUCHTSDELIKTE. 1930. 97 pp.
Heft 15. Flatau, Georg UNFÄLLE-NEUROSEN. 1931. 48 pp.

487. *Action et pensée.* [Bulletin of the Société internationale de psychagogie (et de psychothérapie).]

TITLE VARIATIONS: Subtitled *Revue mensuelle*, 1925–1930; *Revue trimestrielle*, 1931–1950 +.

DATES OF PUBLICATION: Année 1–26, 1925–December 1950 +.

FREQUENCY: **Monthly,** Année 1–6, Numéro 10, 1925. October/December 1930. **Quarterly,** Année 7–26, Numéro 4, January 1931–December 1950 +.

NUMBERING VARIATIONS: None.

PUBLISHER: **Geneva:** Institut de Psychologie, 1925–1950 +.

PRIMARY EDITORS: Rédaction: Institut de Psychologie, 1925–1942 (?); **Charles Baudouin,** 1946–1950 +.

488. *Akademiia nauk SSSR (Leningrad). Fiziologicheskii institut. Fiziologicheskii laboratorii akademika I. P. Pavlova. Trudy.*

TITLE VARIATIONS: Superseded by *Akademiia nauk SSSR, Fiziologicheskii institut imeni I. P. Pavlova. Trudy* with Tom 1, 1944.

DATES OF PUBLICATION: Tom 1–10, 1925–1941.

FREQUENCY: Irregular.

NUMBERING VARIATIONS: None.

PUBLISHER: **Leningrad:** Akademiia nauk SSSR. Fiziologicheskii laboratorii akademika I. P. Pavlova, 1925–1941.

PRIMARY EDITOR: **I. P. Pavlov,** 1925–1933; none listed, 1934–1941.

489. *Allgemeiner deutscher Lehrerinnenverein. Pädagogisch-psychologische Schriftenreihe.*

TITLE VARIATIONS: None.

DATES OF PUBLICATION: Heft 1–6, 1925–1931.

FREQUENCY: Irregular. *See* Contents *below.*

NUMBERING VARIATIONS: None.

PUBLISHER: **Berlin:** F. A. Herbig, 1925–1931.

PRIMARY EDITORS: None listed.

CONTENTS:
Heft 1. Wurmb, Agnes. HAT DIE BISHERIGE JUGENDPSYCHOLOGISCHE FORSCHUNG ZU ERGEBNISSEN FÜR EINE PSYCHOLOGIE DES WEIBLICHEN GESCHLECHTS GEFÜHRT? 1925. 40 pp.
Heft 2. Barschak, Erna. DIE SCHÜLERIN DER BERUFSSCHULE UND IHRE UMWELT. 1926. 48 pp.

Heft 3. Müchow, Martha. Beiträge zur psychologische Charakteristik der Kindergarten- und Grundschulalteres. 1926. 63 pp.

Heft 4. Schecker, Margarete. Fragen hauswirtschaftlicher Erziehung. 1929. 42 pp.

Heft 5. Bäumer, Gertrud. Nationale und internationale Erziehung in der Schule. 1929. 28 pp.

Heft 6. Köhler, Elsa, and Ingeborg Hamberg. Zur Psychologie und Pädagogik der geistigen Aktivität. 1931. 63 pp.

490. *Bibliothéque de psychologie de l'enfant et de pédagogie.* [*1.*]

TITLE VARIATIONS: None.

DATES OF PUBLICATION: Volume I–VII, 1925–1935.

FREQUENCY: Irregular. *See* Contents *below.*

NUMBERING VARIATIONS: None.

PUBLISHER: **Paris:** Librairie Félix Alcan, 1925–1935.

PRIMARY EDITORS: None listed.

CONTENTS:

Volume I. Guillaume, Paul. L'Imitation chez l'enfant. 1925. 23 pp.

Volume II. Wallon, Henri. L'Enfant turbulent. 1925. 653 pp.

Volume III. Piaget, Jean. La Representation du monde chez l'enfant. 1926. 424 pp.

Volume IV. Piaget, Jean. La Causalité physique chez l'enfant. 1927. 347 pp.

Volume V. Decroly, Ovid, and R. Buyse. La Pratique des tests mentaux. 1928. 402 pp.

Volume VI. Piaget, Jean. Le Jugement moral chez l'enfant. 1932. 478 pp.

Volume VII. Rey, André. L'Intelligence pratique chez l'enfant. 1935. 234 pp.

491. *Charakterologische Jahrbücher.*

TITLE VARIATIONS: Each volume carries a distinctive title. Jahrgang 1 is titled Der Charakter. Jahrgang 2 is titled Beruf und Charakter.

DATES OF PUBLICATION: Jahrgang 1–2, 1925–1926.

FREQUENCY: Annual.

NUMBERING VARIATIONS: None.

PUBLISHER: **Berlin:** Verlag Kreusch, 1925–1926.

PRIMARY EDITOR: **Max von Kreusch,** 1925–1926.

492. *Educational Measurement Review.*

TITLE VARIATIONS: None.

DATES OF PUBLICATION: Volume 1–2, Number 4/5, January 1925–July–September 1926.

FREQUENCY: Bimonthly.

NUMBERING VARIATIONS: Title ceased with a double issue, Volume 2, Number 4/5, 1926.

PUBLISHER: **Los Angeles:** Southern California Educational Research Association, January–May, 1925. **Los Angeles:** California Educational Research Association, Southern Section, July 1925–September 1926.

PRIMARY EDITOR: **J. Harold Williams,** 1925–1926.

EDITORIAL BOARD: W. Hardin Hughes, 1925–1926; Marvin L. Darsie, 1925–1926; M. J. Stormzand, 1925–1926.

493. *Encéphale; journal de neurologie, de psychiatrie, de biologie et de physiologie pathologique du système nerveux.*

TITLE VARIATIONS: Continues *Encéphale; journal de neurologie et de psychiatrie.* Continued by *Encéphale; journal de neurologie et de psychiatrie* with Année 22, 1927.

DATES OF PUBLICATION: Année 20–21, 1925–1926.

FREQUENCY: Monthly (except July/August and September/October).

NUMBERING VARIATIONS: None.

PUBLISHER: **Paris:** H. Delarue, Librairie-éditeur, 1925–1926.

PRIMARY EDITORS: **A. Antheaume,** 1925; **Henri Claude,** 1925; **E. Toulouse,** 1925.

EDITORIAL BOARD: J. Lhermitte, 1925–1926; J. Abadie, 1925–1926; D. Anglade, 1925–1926; A. André-Thomas, 1925–1926; L. Bour, 1925–1926; A. Barbe, 1925–1926; J. Capgras, 1925–1926; R. Cestan, 1925–1926; L. Cornil, 1925–1926; Mme. Dejerine, 1925–1926; G. Étienne, 1925–1926; J. Euzière, 1925–1926; J. Froment, 1925–1926; G. Genil-Perrin, 1925–1926; G. Guillain, 1925–1926; P. Guiraud, 1925–1926; A. Hesnard, 1925–1926; G. Heuyer, 1925–1926; M. Klippel, 1925–1926; M. Laignel-Lavastine, 1925–1926; J. Lévi-Valensi, 1925–1926; J. Lépine, 1925–1926; B.-J. Logre, 1925–1926; R. Mignot, 1925–1926; G. Raviart, 1925–1926; H. Roger, 1925–1926; Rogues de Fursac, 1925–1926; J. Roubinovitch, 1925–1926; P. Sainton, 1925–1926; J. Séglas, 1925–1926; P. Sérieux, 1925–1926; J. Sicard, 1925–1926; J. Tinel, 1925–1926; C.-L. Trepsat, 1925–1926; H. Verger, 1925–1926.

494. *Évolution psychiatrique. Psychanalyse. Psychologie clinique.*

TITLE VARIATIONS: Continued by *Évolution psychiatrique. Cahiers de psychologie clinique et de psychopathologie générale* with Série 2, Numéro 1, October 1929.

DATES OF PUBLICATION: [Tome 1]–2, 1925–1927.

FREQUENCY: Irregular.

NUMBERING VARIATIONS: Tome number lacking, 1925.

PUBLISHER: **Paris:** Payot, 1925–1927.

PRIMARY EDITORS: **A. Hesnard,** 1925–1927; **R. Laforgue,** 1925–1927.

495. *Forschungen zur Völkerpsychologie und Soziologie.*

TITLE VARIATIONS: None.

DATES OF PUBLICATION: Band 1–14, 1925–1935.

FREQUENCY: Irregular. *See* Contents *below.*

NUMBERING VARIATIONS: None.

PUBLISHER: **Leipzig:** C. L. Hirschfeld, 1925–1935. Also: **Stuttgart:** W. Kohlhammer, 1931–1935.

PRIMARY EDITOR: **Richard Thurnwald,** 1925–1935.

CONTENTS:

Band 1. Alverdes, Friedrich. TIERSOZIOLOGIE. 1925. 152 pp.

Band 2. PARTEI UND KLASSE IM LEBENSPROZESS DER GESELLSCHAFT. 1926. 119 pp.

Band 3. VÖLKERPSYCHOLOGISCHE CHARAKTERSTUDIEN. 1927. 338 pp.

Band 4. DIE NEUE JUGEND. 1927. 340 pp.

Band 5. Winthuis, Joseph. DAS ZWEIGESCHLECHTERWESEN BEI DEN ZENTRALAUSTRALIERN UND ANDEREN VÖLKERN. 1928. 297 pp.

Band 6. Kelchner, Mathilde. KUMMER UND TROST JUGENDLICHER ARBEITERINNEN. 1929. 90 pp.

Band 7. Stegmann von Pritzwald, Friedrich P. ZUR GESCHICHTE DER HERRSCHERBEZEICHNUNGEN VON HOMER BIS PLATO. 1930. 179 pp.

Band 8. Schmölders, Günter. DIE PROHIBITION IN DER VEREINIGTEN STAATEN. 1930. 266 pp.

Band 9. Ichheiser, Gustav. KRITIK DES ERFOLGES. 1930. 65 pp.

Band 10, Halbband 1. Legewie, H., Theodor Geiger, Erich Wasmann, and Eugen Schwiedland. ARBEITEN ZUR BIOLOGISCHEN GRUNDLEGUNG DER SOZIOLOGIE. 1931. 378 pp.

———, **Halbband 2.** Rapaies, Raymond, Walter Zimmermann, Paul Krische, Thorleif Schjelderup-Ebbe, Gerhard Heberer, and K. F. Wolff. ARBEITEN ZUR BIOLOGISCHEN GRUNDLEGUNG DER SOZIOLOGIE. 1931. 220 pp.

Band 11. Baldus, Herbert. INDIANERSTUDIEN IM NORDÖSTLICHEN CHACO. 1931. 230 pp.

Band 12. Alverdes, Friedrich. TIERPSYCHOLOGIE IN IHREN BEZIEHUNGEN ZUR PSYCHOLOGIE DER MENSCHEN. 1932. 120 pp.

Band 13. Koty, John. BEHANDLUNG DER ALTEN UND KRANKEN BEI DER NATURVÖLKERN. 1934. 373 pp.

Band 14. Thurnwald, Hilde, DIE SCHWARZE FRAU IM WANDEL AFRIKAS. 1935. 167 pp.

496. *ha-Hinuch. Yarhon Pedagog' la-Morim ve-la-horim.*

TITLE VARIATIONS: Also called *Hahinuch.* (*Pedagogy-Psychology Quarterly.*)

DATES OF PUBLICATION: Volume 1–11, Number 2, 1925–1938.

FREQUENCY: Quarterly.

NUMBERING VARIATIONS: Multinumber issues present.

PUBLISHER: **Tel-Aviv:** Histadrut ha-Morim be-Erets Yisrael, printed by Defus Eilan ve-Shoshani, 1925–1935. **Tel-Aviv:** Published by the Teachers Association of Palestine, 1936–1938.

PRIMARY EDITORS: **D. Levin** (or Lewin), 1925–(1935); **Shneerson**, (1936)–1938; **F. Lewin** (1936)–1938; **D. Levy** (1936)–1938; **M. Jacob** (1936)–1938.

NOTE: Information on this title was compiled from *Kiryat Sefer*, 1927, p. 88; and the *Bibliographie de la Philosophie* published by the International Institute of Philosophical Collaboration, Paris. Paris: Librairie philosophique J. Vrin, 1937–1953.

497. *Hygiène mentale. Journal d'assistance psychiatrique, d'anthropologie criminelle et d'intérêts professionnels.*

TITLE VARIATIONS: Continues *Informateur des aliénistes et de neurologistes. Journal d'information, d'intérêts professionnels et d'assistance.* Continued by *Hygiène mentale. Journal d'assistance psychiatrique et de psychiatrie appliquée* with Anée 23, 1928.

DATES OF PUBLICATION: Année 20, Numéro 5–Année 22, May 1925–1927.

FREQUENCY: Monthly, (except July/August and September/October).

NUMBERING VARIATIONS: None.

PUBLISHER: **Paris:** H. Delarue, Librarie-éditeur, 1925–1927.

PRIMARY EDITORS: **A. Antheaume**, 1925–1927; **E. Toulouse**, 1925–1927.

498. *Jenaer Beiträge zur Jugend- und Erziehungs- Psychologie.*

TITLE VARIATIONS: None.

DATES OF PUBLICATION: Heft 1–12, 1925–1929.

FREQUENCY: Irregular. *See* Contents *below.*

NUMBERING VARIATIONS: None.

PUBLISHER: **Langensalza, Germany:** Julius Beltz, 1925–1929.

PRIMARY EDITORS: **Annelies Argelander**, 1925–1929; **Wilhelm Peters**, 1925–1929; **Otto Scheibner**, 1925–1929.

CONTENTS:

Heft 1. Bracken, Helmut von. PERSÖNLICHKEITSERFASSUNG AUF GRUND VON PERSÖNLICHKEITSBESCHREIBUNGEN; and Peters, W. PSYCHOLOGIA ANSTALT DER UNIVERSITÄT JENA. 1925. 60 pp.

Heft 2. Meister, Hermann. DIE RETENTION DES SCHULWISSENS IN IHRER BEZIEHUNG ZUR PERSÖNLICHKEIT. (1926.) 59 pp.

Heft 3. Deuzing, Hans. DER SPRACHLICHE AUSDRUCK DER SCHULKINDES. and Argelander, A[nnelies]. ÜBER DEN SPRACHLICHEN AUSDRUCK DER SCHULKINDES IN DER FREIEN ERZÄHLUNG. 1927. 79 pp.

Heft 4. Burt Cyril DIE VERTEILUNG DER SCHULFÄHIGKEITEN UND IHRE GEGENSEITIGEN BEZIEHUNGEN. 1927. 120 pp.

Heft 5. Wolberg, Dina. ZUR DIFFERENTIELLEN PSYCHOLOGIE DER JUDEN. 1927. 32 pp.

Heft 6. Liedloff, Werner. BEITRÄGE ZUR PSYCHOLOGIE DER MATHEMATISCHEN SCHULBEGABUNG. 1928. 94 pp.

Heft 7. Argelander, Annelies. DER EINFLUSS DER UMWELT AUF DER GEISTIGE ENTWICKLUNG. 1928. 39 pp.

Heft 8. Lämmermann, Hans. VON DER TÄTIGKEIT DES SCHUL-PSYCHOLOGEN. 1929. 44 pp.

Heft 9. Kniese, Fritz. PSYCHOLOGISCHE LEISTUNGSPRÜFUNGEN AN MITTELDEUTSCHEN VOLKSSCHÜLERN UND WAISENHAUSKINDERN. and Groetenherdt, Karl. DIE GEISTIGE LEISTUNGSFÄHIGKEIT DER PUBESZENTEN. 1929. 81 pp.

Heft 10. Hauck, Erich. ZUR DIFFERENTIELLEN PSYCHOLOGIE DES INDUSTRIE- UND LANDKINDES. 1929. 65 pp.

Heft 11. Ruelius, Alwin. ARBEITSVERSUCHE AN HILFSSCHÜLERN. 1929. 46 pp.

Heft 12. Thyen, Hermann. ÜBER GESCHLECHTSUNTERSCHIEDE DER INTELLEKTUELLEN LEISTUNGSFÄHIGKEIT AUF GRUND STATISTISCHER ERHEBUNGEN AN HÖHEREN KOEDUKATIONSSCHULEN. 1929. 76 pp.

499. *Journal of Abnormal and Social Psychology.*

TITLE VARIATIONS: Continues *Journal of Abnormal Psychology and Social Psychology.*

DATES OF PUBLICATION: Volume 20–45+, 1925–1950+.

FREQUENCY: Quarterly.

NUMBERING VARIATIONS: Multinumber issues present. Volume 38, Number 2, Supplement issued April 1943.

PUBLISHER: **Albany, New York:** Boyd Printing Company, Inc., 1925–1929. **Princeton, New Jersey:** American Psychological Association, 1929–1937. **Columbus, Ohio:** American Psychological Association, 1938–1939. **Evanston, Illinois:** American Psychological Association, Inc. 1940–1945. **Albany** and **Washington, D.C.** American Psychological Association, Inc., 1946–1950+.

PRIMARY EDITORS: **Morton Prince,** 1925–1929; **Henry T. Moore,** 1925–1937; **Adolf Meyer,** 1925–1937; **William McDougall,** 1925–1937; **Floyd H. Allport,** 1925–1937; **J. Ramsay Hunt,** 1925–1937; **Henry Herbert Goddard,** 1925–1937; **Franklin H. Giddings,** 1925–1931; **James Drever,** 1925–1937; **Gordon W. Allport,** 1937–1949; **J. McV. Hunt,** 1950+.

EDITORIAL BOARD: Edna Heidbreder, 1938–1949; Floyd H. Allport, 1938–1949; Ruth Benedict, 1938–1948; Henry E. Garrett, 1938–1949; James Q. Holsopple, 1938–1944; Carney Landis, 1938–1949; Henry T. Moore,

1938–1949; David Slight, 1938–1944; Stanley Estes, 1940–1949; Honorio Delgado, 1941–1949; Luberta Harden McCabe, 1942–1949; Allen L. Edwards, 1945–1949; Robert W. White, 1945–1950+; David Shakow, 1950+; Ross Stagner, 1950+; Elizabeth Collins Wesman, 1950+; Gordon W. Allport; 1950+; Hadley Cantril, 1950+; John Dollard, 1950+; Leonard W. Doob, 1950+; Charles M. Harsh, 1950+; William A. Hunt, 1950+; Arthur Jenness, 1950+; W. Ernst Kris, 1950+; Donald W. MacKinnon, 1950+; Quinn McNemar, 1950+; O. Hobart Mowrer, 1950+; Theodore M. Newcomb, 1950+; Saul Rosenzweig, 1950+; Harold Seashore, 1950+.

500. *Leningrad. Gosudarstvennyi refleksologicheskii institut po izucheniiu mozga. Novoe v refleksologii i fiziologii nervnoi sistemy.*

TITLE VARIATIONS: Continued by [*Leningrad.*] *Gosudarstvenyi institut po izucheniiu mozga. Novoe v refleksologii i fiziologii nervnoi sistemy* with Tom 2, 1926.

DATES OF PUBLICATION: Tom 1, 1925.

FREQUENCY: Irregular.

NUMBERING VARIATIONS: Tom 1 is unnumbered.

PUBLISHER: **Leningrad:** Gosudarstvennyi refleksologicheskii institut po izucheniiu mozga, 1925.

PRIMARY EDITORS: Unknown.

NOTE: Information on this title was compiled from entries in *A Half Century of Soviet Serials.*

501. *Mental Measurement Monographs.*

TITLE VARIATIONS: None.

DATES OF PUBLICATION: Serial Number 1–11, 1925–August 1936.

FREQUENCY: Irregular. *See* Contents *below.*

NUMBERING VARIATIONS: None.

PUBLISHER: **Baltimore:** Williams & Wilkins Company, 1925–1936.

PRIMARY EDITORS: **Buford Johnson,** 1925–1936; **Knight Dunlap,** 1925–1936; **John E. Anderson,** 1925–1936; **John E. Coover,** 1925–1936; **Donald G. Paterson,** 1925–1936; **Joseph Peterson,** 1925–1936.

CONTENTS:

Serial Number 1. Seago, Dorothy W. AN ANALYSIS OF LANGUAGE FACTORS IN INTELLIGENCE TESTS. [1925.] 124 pp.

Serial Number 2. Kirkpatrick, Clifford. INTELLIGENCE AND IMMIGRATION. 1926. 127 pp.

Serial Number 3. Boody, Bertha May. A PSYCHOLOGICAL STUDY OF IMMIGRANT CHILDREN AT ELLIS ISLAND. 1926. 163 pp.

Serial Number 4. Blackwood, Beatrice. A STUDY OF MENTAL TESTING IN RELATION TO ANTHROPOLOGY. 1927. 120 pp.

Serial Number 5. Peterson, Joseph, and Lyle H. Lanier. STUDIES IN THE COMPARATIVE ABILITIES OF WHITES AND NEGROES. 1929. 156 pp.

Serial Number 6. Wallin, J. E. Wallace. A STATISTICAL STUDY OF THE INDIVIDUAL TESTS IN AGES VIII AND IX IN THE STANFORD-BINET SCALE. 1929. 58 pp.

Serial Number 7. McFadden, John Holman. DIFFERENTIAL RESPONSES OF NORMAL AND FEEBLEMINDED SUBJECTS OF EQUAL MENTAL AGE, ON THE KENT–ROSANOFF FREE ASSOCIATION TEST AND THE STANFORD REVISION OF THE BINET–SIMON INTELLIGENCE TEST. 1931. 85 pp.

Serial Number 8. Shaffer, G. Wilson. ALERTNESS AND MOTOR ABILITIES OF ATHLETES AND NON-ATHLETES. 1931. 65 pp.

Serial Number 9. Kent, Grace H. ORAL TEST FOR EMERGENCY USE IN CLINICS. 1932. 50 pp.

Serial Number 10. Betts, Evelyn W. TIME-LIMIT VS. WORK-LIMIT IN LEARNING. 1934. 58 pp.

Serial Number 11. Fernald, Grace M. ON CERTAIN LANGUAGE DISABILITIES, THEIR NATURE AND TREATMENT. WITH A SECTION ON REMEDIAL READING IN THE LOS ANGELES CITY SCHOOLS, BY HELEN B. KELLER. 1936. 121 pp.

502. *Mental Welfare.*

TITLE VARIATIONS: Continues *Studies in Mental Inefficiency.*

DATES OF PUBLICATION: Volume 6–20, 1925–1939.

FREQUENCY: Quarterly.

NUMBERING VARIATIONS: None.

PUBLISHER: **London:** Central Association for Mental Welfare, 1925–1939.

PRIMARY EDITORS: **A. L. Hargrove,** 1925, 1939; **Mrs. Welfare,** 1925–1939; **Lucy E. Beach,** 1925–1927.

503. *Milan. Università Cattolica del Sacro Cuore. Istituto di psicologia sperimentale. Contributi.*

TITLE VARIATIONS: Also cited as *Contributi del laboratorio di psicologia e biologia,* Série 1–4, and as *Contributi del laboratorio di psicologia,* Série 5–14 + .

DATES OF PUBLICATION: Série 1–14 + , 1925–1950 + .

FREQUENCY: Irregular. Série 1, 1925; Série 2, no date on publication; Série 3, 1928; Série 4, 1929; Série 5, 1931; Série 6, 1935; Série 7, 1938; Série 8, 1940; Série 9, 1941; Série 10, (1942); Série 11, (1943); Série 12, 1944; Série 13, 1944, Série 14, 1950.

NUMBERING VARIATIONS: Série 1–2 also numbered as [*Milan.*] *Università Cattolica del Sacro Cuore. Pubblicazioni. Série prima: Scienze filosofiche,* Volume 1, Fasicule 4 and Volume 11. Série 3–11 also numbered as [*Milan.*] *Università Cattolica del Sacro Cuore. Pubblicazioni. Série sesta: Scienze biologiche,* Volume 4, 5, 6, 8, 10, 12–15. Séries 12–14 + also numbered as [*Milan.*] *Università Cattolica del Sacro Cuore. Pubblicazioni. Nuova série. (Série II),* Volume 1, 3, 35. Only Série 13 is monographic. *See* Contents *below.*

PUBLISHER: **Milano:** Società editrice "Vita e Pensiero," 1925–1950+.

PRIMARY EDITORS: [A. Gemelli], 1925–1950+.

CONTENTS:
Série 13. Alabastro, A., and A. Sidlauskajte. NUOVE RICERCHE SUI FAN-
CIULLI INSTABILI. 1944. 222 pp.

504. *Moscow. Gosudarstvennyi institut muzykal'noi nauki. Fiziologo-psikhologicheskaia sektsiia. Sbornik rabot.*

TITLE VARIATIONS: None.

DATES OF PUBLICATION: Number 1, 1925.

FREQUENCY: Irregular.

NUMBERING VARIATIONS: None.

PUBLISHER: **Moscow:** Gosudarstvennoye izdatel'stvo, Muzykal'nyi sektor,
1925.

PRIMARY EDITORS: None listed.

505. *Pedagogical Seminary and Journal of Genetic Psychology.*

TITLE VARIATIONS: Subtitled *Child Behavior, Differential and Genetic Psychology,* 1928; and *Child Behavior, Animal Behavior and Comparative Psychology,* 1929. Continues *Pedagogical Seminary. An International Record of
Educational Literature, Institutions and Progress.*

DATES OF PUBLICATION: Volume 32–80+, 1925–1950+.

FREQUENCY: **Quarterly,** Volume 32–36, 1925–1929. **Quarterly,** 2 volumes per
year, Volume 37–76+, 1930–1950+.

NUMBERING VARIATIONS: Volume 39 only volume issued in 1931.

PUBLISHER: **Worcester, Massachusetts:** Clark University, 1925–1927.
Worcester: Clark University Press, 1928–1936. **Provincetown, Massachusetts:**
The Journal Press, 1937–1950+.

PRIMARY EDITORS: **Carl Murchison,** 1925–1950+; **Luberta M. Harden,**
1930–1934.

EDITORIAL BOARD: Bird T. Baldwin, 1925–1927; William H. Burnham,
1925–1940; Cyril Burt, 1925–1950+; Éd Claparède, 1925–1940; Edmund S.
Conklin, 1925–1926, 1929–1942; Arnold Gesell, 1925–1926, 1928–1950+; William Healy, 1925–1950+; Walter S. Hunter, 1925–1934; K. S. Lashley,
1925–1950+; Henri Piéron, 1925–1950+; Sante de Sanctis, 1925–1950+; William Stern, 1925–1937; Lewis M. Terman, 1925–1950+; E. L. Thorndike,
1925–1949; John B. Watson, 1925–1950+; Helen Thompson Woolley,
1925–1947; Truman L. Kelley, 1927–1950+; Calvin P. Stone, 1927–1950+;
Godfrey Thomson, 1927–1950+; John E. Anderson, 1928–1950+; Charlotte
Bühler, 1928–1950+; Leta S. Hollingworth, 1928–1939; Buford Johnson,
1928–1950+; Yoshihide Kubo, 1928–1943; A. R. Luria, 1928–1950+; Toshio
Nogami, 1928–1943; Ivan P. Pavlov, 1928–1935; C. J. Warden, 1928–1950+;
Harold E. Jones, 1930–1950+; Leonard Carmichael, 1932–1950+; George D.

Stoddard, 1939–1950+; Arthur T. Jersild, 1948–1950+; Robert R. Sears, 1948–1950+.

506. *Plus ultra. Revista de estudios psicológicos.*

TITLE VARIATIONS: None.

DATES OF PUBLICATION: Años 1–2, 1925–1927.

FREQUENCY: Monthly.

NUMBERING VARIATIONS: None.

PUBLISHER: **Madrid:** Publisher unknown, 1925–1927.

PRIMARY EDITORS: Unknown.

NOTE: Information is from serials holdings of the National Library in Madrid.

507. *Practical Psychologist.* [Official organ of the Federation of Practical Psychology Clubs of Great Britain.]

TITLE VARIATIONS: None.

DATES OF PUBLICATION: Volume 1–2, Number 6, January 1925–[December 1925].

FREQUENCY: Monthly.

NUMBERING VARIATIONS: Volume 1, Number 4–Volume 2, Number 6 not dated.

PUBLISHER: **London:** Head Offices of the Practical Psychologist, 1925.

PRIMARY EDITORS: **Anna Maud Hallam,** 1925; **F. S. Hayburn,** 1925.

508. *Psikhologiia i marksizm.*

TITLE VARIATIONS: Continued by *Problemy sovremennoi psikhologii; Uchenye zapiski* with [Tom 2], 1926.

DATES OF PUBLICATION: [Tom 1], 1925.

FREQUENCY: Annual.

NUMBERING VARIATIONS: Numbered by date only.

PUBLISHER: **Moscow:** Moskovskii gosudarstvennyi institut eksperimental'noi psikhologii, 1925.

PRIMARY EDITORS: Unknown.

NOTE: Information on this title was compiled from entries in *A Half Century of Soviet Serials.*

509. *Psikhonevrologicheskii zhurnal.*

TITLE VARIATIONS: None.

DATES OF PUBLICATION: Tom 1, 1925.

FREQUENCY: Annual.

NUMBERING VARIATIONS: None.

PUBLISHER: **Omsk:** Omskoe psikhonevrologicheskoe obshchestvo, 1925.

PRIMARY EDITORS: Unknown.

NOTE: Information on this title was compiled from entries in A *Half Century of Soviet Serials.*

510. *Psychologie und Medizin. Vierteljahrsschrift für Forschung und Anwendung auf ihren Grenzgebieten.*
[Organ of the Berliner Gesellschaft für Psychologie und Charakterologie (Psychologische Gesellschaft zu Berlin); the Arbeitsgemeinschaft für praktische Psychologie in Berlin; and the Arbeitsgemeinschaft für Psychologie der Leibesübungen.]

TITLE VARIATIONS: Subtitled *Zeitschrift für Forschung und Anwendung auf ihren Grenzgebieten,* Band 4. Supersedes *Zeitschrift für Psychotherapie und Medizinische Psychologie.*

DATES OF PUBLICATION: Band 1–4, October 1925–May 1932.

FREQUENCY: **Quarterly,** Band 1–3, 1925–1928. **Irregular,** Band 4, September 1929–May 1932 (8 hefte).

NUMBERING VARIATIONS: None.

PUBLISHER: **Stuttgart:** Verlag von Ferdinand Enke, 1925–1929. **Berlin:** Belle-Alliance-Druck Noffz & Zimmermann, September 1929–1932.

PRIMARY EDITOR: **Robert Werner Schulte,** 1925–1932.

511. *Psychotechnische Forschungen zur Berufsberatung.*
TITLE VARIATIONS: None.

DATES OF PUBLICATION: Heft 1–3, 1925–1931.

FREQUENCY: Irregular. *See* Contents *below.*

NUMBERING VARIATIONS: Also numbered as part of *Deutsche Psychologie. Arbeitenreihe;* as part of *Deutsche Psychologie. Arbeitenreihe zur Kulturpsychologie und Psychologie der Praxis;* and as *Beiträge zur Sozialpsychologie der Berufe. See* Contents *below.*

PUBLISHER: **Halle:** C. Marhold, 1925–1931.

PRIMARY EDITOR: **Fritz Giese,** 1925–1931.

CONTENTS:

Heft 1. Lang, Emmy PSYCHOLOGISCHE MASSENPRÜFUNGEN FÜR ZWECKE DER BERUFSBERATUNG; and, Rüssel, Arnulf. DIE EIGNUNGSPRÜFUNG ALS ERLEBNIS DER JUGENDLICHEN. 1925. 68 pp. (also as *Deutsche Psychologie. Arbeitenreihe,* Band 4, Heft 1.)

Heft 2. Wagner Erich. BERUFSUMWELT UND GEISTIGE LEISTUNG BEI JUGENDLICHEN. 1930. 68 pp. (Also as *Beiträge zur Sozialpsychologie der Berufe,* Heft 1; and as *Deutsche Psychologie. Arbeitenreihe zur Kulturpsychologie und Psychologie der Praxis. Psychotechnik,* Band 7, Heft 1.)

Heft 3. Hirsch, Georg. DIE FAULHEIT. 1931. 153 pp. (Also as *Beiträge zur*

Sozialpsychologie der Berufe, Heft 1; and as *Deutsche Psychologie. Arbeiten-reihe zur Kulturpsychologie und Psychologie der Praxis. Psychotechnik*, Band 7, Heft 2.)

512. *Psychotechnische Zeitschrift.*

TITLE VARIATIONS: Continued by *Zeitschrift für Arbeitspsychologie und praktische Psychologie im Allgemeinen* with Band 11, 1938.

DATES OF PUBLICATION: Band 1–10, October 1925–December 1936.

FREQUENCY: Bimonthly (Irregular). *See* Numbering Variations *below.*

NUMBERING VARIATIONS: Band 1, October 1925–October 1926. Band 2, February–December, 1927. Band 7, 1932, April (Heft 1), June (Heft 2/3). Combined issues in Band 7–10, 1932–1936.

PUBLISHER: **Munich:** Druck und Verlag von R. Oldenbourg, October 1925–1932. **Dresden:** Kommissionsverlag: Franz Bungartz, 1933–1936.

PRIMARY EDITOR: **Hans Rupp,** 1925–1936.

513. *Quellen und Studien zur Jugendkunde.*

TITLE VARIATIONS: None.

DATES OF PUBLICATION: Heft 1–13, 1925–1937.

FREQUENCY: Irregular. *See* Contents *below.*

NUMBERING VARIATIONS: Heft 2–4 published before Heft 1.

PUBLISHER: **Jena:** Verlag von Gustav Fischer, 1925–1937.

PRIMARY EDITOR: **Charlotte Bühler,** 1925–1937.

CONTENTS:
Heft 1. Bühler, Charlotte, ed. ZWEI MÄDCHENTAGEBÜCHER. 1927. 145 pp.
Heft 2. Busemann, A. DIE SPRACHE DER JUGEND ALS AUSDRUCK DER ENT-WICKLUNGSRHYTHMIK. 1925. 98 pp.
Heft 3. Bühler, Charlotte, ed. ZWEI KNABENTAGEBÜCHER. 1925. 169 pp.
Heft 4. Hetzer, Hildegard, and Lucia Večerka. SOZIALES VERHALTEN PU-BERTIERENDER MÄDCHEN. 1926. 121 pp.
Heft 5. Bühler, Charlotte, Hildegard Hetzer, and Beatrix Tudor-Hart. SOZIOLOGISCHE UND PSYCHOLOGISCHE STUDIEN ÜBER DAS ERSTE LEBENSJAHR. 1927. 250 pp.
Heft 6. Winkler-Hermaden, Viktor. PSYCHOLOGIE DES JUGENDFÜHRERS. 1927. 126 pp.
Heft 7. Hetzer, Hildegard. KIND UND SCHAFFEN. EXPERIMENTE ÜBER KONSTRUKTIVE BETÄTIGUNGEN IM KLEINKINDALTER. 1931. 108 pp.
Heft 8. Lazarsfeld, Paul F., ed. JUGEND UND BERUF. KRITIK UND MATE-RIAL. 1931. 206 pp.
Heft 9. Bühler, Charlotte, ed. JUGENDTAGEBUCH UND LEBENSLAUF. ZWEI MÄDCHENTAGEBÜCHER. 1932. 262 pp.
Heft 10. Argelander, Annelies, and Ilse Weitsch. AUS DEM SEELENLEBEN

VERWAHRLOSTER MÄDCHEN AUF GRUND IHRER TAGEBUCHAUFZEICHNUNGEN. 1933. 126 pp.

Heft 11. Bühler, Charlotte. DREI GENERATIONEN IM JUGENDTAGEBUCH. 1934. 184 pp.

Heft 12. Frankl, Liselotte. LOHN UND STRAFE; IHRE ANWENDUNG IN DER FAMILIENERZIEHUNG. Mit einer Einführung von Charlotte Büher. 1935. 116 pp.

Heft 13. Baar, Edeltrud. DIE GEISTIGE WELT DES SCHULKINDES. 1937. 129 pp.

514. *Sovremennaia psikhonevrologiia.*

TITLE VARIATIONS: Continued by *Sovetskaia psikhonevrologiia* with Tom 11, Vypusk 2, 1931.

DATES OF PUBLICATION: Tom 1–11, Vypusk 1, 1925–1931.

FREQUENCY: **8 issues,** Tom 1, 1925. **Bimonthly,** Tom 2–11, Vypusk 1, 1926–1931.

NUMBERING VARIATIONS: Multinumber issues present.

PUBLISHER: **Kiev:** Narodnyi komitet zdravookhraneniia Ukrainskoi SSR, 1925–1931.

PRIMARY EDITORS: Unknown.

NOTE: Information on this title was compiled from entries in *Half a Century of Soviet Serials.*

515. *Ukrains'kyi visnyk refleksologii ta eksperymental'noi pedagogiky.*

TITLE VARIATIONS: Continued by *Ukrains'kyi visnyk eksperymental'noi pedagogiky ta refleksologii* with Vypusk 1, 1927.

DATES OF PUBLICATION: Vypusk 1–3, 1925–1926.

FREQUENCY: Irregular.

NUMBERING VARIATIONS: None.

PUBLISHER: **Kharkov:** Urkains'kii nauchno-issledovatel'skii institut pedagogiki, 1925–1926.

PRIMARY EDITOR: **V. P. Protopopov,** 1925–1926.

EDITORIAL COMMITTEE: M. S. Volobiv, 1925–1926; A. S. Zaluzhnii, 1925–1926; O. I. Popov, 1925–1926; I. P. Sokolians'kii, 1925–1926; I. M. Murakhivs'ka, 1925–1926.

516. *Washington, D.C. National Research Council. Committee on Child Development. Conference on Research in Child Development. Proceedings.*

TITLE VARIATIONS: None.

DATES OF PUBLICATION: 1st–4th, 1925–1933.

FREQUENCY: **Biennial,** 1st–3rd, 1925–1929. **Irregular,** 4th, 1933.

NUMBERING VARIATIONS: None.

PUBLISHER: **Washington, D.C.:** Committee on Child Development, National Research Council, 1925–1933.

PRIMARY EDITORS: Members of the Committee on Child Development: **Robert S. Woodworth,** 1925–1933; **George M. Stratton,** 1925–1929; **Bird T. Baldwin,** 1925–1927; **John E. Anderson,** 1925–1933; **A. V. Kidder,** 1927; **Leslie Ray Marston,** 1927; **E. V. McCollum,** 1929–1933; **T. Wingate Todd,** 1929; **Martha M. Eliot,** 1929–1933; **Mervin A. Durea,** 1929; **Knight Dunlap,** 1929; **Kenneth D. Blackfan,** 1933; **Francis G. Blake,** 1933; **Robert S. Lynd,** 1933; **R. E. Scammon,** 1933; **Mandel Sherman,** 1933; **G. D. Stoddard,** 1933; **A. T. Pottenberger,** 1933.

CONTENTS:

    1. FIRST CONFERENCE ON RESEARCH IN CHILD DEVELOPMENT, BRONXVILLE, NEW YORK, OCTOBER 23–25, 1925. 39 pp.

    2. SECOND CONFERENCE ON RESEARCH IN CHILD DEVELOPMENT, WASHINGTON, D.C., MAY 5–7, 1927. 123 pp.

    3. THIRD CONFERENCE ON RESEARCH IN CHILD DEVELOPMENT, UNIVERSITY OF TORONTO, TORONTO, CANADA, MAY 2–4, 1929. 351 pp. (2 Volumes).

    4. FOURTH CONFERENCE ON RESEARCH IN CHILD DEVELOPMENT, THE UNIVERSITY OF CHICAGO, CHICAGO, ILLINOIS, JUNE 22–24, 1933. 179 pp.

517. *Zeitschrift für angewandte Psychologie.* [2.] [Organ of the Schweizerische Vereinigung der Freunde Coués.]

TITLE VARIATIONS: Also called *Revue de psychologie appliquée.* [3]. Continued by *Schweizerische Zeitschrift für angewandte Psychologie* with Jahrgang 2, 1926.

DATES OF PUBLICATION: Jahrgang 1, Heft 1–12, 1925.

FREQUENCY: Monthly.

NUMBERING VARIATIONS: Multinumber issue: Heft 4/5, 1925.

PUBLISHER: **Zurich:** A. Funk, 1925.

PRIMARY EDITOR: **Arnold Funk,** 1925.

518. *Zeitschrift für Menschenkunde. Blätter für Charakterologie und angewandte Psychologie.*

TITLE VARIATIONS: Continued by *Zeitschrift für Menschenkunde. Blätter für Charakterologie und Zentralblatt für Graphologie* with Jahrgang 11, 1935.

DATES OF PUBLICATION: Jahrgang 1–10, May 1925–November 1934.

FREQUENCY: **Bimonthly,** Jahrgang 1–5, 1925–1929. **Quarterly,** Jahrgang 6–10, 1930–1934.

NUMBERING VARIATIONS: None.

PUBLISHER: **Heidelberg:** Niels Kampmann, 1925. **Freiburg:** Niels Kampmann, 1926–1934.

PRIMARY EDITORS: **Hans von Hattingberg**, 1925–1934; **Niels Kampmann**, 1925–1934.

519. *Zeitschrift für pädagogische Psychologie, experimentelle Pädagogik und jugendkundliche Forschung.*

TITLE VARIATIONS: Continues *Zeitschrift für pädagogische Psychologie und experimentelle Pädagogik*. Continued by *Zeitschrift für pädagogische Psychologie und Jugendkunde* with Jahrgang 34, Heft 9, September 1933.

DATES OF PUBLICATION: Jahrgang 26–34, Heft 8, 1925–August 1933.

FREQUENCY: Monthly.

NUMBERING VARIATIONS: Multinumber issues present. Supplement, 1926, numbered in *Pädagogische Monographien*. One issue also numbered in subseries *Studien über Spielgaben und Lernspiele*.

PUBLISHER: **Leipzig:** Quelle & Meyer, 1925–1933.

PRIMARY EDITORS: **Otto Scheibner**, 1925–1933; **William Stern**, 1925–1933; **Aloys Fischer**, 1925–1933; **Oswald Kroh**, 1933.

520. *Zeitschrift für Völkerpsychologie und Soziologie [1].*

TITLE VARIATIONS: Continued by *Sociologus. Zeitschrift für Völkerpsychologie und Soziologie* with Band 8, 1932.

DATES OF PUBLICATION: Band 1–7, 1925–1931.

FREQUENCY: Quarterly.

NUMBERING VARIATIONS: None.

PUBLISHER: **Leipzig:** C. L. Hirschfeld, 1925–1931.

PRIMARY EDITORS: **Richard Thurnwald**, 1925–1931; **Otto Bobertag**, 1930; **W. E. Mühlmann**, 1931; **F. Alverdes**, 1925–1931; **R. Bolte**, 1925–1931; **B. Malinowski**, 1925–1931; **E. Schwiedland**, 1925–1931; **G. A. Jaederholm**, 1926–1929; **W. F. Ogburn**, 1926–1931; **E. Schultz-Ewerth**, 1926–1931; **S. R. Steinmetz**, 1926–1931; **P. A. Sorokin**, 1930–1931.

1926

521. *Allgemeiner ärztlicher Kongress für Psychotherapie.*
ericht. [Sponsored by the Allgemeine ärztliche Gesellschaft für Psychotherapie.]

TITLE VARIATIONS: None.

DATES OF PUBLICATION: 1st–6th, 1926–1931.

FREQUENCY: Annual.

NUMBERING VARIATIONS: None.

PUBLISHER: **Leipzig:** S. Hirzel, 1926–1931.

PRIMARY EDITORS: *See* Contents *below.*

CONTENTS:

    1st. Baden-Baden 17.–19. IV [April] 1926. Edited by Wladimir Eliasberg. 1927. 327 pp.

    2nd. Bad Nauheim 27.–30. IV [April] 1927. Edited by Wladimir Eliasberg. 1927. 369 pp.

    3rd. Baden-Baden 20.–22. IV [April] 1928. Edited by Wladimir Eliasberg. 1929. 326 pp.

    4th. Bad Nauheim 11.–14. IV. [April] 1929. Edited by Walter Cimbal. 1929. 200 pp.

    5th. Baden-Baden 26.–29. IV. [April] 1930. Edited by Ernst Kretschmer and Walter Cimbal. 1930. 307 pp.

    6th. Dresden 1931. Edited by Ernst Kretschmer and Walter Cimbal. 1931. 267 pp.

522. *Almanach.*

TITLE VARIATIONS: Continued by *Almanach der Psychoanalyse* with Band 5, 1930.

DATES OF PUBLICATION: Band 1–4, 1926–1929.

FREQUENCY: Annual.

NUMBERING VARIATIONS: None.

PUBLISHER: **Vienna:** Internationaler psychoanalytischer Verlag, 1926–1929.

PRIMARY EDITOR: **Adolf Josef Storfer,** 1926–1929.

523. *Archives of Psychoanalysis; A Quarterly Devoted to the Theory and Treatment of the Neuroses and Psychoses.*

TITLE VARIATIONS: None.

DATES OF PUBLICATION: Volume 1, Number 1–4, October 1926–July 1927.

FREQUENCY: Quarterly.

NUMBERING VARIATIONS: Continuous pagination.

PUBLISHER: **Stamford, Connecticut:** The Psychoanalytic Institute, 1926–1927.

PRIMARY EDITOR: **L. Pierce Clark,** 1926–1927.

524. *Catholic University of America. Studies in Psychology and Psychiatry.*

TITLE VARIATIONS: None.

DATES OF PUBLICATION: Volume 1–8, Number 1, 1926–1950 + .

FREQUENCY: Irregular.

NUMBERING VARIATIONS: None.

Year 1926

PUBLISHER: **Baltimore:** Williams and Wilkins Company, 1926–1938. **Washington, D.C.:** Catholic University of America Press, 1939–1950+.

PRIMARY EDITORS: **Edward A. Pace,** 1926–1938; **Thomas Verner Moore,** 1939–1941; [None listed, 1942–1947]; **John W. Stafford,** 1948+.

EDITORIAL BOARD: Cornelius Joseph Connolly, 1926–1938; Thomas George Foran, 1926–1938; Paul Hanly Furfey, 1926–1938; John Albert Haldi, 1926–1929; Thomas Verner Moore, 1926–1938; John William Rauth, 1926–1938; Francis Augustine Walsh, 1926–1938.

CONTENTS:

Volume 1, Number 1. Dunn, Miriam Frances. THE PSYCHOLOGY OF REASONING. 1926. 141 pp.

————, **Number 2.** Rauth, John William. DIASTATIC ACTIVITY OF THE BLOOD SERUM IN MENTAL DISORDERS. 1926. 32 pp.

————, **Number 3.** Mullen, Joseph J. PSYCHOLOGICAL FACTORS IN THE PASTORAL TREATMENT OF SCRUPLES. 1927. 165 pp.

————, **Number 4.** Linfert, Harriette Elise, and Helen M. Hierholzer. A SCALE FOR MEASURING THE DEVELOPMENT OF INFANTS DURING THE FIRST YEAR OF LIFE. 1928. 33 pp.

Volume 2, Number 1. Philip, Brother R. (F.S.C.). THE MEASUREMENT OF ATTENTION. 1928. 81 pp.

————, **Number 2.** Moore, Thomas Verner. THE REASONING ABILITY OF CHILDREN IN THE FIRST YEARS OF SCHOOL LIFE. 1929. 34 pp.

————, **Number 3.** McDonough, Sister M. Rosa. THE EMPIRICAL STUDY OF CHARACTER. PART I. 1929. 144 pp.

————, **Number 4.** McDonough, Sister M. Rosa. THE EMPIRICAL STUDY OF CHARACTER. PART II. 1929. Pp. 147–222.

————, **Number 5.** Reinhart, Sister Miriam. A SCALE FOR MEASURING THE G-FACTORS IN INTELLIGENCE. 1931. 42 pp.

Volume 3, Number 1. Moore, Thomas Verner. MULTIPLE CORRELATION AND THE CORRELATION BETWEEN GENERAL FACTORS. 1931. 32 pp.

————, **Number 2.** Moore, Thomas Verner. PARTIAL CORRELATION. 1932. 40 pp.

————, **Number 3.** Moore, Thomas Verner. THE ESSENTIAL PSYCHOSES AND THEIR FUNDAMENTAL SYNDROMES. 1933. 128 pp.

————, **Number 4.** Sullivan, Sister Celestine. A SCALE FOR MEASURING DEVELOPMENTAL AGE IN GIRLS. 1934. 65 pp.

————, **Number 5.** Monoghan, Edward A. MAJOR FACTORS IN COGNITION. 1935. 48 pp.

————, **Number 6.** Reiman, M. Gertrude. THE PROGNOSTIC VALUE OF MENTAL SYMPTOMS IN THE PSYCHOSES. 1935. 40 pp.

Volume 4, Number 1. Mary, Sister (I.H.M.), and Margaret Mary Hughes. THE MORAL AND RELIGIOUS DEVELOPMENT OF THE PRESCHOOL CHILD. 1936. 51 pp.

————, **Number 2.** McManama, Sister Maurice. A GENETIC STUDY OF THE COGNITIVE GENERAL FACTOR IN HUMAN INTELLIGENCE. 1936. 35 pp.

————, **Number 3.** Moore, Thomas Verner. CONSCIOUSNESS AND THE NERVOUS SYSTEM. 1938. 94 pp.

————, **Number 4.** Gannon, Joseph Timothy. A STATISTICAL STUDY OF CERTAIN DIAGNOSTIC PERSONALITY TRAITS OF COLLEGE MEN. 1939. 45 pp.

————, **Number 5.** Connolly, C. J. PHYSIQUE IN RELATION TO PSYCHOSIS. 1939. 24 pp.

————, **Number 6.** Noble, Sister Mary Alfred (C.S.J.). FACTORIAL DIFFERENTIATION BY MAXIMAL DIFFERENCES. 1940. 40 pp.

————, **Number 7.** Dunkerley, Mother Mary Dorothea (O.S.U.). A STATISTICAL STUDY OF LEADERSHIP AMONG COLLEGE WOMEN. 1940. 65 pp.

————, **Number 8.** Holland, Sister Regis. THE DEVELOPMENT OF LOGICAL AND ROTE MEMORY. 1940. 45 pp.

Volume 5, Number 1. Forrest, Sister Helen de Sales. CORRELATIONS BETWEEN THE CONSTANTS IN THE CURVE OF LEARNING. 1941. 43 pp.

————, **Number 2.** Krause, Lawrence J. THE CORRELATION OF ADJUSTMENT AND ACHIEVEMENT IN DELINQUENT BOYS. 1941. 74 pp.

————, **Number 3.** Barrett, Sister Mary Constance. AN EXPERIMENTAL STUDY OF THE THOMISTIC CONCEPT OF THE FACULTY OF IMAGINATION. 1941. 51 pp.

————, **Number 4.** McCarthy, Thomas J. PERSONALITY TRAITS OF SEMINARIANS. 1942. 46 pp.

————, **Number 5.** Moynihan, James F. (S.J.). THE CONCEPT OF THE SYNTHETIC SENSE AND A TECHNIQUE OF ITS MEASUREMENT. 1942. 48 pp.

————, **Number 6.** Devlin, William J. (S.J.). THE EFFECT OF CERTAIN PHARMACOLOGICAL PREPARATIONS ON THE EMOTIONS OF NORMAL AND PSYCHOTIC INDIVIDUALS. 1942. 56 pp.

————, **Number 7.** Peters, Sister Richarda (O.S.B.). A STUDY OF THE INTERCORRELATIONS OF PERSONALITY TRAITS AMONG A GROUP OF NOVICES IN RELIGIOUS COMMUNITIES. 1942. 38 pp.

————, **Number 8.** Kremer, Alphonse H. THE NATURE OF PERSISTENCE. 1942. 40 pp.

Volume 6, Number 1. Hsü, En Hsi. THE CONSTRUCTION OF A TEST FOR MEASURING CHARACTER TRAITS. 1943. 55 pp.

————, **Number 2.** McAndrew, Sister M. Bernardina (I.H.M.). AN EXPERIMENTAL INVESTIGATION OF YOUNG CHILDREN'S IDEAS OF CAUSALITY. 1943. 65 pp.

————, **Number 3.** Robitaille, Henry J. THE DEVELOPMENT OF A TEST FOR REASONING ABILITY AND ITS APPLICATION TO STUDENTS MAJORING IN SCIENCE, CLASSICS AND COMMERCIAL COURSES. 1943. 64 pp.

————, **Number 4.** Betke, Sister Mary Angela. DEFECTIVE MORAL REASONING IN DELINQUENCY. A PSYCHOLOGICAL STUDY. 1944. 95 pp.

————, **Number 5.** Lorang, Sister Mary Corde. THE EFFECT OF READING ON MORAL CONDUCT AND EMOTIONAL EXPERIENCE. 1945. 122 pp.

————, **Number 6.** Keckeissen, Sister Mary Gertrude. AN EMPIRICAL STUDY OF MORAL PROBLEMS AND CHARACTER TRAITS OF HIGH SCHOOL PUPILS. 1945. 31 pp.

————, **Number 7.** Collins, William J. THE EFFECTS OF CERTAIN PARASYMPATHOMIMETIC SUBSTANCES ON THE EMOTIONS OF NORMAL AND PSYCHOTIC INDIVIDUALS. 1946. 68 pp.

————, **Number 8.** Keneally, Katherine G. THE CONSTRUCTION AND EVALUATION OF A DIAGNOSTIC TEST OF STUDY SKILLS FOR GRADES 4, 5, AND 6. 1947. 60 pp.

Volume 7, Number 1. Lhota, Brian. VOCATIONAL INTERESTS OF CATHOLIC PRIESTS. 1948. 40 pp.

————, **Number 2.** Dowd, Sister Mary Amadeus. CHANGES IN MORAL REASONING THROUGH THE HIGH SCHOOL YEARS. 1948. 120 pp.

————, **Number 3.** Bier, William C. (S.J.). A COMPARATIVE STUDY OF A SEMINARY GROUP AND FOUR OTHER GROUPS ON THE MINNESOTA MULTIPHASIC PERSONALITY INVENTORY. 1948. 107 pp.

————, **Number 4.** Grimes, Francis V. AN EXPERIMENTAL ANALYSIS OF THE NATURE OF SUGGESTIBILITY AND OF ITS RELATION TO OTHER PSYCHOLOGICAL FACTORS. 1948. 45 pp.

————, **Number 5.** Frawley, Patrick J. A STUDY OF JUDGMENT—A FACTORIAL ANALYSIS OF THE ANCHORING EFFECTS. 1948. 132 pp.

Volume 8, Number 1. Harney, Sister Maureen. SOME PSYCHOLOGICAL AND PHYSICAL CHARACTERISTICS OF RETARDED GIRLS BEFORE AND FOLLOWING TREATMENT WITH GLUTAMIC ACID. 1950. 64 pp.

525. *College Entrance Examination Board. Commission on Scholastic Aptitude. Annual Reports.*

TITLE VARIATIONS: None.

DATES OF PUBLICATION: 1st–15th. 1926–1940.

FREQUENCY: Annual.

NUMBERING VARIATIONS: All reports are published as a section of the *College Entrance Examination Board. Annual Report*. The Commission was established in 1925 and the first report was published in the *26th Annual Report* of the CEEB. Reports are also published as Appendices to the *CEEB Annual Report*. See 2nd, 1927; 3rd, 1928; 5th, 1930; 6th, 1931; etc.

PUBLISHER: **New York:** Published by the Board, 1926–1940.

PRIMARY EDITORS: Secretary of the College Entrance Examination Board acts as editor.

526. *Genetic Psychology Monographs.*

TITLE VARIATIONS: None. Subtitled *Child Behavior, Differential and Genetic Psychology*, 1926–1929; and *Child Behavior, Animal Behavior, and Comparative Psychology*, 1929–1950+.

DATES OF PUBLICATION: Volume 1–42+, 1926–1950+.

FREQUENCY: **Bimonthly,** 1926–1927; **Monthly,** 1928–1934; **Bimonthly,** 1935–1936; **Quarterly,** 1937–1940; **Quarterly** (2 issues per volume, 2 volumes per year), 1941–1950+.

NUMBERING VARIATIONS: None.

PUBLISHER: **Worcester, Massachusetts:** Clark University Press, 1926–1936. **Provincetown, Massachusetts:** The Journal Press, 1937–1950+.

526. *(Continued)*

PRIMARY EDITOR: **Carl Murchison,** 1926–1950 + .

ASSISTANT EDITOR: Luberta M. Harden, 1930–1934.

EDITORIAL BOARD: John E. Anderson, 1928–1950+; Bird T. Baldwin, 1926–1928; Charlotte Bühler, 1928–1950 +; William H. Burnham, 1926–1941; Cyril Burt, 1926–1950+; Leonard Carmichael, 1932–1950+; Éd. Claparède, 1926–1940; Edmund S. Conklin, 1926, 1928–1942; Sante de Sanctis, 1926–1950 +; Arnold Gesell, 1926, 1928–1950 +; William Healy, 1926–1950 +; Leta S. Hollingworth, 1928–1940; Walter S. Hunter, 1926–1933; Arthur T. Jersild, 1948–1950+; Buford Johnson, 1928–1950+; Harold E. Jones, 1930–1950+; Truman L. Kelley, 1927–1950+; Yoshihide Kubo, 1928–1943; K. S. Lashley, 1926–1950+; A. R. Luria, 1928–1950+; Toshio Nogami, 1928–1943; Ivan P. Pavlov, 1928–1940; Henri Piéron, 1926–1950+; Robert R. Sears, 1949–1950+; William Stern, 1926–1937; George D. Stoddard, 1939–1950+; Calvin P. Stone, 1927–1950+; Lewis M. Terman, 1926–1950+; Godfrey Thomson, 1927–1950+; E. L. Thorndike, 1926–1949; C. J. Warden, 1928–1950+; John B. Watson, 1926–1950+; Helen Thompson Woolley, 1926–1947.

CONTENTS:
   Volume 1, Number 1. Stutsman, Rachel. PERFORMANCE TESTS FOR CHILDREN OF PRE-SCHOOL AGE. 1926. Pp. 1–67.
   ———, **Number 2.** Klüver, Heinrich. AN EXPERIMENTAL STUDY OF THE EIDETIC TYPE. 1926. Pp. 69–230.
   ———, **Number 3/4.** Hirsch, Nathaniel D. Mttron. A STUDY OF NATIO-RACIAL MENTAL DIFFERENCES. 1926. Pp. 231–406.
   ———, **Number 5.** Bridges, J. W., and K. M. Banham Bridges. A PSYCHOLOGICAL STUDY OF JUVENILE DELINQUENCY BY GROUP METHODS. 1926. Pp. 407–506.
   ———, **Number 6.** Gesell, Arnold. THE INFLUENCE OF PUBERTY PRAECOX UPON MENTAL GROWTH. 1926. Pp. 507–538.
   Volume 2, Number 1/2. Yerkes, Robert M. THE MIND OF A GORILLA. 1927. Pp. 1–193.
   ———, **Number 3.** Dunlap, Knight. THE ROLE OF EYE-MUSCLES AND MOUTH-MUSCLES IN THE EXPRESSION OF THE EMOTIONS. 1927. Pp. 195–233.
   ———, **Number 4.** Willoughby, Raymond Royce. FAMILY SIMILARITIES IN MENTAL-TEST ABILITIES. (WITH A NOTE ON THE GROWTH AND DECLINE OF THESE ABILITIES). 1927. Pp. 235–277.
   ———, **Number 5.** Burnside, Lenoir H. COORDINATION IN THE LOCOMOTION OF INFANTS. 1927. Pp. 279–372.
   ———, **Number 6.** Yerkes, Robert M. THE MIND OF A GORILLA: PART II. MENTAL DEVELOPMENT. 1927. Pp. 375–551.
   Volume 3, Number 1. Liggett, John Riley. AN EXPERIMENTAL STUDY OF THE OLFACTORY SENSITIVITY OF THE WHITE RAT. 1928. Pp. 1–64.
   ———, **Number 2.** Tinker, Miles A. A PHOTOGRAPHIC STUDY OF EYE MOVEMENTS IN READING FORMULAE. 1928. Pp. 65–182.

————, **Number 3.** Hirsch, Nathaniel D. Mttron. AN EXPERIMENTAL STUDY OF THE EAST KENTUCKY MOUNTAINEERS. A STUDY IN HEREDITY AND ENVIRONMENT. 1928. Pp. 183–244.

————, **Number 4.** Avery, George T. RESPONSES OF FOETAL GUINEA PIGS PREMATURELY DELIVERED. 1928. Pp. 245–332.

————, **Number 5.** Jensen, Milton B. OBJECTIVE DIFFERENTIATION BETWEEN THREE GROUPS IN EDUCATION (TEACHERS, RESEARCH WORKERS, AND ADMINISTRATORS). 1928. Pp. 333–454c.

————, **Number 6.** Jenkins, Marion. THE EFFECT OF SEGREGATION ON THE SEX BEHAVIOR OF THE WHITE RAT AS MEASURED BY THE OBSTRUCTION METHOD. 1928. Pp. 455–571.

Volume 4, Number 1. Bott, E. A., W. E. Blatz, Nellie Chant, and Helen Bott. OBSERVATION AND TRAINING OF FUNDAMENTAL HABITS IN YOUNG CHILDREN. 1928. Pp. 1–161.

————, **Number 2/3.** Burch, Mary Crowell. DETERMINATION OF A CONTENT OF THE COURSE IN LITERATURE OF A SUITABLE DIFFICULTY FOR JUNIOR AND SENIOR HIGH SCHOOL STUDENTS. 1928. Pp. 163–332.

————, **Number 4/5.** Monroe, Marion. METHODS FOR DIAGNOSIS AND TREATMENT OF CASES OF READING DISABILITY. BASED ON THE COMPARISON OF THE READING PERFORMANCE OF ONE HUNDRED AND TWENTY NORMAL AND ONE HUNDRED AND SEVENTY-FIVE RETARDED READERS. Foreword by Samuel T. Orton. 1928. Pp. 333–456.

————, **Number 6.** Greene, Edward Barrows. THE RELATIVE EFFECTIVENESS OF LECTURE AND INDIVIDUAL READING AS METHODS OF COLLEGE TEACHING. 1928. Pp. 457–563.

Volume 5, Number 1. Stone, Calvin P. THE AGE FACTOR IN ANIMAL LEARNING: I. RATS IN THE PROBLEM BOX AND THE MAZE. 1929. Pp. 1–130.

————, **Number 2.** Hamilton, E. Louise. THE EFFECT OF DELAYED INCENTIVE ON THE HUNGER DRIVE IN THE WHITE RAT. 1929. Pp. 131–207.

————, **Number 3.** Smith, Josephine Mitchell. WHICH HAND IS THE EYE OF THE BLIND? 1929. Pp. 209–252.

————, **Number 4.** Ekdahl, Adolph Gustavus. THE EFFECT OF ATTITUDE UPON FREE WORD ASSOCIATION-TIME. 1929. Pp. 253–338.

————, **Number 5.** Cole, Lawrence E. THE LOCALIZATION OF TACTUAL SPACE: A STUDY OF AVERAGE AND CONSTANT ERRORS UNDER DIFFERENT TYPES OF LOCALIZATION. 1929. Pp. 335–450.

————, **Number 6.** Nissen, Henry W. THE EFFECTS OF GONADECTOMY, VASOTOMY, AND INJECTIONS OF PLACENTAL AND ORCHIC EXTRACTS ON THE SEX BEHAVIOR OF THE WHITE RAT. 1929. Pp. 451–550.

Volume 6, Number 1. Gesell, Arnold, and Helen Thompson. LEARNING AND GROWTH IN IDENTICAL INFANT TWINS: AN EXPERIMENTAL STUDY BY THE METHOD OF CO-TWIN CONTROL. 1929. Pp. 1–124.

————, **Number 2.** Stone, Calvin P. THE AGE FACTOR IN ANIMAL LEARNING: II. RATS ON A MULTIPLE LIGHT DISCRIMINATION BOX AND A DIFFICULT MAZE. 1929. Pp. 125–202.

————, **Number 3.** McGinnis, Esther. THE ACQUISITION AND INTERFERENCE OF MOTOR HABITS IN YOUNG CHILDREN. 1929. Pp. 203–311.

526. *(Continued)*

————, **Number 4.** Mueller, A. D. A Vocational and Socio-educational Survey of Graduates and Non-Graduates of Small High Schools of New England. 1929. Pp. 313–395.

————, **Number 5.** Washburn, Ruth Wendell. A Study of the Smiling and Laughing of Infants in the First Year of Life. 1929. Pp. 397–537.

Volume 7, Number 1. Duffy, Elizabeth. Tensions and Emotional Factors in Reaction. 1930. Pp. 1–79.

————, **Number 2.** Taylor, Howard Rice. Teacher Influence on Class Achievement: A Study of the Relationship of Estimated Teaching Ability to Pupil Achievement in Reading and Arithmetic. 1930. Pp. 81–175.

————, **Number 3/4.** Ewert, P. Harry. A Study of the Effect of Inverted Retinal Stimulation upon Spatially Coordinated Behavior. 1930. Pp. 177–363.

————, **Number 5.** Lord, Elizabeth Evans. A Study of the Mental Development of Children with Lesion in the Central Nervous System. 1930. Pp. 365–486.

————, **Number 6.** Hirsch, Nathaniel D. Mttron. An Experimental Study upon Three Hundred School Children over a Six-year Period. 1930. Pp. 487–549.

Volume 8, Number 1. Irwin, Orvis C. The Amount and Nature of Activities of Newborn Infants under Constant External Stimulating Conditions during the First Ten Days of Life. 1930. Pp. 1–92.

————, **Number 2.** Porteus, S. D., with the Assistance of Doris M. Dewey and Robert G. Bernreuter. Race and Social Differences in Performance Tests. 1930. Pp. 93–208.

————, **Number 3.** Strayer, Lois Curry. Language and Growth: The Relative Efficacy of Early and Deferred Vocabulary Training, Studied by the Method of Co-twin Control. 1930. Pp. 209–319.

————, **Number 4.** McGinnis, John M. Eye-Movements and Optic Nystagmus in Early Infancy. 1930. Pp. 321–430.

————, **Number 5/6.** Farwell, Louise. Reactions of Kindergarten, First-, and Second-grade Children to Constructive Play Materials. 1930. Pp. 431–562.

Volume 9, Number 1/2. Hsiao, Hsiao Hung. The Status of the First-Born with Special Reference to Intelligence. 1931. Pp. 1–118.

————, **Number 3/4.** Davidson, Helen P. An Experimental Study of Bright, Average, and Dull Children at the Four-year Mental Level. 1931. Pp. 119–289.

————, **Number 5.** Farnsworth, Paul R. An Historical, Critical, and Experimental Study of the Seashore–Kwalwasser Test Battery. 1931. Pp. 291–393.

————, **Number 6.** Wilson, F. T. A Comparison of Difficulty and Improvement in the Learning of Bright and Dull Children in Reproducing a Descriptive Selection. 1931. Pp. 395–435.

Volume 10, Number 1. McGraw, Myrtle B. A Comparative Study of a Group of Southern White and Negro Infants. 1931. Pp. 1–105.

————, **Number 2/3.** Halverson, H. M. An Experimental Study of Pre-

526. *(Continued)*

————, **Number 4.** Coronios, J. D. DEVELOPMENT OF BEHAVIOR IN THE FETAL CAT. 1933. Pp. 283–386.

————, **Number 5.** LaBrant, Lou L. A STUDY OF CERTAIN LANGUAGE DEVELOPMENTS OF CHILDREN IN GRADES FOUR TO TWELVE, INCLUSIVE. 1933. Pp. 387–491.

————, **Number 6.** Hilgard, Josephine Rohrs. THE EFFECT OF EARLY AND DELAYED PRACTICE ON MEMORY AND MOTOR PERFORMANCES STUDIED BY THE METHOD OF CO-TWIN CONTROL. 1933. Pp. 493–567.

Volume 15, Number 1. Farnsworth, Paul R. STUDIES IN THE PSYCHOLOGY OF TONE AND MUSIC. 1934. Pp. 1–94.

————, **Number 2.** Beebe, Elinor Lee. MOTOR LEARNING OF CHILDREN IN EQUILIBRIUM IN RELATION TO NUTRITION. 1934. Pp. 95–243.

————, **Number 3.** Rowley, Jean B. DISCRIMINATION LIMENS OF PATTERN AND SIZE IN THE GOLDFISH CARASSIUS AURATUS. 1934. Pp. 245–302.

————, **Number 4.** Riess, Bernard F. LIMITS OF LEARNING ABILITY IN THE WHITE RAT AND THE GUINEA PIG. 1934. Pp. 303–368.

————, **Number 5/6.** Fjeld, Harriet Anderson. THE LIMITS OF LEARNING ABILITY IN RHESUS MONKEYS. 1934. Pp. 369–537.

Volume 16, Number 1. Conrad, Herbert S. A STATISTICAL STUDY OF RATINGS ON THE CALIFORNIA BEHAVIOR INVENTORY FOR NURSERY-SCHOOL CHILDREN. 1934. Pp. 1–78.

————, **Number 2.** Frandsen, Arden. AN EYE-MOVEMENT STUDY OF OBJECTIVE EXAMINATION QUESTIONS. 1934. Pp. 79–138.

————, **Number 3.** Klineberg, Otto, S. E. Asch, and Helen Block. AN EXPERIMENTAL STUDY OF CONSTITUTIONAL TYPES. 1934. Pp. 139–221.

————, **Number 4.** Durost, Walter N. THE DEVELOPMENT OF A BATTERY OF OBJECTIVE GROUP TESTS OF MANUAL LATERALITY, WITH THE RESULTS OF THEIR APPLICATION TO 1300 CHILDREN. 1934. Pp. 223–335.

————, **Number 5/6.** Carmichael, Leonard. AN EXPERIMENTAL STUDY IN THE PRENATAL GUINEA-PIG OF THE ORIGIN AND DEVELOPMENT OF REFLEXES AND PATTERNS OF BEHAVIOR IN RELATION TO THE STIMULATION OF SPECIFIC RECEPTOR AREAS DURING THE PERIOD OF ACTIVE FETAL LIFE. 1934. Pp. 337–491.

Volume 17, Number 1. Thorndike, Robert Ladd. ORGANIZATION OF BEHAVIOR IN THE ALBINO RAT. 1935. Pp. 1–70.

————, **Number 2.** Crawford, Meredith Pullen. BRIGHTNESS DISCRIMINATION IN THE RHESUS MONKEY. 1935. Pp. 71–162.

————, **Number 3.** Koch, Adolph Meyer. THE LIMITS OF LEARNING ABILITY IN CEBUS MONKEYS. 1935. Pp. 163–234.

————, **Number 4.** Leahy, Alice M. NATURE-NURTURE AND INTELLIGENCE. 1935. Pp. 235–308.

————, **Number 5.** Sullivan, Ellen B., and Laurence Gahagan. ON INTELLIGENCE OF EPILEPTIC CHILDREN. 1935. Pp. 309–376.

————, **Number 6.** Cockrell, Dura-Louise. A STUDY OF THE PLAY OF CHILDREN OF PRESCHOOL AGE BY AN UNOBSERVED OBSERVER. 1935. Pp. 377–469.

Volume 18, Number 1. McNemar, Quinn, and Lewis M. Terman. SEX DIFFERENCES IN VARIATIONAL TENDENCY. 1936. Pp. 1–66.

————, **Number 2.** Key, Cora B., Margaret R. White, Marjorie Pyles Honzik, Adelia Boynton Heiney, and Doris Erwin. THE PROCESS OF LEARNING TO DRESS AMONG NURSERY-SCHOOL CHILDREN. 1936. Pp. 67–164.

————, **Number 3.** Baller, Warren Robert. A STUDY OF THE PRESENT SOCIAL STATUS OF A GROUP OF ADULTS, WHO, WHEN THEY WERE IN ELEMENTARY SCHOOLS, WERE CLASSIFIED AS MENTALLY DEFICIENT. 1936. Pp. 165–244.

————, **Number 4.** Anastasi, Anne. THE INFLUENCE OF SPECIFIC EXPERIENCE UPON MENTAL ORGANIZATION. 1936. Pp. 245–355.

————, **Number 5/6.** Bender, Lauretta, Sylvan Keiser, and Paul Schilder. STUDIES IN AGGRESSIVENESS. 1936. Pp. 357–564.

Volume 19, Number 1. Dabrowski, Casimir. PSYCHOLOGICAL BASES OF SELF-MUTILATION. 1937. Pp. 1–104; and Gilkinson, Howard. MASCULINE TEMPERAMENT AND SECONDARY SEX CHARACTERISTICS: A STUDY OF THE RELATIONSHIP BETWEEN PSYCHOLOGICAL AND PHYSICAL MEASURES OF MASCULINITY. 1937. Pp. 105–154.

————, **Number 2.** Nottingham, Ruth D. A PSYCHOLOGICAL STUDY OF FORTY UNMARRIED MOTHERS. 1937. Pp. 155–228; and Bender, Lauretta. BEHAVIOR PROBLEMS IN THE CHILDREN OF PSYCHOTIC AND CRIMINAL PARENTS. 1937. Pp. 229–339.

————, **Number 3.** Anderson, Harold H. DOMINATION AND INTEGRATION IN THE SOCIAL BEHAVIOR OF YOUNG CHILDREN IN AN EXPERIMENTAL PLAY SITUATION. 1937. Pp. 341–408.

————, **Number 4.** Ames, Louise Bates. THE SEQUENTIAL PATTERNING OF PRONE PROGRESSION IN THE HUMAN INFANT. 1937. Pp. 409–460.

Volume 20, Number 1. Cabot, P. S. de Q. THE RELATIONSHIP BETWEEN CHARACTERISTICS OF PERSONALITY AND PHYSIQUE IN ADOLESCENTS. 1938. Pp. 3–120.

————, **Number 2.** Masten, Isabel Young. BEHAVIOR PROBLEMS OF ELEMENTARY SCHOOL CHILDREN: A DESCRIPTIVE AND COMPARATIVE STUDY. 1938. Pp. 123–181; and Gridley, Pearl Farwell. GRAPHIC REPRESENTATION OF A MAN BY FOUR-YEAR-OLD CHILDREN IN NINE PRESCRIBED DRAWING SITUATIONS. 1938. Pp. 183–350.

————, **Number 3.** Tolman, Ruth Sherman. DIFFERENCES BETWEEN TWO GROUPS OF ADULT CRIMINALS. 1938. Pp. 353–458.

————, **Number 4.** Troup, Evelyn. A COMPARATIVE STUDY BY MEANS OF THE RORSCHACH METHOD OF PERSONALITY DEVELOPMENT IN TWENTY PAIRS OF IDENTICAL TWINS. 1938. Pp. 461–556; and Swan, Carla. INDIVIDUAL DIFFERENCES IN THE FACIAL EXPRESSIVE BEHAVIOR OF PRESCHOOL CHILDREN: A STUDY BY THE TIME-SAMPLING METHOD. 1938. Pp. 557–650.

Volume 21, Number 1. Gould, Rosalind. AN EXPERIMENTAL ANALYSIS OF "LEVEL OF ASPIRATION." 1939. Pp. 3–115.

————, **Number 2.** Smith, Madorah E. SOME LIGHT ON THE PROBLEM OF BILINGUALISM AS FOUND FROM A STUDY OF THE PROGRESS IN MASTERY OF ENGLISH AMONG PRE-SCHOOL CHILDREN OF NON-AMERICAN ANCESTRY IN HAWAII. 1939. Pp. 119–284.

————, **Number 3.** Anderson, Harold H. DOMINATION AND SOCIAL INTEGRATION IN THE BEHAVIOR OF KINDERGARTEN CHILDREN AND TEACHERS. 1939. Pp. 287–385; and Galt, William Egleston. THE CAPACITY OF THE RHESUS

526. *(Continued)*

AND CEBUS MONKEY AND THE GIBBON TO ACQUIRE DIFFERENTIAL RESPONSE TO COMPLEX VISUAL STIMULI. 1939. Pp. 387–457.

———, **Number 4.** Campbell, Elise Hatt. THE SOCIAL-SEX DEVELOPMENT OF CHILDREN. 1939. Pp. 461–552.

Volume 22, Number 1. Chapple, Eliot D., with the collaboration of Conrad M. Arensberg. MEASURING HUMAN RELATIONS: AN INTRODUCTION TO THE STUDY OF THE INTERACTION OF INDIVIDUALS. 1940. Pp. 3–147.

———, **Number 2.** Fite, Mary Delafield. AGGRESSIVE BEHAVIOR IN YOUNG CHILDREN AND CHILDREN'S ATTITUDES TOWARD AGGRESSION. 1940. Pp. 151–319.

———, **Number 3.** Nelson, Erland. STUDENT ATTITUDES TOWARD RELIGION. 1940. Pp. 323–423; Jacob, Joseph Simeon. THE PREDICTION OF THE OUTCOME-ON-FURLOUGH OF DEMENTIA PRAECOX PATIENTS. 1940. Pp. 425–453; and Read, Katherine H. SIGNIFICANT CHARACTERISTICS OF PRESCHOOL CHILDREN AS LOCATED IN THE CONRAD INVENTORY. 1940. Pp. 455–489.

———, **Number 4.** McCay, Jeanette B., Ethel B. Waring, and Paul J. Kruse. LEARNING BY CHILDREN AT NOON-MEAL IN A NURSERY SCHOOL: TEN "GOOD" EATERS AND TEN "POOR" EATERS. 1940. Pp. 491–555; and Erikson, Erik Homburger. STUDIES IN THE INTERPRETATION OF PLAY: I. CLINICAL OBSERVATION OF PLAY DISRUPTION IN YOUNG CHILDREN. 1940. Pp. 557–671.

Volume 23, Number 1. Young, Florene M. AN ANALYSIS OF CERTAIN VARIABLES IN A DEVELOPMENTAL STUDY OF LANGUAGE. 1941. Pp. 3–141; Dennis, Wayne. INFANT DEVELOPMENT UNDER CONDITIONS OF RESTRICTED PRACTICE AND OF MINIMUM SOCIAL STIMULATION. 1941. Pp. 143–189; and Balinsky, Benjamin. AN ANALYSIS OF THE MENTAL FACTORS OF VARIOUS AGE GROUPS FROM NINE TO SIXTY. 1941. Pp. 191–234.

———, **Number 2.** Bennett, Mary Woods. FACTORS INFLUENCING PERFORMANCE ON GROUP AND INDIVIDUAL TESTS OF INTELLIGENCE: I. RATE OF WORK. 1941. Pp. 237–318; and Amen, Elisabeth W. INDIVIDUAL DIFFERENCES IN APPERCEPTIVE REACTION: A STUDY OF THE RESPONSE OF PRESCHOOL CHILDREN TO PICTURES. 1941. Pp. 319–385.

Volume 24, Number 1. Gesell, Arnold, and Helen Thompson. TWINS T AND C FROM INFANCY TO ADOLESCENCE: A BIOGENETIC STUDY OF INDIVIDUAL DIFFERENCES BY THE METHOD OF CO-TWIN CONTROL. 1941. Pp. 3–121; Billig, Albert Leroy. FINGER NAIL-BITING: ITS INCIPIENCY, INCIDENCE, AND AMELIORATION. 1941. Pp. 123–218; and Fromme, Allan. AN EXPERIMENTAL STUDY OF THE FACTORS OF MATURATION AND PRACTICE IN THE BEHAVIORAL DEVELOPMENT OF THE EMBRYO OF THE FROG, RANA PIPIENS. 1941. Pp. 219–256.

———, **Number 2.** Richards T. W., and Marjorie Powell Simons. THE FELS CHILD BEHAVIOR SCALES. 1941. Pp. 259–309; Smith, Mary Katherine. MEASUREMENT OF THE SIZE OF GENERAL ENGLISH VOCABULARY THROUGH THE ELEMENTARY GRADES AND HIGH SCHOOL. 1941. Pp. 311–345; and Farnsworth, Paul R. STEREOTYPES IN THE FIELD OF MUSICAL EMINENCE. 1941. Pp. 347–381.

Volume 25, Number 1. Flanagan, John C. A STUDY OF FACTORS DETERMINING FAMILY SIZE IN A SELECTED PROFESSIONAL GROUP. 1942. Pp. 3–99; Walters, Sister Annette. A GENETIC STUDY OF GEOMETRICAL-OPTICAL ILLU-

SIONS. 1942. Pp. 101–155; and Read, Katherine H., and Herbert S. Conrad. INTERPRETATION OF BEHAVIOR-RATINGS IN TERMS OF FAVORABLE AND UNFAVOR-ABLE DEVIATIONS: A STUDY OF SCORES FROM THE READ-CONRAD BEHAVIOR IN-VENTORY. 1942. Pp. 157–215.

————, **Number 2.** Schoolland, John B. ARE THERE ANY INNATE BEHAV-IOR TENDENCIES? 1942. Pp. 219–287; and Hudgins, C. V., and F. C. Numbers. AN INVESTIGATION OF THE INTELLIGIBILITY OF THE SPEECH OF THE DEAF. 1942. Pp. 289–392.

Volume 26, Number 1. Miller, Vernon L. THE CRITICAL FREQUENCY LIMEN FOR VISUAL FLICKER IN CHILDREN BETWEEN THE AGES OF 6 AND 18. 1942. Pp. 3–53; and Wentworth, K. L. SOME FACTORS DETERMINING HANDEDNESS IN THE WHITE RAT. 1942. Pp. 55–117.

————, **Number 2.** Frenkel-Brunswik, Else. MOTIVATION AND BEHAVIOR. 1942. Pp. 121–265.

Volume 27, Number 1. Maddy, Nancy Ruth. COMPARISON OF CHILDREN'S PERSONALITY TRAITS, ATTITUDES, AND INTELLIGENCE WITH PARENTAL OCCU-PATION. 1943. Pp. 3–65.

————, **Number 2.** Pignatelli, Myrtle Luneau. A COMPARATIVE STUDY OF MENTAL FUNCTIONING PATTERNS OF PROBLEM AND NON-PROBLEM CHILDREN, SEVEN, EIGHT, AND NINE YEARS OF AGE. 1943. Pp. 67–162.

Volume 28, Number 1. Edelston, H. SEPARATION ANXIETY IN YOUNG CHILDREN: A STUDY OF HOSPITAL CASES. 1943. Pp. 3–95.

————, **Number 2.** Bradley, William Arthur Jr. CORRELATES OF VOCA-TIONAL PREFERENCES. 1943. Pp. 99–169.

Volume 29, Number 1. Porteus, Stanley D., and Richard DeMonbrun Kepner. MENTAL CHANGES AFTER BILATERAL PREFRONTAL LOBOTOMY. 1944. Pp. 3–115.

————, **Number 2.** Price, Bronson, Wencel J. Kostir, and W. Mark Tay-lor. A TWIN-CONTROLLED EXPERIMENT ON THE LEARNING OF AUXILIARY LAN-GUAGES. 1944. Pp. 117–154.

Volume 30, Number 1. Clark, Ruth Millburn. A METHOD OF ADMINIS-TERING AND EVALUATING THE THEMATIC APPERCEPTION TEST IN GROUP SITUA-TIONS. 1944. Pp. 3–55.

————, **Number 2.** Temple, Rita, and Elisabeth W. Amen. A STUDY OF ANXIETY REACTIONS IN YOUNG CHILDREN BY MEANS OF A PROJECTIVE TECH-NIQUE. 1944. Pp. 59–114.

Volume 31, Number 1. Weinstein, Benjamin. THE EVOLUTION OF INTEL-LIGENT BEHAVIOR IN RHESUS MONKEYS. 1945. Pp. 3–48.

————, **Number 2.** Werner, Heinz. PERCEPTUAL BEHAVIOR OF BRAIN-INJURED, MENTALLY DEFECTIVE CHILDREN: AN EXPERIMENTAL STUDY BY MEANS OF THE RORSCHACH TECHNIQUE. 1945. Pp. 51–110.

Volume 32, Number 1. Murray, Henry A., and Christiana D. Morgan. A CLINICAL STUDY OF SENTIMENTS. I. 1945. Pp. 3–149.

————, **Number 2.** Murray, Henry A., and Christiana D. Morgan. A CLINICAL STUDY OF SENTIMENTS. II. 1945. Pp. 153–311.

Volume 33, Number 1. Waehner, Trude S. INTERPRETATION OF SPONTA-NEOUS DRAWINGS AND PAINTINGS. 1946. Pp. 3–70; and Franck, Kate. PREF-

526. *(Continued)*

ERENCE FOR SEX SYMBOLS AND THEIR PERSONALITY CORRELATES. 1946. Pp. 73–123.

————, **Number 2.** Wells, F. L., and W. L. Woods. OUTSTANDING TRAITS: IN A SELECTED COLLEGE GROUP, WITH SOME REFERENCE TO CAREER INTERESTS AND WAR RECORDS. 1946. Pp. 127–249.

Volume 34, Number 1. Despert, J. Louise, and Helen Oexle Pierce. THE RELATION OF EMOTIONAL ADJUSTMENT TO INTELLECTUAL FUNCTION. 1946. Pp. 3–56; and Spitz, Rene A., with the assistance of K. M. Wolf. THE SMILING RESPONSE: A CONTRIBUTION TO THE ONTOGENESIS OF SOCIAL RELATIONS. 1946. Pp. 57–125.

————, **Number 2.** Napoli, Peter J. FINGER-PAINTING AND PERSONALITY DIAGNOSIS. 1946. Pp. 129–231.

Volume 35, Number 1. Henry, William E. THE THEMATIC APPERCEPTION TECHNIQUE IN THE STUDY OF CULTURE–PERSONALITY RELATIONS. 1947. Pp. 3–135.

————, **Number 2.** Dorkey, Margaret, and Elisabeth W. Amen. A CONTINUATION STUDY OF ANXIETY REACTIONS IN YOUNG CHILDREN BY MEANS OF A PROJECTIVE TECHNIQUE. 1947. Pp. 139–183; and Cawley, Sister Anne Mary. A STUDY OF THE VOCATIONAL INTEREST TRENDS OF SECONDARY SCHOOL AND COLLEGE WOMEN. 1947. Pp. 185–247.

Volume 36, Number 1. Porteus, Stanley D., and Henry N. Peters. MAZE TEST VALIDATION AND PSYCHOSURGERY. 1947. Pp. 3–86.

————, **Number 2.** Jolles, Isaac. THE DIAGNOSTIC IMPLICATIONS OF RORSCHACH'S TEST IN CASE STUDIES OF MENTAL DEFECTIVES. 1947. Pp. 89–198.

Volume 37, Number 1. Warner, W. Lloyd, and William E. Henry. THE RADIO DAY TIME SERIAL: A SYMBOLIC ANALYSIS. 1948. Pp. 3–71; and Grace, Gloria Laver. THE RELATION OF PERSONALITY CHARACTERISTICS AND RESPONSE TO VERBAL APPROVAL IN A LEARNING TASK. 1948. Pp. 73–103.

————, **Number 2.** Lashley, K. S. THE MECHANISM OF VISION: XVIII. EFFECTS OF DESTROYING THE VISUAL "ASSOCIATIVE AREAS" OF THE MONKEY. 1948. Pp. 107–166; and Castelnuova-Tedesco, Peter. A STUDY OF THE RELATIONSHIP BETWEEN HANDWRITING AND PERSONALITY VARIABLES. 1948. Pp. 167–220.

Volume 38, Number 1. Lind, Melva. MODERN LANGUAGE LEARNING: THE INTENSIVE COURSE AS SPONSORED BY THE UNITED STATES ARMY AND IMPLICATIONS FOR THE UNDERGRADUATE COURSE OF STUDY. 1948. Pp. 3–82; and Tolcott, Martin Arnold. CONFLICT: A STUDY OF SOME INTERACTIONS BETWEEN APPETITE AND AVERSION IN THE WHITE RAT. 1948. Pp. 83–142.

————, **Number 2.** Shneidman, Edwin S. SCHIZOPHRENIA AND THE MAPS TEST: A STUDY OF CERTAIN FORMAL PSYCHO-SOCIAL ASPECTS OF FANTASY PRODUCTION IN SCHIZOPHRENIA AS REVEALED BY PERFORMANCE ON THE MAKE A PICTURE STORY (MAPS) TEST. 1948. Pp. 145–223; and Ingersoll, Hazel L. A STUDY OF THE TRANSMISSION OF AUTHORITY PATTERNS IN THE FAMILY. 1948. Pp. 225–302.

Volume 39, Number 1. Blum, Gerald S. A STUDY OF THE PSYCHOANALYTIC

THEORY OF PSYCHOSEXUAL DEVELOPMENT. 1949. Pp. 3–99; and Shoben, Edward Joseph Jr. THE ASSESSMENT OF PARENTAL ATTITUDES IN RELATION TO CHILD ADJUSTMENT. 1949. Pp. 101–148.

————, **Number 2.** Feifel, Herman. QUALITATIVE DIFFERENCES IN THE VOCABULARY RESPONSES OF NORMALS AND ABNORMALS. 1949. Pp. 151–204; Eiserer, Paul E. THE RELATIVE EFFECTIVENESS OF MOTION AND STILL PICTURES AS STIMULI FOR ELICITING FANTASY STORIES ABOUT ADOLESCENT–PARENT RELATIONSHIPS. 1949. Pp. 205–278; and Searle, Lloyd V. THE ORGANIZATION OF HEREDITARY MAZE-BRIGHTNESS AND MAZE-DULLNESS. 1949. Pp. 279–325.

Volume 40, Number 1. Biber, Barbara, and Claudia Lewis. AN EXPERIMENTAL STUDY OF WHAT YOUNG SCHOOL CHILDREN EXPECT FROM THEIR TEACHERS. 1949. Pp. 3–97; Curtis, Hazen Alonzo. A STUDY OF THE RELATIVE EFFECTS OF AGE AND OF TEST DIFFICULTY UPON FACTOR PATTERNS. 1949. Pp. 99–148; and, Seaton, James Kirk. A PROJECTIVE EXPERIMENT USING INCOMPLETE STORIES WITH MULTIPLE-CHOICE ENDINGS. 1949. Pp. 149–228.

————, **Number 2.** Milner, Esther. EFFECTS OF SEX ROLE AND SOCIAL STATUS ON THE EARLY ADOLESCENT PERSONALITY. 1949. Pp. 231–325; and Radke, Marian, Helen G. Trager, and Hadassah Davis. SOCIAL PERCEPTIONS AND ATTITUDES OF CHILDREN. 1949. Pp. 327–447.

Volume 41, Number 1. Blum, Lucille Hollander. SOME PSYCHOLOGICAL AND EDUCATIONAL ASPECTS OF PEDIATRIC PRACTICE: A STUDY OF WELL-BABY CLINICS. 1950. Pp. 3–97; Hudson, Bradford B. ONE-TRIAL LEARNING IN THE DOMESTIC RAT. 1950. Pp. 99–145; and Ellis, Albert. AN INTRODUCTION TO THE PRINCIPLES OF SCIENTIFIC PSYCHOANALYSIS. 1950. Pp. 147–212.

————, **Number 2.** Springer, Doris V. AWARENESS OF RACIAL DIFFERENCES BY PRESCHOOL CHILDREN IN HAWAII. 1950. Pp. 215–270; Witryol, Sam L. AGE TRENDS IN CHILDREN'S EVALUATION OF TEACHER-APPROVED AND TEACHER-DISAPPROVED BEHAVIOR. 1950. Pp. 271–326; and Stubbins, Joseph THE RELATIONSHIP BETWEEN LEVEL OF VOCATIONAL ASPIRATION AND CERTAIN PERSONAL DATA: A STUDY OF SOME TRAITS AND INFLUENCES BEARING ON THE PRESTIGE LEVEL OF VOCATIONAL CHOICE. 1950. Pp. 327–408.

Volume 42, Number 1. Farberow, Norman L. PERSONALITY PATTERNS OF SUICIDAL MENTAL HOSPITAL PATIENTS. 1950. Pp. 3–79; and Rabban, Meyer. SEX-ROLE IDENTIFICATION IN YOUNG CHILDREN IN TWO DIVERSE SOCIAL GROUPS. 1950. Pp. 81–158.

————, **Number 2.** Shapiro, David. A STUDY OF THE INFLUENCE OF THE SOCIAL FIELD ON INDIVIDUAL BEHAVIOR: AS REVEALED IN THE EXPRESSION OF HOSTILITY AND WARMTH BY NEUROTICS AND PARANOID SCHIZOPHRENICS IN DISCUSSION GROUP SITUATIONS. 1950. Pp. 161–230; and Hefferline, Ralph Franklin. AN EXPERIMENTAL STUDY OF AVOIDANCE. 1950. Pp. 231–334.

527. *Indian Journal of Psychology.* [Official organ of the Indian Psychological Association.]

TITLE VARIATIONS: None.

DATES OF PUBLICATION: Volume 1–25 + , 1926–1950 + .

FREQUENCY: Quarterly.

NUMBERING VARIATIONS: Multinumber issues present.

PUBLISHER: **Calcutta:** Calcutta University Press, 1926–1950+.

PRIMARY EDITORS: **M. N. Banerji,** 1930–1938; **H. P. Maiti,** 1939–1945; **S. C. Mitra,** 1944, 1946–1947; **J. M. Sen,** 1948–1950+.

EDITORIAL BOARD: Owen Berkeley-Hill, 1926–1937; Haridas Bhattacharya, 1926–1929; G. C. Chatterjee, 1926–1929, 1945–1950+; J. M. Sen, 1926–1928, 1939–1947; Michael West, 1930–1932; Narendranath Sengupta, 1926–1938; S. C. Mitra, 1929, 1948–1950+; P. S. Naidu, 1945–1950+; Haripada Maiti, 1930–1938; M. V. Gopalswami, 1930–1938; Jumna Prosad, 1933–1938; I. Latif, 1939–1944; N.S.N. Sastry, 1939–1950+.

528. *Industrial Psychology Monthly: The Magazine of Manpower.*

TITLE VARIATIONS: Titled *Industrial Psychology; Human Engineering for Executives,* Volume 1, 1926.

DATES OF PUBLICATION: Volume 1–3, 1926–December 1928.

FREQUENCY: Monthly.

NUMBERING VARIATIONS: Volume 2, Number 4–6 incorrectly labeled Volume 3, Number 4–6.

PUBLISHER: **Hamilton, New York:** Industrial Psychology, 1926–1928.

PRIMARY EDITORS: **Donald A. Laird,** 1926–1928; **Paul R. Martino,** 1926; **Hilda Drexel,** 1926; **V. N. Barrington,** 1926; **R. F. Dixon,** 1926.

EDITORIAL BOARD: Percy S. Brown, 1926; William Forster, 1926; Douglas Fryer, 1926; Keppele Hall, 1926; Harry Dexter Kitson, 1926; J. M. Lahy, 1926; Donald A. Laird, 1926; Fred Moss, 1926; Lorine Pruette, 1926; A. J. Snow, 1926; Erich Stern, 1926; Charles S. Myers, 1926; Morris S. Viteles, 1926.

529. *Kharkov. Ukrainskii psikhonevrologicheskii institut. Trudy.*

TITLE VARIATIONS: Institute also cited as Ukrainskii derzhavnii psikhonevrologicheskii institut; and as Institut psychoneurologique ukrainien. Vypusk 4, 1927 and 14, 1930 issued by the institute under the name Ukrainskii gosudarstvennyi psikhonevrologicheskii institut. Superseded by *Vseukrainskaia psikhonevrologicheskaia akademiia. Trudy* with Novaia seriia, Tom 1, 1935.

DATES OF PUBLICATION: Vypusk 1–21, 1926–1932.

FREQUENCY: Irregular.

NUMBERING VARIATIONS: Vypusk 1, 1926 issued unnumbered. Vypusk 1, 1926 and Vypusk 10, 1929 also numbered as *Kharkov. (Pervii) ukrainskii institut ochrany materinstva i detstva. Trudy,* Vypusk [1] and 3, respectively, and as *Materialy po antropologii ukrainy,* Vypusk 1 and 4, respectively. Vypusk 12, 1930 issued jointly with Khar'kovskii meditsinskii institut. Kafedra sotsial'noi gigieny.

PUBLISHER: **Kharkov:** Gosudarstvennoe izdatel'stvo ukrainy, 1926–1932.

PRIMARY EDITOR: **A. I. Geimanovich** (Director of the Institute), 1926–1932.

530. *Krakow. Uniwersytet Jagielloński. Zakład psychológii doświadczalnej. Praca.*

TITLE VARIATIONS: Also titled *Travaux du laboratoire de psychologie expérimentale de l'université de cracovie.*

DATES OF PUBLICATION: Tom 1–2, 1926–1928.

FREQUENCY: Irregular.

NUMBERING VARIATIONS: None.

PUBLISHER: **Krakow:** Académie polonaise des sciences et de lettres; and **Paris:** Librairie Félix Alcan, 1926. **Paris:** Librairie Félix Alcan, 1928.

PRIMARY EDITOR: **Władysław Heinrich,** 1926–1928.

531. *Leningrad. Gosudarstvennyi institut po izucheniiu mozga. Novoe v refleksologii i fiziologii nervnoi sistemy.*

TITLE VARIATIONS: Also called *Beiträge zur Reflexologie und Physiologie des Nervensystems.* Continues *[Leningrad.] Gosudarstvennyi refleksologicheskii institut po izucheniiu mozga. Novoe v refleksologii i fiziologii nervnoi sistemy.*

DATES OF PUBLICATION: Tom 2–3, 1926–1929.

FREQUENCY: Irregular.

NUMBERING VARIATIONS: Each Tom consists of 5 parts with continuous pagination.

PUBLISHER: **Leningrad:** Gosudarstvennyi institut po izucheniiu mozga, 1926–1929.

PRIMARY EDITOR: **V. M. Bekhterev,** 1926–1929.

SECTION EDITORS: N. M. Shchelovanov, 1926–1929; A. A. Ukhtomskii, 1926; L. L. Vasil'ev, 1926–1929; M. V. Lange, 1926; V. N. Myasishchev, 1926–1929; V. N. Osipova, 1926–1929; A. L. Shnirman, 1926–1929.

NOTE: Information on this title was compiled from entries in *A Half Century of Soviet Serials.*

532. *London. National Institute of Industrial Psychology. Institute Report.*

TITLE VARIATIONS: Continued by *[London.] National Institute of Industrial Psychology. Report* with Number 2, 1927.

DATES OF PUBLICATION: Number 1, 1926.

FREQUENCY: Annual.

NUMBERING VARIATIONS: None.

PUBLISHER: **London:** National Institute of Industrial Psychology, 1926.

PRIMARY EDITOR: Secretary acts as editor.

533. London. National Institute of Industrial Psychology. Report.

TITLE VARIATIONS: None.

DATES OF PUBLICATION: Number 1–8, 1926–1939. Suspended publication with 1940–1952.

FREQUENCY: Irregular. *See* Contents *below.*

NUMBERING VARIATIONS: None.

PUBLISHER: **London:** National Institute of Industrial Psychology, 1926–1953 +.

PRIMARY EDITORS: Members of the Council and Advisory Board of the National Institute of Industrial Psychology act as editors.

CONTENTS:
Number 1. OCCUPATION ANALYSIS. 1926. 36 pp.
Number 2. Dunlop, W. R. AN INVESTIGATION OF CERTAIN PROCESSES AND CONDITIONS ON FARMS. 1927. 71 pp.
Number 3. Earle, F. M., A. Macrae et al. TESTS OF MECHANICAL ABILITY. 1929. 42 pp.
Number 4. Earle, F. M., F. Gaw et al. THE MEASUREMENT OF MANUAL DEXTERITIES. 1930. 88 pp.
Number 5. AN ACCOUNT OF THE RESEARCH WORK CARRIED OUT BY THE N.I.I.P., 1921–1934. 1934. 37 pp.
Number 6. Earle, F. M., and J. Kilgour. A VOCATIONAL GUIDANCE RESEARCH IN FIFE. 1935. 101 pp.
Number 7. Seymour, W. Douglas. IMPROVING THE BLACKBOARD. 1938. 35 pp.
Number 8. Ramsay, J., R. E. Rawson et al. REST-PAUSES AND REFRESHMENTS IN INDUSTRY. 1939. 52 pp.

534. Minnesota. University. Institute of Child Welfare. Report.

TITLE VARIATIONS: Institute of Child Welfare later called: Institute of Child Development.

DATES OF PUBLICATION: 1926/1927–1948/1950 +. None published 1940/1942.

FREQUENCY: Annual/biennial.

NUMBERING VARIATIONS: Numbered by date only.

PUBLISHER: **Minneapolis:** Institute of Child Welfare, University of Minnesota, 1926–1950 +.

PRIMARY EDITOR: Director of the Institute.

535. Minnesota. University. Institute of Child Welfare. Scientific Publications.

TITLE VARIATIONS: None.

DATES OF PUBLICATION: Volume 1–3, 1926–1934.

FREQUENCY: Irregular. *See* Contents *below.*

NUMBERING VARIATIONS: None.

PUBLISHER: Various. *See* Note *below.*

PRIMARY EDITORS: None listed.

CONTENTS:
 Volume 1. SCIENTIFIC PUBLICATIONS, 1926–1931. ANATOMICAL, PHYSIO-LOGICAL AND MOTOR STUDIES. 26 studies. May 1932.
 Volume 2. SCIENTIFIC PUBLICATIONS, 1926–1931. PSYCHOLOGICAL STUD-IES OF PRE-SCHOOL CHILDREN. 42 studies. May 1932.
 Volume 3. SCIENTIFIC PUBLICATIONS, 1932–1934. STUDIES OF ALL TYPES. 34 studies. May 1934.

NOTE: No original publications. Compilation of reprints of articles by John E. Anderson, Florence L. Goodenough, Richard E. Scammon, and others.

536. *Monatsschrift für Kriminalpsychologie und Strafrechtsreform. Beiheft.*

TITLE VARIATIONS: None.

DATES OF PUBLICATION: Heft 1–3, 1926–1930.

FREQUENCY: Irregular. *See* Contents *below.*

NUMBERING VARIATIONS: None.

PUBLISHER: **Heidelberg:** Carl Winter Verlag, 1926–1930.

PRIMARY EDITORS: **Alfred Kloss**, 1926–1930; **Karl von Lilienthal**, 1926–1927; **Gustav Aschaffenburg**, 1926–1930; **Hans von Hentig**, 1926–1930.

CONTENTS:
 Heft 1. BEITRÄGE ZUR KRIMINALPSYCHOLOGIE UND STRAFRECHTSREFORM. 1926. 106 pp.
 Heft 2. Luz, Walter. DAS VERBRECHEN IN DER DARSTELLUNG DES VERBRECHERS. 1927. 215 pp.
 Heft 3. RECHTSSTAATSIDEE UND ERZIEHUNGSSTRAFE. 1930. 161 pp.

537. *Mysore. University. Maharaja's College. Psychological Laboratory. Psychological Studies.*

TITLE VARIATIONS: None.

DATES OF PUBLICATION: Volume 1, July 1926.

FREQUENCY: Irregular.

NUMBERING VARIATIONS: None.

PUBLISHER: **Mysore:** Psychological Laboratory, Maharaja's College, University of Mysore, 1926.

PRIMARY EDITOR: **M. V. Gopalaswami**, 1926.

538. *Neue psychologische Studien.*

TITLE VARIATIONS: Each Band carries a distinctive title. *See* Contents *below.* Supersedes *Psychologische Studien.*

538. *(Continued)*

DATES OF PUBLICATION: Band 1–15, Heft 2, 1926–1943. Suspended publication 1944–1952.

FREQUENCY: Irregular. *See* Contents *below.*

NUMBERING VARIATIONS: Numbering does not follow a strictly chronological order. Number of Hefte per volume varies from 3 to 6. Also numbered as *Leipzig. Sächsische staatliche Forschungsinstitute. Forschungsinstitut für Psychologie. Abhandlungen;* and *Charakter und Persönlichkeit. See* Contents *below.*

PUBLISHER: **Munich:** C. H. Beck'sche Verlag, 1926–1930. **Munich:** C. H. Beck, 1931–1943.

PRIMARY EDITOR: **Felix Emil Krueger,** 1926–1943.

VOLUME EDITORS: *See* Contents *below.*

CONTENTS:
Band 1. Krueger, Felix Emil, ed. KOMPLEXQUALITÄTEN, GESTALTEN UND GEFÜHLE. Contains:
———, Heft 1. Krueger, Felix. ZUR EINFÜHRUNG—ÜBER PSYCHISCHE GANZHEIT. 1926. Pp. 1–122. (Also as *Leipzig. Sächsische staatliche Forschungsinstitute. Forschungsinstitut für Psychologie. Abhandlungen,* Stück 8.)
———, Heft 2. Sander, Friedrich. ÜBER RÄUMLICHE RHYTHMIK. EXPERIMENTELLE UNTERSUCHUNGEN ÜBER RHYTHMUSARTIGE REIHEN- UND GRUPPENBILDUNGEN BEI SIMULTANEN GESICHTSEINDRÜCKEN; Sander, Friedrich. OPTISCHE TÄUSCHUNGEN UND PSYCHOLOGIE; and Ipsen, Gunther. ÜBER GESTALTAUFFASSUNG. ERÖRTERUNG DES SANDERSCHEN PARALLELOGRAMMS. 1926. Pp. 123–278. (Also as *Leipzig. Sächsische staatliche Forschungsinstitute. Forschungsinstitut für Psychologie. Abhandlungen.* Stück 9–11.)
———, Heft 3. Ipsen, Gunther. ZUR THEORIE DES ERKENNENS. UNTERSUCHUNGEN ÜBER GESTALT UND SINN SINNLOSER WÖRTER. 1926. Pp. 279–472. (Also as *Leipzig. Sächsische staatliche Forschungsinstitute. Forschungsinstitut für Psychologie. Abhandlungen,* Stück 12.)
———, Heft 4. Herrmann, Johannes. GESAMTERLEBNISSE BEI GERÜCHEN; Würdemann, Wilhelm. ÜBER DIE BEDEUTUNG DES GEFÜHLS FÜR DAS BEHALTEN UND ERINNERN; Lenk, Erhard. ÜBER DIE OPTISCHE AUFFASSUNG GEOMETRISCH-REGELMÄSSIGER GESTALTEN; and Rudert, Johannes. KASUISTISCHER BEITRAG ZUR LEHRE VON DER FUNKTIONELLEN ASYMMETRIE DER GROSSHIRNHEMISPHÄREN. 1926. Pp. 473–692. (Also as *Leipzig. Sächsische staatliche Forschungsinstitute. Forschungsinstitut für Psychologie. Abhandlungen,* Stück 13–16.)
Band 2. Krueger, Felix, and August Kirschmann, eds. LICHT UND FARBE. Contains:
———, Heft 1. Krueger, Felix. VORBEMERKUNGEN; Bergfeld, Emil. DIE STRECKENEINTEILUNG UND DIE GEBRÄUCHLICHSTEN ZAHLENSYSTEME. NEUE VERSUCHE ZUR DEZIMALGLEICHUNG; Schjelderup-Ebbe, Thorleif. DER KONTRAST AUF DEM GEBIETE DES LICHT- UND FARBENSINNS. I. TEIL. 1926. Pp. 1–126. (Also as *Leipzig. Sächsische staatliche Forschungsinstitute. Forschungsinstitut für Psychologie. Abhandlungen,* Stück 17–18.)

————, **Heft 2.** Kirschmann, August. FARBENTERMINOLOGIE; Donath, Friedrich. DIE FUNKTIONALE ABHÄNGIGKEIT ZWISCHEN REIZ UND EMPFINDUNG BEI DER FARBENSÄTTIGUNG; Ehrler, Fritz. ÜBER DAS FARBENGEDÄCHTNIS UND SEINE BEZIEHUNGEN ZUR ATELIER- UND FREILICHTMALEREI. 1926. Pp. 127–308. (Also as *Leipzig. Sächsische staatliche Forschungsinstitute. Forschungsinstitut für Psychologie. Abhandlungen*, Stück 19–21.)

————, **Heft 3.** Weissenborn, Friedrich. DIE LAGE DER QUALITÄTEN IM FARBENKREIS UND IHRE KOMPLEMENTÄRVERHÄLTNISSE, NACH DER SCHWELLENMETHODE UNTERSUCHT; Fiedler, Kurt. DAS SCHWARZ-WEISS-PROBLEM; and Kirschmann, August. DAS UMGEKEHRTE SPEKTRUM UND SEINE FARBEN SOWIE SEINE BEDEUTUNG FÜR DIE OPTISCHE WISSENSCHAFT. 1926. Pp. 309–442. (Also as *Leipzig. Sächsische staatliche Forschungsinstitute. Forschungsinstitut für Psychologie. Abhandlungen*, Stück 22–24.)

Band 3. Krueger, Felix, ed. GRENZFRAGEN DER PHILOSOPHIE. Contains:

————, **Heft 1.** Krueger, Felix. WISSENSCHAFTEN UND DER ZUSAMMENHANG DES WIRKLICHEN. GELEITWORT DES HERAUSGEBERS; Buchholz, Heinrich. DAS PROBLEM DER KONTINUITÄT; and Buchholz, Heinrich. DIE UNMÖGLICHKEIT ABSOLUTER METRISCHER PRÄZISION UND DIE ERKENNTNISTHEORETISCHEN KONSEQUENZEN DIESER UNMÖGLICHKEIT. 1927. Pp. 1–133. (Also as *Leipzig. Sächsische staatliche Forschungsinstitute. Forschungsinstitut für Psychologie. Abhandlungen*, Stück 25–26.)

————, **Heft 2.** Bergfeld, Emil. DIE AXIOME DER EUKLIDISCHEN GEOMETRIE PSYCHOLOGISCH UND ERKENNTNISTHEORETISCH UNTERSUCHT. 1927. Pp. 135–218. (Also as *Leipzig. Sächsische staatliche Forschungsinstitute. Forschungsinstitut für Psychologie. Abhandlungen*, Stück 27.)

————, **Heft 3.** Fischer, Hugo. ERLEBNIS UND METAPHYSIK. ZUR PSYCHOLOGIE DES METAPHYSISCHEN SCHAFFENS. 1928. Pp. 219–440. (Also as *Leipzig. Sächsische staatliche Forschungsinstitute. Forschungsinstitut für Psychologie. Abhandlungen*, Stück 32.)

————, **Heft 4.** Weidauer, Friedrich. ZUR SYLLOGISTIK. 1928. Pp. 441–644. (Also as *Leipzig. Sächsische staatliche Forschungsinstitute. Forschungsinstitut für Psychologie. Abhandlungen*, Stück 33.)

Band 4. Krueger, Felix, and Friedrich Sander, eds. GESTALT UND SINN. Contains:

————, **Heft 1.** Lippert, Elisabeth. UNTERSCHIEDSEMPFINDLICHKEIT BEI MOTORISCHEN GESTALTBILDUNGEN DES ARMES; and Schneider, Carl. UNTERSUCHUNGEN ÜBER DIE UNTERSCHIEDSEMPFINDLICHKEIT VERSCHIEDEN GEGLIEDERTER OPTISCHER GESTALTEN. 1928. Pp. 1–159. (Also as *Leipzig. Sächsische staatliche Forschungsinstitute. Forschungsinstitut für Psychologie. Abhandlungen*, Stück 30 and 31.)

————, **Heft 2.** Biemüller, Wilhelm. WIEDERGABE DER GLIEDERANZAHL UND GLIEDERUNGSFORM OPTISCHER KOMPLEXE; and Heiss, Alfred. ZUM PROBLEM DER ISOLIERENDEN ABSTRAKTION. GENETISCH VERGLEICHENDE STUDIEN. 1930. Pp. 161–318. (Also as *Leipzig. Sächsische staatliche Forschungsinstitute. Forschungsinstitut für Psychologie. Abhandlungen*, Stück 36.)

————, **Heft 3.** Sander, Friedrich. GESTALTPSYCHOLOGIE UND KUNSTTHEORIE. EIN BEITRAG ZUR PSYCHOLOGIE ARCHITEKTONISCHER GESTALTEN; and

538. *(Continued)*

Wohlfahrt, Erich. Der Auffassungsvorgang an kleinen Gestalten. Ein Beitrag zur Psychologie des Vorgestalterlebnisses. 1932. Pp. 319–414. (Also as *Leipzig. Sächsische staatliche Forschungsinstitute. Forschungsinstitut für Psychologie. Abhandlungen,* Stück 48.)

Band 5. Krueger, Felix, and Otto Klemm, eds. Angewandte Psychologie. Contains:

————, **Heft 1.** Gerichtliche Psychologie: Klemm, Otto. Erfahrungen bei einer Eignungsprüfung an Kriminalbeamten; Klemm, Otto. Zufall oder Geschicklichkeit? Benscher, Ilse. Zur Psychologie des Gedankenlesens; Klemm, Otto. Über die Atmungssymptomatik bei Untersuchungsgefangenen; and Klemm, Otto. Dunkles beim Hellsehen. 1929. Pp. 1–142. (Also as *Leipzig. Sächsische staatliche Forschungsinstitute. Forschungsinstitut für Psychologie. Abhandlungen,* Stück 34.)

————, **Heft 2.** Leistungsforschung: Klemm, Otto. Gedanken über Leibesübungen; Benscher, Ilse, and Otto Klemm. Korrelationstheoretisches zur Ganzheit; Tauscher, Erwin. Über die Korrelation zwischen Handgeschicklichkeit und Intelligenz; Ulbricht, Oswald. Über die optimalen Bedingungen bei der Arbeit an Drehkurbeln; Doležal, Jan. Über die Bewegungsform bei der Arbeit an Drehkurbeln; and Wilsdorf, Otto-Hermann. Griffstudien an der Spulmaschine. 1930. Pp. 145–346. (Also as *Leipzig. Sächsische staatliche Forschungsinstitute. Forschungsinstitut für Psychologie. Abhandlungen,* Stück 35.)

————, **Heft 3.** Zur Eignungsprüfung für den Lenkerberuf; Du Preez, Nicolaas. Beiträge zur Eignungsprüfung für den Lenkerberuf; Ehrhardt, Adolf. Das Ranschburgsche Phänomen bei Reaktionsbewegungen; and Herrmann, Johannes. Die Bedeutung der persönlichen Gleichung für die Lenkertätigkeit. Mit einem Beitrag zur Theorie der Zeitverschiebungen. 1931. Pp. 347–470. (Also as *Leipzig. Sächsische staatliche Forschungsinstitute. Forschungsinstitut für Psychologie. Abhandlungen,* Stück 42.)

Band 6. Krueger, Felix, ed. Psychologische Optik. Contains:

————, **Heft 1.** Podestà, Hans. Beiträge zur Systematik der Farbenempfindungen; Gebhardt, Martin. Goethe und das umgekehrte Spektrum; Weissenborn, Fritz. August Kirschmanns schiefer Farbenkegel, verglichen mit einigen vorher und nachher entstandenen Farbensystemen; and Kiesow, Friedrich. Über die Entstehung der Braunempfindung. 1930. Pp. 1–130. (Also as *Leipzig. Sächsische staatliche Forschungsinstitute. Forschungsinstitut für Psychologie. Abhandlungen,* Stück 39.)

————, **Heft 2.** Schwarz, Georg. Über konzentrische Gesichtsfeldeinengung bei psychisch Normalen. 1930. Pp. 131–252. (Also as *Leipzig. Sächsische staatliche Forschungsinstitute. Forschungsinstitut für Psychologie. Abhandlungen,* Stück 40.)

————, **Heft 3.** Heuss, Eugen. Zur Metaphysik des Lichtes; Wirth, Wilhelm. Die Konstanz des üblichen Masses für den simultanen Hellig-

KEITSKONTRAST; Rüssel, Arnulf. ÜBER HELLIGKEITSKONSTANZ DER SEHDINGE; Angyal, Andreas. DIE LAGEBEHARRUNG DER OPTISCH VORGESTELLTEN RÄUMLICHEN UMGEBUNG; Grund, Erich. DAS LESEN DES WORTANFANGES BEI VOLKSSCHULKINDERN VERSCHIEDENER ALTERSSTUFEN. TACHISTOSKOPISCH UNTERSUCHT; and Schneider, Karl Max. BEOBACHTUNGEN ÜBER DIE PUPILLENGESTALT BEI EINIGEN LEBENDEN SÄUGETIEREN. 1930. Pp. 253–356. (Also as *Leipzig. Sächsische staatliche Forschungsinstitute. Forschungsinstitut für Psychologie. Abhandlungen,* Stück 41.)

————, **Heft 4.** Klemm, Otto. DIE BINOKULARE ZEITPARALLAXE; Dürckheim, Graf Karlfried von. UNTERSUCHUNGEN ZUR GELEBTEN RAUM. (ERLEBNISWIRKLICHKEIT UND IHR VERSTÄNDNIS. SYSTEMATISCHE UNTERSUCHUNGEN II); and Krueger, Felix. AUGUST KIRSCHMANN. 1932. Pp. 357–513. (Also as *Leipzig. Sächsische staatliche Forschungsinstitute. Forschungsinstitut für Psychologie. Abhandlungen,* Stück 46.)

Band 7. Krueger, Felix, and Hans Volkelt, eds. EXPERIMENTELLE KINDESPSYCHOLOGIE. Contains:

————, **Heft 1.** Rüssel, Arnulf. ÜBER FORMAUFFASSUNG ZWEI-BIS FÜNFJÄHRIGER KINDER. 1931. 108 pp. (Also as *Leipzig. Sächsische staatliche Forschungsinstitute. Forschungsinstitut für Psychologie. Abhandlungen,* Stück 43.)

————, **Heft 2.** Haubold, Marianne. BILDBETRACHTUNG DURCH KINDER UND JUGENDLICHE. (VERSUCHE ÜBER DAS UNTERSCHEIDEN VON BILDERN VERSCHIEDENEN STILES). 1933. 108 pp. (Also as *Leipzig. Sächsische staatliche Forschungsinstitute. Forschungsinstitut für Psychologie. Abhandlungen,* Stück 53.)

————, **Heft 3.** Burkhardt, Heinz. ÜBER VERLAGERUNG RÄUMLICHER GESTALTEN. 1934. 158 pp. (Also as *Leipzig. Sächsische staatliche Forschungsinstitute. Forschungsinstitut für Psychologie. Abhandlungen,* Stück 54.)

————, **Heft 4.** Rabe, Johannes. UMGANG MIT KÖRPERN VON VERSCHIEDENER FORM UND FARBE IN FRÜHESTER KINDHEIT. Introduction by Hans Volkelt and Johannes Rabe; and Iwai, Katsujiro, and Arnulf Rüssel. DER UMGANG DES KINDES MIT VERSCHIEDEN GEFORMTEN KÖRPERN IM 9. BIS 12. LEBENSMONAT. 1938. 181 pp.

————, **Heft 5.** Wittke, Erich. DAS TASTMASS SEHENDER UND BLINDER KINDER UND ERWACHSENER. 1943. 46 pp.

————, **Heft 6.** Hecker, Walther. ÜBER DIE SITTLICHE ENTWICKLUNG VON SCHULKINDERN UND FRÜHJUGENDLICHEN. 1937. 150 pp.

Band 8. Krueger, Felix, and Hans Volkelt, eds. DAS BILDNERISCH GESTALTENDE KIND. Contains:

————, **Heft 1.** Müssler, Marianne. DAS BAUEN DES KINDES MIT ZWEIFARBIGEN MATERIAL. 1933. 124 pp. (Also as *Leipzig. Sächsische staatliche Forschungsinstitute. Forschungsinstitut für Psychologie. Abhandlungen,* Stück 50.)

————, **Heft 2.** Brandner, Margarete. DER UMGANG DES KLEINKINDES MIT WÜRFELN BIS ZU DEN FRÜHESTEN FORMEN DES BAUENS. EIN BEITRAG ZUR PSYCHOLOGIE DER ENTSTEHUNG DER DINGWAHRNEHMUNG UND DES GEGENSTANDS- UND WERKBEWUSSTSEINS DURCH HANDELNDES GESTALTEN. 1939. 217 pp.

538. *(Continued)*

————, **Heft 3.** Cappeller, Richard. FREIER UMGANG DREI- BIS SECHSJÄHRIGER KINDER MIT MONTESSORI-MATERIAL. EIN BEITRAG ZUR KRITIK DER MONTESSORI-ERZIEHUNG UND ZUR PSYCHOLOGIE DES GESTALTERISCHEN SPIELES. With Appendices by Hans Volkelt. 1939. 189 pp.

————, **Heft 4.** Lippert, Elisabeth O. DAS MEHRFARBIGE BAUEN DES KINDES. EINE UNTERSUCHUNG ÜBER DAS KINDLICHE FARBERLEBEN UND EIN BEITRAG ZUR PSYCHOLOGIE UND PÄDAGOGIK DER FARBVERWENDUNG IM BILD- NERISCHEN GESTALTEN DES VORSCHULPFLICHTIGEN UND DES SCHULKINDES. 1940. 138 pp.

Band 9. Krueger, Felix, and Otto Klemm, eds. MOTORIK. Contains:

————, **Heft 1.** Voigt, Erich. ÜBER DEN AUFBAU VON BEWEGUNGSGESTALTEN; and Haferkorn, Walter. ÜBER DIE ZEITLICHE EING- LIEDERUNG VON WILLKÜRBEWEGUNGEN. 1933. Pp. 1–63. (Also as *Leipzig. Sächsische staatliche Forschungsinstitute. Forschungsinstitut für Psychologie. Abhandlungen,* Stück 49.)

————, **Heft 2.** Kern, Gerhard. MOTORISCHE UMREISSUNG OPTISCHER GESTALTEN; Stimpel, Edmund. DER WURF; and Drill, Rudolf. DER HAMMER- SCHLAG. 1933. Pp. 65–208. (Also as *Leipzig. Sächsische staatliche Forschungs- institute. Forschungsinstitut für Psychologie. Abhandlungen,* Stück 51.)

————, **Heft 3.** Oeser, Max. ÜBER DEN SPEERWURF; Pankauskas, Johan- nes. VERGLEICH ISOLIERTER UND RHYTHMISCH GEBUNDENER ZEITSTRECKEN; and Fukutomi, Ichiro. ÜBER DAS δ-PHÄNOMEN UND DIE SUBJEKTIVE BEDINGTHEIT DER SCHEINBEWEGUNGEN. 1936. Pp. 209–350.

————, **Heft 4.** Steger, Gerhard. ÜBER DEN DISKUSWURF; and Klemm, Otto. ZWÖLF LEITSÄTZE ZU EINER PSYCHOLOGIE DER LEIBESÜBUNGEN. 1938. Pp. 351–398.

Band 10. Krueger, Felix, and Karlfried Graf von Dürckheim-Montmartin, eds. ERLEBNISWIRKLICHKEIT UND STRUKTUR. Contains:

————, **Heft 1.** Riedel, Gerhard. ÜBER DIE ABHÄNGIGKEIT OPTISCHER KONTRASTE VON GESTALTBEDINGUNGEN; and Kunz-Henriquez, Guillermina. ÜBER DIE ÄNDERUNGSEMPFINDLICHKEIT FÜR OPTISCHE GESTALTEN. 1937. 102 pp. (Also as part of *Leipzig. Sächsische staatliche Forschungsinstitute. For- schungsinstitut für Psychologie. Abhandlungen,* Stück 52.)

————, **Heft 2.** Viergutz, Felix. DAS BESCHREIBEN. EXPERIMENTELLE UNTERSUCHUNG DES BESCHREIBENS VON GEGENSTÄNDEN. 1933. 92 pp. (Also as part of *Leipzig. Sächsische staatliche Forschungsinstitute. Forschungsinstitut für Psychologie. Abhandlungen,* Stück 52.)

————, **Heft 3.** Meyer, Edith. ORDEN UND ORDNUNG BEI DREI- BIS SECHSJÄHRIGEN KINDERN. 1934. 100 pp. (Also as *Leipzig. Sächsische staatliche Forschungsinstitute. Forschungsinstitut für Psychologie. Abhandlungen,* Stück 55.)

————, **Heft 4.** Schadeberg, Walter. ÜBER DEN EINSTELLUNGSCHARAK- TER KOMPLEXER ERLEBNISSE. 1934. 69 pp. (Also as *Leipzig. Sächsische staa- tliche Forschungsinstitute. Forschungsinstitut für Psychologie. Abhandlungen,* Stück 58.)

————, **Heft 5.** Hippius, Rudolf. ERKENNENDES TASTEN ALS WAHRNEH-MUNG UND ALS ERKENNTNISVORGANG. 1934. 163 pp. (Also as *Leipzig. Sächsische staatliche Forschungsinstitute. Forschungsinstitut für Psychologie. Abhandlungen,* Stück 59.)

Band 11. Krueger, Felix, and Johannes Rudert, eds. PSYCHOLOGIE DES SCHREIBENS UND DER HANDSCHRIFT. Contains:

————, **Heft 1.** Tittel, Käthe. UNTERSUCHUNGEN ÜBER SCHREIB-GESCHWINDIGKEIT. EIN BEITRAG ZUR EXPERIMENTELLEN GRAPHOLOGIE. 1934. 58 pp. (Also as *Leipzig. Sächsische staatliche Forschungsinstitute. Forschungs-institut für Psychologie. Abhandlungen,* Stück 56.)

————, **Heft 2.** Werner, Rudolf. ÜBER DEN ANTEIL DES BEWUSSTSEINS BEI SCHREIBVORGÄNGEN; and Dietrich, Werner. STATISTISCHE UNTERSUCHUNG-EN ÜBER DEN ZUSAMMENHANG VON SCHRIFTMERKMALEN. 1937. 144 pp.

————, **Heft 3.** Wirtz, Joseph. DRUCK- UND GESCHWINDIGKEITSVERLAUF VON GANZHEITLICHEN SCHREIBBEWEGUNGSWEISEN; and Walther, Johannes. DIE PSYCHOLOGISCHE UND CHARAKTEROLOGISCHE BEDEUTUNG DER HAND-SCHRIFTLICHEN BINDUNGSARTEN. 1938. 158 pp.

Band 12. Klemm, Otto, Hans Volkelt, and Karlfried Graf von Dürckheim-Montmartin, eds. GANZHEIT UND STRUKTUR. FESTSCHRIFT ZUM 60. GEBURTS-TAG FELIX KRUEGERS. Contains:

————, **Heft 1.** Klemm, Otto, ed. WEGE ZUR GANZHEITSPSYCHOLOGIE. 1934. (2nd ed, 1953.) 214 pp. (Also as *Leipzig. Sächsische staatliche Forschungs-institute. Forschungsinstitut für Psychologie. Abhandlungen,* Stück 60.)

————, **Heft 2.** Volkelt, Hans, ed. SEELISCHE STRUKTUREN. 1934. 134 pp. (Also as *Leipzig. Sächsische staatliche Forschungsinstitute. Forschungsinstitut für Psychologie. Abhandlungen,* Stück 61.)

————, **Heft 3.** Dürckheim-Montmartin, Karlfried Graf von, ed. GEI-STIGE STRUKTUREN. 1934. 134 pp. (Also as *Leipzig. Sächsische staatliche For-schungsinstitute. Forschungsinstitut für Psychologie. Abhandlungen,* Stück 62.)

Band 13. Krueger, Felix, and Arnulf Rüssel, ed. PATHOLOGISCHE VER-GLEICHUNG. Contains:

————, **Heft 1.** Rüssel, Arnulf. ZUR PSYCHOLOGIE DER OPTISCHEN AG-NOSIEN. 1936. 92 pp. (Also as *Leipzig. Sächsische staatliche Forschungsinstitute. Forschungsinstitut für Psychologie. Abhandlungen,* Stück 65.)

————, **Heft 2.** Mantell, Ursula. AKTUALGENETISCHE UNTERSUCHUNGEN AN SITUATIONSDARSTELLUNGEN (UNTER BERÜCKSICHTIGUNG DER KÜNSTLERISCHEN FORMUNG). 1936. 96 pp. (Also as *Leipzig. Sächsische staatliche Forschungsin-stitute. Forschungsinstitut für Psychologie. Abhandlungen,* Stück 65.)

————, **Heft 3.** Sommer, Walter. ZERFALL OPTISCHER GESTALTEN. ER-LEBNISFORMEN UND STRUKTUR-ZUSAMMENHÄNGE; and Johnson, Hiram Kellogg. GEFÜHLSVERLUST ALS KRANKHEITSSYMPTOM. EINE GANZHEITPSYCHOLOGISCHE DEUTUNG. Adapted by A. Wellek. 1937. 86 pp.

Band 14. Krueger, Felix, Arnulf Rüssel, and Albert Wellek, eds. PHAN-TASIE UND KUNST. Contains:

————, **Heft 1.** Wellek, Albert. GEFÜHL UND KUNST; and Sandig, Hans. BEOBACHTUNGEN AN ZWEIKLÄNGEN IN GETRENNTOHRIGER UND BEIDOHRIGER DARBIETUNG. EIN BEITRAG ZUR THEORIE DER KONSONANZ. 1939. 131 pp.

———, **Heft 2.** Schmidt, Erich M. ÜBER DEN AUFBAU RHYTHMISCHER GESTALTEN. 1939. 98 pp.

Band 15. Krueger, Felix, Ehrig Wartegg, and Albert Wellek, eds. CHARAKTER UND PERSÖNLICHKEIT. DIE GENETISCHE GANZHEITSPSYCHOLOGIE. Contains:

———, **Heft 1.** Bönisch, Rolf. ÜBER DEN ZUSAMMENHANG SEELISCHER TEILSTRUKTUREN. 1939. 144 pp. (Also as *Charakter und Persönlichkeit.* Heft 1.)

———, **Heft 2.** Schmidt-Durban, Wilfried. EXPERIMENTELLE UNTERSUCHUNGEN ZUR TYPOLOGIE DER WAHRNEHMUNG. 1939. 87 pp. (Also as *Charakter und Persönlichkeit,* Heft 2.)

539. *Obozrenie psikhiatrii, nevrologii i refleksologii imeni V. M. Bekhtereva.*

TITLE VARIATIONS: Continues *Obozrenie psikhiatrii, nevrologii i eksperimental'noi psikhologii.*

DATES OF PUBLICATION: Tom 1–5, 1926–1930.

FREQUENCY: Tom 1 (5 issues), 1926. Tom 2 (3 issues), 1927. Tom 3 (2 issues), 1928. Tom 4–5 (5 issues per year). 1929–1930.

NUMBERING VARIATIONS: Multinumber issues present.

PUBLISHER: **Leningrad:** Gosudarstvennyi refleksologicheskii institut po izucheniiu mozga, 1926–1930.

EDITORIAL COMMITTEE: M. I. Astvatsaturov, 1926–1930; L. V. Blumenau, 1926–1930; S. A. Brushtein, 1926–1930; L. L. Vasil'ev, 1926–1930; A. V. Gerver, 1926–1930; A. S. Griboedov, 1926–1930; Z. A. Gize, 1926–1930; R. Ia. Golant, 1926–1930; B. E. Maksimov, 1926–1930; V. M. Narbut, 1926–1930; M. P. Nikitin, 1926–1930; L. G. Orshanskii, 1926–1930; V. P. Osipov, 1926–1930; P. A. Ostankov, 1926–1930; K. I. Povarnin, 1926–1930; G. V. Reitts, 1926–1930; N. Ia. Smelov, 1926–1930; V. V. Sreznevskii, 1926–1930.

540. *Ohio. State University. Contributions in Principles of Education.*

TITLE VARIATIONS: None.

DATES OF PUBLICATION: Number 1–3, 1926–1928.

FREQUENCY: Irregular. See Contents *below.*

NUMBERING VARIATIONS: None.

PUBLISHER: **Columbus, Ohio:** Ohio State University Press, 1926–1928.

PRIMARY EDITORS: None listed.

CONTENTS:

Number 1. Hullfish, H. Gordon. ASPECTS OF THORNDIKE'S PSYCHOLOGY IN THEIR RELATION TO EDUCATIONAL THEORY AND PRACTICE. 1926. 113 pp.

Number 2. Alberty, H. B. A STUDY OF THE PROJECT METHOD IN EDUCATION. 1927. 111 pp.

Number 3. Orata, Pedro Tamesis. THE THEORY OF IDENTICAL ELEMENTS; BEING A CRITIQUE OF THORNDIKE'S THEORY OF IDENTICAL ELEMENTS AND A RE-INTERPRETATION OF THE PROBLEM OF TRANSFER OF TRAINING. 1928. 204 pp.

541. *Polskie archiwum psychologji. Kwartalnik poświęcony zagadnieniom psychologji teoretycznej i stosowanej wydawany przez zwiazek polskiego nauczycielstwa szkól powszechnych.*

TITLE VARIATIONS: Subtitle varies. Continued by *Psychologia wychowawcza* with Tom 11, 1938.

DATES OF PUBLICATION: Tom 1–10, 1926–August 1938. Suspended publication 1929.

FREQUENCY: Quarterly.

NUMBERING VARIATIONS: Multinumber issues present.

PUBLISHER: **Warsaw:** Skład głowny w zwiazku polskiego nauczycielstwa szkól powszechnych, 1926–1931. **Warsaw:** Skład główny w naszej księgarni, 1932. **Warsaw:** Związek nauczyciełstwa polskiego, 1933–1938.

PRIMARY EDITORS: **Jozefy Joteko,** 1926–1927; **K. Makuch,** 1927–1932; **Stefan Baley,** 1933–1938.

EDITORIAL BOARD: Stefan Baley, 1930–1932; Marja Grzegorzewska, 1930–1932; Jakob Segal, 1930–1932; none listed, 1933–1938.

542. *Problemy sovremennoi psikhologii; Uchenye zapiski.*

TITLE VARIATIONS: Continues *Psikhologiia i marksizm.*

DATES OF PUBLICATION: Tom [2]–6, 1926–1930.

FREQUENCY: Annual.

NUMBERING VARIATIONS: Tom 2 is unnumbered.

PUBLISHER: **Moscow:** Moskovskii gosudarstvennyi institut eksperimental'noi psikhologii, 1926–1930.

PRIMARY EDITOR: **I. Sapir** [Secretary], 1926–1930.

NOTE: Information on this title was compiled from entries in *A Half Century of Soviet Serials.*

543. *Psyche Miniatures; General Series.* [Published in connection with the Orthological Institute, Cambridge.]

TITLE VARIATIONS: None.

DATES OF PUBLICATION: Number 1–96, 1926–1950. Suspended publication 1943–1949.

FREQUENCY: Irregular. *See* Contents *below.*

NUMBERING VARIATIONS: Published in connection with *Psyche. A Quarterly Review of Psychology.* Some numbers also published in New York by W. W. Norton & Co. in the unnumbered series entitled the *New Science Series.*

543. *(Continued)*

PUBLISHER: **London:** Kegan Paul, Trench, Trubner & Co., Ltd., 1926–1942. **London:** Basic English Publishing Company, 1950.

PRIMARY EDITOR: **Charles Kay Ogden,** 1926–1950.

CONTENTS:

Number 1. Richards, Ivor A. SCIENCE AND POETRY. 1926. 83 pp.

Number 2. Florence, Philip Sargant. OVER-POPULATION, THEORY AND STATISTICS. 1926. 66 pp.

Number 3. Rignano, Eugenio. MAN NOT A MACHINE; A STUDY OF THE FINALISTIC ASPECTS OF LIFE. Foreword by Hans Driesch. 1926. 77 pp.

Number 4. Thompson, Richard Lowe. THE HUNTER IN OUR MIDST. 1926. 89 pp.

Number 5. Massingham, Harold John. FEE, FI, FO, FUM; OR, THE GIANTS IN ENGLAND. 1926. 175 pp.

Number 6. Malinowski, Bronislaw. MYTH IN PRIMITIVE PSYCHOLOGY. 1926. 128 pp.

Number 7. Rowse, Alfred Leslie. ON HISTORY; A STUDY OF PRESENT TENDENCIES. 1927. 102 pp.

Number 8. Malinowski, Bronislaw. THE FATHER IN PRIMITIVE PSYCHOLOGY. 1927. 93 pp.

Number 9. Florence, Philip Sargant. ECONOMICS AND HUMAN BEHAVIOUR, A REJOINDER TO SOCIAL PSYCHOLOGISTS. 1927. 117 pp.

Number 10. Herrick, Charles Judson. FATALISM OR FREEDOM; A BIOLOGIST'S ANSWER. 1927. 106 pp.

Number 11. Wheeler, William Morton. EMERGENT EVOLUTION AND THE SOCIAL. 1927. 57 pp.

Number 12. Needham, Joseph. MAN A MACHINE; IN ANSWER TO A ROMANTICAL AND UNSCIENTIFIC TREATISE WRITTEN BY SIG. EUGENIO RIGNANO & ENTITLED "MAN NOT A MACHINE". 1927. 111 pp.

Number 13. Claremont, Claude Albert. INTELLIGENCE AND MENTAL GROWTH. 1927. 138 pp.

Number 14. Bousfield, William Robert. THE BASIS OF MEMORY. 1928. 132 pp.

Number 15. Fox, Harold Munro. SELENE; OR, SEX AND THE MOON. 1928. 84 pp.

Number 16. Stefansson, Vilhjalmur. THE STANDARDIZATION OF ERROR. 1928. 110 pp.

Number 17. Reiser, Oliver Leslie. THE ALCHEMY OF LIGHT AND COLOUR. 1928. 86 pp.

Number 18. Smith, Grafton Elliot, Bronislaw Malinowski, Herbert J. Spinden, and A. Goldenweiser. CULTURE, THE DIFFUSION CONTROVERSY. 1928. 89 pp.

Number 19. Watson, John B., and William McDougall. THE BATTLE OF BEHAVIORISM. AN EXPOSITION AND AN EXPOSURE. 1928. 103 pp.

Number 20. Warden, Carl John. AN OUTLINE OF COMPARATIVE PSYCHOLOGY. 1928. 147 pp.

Number 21. Morris, Margaret. THE NOTATION OF MOVEMENT; TEXT, DRAWINGS AND DIAGRAMS. 1928. 103 pp.

Number 22. Klüver, Heinrich. MESCAL. THE "DIVINE" PLANT AND ITS PSYCHOLOGICAL EFFECTS. Introduction by Macdonald Critchley. 1928. 111 pp.

Number 23. Evans, Montogomery, II. PRODIGAL SONS; OR, THE FUTURE OF CASTE. 1928. 88 pp.

Number 24. Jeffreys, Harold. THE FUTURE OF THE EARTH. 1929. 72 pp.

Number 25. Florence, Philip Sargant. UPLIFT IN ECONOMICS. A PLEA FOR THE EXCLUSION OF MORAL IMPLICATIONS FROM ECONOMICS AND THE POLITICAL SCIENCES. 1929. 100 pp.

Number 26. Hatfield, Henry Stafford. THE CONQUEST OF THOUGHT BY IN-VENTION IN THE MECHANICAL STATE OF THE FUTURE. 1929. 117 pp.

Number 27. Bennett, Edward Stanley. A PHILOSOPHY IN OUTLINE. 1931. 100 pp.

Number 28. Dingwall, Eric John. GHOSTS AND SPIRITS IN THE ANCIENT WORLD. 1930. 124 pp.

Number 29. Ogden, C. K. BASIC ENGLISH. A GENERAL INTRODUCTION WITH RULES AND GRAMMAR. 1930. 100 pp.

Number 30. Ogden, C. K. BRIGHTER BASIC; EXAMPLES OF BASIC ENGLISH FOR YOUNG PERSONS OF TASTE AND FEELING. 1931. 100 pp.

Number 31. Ogden, C. K. THE BASIC VOCABULARY, A STATISTICAL ANAL-YSIS, WITH SPECIAL REFERENCE TO SUBSTITUTION AND TRANSLATION. 1930. 96 pp.

Number 32. Frank, Leonhard. CARL AND ANNA. Translated into Basic English by L. W. Lockhart. 1930. 144 pp.

Number 33. Ogden, C. K. BASIC ENGLISH APPLIED (SCIENCE). WITH SPECIMEN TRANSLATIONS IN CHEMISTRY, PHYSICS AND BIOLOGY by R. Michaelis. 1930. 86 pp.

Number 34. Lockhart, Leonora Wilhelmina. THE BASIC TRAVELLER AND OTHER EXAMPLES OF BASIC ENGLISH. Introduction by C. K. Ogden. 1931. 119 pp. (Re-titled: EVERYDAY BASIC ("THE BASIC TRAVELLER"). EXAMPLES OF BASIC ENGLISH, in 1934 edition).

Number 35. Wisdom, John. INTERPRETATION AND ANALYSIS IN RELATION TO BENTHAM'S THEORY OF DEFINITION. 1931. 136 pp.

Number 36. Ogden, C. K. DEBABELIZATION, WITH A SURVEY OF CON-TEMPORARY OPINION ON THE PROBLEM OF A UNIVERSAL LANGUAGE. 1931. 171 pp.

Number 37. Shenton, Herbert N., Edward Sapir, and Otto Jesperson. INTERNATIONAL COMMUNICATION; A SYMPOSIUM ON THE LANGUAGE PROBLEM. 1931. 120 pp.

Number 38. Lockhart, Leonora Wilhelmina. WORD ECONOMY, A STUDY IN APPLIED LINGUISTICS. 1931. 94 pp.

Number 39. Buchanan, Scott Milross. SYMBOLIC DISTANCE IN RELATION TO ANALOGY AND FICTION. 1932. 110 pp.

Number 40. Burrow, Trigant. THE STRUCTURE OF INSANITY. A STUDY IN PHYLOPATHOLOGY. 1932. 80 pp.

Number 41. Ogden, C. K. OPPOSITION. A LINGUISTIC AND PSYCHOLOGI-CAL ANALYSIS. 1932. 103 pp.

543. *(Continued)*

Number 42. Ogden, C. K. THE BASIC DICTIONARY, BEING THE 7,500 MOST USEFUL WORDS WITH THEIR EQUIVALENTS IN BASIC ENGLISH, FOR THE USE OF TRANSLATORS, TEACHERS AND STUDENTS. 1932 (2nd edition). 106 pp.

Number 43. Ogden, C. K. THE A B C OF BASIC ENGLISH (IN BASIC), WITH AN ACCOUNT OF THE SOUNDS OF BASIC ENGLISH by A. Lloyd James. 1932. 187 pp.

Number 44. Ogden, C. K. THE BASIC WORDS, A DETAILED ACCOUNT OF THEIR USES. 1932. 96 pp.

Number 45. Poe, Edgar Allan. THE GOLD INSECT, BEING THE "GOLD BUG" PUT INTO BASIC ENGLISH by A. P. Rossiter. 1932. 81 pp.

Number 46. Ogden, C. K. JEREMY BENTHAM, 1832–2032; BEING THE BENTHAM CENTENARY LECTURE, DELIVERED IN UNIVERSITY COLLEGE, LONDON, ON JUNE 6TH, 1932 WITH NOTES AND APPENDICES. 1932. 121 pp.

Number 47. Steed, Henry Wickham. INTERNATIONAL TALKS IN BASIC ENGLISH, PUT INTO BASIC by C. K. Ogden. 1932. 105 pp.

Number 48. Ogden, C. K. BASIC BY EXAMPLES. 1933. 128 pp.

Number 49. Galt, William. PHYLOANALYSIS. A STUDY IN THE GROUP OR PHYLETIC METHOD OF BEHAVIOUR-ANALYSIS. Preface by Trigant Burrow. 1933. 151 pp.

Number 50. Plutarch. JULIUS CAESAR, FROM THE HISTORIES OF JULIUS CAESAR AND BRUTUS IN NORTH'S PLUTARCH; PUT INTO BASIC by A. P. Rossiter. 1933. 143 pp.

Number 51. Hearn, Lafcadio. JAPANESE STORIES; PUT INTO BASIC by T. Takata. 1933. 167 pp.

Number 52. Salzedo, S. L. BASIC FOR BUSINESS. 1933. 101 pp.

Number 53. Garnett, James Clerk Maxwell. THE ORGANIZATION OF PEACE; PUT INTO BASIC by L. W. Lockhart. 1933. 123 pp.

Number 54. Tumura, Kyôson. THAT NIGHT ("SONO YO" IN BASIC ENGLISH); PUT INTO BASIC by F. J. Daniels. 1933. 96 pp.

Number 55. Sewell, Anna. BLACK BEAUTY, THE STORY OF A HORSE; PUT INTO BASIC by Winifred A. Holl. 1933. 98 pp.

Number 56. Lamb, Charles. LAMB'S STORIES FROM SHAKESPEARE; PUT INTO BASIC ENGLISH by T. Takata. 1932. 107 pp.

Number 57. Lockhart, Leonora Wilhelmina. BASIC FOR ECONOMICS. 1933. 139 pp.

Number 58. Bible. ENGLISH (BASIC ENGLISH). SELECTIONS. STORIES FROM THE BIBLE; PUT INTO BASIC ENGLISH by C. K. Ogden. 1933. 127 pp.

Number 59. Defoe, Daniel. ROBINSON CRUSOE; PUT INTO BASIC by T. Takata. 1933. 87 pp.

Number 60. Pearl, Raymond. CONSTITUTION AND HEALTH. 1933. 97 pp.

Number 61. Faraday, Michael. THE CHEMICAL HISTORY OF A CANDLE, PUT INTO BASIC ENGLISH by Phyllis Rossiter. 1933. 152 pp.

Number 62. Richards, Ivor A. BASIC RULES OF REASON. 1933. 138 pp.

Number 63. Carnap, Rudolf. THE UNITY OF SCIENCE. 1934. 101 pp.

Number 64. Holden, Inez. DEATH IN HIGH SOCIETY AND OTHER STORIES. 1934. 105 pp.

Number 65. Salzedo, S. L. A Basic Astronomy. 1934. 96 pp.

Number 66. Tolstoï, Leo. Stories for the Young; Put into Basic by J. Rantz. 1934. 94 pp.

Number 67. Swift, Jonathan. Gulliver in Lilliput; Put into Basic by C. Hughes Hartmann. 1935. 111 pp.

Number 68. The Basic St. Mark. 1935. 104 pp.

Number 69. Rossiter, Arthur Percival. Statement and Suggestion; The Basic English System as an Instrument for Reading Verse. 1935. 135 pp.

Number 70. Carnap, Rudolf. Philosophy and Logical Syntax. 1935. 100 pp.

Number 71. Perrault, Charles. Stories from France; Put into Basic by H. Walpole. 1935. 95 pp.

Number 72. Richards, Ivor A. Basic in Teaching: East and West. 1935. 112 pp.

Number 73. Ogden, C. K. Brighter Basic; Examples of Basic English for Young Persons of Taste and Feeling. 1935. 118 pp. [2nd ed. of Number 30.]

Number 74. Stevenson, Robert Louis. Keawe's Bottle; Being "The Bottle Imp" Put into Basic English by L. W. Lockhart. 1935. 73 pp.

Number 75. Searight, Kenneth. Sona; An Auxiliary Neutral Language. 1935. 119 pp.

Number 76. Franklin, Benjamin. Wise Words of an Early American; A Selection from the Writings of Benjamin Franklin. 1935. 109 pp.

Number 77. Haldane, John Burdon Sanderson. Science and Well-Being; Put into Basic by W. Empson. 1935. 117 pp.

Number 78. Ogden, C. K., with contributions by Paul D. Hugon and L. W. Lockhart. Basic English versus the Artificial Languages. 1935. 184 pp.

Number 79. Hawthorne, Nathaniel; Washington Irving; and Edgar Allen Poe. The Three Signs and Other American Stories Put into Basic English. 1935. 95 pp.

Number 80. Haldane, John Burdon Sanderson. The Outlook of Science; Put into Basic by W. Empson. 1935. 143 pp.

Number 81. Ogden, C. K. Basic Step by Step. 1935. 264 pp.

Number 82. Tourgenieff, Ivan. The Two Friends; Put into Basic by Noel Evans. 1936. 115 pp.

Number 83. Neurath, Otto. International Picture Language, The First Rules of Isotype. 1936. 117 pp.

Number 84. Rantz, J. The Sounds and Forms of Basic English. 1936. 123 pp.

Number 85. Walpole, Ellen. From Pictures to Letters; First Steps in the Teaching of Reading and Writing. 1937. 243 pp.

Number 86. Neurath, Otto. Basic by Isotype. 1937. 130 pp.

Number 87. Andersen, Hans. Stories from Hans Anderson; Put into Basic English by C. Hughes Hartmann. 1937. 121 pp.

Number 88. The Song of Songs; Put into Basic English by Ma Than É, with Ecclesiastes. 1937. 77 pp.

Number 89. Ch'u, Ta-Kao. STORIES FROM CHINA; PUT INTO BASIC ENG-
LISH. 1937. 84 pp.

Number 90. Rossiter, Phyllis Mary. BASIC FOR GEOLOGY. 1937. 164 pp.

Number 91. Plato. THE MENO; PUT INTO BASIC by J. Rantz. 1938. 87 pp.

Number 92. Bible. NEW TESTAMENT. JOHN. ENGLISH (BASIC ENGLISH).
THE BASIC ST. JOHN by Edwin W. Smith. 1938. 119 pp.

Number 93. Griffith, C.L.T. THE STORY OF LETTERS AND NUMBERS, WITH
40 FULL-PAGE PICTURES. 1939. 199 pp.

Number 94. Collodi, C. PINOCCHIO; PUT INTO BASIC by Margaret Bottrall;
Pictures by James Forsyth. 1940. 86 pp.

Number 95. Ogden, C. K., with the help of a Committee of the Orthological Institute. BASIC FOR SCIENCE. 1942. 314 pp.

Number 96. Von der Porten, Walter. BETWEEN THE LINES; OLD GREEK
STORIES IN NEW DRESS by W. Repton (pseud.). 1950. 107 pp.

544. *Psyche Miniatures; Medical Series.* [Published in connection with the Orthological Institute, Cambridge.]

TITLE VARIATIONS: None.

DATES OF PUBLICATION: Number 1–14, 1926–1931.

FREQUENCY: Irregular. *See* Contents *below.*

NUMBERING VARIATIONS: Published in conjunction with *Psyche. A Quarterly
Review of Psychology.* Some numbers also published in New York by W. W.
Norton & Co. in the unnumbered *New Science Series.*

PUBLISHER: **London:** Kegan Paul, Trench, Trubner & Co., Ltd., 1926–1931.

PRIMARY EDITOR: **Charles Kay Ogden,** 1926–1931.

CONTENTS:

Number 1. Crookshank, F. G. MIGRAINE AND OTHER COMMON NEUROSES;
A PSYCHOLOGICAL STUDY. 1926. 101 pp.

Number 2. Wilson, S. A. Kinnier. APHASIA. 1926. 108 pp.

Number 3. Ray, Matthew Burrow. RHEUMATIC; DISEASES. 1927. 91 pp.

Number 4. Miller, Emmanuel. TYPES OF MIND AND BODY. 1926. 132 pp.

Number 5. O'Donovan, William James. DERMATOLOGICAL NEUROSES.
1927. 99 pp.

Number 6. Crookshank, F. G. DIAGNOSIS: AND SPIRITUAL HEALING.
1927. 101 pp.

Number 7. Culpin, Millais. MEDICINE: AND THE MAN. 1927. 66 pp.

Number 8. Rolleston, Humphrey. IDIOSYNCRACIES. 1927. 119 pp.

Number 9. Hurst, Arthur F. THE CONSTITUTIONAL FACTOR IN DISEASE.
1927. 93 pp.

Number 10. Blondel, Charles. THE TROUBLED CONSCIENCE AND THE IN-
SANE MIND. Introduction by F. G. Crookshank. 1928. 91 pp.

Number 11. Critchley, Macdonald. MIRROR-WRITING. 1928. 80 pp.

Number 12. Gillespie, Robert Dick. HYPOCHONDRIA. 1929. 104 pp.

Number 13. Crookshank, F. G. INDIVIDUAL DIAGNOSIS. 1930. 89 pp.
Number 14. Crookshank, F. G. INDIVIDUAL SEXUAL PROBLEMS. 1931.
150 pp.

545. *Psychologische Monographien.*

TITLE VARIATIONS: None.

DATES OF PUBLICATION: Heft 1–5, 1926–1933.

FREQUENCY: Irregular. *See* Contents *below.*

NUMBERING VARIATIONS: None.

PUBLISHER: **Leipzig:** S. Hirzel, 1926–1933.

PRIMARY EDITOR: **Karl Bühler,** 1926–1933.

CONTENTS:
Heft 1. Willwoll, Alexander. BEGRIFFSBILDUNG. 1926. 148 pp.
Heft 2. Köhler, Elsa. DIE PERSÖNLICHKEIT DER DREIJÄHRIGEN KINDES.
1926. 240 pp.
Heft 3. Bühler, Charlotte. KINDHEIT UND JUGEND. 2ND AUFL. 1930.
308 pp.
Heft 4. Bühler, Charlotte. DER MENSCHLICHE LEBENSLAUF ALS PSYCHO-
LOGISHES PROBLEM. 1933. 328 pp.
Heft 5. Lazarsfeld-Jahoda, Marie, and Hans Zeisl. DIE ARBEITSLOSEN VON
MARIENTHAL. 1933. 123 pp.

546. *Religionspsychologie.* [Publication of the Wiener religionspsychologisches Forschungs-Institut.]

TITLE VARIATIONS: Superseded by *Zeitschrift für Religionspsychologie. Sonderhefte* with Heft 1, 1929.

DATES OF PUBLICATION: Heft 1–4, 1926–1928.

FREQUENCY: Semiannual.

NUMBERING VARIATIONS: None.

PUBLISHER: **Vienna:** W. Braumüller, 1926–1928.

PRIMARY EDITOR: **Karl Beth,** 1926–1928.

CONTENTS:
Heft 1. RELIGIONSPSYCHOLOGIE. Contributions by Rudolf Otto, James B.
Pratt, Paul Schilder et al. 1926. 176 pp.
Heft 2. RELIGIONSPSYCHOLOGIE. Contributions by Karl Küssner, Walter
Frühauf, Robert H. Thouless et al. 1927. 198 pp.
Heft 3. RELIGIONSPSYCHOLOGIE. Contributions by Karl Beth, Elly Adolf,
Friedrich Niebergall et al. 1927. 192 pp.
Heft 4. RELIGIONSPSYCHOLOGIE. Contributions by Wolfgang von Weisl,
Carl Schneider, Friedrich Zöller, and Victor Kichner. 1928. 120 pp.

547. *Schweizerische Zeitschrift für angewandte Psychologie.*
[Organ of the Schweizerische Vereiningung der Freunde
Coués.]

TITLE VARIATIONS: Continues *Zeitschrift für angewandte Psychologie.* [2].

DATES OF PUBLICATION: Jahrgang 2–5, 1926–1929.

FREQUENCY: Monthly.

NUMBERING VARIATIONS: None.

PUBLISHER: **Zurich:** Schweizerische Vereinigung der Freunde Coués, Bahn-hofstrasse 76, 1926–1929.

PRIMARY EDITOR: **B. Deuss,** 1926–1929.

548. *Sexualpsychologie; Dokumente zur Geschichte der Sexualität.*

TITLE VARIATIONS: None.

DATES OF PUBLICATION: Heft 1–3, 1926–1928.

FREQUENCY: Irregular. *See* Contents *below.*

NUMBERING VARIATIONS: None.

PUBLISHER: **Lörrach, Germany:** Grenzland Verlag, 1926. **Lörrach:** J. Umbach, 1928.

PRIMARY EDITOR: **Fritz Dorsch,** 1926–1928.

CONTENTS:
   Heft 1. Fischer, Friederich Christoph Jonathan. ÜBER DIE PROBENÄCHTE DER DEUTSCHEN BAUERMÄDCHEN. 1926. 63 pp.
   Heft 2. Luther, Martin. SEXUALETHISCHE ANWEISUNGEN. 1926. 87 pp.
   Heft 3. Augustinus, Sanktus Aurelius. ÜBER DIE ERBSÜNDE. 1928. 97 pp.

549. *Shinrigaku Kenkyū. Shin Shirīzu.* [Psychological Research. New Series.]

TITLE VARIATIONS: Also cited in English as *Japanese Journal of Psychology. New Series.* Supersedes *Shinrigaku Kenkyū* [Psychological Research]; *Nihon Shinrigaku Zasshi* [Japanese Journal of Psychology]. [2]. and *Shinri Kenkyū* [Psychological Research].

DATES OF PUBLICATION: Volume 1–20, February 1926–December 1950+. Suspended publication, 1944–1948.

FREQUENCY: **Bimonthly,** Volume 1–18, 1926–1944. **Quarterly,** Volume 19–20+, 1944–1950+.

NUMBERING VARIATIONS: Multinumber issues present. Contains *Nippon Shinrigakkai. Nenkai. Hōkoku.* [*Japanese Psychological Society. Congress. Reports*], 1927–1943.

PUBLISHER: **Tokyo:** Tōkyō Teikoku Daigaku [Tokyo Imperial University], 1926–1944. **Tokyo:** Nihon Shinrigakkai [Japanese Psychological Society], 1948–1950+.

PRIMARY EDITORS: **Koreshige Masuda,** 1927–1933; **K. Matsumoto,** 1934–1936; **H. Umezdu,** 1936; **M. Kido,** 1927–1941; **S. Takagi,** 1936–1941; **M. Sagara,** 1942–1944, 1948–1950+; **T. Obonai,** 1948–1949; **Y. Togawa,** 1942–1944, 1948–1949; **O. Miyagi,** 1948–1950+; **M. Yokoyama,** 1948–1950+; **K. Yuki,** 1950; **Y. Umezu,** 1950+.

EDITORIAL BOARD: T. Chiba, 1927–1940; G. Kuroda, 1927–1939; Y. Kuwata, 1927–1941, 1950+; H. Hayami, 1927–1939; M. Matsumoto, 1927–1941; T. Nogami, 1927–1941; Y. Takahashi, 1927–1939; K. Tanaka, 1927–1941; K. Sakuma, 1927–1941, 1948–1949; S. Takagi, 1950+; R. Iinuma, 1940–1941; Y. Kubo, 1940–1941; R. Kuroda, 1940–1941; T. Tiba, 1941; Mutsuo Aizawa, 1942–1943; Yoshiharu Akishige, 1942–1944, 1950+; Toshitada Ishii, 1942–1944; Y. Koga, 1942–1944, 1948–1950+; Taro Sonohara, 1942–1944; K. Takagi, 1942–1943, 1948; Y. Togawa, 1950+; O. Miyagi, 1942–1944; A. Yoda, 1942–1944, 1948–1950+; Yoshio Ueno, 1942–1944; Hiroshi Kareko, 1944; Ken Kato, 1944; T. Amano, 1943–1944; M. Imada, 1948–1950+; M. Kido, 1948–1949; T. Yatabe, 1948–1950+; Y. Usizima, 1948–1950+; H. Chiwa, 1948–1950+; T. Yamashita, 1948–1949; T. Watanabe, 1948–1950+; T. Obonai, 1950+; K. Yuki, 1948–1950+; G. Ohwaki, 1948–1950+.

550. *Zeitschrift für Parapsychologie.*

TITLE VARIATIONS: Continues *Psychische Studien.*

DATES OF PUBLICATION: Band 53–61, 1926–1934.

FREQUENCY: Monthly.

NUMBERING VARIATIONS: Band 53–61 also numbered [Reihe 3], Band 1–9.

PUBLISHER: **Leipzig:** O. Mutze, 1926–1934.

PRIMARY EDITORS: **Paul Sünner,** 1926–1934; **Rudolf Bernoulli,** 1926–1934; **Rudolf Lambert,** 1926–1934.

551. *Zeitschrift für psychoanalytische Pädagogik.*

TITLE VARIATIONS: None.

DATES OF PUBLICATION: Jahrgang 1–11, October 1926–1937.

FREQUENCY: **Monthly,** Jahrgang 1, 1926–1927. **Bimonthly,** Jahrgang 2–11, 1928–1937.

NUMBERING VARIATIONS: Multinumber issue present.

PUBLISHER: **Vienna:** Internationaler psychoanalytischer Verlag, 1926–1937.

PRIMARY EDITORS: **Heinrich Meng,** 1926–1930; **Ernst Schneider,** 1926–1930; **August Aichorn,** 1931–1937; **Paul Federn,** 1931–1937.

552. *Zeitschrift für Seelenleben und neuere Psychologie und verwandte Gebiete.*

TITLE VARIATIONS: Title varies slightly. Continues *Zeitschrift für Seelenleben.* Continued by *Zeitschrift für Seelenleben. Neuere Psychologie und verwandte*

Gebiete, psychologische Forschung und geisteskundliche Heilfragen with Jahrgang 44, 1940.

DATES OF PUBLICATION: Jahrgang 30–43, 1926–1939.

FREQUENCY: **Biweekly,** Jahrgang 30–38, 1926–1934. **Monthly,** Jahrgang 39–43, 1935–1939.

NUMBERING VARIATIONS: None.

PUBLISHER: **Leipzig:** D. Mutze, 1926–1939.

PRIMARY EDITORS: **Rudolf Feilgenhauer,** 1926–1939; **Fritz Feilgenhauer,** 1935–1939.

553. *Zeitschrift für Sexualwissenschaft und Sexualpolitik.*
[Organ of the Internationale Gesellschaft für Sexualforschung.]

TITLE VARIATIONS: Continues *Zeitschrift für Sexualwissenschaft.*

DATES OF PUBLICATION: Band 13–18, April 1926–March 1932.

FREQUENCY: 8 Hefte per year.

NUMBERING VARIATIONS: None.

PUBLISHER: **Berlin:** A. Marcus & E. Weber, 1926–1932.

PRIMARY EDITOR: **Max Marcuse,** 1926–1932.

554. *Zeitschrift für Volkerpsychologie und Soziologie. Beilage.*

TITLE VARIATIONS: None.

DATES OF PUBLICATION: Heft 1, 1926.

FREQUENCY: Irregular. *See* Contents *below.*

NUMBERING VARIATIONS: None.

PUBLISHER: **Halle:** Verlag von Wilhelm Knapp.

PRIMARY EDITORS: None listed.

CONTENTS:

   Heft 1. Karo, Georg. DER GEISTIGE KRIEG GEGEN DEUTSCHLAND. 1926. (2nd ed.). 39 pp.

1927

555. *Bibliothèque de psychologie de l'enfant et de pédagogie.* [2.]

TITLE VARIATIONS: None.

DATES OF PUBLICATION: Volume 1–2, 1927–1936.

FREQUENCY: Irregular.

NUMBERING VARIATIONS: None.

PUBLISHER: **Paris**: Librairie Félix Alcan, 1927–1936.

PRIMARY EDITORS: None listed.

CONTENTS:
Volume 1. Luquet, Georges Henri. LE DESSIN ENFANTIN. 1927. 260 pp.
Volume 2. Guillaume, Paul. LA FORMATION DES HABITUDES. 1936. 206 pp.

556. *Child Development Abstracts and Bibliography.*

TITLE VARIATIONS: Titled *Selected Child Development Abstracts,* Volume 1, June–December 1927.

DATES OF PUBLICATION: Volume 1–24+, June/September/December 1927–October/December 1950+.

FREQUENCY: Bimonthly.

NUMBERING VARIATIONS: Volume 1 issued as Numbers 1/3, June/September/December 1927. Double-numbered issues published 1942–1950+.

PUBLISHER: **Washington, D.C.**: Committee on Child Development, National Research Council, 1927–1932. **Washington, D.C.**: Committee on Child Development, Division of Anthropology and Psychology, National Research Council, 1933–1935. **Washington, D.C.**: Society for Research in Child Development, National Research Council, 1936–1945 (April). **Washington, D.C.**: Society for Research in Child Development and Committee on Child Development, Division of Anthropology and Psychology, National Research Council, 1945 (June)–1948. **Washington, D.C.**: Child Development Publications in Cooperation with Children's Bureau, Federal Security Agency, 1949–1950+.

PRIMARY EDITORS: None listed 1927–1944; **Antonio Ciocco,** 1945–1947; **Beulah Brewer,** 1945–1947; **Hermine Grimm** (Bird), 1945–1946; **Isidore Altman,** 1947–1950+; **Hazelle I. Freiss,** 1947–1948; **Samuel S. Herman,** 1950+.

EDITORIAL BOARD: Leslie Ray Marston, 1927–1928; W. E. Blatz, 1927–1935; Clayton T. J. Dodge, 1927–1935; Julia Outhouse, 1927–1935; W. W. Swingle, 1927; Rowland Godfrey Freeman, Jr., 1927–1932; M. M. Kunde, 1928–1935; Mervin A. Durea, 1928–1929; F. L. Wells, 1928–1935; J. Allan Hicks, 1930–1932; Mandel Sherman, 1932–1935; J. E. Anderson, 1933; R. S. Woodworth, 1933; Martha M. Eliot, 1933; G. D. Stoddard, 1933; E. V. McCollum, 1933; R. E. Scammon, 1934; Francis G. Blake, 1934; Robert S. Lynd, 1934; C. E. Palmer, 1935–1940; R. C. Foster, 1935–1940; A. P. Weinbach, 1936–1941; W. M. Krogman, 1936–1950+; Edith Boyd, 1936–1940; C. R. Garvey, 1936; Arthur T. Jersild, 1936–1950+; Ralph H. Ojemann, 1936–1950+; Beulah Brewer, 1936–1945; Sander E. Lachman, 1937–1944; Marian M. Crane, 1941–1943, 1947–1950+; James A. Nolan, 1941–1946; Antonio Ciocco, 1941–1945, 1949–1950+; Carl D. Wells, 1941–1943; Harold Blumberg, 1942–1946; P. S. de Q. Cabot, 1943–1950+; Barbara A. Hewell, 1944–1946; Arthur Lichtenstein, 1945–1950+; Isidore Altman, 1945–1946.

557. *Educational Research Monographs.*

TITLE VARIATIONS: Continues *Journal of Educational Research. Monographs.*

DATES OF PUBLICATION: Number 9–10, 1927.

FREQUENCY: Irregular. *See* Contents *below.*

NUMBERING VARIATIONS: None.

PUBLISHER: **Bloomington, Illinois:** Public School Publishing Company, 1927.

PRIMARY EDITOR: **Guy M. Whipple,** 1927.

CONTENTS:

    Number 9. West, Paul V. CHANGING PRACTICE IN HANDWRITING INSTRUCTION. SUGGESTIONS AND DISCUSSIONS BASED UPON A SURVEY OF PRESENT PRACTICES AND PROBLEMS. [1927.] 142 pp.

    Number 10. Nolan, Aretas Wilbur. THE CASE METHOD IN THE STUDY OF TEACHING WITH SPECIAL REFERENCE TO VOCATIONAL AGRICULTURE. A CASE BOOK FOR TEACHERS OF AGRICULTURE. 1927. 266 pp.

558. *Encéphale; journal de neurologie et de psychiatrie.* [2.]

TITLE VARIATIONS: Continues *Encéphale; journal de neurologie, de psychiatrie, de biologie et de physiologie pathologique du système nerveux.* Continued by *Encéphale; journal de neurologie et de psychiatrie et l'hygiène mentale* with Année 37, 1948.

DATES OF PUBLICATION: Année 22–36, 1927–1947.

FREQUENCY: Monthly (except July/August and September/October).

NUMBERING VARIATIONS: Multinumber issues 1939–1947.

PUBLISHER: **Paris:** H. Delarue, Libraire-éditeur, 1927. **Paris:** G. Doin et Cie, éditeurs, 1928–1947.

PRIMARY EDITORS: **A. Antheaume,** 1927; **Henri Claude,** 1927–1945; **E. Toulouse,** 1927; **Jean L'hermitte,** 1928–1947; **Albert Brousseau,** 1941–1945; **Paul Meignant,** 1941–1945; **Jean Delay,** 1946–1947.

EDITORIAL BOARD: J. Lhermitte, 1927; J. Abadie, 1927–1940; D. Anglade, 1927–1940; A. André-Thomas, 1927–1940; L. Bour, 1927–1940; A. Barbé, 1927–1940; J. Capgras, 1927–1940; R. Cestan, 1927–1933; L. Cornil, 1927–1940; Mme Dejerine, 1927; G. Étienne, 1927–1935, 1939–1940; J. Euzière, 1927–1940; J. Froment, 1927–1940; G. Genil-Perrin, 1927–1940; G. Guillain, 1927–1940; P. Guiraud, 1927–1940; A. Hesnard, 1927–1940; G. Heuyer, 1927–1940; M. Klippel, 1927–1940; M. Laignel-Lavastine, 1927–1940; J. Lévi-Valensi, 1927–1940; J. Lépine, 1927–1940; B-J. Logre, 1927–1940; R. Mignot, 1927–1940; G. Raviart, 1927–1940; H. Roger, 1927–1940; J. Rogues de Fursac, 1927–1940; J. Roubinovitch, 1927–1940; P. Sainton, 1927–1940; J. Séglas, 1927–1940; P. Sérieux, 1927–1940; J. Sicard, 1927–1928; J. Tinel, 1927–1940; Trepsat, 1927–1928; H. Verger, 1927–1930; Paul Schiff, 1928–1940; G. Petit, 1928–1940; A. Porot, 1928–1940; G. Roussy, 1929–1940; Barre, 1931–1940; P. Delmas-Marsalet, 1934–1940; Mourgue, 1934–1940; Riser, 1934–1940; Albert Brousseau, 1934–1940.

559. *Iowa. University. Studies in Character.*

TITLE VARIATIONS: None.

DATES OF PUBLICATION: Volume 1–4, Number 2, August 1, 1927–December 15, 1931.

FREQUENCY: Irregular. *See* Contents *below.*

NUMBERING VARIATIONS: Also numbered as [*Iowa. University.*] *Studies. First Series;* and [*Iowa. University.*] *Studies. New Series. See* Contents *below.*

PUBLISHER: **Iowa City:** University of Iowa, Institute of Character Research, 1927–1931.

PRIMARY EDITORS: **Edwin D. Starbuck,** 1927–1930; **James C. Manry,** 1931.

CONTENTS:

Volume 1, Number 1. Manry, James C. WORLD CITIZENSHIP. August 1, 1927. 67 pp. (Also as [*Iowa. University.*] *Studies. First Series,* Number 136.)

————, **Number 2.** Shuttleworth, Frank K. THE MEASUREMENT OF THE CHARACTER AND ENVIRONMENTAL FACTORS INVOLVED IN SCHOLASTIC SUCCESS. October 1, 1927. 80 pp. (Also as [*Iowa. University.*] *Studies. First Series,* Number 140.)

————, **Number 3.** Searles, Herbert Leon. THE STUDY OF RELIGION IN STATE UNIVERSITIES. October 15, 1927. 91 pp. (Also as [*Iowa. University.*] *Studies. First Series,* Number 141.)

————, **Number 4.** Slaght, W. E. UNTRUTHFULNESS IN CHILDREN: ITS CONDITIONING FACTORS AND ITS SETTING IN CHILD NATURE. February 15, 1928. 79 pp. (Also as [*Iowa. University.*] *Studies. First Series,* Number 149.)

Volume 2, Number 1. Franklin, Samuel P. MEASUREMENT OF THE COMPREHENSION DIFFICULTY OF THE PRECEPTS AND PARABLES OF JESUS. May 15, 1928. 63 pp. (Also as [*Iowa. University.*] *Studies. First Series,* Number 155.)

————, **Number 2.** Howells, Thomas H. A COMPARATIVE STUDY OF THOSE WHO ACCEPT AS AGAINST THOSE WHO REJECT RELIGIOUS AUTHORITY. November 15, 1928. 80 pp. (Also as [*Iowa. University.*] *Studies. First Series,* Number 167.)

————, **Number 3.** Sinclair, Robert Daniel. A COMPARATIVE STUDY OF THOSE WHO REPORT THE EXPERIENCE OF THE DIVINE PRESENCE AND THOSE WHO DO NOT. December 1, 1928. 68 pp. (Also as [*Iowa. University.*] *Studies. First Series,* Number 168.)

————, **Number 4.** Case, Ralph Thomas. A STUDY OF THE PLACEMENT IN THE CURRICULUM OF SELECTED TEACHINGS OF THE OLD TESTAMENT PROPHETS. August 1, 1930. 54 pp. (Also as [*Iowa. University.*] *Studies. First Series,* Number 184.)

Volume 3, Number 1. Lockhart, Earl G. THE ATTITUDES OF CHILDREN TOWARD LAW. August 15, 1930. 61 pp. (Also as [*Iowa. University.*] *Studies. First Series,* Number 185.)

————, **Number 2.** Hightower, Pleasant Roscoe. BIBLICAL INFORMATION IN RELATION TO CHARACTER AND CONDUCT. September 1, 1930. 72 pp. (Also as [*Iowa. University.*] *Studies. First Series,* Number 186.)

————, **Number 3.** Beiswanger, George W. THE CHARACTER VALUE OF THE OLD TESTAMENT STORIES. September 15, 1930. 63 pp. (Also as [*Iowa. University.*] *Studies. First Series,* Number 187.)

————, **Number 4.** Andrews, Elizabeth Gordon. THE DEVELOPMENT OF

IMAGINATION IN THE PRESCHOOL CHILD. November 15, 1930. 64 pp. (Also as [*Iowa. University.*] *Studies. First Series,* Number 191.)

    Volume 4, Number 1. Carlson, Harold S. INFORMATION AND CERTAINTY IN POLITICAL OPINIONS: A STUDY OF UNIVERSITY STUDENTS DURING A CAMPAIGN. August 15, 1931. 48 pp. (Also as [*Iowa. University.*] *Studies. New Series,* Number 209.)

    ————, **Number 2.** Minard, Ralph D. RACE ATTITUDES OF IOWA CHILDREN. December 15, 1931. 101 pp. (Also as [*Iowa. University.*] *Studies. New Series,* Number 217.)

560. *Kyoiku Shinri Kenkyū.* [Educational Psychological Research.]

TITLE VARIATIONS: None.

DATES OF PUBLICATION: Volume 1–15, 1927–1940.

FREQUENCY: Unknown.

NUMBERING VARIATIONS: None.

PUBLISHER: **Tokyo:** Tōkyō Bunrika Daigaku [Tokyo University of Liberal Arts and Sciences], 1927–1940.

PRIMARY EDITORS: None listed.

NOTE: Information for this entry was obtained from *Gakujutsu Zasshi Sōgō Mokuroku. Jimbun Kagaku Wabun Hen.* [Union List of Scholarly Journals. Japanese Language Section. Humanities Part.] Tokyo, 1973.

561. *London. National Institute of Industrial Psychology. (Annual) Report.*

TITLE VARIATIONS: Continues [*London.*] *National Institute of Industrial Psychology. Institute Report.*

DATES OF PUBLICATION: Number 2–25+, 1927–1950/1951+.

FREQUENCY: **Annual,** Number 2–15, 1927–1938. **Biennial,** Number 16–20, 1939–1946. **Annual,** Number 21–25+, 1946/1947–1950/1951.

NUMBERING VARIATIONS: None.

PUBLISHER: **London:** National Institute of Industrial Psychology, 1927–1950+.

PRIMARY EDITORS: Secretary acts as editor.

562. *London. National Laboratory of Psychical Research. Proceedings.*

TITLE VARIATIONS: None.

DATES OF PUBLICATION: Volume 1, Part 1–2, January 1927–April 1929.

FREQUENCY: Irregular.

NUMBERING VARIATIONS: None.

PUBLISHER: **London:** National Laboratory of Psychical Research, 1927–1929.

PRIMARY EDITORS: None listed.

563. *Los Angeles City School District. Department of Psychology and Educational Research. Yearbook.*

TITLE VARIATIONS: Continues *Los Angeles City School District. Division of Educational Research. Yearbook.*

DATES OF PUBLICATION: 3rd–4th, 1927/1929–1929/1931.

FREQUENCY: Biennial.

NUMBERING VARIATIONS: Also numbered as *Los Angeles City School District. Publications,* Number 185 and 211.

PUBLISHER: **Los Angeles:** Los Angeles City School District, 1927–1931.

PRIMARY EDITOR: **Elizabeth L. Woods,** 1927–1931.

564. *Minnesota. University. Institute of Child Welfare. Monograph Series.*

TITLE VARIATIONS: None.

DATES OF PUBLICATION: Number 1–24+, 1927–1950+.

FREQUENCY: Irregular.

NUMBERING VARIATIONS: None.

PUBLISHER: **Minneapolis:** University of Minnesota Press, 1927–1950+.

PRIMARY EDITOR: None listed. However, John E. Anderson, Director of the Institute of Child Welfare who contributed an "Editor's Preface" to Number 8 and Forewords to all numbers except 1, 7 and 10, can be considered primary editor, 1927–1950+.

CONTENTS:

Number 1. Foster, Josephine C., and John E. Anderson. THE YOUNG CHILD AND HIS PARENTS. A STUDY OF ONE HUNDRED CASES. 1927. 190 pp. (Also a rev. ed., 1930. 247 pp.)

Number 2. Goodenough, Florence L. THE KUHLMAN–BINET TESTS FOR CHILDREN OF PRESCHOOL AGE. A CRITICAL STUDY AND EVALUATION. (1928). 146 pp.

Number 3. Olson, Willard C. THE MEASUREMENT OF NERVOUS HABITS IN NORMAL CHILDREN. (1929). 97 pp.

Number 4. McCarthy, Dorothea A. THE LANGUAGE DEVELOPMENT OF THE PRESCHOOL CHILD. (1930). 174 pp.

Number 5. Atkins, Ruth Ellen. THE MEASUREMENT OF THE INTELLIGENCE OF YOUNG CHILDREN BY AN OBJECT-FITTING TEST. (1931). 89 pp.

Number 6. Shirley, Mary M. THE FIRST TWO YEARS. A STUDY OF TWEN-TY-FIVE BABIES. VOLUME I. POSTURAL AND LOCOMOTOR DEVELOPMENT. (1931). 227 pp.

Number 7. Shirley, Mary M. THE FIRST TWO YEARS. A STUDY OF TWENTY-FIVE BABIES. VOLUME II. INTELLECTUAL DEVELOPMENT. (1933). 513 pp.

Number 8. Shirley, Mary M. THE FIRST TWO YEARS. A STUDY OF TWENTY-FIVE BABIES. VOLUME III. PERSONALITY MANIFESTATIONS. (1933). 228 pp.

Number 9. Goodenough, Florence L. ANGER IN YOUNG CHILDREN. (1931). 278 pp.

Number 10. Boyd, Edith. THE GROWTH OF THE SURFACE AREA OF THE HUMAN BODY. Foreward by Richard E. Scammon. 1935. 145 pp.

Number 11. Leahy, Alice M. THE MEASUREMENT OF URBAN HOME ENVIRONMENT. VALIDATION AND STANDARDIZATION OF THE MINNESOTA HOME STATUS INDEX. (1936). 70 pp.

Number 12. Rundquist, Edward A., and Raymond F. Sletto. PERSONALITY IN THE DEPRESSION. A STUDY IN THE MEASUREMENT OF ATTITUDES. 1936. 398 pp.

Number 13. Deutsche, Jean Marquis. THE DEVELOPMENT OF CHILDREN'S CONCEPTS OF CAUSAL RELATIONS. 1937. 104 pp.

Number 14. Davis, Edith A. THE DEVELOPMENT OF LINGUISTIC SKILL IN TWINS, SINGLETONS WITH SIBLINGS, AND ONLY CHILDREN FROM AGE FIVE TO TEN YEARS. 1937. 165 pp.

Number 15. Wolf, Theta Holmes. THE EFFECT OF PRAISE AND COMPETITION ON THE PERSISTING BEHAVIOR OF KINDERGARTEN CHILDREN. 1938. 138 pp.

Number 16. Katz, Evelyn. SOME FACTORS AFFECTING RESUMPTION OF INTERRUPTED ACTIVITIES BY PRESCHOOL CHILDREN. 1938. 52 pp.

Number 17. Davis, Edith A., and Esther McGinnis. PARENT EDUCATION. A SURVEY OF THE MINNESOTA PROGRAM. 1939. 153 pp.

Number 18. Garvey, Chester Roy. THE ACTIVITY OF YOUNG CHILDREN DURING SLEEP. AN OBJECTIVE STUDY. 1939. 102 pp.

Number 19. Morgan, Winona L. THE FAMILY MEETS THE DEPRESSION. A STUDY OF A GROUP OF HIGHLY SELECTED FAMILIES. 1939. 126 pp.

Number 20. Goodenough, Florence L., and Katherine M. Maurer. THE MENTAL GROWTH OF CHILDREN FROM TWO TO FOURTEEN YEARS. A STUDY OF THE PREDICTIVE VALUE OF THE MINNESOTA PRESCHOOL SCALES. 1942. 130 pp.

Number 21. Maurer, Katherine M. INTELLECTUAL STATUS AT MATURITY AS A CRITERION FOR SELECTING ITEMS IN PRESCHOOL TESTS. 1946. 166 pp.

Number 22. Radke, Marian J. THE RELATION OF PARENTAL AUTHORITY TO CHILDREN'S BEHAVIOR AND ATTITUDES. 1946. 123 pp.

Number 23. Ford, Mary. THE APPLICATION OF THE RORSCHACH TEST TO YOUNG CHILDREN. 1946. 114 pp.

Number 24. Templin, Mildred C. THE DEVELOPMENT OF REASONING IN CHILDREN WITH NORMAL AND DEFECTIVE HEARING. 1950. 143 pp.

565. *Moscow. Akademiia kommunisticheskogo vospitaniia. Psikhologicheskaia laboratoriia. Trudy.*

TITLE VARIATIONS: Continued by [*Moscow.*] *Akademiia kommunisticheskogo vospitaniia. Psikhologicheskaia laboratoriia. Raboty* with Tom 2, 1928.

DATES OF PUBLICATION: Tom 1, 1927.

FREQUENCY: Annual.

NUMBERING VARIATIONS: None.

PUBLISHER: **Moscow:** Akademiia kommunisticheskogo vospitaniia, Psikhologicheskaia laboratoriia, Gosudarstvenoe izdatel'stvo, 1927.

PRIMARY EDITORS: None listed. However, A. B. Zalkind, who contributed an Introduction, can probably be considered primary editor, 1927.

NOTE: Information on this title was compiled from entries in *Half a Century of Soviet Serials.*

566. *Personnel Journal.*

TITLE VARIATIONS: Subtitled: *The Magazine of Labor Relations and Personnel Practices,* 1938 + . Continues *Journal of Personnel Research.*

DATES OF PUBLICATION: Volume 6–28 + , 1927/1928–1949/1950 + .

FREQUENCY: **Bimonthly,** Volume 6–13, June 1927–1935. **Monthly** (except July and August), Volume 14–25, May 1935–April 1948. **Monthly** (combined issue July & August), Volume 27–28 + , May 1948–April 1950 + .

NUMBERING VARIATIONS: Volume 14, Number 7/8, January/February 1936 joint issue.

PUBLISHER: **Baltimore:** Williams & Wilkins Company, 1927–1934. **Baltimore:** Personnel Research Federation by Williams & Wilkins Company, 1934–1935. **New York:** Personnel Research Federation, 1935–1946. **New York:** Personnel Journal, Inc., 1946–1947. **Swarthmore, Pennsylvania:** Personnel Journal, Inc., 1947–1950 + .

PRIMARY EDITORS: **Walter V. Bingham,** 1927–1935; **Clarence S. Yoakum,** 1927–1935; **Max Freyd,** 1927–1931; **O. Milton Hall,** 1931–1934; **Charles S. Slocombe,** 1935–1946; **Edward N. Hay,** 1947–1950 + .

EDITORIAL BOARD: Alfred D. Flinn, 1927–1929; Howard W. Haggard, 1927–1946; Wesley C. Mitchell, 1927–1946; Leonard Outhwaite, 1927–1929; Edward K. Strong, Jr., 1927–1946; Louis L. Thurstone, 1927–1946; Mary van Kleeck, 1927–1946; Frankwood E. Williams, 1927–1936; Joseph H. Willits, 1927–1936; Matthew Woll, 1927–1934; Douglas Fryer, 1929–1946; Morris S. Viteles, 1929–1940; Walter V. Bingham, 1935–1946; Clarence S. Yoakum, 1935–1943.

567. *Psyche Monographs.*

TITLE VARIATIONS. None.

DATES OF PUBLICATION: Number 1–13, 1927–1940.

FREQUENCY: Irregular.

NUMBERING VARIATIONS: Published in conjunction with *Psyche. A Quarterly Review of Psychology,* 1927–1932; and *Psyche. An Annual of General and Linguistic Psychology,* 1933–1940.

PUBLISHER: **London:** Kegan Paul, Trench, Trubner & Co., Ltd., 1927–1940.

PRIMARY EDITOR: None listed. However, **C. K. Ogden,** primary editor of *Psyche* (*see* Numbering Variations *above*) can be considered primary editor, 1927–1940.

CONTENTS:

Number 1. Bugnion, Édouard. THE ORIGIN OF INSTINCT; A STUDY OF THE WAR BETWEEN THE ANTS AND THE TERMITES. Translated by C. K. Ogden. 1927. 44 pp.

Number 2. Dixon, Edward T. THE GUIDANCE OF CONDUCT. 1928. 216 pp.

Number 3. Welch, Livingston. IMAGINATION AND HUMAN NATURE. 1935. 223 pp.

Number 4. Schilder, Paul. THE IMAGE AND APPEARANCE OF THE HUMAN BODY. STUDIES IN THE CONSTRUCTIVE ENERGIES OF THE PSYCHE. 1935. 353 pp.

Number 5. Allen, Arthur Henry Burlton. THE SELF IN PSYCHOLOGY; A STUDY IN THE FOUNDATIONS OF PERSONALITY. 1935. 282 pp.

Number 6. Wandell, Samuel Henry. AARON BURR IN LITERATURE; BOOKS, PAMPHLETS, PERIODICALS, AND MISCELLANY RELATING TO AARON BURR AND HIS LEADING POLITICAL CONTEMPORARIES, WITH OCCASIONAL EXCERPTS FROM PUBLICATIONS, BIBLIOGRAPHICAL, CRITICAL AND HISTORICAL NOTES, ETC. Introduction by Walter F. McCaleb. 1936. 302 pp.

Number 7. Harding, Rosamond Evelyn Mary. TOWARDS A LAW OF CREATIVE THOUGHT. 1936. 178 pp.

Number 8. Jones, Chester Henry. THE WRITINGS AND DIARY OF CHESTER JONES, Edited with an Introduction by L. Haden Guest. 1936. 221 pp.

Number 9. Benjamin, Abram Cornelius. THE LOGICAL STRUCTURE OF SCIENCE. 1936. 344 pp.

Number 10. O'Neill, F. R. THE RELATION OF ART TO LIFE; A SKETCH OUTLINE OF AN ART PHILOSOPHY. 1938. 232 pp.

Number 11. Miller, James Wilkinson. THE STRUCTURE OF ARISTOTELIAN LOGIC. 1938. 97 pp.

Number 12. O'Neill, F. R. THE SOCIAL VALUE OF ART; A PSYCHOLOGICAL AND LINGUISTIC APPROACH TO AN UNDERSTANDING OF ART ACTIVITY. 1939. 232 pp.

Number 13. Macdermott, Mary Marshall. VOWEL SOUNDS IN POETRY; THEIR MUSIC AND TONE-COLOUR. 1940. 148 pp.

568. *Psychological Abstracts.*

TITLE VARIATIONS: None.

DATES OF PUBLICATION: Volume 1–24+, 1927–1950+.

FREQUENCY: Monthly (2 issues during December).

NUMBERING VARIATIONS: A 13th issue which is the index issue for the year is published in December.

PUBLISHER: **Lancaster, Pennsylvania:** American Psychological Association, 1927–1932 and 1937–1941. **Worcester, Massachusetts:** American Psychological Association, 1933–1936. **Lancaster:** American Psychological Association, Inc., 1942–1950+.

PRIMARY EDITORS: **Walter S. Hunter,** 1927–1946; **Raymond R. Willoughby,** 1927–1939; **H. L. Ansbacher,** 1940–1943; **C. M. Louttit,** 1947–1950+; **Allen J. Sprow,** 1949–1950+.

569. *Revue française de psychanalyse.* [Official organ of the Société psychanalytique de Paris.]

TITLE VARIATIONS: None.

DATES OF PUBLICATION: Tome 1–14+, July 1927–October/December 1950+. Suspended publication 1940–1947.

FREQUENCY: Quarterly.

NUMBERING VARIATIONS: All four issues of Tome 1 were published July–December 1927. Tome 11 is complete with issue Numéro 1, 1939.

PUBLISHER: **Paris:** G. Doin et Cie, éditeurs, 1927–1931/1931. **Paris:** Denoël et Steele, éditeurs, 1932–1939. **Paris:** Presses universitaires de France, 1948–1950+.

PRIMARY EDITORS: [**Marie Bonaparte,** 1927–1950+.]

570. *Ukrains'kyi visnyk eksperymental'noi pedagogiky ta refleksologii.*

TITLE VARIATIONS: Continues *Ukrains'kyi visnyk refleksologii ta eksperymental'noi pedagogiky.* Continued by *Za Markso-Lenins'ku pedagogiku* with Vypusk 1, 1931.

DATES OF PUBLICATION: Vypusk 1–18, 1927–1930.

FREQUENCY: **Quarterly,** Vypusk 1–12, 1927–1929. **Bimonthly,** Vypusk 13–18, 1929–1930.

NUMBERING VARIATIONS: Also numbered Tom 1–5, Vypusk 3, 1927–1930; and also numbered continuously with *Ukrains'kyi visnyk refleksologii ta eksperymental'noi pedagogiky.* Multinumber issues present.

PUBLISHER: **Kharkov:** Ukrainskii nauchno-issledovatel'skii institut pedagogiki, 1927–1930.

PRIMARY EDITOR: **V. P. Protopopov,** 1927–1930.

EDITORIAL COMMITTEE: M. S. Volobiv, 1927–1930; A. S. Zaluzhnii, 1927–1930; O. I. Popov, 1927–1930; I. P. Sokolians'kii, 1927–1930; I. M. Murakhivs'ka, 1927; S. D. Stril'bits'kii, 1929–1930; M. T. Gerasimovich, 1928–1930; Iu. P. Gorbenko, 1930.

571. *Vergleichende Untersuchungen zur Psychologie, Typologie und Pädagogik des ästhetischen Erlebens.*

TITLE VARIATIONS: None.

DATES OF PUBLICATION: Heft 1–4, 1927.

FREQUENCY: Quarterly.

NUMBERING VARIATIONS: Heft 2 never published.

PUBLISHER: **Göttingen:** Bandenhoeck & Ruprecht, 1927.

PRIMARY EDITOR: **Oswald Kroh,** 1927.

CONTENTS:
    Heft 1. Heckel, Richard. OPTISCHE FORMEN UND ÄSTHETISCHES ERLEBEN. 1927. 104 pp.
    Heft 3. Fromm, Hermann. SPRACHLICHE FORMGEBUNG UND ÄSTHETISCHE WERTUNG. 1927. 46 pp.

Heft 4. Walker, Erwin. Das musikalische Erlebnis und seine Entwicklung. 1927. 160 pp.

1928

572. Allgemeine ärztliche Zeitschrift für Psychotherapie und psychische Hygiene einschliesslich der klinischen und sozialen Grenzgebiete. [Organ of the Allgemeine ärztliche Gesellschaft für Psychotherapie.]

TITLE VARIATIONS: Continued by *Zentralblatt für Psychotherapie und ihre Grenzgebiete einschliesslich der medizinischen Psychologie und psychischen Hygiene* with Band 3, 1930.

DATES OF PUBLICATION: Band 1–2, 1928–1929.

FREQUENCY: **10 Hefte,** Band 1, 1928. **Monthly,** Band 2, 1929.

NUMBERING VARIATIONS: None.

PUBLISHER: **Leipzig:** S. Hirzel, 1928–1929.

PRIMARY EDITORS: **Robert Sommer,** 1928–1929; **Wladimir Eliasberg,** 1928–1929; **Rudolf Allers,** 1928–1929.

573. Beiträge zur Massenpsychologie.

TITLE VARIATIONS: None.

DATES OF PUBLICATION: Heft 1–3, 1928–1929.

FREQUENCY: Semiannual.

NUMBERING VARIATIONS: None.

PUBLISHER: **Halle:** C. Marhold, 1928–1929.

PRIMARY EDITOR: **Paul Plaut,** 1928–1929.

CONTENTS:
Heft 1. Schneersohn, Fischel. Neue Wege der Sozialpsychologie. 1928. 79 pp.
Heft 2. Bekhterev, Vladimir Michailovich. Die kollektive Reflexologie. 1928. 66 pp.
Heft 3. Plaut, Paul. Aussage und Umwelt in Sittlichkeitsprozessen. 1929. 77 pp.

574. Beiträge zur Philosophie und Psychologie.

TITLE VARIATIONS: None.

DATES OF PUBLICATION: Heft 1–11, 1928–1932.

FREQUENCY: Irregular. *See* Contents *below.*

NUMBERING VARIATIONS: Heft 9 published 1932. Heft 10 published 1931.

PUBLISHER: **Stuttgart:** W. Kohlhammer, 1928–1932.

PRIMARY EDITOR: **Traugott Konstantin Oesterreich,** 1928–1932.

CONTENTS:

Heft 1. Oesterreich, Traugott Konstantin. DIE PROBLEME DER EINHEIT UND DER SPALTUNG DES ICH. 1928. 37 pp.

Heft 2. Rösel, Richard. DIE PSYCHOLOGISCHEN GRUNDLAGEN DER YOGA-PRAXIS. 1928. 135 pp.

Heft 3. Schumacher, Karl. EIN VERGLEICH DER BUDDHISTISCHEN VERSEN-KUNG MIT DEN JESUITISCHEN EXERZITIEN. 1928. 78 pp.

Heft 4. Grabert, Herbert. DIE EKSTATISCHEN ERLEBNISSE DER MYSTIKER UND PSYCHOPATHEN. 1929. 108 pp.

Heft 5. Oesterreich, Traugott Konstantin. DAS MÄDCHEN AUS DER FREMDE. 1929. 178 pp.

Heft 6. Niemeier, Gottfried. DIE METHODEN UND GRUNDAUFFASSUNGEN DER RELIGIONSPHILOSOPHIE DER GEGENWART. 1930. 205 pp.

Heft 7. Steiger, Kurt. DIE STRUKTUR MÄNNLICHER DURCHSCHNITTS-RELIGIOSITÄT. 1930. 140 pp.

Heft 8. Oesterreich, Traugott Konstantin. PSYCHOLOGISCHES GUTACHTEN IN EINEM HELLSEHERPROZESS. 1930. 117 pp.

Heft 9. Prince, Morton, and Walter F. Prince. DIE SPALTUNG DER PERSÖNLICHKEIT. Translation and Bibliography by Willy Herms. Introduction by T. K. Oesterreich. 1932. 271 pp.

Heft 10. Heyer, Gustav Richard. SEELEN-RÄUME. PSYCHOTHERAPEU-TISCHE BEOBACHTUNGEN ZUM KOLLEKTIV-SEELISCHEN. 1931. 37 pp.

Heft 11. Müllensiefen, Paul. FAUST ALS NAPOLEON. 1932. 43 pp.

575. *California. University. Institute of Child Welfare. Bulletin.*

TITLE VARIATIONS: Titled *Research Bulletin. An Informational Publication on the Institute and Its Works*, Number 1 and 2.

DATES OF PUBLICATION: Number 1–14, March 1928–June 1942.

FREQUENCY: **Annual,** Number 1–6, 1928–1933. **Irregular,** Number 7–14, 1934–1942.

NUMBERING VARIATIONS: Bulletins 9, 10, 11 issued in 1938. Bulletins 12, 13 issued 1940. Bulletin 14, 1942.

PUBLISHER: **Berkeley, California:** University of California, Institute of Child Welfare, 1928–1942.

PRIMARY EDITORS: None listed. However, the Director of the Institute can generally be considered to be primary editor.

576. *Chiao yü yen Chiu.* [Studies in Education].

TITLE VARIATIONS: None.

DATES OF PUBLICATION: Number 1–110, February 1928–September 1948.

FREQUENCY: Monthly.

NUMBERING VARIATIONS: None.

PUBLISHER: **Canton:** Kuo li Chung-shan ta hsüeh [National Sun Yat-sen University], 1928–1948.

PRIMARY EDITORS: None listed.

NOTE: Kuo li Chung-shan ta hsüeh [National Sun Yat-sen University] is also called Chung-shan ta hsüeh [Sun Yat-sen University]. Information on this title was partially compiled from *Chuan-kuo Chung-wen Chi-kan lien-ho mu-lu, 1833–1949.* [Union List of Chinese Periodicals in China, 1833–1949.] Peking: Peking Library, 1961.

577. *Chiao yü yü hsin li.* [Education and Psychology.] [*1.*]

TITLE VARIATIONS: None.

DATES OF PUBLICATION: Volume 1, Number 1, May 1928.

FREQUENCY: Semiannual.

PUBLISHER: **Peking:** Ch'ing-hua hsüeh hsi'ao. Chiao yü hsin li hsüeh hsi [Ch'ing-hua College. Department of Educational Psychology], 1928.

PRIMARY EDITORS: None listed.

NOTE: Ch'ing-hua hsüeh hsi'ao [Ch'ing-hua College] later called Ch'ing-hua ta hsüeh [Ch'ing-hua University] and Kuo li Ch'ing-hua ta hsuëh [National Ch'ing-hua University]. English name also as National Tsing-hua University. Information on this title was partially compiled from *Chuan-kuo Chung-wen Chi-kan lien-ho mu-lu, 1833–1949.* [Union List of Chinese Periodicals in China, 1833–1949.] Peking, Peking Library, 1961.

578. *Deutsche Psychologie. Arbeitenreihe zur Kulturpsychologie und Psychologie der Praxis. Psychotechnik.*

TITLE VARIATIONS: Continues *Deutsche Psychologie: Arbeitenreihe.*

DATES OF PUBLICATION: Band 5, Heft 2–Band 7, Heft 4, 1928–1932.

FREQUENCY: Irregular. *See* Contents *below.*

NUMBERING VARIATIONS: Band 6, Heft 2–6 never published. Some issues also numbered as *Beiträge zur Sozialpsychologie der Berufe; Beiträge zur Objektspsychotechnik;* and *Psychotechnische Forschungen zur Berufsberatung. See* Contents *below.*

PUBLISHER: **Halle:** Carl Marhold Verlagsbuchhandlung, 1928–1932.

PRIMARY EDITOR: **Fritz Giese,** 1928–1932.

CONTENTS:
Band 5, Heft 2. Giese, Fritz. ERLEBNISFORMEN DES ALTERNS. 1928. 90 pp.

————, **Heft 3.** Helfenberger, Alfons. KORRELATIONSFORSCHUNGEN ZUR PSYCHOTECHNIK. 1928. 50 pp.

————, **Heft 4.** Kölle, Hermann. PSYCHOTECHNISCHE SCHULUNGSME-THODEN FÜR POLIZEIBEAMTE. 1929. 50 pp.

————, **Heft 5.** Anschütz, Georg. DAS FARBE-TON-PROBLEM IM PSY-CHISCHEN GESAMTBEREICH. 1929. 104 pp.

————, **Heft 6.** Mehmke, Rudolf L. ARBEITSGESINNUNG IM WANDEL DER ZEITEN. 1930. 116 pp.

Band 6, Heft 1. Kuhn, Heinrich. ARBEITSLEISTUNG UND BELEUCHTUNG. 1927. 80 pp. (Also as *Beiträge zur Objektspsychotechnik*, Heft 1).

Band 7, Heft 1. Wagner, Erich. BERUFSUMWELT UND GEISTIGE LEISTUNG BEI JUGENDLICHEN. 1930. 68 pp. (Also as *Beiträge zur Sozialpsychologie der Berufe*, Heft 1; and as *Psychotechnische Forschungen zur Berufsberatung*, Heft 2.)

————, **Heft 2.** Hirsch, Georg. DIE FAULHEIT. 1931. 153 pp. (Also as *Beiträge zur Sozialpsychologie der Berufe*, Heft 1; and as *Psychotechnische Forschungen zur Berufsberatung*, Heft 3.)

————, **Heft 3.** Giese, Fritz, and Cläre Cordemann. PSYCHOLOGISCHE BEOBACHTUNGSTECHNIK BEI ARBEITSPROBEN. 1931. 82 pp. (Also as *Beiträge zur Sozialpsychologie der Berufe*, Heft 1.)

————, **Heft 4.** Klatt, Georg. PSYCHOLOGIE DES ALKOHOLISMUS. 1932. 79 pp. (Also as *Beiträge zur Sozialpsychologie der Berufe*, Heft 1.)

579. *Gesellschaft für Tierpsychologie. Kurzmitteilungen.*

TITLE VARIATIONS: None.

DATES OF PUBLICATIONS: Number 1–4, July 1928–1930.

FREQUENCY: **Annual,** Numbers 1 and 4, 1928 and 1930. **Semiannual,** Numbers 2 and 3, 1929.

NUMBERING VARIATIONS: None.

PUBLISHER: **Stuttgart:** Gesellschaft für Tierpsychologie, Richard Jordan Verlag, 1928–1930.

PRIMARY EDITOR: **Richard Jordan,** 1928–1930.

580. *Great Britain. Industrial Health Research Board. Annual Report.*

TITLE VARIATIONS: Continues [*Great Britain.*] *Industrial Fatigue Research Board. Annual Report.*

DATES OF PUBLICATION: Number 9–19, December 31, 1928–June 30, 1939.

FREQUENCY: Annual.

NUMBERING VARIATIONS: 9th and 10th reports dated December 31, 1928 and 1929. 11th–19th reports dated 30 June 1931–1939.

PUBLISHER: **London:** His Majesty's Stationery Office, 1929–1939.

PRIMARY EDITORS: **D. R. Wilson,** 1928–1929; **David Munro,** 1930–1939.

581. *Hygiène mentale. Journal d'assistance psychiatrique et de psychiatrie appliquée.*

TITLE VARIATIONS: Continues *Hygiène mentale. Journal d'assistance psychiatrique, d'anthropologie criminelle et d'intérêts professionnels.* Continued by *Hygiène mentale. Journal de psychiatrie appliquée* with Année 24, 1929.

DATES OF PUBLICATION: Année 23, Numéro 1–10, January–December 1928.

FREQUENCY: Monthly (except July/August and September/October).

NUMBERING VARIATIONS: None.

PUBLISHER: **Paris:** Doin et Cie, éditeurs, 1928.

PRIMARY EDITORS: **H. Claude,** 1928; **Jean Lhermitte,** 1928.

582. *Imago; Zeitschrift für Anwendung der Psychoanalyse auf die Natur- und Geisteswissenschaften.*

TITLE VARIATIONS: Continues *Imago; Zeitschrift für Anwendung der Psychoanalyse auf die Geisteswissenschaften.* Continued by *Imago; Zeitschrift für psychoanalytische Psychologie, ihre Grenzgebiete und Anwendungen* with Jahrgang 19, 1933.

DATES OF PUBLICATION: Jahrgang 14–18, 1928–1932.

FREQUENCY: Quarterly.

NUMBERING VARIATIONS: None.

PUBLISHER: **Leipzig** and **Vienna:** Internationaler psychoanalytischer Verlag, 1928–1932.

PRIMARY EDITORS: **Hanns Sachs,** 1928–1932; **A. J. Storfer,** 1928–1932; **Sandor Rado,** 1928–1932.

583. *International Journal of Psycho-Analysis. Supplements.*

TITLE VARIATIONS: None.

DATES OF PUBLICATION: Number 1–4, 1928–1930.

FREQUENCY: Irregular. *See* Contents *below.*

NUMBERING VARIATIONS: Some issues also numbered as *International Journal of Psycho-Analysis. Research Supplement. See* Contents *below.*

PUBLISHER: **London:** Published for the Institute of Psycho-Analysis by Bailliere, Tindall & Cox, 1928–1930.

PRIMARY EDITOR: **Ernest Jones,** 1928–1930.

CONTENTS:

    Number 1. Jones, Ernest. A GLOSSARY OF TECHNICAL TERMS FOR USE OF TRANSLATORS OF PSYCHO-ANALYTIC WORKS. 1928. 16 pp.

    Number 2. Rickman John, THE DEVELOPMENT OF THE PSYCHO-ANALYTICAL THEORY OF THE PSYCHOSES, 1893–1926. 1928. 106 pp. (Also as *International Journal of Psycho-Analysis. Research Supplement,* Number 2.)

Number 3. Glover, Edward. THE TECHNIQUE OF PSYCHO-ANALYSIS. 1928. 141 pp. (Also as *International Journal of Psycho-Analysis. Research Supplement*, Number 3.)

Number 4. Bryan, Douglas. COMPLETE INDEX TO VOLUMES I–X. [1930.] 118 pp.

584. *Jeugd en beroep. Tijdschrift voor jeugdpsychologie, voorlichting bij beroepskeuze en beroepsvorming.* [Organ of the Vereniging tot bevordering der voorlichting bij beroepskeuze.]

TITLE VARIATIONS: None.

DATES OF PUBLICATION: Jaargang 1–3, January 1928–December 1930.

FREQUENCY: Monthly.

NUMBERING VARIATIONS: None.

PUBLISHER: **Purmerend, Netherlands:** J. Muusses, 1928–1930.

PRIMARY EDITORS: None listed.

585. *Journal of General Psychology; Experimental, Theoretical, Clinical, and Historical Psychology.*

TITLE VARIATIONS: None.

DATES OF PUBLICATION: Volume 1–42+, 1928–1950+.

FREQUENCY: Quarterly (2 volumes per year).

NUMBERING VARIATIONS: None.

PUBLISHER: **Worcester, Massachusetts:** Clark University Press, 1928–1936. **Provincetown, Massachusetts:** Journal Press, 1937–1950+.

PRIMARY EDITORS: **Edward Bradford Titchener,** 1928; **Carl Murchison,** 1928–1950+; **Luberta M. Harden,** 1930–1934.

EDITORIAL BOARD: Frank Angell, 1928–1939; V. M. Borovskii, 1928–1949; F. C. Bartlett, 1928–1950+; Harvey Carr, 1929–1950+; G. S. Brett, 1928–1944; W. J. Crozier, 1928–1950+; Karl Bühler, 1928–1950+; Georges Dumas, 1928–1946; Raymond Dodge, 1928–1941; Pierre Janet, 1928–1946; James Drever, 1928–1950+; Felix Krueger, 1928–1946; Knight Dunlap, 1928–1949; A. Michotte, 1928–1950+; Shepherd Ivory Franz, 1928–1934; A. L. Schniermann, 1928–1949; H. L. Hollingworth, 1928–1950+; T. A. Hunter, 1928–1950+; F. Kiesow, 1928–1950+; Otto Klemm, 1928–1939; William McDougall, 1928–1939; Walter Miles, 1928–1950+; John Paul Nafe, 1928–1950+; C. E. Spearman, 1928–1945; Edward C. Tolman, 1928–1950+; John B. Watson, 1928–1950+; Albert P. Weiss, 1928–1931; H. P. Weld, 1928–1950+; Raymond H. Wheeler, 1928–1950+; R. W. Wilcocks, 1928–1950+; Clark Wissler, 1928–1931; Robert M. Yerkes, 1928–1936; Matataro Matsumoto, 1931–1943; Kanae Sakuma, 1931–1943; Clark L. Hull, 1935–1950+; Samuel Renshaw, 1935–1950+.

586. *Journal of Juvenile Research.*

TITLE VARIATIONS: Continues *Journal of Delinquency.*

DATES OF PUBLICATION: Volume 12, Number 3/4–Volume 22, Number 3/4, September/December 1928–July/October 1938.

FREQUENCY: Quarterly.

NUMBERING VARIATIONS: Multinumber issues present.

PUBLISHER: **Whittier, California:** California Bureau of Juvenile Research, Whittier State School, 1928–1931. **Los Angeles:** California Bureau of Juvenile Research, 1931–1932. **Claremont:** California Bureau of Juvenile Research, 1932–1937. **Stanford:** California Bureau of Juvenile Research, 1937–1938.

PRIMARY EDITORS: **Norman Fenton,** 1928–1938; **Jessie C. Fenton,** 1929–1938; **Dorothy K. Tyson,** 1931–1938; **Cornelia R. Keough,** 1933–1934; **Ramona Wallace,** 1934–1938; **Marjorie Pirie,** 1935; **Sybil M. Kilduff,** 1936; **Sybil K. Richardson,** 1936–1938; **Dorothy K. Thompson,** 1938.

587. *Loyola Educational Index; A Readers' Guide to Education and Psychology.*

TITLE VARIATIONS: None.

DATES OF PUBLICATION: Volume 1, Number 1–4, February–December 1928.

FREQUENCY: Issued in February, April, June, October, and cumulated in December.

NUMBERING VARIATIONS: None.

PUBLISHER: **Chicago:** Loyola University Press, 1928.

PRIMARY EDITORS: **Austin G. Schmidt,** 1928; **Florence H. McIntosh,** 1928; **May Feehan,** 1928; **Raphael C. McCarthy,** 1928.

588. *Magyar Psychológiai Szemle.*

TITLE VARIATIONS: Also called *Ungarische Zeitschrift für Psychologie; Hungarian Psychological Review; Revue psychologie hongroise;* and *Rivista ungherese di psicologia.* Subtitle varies.

DATES OF PUBLICATION: Évfolyam 1–16, July/December 1928–1947. Suspended publication 1943–1946.

FREQUENCY: Quarterly (Irregular).

NUMBERING VARIATIONS: Multinumber issues (varying from 1-4 numbers per issue) present.

PUBLISHER: **Budapest:** Kiadja a Magyar Psychologiai Táraság, 1928–1947.

PRIMARY EDITORS: **IstV́an Boda,** 1928–1932; **Hildebrand Várkonyi,** 1933–1940; **Tibor Lehoczky,** 1941–1942; **Lászlō Mátrai,** 1941–1942; **Lajos Kardos,** 1947; **Ferenc Lenard,** 1947.

589. **Minnesota. University. Institute of Child Welfare. Circulars. (Series 1.)**

TITLE VARIATIONS: Superseded by *Minnesota. University. Institute of Child Welfare. Circulars. Series 2* with Number 1, 1930.

DATES OF PUBLICATION: Number 1–2, 1928–1929.

FREQUENCY: Annual.

NUMBERING VARIATIONS: None.

PUBLISHER: **Minneapolis:** Institute of Child Welfare, University of Minnesota, 1928–1929.

PRIMARY EDITORS: None listed.

CONTENTS:
    Number 1. Parental Education Department. A MANUAL FOR THE ORGANIZATION OF STUDY GROUPS. 1928. 19 pp.
    Number 2. PUBLICATIONS OF THE INSTITUTE OF CHILD WELFARE. 1929. 7 pp.

590. **Moscow. Akademiia kommunisticheskogo vospitaniia. Psikhologicheskaia laboratoriia. Raboty.**

TITLE VARIATIONS: Continues [*Moscow.*] *Akademiia kommunisticheskogo vospitaniia. Psikhologicheskaia laboratoriia. Trudy.*

DATES OF PUBLICATION: Tom 2–5, 1928–1931.

FREQUENCY: Annual.

NUMBERING VARIATIONS: None.

PUBLISHER: **Moscow:** Akademiia kommunisticheskogo vospitaniia. Psikhologicheskaia laboratoriia, Gosudarstvenoe izdatel'stvo, 1928–1931.

PRIMARY EDITORS: None listed. However, A. B. Zalkind, who contributed an Introduction to every volume, can probably be considered primary editor, 1928–1931.

NOTE: Information on this title was compiled from entries in *A Half Century of Soviet Serials.*

591. **Rochester (New York). University. Eastman School of Music. Studies in Psychology.**

TITLE VARIATIONS: None.

DATES OF PUBLICATION: Volume 1, Number 2–4, 1928–1929.

FREQUENCY: Irregular. *See* Contents *below.*

NUMBERING VARIATIONS: Volume 1, Number 1 never published. Volume 1, Number 2–3 not numbered on publication. Some issues also numbered in *Personnel Journal* or *Psychological Monographs*. *See* Contents *below.*

PUBLISHER: **Rochester, New York:** University of Rochester, Eastman School of Music, 1928–1929.

PRIMARY EDITOR: **Hazel M. Stanton,** 1928–1929.

CONTENTS:
[**Volume 1, Number 2.**] Stanton, Hazel M. MEASURING MUSICAL TALENT. SEASHORE TESTS AS ADMINISTRATIVE AIDS. (Also in *Personnel Journal,* Volume 7, Number 4, 1928, pp. 286–292.)
——, [**Number 3.**] Stanton, Hazel M. SEASHORE MEASURES OF MUSICAL TALENT. (Also in *Psychological Monographs,* Volume 39, Number 2, 1928, pp. 135–144.)
——, **Number 4.** Stanton, Hazel M. PROGNOSIS OF MUSICAL ACHIEVEMENT. 1929. 89 pp.

592. *Schriften zur landwirtschaftlichen Arbeitsforschung auf psychologischer Grundlage.*

TITLE VARIATIONS: None.

DATES OF PUBLICATION: Heft 1–2, 1928–1929.

FREQUENCY: Annual.

NUMBERING VARIATIONS: None.

PUBLISHER: **Leipzig:** Johann Ambrosius Barth, 1928–1929.

PRIMARY EDITOR: **Max Schönberg,** 1928–1929.

CONTENTS:
Heft 1. Schönberg, Max. EIN NEUES ZIEL DER LANDWIRTSCHAFTLICHEN ARBEITSFORSCHUNG. 1928. 82 pp.
Heft 2. Schönberg, Max. DIE KUNST DER WIRTSCHAFTSBERATUNG IN DER LANDWIRTSCHAFT. 1929. 89 pp.

593. *Schriften zur Psychologie der Strafrechtspflege.*

TITLE VARIATIONS: None.

DATES OF PUBLICATION: Stück 1–3, 1928–1930.

FREQUENCY: Irregular. *See* Contents *below.*

NUMBERING VARIATIONS: None.

PUBLISHER: **Mannheim:** J. Bensheimer, 1928–1930.

PRIMARY EDITOR: **Max Alsberg,** 1928–1930.

CONTENTS:
Stück 1. Alsberg, Max. DER PROZESS DES SOKRATES IM LICHTE MODERNER JURISPRUDENZ UND PSYCHOLOGIE. 1928. 29 pp.
Stück 2. Alsberg, Max. DIE PHILOSOPHIE DER VERTEIDIGUNG. 1930. 32 pp.
Stück 3. Alsberg, Max. DAS WELTBILD DER STRAFRICHTERS. 1930. 30 pp.

594. *Schriften zur Psychologie und Soziologie von Sexualität und Verbrechen.*

TITLE VARIATIONS: None.

DATES OF PUBLICATION: Stück 1–3, 1928–1932.

FREQUENCY: Irregular. *See* Contents *below.*

NUMBERING VARIATIONS: None.

PUBLISHER: **Stuttgart:** J. Püttmann, 1928–1932.

PRIMARY EDITORS: **Hertha Riese,** 1928–1932; **Walther Riese,** 1928–1932.

CONTENTS:

Stück 1. Fuerst, Bruno et al. WIECHMANN. DER FALL. ZUR PSYCHOLOGIE UND SOZIOLOGIE DES FAMILIENMORDES. 1928. 165 pp.

Stück 2. Fürth, Henriette. DIE REGELUNG DER NACHKOMMENSCHAFT ALS EUGENISCHES PROBLEM. 1929. 143 pp.

Stück 3. Noack, Victor. DAS SOZIALE SEXUALVERBRECHEN. 1932. 80 pp.

595. *Schriften zur Seelenforschung.*

TITLE VARIATIONS: Continues *Kleine Schriften zur Seelenforschung.*

DATES OF PUBLICATION: Heft 19–20, 1928–1933.

FREQUENCY: Irregular. *See* Contents *below.*

NUMBERING VARIATIONS: Heft 19 issued as Lieferung 1–2. Heft 19, Lieferung 2 issued after Heft 20.

PUBLISHER: **Stuttgart:** J. Püttmann, 1928–1933.

PRIMARY EDITORS: **Arthur Kronfeld,** 1928; **Carl Schneider,** 1933.

CONTENTS:

Heft 19, Lieferung 1. Fischer, Edmund. KINDERTRÄUME. EINE PSYCHO-LOGISCH-PÄDAGOGISCHE STUDIE. 1928. Pp. 1–64.

————, **Lieferung 2.** Fischer, Edmund. KINDERTRÄUME. EINE PSYCHO-LOGISCH-PÄDAGOGISCHE STUDIE. 1933. Pp. 65–128.

Heft 20. Achelis, Werner. DAS PROBLEM DES TRAUMES. EINE PHILO-SOPHISCHE ABHANDLUNG. 1928. 39 pp.

596. *Tijdschrift voor parapsychologie. Gewijd aan de studie van het occultisme in zijn vollen omvang.* [Organ of the Studievereniging voor "psychical research".]

TITLE VARIATIONS: None.

DATES OF PUBLICATION: Jaargang 1–18+, November 1928–1950+. Suspended publication 1942–1945.

FREQUENCY: Bimonthly.

NUMBERING VARIATIONS: None.

PUBLISHER: **Amsterdam: Emil Wegelin, 1928–1930. Bussum: Emil Wegelin, 1930–1941. The Hague: H. P. Leopold, 1946–1950+.**

PRIMARY EDITORS: None listed, 1928–1941; **W.H.C. Tenhaeff, 1946–1950+.**

EDITORIAL BOARD: **Ir. J. Bethlem, 1946–1950+; H. Th. Fischer, 1946–1950+; H. M. Haye, 1946–1950+; G. Zorab, 1946–1950+.**

597. *Zeitschrift für individualpsychologische Pädagogik und Psychohygiene.*

TITLE VARIATIONS: None.

DATES OF PUBLICATION: Jahrgang 1, Heft 1–9/10, March–December 1928.

FREQUENCY: Monthly.

NUMBERING VARIATIONS: Multinumbered issue present.

PUBLISHER: **Berlin:** A. Hoffmann's Verlag, 1928.

PRIMARY EDITORS: **Manes Sperber, 1928; Herman Laasch, 1928.**

598. *Zeitschrift für Religionspsychologie. Beiträge zur religiösen Seelenforschung und Seelenführung.* [Publication of the Internationale religionspsychologische Gesellschaft.]

TITLE VARIATIONS: None.

DATES OF PUBLICATION: Band 1–11, 1928/1929–April 1938.

FREQUENCY: **Quarterly,** Band 1–3, 1928/1929–1930. **Bimonthly,** Band 4–6, 1931–1933. **Quarterly,** Band 7–11, 1935/1936–1938.

NUMBERING VARIATIONS: Multinumber issues present.

PUBLISHER: **Gütersloh, Germany:** C. Bertelsmann, 1928/1929–1930. **Dresden:** C. L. Ungelenk, 1931–1933. **Vienna:** Internationale religionspsychologische Gesellschaft 1935/1936–1938.

PRIMARY EDITOR: **Karl Beth, 1928/1929–1938.**

599. *Zhurnal psikhologii, pedologii i psikhotekhniki. Seriia A. Psikhologiia.*

TITLE VARIATIONS: Continued by *Psikhologiia* with Tom 2, 1929.

DATES OF PUBLICATION: Tom 1, Vypusk 1–3, 1928.

FREQUENCY: Triannual.

NUMBERING VARIATIONS: None.

PUBLISHER: **Moscow** and **Leningrad:** Glavnoe upravlenie nauchnymi uchrezhdeniiami (Glavnauka). Gosudarstvennoe izdatel'stvo (Gosizdat), 1928.

PRIMARY EDITORS: **K. N. Kornilov, 1928; V. A. Artemov, 1928; V. M. Borovskii, 1928; Z. I. Chuchmarev, 1928; N. A. Rybnikov, 1928; I. D. Sapir, 1928; I. N. Shpil'rein, 1928; S. M. Vacileiskii, 1928.**

600. *Zhurnal psikhologii, pedologii i psikhotekhniki. Seriia B. Pedologii.*

TITLE VARIATIONS: Continued by *Pedologiia* with Tom 2, 1929.

DATES OF PUBLICATION: Tom 1, Vypusk 1–2, 1928.

FREQUENCY: Semiannual.

NUMBERING VARIATIONS: None.

PUBLISHER: **Moscow:** Glavnoe upravlenie nauchnymi uchrezhdeniiami RSFSR, 1928.

PRIMARY EDITOR: **A. B. Zalkind,** 1928.

NOTE: Information on this title was compiled from entries in *Half a Century of Soviet Serials.*

601. *Zhurnal psikhologii, pedologii i psikhotekhniki. Seriia V. Psikhofiziologiia truda i psikhotekhnika.*

TITLE VARIATIONS: Continued by *Psikhotekhnika i psikhofiziologiia truda* with Tom 2, 1929.

DATES OF PUBLICATION: Tom 1, Vypusk 1–4, 1928.

FREQUENCY: Quarterly.

NUMBERING VARIATIONS: None.

PUBLISHER: **Moscow:** Vsesoiuznyi obshchestvo psikhotekhniki i prikladnoi psikhofiziologii, 1928.

PRIMARY EDITORS: Unknown.

NOTE: Information on this title was compiled from entries in *Half a Century of Soviet Serials.*

1929

602. *Archiv für die gesamte Psychologie. Ergänzungsband.*
[Organ of the Deutsche Gesellschaft für Psychologie.]

TITLE VARIATIONS: None.

DATES OF PUBLICATION: Heft 1–4, 1929–1937.

FREQUENCY: Irregular. *See* Contents *below.*

NUMBERING VARIATIONS: None.

PUBLISHER: **Leipzig:** Akademische Verlagsgesellschaft, 1929–1937.

PRIMARY EDITOR: **Wilhelm Wirth,** 1929–1937.

CONTENTS:

Heft 1. Rieffert, Johann Baptist. PRAGMATISCHE BEWUSSTSEINSTHEORIE AUF EXPERIMENTELLER GRUNDLAGE. 1929. 229 pp.

Heft 2. Ach, N., H. Gerdessen, F. Kohlhagen, and S. Margaritzky. FI-
NALE QUALITÄT (GEFÜGIGKEIT). 1932. 366 pp.

Heft 3. Blumenfeld, Walter. URTEIL UND BEURTEILUNG. 1931. 623 pp.

Heft 4. Skramlik, Emil von. PSYCHOPHYSIOLOGIE DER TASTSINNE. TEIL 1
AND 2. 1937. 935 pp. (Also called *Beiträge zur Psychophysiologie der Sinnes-
leistungen.*)

603. *Archiv für Religionspsychologie und Seelenführung.*

TITLE VARIATIONS: Continues *Archiv für Religionspsychologie.*

DATES OF PUBLICATION: Band 4–5, 1929–1930.

FREQUENCY: Annual.

NUMBERING VARIATIONS: None.

PUBLISHER: **Leipzig:** Gesellschaft für Religionspsychologie, 1929. **Leipzig:** Internationale Gesellschaft für Religionspsychologie, 1930.

PRIMARY EDITORS: **Wilhelm Stählin,** 1929–1930; **Werner Grühn,** 1929–1930.

EDITORIAL BOARD: H. Höffding, 1929–1930; A. Messer, 1929–1930; A. Dyroff, 1929–1930; S. Behn, 1929–1930; G. Berguer, 1929–1930; K. Bühler,
1929–1930; A. Gemelli, 1929–1930; J. W. Hauer, 1929–1930; Felix Krueger,
1929–1930; F. Künkel, 1929–1930; L. Lévy-Bruhl, 1929–1930; J. Lindworsky,
1929–1930; H. Restorff, 1929–1930; J. H. Schultz, 1929–1930; C. Schweitzer,
1929–1930; R. Sommer, 1929–1930; E. Stange, 1929–1930; E. D. Starbuck,
1929–1930; R. H. Thouless, 1929–1930; B. Vasady, 1929–1930; G. Wunderle,
1929–1930.

604. *Cluj (Rumania). Universitatea. Institutul de psihologie experimentală, comparată şi aplicată. Studii şi cercetări psihologice.*

TITLE VARIATIONS: None.

DATES OF PUBLICATION: Număr 1–28, 1929–1941.

FREQUENCY: *See* Contents *below.*

NUMBERING VARIATIONS: Număr 1, 19 and 20 all have an extra publication
with an "A" suffix.

PUBLISHER: **Cluj, Rumania:** Tip. "Cartea Româneăsca" S. A., 1929–1930.
Cluj: Editura institutului de psihologie al universităţii, 1931–1940. **Sibiu, Rumania:** Editura institutului de psihologie al universităţii, 1941.

PRIMARY EDITOR: **F. Ştefănescu-Goăngă,** 1929–1941.

CONTENTS:

Număr 1. Ştefănescu-Goăngă, Florian. SELECŢIA CAPACITĂŢILOR ŞI ORIEN-
TAREA PROFESIONALĂ. 1929. 74 pp.

Număr 1a. Rusu, Liviu. SELECTIA COPIILOR DOTAŢI (EPUIZATĂ). 1929.
228 pp.

Year 1929

Număr 2. Mărgineanu, Nicolae. PSIHOLOGIA EXERCIȚIULUI. 1929. 212 pp.

Număr 3. Rusu, Liviu, Lucian Bologa, Nicolae Mărgineanu, Alexandru Roșca, and Dimitrie Tudoranu. PSIHOLOGIA CONFIGURAȚIEI. 1929. 151 pp.

Număr 4. Mărgineanu, Nicolae. PSIHOTEHNICA IN GERMANIA. 1929. 82 pp.

Număr 5. Roșca, Alexandru. MĂSURAREA INTELIGENȚII SI DEBILITATEA MINTALĂ. 1930. 187 pp.

Număr 6. Bologa, Lucian. PSIHOLOGIA VIEȚII RELIGIOASE. 1930. 331 pp.

Număr 7. Mărgineanu, Nicolae. PSIHOLOGIA GERMANĂ CONTIMPORANĂ. 1930. 348 pp.

Număr 8. Rusu, Liviu. APTITUDINEA TEHNICĂ ȘI INTELIGENȚA PRACTICĂ. 1931. 141 pp.

Număr 9. Mărgineanu, Nicolae. PSIHOLOGIA INVĂȚĂRII. 1931. 166 pp.

Număr 10. Roșca, Alexandru. PSIHOPATOLOGIA DEVIAȚILOR MORALE. 1931. 110 pp.

Număr 11. Roșca, Alexandru. DEBILITATEA MINTALĂ. 1931. 76 pp.

Număr 12. Pârlog, Cristea. PSIHOLOCIA DESEMNULUI. 1932. 170 pp.

Număr 13. Tudoranu, Dimitrie. PSIHOLOGIA TEMPERAMENTULUI. 1932.

Număr 14. Mărgineanu, Nicolae. PSIHOLOGIA FRANCEZĂ CONTEMPORANĂ. 1932. 169 pp.

Număr 15. Roșca, Alexandru. DELINCVENTUL MINOR. 1933.

Număr 16. Bologă, Lucian. LECTURA TINERETULUI. 1933. 116 pp.

Număr 17. Roșca, Alexandru. PSIHOLOGIA MARTORULUI. 1934. 160 pp.

Număr 18. Beniuc, Mihăil. INVĂȚAREA ȘI INTELIGENȚA LA ANIMALE. 1934. 88 pp.

Număr 19. Tudoranu, Dimitrie. PSIHOLOGIA RECLAMEI. (1935).

Număr 19a. Roșca, Alexandru. ORIENTAREA PROFESIONALĂ A ANORMALILOR. 1936. 102 pp.

Număr 20. Ștefănescu-Goangă, F., Alexandru Roșca, and S. Cupcea. INSTABILITATEĂ EMOTIVĂ. 1936. 200 pp.

Număr 20a. Rusu, Liviu. ESTETICA POEZIEI LIRICE. (1937.)

Număr 21. Mărgineanu, Nicolae. ELEMENTE DE PSIHOMETRIE. 1938. 376 pp.

Număr 22. Mărgineanu, Nicolae. ANALIZA FACTORILOR PSIHICE. 1938. 216 pp.

Număr 23. Ștefănescu-Goangă, F., Alexandru Roșca, and S. Cupcea. ADAPTAREA SOCIALĂ. 1938. 180 pp.

Număr 24. Roșca, Alexandru. IGIENA MENTALĂ SCOLARĂ. 1939. 173 pp.

Număr 25. Ștefănescu-Goangă, F. MĂSURAREA INTELIGENȚEI. 1940. 94 pp.

Număr 26. Barbu, Zevedei. CONTRIBUȚIUNI LA PSIHOLOGIA ONESTITĂȚII. 1940. 105 pp.

Număr 27. Roșca, Alexandru. COPII SUPERIOR INZESTRAȚI. 1941. 207 pp.

Număr 28. Mărgineanu, Nicolae. PSIHOLOGIA PERSOANEI. 1941. (2nd ed., 1944, 557 pp.)

605. *Columbia University. Teachers College. Child Development Institute. Child Development Monographs.*

TITLE VARIATIONS: None.

DATES OF PUBLICATION: Number 1–32, 1929–1945.

FREQUENCY: Irregular. *See* Contents *below.*

NUMBERING VARIATIONS: None.

PUBLISHER: **New York:** Columbia University Teachers College. Bureau of Publications, 1929–1945.

PRIMARY EDITORS: **Helen T. Woolley,** 1929–1930; **Lois Hayden Meek,** 1930–1939; **Arthur T. Jersild,** 1939–1945.

CONTENTS:

Number 1. Thomas, Dorothy Swaine, and associates. SOME NEW TECHNIQUES FOR STUDYING SOCIAL BEHAVIOR. 1929. 203 pp.

Number 2. Rose, Mary Swartz, and Cora E. Gray, with the cooperation of Katherine L. Foster. THE RELATION OF DIET TO HEALTH AND GROWTH OF CHILDREN IN INSTITUTIONS WITH A METHOD OF EVALUATING DIETARIES AND A THREE-WEEKS DIETARY CONFORMING TO THE STANDARDS PROPOSED. 1930. 128 pp.

Number 3. Barker, Margaret. A TECHNIQUE FOR STUDYING THE SOCIAL–MATERIAL ACTIVITIES OF YOUNG CHILDREN. 1930. 69 pp.

Number 4. Nelson, Janet Fowler. PERSONALITY AND INTELLIGENCE. A STUDY OF SOME RESPONSES OTHER THAN INTELLECTUAL NOTED IN A SIMPLE MENTAL TEST SITUATION. 1931. 62 pp.

Number 5. Loomis, Alice Marie. A TECHNIQUE FOR OBSERVING THE SOCIAL BEHAVIOR OF NURSERY SCHOOL CHILDREN. 1931. 100 pp.

Number 6. Rust, Metta Maund. THE EFFECT OF RESISTANCE ON INTELLIGENCE TEST SCORES OF YOUNG CHILDREN. 1931. 80 pp.

Number 7. Beaver, Alma Perry. THE INITIATION OF SOCIAL CONTACTS BY PRESCHOOL CHILDREN. A STUDY OF TECHNIQUE IN RECORDING SOCIAL BEHAVIOR. 1932. 65 pp.

Number 8. Arrington, Ruth E. INTERRELATIONS IN THE BEHAVIOR OF YOUNG CHILDREN. 1932. 156 pp.

Number 9. Leonard, Eugenie Andruss. PROBLEMS OF FRESHMAN COLLEGE GIRLS: A STUDY OF MOTHER-DAUGHTER RELATIONSHIPS AND SOCIAL ADJUSTMENTS OF GIRLS ENTERING COLLEGE. 1932. 139 pp.

Number 10. Jersild, Arthur T., assisted by Wilhelmina Bennett, Ruth Bush, Ruth Ortleb, and Sylvia Bienstock. TRAINING AND GROWTH IN THE DEVELOPMENT OF CHILDREN. A STUDY OF THE RELATIVE INFLUENCE OF LEARNING AND MATURATION. 1932. 73 pp.

Number 11. Caille, Ruth Kennedy. RESISTANT BEHAVIOR OF PRESCHOOL CHILDREN. 1933. 142 pp.

Number 12. Jersild, Arthur T., Frances V. Markey, and Catherine L. Jersild. CHILDREN'S FEARS, DREAMS, WISHES, DAYDREAMS, LIKES, DISLIKES, PLEASANT AND UNPLEASANT MEMORIES. A STUDY BY THE INTERVIEW METHOD OF 400 CHILDREN AGED 5 TO 12. 1933. 172 pp.

Number 13. Driscoll, Gertrude Porter. THE DEVELOPMENTAL STATUS OF THE PRESCHOOL CHILD AS A PROGNOSIS OF FUTURE DEVELOPMENT. 1933. 111 pp.

Number 14. Brackett, Catherine Williams. LAUGHING AND CRYING OF PRESCHOOL CHILDREN. A STUDY OF THE SOCIAL AND EMOTIONAL BEHAVIOR OF YOUNG CHILDREN AS INDICATED BY LAUGHING AND CRYING. 1934. 91 pp.

Number 15. Fisher, Mary Shattuck. LANGUAGE PATTERNS OF PRESCHOOL CHILDREN. 1934. 88 pp.

Number 16. Robb, Elda. THE ENERGY REQUIREMENT OF NORMAL THREE- AND FOUR-YEAR-OLD CHILDREN UNDER STANDARD BASAL METABOLISM CONDITIONS AND DURING PERIODS OF QUIET PLAY. 1934. 57 pp.

Number 17. Rose, Mary Swartz, and Gertrude M. Borgeson. CHILD NUTRITION ON A LOW-PRICED DIET WITH SPECIAL REFERENCE TO THE SUPPLEMENTARY VALUE OF AN EGG A DAY, THE EFFECT OF ADDING ORANGE JUICE AND OF REPLACING EGG BY LIVER. 1935. 109 pp.

Number 18. Markey, Frances V. IMAGINATIVE BEHAVIOR OF PRESCHOOL CHILDREN. 1935. 139 pp.

Number 19. Rood, Dorothy. THE NURSE AND PARENT EDUCATION. 1935. 87 pp.

Number 20. Jersild, Arthur T., and Frances B. Holmes. CHILDREN'S FEARS. 1935. 356 pp.

Number 21. Jersild, Arthur T., and Frances V. Markey. CONFLICTS BETWEEN PRESCHOOL CHILDREN. 1935. 181 pp.

Number 22. Jersild, Arthur T., and Sylvia F. Bienstock. DEVELOPMENT OF RHYTHM IN YOUNG CHILDREN. 1935. 97 pp.

Number 23. McFarland, Margaret B. RELATIONSHIPS BETWEEN YOUNG SISTERS AS REVEALED IN THEIR OVERT RESPONSES. 1938. 230 pp.

Number 24. Borgeson, Gertrude M. TECHNIQUES USED BY THE TEACHER DURING THE NURSERY SCHOOL LUNCHEON PERIOD. 1938. 214 pp.

Number 25. Jersild, Arthur T. THE INFLUENCE OF NURSERY SCHOOL EXPERIENCE ON CHILDREN'S SOCIAL ADJUSTMENTS. 1939. 112 pp.

Number 26. Jones, Theresa Dower. THE DEVELOPMENT OF CERTAIN MOTOR SKILLS AND PLAY ACTIVITIES IN YOUNG CHILDREN. A GENETIC STUDY OF THE MOTOR DEVELOPMENT OF PRESCHOOL CHILDREN AS REVEALED BY THEIR USE OF WHEEL PLAY MATERIALS. 1939. 180 pp.

Number 27. Williams, Alice Marietta. CHILDREN'S CHOICES IN SCIENCE BOOKS; A STUDY TO DISCOVER SOME ELEMENTS OF A BOOK IN THE FIELD OF SCIENCE THAT APPEAL TO CHILDREN. 1939. 163 pp.

Number 28. Preston, Ralph C. CHILDREN'S REACTIONS TO A CONTEMPORARY WAR SITUATION. 1942. 96 pp.

Number 29. Baker, H. V. CHILDREN'S CONTRIBUTIONS IN ELEMENTARY SCHOOL GENERAL DISCUSSION. 1942. 150 pp.

Number 30. McKinnon, Kathern Mae. CONSISTENCY AND CHANGE IN BEHAVIOR MANIFESTATIONS AS OBSERVED IN A GROUP OF SIXTEEN CHILDREN DURING A FIVE-YEAR PERIOD. 1942. 144 pp.

Number 31. Lafore, Gertrude Gilmore. PRACTICES OF PARENTS IN DEALING WITH PRESCHOOL CHILDREN. 1945. 150 pp.

Number 32. Sandin, Adolph Angus. SOCIAL AND EMOTIONAL ADJUST-
MENTS OF REGULARLY PROMOTED AND NON-PROMOTED PUPILS. 1944. 142 pp.

606. *Debrecen (Hungary). Tudomány-egyetem. Pedagógiai Szemináriumából és Pszihológiai Intézét. Közlemenyék.*

TITLE VARIATIONS: None.

DATES OF PUBLICATION: Szám 1–26, [192?]–1941.

FREQUENCY: Irregular. *See* Contents *below.*

NUMBERING VARIATIONS: None.

PUBLISHER: **Debrecen:** Városi Nyomda, 1937 (Szám 18). **Debrecen:** Külön-
lenyomat a Mitrovics Gyula Tudományos Müködesének 50. Évforduloja Al-
kalmából Kiadott Emlékkönyvböl, 1939 (Szám 21). **Debrecen:** Csuka Lászlo
Könyvnyomdája, 1941 (Szám 24). **Debrecen:** A Debreceni Református
Kollégium Tanárképzö intézete Dolgozatainak 23, 1941 (Szám 26).

PRIMARY EDITOR: **Gyula Mitrovics,** 1937–1941.

CONTENTS:
Szám 18. Zombor, Zoltán. A Kisérleti Lélektan Neveléstörténeti
Jelentösége és a Reakciós Idö Mérések Pedagógiai Vonatkozásai. 1937. 41 pp.
Szám 21. Faragó, Tibor. A Matematikában Tehetséges Tanuló. 1939. n.p.
Szám 24. Tömöry, Ödön. A Középiskolai Vallásos Nevelés Elmélete és
Módszere. 1941. n.p.
Szám 26. Sipka, Sándor. Középiskolai Oktatásunk Nemzeti Célkitüzései,
1941. 64 pp.

NOTE: Information on this entry is incomplete. The compilers have information
for all volumes known to be in the United States. First year of publication is
uncertain. The entry has been placed here since approximatè first date of issue
is 1929.

607. *Évolution psychiatrique. Cahiers de psychologie clinique et de psychopathologie générale.*

TITLE VARIATIONS: Continues *Évolution psychiatrique. Psychanalyse. Psychologie clinique.*

DATES OF PUBLICATION: Série 2, Numéro 1–[Unnumbered], October
1929–1950 +. Suspended publication 1940–1946, 1948–1949.

FREQUENCY: Quarterly (Irregular).

NUMBERING VARIATIONS: Série 2 only appears on Numéro 1–4. Numéro 5–6
also numbered Tome 3, Fasicule 1–2. Issues from 1934–1950 + are unnumbered except by date.

PUBLISHER: **Paris:** Payot, 1929–1939. **Paris:** Desclée de Brouwer & Cie, 1947.
Paris: Centre d'éditions psychiatriques, 1950 +.

PRIMARY EDITORS: **A. Hesnard,** 1925–1935; **Réné Laforgue,** 1925–1935; none
listed, 1936–1939; **E. Minkowski,** 1947–1950 +; **Henri Ey,** 1947–1950 +.

EDITORIAL BOARD: A. Borel, 1947–1950+; M. Cenac, 1947–1950+; O. Codet, 1947; O. Laurent-Lucas-Championniere, 1950+; P. Male, 1947–1950+; F. Minkowska, 1947–1950; M. Montassut, 1947–1950+; G. Parcheminey, 1947–1950+; J. Rouart, 1947–1950+; P. Rube, 1947–1950; J. Lacan, 1947–1950.

EDITORIAL SECRETARY: J. Rondepierre, 1947–1950; P. Sivadon, 1950+.

608. *Hygiène mentale. Journal de psychiatrie appliquée.*

TITLE VARIATIONS: Continues *Hygiène mentale. Journal d'assistance psychiatrique et de psychiatrie appliquée.* Continued by *Encéphale; journal de neurologie et de psychiatrie et l'hygiène mentale* with Année 37–38, 1948–1949.

DATES OF PUBLICATION: Année 24–36, January 1929–1947.

FREQUENCY: Monthly (except July/August and September/October).

NUMBERING VARIATIONS: Multinumber issues present in Année 35–36, 1942–1947.

PUBLISHER: **Paris:** Gaston Doin et Cie, éditeurs, 1929–1947.

PRIMARY EDITORS: **Henri Claude,** 1929–1945; **Jean Lhermitte,** 1929–1947; **R. Mignot,** 1930–1933; **G. Genil-Perrin,** 1930–1933; **A. Brousseau,** 1934–1947.

609. *Iowa. University. Child Welfare Research Station. Report.*

TITLE VARIATIONS: None.

DATES OF PUBLICATION: 1929/1930–1948/1949.

FREQUENCY: Annual.

NUMBERING VARIATIONS: None.

PUBLISHER: **Iowa City, Iowa:** University of Iowa. Iowa Child Welfare Station, 1930–1949.

PRIMARY EDITORS: **George D. Stoddard,** 1929–1941; **Robert R. Sears,** 1942–1949.

610. *Krakow. Naukowe towarzystwo pedagogiczne. Psychologia niewidomych.*

TITLE VARIATIONS: None.

DATES OF PUBLICATION: Tom 1, 1929.

FREQUENCY: Irregular.

NUMBERING VARIATIONS: None.

PUBLISHER: **Warzaw:** Wydawnictwo naukowego towarzystwa pedagogicznego, 1929.

PRIMARY EDITOR: **Marja Grzegorzewska,** 1929.

CONTENTS:

 Tom 1. Grzegorzewska, Marja. Psychologia niewidomych. 1929. 348 pp.

611. *Monographien zur Grundlegung der philosophischen Anthropologie und Wirklichkeitsphilosophie.*

TITLE VARIATIONS: None.

DATES OF PUBLICATION: Heft 1–4, 1929–1930.

FREQUENCY: Semiannual.

NUMBERING VARIATIONS: None.

PUBLISHER: **Berlin:** O. Elsner Verlagsbuchhandlung, 1929–1930.

PRIMARY EDITOR: **Erich Jaensch,** 1929–1930.

CONTENTS:

Heft 1. Jaensch, E. WIRKLICHKEIT UND WERT IN DER PHILOSOPHIE UND KULTUR DER NEUZEIT. PROLEGOMENA ZUR PHILOSOPHISCHEN FORSCHUNG AUF DER GRUNDLAGE PHILOSOPHISCHER ANTHROPOLOGIE NACH EMPIRISCHER METHODE. 1929. 254 pp.

Heft 2. Jaensch, E. GRUNDFORMEN MENSCHLICHEN SEINS. (MIT BERÜCK-SICHTIGUNG IHRER BEZIEHUNGEN ZU BIOLOGIE UND MEDIZIN, ZU KULTUR-PHILOSOPHIE UND PÄDAGOGIK.) 1929. 524 pp.

Heft 3. Drinkuth, Rudolf. ORGANISCHE ERZIEHUNG. 1930. 66 pp.

Heft 4. Weber, Hermann. DIE THEOLOGIE CALVINS. 1930. 64 pp.

612. *Oregon. University. Publications. Psychology Series.*

TITLE VARIATIONS: Continued by [*Oregon. University.*] *Studies in Psychology* with Volume 1, Number 4, December 1933.

DATES OF PUBLICATION: Volume 1, Number 1–3, January 1929–December 1931.

FREQUENCY: Irregular. *See* Contents *below.*

NUMBERING VARIATIONS: None.

PUBLISHER: **Eugene, Oregon:** Published by the University, University Press, 1929–1931.

PRIMARY EDITORS: None listed.

EDITORIAL BOARD: Eric W. Allen, 1931; C. E. Carpenter, 1931; M. H. Douglass, 1931; D. E. Faville, 1931; Robert C. Hall, 1931; C. L. Huffaker, 1931; E. L. Packard, 1931; P. A. Parsons, 1931; Charles G. Howard, 1931; John H. Mueller, 1931.

CONTENTS:

Volume 1, Number 1. Crosland, Harold R. THE PSYCHOLOGICAL METHODS OF WORD-ASSOCIATION AND REACTION-TIME AS TESTS OF DECEPTION. January 1929. 104 pp.

————, **Number 2.** Conklin, Edmund S. VOLUME-YEAR CHECK LIST OF PSYCHOLOGICAL AND ALLIED JOURNALS. January 1931. Pp. 105–128.

————, **Number 3.** Crosland, Harold R., and Lester F. Beck. OBJECTIVE MEASUREMENTS OF EMOTION. A SYMPOSIUM OF THREE EXPERIMENTAL PAPERS. December 1931. Pp. 129–202.

613. *Pedologiia.*

TITLE VARIATIONS: Continues *Zhurnal psikhologii, pedologii i psikhotekhniki. Seriia B. Pedologii.*

DATES OF PUBLICATION: Tom 2–5, 1929–1932.

FREQUENCY: **Quarterly,** Tom 2, 1929. **Bimonthly,** Tom 3, 1930. **Eight issues,** Tom 4, 1931. **Quarterly,** Tom 5, 1932.

NUMBERING VARIATIONS: Issues also assigned whole numbers, Nomer 3–24.

PUBLISHER: **Moscow:** Tsentral'naia mezhduvedomstvennaia komissiia SSSR, 1929–1931. **Moscow:** Sektor nauki narodnogo komissariata prosveschcheniia RSFSR, 1932.

PRIMARY EDITORS: **A. B. Zalkind,** 1929–1931; **R. G. Vilenkina,** 1932.

NOTE: Information on this title was compiled from entries in *A Half Century of Soviet Serials.*

614. *Psikhologiia.*

TITLE VARIATIONS: Continues *Zhurnal psikhologii, pedologii i psikhotekhniki. Seriia A. Psikhologiia.*

DATES OF PUBLICATION: Tom 2–5, 1929–1932.

FREQUENCY: **Triannual,** Tom 2, 1929. **Quarterly,** Tom 3–5, 1930–1932.

NUMBERING VARIATIONS: Tom 4, Vypusk 2 incorrectly numbered Tom 5, Vypusk 2.

PUBLISHER: **Moscow** and **Leningrad:** Glavnoe upravlenie nauchnymi uchrezhleniiami (glavnauka). Gosudarstvennoe izdatel'stvo (Gosizdat), 1929–1930. **Moscow** and **Leningrad:** Sektor nauki, Narodnyi komitet prosveshcheniia. Gosudarstvennoe sotsial'no-ekonomicheskoe izdatel'stvo, 1931. **Moscow** and **Leningrad:** Gosudarstvennoe sotsial'no-ekonomicheskoe izdatel'stvo, 1932.

PRIMARY EDITORS: **K. N. Kornilov,** 1929–1930; none listed, 1931; **V. Kolbanovskii,** 1932.

EDITORIAL BOARD: V. A. Artemov, 1929–1930; V. M. Borovskii, 1929–1932; Z. I. Chuchmarev, 1929; T. L. Kogan, 1931–1932; K. N. Kornilov, 1931–1932; N. F. Kurmanov, 1930; A. R. Luriia, 1931–1932; N. A. Rybnikov, 1929–1930; I. D. Sapir, 1929–1931; F. Shemiakin, 1932; I. N. Shpil'rein, 1929–1932; A. A. Talankin, 1931–1932; S. M. Vacileiskii, 1929; A. V. Vedenov, 1931–1932; L. S. Vygotskii, 1930–1932; A. B. Zalkind, 1931.

615. *Psikhotekhnika i psikhofiziologiia truda.*

TITLE VARIATIONS: Continues *Zhurnal psikhologii, pedologii i psikhotekhniki. Seriia V. Psikhofiziologiia truda i psikhotekhnika.* Continued by *Sovetskaia psikhotekhnika* with Tom 5, 1932.

DATES OF PUBLICATION: Tom 2–4, 1929–1931.

FREQUENCY: **Quarterly,** Tom 2, 1929. **Bimonthly,** Tom 3–4, 1930–1931.

NUMBERING VARIATIONS: Multinumber issues present.

PUBLISHER: **Moscow:** Vsesoiuznyi obshchestvo psikhotekhniki i prikladnoi psikhofiziologii, 1929–1931.

PRIMARY EDITORS: Unknown.

NOTE: Information on this title was compiled from entries in *A Half Century of Soviet Serials.*

616. *Psychoanalytische Bewegung.*

TITLE VARIATIONS: None.

DATES OF PUBLICATION: Band 1–5, May/June 1929–1933.

FREQUENCY: Bimonthly.

NUMBERING VARIATIONS: Band 1 has only 4 Hefte.

PUBLISHER: **Vienna:** Internationaler psychoanalytischer Verlag, 1929–1933.

PRIMARY EDITOR: **Adolf Josef Storfer,** 1929–1933.

617. *Psychological Register.*

TITLE VARIATIONS: None.

DATES OF PUBLICATION: Volume 2–3, 1929–1932.

FREQUENCY: Irregular.

NUMBERING VARIATIONS: Issued in the unnumbered *International University Series in Psychology.* Volume 1 never published. Volume 3 is a revised and expanded edition of Volume 2.

PUBLISHER: **Worcester, Massachusetts:** Clark University Press, 1929–1932.

PRIMARY EDITOR: **Carl Murchison,** 1929–1932.

ASSISTANT EDITOR: **Luberta Harden,** 1932.

EDITORIAL BOARD: Anathon A. F. Aall, 1932; F. C. Bartlett, 1929–1932; Stefan Błachowski, 1929–1932; Theophilas Boreas, 1932; Karl Bühler, 1929–1932; Ramiro Bujas, 1932; Édouard Claparède, 1932; Paul Dahle, 1932; Sante de Sanctis, 1929–1932; James Drever, 1932; Julio Endara, 1932; Henry Halvorsen, 1932; Thorleif G. Hegge, 1929; Thomas A. Hunter, 1932; Gustav A. Jaederholm, 1932; Spiro S. Kasandjiev, 1932; David Katz, 1932; Kurt Lewin, 1932; H. Tasman Lovell, 1932; Alexander R. Luria, 1932; Matataro Matsumoto, 1929–1932; Albert E. Michotte, 1932; E. Lopez Mira, 1932; José Carlos Montaner, 1932; Enrique Mouchet, 1932; Henri Piéron, 1929–1932; Viktor P. Protopopov, 1932; Constantin Rădulescu-Motru, 1932; Konstantin Ramul, 1932; Paul Ranschburg, 1932; Franciscus M.J.A. Roels, 1932; Henrique de Brito Belford Roxo, 1932; Edgar J. Rubin, 1932; Hans W. Ruin, 1932; Friedrich Sander, 1932; A. L. Schniermann, 1929–1932; Mustafa Sekip, 1932; N. Sengupta, 1932; František Seřacký, 1932; Eugene Shen, 1932; C. Spearman, 1932; Dimitry Uznadze, 1932; Raymond W. Wilcocks, 1932;

618. *Psychologische Rundschau; Schweizerische Monatsschrift für das Gesamtgebiet der modernen Psychologie.*
TITLE VARIATIONS: None.
DATES OF PUBLICATION: Jahrgang 1–4, Nummer 6, 1929–1933.
FREQUENCY: Monthly.
NUMBERING VARIATIONS: None.
PUBLISHER: **Basel:** E. Birkhäuser & Cie, 1929–1933.
PRIMARY EDITOR: **K. F. Schaer,** 1929–1933.

619. *Revue de psychologie concrète. Publication internationale pour recherches de psychologie positive.*
TITLE VARIATIONS: None.
DATES OF PUBLICATION: Numéro 1–2, February and July 1929.
FREQUENCY: Quarterly (Irregular).
NUMBERING VARIATIONS: None.
PUBLISHER: **Paris:** Les Revues, 47, rue monsier-le-prince, 1929.
PRIMARY EDITOR: **G. Politzer,** 1929.

620. *Revue de psychothérapie et de psychologie appliquée.* [2.]
TITLE VARIATIONS: Continues *Revue de psychologie appliquée.* Superseded by [*Paris.*] *École de psychologie. Bulletin* with Numéro 1, 1935.
DATES OF PUBLICATION: Série 4, Année 38–43, Numéro 8, January 1929–November/December 1934.
FREQUENCY: Monthly (except August and September).
NUMBERING VARIATIONS: Also numbered in Series. Série 4 listed on Année 38 and 39 only.
PUBLISHER: **Paris:** Société de psychothérapie, d'hypnologie et de psychologie, Rédaction et administration, 8 boulevard de courcelles, 1929–1933. **Paris:** Société de psychothérapie, d'hypnologie et de psychologie, Rédaction et administration, 11 rue du printemps, 1934.
PRIMARY EDITORS: **E. Bérillon,** 1929–1934; **Paul Farez,** 1929–1934; **Pierre Vachet,** 1929–1934; **Marcel Viard,** 1934.

621. *Studien zur psychologischen Ästhetik und Kunstpsychologie mit pädagogischen Anwendungen.*
TITLE VARIATIONS: None.
DATES OF PUBLICATION: Stück [1?]–6, [1929?]–1931.
FREQUENCY: Irregular. *See* Contents *below.*

NUMBERING VARIATIONS: Also numbered as *Friedrich Manns pädagogisches Magazin. See* Contents *below.*

PUBLISHER: **Langensalza, Germany:** H. Beyer & Söhne, 1929–1931.

PRIMARY EDITOR: **Erich Rudolf Jaensch,** 1929–1931.

CONTENTS:

Stück 2. Metz, Paul. Die eidetische Anlage der Jugendlichen in ihrer Beziehung zur künstlerischen Gestaltung. 1929. 116 pp. (Also as *Friedrich Manns pädagogisches Magazin,* Heft 1252.)

Stück 4. Nolte, Reinhard. Analyse der freien Märchenproduktion. 1931. 144 pp. (Also as *Friedrich Manns pädagogisches Magazin,* Heft 1256.)

Stück 6. Leinweber, Berthold. Empirisch–psychologische Beiträge zur Typologie des dichterischen Schaffens. 1929. 96 pp. (Also as *Friedrich Manns pädagogisches Magazin,* Heft 1275.)

NOTE: Information on this entry is incomplete. The compilers were unable to locate or identify all issues. Entry is placed here since approximate date of first issue is 1929.

622. *Tashkent. Universitet. Trudy. Seriia 1c. Psikhologiia.*

TITLE VARIATIONS: Full name of the University is Sredne-aziatskii gosudarstvennyi universitet. Also called Turkestanskii gosudarstvennyi universitet. French name is L'Université de l'Asie centrale. Latin title is *Universitas Asiae Mediae.*

DATES OF PUBLICATION: Vypusk 1–3, 1929–1930.

FREQUENCY: Irregular. *See* Contents *below.*

NUMBERING VARIATIONS: None.

PUBLISHER: **Tashkent:** Izdatel'stvo sredne-aziatskogo gosudarstvennogo universiteta, 1929–1930.

PRIMARY EDITORS: None listed.

CONTENTS:

Vypusk 1. Baranova, T. Materialy po razvitiiu risunka i iunoshestva i vzroslykh. II. Risunok uzbechek. 1929. 35 pp.

Vypusk 2. Baranova, T., and F. Rosenfeld. Opyt izucheniia umstvennogo razvitiia uchashchikhsia srednei azii. 1929. 97 pp.

Vypusk 3. Instituta pedagogiki i psikhologii SAGU. Metody izucheniia rebenka srednei azii. C predisloviem T. Baranova. 1930.

623. *Tidskrift för psykologisk och pedagogisk forskning.*

TITLE VARIATIONS: None.

DATES OF PUBLICATION: Band 1–3, Nummer 2, 1929–1931.

FREQUENCY: **Triannual,** Band 1–2, 1929–1930. **Irregular,** Band 3, Nummer 1–2, 1931.

NUMBERING VARIATIONS: Supplement issued in 1930. *See* Contents *below.*

PUBLISHER: **Helsingfors:** Allmänna pressbyrån, 1929–1931.

PRIMARY EDITOR: **Karl Bruhn,** 1929–1931.

CONTENTS:

Supplement. Hassler-Göransson, Carita. EXPERIMENTELLA OCH STATIS-
TISKA STUDIER ÖVER ORDFÖRRÅD OCH RÄTTSTAVNINGSFÄRDIGHET. 1930. 93 pp.

624. *Voprosy geneticheskoi refleksologii i pedologii mladenschestva.*

TITLE VARIATIONS: None.

DATES OF PUBLICATION: Tom 1, 1929.

FREQUENCY: Irregular.

NUMBERING VARIATIONS: None.

PUBLISHER: **Moscow** and **Leningrad:** Unknown, 1929.

PRIMARY EDITORS: Unknown.

NOTE: Above entry based on partial information. The compilers were unable
to examine this title.

625. *Voprosy pedologii i detskoi psikhonevrologii.*

TITLE VARIATIONS: None.

DATES OF PUBLICATION: Tom 1–4, Vypusk 3, [192?]–1932.

FREQUENCY: Unknown.

NUMBERING VARIATIONS: None.

PUBLISHER: **Moscow:** Unknown.

PRIMARY EDITORS: Unknown.

NOTE: Information on this entry is incomplete. The compilers were unable to
examine this title. First year of publication is uncertain. The entry has been
placed here since approximate first date of issue is 1929.

626. *World Book Company. Department of Research and Test Service. Test Service Bulletin.*

TITLE VARIATIONS: Department was evenutally renamed Division of Test Research and Service.

DATES OF PUBLICATION: Number 1–70+, [192?]–1950+.

FREQUENCY: Irregular.

NUMBERING VARIATIONS: None.

PUBLISHER: **Yonkers-on-Hudson, New York:** World Book Company, dates
uncertain.

PRIMARY EDITORS: **Walter N. Durost,** to 1950+; **Arthur S. Otis,** to 1950+;
Roger T. Lennon, to 1950+.

NOTE: Above entry is based on partial information. The compilers were unable
to examine this title. First year of publication is uncertain. The entry has been
placed here since approximate first date of issue is 1929.

627. **World Book Company. Department of Research and Test Service. Test Service Notebook.**

TITLE VARIATIONS: Department was eventually renamed Division of Test Research and Service.

DATES OF PUBLICATION: Number 1–[?], [192?]–1950 + .

FREQUENCY: Irregular.

NUMBERING VARIATIONS: None.

PUBLISHER: **Yonkers-on-Hudson, New York:** World Book Company, dates uncertain.

PRIMARY EDITORS: **Roger T. Lennon** (Director), to 1950 + ; **Walter N. Durost** (Consultant), to 1950 + ; **Arthur S. Otis** (Consultant), to 1950 + .

NOTE: Above entry is based on partial information. The compilers were unable to examine this title. First year of publication is uncertain. The entry has been placed here since approximate first date of issue is 1929.

628. *Zeitschrift für Religionspsychologie. Sonderhefte.*

TITLE VARIATIONS: Also titled *Religionspsychologie. Beihefte*, Heft 1–2.

DATES OF PUBLICATION: Heft 1–5, 1929–1937.

FREQUENCY: Irregular. *See* Contents *below*.

NUMBERING VARIATIONS: None.

PUBLISHER: **Gütersloh, Germany:** C. Bertelsmann, 1929. **Vienna:** Verlag der Internationalen religionspsychologischen Gesellschaft, 1935–1937.

PRIMARY EDITOR: **Karl Beth,** 1929–1937.

CONTENTS:

Heft 1. Römer, Alfred. DAS BEDÜRFNIS NACH SINNHAFTIGKEIT DES LEBENS. PSYCHOLOGISCHE ERHEBUNGEN UNTER DEN BESUCHERN VON VÖLKSBILDUNGSKURSEN. 1929. 105 pp.

Heft 2. Thimme, Wilhelm. AUGUSTINS SELBSTBILNIS IN DEN KONFESSIONEN. EINE RELIGIONSPSYCHOLOGISCHE STUDIE. 1929. 112 pp.

Heft 3. Weindl, Theodor. MONOTHEISMUS UND DUALISMUS IN INDIEN, IRAN UND PALÄSTINA ALS RELIGION JUNGER, KRIEGERISCH-NOMADISTISCHEN VÖLKER. 1935. 137 pp.

Heft 4. Kiefer, Robert. NIETZSCHE ALS RELIGIONSPSYCHOLOGE. 1937. 75 pp.

Heft 5. Adolf, Helen. WORTGESCHICHTLICHE STUDIEN ZUM LEIB/SEELE-PROBLEM. 1937. 114 pp.

629. *Zeitschrift für Volkskunde.*

TITLE VARIATIONS: Continues *Verein für Volkskunde. Zeitschrift. Neue Folge der Zeitschrift für Völkerpsychologie und Sprachwissenschaft.*

DATES OF PUBLICATION: Band 39–49, 1929/1930–1940. Suspended publication 1941–1952.

FREQUENCY: **Triannual,** Neue Folge, Band 1–6, 1929/1930–1934. **Quarterly,** Neue Folge, Band 7–11, 1935–1940.

NUMBERING VARIATIONS: Also numbered Neue Folge, Band 1–11.

PUBLISHER: **Berlin:** W. de Gruyter & Co. 1929/1930–1939. **Bin-Dahlem:** Ahnenerbe-Stiftung Verlag, 1940.

PRIMARY EDITORS: **Johannes Bolte,** 1929–1930; **Fritz Böhm,** 1929–1937; **Heinrich Harmjanz,** 1937–1940; **Gunther Ipsen,** 1937–1939; **Erich Röhr,** 1937–1940.

....
....

....
.. ..
....

....
.. ..
.. ..

1930-1939

630. *Acta Psychologica Keijo.*

TITLE VARIATIONS: None.

DATES OF PUBLICATION: Volume 1–3, Number 2, December 1930–March 1939.

FREQUENCY: Irregular. In 1930, 1 issue; 1931, 2; 1932, 1; 1933, 2; 1934, 1; 1935, 1; 1936, 1; 1937, 1; 1939, 1.

NUMBERING VARIATIONS: None.

PUBLISHER: **Keijo:** Keijo Teikoku Daigaku [Keijo Imperial University], 1930–1939.

PRIMARY EDITOR: [**Ryo Kuroda,**] 1930–1939.

NOTE: Abstracts of some articles are in English.

631. *Almanach der Psychoanalyse.*

TITLE VARIATIONS: Continues *Almanach.*

DATES OF PUBLICATION: Band 5–13, 1930–1938.

FREQUENCY: Annual.

For serial publications that began before 1930 and were still being published during the decade 1930 to 1939, *see also* entries 32, 50, 73, 74, 79, 84, 90, 96, 112, 119, 121, 122, 131, 135, 140, 153, 163, 169, 177, 181, 190, 196, 210, 215, 223, 229, 234, 236, 237, 249, 251, 267, 270, 275, 281, 285, 288, 290, 295, 306, 309, 313, 317, 320, 324, 327, 333, 334, 346, 350, 353, 354, 355, 356, 357, 359, 361, 366, 368, 369, 370, 373, 374, 376, 377, 378, 380, 383, 392, 393, 394, 397, 398, 399, 400, 401, 402, 410, 411, 412, 413, 414, 416, 417, 419, 420, 422, 423, 425, 426, 427, 428, 432, 433, 438, 439, 441, 445, 447, 449, 450, 451, 455, 456, 458, 459, 460, 461, 463, 465, 466, 472, 473, 479, 481, 482, 483, 486, 487, 488, 489, 490, 495, 496, 499, 501, 502, 503, 505, 510, 511, 512, 513, 514, 516, 518, 519, 520, 521, 524, 525, 526, 527, 529, 533, 534, 535, 536, 538, 539, 541, 542, 543, 544, 549, 550, 551, 552, 553, 555, 556, 558, 559, 560, 561, 563, 564, 566, 567, 568, 569, 570, 574, 575, 576, 578, 579, 580, 582, 583, 584, 585, 586, 588, 590, 593, 594, 595, 596, 598, 602, 603, 604, 605, 606, 607, 608, 609, 611, 612, 613, 614, 615, 616, 617, 618, 620, 621, 622, 623, 625, 626, 627, 628, 629.

NUMBERING VARIATIONS: None.

PUBLISHER: **Vienna:** Internationaler psychoanalytischer Verlag, 1930–1938.

PRIMARY EDITOR: **Adolf Josef Storfer,** 1930–1938.

632. *American Journal of Orthopsychiatry; A Journal of Human Behavior.* [Official organ of the American Orthopsychiatric Association.]

TITLE VARIATIONS: None.

DATES OF PUBLICATION: Volume 1–20+, October 1930–October 1950+.

FREQUENCY: Quarterly.

NUMBERING VARIATIONS: Volume 1 has five issues.

PUBLISHER: **Menasha, Wisconsin:** George Banta Publishing Company [for] American Orthopsychiatric Association, 1930–1950+.

PRIMARY EDITORS: **Lawson G. Lowrey,** 1930–1948; **Herman Adler,** 1930–1935; **Augusta Bronner,** 1930–1937; **Porter R. Lee,** 1930–1937; **Harvey Zorbaugh,** 1930–1935; **William Healy,** 1936–1937; **Samuel J. Beck,** 1936–1944; **Bertha C. Reynolds,** 1936–1937; **Phyllis Bartelme,** 1938; **Anna Belle Tracy,** 1938–1940; **Ira S. Wile,** 1938–1943; **Helen Witmer,** 1938–1940; **Forrest N. Anderson,** 1939–1943; **Richard L. Jenkins,** 1942–1944; **Irma E. Mohr,** 1942–1944; **W. Mason Mathews,** 1942–1943; **Jules Henry,** 1944; **Milton E. Kirkpatrick,** 1944; **Jean Walker MacFarlane,** 1944; **Victoria Sloane,** 1945–1949; **George E. Gardner,** 1949–1950+.

EDITORIAL BOARD: Samuel J. Beck, 1945–1947, 1950+; Jules Henry, 1945–1950+; Richard L. Jenkins, 1945–1950+; Milton E. Kirkpatrick, 1945; Jean Walker MacFarlane, 1945; Irma E. Mohr, 1945; Arthur L. Beeley, 1946–1947; Louis A. Lurie, 1946–1950+; Adolf G. Woltmann, 1946–1950+; Helen Speyer, 1946–1950+; Sol W. Ginsburg, 1948–1950+; Nina Ridenour, 1950+; David Shakow, 1950+.

633. *Buenos Aires. Sociedad de psicología. Boletín.*

TITLE VARIATIONS: Superseded by [*Buenos Aires.*] *Sociedad de psicología. Anales* with Tomo 1, 1933/1935.

DATES OF PUBLICATION: Tomo 1, 1930–1932.

FREQUENCY: Irregular.

NUMBERING VARIATIONS: None.

PUBLISHER: **Buenos Aires:** Talleres gráficos de la penitenciaria nacional, 1933.

PRIMARY EDITORS: **Osvaldo Loudet,** 1933; **Américo Foradori,** 1933.

634. *Child Development.*

TITLE VARIATIONS: None.

DATES OF PUBLICATION: Volume 1–21+, 1930–1950+.

FREQUENCY: Quarterly.

NUMBERING VARIATIONS: Double-number issues 1944–1948.

PUBLISHER: **Baltimore:** Williams & Wilkins Co., 1930–1935. **Washington, D.C.:** Society for Research in Child Development, National Research Council, 1936–1948. **Evanston, Illinois:** Child Development Publications (of the Society for Research in Child Development), 1949–1950 + .

EDITORIAL BOARD: Buford Johnson, 1930–1937; **John E. Anderson,** 1930–1935; **E. V. McCollum,** 1930–1950 + ; **Edwards A. Park,** 1930–1935; **Mandel Sherman,** 1930–1947, 1949; **T. Wingate Todd,** 1930–1938; **Frederick F. Tisdall,** 1936–1949; **Harold E. Jones,** 1936–1950 + ; **F. Stuart Chapin,** 1936–1941; **Carroll E. Palmer,** 1938–1948; **Richard E. Scammon,** 1939–1950 + ; **T. W. Richards,** 1949–1950 + .

635. *International Congress on Mental Hygiene. Proceedings.*

TITLE VARIATIONS: *See* Contents *below.*

DATES OF PUBLICATION: 1st–3rd + , 1930–1948 + . Proceedings from the 4th Congress were published in 1952.

FREQUENCY: Irregular. *See* Contents *below.*

NUMBERING VARIATIONS: None.

PUBLISHER: *See* Contents *below.*

PRIMARY EDITORS: *See* Contents *below.*

CONTENTS:

    1st. Washington, D.C., 1930. PROCEEDINGS OF THE FIRST INTERNATIONAL CONGRESS ON MENTAL HYGIENE, HELD AT WASHINGTON, D.C., MAY 5TH TO 10TH, 1930. Edited by Frankwood E. Williams. New York: The International Committee for Mental Hygiene, Inc., 1932. 2 Volumes. 803 pp., 840 pp.

    2nd. Paris, 1937. IIe CONGRÈS INTERNATIONAL D'HYGIÈNE MENTALE, 19–23 JUILLET 1937. COMPTES RENDUS. Edited by René Charpentier. Cahors: Imprimerie A. Coueslant, 1937. 2 Volumes. 437 pp., 461 pp.

    3rd. London, 1948. INTERNATIONAL CONGRESS ON MENTAL HEALTH. PROCEEDINGS. 4 Volumes: I. HISTORY, DEVELOPMENT AND ORGANISATION; II. PROCEEDINGS OF THE INTERNATIONAL CONFERENCE ON CHILD PSYCHIATRY, 11TH–14TH AUGUST; III. PROCEEDINGS OF THE INTERNATIONAL CONFERENCE ON MEDICAL PSYCHOTHERAPY, 11TH–14TH AUGUST; IV. PROCEEDINGS OF THE INTERNATIONAL CONFERENCE ON MENTAL HYGIENE, 16TH–21ST AUGUST. Edited by J. C. Flugel. Associate editors: E. M. Goldberg, Mary Cockett. Programme Secretary: S. Clement Brown. London: H. K. Lewis; New York: Columbia University Press, 1948. 154 pp., 142 pp., 129 pp., 330 pp.

636. *Internationale Zeitschrift für Individualpsychologie. Beihefte.*

TITLE VARIATIONS: None.

DATES OF PUBLICATION: Band 1–6, 1930–1931.

FREQUENCY: Irregular. *See* Contents *below*.

NUMBERING VARIATIONS: None.

PUBLISHER: **Leipzig:** Verlag von S. Hirzel, 1930–1931.

PRIMARY EDITORS: **Alfred Adler,** 1930–1931; **Lad. Zilahi,** 1930–1931.

CONTENTS:
> **Band 1.** Adler, Alfred. DAS PROBLEM DER HOMOSEXUALITÄT: EROTISCHES TRAINING UND EROTISCHER RÜCKZUG. .1930. 110 pp.
> **Band 2.** Wexberg, Erwin. EINFÜHRUNG IN DIE PSYCHOLOGIE DES GESCHLECHTSLEBENS. 1930. 120 pp.
> **Band 3.** Dreikurs, Rudolf. SEELISCHE IMPOTENZ. 1931. 131 pp.
> **Band 4.** Holub, Arthur. DIE LEHRE VON DER ORGANMINDERWERTIGKEIT. 1931. 91 pp.
> **Band 5.** Birnbaum, Ferdinand. DIE SEELISCHEN GEFAHREN DES KINDES. 1931. 123 pp.
> **Band 6.** Künkel, Fritz. EINE ANGSTNEUROSE UND IHRE BEHANDLUNG. 1931. 70 pp.

637. *Journal of Social Psychology; Political, Racial, and Differential Psychology.*

TITLE VARIATIONS: Subtitle ceases with Volume 30, 1949.

DATES OF PUBLICATION: Volume 1–31+, February 1930–1950+.

FREQUENCY: Quarterly.

NUMBERING VARIATIONS: Volumes 10–20 contain the continuation of *Society for Psychological Study of Social Issues. Bulletin.*

PUBLISHER: **Worcester, Massachusetts:** Clark University Press, 1930–1936. **Provincetown, Massachusetts:** The Journal Press, 1937–1950+.

PRIMARY EDITORS: **John Dewey,** 1930–1940; **Carl Murchison,** 1930–1950+; **Luberta M. Harden,** 1930–1933.

EDITORIAL BOARD: Franz Boas, 1930–1942; Floyd H. Allport, 1930–1950+; Trigant Burrow, 1930–1950+; Havelock Ellis, 1930–1938; Franklin H. Giddings, 1930–1934; G. Dawes Hicks, 1930–1940; A. Hrdlicka, 1930–1943; Charles H. Judd, 1930–1946; K. Kornilov, 1930–1950+; L. Lévy-Bruhl, 1930–1950+; Mark A. May, 1930–1950+; William McDougall, 1930–1938; Raymond Pearl, 1930–1940; Walter B. Pillsbury, 1930–1950+; A. T. Poffenberger, 1930–1950+; Bertrand Russell, 1930–1950+; Carl E. Seashore, 1930; Guiseppe Sergi, 1930–1937; L. L. Thurstone, 1930–1950+; Clark Wissler, 1930–1947; David Katz, 1931–1950+; Richard Müller-Freienfels, 1931–1945; Edward Sapir, 1931–1938; Kimball Young, 1931–1950+; Gardner Murphy, 1935–1950+; Edward F. Robinson, 1935–1936; Harold E. Burtt, 1938–1950+; Goodwin Watson, 1938–1950+; Paul Thomas Young, 1938–1950+; John Dewey, 1941–1950+.

638. *Kwartalnik psychologiczny.*

TITLE VARIATIONS: None.

DATES OF PUBLICATION: Tom 1–12, Numer 1, 1930–1939.

FREQUENCY: Quarterly.

NUMBERING VARIATIONS: Multinumber issues present.

PUBLISHER: **Poznan:** Poznańskie towarzystwo psychologiczne, 1930–1933. **Poznan:** Poznańskie towarzystwo psychologiczne z zasiłku funduszu kultury narodowej, 1934–1939.

PRIMARY EDITOR: **Stefan Błachowski,** 1930–1939.

NOTE: Although this cannot be verified in the United States, a Tom 13/14 may also have been issued in 1947/1948.

639. *Mentsh vissenshaft.*

TITLE VARIATIONS: English title is *Psychological Science of Man. A Quarterly Journal in Yiddish for Research into the Normal and Abnormal Psychical Life.*

DATES OF PUBLICATION: Volume 1, Number 1–2/3, April 1930–March 1931.

FREQUENCY: Irregular.

NUMBERING VARIATIONS: Multinumber issue present.

PUBLISHER: **New York:** F. Schneersohn, 22 W. 88th St., Science of Man Press, 1930–1931.

PRIMARY EDITOR: **F. Schneersohn,** 1930–1931.

640. *Minnesota. University. Institute of Child Welfare. Circulars. (Series 2).*

TITLE VARIATIONS: Supersedes [*Minnesota. University.*] *Institute of Child Welfare. Circulars. (Series 1).*

DATES OF PUBLICATION: Number 1–6, 1930–1936.

FREQUENCY: Irregular. *See* Contents *below.*

NUMBERING VARIATIONS: None.

PUBLISHER: **Minneapolis:** Institute of Child Welfare, 1930–1936.

PRIMARY EDITORS: None listed.

CONTENTS:

Number 1. McGinnis, Esther. A MANUAL FOR THE ORGANIZATION OF STUDY GROUPS. September 1931 (rev. ed.). 25 pp.

Number 2. PUBLICATIONS OF THE INSTITUTE OF CHILD WELFARE. January 1930 (rev. ed.). 8 pp.

Number 3. Chapin, F. Stuart. SCALE FOR RATING LIVING ROOM EQUIPMENT. January 1930. 4 pp.

Number 4. THE SLEEP OF YOUNG CHILDREN. REPORT TO THE PARENTS WHO PARTICIPATED IN THE STUDY. February 1930. 11 pp.

Number 5. Howard, Ruth W. A DEVELOPMENTAL STUDY OF TRIPLETS. REPORT TO THE PARTICIPANTS IN THE STUDY. July 1934. 14 pp.

Number 6. Foster, Josephine C., and John E. Anderson. UNPLEASANT DREAMS IN CHILDHOOD: PARENTS' VERSION. REPORT TO THE PARENTS WHO PARTICIPATED IN THE STUDY. June 1936. 8 pp.

641. *Perm. Ural'skaia oblastnaia psikhiatricheskaia lechebnitsa. Trudy.*

TITLE VARIATIONS: None.

DATES OF PUBLICATION: Vypusk 1, 1930/1931.

FREQUENCY: Irregular.

NUMBERING VARIATIONS: None.

PUBLISHER: **Perm:** Ural'skaia oblastnaia psikhiatricheskaia lechebnitsa, 1930/1931.

PRIMARY EDITORS: Unknown.

NOTE: Information on this title was compiled from entries in *Half a Century of Soviet Serials.*

642. *Religionspsychologische Reihe; Studien über Aufbau und Führung des Charakters und des religiösen Lebens.*

TITLE VARIATIONS: None.

DATES OF PUBLICATION: Band 1–2, 1930–1931.

FREQUENCY: Annual.

NUMBERING VARIATIONS: None.

PUBLISHER: **Gütersloh, Germany:** Druck und Verlag von C. Bertelsmann, 1930–1931.

PRIMARY EDITOR: **Johannes Neumann,** 1930–1931.

CONTENTS:

Band 1. Neumann, Johannes, ed. EINFÜHRUNG IN DIE PSYCHOTHERAPIE FÜR PFARRER. 1930. [2. Teil.] Pp. 1–185, 187–347.

Band 2. Neumann, Johannes, ed. DIE ENTWICKLUNG ZUR SITTLICHEN PERSÖNLICHKEIT. 1931. [4. Teil.] Pp. 1–225, 229–253, 257–378, 381–455.

643. *Riga. Jaunatnes un Arodu Piemērotibas Pētišanas Institūta. Zinojumi. A.*

TITLE VARIATIONS: Also titled *Psycho-physiologische Arbeiten*, Burtn. 1, 1930.

DATES OF PUBLICATION: Burtn. 1–2, 1930.

FREQUENCY: Semiannual.

NUMBERING VARIATIONS: None.

PUBLISHER: **Riga, Latvia:** Jaunatnes un Arodu Piemērotibas Pētišanas Institūta, 1930.

PRIMARY EDITOR: **M. Moeller,** 1930.

644. *Riga. Jaunatnes un Arodu Piemērotibas Pētišanas Institūta. Zinojumi. B.*

TITLE VARIATIONS: None.

DATES OF PUBLICATION: Burtn. 1, 1930.

FREQUENCY: Irregular.

NUMBERING VARIATIONS: None.

PUBLISHER: **Riga, Latvia:** Jaunatnes un Arodu Piemērotibas Pētišanas Institūta, 1930.

PRIMARY EDITORS: **R. Drille,** 1930; **M. Moeller,** 1930.

645. *Schriftenreihe der psychologischen Rundschau.*

TITLE VARIATIONS: None.

DATES OF PUBLICATION: Heft 1–3, 1930–1931.

FREQUENCY: Irregular. *See* Contents *below.*

NUMBERING VARIATIONS: Also numbered as articles in *Psychologische Rundschau. See* Contents *below.*

PUBLISHER: **Basel:** E. Birkhäuser & Cie, 1930–1931.

PRIMARY EDITOR: **K. F. Schaer,** 1930–1931.

CONTENTS:

Heft 1. Carrard, Alfred. ZUR PSYCHOLOGIE DER FÜHRUNG. EIN BEITRAG ZUR FRAGE DER ERTÜCHTIGUNG DER VORGESETZTEN. 1930. 21 pp. (Also as *Psychologische Rundschau,* Volume 1, 1929, pp. 301–307.)

Heft 2. Römer, Georg August. DIE WISSENSCHAFTLICHE ERSCHLIESSUNG DER INNENWELT EINER PERSÖNLICHKEIT. 1931. 42 pp. (Also, under a slightly different title, as *Psychologische Rundschau,* Volume 2, 1930, pp. 4–12, 33–41.)

Heft 3. Harms, Ernst. ZUR PÄDAGOGIK DER PSYCHOLOGIE. 1931. 14 pp. (Also as *Psychologische Rundschau,* Volume 3, 1931, pp. 41–46, 73–78.)

646. *Smith College. William Allan Neilson Research Laboratory. Studies in Psychology.*

TITLE VARIATIONS: None.

DATES OF PUBLICATION: Number 1–4, 1930–1933.

FREQUENCY: Annual.

NUMBERING VARIATIONS: All issues consist of repaginated reprints of articles published in the *Psychologische Forschung.* Some portions of issues are also numbered as *Beiträge zur Psychologie der Gestalt- und Bewegungserlebnisse*. *See* Contents *below*.

PUBLISHER: **Berlin:** Julius Springer; and **Northampton, Massachusetts:** Smith College, 1930–1933.

PRIMARY EDITOR: **Kurt Koffka,** 1930–1933.

CONTENTS:

Number 1. Huang, I. CHILDREN'S EXPLANATIONS OF STRANGE PHENOMENA. 1930. Pp. 1–118. (Also as *Psychologische Forschung*, Band 14, 1930. Pp. 63–180.)

Number 2. Koffka, K., and Alexander Mintz. ON THE INFLUENCE OF TRANSFORMATION AND CONTRAST ON COLOUR- AND BRIGHTNESS-THRESHOLDS. Pp. 119–134. (Also as *Psychologische Forschung*, Band 14, pp. 183–198; and as *Beiträge zur Psychologie der Gestalt- und Bewegungserlebnisse*, Heft 19); Sturm, Marthe. A STUDY OF THE DIRECTION IN THE MOVEMENT-AFTER-IMAGE. Pp. 135–159. (Also as *Psychologische Forschung*, Band 14, pp. 269–293; and as *Beiträge zur Psychologie der Gestalt- und Bewegungserlebnisse*, Heft 20); Harrower, Molly R. SOME EXPERIMENTS ON THE NATURE OF γ-MOVEMENT. Pp. 160–168. (Also as *Psychologische Forschung*, Band 13, pp. 55–63; and as *Beiträge zur Psychologie der Gestalt- und Bewegungserlebnisse*, Heft 18); and Mintz, Alexander. A NOTE ON THE "BLACK-WHITE PROBLEM". Pp. 169–175. (Also as *Psychologische Forschung*, Band 13, pp. 128–134.) 1931.

Number 3. Koffka, K., and M. R. Harrower. COLOUR AND ORGANIZATION. 1932. Pp. 177–303. (Also as *Psychologische Forschung*, Band 15, pp. 145–275; and as *Beiträge zur Psychologie der Gestalt- und Bewegungserlebnisse*, Heft 21–22.)

Number 4. Koffka, K. SOME REMARKS ON THE THEORY OF COLOUR CONSTANCY. Pp. 305–329. (Also as *Psychologische Forschung*, Band 16, pp. 329–354; and as *Beiträge zur Psychologie der Gestalt- und Bewegungserlebnisse*, Heft 23); Heider, Grace Moore. NEW STUDIES IN TRANSPARENCY, FORM AND COLOR. Pp. 330–371. (Also as *Psychologische Forschung*, Band 17, pp. 13–55; and as *Beiträge zur Psychologie der Gestalt- und Bewegungserlebnisse*, Heft 24); Heider, Fritz. REMARKS ON THE BRIGHTNESS PARADOX DESCRIBED BY METZGER. Pp. 372–380. (Also as *Psychologische Forschung*, Band 17, pp. 121–129); and Harrower, M. R. ORGANIZATION IN HIGHER MENTAL PROCESSES. Pp. 381–444. (Also as *Psychologische Forschung*, Band 17, pp. 56–120; and as *Beiträge zur Psychologie der Gestalt- und Bewegungserlebnisse*, Heft 25.) 1933.

647. *Test Service Bulletin.* [*1.*]

TITLE VARIATIONS: None.

DATES OF PUBLICATION: Number 1–40+. February 1930–1948/1950+.

FREQUENCY: Irregular.

NUMBERING VARIATIONS: Many combined numbers. Number 36–40, 1948–1950 contain articles reprinted from earlier issues.

PUBLISHER: **New York:** Psychological Corporation, 1930–1950+.

PRIMARY EDITORS: **W. Bennett,** 1930–1935; none listed, 1936–September 1938; **George K. Bennett,** 1938–1946; **Harold G. Seashore,** 1947–1950+.

648. *World Book Company. Department of Research and Test Service. Test Method Help.*

TITLE VARIATIONS: None.

DATES OF PUBLICATION: Number 1–4, 1930–1938.

FREQUENCY: Irregular. *See* Contents *below.*

NUMBERING VARIATIONS: None.

PUBLISHER: **Yonkers-on-Hudson, New York:** World Book Company, 1930–1938.

PRIMARY EDITORS: **Walter N. Durost,** 1930–1938; **Arthur S. Otis,** 1930–1938.

CONTENTS:

> **Number 1.** Otis, Arthur S., and Jacob S. Orleans. MANUAL FOR TRANSMUTING STANDARDIZED TEST SCORES INTO TERMS OF SCHOOL MARKS. 1930. 17 pp.
> **Number 2.** Unknown.
> **Number 3.** Unknown.
> **Number 4.** Otis, Arthur S., and Walter N. Durost. STATISTICAL METHODS APPLIED TO TEST SCORES. 1938. 32 pp.

NOTE: Above entry is based on partial information. The compilers were unable to examine this title.

649. *Zentralblatt für Psychotherapie und ihre Grenzgebiete einschliesslich der medizinischen Psychologie und psychischen Hygiene.* [Organ of the Allgemeine ärztliche Gesellschaft für Psychotherapie.]

TITLE VARIATIONS: Continues *Allgemeine ärztliche Zeitschrift für Psychotherapie und psychische Hygiene.*

DATES OF PUBLICATION: Band 3–16, Heft 1/2, 1930–January 1944.

FREQUENCY: **Monthly,** Band 3, 1930. **Bimonthly,** Band 4–16, 1931–1944.

NUMBERING VARIATIONS: Multinumber Hefte present. Double numbers in war years.

PUBLISHER: **Leipzig:** S. Hirzel, 1930–1944.

PRIMARY EDITORS: **E. Kretschmer,** 1930; **Robert Sommer,** 1930; **Rudolf Allers,** 1930; **A. Kronfeld,** 1930; **H. H. Schultz,** 1930; **Carl Gustav Jung,** 1931–1940; **Matthias Heinrich Göring,** 1936–1944.

1931

650. *Abhandlungen und Monographien zur Philosophie des Wirklichen.*

TITLE VARIATIONS: None.

DATES OF PUBLICATION: Heft 1/2–9, 1931–1939.

FREQUENCY: Irregular. *See* Contents *below.*

NUMBERING VARIATIONS: Heft 1/2 is the only multinumber issue.

PUBLISHER: **Leipzig:** Johann Ambrosius Barth, 1931–1939.

PRIMARY EDITOR: **Erich Rudolf Jaensch,** 1931–1939.

CONTENTS:

Heft 1/2. Jaensch, E. R. VORFRAGEN DER WIRKLICHKEITSPHILOSOPHIE; and Oppenheimer, Friedrich. DER KAUSALBEGRIFF IN DER NEUESTEN PHYSIK. 1931. 256 pp.

Heft 3. Grünhut, Laszlo. DAS WESEN UND DER WERT DES SEINS UND DER GRENZEN DES REINEN VERNUNFT. 1931. 271 pp.

Heft 4. Wiedling, Hans. DIE WIRKLICHKEIT DER ETHIK. 1931. 120 pp.

Heft 5. Schlink, Edm. EMOTIONALE GOTTESERLEBNISSE. 1931. 168 pp.

Heft 6. Mandel, Herm. METAPSYCHOLOGIE. 1935. 189 pp.

Heft 7. Mandel, Herm. WIRKLICHKEITSETHIK. 1937. 143 pp.

Heft 8. Vahiduddin, Syed. INDISCH-MOSLEMISHE WERTERLEBNISSE ALS PARALLELE ZU EUROPÄISCHEN KULTURWANDLUNGEN. 1937. 59 pp.

Heft 9. Schwarze, Karl. ERNST MORITZ ARNDT UND SEIN KAMPF GEGEN DEN GEISTESIDEALISMUS. 1939. 74 pp.

651. *Archiv für angewandte Psychologie.*

TITLE VARIATIONS: None.

DATES OF PUBLICATION: Band 1–2, 1931.

FREQUENCY: Semiannual.

NUMBERING VARIATIONS: None.

PUBLISHER: **Berlin:** Verlag des Archivs für angewandte Psychologie, 1931.

PRIMARY EDITOR: **Fritz Miroslav Feller,** 1931.

CONTENTS:

Band 1. Feller, Fritz Miroslav. ANTISEMITISMUS; VERSUCH EINER PSYCHO-ANALYTISCHEN LÖSUNG DES PROBLEMS. 1931. 43 pp.

Band 2. Feller, Fritz Miroslav. GESAMMELTE SCHRIFTEN ZUR EINFÜHRUNG DER PSYCHOANALYSE IN DIE WERBEPRAXIS. 1931. 160 pp.

652. *Archivio generale di biopsicologia, biopsicopatologia e biopsicoterapia. Periodico internazionale di scienza medica esatta.* [Official organ of the Istituto di biopsicoterapia di Roma.]

TITLE VARIATIONS: None.

DATES OF PUBLICATION: Volume 1–2, November 1931–January 1933.

FREQUENCY: **Irregular,** Volume 1, November 1931. **Quarterly,** Volume 2, March 1932–January 1933.

NUMBERING VARIATIONS: Volume 1 is complete in 1 issue. Multinumber issue present.

PUBLISHER: **Rome:** Tipografia (La Precisa) Cesare Calandri, 1931–1933.

PRIMARY EDITOR: **Casimiro Frank,** 1931–1933.

653. *British Journal of Educational Psychology.*

TITLE VARIATIONS: Incorporates *Forum of Education.*

DATES OF PUBLICATION: Volume 1–20 +, 1931–1950 +.

FREQUENCY: Triannual.

NUMBERING VARIATIONS: None.

PUBLISHER: **Birmingham:** British Psychological Society, Education Section, 1931. **Birmingham:** British Psychological Society and the Training College Association, 1932–1945. **Birmingham:** British Psychological Society and the Association of Teachers in Colleges and Departments of Education, 1946–1950 +.

PRIMARY EDITOR: **C. W. Valentine,** 1931–1950 +.

EDITORIAL BOARD: John Adams, 1931–1934; R. L. Archer, 1931–1950 +; Cyril Burt, 1931–1950 +; James Drever, 1931–1950; Susan Isaacs, 1931–1948; H. Crichton-Miller, 1931–1950; T. Percy Nunn, 1931–1944; H. Bompas Smith, 1931–1950 +; C. E. Spearman, 1931–1945; Godfrey Thomson, 1931–1950 +; Helen M. Wodehouse, 1931–1950 +; Charlotte Bühler, 1931–1948; I. Meyerson, 1931–1950 +; Peter Petersen, 1931–1950 +; Jean Piaget, 1931–1950 +; William Stern, 1931–1937; L. M. Terman, 1931–1950 +; E. L. Thorndike, 1931–1949; L. Wynn-Jones, 1932–1950; P. B. Ballard, 1933–1950 +; Herbert Russell Hamley, 1935–1949; Arnold Gesell, 1938–1950 +; P. E. Vernon, 1946–1950 +; Fred J. Schonell, 1948–1950 +; L. Carmichael, 1950 +.

654. *Buenos Aires. Universidad nacional. Facultad de filosofia y letras. Archivos del laboratorio de facultad de filosofia y letras psicológicas.*

TITLE VARIATIONS: None.

DATES OF PUBLICATION: [Número 1,] 1931.

FREQUENCY: Irregular.

NUMBERING VARIATIONS: Publication unnumbered on title page.

PUBLISHER: **Buenos Aires:** Imprinta de la Universidad, 1931.

PRIMARY EDITORS: None listed.

655. *Deutsche Gesellschaft für Psychologie. Kongress. Bericht.*

TITLE VARIATIONS: Continues *Kongress für experimentelle Psychologie. Bericht.*

DATES OF PUBLICATION: Nummer 12–17/18+, 1931–1948/1951+. Suspended publication, 1939–1947.

FREQUENCY: **Biennial,** Nummer 12–13, 1931–1933, Nummer 15–16, 1936–1938. **Annual,** Nummer 14, 1934. Irregular, Nummer 17/18, 1948/1951.

NUMBERING VARIATIONS: Nummer 17/18, 1948/1951 published as a single issue in 1952.

PUBLISHER: **Jena:** Deutsche Gesellschaft für Psychologie, Verlag von Gustav Fischer, 1931–1936. **Leipzig:** Deutsche Gesellschaft für Psychologie, Verlag von Johann Ambrosius Barth, 1938. **Göttingen:** Deutsche Gesellschaft für Psychologie, Verlag für Psychologie, 1948/1951+.

PRIMARY EDITORS: **Gustav Kafka,** 1931; **Otto Klemm,** 1933–1938; **Albert Wellek,** 1948?–1951+.

NOTE: Numbers for 1934, 1936, 1938 also have distinctive titles: PSYCHOLOGIE DES GEMEINSCHAFTSLEBENS, 1934; GEFÜHL UND WILLE, 1936; CHARAKTER UND ERZIEHUNG, 1938.

656. *Duke University. Psychological Monographs.*

TITLE VARIATIONS: Superseded by [*Duke University.*] *Contributions to Psychological Theory* with Number 1, 1934.

DATES OF PUBLICATION: Number 1–3, 1931–1934.

FREQUENCY: Irregular. *See* Contents *below.*

NUMBERING VARIATIONS: One issue also numbered as [*Duke University.*] *Contributions to Psychological Theory. See* Contents *below.*

PUBLISHER: **Durham, North Carolina:** Duke University Press, 1931–1934.

PRIMARY EDITORS: None listed.

CONTENTS:
  Number 1. Lundholm, Helge. THE MANIC-DEPRESSIVE PSYCHOSIS. 1931. 86 pp.
  Number 2. Lundholm, Helge. SCHIZOPHRENIA. 1932. 117 pp.
  Number 3. Lundholm, Helge. CONATION AND OUR CONSCIOUS LIFE. PROLEGOMENA TO A DOCTRINE OF URGE PSYCHOLOGY. 1934. 96 pp. (Also as [*Duke University.*] *Contributions to Psychological Theory,* Number 1.)

657. *Individual Psychology Publications. Medical Pamphlets.*

TITLE VARIATIONS: Continued by *Individual Psychology Pamphlets* with Number 9, 1933.

DATES OF PUBLICATION: Number 1–8, 1931–1933.

FREQUENCY: Quarterly.

NUMBERING VARIATIONS: Supplementary pamphlets, dealing with special subjects and published on behalf of individual authors, are numbered with the addition of a roman letter to the arabic numeral denoting the quarterly issue with which they are linked. *See* Contents *below.*

PUBLISHER: **London:** C. W. Daniel Company for the Medical Society of Individual Psychology (London), 1931–1933.

PRIMARY EDITORS: **F. G. Crookshank,** 1931–1933; **Hilda Weber,** 1931–1933; **W. Beran Wolfe,** 1931–1933.

CONTENTS:

Number 1. Adler, Alfred. THE CASE OF MRS. A. (THE DIAGNOSIS OF A LIFE-STYLE). 1931. 48 pp.

Number 2. Brown, W. Langdon, F. G. Crookshank, J. C. Young, George Gordon, and C. M. Bevan-Brown. ANOREXIA NERVOSA. A DISCUSSION. 1931. 63 pp.

Number 3. Adler, Alfred, Rudolf Dreikurs, Erwin Wexberg, ———— Hervat, J. C. Young, F. G. Crookshank, Mary C. Luff et al. INDIVIDUAL PSYCHOLOGY AND SEXUAL DIFFICULTIES (1). 1932. 72 pp.

Number 3a. Crookshank, F. G. INDIVIDUAL PSYCHOLOGY, MEDICINE, AND THE BASES OF SCIENCE. January 1932. 72 pp.

Number 4. Brown, W. Langdon, O. H. Woodcock, J. C. Young, S. Vere Pearson, M. B. Ray, M. Robb, and F. G. Crookshank. INDIVIDUAL PSYCHOLOGY AND PSYCHOSOMATIC DISORDERS (1). April 1932. 71 pp.

Number 5. Adler, Alfred, W. Beran Wolfe, C.L.C. Burns, and J. C. Young. INDIVIDUAL PSYCHOLOGY AND SOCIAL PROBLEMS (1). July 1932. 64 pp.

Number 6. Wexberg, Erwin, Olga Knopf, and H. C. Squires. INDIVIDUAL PSYCHOLOGY AND PRACTICE (1). October 1932. 64 pp.

Number 7. Seif, Leonhard, Doris Rayner, and Agnes Zilahi. INDIVIDUAL PSYCHOLOGY AND THE CHILD (1). January 1933. 64 pp.

Number 8. Hutton, Laura, Hilda Weber, and W. Beran Wolfe. INDIVIDUAL PSYCHOLOGY AND THE CHILD (II). April 1933. 64 pp.

Number 8a. Seif, Leonhard. INDIVIDUAL PSYCHOLOGY AND LIFE-PHILOSOPHY. 1933.

658. *Monographien zur Ethno-Psychologie.*

TITLE VARIATIONS: None

DATES OF PUBLICATION: Stück 1, 1931.

FREQUENCY: Irregular. *See* Contents *below.*

NUMBERING VARIATIONS: None.

PUBLISHER: **Neubrandenburg, Germany:** G. Feller, 1931.

PRIMARY EDITORS: **Felix Bryk,** 1931. **C. L. Hansen,** 1931.

CONTENTS:

Stück 1. Bryk, Felix. DIE BESCHNEIDUNG BEI MANN UND WEIB. 1931. 319 pp.

659. *New York. National Advisory Council on Radio in Education. Listener's Notebook.*

TITLE VARIATIONS: None.

DATES OF PUBLICATION: Number 1–6, 1931–1932.

FREQUENCY: Monthly.

NUMBERING VARIATIONS: None.

PUBLISHER: **Chicago:** University of Chicago Press, 1931–1932.

PRIMARY EDITORS: **Henry E. Garrett,** 1931; **Florence L. Goodenough,** 1931; **Walter V. Bingham,** 1931–1932; **F. A. Moss,** 1932; **Carl J. Warden,** 1932; **Frank N. Freeman,** 1932.

CONTENTS:
    Number 1. PSYCHOLOGY TODAY. 1931. 43 pp.
    Number 2. CHILD DEVELOPMENT. 1931. 47 pp.
    Number 3. OUR CHANGING PERSONALITIES. 1932. 32 pp.
    Number 4. ANIMAL BEHAVIOR. 1932. 32 pp.
    Number 5. PSYCHOLOGY OF EDUCATION. 1932. 32 pp.
    Number 6. PSYCHOLOGY AND INDUSTRY. 1932. 36 pp.

660. *New York. National Advisory Council on Radio in Education. Psychology Series Lecture.*

TITLE VARIATIONS: None.

DATES OF PUBLICATION: Number 1–30, October 17, 1931–May 21, 1932.

FREQUENCY: Weekly.

NUMBERING VARIATIONS: Number 1–10 unnumbered. Ordered by date of lecture. Number 11 dated January 10, 1932 should be January 9, 1932. Series is divided into 6 subseries: Number 1–5 entitled *Psychology Today;* Number 6–10 entitled *Child Development;* Number 11–15 entitled *Our Changing Personalities;* Number 16–20 entitled *Animal Behavior;* Number 21–25 entitled *Psychology of Education,* and Number 26–30 entitled *Psychology and Industries.* The complete set of 30 lectures was also collected and issued as: Bingham, W. V., ed. *Psychology Today.* Chicago: University of Chicago Press, 1932. 271 pp.

PUBLISHER: **Chicago:** University of Chicago Press, 1931–1932.

EDITORIAL COMMITTEE: **Paul S. Achilles,** 1931–1932; **Arthur I. Gates,** 1931–1932; **Walter V. Bingham,** 1931–1932.

CONTENTS:
    [Number 1.] Angell, James R. PSYCHOLOGY TODAY. October 17, 1931. 8 pp.
    [Number 2.] Miles, Walter R. PSYCHOLOGY: THE MODERN SCIENCE OF HUMAN MANAGEMENT. October 24, 1931. 9 pp.
    [Number 3.] Robinson, Edward S. LEARNING AND FORGETTING. October 31, 1931. 10 pp.

[**Number 4.**] Murphy, Gardner. OUR SOCIAL ATTITUDES. November 7, 1931. 8 pp.

[**Number 5.**] Woodworth, Robert S. OLD PREJUDICES AND NEW SCHOOLS IN PSYCHOLOGY. November 14, 1931. 9 pp.

[**Number 6.**] Gesell, Arnold. THE GROWTH OF THE INFANT MIND. November 21, 1931. 8 pp.

[**Number 7.**] Jones, Harold E. CHILDREN'S FEARS. November 28, 1931. 8 pp.

[**Number 8.**] Goodenough, Florence L. ANGER: ITS CAUSES AND CONTROL. December 5, 1931. 8 pp.

[**Number 9.**] Anderson, John E. SOCIAL BEHAVIOR IN INFANCY AND CHILDHOOD. December 12, 1931. 9 pp.

[**Number 10.**] Hollingworth, Leta S. ADOLESCENCE: THE DIFFICULT AGE. December 19, 1931. 8 pp.

Number 11. Moss, Fred A. TRANSIENT CHANGES IN PERSONALITY. January 9, 1932. 9 pp.

Number 12. Watson, John B. HOW TO GROW A PERSONALITY. January 16, 1932. 9 pp.

Number 13. Landis, Carney. GROWING OLDER. January 23, 1932. 7 pp.

Number 14. Allport, Floyd H. PERSONALITY IN OUR CHANGING SOCIETY. January 30, 1932. 8 pp.

Number 15. Moss, F. A. MENDING BROKEN PERSONALITIES. February 6, 1932. 9 pp.

Number 16. Nissen, Henry W. THE GREAT APES. February 13, 1932. 8 pp.

Number 17. Cannon, Walter B. EFFECTS OF STRONG EMOTIONS. February 20, 1932. 8 pp.

Number 18. Warden, Carl J. ANIMAL DRIVES. February 27, 1932. 8 pp.

Number 19. Hunter, Walter S. HOW ANIMALS LEARN. March 5, 1932. 9 pp.

Number 20. Thorndike, Edward L. INTELLIGENCE OF ANIMALS AND MEN. March 12, 1932. 7 pp.

Number 21. Judd, Charles H. PSYCHOLOGY OF READING. March 19, 1932. 8 pp.

Number 22. Dearborn, Walter F. DIFFICULTIES IN LEARNING. March 26, 1932. 9 pp.

Number 23. Freeman, Frank N. THE BASES OF LEARNING. April 2, 1932. 9 pp.

Number 24. Seashore, Carl E. THE PSYCHOLOGY OF MUSICAL SKILLS. April 9, 1932. 8 pp.

Number 25. Henmon, V.A.C. INDIVIDUAL DIFFERENCES: THEIR MEASUREMENT AND SIGNIFICANCE. April 16, 1932. 10 pp.

Number 26. Thorndike, Edward L. EFFECTS OF PUNISHMENT AND OF REWARD. April 23, 1932. 6 pp.

Number 27. Mayo, Elton. THE PROBLEM OF WORKING TOGETHER. April 30, 1932. 9 pp.

Number 28. Viteles, Morris S. MACHINES AND MONOTONY. May 7, 1932. 9 pp.

Number 29. O'Rourke, L. J. MATCHING MEN AND OCCUPATIONS. May 14, 1932. 13 pp.

Number 30. Bingham, Walter V. MAKING WORK WORTH WHILE. May 21, 1932. 10 pp.

661. *Peking. National Tsing Hua University. Science Reports. Series B: Biological and Psychological Sciences.*

TITLE VARIATIONS: University's Chinese name is Kuo li Ch'ing-hua ta hsüeh [National Ch'ing-hua University]. Also called Ch'ing-hua ta hsüeh [Ch'ing-hua University]; and previously called Ch'ing-hua hsüeh hsi'ao [Ch'ing-hua College].

DATES OF PUBLICATION: Volume 1–2, Number 3, January 1931–March 1937.

FREQUENCY: Irregular. Volume 1, Number 1, January 15, 1931; Number 2, July 1, 1931; Number 3, December 1, 1931; Number 4, July 1, 1932; Number 5, December 1, 1932; Number 6, February 10, 1934; Volume 2, Number 1, May 10, 1934; Number 2, July 10, 1936; Number 3, March 1, 1937.

NUMBERING VARIATIONS: Volume 1, Number 4 incorrectly numbered Volume 2, Number 2.

PUBLISHER: **Peking**: Ch'ing-hua ta hsüeh [Ch'ing-hua University], 1931–1937.

PRIMARY EDITORS: Jointly edited by the faculty members in the departments of Biology and Psychology.

NOTE: Publication is primarily in English. Main entry is therefore in English.

662. *Psychiatrisch-juridisch gezelschap. Verslagen.*

TITLE VARIATIONS: None.

DATES OF PUBLICATION: Nummer 1–30+, 1931–1949+.

FREQUENCY: Irregular. *See* Contents *below.*

NUMBERING VARIATIONS: Nummer 18 never published. Nummer 28 and 29 published without numbers.

PUBLISHER: **Amsterdam:** F. van Rossen, 1931–1949+.

PRIMARY EDITORS: None listed.

CONTENTS:

Nummer 1. Meyers, F. S. DE GEESTELIJKE HYGIËNE EN HARE BETEEKENIS VOOR ONZE SAMENLEVING. 1931. 16 pp.

Nummer 2. Roels, F. DE TAAK VAN DEN PSYCHOLOOG IN HET STRAFPROCESS; Bouman, L. DE ROL VAN DE PSYCHOLOGIE IN HET STRAFGEDING; and Pompe, W. DE BEWARING. 1932. 35 pp.

Nummer 3. van Mesdag, S. BRANDSTICHTING; Siolo, F. DIE PSYCHIATRISCHE BEGUTACHTUNG DES DÜSSELDORFER MÖRDERS PETER KÜRTEN. 1932. 62 pp.

Nummer 4. Staub, Hugo. PSYCHOANALYSE UND STRAFRECHT. 1932. 7 pp.

Nummer 5. Rombouts, J. M. DE KRANKZINNIGHEIDSVERKLARING BIJ PARANOIDE EN QUERULERENDE PERSONEN; and Barnhoorn, J.A.J. MOEILIJKHEDEN BIJ DE PRACTISCHE UITVOERING DER PSYCHOPATHENWET. 1932. 44 pp.

Nummer 6. Stärcke, A. PSYCHO-ANALYTISCHE EN ANDERE BESCHOUWINGEN OVER SCHULD EN STRAF. 1932. 42 pp.

Nummer 7. Frets, G. P. STERILISATIE; and van Bemmelen, J. M. VOOR-EN NADEELEN VAN EEN WETTELIJKE REGELING DER STERILISATIE EN CASTRATIE. 1933. 52 pp.

Nummer 8. Carp, E.A.D.E. and A. J. Marx. HET EXHIBITIONISME IN ZIJN PSYCHOPATHOLOGISCHE EN FORENSISCHE BETEEKENIS. 1933. 35 pp.

Nummer 9. Casparie, J. BESCHOUWINGEN OVER DE CRIMINALITEIT IN OSS E. O. VERGELEKEN BIJ DIE IN ANDERE CENTRA VAN NOORD-BRABANT. 1934. 27 pp.

Nummer 10. Röling, B.V.A. LEIDENDE BEGINSELEN IN EEN WETGEVING TEGEN DE GEVAARLIJKE RECIDIVISTEN. 1934. 23 pp.

Nummer 11. Gerlings, H. Th. WIE WORDEN DOOR ONS STRAFRECHT GEGREPEN?; and Plaut, Paul. SITTLICHKEITSVERBRECHER UND IHRE FORENSISCHE BEGUTACHTUNG. 1935. 38 pp.

Nummer 12. van Geuns, S.J.M. HET PSYCHIATRISCH-PSYCHOLOGISCH ELEMENT IN DE STRAFRECHTSPRAAK; van Loon, F.H.G. PLOTSELINGE INZINKINGEN VAN HET BEWUSTZIJN ALS OORZAAK VAN AUTOONGELUKKEN; Rutgers, V. H. INDRUKKEN VAN HET BEWUSTZIJN ALS OORZAAK VAN AUTO ONGELUKKEN; and Rutgers, V. H. INDRUKKEN VAN HET "XIE CONGRÉS PÉNAL ET PÉNITENTIAIRE INTERNATIONAL" VAN 19–24 AUG. 1935 TE BERLIJN GEH. 1936. 48 pp.

Nummer 13. van Wulfften Palthe, P. M. FORENSISCHE PSYCHIATRIE IN NEDERLANDSCH-INDIË; and Westerterp, M. KORTE BESCHRIJVING VAN DE INRICHTING VAN HET RIJKS ASYL. ALGEMEENE BESCHOUWINGEN OVER PSYCHOPATHENVERZORGING INZONDERHEID IN HET RIJKS ASYL. 1936. 48 pp.

Nummer 14. Querido, Arie. EEN BIJZONDER GEVAL VAN BALDADIGE BRANDALARMEERINGEN. DE GESCHIEDENIS VAN V[ALSCH] A[LARM] M[AKEN]. 1937. 21 pp.

Nummer 15. Tenhaeff, W.H.C. PARAPHYSIOLOGIE EN CRIMINOLOGIE; and van der Esch, P., and J. de Vrieze. KRANKZINNIGHEID ALS REDEN TOT ECHTSCHEIDING. 1937. 52 pp.

Nummer 16. Meyers, F. S. MIJN ERVARINGEN BETR. ZEDENMISDADIGERS. 1938. 32 pp.

Nummer 17. Fortanier, A. H. OVER INDUCTIEPSYCHOSEN; and East, W Norwood. PSYCHIATRY AND THE CRIMINAL LAW. 1938. 35 pp.

Nummer 18. Never published.

Nummer 19. Hutter, A. MELANCHOLISCHE CRIMINALITEIT. 1939. 18 pp.

Nummer 20. van Dael, Jac. DE PSYCHOLOGIE VAN HET GETUIGENIS. 1940. 27 pp.

Nummer 21. Kempe, G. Th. OORLOG EN MISDADIGHEID. 1940. 23 pp.

Nummer 22. Spanjaard, L. GRAPHOLOGIE EN HANDSCHRIFTEN VAN MISDADIGERS; Bouman, Herman. HET MEDISCH BEROEPSGEHEIM; and Hazewinkel-Suringa, D. HET BEROEPSGEHEIM VAN DEN MEDICUS. 1940. 63 pp.

Nummer 23. Tammenoms Bakker, S. P. PSYCHO-PATHOLOGISCHE REAC-TIES IN HET HUIS VAN BEWARING TE AMSTERDAM. 1941. 23 pp.

Nummer 24. Kastein, G. W. NEUROTISCHE REACTIES BIJ VERZEKERDEN. 1941. 39 pp.

Nummer 25. Diepenhorst, I. A., and J. Wiardi. HET VRAAGSTUK VAN DE DOODSTRAF. 1946. 36 pp.

Nummer 26. Tolsma, F. J. MODERNE PSYCHIATRISCHE OPVATTINGEN OM-TRENT DE INDUCTIE-PSYCHOSE NAAR AANLEIDING VAN DEN MOORD IN RELIGIEUSE OPWINDING GEPLEEGD TE MEERKERK. 1947. 25 pp.

Nummer 27. van Oyen, H., A.L.C. Palies, and J. C. Hudig. CASTRATIE VAN PROTESTANTS ETHISCH STANDPUNT BESCHOUWD. 1948. 40 pp.

[Nummer 28 and 29] Published unnumbered.

Nummer 30. Mannheim, H. THE PLACE OF PSYCHIATRY AND PSYCHOLOGY IN THE PRESENT ENGLISH PENAL SYSTEM. 1949. 12 pp.

663. *Psychoanalytische Praxis. Vierteljahrsschrift für die aktive Methode der Psychoanalyse.*

TITLE VARIATIONS: Superseded by *Psychotherapeutische Praxis* with Band 1, 1934.

DATES OF PUBLICATION: Band 1–3, 1931–1933.

FREQUENCY: Quarterly.

NUMBERING VARIATIONS: None.

PUBLISHER: **Leipzig:** Hirzel, 1931–1933.

PRIMARY EDITORS: Wilhelm Stekel, 1931–1933; **Arthur Kronfeld,** 1931–1933.

664. *Schulreifetest.*

TITLE VARIATIONS: Continues *Wiener Arbeiten zur pädagogischen Psychologie.*

DATES OF PUBLICATION: Heft 8–9, 1931–1933.

FREQUENCY: Irregular. *See* Contents *below.*

NUMBERING VARIATIONS: None.

PUBLISHER: **Vienna:** Deutscher Verlaf für Jugend und Volk, 1931–1933.

PRIMARY EDITORS: **Charlotte Bühler,** 1931–1933; **Viktor Fadrus,** 1931–1933.

CONTENTS:

Heft 8. Rada, Margar. DAS REIFENDE PROLETARIERMÄDCHEN. 1931. 81 pp.

Heft 9. Danzinger, Lotte. DER SCHULREIFETEST MIT EINER UNTERSU-CHUNG ÜBER DIE URSACHEN DES VERSAGENS IM ERSTEN SCHULJAHR. 1933. 56 pp.

665. *Sovetskaia psikhonevrologiia.*

TITLE VARIATIONS: Continues *Sovremennaia psikhonevrologiia.*

DATES OF PUBLICATION: Tom 11, Vypusk 2–Tom 21, Typusk 3, 1931–1941.

FREQUENCY: **5 issues,** Tom 11, 1931. **Bimonthly,** Tom 12–15, 1932–1935. **Monthly,** Tom 16, 1936. **8 issues,** Tom 17, 1937. **Bimonthly,** Tom 18–20, 1938–1940. **3 issues,** Tom 21, 1941.

NUMBERING VARIATIONS: Multinumber issues present.

PUBLISHER: **Kharkov:** Medizdat, 1931–1941.

PRIMARY EDITORS: **S. I. Kantorovich,** 1931–1935(?); **M. A. Gol'denberg,** 1931–1941; **O. I. Vol'fovskii,** 1931–1941; **P. Ia. Gal'perin,** 1931–1933.

EDITORIAL BOARD: V. V. Brailovskii, 1931–1935; P. Ia. Budina, 1931–1935; Ch. Z. Vel'vovskii, 1931–1935; A. I. Geimanovich, 1931–1941; A. M. Grinshtein, 1931–1941; E. D. Guk, 1931–1934; E. S. Zatonskaia, 1931–1935; A. B. Iozefovich, 1931–1941; L. A. Kvint, 1931–1935; A. R. Luriia, 1931–1933; E. A. Popov, 1931–1941; V. P. Protopopov, 1931–1941; L. L. Rokhlin, 1931–1935; L. O. Smirnov, 1931–1941; I. N. Filimonov, 1931–1935; T. I. Iudin, 1931–1941; A. I. Iushchenko, 1931–1935; P. Ia. Gal'perin, 1934–1941; Z. Iu. Svetnik, 1934–1935; G. E. Sukhareva, 1934–1935; R. Ia. Shindel'man, 1934–1935; A. F. Neiman, 1939–1941; B. N. Man'kovskii, 1940–1941.

SUBSIDIARY EDITORS: A. L. Abashev, 1931–1935; I. A. Zalkind, 1931–1935; L. G. Karlinskii, 1931–1934; V. G. Lazarev, 1931–1935; B. N. Man'kovskii, 1931–1935; L. I. Aikhenval'd, 1931–1935; G. I. Markelov, 1931–1935; L. A. Mirel'zon, 1931–1935; M. N. Neiding, 1931–1935; E. A. Shevalev, 1931–1935; S. S. Shturman, 1931–1935; E. M. Vilenskii, 1931–1935; N. V. Mirtovskii, 1931–1935; Ia. P. Frumkin, 1934–1935.

NOTE: Portions of this entry were compiled from entries in *A Half Century of Soviet Serials.* Editorial information may be incomplete. The compilers were only able to examine part of this serial.

666. *Understanding the Child. A Magazine for Teachers.*

TITLE VARIATIONS: None.

DATES OF PUBLICATION: Volume 1–19, Number 4, January 1931–October 1950 +. Suspended publication November 1935–March 1937.

FREQUENCY: Quarterly.

NUMBERING VARIATIONS: None.

PUBLISHER: **Boston:** Massachusetts Society for Mental Hygiene, 1931–1935. **Boston:** National Committee for Mental Hygiene, 1937–1940. **Belmont, Massachusetts:** National Committee for Mental Hygiene, 1941–1942. **Chapel Hill, North Carolina:** National Committee for Mental Hygiene, 1943–1950 +. **Lancaster, Pennsylvania:** National Committee for Mental Hygiene, 1945–1950 +.

EDITORIAL BOARD: **J. Mace Andress,** 1931–1935; **E. Stanley Abbot,** 1931–1933; **Henry B. Elkind,** 1931–1942; **Walter F. Dearborn,** 1934–1935; **Judith Andress,** 1934–1935; **Richard D. Allen,** 1937–1945; **Grayson N. Kefauver,** 1937–1945; **Samuel R. Laycock,** 1937–1950 +; **William Line,** 1937–1950 +; **Esther Lloyd-Jones,** 1937–1950 +; **Bruce B. Robinson,** 1937–1950 +; **Herman**

E. Dean, 1937; T. Ernest Newland, 1939–1950+; Katharine W. Taylor, 1939–1950+; W. Carson Ryan, 1943–1950+; James L. Hymes, Jr., 1949–1950+.

667. *Za Markso-Lenins'ku pedagogiku.*

TITLE VARIATIONS: Continues *Ukrains'kyi visnyk eksperymental'noi pedagogiky ta refleksologii.*

DATES OF PUBLICATION: Vypusk 1–6, 1931 and Vypusk 1/2, 1932.

FREQUENCY: Bimonthly.

NUMBERING VARIATIONS: Volume numbering by year only. Multinumber issue present.

PUBLISHER: **Kharkov:** Ukrainskii nauchno-issledovatel'skii institut pedagogiki, 1931–1932.

PRIMARY EDITORS: Unknown.

NOTE: Information on this title was compiled from entries in *A Half Century of Soviet Serials.*

1932

668. *Academia Sinica. National Research Institute of Psychology. Contributions.*

TITLE VARIATIONS: Institute's Chinese name is Chung-yang yen chiu yüan. Hsin li hsüeh yen chiu so [Central Research Institute. Research Institute of Psychology].

DATES OF PUBLICATION: Number 1–3, July 1932–1933.

FREQUENCY: Irregular.

NUMBERING VARIATIONS: None.

PUBLISHER: **Peking:** National Research Institute of Psychology, 1932. **Shanghai:** National Research Institute of Psychology, 1933.

PRIMARY EDITORS: None listed.

CONTENTS:
Number 1. T'ang, Yueh, Kung Ch'in, and Yu Hai Tsang. THE EFFECT OF A VEGETARIAN DIET ON THE LEARNING ABILITY OF ALBINO RATS. 1932. 22 pp.
Number 2. Loo, Yu-Tao. POSTNATAL MYELOGENESIS OF THE CEREBRAL CORTEX. 1932. 14 pp.
Number 3. Chu, Ho-Nien. ON THE CENTRAL NERVOUS SYSTEM OF THE ALBINO RATS FED WITH NORMAL AND VEGETARIAN DIETS. 1933. 16 pp.

NOTE: Publication is in English. Main entry is therefore in English.

669. *Academia Sinica. National Research Institute of Psychology. Monographs.*

TITLE VARIATIONS: Institute's Chinese name is Chung-yang yen chiu yüan. Hsin li hsüeh yen chiu so [Central Research Institute. Research Institute of Psychology].

DATES OF PUBLICATION: Number 1–9, March 1932–November 1935.

FREQUENCY: **Triannual,** Number 1–3, 1932. **Biannual,** Number 4–9, 1933–1935.

NUMBERING VARIATIONS: None.

PUBLISHER: **Peking:** National Research Institute of Psychology, 1932. **Shanghai:** National Research Institute of Psychology, 1933–1934. **Nanking:** National Research Institute of Psychology, 1935.

PRIMARY EDITORS: None listed.

CONTENTS.

Number 1. Tsai, Loh Seng. THE LAWS OF MINIMUM EFFORT AND MAXIMUM SATISFACTION IN ANIMAL BEHAVIOR. 1932. 49 pp.

Number 2. Chu, Ho-Nien. THE CELL MASSES OF THE DIENCEPHALON OF THE OPOSSUM. 1932. 48 pp.

Number 3. Chu, Ho-Nien. THE FIBER CONNECTIONS OF THE DIENCEPHALON OF THE OPOSSUM. 1932. 48 pp.

Number 4. Loo, Yu-Tao. POSTNATAL GROWTH OF THE CEREBRAL CORTEX. 1933. 83 pp.

Number 5. Loo, Yu-Tao. THE CEREBRAL CORTEX OF A CHINESE BRAIN, 1–3. 1933. 80 pp.

Number 6. Loo, Yu-Tao. THE CEREBRAL CORTEX OF A CHINESE BRAIN, 4–5. 1934. 63 pp.

Number 7. Ngowyang, C. DIE CYTOARCHITEKTONIK DES MENSCHLICHEN STIRNHIRNS. TEIL 1. 1934. 69 pp.

Number 8. Loo, Yu-Tao. THE CEREBRAL CORTEX OF A CHINESE BRAIN, 6–7. 1935. 81 pp.

Number 9. Loo, Yu-Tao. THE CEREBRAL CORTEX OF A CHINESE BRAIN, 8–10. 1935. 35 pp.

NOTE: Publication is almost entirely in English. Main entry is therefore in English.

670. *Canton. Sun Yat-sen University. Institute of Educational Research. Psychological Laboratory. Studies. Series A.*

TITLE VARIATIONS: Also cited as *Chung-shan ta hsüeh. Chiao yü hsüeh yen Chiu so* [Sun Yat-sen University. Institute of Educational Research]. *Psychological Laboratory. Studies. Series A.*

DATES OF PUBLICATION: Number 1–3, 1932–1934.

FREQUENCY: Annual.

NUMBERING VARIATIONS: Series A is the only series issued.

PUBLISHER: **Canton:** Chung-shan ta hsüeh, Chiao yü hsüeh yen Chiu so [Sun Yat-sen University. Institute of Educational Research], 1932–1934.

PRIMARY EDITORS: None listed.

NOTE: Publication is in English. Main entry is therefore in English. Chung-shan ta hsüeh [Sun Yat-sen University] is also called Kuo li Chung-shan ta hsüeh [National Sun Yat-sen University].

671. *Character and Personality; An International Quarterly of Psychodiagnostics and Allied Studies.*

TITLE VARIATIONS: Continued by *Character and Personality; An International Psychological Quarterly* with Volume 3, September 1934.

DATES OF PUBLICATION: Volume 1–2, September 1932–June 1934.

FREQUENCY: Quarterly.

NUMBERING VARIATIONS: None.

PUBLISHER: **Durham, North Carolina:** Duke University Press, 1932–1934.

PRIMARY EDITORS: **Robert Saudek,** 1932–1934; **Ernest Seeman,** 1932–1934.

COLLABORATORS: Alfred Adler, 1932–1934; Gordon W. Allport, 1932–1934; Max Alsberg, 1932–1933; P. B. Ballard, 1932–1934; Stefan Błachowski, 1932–1934; Manfred Bleuler, 1932–1934; Charlotte Bühler, 1932; Karl Bühler, 1932; Oswald Bumke, 1932–1934; J. Crepieux-Jamin, 1932–1934; Max Dessoir, 1932–1934; June E. Downey, 1932; James Drever, 1932–1934; Elisabeth Enke, 1932–1934; Willi Enke, 1932–1934; F. N. Freeman, 1932–1934; Max I. Friedlander, 1932–1934; Robert Heindl, 1932–1934; R.W.G. Hingston, 1932–1934; Pierre Janet, 1932–1934; C. G. Jung, 1932–1934; James Kerr, 1932–1934; C. W. Kimmins, 1932–1934; Ernst Kretschmer, 1932–1934; E. Landau, 1932–1934; Johannes Lange, 1932–1934; Lucien Lévy-Bruhl, 1932–1934; Otto Lipmann, 1932–1933; A. R. Luria, 1932–1934; William McDougall, 1932–1934; Jan Meloun, 1932–1934; T. H. Pear, 1932–1934; A. A. Roback, 1932–1934; J. S. Rosenthal, 1932–1934; F. Schwangart, 1932–1934; V. Tille, 1932–1934; Emil Utitz, 1932–1934; Otmar von Verschuer, 1932–1934; Lev. S. Vygotsky, 1932–1934; Aleš Hrdlicka, 1932–1934; Helge Lundholm, 1932–1934; Lewis M. Terman, 1932–1934; E. D. Wiersma, 1932–1934; Hans Driesch, 1933–1934; Havelock Ellis, 1933–1934; Paul Ranschburg, 1933–1934.

672. *Charakter; Eine Vierteljahrsschrift für psychodiagnostische Studien und verwandte Gebiete.*

TITLE VARIATIONS: Also published in English as *Character and Personality; An International Quarterly of Psychodiagnostics and Allied Studies.*

DATES OF PUBLICATION: Band 1, Heft 1–4, September 1932–June 1933.

FREQUENCY: Quarterly.

NUMBERING VARIATIONS: None.

PUBLISHER: **Berlin:** Pan Verlagsgesellschaft, 1932–1933.

PRIMARY EDITOR: **Robert Saudek,** 1932–1933.

EDITORIAL BOARD: See Collaborators listed for *Character and Personality; An International Quarterly of Psychodiagnostics and Allied Studies* (entry number 671).

673. *Chicago. Institute for Psychoanalysis. Leaflet.*

TITLE VARIATIONS: None.

DATES OF PUBLICATION: Number 1, 1932.

FREQUENCY: Irregular.

NUMBERING VARIATIONS: None.

PUBLISHER: **Chicago:** Institute for Psychoanalysis, 1932.

PRIMARY EDITORS: None listed.

CONTENTS:

Number 1. INSTITUTE FOR PSYCHOANALYSIS, CHICAGO; DEDICATED TO INCREASING THE KNOWLEDGE OF THE PSYCHIC PROCESSES OF MAN. 1932. 16 pp.

674. *Human Factor.*

TITLE VARIATIONS: Continues *London. National Institute of Industrial Psychology. Journal.* Continued by *Occupational Psychology* with Volume 12, 1938.

DATES OF PUBLICATION: Volume 6–11, 1932–1937.

FREQUENCY: Monthly.

NUMBERING VARIATIONS: Supplement to Volume 11, 1937 numbered as *London. National Institute of Industrial Psychology. News.*

PUBLISHER: **London:** National Institute of Industrial Psychology, 1932–1937.

PRIMARY EDITORS: **Charles S. Myers,** 1932–1937; **Margaret Horsey,** 1932–1935; **Joan Wynn Reeves,** 1937.

675. *Indiana. University. Department of Psychology. Psychological Clinics. Publications. Series 2.*

TITLE VARIATIONS: Series 1 never published.

DATES OF PUBLICATION: Number 1–28+, 1932–1942+.

FREQUENCY: Irregular.

NUMBERING VARIATIONS: None.

PUBLISHER: Various. *See* Note *below.*

PRIMARY EDITOR: **C. M. Louttit,** 1932–1942+.

CONTENTS:

Number 7. Louttit, C. M., and Willard B. Waskom. INDIANA PSYCHODIAGNOSTIC BLANK. 1933 (Rev. ed. 1934). 12 pp.

Number 8. Louttit, C. M., and Willard B. Waskom. MANUAL FOR THE INDIANA PSYCHODIAGNOSTIC BLANK. 1933. 13 pp.

NOTE: Only Number 7 and Number 8 contain original material. *See* Contents *above*. All other numbers are reprints of articles published in various scientific journals by members of the University Clinic staff.

676. *Iowa. University. Child Welfare Pamphlets.*

TITLE VARIATIONS: None.

DATES OF PUBLICATION: Number 1–79+, August 6, 1932–December 12, 1942+. Suspended publication December 26, 1936–January 19, 1938 and December 12, 1942–February 17, 1951.

FREQUENCY: Irregular. *See* Contents *below*.

NUMBERING VARIATIONS: Also numbered as [*Iowa. University.*] *Bulletin. New Series;* and as [*Iowa. University.*] *Publication. New Series.* Two separate pamphlets given Number 16. *See* Contents *below*.

PUBLISHER: **Iowa City, Iowa:** University [of Iowa], 1932–1942+.

PRIMARY EDITORS: None listed.

CONTENTS:

Number 1. McCloy, C. H. IS MY CHILD UNDERWEIGHT? August 6, 1932. 7 pp. (Also as [*Iowa. University.*] *Bulletin. New Series,* Number 647.)

Number 2. McCloy, Charles Harold. THE CHILD AND HIS CONSTITUTION. 1932. 8 pp. (Also as [*Iowa. University.*] *Bulletin. New Series,* Number 648.)

Number 3. Barnes, M. E. HEALTH PROTECTION OF THE PRESCHOOL CHILD. 1932. 7 pp. (Also as [*Iowa. University.*] *Bulletin. New Series,* Number 649.)

Number 4. Giddings, Mate. LEARNING TO EAT. 1932. 8 pp. (Also as [*Iowa. University.*] *Bulletin. New Series,* Number 651.) Rev. ed. 1939. 14 pp. (Also as [*Iowa. University.*] *Publication. New Series,* Number 1070.)

Number 5. Wellman, Beth L. EDUCATION OF THE PRESCHOOL CHILD. 1932. 8 pp. [*Iowa. University.*] *Bulletin. New Series,* Number 654.)

Number 6. Wellman, Beth L. LEARNING TO TALK. 1932. 7 pp. (Also as [*Iowa. University.*] *Bulletin. New Series,* Number 655.)

Number 7. Wellman, Beth L. LEARNING TO USE HANDS AND FEET. 1932. 7 pp. (Also as [*Iowa. University.*] *Bulletin. New Series,* Number 656.)

Number 8. Stoddard, George D. THE EXCEPTIONAL CHILD: THE DULL, THE BRIGHT, AND THE SPECIALLY TALENTED. 1932. 7 pp. (Also as [*Iowa. University.*] *Bulletin. New Series,* Number 657.)

Number 9. Stoddard, George D. INTELLIGENCE TESTING. 1932. 8 pp. (Also as [*Iowa. University.*] *Bulletin. New Series,* Number 658.)

Number 10. Updegraff, Ruth. HOW THE CHILD'S MIND GROWS. 1932. 8 pp. (Also as [*Iowa. University.*] *Bulletin. New Series,* Number 659.)

Number 11. Anderson, Harold H. DISCIPLINE. 1932. 8 pp. (Also as [*Iowa. University.*] *Bulletin. New Series,* Number 661.)

Number 12. Johnson, Wendell. EDUCATING THE HANDICAPPED. 1932. 11 pp. (Also as [*Iowa. University.*] *Bulletin. New Series,* Number 662). Rev. ed. 1939. 15 pp. (Also as *Iowa. University. Publication. New Series,* Number 1087.)

Number 13. Ojemann, Ralph H., and Lula E. Smith. THE HOUSE AND ITS

FURNISHINGS IN RELATION TO CHILD DEVELOPMENT. 1932. 8 pp. (Also as [*Iowa. University.*] *Bulletin. New Series,* Number 663.)

Number 14. Ojemann, Ralph H. MANAGING THE FAMILY INCOME. 1932. 8 pp. (Also as [Iowa. University.] Bulletin. New Series, Number 664.)

Number 15. Anderson, Harold H. SCHOOL–HOME CO-OPERATION. 1932. 11 pp. (Also as [*Iowa. University.*] *Bulletin. New Series,* Number 665.)

Number 16. Moore, Fred. CHILD HEALTH: A STATE AND NATIONAL DILEMMA. 1933. 13 pp. (Also as [*Iowa. University.*] *Bulletin, New Series,* Number 693.)

Number 16. Ojemann, Ralph H. THE CHILD AND HIS READING. 1941. 12 pp. (Also as [*Iowa. University.*] *Publication. New Series,* Number 1224.)

Number 17. Stoddard, George D. WHAT THE KINDERGARTEN AND NURSERY SCHOOL HAVE IN STORE FOR PARENT AND CHILD. 1933. 7 pp. (Also as [*Iowa. University.*] *Bulletin. New Series,* Number 694.)

Number 18. Furfey, Paul Hanly. UNDERSTANDING YOUR SCHOOL-AGE CHILD. 1933. 13 pp. (Also as [*Iowa. University.*] *Bulletin. New Series,* Number 695.)

Number 19. Walker, Wilma. THE VISITING TEACHER. 1933. 11 pp. (Also as [*Iowa. University.*] *Bulletin. New Series,* Number 696.)

Number 20. Pratt, George K. MENTAL HYGIENE AND THE INDIVIDUAL CHILD. 1933. 10 pp. (Also as [*Iowa. University.*] *Bulletin. New Series,* Number 697.)

Number 21. Edson, Newell W. SEX CONDUCT. 1933. 10 pp. (Also as [*Iowa. University.*] *Bulletin. New Series,* Number 698.)

Number 22. Bridgman, Ralph P. THE QUEST FOR EMOTIONAL HONESTY. 1933. 12 pp. (Also as [*Iowa. University.*] *Bulletin. New Series,* Number 699.)

Number 23. Shaw, Clifford R. JUVENILE DELINQUENCY—A GROUP TRADITION. 1933. 14 pp. (Also as [*Iowa. University.*] *Bulletin. New Series,* Number 700.)

Number 24. Shaw, Clifford R. JUVENILE DELINQUENCY—A CASE HISTORY. 1933. 11 pp. (Also as [*Iowa. University.*] *Bulletin. New Series,* Number 701.)

Number 25. Ojemann, Ralph H. WHAT MONEY MEANS TO THE CHILD. 1933. 10 pp. (Also as [*Iowa. University.*] *Bulletin. New Series,* Number 702.)

Number 26. Scoe, Hjalmar Fletcher. BLADDER CONTROL IN INFANCY AND EARLY CHILDHOOD. 1933. 7 pp. (Also as [*Iowa. University.*] *Bulletin. New Series,* Number 703.)

Number 27. L'Engle, Louise. FEEDING THE FAMILY DURING A DEPRESSION. 1933. 9 pp. (Also as [*Iowa. University.*] *Bulletin. New Series,* Number 704.)

Number 28. Leib, Karl A. EFFECTS OF CHANGING ECONOMIC CONDITIONS UPON CHILDREN. 1933. 9 pp. (Also as [*Iowa. University.*] *Bulletin. New Series,* Number 705.)

Number 29. Williams, Harold M. MUSICAL GUIDANCE OF YOUNG CHILDREN. 1933. 15 pp. (Also as [*Iowa. University.*] *Bulletin. New Series,* Number 707.)

Number 30. Hattendorf, Katharine Wood. PARENTS' ANSWERS TO CHILDREN'S SEX QUESTIONS. 1933. 15 pp. (Also as [*Iowa. University.*] *Bulletin. New Series,* Number 710.)

676. *(Continued)*

Number 31. Stoddard, George D. WHAT MOTION PICTURES MEAN TO THE CHILD. 1933. 8 pp. (Also as [*Iowa. University.*] *Bulletin. New Series,* Number 713.)

Number 32. Dimock, Hedley S. THE MODERN CHILD AND RELIGION. 1934. 11 pp. (Also as [*Iowa. University.*] *Bulletin. New Series,* Number 749.)

Number 33. Richards, Esther Loring. BASIC FACTORS IN CHILD-TEACHER RELATIONSHIPS. 1934. 16 pp. (Also as [*Iowa. University.*] *Bulletin. New Series,* Number 750.)

Number 34. Richards, Esther Loring. THE ORIGIN OF CONDUCT PROBLEMS IN SCHOOL CHILDREN. 1934. 14 pp. (Also as *Iowa. University.*] *Bulletin. New Series,* Number 751.)

Number 35. Dell, Floyd. CHILDREN AND THE MACHINE AGE. 1934. 11 pp. (Also as [*Iowa. University.*] *Bulletin. New Series,* Number 752.)

Number 36. Groves, Ernest R. MARRIAGE AND MODERN LIFE. 1934. 9 pp. (Also as [*Iowa. University.*] *Bulletin. New Series,* Number 747.)

Number 37. Johnson, Wendell. STUTTERING IN THE PRESCHOOL CHILD. 1934. 8 pp. (Also as [*Iowa. University.*] *Bulletin. New Series,* Number 748.) Rev. ed. 1934. 12 pp. (Also as *Iowa. University. Publication. New Series,* Number 748.)

Number 38. Douglas, Paul H. THE IMPACT OF RECENT SOCIAL AND ECONOMIC CHANGES UPON THE FAMILY. 1934. 17 pp. (Also as [*Iowa. University.*] *Bulletin. New Series,* Number 761.)

Number 39. Douglas, Paul H. WHAT IS THE NEW DEAL DOING FOR THE AMERICAN FAMILY? 1934. 18 pp. (Also as [*Iowa. University.*] *Bulletin. New Series,* Number 762.)

Number 40. Trout, David M. HOW THE CHILD BECOMES RELIGIOUS. 1934. 17 pp. (Also as [*Iowa. University.*] *Bulletin. New Series,* Number 763.)

Number 41. Trout, David M. GUIDING THE RELIGIOUS DEVELOPMENT OF THE CHILD. 1934. 17 pp. (Also as [*Iowa. University.*] *Bulletin. New Series,* Number 764.)

Number 42. Trout, David M. CHARACTER THROUGH RELIGIOUS CONTROL. 1934. 15 pp. (Also as [*Iowa. University.*] *Bulletin. New Series,* Number 765.)

Number 43. Zook, George F. THE CHILD IN OUR EDUCATIONAL CRISIS. 1934. 15 pp. (Also as [*Iowa. University.*] *Bulletin. New Series,* Number 766.)

Number 44. Blatz, William E. HUMAN NEEDS AND HOW THEY ARE SATISFIED. 1934. 8 pp. (Also as [*Iowa. University.*] *Bulletin. New Series,* Number 768.)

Number 45. Blatz, William E. THE IMPORTANCE OF FAILURE. 1934. 10 pp. (Also as [*Iowa. University.*] *Bulletin. New Series,* Number 769.)

Number 46. Updegraff, Ruth. A SYLLABUS IN NURSERY SCHOOL EDUCATION. 1935. 16 pp. (Also as [*Iowa. University.*] *Bulletin. New Series,* Number 814.)

Number 47. Winslow, C.E.A. BRINGING HEALTH TO THE CHILD. 1935. 17 pp. (Also as [*Iowa. University.*] *Bulletin. New Series,* Number 815.)

Number 48. Barnes, M. E. COMMUNITY HEALTH. 1935. 8 pp. (Also as [*Iowa. University.*] *Bulletin. New Series,* Number 816.)

Number 49. Allen, Frederick H. WHAT CONSTITUTES A HEALTHY PARENT–CHILD RELATION. 1935. 8 pp. (Also as [*Iowa. University.*] *Bulletin. New Series,* Number 818.)

Number 50. Allen, Frederick H. THE CHILD AS THE THERAPIST SEES HIM. 1935. 9 pp. (Also as [*Iowa. University.*] *Bulletin. New Series,* Number 819.)

Number 51. Thayer, Vivian T. WHAT MAKES A MODERN SCHOOL? 1935. 10 pp. (Also as [*Iowa. University.*] *Bulletin. New Series,* Number 820.)

Number 52. Roberts, Mary Price. WHEN CHILDREN PLAY AT HOME. 1936. 16 pp. (Also as [*Iowa. University.*] *Bulletin. New Series,* Number 876.)

Number 53. Reavis, William C. CULTIVATION OF LEISURE ACTIVITIES. 1936. 10 pp. (Also as [*Iowa. University.*] *Bulletin. New Series,* Number 877.)

Number 54. Hart, Hornell. FAMILY LIFE IN ITS SOCIAL IMPLICATIONS. 1936. 11 pp. (Also as [*Iowa. University.*] *Bulletin. New Series,* Number 879.)

Number 55. Hart, Hornell. THE FAMILY CIRCLE. 1936. 10 pp. (Also as [*Iowa. University.*] *Bulletin. New Series,* Number 880.)

Number 56. Robinson, Bruce B. AID FROM THE CHILD GUIDANCE CLINIC. 1936. 9 pp. (Also as [*Iowa. University.*] *Bulletin. New Series,* Number 881.)

Number 57. Langdon, Grace. THE NURSERY SCHOOL AS A FAMILY AID. 1936. 11 pp. (Also as [*Iowa. University.*] *Bulletin. New Series,* Number 882.)

Number 58. Plant, James S. THE EMOTIONS OF THE CHILD. 1938. 11 pp. (Also as [*Iowa. University.*] *Bulletin. New Series,* Number 952.)

Number 59. Bain, Winifred E. PARENTS LOOK AT MODERN EDUCATION. 1938. 11 pp. (Also as [*Iowa. University.*] *Bulletin. New Series,* Number 953.)

Number 60. Bain, Winifred E. HOW PARENTS MAY JUDGE THE EFFECTIVENESS OF THE SCHOOL'S PROGRAM. 1938. 10 pp. (Also as [*Iowa. University.*] *Bulletin. New Series,* Number 954.)

Number 61. Young, Kimball. THE IMPACT OF SOCIETY UPON THE CHILD. 1938. 15 pp. (Also as [*Iowa. University.*] *Bulletin. New Series,* Number 955.)

Number 62. Overstreet, H. A. THE CHILD IN THE MODERN WORLD. 1938. 5 pp. (Also as [*Iowa. University.*] *Bulletin. New Series,* Number 957.)

Number 63. Plass, Everett D. PRENATAL CARE FOR THE BABY. 1938. 6 pp. (Also as [*Iowa. University.*] *Bulletin. New Series,* Number 958.)

Number 64. Williams, Harold M. FACTORS IN DELINQUENCY. 1938. 11 pp. (Also as [*Iowa. University.*] *Bulletin. New Series,* Number 960.)

Number 65. Osborne, Ernest. INDIVIDUAL ADJUSTMENT THROUGH GROUP ACTIVITY. 1938. 14 pp. (Also as [*Iowa. University.*] *Publication. New Series,* Number 1016.)

Number 66. Bates, Sanford. WHY CHILDREN GO WRONG. 1938. 12 pp. (Also as [*Iowa. University.*] *Publication. New Series,* Number 1017.)

Number 67. Bates, Sanford. YOUR TOWN AND YOUR CHILD. 1938. 15 pp. (Also as [*Iowa. University.*] *Publication. New Series,* Number 1019.)

Number 68. Murphy, Lois Barclay. WHAT LIES BACK OF BEHAVIOR PROBLEMS? 1938. 16 pp. (Also as [*Iowa. University.*] *Publication. New Series,* Number 1020.)

Number 69. Bristow, William H. THE ROLE OF PARENTS AND TEACHERS IN GUIDING CHILDREN. 1939. 17 pp. (Also as [*Iowa. University.*] *Publication. New Series,* Number 1021.)

Number 70. MacLean, Malcolm. THE PARENT AS CULTURAL IMPACT. 1939. 13 pp. (Also as [*Iowa. University.*] *Publication. New Series*, Number 1022.)

Number 71. Christ-Janer, Albert. ART IN CHILD LIFE. 1939. 12 pp. (Also as [*Iowa. University.*] *Publication. New Series*, Number 1024.)

Number 72. Seashore, Carl E. MUSIC BEFORE FIVE. 1939. 11 pp. (Also as [*Iowa. University.*] *Publication. New Series*, Number 1056.)

Number 73. Wood, Grant. ART IN THE DAILY LIFE OF THE CHILD. 1939. 8 pp. (Also as [*Iowa. University.*] *Publication. New Series*, Number 1057.

Number 74. Carr, Charlotte. PROBLEM COMMUNITIES. 1940. 8 pp. (Also as [*Iowa. University.*] *Publication. New Series*, Number 1110.)

Number 75. Nash, Jay B. LEISURE FOR WHAT? 1940. 10 pp. (Also as [*Iowa. University.*] *Publication. New Series*, Number 1111.)

Number 76. Seashore, Carl E. ON THEIR MUSICAL WAY. 1941. 8 pp. (Also as [*Iowa. University.*] *Publication. New Series*, Number 1217.)

Number 77. Taylor, Katharine Whiteside. DO ADOLESCENTS NEED PARENTS? 1941. 7 pp. (Also as [*Iowa. University.*] *Publication. New Series*, Number 1218.)

Number 78. Taylor, Katharine Whiteside. PARENTS, RELAX! 1941. 7 pp. (Also as [*Iowa. University.*] *Publication. New Series*, Number 1208.)

Number 79. Irwin, Orvis C. HOW TO CARE FOR CHILDREN DURING AN AIR RAID. 1942. 8 pp. (Also as [*Iowa. University.*] *Publication. New Series*, Number 1280.)

677. *Iowa. University. Studies in the Psychology of Music.*

TITLE VARIATIONS: None.

DATES OF PUBLICATION: Volume 1–4+, 1932–1936+. Suspended publication 1937–1967.

FREQUENCY: Irregular. *See* Contents *below*.

NUMBERING VARIATIONS: Also numbered as [*Iowa. University.*] *Studies. See* Contents *below*.

PUBLISHER: **Iowa City, Iowa:** Published by the University, 1932–1935. **Iowa City, Iowa:** University Press, 1936.

PRIMARY EDITOR: **Carl E. Seashore,** 1932–1936.

CONTENTS:

Volume 1. Seashore, Carl E. THE VIBRATO. 1932. 382 pp. (Also as [*Iowa. University.*] *Studies. New Series*, Number 225.)

Volume 2. Stanton, Hazel M. MEASUREMENT OF MUSICAL TALENT. 1935. 140 pp. (Also as [*Iowa. University.*] *Studies. New Series*, Number 291.)

Volume 3. Seashore, Carl E. PSYCHOLOGY OF THE VIBRATO IN VOICE AND INSTRUMENT. 1936. 159 pp. (Also as [*Iowa. University.*] *Studies. New Series*, Number 317.)

Volume 4. Seashore, Carl E. OBJECTIVE ANALYSIS OF MUSICAL PERFORMANCE. 1936. 379 pp. (Also as [*Iowa University.*] *Studies. New Series*, Number 330.)

678. *Journal of Experimental Education.*

TITLE VARIATIONS: None.

DATES OF PUBLICATION: Volume 1–19+, September 1932–December 1950+.

FREQUENCY: Quarterly.

NUMBERING VARIATIONS: Volume 1–14, 1932–1945 consistently dedicated issue Number 2, December, to Child Development.

PUBLISHER: **Ann Arbor, Michigan:** Edwards Brothers, Inc. 1932–1936. **Madison, Wisconsin:** Journal of Experimental Education, Box 12, Bascom Hall, University of Wisconsin (Printed by Democrat Printing Company), 1936–1946. **Madison:** Dembar Publications, Inc., 1946–1950+.

PRIMARY EDITOR: **A.S. Barr,** 1932–1950+.

EDITORIAL BOARD: Carter V. Good, 1932–1945; Henry Harap, 1932–1935; Walter S. Monroe, 1932–1936; George D. Stoddard, 1932–1939; J. Paul Leonard, 1935–1937; Edward E. Cureton, 1936–1947; J. Wayne Wrightstone, 1937–1950+; Arthur T. Jersild, 1939–1950+; Palmer O. Johnson, 1945–1950+; H. H. Remmers, 1947–1950+.

679. *Modern Psychologist.*

TITLE VARIATIONS: None.

DATES OF PUBLICATION: Volume 1–10, Number 2, November 1932–April 1938.

FREQUENCY: Monthly.

NUMBERING VARIATIONS: Issues not printed for July and August 1933.

PUBLISHER: **New York:** The Modern Psychologist, Inc., 1932–1938.

PRIMARY EDITOR: **Dagobert D. Runes,** 1932–1938.

680. *Psychoanalytic Quarterly.*

TITLE VARIATIONS: None.

DATES OF PUBLICATION: Volume 1–19+, 1932–1950+.

FREQUENCY: Quarterly.

NUMBERING VARIATIONS: Multinumber issues present.

PUBLISHER: **Albany, New York:** Psychoanalytic Quarterly Press, 1932–1936. **Albany:** Psychoanalytic Quarterly, Inc., 1937–1950+.

PRIMARY EDITORS: **Dorian Feigenbaum,** 1932–1937; **Bertram D. Lewin,** 1932–1940+; **Frankwood E. Williams,** 1932–1934; **Gregory Zilboorg,** 1932–1950+; **Henry Alden Bunker, Jr.,** 1934–1950+; **Raymond Gosselin,** 1934–1950+; **Lawrence S. Kubie,** 1934–1950+; **Carl Binger,** 1937–1946; **Monroe A. Meyer,** 1937–1938; **Flanders Dunbar,** 1939–1940; **A. Kardiner,** 1939–1941; **Sandor Rado,** 1939–1942; **Franz Alexander,** 1939–1950+; **Thomas M. French,** 1939–1950+; **Leon J. Saul,** 1939–1950+; **Helene Deutsch,** 1939–1950+; **Martin W. Peck,** 1939–1940; **Otto Fenichel,** 1939–1946; **Geza Roheim,** 1939–1950+; **Karl A. Menninger,** 1942–1950+; **Herbert A. Wiggers,** 1944–1950+; **Ruth Mack Brunswick,** 1944–1946.

681. Psychoanalytic Review. An American Journal of Psychoanalysis Devoted to an Understanding of Human Conduct.

TITLE VARIATIONS: Continues *Psychoanalytic Review. A Journal Devoted to an Understanding of Human Conduct.* Continued by *Psychoanalytic Review. An Educational American Journal of Psychoanalysis Devoted to an Understanding and Education of Human Behavior* with Volume 27, 1940.

DATES OF PUBLICATION: Volume 19–26, January 1932–October 1939.

FREQUENCY: Quarterly.

NUMBERING VARIATIONS: Each issue also assigned a whole number, Number 73–104.

PUBLISHER: **Lancaster, Pennsylvania** and **Washington, D.C.:** Nervous and Mental Disease Publishing Company, 1932–1937. **New York** and **Albany, New York:** Nervous and Mental Disease Publishing Company, 1938–1939.

PRIMARY EDITORS: **William A. White,** 1932–1937; **Smith Ely Jelliffe,** 1932–1939; **A. A. Brill,** 1938–1939; **J.H.W. van Ophuijsen,** 1938–1939.

682. Psychological Exchange.

TITLE VARIATIONS: None.

DATES OF PUBLICATION: Volume 1–5, Number 1, April 1932–October 1936. Suspended publication May–September 1935.

FREQUENCY: **Bimonthly,** Volume 1–3, Number 6, April 1932–March/April 1935. **Irregular** (October, November, January, February, April, May), Volume 4–5, October 1935–October 1936.

NUMBERING VARIATIONS: None.

PUBLISHER: **New York:** Psychological Exchange, 1932–1936.

PRIMARY EDITORS: **James Hargan,** 1932–1936; **Norman Powell,** 1932–1933.

683. Sociologus. Zeitschrift für Völkerpsychologie und Soziologie.

TITLE VARIATIONS: Continues *Zeitschrift für Völkerpsychologie und Soziologie.*

DATES OF PUBLICATION: Band 8–9, 1932–1933.

FREQUENCY: Quarterly.

NUMBERING VARIATIONS: None.

PUBLISHER: **Leipzig:** C. L. Hirschfeld, 1932. **Stuttgart:** C. L. Hirschfeld, 1933.

PRIMARY EDITORS: **Richard Thurnwald,** 1932–1933; **W. E. Mühlmann,** 1932–1933; **F. Alverdes,** 1932–1933; **L. L. Bernard,** 1932–1933; **R. Bolte,** 1932–1933; **B. Malinowski,** 1932–1933; **W. F. Ogburn,** 1932–1933; **E. Sapir,** 1932–1933; **E. Schultz-Ewerth,** 1932–1933; **E. Schwiedland,** 1932–1933; **P. A. Sorokin,** 1932–1933; **S. R. Steinmetz,** 1932–1933.

684. *Sovetskaia psikhotekhnika.*

TITLE VARIATIONS: Continues *Psikhotekhnika i psikhofiziologiia truda.*

DATES OF PUBLICATION: Tom 5–7, 1932–1934.

FREQUENCY: **Bimonthly,** Tom 5, 1932. **Quarterly,** Tom 6–7, 1933–1934.

NUMBERING VARIATIONS: Multinumber issues present.

PUBLISHER: **Moscow:** Vsesoiuznyi obshchestvo psikhotekhniki i prikladnoi psikhofiziologii, 1932–1934.

PRIMARY EDITORS: Unknown.

NOTE: Information on this title was compiled from entries in *A Half Century of Soviet Serials.*

685. *Zagreb. Univerzítēt. Psihologijski institut. Acta.*

TITLE VARIATIONS: Also cited as *Acta Instituti Psychologici Universitatis Zagrebensis* and *Radovi psihologijskog instituta univerziteta u zagrebu.*

DATES OF PUBLICATION: Sveska 1–3, Broj 3, 1932–1939; Numero 13–16, 1941–1947.

FREQUENCY: Irregular. *See* Contents *below.*

NUMBERING VARIATIONS: Numbering system changed in midseries. *See* Dates of Publication *above.*

PUBLISHER: **Zagreb:** Članovi psihologijskog instituta, 1932–1939. **Zagreb:** Psihologijski zavod sveùčilĩšta, 1941. **Zagreb:** Izdanje psihologijskih zavoda visoke pedagožke škole i sveùčilĩšta, 1943. **Zagreb:** Psihologijski institut sveùčilĩšta, 1947.

PRIMARY EDITOR: **Ramiro Bujas,** 1932–1947.

CONTENTS:

Sveska 1, Broj 1. Bujas, Ramiro. Über den Zusammenhang von Positivem und negativem Nachbild. 1932. 7 pp.

————, **Broj 2.** Bujas, Zoran. Contribution à la recherche des émotions des animaux: la loi psycho-galvanique expérimentée sur un chat. 1932. 20 pp.

————, **Broj 3.** Kučera, Elza. Experimentelle Beiträge zur Charakteristik von Willensstufen. 1933. 36 pp.

————, **Broj 4.** Bujas, Ramiro. Über die Funktion des cortischen Organs. 1933. 21 pp.

————, **Broj 5.** Bujas, Ramiro. Über den blinden Fleck. 1933. 7 pp.

Sveska 2, Broj 1. Bujas, Zoran, with collaboration of Ida Ostojčić. La mesure de la sensibilité différentielle dans le domaine gustatif. 1937. 18 pp.

————, **Broj 2.** Bujas, Ramiro, and Zoran Bujas. Ein Test zur Untersuchung der Lesbarkeit von Druckschriften. 1937. 9 pp.

————, **Broj 3.** Bujas, Ramiro, and Zoran Bujas. Die Distribution der Noten als Mittel zur Bestimmung der Schwere des Lehrplans. 1937. 6 pp.

———, **Broj 4.** Bujas, Zoran. KONTRAST- UND HEMMUNGSERSCHEINUNG-EN BEI DISPARATEN SIMULTANEN GESCHMACKSREIZEN. 1937. 12 pp.

Sveska 3, Broj 1. Bujas, Zoran, and Adela Ostojčić. L'ÉVOLUTION DE LA SENSATION GUSTATIVE EN FONCTION DU TEMPS D'EXCITATION. 1939. 24 pp.

———, **Broj 2.** Bujas, Zoran. DEUX TESTS DE COMPLÈTEMENT. 1939. 8 pp.

———, **Broj 3.** Bujas, Zoran, with the cooperation of Dora Majer and Adela Ostojčić. BEOBACHTUNGEN ÜBER DEN RESTITUTIONSVORGANG BEIM GESCHMACKSINN. 1939. 14 pp.

Numero 13. Bujas, Zoran, and Adela Ostojčić. LA SENSIBILITÉ GUSTATIVE EN FONCTION DE LA SURFACE EXCITÉE. 1941. 19 pp.

Numero 14 Bujas, Zoran. DIE BEZIEHUNG DER KALTEMPFINDUNGEN ZUR GRÖSSE DER REIZFLÄCHE. 1943. 15 pp.

Numero 15. Bujas, Ramiro. LE CONTRASTE SIMULTANÉ EST-IL-EXPLIQUÉ? 1947. 6 pp.

Numero 16. Bujas, Zoran, and Adela Ostojčić. LA PERSISTANCE APPARENTE DES SENSATIONS DU FROID. 1947. 9 pp.

1933

686. *Akademiya navuk BSSR (Minsk). Instytut psykhaneuralogii. Zbornik prats.*

TITLE VARIATIONS: Institute called Psykhaneuralagichny instytut, 1933.

DATES OF PUBLICATION: Tom 1–5, 1933–1936.

FREQUENCY: **Annual,** Tom 1–3, 1933–1935. **Semiannual,** Tom 4–5, 1936.

NUMBERING VARIATIONS: None.

PUBLISHER: **Minsk:** Akademiya navuk BSSR. Psykhaneuralogichny instytut, 1933. **Minsk:** Akademiya navuk BSSR. Instytut psykhaneuralogii, 1934–1936.

PRIMARY EDITOR: **I. D. Sapir,** 1933–1936.

NOTE: Information on this title was compiled from entries in *Half a Century of Soviet Serials.*

687. *American Association on Mental Deficiency. Proceedings and Addresses.*

TITLE VARIATIONS: Continues *American Association for the Study of the Feeble-Minded. Proceedings and Addresses.* Continued in *American Journal of Mental Deficiency* with Volume 45, 1940.

DATES OF PUBLICATION: Number 57–63, 1933–1939.

FREQUENCY: Annual (comprised of four issues published as one volume and containing only the Annual Proceedings).

NUMBERING VARIATIONS: Number 57–63 published in *Journal of Psycho–Asthenics,* Volume 38–44.

PUBLISHER: [**n.p.**]: By the Association, 1933–1934. [**Manchester, New Hampshire**]: By the Association, 1934–1936. [**Philadelphia**]: By the Association, 1936–1939.

PRIMARY EDITORS: **Groves Blake Smith**, 1933–1935; **E. Arthur Whitney**, 1935–1938; **Edward J. Humphreys**, 1938–1939.

688. *Archivos argentinos de psicología normal y patológia, terapia neuro mental y ciencias afines.*

TITLE VARIATIONS: None.

DATES OF PUBLICATION: Tomo 1–2, July/August 1933–December 1935.

FREQUENCY: Irregular.

NUMBERING VARIATIONS: Multinumber issues present.

PUBLISHER: **Buenos Aires**: No publisher given.

PRIMARY EDITORS: None listed.

689. *Arxius de psicología i psiquiatría infantil.*

TITLE VARIATIONS: None.

DATES OF PUBLICATION: Número 1–13, 1933–1935.

FREQUENCY: Quarterly.

NUMBERING VARIATIONS: None.

PUBLISHER: **Barcelona:** Publicacio del tribunal tutelar de menors de Barcelona, 1933–1935.

PRIMARY EDITORS: None listed.

690. *Aus dem Jahresbericht.* [Yearbook of the Psychologischer Club, Zurich.]

TITLE VARIATIONS: None.

DATES OF PUBLICATION: 1st–18th+, 1933/1934–1950/1951+.

FREQUENCY: **Annual.**

NUMBERING VARIATIONS: None.

PUBLISHER: **Zurich:** Psychologischer Club, 1933/1934–1950/1951+.

PRIMARY EDITORS: None listed.

NOTE: Contains directory of members and associates and digests of papers read to the club.

691. *Barcelona. Instituto de psicología aplicada y psicotecnia. Trabajos.*

TITLE VARIATIONS: None.

DATES OF PUBLICATION: Tomo 1–4, Número 3, 1933–1936.

FREQUENCY: Quarterly.

NUMBERING VARIATIONS: None.

PUBLISHER: **Barcelona:** Instituto de psicología aplicada y psicotecnia, 1933–1936.

PRIMARY EDITORS: None listed.

NOTE: Information on this entry is incomplete. The compilers were unable to examine this title.

692. *Buenos Aires. Sociedad de psicología. Anales.*

TITLE VARIATIONS: Supercedes *Buenos Aires. Sociedad de psicología. Boletín.*

DATES OF PUBLICATION: Tomo 1, 1933/1935.

FREQUENCY: Irregular.

NUMBERING VARIATIONS: None.

PUBLISHER: **Buenos Aires:** Sociedad de psicología, 1933/1935.

PRIMARY EDITOR: **Osvaldo Loudet,** 1933/1935.

693. *California. University of California at Los Angeles. Publications in Education, Philosophy and Psychology.*

TITLE VARIATIONS: None.

DATES OF PUBLICATION: Volume 1, Number 1–15, July 1933–1939.

FREQUENCY: Irregular. *See* Contents *below.*

NUMBERING VARIATIONS: Some issues also numbered as *Studies in Cerebral Function. See* Contents *below.*

PUBLISHER: **Los Angeles:** University of California Press, 1933–1939.

PRIMARY EDITORS: **Kate Gordon,** 1933–1934; **D. A. Piatt,** 1939; **John Elof Boodin,** 1933–1934; **Franklin Fearing,** 1939; **W. A. Smith,** 1933–1939.

CONTENTS:

Volume 1, Number 1. Boodin, John Elof. GROUP PARTICIPATION AS THE SOCIOLOGICAL PRINCIPLE PAR EXCELLENCE. 1933. Pp. 1–46.

————, **Number 2.** Davis, Frank C. EFFECT OF MAZE ROTATION UPON SUBJECTS REPORTING DIFFERENT METHODS OF LEARNING AND RETENTION. 1933. Pp. 47–64.

————, **Number 3.** Franz, Shepherd Ivory, and John D. Layman. PERIPHERAL RETINAL LEARNING AND PRACTICE TRANSFER. 1933. Pp. 65–78. (Also as *Studies in Cerebral Function,* Number 1.)

————, **Number 4.** Franz, Shepherd Ivory, and Sybil Kilduff. CEREBRAL DOMINANCE AS SHOWN BY SEGMENTAL VISUAL LEARNING. 1933. Pp. 79–90. (Also as *Studies in Cerebral Function,* Number 2.)

————, **Number 5.** Franz, Shepherd Ivory, and Roy C. Morgan. TRANSFER OF EFFECTS OF LEARNING FROM ONE RETINAL AREA TO OTHER RETINAL AREAS. 1933. Pp. 91–98. (Also as *Studies in Cerebral Function,* Number 3.)

————, **Number 6.** Franz, Shepherd Ivory, and Evelene F. Davis. SIMULTANEOUS READING WITH BOTH CEREBRAL HEMISPHERES. 1933. Pp. 99–106. (Also as *Studies in Cerebral Function*, Number 4.)

————, **Number 7.** McCulloch, T. L. A STUDY OF AN APHASIC'S LEARNING TO READ. 1933. Pp. 107–110. (Also as *Studies in Cerebral Function*, Number 5.)

————, **Number 8.** Franz, Shepherd Ivory, and Amerette G. Eaton. TOUCH LOCALIZATION—CONSTANT ERRORS. 1933. Pp. 111–116. (Also as *Studies in Cerebral Function*, Number 6.)

————, **Number 9.** Franz, Shepherd Ivory, and Amerette G. Eaton. THE POSSIBILITY OF TRAINING IN TACTILE SPACE PERCEPTION. 1933. Pp. 117–120. (Also as *Studies in Cerebral Function*, Number 7.)

————, **Number 10.** Franz, Shepherd Ivory. TRAINING IN TOUCH PERCEPTION AND CROSS-EDUCATION. 1933. Pp. 121–128. (Also as *Studies in Cerebral Function*, Number 8.)

————, **Number 11.** Franz, Shepherd Ivory. DIFFUSION EFFECTS FOLLOWING LOCALIZED TACTILE TRAINING. 1933. Pp. 129–135. (Also as *Studies in Cerebral Function*, Number 9.)

————, **Number 12.** Lenzen, V. F. THE CONCEPT OF REALITY IN THE LIGHT OF QUANTUM THEORY. 1933. Pp. 137–164.

————, **Number 13.** Gengerelli, J. A. THE PRINCIPLE OF MINIMUM PATH IN THE RINGTAIL MONKEY. 1933. Pp. 165–188.

————, **Number 14.** Crook, Mason N., and Marion Thomas. FAMILY RELATIONSHIPS IN ASCENDANCE–SUBMISSION. 1934. Pp. 189–192.

————, **Number 15.** Gengerelli, J. A. THE STRUCTURE OF MENTAL CAPACITIES. 1939. Pp. 193–268.

694. *Chicago. Institute for Psychoanalysis. Report.*

TITLE VARIATIONS: Variously titled *Annual Report; Review for the Year; Five Year Report;* and *Ten Year Report. See* Numbering Variations *below.*

DATES OF PUBLICATION: 1st–18th, 1933/1934–1950 + .

FREQUENCY: Annual.

NUMBERING VARIATIONS: Annual reports were cumulated at five-year intervals. The first *Five Year Report* was issued for 1932–1937. The second *Five Year Report,* for the period 1937–1942, was incorporated into a *Ten Year Report* covering 1932–1942. The third *Five Year Report* was issued for 1942–1947.

PUBLISHER: **Chicago:** Institute for Psychoanalysis, 1933–1950 + .

PRIMARY EDITOR: [**F. G. Alexander**, 1933–1950 + .]

695. *Eranos Jahrbuch.*

TITLE VARIATIONS: None.

DATES OF PUBLICATION: Band 1–19 + ; 1933–1950 + .

FREQUENCY: Annual.

NUMBERING VARIATIONS: None.

PUBLISHER: **Zurich:** Rhein Verlag, 1933–1950+.

PRIMARY EDITOR: **Olga Fröbe-Kapteyn,** 1933–1950+.

696. *Imago; Zeitschrift für psychoanalytische Psychologie, ihre Grenzgebiete und Anwendungen.*

TITLE VARIATIONS: Continues *Imago; Zeitschrift für Anwendung der Psychoanalyse auf die Natur- und Geisteswissenschaften.*

DATES OF PUBLICATION: Jahrgang 19–23, 1933–1937.

FREQUENCY: Quarterly.

NUMBERING VARIATIONS: None.

PUBLISHER: **Leipzig** and **Vienna:** Internationaler psychoanalytischer Verlag, 1933–1937.

PRIMARY EDITORS: **Ernst Kris,** 1933–1937; **Robert Waelder,** 1933–1937.

697. *Individual Psychology Pamphlets.*

TITLE VARIATIONS: Continues *Individual Psychology Publications. Medical Pamphlets.* Continued by *Individual Psychology Medical Pamphlets* with Number 13, 1934.

DATES OF PUBLICATION: Number 9–12, July 1933–April 1934.

FREQUENCY: Quarterly.

NUMBERING VARIATIONS: Supplementary pamphlets, dealing with special subjects and published on behalf of individual authors, are numbered with the addition of a roman letter to the arabic numeral denoting the quarterly issue with which they are linked. *See* Contents *below.*

PUBLISHER: **London:** C. W. Daniel Company for the Medical Society of Individual Psychology (London), 1933–1934.

PRIMARY EDITORS: **F. G. Crookshank,** 1933; **Hilda Weber,** 1933; **Maurice Marcus,** 1933–1934; **J. C. Young,** 1934.

CONTENTS:

Number 9. Fairbairn, J. S., W. McAdam Eccles, Maurice Marcus, Mary Bell Ferguson, and F. G. Crookshank. INDIVIDUAL PSYCHOLOGY AND PSYCHOSOMATIC DISORDERS (II). July 1933. 64 pp.

Number 10. Crookshank, F. G. INDIVIDUAL PSYCHOLOGY AND NIETZSCHE. October 1933. 80 pp.

Number 11. Young, J. C. INDIVIDUAL PSYCHOLOGY, PSYCHIATRY AND HOLISTIC MEDICINE. January 1934. 64 pp.

Number 11a. Seif, Leonhard. INDIVIDUAL PSYCHOLOGY AND LIFE PHILOSOPHY. 1934. 61 pp.

Number 12. Bevan-Brown, C. M., F. G. Layton, O. H. Woodcock, and F. Marjory Edwards. INDIVIDUAL PSYCHOLOGY AND PRACTICE (II). April 1934. 64 pp.

698. *Iowa. University. Educational Psychology Series.*

TITLE VARIATIONS: None.

DATES OF PUBLICATION: Number 1–3, October 1933–November 1936.

FREQUENCY: Irregular. *See* Contents *below.*

NUMBERING VARIATIONS: Also numbered as [*Iowa. University.*] *Studies. New Series;* and as [*Iowa. University.*] *Studies in Education.* Some issues also numbered as *Studies in the Psychology of Learning. See* Contents *below.*

PUBLISHER: **Iowa City, Iowa:** University of Iowa, 1933. **Iowa City:** University [of Iowa], 1934–1936.

PRIMARY EDITOR: **Charles L. Robbins,** 1933–1936.

CONTENTS:

Number 1. Norem G. M., and M. F. Wiederaenders. STUDIES IN THE PSYCHOLOGY OF LEARNING. 1933. 75 pp. (Also as [*Iowa. University.*] *Studies. New Series,* Number 260; and [*Iowa. University.*] *Studies in Education,* Volume 8, Number 6.)

Number 2. McConnell, T. R., Lyle K. Henry, and Clellan Morgan. STUDIES IN THE PSYCHOLOGY OF LEARNING II. 1934. 143 pp. (Also as [*Iowa. University.*] *Studies. New Series,* Number 283; and [*Iowa. University.*] *Studies in Education,* Volume 9, Number 5.)

Number 3. Ruch, G. M., F. B. Knight, E. A. Olander, and G. E. Russell. SCHEMATA FOR THE ANALYSIS OF DRILL IN FRACTIONS. 1936. 58 pp. (Also as [*Iowa. University.*] *Studies. New Series,* Number 327; and [*Iowa. University.*] *Studies in Education,* Volume 10, Number 2.)

699. *Journal belge de neurologie et de psychiatrie.* [Official bulletin of the Société de médecine mentale de belgique; the Société belge de neurologie; the Groupement belge d'études oto-ophtalmologiques et neuro-chirurgicales; and the Congrès belge de neurologie et de psychiatrie.]

TITLE VARIATIONS: Continues *Journal de neurologie et de psychiatrie. [1].* Continued by *Acta neurologica et psychiatrica belgica* with Tome 48, 1948.

DATES OF PUBLICATION: Tome 33–47, 1933–1947.

FREQUENCY: **Monthly,** Tome 33–40, 1933–1040. **Irregular,** Tome 41–46, 1941–1946. **Monthly,** Tome 47, 1947.

NUMBERING VARIATIONS: Multinumber issues 1941–1946.

PUBLISHER: **Brussels:** Des Presses de J. Vromans, 1933–1946. **Brussels:** Des Presses de Jean Vromans, 1947.

EDITORIAL BOARD: A. Leroy, 1933–1946; Rodolphe Ley, 1933–1947; L. van Bogaert, 1933–1947; Ch. Rouvroy, 1947.

700. *Koers; maanblad vir Calvinistiere denke.*

TITLE VARIATIONS: Also called *Koers; Journal de l'afrique du sud de philosophie et de psychologie.* Subtitle varies.

DATES OF PUBLICATION: Jaargang 1–18+, August 1933–1950+.

FREQUENCY: Bimonthly.

NUMBERING VARIATIONS: None.

PUBLISHER: **Potchefstroom, Transvaal:** Von Wiellighstraat 40 Westelake Stem, 1933–1950.

PRIMARY EDITORS: **D. J. van Rooy,** 1933–1937. Editorial staff comprised of professors of Potchefstroom University for Christian Higher Education, 1938–1950+.

701. *Nederlandsch tijdschrift voor psychologie.*

TITLE VARIATIONS: Continued by *Nederlandsch tijdschrift voor psychologie en hare grensgebieden* with Jaargang 4, 1936.

DATES OF PUBLICATION: Jaargang 1–3, May 1933–April 1936.

FREQUENCY: Monthly.

NUMBERING VARIATIONS: None.

PUBLISHER: **Amsterdam:** Academische uitgeverij Amsterdam-Weenen, 1933–1936.

PRIMARY EDITORS: [**L. van der Horst,**] 1933–1936; [**G. Révész,**] 1933–1936.

702. *Occupations: The Vocational Guidance Journal.* [Official organ of the National Vocational Guidance Association.]

TITLE VARIATIONS: Subtitle varies. Continues *Vocational Guidance Magazine.*

DATES OF PUBLICATION: Volume 12–29, June 1933–1950+.

FREQUENCY: **Nine times a year,** October to June, Volume 12–17, June 1933–June 1939. **Eight times a year,** October to May, October 1939–1950+.

NUMBERING VARIATIONS: None.

PUBLISHER: **New York:** National Occupational Conference, 1933–1939. **New York:** National Vocational Guidance Association, Inc., 1939–1949. **Washington, D.C.:** National Vocational Guidance Association, Inc., 1949–1950+.

PRIMARY EDITORS: **Fred C. Smith,** 1933–1937; **Arthur J. Jones,** 1933–1936; **Harry D. Kitson,** 1933–1935, 1936–1950; **Mildred E. Lincoln,** 1933–1934; **Morse A. Cartwright,** 1933–1939; **Marie McNamara,** 1934–1937; **John A. Fitch,** 1935–1938; **Donald M. Cresswell,** 1936–1939; **Leona C. Buchwald,** 1937–1939; **Lynn A. Emerson,** 1937–1939; **Rex B. Cunliffe,** 1938–1939; **Ralph B. Kenney,** 1939–1941; **Clarence W. Failor,** 1941–1943; **Gertrude Wolff,** 1945–1948; **Ruth Bellamy,** 1948–1949; **Nancy Shivers,** 1949–1950+; **Campbell B. Beard,** 1950+.

EDITORIAL BOARD: Fred C. Smith, 1944–1946; Franklin J. Keller, 1933–1936; Robert Hoppock, 1933–1940; Raymond G. Fuller, 1933–1936; Royal J. Davis, 1934; Edwin A. Lee, 1936–1939; Harold C. Whitford, 1938–1939; Leona C. Buchwald, 1939–1940; Warren K. Layton, 1939–1941; Irma E. Voigt, 1939–1942; Roy A. Hinderman, 1940–1944; Dorothy S. Wheeler, 1940–1944;

Arthur F. Dodge, 1941–1946; Forrest H. Kirkpatrick, 1941–1946, 1950+; Christine Melcher, 1943–1945; Georgia Brown, 1944–1946; H. B. McDaniel, 1944–1948; Leonard M. Miller, 1944; C. L. Shartle, 1944–1946; M. R. Trabue, 1945–1948; Garrett Bergen, 1946–1948; Frank S. Endicott, 1946–1949; Dorothy Hay, 1946–1949; Raymond H. Shevenell, 1946–1948; Edward Landy, 1946–1949; Wilson R. G. Bender, 1948–1950; Truman M. Cheney, 1948–1950; Charles R. Foster, 1948–1950; Marguerite E. Stuehrk, 1948–1950; Mary J. Drucker, 1949–1950+; Clifford Erickson, 1949–1950+; Robert Shaffer, 1949–1950+; Edgar L. Harden, 1950+; J. R. MacNeel, 1950+; William D. Wilkins, 1950+.

703. *Oregon. University. Studies in Psychology.*

TITLE VARIATIONS: Continues [*Oregon. University.*] *Publications. Psychology Series.*

DATES OF PUBLICATION: Volume 1, Number 4–7, December 1933–December 1935.

FREQUENCY: Irregular. *See* Contents *below.*

NUMBERING VARIATIONS: All issues also numbered as [*Oregon. University.*] *Publications.* One issue also numbered in *Psychoanalytic Review. See* Contents *below.*

PUBLISHER: **Eugene, Oregon:** University of Oregon, 1933–1935.

PRIMARY EDITORS: None listed.

CONTENTS:

Volume 1, Number 4. Anderson, Irving, and Harold R. Crosland. THE EFFECTS OF EYE-DOMINANCE ON "RANGE OF ATTENTION" SCORES. December 1933. 23 pp. (Also as [*Oregon. University.*] *Publications,* Volume 4, Number 4.)

———, **Number 5.** Anderson, Irving, and Harold R. Crosland. THE EFFECTS OF HANDEDNESS ON "RANGE OF ATTENTION" SCORES. January 1934. 16 pp. (Also as [*Oregon. University.*] *Publications,* Volume 4, Number 5.)

———, **Number 6.** Anderson, Irving, and Harold R. Crosland. THE EFFECTS OF COMBINATIONS OF HANDEDNESS AND EYEDNESS ON LETTER-POSITION, "RANGE OF ATTENTION" SCORES. March 1934. 48 pp. (Also as [*Oregon. University.*] *Publications,* Volume 4, Number 7.)

———, **Number 7.** Smith, S. Stephenson, and Andrei Isotoff. THE ABNORMAL FROM WITHIN: DOSTOEVSKY. December 1935. (Also as [*Oregon. University.*] *Publications,* Volume 5, Number 2; and as *Psychoanalytic Review,* Volume 22, Number 4, October 1935, pp. 361–391.)

704. *Psikhogigienu v massy.*

TITLE VARIATIONS; None.

DATES OF PUBLICATION: Tom 1–2, 1933–1934.

FREQUENCY: 5 times a year.

NUMBERING VARIATIONS: None.

PUBLISHER: **Kharkov:** Institut sotsial'noi psikhonevrologii i psikhogigieny, 1933–1934.

PRIMARY EDITORS: Unknown.

NOTE: Information on this title was compiled from entries in *Half a Century of Soviet Serials.*

705. *Psyche; An Annual of General and Linguistic Psychology.*

TITLE VARIATIONS: Continues *Psyche. A Quarterly Review of Psychology.*

DATES OF PUBLICATON: Volume 13–18+, 1933–1938/1952+. Suspended publication 1938–1951.

FREQUENCY: **Annual,** Volume 13–17, 1933–1937. **Irregular,** Volume 18+, 1938/1952+.

NUMBERING VARIATIONS: Volume 18 contains the years 1938–1952.

PUBLISHER: **Cambridge, England:** The Orthological Institute and **London:** Kegan Paul & Co., 1933–1937. **Cambridge:** The Orthological Institute, 1938/1952+.

PRIMARY EDITOR: **C. K. Ogden,** 1933–1952+.

706. *Psychologie van het ongeloof.*

TITLE VARIATIONS: None.

DATES OF PUBLICATION: Deel 1–8, 1933–1939.

FREQUENCY: Irregular. *See* Contents *below.*

NUMBERING VARIATIONS: None.

PUBLISHER: **Amsterdam:** Boekhandel W. ten Have vd. Hövekers Boekhandel, 1933–1935. **Amsterdam:** W. ten Have, 1936–1939.

PRIMARY EDITOR: **Ph. Kohnstamm,** 1933–1939.

CONTENTS:

Deel 1. Kohnstamm, Ph. ALGEMEENE INLEIDING. 1933. 80 pp.

Deel 2. Künkel, Fr. DE RELIGIEUZE OPVOEDING IN HET GEZIN EN HET ON-GELOOF. TRANSLATED BY A. L. BOESER. 1933. 78 pp.

Deel 3. Kohnstamm, Ph. PSYCHOLOGIE VAN HET ANTI-SEMITISME. 1933. 87 pp.

Deel 4. van der Leeuw, G. HET ONGELOOF EN DE KERK. 1934. 61 pp.

Deel 5. van der Does, L. P., Jr. HET ONGELOOF EN DE HEDENDAAGSCHE MAATSCHAPPIJ. 1934. 80 pp.

Deel 6. Kohnstamm, Ph. HET ONGELOOF EN DE NATUURWETENSCHAP. 1935. 84 pp.

Deel 7. van der Does, J. C. HET ONGELOOF EN DE SCHOOL. 1936. 96 pp.

Deel 8. Rümke, H. C. KARAKTER EN AANLEG IN VERBAND MET HET ONGE-LOOF. 1939. 86 pp.

707. *Psychologist. Practical and Personal Psychology.*

TITLE VARIATIONS: Subtitle varies.

DATES OF PUBLICATION: Volume 1–Volume 18+. January 1933–December 1950+.

FREQUENCY: Monthly.

NUMBERING VARIATIONS: Issues are also assigned whole numbers, Number 1–216+.

PUBLISHER: **London:** Frank J. Allard, at Manfield House, 1933–1950+.

PRIMARY EDITOR: **Frank J. Allard,** 1933–1950+.

708. *Revista de psicología i pedagogía.*

TITLE VARIATIONS: None.

DATES OF PUBLICATION: Volumen 1–5, [Número 3,] February 1933–May 1937.

FREQUENCY: Quarterly.

NUMBERING VARIATIONS: Issues also assigned whole numbers, Número 1–19. Multinumber issue Volumen 4, Número 14/15. This issue is mismarked Volumen 5, Número 14/15, August 1936. Volumen 4, Número 16, November 1936 mismarked Volumen 6, Número 16.

PUBLISHER: **Barcelona:** Publicada per l'institut psicotecnic de la generalitat i el seminari de pedagogía de la universitat, 1933–1937.

PRIMARY EDITORS: **Emilio Mira Lopez,** 1933–1937; **Joaqium Xirau,** 1933–1937.

709. *Rivista di psicologia normale e patologica.* [Official organ of the Società italiana di psicologia and the Istituti universitari di psicologia sperimentale.]

TITLE VARIATIONS. Title lengthened to *Rivista di psicologia normale, patologica e applicata,* 1942+. Continues *Rivista di psicologia.* [2].

DATES OF PUBLICATION: Volume 29–41, 1933–1945.

FREQUENCY: Quarterly.

NUMBERING VARIATIONS: Volume 29–37 also called Série III. Multinumbered issues in Volume 33, 36–41. Volume 38–41 also labeled Série IV.

PUBLISHER. **Bologna:** Nicola Zanichelli editore, 1933–1941. **Florence:** G. C. Sansoni editore, 1942–1945.

PRIMARY EDITORS: **Mario F. Canella,** 1933–1945; **A. Marzi,** 1933–1937, 1942; **V. Petri,** 1933–1939; **C. A. Ferrari,** 1942; **V. Lazzeroni,** 1942–1943; **A. Miotto,** 1942–1943.

EDITORIAL BOARD: E. Bonaventura, 1933–1938, 1943; C. Colucci, 1933–1941; S. de Sanctis, 1933–1935; C. A. Ferrari, 1933–1941, 1943; G. Pellacani, 1933–1943; M. Ponzo, 1933–1943; O. Rossi, 1933–1935; A. Gatti, 1935–1937; L. Galdo, 1938–1943; A. Marzi, 1938–1941, 1943; F. Banissoni, 1938–1943; A. Niceforo, 1940–1943; U. Cerletti, 1940–1943; M. Gozzano, 1940–1943; G. Vidoni, 1940–1943; S. Baglioni, 1942–1943; G. C. Pupilli, 1942–1943; S. Sergi, 1942–1943; P. Rossi, 1943; C. L. Musatti, 1933–1938; A. Gemelli, 1933–1943.

710. S.-A. tydskrif vir sielkunde en opvoedkunde.

TITLE VARIATIONS: S.-A. is an abbreviation for Suid-Afrikaanse.

DATES OF PUBLICATION: 1–2, 1933–1934.

FREQUENCY: Unknown.

NUMBERING VARIATIONS: None.

PUBLISHER: **Johannesburg:** Publisher unknown, 1933–1934.

PRIMARY EDITORS: None listed.

NOTE: Above entry is based on partial information. The compilers were unable to examine this title.

711. San Francisco. Old Age Counseling Center. Publications.

TITLE VARIATIONS: None.

DATES OF PUBLICATION: Number 1–5, 1933.

FREQUENCY: Irregular. *See* Contents *below.*

NUMBERING VARIATIONS: Number 4 listed with 2 different titles. *See* Contents *below.*

PUBLISHER: **San Francisco:** Old Age Counseling Center, 1933.

PRIMARY EDITORS: None listed. However, Lillian J. Martin and Clare de Gruchy may be considered editors, 1933.

CONTENTS:

Number 1. Martin, Lillien J., and Clare de Gruchy. SALVAGING OLD AGE IN INDUSTRY. 1933. 7 pp.

Number 2. Martin, Lillien J., and Clare de Gruchy. SALVAGING OLD AGE IN SOCIAL WORK. 1933.

Number 3. Martin, Lillien J., and Clare de Gruchy. SALVAGING OLD AGE IN FAMILY RELATIONS. 1933.

Number 4a. Martin, Lillien J., and Clare de Gruchy. SALVAGING OLD AGE IN INSTITUTIONS. 1933.

Number 4b. Martin, Lillien J., and Clare de Gruchy. OLD AGE AND THE FUTURE. 1933. 8 pp.

Number 5. Martin, Lillien J., and Clare de Gruchy. SALVAGING THE UN-EMPLOYED. 1933.

712. Schriften zur Wirtschaftspsychologie und zur Arbeitswissenschaft.

TITLE VARIATIONS: Continues *Schriften zur Psychologie der Berufseignung und des Wirtschaftslebens.*

DATES OF PUBLICATION: Heft 45–47, 1933.

FREQUENCY: Irregular. *See* Contents *below.*

NUMBERING VARIATIONS: One issue also numbered in *Zeitschrift für angewandte Psychologie. See* Contents *below.*

PUBLISHER: **Leipzig:** Johann Ambrosius Barth, 1933.

PRIMARY EDITORS: **Otto Lipmann,** 1933; **William Stern,** 1933.

CONTENTS:

Heft 45. Erdelyi, Michael, Otto Lipmann, Isaak N. Spielrein, and William Stern. PRINZIPIENFRAGEN DER PSYCHOTECHNIK. ABHANDLUNGEN ÜBER BEGRIFF UND ZIELE DER PSYCHOTECHNIK UND DER PRAKTISCHEN PSYCHOLOGIE. 1933. 79 pp.

Heft 46. Busse, Hanns. BEKÄMPFUNG DER ARBEITSERMÜDUNG BEI BAND-MONTAGE. 1933. 26 pp.

Heft 47. Lorenz, Edu. ZUR PSYCHOLOGIE DER INDUSTRIELLEN GRUPPEN-ARBEIT. 1933. 45 pp. (Also as *Zeitschrift fur angewandte Psychologie,* Volume 45, 1933, pp. 1–45.)

713. *Sociologus. Zeitschrift für Völkerpsychologie und Soziologie. Beiheft.*

TITLE VARIATIONS: None.

DATES OF PUBLICATION: Heft 1–3, 1933.

FREQUENCY: Irregular. *See* Contents *below.*

NUMBERING VARIATIONS: None.

PUBLISHER: **Leipzig:** C. L. Hirschfeld, 1933.

PRIMARY EDITOR: **Richard Thurnwald,** 1933.

CONTENTS:

Heft 1. Stern, Bernhard J., ed. THE LETTERS OF LUDWIG GUMPLOWICZ TO LESTER F. WARD. 1933. 32 pp.

Heft 2. Schwiedland, Eugen. ZUR SOZIOLOGIE DES UNTERNEHMERTUMS. 1933. 52 pp.

Heft 3. Götz, Berndt. DIE BEDEUTUNG DES OPFERS BEI DEN VÖLKERN. 1933. 82 pp.

714. *Stanford University. Publications. University Series. Education and Psychology.*

TITLE VARIATIONS: None.

DATES OF PUBLICATION: Volume 1–2, Number 1, 1933–1950+ Suspended publication 1936–1949.

FREQUENCY: Irregular. *See* Contents *below.*

NUMBERING VARIATIONS: None.

PUBLISHER: **Stanford, California:** Stanford University Press, 1933–1950+.

PRIMARY EDITORS: None listed.

CONTENTS:

Volume 1, Number 1. Strong, Edward K., and Reginald Bell. VOCATIONAL APTITUDES OF SECOND-GENERATION JAPANESE IN THE UNITED STATES. 1933. 183 pp.

————, **Number 2.** Strong, Edward K. JAPANESE IN CALIFORNIA. 1933. 188 pp.

————, **Number 3.** Bell, Reginald. PUBLIC SCHOOL EDUCATION OF SECOND-GENERATION JAPANESE IN CALIFORNIA. 1935. 116 pp.

Volume 2, Number 1. Farnsworth, Paul Randolph. MUSICAL TASTE: ITS MEASUREMENT AND CULTURAL NATURE. 1950. 94 pp.

715. *Statistical Methodology Reviews.*

TITLE VARIATIONS: *See* Contents *below.*

DATES OF PUBLICATION: Number 1–3, 1933/1938–1941/1950.

FREQUENCY: Irregular. *See* Contents *below.*

NUMBERING VARIATIONS: None.

PUBLISHER: **New Brunswick, New Jersey:** Rutgers University Press, 1938. **Highland Park, New Jersey:** Gryphon Press, 1941. **New York:** John Wiley and Sons, 1951.

PRIMARY EDITOR: **Oscar K. Buros,** 1933/1938–1941/1950.

CONTENTS:

Number 1. RESEARCH AND STATISTICAL METHODOLOGY. BOOKS AND REVIEWS. 1933–1938. (Reprinted from the *Mental Measurements Yearbook,* 1938.)

Number 2. SECOND YEARBOOK OF RESEARCH AND STATISTICAL METHODOLOGY. BOOKS AND REVIEWS. 1941.

Number 3. STATISTICAL METHODOLOGY REVIEWS. 1941–1950.

716. *Studies in Social Eugenics.*

TITLE VARIATIONS: None.

DATES OF PUBLICATION: Number 1–2, 1933–1934.

FREQUENCY: Irregular. *See* Contents *below.*

NUMBERING VARIATIONS: One issue also numbered as *Eugenics Research Association. Monograph. See* Contents *below.*

PUBLISHER: **New York:** Macmillan Company, 1933. **Cold Spring Harbor, New York:** Eugenics Research Association, 1934.

PRIMARY EDITOR: **Frederick H. Osborn,** 1933–1934.

CONTENTS:

Number 1. Schwesinger, Gladys C. HEREDITY AND ENVIRONMENT. STUDIES IN THE GENESIS OF PSYCHOLOGICAL CHARACTERISTICS. 1933. 484 pp.

Number 2. Lorimer, Frank, and Frederick H. Osborn. DYNAMICS OF POPULATION; SOCIAL AND BIOLOGICAL SIGNIFICANCE OF CHANGING BIRTH RATES IN THE UNITED STATES. 1934. 461 pp. (Also as *Eugenics Research Association. Monograph,* Number 9.)

717. *Tohoku Psychologica Folia.*

TITLE VARIATIONS: None.

DATES OF PUBLICATION: Volume 1–12, Number 1/2+, 1933–1950+. Suspended publication, 1945–1948.

FREQUENCY: Quarterly.

NUMBERING VARIATIONS: Double issues in Volume 6, 7, 9, 10, 11, and 12.

PUBLISHER: **Sendai:** Tohoku Teikoku Daigaku [Tohoku Imperial University], 1933–1944. **Sendai:** Tohoku Daigaku [Tohoku University], 1949–1950+.

PRIMARY EDITORS: **Tanenari Chiba,** 1933–1949; **Toshihiko Fujita,** 1933–1949; **Uiti Kuribayasi,** 1933–1950+; **Yosikazu Ohwaki,** 1933–1950+; **M. Masaki,** 1949–1950+; **Seiro Kitamura,** 1950+; **K. Motokawa,** 1950+.

718. *Toronto. University. Studies. Child Development Series.*

TITLE VARIATIONS: None.

DATES OF PUBLICATION: Number 1–18, September 1933–1940.

FREQUENCY: Irregular. *See* Contents *below.*

NUMBERING VARIATIONS: Numbers 11–16 issued bound as a single volume: Blatz, W. E., N. Chant, M. W. Charles, M. I. Fletcher, N.H.C. Ford, A. L. Harris, J. W. MacArthur, M. Mason, and D. A. Millichamp. *Collected Studies on the Dionne Quintuplets.* October, 1937.

PUBLISHER: **Toronto:** University of Toronto Press, 1933–1940.

PRIMARY EDITORS: None listed.

CONTENTS:

Number 1. Bott, Helen. METHOD IN SOCIAL STUDIES OF YOUNG CHILDREN. 1933. 110 pp.

Number 2. Bott, Helen. PERSONALITY DEVELOPMENT IN YOUNG CHILDREN. 1934. 139 pp.

Number 3. Blatz, William E., and Mabel Crews Ringland. THE STUDY OF TICS IN PRE-SCHOOL CHILDREN. 1935. 58 pp.

Number 4. Blatz, William E., and Dorothy A. Millichamp. THE DEVELOPMENT OF EMOTION IN THE INFANT. 1935. 44 pp.

Number 5. OUTLINES FOR PARENT EDUCATION GROUPS: PRE-SCHOOL LEARNING. By the Staff of St. George's School for Child Study. nd. 77 pp.

Number 6. Blatz, W. E., and J.D.M. Griffin. AN EVALUATION OF THE CASE HISTORIES OF A GROUP OF PRE-SCHOOL CHILDREN. 1936. 24 pp.

Number 7. Blatz, William E., Kathleen Drew Allin, and Dorothy A. Millichamp. A STUDY OF LAUGHTER IN THE NURSERY SCHOOL CHILD. 1936. 31 pp.

Number 8. Bott, Helen. ADULT ATTITUDES TO CHILDREN'S MISDEMEANOURS. 1937. 21 pp.

Number 9. Blatz, W. E., S.N.F. Chant, and M. D. Salter. EMOTIONAL EPISODES IN THE CHILD OF SCHOOL AGE. 1937. 45 pp.

Number 10. Bernhardt, Karl S., Dorothy A. Millichamp, Marion W. Charles, and Mary P. McFarland. AN ANALYSIS OF THE SOCIAL CONTACTS OF PRESCHOOL CHILDREN WITH THE AID OF MOTION PICTURES. 1937. 53 pp.

Number 11. MacArthur, John W., and Norma Ford. A BIOLOGICAL STUDY OF THE DIONNE QUINTUPLETS. AN IDENTICAL SET. 1937. 49 pp.

Number 12. Blatz, W. E., and D. A. Millichamp. THE MENTAL GROWTH OF THE DIONNE QUINTUPLETS. 1937. 13 pp.

Number 13. Blatz, W. E., D. A. Millichamp, and M. W. Charles. THE EARLY SOCIAL DEVELOPMENT OF THE DIONNE QUINTUPLETS. 1937. 40 pp.

Number 14. Blatz, W. E., D. A. Millichamp, and N. Chant. THE DEVELOPMENT OF SELF-DISCIPLINE IN THE DIONNE QUINTUPLETS. 1937. 40 pp.

Number 15. Blatz, W. E., D. A. Millichamp, and A. L. Harris. ROUTINE TRAINING OF THE DIONNE QUINTUPLETS (SLEEPING, EATING, ELIMINATION ROUTINE, WASHING, DRESSING, AND PLAY). 1937. 48 pp.

Number 16. Blatz, W. E., M. I. Fletcher, and M. Mason. EARLY DEVELOPMENT IN SPOKEN LANGUAGE OF THE DIONNE QUINTUPLETS. 1937. 13 pp.

Number 17. OUTLINES FOR PARENT EDUCATION GROUPS: DISCIPLINE. By the Staff of the Institute of Child Study. nd. 38 pp.

Number 18. Salter, Mary D. AN EVALUATION OF ADJUSTMENT BASED UPON THE CONCEPT OF SECURITY. 1940. 72 pp.

719. *Yidischer wisnaschaftlicher Institut. Psichologishpedagogishe Sekzye. Shriftn far Psichologye un Pedagogik.*

TITLE VARIATIONS: Institute also called: Yiddish Scientific Institute; and, Zydowski instytut naukowy.

DATES OF PUBLICATION: Tom 1, 1933.

FREQUENCY: Irregular.

NUMBERING VARIATIONS: Also numbered as *Prace zydowskiege instytutu naukowego*, Tom 7, 1933.

PUBLISHER: **Vilna:** Yidischer wisnaschaftlicher Institut, Psichologish-pedagogishe Sekzye, 1933.

PRIMARY EDITOR: **L. Lehrer,** 1933.

720. *Zeitschrift für pädogogische Psychologie und Jugendkunde.*

TITLE VARIATIONS: Continues *Zeitschrift für pädogogische Psychologie, experimentelle Pädagogik und jugendkundliche Forschung.*

DATES OF PUBLICATION: Jahrgang 34, Heft 9–Jahrgang 45, Heft 2, September 1933–February 1944.

FREQUENCY: **Monthly,** Jahrgang 34–35, 1933–1934. **Bimonthly,** Jahrgang 36–43, 1935–1942. **5 numbers,** Jahrgang 44, 1943. **2 numbers,** Jahrgang 45, 1944.

NUMBERING VARIATIONS: Multinumbered issues present.

PUBLISHER: **Leipzig:** Quelle & Meyer, 1933–1940. **Heidelberg:** Quelle & Meyer, 1941–1944.

PRIMARY EDITORS: **Otto Scheibner,** 1933–1944; **Oswald Kroh,** 1933–1944; **Aloys Fischer,** 1933–1937; **A. Hoffmann,** 1933–1940; **Hans Volkelt,** 1933–1940; **E. Jaensch,** 1938–1940; **Gerhard Pfahler,** 1939–1940.

1934

721. Algemeen nederlands tijdschrift voor wijsbegeerte en psychologie.

TITLE VARIATIONS: Continues *Tijdschrift voor wijsbegeerte*.

DATES OF PUBLICATION: Jaargang 27–39+, 1934–1950+. Suspended publication August 1944–April 1946.

FREQUENCY: Bimonthly (5 times yearly).

NUMBERING VARIATIONS: Multinumber issues present.

PUBLISHER: **Assen, Netherlands:** Van Gorcum & Comp., 1934–1950+.

PRIMARY EDITORS: None listed.

722. Association of Consulting Psychologists. Newsletter.

TITLE VARIATIONS: Continued by *Consulting Psychologist* with Volume 2, November 1935.

DATES OF PUBLICATION: Volume 1, Number 1–7, November 1934–June 1935.

FREQUENCY: **Monthly,** Volume 1, Number 1–6, November 1934–April 1935. **Bimonthly,** Volume 1, Number 7, June 1935.

NUMBERING VARIATIONS: Volume 1 only contains 7 issues. Volume 1, Number 1 is a letter from the secretary of the Association of Consulting Psychologists and two enclosures: 1. THE SUGGESTED PLAN FOR EXPANDING THE SCOPE OF THE ASSOCIATION: and 2. DRAFT OF REGULATIONS FOR LICENSING PSYCHOLOGISTS, prepared by Ethel Cornell.

PUBLISHER: **New York:** Association of Consulting Psychologists, 1934–1935.

PRIMARY EDITORS: **Warren G. Findley,** 1934–1935; **Andrew W. Brown,** 1935; **Gladys G. Idle,** 1935; **Percival Symonds,** 1935.

723. Cahiers de pédagogie expérimentale et de psychologie de l'enfant. (Première série).

TITLE VARIATIONS: Series also cited as: [*Université de Genève.*] *Institut des sciences de l'éducation. Cahiers de pédagogie expérimentale et de psychologie de l'enfant.* Superseded by *Cahiers de pédagogie expérimentale et de psychologie de l'enfant. (Nouvelle série)* with Numéro 1, 1946.

DATES OF PUBLICATION: Numéro 1–11, 1934–1938.

FREQUENCY: Irregular. *See* Contents *below.*

NUMBERING VARIATIONS: None.

PUBLISHER: **Neuchâtel:** Delachaux et Niestlé, 1934–1938.

PRIMARY EDITORS: **Pierre Bovet,** 1934–1938; **Édouard Claparède,** 1934–1938.

CONTENTS:

Numéro 1. Claparède, Éd. LE SENTIMENT D'INFÉRIORITÉ CHEZ L'ENFANT. 1934. 28 pp.

Numéro 2. Junod, Charles. RECHERCHES SUR LA FACILITÉ DE LANGAGE. 1934. 16 pp.

Numéro 3. Meili, Richard. TESTS ANALYTIQUES D'INTELLIGENCE. 1934.

Numéro 4. Schmid, Jakob Robert. TYPES DE MAÎTRES. 1934. 20 pp.

Numéro 5. Rey, André. RÉFLEXIONS SUR LE PROBLÈME DU DIAGNOSTIC MENTAL. 1935. 16 pp.

Numéro 6. Piaget, Jean. LES THÉORIES DE L'IMITATION. 1935. 13 pp.

Numéro 7. Szeminska, Alina. ESSAI D'ANALYSE PSYCHOLOGIQUE DU RAISONNEMENT MATHÉMATIQUE. [1935.] 18 pp.

Numéro 8. Meyer, Edith. LA REPRÉSENTATION DES RELATIONS SPATIALES CHEZ L'ENFANT. 1935. 20 pp.

Numéro 9. Inhelder, Bärbel. OBSERVATIONS SUR LE PRINCIPE DE CONSERVATION DANS LA PHYSIQUE DE L'ENFANT. 1936. 20 pp.

Numéro 10. Bovet, Pierre. ÉCOLE NOUVELLES D'AUTREFOIS. 1938. 82 pp.

Numéro 11. Lerner, Eugene. OBSERVATIONS SUR LE RAISONNEMENT MORAL DE L'ENFANT. 1938. 27 pp.

724. Character and Personality; An International Psychological Quarterly.

TITLE VARIATIONS: Continues *Character and Personality; An International Quarterly of Psychodiagnostics and Allied Studies*. Continued by *Journal of Personality* with Volume 14, September 1945.

DATES OF PUBLICATION: Volume 3–13, September 1934–June 1945.

FREQUENCY: Quarterly.

NUMBERING VARIATIONS: None.

PUBLISHER: **Durham, North Carolina:** Duke University Press, 1934–1945.

PRIMARY EDITORS: **Robert Saudek,** 1934–1935; **Karl Zener,** 1934–1945; **Charles E. Spearman,** 1935–1944; **Jan Meloun,** 1935–1944.

COLLABORATORS/EDITORIAL BOARD: None listed, 1937–1938; Alfred Adler, 1934–1936; Gordon W. Allport, 1934–1936, 1939–1945; Francis Aveling, 1939–1943; P. B. Ballard, 1934–1936, 1939–1945; F. C. Bartlett, 1939–1945; Ruth Benedict, 1939–1945; Walter V. Bingham, 1939–1945; Stefan Błachowski, 1934–1936; Manfred Bleuler, 1934–1936, 1939–1945; Warner Brown, 1939–1945; Oluf Brüel, 1939–1945; Oswald Bumke, 1934–1936; Charlotte Bühler, 1939–1945; Karl Bühler, 1939–1945; Cyril L. Burt, 1939–1945; Raymond B. Cattell, 1939–1945; Édouard Claparède, 1939–1945; J. Crepieux-Jamin, 1934–1936; Max Dessoir, 1934–1936; James Drever, 1934–1936, 1939–1945; Elisabeth Enke, 1934–1936; John C. Flugel, 1939–1945; F. N. Freeman, 1934–1936; Max I. Friedlander, 1934–1936; Robert Heindl, 1934–1936; R.W.G. Hingston, 1934–1936; Karl J. Holzinger, 1939–1945; Pryns Hopkins, 1935–1936, 1939–1945; Pierre Janet, 1934–1936; C. G. Jung, 1934–1936; James Kerr, 1934–1936; Charles W. Kimmins, 1934–1936,

1939–1945; Ernst Kretschmer, 1934–1936, 1939–1945; E. Landau, 1934–1936; Johannes Lange, 1934–1936, 1939–1945; Lucien Lévy-Bruhl, 1934–1936; William Line, 1939–1945; Helge Lundholm, 1934–1936, 1939–1945; A. R. Luria, 1934–1936; D. R. MacCalman, 1939–1945; William McDougall, 1934–1936; Edward Mapother, 1939–1940; Jan Meloun, 1934–1935, 1944–1945; Thomas V. Moore, 1939–1945; Charles S. Myers, 1939–1945; T. H. Pear, 1934–1936, 1939–1945; Henri Piéron, 1939–1945; Martin L. Reymert, 1939–1945; A. A. Roback, 1934–1936, 1939–1945; J. S. Rosenthal, 1934–1936; F. Schwangart, 1934–1936; C. G. Seligman, 1939–1943; Constance A. Simmins, 1939–1945; William Stephenson, 1939–1945; Lewis M. Terman, 1934–1936, 1939–1945; Edward L. Thorndike, 1939–1945; Robert H. Thouless, 1939–1945; Louis L. Thurstone, 1939–1945; V. Tille, 1934–1936; Emil Utitz, 1934–1936, 1939–1945; Philip E. Vernon, 1939–1945; Otmar von Verschuer, 1934–1936; Aleš Hrdlicka, 1934–1936; Hans Driesch, 1934–1936; Havelock Ellis, 1934–1936; Paul Ranschburg, 1934–1936; E. D. Wiersma, 1934–1936, 1939–1945; E. H. Wild, 1939–1945; L. Wynn-Jones, 1939–1945; Donald W. MacKinnon, 1940–1945; John Gillin, 1941–1945; Charles Spearman, 1944–1945.

725. *Chiao yü yü hsin li.* [Education and Psychology.] [*2.*]

TITLE VARIATIONS: None.

DATES OF PUBLICATION: Volume 1, Number 1, March 1934.

FREQUENCY: Irregular.

NUMBERING VARIATIONS: None.

PUBLISHER: **Peking:** Fujen ta hsüeh. Chiao yü k'o hsüeh yen Chiu hui [Fujen University. Society of Educational Sciences], 1934.

PRIMARY EDITORS: None listed.

NOTE: Fujen University also called in English: Catholic University, Peking. Information on this title was partially compiled from *Chuan-kuo Chung-wen Chi-kan lien-ho mu-lu, 1833–1949* [Union List of Chinese Periodicals in China, 1833–1949]. Peking, Peking Library, 1961.

726. *Dobutsu Shinri.* [Animal Psychology.] [*1.*]

TITLE VARIATIONS: None.

DATES OF PUBLICATION: Volume 1–4, 1934–1937.

FREQUENCY: Quarterly.

NUMBERING VARIATIONS: None.

PUBLISHER: **[Tokyo:]** Dobutsu Shinrigakai, [Society for Animal Psychology], 1934–1937.

PRIMARY EDITORS: None listed.

NOTE: Information for this entry was found in *Gakujutsu Zasshi Sōgō Mokuroku. Shizen Kagaku Wabun Hen* [Union List of Scholarly Journals. Japanese Language Section. Natural Sciences Part]. Tokyo, 1968.

727. *Duke University. Contributions to Psychological Theory.*

TITLE VARIATIONS: Supersedes *Duke University. Psychological Monographs.*

DATES OF PUBLICATION: Number 1–7, 1934–1942.

FREQUENCY: Irregular. *See* Contents *below.*

NUMBERING VARIATIONS: Issues also numbered as Volume 1–2, Number 3.

PUBLISHER: **Durham, North Carolina:** Duke University Press, 1934–1942.

PRIMARY EDITORS: **Donald K. Adams,** 1934–1942; **Helge Lundholm,** 1934–1942.

CONTENTS:

Number 1. Lundholm, Helge, CONATION AND OUR CONSCIOUS LIFE. PROLEGOMENA TO A DOCTRINE OF URGE PSYCHOLOGY. 1934. 96 pp.

Number 2. McCulloch, Thomas Logan. A STUDY OF THE COGNITIVE ABILITIES OF THE WHITE RAT WITH SPECIAL REFERENCE TO SPEARMAN'S THEORY OF TWO FACTORS. 1935. 66 pp.

Number 3. Wright, Herbert Fletcher. THE INFLUENCE OF BARRIERS UPON STRENGTH OF MOTIVATION. 1937. 143 pp.

Number 4. Lewin, Kurt. THE CONCEPTUAL REPRESENTATION AND MEASUREMENT OF PSYCHOLOGICAL FORCES. 1938. 247 pp.

Number 5. MacColl, Sylvia Hazelton. A COMPARATIVE STUDY OF THE SYSTEMS OF LEWIN AND KOFFKA WITH SPECIAL REFERENCE TO MEMORY PHENOMENA. 1939. 160 pp.

Number 6. Buxton, Claude E. LATENT LEARNING AND THE GOAL GRADIENT HYPOTHESIS. 1940. 75 pp.

Number 7. Henle, Mary. AN EXPERIMENTAL INVESTIGATION OF DYNAMIC AND STRUCTURAL DETERMINANTS OF SUBSTITUTION. 1942. 112 pp.

728. *Hsin li hsüeh pan nien Kan.* [Psychology Semi-Annual.]

TITLE VARIATIONS: None.

DATES OF PUBLICATION: Volume 1–4, Number 1, January 1934–1937.

FREQUENCY: Semiannual.

NUMBERING VARIATIONS: None.

PUBLISHER: **Nanking:** Kuo li Chung-yang ta hsüeh [National Central University], 1934–1937.

PRIMARY EDITORS: None listed.

NOTE: Information on this title was compiled from *Chuan-kuo Chung-wen Chi-kan lien-ho mu-lu, 1833–1949* [Union List of Chinese Periodicals in China, 1833–1949]. Peking, Peking Library, 1961.

729. *Hsin li hsüeh pan nien Kan. Hsin li fu Kan.* [Psychology Semi-Annual. Supplement.]

TITLE VARIATIONS: None.

DATES OF PUBLICATION: Number 1–6, 9–12, 14–41, 43–50, 1934–1937.

FREQUENCY: Irregular.

NUMBERING VARIATIONS: None.

PUBLISHER: **Nanking:** Kuo li Chung-yang ta hsüeh [National Central University], 1934–1937.

PRIMARY EDITORS: None listed.

NOTE: Information on this title was compiled from *Chuan-kuo Chung-wen Chi-kan lien-ho mu-lu, 1833–1949* [Union List of Chinese Periodicals in China, 1833–1949]. Peking, Peking Library, 1961.

730. *Individual Psychology Medical Pamphlets.*

TITLE VARIATIONS: Titled *Individual Psychology Pamphlets. Medical Pamphlets,* Number 13, 1934. Continues *Individual Psychology Pamphlets.*

DATES OF PUBLICATION: Number 13–23, 1934–November 1943.

FREQUENCY: Irregular. *See* Contents *below.*

NUMBERING VARIATIONS: None.

PUBLISHER: **London:** C. W. Daniel Company for the Medical Society of Individual Psychology (London), 1934–1940. **Ashingdon, Rochford, Essex:** C. W. Daniel Company for the Medical Society of Individual Psychology (London), 1943.

PRIMARY EDITOR: **J. C. Young,** 1934–1935; **Maurice Marcus,** 1934–1935; **H. C. Squires,** 1936–1943.

CONTENTS:

Number 13. Adler, Alfred, and F. G. Crookshank. INDIVIDUAL PSYCHOLOGY AND SEXUAL DIFFICULTIES (II). September 1934. 63 pp.

Number 14. Ferguson, Mary, Hilda Weber, O. H. Woodcock, F. V. Bevan-Brown, and J. C. Young. AWARENESS AND THE NEUROSES OF DECLINING YEARS. June 1935. 61 pp.

Number 15. Bevan-Brown, C. M., G.E.S. Ward, and F. G. Crookshank. INDIVIDUAL PSYCHOLOGY: THEORY AND PRACTICE. May 1936. 79 pp.

Number 16. Langdon-Brown, Walter, R. G. Macdonald Ladell, Frank Gray, and F. G. Crookshank. THE PLACE OF PSYCHOLOGY IN THE MEDICAL CURRICULUM AND OTHER PAPERS. October 1936. 64 pp.

Number 17. Baynes, H. G., S. Crown, S. H. Lubner, A. C. Court, M. Marcus, and F. G. Crookshank. THE PARENT-CHILD RELATION: THE PSYCHOLOGICAL BACKGROUND AND OTHER PAPERS. June 1937. 71 pp.

Number 18. Partridge, E. Joyce, H. Crichton-Miller, T. A. Ross, and F. G. Crookshank. THE MANAGEMENT OF EARLY INFANCY; PUBERTY AND ADOLESCENCE; THE PSYCHOLOGICAL APPROACH; and THE NEUROTIC CHARACTER. December 1937. 64 pp.

Number 19. Mairet, Philip, H. C. Squires, Cuthbert Dukes, O. H. Woodcock, Walter Langdon-Brown et al. THE CONTRIBUTION OF ALFRED ADLER. April 1938. 76 pp.

Number 20. Macmurray, John, A.T.M. Wilson, Ralph Noble, and F. G. Crookshank. A PHILOSOPHER LOOKS AT PSYCHOTHERAPY; PSYCHOLOGICAL FAC-

TORS IN ORGANIC DISEASE; PSYCHIATRY AND THE COMMUNITY; and THE FAMILY, SOCIETY, AND EDUCATION. December 1938. 72 pp.

Number 21. Bennet, E. A., George Gordon, W. R. Reynell, Ethel Dukes, and F. G. Crookshank. THE SIGNIFICANCE OF DREAMS; ESCAPE INTO INVALID-ISM; THE INFECTIOUS QUALITY OF NEUROSIS; and THE SEXUAL DEMAND. July 1939. 62 pp.

Number 22. Sandison, A., R. Hargreaves, H. Crichton-Miller, and F. M. Edwards. ESCAPE INTO ACTIVITIES; THE FLIGHT INTO NORMALITY; DISCIPLINE AND LEADERSHIP; and CHINA UNDER WAR CONDITIONS. October 1940. 48 pp.

Number 23. Langdon-Brown, Walter, O. H. Woodcock, Alexander Baldie, Wilhelm Stekel, Allan Worsley, Culver Barker, H. V. Dicks, and Ellis Stungo. EARLY PHASES OF MEDICAL PSYCHOLOGY; HISTORY OF THE SOCIETY; POST WAR PLANNING; ACTIVE PSYCHOTHERAPY IN WAR-TIME; THE APPROACH TO THE PATIENT; and ANALYSIS UNDER HYPNOTICS. November 1943. 71 pp.

731. *Industrielle Psychotechnik; Der Mensch, Eignung, Leistung, Charakter, Verhalten.*

TITLE VARIATIONS: Continues *Industrielle Psychotechnik; Angewandte Psychologie in Industrie, Handel, Verkehr, Verhalten.*

DATES OF PUBLICATION: Jahrgang 11–20, Heft 7/9, January 1934–January/March 1944.

FREQUENCY: Monthly.

NUMBERING VARIATIONS: Multinumber issues in Jahrgang 11–20, 1934–1944.

PUBLISHER: **Berlin:** Buchholz und Weisswange, 1934–1944.

PRIMARY EDITOR: **Walther Moede,** 1934–1944.

732. *Internationale Zeitschrift für Psychoanalyse und "Imago." Beihefte.* [Organ of the Internationale psychoanalytische Vereinigung.]

TITLE VARIATIONS: Supersedes *Internationale Zeitschrift für Psychoanalyse. Beihefte.*

DATES OF PUBLICATION: Stück 1, 1934.

FREQUENCY: Irregular.

NUMBERING VARIATIONS: None.

PUBLISHER: **Vienna:** Internationaler psychoanalytischer Verlag, 1934.

PRIMARY EDITOR: **Sigmund Freud,** 1934.

CONTENTS:

Stück 1. Hermann, Imre. PSYCHOANALYSE ALS METHODE. 1934. 113 pp.

733. *Iowa. University. Research Studies in Educational Measurements.*

TITLE VARIATIONS: None.

DATES OF PUBLICATION: Number 1, 1934.

FREQUENCY: Irregular. *See* Contents *below.*

NUMBERING VARIATIONS: Also numbered as [*Iowa. University.*] *Studies. New Series;* and as [*Iowa. University.*] *Studies in Education. See* Contents *below.*

PUBLISHER: **Iowa City, Iowa:** University of Iowa, 1934.

PRIMARY EDITOR: **Charles L. Robbins,** 1934.

CONTENTS:

    Number 1. RESEARCH STUDIES IN EDUCATIONAL MEASUREMENTS. I: Crawford, John Raymond. AGE AND PROGRESS FACTORS IN TEST NORMS; and Kirkpatrick, James Earl. THE MOTIVATING EFFECT OF A SPECIFIC TYPE OF TESTING PROGRAM. June 15, 1934. 68 pp. (Also as [*Iowa. University.*] *Studies. New Series.* Number 277; and [*Iowa. University.*] *Studies in Education,* Volume 9, Number 4.)

734. *Jikken Shinrigaku Kenkyū.* [Experimental Psychological Research.]

TITLE VARIATIONS: Also cited in English as *Japanese Journal of Experimental Psychology.*

DATES OF PUBLICATION: Volume 1–8, April 1934–1941.

FREQUENCY: **Semiannual,** Volume 1–3, 1934–1936. **Quarterly,** Volume 4–5, Number 1/2, June 1937–October 1938. Unknown, Volume 6–8.

NUMBERING VARIATIONS: Multinumber issues present.

PUBLISHER: **Kyoto:** Kyōto Jikken Shinrigaku Kenkyūkai [Kyoto Society for Research in Experimental Psychology], 1934–1935. **Kyoto:** Kyōto Teikoku Daigaku, Jikken Shinrigaku Kenkyūkai [Kyoto Imperial University, Society for Research in Experimental Psychology], 1936–1938. Unknown, 1939–1941.

EDITORIAL BOARD: **K. Ataka,** 1934–1935; **T. Ibukiyama,** 1934–1935; **M. Kato,** 1934–1935; **S. Maekawa,** 1934–1935; **O. Miyagi,** 1934–1935; **A. Mori,** 1934–1935; **S. Odani,** 1934–1935; **K. Sato,** 1934–1935; **T. Sonohara,** 1934–1935; **A. Tadera,** 1934–1935; **O. Tamaki,** 1934–1935; **Y. Takase,** 1934–1935; **S. Utsunomiya,** 1934–1935; **C. Hasuo,** 1935; **T. Hisada,** 1935; unknown, 1936–1941.

NOTE: Information concerning period of issue beyond Volume 5 is based on data supplied by the National Diet Library of Japan. These volumes are not in their collection, however, and personnel in the Library know of no location in Japan.

735. *Kyoiku Shinri.* [Educational Psychology.]

TITLE VARIATIONS: None.

DATES OF PUBLICATION: Volume 1–2, 1934–1935.

FREQUENCY: Unknown.

NUMBERING VARIATIONS: None.

PUBLISHER: N.p.: Kyoiku Shinri Kenkyūkai [Society for Research in Educational Psychology], 1934–1935.

PRIMARY EDITORS: None listed.

NOTE: Information for this entry was obtained from *Gakujutsu Zasshi Sōgō Mokuroku. Jimbun Kagaku Wabun Hen* [Union List of Scholarly Journals. Japanese Language Section. Humanities Part]. Tokyo, 1973.

736. *Nanking. Kuo li Chung-yang ta hsüeh. Chiao yü hsüeh yüan. Chiao yü Shih yen so. Hsin li Chiao yu Shih yen Chuan pien.* [National Central University. School of Education. Institute for Educational Experimentation. Monograph of Psychology and Education.]

TITLE VARIATIONS: None.

DATES OF PUBLICATION: Volume 1–4, Number 1, February 1934–June 1939.

FREQUENCY: Irregular.

NUMBERING VARIATIONS: None.

PUBLISHER: **Nanking:** Kuo li Chung-yang ta hsüeh, Chiao yü hsüeh yüan, Chiao yü Shih yen so [National Central University, School of Education, Institute for Educational Experimentation], 1934–1939.

PRIMARY EDITOR: Hsiao Hung Hsiao, [1934–1939?].

CONTENTS:
> **Volume 1, Number 1.** Hsiao, Hsiao Hung. [DETERMINANTS IN THE FORMATION OF PERCEPTUAL UNITS.] February 1934. 104 pp.
> ———, **Number 2.** Ai, Joseph Wei. [THE MEASUREMENT OF CHINESE CHARACTERS.] March 1934. 96 pp.
> **Volume 3, Number 1.** Hsiao, Hsiao Hung, and L. T. Tsung. [THE STANDARDIZATION OF MECHANICAL ABILITY TESTS.] 1936. 54 pp.
> ———, **Number 2.** Hsiao, Hsiao Hung. [DETERMINANTS IN THE FORMATION OF PERCEPTUAL UNITS.] 1936. 118 pp.
> **Volume 4, Number 1.** Hsiao, Hsiao Hung. [HSIAO'S REVISION OF GOODENOUGH'S TEST OF INTELLIGENCE IN CHILDREN.] 1939. 51 pp.

NOTE: Incomplete information on this title was found in *Chuan-kuo Chung-wen Chi-kan lien-ho mu-lu, 1833–1949* [Union List of Chinese Periodicals in China, 1833–1949]. Peking, Peking Library, 1961; the U.S. Library of Congress; and the *Cumulative Author Index to Psychological Abstracts*.

737. *Perm. Ural'skii nauchno-issledovatel'skii psikhonevrologicheskii institut. Trudy.*

TITLE VARIATIONS: None.

DATES OF PUBLICATION: Vypusk 1–2, 1934–1935.

FREQUENCY: Annual.

NUMBERING VARIATIONS: None.

PUBLISHER: **Perm:** Ural'skii nauchno-issledovatel'skii psikhonevrologicheskii institut, 1934–1935.

PRIMARY EDITORS: Unknown.

NOTE: Information on this title was compiled from entries in *Half a Century of Soviet Serials.*

738. *Politisch-psychologische Schriftenreihe.*

TITLE VARIATIONS: None.

DATES OF PUBLICATION: Heft 1–3, 1934–1935.

FREQUENCY: Irregular. *See* Contents *below.*

NUMBERING VARIATIONS: None.

PUBLISHER: **Prague:** M. Kacha, 1934. **Copenhagen:** Verlag für Sexual-Politik, 1935.

PRIMARY EDITORS: None listed.

CONTENTS:
    Heft 1. Parell, Ernst. WAS IST KLASSENBEWUSSTSEIN? 1934. 73 pp.
    Heft 2. Reich, Wilhelm. DIALEKTISCHER MATERIALISMUS UND PSYCHO-ANALYSE. 1934. 59 pp.
    Heft 3. Teschitz, Karl. RELIGION, KIRCHE, RELIGIONSSTREIT IN DEUTSCH-LAND. 1935. 112 pp.

739. *Psychotherapeutische Praxis. Vierteljahrsschrift für praktische ärztliche Psychotherapie.*

TITLE VARIATIONS: Supersedes *Psychoanalytische Praxis.*

DATES OF PUBLICATION: Band 1–3, 1934–1937.

FREQUENCY: **Quarterly,** Band 1–2, 1934–1935. **Semiannual,** Band 3, 1936/1937.

NUMBERING VARIATIONS: None.

PUBLISHER: **Leipzig:** Verlag der psychotherapeutischen Praxis, 1934–1935. **Vienna:** Verlag für Medizin, Weidmann & Co., 1936–1937.

PRIMARY EDITORS: **Wilhelm Stekel,** 1934–1937; **Arthur Kronfeld,** 1934–1937.

740. *Revue du cercle de pédagogie.*

TITLE VARIATIONS: Continued by *Revue de pédagogie* with Tome 2, Numéro 9, 1935.

DATES OF PUBLICATION: Tome 1, Numéro 1–8, March–December 1934.

FREQUENCY: Monthly (except August and September).

NUMBERING VARIATIONS: None.

PUBLISHER: **Saint-Gilles, Brussels:** Université libre de Bruxelles, 1934.

EDITORIAL COMMITTEE: Aug. Ley, 1934; Guy Vermeylen, 1934; L. de Meut-

ter, 1934; H. Vanhamme, 1934; Dom Vandezande, 1934; Albert van Waeyen-
berghe, 1934.

741. *Societatea română de cercetări psihologice (Bucharest). Analele de psihologie.*

TITLE VARIATIONS: None.

DATES OF PUBLICATION: Volumul 1–8, 1934–1941.

FREQUENCY: Annual.

NUMBERING VARIATIONS: None.

PUBLISHER: **Bucharest:** Societatea română de cercetări psihologice, 1934–1941.

PRIMARY EDITORS: **C. Rădulescu-Motru,** 1934; **I. M. Nestor,** 1935–1941.

742. *Society for Research in Child Development. Proceedings.*

TITLE VARIATIONS: None.

DATES OF PUBLICATION: 1st–3rd, 1934–1938.

FREQUENCY: Biennial.

NUMBERING VARIATIONS: Publication date lags one year behind date of Proceedings.

PUBLISHER: **Washington, D.C.:** Committee on Child Development, Division
of Anthropology and Psychology, National Research Council, 1935. **Washington, D.C.:** Society for Research in Child Development, National Research
Council, 1937–1939.

PRIMARY EDITORS: None listed.

743. *Soldatentum. Zeitschrift für Wehrpsychologie, Wehrerziehung, Menschenauslese.* [Issued by Reichswehrministerium, 1934–1935; Reichskriegsministerium, 1936–1937; Psychologisches Laboratorium des Reichskriegsministerium, 1938; Hauptstelle der Wehrmacht für Psychologie und Rassenkunde, 1939–1940; and Inspektion des Personalprüfwesens des Heeres, 1941–1942.]

TITLE VARIATIONS: Subtitle varies.

DATES OF PUBLICATION: Jahrgang 1–9, July 1934–November 1942.

FREQUENCY: Bimonthly.

NUMBERING VARIATIONS: None.

PUBLISHER: **Berlin:** Bernard & Graefe, 1934–1942.

PRIMARY EDITORS: **P. von Voss,** 1934–1940; **Max Simoneit,** 1934–1940; **Bodo Graefe,** 1941–1942.

744. *Sprachpsychologische Untersuchungen.*

TITLE VARIATIONS: None.

DATES OF PUBLICATION: Heft 1–2, 1934–1935.

FREQUENCY: Irregular. *See* Contents *below.*

NUMBERING VARIATIONS: Hefte also numbered in *Friedrich Manns pädagogisches Magazin. See* Contents *below.*

PUBLISHER: **Langensalza, Germany:** Beyer, 1934–1935.

PRIMARY EDITOR: **Friedrich Sander,** 1934–1935.

CONTENTS:

Heft 1. Michael, Alfred Arthur. Über die sprachliche Darstellung bewegter Szenen durch schwachsinnige und normale Schulkinder. 1934. 77 pp. (Also as *Friedrich Manns pädagogisches Magazin,* Heft 1410.)

Heft 2. Maesse, Herm. Das Verhältnis von Laut- und Gebärdensprache in der Entwicklung des taubstummen Kindes. 1935. 122 pp. (Also as *Friedrich Manns pädagogisches Magazin,* Heft 1416.)

745. *Woods Schools (Langhorne, Pennsylvania). Child Research Clinic. Pamphlets.*

TITLE VARIATIONS: One of a set of serials collectively referred to as *Woods Schools. Child Research Clinic. Publications.* Also called *Woods Schools. Child Research Clinic. Child Research Clinic Series. See* Numbering Variations *below.*

DATES OF PUBLICATION: Number 1–13, 1934–1939.

FREQUENCY: Irregular. *See* Contents *below.*

NUMBERING VARIATIONS: Issues also numbered as *Woods Schools. Child Research Clinic. Child Research Clinic Series,* Volume 1–3, Number 1, 1934–1939. *See* Contents *below.*

PUBLISHER: **Langhorne, Pennsylvania:** Woods Schools Child Research Clinic, 1934–1939.

PRIMARY EDITOR: **Irene S. Seipt,** 1934–1939.

CONTENTS:

[Volume 1] Number 1. Speech Retardation; A Case Study. 1934. 5 pp.

[————] Number 2. Emotional Instability; A Case Study. 1934. 6 pp.

[————] Number 3. The Scientist Looks at the Emotionally Unstable Child; Fay, Temple. Behavior Problems in Children: The Importance of Training and Conditioning; and, Blumgarten, A.S. The Endocrine Aspects of the Emotionally Unstable Child. 1935. 24 pp.

[————] Number 4. The Scientist Looks at the Emotionally Unstable Child; Potter, Howard W. Family Situations in Relation to the Emotionally Unstable Child; and, Liss, Edward. Play Techniques and Child Analysis. 1935. 22 pp.

[————] Number 5. Toward the Development of Emotional Stability; A Case Study. 1935. 13 pp.

[————] Number 6. Orton, Samuel T. The Development of Speech Understanding in Relation to Intelligence. (A Paper Delivered in November, 1934, at the First Institute on the Exceptional Child.) 1935. 14 pp.

[Volume 2] Number 7. READING DISABILITY; A CASE STUDY. 1935. 19 pp.

[————] Number 8. A NURSERY SCHOOL CHILD; A CASE STUDY. 1935. 13 pp.

[————] Number 9. Levy, John, and O. Spurgeon English. FAMILY SITUATIONS AND THE EXCEPTIONAL CHILD. 1936. 18 pp.

[————] Number 10. LANGUAGE DEVELOPMENT IN A NURSERY SCHOOL CHILD; A CASE STUDY. 1936. 23 pp.

[————] Number 11. THE EXCEPTIONAL CHILD AT HOME AND AT SCHOOL. PART I; Richmond, Winifred. THE EXCEPTIONAL CHILD AT HOME AND AT SCHOOL; and Bentley, John Edward. THE SERVICE TO SCHOOL AND HOME OF THE CHILD GUIDANCE CLINIC. 1937. 32 pp.

[————] Number 12. THE EXCEPTIONAL CHILD AT HOME AND AT SCHOOL. PART II; Watson, Goodwin. THE EXCEPTIONAL CHILD AS A NEGLECTED RESOURCE; and Astor, Frank. EMOTIONAL NEEDS OF THE EXCEPTIONAL CHILD. 1937. 24 pp.

[Volume 3] Number 13. Hankins, Ruth. PRINCIPLES OF TEACHING EXCEPTIONAL CHILDREN IN THE ELEMENTARY SCHOOLS. 1939. 24 pp.

1935

746. *Acta Psychologica.*

TITLE VARIATIONS: Subtitled *Including Netherlands-Scandinavian Journal of Psychology;* 1938–1939, and *Including Netherlands-Scandinavian, Belgium and Switzerland Journal of Psychology,* 1940+.

DATES OF PUBLICATION: Volume 1–7, 1935–1950+.

FREQUENCY: Irregular. Volume 1, 1935; Volume 2, 1936–1937; Volume 3, 1937; Volume 4, 1938–1939 (Volumes 1–4 have 3 issues per volume); Volume 5, 1940–1941; Volume 6, 1949; Volume 7, 1950 (Volumes 5–7 have 4 issues per volume).

NUMBERING VARIATIONS: Volume 1, Number 1 consists of the PAPERS READ TO THE X. INTERNATIONAL CONGRESS OF PSYCHOLOGY AT COPENHAGEN, 1932. Combined issues in Volumes 5, 6 and 7. Volume 7, Number 2–4, 1950 is SPECIAL ISSUE IN HONOUR OF G. RÉVÉSZ ON THE OCCASION OF HIS 70TH BIRTHDAY.

PUBLISHER: The Hague: Martinus Nijhoff, 1935–1939. Amsterdam: North Holland Publishing Company, 1940, 1941, 1949, 1950+.

PRIMARY EDITORS: G. Révész, 1935–1950; H.J.F.W. Brugmans, 1938–1950; D. Katz, 1938–1950; E. Rubin, 1938–1950; Éd. Claparède, Issue 5:1, 1940 only; J. Piaget, 1940–1950; E. Kaila, 1938–1950; A. E. Michotte, 1938–1950; H. Schjelderup, 1938–1950; Frederic Bartlett, 1949–1950.

747. *Buenos Aires. Universidad nacional. Instituto de psicología. Anales.*

TITLE VARIATIONS: None.

DATES OF PUBLICATION: Tomo 1–3, 1935–1941.

FREQUENCY: Triannual.

NUMBERING VARIATIONS: None.

PUBLISHER: **Buenos Aires:** Imprenta de la Universidad, 1935–1941.

PRIMARY EDITOR: **Enrique Mouchet,** 1935–1941.

748. *Chinese National Association of the Mass Education Movement. Research Committee in Educational Psychology. Report.*

TITLE VARIATIONS: Association's Chinese name is Chung-hua p'ing Min Chiao yü Ts'u Chin Hui.

DATES OF PUBLICATION: Number 1, April 1935.

FREQUENCY: Irregular. *See* Contents *below.*

NUMBERING VARIATIONS: None.

PUBLISHER: **Peking:** Chinese National Association of the Mass Education Movement, 1935.

PRIMARY EDITOR: **Siegen K. Chou,** 1935.

CONTENTS:

    Number 1. Chou, Siegen K. EDUCATIONAL MEASUREMENTS IN THE MASS EDUCATION MOVEMENT, 1927–1934. April 1935. 24 pp.

NOTE: Publication is entirely in English. Main entry is therefore in English.

749. *Consulting Psychologist.*

TITLE VARIATIONS: Continues *Association of Consulting Psychologists. Newsletter.* Superseded by *Journal of Consulting Psychology* with Volume 1, 1937.

DATES OF PUBLICATION: Volume 2, Number 1–7, November 1935–May 1936.

FREQUENCY: Monthly.

NUMBERING VARIATIONS: None.

PUBLISHER: **New York:** Association of Consulting Psychologists, November 1935–May 1936.

PRIMARY EDITORS: **Percival M. Symonds,** 1935–1936; **Warren G. Findley,** 1935–1936; **Gladys Idle,** 1935; **Andrew W. Brown,** 1935; **Elaine F. Kinder,** 1936.

750. *Educational, Psychological, and Personality Tests.*

TITLE VARIATIONS: *See* Contents *below.*

DATES OF PUBLICATION: May 1935–August 1937.

FREQUENCY: Annual.

NUMBERING VARIATIONS: Also numbered as *Rutgers University. Bulletin. Studies in Education.* See Contents *below.*

PUBLISHER: **New Brunswick, New Jersey:** Rutgers University, School of Education, 1935–1937.

PRIMARY EDITOR: **Oscar Krisen Buros,** 1935–1937.

CONTENTS:

1935. EDUCATIONAL, PSYCHOLOGICAL, AND PERSONALITY TESTS OF 1933 AND 1934. May 1935. 44 pp. (Also as *Rutgers University. Bulletin,* Volume 11, Number 11. *Studies in Education,* Number 7.)

1936. EDUCATIONAL, PSYCHOLOGICAL, AND PERSONALITY TESTS OF 1933, 1934, AND 1935. July 1936. 83 pp. (Also as *Rutgers University, Bulletin,* Volume 13, Number 1. *Studies in Education,* Number 9.)

1937. EDUCATIONAL, PSYCHOLOGICAL AND PERSONALITY TESTS OF 1936. August 1937. 141 pp. (Also as *Rutgers University. Bulletin,* Volume 14, Number 2A. *Studies in Education,* Number 11.)

751. *International Journal of Individual Psychology.*

TITLE VARIATIONS: None.

DATES OF PUBLICATION: Volume 1–3, 1935–1937.

FREQUENCY: Quarterly.

NUMBERING VARIATIONS: None.

PUBLISHER: **Chicago:** International Publications, Inc. Publishers, 1935–1937.

PRIMARY EDITORS: **Alfred Adler,** 1935–1937; **Edyth Barlow Menser,** 1935–1937; **Erwin O. Krausz,** 1935 (1st–3rd Quarters); **Sydney M. Roth,** 1935–1937; **Alexandra Adler,** 1935 (4th Quarter), 1937.

EDITORIAL BOARD: Felix Asnaourow, 1935–1937; A. R. Radcliffe-Browne, 1935; Ferdinand Birnbaum, 1935–1937; J. Carruthers Young, 1935–1937; Oliver Brachfield, 1935–1937; Lydia Sicher, 1935–1937; Rudolf Dreikurs, 1935–1937; Stefan V. Maday, 1935–1937; D. G. Campbell, 1935; Leonhard Seif, 1935–1937; Ladislaus Zilahi, 1935–1937; P. H. Ronge, 1935–1937; Eyuep Hamdi Bey, 1935–1937; Erwin O. Krausz, 1935; Arthur Holub, 1935–1937; Alexandra Adler, 1935–1937; Demetrios Moraitis, 1935–1937; Franz Plewa, 1935–1937.

752. *Iowa. University. Child Welfare Pamphlets. Narrative Supplements.*

TITLE VARIATIONS: None.

DATES OF PUBLICATION: Story A–H, 1935–1937.

FREQUENCY: Irregular. *See* Contents *below.*

NUMBERING VARIATIONS: None.

PUBLISHER: **Iowa City, Iowa:** Published by the University, 1935–1937.

PRIMARY EDITORS: None listed.

CONTENTS:

Story A. Saltzman, Eleanor. THE FATHERS HAVE EATEN. June 29, 1935. 12 pp.

Story B. Saltzman, Eleanor. I WONDER. July 6, 1935, 9 pp.

Story C. Saltzman, Eleanor. EAST BRANCH AND BEYOND. July 13, 1935. 15 pp.

Story D. Saltzman, Eleanor. HIRED HAND. July 20, 1935. 11 pp.

Story E. Saltzman, Eleanor. THE MOURNERS. July 27, 1935. 8 pp.

Story F. Anderson, Harold H. SIX CENTS. October 12, 1935. 6 pp.

Story G. Saltzman, Eleanor. THE ALL-SEEING EYE. December 30, 1936. 8 pp.

Story H. Saltzman, Eleanor. STRANGER WITHIN THE GATES. January 2, 1937. 6 pp.

753. *Journal of Psychology; The General Field of Psychology.*

TITLE VARIATIONS: None.

DATES OF PUBLICATION: Volume 1–29+, 1935–1950+.

FREQUENCY: **Semiannual,** Volume 1–2, 1935/1936–1936. **Quarterly,** Volume 3–29+, 1937–1950+.

NUMBERING VARIATIONS: None.

PUBLISHER: **Worcester, Massachusetts:** The Journal of Psychology, 1935/1936. **Provincetown, Massachusetts:** The Journal Press, 1936–1950+.

PRIMARY EDITOR: **Carl Murchison,** 1935–1950+.

EDITORIAL BOARD: Gordon Allport, 1935–1950+; Arthur G. Bills, 1935–1950+; Leonard Carmichael, 1935–1950+; Hulsey Cason, 1935–1950+; Herbert S. Conrad, 1935–1950+; Elmer K. Culler, 1935–1950+; John F. Dashiell, 1935–1950+; Roy M. Dorcus, 1935–1950+; Horace B. English, 1935–1950+; Harry Ewert, 1935–1937; Franklin Fearing, 1935–1950+; Frank A. Geldard, 1935–1950+; Clarence H. Graham, 1935–1950+; Ernest R. Hilgard, 1935–1950+; H. M. Johnson, 1935–1950+; Heinrich Klüver, 1935–1950+; Carney Landis, 1935–1950+; John A. McGeoch, 1935–1941; Norman L. Munn, 1935–1950+; John Paul Nafe, 1935–1950+; Donald G. Paterson, 1935–1950+; Lee Edward Travis, 1935–1950+; Robert C. Tryon, 1935–1950+; E. A. Bott, 1936–1950+, K. S. Lashley, 1936–1950+; Michael J. Zigler, 1937–1950+.

754. *Kharkov. Vseukrainskaia psikhonevrologicheskaia akademiia. Trudy.*

TITLE VARIATIONS; Also called Ukrainskaia psikhonevrologicheskaia akademiia in 1935 and Tsentral'nii psikhonevrologicheskii institut from 1937–1939. Supersedes *Kharkov. Ukrainskii psikhonevrologicheskii institut. Trudy.*

DATES OF PUBLICATION: Novaia Seriia, Tom 1–24+, 1935–1949+.

FREQUENCY: Irregular.

NUMBERING VARIATIONS: None.

PUBLISHER: **Kharkov:** Gosudarstvennoe izdatel'stvo ukrainy(?), 1935–1949+.

PRIMARY EDITORS: Unknown.

NOTE: Above entry is based on incomplete information. The compilers were unable to examine this title.

755. *Mensch und Welt. Berner Abhandlungen zur Psychologie und Pädagogik.*

TITLE VARIATIONS: None.

DATES OF PUBLICATION: Stück 1–7, 1935–1941.

FREQUENCY: Irregular. *See* Contents *below.*

NUMBERING VARIATIONS: None.

PUBLISHER: **Bern:** P. Haupt, 1935, 1939–1941. **Bern and Leipzig:** P. Haupt, 1936. **Bern and Leipzig:** P. Haupt, vormals M. Drechsel, 1938–1939.

PRIMARY EDITOR: **Carlo Sganzini,** 1935–1941.

CONTENTS:

Stück 1. Blum, Emil. ARBEITERBILDUNG ALS EXISTENZIELLE BILDUNG. 1935. 151 pp.

Stück 2. Pestalozzi, Johann Heinrich. ABENDSTUNDE EINES EINSIEDLERS. 1935. 74 pp.

Stück 3. Sganzini, Carlo. PHILOSOPHIE UND PÄDAGOGIK. 1936. 31 pp.

Stück 4. Zulliger, Hans. JUGENDLICHE DIEBE IM RORSCHACH-FORM-DEUTVERSUCH. 1938. 166 pp.

Stück 5. Sganzini, Carlo. WAS HEISST DENKEN? 1939. 32 pp.

Stück 6. Münger, Werner. SCHWERERZIEHBARKEIT. 1939. 151 pp.

Stück 7. Zürcher, Werner. ÜBER DIE INTELLIGENZ UND IHREN ORT IM GEFÜGE DES VERHALTENS. 1941. 118 pp.

756. *Moscow. Gosudarstvennyi institut psikhologii. Psikhologicheskie issledovaniia.*

TITLE VARIATIONS: Separately titled *Instinkty, navyki,* Tom 1, and *Reflesky, instinkty i navyki,* Tom 2.

DATES OF PUBLICATION: Tom 1–2, 1935–1936.

FREQUENCY: Annual (Irregular?).

NUMBERING VARIATIONS: None.

PUBLISHER: **Moscow:** Gosudarstvennoe sotsial'no-ekonomicheskoe izdatel'stvo, 1935–1936.

GENERAL EDITOR: **V. N. Kolbanovskii,** 1935–1936.

VOLUME EDITOR: V. M. Borovskii, 1935–1936.

NOTE: Above entry may be based on partial information. The compilers were only able to examine Tom 1–2. Other volumes may exist.

757. Nederlandsche maatschappij tot bevordering der geneeskunst. Commissie inzake oorlagsprophylaxis. Bibliography on War-Problem, War-Psychology, War-Psychiatry.

TITLE VARIATIONS: None.

DATES OF PUBLICATION: Number 1, 1935.

FREQUENCY: Irregular.

NUMBERING VARIATIONS: None.

PUBLISHER: **Haarlem, Netherlands:** Commissie inzake oorlogsprophylaxis der nederlandsche maatschappij tot bevordering der geneeskunst, Koningenneweg 107, 1935.

PRIMARY EDITORS: None listed.

758. Paris. École de psychologie. Bulletin.

TITLE VARIATIONS: Also called *Bulletin de l'école de psychologie et de la société de psychothérapie.* Supersedes *Revue de psychothérapie et de psychologie appliquée.*

DATES OF PUBLICATION: Numéro 1–23, January 1935–January/March 1940.

FREQUENCY: **Bimonthly,** Numéro 1–8, January/February 1935–March/April 1936. **Quarterly,** Numéro 9, May/June/July 1936. **Bimonthly,** Numéro 10–11, September/October 1936–November/December 1936. **Quarterly,** Numéro 12–23, January/March 1937–January/March 1940.

NUMBERING VARIATIONS: Numéro 13 (cover) dated April–May 1937, contents include June. Numéro 18 dated August/October 1938. Numéro 19 dated November/December 1938 and January 1939. Numéro 20 dated February/March 1939.

PUBLISHER: **Paris:** L'École de psychologie et de la société de psychothérapie, 1935–1940.

PRIMARY EDITOR: **Edgar Bérillon,** 1935–1940.

759. Psychologie. Journal de psychologie théorique et pratique.

TITLE VARIATIONS: Subtitle varies.

DATES OF PUBLICATION: Volume 1–5, Numéro 1, 1935–1939; Volume Numbers unknown, 1949–1950 +. Suspended publication 1940–1949.

FREQUENCY: **Quarterly,** Volume 1–5, Numéro 1, 1935–1939. **Bimonthly,** 1949–1950 +.

NUMBERING VARIATIONS: Multinumber issues present.

PUBLISHER: **Brno:** Sdružené pedagogické korporace v Brně Na Rejdišti 2, 1935–1939. **Brno:** Brno Kralova Pole, Palackého 8, 1949–1950 +.

PRIMARY EDITORS: **Mihajlo Roztohar,** 1935–1939; **V. Chmelař,** 1949–1950.

NOTE: Publication apparently appeared in French. Main entry is therefore in French. No Czech or Slovak title is available. This entry was compiled from information in the *Bibliographie de la philosophie* published by the International Institute of Philosophical Collaboration, Paris. Paris: J. Vrin, 1937–1953.

760. *Revue de pédagogie.*

TITLE VARIATIONS: Continues *Revue du cercle de pédagogie.* Continued by *Revue des sciences pédagogiques* with Tome 6, 1939.

DATES OF PUBLICATION: Tome 2–5, 1935–1937/1938.

FREQUENCY: **Bimonthly** (except for May-September when only a July issue appeared), 1935–1936. **Triannual,** 1936–1937/1938.

NUMBERING VARIATIONS: Issues also assigned whole numbers, Numéro 9–24.

PUBLISHER: **Saint-Gilles, Brussels:** Université libre de Bruxelles, 1935–1937/1938.

EDITORIAL COMMITTEE: Aug. Ley, 1935–1937/1938; Bl. Leysens, 1935–1937/1938; F. P. Doms, 1935–1937/1938; Guy Vermeylen, 1935–1937/1938; P. van Gompel, 1935–1937; M. Vanhamme, 1935–1937/1938; Dr. Patte, 1937/1938. R. Vandevelde, 1937/1938; J. Boeckx, 1937/1938.

761. *Société roumaine de neurologie, psychiatrie, psychologie et endocrinologie. Section d'endocrinologie. Bulletins et mémoires.*

TITLE VARIATIONS: Also called *Societatea română de neurologie, psichiatrie, psichologie şi endocrinologie. Section d'endocrinologie. Bulletins et mémoires.*

DATES OF PUBLICATION: Tome 1–3, June 1935–December 1937.

FREQUENCY: Monthly.

NUMBERING VARIATIONS: Tome 1 contains only 6 issues.

PUBLISHER: **Bucharest:** Société roumaine de neurologie, psychiatrie, psychologie et endocrinologie, 1935–1937.

PRIMARY EDITORS: None listed.

762. *Society for Research in Child Development. Monographs.*

TITLE VARIATIONS: None.

DATES OF PUBLICATION: Number 1–48 +, 1935–1950 +.

FREQUENCY: Irregular. *See* Contents *below.*

NUMBERING VARIATIONS: Some issues also numbered [*Chicago. University.*] *Committee on Child Development. Study;* or [*Harvard University.*] *School of Public Health. Center for Research in Child Health and Development. Studies;* or *Brush Foundation. Study of Child Growth and Development.* Issues also bound as volume 1–13. *See* Contents *below.*

Year 1935

PUBLISHER: **Washington, D.C.**: Society for Research in Child Development, National Research Council, 1935–1949. **Evanston, Illinois:** Child Development Publications, 1949–1950+.

EDITORIAL BOARD CHAIRMEN: **John E. Anderson,** 1935–1938; **Lester W. Sontag,** 1938–1949; **Thomas W. Richards,** 1949–1950+.

EDITORIAL BOARD: Frank N. Freeman, 1935–1947; Melville J. Herskovits, 1936–1950+; Willard C. Olson, 1939–1950+; Lydia J. Roberts, 1936–1950+; Lester W. Sontag, 1950+; Harold C. Stuart, 1936–1950+; Alfred H. Washburn, 1936–1950+; F. L. Wells, 1936–1947.

CONTENTS:

[Volume 1] **Number 1.** Bayley, Nancy. THE DEVELOPMENT OF MOTOR ABILITIES DURING THE FIRST THREE YEARS. 1935. 26 pp.

[———] **Number 2.** Meredith, Howard V. PHYSICAL GROWTH OF WHITE CHILDREN; A REVIEW OF AMERICAN RESEARCH PRIOR TO 1900. 1936. 83 pp.

[———] **Number 3.** Flory, Charles D. OSSEOUS DEVELOPMENT IN THE HAND AS AN INDEX OF SKELETAL DEVELOPMENT. 1936. 141 pp. (Also as [*Chicago. University.*] *Committee on Child Development. Study,* Number 1.)

[———] **Number 4.** Jones, Mary Cover, and Barbara Stoddard Burks. PERSONALITY DEVELOPMENT IN CHILDHOOD. A SURVEY OF PROBLEMS, METHODS AND EXPERIMENTAL FINDINGS. 1936. 205 pp.

[———] **Number 5.** Giesecke, Minnie. THE GENESIS OF HAND PREFERENCE. 1936. 102 pp. (Also as [*Chicago. University.*] *Committee on Child Development. Study,* Number 2.)

[———] **Number 6.** Flory, Charles D. THE PHYSICAL GROWTH OF MENTALLY DEFICIENT BOYS. 1936. 119 pp.

[———] **Number 7.** Abernethy, Ethel Mary. RELATIONSHIPS BETWEEN MENTAL AND PHYSICAL GROWTH. 1936. 80 pp.

[Volume 2] **Number 8.** Richard, Herman G. THE RELATION OF ACCELERATED, NORMAL AND RETARDED PUBERTY TO THE HEIGHT AND WEIGHT OF SCHOOL CHILDREN. 1937. 67 pp. (Also as [*Chicago. University.*] *Committee on Child Development. Study,* Number 3.)

[———] **Number 9.** Freeman, Frank N., and Charles D., Flory. GROWTH IN INTELLECTUAL ABILITY AS MEASURED BY REPEATED TESTS. 1937. 116 pp.

[———] **Number 10.** Willoughby, Raymond Royce. SEXUALITY IN THE SECOND DECADE. 1937. 57 pp.

[———] **Number 11.** Van Alstyne, Dorothy, and Emily Osborne. RHYTHMIC RESPONSES OF NEGRO AND WHITE CHILDREN TWO TO SIX, WITH A SPECIAL FOCUS ON REGULATED AND FREE RHYTHM SITUATIONS. 1937. 63 pp.

[———] **Number 12.** Shuttleworth, Frank K. SEXUAL MATURATION AND THE PHYSICAL GROWTH OF GIRLS AGE SIX TO NINETEEN. 1937. 253 pp.

[———] **Number 13.** Preyer, W. EMBRYONIC MOTILITY AND SENSITIVITY. TRANSLATED FROM THE ORIGINAL GERMAN OF "SPECIELLE PHYSIOLOGIE DES EMBRYO" BY G. E. COGHILL AND WOLFRAM K. LEGNER. 1937. 114 pp.

[Volume 3] **Number 14.** Dearborn, Walter F., John W. M. Rothney and Frank K. Shuttleworth. DATA ON THE GROWTH OF PUBLIC SCHOOL CHILDREN (FROM THE MATERIALS OF THE HARVARD GROWTH STUDY). 1938. 136 pp.

762. *(Continued)*

[————] **Number 15.** Greulich, William Walter, Harry G. Day, Sander E. Lachman, John B. Wolfe, and Frank K. Shuttleworth. A HANDBOOK OF METHODS FOR THE STUDY OF ADOLESCENT CHILDREN. 1938. 406 pp.

[————] **Number 16.** Shuttleworth, Frank K. THE ADOLESCENT PERIOD. A GRAPHIC AND PICTORIAL ATLAS. 1938. 246 pp.

[————] **Number 17.** Sontag, L. W., and T. W. Richards. STUDIES IN FETAL BEHAVIOR. I. FETAL HEART RATE AS A BEHAVIORAL INDICATOR. 1938. 72 pp.

[————] **Number 18.** Shuttleworth, Frank K. SEXUAL MATURATION AND THE SKELETAL GROWTH OF GIRLS AGE SIX TO NINETEEN. 1938. 56 pp.

[————] **Number 19.** Macfarlane, Jean Walker. STUDIES IN CHILD GUIDANCE. I. METHODOLOGY OF DATA COLLECTION AND ORGANIZATION. 1938. 254 pp.

[Volume 4] **Number 20.** Stuart, Harold C., and Staff. STUDIES FROM THE CENTER FOR RESEARCH IN CHILD HEALTH AND DEVELOPMENT, SCHOOL OF PUBLIC HEALTH, HARVARD UNIVERISTY. I. THE CENTER, THE GROUP UNDER OBSERVATION, SOURCES OF INFORMATION, AND STUDIES IN PROGRESS. 1939. 261 pp. Also as [*Harvard University.*] *School of Public Health. Center for Research in Child Health and Development. Studies,* Number 1.)

[————] **Number 21.** Slater, Eleanor, with the assistance of Ruth Beckwith and Lucille Behnke. STUDIES FROM THE CENTER FOR RESEARCH IN CHILD HEALTH AND DEVELOPMENT, SCHOOL OF PUBLIC HEALTH, HARVARD UNIVERSITY. II. TYPES, LEVELS, AND IRREGULARITIES OF RESPONSE TO A NURSERY SCHOOL SITUATION OF FORTY CHILDREN OBSERVED WITH SPECIAL REFERENCE TO THE HOME ENVIRONMENT. 1939. 148 pp. Also as [*Harvard University.*] *School of Public Health. Center for Research in Child Health and Development. Studies,* Number 2.)

[————] **Number 22.** Shuttleworth, Frank K. THE PHYSICAL AND MENTAL GROWTH OF GIRLS AND BOYS AGE SIX TO NINETEEN IN RELATION TO AGE AT MAXIMUM GROWTH. 1939. 291 pp.

[————] **Number 23.** Tryon, Caroline McCann. EVALUATIONS OF ADOLESCENT PERSONALITY BY ADOLESCENTS. 1939. 83 pp.

[Volume 5] **Number 24.** Espenschade, Anna. MOTOR PERFORMANCE IN ADOLESCENCE, INCLUDING THE STUDY OF RELATIONSHIPS WITH MEASURES OF PHYSICAL GROWTH AND MATURITY. 1940. 126 pp.

[————] **Number 25.** Coghill, G. E. EARLY EMBRYONIC SOMATIC MOVEMENTS IN BIRDS AND IN MAMMALS OTHER THAN MAN. 1940. 48 pp.

[————] **Number 26.** Stuart, Harold C., Penelope Hill, and Constance Shaw. STUDIES FROM THE CENTER FOR RESEARCH IN CHILD HEALTH AND DEVELOPMENT. SCHOOL OF PUBLIC HEALTH, HARVARD UNIVERSITY. III. THE GROWTH OF BONE, MUSCLE AND OVERLYING TISSUES AS REVEALED BY STUDIES OF ROENTGENOGRAMS OF THE LEG AREA. DESCRIPTION OF A METHOD OF EVALUATING THESE TISSUES, STANDARDS DERIVED FROM A SERIES OF NORMAL CHILDREN EXAMINED PERIODICALLY FROM BIRTH TO SEVEN YEARS AND EXAMPLES OF THE GROWTH OF INDIVIDUAL CHILDREN. 1940. 220 pp. (Also as [*Harvard University.*] *School of Public Health. Center for Research on Child Health and Development. Studies,* Number 3.)

[Volume 6] Number 27. Mitchell, A. Graeme. PEDIATRIC BIBLIOGRAPHY. 1941. 119 pp.

[———] Number 28. Koshuk, Ruth Pearson. SOCIAL INFLUENCES AFFECTING THE BEHAVIOR OF YOUNG CHILDREN. 1941. 71 pp.

[———] Number 29. Ciocco, Antonio, and Carroll E. Palmer. THE HEARING OF SCHOOL CHILDREN. A STATISTICAL STUDY OF AUDIOMETRIC AND CLINICAL RECORDS. 1941. 77 pp.

[———] Number 30. Lerner, Eugene, and Lois Barclay Murphy, eds., with the collaboration of L. Joseph Stone, Evelyn Beyer, and Elinor Whitney Brown. METHODS FOR THE STUDY OF PERSONALITY IN YOUNG CHILDREN. 1941. 289 pp.

[Volume 7] Number 31. Chittenden, Gertrude E. AN EXPERIMENTAL STUDY IN MEASURING AND MODIFYING ASSERTIVE BEHAVIOR IN YOUNG CHILDREN. 1942. 87 pp.

[———] Number 32. Johnston, Philip W. THE RELATION OF CERTAIN ANOMALIES OF VISION AND LATERAL DOMINANCE TO READING DISABILITY. 1942. 147 pp.

[———] Number 33. Greulich, William Walter, Ralph I. Dorfman, Hubert R. Catchpole, Charles I. Solomon, and Charles S. Culotta. SOMATIC AND ENDOCRINE STUDIES OF PUBERAL AND ADOLESCENT BOYS. 1942. 85 pp.

[Volume 8] Number 34. Adkins, Margaret M., Elizabeth A. Cobb, R. Bretney Miller, R. Nevitt Sanford, and Ann H. Stewart, with special contributors Joseph C. Aub, Bertha S. Burke, Ira T. Nathanson, Harold C. Stuart, and Lois Towne. PHYSIQUE, PERSONALITY AND SCHOLARSHIP. A COOPERATIVE STUDY OF SCHOOL CHILDREN. FROM THE PSYCHOLOGICAL CLINIC, HARVARD UNIVERSITY, CAMBRIDGE, MASSACHUSETTS, AND THE DEPARTMENT OF CHILD HYGIENE, HARVARD SCHOOL OF PUBLIC HEALTH, BOSTON, MASSACHUSETTS, WITH THE COLLABORATION OF OTHER DEPARTMENTS OF HARVARD UNIVERSITY. 1943. 705 pp.

[———] Number 35. Ebert, Elizabeth, and Katherine Simmons. THE BRUSH FOUNDATION STUDY OF CHILD GROWTH AND DEVELOPMENT. I. PSYCHOMETRIC TESTS. 1943. 113 pp.

[———] Number 36. Roberts, Katherine Elliott, and Virginia Van Dyne Fleming. PERSISTENCE AND CHANGE IN PERSONALITY PATTERNS. 1943. 206 pp.

[Volume 9] Number 37. Simmons, Katherine. THE BRUSH FOUNDATION STUDY OF CHILD GROWTH AND DEVELOPMENT. II. PHYSICAL GROWTH AND DEVELOPMENT. 1944. 87 pp.

[———] Number 38. Washburn, Ruth Wendell. RE-EDUCATION IN A NURSERY GROUP; A STUDY IN CLINICAL PSYCHOLOGY. 1944. 175 pp.

[———] Number 39. Henry, Charles E. ELECTROENCEPHALOGRAMS OF NORMAL CHILDREN. 1944. 71 pp.

[Volume 10] Number 40. Cureton, Thomas Kirk, Warren J. Huffman, Lyle Welser, Ramon E. Kireilis, and Darrell E. Latham. ENDURANCE OF YOUNG MEN. ANALYSIS OF ENDURANCE EXERCISES AND METHODS OF EVALUATING MOTOR FITNESS. 1945. 284 pp.

[———] Number 41. Antonov, A. N. PHYSIOLOGY AND PATHOLOGY OF THE NEWBORN. BIBLIOGRAPHY OF MATERIAL FOR THE PERIOD 1930–1940. 1947. 217 pp.

[Volume 11] **Number 42.** Wolfenstein, Martha. THE IMPACT OF A CHILDREN'S STORY ON MOTHERS AND CHILDREN. 1947. 54 pp.

[————] **Number 43.** Harris, Esther Kite. THE RESPONSIVENESS OF KINDERGARTEN CHILDREN TO THE BEHAVIOR OF THEIR FELLOWS. 1948. 184 pp.

[Volume 12] **Number 44.** Cooper, Marcia Mann. EVALUATION OF THE MOTHERS' ADVISORY SERVICE. 1948. 42 pp.

[————] **Number 45.** Phillips, E. Lakin, Isabel R. Berman, and Harold B. Hanson. INTELLIGENCE AND PERSONALITY FACTORS ASSOCIATED WITH POLIOMYELITIS AMONG SCHOOL AGE CHILDREN. 1948. 60 pp.

[Volume 13] **Number 46.** Mack, Pauline Beery, and Charles Urbach. A STUDY OF INSTITUTIONAL CHILDREN WITH PARTICULAR REFERENCE TO THE CALORIC VALUE AS WELL AS OTHER FACTORS OF THE DIETARY. 1949. 93 pp.

[————] **Number 47.** Boder, Elena. FURTHER STUDIES ON THE ETIOLOGY AND SIGNIFICANCE OF CONGENITAL CRANIAL OSTEOPOROSIS (CRANIOTABES). I. 1949. 30 pp.

[————] **Number 48.** Krogman, Wilton Marion. A HANDBOOK OF THE MEASUREMENT AND INTERPRETATION OF HEIGHT AND WEIGHT IN THE GROWING CHILD. 1950. 68 pp.

NOTE: Dates for publishers and editors are listed in terms of the publication dates of individual monographs rather than volume years where these do not correspond.

763. *Theoria; A Swedish Journal of Philosophy and Psychology.*

TITLE VARIATIONS: Subtitled *Tidskrift för filosofi och psykologi,* Volume 1–2, 1935–1936.

DATES OF PUBLICATION: Volume 1–16+, 1935–1950+.

FREQUENCY: Triannual (December, April and August).

NUMBERING VARIATIONS: Combined issues in Volumes 1–3, 12, 13, 15 and 17.

PUBLISHER: **Göteborg:** Wettergren & Kerbers Förlag, 1935–1940. **Lund:** C.W.K. Gleerup, 1941–1950+.

PRIMARY EDITORS: **Åke Petzäll,** 1935–1950+; **Gunnar Aspelin,** 1935–1950+; **Konrad Marc-Wogau,** 1935–1950+; **Torgny T. Segerstedt,** 1937–1950+; **Frithiof Brandt,** 1940–1950+; **John Elmgren,** 1940–1950+; **Eino Kaila,** 1940–1950+; **Alf Nyman,** 1940–1950+.

764. *Woods Schools (Langhorne, Pennsylvania). Child Research Clinic. Conference on Education and the Exceptional Child. Proceedings.*

TITLE VARIATIONS: One of a set of serials collectively referred to as *Woods Schools. Child Research Clinic. Publications.* Sometimes also called *Woods Schools. Child Research Clinic. Spring Conference.* Each conference also has a distinctive title. *See* Contents *below.*

DATES OF PUBLICATION: 1st–14th, April 1935–1950+. Suspended publication 1943–1945.

FREQUENCY: Annual.

NUMBERING VARIATIONS: 12th and 13th conference held same year.

PUBLISHER; **Langhorne, Pennsylvania:** Child Research Clinic, the Woods Schools, 1935–1950+.

PRIMARY EDITOR: **Irene S. Seipt,** 1935–1950+.

CONTENTS:
> **1st.** EDUCATION AND THE EXCEPTIONAL CHILD. April 1935. 60 pp.
> **2nd.** MEETING THE CHALLENGE OF THE EXCEPTIONAL CHILD. April 1936. 62 pp.
> **3rd.** CONTRIBUTIONS OF PROGRESSIVE EDUCATION. May 1937. 55 pp.
> **4th.** CHALLENGE OF PROGRESSIVE EDUCATION. 1938 (1939). 69 pp.
> **5th.** TWENTY-FIVE YEARS OF PROGRESS IN EDUCATION. 1939. 51 pp.
> **6th.** CHARACTER EDUCATION AND THE EXCEPTIONAL CHILD. 1940 63 pp.
> **7th.** EDUCATION'S PRESENT RESPONSIBILITY TOWARD THE EXCEPTIONAL CHILD. 1941. 63 pp.
> **8th.** WARTIME ADJUSTMENT OF THE EXCEPTIONAL CHILD. 1942. 50 pp.
> **9th.** LANGUAGE IN RELATION TO PSYCHO-MOTOR DEVELOPMENT. 1946. 49 pp.
> **10th.** AN EDUCATIONAL PHILOSOPHY FOR EXCEPTIONAL CHILDREN. 1947. 53 pp.
> **11th.** NUTRITION IN RELATION TO CHILD DEVELOPMENT AND BEHAVIOR. 1948. 36 pp.
> **12th.** EMOTIONAL CLIMATE OF THE EXCEPTIONAL CHILD. 1949. 50 pp.
> **13th.** SPECIAL CONFERENCE: SOME CONTEMPORARY THINKING ABOUT THE EXCEPTIONAL CHILD. 1949. 64 pp.
> **14th.** EXCEPTIONAL CHILD IN INFANCY AND EARLY CHILDHOOD. 1950. 48 pp.

765. Woods Schools (Langhorne, Pennsylvania). Child Research Clinic. Institute Proceedings.

TITLE VARIATIONS: One of a set of serials collectively referred to as *Woods Schools. Child Research Clinic. Publications.* Each Proceedings also has a distinctive title. *See* Contents *below.*

DATES OF PUBLICATION: 2nd–11th, October 1935–1944. 1st never published; 8th never held.

FREQUENCY: **Annual,** 2nd–7th, 1935–1940. **Irregular,** 9th–11th, 1943–1944.

NUMBERING VARIATIONS: *See* Dates of Publication *above.*

PUBLISHER: **Langhorne, Pennsylvania:** Child Research Clinic, the Woods Schools, 1935–1944.

PRIMARY EDITOR: **Irene S. Seipt,** 1935–1944.

Heft 87. Hemm, Ludwig. DIE UNTEREN FÜHRER IN DER H. J. VERSUCH IHRER PSYCHOLOGISCHEN TYPENGLIEDERUNG. 1940. 106 pp.

Heft 88. Gackstatter, Erwin. ARCHITEKTEN UND MASCHINENBAUER IN TYPOLOGISCHER BELEUCHTUNG. 1940. 123 pp.

768. *Zeitschrift für Menschenkunde. Blätter für Charakterologie und Zentralblatt für Graphologie.*

TITLE VARIATIONS: Continues *Zeitschrift für Menschenkunde. Blätter für Charakterologie und angewandte Psychologie.* Continued by *Zeitschrift für Menschenkunde und Zentralblatt für Graphologie.*

DATES OF PUBLICATION: Jahrgang 11, Heft 1–4, 1935.

FREQUENCY: Quarterly.

NUMBERING VARIATIONS: None.

PUBLISHER: **Kampen, Netherlands:** Niels Kampmann, 1935.

PRIMARY EDITORS: **Hans von Hattingberg,** 1935; **Niels Kampmann,** 1935.

1936

769. *Analytical Psychology Club of New York. Papers.*

TITLE VARIATIONS: None.

DATES OF PUBLICATION: Volume 1–6+, 1936/1938–1948/1950+. Suspended publication 1941–1945.

FREQUENCY: Irregular. Volume 1, 1936/1938; Volume 2, 1938/1939; Volume 3, 1939; Volume 4, 1940; Volume 5, 1946/1948; Volume 6, 1948/1950.

NUMBERING VARIATIONS: None.

PUBLISHER: **New York:** Analytical Psychology Club of New York, Inc., 1936/1938–1948/1950.

PRIMARY EDITORS: Edited by the publications committee.

770. *Centro de estudios psicopedagógicos del Uruguay. Publicaciones.*

TITLE VARIATIONS: None.

DATES OF PUBLICATION: Número 1–3, 1936–1939.

FREQUENCY: Annual.

NUMBERING VARIATIONS: Número 3 also numbered Ano IV, Número 3.

PUBLISHER: **Montevideo:** Centro de estudios psicopedagogicos del Uruguay, 1936–1939.

PRIMARY EDITORS: **Manuel Acuna Friedrich,** 1936; **Julieta Baletti Bianchi,** 1938–1939.

771. *Chung-hua hsin li hsüeh pao.* [Chinese Journal of Psychology.]

TITLE VARIATIONS: None.

DATES OF PUBLICATION: Volume 1, Number 1–4, September 1936–June 1937.

FREQUENCY: Quarterly.

NUMBERING VARIATIONS: None.

PUBLISHER: **Peking:** Kuo li Ch'ing-hua ta hsüeh, Hsin li hsüeh hsi [National Ch'ing-hua University, Department of Psychology]; and Yenching ta hsüeh, Hsin li hsüeh hsi [Yenching University, Department of Psychology], 1936. **Peking:** Chung-kuo hsin li hsüeh hsieh hui [Chinese Psychological Association], 1937.

PRIMARY EDITORS: **C. W. Luh**, 1936–1937; **K. H. Sun**, 1936–1937; **Siegen K. Chou**, 1936–1937.

NOTE: Kuo li Ch'ing-hua ta hsüeh [National Ch'ing-hua University] is also called Ch'ing-hua ta hsüeh [Ch'ing-hua University], Ch'ing-hua hsüeh hsi'ao [Ch'ing-hua College]; and, in English, National Tsing-hua University.

772. *Exposés sur la psycho-biologie de l'enfant.*

TITLE VARIATIONS: Continued by *Psycho-biologie de l'enfant* with Tome 3, 1938.

DATES OF PUBLICATION: Tome 1 and 2, 1936.

FREQUENCY: Irregular. *See* Contents *below.*

NUMBERING VARIATIONS: Also numbered in *Actualités scientifiques et industrielles. See* Contents *below.*

PUBLISHER: **Paris:** Hermann & Cie, 1936.

PRIMARY EDITOR: **Henri Wallon**, 1936.

CONTENTS:

Tome 1. Ombredane, André. LE PROBLÉME DES APTITUDES Á L'ÂGE SCO-LAIRE. 1936. 57 pp. (Also as *Actualités scientifiques et industrielles*, Numéro 439.)

Tome 2. Ombredane, André. LES INADAPTÉS SCOLAIRES. 1936. 84 pp. (Also as *Actualités scientifiques et industrielles*, Numéro 440.)

773. *Freiburg (Switzerland). Universität. Heilpädagogischen Seminar. Arbeiten.*

TITLE VARIATIONS: Continued by *Arbeiten zur Psychologie, Erziehungswissenschaft und Sondererziehungswissenschaft* with Heft 14, 1942.

DATES OF PUBLICATION: Heft 1–13, 1936–1942.

FREQUENCY: Irregular. *See* Contents *below.*

NUMBERING VARIATIONS: None.

PUBLISHER: **Lucerne:** Institut für Heilpädagogik Verlag, 1936–1938. **Olten:**

Verlag Walter, 1938. **Zug:** E. Kalt-Zehnder, 1939. **Solothurn:** St. Antonius-verlag, 1939. **Lucerne:** Verlag der Institut für Heilpädagogik, 1941–1942.

PRIMARY EDITOR: **Jos. Spieler,** 1936–1942.

CONTENTS:

Heft 1. Otter, Paula. DER WERT DER NACHGEHENDEN FÜRSORGE. 1936. 30 pp.

Heft 2. Uffenheimer, Albert. DIE BETTNÄSSER-KRANKHEITEN IM KINDES-UND JUGENDALTER. 1937. 82 pp.

Heft 3. Motta, Beatrice. DAS SCHWÄRMEN BEIM SITTLICH VERWAHRLOSTEN WEIBLICHEN FÜRSORGEZÖGLING. 1937. 41 pp.

Heft 4. Lichtensteiger, Albert. VOM SCHICKSAL DER SITZENBLEIBERS. 1937. 48 pp.

Heft 5. Portmann, Fabienne. DIE ENTWICKLUNG DES R-LAUTES BEIM NOR-MALEN, STAMMELNDEN, SCHWERHÖRIGEN UND TAUBEN KINDE. 1938. 56 pp.

Heft 6. Fellerer, Karl Gustav. MUSIK IN HAUS, SCHULE UND HEIM. 1938. 66 pp.

Heft 7. Haups, Hohanna. DAS SCHWÄRMEN DES SITTLICH VERWAHRLOS-TEN WEIBLICHEN FÜRSORGEZÖGLINGS ALS ERZIEHUNGSAUFGABE. 1938. 97 pp.

Heft 8. Montalta, Eduard. JUGENDVERWAHRLOSUNG, MIT BESONDERER BERÜCKSICHTIGUNG SCHWEIZERISCHER VERHÄLTNISSE. 1939. 232 pp.

Heft 9. Kramer, Josefine. DER STIGMATISMUS. SEINE BEDINGUNGEN UND SEINE BEHANDLUNG. 1939. 63 pp.

Heft 10. Forster, Alice. DAS GEFAHRENMOMENT IN DER MÄDCHENER-ZIEHUNG. 1941. 137 pp.

Heft 11. Pittet, Faustin. DIE STELLUNG DER KIRCHE ZUR EUGENIK UND RASSENHYGIENE. 1942. 24 pp.

Heft 12. Gügler, Alois. DIE ERZIEHLICHE BEHANDLUNG JUGENDLICHER MÄNNLICHER ONANISTEN. 1942. 221 pp.

Heft 13. Englert, Othmar. DIE ABNORMENZÄHLUNG IN DEUTSCHLAND UND IN DER SCHWEIZ. 1942. 102 pp.

774. *Hsin li chi Kan.* [Psychology Quarterly.]

TITLE VARIATIONS: None.

DATES OF PUBLICATION: Volume 1–2, Number 2, April 1936–June 1937.

FREQUENCY: Quarterly.

NUMBERING VARIATIONS: None.

PUBLISHER: **Shanghai:** Ta-hsia ta hsüeh [Ta-hsia University], 1936–1937.

PRIMARY EDITORS: None listed.

NOTE: Information on this title was compiled from *Chuan-kuo Chung-wen Chi-kan lien-ho mu-lu, 1833–1949* [Union List of Chinese Periodicals in China, 1833–1949]. Peking, Peking Library, 1961.

775. *International Congress of Criminal Anthropology and Psychiatry. Proceedings.*

TITLE VARIATIONS: Also called *Congrès international d'anthropologie et psy-chologie. Comptes rendus.*

DATES OF PUBLICATION: 1st–2nd, 1936–1938.

FREQUENCY: Biennial.

NUMBERING VARIATIONS: None.

PUBLISHER: Rome: None listed, 1936–1938.

PRIMARY EDITORS: None listed.

CONTENTS:

1st. CONGRÈS INTERNATIONAL D'ANTHROPOLOGIE ET PSYCHOLOGIE. COMPTES RENDUS. Rome, 1936.

2nd. CONGRÈS INTERNATIONAL D'ANTHROPOLOGIE ET PSYCHOLOGIE. COMPTES RENDUS. Rome, 1938.

776. *Invitational Conference on Testing Problems. Proceedings.*

TITLE VARIATIONS: Also titled *Invitational Conference on Testing Problems. Report.* Issues for 1937–1947 have distinctive titles. *See* Contents *below.*

DATES OF PUBLICATION: [1st]–10th, 1936–1949 +.

FREQUENCY: Irregular. *See* Contents *below.*

NUMBERING VARIATIONS: 1st–6th not numbered. Some issues also numbered in *American Council on Education. Studies. Series I. Reports of Committees and Conferences. See* Contents *below.*

PUBLISHER: **Washington, D.C.:** American Council on Education, 1937–1948. **Princeton, New Jersey:** Educational Testing Service, 1949–1950 +.

PRIMARY EDITORS: *See* Contents *below.*

CONTENTS:

[1st.] THE TESTING MOVEMENT. REPORT OF THE COMMITTEE ON REVIEW OF THE TESTING MOVEMENT. 1937. 39 pp. (Also as *American Council on Education. Studies. Series I,* Number 1.)

[2nd.] COOPERATION AND COORDINATION IN HIGHER EDUCATION. 1938. 110 pp. (Also as *American Council on Education. Studies. Series I,* Number 5.)

[3rd.] COORDINATION OF ACCREDITING ACTIVITIES. 1939. 46 pp. (Also as *American Council on Education. Studies. Series I,* Number 9.)

[4th.] DELIBERATIVE COMMITTEE REPORTS ON SECONDARY EDUCATION. 1940. 37 pp. (Also as *American Council on Education. Studies. Series I,* Number 12.)

[5th.] COOPERATION IN ACCREDITING PROCEDURES. 1941. 56 pp. (Also as *American Council on Education. Studies. Series I,* Number 14.)

[6th.] NEW DIRECTION FOR MEASUREMENT AND GUIDANCE. A Symposium by Ralph W. Tyler et al. 1944. 103 pp. (Also as *American Council on Education. Studies. Series I,* Number 20.)

7th. NATIONAL PROJECTS IN EDUCATIONAL MEASUREMENT. A REPORT OF THE 1946 INVITATIONAL CONFERENCE ON TESTING PROBLEMS, NEW YORK, NOVEMBER 2, 1946. Herschel T. Manuel, Chairman. Edited by K. W. Vaughn. 1947. 80 pp. (Also as *American Council on Education. Studies. Series I,* Number 28.)

8th. Exploring Individual Differences. A Report of the 1947 Invitational Conference on Testing Problems, New York, November 1, 1947. Henry Chauncey, Chairman. 1948. 110 pp. (Also as *American Council on Education. Studies. Series I,* Number 32.)

9th. Proceedings of the 1948 Invitational Conference on Testing Problems, October 30, 1948. John C. Flanagan, Chairman. 1949. 117 pp.

10th. Proceedings of the 1949 Invitational conference on Testing Problems, October 29, 1949. Oscar K. Buros, Chairman. 1950. 94 pp.

777. *Menninger Clinic. Bulletin.*

TITLE VARIATIONS: None.

DATES OF PUBLICATION: Volume 1–14, Number 6+, September 1936–November 1950+.

FREQUENCY: Bimonthly.

NUMBERING VARIATIONS: Volume 1 has 8 issues, 2 in 1936 and 6 in 1937.

PUBLISHER: **Topeka, Kansas:** The Menninger Clinic, 1936–1943. **Topeka:** Menninger Foundation, 1944–1950+.

PRIMARY EDITORS: [**Karl A. Menninger,** 1936–1950+]; [**William C. Menninger,** 1936–1950+.]

EDITORIAL BOARD: Listed for the first time in Volume 14, Number 2, March 1950: Jean Lyle Menninger; H. C. Modlin; Rudolf Ekstein; R. L. Sutherland; Mary Douglas Lee (Assistant).

778. *Menninger Clinic. Monograph Series.*

TITLE VARIATIONS: Titled *Menninger Foundation. Monograph Series,* Number 5–6, 1947–1948.

DATES OF PUBLICATION: Number 1–7+, 1936–1950+.

FREQUENCY: Irregular. *See* Contents *below.*

NUMBERING VARIATIONS: Number 3/4 is a two volume set.

PUBLISHER: **Baltimore:** Williams and Wilkins Company, 1936–1942. **Chicago:** The Year Books Publishers, Inc. 1945–1946. **New York:** International Universities Press, 1947–1948. **New York:** Grune & Stratton, 1950+.

PRIMARY EDITORS: None listed.

CONTENTS:

Number 1. Menninger, W. C. Juvenile Paresis. 1936. 199 pp.

Number 2. Rapaport, David. Emotions and Memory. 1942. 282 pp.

Number 3/4. Rapaport, David, Roy Schafer, and Merton Gill. Manual of Diagnostic Testing. I. Diagnostic Testing of Intelligence and Concept Formation; II. Diagnostic Testing of Personality and Ideational Content. 1944–1946. 239 pp. and 100 pp.

Number 5. Brenman, Margaret, and Merton N. Gill. Hypnotherapy: A Survey of the Literature. 1947. 276 pp.

Number 6. Schafer, Roy. Clinical Application of Psychological Tests. 1948. 346 pp.

Number 7. Menninger, Karl A., and George Devereux. Guide to Psychiatric Books. 1950. 148 pp.

779. *Minnesota. University. Institute of Child Welfare. Leaflets.*

TITLE VARIATIONS: None.

DATES OF PUBLICATION: Number 1–15+, 1936–1950+.

FREQUENCY: Irregular. *See* Contents *below.*

NUMBERING VARIATIONS: Number 13 mismarked Number 2 but dated 1950.

PUBLISHER: **Minneapolis:** Institute of Child Welfare, University of Minnesota, 1936–1950+.

PRIMARY EDITORS: None listed.

CONTENTS:

Number 1. The Institute and Its Activities 1925–1936. 1936. 12 pp.

Number 2. Play Equipment That Can Be Made at Home. 1936. (5 pp.)

Number 3. Play Equipment for Young Children. 1936. 8 pp.

Number 4. Bibliography for Parents on the Young Child and the School-Age Child. 1936. 10 pp.

Number 5. Bibliography for Parents on the Adolescent. 1936. 8 pp.

Number 6. Bibliography on Sex Education. 1936. (5 pp.)

Number 7. Bibliography on Living Together in the Family. 1936. 11 pp.

Number 8. Music for Young Children. 1936. 15 pp.

Number 9. Picture Books, Stories, and Poems for Young Children. 1936. 8 pp.

Number 10. Literature for Children from Six to Sixteen. 1936. 16 pp.

Number 11. Finger Plays for Young Children. 1936. 12 pp.

Number 12. Suggestions for High School Principals Regarding the Education of Youth for Family Living. 1937. 6 pp.

Number 13. Institute of Child Welfare, University of Minnesota. Staff 1950–51. 1950. 2 pp.

Number 14. Group Study and Parent Education. [ca. 1950.] 6 pp.

Number 15. Topics for Lectures, Lecture Series, and Group Study. 1950. 8 pp.

780. *Nederlandsch tijdschrift voor psychologie en hare grensgebieden.*

TITLE VARIATIONS: Continues *Nederlandsch tijdschrift voor psychologie.* Continued by *Nederlandsch tijdschrift voor psychologie en hare grensgebieden* with Nieuwe Reeks, Deel 1, 1946.

DATES OF PUBLICATION: Jaargang 4–11, May 1936–1943/1944.

FREQUENCY: Bimonthly.

NUMBERING VARIATIONS: Multinumber issues present.

PUBLISHER: **Zutphen, Netherlands:** G.J.A. Ruys, 1936–1944.

PRIMARY EDITORS: **L. van der Horst,** 1936–1944; **G. Révész,** 1936–1944.

781. *Practical Psychology Magazine.*

TITLE VARIATIONS: Continued by *Practical Psychology* with Volume 2, Number 1, March 1937.

DATES OF PUBLICATION: Volume 1, Number 1–12, February 1936–February 1937.

FREQUENCY: Monthly.

NUMBERING VARIATIONS: None.

PUBLISHER: **London:** British Union of Practical Psychologists, 1936–1937.

PRIMARY EDITORS: None listed.

782. *Practical Psychology Monthly.*

TITLE VARIATIONS: None.

DATES OF PUBLICATION: Volume 1–3, Number 5, August 1936–March 1938.

FREQUENCY: Monthly (Irregular).

NUMBERING VARIATIONS: None.

PUBLISHER: **Chicago:** Unknown, 1936–1938.

PRIMARY EDITORS: None listed.

NOTE: Above entry based on partial information. The compilers were unable to examine this title.

783. *Psychologist. Practical Psychology Handbooks.*

TITLE VARIATIONS: None.

DATES OF PUBLICATION: Number 1–22+, 1936–1950+. Suspended publication 1943–1948.

FREQUENCY: Irregular. *See* Contents *below.*

NUMBERING VARIATIONS: None.

PUBLISHER: **London:** Frank J. Allard, at Manfield House, 1936–1950+.

PRIMARY EDITORS: None listed.

CONTENTS:

Number 1. McBride, William James. THE INFERIORITY COMPLEX; ITS MEANING AND TREATMENT. 1936. 46 pp.

Number 2. Philp, Howard L. MEMORY. HOW TO MAKE THE MOST OF IT. 1936. 41 pp.

Number 3. "A Psychologist." Nervousness. Its Cause, Prevention and Cure. 1936. 43 pp.

Number 4. Northfield, Wilfrid. Curing Nervous Tension. 1936. 46 pp.

Number 5. McBride, William J. The Conquest of Fear through Psychology. 1939. 47 pp.

Number 6. Graham, J. M. Neurasthemia: Its Nature, Origin and Cure. 1936. 45 pp.

Number 7. Kennedy, John. Worry. Its Cause and Cure. 1937. 59 pp.

Number 8. Northfield, Wilfrid. How to Relax. Methods of Lessening the Strain of Modern Living. 1937. 55 pp.

Number 9. Northfield, Wilfrid. Sound Sleep. Proved Methods of Attaining It. 1937. 47 pp.

Number 10. Kennedy, John. Will-Power. Ways to Develop It. 1938. 56 pp.

Number 11. Graham, J. M. Personality. How It Can Be Developed. 1938. 56 pp.

Number 12. Cardwell, Mary G. How to Keep Well. A Simple Outline of the Proved Laws of Health. 1938. 47 pp.

Number 13. Ladell, R. George Macdonald. The First Five Years from Birth to School. 1939. 48 pp.

Number 14. Chadwick, Mary. Chapters about Childhood. The Psychology of Children from 5–10 years. 1939. 45 pp.

Number 15. Teear, C. H. The Art of Making Friends. 1939. 54 pp.

Number 16. Fletcher, Peter. How To Practise Auto-Suggestion. 1939. 48 pp.

Number 17. Northfield, Wilfrid. Frayed Nerves. Simple Ways of Restoring Their Tone. 1940. 48 pp.

Number 18. Kornhauser, Arthur William. How To Study. (2nd ed.) 1941. 56 pp.

Number 19. Ladell, R. George Macdonald. The Parent's Problem; Or, How to Tell Children about Sex. 1941. 48 pp.

Number 20. Teear, C. H. Mastering Shyness. 1941. 47 pp.

Number 21. Wilde, Reginald W. Psychology: How It Can Help You. 1942. 48 pp.

Number 22. Ladell, R. George Macdonald. Blushing: Its Analysis, Causes and Cure. 1949. 40 pp.

784. *Psychology Digest. Psychological Articles of Lasting Value.*

TITLE VARIATIONS: None.

DATES OF PUBLICATION: Volume 1–3, Number 2, 1936–June 1939.

FREQUENCY: Monthly (Irregular).

NUMBERING VARIATIONS: None.

PUBLISHER: **New York:** Lex Publications, Inc., 1936–1939.

PRIMARY EDITORS: **Eldorado Field,** 1936–1939; **Emile E. Allen,** 1936–1939.

785. *Psychometrika; A Journal Devoted to the Development of Psychology as a Quantitative Rational Science.*[Official journal of the Psychometric Society.]

TITLE VARIATIONS: None.

DATES OF PUBLICATION: Volume 1–15+, March 1936–1950+.

FREQUENCY: **Quarterly,** Volume 1–5, 1936–1940. **Bimonthly,** Volume 6, 1941. **Quarterly,** Volume 7–15+, 1942–1950+.

NUMBERING VARIATIONS: None.

PUBLISHER: N.p.: Psychometric Society, 1936–1937. **Chicago:** Psychometric Corporation, 1938–1940. **Colorado Springs, Colorado:** Psychometric Society, 1941–1950+.

PRIMARY EDITORS: **Paul Horst,** 1936–1941; **Albert K. Kurtz,** 1936–1950+; **Marion W. Richardson,** 1936–1950+; **L. L. Thurstone,** 1937–1950+; **Dorothy C. Adkins,** 1941–1950+; **Harold Gulliksen,** 1942–1949; **Samuel B. Lyerly,** 1950+.

EDITORIAL BOARD: Elmer A. Culler, 1936–1950+; Jack W. Dunlap, 1936; Harold Gulliksen, 1936–1941, 1950+; Paul Horst, 1942–1950+; Clark L. Hull, 1936–1946; Quinn McNemar, 1936–1950+; Nicholas Rashevsky, 1936–1946; Phillip Justin Rulon, 1936–1950+; Samuel A. Stouffer, 1936–1949; L. L. Thurstone, 1936; S. S. Wilks, 1936–1950+; Edward E. Cureton, 1937–1950+; Max D. Engelhart, 1937–1950+; J. P. Guilford, 1937–1950+; Karl J. Holzinger, 1937–1948; Truman L. Kelley, 1937–1950+; Charles Spearman, 1937–1946; William Stephenson, 1937–1950+; Godfrey Thomson, 1937–1950+; Henry E. Garrett, 1941–1950+; Charles M. Harsh, 1941–1950+; Irving Lorge, 1941–1950+; Charles I. Mosier, 1941–1950+; Herbert Woodrow, 1941–1950+; H. S. Conrad, 1945–1950+; Alston S. Householder, 1945–1950+; Ledyard Tucker, 1945–1950+; R. L. Anderson, 1949–1950+; Frederick Mosteller, 1949–1950+; Robert J. Wherry, 1949; George E. Nicholson, 1950+.

786. *Rorschach Research Exchange.*

TITLE VARIATIONS: Continued by *Rorschach Research Exchange and Journal of Projective Techniques* with Volume 11, 1947.

DATES OF PUBLICATION: Volume 1–10, 1936–1946.

FREQUENCY: **5 times a year,** Volume 1, September 1936–July 1937. **Quarterly,** Volume 2–10, September 1937–December 1946.

NUMBERING VARIATIONS: None.

PUBLISHER: **New York:** Rorschach Institute, Inc., 1936–1946.

PRIMARY EDITORS: **Bruno Klopfer,** 1936–1946; **Douglas M. Kelley,** 1941–1943; **Zygmunt Piotrowski,** 1941–1943; **Hanna Faterson,** 1944–1945; **Camilla Kemple,** 1946.

787. Society for the Psychological Study of Social Issues. Bulletin.

TITLE VARIATIONS: Superseded by *Journal of Social Issues* in 1945.

DATES OF PUBLICATION: Volume 1–3, Number 1, 1936–1938 and as a quarterly section in the *Journal of Social Psychology,* Volume 10–20, 1939–1944.

FREQUENCY: **Irregular, 1936–1938. Quarterly, 1939–1944.**

NUMBERING VARIATIONS: Volume 1 consisted of Numbers 1–3, Volume 2 of Numbers 1–4, Volume 3, Number 1 only. Quarterly sections appeared in the *Journal of Social Psychology* in Volume 10, pp. 105–154, 269–308, 407–447, 561–599; Volume 11, pp. 157–227, 415–490; Volume 12, pp. 177–220, 431–465; Volume 13, pp. 203–240, 427–487; Volume 14, pp. 195–261, 373–418; Volume 15, pp. 163–210, 351–412; Volume 16, pp. 107–160, 295–345; Volume 17, pp. 111–162, 307–362; Volume 18, pp. 159–233, 365–419; Volume 19, pp. 145–194, 317–375; Volume 20, pp. 141–180.

PUBLISHER: N.p.: Society for the Psychological Study of Social Issues, 1936–1938. **Provincetown, Massachusetts:** The Journal Press, 1939–1944.

EDITORIAL BOARD CHAIRMEN: None listed, 1936–1938; **Gardner Murphy,** 1939–1941; **Barbara S. Burks,** 1942–1943; **Ronald Lippitt,** 1944.

NEWSLETTER EDITOR: Alvin Zander, 1944.

EDITORIAL ASSISTANT: Claire Selltiz, 1944.

EDITORIAL BOARD: J. F. Brown, 1939–1943; Barbara S. Burks, 1939–1943; Leonard Carmichael, 1939–1943; Violet Edwards, 1944; H. B. English, 1936–1938; George W. Hartmann, 1939–1943; Russell Hogrefe, 1944; E. L. Horowitz, 1942–1943; Harold E. Jones, 1939–1943; Daniel Katz, 1944; Otto Klineberg, 1939–1943; A. W. Kornhauser, 1939–1944; I. Krechevsky, 1936–1943; Eugene Lerner, 1943; Kurt Lewin, 1939–1943; Ralph Linton, 1939–1943; Ronald Lippitt, 1944; Robert S. Lynd, 1939–1943; A. H. Maslow, 1944; Gardner Murphy, 1939–1943; T. C. Schneirla, 1937–1938; Ross Stagner, 1936–1937, 1939–1940. C. L. Stone, 1940–1943; Ruth Valentine, 1942–1944; Goodwin B. Watson, 1939–1944; Gene Weltfish, 1944.

788. Sociometric Review.

TITLE VARIATIONS: Superseded by *Sociometry.*

DATES OF PUBLICATION: [Number 1,] 1936.

FREQUENCY: Irregular.

NUMBERING VARIATIONS: Publication was issued unnumbered.

PUBLISHER: **Hudson, New York:** New York State Training School for Girls, 1936.

PRIMARY EDITOR: [Jacob L. Moreno,] 1936.

ADVISORY RESEARCH BOARD: Gardner Murphy, 1936; Franz Boas, 1936; Barbara S. Burks, 1936; Hadley Cantril, 1936; John L. Childs, 1936; Lyford Edwards, 1936; Helen Jennings, 1936; William H. Kilpatrick, 1936; Helen Merrell Lynd, 1936; Robert S. Lynd, 1936; Lois Barclay Murphy, 1936; Theodore M. Newcomb, 1936; Ralph B. Spence, 1936. *See* Note *below*.

CONTENTS:

[Number 1]. REPORT OF THE RESEARCH STAFF TO THE ADVISORY RESEARCH BOARD. 1936. 62 pp.

NOTE: It is unclear from the publication whether the advisory research board was also intended to act as an advisory editorial committee.

789. *West Virginia. State College. Department of Psychology and Philosophy. Contributions.*

TITLE VARIATIONS: None.

DATES OF PUBLICATION: Number [1]–3, [19?]–1936.

FREQUENCY: Irregular: *See* Contents *below*.

NUMBERING VARIATIONS: Number 3 also numbered as [*West Virginia.*] *State College. Bulletin. See* Contents *below*.

PUBLISHER: **Institute, West Virginia:** West Virginia State College Press, [19?]–1936.

PRIMARY EDITORS: None listed.

CONTENTS:

[Number 1.] Unknown.

Number 2. Canady, Herman George, and William C. Pyant. CURRICULUM BUILDING AND BEHAVIOR ADJUSTMENT IN A SHORT TERM CAMP (A PROPOSAL OF METHOD). 1936. 47 pp.

Number 3. Canady, Herman George. INDIVIDUAL DIFFERENCES AMONG FRESHMEN AT WEST VIRGINIA STATE COLLEGE AND THEIR EDUCATIONAL BEARINGS. 1936. 42 pp. (Also as [*West Virginia.*] *State College. Bulletin*, Series 23, Number 2, April 1936.)

NOTE: Information on this entry is incomplete. The compilers were unable to locate a complete run of this title. Entry is filed here since approximate date of first issue is 1936.

790. *Zeitschrift für Menschenkunde und Zentralblatt für Graphologie.*

TITLE VARIATIONS: Continues *Zeitschrift für Menschenkunde. Blätter für Charakterologie und Zentralblatt für Graphologie.*

DATES OF PUBLICATION: Jahrgang 12–16, Heft 2, 1936–1942.

FREQUENCY: **Quarterly,** Jahrgang 12–15, 1936. **Irregular,** Jahrgang 16, Heft 1, 1940; Heft 2, 1942.

NUMBERING VARIATIONS: None.

PUBLISHER: **Berlin:** Niels Kampmann, 1936–1942.

PRIMARY EDITOR: **Niels Kampmann,** 1936–1942.

791. *Zentralblatt für Psychotherapie und ihre Grenzgebiete einschliesslich der medizinischen Psychologie und psychischen Hygiene. Beihefte.*

TITLE VARIATIONS: None.

DATES OF PUBLICATION: Heft 1–6, 1936–1943.

FREQUENCY: Irregular. *See* Contents *below.*

NUMBERING VARIATIONS: None.

PUBLISHER: **Leipzig:** S. Hirzel, 1936–1943.

PRIMARY EDITORS: **Carl Gustav Jung,** 1936–1940; **Matthias Heinrich Göring,** 1936–1943.

CONTENTS:

Heft 1. Bilz, Rud. PSYCHOGENE ANGINA. 1936. 70 pp.

Heft 2. Heugel, Doroth. AUTOGENES TRAINING ALS ERLEBNIS. PROTO-KOLL EINER PSYCHOLOGISCHEN ENTWICKLUNG. 1938. 70 pp.

Heft 3. Döhl, Ilse, Gustav Hans Graber, and Fritz Mohr. LEIBNITZ, CA-RUS UND NIETZSCHE ALS VORLÄUFER UNSERER TIEFENPSYCHOLOGIE. 1941. 66 pp.

Heft 4. Bilz, Rud. LEBENSGESETZE DER LIEBE. 1943. 126 pp.

Heft 5. Bilz, Rud. JOSEPHINE: MENSCHLICHE REIFUNG IM SINNBILD. 1943. 71 pp.

Heft 6. Staabs, Gerhild von. DER SCENO-TEST; BEITRAG ZUR ERFASSUNG UNBEWUSTER PROBLEMATIK BEI KINDERN UND JUGENDLICHEN. 1943. 59 pp.

1937

792. *American Orthopsychiatric Association. Research Monographs.*

TITLE VARIATIONS: Titled *American Orthopsychiatric Association. Monograph,* Number 1, 1937.

DATES OF PUBLICATION: Number 1–4, 1937–1944.

FREQUENCY: Irregular. *See* Contents *below.*

NUMBERING VARIATIONS: None.

PUBLISHER: **New York:** American Orthopsychiatric Association, 1937–1944.

PRIMARY EDITOR: **Lawson G. Lowrey,** 1937–1944.

CONTENTS:

Number 1. Beck, Samuel J. INTRODUCTION TO THE RORSCHACH METHOD. A MANUAL OF PERSONALITY STUDY. With a Preface by F. L. Wells. 1937. 278 pp.

Number 2. Levy, David M. STUDIES IN SIBLING RIVALRY. 1937. 96 pp.

Number 3. Bender, Lauretta. A VISUAL MOTOR GESTALT TEST AND ITS CLINICAL USE. 1938. 176 pp.

Number 4. Henry, Jules, and Zunia Henry. DOLL PLAY OF PILAGÁ INDIAN CHILDREN. AN EXPERIMENTAL AND FIELD ANALYSIS OF THE BEHAVIOR OF THE PILAGÁ INDIAN CHILDREN. 1944. 133 pp.

793. *American Psychoanalytic Association. Bulletin.*

TITLE VARIATIONS: None.

DATES OF PUBLICATION: Volume 1–6, June 1937–December 1950+. Suspended publication June 1940–February 1948.

FREQUENCY: **Annual,** Volume 1–3, June 1937–June 1940. **Quarterly,** Volume 4–6, February 1948–December 1950+.

NUMBERING VARIATIONS: None.

PUBLISHER: **Washington, D.C.:** American Psychoanalytic Association, 1937–1940. **New York:** American Psychoanalytic Association, 1948–1950+.

PRIMARY EDITORS: **Lawrence S. Kubie,** 1937–1940; **John Frosch,** 1948–1950+; **Nathaniel Ross,** 1948–1950+; **William H. Dunn,** 1948–1950+.

EDITORIAL BOARD: Thomas M. French, 1937–1940; Lewis B. Hill, 1937–1940; Karl A. Menninger, 1937–1940; John M. Murray, 1937–1940; Sandor Rado, 1937–1940; Gregory Zilboorg, 1937–1940; William C. Menninger, 1948–1949; M. Ralph Kaufman, 1948–1950+; George J. Mohr, 1948–1949; Robert P. Knight, 1950+; LeRoy M. A. Maeder, 1950+.

794. *Chicago. Psychological Museum. Topics.*

TITLE VARIATIONS: None.

DATES OF PUBLICATION: Volume 1, Number 1–3, November 10, 1937–January 1938.

FREQUENCY: Monthly.

NUMBERING VARIATIONS: Volume 1, Number 2/3 is a double issue published in January 1938.

PUBLISHER: **Chicago:** Psychological Museum, 1937–1938.

PRIMARY EDITORS: **Arthur Weil,** 1937–1938; **Irene Case Sherman,** 1937–1938; **David P. Boder,** 1937–1938.

795. *Inward Light.*

TITLE VARIATIONS: None.

DATES OF PUBLICATION: Number 1–37+, 1937–1950+.

FREQUENCY: Irregular (2–4 times a year).

NUMBERING VARIATIONS: None.

PUBLISHER: **Philadelphia:** Sponsored by the Friends Conference on Religion and Psychology, 1937–1947. **Washington, D.C.:** Sponsored by the Friends Conference on Religion and Psychology, 1948–1950+.

PRIMARY EDITORS: None listed.

796. *Journal of Consulting Psychology.*

TITLE VARIATIONS: None.

DATES OF PUBLICATION: Volume 1–14+, 1937–1950+.

FREQUENCY: Bimonthly.

NUMBERING VARIATIONS: None.

PUBLISHER: **Lancaster, Pennsylvania:** Association of Consulting Psychologists, Inc., 1937–1938. **Lancaster:** American Association for Applied Psychology, 1939. **Colorado Springs, Colorado:** American Association for Applied Psychology, Inc., 1940–1945. **Colorado Springs:** American Psychological Association, Inc., 1946. **Washington, D.C.:** American Psychological Association, Inc., 1947–1950+.

PRIMARY EDITORS: **Johnnie P. Symonds,** 1937–1946; **Laurance F. Shaffer,** 1947–1950+.

EDITORIAL COMMITTEE: Henry E. Garrett, 1937; Douglas Fryer, 1937–1940; Katherine G. Ecob, 1937; Miles Murphy, 1937; Gladys C. Schwesinger, 1937; Walter V. Bingham, 1938; Emily T. Burr, 1938; Harold E. Burtt, 1938–1946; Edgar A. Doll, 1938–1940, 1947–1950+; Donald G. Paterson, 1938; C. M. Louttit, 1938–1940; Morris S. Viteles, 1938–1940; F. L. Wells, 1938–1946; Bertha M. Luckey, 1939–1950+; Robert A. Brotemarkle, 1938–1939; Paul S. Achilles, 1939; Henry C. Link, 1938–1940; Carroll L. Shartle, 1939–1940; Richard Paynter, 1938–1940; Robert G. Bernreuter, 1940; John E. Anderson, 1938–1939; Carl R. Rogers, 1940–1950+; Frank N. Freeman, 1938–1940; Sadie M. Shellow, 1940; Gertrude Hildreth, 1938–1940; Harold E. Jones, 1941–1946; Percival M. Symonds, 1938–1940; Arthur W. Kornhauser, 1941–1946; William A. Hunt, 1947–1950+; Goodwin Watson, 1941–1946; E. Lowell Kelly, 1947–1950+; Morris Krugman, 1947–1950+; Fred McKinney, 1947–1950+; Catharine C. Miles, 1947–1949; R. Nevitt Sanford, 1947–1950+; Anne Roe, 1950+.

797. *Journal of Parapsychology.*

TITLE VARIATIONS: Continued by *Journal of Parapsychology. A Scientific Quarterly Dealing with Extra-Sensory Perception and Related Topics* with Volume 6, 1942.

DATES OF PUBLICATION: Volume 1–5, March 1937–1941.

FREQUENCY: **Quarterly,** Volume 1–2, 1937–1938. **Semiannual,** Volume 3–4, 1939–1940. **Quarterly,** Volume 5, 1941.

NUMBERING VARIATIONS: None.

PUBLISHER: **Durham, North Carolina:** Duke University Press, 1937–1939. **[New York]:** No publisher listed, 1940–1941.

PRIMARY EDITORS: **William McDougall,** 1937–1938; **Joseph Banks Rhine,** 1937–1938; **Charles E. Stuart,** 1937–1938; **Gardner Murpy,** 1939–1941; **Bernard F. Riess,** 1939–1941; **Ernest Taves,** 1939–1941; **J. L. Woodruff,** 1941.

798. *Jurnal de psihotehnica.*

TITLE VARIATIONS: Also called *Journal roumain pour la psychologie pratique.*

DATES OF PUBLICATION: Volum 1–5, Număr 1, 1937–1941.

FREQUENCY: Quarterly.

NUMBERING VARIATIONS: None.

PUBLISHER: **Bucharest:** Université de Bucarest, Laboratoire de psychologie expérimentale, strada Edgar-Quinet, 1937–1941.

PRIMARY EDITORS: **C. Rădulescu-Motru** (Director), 1937–1941; **I.-M. Nestor,** 1937–1941; **G. C. Bontila,** 1937–1941; **Al. Chiapella,** 1937–1941.

NOTE: Information on this title was found in the *Bibliographie de la philosophie* published by the International Institute of Philosophical Collaboration, Paris. Paris, Librairie philosophique J. Vrin, 1937–1953.

799. *London. National Institute of Industrial Psychology. News.*

TITLE VARIATIONS: Also called *NIIP. News.* Superseded by *Psychology at Work* with Volume 1, Number 1, March 1948.

DATES OF PUBLICATION: December 1937–February 1948.

FREQUENCY: Quarterly.

NUMBERING VARIATIONS: Numbered by date only. Published as a supplement to *Human Factor,* Volume 11, 1937, and to *Occupational Psychology,* Volume 12–22, 1938–1948.

PUBLISHER: **London:** National Institute of Industrial Psychology, 1937–1948.

PRIMARY EDITORS: **Charles S. Myers,** 1938–1947; **Joan Wynn Reeves,** 1938–1941; **Betty Addinsell,** 1942–1944; **Mary Cockett,** 1944–1947; **Alec Rodger,** 1947–1948.

800. *London. University. Institute of Education. Concerning Children. Pamphlet Series.*

TITLE VARIATIONS: None.

DATES OF PUBLICATION: Number 1–10, March 1937–June 1938.

FREQUENCY: Irregular. *See* Contents *below.*

NUMBERING VARIATIONS: None.

PUBLISHER: **London:** University of London, Institute of Education and the Home and School Council of Great Britain, 1937–1938.

PRIMARY EDITOR: **Susan Isaacs,** 1937–1938.

CONTENTS:

Number 1. Shepherd, Flora. WEANING. March 1937. 10 pp.

Number 2. Gutteridge, Mary V. CONCENTRATION IN YOUNG CHILDREN. 1937. 7 pp.

Number 3. Isaacs, Susan. THE FIRST TWO YEARS. 1937. 15 pp.

Number 4. Swaine, G. R. SCHOOL REPORTS. 1937. 11 pp.

Number 5. Yates, Sybille. FRIENDSHIPS IN ADOLESCENCE. 1937. 10 pp.

Number 6. Roe, Frances. THE BEGINNING OF READING IN THE INFANT SCHOOL. 1937. 10 pp.

Number 7. Shepherd, Flora. THE BABY WHO DOES NOT CONFORM TO RULES. 1937. 11 pp.

Number 8. Yates, Sybille. INDEPENDENCE IN ADOLESCENCE. 1938. 7 pp.

Number 9. Griffiths, Ruth. IMAGINATION AND PLAY IN CHILDHOOD. 1938. 11 pp.

Number 10. Boyce, E. R. PLAY IN THE INFANT SCHOOL. June 1938. 15 pp.

801. *Monatsschrift für Kriminalbiologie und Strafrechtsreform.*
[Organ of the Kriminalbiologische Gesellschaft.]

TITLE VARIATIONS: Continues *Monatsschrift für Kriminalpsychologie und Strafrechtsreform.*

DATES OF PUBLICATION: Band 28–35, 1937–1944. Suspended publication, 1944–1953.

FREQUENCY: Irregular, 12 Hefte per year.

NUMBERING VARIATIONS: Multinumbered issues present.

PUBLISHER: **Munich:** J. F. Lehmanns Verlag, 1937–1944.

PRIMARY EDITORS: **Franz Exner,** 1937–1944; **Johs. Lange,** 1937–1940; **Hans Reiter,** 1937–1940; **Rud. Sieverts,** 1937–1940; **Hans Bürger-Prinz,** 1937–1944.

802. *New York. Psychologists' League. Journal.*

TITLE VARIATIONS: None.

DATES OF PUBLICATION: Volume 1–5, Number 1, January/February 1937–February 1942.

FREQUENCY: **Bimonthly,** Volume 1–3, Number 5, January/February 1937–November/December 1939. **Irregular,** Volume 4–5, January/April 1940–February 1942.

NUMBERING VARIATIONS: None.

PUBLISHER: **New York:** Psychologists' League, 1937–1942.

PRIMARY EDITORS: **Samuel Coe,** 1937–1939; **Ruth Lehrer,** 1937–1938; **Florence Sadowsky,** 1938–1939; **H. Rogosin,** 1940–1942.

EDITORIAL BOARD: Samuel Coe, 1940; Solomon E. Asch, 1937–1938; Max Hertzman, 1937–1940; Robert C. Challman, 1938–1940; Philip Eisenberg, 1938–1940; Eugene Horowitz, 1938–1940; H. Rogosin, 1938–1940; David Shakow, 1938–1940; Florence Sadowsky, 1940; H. A. Witkin, 1939–1940.

803. *Practical Psychology.*

TITLE VARIATIONS: Continues *Practical Psychology Magazine.* Continued by *You* with Volume 3, March 1938.

DATES OF PUBLICATION: Volume 2, Number 1–12, March 1937–February 1938.

FREQUENCY: Monthly.

NUMBERING VARIATIONS: None.

PUBLISHER: **London:** British Union of Practical Psychologists, 1937–1938.

PRIMARY EDITORS: None listed.

804. *Psycho-Analytical Epitomes.*

TITLE VARIATIONS: None.

DATES OF PUBLICATION: Number 1–4, 1937–1939.

FREQUENCY: Irregular: *See* Contents *below.*

NUMBERING VARIATIONS: None.

PUBLISHER: **London:** Published by Leonard and Virginia Woolf at the Hogarth Press and the Institute of Psycho-Analysis, 1937. **London:** The Hogarth Press and the Institute of Psycho-Analysis, 1939.

PRIMARY EDITOR: **John Rickman,** 1937–1939.

CONTENTS:

Number 1. Freud, Sigmund. A GENERAL SELECTION FROM THE WORKS OF SIGMUND FREUD. 1937. 329 pp.

Number 2. Klein, M. LOVE, HATE AND REPARATION. 1937. 119 pp.

Number 3. Money-Kyrle, R. E. SUPERSTITION AND SOCIETY. 1939. 163 pp.

Number 4. Freud, Sigmund. CIVILIZATION, WAR AND DEATH. SELECTIONS FROM THREE WORKS. Edited by John Rickman. 1939. 99 pp.

805. *Psychological Record.*

TITLE VARIATIONS: None.

DATES OF PUBLICATION: Volume 1–5+, March 1937–March 1945+. Suspended publication, 1946–1956.

FREQUENCY: Irregular.

NUMBERING VARIATIONS: Volume 1 has 29 numbers; Volume 2 has 20 numbers; Volume 3 has 23 numbers; Volume 4 has 27 numbers; Volume 5 has 13 numbers. Each number contains one article.

PUBLISHER: **Bloomington, Indiana:** Principia Press, 1937–1945.

PRIMARY EDITORS: **J. R. Kantor,** 1937; **C. M. Louttit,** 1937; **Edmund S. Conklin,** 1937–1945; **Helen Koch,** 1937–1940; **B. M. Castner,** 1937–1940; **E. A. Culler,** 1937–1945; **J. G. Peatman,** 1937–1945; **B. F. Skinner,** 1937–1945; **Norman Cameron,** 1937–1940; **C. F. Scofield,** 1937–1945; **J. P. Guilford,**

1937–1945; **Norman C. Meier**, 1937–1945; **J. W. Carter, Jr.**, 1937–1945; **Martin Reymert**, 1940–1945; **G. A. Kelly**, 1940–1945; **Joseph Tiffin**, 1940–1945.

806. *Psychologische Forschungen über den Lebenslauf.*

TITLE VARIATIONS: None.

DATES OF PUBLICATION: Band 1, 1937.

FREQUENCY: Irregular. *See* Contents *below*.

NUMBERING VARIATIONS: None.

PUBLISHER: **Vienna:** Gerold & Co., 1937.

PRIMARY EDITORS: **Charlotte Bühler**, 1937; **Else Frenkel**, 1937.

CONTENTS:
  Band 1. Frenkel, Else, and Edith Weisskopf. Wunsch und Pflicht im Aufbau des menschlichen Lebens. 1937. 163 pp.

807. *Reich der Seele; Arbeiten aus dem Münchener psychologischen Arbeitskreis.*

TITLE VARIATIONS: None.

DATES OF PUBLICATION: Band 1–2, 1937.

FREQUENCY: Semiannual.

NUMBERING VARIATIONS: None.

PUBLISHER: **Munich:** J. F. Lehmann, 1937.

PRIMARY EDITORS: **Gustav Richard Heyer**, 1937; **Friedrich Seifert**, 1937.

808. *Schriften zur Psychologie der Berufe und der Arbeitswissenschaft.*

TITLE VARIATIONS: None.

DATES OF PUBLICATION: Heft 1–5, 1937–1947.

FREQUENCY: Irregular. *See* Contents *below*.

NUMBERING VARIATIONS: None.

PUBLISHER: **Burgdorf, Switzerland:** Baumgartner, 1937–1940. **Zurich:** Verlag Organisator, 1943. **Zurich:** Rascher & Cie, 1946–1947.

PRIMARY EDITOR: **Franziska Baumgarten**, 1937–1947.

CONTENTS:
  Heft 1. Baumgarten, Franziska. Der Jugendliche und das Berufsleben. 1937. 127 pp.
  Heft 2. Baumgarten, Franziska. Die Arbeit des Menschen. 1940. 72 pp.
  Heft 3. Baumgarten, Franziska. Die Psychologie im kaufmännischen Berufe. 1943. 160 pp.
  Heft 4. Baumgarten, Franziska. Die Psychologie der Menschenbehandlung im Betriebe. 1946. 304 pp.

Heft 5. Baumgarten, Franziska. ZUR PSYCHOLOGIE DES MASCHINENARBEIT-ERS. 1947. 82 pp.

809. *Schweizerische pädagogische Schriften. Reihe: Psychologie.*

TITLE VARIATIONS: None.

DATES OF PUBLICATION: Heft 1–3, 1937–1939.

FREQUENCY: Irregular. *See* Contents *below.*

NUMBERING VARIATIONS: Also numbered as *Schweizerische pädagogische Schriften. See* Contents *below.*

PUBLISHER: **Frauenfeld, Switzerland:** Huber, 1937–1939.

PRIMARY EDITORS: None listed.

CONTENTS:

Heft 1. Häberlin, Paul. LEITFADEN DER PSYCHOLOGIE. 1937. 70 pp. (Also as *Schweizerische pädagogische Schriften,* 6.)

Heft 2. Schohaus, Willi. SEELE UND BERUF DES LEHRERS. 1937. 44 pp. (Also as *Schweizerische pädagogische Schriften,* 7.)

Heft 3. Biäsch, Hans. TESTREIHEN ZUR PRÜFUNG VON SCHWEIZERKINDERN VOM 3.–15. ALTERSJAHR. 1939. 171 pp. (Also as *Schweizerische pädagogische Schriften,* 10.)

810. *Sociometry: A Journal of Inter-personal Relations.*

TITLE VARIATIONS: Supersedes *Sociometric Review.*

DATES OF PUBLICATION: Volume 1–13+, 1937–1950+.

FREQUENCY: Quarterly.

NUMBERING VARIATIONS: Volume 1, Number 1–2 dated July-October 1937; Volume 1, Number 3–4 dated January–April 1938; Volume 2, Number 1 dated January 1939. Combined issues in Volumes 8/9, 11/12. Volume 8, Number 3–4 titled GROUP PSYCHOTHERAPY: A SYMPOSIUM. Various articles separately reprinted as *Sociometry Monographs.*

PUBLISHER: **New York:** Beacon Hill, J. L. Moreno, 1937–1940. **New York:** Sociometry, 1941–1942. **New York:** Beacon House, Inc., 1942–1950+.

PRIMARY EDITORS: **J. L. Moreno,** 1937–1950+; **Gardner Murphy,** 1939–1940; **J. G. Franz,** 1939–1941; **George A. Lundberg,** 1941–1946; **Helen H. Jennings,** 1942–1950; **Zerka Toeman,** 1944–1949; **Joan H. Criswell,** 1950+; **Frederic M. Thrasher,** 1950+; **Leona M. Kerstetter,** 1950+; **Edgar Borgatta,** 1950+.

EDITORIAL BOARD: John Dewey, 1941–1950+; Adolf Meyer, 1941–1950; Wesley C. Mitchell, 1941–1949; George P. Murdock, 1941–1950+; Gardner Murphy, 1941–1950+; George Gallup, 1941–1950+; Ernest W. Burgess, 1943–1950+.

SPECIAL EDITORS:
Volume 10, 1947: **Number 1,** Helen H. Jennings. **Number 2,** Merl E. Bonney. **Number 3,** Joan H. Criswell. **Number 4,** Leslie D. Zeleny.
Volume 11, 1948: **Number 1–2,** Stuart C. Dodd. **Number 3–4,** Charles P. Loomis.
Volume 12, 1949: **Number 1–3,** Georges Gurvitch. **Number 4,** Charles P. Loomis.
Volume 13, 1950: **Number 1,** Paul Deutschberger. **Number 2,** Leo Katz. **Number 3–4,** Ralph B. Spence.

811. *Yale University. Laboratories of Primate Biology. Publications.*

TITLE VARIATIONS: Also called [*Yale University.*] *Laboratories of Comparative Psychobiology. Publications;* and [*Yale University.*] *Laboratories of Comparative Psychobiology. Contributions.*

DATES OF PUBLICATION: [1]–[3,] 1937–1941.

FREQUENCY: Irregular. *See* Contents *below.*

NUMBERING VARIATIONS: None.

PUBLISHER: **New Haven, Connecticut:** Yale University, School of Medicine, 1937–1941.

PRIMARY EDITOR: **Robert M. Yerkes,** 1937–1941.

CONTENTS:
[1.] PUBLICATIONS FROM THE YALE LABORATORIES OF PRIMATE BIOLOGY, 1925–1936. 1937. 9 pp.
[2.] PUBLICATIONS FROM THE YALE LABORATORIES OF PRIMATE BIOLOGY, 1925–1939. 1940. 14 pp.
[3.] PUBLICATIONS FROM THE YALE LABORATORIES OF PRIMATE BIOLOGY, 1940/1941. 1941. 4 pp.

NOTE: Each of the above issues is a pamphlet-length bibliography of articles published in other journals by faculty and students of the Yale Laboratories of Primate Biology.

812. *Zeitschrift für Tierpsychologie.* [Issued by the Deutsche Gesellschaft für Tierpsychologie.]

TITLE VARIATIONS: None.

DATES OF PUBLICATION: Band 1–7 +, 1937–1950 +. Suspended publication, May 1944–September 1948.

FREQUENCY: **Triannual,** Band 1–5, April 1937–1944. **Quarterly,** Band 6–7 +, 1948–1950 +.

NUMBERING VARIATIONS: None.

PUBLISHER: **Berlin:** Paul Parey, 1937–1950 +.

PRIMARY EDITORS: Carl Kronacher, 1937; Otto Köhler, 1937–1950+; Konrad Lorenz, 1937–1950+; Otto Antonius, 1938–1944.

1938

813. *American Council on Education. Studies. Series V: Council Staff Reports.*

TITLE VARIATIONS: None.

DATES OF PUBLICATION: Number 1–11, 1938–1947.

FREQUENCY: Annual (two issued 1943).

NUMBERING VARIATIONS: Reports number 5 and 6 were issued in February and May of 1943.

PUBLISHER: **Washington, D.C.:** American Council on Education, 1938–1947.

PRIMARY EDITORS: **Clarence Stephen Marsh,** 1938–1943; **Mary Irwin,** 1944–1947.

CONTENTS:

Number 1. Mann, C. R. LIVING AND LEARNING. September 1938. 90 pp.

Number 2. Thurstone, L. L., Thelma G. Thurstone, and Dorothy C. Adkins. PSYCHOLOGICAL EXAMINATIONS, 1939 NORMS. May 1940. 56 pp.

Number 3. Thurstone, L. L., and Thelma G. Thurstone. PSYCHOLOGICAL EXAMINATIONS, 1940 NORMS. May 1941. 41 pp.

Number 4. Thurstone, L. L., and Thelma G. Thurstone. PSYCHOLOGICAL EXAMINATIONS, 1941 NORMS. May 1942. 42 pp.

Number 5. Marsh, C. S. ACCELERATION IN THE COLLEGES. February 1943. 29 pp.

Number 6. Thurstone, L. L., and Thelma G. Thurstone. PSYCHOLOGICAL EXAMINATION FOR COLLEGE FRESHMEN, 1942 NORMS. May 1943. 32 pp.

Number 7. Goldthorpe, J. Harold. HIGHER EDUCATION, PHILANTHROPY, AND FEDERAL TAX EXEMPTIONS. May 1944. 40 pp.

Number 8. Thurstone, L. L., and Thelma G. Thurstone. PSYCHOLOGICAL EXAMINATION FOR COLLEGE FRESHMEN, 1943 NORMS. June 1944. 28 pp.

Number 9. Thurstone, L. L., and Thelma G. Thurstone. PSYCHOLOGICAL EXAMINATION FOR COLLEGE FRESHMEN, 1944 NORMS. June 1945. 29 pp.

Number 10. Thurstone, L. L., and Thelma G. Thurstone. PSYCHOLOGICAL EXAMINATION FOR COLLEGE FRESHMEN, 1945 NORMS. May 1946. 34 pp.

Number 11. Thurstone, L. L., and Thelma G. Thurstone. PSYCHOLOGICAL EXAMINATION FOR COLLEGE FRESHMEN, 1946 NORMS. June 1947. 23 pp.

814. *Analytical Psychology Club of New York. Newsletter.*

TITLE VARIATIONS: Superseded by *Analytical Psychology Club of New York. Bulletin* with Volume 1, February 1939.

DATES OF PUBLICATION: Issues 1–8, June 1938–January 1939.

FREQUENCY: Monthly.

NUMBERING VARIATIONS: None.

PUBLISHER: **New York:** Analytical Psychology Club of New York, Inc., 1938–1939.

PRIMARY EDITORS: Edited by publications committee.

815. *Bulletin of Animal Behaviour.*

TITLE VARIATIONS: None.

DATES OF PUBLICATION: Number 1–8+, October 1938–June 1950+. (Ceased publication in 1951.)

FREQUENCY: Irregular.

NUMBERING VARIATIONS: Two special numbers were published. *See* Contents *below.*

PUBLISHER: **London:** Institute for the Study of Animal Behaviour, Zoological Society, 1938–1948. **London:** Association for the Study of Animal Behaviour, 1950–1951.

PRIMARY EDITORS: **S. Zuckerman,** 1938–1941; **J.W.B. Douglas,** 1938–1941; none listed, 1942–1950+.

CONTENTS:
>   **Number 5.** Frisch, Karl von. THE DANCES OF THE HONEY BEE. 1947. 32 pp.
>   **Number 7.** Thorpe, William Homan. THE MODERN CONCEPT OF INSTINCTIVE BEHAVIOR. 1948. 12 pp.

816. *Florence. Università. Istituto di psicologia. Studi e ricerche di psicologia.*

TITLE VARIATIONS: Continues [*Florence. Università.*] *Laboratorio di psicologia sperimentale. Ricerche di psicologia.*

DATES OF PUBLICATION: Parte 1–30, 1938–1947.

FREQUENCY: Irregular.

NUMBERING VARIATIONS: None.

PUBLISHER: **Florence:** Istituto di psicologia, 1938–1947.

PRIMARY EDITOR: **Alberto Marzi,** 1938–1947.

817. *Journal of Neurology and Psychiatry.*

TITLE VARIATIONS: Continues *Journal of Neurology and Psychopathology.* Continued by *Journal of Neurology, Neurosurgery and Psychiatry* with New Series, Volume 7, 1944.

DATES OF PUBLICATION: New Series, Volume 1–6, January 1938–July/October 1943.

FREQUENCY: Quarterly.

NUMBERING VARIATIONS: Multinumber issues present.

PUBLISHER: **London:** British Medical Association, 1938–1943.

PRIMARY EDITORS: **E. Arnold Carmichael,** 1938–1943; **D. Denny-Brown,** 1938–1943; **Aubrey Lewis,** 1938–1943; **G. Jefferson,** 1938–1943; **A. Meyer,** 1938–1943; **R. A. McCance,** 1938–1943.

EDITORIAL BOARD: E. D. Adrian, 1938–1943; W. Russell Brain, 1938–1943; E. Bramwell, 1938–1943; William Brown, 1938–1943; Hugh Cairns, 1938–1943; C. Macfie Campbell, 1938–1943; A. Feiling, 1938–1943; R. A. Fisher, 1938–1943; R. D. Gillespie, 1938–1943; F. L. Golla, 1938–1943; R. G. Gordon, 1938–1943; J. G. Greenfield, 1938–1943; Bernard Hart, 1938–1943; R. Foster Kennedy, 1938–1943; E. Mapother, 1938–1939; R. M. Stewart, 1938–1943; C. P. Symonds, 1938–1943; H. H. Woollard, 1938; C. C. Worster-Drought, 1938–1943; W. E. Le Gros Clark, 1939–1943.

818. *Mental Measurements Yearbook.*

TITLE VARIATIONS: Titled *The Nineteen Thirty Eight Mental Measurements Yearbook of the School of Education, Rutgers University,* Volume 1, 1938; *The Nineteen Forty Mental Measurements Yearbook,* Volume 2, 1940; and *The Third Mental Measurements Yearbook,* Volume 3, 1949. Continues *Educational, Psychological, and Personality Tests* of 1933/1934, 1933/1934/1935, and 1936.

DATES OF PUBLICATION: Volume 1–3+, 1938–1949+.

FREQUENCY: Irregular.

NUMBERING VARIATIONS: None.

PUBLISHER: **New Brunswick, New Jersey:** Rutgers University Press, 1938. **Highland Park, New Jersey:** The Mental Measurements Yearbook, 1941. **New Brunswick:** Rutgers University Press, 1949.

PRIMARY EDITOR: **Oscar Krisen Buros,** 1938–1949+.

819. *Occupational Psychology.*

TITLE VARIATIONS: Continues *Human Factors.*

DATES OF PUBLICATION: Volume 12–24+, 1938–1950+.

FREQUENCY: Quarterly.

NUMBERING VARIATIONS: Supplement to Volume 12–22 also numbered as [*London.*] *National Institute of Industrial Psychology. News.*

PUBLISHER: **London:** National Institute of Industrial Psychology, 1938–1950+.

PRIMARY EDITORS: **Charles S. Myers,** 1938–1947; **Joan Wynn Reeves,** 1938–1941; **Betty Addinsell,** 1942–1944; **Mary Cockett,** 1944–1947; **Alec Rodger,** 1947–1950+.

EDITORIAL BOARD: F. C. Bartlett, 1947–1950+; D. W. Harding, 1947–1950+; Cyril Burt, 1947–1950+; C. A. Mace, 1947–1950+.

820. *Parent Education Bulletin.*

TITLE VARIATIONS: Continued by [*Toronto. University.*] *Institute of Child Study. Bulletin* with Volume 1, Number 2, 1939.

DATES OF PUBLICATION: Volume 1, Number 1, December 1938.

FREQUENCY: Monthly.

NUMBERING VARIATIONS: None.

PUBLISHER: **Toronto:** University of Toronto, Institute of Child Study, 1938.

PRIMARY EDITORS: None listed.

NOTE: Above entry is based on partial information. The compilers were unable to examine this title.

821. *Psycho-biologie de l'enfant.*

TITLE VARIATIONS: Continues *Exposés sur la psycho-biologie de l'enfant.*

DATES OF PUBLICATION: Tome 3–5, 1938–1948. Suspended publication 1939–1946.

FREQUENCY: Irregular. *See* Contents *below.*

NUMBERING VARIATIONS: Also number in *Actualités scientifiques et industrielles. See* Contents *below.*

PUBLISHER: **Paris:** Hermann & Cie, 1938. **Paris:** Hermann, 1947–1948.

PRIMARY EDITOR: **Henri Wallon,** 1938–1948.

CONTENTS:

    Tome 3. Loosli-Usteri, Marguerite. LE DIAGNOSTIC INDIVIDUEL CHEZ L'ENFANT AU MÔYEN DU TEST DE RORSCHACH. 1938. 90 pp. (Also as *Actualités scientifiques et industrielle,* Numéro 639.)

    Tome 4. Bergeron, Marcel. LES MANIFESTATIONS MOTRICES SPONTANÉES CHEZ L'ENFANT, ÉTUDE PSYCHO-BIOLOGIQUE. 1947. 105 pp. (Also as *Actualités scientifiques et industrielles,* Numéro 1025.)

    Tome 5. Loosli-Usteri, Marguerite. LE DIAGNOSTIC INDIVIDUEL CHEZ L'ENFANT AU MÔYEN DU TEST DE RORSCHACH. 2nd rev. ed. 1948. 128 pp. (Also as *Actualités scientifiques et industrielles,* Numéro 1055.)

822. *Psychologia wychowawcza.*

TITLE VARIATIONS: Continues *Polskie archiwum psychologiji* with Tom 11, 1938.

DATES OF PUBLICATION: Tom 11, Numer 1–4, September/October 1938–July/August 1939.

FREQUENCY: Quarterly.

NUMBERING VARIATIONS: Multinumber issue present.

PUBLISHER: **Warsaw:** Związek nauczycielstwa polskiego, 1938–1939.

PRIMARY EDITOR: **Marja Grzegorzewska,** 1938–1939.

823. *Psychometric Monographs.*

TITLE VARIATIONS: None.

DATES OF PUBLICATION: Number 1–4+, 1938–1944+. Suspended publication, 1945–1950.

FREQUENCY: Irregular. *See* Contents *below.*

NUMBERING VARIATIONS: Number 3, 1940, published prior to Number 2, 1941.

PUBLISHER: **Chicago:** University of Chicago Press for the Psychometric Society, 1938–1944+.

EDITORIAL BOARD CHAIRMEN: **Paul Horst,** 1938–1944; **J. P. Guilford,** 1944+.

EDITORIAL BOARD: Jack Dunlap, 1938–1940; J. P. Guilford, 1938–1944; Harold Gulliksen, 1938–1944+; Paul Horst, 1944+; Frederic Kuder, 1944+; Irving Lorge, 1938–1940; L. L. Thurstone, 1944+.

CONTENTS:
> **Number 1.** Thurstone, Louis Leon. PRIMARY MENTAL ABILITIES. 1938. 121 pp.
> **Number 2.** Thurstone, Louis Leon, and Thelma Gwinn Thurstone. FACTORIAL STUDIES OF INTELLIGENCE. 1941. 94 pp.
> **Number 3.** Wolfle, Dael. FACTOR ANALYSIS TO 1940. 1940. 69 pp.
> **Number 4.** Thurstone, Louis Leon. A FACTORIAL STUDY OF PERCEPTION. 1944. 148 pp.

824. *Revista de psihologie. Teoretică şi aplicată.*

TITLE VARIATIONS: None.

DATES OF PUBLICATION: Volumul 1–11, January/March 1938–June/December 1948.

FREQUENCY: Quarterly.

NUMBERING VARIATIONS: Issued half-yearly with multinumber issues, 1946–1948.

PUBLISHER: **Cluj, Transylvania:** Editura Institutului de psihologie al universităţii, 1938–1939. **Sibiu, Romania:** Editura Institutului de psihologie al universităţii, 1940–1948.

PRIMARY EDITORS: **F. Ştefănescu-Goangă,** 1938–1948; **N. Mărgineanu,** 1941; **A. Rosca,** 1941–1948; **D. Todoranu,** 1943–1947.

EDITORIAL BOARD: Z. Barbu, 1941–1943, 1946; M. Beniuc, 1941–1946; S. Cupcea, 1941–1946; L. Rusu, 1941–1946; D. Todoranu, 1941–1942; A. Chircev, 1942–1946; L. Bologă, 1944–1946; G. Em. Marica, 1944–1946; M. Peteanu, 1944–1946.

825. *Toronto. University. Institute of Child Study. Parent Education Bulletin.*

TITLE VARIATIONS: Continued by [*Toronto. University.*] *Institute of Child Study. Bulletin* with Number 45, Fall 1949.

DATES OF PUBLICATION: Number 1–44, December 1938–Summer 1949.

FREQUENCY: **Five times yearly,** Number 1–28, December 1938–June 1944. **Quarterly,** Number 29–44, Fall 1944–Summer 1949.

NUMBERING VARIATIONS: Combined issues present.

PUBLISHER: **Toronto:** University of Toronto, St. George's School for Child Study, Institute of Child Study, Parent Education Division, 1938–1944. **Toronto:** University of Toronto, Institute of Child Study, 1944–1949.

PRIMARY EDITOR: **Karl S. Bernhardt,** 1938–1949.

826. *You.*

TITLE VARIATIONS: Continues: *Practical Psychology.*

DATES OF PUBLICATION: Volume 3, Number 1–12, March 1938–February 1939.

FREQUENCY: Monthly.

NUMBERING VARIATIONS: None.

PUBLISHER: **London:** British Union of Practical Psychologists, 1938–1939.

PRIMARY EDITORS: None listed.

827. *Zeitschrift für Arbeitspsychologie und praktische Psychologie im Allgemeinen.*

TITLE VARIATIONS: Continues *Psychotechnische Zeitschrift.*

DATES OF PUBLICATION: Band 11–12, 1938–1939.

FREQUENCY: Bimonthly.

NUMBERING VARIATIONS: None.

PUBLISHER: **Neustadt in Sachsen, Germany:** Julius Missbach, Buchdruckerei, 1938–1939.

PRIMARY EDITOR: **Hans Rupp,** 1938–1939.

1939

828. *American Council on Education. Studies. Series VI: Student Personnel Work.*

TITLE VARIATIONS: Series VI also called *Personnel Work in Colleges and Universities.*

DATES OF PUBLICATION: Number 1–15 +, 1939–1950 +.

FREQUENCY: Irregular. *See* Contents *below.*

NUMBERING VARIATIONS: Number 1 and 2 also numbered as Volume 3, Number 1 and 2; Number 3 also numbered as Volume 4, Number 3.

PUBLISHER: **Washington, D.C.:** American Council on Education, 1939–1950 + .

PRIMARY EDITORS: **Clarence Stephen Marsh,** 1939–1943; **Mary Irwin,** 1945–1950 + .

CONTENTS:

Number 1. Bragdon, Helen D., A. J. Brumbaugh, Basil H. Pillard, and E. G. Williamson. EDUCATIONAL COUNSELING OF COLLEGE STUDENTS. 1939. 61 pp.

Number 2. Cowley, W. H. et al. OCCUPATIONAL ORIENTATION OF COLLEGE STUDENTS. 1939. 74 pp.

Number 3. Lloyd-Jones, Esther. SOCIAL COMPETENCE AND COLLEGE STUDENTS. 1940. 89 pp.

Number 4. Merriam, Thornton W. et al. RELIGIOUS COUNSELING OF COLLEGE STUDENTS. 1943. 77 pp.

Number 5. COUNSELING AND POSTWAR EDUCATIONAL OPPORTUNITIES. 1944. 13 pp.

Number 6. Blaesser, Willard W. et al. STUDENT PERSONNEL WORK IN THE POSTWAR COLLEGE. 1945. 95 pp.

Number 7. Sharpe, Russell T. et al. FINANCIAL ASSISTANCE FOR COLLEGE STUDENTS. 1946. 113 pp.

Number 8. Mueller, Kate Heyner et al. COUNSELING FOR MENTAL HEALTH. 1947. 64 pp.

Number 9. Darley, John G. et al. USE OF TESTS IN COLLEGE. 1947. 82 pp.

Number 10. Shank, Donald J. et al. THE TEACHER AS COUNSELOR. 1948. 48 pp.

Number 11. La Barre, Corinne. GRADUATE TRAINING FOR EDUCATIONAL PERSONNEL WORK. 1948. 54 pp.

Number 12. Kirkpatrick, Forrest H. et al. HELPING STUDENTS FIND EMPLOYMENT. 1949. 37 pp.

Number 13. Committee on Student Personnel Work. E. G. Williamson, Chairman. THE STUDENT PERSONNEL POINT OF VIEW. 1949. 20 pp.

Number 14. Strozier, Robert M. et al. HOUSING FOR STUDENTS. 1950. 68 pp.

Number 15. Blegen, Theodore C. et al. COUNSELING FOREIGN STUDENTS. 1950. 54 pp.

829. *American Imago; A Psychoanalytic Journal for the Arts and Sciences.*

TITLE VARIATIONS: None.

DATES OF PUBLICATION: Volume 1–7 + , November 1939–1950 + . Suspended publication, September 1942–January 1946.

FREQUENCY: Quarterly.

NUMBERING VARIATIONS: Multinumber issues present.

PUBLISHER: **Boston:** Hanns Sachs, Boston, 1939–1947. **Boston:** George B. Wilbur, 1947–1950+.

PRIMARY EDITORS: **Sigmund Freud,** 1939; **Hanns Sachs,** 1939–1947; **George B. Wilbur,** 1947–1950+.

830. *Analytical Psychology Club of New York. Bulletin.*

TITLE VARIATIONS: Also called *APC of New York. Bulletin.* Supersedes *Analytical Psychology Club of New York. Newsletter.*

DATES OF PUBLICATION: Volume 1–12+, February 1939–December 1950+.

FREQUENCY: **Bimonthly,** Volume 1, Number 1–6, February–November 1939. **Monthly,** (except July, August and September), Volume 2–10, Number 1–9, January 1940–December 1948. **Monthly,** (except June, July, August and September), Volume 11–12, Number 1–8+, January 1949–December 1950+.

NUMBERING VARIATIONS: None.

PUBLISHER: **New York:** Published by the Analytical Psychology Club of New York, Inc., 1939–1950+.

PRIMARY EDITORS: Publications committee of the APC of New York, chaired in succession by **Hildegard Nagel, Ellen Thayer,** and **Jane Abott Pratt.**

831. *Arbeiten zur Pädagogik und psychologischen Anthropologie.*

TITLE VARIATIONS: None.

DATES OF PUBLICATION: Band 1, 1939.

FREQUENCY: Irregular. *See Contents below.*

NUMBERING VARIATIONS: Also published as *Friedrich Manns pädagogisches Magazin,* Heft 1433.

PUBLISHER: **Langensalza, Germany:** Hermann Beyer und Söhne (Beyer und Mann), 1939.

PRIMARY EDITOR: **Erich R. Jaensch,** 1939.

CONTENTS:
> **Band 1.** Jaensch, Erich. DAS WAHRHEITSPROBLEM BEI DER VÖLKISCHEN NEUGESTALTUNG VON WISSENSCHAFT UND ERZIEHUNG. 1939. 40 pp.

832. *Archivio di psicologia, neurologia, psichiatria e psicoterapia.*

TITLE VARIATIONS: Supersedes *Archivio generale di neurologia, psichiatria e psicoanalisi.*

DATES OF PUBLICATION: Anno 1–11+, November 1939–December 1950+.

FREQUENCY: **Quarterly,** Anno 1–10, November 1939–December 1949. **Bimonthly,** Anno 11+, February 1950–December 1950+.

NUMBERING VARIATIONS: Multinumber issues present.

PUBLISHER: **Milan:** Piazza S. Ambrogio, 1939 (Fascicolo 1/2). **Milan:** Redazione e amministrazione, Via Ludovico Mecchi, 1940–1943. **Milan:** Redazione e amministrazione, Piazza S. Ambrogio, N. 9, 1943–1950 + .

PRIMARY EDITOR: **Agostino Gemelli,** 1939–1950 + .

EDITORIAL BOARD: Ferruccio Banissoni, 1939–1950 + ; Carlo Besta, 1939–1940; Ugo Cerletti, 1939–1945; Lionello De Lisi, 1939–1950 + ; Eugenio Medea, 1939–1950 + ; Mario Ponzo, 1939–1950 + ; Carlo Berlucchi, 1942–1950 + ; Giuseppe Corberi, 1946–1950 + ; Angiola Massucco Costa, 1946–1950 + ; G. E. Morselli, 1946–1950 + .

833. *Beiträge zur Geschichte der Psychologie.*

TITLE VARIATIONS: None.

DATES OF PUBLICATION: Heft 1–2, July 1939–May 1940.

FREQUENCY: Semiannual.

NUMBERING VARIATIONS: Also numbered as part of *Zeitschrift für Psychologie und Physiologie der Sinnesorgane.* Abteilung I. *Zeitschrift für Psychologie.* *See* Contents *below.*

PUBLISHER: **Leipzig:** Johann Ambrosius Barth, 1939–1940.

PRIMARY EDITOR: **Friedrich Sander,** 1939–1940.

CONTENTS:

Heft 1. Wagner, Karl. ÜBER DIE GRUNDLAGEN DER PSYCHOLOGISCHEN FORSCHUNG FRIEDRICH NIETZSCHES. (Also as *Zeitschrift für Psychologie und Physiologie der Sinnesorgane.* Abteilung I. *Zeitschrift für Psychologie*, Band 146, 1939, pp. 1–68.)

Heft 2. Trebeck, Richard. DIE ANTHROPOLOGIE DES JOHANN CASPAR LAVATER. (Also as *Zeitschrift für Psychologie und Physiologie der Sinnesorgane.* Abteilung I. *Zeitschrift für Psychologie*, Band 147, 1940, pp. 274–327.)

834. *Études de psychologie et de philosophie.*

TITLE VARIATIONS: None.

DATES OF PUBLICATION: Numéro 1–2 + , 1939–1950 + .

FREQUENCY: Irregular. *See* Contents *below.*

NUMBERING VARIATIONS: None.

PUBLISHER: **Paris:** Librairie philosophique J. Vrin, 1939–1950 + .

PRIMARY EDITORS: **Paul Guillaume,** 1939–1950 + ; **I. Meyerson,** 1939.

CONTENTS:

Numéro 1. Lalo, Charles. L'ART LOIN DE LA VIE. 1939. 295 pp.

Numéro 2. Tilquin, André. LE BEHAVIORISME; ORIGINE ET DÉVELOPPEMENT DE LA PSYCHOLOGIE DE REACTION EN AMÉRIQUE. 1942. 531 pp. (Reissued in 1950.)

835. *Guild of Pastoral Psychology. Lectures.*

TITLE VARIATIONS: None.

DATES OF PUBLICATION: Number 1–66+, 1939–1950+.

FREQUENCY: Irregular. *See* Contents *below.*

NUMBERING VARIATIONS: Number 12/13 joint number publication. Dates of numbers 2, 5, 35, 39, 43, 45, 50 are not in chronological sequence. Two issues also numbered in *Guild of Pastoral Psychology. Miscellany. See* Contents *below.*

PUBLISHER: **London:** Guild of Pastoral Psychology, 1939–1950+.

PRIMARY EDITORS: None listed.

CONTENTS:

Number 1. Kirsch, James. RELIGIOUS ASPECTS OF THE UNCONSCIOUS. February 1939. 28 pp.

Number 2. Peacey, W. H. PASTORAL PSYCHOLOGY AND THE GOSPEL. January 1939. 15 pp.

Number 3. Westmann, H. OLD TESTAMENT AND ANALYTICAL PSYCHOLOGY. April 1939. 24 pp.

Number 4. Fordham, Michael. ANALYSIS OF CHILDREN. June 1939. 18 pp.

Number 5. Adler, Gerhard. CONSCIOUSNESS AND CURE. May 1938. 20 pp.

Number 6. Jacoby, H. J. CHANGES OF CHARACTER PRODUCED BY RELIGIOUS CONVERSIONS, AS SHOWN IN CHANGES OF HANDWRITING. 1940. 26 pp.

Number 7. Kitchin, Kathleen F. THE THIRD REICH: A PLEA FOR THE GUARDIAN ANGEL.

Number 8. Slade, Peter. VALUE OF DRAMA IN RELIGION, EDUCATION AND THERAPY. May 1940. 16 pp.

Number 9. AUTUMN, 1940. By various members.

Number 10. Westmann, H. THE GOLDEN CALF. March 1941. 16 pp.

Number 11. Woods, Charlotte E. THE PSYCHOLOGY OF SIN. May 1941. 20 pp.

Number 12/13. TECHNIQUE I AND II. By the Staff of the South-West London Pastoral Centre. 1941.

Number 14. Boyd, Canon F. TECHNIQUE III. 1941.

Number 15. Dossetor, R. F. GAWAIN AND THE GREEN KNIGHT. 1941.

Number 16. ANALYTIC FUNCTION. By Three Members. 35 pp.

Number 17. Matland, Adeline M. PASTORAL PSYCHOLOGY. 1942. 20 pp.

Number 18. Peacey, W. H. PATTERNS. 1942. 24 pp.

Number 19. White, V. FRONTIERS OF THEOLOGY AND PSYCHOLOGY. October 1942. 28 pp.

Number 20. Segal, A. ART IN PSYCHOLOGY. December 1942.

Number 21. Howe, E. Graham. WAR AND THE HEALER. February 1943.

Number 22. Howe, E. Graham. BALD-HEAD. April 1943. 32 pp.

Number 23. Collard, Phyllis. THE RING AND THE LAMP. July 1943. 28 pp.

Number 24. Lander, K. Forsaith. A MAP OF THE PSYCHE. September 1943. 40 pp.

Number 25. Lucas, Peter D. WUTHERING HEIGHTS. December 1943. 34 pp.

Number 26. Howe, E. Graham. SPIRITUAL APPROACH TO MEDICAL PSYCHOLOGY.

Number 27. Layard, John. INCARNATION AND INSTINCT. April 1944. 20 pp.

Number 28. Collier, Howard E. THE PLACE OF WORSHIP IN MODERN MEDICINE. June 1944. 22 pp.

Number 29. Witcutt, W. P. THE CHILD IN PARADISE. July 1944. 32 pp.

Number 30. MISCELLANY I. September 1944. 32 pp.

Number 31. White, Victor. WALTER HILTON: AN ENGLISH SPIRITUAL GUIDE. October 1944. 20 pp.

Number 32. Lander, K. Forsaith. THE ANIMA. November 1944.

Number 33. Gledhill, Rolf. ILONDS: THEIR USE AND VALUE IN DIAGNOSIS. December 1944. 20 pp.

Number 34. MISCELLANY II. March 1945. 35 pp.

Number 35. Kitchin, Derek. MATTHEW ARNOLD AND THE SCHOLAR GYPSY. February 1945. 27 pp.

Number 36. Metman, Philip. THE PROBLEM OF ESSENCE AND FORM IN CHRISTIANITY. April 1945. 19 pp.

Number 37. Westmann, H. ECONOMIC PLANNING AND THE UNIQUENESS OF MAN. July 1945. 16 pp.

Number 38. Moore, W. I. RELIGIOUS EDUCATION: AN EXPERIMENT. September 1945. 24 pp.

Number 39. Zimmer, Henry R. INTEGRATING THE EVIL: A CELTIC MYTH AND A CHRISTIAN LEGEND. Spring 1943. 38 pp.

Number 40. Duncan-Johnstone, L. A. A PSYCHOLOGICAL STUDY OF WILLIAM BLAKE. December 1945. 23 pp.

Number 41. Metman, Eva. THE GREEN SNAKE AND THE FAIR LILY. April 1946. 30 pp.

Number 42. Wolff, Toni. CHRISTIANITY WITHIN. May 1946. 15 pp.

Number 43. Adler, Gerhard. PSYCHOLOGY AND THE ATOMIC BOMB. April 1946. 22 pp.

Number 44. Metman, Philip. PATTERNS OF INITIATION. 1946. 20 pp.

Number 45. Kraemer, William P. THE FAMILY CLINIC. July 1947. 23 pp.

Number 46. Fordham, Michael. ANALYTICAL PSYCHOLOGY AND RELIGIOUS EXPERIENCE. March 1947. 20 pp.

Number 47. Schaerf, Rivkah. KING SAUL AND THE SPIRIT OF GOD. 1947. 35 pp.

Number 48. Hone, Margaret E. ASTROLOGY IN RELATION TO PASTORAL PSYCHOLOGY. June 1947. 20 pp.

Number 49. Jung, C. G. THE PSYCHOLOGY OF THE SPIRIT. (An Abstract by Eva Metman.) 1947. 24 pp.

Number 50. Barker, Culver. SOME POSITIVE VALUES OF NEUROSIS. February 1947. 20 pp.

Number 51. Hannah, Barbara. THE PROBLEM OF WOMEN'S PLOTS IN "THE EVIL VINEYARD". February 1948. 58 pp.

Number 52. Baumann, Carol. EUGENE N. MARAIS AND THE PROBLEM OF ANIMAL PSYCHE. March 1948. 24 pp.

Number 53. Heider, Werner. LIVING SYMBOLS IN LITERATURE. April 1948. 36 pp.

Number 54. Abenheimer, Karl. THE PROBLEM OF INDIVIDUATION IN FRIEDRICH NIETZSCHE'S WRITINGS. May 1948. 27 pp.

Number 55. Hoppin, Hector. THE PSYCHOLOGY OF THE ARTIST. July 1948. 29 pp.

Number 56. Howe, E. Graham. PSYCHOTHERAPY AND THE EXPERIENCE OF CONVERSION. October 1948. 24 pp.

Number 57. Sumner, M. Oswald. ST. JOHN OF THE CROSS AND MODERN PSYCHOLOGY. December 1948. 31 pp.

Number 58. Lambert, Kenneth. PSYCHOLOGY AND PERSONAL RELATIONSHIP. February 1949. 27 pp.

Number 59. White, Victor. NOTES ON GNOSTICISM. April 1949. 27 pp.

Number 60. Bertine, Eleanor. MEN AND WOMEN. August 1949. 31 pp.

Number 61. Metman, Philip. VARIATIONS ON THE THEME OF MAN AND WOMAN. November 1949. 16 pp.

Number 62. Neill, Stephen. A CHRISTIAN APPROACH TO PSYCHOLOGY. December 1949. 20 pp.

Number 63. Sumner, M. Oswald. ST. JOHN CLIMACUS: THE PSYCHOLOGY OF THE DESERT FATHERS. January 1950. 23 pp.

Number 64. Metman, Philip. EROS AND AGAPE. August 1950. 25 pp.

Number 65. Buck, Alice E. GROUP PSYCHOLOGY AND THERAPY. September 1950. 20 pp.

Number 66. Allenby, Amy I. RELATIONSHIP AS BASIS OF THE RELIGIOUS ATTITUDE. 1950.

836. *Internationale Zeitschrift für Psychoanalyse und "Imago."* [Organ of the Internationale psychoanalytische Vereinigung.]

TITLE VARIATIONS: Continues *Internationale Zeitschrift für Psychoanalyse.*

DATES OF PUBLICATION: Volume 24–26, 1939–1941.

FREQUENCY: Quarterly.

NUMBERING VARIATIONS: Multinumber issues present in all volumes.

PUBLISHER: **London:** Imago Publishing Co., 1939–1941.

PRIMARY EDITORS: **Edward Bibring,** 1939–1941; **Heinz Hartmann,** 1939–1941; **Wilhelm Hoffer,** 1939–1941; **Ernst Kris,** 1939–1941; **Robert Waelder,** 1939–1941.

EDITORIAL BOARD: Sigmund Freud, 1939; Girindrashekhar Bose, 1939–1941; M. Eitingon, 1939–1941; Thomas M. French, 1939; Lewis B. Hill, 1939–1940; S. Hollos, 1939–1941; Ernest Jones, 1939–1941; J. W. Kannabich, 1939–1941; M. R. Kaufman, 1939; Bertram D. Lewin, 1939; Kiyayasu Marui, 1939–1941; K. A. Menninger, 1939–1940; S.J.R. de Monchy, 1939–1941; Edouard Pichon, 1939; Philipp Sarasin, 1939–1941; Harald K. Schjelderup, 1939–1941; Alfhild Tamm, 1939–1941; Edoardo Weiss, 1939; Y. K. Yabe, 1939–1941; Anna Freud, 1940–1941; S. G. Biddle, 1940–1941; Helene Deutsch, 1940–1941; S. Lawrence, 1940; Helen V. Maclean, 1940; Charles Odier, 1940–1941; A. A. Brill, 1941; F. Fromm-Reichmann, 1941; Robert P. Knight, 1941; David M. Levy, 1941; George J. Mohr, 1941; Adolf Stern, 1941.

837. Journal of Criminal Psychopathology.

TITLE VARIATIONS: Continued by *Journal of Clinical Psychopathology and Psychotherapy* with Volume 6, 1944.

DATES OF PUBLICATION: Volume 1–5, 1939–1944.

FREQUENCY: Quarterly.

NUMBERING VARIATIONS: None.

PUBLISHER: **Woodbourne, New York:** Published by the Woodbourne Institution for Defective Delinquents, New York State Department of Corrections, 1939 (Issue 1). **Woodbourne:** Journal Press, 1939. **Hurleyville, New York:** Medical Journal Press, 1940. **Monticello, New York:** Medical Journal Press, 1941–1944.

PRIMARY EDITOR: **V. C. Branham,** 1939–1944.

EDITORIAL BOARD: Franz Alexander, 1940–1944; Julius Bauer, 1940–1943; A. A. Brill, 1940–1944; J. F. Brown, 1940–1942; Bernard Glueck, 1940–1944; Harry B. Haines, 1940–1942; Leland E. Hinsie, 1940–1943; Ben Karpman, 1940–1941; Ralph Linton, 1940–1943; Sandor Lorand, 1940–1944; C. P. Oberndorf, 1940–1944; Geza Roheim, 1940–1944; Lowell S. Selling, 1940–1944; Paul Schilder, 1940; George Devereux, 1940–1944; Merrill Moore, 1941–1944; Gregory S. Zilboorg, 1941–1944; Sydney B. Maughs, 1941–1942; Walter Bromberg, 1941–1944; Paul L. Schroeder, 1943–1944; Margaret Mead, 1943–1944; Erich Fromm, 1943–1944; Fritz Wittels, 1943–1944; Edmund Bergler, 1944; Philip Q. Roche, 1944.

838. Jurnal de psihologie militara.

TITLE VARIATIONS: Also called *Journal de psychologie militaire.*

DATES OF PUBLICATION: Volum 1, Număr 1–2, 1939.

FREQUENCY: Irregular.

NUMBERING VARIATIONS: None.

PUBLISHER: **Bucharest:** Université de Bucarest, Laboratoire de psychologie expérimentale, strada Edgar-Quinet, 1939.

PRIMARY EDITOR: **C. Rădulescu-Motru,** 1939.

NOTE: Information on this title was found in the *Bibliographie de la philosophie* published by the International Institute of Philosophical Collaboration, Paris. Paris, Librairie philosophique J. Vrin, 1937–1953.

839. Lehigh University. Studies. Psychology Series.

TITLE VARIATIONS: None.

DATES OF PUBLICATION: Number 1–5, 1939–1942.

FREQUENCY: Irregular.

NUMBERING VARIATIONS: Number 4–5 also as [*Lehigh University.*] *Publications. Circular 174–175.*

PUBLISHER: Various. *See* Note *below.*

PRIMARY EDITORS: None listed.

NOTE: No original publications. Compilation of reprints of articles by James Larmour Graham and William Leroy Jenkins.

840. *Louvain. Université catholique. Institut de psychologie appliquée et de pédagogie. Extraits de dissertations.*

TITLE VARIATIONS: Continued by [*Louvain.*] *Université catholique. Institut de psychologie appliquée et de pédagogie. Extraits de dissertations* with Série A, Numéro 1, 1947; and Série B, Numéro 1, 1947.

DATES OF PUBLICATION: Numéro 1–5, 1939–1941.

FREQUENCY: Irregular. *See* Contents *below.*

NUMBERING VARIATIONS: Some issues also numbered in [*Montréal. Université.*] *Institut pédagogique Saint-Georges. Bulletin; Revue belge de pédagogie; Année psychologique;* or *Journal de psychologie normale et pathologique. See* Contents *below.*

PUBLISHER: Louvain: E. Nauwelaerts, 2, place Cardinal Mercier, 1939–1941.

PRIMARY EDITORS: None listed.

CONTENTS:
Numéro 1. Chrysostome, Frère (F.É.C.). LA NOTION DE RELATION CHEZ L'ENFANT. (Also in [*Montréal. Université.*] *Institut pédagogique Saint-Georges. Bulletin,* Numéro 1, 1939. 25 pp.)
Numéro 2. M. -Leo, Frère (F.É.C.). ADAPTATION À LA BELGIQUE DES "PREMIERS TESTS DE LECTURE" DU PROFESSEUR A. I. GATES. (Also in [*Montréal. Université.*] *Institut pédagogique Saint-Georges. Bulletin,* Numéro 2, 1939. 87 pp.)
Numéro 3. Célis, S. DÉFICIENCES POUR LA LECTURE. (Also in *Revue belge de pédagogie,* Tome 21, 1939/1940; pp. 73–80.)
Numéro 4. Pollet, A. M. EXAMEN CRITIQUE DE L'ÉCHELLE D'EXÉCUTION DE PINTNER ET PATERSON. (Also in *Année psychologique,* Année 39, 1940, pp. 136–169.)
Numéro 5. Stoffels, M. J. LA RÉACTION DITE DE COLÉRE CHEZ LES NOU-VEAU-NÉS. (Also in *Journal de psychologie normale et pathologique,* Année 37/38, 1940/1941, pp. 92–148.)

841. *Montreal. Université. Institut pédagogique Saint-Georges. Bulletin.*

TITLE VARIATIONS: None.

DATES OF PUBLICATION: Numéro 1–10+, 1939–1950+.

FREQUENCY: Irregular. *See* Contents *below.*

NUMBERING VARIATIONS: Some issues also numbered in [*Louvain.*] *Université catholique. Institut de psychologie appliquée et de pédagogie. Extraits de dissertations. See* Contents *below.*

PUBLISHER: **Montreal:** Université de Montréal. Institut pédagogique Saint-Georges, 1939–1950+.

PRIMARY EDITORS: None listed.

CONTENTS:

Numéro 1. Chrysostome, Frère (F.É.C.). LA NOTION DE RELATION CHEZ L'ENFANT. 1939. 25 pp. (Also as [*Louvain.*] *Université catholique. Institut de psychologie appliquée et de pédagogie. Extraits de dissertations*, Numéro 1, 1939.)

Numéro 2. M.-Leo, Frère (F.É.C.) ADAPTATION À LA BELGIQUE DES "PREMIERS TESTS DE LECTURE" DU PROFESSEUR A. I. GATES. 1939. 87 pp. (Also as [*Louvain.*] *Université catholique. Institut de psychologie appliquée et de pédagogie. Extraits de dissertations,* Numéro 2, 1939.)

Numéro 3. Chrysostome, Frère (F.É.C.), and Jean Martin: UNE ÉTUDE CRITIQUE DU TEST D'INTELLIGENCE LOGIQUE DE J.-M. LAHY. 1939. 57 pp.

Numéro 4. Dayhaw, Lawrence T. UNE ÉCHELLE DE VOCABULAIRE. 1941. 49 pp.

Numéro 5. M.-Luc, Frère (F.É.C.). LA MÉTHODE DE RORSCHACH APPLIQUÉE À UN GROUPE DE DÉLINQUANTS ET À UN GROUPE CONTRÔLE. 1942. 57 pp.

Numéro 6. Bertrand, Frère (des Frères de Saint-Gabriel). TEST DE VOCABULAIRE. ÉTUDE EXPÉRIMENTALE DU VOCABULAIRE COMPRIS PAR LES ENFANTS DANS LES LIVRES ÉCRITS POUR LES ADULTES. 1944. 47 pp.

Numéro 7. L'Archevêque, Paul. ÉPREUVE COLLECTIVE D'HABILETÉ MENTALE GÉNÉRALE. FORMES A ET B. 1944. 90 pp.

Numéro 8. Gédéon, Frère (S-C.) L'INTELLIGENCE DES RELATIONS SPATIALES. APTITUDE AUX MATHÉMATIQUES ET AUX SCIENCES. 1945. 109 pp.

Numéro 9. Dominique, Frère (É.C.). LES ENFANTS DEFICIENTS DE L'OUÏE ET LEUR DÉVELOPPEMENT MENTAL ET SOCIAL. ENQUÊTE FAITE SUR LES ENFANTS DES ÉCOLES ÉLÉMENTAIRES DE LA COMMISSION DES ÉCOLES CATHOLIQUES DE MONTRÉAL. 1946. 67 pp.

Numéro 10. Grégoire, Frère (É.C.). LA VALEUR DU COLORIAGE DES CROQUIS EN PÉDAGOGIE CATHÉCHISTIQUE. 1950. 80 pp.

842. *Psicotecnia.* [Organ of the Instituto nacional de psicotecnia.]

TITLE VARIATIONS: Superseded by *Revista de psicología general y applicada* with Volumen 1, Número 1, 1946.

DATES OF PUBLICATION: Volumen 1–6, October 1939–October 1945.

FREQUENCY: Quarterly.

NUMBERING VARIATIONS: Five issues present in Volumen 1.

PUBLISHER: **Madrid:** Instituto nacional de psicotecnia, Plaza de Santa Barbara, 10, 1939–1945.

PRIMARY EDITORS: None listed.

843. *Psychological Cinema Register.*

TITLE VARIATIONS: None.

DATES OF PUBLICATION: Number 1–6+, 1939–1949+.

FREQUENCY: Irregular.

NUMBERING VARIATIONS: Number 5 also numbered as *Pennsylvania State College. Bulletin,* Volume 38, Number 26; Number 5 Supplement also numbered as *Pennsylvania State College. Bulletin,* Volume 40, Number 10; Number 6 also numbered as *Pennsylvania State College. Bulletin,* Volume 43, Number 7.

PUBLISHER: **Bethlehem, Pennsylvania:** Psychological Cinema Register, 1939–1941. **State College, Pennsylvania:** Pennsylvania State College. Audio-Visual Aids Library, 1944/1945–1949+.

PRIMARY EDITORS: **Adelbert Ford,** 1939–1941; **Edward B. Van Ormer,** 1944/1945; **Clarence R. Carpenter,** 1949+.

EDITORIAL BOARD: Lester F. Beck, 1944/1945; Clarence R. Carpenter, 1944/1945; Adelbert Ford, 1944/1945; Alexander H. Leighton, 1944/1945; George M. Lott, 1949+; O. H. Mowrer, 1944/1945; Bruce V. Moore, 1944/1945–1949+; Hugh G. Pyle, 1949+.

844. *Psychological Corporation. Report.*

TITLE VARIATIONS: None.

DATES OF PUBLICATION: Number 18–29+, 1939–1950+.

FREQUENCY: Annual.

NUMBERING VARIATIONS: Number 18–20, 1939–1941 were published in the *Journal of Applied Psychology,* Volume 24–26, 1940–1942. Number 21–29+ 1942–1950+ were published separately. Number 1–17, 1922–1938 may have appeared in mimeographed form but apparently were not officially published.

PUBLISHER: **Lancaster, Pennsylvania:** Science Press Printing Company, 1939–1941. **New York:** Psychological Corporation, 1942–1950+.

PRIMARY EDITORS: **Paul S. Achilles,** 1939–1941; none listed, 1942–1950+.

845. *Psychosomatic Medicine. Experimental and Clinical Studies.*

TITLE VARIATIONS: None.

DATES OF PUBLICATION: Volume 1–12+, January 1939–November/December 1950+.

FREQUENCY: **Quarterly,** Volume 1–6, 1939–1944. **Bimonthly,** Volume 7–12+, 1945–1950+.

NUMBERING VARIATIONS: None.

PUBLISHER: **Washington, D.C.:** National Research Council, Division of Anthropology and Psychology, Committee on Problems of Neurotic Behavior, 1939–1941. **Baltimore:** Williams & Wilkins Company, with the Sponsorship of the Committee on Problems of Neurotic Behavior, Division of Anthropology and Psychology, National Research Council, 1942–1944. **New York:** American Society for Research in Psychosomatic Problems, Inc., 1945–1946. **New York:**

Paul B. Hoeber, Inc., Medical Book Department of Harper & Brothers under the Editorial Supervision of the American Society for Research in Psychosomatic Problems, Inc., 1947–1948. **New York:** Paul B. Hoeber, Inc., Medical Book Department of Harper & Brothers under the Editorial Supervision of the American Psychosomatic Society, Inc., 1949–1950+.

PRIMARY EDITORS: **Flanders Dunbar,** 1939–1947; **Ruth Potter,** 1945–1947; **Carl Binger,** 1948–1950+.

EDITORIAL BOARD: Franz Alexander, 1939–1947, 1948–1950+; Dana W. Atchley, 1939–1947, 1948–1950+; Clark L. Hull, 1939–1942; Stanley Cobb, 1939–1942, 1948–1950+; Grover F. Powers, 1939–1944; Hallowell Davis, 1939–1947, 1948–1950+; Theodore P. Wolfe, 1939; Flanders Dunbar, 1939–1947; Roy G. Hoskins, 1943–1947; Howard S. Liddell, 1939–1947, 1948–1950+; John C. Whitehorn, 1943–1947; C. Anderson Aldrich, 1945–1947; Martin Grotjahn, 1945–1947; Walter Bauer, 1948–1950+; George E. Daniels, 1948–1950+; Lawrence S. Kubie, 1948–1950+; David M. Levy, 1948–1950+; Milton J. E. Senn, 1948–1950+; Edward Weiss, 1948–1950+; Harold G. Wolff, 1948–1950+; Leon J. Saul, 1948–1950+.

846. *Psychosomatic Medicine Monographs.*

TITLE VARIATIONS: Also called *Psychosomatic Monographs.*

DATES OF PUBLICATION: Series 1, Number 1–7, 1939–1944. Series 2, Number 8–[10]+, 1945–1950+.

FREQUENCY: Irregular. *See* Contents *below.*

NUMBERING VARIATIONS: Series 1 also given volume numbering. *See* Contents *below.* After Number 9, monographs are not numbered.

PUBLISHER: **Washington, D.C.:** National Research Council, Division of Anthropology and Psychology, Committee on Problems of Neurotic Behavior, 1939–1942. **New York:** Paul B. Hoeber, Inc. under Sponsorship of the Committee on Problems of Neurotic Behavior, Division of Anthropology and Psychology, National Research Council, 1944. **New York:** American Society for Research in Psychosomatic Problems, 1945–1946. **New York:** Paul B. Hoeber, Inc., Medical Book Department of Harper & Brothers under the Editorial Supervision of the American Psychosomatic Society, 1950.

PRIMARY EDITORS: **Flanders Dunbar,** 1939–1946; **Ruth Potter,** 1945–1946; **Carl Binger,** 1950.

EDITORIAL BOARD: C. Anderson Aldrich, 1945–1946; Franz Alexander, 1939–1950; Dana W. Atchley, 1939–1950; Stanley Cobb, 1939–1942; Hallowell Davis, 1939–1950; Roy G. Hoskins, 1944–1946; Martin Grotjahn, 1945–1946; Clark Hull, 1939–1942; Howard S. Liddell, 1939–1950; Grover F. Powers, 1939–1944; Theodore P. Wolfe, 1939; John C. Whitehorn, 1944–1946; Walter Bauer, 1950; George E. Daniels, 1950; Lawrence S. Kubie, 1950; David M. Levy, 1950; Milton J. E. Senn, 1950; Edward Weiss, 1950; Harold G. Wolff, 1950; Leon J. Saul, 1950.

Year 1939

CONTENTS:

[**Volume 1, Number 1**] **Number 1.** White, Benjamin V., Stanley Cobb, and Chester M. Jones. MUCOUS COLITIS: A PSYCHOLOGICAL AND MEDICAL STUDY OF SIXTY CASES. 1939. 103 pp.

[——, **Number 2/3**] **Number 2.** Kardiner, Abraham. THE TRAUMATIC NEUROSES OF WAR. 1941. 258 pp.

[——, **Number 4**] **Number 3.** French, Thomas M., and Franz Alexander. PSYCHOGENIC FACTORS IN BRONCHIAL ASTHMA, PART 1. 1941. 92 pp.

[**Volume 2, Number 1/2**] **Number 4.** French, Thomas M., and Franz Alexander. PSYCHOGENIC FACTORS IN BRONCHIAL ASTHMA, PART 2. 1941. 236 pp.

[——, **Number 3/4**] **Number 5.** Anderson, O. D., and Richard Parmenter. A LONG-TERM STUDY OF THE EXPERIMENTAL NEUROSIS IN THE SHEEP AND DOG. 1941. 150 pp.

[**Volume 3, Number 1/2**] **Number 6.** Benedek, Therese, and Boris B. Rubenstein. THE SEXUAL CYCLE IN WOMEN. 1942. 307 pp.

[——, **Number 3/4**] **Number 7.** Gantt, W. Horsley. EXPERIMENTAL BASIS FOR NEUROTIC BEHAVIOR. 1944. 211 pp.

Number 8. Binger, Carl, N. W. Ackerman, A. E. Cohn, H. A. Schroeder, and J. M. Steele. PERSONALITY IN ARTERIAL HYPERTENSION. 1945. 228 pp.

Number 9. Ruesch, Jurgen. CHRONIC DISEASES AND PSYCHOLOGICAL INVALIDISM. 1946. 191 pp.

[**Number 10.**] Klein, Henriette R. ANXIETY IN PREGNANCY AND CHILDBIRTH. 1950. 111 pp.

847. *Revue des sciences pédagogiques.*

TITLE VARIATIONS: Continues *Revue de pédagogie*. Continued by *Revue belge de psychologie et de pédagogie* with Tome 12+, 1950+.

DATES OF PUBLICATION: Tome 6–11, 1939–1949. Suspended publication, 1940–1944.

FREQUENCY: Quarterly.

NUMBERING VARIATIONS: Issues also assigned whole numbers, Numéro 25–48.

PUBLISHER: **Brussels:** Fondation universitaire de Belgique, 1939–1949.

PRIMARY EDITORS: None listed.

848. *Rutgers University. Studies in Psychology.*

TITLE VARIATIONS: None.

DATES OF PUBLICATION: Number 1, 1939.

FREQUENCY: Irregular. *See* Contents *below*.

NUMBERING VARIATIONS: None.

PUBLISHER: **New Brunswick:** Rutgers University Press, 1939.

PRIMARY EDITORS: None listed.

CONTENTS:

Number 1. Fay, Jay Wharton. AMERICAN PSYCHOLOGY BEFORE WILLIAM JAMES. 1939. 240 pp.

849. *Society for Personnel Administration. Pamphlet Series.*

TITLE VARIATIONS: Also called *General Series Pamphlets.*

DATES OF PUBLICATION: Number 1–4 +, April 1939–1941. Suspended publication 1942–1952.

FREQUENCY: Irregular. *See* Contents *below.*

NUMBERING VARIATIONS: None.

PUBLISHER: **Washington, D.C.:** Society for Personnel Administration, 1939–1941 +.

PRIMARY EDITORS: **Max Freyd,** 1939–1940; **Richard W. Cooper,** 1941.

CONTENTS:

Number 1. Bingham, W. V. ADMINISTRATIVE ABILITY: ITS DISCOVERY AND DEVELOPMENT. April 1939. 17 pp.

Number 2. Ordway, Samuel H., and James C. O'Brien. AN APPROACH TO MORE OBJECTIVE ORAL TESTS. June 1939. 31 pp.

Number 3. Hall, Milton. TRAINING YOUR EMPLOYEES. 1940. 26 pp.

Number 4. Appley, L. A. HUMAN ELEMENT IN PERSONNEL MANAGEMENT AND THE RESPONSIBILITIES OF THE ADMINISTRATOR. 1941. 34 pp.

850. *Society for the Psychological Study of Social Issues. Yearbook.*

TITLE VARIATIONS: Each volume is individually titled. *See* Contents *below.*

DATES OF PUBLICATION: Number 1–3, 1939–1945.

FREQUENCY: Irregular. *See* Contents *below.*

NUMBERING VARIATIONS: None.

PUBLISHER: **New York:** Cordon Company for the Society, 1939. **New York:** Reynal and Hitchcock for the Society, 1942. **Boston:** Houghton Mifflin Company for the Society, 1945.

PRIMARY EDITORS: *See* Contents *below.*

CONTENTS:

Number 1. Hartmann, George W., and Theodore Newcomb, eds. Industrial CONFLICT: A PSYCHOLOGICAL INTERPRETATION. 1939. 583 pp.

Number 2. Watson, Goodwin, ed. CIVILIAN MORALE. 1942. 463 pp.

Number 3. Murphy, Gardner, ed. HUMAN NATURE AND ENDURING PEACE. 1945. 475 pp.

1940-1950

851. *American Journal of Mental Deficiency.*

TITLE VARIATIONS: Continues *Journal of Psycho-Asthenics*, and *American Association on Mental Deficiency. Proceedings and Addresses* (published in the *Journal of Psycho-Asthenics*). Contains *American Association on Mental Deficiency Conference Proceedings.*

DATES OF PUBLICATION: Volume 45–55+, July 1940–1950+.

FREQUENCY: Quarterly.

NUMBERING VARIATIONS: None.

PUBLISHER: **Albany, New York:** American Association on Mental Deficiency, 1940–April 1943. **Coldwater, Michigan:** Coldwater State Home and Training School, July 1943–1944. **Columbus, Ohio:** Bureau of Mental Hygiene, July 1944–1946. **Columbus:** Bureau of Special and Adult Education, Ohio State University, July 1946–1948. **New York:** 224 East 28th St., July 1948–1950+.

PRIMARY EDITORS: **Edward J. Humphreys,** 1940–1948; **C. Roger Myers,** 1945–1946; **Arthur T. Hopwood,** 1945–1950+; **Mary Vanuxem,** 1945; **Winifred R. Wardell,** 1945–1950+; **N. A. McCormick,** 1946–1948; **E. Arthur Whitney,** 1946–1950+; **Richard H. Hungerford,** 1948–1950+; **Louis E. Rosenzweig,** 1948–1950+; **Barbara May,** 1948–1950+; **Horace Mann,** 1948–1950+; **Arthur J. Present,** 1948–1950+; **Marie M. Weiss,** 1950+.

For serial publications that began before 1940 and were still being published during the time period 1940 to 1950, *see also* entries 32, 50, 73, 74, 79, 84, 90, 96, 112, 119, 122, 135, 169, 177, 181, 190, 196, 215, 223, 229, 237, 242, 267, 275, 281, 285, 288, 295, 320, 324, 327, 334, 346, 350, 354, 359, 361, 366, 368, 373, 378, 394, 397, 399, 400, 416, 417, 419, 420, 422, 426, 428, 432, 433, 438, 441, 455, 456, 460, 479, 487, 488, 499, 503, 505, 524, 525, 526, 527, 534, 538, 549, 556, 558, 560, 561, 564, 566, 567, 568, 569, 575, 576, 585, 588, 596, 604, 605, 606, 607, 608, 609, 629, 632, 634, 635, 637, 647, 649, 653, 655, 662, 665, 666, 675, 676, 677, 678, 680, 685, 690, 694, 695, 699, 700, 702, 705, 707, 709, 714, 715, 717, 718, 720, 721, 724, 727, 730, 731, 734, 741, 743, 746, 747, 753, 754, 755, 758, 759, 762, 763, 764, 765, 766, 767, 769, 773, 776, 777, 778, 779, 780, 783, 785, 786, 787, 790, 791, 792, 793, 795, 796, 797, 798, 799, 801, 802, 805, 808, 810, 811, 812, 813, 815, 816, 817, 818, 819, 821, 823, 824, 825, 828, 829, 830, 832, 833, 834, 835, 836, 837, 839, 840, 841, 842, 843, 844, 845, 846, 847, 849, 850.

EDITORIAL BOARD: Lionel S. Penrose, 1940–1950+; Horatio M. Pollock, 1940–1950+; Clemens E. Benda, 1940–1950+; George A. Jervis, 1940–1950+; George S. Stevenson, 1940–1950+; Thorleif G. Hegge, 1940–1950+; Meta Anderson, 1940–1942; Elise H. Martens, 1940–1950+; Stanley P. Davies, 1940–1950+; Agnes K. Hanna, 1940–1944; H. H. Ramsay, 1940–1950+; William J. Ellis, 1940–1945.

852. *Beiträge zur Psychologie des gehaltserfüllten Lebens.*

TITLE VARIATIONS: None.

DATES OF PUBLICATION: Heft 1, November 1940.

FREQUENCY: Irregular.

NUMBERING VARIATIONS: Also numbered as part of *Zeitschrift für Psychologie. See* Contents *below.*

PUBLISHER: **Leipzig:** Johann Ambrosius Barth, 1940.

PRIMARY EDITOR: **B. Petermann,** 1940.

CONTENTS:

Heft 1. Gostischa, Emil. DIE SPRACHLICHE ENTFALTUNG SOZIALER LEBEN-DIGKEIT BEIM KINDE. (Also as *Zeitschrift für Psychologie,* Band 149, 1940, pp. 127–204.)

853. *Canadian Psychological Association. Bulletin.*

TITLE VARIATIONS: None.

DATES OF PUBLICATION: Volume 1–6, October 1940–October/December, 1946.

FREQUENCY: Quarterly (Irregular). *See* Numbering Variations *below.*

NUMBERING VARIATIONS: Volume 1, Number 1 issued October 1940; Number 2 issued December 1940; Numbers 3–6 issued quarterly 1941. Volume 1 has 6 issues. Volume 6, special issue, dated October 1946.

PUBLISHER: **Kingston, Ontario:** Canadian Psychological Association, October 1940–April 1942. **Toronto:** Canadian Psychological Association, October 1942–October/December 1946.

PRIMARY EDITORS: **D. O. Hebb,** 1940–1942; **H. M. Estall,** 1940–1942; **J. A. Irving,** 1940–April 1946; **S. R. Laycock,** 1940–April 1946; **R. B. Liddy,** 1940–April 1946; **Jean Martin,** 1940–1942; **C. A. Krug,** 1940; **T. W. Cook,** 1941–April 1946; **J. A. Long,** 1942–1946; **K. M. Hobday,** 1942–1946; **G. Humphrey,** 1942–April 1946; **R. Vinette,** 1943–April 1946; **C. Bilodeau,** 1943–April 1946; **J. Tuckman,** 1946; **Marion MacDonald,** 1946.

854. *Chiao yü hsin li yen Chiu.* [Studies in Educational Psychology.]

TITLE VARIATIONS: Also called *Chung-yang ta hsüeh. Chiao yü hsin li yen Chiu* [Central University. Studies in Educational Psychology]; and *Kuo li*

Chung-yang ta hsüeh. Chiao yü hsin li yen Chiu [National Central University. Studies in Educational Psychology].

DATES OF PUBLICATION: Volume 1–3, Number 2, March 1940–June 1945.

FREQUENCY: Quarterly.

NUMBERING VARIATIONS: None.

PUBLISHER: **Chungking:** Chung-yang ta hsüeh [Central University], 1940–1945.

PRIMARY EDITORS: None listed.

NOTE: Information on this title was partially compiled from *Chuan-kuo Chung-wen Chi-kan lien-ho mu-lu, 1833–1949* [Union List of Chinese Periodicals in China, 1833–1949]. Peking, Peking Library, 1961.

855. *Chinese Journal of Educational Psychology.*

TITLE VARIATIONS: Subtitled *English Abstracts of Important Articles.*

DATES OF PUBLICATION: Volume 1, Number 1–4, March 1940–June 1945.

FREQUENCY: Irregular. Number 1, March 1940; Number 2, June 1940; Number 3, June 1944; and Number 4, June 1945.

NUMBERING VARIATIONS: None.

PUBLISHER: **Chungking:** National Central University, Institute of Educational Psychology, 1940–1945.

PRIMARY EDITORS: [J. W. Ai,] 1940–1945.

NOTE: Publication is entirely in English. Main entry is therefore in English. National Central University [Kuo li Chung-yang ta hsüeh] is also called Central University [Chung-yang ta hsüeh].

856. *Constitutional Psychology Series.*

TITLE VARIATIONS: None.

DATES OF PUBLICATION: Volume 1–2, 1940–1942.

FREQUENCY: Irregular.

NUMBERING VARIATIONS: None.

PUBLISHER: **New York** and **London:** Harper Brothers Publishers, 1940. **New York:** Harper & Row, 1942.

PRIMARY EDITOR: **William H. Sheldon,** 1940–1942.

CONTENTS:
   Volume 1. Sheldon, William H. THE VARIETIES OF HUMAN PHYSIQUE. AN INTRODUCTION TO CONSTITUTIONAL PSYCHOLOGY. With the collaboration of S. S. Stevens and W. B. Tucker. 1940. 347 pp.
   Volume 2. Sheldon, William H. THE VARIETIES OF TEMPERAMENT. A PSYCHOLOGY OF CONSTITUTIONAL DIFFERENCES. With S. S. Stevens. 1942. 520 pp.

857. *Foster Parents' Plan for War Children. Report.*

TITLE VARIATIONS: Subtitled *First Year Report on Hampstead Nursery Colony*, 1940; *Report on Hampstead Nurseries*, 1940–1942; *Freud-Burlingham Report*, 1942–1945; *Report on Hostel for Children Rescued from Concentration Camps*, 1946; *Half-yearly Report on Hampstead Nurseries. After-Care*, 1947–1950+.

DATES OF PUBLICATION: 1940–1950+.

FREQUENCY: Irregular, 1940; Monthly, 1941–1946; Biannual, 1947–1950+.

NUMBERING VARIATIONS: Numbered only by date. 1940 issues undated. January–March, August–November, 1942 undated. January, 1946 apparently never issued.

PUBLISHER: **New York:** Foster Parents' Plan for War Children, Inc., 1940–1950+.

PRIMARY EDITORS: **Anna Freud,** 1940–1950+; **Dorothy T. Burlingham,** 1940–1950+.

858. *Fukushima. Fukushima Daigaku. Gakugeigakubu. Ronshu. III. Kyoiku. Shinrigaku.* [Fukushima University. Faculty of Arts and Sciences. Bulletin. Series III. Education. Psychology].

TITLE VARIATIONS: None.

DATES OF PUBLICATION: Number 1–2+, March 1940–March 1950+. Suspended publication 1941–1949.

FREQUENCY: Annual.

NUMBERING VARIATIONS: None.

PUBLISHER: **Fukushima:** Fukushima Daigaku. Gakugeigakubu [Fukushima University. Faculty of Arts and Sciences], 1940–1950+.

PRIMARY EDITOR: None listed.

NOTE: Information on this title was found in: Japan. Higher Education and Science Bureau. *Bibliographical List of Japanese Learned Journals.* Number 2. *Humanities and Social Sciences.* 1959.

859. *Great Britain. Industrial Health Research Board. (War) Emergency Reports.*

TITLE VARIATIONS: None.

DATES OF PUBLICATION: Number 1–5, 1940–1944.

FREQUENCY: Irregular. *See* Contents *below.*

NUMBERING VARIATIONS: None.

PUBLISHER: **London:** His Majesty's Stationery Office, 1940–1944.

PRIMARY EDITOR: **R.S.F. Schilling,** 1940–1944.

CONTENTS:

    Number 1. INDUSTRIAL HEALTH IN WAR. 1940. 36 pp.

    Number 2. HOURS OF WORK, LOST TIME AND LABOUR WASTAGE. 1942. 26 pp.

    Number 3. THE PERSONAL FACTOR IN ACCIDENTS. 1942. 19 pp.

    Number 4. Wyatt S., R. Marriott, and D.E.R. Hughes. A STUDY OF AB-SENTEEISM AMONG WOMEN. 1943. 12 pp.

    Number 5. Wyatt, S., assisted by R. Marriott, W. M. Dawson, D.E.R. Hughes, and F. G. L. Stock. A STUDY OF VARIATIONS IN OUTPUT. 1944. 16 pp.

860. *Harvard University. Graduate School of Education. Harvard Education Papers.*

TITLE VARIATIONS: None.

DATES OF PUBLICATION: Number 1–2, 1940–1946.

FREQUENCY: Irregular. *See* Contents *below.*

NUMBERING VARIATIONS: None.

PUBLISHER: **Cambridge, Massachusetts:** Harvard University, Graduate School of Education, 1940–1946.

PRIMARY EDITORS: None listed.

CONTENTS:

    Number 1. Kelley, Truman L. TALENTS AND TASKS. THEIR CONJUNCTION IN A DEMOCRACY FOR WHOLESOME LIVING AND NATIONAL DEFENSE. July 1940. 48 pp.

    Number 2. Davis, Frederick B. ITEM-ANALYSIS DATA. 1946. 42 pp.

861. *Individual Psychology News.*

TITLE VARIATIONS: Continued by *Individual Psychology Bulletin* with Volume 2, October 1941.

DATES OF PUBLICATION: Volume 1, Number 1–12, 1940–1941.

FREQUENCY: Monthly.

NUMBERING VARIATIONS: None.

PUBLISHER: **Chicago:** Individual Psychology Association, 1940–1941.

PRIMARY EDITORS: **Rudolf Dreikurs,** 1940–1941; **Catherine Brown,** 1940–1941.

862. *International Journal of Psycho-Analysis. Research Supplement.*

TITLE VARIATIONS: None.

DATES OF PUBLICATION: Number 1–4, 1940–1943.

FREQUENCY: Irregular. *See* Contents *below.*

NUMBERING VARIATIONS: Number 4 published before Number 1. Number

2 and 3 previously published as *International Journal of Psycho-Analysis. Supplements* and here renumbered. Dates given above are for original titles only. *See* Contents *below.*

PUBLISHER: **London:** Bailliere, Tindall & Cox for the Institute of Psycho-Analysis, 1940–1943.

PRIMARY EDITORS: None listed.

CONTENTS:

Number 1. Strachey, Alix. A NEW GERMAN-ENGLISH PSYCHO-ANALYTICAL VOCABULARY. 1943. 84 pp.

Number 2. Rickman, John. THE DEVELOPMENT OF THE PSYCHO-ANALYTICAL THEORY OF THE PSYCHOSES, 1893–1926. 1928. 106 pp. (Also as *International Journal of Psycho-Analysis. Supplements*, Number 2.)

Number 3. Glover, Edward. THE TECHNIQUE OF PSYCHO-ANALYSIS. 1928. 141 pp. (Also as *International Journal of Psycho-Analysis. Supplements*, Number 3.)

Number 4. Glover, Edward. AN INVESTIGATION OF THE TECHNIQUE OF PSYCHO-ANALYSIS. 1940. 188 pp.

863. *Istanbul. Üniversite. Pedagoji enstitüsü. Psikoloji ve pedagoji çalişmalari.*

TITLE VARIATIONS: None.

DATES OF PUBLICATION: Cilt 1–[?], 1940–[?].

FREQUENCY: Irregular.

NUMBERING VARIATIONS: None.

PUBLISHER: **Istanbul:** Türkiye Basimevi, 1940.

PRIMARY EDITOR: **Wilhelm Peters,** 1940–[?].

CONTENTS: Unknown.

NOTE: Information on this entry is incomplete. The compilers were unable to examine this title.

864. *Kansas. Fort Hays Kansas State College. Studies. Psychology Series.*

TITLE VARIATIONS: None.

DATES OF PUBLICATION: Number 1, August 1, 1940.

FREQUENCY: Irregular. *See* Contents *below.*

NUMBERING VARIATIONS: Also numbered as *Fort Hays Kansas State College. Studies. General Series. See* Contents *below.*

PUBLISHER: **Topeka:** Kansas State Printing Plant, W. C. Austin, State Printer, 1940.

PRIMARY EDITOR: **F. B. Streeter,** 1940.

CONTENTS:
Number 1. Kelly, George A. STUDIES IN CLINICAL PSYCHOLOGY. 1940. 38 pp. (Also as *Fort Hays Kansas State College. Studies. General Series*, Number 2.)

865. *Pædagogisk-psykologisk Tidsskrift.* [Organ of the Social-Pædagogisk Forening for Ny Opdragelse; later Danmarks Social-Pædagogisk Forening.]

TITLE VARIATIONS: None.

DATES OF PUBLICATION: Bind 1–10+, September 1940–December 1950+.

FREQUENCY: Bimonthly.

NUMBERING VARIATIONS: Bind 1 has 8 Hefte 1940–1941. Multinumber issues present.

PUBLISHER: **Copenhagen:** Ejnar Munksgaards Forlag, 1940–1950+.

PRIMARY EDITOR: **Georg Christensen,** 1940–1950+.

866. *Peking. Catholic University. College of Education. Publications.*

TITLE VARIATIONS: Also called *Fujen University. College of Education. Publications.* University's Chinese name is Fujen ta hsüeh [Fujen University].

DATES OF PUBLICATION: Number 1, 1940.

FREQUENCY: Irregular. *See* Contents *below.*

NUMBERING VARIATIONS: None.

PUBLISHER: **Peking:** Catholic University [Fujen ta hsüeh], 1940.

PRIMARY EDITORS: [Charles K. A. Wang,] 1940.

CONTENTS:
Number 1. Wang, Charles K. A. AN ANNOTATED BIBLIOGRAPHY OF MENTAL TESTS AND SCALES. Volume 2. 1940. 698 pp.

NOTE: Publication is entirely in English. Main entry is therefore in English.

867. *Psychoanalytic Review. An Educational American Journal of Psychoanalysis Devoted to an Understanding and Education of Human Behavior.*

TITLE VARIATIONS: Continues *Psychoanalytic Review. An American Journal of Psychoanalysis Devoted to an Understanding of Human Conduct.*

DATES OF PUBLICATION: Volume 27–37+, January 1940–October 1950+.

FREQUENCY: Quarterly.

NUMBERING VARIATIONS: Each issue also assigned a whole number, Number 105–148.

PUBLISHER: **New York** and **Albany, New York:** Nervous and Mental Disease Publishing Company, 1940–1945. **New York:** Coolidge Foundation Publishers, 1946–1950+.

PRIMARY EDITORS: **Smith Ely Jelliffe,** 1940–1944; **A. A. Brill,** 1940–1947; **J.H.W. van Ophuijsen,** 1940–1950+; **Ben Karpman,** 1940–1950+; **A. N. Foxe,** 1944–1950+; **Nolan D. C. Lewis,** 1945–1950+; **S. Rado,** 1948–1950+.

868. *West Virginia. State College. Departments of Psychology and Education. Contributions.*

TITLE VARIATIONS: None.

DATES OF PUBLICATION: Number 1, 1940.

FREQUENCY: Irregular.

NUMBERING VARIATIONS: Also numbered as *West Virginia. State College. Bulletin. See* Contents *below.*

PUBLISHER: **Charleston, West Virginia:** Jarrett Printing Company for West Virginia State College, 1940.

PRIMARY EDITORS: None listed.

CONTENTS:
    Number 1. Goodlett, Carlton B., and Vivian R. Greene. THE MENTAL ABILITIES OF TWENTY-NINE DEAF AND PARTIALLY DEAF NEGRO CHILDREN. 1940. 23 pp. (Also as *West Virginia. State College. Bulletin*, Series Number 4, June 1940.)

869. *Zeitschrift für Psychologie.* [Organ of the Deutsche Gesellschaft für Psychologie.]

TITLE VARIATIONS: Continues *Zeitschrift für Psychologie und Physiologie der Sinnesorgane. Abteilung I. Zeitschrift für Psychologie.*

DATES OF PUBLICATION: Band 148–156+, 1940–1944+. Suspended publication 1945–1953.

FREQUENCY: Monthly.

NUMBERING VARIATIONS: Multinumber issues. 6 numbers to a volume, 2 volumes per year 1940–1943. Band 156 has only Heft 1/3, March 1944.

PUBLISHER: **Leipzig:** Johann Ambrosius Barth, 1940–1944.

PRIMARY EDITOR: **Oswald Kroh,** 1940–1944.

870. *Zeitschrift für Seelenleben. Neuere Psychologie und verwandte Gebiete, psychologische Forschung und geisteskundliche Heilfragen.*

TITLE VARIATIONS: Continues *Zeitschrift für Seelenleben und neuere Psychologie und verwandte Gebiete.*

DATES OF PUBLICATION: Jahrgang 44–45, 1940–1941.

FREQUENCY: **Monthly,** Jahrgang 44, Heft 1–12, 1940. **Bimonthly,** Jahrgang 45, Heft 1–6, 1941.

NUMBERING VARIATIONS: None.

PUBLISHER: **Leipzig:** Mutze, 1940–1941

PRIMARY EDITORS: **Rudolf Feilgenhauer,** 1940–1941; **Fritz Feilgenhauer,** 1940.

871. *Zeitschrift für Sinnesphysiologie.*

TITLE VARIATIONS: Continues *Zeitschrift für Psychologie und Physiologie der Sinnesorgane. Abteilung II. Zeitschrift für Sinnesphysiologie.*

DATES OF PUBLICATION: Band 69–70, October 1940–December 1943.

FREQUENCY: Irregular (6 Hefte to a volume).

NUMBERING VARIATIONS: Multinumbered issues.

PUBLISHER: **Leipzig:** Johann Ambrosius Barth, 1940–1943.

PRIMARY EDITOR: **Martin Gildemeister,** 1940–1943.

EDITORIAL BOARD: A. Kohlrausch, 1940–1943; A. von Tschermak, 1940–1943; Theodor Ziehen, 1940–1943.

872. *Zentralblatt für Psychotherapie und ihre Grenzgebiete einschliesslich der medizinischen Psychologie und psychischen Hygiene. Sonderheft.*

TITLE VARIATIONS: None.

DATES OF PUBLICATION: Heft 1–2, 1940.

FREQUENCY: Irregular. *See* Contents *below.*

NUMBERING VARIATIONS: None.

PUBLISHER: **Leipzig:** S. Hirzel, 1940.

PRIMARY EDITOR: **Matthias Heinrich Göring,** 1940.

CONTENTS:

Heft 1. SONDERHEFT DES DEUTSCHEN INSTITUTS FÜR PSYCHOLOGISCHE FORSCHUNG UND PSYCHOTHERAPIE. 1940. 27 pp.

Heft 2. Göring, Matthias Heinrich. ERZIEHUNGSHILFE. 1940. 68 pp.

1941

873. *American Journal of Psychoanalysis.*

TITLE VARIATIONS: None.

DATES OF PUBLICATION: Volume 1–10+, 1941–1950+.

FREQUENCY: Annual.

NUMBERING VARIATIONS: Each issue of Volume 1–6 is assigned Number 1. (Only one issue published per year.)

PUBLISHER: **New York:** Association for the Advancement of Psychoanalysis, 1941–1950+.

PRIMARY EDITORS: **Karen Horney,** 1948–1950+; **Muriel Ivimey,** 1946–1950+; **Elizabeth Kilpatrick,** 1943–1950+; **Harold Kelman,** 1948–1950+; **Bernard S. Robbins,** 1942; **Judah Marmor,** 1942–1943; **Janet McK. Rioch,** 1942; **Sidney Tarachow,** 1942; **Edward S. Tauber,** 1942; **Charles R. Hulbeck,** 1943–1945; **Valer Barbu,** 1945–1947

874. *Anales de psicotecnia.* [Organ of the Comisión de información estudios psicotécnicos.]

TITLE VARIATIONS: None.

DATES OF PUBLICATION: Tomo 1–2, December 1941–December 1942.

FREQUENCY: Annual.

NUMBERING VARIATIONS: None.

PUBLISHER: **Rosario, Argentina:** Instituto cultural "Joaquin V. Gonzalez" filial Rosario. Comisión de información y estudios psicotécnicos, 1941–1942.

PRIMARY EDITORS: **Velex Sarsfield,** 1941; **Elias Diaz Molano,** 1942.

875. *Educational and Psychological Measurement.*

TITLE VARIATIONS: Subtitled *A Quarterly Journal Devoted to the Development and Application of Measures of Individual Differences,* Volume 1–4, 1941–1944.

DATES OF PUBLICATION: Volume 1–10+, 1941–1950+.

FREQUENCY: Quarterly.

NUMBERING VARIATIONS: None.

PUBLISHER: **Chicago:** Science Research Associates, 1941–1944. **Washington, D.C.:** Educational and Psychological Measurement Office, 1945–1948. **Durham, North Carolina:** Educational and Psychological Measurement, 1949–1950+.

PRIMARY EDITORS: **G. Frederic Kuder,** 1941–1950+; **Dorothy C. Adkins,** 1941–1950+; **Forrest A. Kingsbury,** 1941–1948; **M. W. Richardson,** 1941–1950+; **Grace E. Manson,** 1943–1944; **Fred McKinney,** 1945–1948; **Marcia M. Mathews,** 1949–1950+; **John H. Rohrer,** 1949–1950+.

876. *Individual Psychology Bulletin.*

TITLE VARIATIONS: Continues *Individual Psychology News.*

DATES OF PUBLICATION: Volume 2–8, 1941–1950+.

FREQUENCY: Quarterly.

NUMBERING VARIATIONS: Multinumber issues present.

PUBLISHER: **Chicago:** Individual Psychology Association, 1941–1944. **Chicago:** Individual Psychology Association of Chicago, Inc., 1945–1950+.

PRIMARY EDITORS: **Rudolf Dreikurs,** 1941–1950+; **Catherine Brown,** 1941–1945; **Mary Budd,** 1941–1945; **Arthur Zweibel,** 1946–1950+.

877. *Kyoiku Shinri Kenkyū Kijō.* [Educational Psychological Research Record.]

TITLE VARIATIONS: None.

DATES OF PUBLICATION: Number 1, 1941.

FREQUENCY: Irregular.

NUMBERING VARIATIONS: None.

PUBLISHER: **Tokyo:** Tōkyō Bunrika Daigaku [Tokyo University of Liberal Arts and Sciences], 1941.

PRIMARY EDITORS: None listed.

NOTE: Information for this entry was obtained from *Gakujutsu Zasshi Sōgō Mokuroku. Jimbun Kagaku Wabun Hen* [Union List of Scholarly Journals. Japanese Language Section. Humanities Part]. Tokyo, 1973.

878. *Nervous Child; Quarterly Journal of Psychopathology, Psychotherapy, Mental Hygiene and Guidance of the Child.*

TITLE VARIATIONS: None.

DATES OF PUBLICATION: Volume 1–8+, Winter 1941/42–October 1950+.

FREQUENCY: Quarterly.

NUMBERING VARIATIONS: Multinumber issues present.

PUBLISHER: **New York:** Philosophical Library, 1941–1942. **New York:** Grune & Stratton, 1942–1945. **Baltimore:** Child Care Publications, 1946–1947. **New York** and **Baltimore:** Child Care Publications, 1948–1950+.

PRIMARY EDITORS: **Ernest Harms,** 1941–1950+; **Adolf G. Woltman,** 1941–1945; **Violet de Laszlo,** 1942–1945.

EDITORIAL BOARD: Lauretta Bender, 1941–1945; Robert G. Bernreuter, 1941–1945; Bernard Glueck, 1941–1950+; Leo Kanner, 1941–1950+; Kurt Lewin, 1941–1945; C. M. Louttit, 1941–1950+; Thomas V. Moore, 1941–1945; Martin L. Reymert, 1941–1950+; Augusta Runes, 1941–1942; Edward A. Strecker, 1941–1950+; Erwin Wexberg, 1941–1950+; Ira S. Wile, 1941–1943; Harry Bakwin, 1942–1950; J. Louise Despert, 1942–1950+; Frederic J. Farnell, 1942–1950+; Margaret Mahler-Schoenberger, 1942–1945; Edith Neumann, 1942–1945; Jacob Panken, 1942–1950+; Karl A. Menninger, 1943–1950; Margaret Naumberg, 1943–1945; Florence Brown Sherbon, 1943–1946; Herbert D. Williams, 1943–1950+; Lewis R. Wolberg, 1943–1947; Charlotte Bühler, 1946–1950+; Violet de Laszlo, 1946–1950+; Gerald H. J. Pearson, 1946–1950+; Lowell S. Selling, 1946–1950+; Frederick C. Thorne,

1946–1950+; Eugenia S. Cameron, 1947–1950; Henry C. Schumacher, 1947–1950+; Alexandra Adler, 1948–1950+; Jacob H. Conn, 1948–1950+.

879. *New Public Personnel Studies.*

TITLE VARIATIONS: Continues *Public Personnel Studies.*

DATES OF PUBLICATION: Volume 10, Number 1–10, June 1941–March/April 1942.

FREQUENCY: Monthly.

NUMBERING VARIATIONS: Volume 10, Number 4, mismarked August (instead of September), 1941.

PUBLISHER: **Washington, D.C.:** Bureau of Public Personnel Administration, 1941–1942.

PRIMARY EDITORS: **Fred Telford,** 1941–1942; **Beverly Emmert,** 1941–1942.

EDITORIAL BOARD: Charles P. Messick, 1941–1942; Harvey Walker, 1941–1942.

880. *Sociometry Monographs.*

TITLE VARIATIONS: None.

DATES OF PUBLICATION: Number 1–21+; 1941–1949+.

FREQUENCY: Irregular. *See* Contents *below.*

NUMBERING VARIATIONS: Most numbers are reprinted from *Sociometry* and other journals. *See* Contents *below.*

PUBLISHER: **New York:** Beacon House, Inc., 1941–1949+.

PRIMARY EDITORS: None listed.

CONTENTS:

Number 1. Cottrell, Leonard S., Jr., and Ruth Gallagher. DEVELOPMENTS IN SOCIAL PSYCHOLOGY, 1930–1940. 1941. 58 pp.

Number 2. Moreno, J. L. SOCIOMETRY AND THE CULTURAL ORDER. 1943. (Also as *Sociometry,* Volume 6, 1943, pp. 299–344.)

Number 3. Moreno, J. L., and Helen H. Jennings. SOCIOMETRIC MEASUREMENT OF SOCIAL CONFIGURATIONS BASED ON DEVIATION FROM CHANCE. 1945. 35 pp. (Also as STATISTICS OF SOCIAL CONFIGURATION in *Sociometry,* Volume 1, 1937, pp. 342–374.)

Number 4. Moreno, J. L. FOUNDATIONS OF SOCIOMETRY. AN INTRODUCTION n.d. (Also as *Sociometry,* Volume 4, 1941, pp. 15–35.)

Number 5. Moreno, J. L. GROUP METHOD AND GROUP PSYCHOTHERAPY. n.d. 104 pp. (Also as A PRELIMINARY REPORT IN COLLABORATION WITH E. STAGG WHITIN AND HELEN H. JENNINGS FOR THE NATIONAL COMMITTEE ON PRISONS AND PRISON LABOR; 1932.)

Number 6. Bronfenbrenner, Urie. THE MEASUREMENT OF SOCIOMETRIC STATUS, STRUCTURE AND DEVELOPMENT. 1945. 80 pp. (Also as *Sociometry,* Volume 6, 1943, pp. 363–397, and Volume 7, 1944, pp. 40–75, 283–289.)

Number 7. Moreno, J. L., and Helen H. Jennings. SOCIOMETRIC CONTROL STUDIES OF GROUPING AND REGROUPING. WITH REFERENCE TO AUTHORITATIVE AND DEMOCRATIC METHODS OF GROUPING. 1947. 23 pp. (Also as *Sociometry,* Volume 7, 1944, pp. 397–414.)

Number 8. Ichheiser, Gustav. DIAGNOSIS OF ANTISEMITISM. TWO ESSAYS. 1946. 27 pp. (Also as *Sociometry,* Volume 7, 1944, pp. 376–383, and Volume 9, 1946, pp. 92–108.)

Number 9. Bonney, Merl E. POPULAR AND UNPOPULAR CHILDREN, A SOCIOMETRIC STUDY. 1947. 81 pp.

Number 10. Kaufman, Harold F. DEFINING PRESTIGE IN A RURAL COMMUNITY 1946. 26 pp. (Also as *Sociometry,* Volume 8, 1945, pp. 199–207, and Volume 9, 1946, pp. 71–85.)

Number 11. Northway, Mary L., Esther B. Frankel, and Reva Potashin. PERSONALITY AND SOCIOMETRIC STATUS. 1947. 73 pp. (Also as *Sociometry,* Volume 9, 1946, pp. 48–70, 187–198, 210–225, 233–248.)

Number 12. Moreno, J. L. PSYCHOLOGICAL ORGANIZATION OF GROUPS IN THE COMMUNITY. 1947. 25 pp. (Also in *American Association on Mental Deficiency, Fifty-seventh Annual Session. Proceedings and Addresses.* 1933.)

Number 13. Moreno, J. L., Helen H. Jennings, and Joseph H. Sargent. TIME AS A MEASURE OF INTER-PERSONAL RELATIONS. 1947. (Also as *Sociometry,* Volume 3, 1940, pp. 62–80.)

Number 14. Jennings, Helen H. SOCIOMETRY OF LEADERSHIP. BASED ON THE DIFFERENTIATION OF PSYCHEGROUP AND SOCIOGROUP. 1947. 28 pp. (Also as *Sociometry,* Volume 10, 1947, pp. 32–49, 71–79.)

Number 15. Infield, Henrik F. SOCIOMETRIC STRUCTURE OF A VETERAN'S COOPERATIVE LAND SETTLEMENT. 1947. 23 pp. (Also as A VETERAN'S COOPERATIVE LAND SETTLEMENT AND ITS SOCIOMETRIC STRUCTURE, in *Sociometry,* Volume 10, 1947, pp. 50–70.)

Number 16. Loomis, Charles P. POLITICAL AND OCCUPATIONAL CLEAVAGES IN A HANOVERIAN VILLAGE, GERMANY. A SOCIOMETRIC STUDY. 1947. (Also as *Sociometry,* Volume 9, 1946, pp. 316–333.)

Number 17. Lewin, Kurt. THE RESEARCH CENTER FOR GROUP DYNAMICS. With comments and bibliography by Ronald Lippitt. n.d. 32 pp. (Parts of this number also as *Sociometry,* Volume 8, 1945, pp. 126–136, and Volume 10, 1947, pp. 87–97).

Number 18. Deutschberger, Paul. INTERACTION PATTERNS IN CHANGING NEIGHBORHOODS: NEW YORK AND PITTSBURGH. A SOCIOMETRIC STUDY. 1947. 15 pp. (Also as *Sociometry,* Volume 9, 1946, pp. 303–315.)

Number 19. Loomis, C. P., J. A. Beegle, and T. W. Longmore. CRITIQUE OF CLASS AS RELATED TO SOCIAL STRATIFICATION. 1948. 21 pp. (Also as *Sociometry,* Volume 10, 1947, pp. 319–337.)

Number 20. Loomis, Charles P., and Harold B. Pepinsky. SOCIOMETRY, 1937–1947: THEORY AND METHODS. 1949. 27 pp. (Also as *Sociometry,* Volume 11, 1948, pp. 262–286.)

Number 21. Moreno, J. L. THE THREE BRANCHES OF SOCIOMETRY. 1949. 10 pp. (Also as *Sociometry,* Volume 11, 1948, pp. 121–128.)

881. Spring.

TITLE VARIATIONS: Also called *Analytical Psychology Club of New York. Annual*; and *APC of New York. Annual*.

DATES OF PUBLICATION: Volume 1–10+, 1941–1950+.

FREQUENCY: Annual.

NUMBERING VARIATIONS: None.

PUBLISHER: **New York:** Analytical Psychology Club of New York, Inc., 1941–1950+.

PRIMARY EDITORS: Publications Committee of the APC of New York, chaired in succession by **Hildegard Nagel, Ellen Thayer,** and **Jane Abott Pratt.**

1942

882. Akademiia nauk Gruzinskoi SSR (Tiflis.) Institut psikhologii. Trudy.

TITLE VARIATIONS: Also titled *Psikhologiia*, Tom 1–5, 1942–1948.

DATES OF PUBLICATION: Tom 1–7+, 1942–1950+.

FREQUENCY: Annual.

NUMBERING VARIATIONS: None.

PUBLISHER: **Tiflis:** Akademiia nauk Gruzinskoi SSR, Institut psikhologii, 1942–1950+.

PRIMARY EDITORS: None listed.

NOTE: Information on this title was compiled from entries in *Half a Century of Soviet Serials*.

883. Arbeiten zur Psychologie, Erziehungswissenschaft und Sondererziehungswissenschaft.

TITLE VARIATIONS: Continues *Arbeiten aus der heilpädagogischen Seminar der Universität Freiburg (Schweiz)*.

DATES OF PUBLICATION: Heft 14–20, 1942–1944.

FREQUENCY: Irregular. *See* Contents *below*.

NUMBERING VARIATIONS: Heft 19 never issued.

PUBLISHER: **Lucerne:** Verlag der Institut für Heilpädagogik, 1942–1943. **Olten:** O. Walter, 1944. **Lucerne:** Verlag des Instituts für Heilpädagogik, 1944.

PRIMARY EDITOR: **Jos. Spieler,** 1942–1944.

CONTENTS:
> **Heft 14.** Spieler, Jos., ed. JUGENDRECHTSPFLEGE UND ANSTALTSFÜHRUNG. 1942. 62 pp.
>> **Heft 15.** Rudin, Jos. DER ERLEBNISDRANG. 1942. 141 pp.
>> **Heft 16.** Spieler, Jos. ERZIEHGSMITTEL. 1943. 23 pp.

Heft 17. Spieler, Jos. SCHWEIGENDE UND SPRACHSCHEUE KINDER. 1944, 107 pp.

Heft 18. Strässle, Theo. DER SCHULKONFLIKT, SEINE PSYCHOLOGIE UND PÄDAGOGIK IM VOLKSSCHULALTER. 1944. 153 pp.

Heft 19. Never issued.

Heft 20. Spieler, Jos., ed. DIE ERZIEHUNGSMITTEL. 1944. 492 pp.

884. *Aviation Psychology Abstract Series.*

TITLE VARIATIONS: None.

DATES OF PUBLICATION: Number 1–196, January 1942–April 1946.

FREQUENCY: Irregular. *See* Contents *below.*

NUMBERING VARIATIONS: None.

PUBLISHER: **Washington, D.C.:** Psychology Section, Medical Research Division, Office of the Air Surgeon, Army Air Forces, 1942–1946.

PRIMARY EDITORS: None listed.

CONTENTS:

Number 1. SUSPENSION AT ELEMENTARY FLYING TRAINING. FREQUENCY OF FAULTS. January 1942. 1 p.

Number 2. TEST OF STEREOSCOPIC DEPTH PERCEPTION. February 1942. 1 p.

Number 3. NOTES ON FIGHTER TRAINING. February 1942. 1 p.

Number 4. RESUME OF STATISTICAL WORK AT THE BOMBARDIER-NAVIGATOR SECTION. February 1942. 4 pp.

Number 5. STATISTICS ON HICKS AND CORSICANA PILOTS. February 1942. 1 p.

Number 6. VALIDATION OF NIGHT VISION TESTS. March 1942. 2 pp.

Number 7. PILOTS TRAINED WITH AND WITHOUT CAA TRAINING. February 1942. 1 p.

Number 8. IN FAVOR OF A NEW APPROACH TO THE PROBLEM OF PILOT SELECTION. February 1942. 1 p.

Number 9. THE WICKES APTITUDE TESTER. February 1942. 1 p.

Number 10. THE REPORT OF A COMMITTEE OF EDUCATIONAL CONSULTANTS TO THE CHIEF OF THE AIR CORPS. March 1942. 1 p.

Number 11. A SUMMARY OF MANUAL AND MECHANICAL ABILITY TESTS. March 1942. 1 p.

Number 12. THE SELECTION AND TRAINING OF NAVY AIRCREW. March 1942. 2 pp.

Number 13. THE SELECTION OF FLYING PERSONNEL FROM THE PSYCHIATRIC ASPECT. April 1942. 3 pp.

Number 14. A REPORT ON THE RECEPTION OF STATIONARY AND MOVING AIRPLANE SILHOUETTES IN PLAIN AND CLOUDED FIELDS. April 1942. 2 pp.

Number 15. PILOT WASTAGE IN GREAT BRITAIN. April 1942. 1 p.

Number 16. THE ELECTROENCEPHALOGRAM AS A MEANS OF ASSESSING RAF CADETS. April 1942. 1 p.

Number 17. LEARNING THE TWO-HAND COORDINATION TEST. April 1942. 2 pp.

884. *(Continued)*

Number 18. SELECTION AND CLASSIFICATION IN THE RAF. April 1942. 1 p.

Number 19. PRE-SELECTION AND CLASSIFICATION IN THE SOUTH AFRICAN AIR FORCE. April 1942. 2 pp.

Number 20. REPORT ON AIRCREW PERSONNEL SELECTION IN THE RAF. October 1942. 6 pp.

Number 21. GETTING RESULTS FROM A PROGRAM OF TESTING FOR SALES ABILITY. April 1942. 1 p.

Number 22. A REPORT ON THE HUMM-WADSWORTH TEMPERAMENT SCALE. April 1942. 2 pp.

Number 23. THE TROUBLEMAKER OR NEUROTIC INVENTORY. April 1942. 1 p.

Number 24. A REPORT OF RESEARCH ON INTENSE AUDITORY STIMULATION. April 1942. 2 pp.

Number 25. INTELLIGENCE TESTING OF FLYING CADET APPLICANTS. May 1942. 2 pp.

Number 26. THE PRESENT STATUS OF THE BOMBARDIER AND NAVIGATOR STUDY. July 1942. 1 p.

Number 27. THE PERCEPTION OF VISUAL VELOCITY. August 1942. 2 pp.

Number 28. RELIABILITY OF FORT BELVOIR NIGHT VISION TESTS. August 1942. 2 pp.

Number 29. PRELIMINARY REPORT OF A MODIFIED APPARATUS AND METHOD FOR THE MEASUREMENT OF MANUAL STEADINESS. September 1942. 5 pp.

Number 30. AUDITORY SENSITIVITY UNDER CONDITIONS OF ANOXIA: A STUDY OF SPEECH INTELLIGIBILITY. August 1942. 2 pp.

Number 31. APTITUDE TESTS FOR ANTIAIRCRAFT PERSONNEL. September 1942. 2 pp.

Number 32. PROGRESS REPORT ON TEST OF STEREOSCOPIC VISION FOR THE SELECTION OF RANGE-FINDER OPERATORS. September 1942. 6 pp.

Number 33. REPORT ON PRE-SELECTION TESTS FOR PILOTS. September 1942. 2 pp.

Number 34. STUDIES ON THE SELECTION OF CAA PILOTS. October 1942. 2 pp.

Number 35. THE VALUE OF BIOGRAPHICAL INFORMATION FOR PREDICTING SUCCESS IN AERONAUTICAL TRAINING. September 1942. 4 pp.

Number 36. REPORT ON PRE-SELECTION TESTS. September 1942. 3 pp.

Number 37. AN EXPERIMENTAL STUDY OF FATIGUE. September 1942. 2 pp.

Number 38. AN APPARATUS FOR STUDYING DARK ADAPTATION. September 1942. 1 p.

Number 39. SUMMARY OF STUDIES ON AIRSICKNESS. September 1942. 4 pp.

Number 40. AN APPARATUS FOR STUDYING SENSORY-MOTOR COORDINATION. October 1942. 1 p.

Number 41. AN AUTOMATIC LANDING MACHINE. October 1942. 1 p.

Number 42. REPORT ON FAILURES IN FLYING SCHOOL. n.d. 3 pp.

Number 43. A RATING SCALE FOR MEASURING WAR NEUROSIS. October 1942. 2 pp.

Number 44. PRELIMINARY STUDIES IN THE SELECTION OF AIRCREW IN THE RCAF. November 1942. 8 pp.

Number 45. EXPERIMENTAL STUDIES IN THE SELECTION OF C.P.T. AVIATORS AT NORTHWESTERN UNIVERSITY. January 1943. 14 pp.

Number 46. THE RELATIONSHIP BETWEEN REACTIONS TO DISTURBING STIMULI AND FLYING ABILITY. November 1942. 4 pp.

Number 47. THE EFFECT OF NOISE AND VIBRATION ON CERTAIN PSYCHO-MOTOR RESPONSES. October 1942. 10 pp.

Number 48. PSYCHOLOGICAL TESTING IN A EUROPEAN ARMY. October 1942. 2 pp.

Number 49. THE EFFECTIVENESS OF INSTRUCTIONAL AIDS IN FLIGHT TRAINING. November 1942. 4 pp.

Number 50. PREDICTION OF SUCCESS IN PILOT TRAINING FROM A BIOGRAPHICAL INVENTORY AND A PERSONAL HISTORY INTERVIEW. November 1942. 5 pp.

Number 51. "ABILITY TO TAKE IT" TESTS. November 1942. 7 pp.

Number 52. RETEST RELIABILITIES ON CERTAIN PSYCHOMOTOR MEASURES AND ON A BIOGRAPHICAL INVENTORY. December 1942. 2 pp.

Number 53. SUMMARY OF RESULTS IN THE CAA NATIONAL TESTING SERVICE. November 1942. 4 pp.

Number 54. PSYCHOLOGICAL PROBLEMS OF AVIATION IN WORLD WAR I. November 1942. 5 pp.

Number 55. STUDIES FROM THE CLASSIFICATION DIVISION, ARMY AIR FORCES TECHNICAL TRAINING COMMAND. January 1943. 6 pp.

Number 56. SELECTION OF OFFICER CANDIDATES IN GREAT BRITAIN. December 1942. 2 pp.

Number 57. FLYING APTITUDE TESTS IN THE R.A.F. December 1942. 3 pp.

Number 58. DESCRIPTION OF TWO PSYCHOMOTOR APPARATUS TESTS. December 1942. 3 pp.

Number 59. DESCRIPTION OF FOUR VISUAL-MOTOR DEVICES. January 1943. 7 pp.

Number 60. PRELIMINARY VALIDATION DATA ON THE CAA NATIONAL TESTING SERVICE BATTERY. January 1943. 4 pp.

Number 61. SECOND REPORT ON THE CAA NATIONAL TESTING SERVICE BATTERY. January 1943. 4 pp.

Number 62. DESCRIPTION OF THREE PSYCHOMOTOR TESTS FOR SELECTING ANTIAIRCRAFT PERSONNEL. January 1943. 2 pp.

Number 63. CORRELATIONS BETWEEN FLIGHT CRITERIA AND PRE-TRAINING RATINGS BY INTERVIEWERS. January 1943. 2 pp.

Number 64. VALIDATION DATA ON THE RCAF SELECTION AND CLASSIFICATION TESTS. January 1943. 7 pp.

Number 65. VALIDITY DATA ON CERTAIN SUGGESTED MEASURES OF SUCCESS IN PILOT TRAINING. January 1943. 2 pp.

884. *(Continued)*

Number 66. VERBAL REPORTS OF FLYING PYSCHOLOGISTS ON THE VISUAL CUES EMPLOYED IN LANDING. February 1943. 4 pp.

Number 67. ANALYSIS OF EYE MOVEMENTS DURING LANDING. February 1943. 2 pp.

Number 68. PHOTOGRAPHIC METHODS FOR THE ANALYSIS OF FLIGHT PERFORMANCE. February 1943. 2 pp.

Number 69. RELATION BETWEEN TEST SCORES AND CRITERIA OF FLYING COMPETENCE. February 1943. 3 pp.

Number 70. DESCRIPTION AND VALIDATION OF TESTS USED IN THE SELECTION OF STEREOSCOPIC RANGE FINDER OPERATORS. February 1943. 6 pp.

Number 71. THE FLIGHT INSTRUCTOR'S VOCABULARY. February 1943. 3 pp.

Number 72. SELECTION AND CLASSIFICATION OF AIRCREW IN THE SOUTH AFRICAN AIR FORCE. June 1943. 20 pp.

Number 73. DESCRIPTIONS OF AND RESULTS WITH PENCIL AND PAPER TESTS IN THE SOUTH AFRICAN AIR FORCE. July 1943. 2 pp.

Number 74. A TEST OF LISTENING ABILITY IN NOISE. July 1943. 2 pp.

Number 75. VALIDITY AND RELIABILITY STUDIES OF PILOT SELECTION TESTS. August 1943. 1 p.

Number 76. THE USE OF THE LINK TRAINER AS A SELECTION DEVICE IN THE R.C.A.F. August 1943. 4 pp.

Number 77. AVIATION PSYCHOLOGY IN THE U.S. NAVY. October 1943. 2 pp.

Number 78. PREDICTION OF ASSIGNMENT TO FIGHTER OR BOMBER PILOT TRAINING IN THE S.A.A.F. October 1943. 1 p.

Number 79. VALIDATION DATA IN THE NATIONAL TESTING SERVICE. October 1943. 2 pp.

Number 80. DESCRIPTION OF A DISTANCE PERCEPTION TEST. October 1943. 3 pp.

Number 81. ABSTRACTS OF PROJECT REPORTS FROM THE SCHOOL OF AVIATION MEDICINE. October 1943. 6 pp.

Number 82. DESCRIPTION OF A COMPLEX TASK DEVICE. November 1943. 3 pp.

Number 83. DESCRIPTION OF AND RESULTS WITH PERSONALITY TESTS. November 1943. 5 pp.

Number 84. HISTORY AND RESULTS IN THE AVIATION PSYCHOLOGY PROGRAM OF THE NAVY DEPARTMENT. November 1943. 5 pp.

Number 85. CIVILIAN WAR PROJECTS IN PSYCHOLOGY: THE COMMITTEE ON SERVICE PERSONNEL–SELECTION AND TRAINING. November 1943. 4 pp.

Number 86. THE RELATIONSHIP OF SPEED TO SOLO TO SUBSEQUENT ACHIEVEMENT IN THE RAF. December 1943. 3 pp.

Number 87. AIRCREW SELECTION PROCEDURES IN THE RAF. January 1944. 3 pp.

Number 88. A FURTHER REPORT ON THE USE OF THE LINK TRAINER AS A SELECTION DEVICE IN THE RCAF. January 1944. 5 pp.

Number 89. AIRCREW SELECTION TESTS IN THE ROYAL AUSTRALIAN AIR FORCE. January 1944. 4 pp.

Number 90. SELECTION OF GROUND CREW IN THE ROYAL CANADIAN AIR FORCE. January 1944. 2 pp.

Number 91. SELECTION OF GROUND CREW IN THE ROYAL AIR FORCE. January 1944. 2 pp.

Number 92. SELECTION OF GROUND CREW IN THE ROYAL AUSTRALIAN AIR FORCE. January 1944. 2 pp.

Number 93. SELECTION OF GROUND CREW IN THE ROYAL NEW ZEALAND AIR FORCE. January 1944. 2 pp.

Number 94. FURTHER ABSTRACTS OF PROJECT REPORTS FROM THE SCHOOL OF AVIATION MEDICINE. January 1944. 4 pp.

Number 95. SCREENING FOR ARCTIC DUTY. February 1944. 3 pp.

Number 96. THE RELATIONSHIP BETWEEN VISUAL ACUITY AND STEREOSCOPIC VISION. February 1944. 2 pp.

Number 97. SELECTION TESTS AND RESULTS IN THE RCAF. February 1944. 3 pp.

Number 98. THE EFFECT OF SPECIAL INSTRUCTIONS ON PERFORMANCE IN A FATIGUING TASK. February 1944. 2 pp.

Number 99. SELECTION AND TRAINING IN THE GERMAN AIR FORCE. February 1944. 4 pp.

Number 100. RATING SCALE RESULTS ON FATIGUE IN OPERATIONAL FLYING IN THE RAF. March 1944. 2 pp.

Number 101. SELECTION OF GROUND CREW IN THE SOUTH AFRICAN AIR FORCE. March 1944. 4 pp.

Number 102. SELECTION OF NON-FLYING CREW IN THE FLEET AIR ARM. March 1944. 1 p.

Number 103. PSYCHOLOGISTS IN BRITISH MILITARY SERVICE. March 1944. 2 pp.

Number 104. TESTING IN THE BRITISH ARMY. March 1944. 2 pp.

Number 105. THE RAF SELECTION SYSTEM. June 1944. 17 pp.

Number 106. ORGANIZATION, SELECTION AND TRAINING IN THE CANADIAN ARMY. March 1944. 3 pp.

Number 107. AN INVESTIGATION OF PSYCHOLOGICAL BREAKDOWN IN THE ROYAL AIR FORCE. March 1944. 8 pp.

Number 108. RESEARCH AND DEVELOPMENT OF THE NAVY'S APTITUDE TESTING PROGRAM. March 1944. 2 pp.

Number 109. A PRELIMINARY REPORT ON A STUDY OF LEADERSHIP IN OFFICER CANDIDATE SCHOOL. March 1944. 2 pp.

Number 110. TRAINING RESEARCH ON INTERCOMMUNICATION IN THE AAF. March 1944. 1 p.

Number 111. DESCRIPTION AND VALIDATION OF THE SHIPLEY PERSONAL INVENTORY. April 1944. 3 pp.

Number 112. ORGANIZATION, FUNCTIONS, AND PERSONNEL IN THE STANDARDS AND CURRICULUM SECTION, BUREAU OF NAVAL PERSONNEL, TRAINING ACTIVITY. August 1944. 4 pp.

Number 113. BRITISH STUDIES OF INSTRUMENT LANDINGS. April 1944. 2 pp.

884. (*Continued*)

Number 114. British Investigations of the Operation of Control Mechanisms. April 1944. 2 pp.

Number 115. Group Target Test. July 1944. 2 pp.

Number 116. Civilian War Projects in Psychology: The CAA-NRC Committee on Selection and Training of Aircraft Pilots. April 1944, 3 pp.

Number 117. Attrition Rates and Related Factors in Flying Training in the U.S. Navy. April 1944. 3 pp.

Number 118. The RAF Experiment on the Assessment of Temperament in Connection with Aircrew Selection. June 1944. 8 pp.

Number 119. Psychological Organization and Personnel in the RAF. April 1944. 2 pp.

Number 120. Night Flying Accidents and Autokinetic Movement. May 1944. 2 pp.

Number 121. Abstracts of Reports from the Aero-medical Laboratory, Wright Field. May 1944. 4 pp.

Number 122. Data from the RCAF Testing Program. May 1944. 4 pp.

Number 123. The Cornell Selectee Index. May 1944. 1 p.

Number 124. The Association between Ratings on Specific Maneuvers and Success of Failure in Flying Training of RAF Cadets. May 1944. 2 pp.

Number 125. Tests and Selection Procedures for Naval Aircrew other than Pilots. May 1944. 3 pp.

Number 126. Validity of the Somatotype and Anthropometric Variables in Flying Training. May 1944. 3 pp.

Number 127. Preliminary Analysis of Combat Leadership Ratings and Other Leadership Studies. July 1944. 4 pp.

Number 128. The Effect of Length and Repetition of Operating Periods on Efficiency of Radar Performance. May 1944. 2 pp.

Number 129. Description of and Validation Data on the RCAF Flight Test, Link Test, and Instructors' Ratings. May 1944. 8 pp.

Number 130. Description and Validation of the RCAF Aircrew Information Sheet. May 1944. 3 pp.

Number 131. Results of Psychological Testing for Nonflying Crew in the Royal Navy. June 1944. 1 p.

Number 132. The Psychological Program at the U.S. Coast Guard Academy. September 1944. 2 pp.

Number 133. An Experimental Study of Tank Driving Controls. October 1944. 2 pp.

Number 134. Summary of Selection and Classification Procedures for Aircrew in the RAF, RCAF, U.S. Navy, and USAAF. September 1944. 6 pp.

Number 135. U.S. Navy Night Vision Training. October 1944. 2 pp.

Number 136. The Royal Australian Air Force Flight Test. October 1944. 3 pp.

Number 137. VALIDITY OF THE SCHNEIDER INDEX FOR PREDICTING SUCCESS IN PRIMARY FLYING TRAINING. October 1944. 2 pp.

Number 138. AAF NIGHT VISION TRAINER. October 1944. 1 p.

Number 139. PSYCHOLOGICAL ACTIVITIES AT A MARITIME SERVICE TRAINING STATION. October 1944. 2 pp.

Number 140. ITEM ANALYSIS OF A MOTION SICKNESS QUESTIONNAIRE IN PREDICTING SUSCEPTIBILITY TO SEASICKNESS. November 1944. 1 p.

Number 141. RESULTS FROM THE ROYAL AUSTRALIAN AIR FORCE TESTING PROGRAM. November 1944. 2 pp.

Number 142. REPORT FROM THE ARMY–NAVY–OSRD VISION COMMITTEE: THE INFLUENCE OF SUNLIGHT ON NIGHT VISION. November 1944. 2 pp.

Number 143. A SHIPBOARD STUDY OF NIGHT LOOKOUTS. November 1944. 2 pp.

Number 144. THE DEVELOPMENT AND STANDARDIZATION OF THE ARMY GENERAL CLASSIFICATION TEST–3. November 1944. 3 pp.

Number 145. DESCRIPTION OF AND VALIDATION DATA ON NIGHT VISION TESTS. November 1944. 4 pp.

Number 146. INSTRUMENT CONTROLS AND DISPLAY–EFFICIENT HUMAN MANIPULATION. December 1944. 7 pp.

Number 147. VALIDITY OF THE SMA #3 TEST. December 1944. 2 pp.

Number 148. SUMMARY OF RESULTS IN THE PENSACOLA STUDY OF NAVAL AVIATORS. November 1944. 3 pp.

Number 149. A FURTHER REPORT ON THE RAF EXPERIMENT ON THE ASSESSMENT OF TEMPERAMENT IN CONNECTION WITH AIRCREW SELECTION. December 1944. 2 pp.

Number 150. SELECTION AND CLASSIFICATION OF AIRCREW IN THE ROYAL NAVY. January 1945. 2 pp.

Number 151. SELECTION AND CLASSIFICATION IN THE RHODESIAN AIR TRAINING GROUP. January 1945. 5 pp.

Number 152. PHYSIOLOGICAL STUDY OF AVIATORS DURING COMBAT FLYING. January 1945. 2 pp.

Number 153. ORGANIZATION AND PSYCHOLOGICAL RESEARCH AT THE U.S. SUBMARINE BASE, NEW LONDON, CONNECTICUT. February 1945. 2 pp.

Number 154. REDISTRIBUTION OF RETURNED AIRCREW IN THE ROYAL AIR FORCE. February 1945. 2 pp.

Number 155. THE SELECTION OF CONTROL TOWER OPERATORS IN THE AAF, U.S. NAVY, AND CAA. February 1945. 4 pp.

Number 156. VALIDATION OF AGO TESTS IN AAF TECHNICAL SCHOOLS. March 1945. 6 pp.

Number 157. A STUDY OF PREDICTION OF SUCCESS IN MARINE OFFICER CANDIDATE SCHOOL BY RATINGS. March 1945. 2 pp.

Number 158. SUMMARY OF RESEARCH FROM NDRC PROJECT N–106 and TEST AND RESEARCH SECTION, SUPERS, USN. March 1945. 2 pp.

Number 159. STUDIES IN EXPERIMENTAL THERAPEUTIC TECHNIQUES WITH ANIMALS. April 1945. 3 pp.

Number 160. OUTLINE OF JAPANESE PSYCHOLOGICAL RESEARCH PROJECTS IN OCTOBER 1942. April 1945. n.p.

884. *(Continued)*

Number 161. EXPERIMENTAL STUDIES IN ESTIMATING THE MEAN POINT OF IMPACT IN BOMBING. April 1945. 2 pp.

Number 162. ANNUAL REPORT OF THE COMMITTEE ON SELECTION AND TRAINING OF AIRCRAFT PILOTS, 1 APRIL 1945. May 1945. 4 pp.

Number 163. PREDICTION OF SUCCESS IN TRAINING AND MEASUREMENT OF ACHIEVEMENT AT NAVAL TRAINING SCHOOL (TACTICAL RADAR). May 1945. 2 pp.

Number 164. A STUDY OF VETERANS' READJUSTMENT TO CIVILIAN LIFE. May 1945. 3 pp.

Number 165. RCAF STUDY OF LEARNING TO FLY THE AT–6 WITHOUT PREVIOUS FLYING EXPERIENCE. June 1945. 6 pp.

Number 166. A NEW CAMBRIDGE UNIT OF RESEARCH IN APPLIED PSYCHOLOGY. June 1945. 4 pp.

Number 167. SOVIET PSYCHOLOGY IN WARTIME. June 1945. 6 pp.

Number 168. THE PREDICTION OF SUCCESS IN PARACHUTE SCHOOL BY THE PERSONAL INVENTORY. June 1945. 2 pp.

Number 169. NAVAL SPEECH INTELLIGIBILITY RESEARCH PROGRAM. June 1945. 2 pp.

Number 170. SUB-COMMITTEE ON METHODS OF MEASURING FLYING PERFORMANCE. June 1945. 4 pp.

Number 171. RECENT RESEARCH ON THE MEASUREMENT OF FLYING ABILITY IN THE RAF. June 1945. 3 pp.

Number 172. THE RELATIONSHIP BETWEEN PHYSICAL FITNESS TESTS AND SUCCESS IN U.S. NAVY FLIGHT TRAINING. June 1945. 2 pp.

Number 173. INSTRUMENT LIGHTING IN AIRCRAFT AND VEHICLES. June 1945. 2 pp.

Number 174. DISCUSSION OF RAF PROGRAM FOR TRAINING RESEARCH. July 1945. 5 pp.

Number 175. EARLY BRITISH STUDIES OF THE SELECTION OF RADIO OPERATORS, WIRELESS OPERATORS, AND SECTOR CONTROLLERS. July 1945. 4 pp.

Number 176. BRITISH PROPOSAL FOR MODIFICATION OF THE BEAM APPROACH INDICATOR. August 1945. 2 pp.

Number 177. ORGANIZATION, FUNCTIONS, AND RESEARCH OF THE EXPERIMENTAL SECTION, INFORMATION AND EDUCATION DIVISION, ARMY SERVICE FORCES. August 1945. 2 pp.

Number 178. A BRITISH STUDY OF TWO ATTITUDE INDICATORS. August 1945. 3 pp.

Number 179. THE ROYAL NEW ZEALAND AIR FORCE SELECTION PROGRAM. August 1945. 4 pp.

Number 180. SUMMARY OF RECENT RESEARCH FROM THE RCAF AND THE NATIONAL RESEARCH COUNCIL OF CANADA. August 1945. 4 pp.

Number 181. THE ROYAL AUSTRALIAN AIR FORCE TESTING PROGRAM AS OF JUNE 1945. August 1945. 2 pp.

Number 182. FLIGHT TEST OF TWO INSTRUMENT PANELS. August 1945. 2 pp.

Number 183. NIGHT VISION TRAINING IN THE ARMY AIR FORCES. August 1945. 4 pp.

Number 184. ALTITUDE TRAINING PROGRAM IN THE ARMY AIR FORCES. August 1945. 4 pp.

Number 185. TESTING IN THE JAPANESE ARMY. August 1945. 2 pp.

Number 186. STUDIES OF COMBAT BOMBING ACCURACY IN THE AAF. August 1945. 3 pp.

Number 187. GERMAN RESEARCH ON THE SELECTION AND TRAINING OF REMOTE CONTROLLED BOMB OPERATORS. August 1945. 6 pp.

Number 188. AVIATION PSYCHOLOGY IN THE GERMAN AIR FORCE. August 1945. 26 pp.

Number 189. RELATIONSHIP BETWEEN TEST SCORES AND ACCIDENTS IN THE SOUTH AFRICAN AIR FORCE. September 1945. 2 pp.

Number 190. SUMMARY OF SELECTED RESEARCH STUDIES CONCERNING LEADERSHIP. September 1945. 41 pp.

Number 191. VALIDATION OF DRAPER RATING AGAINST OPERATIONAL TRAINING AND COMBAT CRITERIA. October 1945. 6 pp.

Number 192. REDISTRIBUTION AND RECLASSIFICATION PROCEDURES FOR NAVAL AIRCREW. November 1945. 2 pp.

Number 193. VALIDATION OF SELECTION TESTS AGAINST COMBAT RATINGS IN THE U.S. NAVY. November 1945. 4 pp.

Number 194. SELECTION AND CLASSIFICATION OF AIRCREW BY THE JAPANESE February 1946. 20 pp.

Number 195. THE PREDICTION OF FAILURE IN FLYING TRAINING AND IN OPERATIONS BY THE BRIEF PSYCHIATRIC INTERVIEW. March 1946. 5 pp.

Number 196. VALIDATION OF OFFICER SELECTION TESTS BY MEANS OF COMBAT PROFICIENCY RATINGS. April 1946. 2 pp.

885. *Brief Psychotherapy Council. Proceedings.*

TITLE VARIATIONS: Also called *Chicago. Institute for Psychoanalysis. Brief Psychotherapy Council. Proceedings.*

DATES OF PUBLICATION: 1st–3rd, 1942–1946.

FREQUENCY: Biennial.

NUMBERING VARIATIONS: None.

PUBLISHER: **Chicago:** Institute for Psychoanalysis, 1942–1946.

PRIMARY EDITORS: None listed.

CONTENTS:

1st. Chicago, 1942. PROCEEDINGS OF THE BRIEF PSYCHOTHERAPY COUNCIL, OCTOBER 25–26, 1942. 1942. 71 pp.

2nd. Chicago, 1944. PROCEEDINGS OF THE SECOND BRIEF PSYCHOTHERAPY COUNCIL, JANUARY 1944: Volume 1. WAR PSYCHIATRY. 1944. 55 p.; Volume 2. PSYCHOSOMATIC MEDICINE. 1944. 64 p.; Volume 3. PSYCHOTHERAPY FOR CHILDREN AND GROUP PSYCHOTHERAPY. 1944. 58 pp.

3rd. Chicago, 1946. PROCEEDINGS OF THE THIRD PSYCHOTHERAPY COUNCIL, October 18–19, 1946. 1947. 176 pp.

886. *Journal of Parapsychology. A Scientific Quarterly Dealing with Extra-Sensory Perception and Related Topics.*
TITLE VARIATIONS: Continues *Journal of Parapsychology*. Continued by *Journal of Parapsychology. A Scientific Quarterly Dealing with Extra-Sensory Perception, the Psychokinetic Effect, and Related Topics* with Volume 8, 1944.
DATES OF PUBLICATION: Volume 6–7, 1942–1943.
FREQUENCY: Quarterly.
NUMBERING VARIATIONS: None.
PUBLISHER: **Durham, North Carolina:** Duke University Press, 1942–1943.
PRIMARY EDITORS: **Joseph Banks Rhine,** 1942–1943; **Charles E. Stuart,** 1942–1943; **J. G. Pratt,** 1942–1943; **J. A. Greenwood,** 1942–1943; **Dorothy H. Pope,** 1942–1943.

887. *Lima. Instituto psicopedagógico nacional. Boletín.*
TITLE VARIATIONS: None.
DATES OF PUBLICATION: Año 1–9+, 1942–1950+.
FREQUENCY: Semiannual.
NUMBERING VARIATIONS: None.
PUBLISHER: **Lima, Peru:** Instituto psicopedagógico nacional, 1942–1950+.
PRIMARY EDITORS: **[Walter Blumenfeld,]** 1942–1949; **[Luis Felipe Alarco,]** 1942–1949; **Carmela Vinatea Lujan,** 1950+; **Emiliano Pisculich Ramirez,** 1950+; **Maria Gómez Calderon,** 1950+; **Juan G. Zela Koort,** 1950+.

888. *Psykologien og Erhvervslivet; Tidsskrift for anvendt Psykologi.*
TITLE VARIATIONS: None.
DATES OF PUBLICATION: Aargang 1–6+, May 1942–December 1949+. None published 1945, 1947 and 1950.
FREQUENCY: Semiannual (Irregular).
NUMBERING VARIATIONS: None.
PUBLISHER: **Copenhagen:** Psykoteknisk Institut, 1942–1944. **Copenhagen:** Nyt nordisk Forlag, 1946–1949+.
PRIMARY EDITORS: **Poul Bahnsen,** 1942–1949+; **Aage Madsen,** 1942–1949+.

889. *Schweizerische Zeitschrift für Psychologie und ihre Anwendungen.* [Affiliated with the Schweizerische Gesellschaft für Psychologie und ihre Anwendungen (also called La Société suisse de psychologie et de psychologie appliquée).]
TITLE VARIATIONS: Also called *Revue suisse de psychologie et de psychologie appliquée.*

DATES OF PUBLICATION: Band 1–9+, 1942–1950+.

FREQUENCY: Quarterly.

NUMBERING VARIATIONS: None.

PUBLISHER: **Bern:** Huber, 1942–1950+.

PRIMARY EDITOR: **W. Morgenthaler,** 1942–1950+.

ASSOCIATE EDITORS: Jean Piaget, 1942–1950+. H. Christoffel, 1942–1950+.

890. *Tidskrift för psykologi och pedagogik.*

TITLE VARIATIONS: None.

DATES OF PUBLICATION: Årgang 1–3, 1942/1943–1946. Suspended publication 1945.

FREQUENCY: Quarterly.

NUMBERING VARIATIONS: Årgang 1 published 1942/1943. Årgang 2 published 1943/1944. Årgang 3 published 1946.

PUBLISHER: **Göteborg:** [Elanders Boktr.,] 1942–1946.

PRIMARY EDITORS: None listed.

1943

891. *Applied Psychology Monographs.*

TITLE VARIATIONS: Superseded by *Psychological Monographs: General and Applied* with Number 288, 1948.

DATES OF PUBLICATION: Number 1–17, March 1943–1948.

FREQUENCY: Irregular. *See* Contents *below.*

NUMBERING VARIATIONS: None.

PUBLISHER: **Stanford, California:** Stanford University Press for the American Association for Applied Psychology, March, 1943–September, 1945. **Stanford, California:** Stanford University Press for the American Psychological Association, June, 1946–1948.

PRIMARY EDITOR: **H. S. Conrad,** 1943–1948.

EDITORIAL BOARD: P. S. Achilles, 1946–1948; R. G. Bernreuter, 1943–1948; E. A. Doll, 1943–1948; A. W. Kornhauser, 1943–1948; Harriet E. O'Shea, 1943–1948; C. R. Rogers, 1943–1948; F. L. Ruch, 1943–1948; P. M. Symonds, 1943–1948; L. M. Terman, 1943–1948.

CONTENTS:

Number 1. Cronbach, Lee J. EXPLORING THE WARTIME MORALE OF HIGH-SCHOOL YOUTH. March, 1943. 79 pp.

Number 2. Carter, Harold D. VOCATIONAL INTERESTS AND JOB ORIENTATION. A TEN-YEAR REVIEW. Foreword by Edward K. Strong, Jr. May 1944. 85 pp.

Number 3. Pintner, Rudolf, Anna Dragositz, and Rose Kushner. SUPPLEMENTARY GUIDE FOR THE REVISED STANFORD-BINET SCALE (FORM L). Foreword by Lewis M. Terman and Maud A. Merrill. June 1944. 135 pp.

Number 4. Peatman, John Gray, and Tore Hallonquist. THE PATTERNING OF LISTENER ATTITUDES TOWARD RADIO BROADCASTS. METHODS AND RESULTS. January 1945. 58 pp.

Number 5. Kerr, Willard A. EXPERIMENTS ON THE EFFECTS OF MUSIC ON FACTORY PRODUCTION. January 1945. 40 pp.

Number 6. Anderson, Harold H., and Helen M. Brewer. STUDIES OF TEACHERS' CLASSROOM PERSONALITIES, I. DOMINATIVE AND SOCIALLY INTEGRATIVE BEHAVIOR OF KINDERGARTEN TEACHERS. Foreword by Harold E. Jones. July 1945. 157 pp.

Number 7. Munroe, Ruth Learned. PREDICTION OF THE ADJUSTMENT AND ACADEMIC PERFORMANCE OF COLLEGE STUDENTS BY A MODIFICATION OF THE RORSCHACH METHOD. Foreword by Gardner Murphy. September 1945. 104 pp.

Number 8. Anderson, Harold H., and Joseph E. Brewer. STUDIES OF TEACHERS' CLASSROOM PERSONALITIES, II. EFFECTS OF TEACHERS' DOMINATIVE AND INTEGRATIVE CONTACTS ON CHILDREN'S CLASSROOM BEHAVIOR. Foreword by Frank N. Freeman. June 1946. 128 pp.

Number 9. Newman, Frances Burks. THE ADOLESCENT IN SOCIAL GROUPS. STUDIES IN THE OBSERVATION OF PERSONALITY. Introduction by Harold E. Jones. 1946. 94 pp.

Number 10. Finch, F. H. ENROLLMENT INCREASES AND CHANGES IN THE MENTAL LEVEL OF THE HIGH-SCHOOL POPULATION. Foreword by W. S. Miller. June 1946. 75 pp.

Number 11. Anderson, Harold H., Joseph E. Brewer, and Mary Frances Reed. STUDIES OF TEACHERS' CLASSROOM PERSONALITIES, III. FOLLOW-UP STUDIES OF THE EFFECTS OF DOMINATIVE AND INTEGRATIVE CONTACTS ON CHILDREN'S BEHAVIOR. Foreword by J. Wayne Wrightstone. December 1946. 156 pp.

Number 12. Killinger, George C., ed. THE PSYCHOBIOLOGICAL PROGRAM OF THE WAR SHIPPING ADMINISTRATION. Foreword by Edward Macauley. Introductory Chapter by Justin K. Fuller. 1947. 351 pp.

Number 13. Muench, George A. AN EVALUATION OF NON-DIRECTIVE PSYCHOTHERAPY BY MEANS OF THE RORSCHACH AND OTHER INDICES. Foreword by Carl R. Rogers. July 1947. 163 pp.

Number 14. Smith, Henry Clay. MUSIC IN RELATION TO EMPLOYEE ATTITUDES, PIECEWORK PRODUCTION, AND INDUSTRIAL ACCIDENTS. Foreword by Joseph Tiffin. August 1947. 59 pp.

Number 15. Pepinsky, Harold B. THE SELECTION AND USE OF DIAGNOSTIC CATEGORIES IN CLINICAL COUNSELING. Foreword by Walter W. Cook. February 1948. 140 pp.

Number 16. Friend, Jeannette G., and Ernest A. Haggard. WORK ADJUSTMENT IN RELATION TO FAMILY BACKGROUND. A CONCEPTUAL BASIS FOR COUNSELING. A REPORT OF AN INVESTIGATION SPONSORED BY THE FAMILY SOCIETY OF GREATER BOSTON. June 1948. 150 pp.

Number 17. Nahm, Helen. AN EVALUATION OF SELECTED SCHOOLS OF NURSING, WITH RESPECT TO CERTAIN EDUCATIONAL OBJECTIVES. Foreword by Walter W. Cook. 1948. 97 pp.

892. *Chicago. University. Psychometric Laboratory. Reports.*

TITLE VARIATIONS: None.

DATES OF PUBLICATION: Number 1–61+; November, 1943–December, 1950+.

FREQUENCY: Irregular. *See* Contents *below.*

NUMBERING VARIATIONS: Number 33 never issued.

PUBLISHER: **Chicago:** University of Chicago Psychometric Laboratory, 1943–1950+.

PRIMARY EDITOR: **Louis Leon Thurstone**, 1943–1950+.

CONTENTS:

Number 1. Thurstone, L. L. NOTE ABOUT FACTOR ANALYSIS OF READING TESTS. 1943.

Number 2. Thurstone, L. L. IN SEARCH OF NEW TESTS. 1943. (Also as *Psychometrika,* Volume 9, Number 1, March 1944, p. 69.)

Number 3. Thurstone, L. L. A CODE APTITUDE TEST. ADAPTED FOR MACHINE SCORING. 1944. 26 pp.

Number 4. Thurstone, L. L. THE CENTROID METHOD OF FACTORING. (1944.) (Also as Chapter VIII in Thurstone, L. L. *Multiple-Factor Analysis.* Chicago: University of Chicago Press, 1947, pp. 149–175.)

Number 5. Thurstone, L. L. ALTERNATIVE METHODS OF ROTATION. (1944). (Also as Chapter XVII in Thurstone, L. L. *Multiple-Factor Analysis.* Chicago: University of Chicago Press, 1947, pp. 377–410.)

Number 6. Thurstone, L. L. SECOND-ORDER FACTORS. 1944. (Also as *Psychometrika,* Volume 9, Number 2, June 1944, pp. 71–100.)

Number 7. Thurstone, L. L. DATA FOR COMPANY 19 AT THE NAVAL TRAINING SCHOOL AFTER SIX WEEKS OF INSTRUCTION. 1944.

Number 8. Thurstone, L. L. SUPPLEMENTARY REPORT ON CODE APTITUDE TEST. ADDITIONAL DATA FOR THREE COMPANIES AT THE NAVAL TRAINING SCHOOL, THE UNIVERSITY OF CHICAGO, SUPPLEMENTING REPORT NUMBER 3 OF JANUARY, 1944. 1944.

Number 9. Thurstone, L. L., Ledyard Tucker, and Virginia Brown. DEFINITIONS OF TERMS IN FACTOR ANALYSIS PREPARED FOR A DICTIONARY OF EDUCATION; and Thurstone, L. L. GENERAL COMMENTS ON DEFINITIONS IN FACTOR ANALYSIS. 1944.

Number 10. Thurstone, L. L. THE PSYCHOMETRIC LABORATORY. RECENT, CURRENT, AND PROPOSED STUDIES AND THE ANNUAL BUDGET. 1944.

Number 11. Brown, Virginia. FREQUENCY DISTRIBUTIONS FOR CODE APTITUDE TEST. 1944.

Number 12. Thurstone, L. L. GRAPHICAL METHOD OF FACTORING THE CORRELATION MATRIX. 1944. (Also as *Proceedings of the National Academy of Sciences,* Volume 30, Number 6, June, 1944, pp. 129–134.)

892. *(Continued)*

Number 13. Brown, Virginia. CODE APTITUDE TEST SCORES FOR COMPANY 31 AT THE NAVAL TRAINING SCHOOL. 1944.

Number 14. Tucker, Ledyard R. THE DETERMINATION OF SUCCESSIVE PRINCIPAL COMPONENTS WITHOUT COMPUTATION OF TABLES OF RESIDUAL CORRELATION COEFFICIENTS. 1944.

Number 15. Brown, Virginia M. PROGRESS REPORT ON CODE APTITUDE TESTS. FINAL REPORT ON COMPANIES 19 AND 20 AT THE NAVAL TRAINING SCHOOL, UNIVERSITY OF CHICAGO. 1944. 5 pp.

Number 16. Brown, Virginia M. FINAL PROGRESS REPORT ON CODE APTITUDE TESTS. FINAL REPORT ON COMPANIES 21 AND 22 AT THE NAVAL TRAINING SCHOOL, UNIVERSITY OF CHICAGO. 1944. 3 pp.

Number 17. Thurstone, L. L. FACTOR ANALYSIS OF THE ALLERGIES. ANALYSIS OF DATA COLLECTED BY PROFESSOR T. GAYLORD ANDREWS, DEPARTMENT OF PSYCHOLOGY, THE UNIVERSITY OF CHICAGO. 1944. 7 pp.

Number 18. Thurstone, L. L. THEORIES OF INTELLIGENCE. 1945. 9 pp.

Number 19. Thurstone, L. L. A MULTIPLE GROUP METHOD OF FACTORING THE CORRELATION MATRIX. 1945. (Also as *Psychometrika*, Volume 10, Number 2, June, 1945, pp. 73–78.)

Number 20. Thurstone, L. L. A SINGLE PLANE METHOD OF ROTATION. 1946. (Also as *Psychometrika*, Volume 11, Number 2, June, 1946, pp. 71–79.)

Number 21. Thurstone, L. L. TESTS FOR PRIMARY MENTAL ABILITIES. 1945. (Also in Kaplan, Oscar J., ed. *The Encyclopedia of Vocational Guidance*. New York: Philosophical Library, 1948, pp. 1099–1102.)

Number 22. Thurstone, L. L. INTELLIGENCE QUOTIENTS FOR SUPERIOR ADULTS. 1945. 2 pp.

Number 23. Thurstone, L. L. THE PREDICTION OF CHOICE. 1945. 14 pp.

Number 24. Thurstone, L. L. FACTOR ANALYSIS AND BODY TYPES. 1945. 7 pp.

Number 25. Thurstone, L. L. NOTE ON THE PREDICTION OF CHOICE WITH CORRELATED RATINGS. 1945. 3 pp.

Number 26. Thurstone, L. L. PSYCHOPHYSICS. 1945. (Also in Harriman, P. L., ed. *Encyclopedia of Psychology*. New York: Philosophical Library, 1946, pp. 640–644).

Number 27. Thurstone, L. L. PRIMARY ABILITIES. 1945. (Also in Harriman, P. L., ed. *Encyclopedia of Psychology*. New York: Philosophical Library, 1946, pp. 544–546.)

Number 28. Thurstone, L. L. A NOTE ON THE EXPERIMENTAL STUDY OF ENGLISH STYLE. 1945. (Also as *American Psychologist*, Volume 1, Number 2, February, 1946, pp. 62–63).

Number 29. Thurstone, L. L. ANALYSIS OF BODY MEASUREMENTS. 1946. 13 pp.

Number 30. Thurstone, L. L. THE SELECTION OF TALENT. MEMORANDUM FOR PROFESSOR STEPHEN M. COREY, CHAIRMAN, COMMITTEE IV OF THE COLUMBIA TEACHERS COLLEGE LECTURE CONFERENCE. 1946. 5 pp.

Number 31. Thurstone, L. L. COMMENT ON GWYNNE NETTLER'S PAPER

"KNOWN-GROUP VALIDATION IN THE MEASUREMENT OF ATTITUDES TOWARD THE JAPANESE IN AMERICA." 1946. (Also as *American Journal of Sociology,* Volume 52, Number 1, July, 1946, pp. 39–40.)

Number 32. Thurstone, L. L. NOTE ON THE ANALYSIS OF READING TESTS. 1946. 3 pp. (Also as *Psychometrika.* Volume 11, September, 1946, pp. 185–188.)

Number 33. Cancelled.

Number 34. Thurstone, L. L. THE CALIBRATION OF TEST ITEMS. 1946. 3 pp.

Number 35. Thurstone, L. L. MECHANICAL APTITUDE. NO. 1. RESEARCH PLAN FOR THE PROJECT. 1946.

Number 36. Thurstone, L. L. NAVY MECHANICAL APTITUDE PROJECT. NO. 2. PROGRESS REPORT. 1947.

Number 37. Thurstone, L. L. THE OBJECTIVE STUDY OF TEMPERAMENT. 1947.

Number 38. Thurstone, L. L. REPORT FOR DR. JOHN G. LYNN, PSYCHIATRIC INSTITUTE, GRASSLANDS HOSPITAL, VALHALLA, NEW YORK. DATA ON PRIMARY MENTAL ABILITIES TESTS FOR PATIENTS. 1947.

Number 39. Thurstone, L. L. AN INTEREST SCHEDULE. 1947. 10 pp.

Number 40. Thurstone, L. L. PSYCHOPHYSICAL METHODS. 1947. 29 pp. (Also in Andrews, T. G. *Methods of Psychology.* New York: John Wiley and Sons, 1947, pp. 124–157.)

Number 41. Thurstone, L. L. THE IMPROVEMENT OF SCHOOL EXAMINATIONS. 1947. 3 pp.

Number 42. Thurstone, L. L. THE DIMENSIONS OF TEMPERAMENT. ANALYSIS OF GUILFORD'S THIRTEEN PERSONALITY SCORES. 1947. 10 pp.

Number 43. Chapman, Robert L. THE MACQUARRIE TEST OF MECHANICAL ABILITY. PRINCIPAL AXES SOLUTION OF GOODMAN DATA. 1947. 5 pp.

Number 44. Thurstone, L. L. PSYCHOLOGICAL IMPLICATIONS OF FACTOR ANALYSIS. 1947. 10 pp.

Number 45. Degan, James W. A NOTE ON THE EFFECTS OF SELECTION IN FACTOR ANALYSIS. 1947. 2 pp.

Number 46. Thurstone, L. L. THE RORSCHACH IN PSYCHOLOGICAL SCIENCE. 1947. 5 pp.

Number 47. Thurstone, Thelma Gwinn, and L. L. Thurstone. MECHANICAL APTITUDE. REPORT OF THE FIRST YEAR OF THE STUDY. 1947. 7 pp.

Number 48. Thurstone, L. L. THE EDGE-MARKING METHOD OF ANALYZING DATA. 1948. 11 pp.

Number 49. Yela, Mariano. APPLICATION OF THE CONCEPT OF SIMPLE STRUCTURE TO ALEXANDER'S DATA. 1948. 15 pp.

Number 50. Thurstone, L. L. PRIMARY MENTAL ABILITIES. PAPER PRESENTED TO THE SYMPOSIUM ON HUMAN INDIVIDUALITY AT THE CENTENNIAL MEETING OF THE AMERICAN ASSOCIATION FOR THE ADVANCEMENT OF SCIENCE, WASHINGTON, D.C., SEPTEMBER 14, 1948. 1948. 10 pp.

Number 51. Thurstone, L. L. PSYCHOLOGICAL ASSUMPTIONS IN FACTOR ANALYSIS. PAPER READ AT THE TWELFTH INTERNATIONAL CONGRESS OF PSYCHOLOGY IN EDINBURGH, JULY 24, 1948. 1949. 3 pp.

Number 52. Thurstone, L. L. EXPERIMENTAL METHODS IN FOOD TASTING.

PAPER READ AT A RESEARCH CONFERENCE SPONSORED BY THE COUNCIL ON RE-SEARCH OF THE AMERICAN MEAT INSTITUTE, MARCH 24, 1950, AT THE UNIVER-SITY OF CHICAGO, CHICAGO, ILLINOIS. 1950. 5 pp.

Number 53. Thurstone, L. L. THE FACTORIAL DESCRIPTION OF TEM-PERAMENT. PAPER READ AT THE NATIONAL ACADEMY OF SCIENCES IN WASH-INGTON, D.C. ON APRIL 24, 1950. 1950. 3 pp.

Number 54. Thurstone, Thelma Gwinn, and L. L. Thurstone. MECHAN-ICAL APTITUDE II. DESCRIPTION OF GROUP TESTS. 1949. 33 pp.

Number 55. Thurstone, L. L. MECHANICAL APTITUDE III. ANALYSIS OF GROUP TESTS. 1949. 20 pp.

Number 56. Thurstone, Thelma Gwinn, and L. L. Thurstone. MECHAN-ICAL APTITUDE IV. DESCRIPTION OF INDIVIDUAL TESTS. 1949. 27 pp.

Number 57. Thurstone, L. L. MECHANICAL APTITUTE V. INDIVIDUAL AND GROUP TESTS OF MECHANICAL APTITUDE. 1950. 7 pp.

Number 58. Degan, James W. MECHANICAL APTITUDE VI. A RE-ANALYSIS OF THE ARMY AIR FORCE BATTERY OF MECHANICAL TESTS. 1950. 13 pp.

Number 59. Thurstone, L. L. SOME PRIMARY ABILITIES IN VISUAL THINK-ING. PAPER READ BEFORE THE AMERICAN PHILOSOPHICAL SOCIETY IN PHILA-DELPHIA ON APRIL 21, 1950. 1950. 7 pp.

Number 60. Thurstone, L. L. APPARATUS FOR STUDYING CONTINUOUS APPARENT MOVEMENT. 1950. 3 pp.

Number 61. Thurstone, L. L., CREATIVE TALENT. 1950. 10 pp. (Also in Thurstone, L. L., ed. *Applications of Psychology. Essays to Honor Walter V. Bingham.* New York: Harper and Bros., 1952, pp. 18–37. Also in *Proceedings of the 1950 Invitational Conference on Testing Problems.* Princeton, New Jersey: Educational Testing Service, 1951, pp. 55–69.)

893. *Jen shih hsin li yen chiu she ts'ung shu.* [Personnel Psychology Research Society. Collectanea.]

TITLE VARIATIONS: None.

DATES OF PUBLICATION: Volume 1–7, 1943–1947.

FREQUENCY: Irregular.

NUMBERING VARIATIONS: None.

PUBLISHER: **Shanghai:** Shang wu yin shu kuan [Commercial Press], 1943–1947.

PRIMARY EDITOR: **Hsiao Hung Hsiao,** 1943–1947.

894. *Journal of Education and Psychology.*

TITLE VARIATIONS: None.

DATES OF PUBLICATION: Volume 1–8, Number 3+, April 1943–October 1950+.

FREQUENCY: Quarterly.

NUMBERING VARIATIONS: None.

PUBLISHER: **Baroda, India:** Secondary Teachers' College, 1943–1950 + .

PRIMARY EDITORS: **T.K.N. Menon,** 1943–1950 + ; **L. J. Bhatt,** 1947–1950 + .

895. *Mendoza (Argentina). Universidad nacional de Cuyo. Instituto de psicología experimental. Publicaciones.*

TITLE VARIATIONS: None.

DATES OF PUBLICATION: Volumen 1–2, Número 1, 1943–December 1947.

FREQUENCY: Irregular. *See* Contents *below.*

NUMBERING VARIATIONS: None.

PUBLISHER: **Mendoza, Argentina:** Instituto de psicología experimental [by] Best Hermanos, 1943. **Mendoza:** Ministerio de justicia e instrucción pública, Universidad nacional de Cuyo, Instituto de psicología experimental, 1943. **Mendoza:** Ministerio de justicia e instrucción pública, Universidad nacional de Cuyo, Facultad de filosofía y letras, Instituto de psicología experimental, 1945–1947.

PRIMARY EDITOR: **Horacio J. A. Rimoldi,** 1943–1947.

CONTENTS:

Volumen 1, Número 1. Rimoldi, Horacio J. A. ADECUACIÓN AL TRABAJO (PAPEL DE CIERTOS FACTORES PSÍQUICOS Y FÍSICOS). 1943. Pp. 1–38.

———, **Número 2.** Rimoldi, Horacio J. A., and Nuria Cortada. ESTUDIO COMPARATIVO SOBRE ALGUNAS FUNCIONES PSICOMOTORAS (DÉBILES FÍSICOS Y NORMALES). October 1943. Pp. 43–79.

———, **Número 3.** Rimoldi, Horacio J. A., Nuria Cortada, and Emma Susana Velasco. ENSAYO DE TIPIFICACIÓN DE UNA PRUEBA MENTAL (PROGRESSIVE MATRICES DE RAVEN). September 1945. Pp. 81–114.

———, **Número 4.** Rimoldi, Horacio J. A., Lydia Bührer, Raquel de San Martín, Nuria Cortada, and Emma Susana Velasco. DESARROLLO INTELECTUAL ENTRE LOS 11 Y LOS 14 AÑOS. December 1945. Pp. 117–237.

Volumen 2, Número 1. Rimoldi, Horacio J. A., Emma Susana Velasco, Raquel de San Martin, and Lydia Bührer. TIPIFICACIÓN DE LOS "PROGRESSIVE MATRICES" DE RAVEN. December 1947. Pp. 1–24.

896. *Montevideo. Laboratorio de psicopedagogía Sebastian Morey Otero. Boletín.*

TITLE VARIATIONS: None.

DATES OF PUBLICATION: Año 1–3/4, March 1943–March 1947.

FREQUENCY: **Annual,** Año 1–2, 1943–1944. **Biennial,** Año 3/4, 1947. Suspended publication March 1944–February 1947.

NUMBERING VARIATIONS: Issues also numbered, Número 1–3/4.

PUBLISHER: **Montevideo, Uruguay:** "Impresora Uruguaya" S.A., 1943. **Montevideo:** Imprenta nacional, 1944–1947.

PRIMARY EDITOR: **Maria A. Carbonell de Grompone,** 1943–1947.

897. *New Zealand. Department of Scientific and Industrial Research. Industrial Psychology Division. Report.*

TITLE VARIATIONS: None.

DATES OF PUBLICATION: Number 1, 1943.

FREQUENCY: Irregular. *See* Contents *below.*

NUMBERING VARIATIONS: None.

PUBLISHER: **Wellington, New Zealand:** Department of Scientific and Industrial Research, Industrial Psychology Division, 1943.

PRIMARY EDITORS: None listed.

CONTENTS:

Number 1. New Zealand Department of Scientific and Industrial Research. Industrial Psychology Division. INDUSTRIAL ABSENTEEISM. 1943. 52 pp.

898. *Oregon. University. Monographs. Studies in Psychology.*

TITLE VARIATIONS: None.

DATES OF PUBLICATION: Number 1–2 +, 1943–1945 +. Suspended publication, 1946–1959.

FREQUENCY: Irregular. *See* Contents *below.*

NUMBERING VARIATIONS: None.

PUBLISHER: **Eugene, Oregon:** University of Oregon, 1943–1945 +.

PRIMARY EDITORS: None listed.

CONTENTS:

Number 1. Leeper, Robert. LEWIN'S TOPOLOGICAL AND VECTOR PSYCHOGY. March 1943. 218 pp.

Number 2. Moore, Arthur Russell. THE INDIVIDUAL IN SIMPLER FORMS. April 1945. 143 pp.

899. *Psychologische Praxis; Schriftenreihe für Erziehung und Jugendpflege.*

TITLE VARIATIONS: None.

DATES OF PUBLICATION: Heft 1–9 +, 1943–1950 +.

FREQUENCY: Irregular. *See* Contents *below.*

NUMBERING VARIATIONS: None.

PUBLISHER: **Basel:** S. Karger, 1943–1950 +.

PRIMARY EDITOR: **Ernst Probst,** 1943–1950 +.

CONTENTS:

Heft 1. Heymann, Karl. SEELISCHE FRÜHFORMEN. 1943. 58 pp.

Heft 2. Huber, Fritz. DAS PFLEGEKIND. 1944. 56 pp.

Heft 3. Probst, Ernst. KINDER UND JUGENDLICHE ALS ZEUGEN. 1945. 55 pp. (2nd ed. 1950.)

Heft 4. Meili, Rich. Psychologie der Berufsberatung. 1945. 64 pp.

Heft 5. Heymann, Karl. Entwurzelte und disharmonische Kinder. 1946. 56 pp.

Heft 6. Stirnimann, Fritz. Das Kind und seine früheste Umwelt. 1947. 72 pp.

Heft 7. Probst, Ernst. Der Binet-Simon-Test zur Prüfung der Intelligenz bei Kindern. 1948. 39 pp.

Heft 8. Heymann, Karl. Kritische Phasen der Kindheit. 1949. 52 pp.

Heft 9. Probst, Ernst. Erziehungshilfe bei ungünstig Veranlagten. 1950. 54 pp.

900. *Revista de psicoanálisis.*

TITLE VARIATIONS: None.

DATES OF PUBLICATION: Tomo 1–7+, July 1943–April/May/June 1950+.

FREQUENCY: Quarterly.

NUMBERING VARIATIONS: None.

PUBLISHER: **Buenos Aires:** Asociación psicoanalítica Argentina, 1943–1950+.

PRIMARY EDITOR: **Arnaldo Rascovsky,** 1947–1950+.

EDITORIAL BOARD: Celes Ernesto Carcamo, 1943–1950+; Marie Langer, 1943–1950+; Enrique Pichon Riviere, 1943–1950+; Guillermo Ferrari Hardoy, 1943–1950+; Angel Garma, 1943–1950+; Arnaldo Rascovsky, 1943–1946; Emilio Antona, 1943–1947; Luis Rascovsky, 1944–1950+; E. Eduardo Krapf, 1947–1950+; Luisa G. de Alvarez de Toledo, 1947–1950+; Alberto Tallaferro, 1947–1950+; Arminda A. de Pichon-Riviere, 1948–1950+; Enrique Racker, 1948–1950+; Teodoro Schlossberg, 1948–1950+; Matilde Wencelblat de Rascovsky, 1948–1950+; Elisabeth Goode. 1950+; Danilo Perestrello, 1950+; Simon Wencelblat, 1950+.

901. *Schweizerische Zeitschrift für Psychologie und ihre Anwendungen. Beiheft.* [Affiliated with the Schweizerische Gesellschaft für Psychologie und ihre Anwendungen (also called La Société suisse de psychologie et de psychologie appliquée).]

TITLE VARIATIONS None.

DATES OF PUBLICATION: Heft 1–19+, 1943–1950+

FREQUENCY: Irregular. *See* Contents *below.*

NUMBERING VARIATIONS: Heft 1 issued after Heft 2. Some issues also numbered as *Rorschachiana* or as *Graphologia*. See *Contents* below.

PUBLISHER: **Bern:** Huber, 1943–1950+.

PRIMARY EDITOR: **W. Morgenthaler,** 1943–1950+.

CONTENTS:

Heft 1. Morgenthaler, Walt. Letzte Aufzeichnungen von Selbstmördern. 1945. 148 pp.

Heft 2. Spreng, Hanns. PSYCHOLOGISCHE KURZPRÜFUNGEN. 1943. 82 pp.

Heft 3. Loosli-Usteri, Marguerite. DE L'ANXIÉTÉ –ENFANTINE. ÉTUDE PSYCHOLOGIQUE ET PÉDAGOGIQUE. 1943. 148 pp.

Heft 4. Moor, Paul. THEORETISCHE GRUNDLEGUNG DER HEILPÄDAGOGISCHEN PSYCHOLOGIE. 1943. 124 pp.

Heft 5. Rutishauser, Eug. PSYCHOLOGIE DER VERWAHRLOSUNG. VERSUCH EINER AUFHELLUNG DES PHÄNOMENS. 1944. 86 pp.

Heft 6. GRAPHOLOGIA I. With contributions by Max Pulver, K. Roman-Goldzieher, Oluf Brüel, and O. Lippuner. 1945. 72 pp.

Heft 7. RORSCHACHIANA I. With contributions by Elsa Josephy, M. Laignel-Lavastine, F. Minkowska, M. Bouvet, P. Neveu, Gina Zangger, F. Tosquelles, Ewald Bohm, and W. Morgenthaler. 1945. 143 pp.

Heft 8. Graber, Gustav Hans. EINHEIT UND ZWIESPALT DER SEELE. 1945. 124 pp.

Heft 9. Schneeberger, Fritz. SCHWIERIGE SCHÜLER UND IHRE ERFASSUNG. 1946. 104 pp.

Heft 10. Sperisen, Walter. DIE ARBEITSSCHEU. EINE PSYCHOLOGISCH-PÄDAGOGISCHE STUDIE. 1946. 160 pp.

Heft 11. Menninger-Lerchenthal, Erich. DER EIGENE DOPPELGÄNGER. 1946. 96 pp.

Heft 12. Sechehaye, M.-A. LA RÉALISATION SYMBOLIQUE. 1947. 96 pp.

Heft 13. RORSCHACHIANA II. With contributions by Marguerite Loosli-Usteri, Peter Mohr, Hans Huber, Jr., W. Morgenthaler, Adolf Friedemann, M. Schachter, D. A. van Krevelen, Amélie Leuzinger-Schuler, Aarre Tuompo, Hildegard Hiltmann, and the Rorschach-Kommission. 1947. 136 pp.

Heft 14. SEMAINES INTERNATIONALES D'ÉTUDE POUR L'ENFANCE VICTIME DE LA GUERRE. With contributions by Therese Wagner-Simon, O. L. Forel, Tien-Ling Chang, P. Moor, R. Fau, Charlotte Memin, A. Aichhorn, Hans Zulliger, R. Dottrens, and L. Le Guillant. 1948. 168 pp.

Heft 15. Krueger, Felix. LEHRE VON DEM GANZEN. 1948, 104 pp.

Heft 16. Bitter, Wilhelm. DIE ANGSTNEUROSE. 1948. 191 pp.

Heft 17. Sechehaye, M.-A. DIAGNOSTICS PSYCHOLOGIQUES. 1949. 119 pp.

Heft 18. GRAPHOLOGIA II. With contributions by Max Pulver, Oskar R. Schlag, Heinz Hector, Helen Schmidheiny, Clothilde Philipp, Robert Bossard, Freddy Sulzer, and David Katz. 1949. 92 pp.

Heft 19. RORSCHACHIANA III. With contributions by Ernst Schneider, M. Schachter, Ewald Bohm, Theodor Schlarmann, K. W. Bash, Renée Stora, Charlotte Spitz, Nancy Bratt-Oestergaard, and E. Liefmann. 1950, 127 pp.

1944

902. *Akademiia nauk SSSR. Fiziologicheskii institut imeni I. P. Pavlova. Trudy.*

TITLE VARIATIONS: Supersedes *Akademiia nauk SSSR (Leningrad). Fiziologicheskii institut. Fiziologicheskii laboratorii akademika I. P. Pavlova. Trudy.*

DATES OF PUBLICATION: Tom 1–6, 1944–1950.

FREQUENCY: Annual.

NUMBERING VARIATIONS: Also cited as Tom 11–16 of *Akademiia nauk SSSR (Leningrad). Fiziologicheskii institut. Fiziologicheskii laboratorii akademika I.P. Pavlova. Trudy.*

PUBLISHER: **Moscow:** Akademiia nauk SSSR. Fiziologicheskii institut imeni I. P. Pavlova, 1944–1950.

PRIMARY EDITOR: **L. A. Orbeli,** 1944–1950.

NOTE: Information on this entry was found in Bruhn, Peter. *Gesamtverzeichnis Russischer und Sowjetischer Periodika und Serienwerke in Bibliotheken der Bundesrepublik Deutschland und West-Berlins.* Berlin, Freien Universität, Osteuropa-Instituts, 1962. Band I.

903. *American Psychopathological Association. Proceedings of the Annual Meeting.*

TITLE VARIATIONS: Issues have distinctive titles. *See* Contents *below.*

DATES OF PUBLICATION: 33rd–34th, 36th–40th Annual Meeting, 1944–1950 +.

FREQUENCY: Annual.

NUMBERING VARIATIONS: Annual meetings 1–32 and 35 did not have published proceedings.

PUBLISHERS: **New York:** King's Crown Press, 33rd Annual Meeting, 1945. **New York:** Grune & Stratton, 34th and 36th–40th Annual Meetings, 1946–1952.

PRIMARY EDITORS: *See* Contents *below.*

CONTENTS:

33rd. TRENDS OF MENTAL DISEASE. PAPERS PRESENTED AT A SYMPOSIUM ARRANGED AS PART OF THE THIRTY-THIRD ANNUAL MEETING OF THE AMERICAN PSYCHOPATHOLOGICAL ASSOCIATION, HELD IN NEW YORK, JUNE 9, 1944. 1945. 114 pp.

34th. CURRENT THERAPIES OF PERSONALITY DISORDERS; THE PROCEEDINGS OF THE THIRTY-FOURTH ANNUAL MEETING OF THE AMERICAN PSYCHOPATHOLOGICAL ASSOCIATION HELD IN NEW YORK CITY, APRIL 1945. Edited by Bernard Glueck. 1946. 296 pp.

36th. EPILEPSY: PSYCHIATRIC ASPECTS OF CONVULSIVE DISORDERS; THE PROCEEDINGS OF THE THIRTY-SIXTH ANNUAL MEETING OF THE AMERICAN PSYCHOPATHOLOGICAL ASSOCIATION HELD IN NEW YORK CITY, MAY 1946. Edited by Paul H. Hoch and Robert P. Knight. 1947. 214 pp.

37th. FAILURES IN PSYCHIATRIC TREATMENT; THE PROCEEDINGS OF THE THIRTY-SEVENTH ANNUAL MEETING OF THE AMERICAN PSYCHOPATHOLOGICAL ASSOCIATION HELD IN NEW YORK CITY, JUNE 1947. Edited by Paul H. Hoch. 1948. 241 pp.

38th. PSYCHOSEXUAL DEVELOPMENT IN HEALTH AND DISEASE; THE PROCEEDINGS OF THE THIRTY-EIGHTH ANNUAL MEETING OF THE AMERICAN PSYCHOPATHOLOGICAL ASSOCIATION HELD IN NEW YORK CITY, JUNE 1948. Edited by Paul H. Hoch and Joseph Zubin. 1949. 283 pp.

39th. ANXIETY; THE PROCEEDINGS OF THE THIRTY-NINTH ANNUAL MEET-
ING OF THE AMERICAN PSYCHOPATHOLOGICAL ASSOCIATION HELD IN NEW YORK
CITY, JUNE 1949. Edited by Paul H. Hoch and Joseph Zubin. 1950. 254 pp.

40th. RELATION OF PSYCHOLOGICAL TESTS TO PSYCHIATRY; THE PROCEED-
INGS OF THE FORTIETH ANNUAL MEETING OF THE AMERICAN PSYCHOPATHOL-
OGICAL ASSOCIATION HELD IN NEW YORK CITY, JUNE 1950. Edited by Paul H.
Hoch and Joseph Zubin. 1952. 301 pp.

904. *Chile. Universidad. Instituto de psicología. Archivos.*

TITLE VARIATIONS: none.

DATES OF PUBLICATION: Volume 1, 1944. Suspended publication, 1945-
1962.

FREQUENCY: Irregular.

NUMBERING VARIATIONS: None.

PUBLISHER: **Santiago:** Prensas de la Universidad de Chile, 1944.

PRIMARY EDITORS: None listed.

905. *Dobutsu Shinrigaku Nenpo.* [Annual of Animal Psychology.]

TITLE VARIATIONS: None.

DATES OF PUBLICATION: Number 1–7+, 1944–1950+.

FREQUENCY: Annual.

NUMBERING VARIATIONS: None.

PUBLISHER: **Tokyo:** Nihon Dobutsu Shinrigakkai [Japanese Society for Animal
Psychology], 1944–1950+.

PRIMARY EDITORS: None listed.

NOTE: Information for this entry was found in *Gakujutsu Zasshi Sōgō Mokuroku. Shizen Kagaku Wabun Hen* [Union List of Scholarly Journals. Japanese
Language Section. Natural Sciences Part]. Tokyo, 1968.

906. *Journal of Clinical Psychopathology and Psychotherapy.*

TITLE VARIATIONS: Continues *Journal of Criminal Psychopathology.* Continued by *Journal of Clinical Psychopathology* with Volume 7, Number 3, 1946.

DATES OF PUBLICATION: Volume 6–7, Number 2, July 1944–October 1945.

FREQUENCY: Quarterly.

NUMBERING VARIATIONS: Volume 6, Number 3/4 is a double issue.

PUBLISHER: **Monticello, New York:** Medical Journal Press, 1944–1945.

PRIMARY EDITOR: **V. C. Branham,** 1944–1945.

EDITORIAL BOARD: Franz Alexander, 1944–1945; Walter Bromberg,
1944–1945; George Devereux, 1944; Arthur N. Foxe, 1944–1945; Erich
Fromm, 1944–1945; Bernard Glueck, 1944–1945; Sandor Lorand, 1944; Mar-

garet Mead, 1944–1945; Merrill Moore, 1944–1945; Robert V. Seliger, 1944–1945; Lowell S. Selling, 1944–1945; Paul L. Schroeder, 1944–1945; Philip Q. Roche, 1944–1945; Robert M. Lindner, 1944–1945; P. L. Goitein, 1945.

907. *Journal of Neurology, Neurosurgery and Psychiatry.*

TITLE VARIATIONS: Continues *Journal of Neurology and Psychiatry.*

DATES OF PUBLICATION: New Series, Volume 7–13+, January/April 1944–1950+.

FREQUENCY: Quarterly.

NUMBERING VARIATIONS: Multinumber issues present in Volume 7 and 8.

PUBLISHER: **London:** British Medical Association, 1944–1950+.

PRIMARY EDITORS: **E. Arnold Carmichael,** 1944–1950+; **D. Denny-Brown,** 1944–1947; **G. Jefferson,** 1944–1950+; **Aubrey Lewis,** 1944–1950+; **A. Meyer,** 1944–1950+; **R. A. McCance,** 1944–1950+; **Denis Williams,** 1944–1950+; **W. Ritchie Russell,** 1948–1950+.

EDITORIAL BOARD: E. D. Adrian, 1944–1950+; F. C. Bartlett, 1944–1950+; W. Russell Brain, 1944–1950+; G. L. Brown, 1944–1950+; Hugh Cairns, 1944–1950+; W. E. Le Gros Clark, 1944–1950+; N. M. Dott, 1944–1950+; A. Feiling, 1944–1950+; R. A. Fisher, 1944–1950+; R. D. Gillespie, 1944–1945; F. L. Golla, 1944–1950+; R. G. Gordon, 1944–1949; J. G. Greenfield, 1944–1950+; W. R. Henderson, 1944–1950+; D.W.C. Northfield, 1944–1950+; W. Ritchie Russell, 1944–1947; Eliot Slater, 1944–1950+; R. M. Stewart, 1944–1947; C. P. Symonds, 1944–1950+; J. Z. Young, 1944–1950+; Editor of the British Medical Journal; 1944–1950+; Dorothy Russell, 1947–1950+; D. Denny-Brown, 1948–1950+; J. W. Aldren Turner, 1950+.

908. *Journal of Parapsychology. A Scientific Quarterly Dealing with Extra-Sensory Perception, the Psychokinetic Effect, and Related Topics.*

TITLE VARIATIONS: Continues *Journal of Parapsychology. A Scientific Quarterly Dealing with Extra-Sensory Perception and Related Topics.*

DATES OF PUBLICATION: Volume 8–14+, 1944–1950+.

FREQUENCY: Quarterly.

NUMBERING VARIATIONS: None.

PUBLISHER: **Durham, North Carolina:** Duke University Press, 1944–1950+.

PRIMARY EDITORS: **Joseph Banks Rhine,** 1944–1950+; **Charles E. Stuart,** 1944–1946; **J. G. Pratt,** 1944–1950+; **J. A. Greenwood,** 1944–1950+; **Dorothy H. Pope,** 1944–1950+; **T.N.E. Grenville,** 1945–1950+; **Betty M. Humphrey,** 1945–1950+.

EDITORIAL BOARD: Hornell Hart, 1948–1950+; H. H. Price, 1948–1950+; Gardner Murphy, 1948–1950+; Robert H. Thouless, 1948–1950+.

909. *Mexico City. Instituto científico de la opinión pública mexicana. Boletín.*

TITLE VARIATIONS: Institute is also called Instituto de estudios de psicología social y opinión pública; Institute for Studies in Social Psychology and Public Opinion; and Scientific Institute of Mexican Public Opinion.

DATES OF PUBLICATION: Número 19(?)–32, 1944(?)–November 1947. *See* Note *below.*

FREQUENCY: Irregular.

NUMBERING VARIATIONS: None.

PUBLISHER: **Mexico City:** Instituto científico de la opinión pública mexicana, 1944(?)–1947.

PRIMARY EDITORS: None listed.

NOTE: Information on this entry is incomplete. The *National Union List of Serials* lists the above numbers. However, neither the Biblioteca nacional de Mexico nor any of the institutions in the *National Union List of Serials* are able to locate this title. Entry is filed here since approximate date of first known issue is 1944.

910. *Psychodrama and Group Psychotherapy Monographs.*

TITLE VARIATIONS: Also cited as *Psychodrama Monographs.*

DATES OF PUBLICATION: Number 1–27 +, 1944–1950 +.

FREQUENCY: Irregular. *See* Contents *below.*

NUMBERING VARIATIONS: Some issues also published in *Sociometry,* in *Sociatry,* and in *Group Psychotherapy. See* Contents *below.*

PUBLISHER: **New York:** Beacon House, 1944–1950 +.

PRIMARY EDITOR: **Jacob L. Moreno,** 1944–1950 +.

CONTENTS:

Number 1. Moreno, J. L. SOCIODRAMA, A METHOD FOR THE ANALYSIS OF SOCIAL CONFLICTS. 1944. 16 pp.

Number 2. Moreno, J. L. PSYCHODRAMATIC TREATMENT OF PERFORMANCE NEUROSIS; CASE HISTORY OF A MUSICIAN. 1944. 31 pp. (Also titled as CREATIVITY AND CULTURAL CONSERVES—WITH SPECIAL REFERENCE TO MUSICAL EXPRESSION, *Sociometry,* Volume 2, 1939, pp. 1–36.)

Number 3. Moreno, J. L. THE THEATRE OF SPONTANEITY. 1947. 113 pp.

Number 4. Moreno, J. L. SPONTANEITY TEST AND SPONTANEITY TRAINING. 1944. 24 pp.

Number 5. Moreno, J. L. PSYCHODRAMATIC SHOCK THERAPY; A SOCIOMETRIC APPROACH TO THE PROBLEM OF MENTAL DISORDERS. 1944. 30 pp. (Also as *Sociometry,* Volume 2, 1939, pp. 1–30.)

Number 6. Moreno, J. L. MENTAL CATHARSIS AND THE PSYCHODRAMA. 1944. Pp. 209–244. (Also as *Sociometry,* Volume 3, 1940, pp. 209–244.)

Number 7. Moreno, J. L. PSYCHODRAMATIC TREATMENT OF MARRIAGE PROBLEMS. 1945. 23 pp. (Also as *Sociometry*, Volume 3, 1940, pp. 1–23.)

Number 8. Moreno, J. L., and Florence B. Moreno. SPONTANEITY THEORY OF CHILD DEVELOPMENT. 1944. 48 pp. (Major part also as *Sociometry*, Volume 7, 1944, pp. 89–128.)

Number 9. Hendry, Charles E., Ronald Lippitt, and Alvin Zander. REALITY PRACTICE AS EDUCATIONAL METHOD, SOME PRINCIPLES AND APPLICATIONS. 1944. 36 pp. (Also as *Sociometry*, Volume 7, 1944, pp. 129–151 and 196–204.)

Number 10. Shoobs, Nahum E. PSYCHODRAMA IN THE SCHOOLS. 1944. 19 pp. (Also as *Sociometry*, Volume 7, 1944, pp. 152–168.)

Number 11. Moreno, J. L. PSYCHODRAMA AND THERAPEUTIC MOTION PICTURES. 1945. 22 pp. (Abridged as *Sociometry*, Volume 7, 1944, pp. 230–244.)

Number 12. Toeman, Zerka. ROLE ANALYSIS AND AUDIENCE STRUCTURE, WITH SPECIAL EMPHASIS ON PROBLEMS OF MILITARY ADJUSTMENT. 1944. 19 pp. (Also as *Sociometry*, Volume 7, 1944; pp. 205–221.)

Number 13. Moreno, J. L. A CASE OF PARANOIA TREATED THROUGH PSYCHODRAMA. 1945. 20 pp. (Also as *Sociometry*, Volume 7, 1944, pp. 312–327.)

Number 14. del Torto, John, and Paul Cornyetz. PSYCHODRAMA AS EXPRESSIVE AND PROJECTIVE TECHNIQUE. 1945. 22 pp. (Also as *Sociometry*, Volume 7, 1944, pp. 356–375.)

Number 15. Moreno, J. L. PSYCHODRAMATIC TREATMENT OF PSYCHOSES. 1945. 18 pp. (Also as *Sociometry*, Volume 3, 1940, pp. 115–132.)

Number 16. Moreno, J. L. PSYCHODRAMA AND THE PSYCHOPATHOLOGY OF INTER-PERSONAL RELATIONS. 1945. 68 pp. (Also titled as INTER-PERSONAL THERAPY AND THE PSYCHOPATHOLOGY OF INTER-PERSONAL RELATIONS, *Sociometry*, Volume 1, 1937, pp. 9–76.)

Number 17. Meiers, Joseph I. ORIGINS AND DEVELOPMENT OF GROUP PSYCHOTHERAPY; A HISTORICAL SURVEY, 1930–1945. 1946. 44 pp.

Number 18. Fantel, Ernest. PSYCHODRAMA IN AN EVACUATION HOSPITAL. 1946. 23 pp. (Also as part of *Sociometry*, Volume 8, 1945, pp. 363–383.)

Number 19. Pratt, Joseph H. THE GROUP METHOD IN THE TREATMENT OF PSYCHOSOMATIC DISORDERS. 1946. 10 pp. (Also as part of *Sociometry*, Volume 8, 1945, pp. 323–331.)

Number 20. Moreno, J. L. LIFE-SITUATION TEST. 1947. 11 pp. (Also as *Sociometry*, Volume 3, 1940, pp. 317–327.)

Number 21. Moreno, J. L. THE FUTURE OF MAN'S WORLD. 1947. 21 pp.

Number 22. Lippitt, Rosemary. PSYCHODRAMA IN THE HOME. 1947. 22 pp. (Also as *Sociatry*, Volume 1, 1947, pp. 148–167.)

Number 23. Moreno, J. L. OPEN LETTER TO GROUP PSYCHOTHERAPISTS; AN INTRODUCTION TO SOCIATRY. 1947. Pp. 7–30. (Also as *Sociatry*, Volume 1, 1947, pp. 7–30.)

Number 24. Macdonald, Margherita Anne. PSYCHODRAMA EXPLORES A PRIVATE WORLD. With comments by J. L. Moreno. 1947. 24 pp. (Also as *Sociatry*, Volume 1, 1947, pp. 97–118.)

Number 25. Haas, Robert B. ACTION COUNSELING AND PROCESS ANALYSIS; A PSYCHODRAMATIC APPROACH. 1948. 32 pp. (Also as part of *Sociatry*, Volume 1, 1947, pp. 256–332.)

Number 26. Herriott, Francis. PSYCHODRAMATIC DIAGNOSIS OF MENTAL PATIENTS. 1949. 16 pp. (Also titled as DIAGNOSTIC EXAMINATION OF MENTAL PATIENTS ON THE PSYCHODRAMATIC STAGE, *Sociometry*, Volume 3, 1940, pp. 383–398.)

Number 27. Moreno, J. L., and James M. Enneis. HYPNODRAMA AND PSYCHODRAMA. 1950. 56 pp. (Also as *Group Psychotherapy*, Volume 3, 1950, pp. 1–54.)

911. *Recent Progress in Psychiatry.* [Published under the auspices of the Royal Medicopsychological Association.]

TITLE VARIATIONS: None.

DATES OF PUBLICATION: Volume 1–2+, 1944–1950+.

FREQUENCY: Irregular.

NUMBERING VARIATIONS: Volume 1 issued as *Journal of Mental Science*, Volume 90, Number 1, January 1944.

PUBLISHER: **London:** Journal of Mental Science by J. & A. Churchill, 1944–1950+.

PRIMARY EDITORS: **G.W.T.H.** Fleming, 1944–1950+; **Alexander Walk,** 1944–1950+; **P. K. McCowan,** 1950+.

912. *Schriftenreihe zur Völkerpsychologie.*

TITLE VARIATIONS: None.

DATES OF PUBLICATION: Heft 1/2–3/4, 1944–1947.

FREQUENCY: Irregular. *See* Contents *below.*

NUMBERING VARIATIONS: None.

PUBLISHER: **Stuttgart:** Hippokrates Verlag, 1944–1947.

PRIMARY EDITOR: **Willy Hellpach,** 1944–1947.

CONTENTS:

Heft 1/2. Hellpach, Willy. VÖLKERENTWICKLUNG UND VÖLKERGESCHICHTE UNTERM WALTEN UND WIRKEN VON BINDENDEM GESETZ UND SCHÖPFERISCHER FREIHEIT IN VÖLKERSEELENLEBEN. 1944. 120 pp.

Heft 3/4. Hellpach, Willy. DAS MAGETHOS. 1947. 96 pp.

1945

913. *Akademiia pedagogicheskikh nauk RSFSR (Moscow). Izvestiia. Otdelenie psikhologii.*

TITLE VARIATIONS: None.

DATES OF PUBLICATION: Tom 1–40+, 1945–1950+.

FREQUENCY: Irregular.

NUMBERING VARIATIONS: None.

PUBLISHER: **Moscow:** Akademiia pedagogicheskikh nauk RSFSR, 1945–1950+.

PRIMARY EDITORS: Unknown.

NOTE: Information on this title was compiled from entries in *Gesamtverzeichnis russischer und sowjetischer Periodika und Serienwerke in Bibliotheken der Bundesrepublik Deutschland und West-Berlins.* Berlin, 1962. Band I.

914. *Bulletin of Industrial Psychology and Personnel Practice.*

TITLE VARIATIONS: Running titled *Industrial Psychology and Personnel Practice*, October 1945–1950+.

DATES OF PUBLICATION: Volume 1–5+, October 1945–1950+.

FREQUENCY: Quarterly.

NUMBERING VARIATIONS: None.

PUBLISHER: **Melbourne:** Industrial Welfare Division, Department of Labour and National Service, 1945–1949. **Melbourne:** Department of Labour and National Service, 1950+.

PRIMARY EDITORS: None listed.

915. *Egyptian Journal of Psychology.*

TITLE VARIATIONS: None.

DATES OF PUBLICATION: Volume 1–5+, June 1945–February 1950+.

FREQUENCY: Triannual.

NUMBERING VARIATIONS: None.

PUBLISHER: **Cairo, Egypt:** Society of Integrative Psychology, by Al Maaref Printing and Publishing House, 1945–1950+.

PRIMARY EDITORS: **Youssef Mourad,** 1945–1950+; **Mostapha Ziwer,** 1945–1950+.

916. *Harvard University. Psycho-acoustic Laboratory. Reports.*

TITLE VARIATIONS: None.

DATES OF PUBLICATION: Number 1–114+, October 1945–1950+.

FREQUENCY: Irregular. *See* Contents *below.*

NUMBERING VARIATIONS: Numbering is not perfectly chronological. Some titles are numbered in *Journal of the Acoustical Society of America* or other journals. *See* Contents *below.*

PUBLISHER: **Cambridge, Massachusetts:** Psycho-acoustic Laboratory, Harvard University, 1945–1950+. (Also various publishers. *See* Contents *below.*)

PRIMARY EDITORS: None listed.

CONTENTS:

Number 1. Forbes, T. W. AUDITORY SIGNALS FOR INSTRUMENT FLYING. (Also as *Journal of the Aeronautical Sciences,* Volume 13, 1946, pp. 255–258.)

Number 2. Wiener, F. M., and A. S. Filler. THE RESPONSE OF CERTAIN EARPHONES ON THE EAR AND ON CLOSED COUPLERS. 1 December 1945.

916. (*Continued*)

Number 3. Dienel, H. F. THE MEASUREMENT OF ACOUSTIC ATTENUATION CHARACTERISTICS OF SOUNDPROOFING MATERIALS. 11 January 1946.

Number 4. DiMattia, A. L., and F. M. Wiener. ON THE ABSOLUTE PRESSURE CALIBRATION OF CONDENSOR MICROPHONES BY THE RECIPROCITY METHOD. 10 December 1945. (Also as *Journal of the Acoustical Society of America,* Volume 18, 1946, pp. 341–344.)

Number 5. Wiener, F. M., D. A. Ross, and A. S. Filler. THE PRESSURE DISTRIBUTION IN THE AUDITORY CANAL IN A PROGRESSIVE SOUND FIELD. 1 December 1945. (Also as *Journal of the Acoustical Society of America,* Volume 18, 1946, pp. 401–408.)

Number 6. Beranek, L. L., et al. AUDIO CHARACTERISTICS OF COMMUNICATION EQUIPMENT. 1 February 1946.

Number 7. Davis, Hallowell, C. V. Hudgins, R. J. Marquis, R. H. Nichols, Jr., G. E. Peterson, D. A. Ross, and S. S. Stevens. THE SELECTION OF HEARING AIDS. 31 December 1945. (Also as *Laryngoscope,* Volume 56, 1946, pp. 85–115 and 135–163.)

Number 8. Mullin, C. J., and H. W. Rudmose. GENERATION OF RF NOISE BY MEANS OF SHORT PULSES. 28 October 1945.

Number 9. Licklider, J.C.R., and S. J. Goffard. THE PERFORMANCE OF COUNTER-MODULATION AND STATIC-CANCELLING CIRCUITS IN AIRCRAFT RADIO RECEIVER AN/APR–15.) 1 March 1946.

Number 10. Goffard, S. J., and J.C.R. Licklider. EFFECTS OF STATIC ON RADIO RANGE PERFORMANCE: LABORATORY TESTS OF THE IMPROVEMENT PROVIDED BY NOISE-REDUCING CIRCUITS. 21 March 1946.

Number 11. Gross, N. B., and J.C.R. Licklider. THE EFFECTS OF TILTING AND CLIPPING UPON THE INTELLIGIBILITY OF SPEECH. 15 April 1946.

Number 12. Shaw, W. A., and D. E. Yates. OBSERVATIONS ON METHODS OF MEASURING THE ACOUSTIC INSULATION OF EARPHONE SOCKETS. 1 August 1946.

Number 13. Wiener, F. M., and R. J. Marquis. NOISE LEVELS DUE TO AN AIRPLANE PASSING OVERHEAD. (Also as *Journal of the Acoustic Society of America,* Volume 18, 1946, pp. 450–452.)

Number 14. Stevens, S. S., Joseph Miller, and Ida Truscott. MASKING OF SPEECH BY SINE WAVES, SQUARE WAVES, AND REGULAR AND MODULATED PULSES. (Also as *Journal of the Acoustical Society of America,* Volume 18, 1946, pp. 418–424.)

Number 15. Cunningham, W. J., S. J. Goffard, and J.C.R. Licklider. THE INFLUENCE OF AMPLITUDE LIMITING AND FREQUENCY SELECTIVITY UPON THE PERFORMANCE OF RADIO RECEIVERS IN NOISE. (Also as *Proceedings of the Institute of Radio Engineers,* Volume 35, 1947, pp. 1021–1025.)

Number 16. Kryter, K. D., J.C.R. Licklider, and S. S. Stevens. PREMODULATION CLIPPING IN AM VOICE COMMUNICATION. (Also as *Journal of the Acoustical Society of America,* Volume 19, 1947, pp. 125–131.)

Number 17. Miller, G. A., and Shirley Mitchell. EFFECTS OF DISTORTION

Year 1945

ON THE INTELLIGIBILITY OF SPEECH AT HIGH ALTITUDES. (Also as *Journal of the Acoustical Society of America*, Volume 19, 1947, pp. 120–125.)

Number 18. Egan, J. P., and F. M. Wiener. ON THE INTELLIGIBILITY OF BANDS OF SPEECH IN NOISE. (Also as *Journal of the Acoustical Society of America*, Volume 18, 1946, pp. 435–441.

Number 19. Licklider, J.C.R. EFFECTS OF AMPLITUDE DISTORTION UPON THE INTELLIGIBILITY OF SPEECH. (Also as *Journal of the Acoustical Society of America*, Volume 18, 1946, pp. 429–434.)

Number 20. Davis, Hallowell, S. S. Stevens, R. H. Nichols, Jr., C. V. Hudgins, R. J. Marquis, G. E. Peterson, and D. A. Ross. HEARING AIDS: AN EXPERIMENTAL STUDY OF DESIGN OBJECTIVES. Cambridge: Harvard University Press, 1947. 197 pp.

Number 21. Kryter, K. D. EFFECTS OF EAR PROTECTIVE DEVICES ON THE INTELLIGIBILITY OF SPEECH IN NOISE. (Also as *Journal of the Acoustical Society of America*, Volume 18, 1946, pp. 413–417.)

Number 22. Shaw, W. A., E. B. Newman, and I. J. Hirsch. THE DIFFERENCE BETWEEN MONAURAL AND BINAURAL THRESHOLDS. (Also as *Journal of Experimental Psychology*. Volume 37, 1947, pp. 229–242.)

Number 23. Miller, G. A. THE MASKING OF SPEECH. (Also as *Psychological Bulletin*, Volume 44, 1947, pp. 105–129.)

Number 24. Wiener, F. M. SPECIFICATIONS FOR A STANDARD PRESSURE MICROPHONE. 1 February 1947.

Number 25. Wiener, F. M. SOUND DIFFRACTION BY RIGID SPHERES AND CIRCULAR CYLINDERS. (Also as *Journal of the Acoustical Society of America*, Volume 19, 1947, pp. 444–451.)

Number 26. Hudgins, C. V., J. E. Hawkins, J. E. Karlin, and S. S. Stevens. DEVELOPMENT OF RECORDED AUDITORY TESTS FOR MEASURING HEARING LOSS FOR SPEECH. (Also as *Laryngoscope*, Volume 57, 1947, pp. 57–89.)

Number 27. Hudgins, C. V., R. J. Marquis, R. H. Nichols, Jr., G. E. Peterson, and D. A. Ross. THE COMPARATIVE PERFORMANCE OF AN EXPERIMENTAL HEARING AID AND TWO COMMERCIAL INSTRUMENTS. (Also as *Journal of the Acoustical Society of America*, Volume 20, 1948, pp. 241–258.)

Number 28. Miller, G. A. SENSITIVITY TO CHANGES IN INTENSITY OF WHITE NOISE AND ITS RELATION TO MASKING AND LOUDNESS. (Also as *Journal of the Acoustical Society of America*, Volume 19, 1947, pp. 609–619.)

Number 29. Licklider, J.C.R., and E. B. Newman. STATIC FOR RADIO RECEIVER TESTS. (Also as *Electronics*, Volume 20, June 1947, pp. 98–101.)

Number 30. Wiener, F. M. ON THE DIFFRACTION OF A PROGRESSIVE SOUND WAVE BY THE HUMAN HEAD. (Also as *Journal of the Acoustical Society of America*, Volume 19, 1947, pp. 143–146.)

Number 31. Brogden, W. J., and G. A. Miller. PHYSIOLOGICAL NOISE GENERATED UNDER EARPHONE CONDITIONS. (Also as *Journal of the Acoustical Society of America*, Volume 19, 1947, pp. 620–623).

Number 32. Licklider, J.C.R., and S. J. Gofford. EFFECTS OF IMPULSIVE INTERFERENCE UPON AM VOICE COMMUNICATION. (Also as *Journal of the Acoustical Society of America*, Volume 19, 1947, pp. 653–663.)

916. *(Continued)*

Number 33. Goffard, S. J., and J. P. Egan. PROCEDURES FOR MEASURING THE INTELLIGIBILITY OF SPEECH: SOUND-POWERED TELEPHONE SYSTEMS. 1 February 1947.

Number 34. Miller, G. A., F. M. Wiener, and S. S. Stevens. TRANSMISSION AND RECEPTION OF SOUNDS UNDER COMBAT CONDITIONS. SUMMARY TECHNICAL REPORT OF NDRC DIVISION 17, SECTION 17–3, VOLUME 17–3. Washington, D.C., 1947. 396 pp.

Number 35. Nichols, R. H., Jr., R. J. Marquis, W. G. Wiklund, A. S. Filler, C. V. Hudgins, and G. E. Peterson. THE INFLUENCE OF BODY-BAFFLE EFFECTS ON THE PERFORMANCE OF HEARING AIDS. (Also as *Journal of the Acoustical Society of America*, Volume 19, 1947, pp. 943–951.)

Number 36. Egan, J. P. ARTICULATION TESTING METHODS. (Also in *Laryngoscope*, Volume 58, 1948, pp. 955–991.)

Number 37. Licklider, J.C.R., Dalbir Bindra, and Irwin Pollack. THE INTELLIGIBILITY OF RECTANGULAR SPEECH WAVES. (Also as *American Journal of Psychology*, Volume 61, 1948, pp. 1–20.)

Number 38. Egan, J. P. THE EFFECT OF NOISE IN ONE EAR UPON THE LOUDNESS OF SPEECH IN THE OTHER EAR. (Also as *Journal of the Acoustical Society of America*, Volume 20, 1948, pp. 58–62.)

Number 39. Rosenblith, W. A., G. A. Miller, J. P. Egan, I. J. Hirsch, and G. J. Thomas. AN AUDITORY AFTERIMAGE? (Also as *Science*, Volume 106, 1947, pp. 333–334.)

Number 40. Stevens, S. S., J. P. Egan, and G. A. Miller. METHODS OF MEASURING SPEECH SPECTRA. (Also as *Journal of the Acoustical Society of America*, Volume 19, 1947, pp. 741–780.)

Number 41. Pollack, Irwin. THE ATONAL INTERVAL. (Also as *Journal of the Acoustical Society of America*, Volume 20, 1948, pp. 146–149.)

Number 42. Miller, G. A. THE PERCEPTION OF SHORT BURSTS OF NOISE. (Also as *Journal of the Acoustical Society of America*, Volume 20, 1948, pp. 160–170.)

Number 43. Miller, G. A., and W. G. Taylor. THE PERCEPTION OF REPEATED BURSTS OF NOISE. (Also as *Journal of the Acoustical Society of America*, Volume 20, 1948, pp. 171–182.)

Number 44. Licklider, J.C.R., and Irwin Pollack. EFFECTS OF DIFFERENTIATION, INTEGRATION, AND INFINITE PEAK CLIPPING UPON THE INTELLIGIBILITY OF SPEECH. (Also as *Journal of the Acoustical Society of America*, Volume 20, 1948, pp. 42–51.)

Number 45. Miller, G. A., and W. R. Garner. THE MASKING OF TONES BY REPEATED BURSTS OF NOISE. (Also as *Journal of the Acoustical Society of America*, Volume 20, 1948, pp. 691–696.)

Number 46. Pollack, Irwin. MONAURAL AND BINAURAL THRESHOLD SENSITIVITY FOR TONES AND FOR WHITE NOISE. (Also as *Journal of the Acoustical Society of America*, Volume 20, 1948, pp. 52–57.)

Number 47. Hirsch, I. J. BINAURAL SUMMATION AND INTERAURAL INHIBITION AS A FUNCTION OF THE LEVEL OF MASKING NOISE. (Also as *American Journal of Psychology*, Volume 61, 1948, pp. 205–213.)

Number 48. Pollack, Irwin. EFFECTS OF HIGH-PASS AND LOW-PASS FIL-TERING ON THE INTELLIGIBILITY OF SPEECH IN NOISE. (Also as *Journal of the Acoustical Society of America*, Volume 20, 1948, pp. 259–266.)

Number 49. Licklider, J.C.R., and E. Dzendolet. OSCILLOGRAPHIC SCAT-TERPLOTS ILLUSTRATING VARIOUS DEGREES OF CORRELATION. (Also as *Science*, Volume 107, 1948, pp. 121–124.)

Number 50. Miller, G. A., and J.C.R. Licklider. THE INTELLIGIBILITY OF INTERRUPTED SPEECH. (Also as *Journal of the Acoustical Society of America*, Volume 22, 1950, pp. 167–173.)

Number 51. Hirsch, I. J. THE INFLUENCE OF INTERAURAL PHASE ON IN-TERAURAL SUMMATION AND INHIBITION. (Also as *Journal of the Acoustical Society of America*, Volume 20, 1948, pp. 536–544.)

Number 52. Licklider, J.C.R. THE INFLUENCE OF INTERAURAL PHASE RE-LATIONS UPON THE MASKING OF SPEECH BY WHITE NOISE. (Also as *Journal of the Acoustical Society of America*, Volume 20, 1948, pp. 150–159.)

Number 53. Hirsch, I. J. BINAURAL SUMMATION—A CENTURY OF INVES-TIGATION. (Also as *Psychological Bulletin*, Volume 45, 1948, pp. 193–206.)

Number 54. Wiener, F. M. NOTES ON SOUND DIFFRACTION BY RIGID CIR-CULAR CONES. (Also as *Journal of the Acoustical Society of America*, Volume 20, 1948, pp. 367–369.)

Number 55. Békésy, G. von, and W. A. Rosenblith. THE EARLY HISTORY OF HEARING—OBSERVATIONS AND THEORIES. (Also as *Journal of the Acoustical Society of America*, Volume 20, 1948, pp. 727–748.)

Number 56. Békésy, G. von. VIBRATION OF THE HEAD IN A SOUND FIELD AND ITS ROLE IN HEARING BY BONE CONDUCTION. (Also as *Journal of the Acoustical Society of America*, Volume 20, 1948, pp. 747–760.)

Number 57. Pollack, Irwin. LOUDNESS AS A DISCRIMINABLE ASPECT OF BANDS OF NOISE. (Also as *American Journal of Psychology*, Volume 62, 1949, pp. 285–289.)

Number 58. Hirsch, I. J., and Irwin Pollack. THE ROLE OF INTERAURAL PHASE IN LOUDNESS. (Also as *Journal of the Acoustical Society of America*, Volume 20, 1948, pp. 761–766.)

Number 59. Pollack, Irwin. SPECIFICATION OF SOUND-PRESSURE LEVELS. (Also as *American Journal of Psychology*, Volume 62, 1949, pp. 412–417.)

Number 60. Pollack, Irwin. THE EFFECT OF WHITE NOISE ON THE LOUD-NESS OF SPEECH OF ASSIGNED AVERAGE LEVEL. (Also as *Journal of the Acoustical Society of America*, Volume 21, 1949, pp. 255–258.)

Number 61. Galambos, Robert, and Hallowell Davis. ACTION POTENTIALS FROM SINGLE AUDITORY-NERVE FIBERS? (Also as *Science*, Volume 108, 1948, p. 513.)

Number 62. Thomas, G. J. EQUAL VOLUME JUDGMENTS OF TONES. (Also as *American Journal of Psychology*, Volume 62, 1949, pp. 182–201.)

Number 63. Békésy, G. von. THE STRUCTURE OF THE MIDDLE EAR AND THE HEARING OF ONE'S OWN VOICE BY BONE CONDUCTION. (Also as *Journal of the Acoustical Society of America*, Volume 21, 1949, pp. 217–232.)

Number 64. Békésy, G. von. THE VIBRATION OF THE COCHLEAR PARTITION IN ANATOMICAL PREPARATIONS AND IN MODELS OF THE INNER EAR. (Also as

916. *(Continued)*

Akustische Zeitschrift, Volume 7, 1942, pp. 173–186; and in *Journal of the Acoustical Society of America,* Volume 21, 1949, pp. 233–245.)

Number 65. Licklider, J.C.R., and J. C. Webster. THE DISCRIMINABILITY OF INTERAURAL PHASE RELATIONS IN TWO-COMPONENT TONES. (Also as *Journal of the Acoustical Society of America,* Volume 22, 1950, pp. 191–195.)

Number 66. Békésy, G. von. ON THE RESONANCE CURVE AND THE DECAY PERIOD AT VARIOUS POINTS ON THE COCHLEAR PARTITION. (Also as *Akustische Zeitschrift,* Volume 8, 1943, pp. 66–76; and in *Journal of the Acoustical Society of America,* Volume 21, 1949, pp. 245–254.)

Number 67. Hirsch, I. J. THE RELATION BETWEEN LOCALIZATION AND INTELLIGIBILITY. (Also as *Journal of the Acoustical Society of America,* Volume 22, 1950, pp. 196–200.)

Number 68. Hirsch, I. J., and F. A. Webster. SOME DETERMINANTS OF INTERAURAL PHASE EFFECTS. (Also as *Journal of the Acoustical Society of America,* Volume 21, 1949, pp. 496–501.)

Number 69. Wallach, Hanz, E. B. Newman, and M. R. Rosenzweig. THE PRECEDENCE EFFECT IN SOUND LOCALIZATION. (Also as *American Journal of Psychology,* Volume 62, 1949, pp. 315–336.)

Number 70. Békésy, G. von. THE MOON ILLUSION AND SIMILAR AUDITORY PHENOMENA. (Also as *American Journal of Psychology,* Volume 62, 1949, pp. 540–552.)

Number 71. Howes, D. H. THE LOUDNESS OF MULTICOMPONENT TONES. (Also as *American Journal of Psychology,* Volume 63, 1950, pp. 1–30.)

Number 72. Smith, M. H., and J.C.R. Licklider. STATISTICAL BIAS IN COMPARISONS OF MONAURAL AND BINAURAL THRESHOLDS: BINAURAL SUMMATION OR BINAURAL SUPPLEMENTATION. (Also as *Psychological Bulletin,* Volume 46, 1949, pp. 278–284.)

Number 73. Hawkins, J. E., Jr., and S. S. Stevens. THE MASKING OF PURE TONES AND OF SPEECH BY WHITE NOISE. (Also as *Journal of the Acoustical Society of America,* Volume 22, 1950, pp. 6–13.)

Number 74. Miller, G. A., G. A. Heise, and William Lichten. THE INTELLIGIBILITY OF SPEECH AS A FUNCTION OF THE CONTEXT OF THE TEST MATERIALS. (Also as *Journal of Experimental Psychology,* Volume 41, 1951, pp. 329–335.)

Number 75. Békésy, G. von. AN INTERCHANGEABLE PENCIL-TYPE MICRO-MANIPULATOR. (Also as *Science,* Volume 111, 1950, pp. 667–669.)

Number 76. Stevens, S. S. MATHEMATICS, MEASUREMENT, AND PSYCHOPHYSICS. (Also as Chapter 1, *Handbook of Experimental Psychology.* New York: Wiley, 1951, pp. 1–49.

Number 77. Miller, G. A. SPEECH AND LANGUAGE (Also as Chapter 21, *Handbook of Experimental Psychology.* New York: Wiley, 1951, pp. 789–810.)

Number 78. Licklider, J.C.R., BASIC CORRELATES OF THE AUDITORY STIMULUS. (Also as Chapter 25, *Handbook of Experimental Psychology.* New York: Wiley, 1951, pp. 985–1039.)

Number 79. Licklider, J.C.R., and G. A. Miller. THE PERCEPTION OF

SPEECH. (Also as Chapter 26, *Handbook of Experimental Psychology.* New York: Wiley, 1951, pp. 1040–1074.)

Number 80. Békésy, G. von, and W. A. Rosenblith. THE MECHANICAL PROPERTIES OF THE EAR. (Also as Chapter 27, *Handbook of Experimental Psychology.* New York: Wiley, 1951, pp. 1075–1115.)

Number 81. Kahana, Lawrence, W. A. Rosenblith, and Robert Galambos. EFFECT OF TEMPERATURE CHANGE ON THE ROUND WINDOW RESPONSE IN THE HAMSTER. (Also as *American Journal of Physiology,* Volume 163, 1950, pp. 213–223.)

Number 82. Békésy, G. von. SUGGESTIONS FOR DETERMINING THE MOBILITY OF THE STAPES BY MEANS OF AN ENDOTOSCOPE FOR THE MIDDLE EAR. (Also as *Laryngoscope,* Volume 60, 1950, pp. 97–110.)

Number 83. Rosenblith, W. A., Robert Galambos, and I. J. Hirsh. THE EFFECT OF EXPOSURE TO LOUD TONES UPON ANIMAL AND HUMAN RESPONSES TO ACOUSTIC CLICKS. (Also as *Science,* Volume 111, 1950, pp. 569–571.)

Number 84. Hirsh, I. J. BINAURAL HEARING AIDS. (Also as *Journal of Speech and Hearing Disorders,* Volume 15, 1950, pp. 114–123.)

Number 85. Thomas, G. J. VOLUME AND LOUDNESS OF NOISE. (Also as *American Journal of Psychology,* Volume 60, 1952, pp. 588–593.)

Number 86. Licklider, J.C.R. A GRIDLESS, WIRELESS RAT-SHOCKER. (Also as *Journal of Comparative and Physiological Psychology,* Volume 44, 1951, pp. 334–337.)

Number 87. Licklider, J.C.R., J. C. Webster, and J. M. Hedlun. ON THE FREQUENCY LIMITS OF BINAURAL BEATS. (Also as *Journal of the Acoustical Society of America,* Volume 22, 1950, pp. 468–473.)

Number 88. Miller, G. A., W. A. Rosenblith, Robert Galambos, I. J. Hirsh, and Shirley K. Hirsh. A BIBLIOGRAPHY IN AUDITION. Cambridge: Harvard University Press, 1950. 2 Volumes.

Number 89. Webster, F. A. INFLUENCE OF INTERAURAL PHASE RELATIONS ON MASKED THRESHOLDS: I. THE ROLE OF INTERAURAL TIME DEVIATION. (Also as *Journal of the Acoustical Society of America,* Volume 23, 1951, pp. 452–462.)

Number 90. Webster, F. A. INFLUENCE OF INTERAURAL PHASE RELATIONS ON MASKED THRESHOLDS: II. MASKING TONES, PULSES, AND NARROW-BAND NOISE. 1951.

Number 91. Miller, G. A., and G. A. Heise. THE THRILL THRESHOLD. (Also as *Journal of the Acoustical Society of America,* Volume 22, 1950, pp. 637–638.)

Number 92. Heise, G. A., and G. A. Miller. AN EXPERIMENTAL STUDY OF AUDITORY PATTERNS. (Also as *American Journal of Psychology,* Volume 64, 1951, pp. 68–77.

Number 93. Heise, G. A., and G. A. Miller. PROBLEM SOLVING BY SMALL GROUPS USING VARIOUS COMMUNICATION NETS. (Also as *Journal of Abnormal and Social Psychology,* Volume 46, 1951, pp. 327–335.)

Number 94. Newman, E. B. COMPUTATIONAL METHODS USEFUL IN ANALYZING SERIES OF BINARY DATA. (Also as *American Journal of Psychology,* Volume 64, 1951, pp. 252–262.)

Number 95. Hirsh, I. J., W. A. Rosenblith, and W. D. Ward. MASKING

916. *(Continued)*

OF CLICKS BY TONES AND BANDS OF NOISE. (Also as *Journal of the Acoustical Society of America*, Volume 22, 1950, pp. 631–637.)

Number 96. Williams, C. M., and Robert Galambos. OSCILLOSCOPIC AND STROBOSCOPIC ANALYSIS OF THE FLIGHT SOUNDS OF DROSOPHILA. (Also as *Biological Bulletin*, Volume 99, 1950, pp. 300–307.)

Number 97. Galambos, Robert, W. A. Rosenblith, and M. R. Rosenzweig. PHYSIOLOGICAL EVIDENCE FOR A COCHLEO-COCHLEAR PATHWAY IN THE CAT. (Also as *Experientia*, Volume 6, 1950, pp. 438–440.)

Number 98. Licklider, J.C.R. THE INTELLIGIBILITY OF AMPLITUDE-DICHOTOMIZED, TIME-QUANTIZED SPEECH WAVES. (Also as *Journal of the Acoustical Society of America*, Volume 22, 1950, pp. 820–823.)

Number 99. Miller, G. A. LANGUAGE ENGINEERING. (Also as *Journal of the Acoustical Society of America*, Volume 22, 1950, pp. 720–725.)

Number 100. Miller, G. A. LANGUAGE AND COMMUNICATION. New York: McGraw-Hill, 1951. 298 pp.

Number 101. Galambos, Robert. NEUROPHYSIOLOGY OF THE AUDITORY SYSTEM. (Also as *Journal of the Acoustical Society of America*, Volume 22, 1950, pp. 785–791.)

Number 102. Rosenblith, W. A. AUDITORY MASKING AND FATIGUE. (Also as *Journal of the Acoustical Society of America*, Volume 22, 1950, pp. 792–800.)

Number 103. Rosenzweig, M. R., and W. A. Rosenblith. SOME ELECTRO-PHYSIOLOGICAL CORRELATES OF THE PERCEPTION OF SUCCESSIVE CLICKS. (Also as *Journal of the Acoustical Society of America*, Volume 22, 1950, pp. 878–880.)

Number 104. Békésy, G. von. MICROPHONICS PRODUCED BY TOUCHING THE COCHLEAR PARTITION WITH A VIBRATING ELECTRODE. (Also as *Journal of the Acoustical Society of America*, Volume 23, 1951, pp. 29–35.)

Number 105. Békésy, G. von. THE COARSE PATTERN OF THE ELECTRICAL RESISTANCE IN THE COCHLEA OF THE GUINEA PIG (ELECTROANATOMY OF THE COCHLEA). (Also as *Journal of the Acoustical Society of America*, Volume 23, 1951, pp. 18–28.)

Number 106. Miller, G. A. RELATION BETWEEN AUTOCORRELATION FUNCTION AND TRANSITIONAL PROBABILITIES FOR BINARY DATA. 15 November 1950.

Number 107. McGill, W. J., and W. A. Rosenblith. ELECTRICAL RESPONSES TO TWO CLICKS: A SIMPLE STATISTICAL INTERPRETATION. (Also as *Bulletin of Mathematical Biophysics*, Volume 13, 1951, pp. 69–77.)

Number 108. Békésy, G. von. MICROMANIPULATOR WITH INCREASED MOBILITY. (Also as *Transactions of the American Microscopical Society*, Volume 71, 1952, pp. 306–310.)

Number 109. Newman, E. B. The Pattern of Vowels and Consonants in Various Languages. (Also as *American Journal of Psychology*, Volume 64, 1951, pp. 369–379.)

Number 110. Rose, J. E., and Robert Galambos. MICROELECTRODE STUDIES ON THE MEDIAL GENICULATE BODY OF THE CAT: I. THE THALAMIC REGION ACTIVATED BY CLICK STIMULI AND THE SIGNIFICANCE OF THE MORPHOLOGICAL SUBSTRATE FOR THE PATTERN OF ELECTRICAL RESPONSE. (Also as *Journal of Neurophysiology*, Volume 15, 1952, pp. 343–357.)

Number 111. Galambos, Robert, J. E. Rose, R. B. Bromiley, and J. R. Hughes. MICROELECTRODE STUDIES ON THE MEDIAL GENICULATE BODY OF THE CAT: II. THE RESPONSE TO CLICKS. (Also as *Journal of Neurophysiology,* Volume 15, 1952, pp. 359–380.)

Number 112. Galambos, Robert, and J. E. Rose. MICROELECTRODE STUDIES ON THE MEDIAL GENICULATE BODY OF THE CAT: III. THE RESPONSE TO PURE TONES. (Also as *Journal of Neurophysiology,* Volume 15, 1952, pp. 381–400.)

Number 113. McGill, W. J., and W. A. Rosenblith. A GENERALIZED RECOVERY CURVE FOR NEURAL RESPONSES TO PAIRS OF CLICKS. [1950?].

Number 114. Békésy, G. von. D-C POTENTIALS AND ENERGY BALANCE OF THE COCHLEAR PARTITION. (Also as *Journal of the Acoustical Society of America,* Volume 22, 1950, pp. 576–582.)

917. *Hverdagens Psykologi.*

TITLE VARIATIONS: Also cited as *Statsradiofoniens Studiekredse.*

DATES OF PUBLICATION: Nummer 1–2, 1945.

FREQUENCY: Irregular. *See* Contents *below.*

NUMBERING VARIATIONS: None.

PUBLISHER: **Copenhagen:** Statsradiofonien, 1945.

PRIMARY EDITORS: None listed.

CONTENTS:

Nummer 1. DE MENNESKELIGE TEMPERAMENTER. 1945. 12 pp.
Nummer 2. HVAD VI VED OM HINANDEN. 1945. 8 pp.

918. *Journal of Clinical Psychology.*

TITLE VARIATIONS: None.

DATES OF PUBLICATION: Volume 1–6+, 1945–1950+.

FREQUENCY: Quarterly.

NUMBERING VARIATIONS: None.

PUBLISHER: **Burlington, Vermont:** University of Vermont, Medical College Building, 1945–1949. **Brandon, Vermont:** Journal of Clinical Psychology, 1950+.

PRIMARY EDITOR: **Frederick C. Thorne,** 1945–1950 | .

EDITORIAL BOARD: Jerry W. Carter, Jr., 1945–1950+; Samuel W. Hamilton, 1945–1950+; William A. Hunt, 1945–1950+; George A. Kelly, 1945–1949; Elaine F. Kinder, 1945–1950+; C. M. Louttit, 1945–1950+; Robert R. Sears, 1945–1947; Robert I. Watson, 1948–1950+.

919. *Journal of Clinical Psychopathology. Monograph Series.*

TITLE VARIATIONS: None.

DATES OF PUBLICATION: Number 1, 1945.

FREQUENCY: Irregular. *See* Contents *below.*

NUMBERING VARIATIONS: None.

PUBLISHER: **Monticello, New York:** Medical Journal Press, 1945.

PRIMARY EDITOR: **V. C. Branham,** 1945.

CONTENTS:

 Number 1. Róheim, Géza. WAR, CRIME AND THE COVENANT. With an Introduction by A. A. Brill. 1945. 160 pp.

920. *Journal of Personality.*

TITLE VARIATIONS: Continues *Character and Personality.*

DATES OF PUBLICATION: Volume 14–18+, September 1945–June 1950+.

FREQUENCY: Quarterly.

NUMBERING VARIATIONS: None.

PUBLISHER: **Durham, North Carolina:** Duke University Press, 1945–1950+.

PRIMARY EDITOR: **Karl Zener,** 1945–1950+.

EDITORIAL BOARD: Gordon W. Allport, 1945–1950+; P. B. Ballard, 1945–1948; F. C. Bartlett, 1945–1948; Ruth Benedict, 1945–1948; Walter V. Bingham, 1945–1948; Manfred Bleuler, 1945–1948; Warner Brown, 1945–1948; Oluf Brüel, 1945–1948; Charlotte Bühler, 1945–1948; Karl Bühler, 1945–1948; Cyril L. Burt, 1945–1948; Raymond B. Cattell, 1945–1948; Édouard Claparède, 1945–1948; James Drever, 1945–1948; John C. Flugel, 1945–1948; John Gillin, 1945–1950+; Karl J. Holzinger, 1945–1948; Pryns Hopkins, 1945–1948; Charles W. Kimmins, 1945–1948; Ernst Kretschmer, 1945–1948; Johannes Lange, 1945–1948; William Line, 1945–1948; Helge Lundholm, 1945–1950+; D. R. MacCalman, 1945–1948; Donald W. MacKinnon, 1945–1950+; Jan Meloun, 1945–1948; Thomas V. Moore, 1945–1948; Charles S. Myers, 1945–1948; T. H. Pear, 1945–1948; Henri Piéron, 1945–1948; Martin L. Reymert, 1945–1948; A. A. Roback, 1945–1948; Constance A. Simmins, 1945–1948; William Stephenson, 1945–1948; Lewis M. Terman, 1945–1948; Edward L. Thorndike, 1945–1948; Robert H. Thouless, 1945–1948; Louis L. Thurstone, 1945–1948; Emil Utitz, 1945–1948; Philip E. Vernon, 1945–1948; D. Wiersma, 1945–1948; E. H. Wild, 1945–1948; L. Wynn-Jones, 1945–1948; Karl Zener, 1948–1950+; Merton Gill, 1948–1950+; Donald O. Hebb, 1948–1950+; David Krech, 1948–1950+; George F. J. Lehner, 1948–1950+; Leo Postman, 1948–1950+; Robert R. Sears, 1948–1950+; David Shakow, 1948–1950+; Joseph Zubin, 1948–1950+

921. *Journal of Social Issues.*

TITLE VARIATIONS: Supersedes *Society for the Psychological Study of Social Issues. Bulletin.*

DATES OF PUBLICATION: Volume 1–6+, 1945–1950+.

FREQUENCY: Quarterly.

NUMBERING VARIATIONS: None.

PUBLISHER: **New York:** Published for the Society for the Psychological Study of Social Issues by Association Press, 1945. (Issue 1). **New York:** Published by the Society for the Psychological Study of Social Issues, Affiliated with the American Psychological Association, 1945. (Issues 2 and 3.) **New York:** Published by the Society for the Psychological Study of Social Issues, A Division of the American Psychological Association, 1945–1950+.

PRIMARY EDITORS: **Ronald Lippitt,** 1945–1950+; **Harold H. Kelley,** 1949.

EXECUTIVE EDITORIAL COMMITTEE: Ronald Lippitt, 1945–1950+; Violet Edwards, 1945–1946; Russell Hogrefe, 1945–1946; Daniel Katz, 1945–1946; Lillian Kay, 1945–1946; Arthur Kornhauser, 1945–1946; Abe Maslow, 1945–1946; Claire Selltiz, 1945–1946; Ruth Valentine, 1945–1946; Goodwin Watson, 1945–1946; Gene Weltfish, 1945–1946; Alvin Zander, 1945–1946; Gordon Allport, 1947–1948; Thelma Alper, 1947–1948; Robert F. Bales, 1947–1948; Jerome Bruner, 1947–1948; Robert Chin, 1947–1948; Mason Haire, 1947–1948; Florence Kluckhohn, 1947–1948; Brewster Smith, 1947–1948; Robert Angell, 1949–1950; Roger Heyns, 1949–1950; Max Hutt, 1949–1950; George Katona, 1949–1950; Harold Kelley, 1949–1950; Jacob Kounin, 1949–1950; Alfred Lee, 1949–1950; Eleanor Maccoby, 1949–1950; Norman R. F. Maier, 1949–1950; Horace Miner, 1949–1950; Theodore Newcomb, 1949–1950.

ADVISORY EDITORIAL BOARD: Roger Barker, 1945–1949; Ruth Benedict, 1945–1948; Merl E. Bonney, 1945–1949; Tamara Dembo, 1945–1949; Franklin Fearing, 1945–1949; John R. P. French, Jr., 1945–1949; Lucien Hanks, Jr., 1945–1949; Robert Leeper, 1945–1949; Fritz Redl, 1945–1949; Robert F. Bales, 1949–1950; Melvin W. Barnes, 1949–1950; Urie Bronfenbrenner, 1949–1950; Isidor Chein, 1949–1950; Fred Covey, 1949–1950; Kermit Eby, 1949–1950; James H. Elder, 1949–1950; Lawrence K. Hall, 1949–1950; Robert F. Holt, 1949–1950; Lloyd G. Humphreys, 1949–1950; David Krech, 1949–1950; Robert K. Merton, 1949–1950; Herbert A. Thelen, 1949–1950; Ruth S. Tolman, 1949–1950; Ralph K. White, 1949–1950.

NOTE: Each issue of this publication has a special editor or editors appropriate to the subject under discussion.

922. *Massachusetts Institute of Technology. Research Center for Group Dynamics. Publication(s).*

TITLE VARIATIONS: Superseded in 1951 by *Michigan. University. Research Center for Group Dynamics. Publication(s).*

DATES OF PUBLICATION: Number 1–3, 1945–1946.

FREQUENCY: Irregular. *See* Contents *below.*

NUMBERING VARIATIONS: All issues were reprinted from various other journals. *See* Contents *below.*

PUBLISHER: **Cambridge, Massachusetts:** Massachusetts Institute of Technology. Research Center for Group Dynamics, 1945–1946.

PRIMARY EDITORS: None listed.

CONTENTS:

Number 1. Lewin, Kurt. THE RESEARCH CENTER FOR GROUP DYNAMICS AT MASSACHUSETTS INSTITUTE OF TECHNOLOGY. (Also as *Sociometry*, Volume 8, Number 2, 1945, pp. 126–136.)

Number 2. Festinger, Leon. THE SIGNIFICANCE OF DIFFERENCE BETWEEN MEANS WITHOUT REFERENCE TO THE FREQUENCY DISTRIBUTION FUNCTION. (Also as *Psychometrika*, Volume 11, Number 2, June 1946, pp. 97–105.)

Number 3. Lewin, Kurt, Paul Crabbe, Ronald Lippitt, and Marian Radke. CHANGING BEHAVIOR AND ATTITUDES. (Also under different titles as *Journal of Social Issues*, December 1945, pp. 1–12; and *Annals of the American Academy of Political and Social Science*, March 1946, pp. 167–176.)

923. *Mexico City. Instituto científico de la opinión pública mexicana. Problemas y resultados de las investigaciones de la opinión pública. Monografías.*

TITLE VARIATIONS: Institute is also called Instituto de estudios de psicología social y opinión pública; Institute for Studies in Social Psychology and Public Opinion; and Scientific Institute of Mexican Public Opinion.

DATES OF PUBLICATION: Número 1–3, 1945–[1946?].

FREQUENCY: Irregular. *See* Contents *below.*

NUMBERING VARIATIONS: Número 4–9 were announced but apparently never published.

PUBLISHER: **Mexico City:** Instituto científico de la opinión pública mexicana, 1945–[1946?].

PRIMARY EDITOR: **Laszlo Radvanyi,** 1945–[1946?].

CONTENTS:

Número 1. Radvanyi, Laszlo. PUBLIC OPINION MEASUREMENT. A SURVEY. 1945. 88 pp.

Número 2. Field, Harry. MIDIENDO LA OPINIÓN PÚBLICA. [1946.] 56 pp.

Número 3. Roper, Elmo. TÉCNICA Y RESULTADOS DE ENCUESTAS DE LA OPINION. [1946?] 48 pp.

924. *Monografías de psicología normal y patológica.*

TITLE VARIATIONS: None.

DATES OF PUBLICATION: Número 1–6+, 1945–1947+. Número 7+ apparently published after 1950.

FREQUENCY: Irregular. *See* Contents *below.*

NUMBERING VARIATIONS: None.

PUBLISHER: **Madrid:** Espasa-Calpe S. A., 1945–1947+.

PRIMARY EDITORS: **José Germain,** 1945–1947+; **José M. Sacristan,** 1945–1947+.

CONTENTS:

Número 1. Katz, David. Psicología de la forma (Gestaltpsycholo-gie). Translated by José M. Sacristan. 1945. 125 pp.

Número 2. Müller, Johannes. Los fenómenos fantásticos de la visión. 1946. 104 pp.

Número 3. Mallart y Cutó, José. Orientación funcional y formación profesional. 1946. 176 pp.

Número 4. Jacobi, Jolande. La psicología de C. G. Jung. 1947. 212 pp.

Número 5. Adrian, E. D. La base de la sensación. 1947. 110 pp.

Número 6. Katz, David. Animales y hombres. 1947. 261 pp.

925. *Occasional Papers on Eugenics.*

TITLE VARIATIONS: Also called *Eugenics Society. Occasional Papers on Eugenics* and *Eugenics Education Society. Occasional papers on Eugenics.*

DATE OF PUBLICATION: Number 1–4, 1945–1947.

FREQUENCY: **Annual,** Number 1–2, 1945–1946. **Semiannual,** Number 3–4, 1947.

NUMBERING VARIATIONS: *See* Contents *below.*

PUBLISHER: **London:** Hamish Hamilton Medical Books, 1945–1946. **London:** The Eugenics Society and Hamish Hamilton Medical Books, 1947.

PRIMARY EDITORS: None listed.

CONTENTS:

Number 1. Blacker, C. P. Eugenics in Prospect and Retrospect. 1945. 33 pp. (Galton Lecture 1945.)

Number 2. Burt, Cyril. Intelligence and Fertility. The Effect of the Differential Birthrate on Inborn Mental Characteristics. 1946. 43 pp.

Number 3. Thomson, Godfrey, The Trend of National Intelligence. 1947. 35 pp. (Galton Lecture 1946.)

Number 4. Terman, Lewis. Psychological Approaches to the Biography of Genius. 1947. 24 pp.

926. *Psicoanalisi applicata alla medicina, pedagogia, sociologia, letteratura ed arte.*

TITLE VARIATIONS: None.

DATES OF PUBLICATION: Anno 1–2, July/September 1945–1946.

FREQUENCY: Quarterly.

NUMBERING VARIATIONS: Anno 1 has only 2 numbers. Multinumber issue present in Anno 2.

PUBLISHER: **Rome:** Editrice "Scienza moderna," 1945–1946.

PRIMARY EDITORS: **J. Flescher,** 1945–1946; **N. Perrotti,** 1945–1946.

927. *Psychoanalytic Study of the Child.*

TITLE VARIATIONS: None.

DATES OF PUBLICATION: Volume 1–5+, 1945–1950+.

FREQUENCY: **Annual,** Volume 1–2, 5+, 1945–1946, 1950+. **Triennial,** Volume 3/4, 1949.

NUMBERING VARIATIONS: Volume 3/4 joint issue for years 1947/1948 published in 1949.

PUBLISHER: **New York:** International Universities Press, 1945–1950+.

PRIMARY EDITORS: **Anna Freud,** 1945–1950+; **Heinz Hartmann,** 1945–1950+; **Ernst Kris,** 1945–1950+; **Ruth S. Eissler,** 1950+.

EDITORIAL BOARD: Otto Fenichel, 1945; Phyllis Greenacre, 1945–1950+; Willie Hoffer, 1945–1950+; Edward Glover, 1945–1950+; Edith B. Jackson, 1945–1950+; Lawrence S. Kubie, 1945–1950+; Bertram D. Lewin, 1945–1950+; Marian C. Putnam, 1945–1950+; Rene A. Spitz, 1945–1950+; Rudolph M. Loewenstein, 1946–1950+.

928. *Psychological and Social Series. Papers.*

TITLE VARIANTS: None.

DATES OF PUBLICATION: Number 1–7, 1945–1948.

FREQUENCY: Irregular. *See* Contents *below.*

NUMBERING VARIANTS: None.

PUBLISHER: **London:** Psychological and Social Series, 10, Nottingham Place, 1945–1947. **London:** George Allen & Unwin, 1948.

PRIMARY EDITORS: **Melitta Schmideberg,** 1945–1948; **Marjorie E. Franklin,** 1945–1948.

CONTENTS:

Number 1. Franklin, Marjorie E. THE USE AND MISUSE OF PLANNED ENVIRONMENTAL THERAPY. 1945. 15 pp.

Number 2. Warburg, Joan. PLAY THERAPY. 1946. 15 pp.

Number 3. Perry, Ethel. THE PSYCHO-ANALYSIS OF A DELINQUENT: INTERPLAY BETWEEM PHANTASY AND REALITY IN THE LIFE OF A LAW BREAKER. 1946. 16 pp.

Number 4. Wills, William David. ELIMINATING PUNISHMENT IN THE RESIDENTIAL TREATMENT OF TROUBLESOME BOYS AND YOUNG MEN. 1946. 32 pp.

Number 5. Schmideberg, Melitta. KNOWLEDGE, THINKING AND INTUITION. 1946. 16 pp.

Number 6. Schmideberg, Melitta. FOLKLORE OF PARENTHOOD. 1947. 20 pp.

Number 7. Schmideberg, Melitta. CHILDREN IN NEED. Introduction by Edward Glover. 1948. 196 pp.

929. *Psychologische bibliotheek (Amsterdam).* [2.]

TITLE VARIATIONS: Continued by *Psychologische reeks.* [2] with Deel 6, 1949.

DATES OF PUBLICATION: Deel 1–6, 1945–1948.

FREQUENCY: Irregular. *See* Contents *below.*

NUMBERING VARIATIONS: Two separate issues were numbered Deel 6. One is listed with this series and the other is listed with *Psychologische reeks.* [2]. *See* Contents *below.*

PUBLISHER: **Amsterdam:** N. V. noord-hollandsche uitgevers maatschappij, 1945–1948.

PRIMARY EDITOR: **G. Révész**, 1945–1948.

CONTENTS:

Deel 1. Révész, G. DE BETEEKENIS DER PSYCHOLOGIE. 1945. 58 pp.

Deel 2. Vuyk, R. EXPERIMENTEEL ONDERZOEK OVER ANALOGIEVORMING EN INDUCTIE BIJ VIJF-EN ZESJARIGE KINDEREN. 1946. 128 pp.

Deel 3. Duijker, H.C.J. EXTRALINGUALE ELEMENTEN IN DE SPRAAK. 1946. 162 pp.

Deel 4. Groot, A. D. de. HET DENKEN VAN DEN SCHAKER: EEN EXPERI-MENTEEL-PSYCHOLOGISCHE STUDIE. 1946. 315 pp.

Deel 5. Have, T. T. ten. HET PSYCHODIAGNOSTISCHE ONDERZOEK. EN ZIJN PRACTISCHE BETEKENIS. 1947. 112 pp.

Deel 6. Révész, G., and H. W. Ouweleen. PROBLEMEN DER SELECTIE VAN STUDENTEN AAN DE UNIVERSITEITEN EN HOGESCHOLEN. 1948. 46 pp.

930. *Psychologische reeks.* [*1.*]

TITLE VARIATIONS: None.

DATES OF PUBLICATION: Deel 1–4, 1945–1946.

FREQUENCY: Irregular. *See* Contents *below.*

NUMBERING VARIATIONS: None.

PUBLISHER: **Deinze, Belgium:** Uitgeverij "Caeciki," 1945. **Deinze:** Caecilia boekhandel, 1946.

PRIMARY EDITORS: None listed.

CONTENTS:

Deel 1. Coetsier, L. NIEUWE NORMEN BIJ HET INTELLIGENTIE-ONDER-ZOEK. 1945. 140 pp.

Deel 2. Mortier, V. INTELLIGENTIE-ONDERZOEK EN LEERPROGNOSE. 1946. 242 pp.

Deel 3. Wens, M. ASPECTEN VAN HET PROBLEEM: "METRISCH" INTELLI-GENTIE-ONDERZOEK. 1946. 212, 63 pp.

Deel 4. Vansteenkiste, E. ONTWERP VAN EEN TYPOLOGISCHE PERSONALIS-TICK. 1946. 78 pp.

931. *Revista de psicoanálisis. Monografías.* [Official organ of the Asociación psicoanalítica argentina.]

TITLE VARIATIONS: None.

DATES OF PUBLICATION: Número 1–2, 1945.

FREQUENCY: Irregular. *See* Contents *below.*

NUMBERING VARIATIONS: None.

PUBLISHER: **Buenos Aires:** Asociación psicoanalítica argentina, 1945.

PRIMARY EDITORS: None listed.

CONTENTS:
> **Número 1.** Reik, Theodor. COMO SE ILEGA A SER PSICÓLOGO. 1945.
> **Número 2.** Sterba, Richard. INTRODUCCIÓN A LA TEORÍA PSICOANALÍTICA DE LA LIBIDO. 1945.

932. *Yearbook of Psychoanalysis.*

TITLE VARIATIONS: None.

DATES OF PUBLICATION: Volume 1–6+, 1945–1950+.

FREQUENCY: Annual.

NUMBERING VARIATIONS: None.

PUBLISHER: **New York:** International Universities Press, 1945–1950+.

PRIMARY EDITOR: **Sandor Lorand,** 1945–1950+.

EDITORIAL BOARD: A. A. Brill, 1945; Henry Alden Bunker, 1945–1950+; Bertram D. Lewin, 1945–1950+; C. P. Oberndorf, 1945–1950+; Ernest Jones, 1946–1950+.

1946

933. *American Jewish Congress. Commission on Community Interrelations. Reports.*

TITLE VARIATIONS: Also called *C.C.I. Reports.*

DATES OF PUBLICATION: Number 1–2, 1946.

FREQUENCY: Irregular. *See* Contents *below.*

NUMBERING VARIATIONS: None.

PUBLISHER: **New York:** American Jewish Congress, Commission on Community Interrelations, 1946.

PRIMARY EDITORS: None listed.

CONTENTS:
> **Number 1.** Allport, Gordon W., and Bernard M. Kramer. SOME ROOTS OF PREJUDICE. 1946. Pp. 9–39. (Reprinted from the *Journal of Psychology,* Volume 22, 1946.)
> **Number 2.** Lippitt, Ronald, and Marian Radke. NEW TRENDS IN THE INVESTIGATION OF PREJUDICE. 1946. Pp. 167–176. (Reprinted from the *Annals of the American Academy of Political and Social Science,* March 1946.)

934. *American Psychologist.* [Professional journal of the American Psychological Association.]

TITLE VARIATIONS: None.

DATES OF PUBLICATION: Volume 1–5+, 1946–1950+.

FREQUENCY: Monthly.

NUMBERING VARIATIONS: None.

PUBLISHER: **Baltimore:** American Psychological Association, Inc., 1946–1949. **Lancaster, Pennsylvania:** American Psychological Association, Inc., 1950+.

PRIMARY EDITORS: **Dael Wolfle,** 1946–1950; **Lorraine Bouthilet,** 1946; **Eugenia Norris,** 1947; **Helen M. Wolfle,** 1948–1950+; **Theodore M. Newcomb,** 1949–1950; **Robert R. Sears,** 1949–1950; **Ruth S. Tolman,** 1949–1950+; **Carl I. Hovland,** 1950+; **Jean W. Macfarlane,** 1950+.

935. *Bulletin of Military Clinical Psychologists.*

TITLE VARIATIONS: None.

DATES OF PUBLICATION: Volume 1, Number 1–3, April, June and August 1946.

FREQUENCY: Bimonthly.

NUMBERING VARIATIONS: None.

PUBLISHER: **Washington, D.C.:** Association of Military Clinical Psychologists (under the Auspices of the Surgeon General's Office, Neuropsychiatry Consultant's Division, Clinical Psychology Branch), 1946.

PRIMARY EDITOR: **Howard H. Kendler,** 1946.

EDITORIAL BOARD: Paul C. Greene, 1946; Max L. Hutt, 1946; E. O. Milton, 1946; Howard L. Siple, 1946; Alfred Udow, 1946.

936. *Cahiers de pédagogie expérimentale et de psychologie de l'enfant. (Nouvelle série).*

TITLE VARIATIONS: Supersedes *Cahiers de pédagogie expérimentale et de psychologie de l'enfant. (Première série).*

DATES OF PUBLICATION: Numéro 1–6+, 1946–1949+.

FREQUENCY: Irregular. *See* Contents *below.*

NUMBERING VARIATIONS: None.

PUBLISHER: **Neuchâtel:** L'institut des sciences de l'éducation de l'université de Genève, 1946–1949+.

PRIMARY EDITORS: None listed.

CONTENTS:

    Numéro 1. Dottrens, Robert. LA PÉDAGOGIE EXPÉRIMENTALE ET L'ENSEIGNEMENT DE LA LANGUE MATERNELLE. 1946. 18 pp.

Numéro 2. Piaget, J., and B. Inhelder. EXPÉRIENCES SUR LA CONSTRUC-TION PROJECTIVE DE LA LIGNE DROITE CHEZ L'ENFANT DE 2 À 8 ANS. (1947). 17 pp.

Numéro 3. Rossello, P. PEUT-ON FAIRE DE L'ÉCOLE ACTIVE SI LE MAÎTRE N'EST PAS UN HOMME D'ACTION? 1948. 10 pp.

Numéro 4. Dottrens, Robert, and Dino Massarenti. VOCABULAIRE FON-DAMENTAL DU FRANÇAIS. 1948. 68 pp.

Numéro 5. Roller, Samuel. LES ENSEIGNEMENTS D'UNE DICTÉE. (1949). 50 pp.

Numéro 6. Dubosson, Jacques. EXERCISES SENSORIELS. 1949. 51 pp.

937. Ciudad Trujillo. Instituto de investigaciones psicopedagógicas. Boletín.

TITLE VARIATIONS: None.

DATES OF PUBLICATION: Año 1–2, May 1946–June 1947. Nueva Serie, Año 1, July/September 1948–July/December 1950+. Suspended publication, July 1947–June 1948, and January 1949–April 1950.

FREQUENCY: **Irregular,** Año 1, 1946. **Bimonthly,** Año 2, 1947. **Quarterly,** Nueva Serie, Año 1, 1948. **Semiannual,** Serie 3, 1950+.

NUMBERING VARIATIONS: Issues in Año 1–2, May 1946–June 1947 also assigned whole numbers, Número 1–14. Issues in Nueva Serie, Año 1, July/September 1948–October/December 1948 also assigned whole numbers, Número 1–2. Issues in Nueva Serie, Año 1, July/December 1950 also assigned whole numbers, Número 3–4, 3ª epoca.

PUBLISHER: **Ciudad Trujillo, Dominican Republic:** Instituto de investigaciones psicopedagógicas, 1946–1950+.

PRIMARY EDITORS: **S. Colombino Henriquez,** 1946–1950; **Gregorio B. Palacin Iglesias,** 1946–1947; **Malaquias Gil Arantigui,** 1946–1950+; **Luis Pichardo Cabral,** 1946–1950+; **Ismael H. Abreu Rodríquez,** 1946–1947; **Mario Martínez,** 1947–1948; **Luis N. Nunez Molina,** 1950; **Julian Diaz Valdepares,** 1950+; **Lilia M. Portalatin,** 1950+; **Antonia S. de Gallardo,** 1950+; **Museta P. de Thormann,** 1950+.

938. Georgia Psychological Association. Bulletin.

TITLE VARIATIONS: None.

DATES OF PUBLICATION: Volume 1–4+, December 1946–November 1950+.

FREQUENCY: **Irregular,** Volume 1, 1946–1947. **Bimonthly,** Volume 2–4+, 1948–1950+.

NUMBERING VARIATIONS: Volume 1, Number 1–2 were numbered after the fact. Joint issue Volume 4, Number 4/5, July/September 1950.

PUBLISHER: **Atlanta:** Georgia Psychological Association, 1946–1950+.

PRIMARY EDITORS: **Hermon W. Martin,** 1946–1947; **Robert C. Topper,** 1947; **Joseph E. Moore,** 1948; **Euri Belle Bolton,** 1948–1950+; **Austin S. Edwards,** 1949; **M. C. Langhorne,** 1950.

939. *Hamburg. Graphologischer Forschungskreis. Rundbrief für der Mitarbeiter und Mitglieder.*

TITLE VARIATIONS: None.

DATES OF PUBLICATION: Jahrgang 1–4, Numer 1, March 1946–February 1949.

FREQUENCY: Bimonthly.

NUMBERING VARIATIONS: Issues also assigned whole numbers, Heft 1–19.

PUBLISHER: **Hamburg:** Graphologischer Forschungskreis, 1946–1949.

PRIMARY EDITOR: **Günter Elster**, 1946–1949.

940. *Internationale Bibliothek für Psychologie und Soziologie.*

TITLE VARIATIONS: None.

DATES OF PUBLICATION: Heft 1–10+, 1946–1950+.

FREQUENCY: Irregular. *See* Contents *below.*

NUMBERING VARIATIONS: None.

PUBLISHER: **Zurich:** Pan-Verlag, 1946–1950+.

PRIMARY EDITOR: **Paul Reiwald**, 1946–1950+.

CONTENTS:

Heft 1. Reiwald, Paul. VOM GEIST DER MASSEN. 1946. 631 pp.

Heft 2. Walter, Emil Jak. PSYCHOLOGISCHE GRUNDLAGEN DER GESCHICHTLICHEN UND SOZIALEN ENTWICKLUNG. 1947. 172 pp.

Heft 3. Segerstedt, Torgny T. DIE MACHT DER WORTES. 1947. 174 pp.

Heft 4. Whyte, Lancelot Law. DIE NÄCHSTE STUFE DER MENSCHHEIT. 1946. 339 pp.

Heft 5. Reiwald, Paul. DIE GESELLSCHAFT UND IHRE VERBRECHER. 1948. 320 pp.

Heft 6. Grabowsky, Adolf. DIE POLITIK. 1948. 452 pp.

Heft 7. Burnham, James. DIE MACHIAVELLISTEN. 1949. 270 pp.

Heft 8. Malinowski, Bronislaw. EINE WISSENSCHAFTLICHE THEORIE DER KULTUR UND ANDERE AUFSÄTZE. 1949. 264 pp.

Heft 9. Osborn, Fairfield. UNSERE AUSGEPLÜNDERTE ERDE. 1950. 168 pp.

Heft 10. Neill, Alexander Sutherland. SELBSTVERWALTUNG IN DER SCHULE. 1950. 176 pp.

941. *Journal of Clinical Psychopathology.*

TITLE VARIATIONS: Continues *Journal of Clinical Psychopathology and Psychotherapy.* Continued by *Journal of Clinical and Experimental Psychopathology* with Volume 12, 1951.

DATES OF PUBLICATION: Volume 7, Number 3–Volume 11, Number 4, January 1946–October 1950.

FREQUENCY: Quarterly.

NUMBERING VARIATIONS: None.

PUBLISHER: **Monticello, New York:** Medical Journal Press, 1946–1948. **Washington, D.C.:** Washington Institute of Medicine, 1948–1950.

PRIMARY EDITORS: **V. C. Branham,** 1946–1948; **Ben Karpman,** 1948–1950.

EDITORIAL BOARD: Walter Bromberg, 1946–1950; Arthur N. Foxe, 1946–1950; Erich Fromm, 1946–1950; Angel Garma, 1946; Bernard Glueck, 1946–1950; P. Lionel Goitein, 1946, 1948–1950; Robert M. Lindner, 1946–1950; Margaret Mead, 1946–1950; Merrill Moore, 1946–1950; Philip Q. Roche, 1946–1950; Paul L. Schroeder, 1946–1950; Robert V. Seliger, 1946–1950; Lowell S. Selling, 1946–1950; Dorothy Seago, 1946–1948; Edmund Bergler, 1948–1950; Frank S. Caprio, 1948–1950; Hervey M. Cleckley, 1948–1950; Jacob H. Conn, 1948–1950; George Devereux, 1948–1950; Rudolph Dreikurs, 1948–1950; Wladimir Eliasberg, 1948–1950; Leonard Gilman, 1948–1950; Leo Kanner, 1948–1950; Samuel B. Kutash, 1948–1950; Philip Litvin, 1948–1950; Louis S. London, 1948–1950; Sidney B. Maughs, 1948–1950; Wendell Muncie, 1948–1950; Horace K. Richardson, 1948–1950; R. Burke Suitt, 1948–1950; Valentine Ujhely, 1948–1950; Leopold E. Wexberg, 1948–1950; Lawrence F. Woolley, 1948–1950; Joseph Borkin, 1950.

942. *Kansas. University. Journal of Psychology.*

TITLE VARIATIONS: None.

DATES OF PUBLICATION: Volume 1, Number 1, June 1946.

FREQUENCY: Irregular.

NUMBERING VARIATIONS: None.

PUBLISHER: **Lawrence, Kansas:** University of Kansas, Department of Psychology, 1946.

PRIMARY EDITORS: **Evan R. Stevens, Jr.,** 1946; **George H. Yeckel,** 1946.

EDITORIAL BOARD: Verlyn L. Norris, 1946; Raymond E. Hartley, 1946; Robert W. Parkinson, 1946; Edward B. Swain, 1946; Jean A. Murray, 1946.

943. *Lima. Instituto psicopedagógico nacional. Boletín. Supplemento.*

TITLE VARIATIONS: None.

DATES OF PUBLICATION: Año 1, Número 1, 1946.

FREQUENCY: Irregular. *See* Contents *below.*

NUMBERING VARIATIONS: Número 1 dated 1947.

PUBLISHER: **Lima:** Editora Médica Peruana, S. A., 1947.

PRIMARY EDITORS: None listed.

CONTENTS:

Número 1. Pisculich Ramirez, Emiliano, with the collaboration of Enriqueta Arroyo C. LA EDUCACIÓN DE LOS NIÑOS ANORMALES. 1947. 138 pp.

944. *Louvain. Université. Laboratoire de psychologie expérimentale. Travaux.*

TITLE VARIATIONS: None.

DATES OF PUBLICATION: Numéro 1, 1946.

FREQUENCY: Irregular. *See* Contents *below.*

NUMBERING VARIATIONS: *See* Contents *below.*

PUBLISHER: **Louvain:** Institut supérieur de philosophie, 1946.

PRIMARY EDITORS: None listed.

CONTENTS:

Numéro 1. Fraisse, P. CONTRIBUTION À L'ÉTUDE DU RYTHME EN TANT QUE FORME TEMPORELLE. (Also as *Journal de psychologie,* Année 39, Numéro 3, 1941, pp. 283–304.)

945. *Nederlandsch tijdschrift voor de psychologie en haar grensgebieden.*

TITLE VARIATIONS: Continues *Nederlandsch tijdschrift voor psychologie en hare grensgebieden.*

DATES OF PUBLICATION: Nieuwe Reeks, Deel 1–5+, 1946–1950+.

FREQUENCY OF ISSUE: Bimonthly.

NUMBERING VARIATIONS: None.

PUBLISHER: **Amsterdam:** V. Noord-Hollandsche uitgevers maatschappij, 1946–1950+.

PRIMARY EDITORS: **L. van der Horst,** 1946–1950+; **G. Révész,** 1946–1950+; **Maria C. Bos,** 1946–1950+; **H.J.F.W. Brugmans,** 1946–1950+; **E.A.D.E. Carp,** 1946–1950+; **H. C. Rümke,** 1946–1950+.

946. *Parapsychology Bulletin.*

TITLE VARIATIONS: None.

DATES OF PUBLICATION: Number 1–20+, March 1946–November 1950+.

FREQUENCY: Quarterly.

NUMBERING VARIATIONS. Issued in connection with the *Journal of Parapsychology.*

PUBLISHER: **Durham, North Carolina:** Duke University Press, 1946–1950.

PRIMARY EDITOR: **Dorothy H. Pope,** 1946–1950+.

947. *Praktisk Psykologi.* [Organ of the Psykotekniska Institutet, Stockholms Högskola.]

TITLE VARIATIONS: None.

DATES OF PUBLICATION: Nummer 1–4, 1946–1948.

FREQUENCY: **Semiannual,** Nummer 1–2, 1946. **Annual,** Nummer 3–4, 1947–1948.

NUMBERING VARIATIONS: None.

PUBLISHER: **Stockholm:** Hugo Gebers Förlag, 1946–1948.

PRIMARY EDITOR: **Valdemar Fellenius,** 1946–1948.

EDITORIAL BOARD: David Katz, 1946–1948; Bror Jonzon, 1946–1948; Einar Tegen, 1946–1948; Yngve Zotterman, 1946–1948; Ejnar Neymark, 1946–1948.

948. *Psyché. Revue internationale de psychanalyse et des sciences de l'homme.*

TITLE VARIATIONS: Subtitled *Bulletin de la ligue d'hygiène mentale,* 1948.

DATES OF PUBLICATION: Année 1–5+, November 1946–December 1950+.

FREQUENCY: Monthly.

NUMBERING VARIATIONS: Issues are assigned whole numbers, Numéro 1–50+. Double-number issues are 9/10, 13/14, 18/19, 21/22, 23/24, 27/28, 30/31, 35/36, 37/38, 45/46.

PUBLISHER: **Paris:** "Psyché," 1946–1950+.

PRIMARY EDITORS: **Maxime Clouzet,** 1946–1947; **Maryse Choisy (Clouzet),** 1947–1950+.

EDITORIAL BOARD: Maryse Choisy, 1946–1947; Henriette Brunot, 1946–1950+; Gisèle Galy, 1946–1950+; André Berge, 1946–1949; Georges Mauco, 1946–1949; André Gybal, 1946–1950+; Hélène Tubiana-Vuillet, 1946–1948; Pierre Salzy, 1947–1950+; Yves Porc'her, 1948–1950+.

949. *Psychologica belgica. Annales de la société belge de psychologie.*

TITLE VARIATIONS: None.

DATES OF PUBLICATION: Volume 1, 1946/1953.

FREQUENCY: Irregular.

NUMBERING VARIATIONS: None.

PUBLISHER: **Louvain:** Éditions E. Nauwelaerts pour la Société belge de psychologie, 1946/1953.

PRIMARY EDITOR: **J. Nuttin,** 1946/1953.

950. *Psychologický sbornik. Časopis psychologickêho ústavu SAVU.*

TITLE VARIATIONS: None.

DATES OF PUBLICATION: Ročnik 1–5, Čislo 1, 1946–1950+.

FREQUENCY: Quarterly.

NUMBERING VARIATIONS: None.

PUBLISHER: **Bratislava:** Matica Slovenska Turč Sv. Martin, 1946–[1948]. **Bratislava:** Slovenska akademia vied a umeni, 1949–1950+.

PRIMARY EDITOR: **Anton Jurouský,** 1946–1950+.

NOTE: Information on this title was found in the *Bibliographie de la philosophie* published by the International Institute of Philosophical Collaboration, Paris. Paris: Librairie philosophique J. Vrin, 1937–1950+.

951. *Revista de psicología general y aplicada.*

TITLE VARIATIONS: Supersedes *Psicotecnia.*

DATES OF PUBLICATION: Volumen 1–5+, 1946–1950+.

FREQUENCY: **Semiannual,** Volumen 1–2, 1946–1947. **Quarterly,** Volumen 3–5+, 1948–1950+.

NUMBERING VARIATIONS: Issues are assigned whole numbers, Número 1–16+.

PUBLISHER: **Madrid:** Publicación del instituto nacional de psicotecnia, 1946–1950+.

PRIMARY EDITORS: **José Germain** (Director), 1946–1950+; **Julian Marias,** 1947–1950+; **José Mallart,** 1947–1950+; **Mariano Yela,** 1947–1950+; **Eusebio Marti Lamich,** 1947–1950+; **José Lopez Mora,** 1947–1950+.

952. *Revista mexicana de higiene mental.* [Organ of the Liga mexicana de higiene mental.]

TITLE VARIATIONS: Continued by *Psiquis; Revista mexicana de higiene mental* with Volumen 2, August 1947.

DATES OF PUBLICATION: Volumen 1, Número 1–7/8, November 1946–June/July 1947.

FREQUENCY: **Bimonthly,** Volumen 1, Número 1, November 1946. **Monthly,** Volumen 1, Número 2-Número 7/8, January 1947–June/July 1947.

NUMBERING VARIATIONS: Issue 7/8 is only multinumber issue.

PUBLISHER: **Mexico City:** Revista mexicana de higiene mental, Gomez Farias 56, 1946–1947.

PRIMARY EDITORS: **Roman Robledo Vazquez,** 1946–1947; **Enrique Felix,** 1947; **Ernesto Julio Teissier,** 1947.

EDITORIAL BOARD: Emma Dolujanoff, 1946–1947; Eva Esteva McMaster, 1946–1947; Sara Margarita Zendejas, 1946–1947; Ramon Parres, 1946–1947; Santiago Ramirez, 1946–1947; Modesto Sanchez, 1946–1947; Hector Prado Huante, 1947.

953. *Revue de psychologie des peuples.* [Organ of the Institut havrais de sociologie économique et de psychologie des peuples.]

TITLE VARIATIONS: None.

DATES OF PUBLICATION: Année 1–5+, May 1946–1950+.

FREQUENCY: Quarterly.

NUMBERING VARIATIONS: None.

PUBLISHER: **Le Havre:** Ancienne imprimerie Marcel Étaix pour l'Institut havrais de sociologie économique et de psychologie des peuples, 1946–1950+.

PRIMARY EDITORS: **Abel Miroglio,** 1946–1950+.

954. *Revue de psychologie. Revue trimestrielle.*

TITLE VARIATIONS: None.

DATES OF PUBLICATION: Volume 1, Numéro 1–3+, September 1946–October 1949+. (Ceased publication with Volume 1, Número 4, July 1952.)

FREQUENCY: Irregular.

NUMBERING VARIATIONS: None.

PUBLISHER: **Montreal:** Institut de psychologie, Université de Montréal, 1946–1949+.

PRIMARY EDITORS: **Edmour Lemay,** 1946–1947; **J.E.A. Marcotte,** 1946–1949+; **Julien Beausoleil,** 1949+.

EDITORIAL BOARD: Noël Mailloux, 1946–1949+; Irenée Lussier, 1946–1949+; Antonio Barbeau, 1946–1947; Miguel Prados, 1946–1949+; Roland Vinette, 1946–1949+; Adrien Pinard, 1946–1949+; Blaise Laurier, 1946–1949+; Wilfrid Éthier, 1946–1949+.

955. *South African Psychological Review.* [Organ of the Psychological Society, Johannesburg.]

TITLE VARIATIONS: None.

DATES OF PUBLICATION: Volume 1–3, Number 2, 1946–1948.

FREQUENCY: Quarterly (Irregular).

NUMBERING VARIATIONS: Volume 3 is complete with 2 issues.

PUBLISHER: **Johannesburg:** Psychological Society, 1946–1948.

PRIMARY EDITORS: None listed.

956. *TAT Newsletter.*

TITLE VARIATIONS: TAT stands for Thematic Apperception Test.

DATES OF PUBLICATION: Volume 1–4, Number 3+, 1946–Winter 1950+.

FREQUENCY: Quarterly.

NUMBERING VARIATIONS: August 1949 *TAT Newsletter* was published within *Rorschach Research Exchange* and *Journal of Projective Techniques*, Volume 13, Number 4, Fall 1949.

PUBLISHER: **Topeka, Kansas:** Menninger Clinic, 1946. **Topeka:** Menninger Foundation, 1947–1950+; and, **New York:** Society for Projective Techniques and Rorschach Institute, Inc., 1949–1950+.

PRIMARY EDITOR: **Robert R. Holt,** 1946–1950+.

957. *Zdrowie psychiczne.*

TITLE VARIATIONS: None.

DATES OF PUBLICATION: 1–[?], 1946–[?].

FREQUENCY: Unknown.

NUMBERING VARIATIONS: None.

PUBLISHER: **Warsaw:** Państwowy instytut higieny psychicznej, 1946–[?].

PRIMARY EDITORS: None listed.

NOTE: Information on this title is incomplete. The compilers were unable to examine this title.

1947

958. *American Journal of Psychotherapy.* [Official organ of the Association for the Advancement of Psychotherapy.]

TITLE VARIATIONS: None.

DATES OF PUBLICATION: Volume 1–4+, January 1947–October 1950+.

FREQUENCY: Quarterly.

NUMBERING VARIATIONS: None.

PUBLISHER: **New York:** Association for the Advancement of Psychotherapy, 1947–1950.

PRIMARY EDITOR: **Emil A. Gutheil,** 1947–1950+.

959. *Association for Physical and Mental Rehabilitation. Journal.* [*1.*]

TITLE VARIATIONS: Continued by *Physical and Mental Rehabilitation Journal* with Volume 2, 1948.

DATES OF PUBLICATION: [Volume 1,] Number 1–3, November 1947–March 1948.

FREQUENCY: Bimonthly.

NUMBERING VARIATIONS: Volume number not listed on first volume.

PUBLISHER: **Columbia, South Carolina:** Association for Physical and Mental Rehabilitation, 1947–1948.

PRIMARY EDITORS: None listed.

960. *Australasian Journal of Philosophy.*

TITLE VARIATIONS: Continues *Australasian Journal of Psychology and Philosophy.*

DATES OF PUBLICATION: Volume 25–28 +, August 1947–1950 +.

FREQUENCY: Triannual.

NUMBERING VARIATIONS: Volume 25, Number 1/2, August 1947 is a double-number issue.

PUBLISHER: **Glebe, New South Wales:** Australasian Association of Psychology and Philosophy, 1947–1950 +.

PRIMARY EDITORS: **J. A. Passmore,** 1947–1949; **A. K. Stout,** 1950 +.

961. *Barcelona. Instituto psicotécnico. Anales.*

TITLE VARIATIONS: None.

DATES OF PUBLICATION: Número 1, 1947/1948.

FREQUENCY: Annual.

NUMBERING VARIATIONS: None.

PUBLISHER: **Barcelona:** Instituto psicotécnico, 1947/1948.

PRIMARY EDITORS: None listed.

NOTE: Information on this title is incomplete. It is possible that an issue may have been issued about 1945.

962. *Behaviour. An International Journal of Comparative Ethology.*

TITLE VARIATIONS: None.

DATES OF PUBLICATION: Volume 1–3 +, 1947/1948–1950/1951 +.

FREQUENCY: Irregular.

NUMBERING VARIATIONS: Volume 1, Number 3/4 and Volume 2, Number 1/2 were published as double numbers.

PUBLISHER: **Leiden:** E. J. Brill, 1947–1950 +.

PRIMARY EDITORS: **G. P. Baerends,** 1950 +; **F. A. Beach,** 1947–1950 +. **C. R. Carpenter,** 1947–1950 +; **H. Hediger,** 1947–1950 +; **O. Koehler,** 1947–1950 +; **P. Palmgren,** 1947–1950 +; **W. H. Thorpe,** 1947–1950 +; **N. Tinbergen,** 1947–1950 +.

963. *British Journal of Psychology. Statistical Section.*

TITLE VARIATIONS: None.

DATES OF PUBLICATION: Volume 1–3 +, 1947–1950 +.

FREQUENCY: Triannual.

NUMBERING VARIATIONS: None.

PUBLISHER: **London:** British Psychological Society by University of London Press, 1947–1950+.

PRIMARY EDITORS: **Cyril Burt,** 1947–1950+; **Godfrey Thomson,** 1947–1950+; **D. W. Harding,** 1947–1948; **H. G. Maule,** 1949–1950+; **Charlotte Banks,** 1950+; **Arthur Summerfield,** 1950+.

EDITORIAL BOARD: A. C. Aitken, 1947–1950+; M. S. Bartlett, 1947–1950+; W. G. Emmett, 1947–1950+; M. G. Kendall, 1947–1950+; D. N. Lawley, 1947–1950+; L. S. Penrose, 1947–1950+; J. Fraser Roberts, 1947–1950+; A. Rodger, 1947–1950+; B. Babington Smith, 1947–1950+; W. Stephenson, 1947–1950+; P. E. Vernon, 1947–1950+; E. S. Pearson, 1950+.

964. *Canadian Journal of Psychology.* [Journal of the Canadian Psychological Association.]

TITLE VARIATIONS: Supersedes *Canadian Psychological Association. Bulletin.*

DATES OF PUBLICATION: Volume 1–4+, 1947–1950+.

FREQUENCY: Quarterly.

NUMBERING VARIATIONS: None.

PUBLISHER: **Toronto:** University of Toronto Press (for the Canadian Psychological Association), 1947–1950+.

PRIMARY EDITORS: **John A. Long,** 1947–1950+; **Kathleen M. Hobday,** 1947–1950+.

EDITORIAL BOARD: D. O. Hebb, 1950+; J. Blackburn, 1950+; R. B. Malmo, 1950+; N. W. Morton, 1950+; C. R. Myers, 1950+.

965. *Current Trends in Psychology.*

TITLE VARIATIONS: Volume titles vary. *See* Contents *below.*

DATES OF PUBLICATION: 1947–1950+.

FREQUENCY: Annual.

NUMBERING VARIATIONS: Series is numbered only by year.

PUBLISHER: **Pittsburgh:** University of Pittsburgh Press, 1947–1950+.

PRIMARY EDITOR: **Wayne Dennis,** 1947–1950+.

CONTENTS:

1947. Dennis, Wayne, B. F. Skinner, Robert R. Sears, E. Lowell Kelly, Carl Rogers, John C. Flanagan, Clifford T. Morgan, and Rensis Likert. CURRENT TRENDS IN PSYCHOLOGY. 225 pp.

1948. Dennis, Wayne, Ronald Lippitt, K. T. Behanan, J. S. Bruner, L. Postman, J. L. Moreno, Robert K. Merton, Paul F. Lazarsfeld, and James G. Miller. CURRENT TRENDS IN SOCIAL PSYCHOLOGY. 299 pp.

1949. Dennis, Wayne, Carroll L. Shartle, John C. Flanagan, Orlo L. Crissey, William McGehee, Brent Baxter, Daniel Katz, and Harold C. Taylor. CURRENT TRENDS IN INDUSTRIAL PSYCHOLOGY. 198 pp.

1950. Dennis, Wayne, Robert Felix, Carlyle Jacobsen, Robert A. Patton, Y. D. Koskoff, Paul E. Huston, Nathan W. Shock, and Hans J. Eysenck. CUR-RENT TRENDS IN THE RELATION OF PSYCHOLOGY TO MEDICINE. 180 pp.

966. *Dobutsu Shinri.* [Animal Psychology.] [2.]

TITLE VARIATIONS: None.

DATES OF PUBLICATION: Number 1–2, 1947–1948.

FREQUENCY: Annual.

NUMBERING VARIATIONS: None.

PUBLISHER: **Kyoto:** Dobutsu Shinrigakkai [Society for Animal Psychology], 1947–1948.

PRIMARY EDITORS: None listed.

NOTE: Information for this entry found in *Gakujutsu Zasshi Sōgō Mokuroku. Shizen Kagaku Wabun Hen* [Union List of Scholarly Journals. Japanese Language Section. Natural Sciences Part]. Tokyo, 1968.

967. *Dobutsu Shinri Nenpo.* [Annual of Animal Psychology.]

TITLE VARIATIONS: None.

DATES OF PUBLICATION: Number 1–2, 1947–1948.

FREQUENCY: Annual.

NUMBERING VARIATIONS: None.

PUBLISHER: **Tokyo:** Dobutsu Shinrigakkai [Society for Animal Psychology], 1947–1948.

PRIMARY EDITORS: None listed.

NOTE: Information for this entry was found in *Gakujutsu Zasshi Sōgō Mokuroku. Shizen Kagaku Wabun Hen* [Union List of Scholarly Journals. Japanese Language Section. Natural Sciences Part]. Tokyo, 1968.

968. *France. Centre national de la recherche scientifique. Bulletin analytique: Philosophie.*

TITLE VARIATIONS: None.

DATES OF PUBLICATION: Volume 1–4+, 1947–1950+.

FREQUENCY: Quarterly.

NUMBERING VARIATIONS: None.

PUBLISHER: **Paris:** Centre de documentation du C.N.R.S., 1947–1950+.

PRIMARY EDITOR: **R. Bayer,** 1947–1950+.

NOTE: This classified index to periodicals covers philosophy, psychology, pedagogy, sociology, religion, logic, aesthetics, etc.

969. *Group for the Advancement of Psychiatry. Report.*

TITLE VARIATIONS: None.

DATES OF PUBLICATION: Number 1–17+, September 1947–September 1950+.

FREQUENCY: Irregular. *See* Contents *below.*

NUMBERING VARIATIONS: None.

PUBLISHER: **Topeka, Kansas:** Group for the Advancement of Psychiatry, 1947–1950+.

PRIMARY EDITORS: None listed.

CONTENTS:

Number 1. Committee on Therapy. SHOCK THERAPY. 1947. 2 pp.

Number 2. Committee on Psychiatric Social Work. THE PSYCHIATRIC SOCIAL WORKER IN THE PSYCHIATRIC HOSPITAL. 1948. 14 pp.

Number 3. Committee on Medical Education. REPORT ON MEDICAL EDUCATION. 1948. 12 pp.

Number 4. Committee on Forensic Psychiatry. COMMITMENT PROCEDURES. 1948. 4 pp.

Number 5. Group for the Advancement of Psychiatry. PUBLIC PSYCHIATRIC HOSPITALS. 1948. 20 pp.

Number 6. Research Committee. RESEARCH ON PREFRONTAL LOBOTOMY. 1948. 10 pp.

Number 7. Hospital Committee. STATISTICS PERTINENT TO PSYCHIATRY IN THE UNITED STATES. 1949. 10 pp.

Number 8. Committee on Cooperation with Lay Groups. AN OUTLINE FOR EVALUATION OF A COMMUNITY PROGRAM IN MENTAL HYGIENE. 1949. 8 pp.

Number 9. Committee on Forensic Psychiatry. PSYCHIATRICALLY DEVIATED SEX OFFENDERS. 1949. 8 pp.

Number 10. Committee on Clinical Psychology. THE RELATION OF CLINICAL PSYCHOLOGY TO PSYCHIATRY. 1949. 7 pp.

Number 11. Committee on International Relations. THE POSITION OF PSYCHIATRISTS IN THE FIELD OF INTERNATIONAL RELATIONS. 1950. 4 pp.

Number 12. Committee on Child Psychiatry. BASIC CONCEPTS IN CHILD PSYCHIATRY. 1950. 8 pp.

Number 13. Committee on Social Issues. THE SOCIAL RESPONSIBILITY OF PSYCHIATRY, A STATEMENT OF ORIENTATION. 1950. 7 pp.

Number 14. Committee on Hospitals. THE PROBLEM OF THE AGED PATIENT IN THE PUBLIC PSYCHIATRIC HOSPITAL. 1950. 7 pp.

Number 15. Committee on Therapy. REVISED ELECTRO-SHOCK THERAPY REPORT. 1950. 4 pp.

Number 16. Committee on Psychiatric Social Work. PSYCHIATRIC SOCIAL WORK IN THE PSYCHIATRIC CLINIC. 1950. 6 pp.

Number 17. Committee on Academic Education. THE ROLE OF PSYCHIATRISTS IN COLLEGES AND UNIVERSITIES. 1950. 8 pp.

970. *Hoja de psicología.*

TITLE VARIATIONS: None.

DATES OF PUBLICATION: Número 1–7+, 1947–1950+.

FREQUENCY: Semiannual.

NUMBERING VARIATIONS: Número 3/4 joint issue 1948–1949.

PUBLISHER: **Montevideo, Uruguay:** Centro de estudios psicológicos de Montevideo, 1947–1950+.

PRIMARY EDITOR: **Waclaw Radecki,** 1947–1950+.

EDITORIAL BOARD: Heriberto D. Staffa, 1947–1949; Maria Dolores Nieto, 1947–1950+; Maria Esther Dominquez, 1947–1950+; Enrique Failde Nogues, 1947–1950+; Dario D. Sorín, 1947–1950+; Maria Celia Torres De Lago, 1947–1948; Federico C. Marchesi, 1947–1950+; Carlos Antonelli, 1948–1949; Gladys Corbi, 1948–1950+; Carlos A. Tuboras, 1948–1950+; Nicolas Altuchow, 1950+; Primitivo Amilcar Techera, 1948–1950+.

971. *Human Relations. A Quarterly Journal of Studies towards the Integration of the Social Sciences.*

TITLE VARIATIONS: None.

DATES OF PUBLICATION: Volume 1–3+, June 1947–1950+.

FREQUENCY: Quarterly.

NUMBERING VARIATIONS: Volume 1 issued June 1947–August 1948.

PUBLISHER: **London:** The Tavistock Institute of Human Relations, 1947–1950+. **Cambridge, Massachusetts:** The Research Center for Group Dynamics, 1947. **Ann Arbor, Michigan:** Research Center for Group Dynamics, 1948–1950+.

PRIMARY EDITORS: **Thomas Fairley,** 1947–1948; **John Harvard-Watts,** 1949–1950+.

EDITORIAL BOARD: *England:* Elliott Jaques, 1947–1950+; John Rickman, 1947–1950+; J. D. Sutherland, 1947–1948; Eric Trist, 1947–1950+; A.T.M. Wilson, 1947–1950+; B. S. Morris, 1949–1950+. *United States:* Dorwin Cartwright, 1947–1950+; Leon Festinger, 1947–1950+; Kurt Lewin, 1947–1948; Ronald Lippitt, 1947–1950+; Marian Radke, 1947–1948; John R. P. French, Jr., 1949–1950+; Alvin Zander, 1949–1950.

972. *Impuls; Organ for Psykologi-interesserte.*

TITLE VARIATIONS: None.

DATES OF PUBLICATION: Årgang 1–4+, September 8, 1947–December 1950+.

FREQUENCY: **Irregular,** Årgang 1, 1947. **Seven issues,** Årgang 2, 1948. **Bimonthly,** Årgang 3–4+, 1949–1950+.

NUMBERING VARIATIONS: None.

PUBLISHER: **Oslo, Norway:** Psykologisk Institutt, Universitetet Oslo, 1947–1950+.

PRIMARY EDITORS: **Arvid Ås,** 1947–1948; **Gudrun Ødegaard,** 1947–1948; **Bjørn Roksand,** 1948–1949; **Arnljot Gjesvik,** 1948–1949; **Erling Bjordal,** 1949; **Gerdt Henrik Vedeler,** 1949; **Bjørn Killingmo,** 1949–1950; **Svein Meldal Hile,** 1949–1950; **Arne Ebeltoft,** 1950+; **Einar Moe,** 1950+.

973. *International Journal of Opinion and Attitude Research.*

TITLE VARIATIONS: None.

DATES OF PUBLICATION: Volume 1–4+, March, 1947–Winter, 1950/1951.

FREQUENCY: Quarterly.

NUMBERING VARIATIONS: None.

PUBLISHER: None listed, 1947. **Mexico City:** Las ciencas sociales, S. de R. L., 1948–1950/1951+.

PRIMARY EDITOR: **Laszlo Radvanyi,** 1947–1950/1951+.

ASSISTANT EDITOR: Lena Jaeck, 1947–1950/1951+.

EDITORIAL BOARD: Gordon W. Allport, 1950+; Herbert Blumer, 1950+; Jerome S. Bruner, 1950+; Don Cahalan, 1950+; Angus Campbell, 1950+; Hadley Cantril, 1950+; Dorwin Cartwright, 1950+; F. Stuart Chapin, 1950+; Leo P. Crespi, 1950+; Richard S. Crutchfield, 1950+; Leonard W. Doob, 1950+; H. J. Eysenck, 1950+; Louis Guttman, 1950+; Daniel Katz, 1950+; David Krech, 1950+; Alfred McClung Lee, 1950+; Curtis D. MacDougall, 1950+; Louis Moss, 1950+; Frederick Mosteller, 1950+; Wilbur Schramm, 1950+.

974. *Jido Shinri.* [Child Psychology.]

TITLE VARIATIONS: None.

DATES OF PUBLICATION: Volume 1–4+, 1947–1950+.

FREQUENCY: Monthly.

NUMBERING VARIATIONS: None.

PUBLISHER: **Tokyo:** Kaneko Shoten, Jido Shinri Kyokai [Kaneko Bookstore for the Association for Child Psychology], 1947–1950+.

PRIMARY EDITORS: None listed.

NOTE: Information on this entry was obtained from *Gakujutsu Zasshi Sōgō Mokuroku. Jimbun Kagaku Wabun Hen* [Union List of Scholarly Journals. Japanese Language Section. Humanities Part]. Tokyo, 1973.

975. *Journal of Child Psychiatry, Neurology and Clinical Psychology of the Child.*

TITLE VARIATIONS: None.

DATES OF PUBLICATION: Volume 1, Section 1–3+, 1947/1948–1950+.

FREQUENCY: Irregular.

NUMBERING VARIATIONS: None.

PUBLISHER: **New York:** Published by the Journal of Child Psychiatry Division of Child Care Publications, 1947/1948–1950+.

PRIMARY EDITOR: **Ernest Harms,** 1947–1950+.

EDITORIAL BOARD: J. Louise Despert, 1947–1950+; Frederic J. Farnell, 1947–1950+; C. M. Louttit, 1947–1950+; Leo Kanner, 1947–1950+; Bernard

L. Pacella, 1947; Veronica O'Brien, 1948–1950+; Wintrop M. Phelps, 1948–1950+.

976. *Journal of Comparative and Physiological Psychology.*

TITLE VARIATIONS: Continues *Journal of Comparative Psychology.*

DATES OF PUBLICATION: Volume 40–43+, 1947–1950+.

FREQUENCY: Bimonthly.

NUMBERING VARIATIONS: None.

PUBLISHER: **Baltimore** and **Washington, D.C.**: American Psychological Association, Inc., 1947–1950+.

PRIMARY EDITOR: **Calvin P. Stone**, 1947–1950+.

977. *Kyoto. Kyōto Daigaku. Bungakubu. Shinrigaku kenkyūshitsu.* **Shinri.** [University of Kyoto. Faculty of Letters. Psychological Research Laboratory. Psychology.]

TITLE VARIATIONS: Also cited simply as *Shinri* [Psychology]; and in English as *University of Kyoto. Studies in Psychology.*

DATES OF PUBLICATION: Number 1–5, 1947–1949.

FREQUENCY: Irregular.

NUMBERING VARIATIONS: None.

PUBLISHER: **Kyoto:** Kyōto Daigaku, Bungakubu, Shinrigaku kenkyūshitsu [University of Kyoto, Faculty of Letters, Psychological Research Laboratory], 1947–1949.

PRIMARY EDITOR: **Tatsuro Yatabe**, 1947–1949.

NOTE: English language abstracts of this publication were also published as *Kyoto. University. Faculty of Letters. Psychological Research Laboratory. Psychology. Abstracts.* Information on this title was found in *Gakujutsu Zasshi Sōgō Mokuroku. Jimbun Kagaku Wabun Hen* [Union List of Scholarly Journals. Japanese Language Section. Humanities Part]. Tokyo, 1973.

978. *Louvain. Université catholique. Institut de psychologie appliquée et de pédagogie. Extraits de dissertations. Série A.*

TITLE VARIATIONS: Continues [*Louvain.*] *Université catholique. Institut de psychologie appliquée et de pédagogie. Extraits de dissertations.*

DATES OF PUBLICATION: Numéro 1–4+, 1947–1950+.

FREQUENCY: Irregular. *See* Contents *below.*

NUMBERING VARIATIONS: None.

PUBLISHER: Varies. *See* Contents *below.*

PRIMARY EDITORS: None listed.

CONTENTS:

Numéro 1. Knops, L. CONTRIBUTION À L'ÉTUDE DE LA "NAISSANCE" ET DE LA "PERMANENCE" PHÉNOMÉNALES DANS LE CHAMP VISUEL. Paris: J. Vrin, 1947. Pp. 562–610.

Numéro 2. Chuan-Ting, Lin. LES RÉACTIONS CHEZ LES NOUVEAU-NÉS AVANT ET APRÉS LE REPAS. Louvain: E. Nauwelaerts, 1949. 72 pp.

Numéro 3. Degardin, E. ÉTUDE CRITIQUE DES ÉCHELLES DE MOTRICITÉ. Paris: Presses universitaires de France, 1949. Pp. 215–244.

Numéro 4. Gille, A. ÉTUDE DE LA VALEUR PRATIQUE DES ÉPREUVES R. B. NOUVELLE CONTRIBUTION CRITIQUE CONCERNANT UNE BATTERIE DE TESTS MENTAUX COLLECTIFS UTILISABLES EN ORGANISATION SCOLAIRE. Tournai: Casterman, 1950. 52 pp.

979. *Louvain. Université catholique. Institut de psychologie appliquée et de pédagogie. Extraits de dissertations. Série B.*

TITLE VARIATIONS: Continues [*Louvain.*] *Université catholique. Institut de psychologie appliquée et de pédagogie. Extraits de dissertations.*

DATES OF PUBLICATION: Numéro 1–5, 1947–1949.

FREQUENCY: Irregular. *See* Contents *below.*

NUMBERING VARIATIONS: None.

PUBLISHER: Varies. *See* Contents *below.*

PRIMARY EDITORS: None listed.

CONTENTS:

Numéro 1. Lambert, J. L'ANALYSE DES FAUTES D'ORTHOGRAPHE D'USAGE. Namur: La Procure, 1947. 74 pp.

Numéro 2. Zuza, Fr. ALFRED BINET ET LA PÉDAGOGIE EXPÉRIMENTALE. Préface de Th. Simon. Louvain: E. Nauwelaerts; Paris: J. Vrin, 1948. 212 pp.

Numéro 3. Vandeputte, J. PSYCHOLOGISCHE ONTLEDING VAN MEISJES. Leuven: E. Nauwelaerts, 1949. 62 pp.

Numéro 4. Pirenne, A. PROGRAMME D'ORTHOGRAPHE D'USAGE POUR LES ÉCOLES PRIMAIRES. Namur: La Procure, 1949. 159 pp.

Numéro 5. Defrenne, L. RECHERCHE PSYCHOPÉDAGOGIQUE SUR LE VOCABULAIRE GÉOGRAPHIQUE. Tournai: Casterman, 1949. 25 pp

980. *Menninger Foundation. News Letter.*

TITLE VARIATIONS: Continued by *Menninger Quarterly* with Volume 4, Number 1, Winter 1950.

DATES OF PUBLICATION: Volume 1–3, April 1947–Annual Meeting Issue 1949.

FREQUENCY: **Bimonthly,** Volume 1, Number 1–6, April 1947–February 1948. **Irregular,** Volume 2, Number 1–9, May 1948–March/April 1949. **Quarterly,** Volume 3, Number 1–4, May 1949–Annual Meeting Issue (November) 1949.

NUMBERING VARIATIONS: None.

PUBLISHER: **Topeka, Kansas:** Menninger Foundation, 1947–1949.

PRIMARY EDITORS: None listed.

981. *Mens en onderneming.* [Organ of the Instituut voor preventieve geneeskunde.]

TITLE VARIATIONS: Also called *Psychologisch centrum van de nederlandse steenkolenmijnen. Mededelingen*, 1947–1948.

DATES OF PUBLICATION: Jaargang 1–4+, April 1947–December 1950+.

FREQUENCY: Bimonthly.

NUMBERING VARIATIONS: None.

PUBLISHER: **Haarlem:** H. D. Tjeenk Willink & Zoon N.V., 1947–1950+.

PRIMARY EDITORS: **J.L.M. Herold,** 1947–1950+; **W.J.P. Willems,** 1947–1948; **R. Remmelts,** 1949–1950+; **J. P. Bijl,** 1949–1950+; **J. Koekebakker,** 1949–1950+.

982. *Mensch und Arbeit. Internationale Zeitschrift für Arbeitspädagogik, Arbeitspsychologie, Arbeitstechnik und Betriebswirtschaft.*

TITLE VARIATIONS: None.

DATES OF PUBLICATION: Band 1–3+, 1947–1950+.

FREQUENCY: Bimonthly.

NUMBERING VARIATIONS: None.

PUBLISHER: **Vienna:** Arbeitsgemeinschaft für Psychotechnik in Oesterreich, Psychotechnisches Institut, 1947–1950+.

PRIMARY EDITOR: **Karl Hackl,** [1947]–1950+.

983. *Mensch und Arbeit. Internationale Zeitschrift für Arbeitspädagogik, Arbeitspsychologie, Arbeitstechnik und Betriebswirtschaft. Beihefte.*

TITLE VARIATIONS: None.

DATES OF PUBLICATION: Stück 1+, 1947+. Stück 2 issued 1953.

FREQUENCY: Irregular. *See* Contents *below.*

NUMBERING VARIATIONS: None.

PUBLISHER: **Vienna:** Arbeitsgemeinschaft für Psychotechnik in Oesterreich, Psychotechnisches Institut, 1947+.

PRIMARY EDITORS: None listed.

CONTENTS:

    Stück 1. Meissner, Fritz. Revolution durch die Technik? 1947. 78 pp.

984. *Messenger.*

TITLE VARIATIONS: None.

DATES OF PUBLICATION: Volume 1, Number 1/2, January 1947.

FREQUENCY: Irregular.

NUMBERING VARIATIONS: Multinumber issue present.

PUBLISHER: **Hastings, Nebraska:** Association for the Advancement of Mental Health in the State of Nebraska, 1947.

PRIMARY EDITOR: **Mrs. Willard Roley,** 1947.

985. *New York. Josiah Macy, Jr. Foundation. Conference on Training in Clinical Psychology. Transactions.*

TITLE VARIATIONS: None.

DATES OF PUBLICATION: 1st, 1947.

FREQUENCY: Annual.

NUMBERING VARIATIONS: None.

PUBLISHER: **New York:** Josiah Macy, Jr. Foundation, 1947.

PRIMARY EDITOR: **Molly R. Harrower,** 1947.

CONTENTS:

    1st. TRAINING IN CLINICAL PSYCHOLOGY. TRANSACTIONS OF THE FIRST CON FERENCE MARCH 27–28, 1947, NEW YORK. Chairman: Lawrence S. Kubie. 1947. 88 pp.

986. *Nordisk Psykologmøte. Förhandlingar.*

TITLE VARIATIONS: None.

DATES OF PUBLICATION: Nummer 1–2+, 1947–1950+.

FREQUENCY: Triannual.

NUMBERING VARIATIONS: None.

PUBLISHER: **Oslo, Norway:** Skrivemaskinstua, 1947. **Borås, Norway:** J. F. Bjørsells Boktryckeri, 1950.

PRIMARY EDITORS: **Emil Østlyngen,** 1947; **John Ermgren,** 1950; **Erik Malmstrøm,** 1950; **Marianne Setterberg,** 1950.

CONTENTS:

    Nummer 1. SEKSJONSFOREDRAG MED REFERAT AV TILHØRENDE ORDSKIF- TER VED NORDISK PSYKOLOGMØTE I OSLO. 1947. 111 pp.

    Nummer 2. ANDRA NORDISKA PSYKOLOGMÖTET I GÖTEBORG, 1950. FÖRHANDLINGAR. 196 pp.

987. *Paris. Université. Groupe d'études de psychologie. Bulletin.*

TITLE VARIATIONS: None.

DATES OF PUBLICATION: Année 1–4, Numéro 3+, August 1947–December 1950+.

FREQUENCY: Monthly (Irregular).

NUMBERING VARIATIONS: Multinumber issues present.

PUBLISHER: **Paris:** Groupe d'études de psychologie de l'université de Paris, 17, rue de la Sorbonne, 1947–1950+.

PRIMARY EDITORS: None listed.

988. *Personnel-O-Gram.*

TITLE VARIATIONS: None.

DATES OF PUBLICATION: Volume 1–4+, October 1947–May 1950+.

FREQUENCY: Quarterly.

NUMBERING VARIATIONS: None.

PUBLISHER: **Lexington, Kentucky:** University of Kentucky, 1947–1950+.

PRIMARY EDITOR: **Leslie L. Martin,** 1947–1950+.

989. *Praktische Psychologie.*

TITLE VARIATIONS: Also called *Psychologische Übungsblätter.*

DATES OF PUBLICATION: Blätter 1–6, 1947–1948.

FREQUENCY: Irregular.

NUMBERING VARIATIONS: None.

PUBLISHER: **Bad Homburg, Germany:** Siemens-Studien-Gesellschaft für praktische Psychologie, 1948.

PRIMARY EDITOR: **Adolf Zeddies,** 1947–1948.

990. *Psiquis; revista mexicana de higiene mental.* [Organ of the Liga mexicana de salud mental and of the Sociedad mexicana de psicología.]

TITLE VARIATIONS: Subtitled *Revista mexicana de psicología y de higiene mental* after January 1948 and *Revista mexicana de psicología y de salud mental* after March 1949. Continues *Revista mexicana de higiene mental.*

DATES OF PUBLICATION: Volumen 2–6, Número 2/3+, August 1947–November/December 1950+.

FREQUENCY: Monthly.

NUMBERING VARIATIONS: Issues in Volumen 2 also assigned whole numbers, Número 9–13. Volumen 3–6 have multinumbered issues and either 6 or 12 issue numbers per volume.

PUBLISHER: **Mexico City:** Revista mexicana de higiene mental, 1947. **Mexico City:** Editorial psiquis, 1948–1950+.

PRIMARY EDITORS: **Enrique Felix,** 1947–1948; **Emma Dolujanoff,** 1947–1950+;

Hector Prado Huante, 1947–1948; Santiago Ramirez, 1947–1948+; Sara Margarita Zendejas, 1947–1950; Victoria Morales, 1947; Silvia Galindo, 1947; Maria Guadalupe Odriozola, 1947; Arturo del Moral, Jr., 1948; Luis Chavez Aldape, 1948; Javier Alba, 1948; Francisco M. Zendejas, 1948.

991. *Psyche; Eine Zeitschrift für Tiefenpsychologie und Menschenkunde in Forschung und Praxis.*

TITLE VARIATIONS: Subtitle varies.

DATES OF PUBLICATION: Band 1–3+, 1947–1950+.

FREQUENCY: **Quarterly**, Band 1–2, July 1947–1949. **Monthly**, Band 3+, July 1949–1950+.

NUMBERING VARIATIONS: None.

PUBLISHER: **Heidelberg:** Verlag L. Schneider, 1947–1950+.

PRIMARY EDITORS: **Hans Kunz**, 1947–1950+; **Alexander Mitscherlich**, 1947–1950+; **Fel. Schottlaender**, 1947–1950+.

992. *Psychoanalysis and the Social Sciences.*

TITLE VARIATIONS: None.

DATES OF PUBLICATION: Volume 1–2+, 1947–1950+.

FREQUENCY: Irregular.

NUMBERING VARIATIONS: None.

PUBLISHER: **New York:** International Universities Press, Inc., 1947–1950+.

PRIMARY EDITORS: **Geza Roheim**, 1947–1950+; **Gertrud M. Kurth**, 1950+.

EDITORIAL BOARD: Marie Bonaparte, 1947–1950; Henry A. Bunker, 1947–1950; John Dollard, 1947–1950; Erik H. Erikson, 1947–1950; Paul Federn, 1947–1950; J. C. Flugel, 1947–1950; Angel Garma, 1947–1950; Heinz Hartmann, 1947–1950; Imre Hermann, 1947–1950; Edward Hitschmann, 1947–1950; Ernest Jones, 1947–1950; Clyde Kluckhohn, 1947–1950; Ernst Kris, 1947–1950; R. Money-Kyrle, 1947–1950; Sandor Lorand, 1947–1950; Karl A. Menninger, 1947–1950; Herman Nunberg, 1947–1950; Clarence P. Oberndorf, 1947–1950; Oskar Pfister, 1947–1950; Fritz Wittels, 1947–1950; Gregory Zilboorg, 1947–1950.

993. *Psychosociologie.*

TITLE VARIATIONS: None.

DATES OF PUBLICATION: June 1947.

FREQUENCY: Irregular.

NUMBERING VARIATIONS: Issue numbered by date only.

PUBLISHER: **Paris:** Société française de psychosociologie, 1947.

PRIMARY EDITOR: **Roger Frétigny**, 1947.

994. *Psychotechniek.* [Organ of the Psychotechnisch laboratorium (Amsterdam).]

TITLE VARIATIONS: None.

DATES OF PUBLICATION: Nummer 1/2+, 1947+. Nummer 3/4 issued 1953.

FREQUENCY: Irregular. *See* Contents *below.*

NUMBERING VARIATIONS: None.

PUBLISHER: **Groningen:** J. B. Wolters, 1947+.

PRIMARY EDITOR: **Ph. M. van der Heyden,** 1947+.

CONTENTS:

    Nummer 1/2. Heyden, Ph. M. van der. MENS EN MAATSCHAPPIJ ALS ARBEIDSVELD DER PSYCHOTECHNIEK. (1. MENS EN LEVENSMILIEU. 2. HET ARBEIDSVELD DER PSYCHOTECHNIEK.) 1947. 245 pp.

995. *Rorschach Research Exchange and Journal of Projective Techniques.*

TITLE VARIATIONS: Continues *Rorschach Research Exchange.* Continued by *Journal of Projective Techniques* with Volume 14, 1950.

DATES OF PUBLICATION: Volume 11–13, 1947–1949.

FREQUENCY: Quarterly.

NUMBERING VARIATIONS: Volume 11, Number 2–4 is a single issue. Volume 13, 1949 contains August 1949 *TAT Newsletter.*

PUBLISHER: **New York:** Rorschach Institute, Inc., 1947. **New York:** Society for Projective Techniques and Rorschach Institute, Inc., 1948–1949.

PRIMARY EDITORS: **Bruno Klopfer,** 1947–1949; **Camilla Kemple,** 1947–1948; **Edward M. L. Burchard,** 1947–1948; **Hanna Faterson,** 1947–1948; **Marguerite R. Hertz,** 1947–1949; **Florence R. Miale,** 1947–1948; **Miriam G. Siegel,** 1947–1949; **Winafred B. Lucas,** 1949; **Walther Joel,** 1949; **Mortimer M. Meyer,** 1949; **Edwin S. Shnudman,** 1949; **Jeanne M. Reitzel,** 1949; **Theodora M. Abel,** 1949; **Bertram R. Forer,** 1949; **Evelyn Troup,** 1949.

EDITORIAL BOARD: Elizabeth Anderson, 1947–1949; Susan Deri, 1947–1949; Lawrence K. Frank, 1947–1949; Max L. Hutt, 1947–1949; Nolan D. C. Lewis, 1947–1949; Karen Machover, 1947–1949; Gardner Murphy, 1947–1949; Lois B. Murphy, 1947–1949; L. Joseph Stone, 1947–1949; Frederick Wyatt, 1947–1949; Franklin G. Ebaugh, 1949; Robert R. Holt, 1949.

996. *Samiksa. Journal of the Indian Psychoanalytic Society.*

TITLE VARIATIONS: None.

DATES OF PUBLICATION: Volume 1–4+, 1947–1950+.

FREQUENCY: Quarterly.

NUMBERING VARIATIONS: None.

PUBLISHER: **Calcutta:** Printed at the Sreekrisha Printing Works and published by A. Datta, Assistant Secretary, Indian Psychoanalytic Society, 1947–1948. **Calcutta:** Printed at Orient Printing & Publishing House Ltd. and published by A. Datta, Assistant Secretary, Indian Psychoanalytic Society, 1949–1950 +. PRIMARY EDITOR: **G. Bose**, 1947–1950 +.

997. *Sociatry. Journal of Group and Intergroup Therapy.*

TITLE VARIATIONS: Continued by *Group Psychotherapy; Journal of Socio-Psychopathology and Sociatry* with Volume 3, 1950.

DATES OF PUBLICATION: Volume 1–2, March 1947–March 1949. Publication suspended April 1949–March 1950.

FREQUENCY: Quarterly.

NUMBERING VARIATIONS: Volume 2, Number 3/4, dated 1948 instead of 1948–1949. Volume 2 contains double issues 1/2 and 3/4.

PUBLISHER: **New York:** Beacon House, Inc., 1947–1949.

PRIMARY EDITORS: **J. L. Moreno**, 1947–1949; **Zerka Toeman**, 1947–1949.

998. *Studia Psychologica et Paedagogica. Series Altera. Investigationes.*

TITLE VARIATIONS: None.

DATES OF PUBLICATION: Number 1–4 +, 1947–1949 +.

FREQUENCY: Irregular. *See* Contents *below.*

NUMBERING VARIATIONS: None.

PUBLISHER: **Lund, Sweden:** C.W.K. Gleerup, 1947–1949 +.

PRIMARY EDITORS: None listed.

CONTENTS:

Number 1. Edlund, Sven. DISKUSSIONEN OM BEGÅVNINGSURVALET UNDER REFORMATIONS- OCH STORMAKSTIDEN, I. 1947. 341 pp.

Number 2. Agrell, Jan. NYINRÄTTADE PROFESSURER INOM FILOSOFISKA FAKULTETEN I LUND UNDER 1800-TALETS FÖRSTA HÄLFT. 1949. 453 pp.

Number 3. Smith, Gudmund. PSYCHOLOGICAL STUDIES IN TWIN DIFFERENCES WITH REFERENCE TO AFTERIMAGES AND EIDETIC PHENOMENA AS WELL AS MORE GENERAL PERSONALITY CHARACTERISTICS. 1949. 251 pp.

Number 4. Husen, Torsten. OM INNEBÖRDEN AV PSYKOLOGISKA MÄTNINGAR. 1949. 78 pp.

NOTE: Monographs appear in either Swedish or English.

999. *United States. Army Air Forces. Aviation Psychology Program. Research Reports.*

TITLE VARIATIONS: None.

DATES OF PUBLICATION: Number 1–19, 1947–1948.

FREQUENCY: Irregular. *See* Contents *below.*

NUMBERING VARIATIONS: None.

PUBLISHER: **Washington, D.C.:** United States Government Printing Office, 1947–1948.

PRIMARY EDITORS: None listed.

CONTENTS:

Number 1. Flanagan, John C., ed. THE AVIATION PSYCHOLOGY PROGRAM IN THE ARMY AIR FORCES. 1948. 316 pp.

Number 2. DuBois, Philip H., ed. THE CLASSIFICATION PROGRAM. 1947. 394 pp.

Number 3. Thorndike, Robert L., ed. RESEARCH PROBLEMS AND TECHNIQUES. 1947. 163 pp.

Number 4. Melton, Arthur W., ed. APPARATUS TESTS. 1947. 1056 pp.

Number 5. Guilford, J. P., and John I. Lacey, eds. PRINTED CLASSIFICATION TESTS. 1947. 919 pp.

Number 6. Davis Frederick B., ed. THE AAF QUALIFYING EXAMINATION. 1947. 266 pp.

Number 7. Gibson, James J., ed. MOTION PICTURE TESTING AND RESEARCH. 1947. 267 pp.

Number 8. Miller, Neal E., ed. PSYCHOLOGICAL RESEARCH ON PILOT TRAINING. 1947. 488 pp.

Number 9. Kemp, Edward H., and A. Pemberton Johnson, eds. PSYCHOLOGICAL RESEARCH ON BOMBARDIER TRAINING. 1947. 294 pp.

Number 10. Carter, Launor F., ed. PSYCHOLOGICAL RESEARCH ON NAVIGATOR TRAINING. 1947. 186 pp.

Number 11. Hobbs, Nicholas, ed. PSYCHOLOGICAL RESEARCH ON FLEXIBLE GUNNERY TRAINING. 1947. 508 pp.

Number 12. Cook, Stuart W., ed. PSYCHOLOGICAL RESEARCH ON RADAR OBSERVER TRAINING. 1947. 340 pp.

Number 13. Dailey, John T., ed. PSYCHOLOGICAL RESEARCH ON FLIGHT ENGINEER TRAINING. 1947. 227 pp.

Number 14. Wickert, Frederic, ed. PSYCHOLOGICAL RESEARCH ON PROBLEMS OF REDISTRIBUTION. 1947. 298 pp.

Number 15. Bijou, Sidney W., ed. THE PSYCHOLOGICAL PROGRAM IN AAF CONVALESCENT HOSPITALS. 1947. 256 pp.

Number 16. Crawford, Meredith P., Richard T. Sollenberger, Lewis B. Ward, Clarence W. Brown, and Edwin E. Ghiselli, eds. PSYCHOLOGICAL RESEARCH ON OPERATIONAL TRAINING IN THE CONTINENTAL AIR FORCES. 1947. 367 pp.

Number 17. Lepley, William M., ed. PSYCHOLOGICAL RESARCH IN THE THEATERS OF WAR. 1947. 202 pp.

Number 18. Deemer, Walter L., Jr., ed. RECORDS, ANALYSIS, AND TEST PROCEDURES. 1947. 621 pp.

Number 19. Fitts, Paul M., ed. PSYCHOLOGICAL RESEARCH ON EQUIPMENT DESIGN. 1947. 276 pp.

1000. *Wiener Zeitschrift für Philosophie, Psychologie, Pädagogik.*

TITLE VARIATIONS: None.

DATES OF PUBLICATION: Band 1–3+, January 1947–1950/1951.

FREQUENCY: **Semiannual,** Band 1, 1947. **Quarterly,** Band 2–3+, 1948/ 1949–1950/1951+.

NUMBERING VARIATIONS: Band 1 has only 2 Hefte.

PUBLISHER: **Vienna:** Universum, 1947. **Vienna:** A. Sexl, 1948–1949. **Vienna** and **Cologne:** A. Sexl, 1950+.

PRIMARY EDITORS: **A. Dempf,** 1947–1950+; **Th. Erismann,** 1947–1950+; **R. Meister,** 1947–1950+; **H. Rohracher,** 1947–1950+.

1948

1001. *A.A.M.D. News.* [Published by the American Association on Mental Deficiency.]

TITLE VARIATIONS: None.

DATES OF PUBLICATION: Volume 1–3, Number 1/2+, October 1948–October/ December 1950+.

FREQUENCY: **Quarterly,** Volume 1, 1948–1949. **Bimonthly,** Volume 2–3, 1949–1950+.

NUMBERING VARIATIONS: Multinumber issues present.

PUBLISHER: **Washington Crossing, New Jersey:** American Association on Mental Deficiency, 1948–1950+.

PRIMARY EDITOR: **Lloyd N. Yepsen,** 1948–1950+.

EDITORIAL CONSULTANT: Edward J. Humphreys, 1948–1950+.

1002. *Acta neurologica et psychiatrica belgica.*

TITLE VARIATIONS: Continues *Journal belge de neurologie et de psychiatrie.*

DATES OF PUBLICATION: Tome 48–50+, 1948–1950+.

FREQUENCY: Monthly.

NUMBERING VARIATIONS: None.

PUBLISHER: **Brussels:** Les éditions "acta medica belgica," 1948–1950+.

PRIMARY EDITORS: None listed.

1003. *American Psychological Association. Directory.*

TITLE VARIATIONS: Continues *American Psychological Association. Yearbook.*

DATES OF PUBLICATION: 1948–1950+.

FREQUENCY: Annual.

NUMBERING VARIATIONS: Numbered by date only.

PUBLISHER: **Washington, D.C.**: American Psychological Association, Inc., 1948–1950+.

PRIMARY EDITORS: **Helen Morrill Wolfle**, 1948–1949; **Jane D. Hildreth**, 1950+.

1004. *Bibliotheca Psychiatrica et Neurologica.*

TITLE VARIATIONS: Continues *Abhandlungen aus der Neurologie, Psychiatrie, Psychologie und ihren Grenzgebieten.*

DATES OF PUBLICATION: Band 88+, 1948+. Band 89 published 1951.

FREQUENCY: Irregular. *See* Contents *below.*

NUMBERING VARIATIONS: Supplement to *Monatsschrift für Psychiatrie und Neurologie.*

PUBLISHER: **Basel** and **New York:** S. Karger, 1948+.

PRIMARY EDITOR: **J. Kläsi**, 1948+.

CONTENTS:
 Band 88. Massion-Verniory, L. LES REFLEXES DE PREHENSION. 1948. 87 pp.

1005. *Bibliothèque des archives de philosophie. (Nouvelle série). Deuxième section: Logique et psychologie.*

TITLE VARIATIONS: None.

DATES OF PUBLICATION: Numéro 1+, 1948+. Numéro 2 issued in 1957.

FREQUENCY: Irregular. *See* Contents *below.*

NUMBERING VARIATIONS: None.

PUBLISHER: **Paris:** Beauchesne et ses fils, 1948+.

PRIMARY EDITORS: None listed.

CONTENTS:
 Numéro 1. Stocker, Arnold. LE TRAITEMENT MORAL DES NERVEUX. 1948. 220 pp.

1006. *Bildung und Erziehung. Monatsschrift für Pädagogik mit besonderer Betonung der pädagogischen Psychologie, der vergleichenden Erziehungswissenschaft und der pädagogischen Bibliographie.*

TITLE VARIATIONS: Supersedes *Pädagogisches Zentralblatt.*

DATES OF PUBLICATION: Band 1–3, Heft 3+, October 1948–December 1950+.

FREQUENCY: Monthly.

NUMBERING VARIATIONS: None.

PUBLISHER: **Stuttgart:** Klett, 1948–1950+.

PRIMARY EDITORS: **Frz. Hilker,** 1948–1950+; **Erich Hylla,** 1948–1950+.

1007. *Brazil. Universidade. Instituto de psicologia (Rio de Janeiro). Monografias psicológicas.*

TITLE VARIATIONS: None.

DATES OF PUBLICATION: Número 1–7+, 1948–1949+. Número 8 issued in 1951.

FREQUENCY: Irregular. *See* Contents *below.*

NUMBERING VARIATIONS: None.

PUBLISHER: **Rio de Janeiro:** Universidade do Brasil, Instituto de psicologia, Oficina gráfica da Universidade do Brasil, 1948–1949+.

PRIMARY EDITORS: **Nilton Campos,** 1948–1949+.

CONTENTS:

Número 1. Campos, Nilton. FUNDAMENTALS OF THE PHENOMENOLOGICAL ATTITUDE IN MODERN PSYCHOLOGY. 1948. 15 pp.

Número 2. Schneider, E. TEORIAS EMERGENTISTAS DA PERSONALIDADE. 1948. 44 pp.

Número 3. Vianna Guerra, C. SIFILIS INATA E INTELIGÊNCIA. 1948. 20 pp.

Número 4. Schneider, E. ORIENTAÇÃO, SELEÇÃO E FORMAÇÃO PROFISSIONAL NO BRASIL. 1949. 63 pp.

Número 5. Vianna Guerra, C. ASPECTOS DO DESENVOLVIMENTO DE LACTENTES DE BERÇÁRIO. 1949.

Número 6. Gomes Penna, Antonio. NOTAS SOBRE O BEHAVIORISMO. 1949.

Número 7. Alves Garcia, J. A UTILIDADE E A NOCIVIDADE DAS EMOÇÕES. 1949.

1008. *British Psychological Society. Bulletin.*

TITLE VARIATIONS: None.

DATES OF PUBLICATION: Volume 1, Number 1–9+, July 1948–July 1950+.

FREQUENCY: Quarterly.

NUMBERING VARIATIONS: None.

PUBLISHER: **London:** British Psychological Society, 1948–1950+.

PRIMARY EDITOR: **Frederick Laws,** 1948–1950+.

1009. *Collection de psychologie scientifique.*

TITLE VARIATIONS: None.

DATES OF PUBLICATION: Numéro 1, 1948.

FREQUENCY: Irregular. *See* Contents *below.*

NUMBERING VARIATIONS: None.

PUBLISHER: **Paris:** Dervy, 1948.

PRIMARY EDITOR: **Bertrand de Cressac de Bachelerie,** 1948.

CONTENTS:

Numéro 1. Cressac de Bachelerie, Bertrand de. LA MÉTAPSYCHIQUE DE-
VANT LA SCIENCE. (1948). 188 pp.

1010. *Congrès international de psychologie religieuse. Travaux.*

TITLE VARIATIONS: Congress Proceedings 1–4 were published without numbering as *Études carmélitaines.* Each Congress has a separate title. *See* Contents
below.

DATES OF PUBLICATION: 5e–6e+, 1948–1950+.

FREQUENCY: Irregular. *See* Contents *below.*

NUMBERING VARIATIONS: None.

PUBLISHER: **Bruges:** Desclée de Brouwer, 1949–1951.

PRIMARY EDITORS: *See* Contents *below.*

CONTENTS:

5e. Avon-Fontainebleau, 1948. TROUBLE ET LUMIÈRE—PAR CHARLES JOUR-
NET ET AL. LES TRAVAUX, EN PARTIE, DU CINQUIÈME CONGRÈS INTERNATIONAL
DE PSYCHOLOGIE RELIGIEUSE TENU À AVON LES 18–19–20 SEPTEMBRE 1948.
1949. 219 pp.

6^e. Avon, 1950. DIRECTION SPIRITUELLE ET PSYCHOLOGIE. 1951. 363 pp.

1011. *Connecticut Psychologist.*

TITLE VARIATIONS: None.

DATES OF PUBLICATION: Volume 1–3, Number 3+, November 1948–October
1950+.

FREQUENCY: **Irregular,** Volume 1–2, 1948–1949. **Triannual,** Volume 3+,
1950+.

NUMBERING VARIATIONS: Volume 1 has 1 issue; Volume 2, 2 issues; Volume
3, 3 issues.

PUBLISHER: **Hartford:** Connecticut State Psychological Society, 1948. **New
Haven:** Connecticut State Psychological Society, 1949–1950+.

PRIMARY EDITORS: **C. Winfield Scott,** 1948–1950+; **Sol Garfield,** 1948; **Wilbert S. Ray,** 1948–1949; **Marion A. Bills,** 1949; **David C. McClelland,** 1949;
Milton Cotzin, 1950+; **Dwane R. Collins,** 1950+.

1012. *Encéphale; journal de neurologie et de psychiatrie et l'hygiène mentale.*

TITLE VARIATIONS: Continues *Encèphale; journal de neurologie et de psychiatrie,* and *Hygiène mentale. Journal de psychiatrie appliquée.* Continued by
Encéphale; journal de neurologie, de psychiatrie et de médecine psycho-soma-

tique, and *Hygiène mentale. Organe de la ligue française d'hygiène mentale* with Année 39+, 1950+.

DATES OF PUBLICATION: Année 37–38, 1948–1949.

FREQUENCY: Monthly (except July and August).

NUMBERING VARIATIONS: None.

PUBLISHER: **Paris:** G. Doin & Cie, éditeurs, 1948–1949.

PRIMARY EDITORS: **Jean Lhermitte,** 1948–1949; **Jean Delay,** 1948–1949.

1013. *Enfance; psychologie, pédagogie, neuro-psychiatrie, sociologie.*

TITLE VARIATIONS: None.

DATES OF PUBLICATION: Année 1–3+, 1948–1950+

FREQUENCY: Bimonthly (5 issues per year).

NUMBERING VARIATIONS: None.

PUBLISHER: **Paris:** Laboratoire de psychobiologie de l'enfant, by Presses universitaires de France, 1948–1950+.

PRIMARY EDITOR: **Henri Wallon,** 1948–1950+.

EDITORIAL BOARD: M. Bergeron, 1948–1950+; G. Friedmann, 1948–1950+; R. Gal, 1948–1950+; R. Girard, 1948–1950+; M. Lebrun, 1948–1950+; Suzanne Roubakine, 1948–1950+; R. Zazzo, 1948–1950+; Fernande Seclet-Riou, 1948–1950+.

1014. *Études de psychologie pédagogique.*

TITLE VARIATIONS: None.

DATES OF PUBLICATION: Numéro 1, 1948.

FREQUENCY: Irregular. *See* Contents *below.*

NUMBERING VARIATIONS: None.

PUBLISHER: **Louvain:** E. Nauwelaerts; **Paris,** J. Vrin, 1948.

PRIMARY EDITOR: **Arthur Fauville,** 1948.

CONTENTS:
   Numéro 1. Fauville, A. ÉLÉMENTS DE PSYCHOLOGIE DE L'ENFANT ET DE L'ADOLESCENT. 1948. 172 pp.

1015. *Études et recherches de pédagogie expérimentale.*

TITLE VARIATIONS: None.

DATES OF PUBLICATION: Numéro 1–2, 1948–1950.

FREQUENCY: Irregular. *See* Contents *below.*

NUMBERING VARIATIONS: None.

PUBLISHER: **Louvain:** E. Nauwelaerts; **Paris,** J. Vrin, 1948–1950.

PRIMARY EDITOR: **R. Buyse,** 1948–1950.

CONTENTS:
   Numéro 1. Zuza, F. ALFRED BINET ET LA PÉDAGOGIE EXPÉRIMENTALE. Préface de Théodore Simon. 1948. 212 pp.
   Numéro 2. Piscart, R. ÉCHELLE OBJECTIVE D'ÉCRITURE POUR ÉCOLIERS BELGES D'EXPRESSION FRANÇAISE. 1950. 71 pp.

1016. *Industrial Relations Research Association. Proceedings.*

TITLE VARIATIONS: None.

DATES OF PUBLICATION: 1st–3rd+, 1948–1950+.

FREQUENCY: Annual.

NUMBERING VARIATIONS: Proceedings also numbered as *Industrial Relations Research Association. Publications* 1, 4 and 6. Proceedings for 1948 also numbered Volume 1, Number 1.

PUBLISHER: **Champaign, Illinois:** Industrial Relations Research Association, 1948–1950+.

PRIMARY EDITOR: **M. Derber,** 1948–1950.

CONTENTS:
   1st. INDUSTRIAL RELATIONS RESEARCH ASSOCIATION. PROCEEDINGS OF THE 1ST ANNUAL MEETING, CLEVELAND, OHIO. DECEMBER 29–30, 1948. 1949. 255 pp.
   2nd. INDUSTRIAL RELATIONS RESEARCH ASSOCIATION. PROCEEDINGS OF THE 2ND ANNUAL MEETING, NEW YORK CITY. DECEMBER 29–30, 1949. 1950. 299 pp.
   3rd. INDUSTRIAL RELATIONS RESEARCH ASSOCIATION. PROCEEDINGS OF THE 3RD ANNUAL MEETING, CHICAGO, ILLINOIS, DECEMBER 28–29, 1950. 1951. 388 pp.

1017. *Johannesburg. South African Council for Scientific and Industrial Research. National Institute for Personnel Research. Bulletin.*

TITLE VARIATIONS: None.

DATES OF PUBLICATION: Volume 1–2, Number 3+, November 1948–October 1950+.

FREQUENCY: Quarterly.

NUMBERING VARIATIONS: None.

PUBLISHER: **Johannesburg:** South African Council for Scientific and Industrial Research, National Institute for Personnel Research, 1948–1950+.

PRIMARY EDITORS: **A. Biggs,** 1948–1949; **N. Unger,** 1949–1950.

1018. *Journal of Clinical Psychology. Monograph Supplement.*

TITLE VARIATIONS: Titled *Clinical Psychology Monographs*, Number 1–2, 1948.

DATES OF PUBLICATION: Number 1–7+, January 1948–January 1950+.

FREQUENCY: Irregular. *See* Contents *below.*

NUMBERING VARIATIONS: Some issues are also numbered in *Journal of Clinical Psychology. See* Contents *below.* Number 6 incorrectly dated 1948 instead of 1949.

PUBLISHER: **Burlington, Vermont:** University of Vermont, Medical College, 1948–1950+.

PRIMARY EDITOR: **Frederick C. Thorne,** 1948–1950+.

EDITORIAL BOARD: Jerry W. Carter, Jr., 1948–1950+; Samuel W. Hamilton, 1948–1950+; William A. Hunt, 1948–1950+; George A. Kelly, 1948–1949; Elaine F. Kinder, 1948–1950+; C. M. Louttit, 1948–1950+; Robert I. Watson, 1948–1950+.

CONTENTS:

Number 1. Billingslea, Fred Y. THE BENDER-GESTALT: AN OBJECTIVE SCORING METHOD AND VALIDATING DATA. January 1948. 27 pp. (Also as *Journal of Clinical Psychology*, Volume 4, Number 1.)

Number 2. Carter, Jerry W., Jr., and J. W. Bowles. A MANUAL ON QUALITATIVE ASPECTS OF PSYCHOLOGICAL EXAMINING. April 1948. 41 pp. (Also as *Journal of Clinical Psychology*, Volume 4, Number 2.)

Number 3. TRAINING IN CLINICAL PSYCHOLOGY. TRANSACTIONS OF THE FIRST CONFERENCE, MARCH 27–28, 1947, NEW YORK, NEW YORK. Sponsored by the Josiah Macy, Jr. Foundation. July 1948. 88 pp.

Number 4. Carter, Jerry W., Jr., ed. CRITICAL EVALUATION OF NONDIRECTIVE COUNSELING AND PSYCHOTHERAPY. (A SYMPOSIUM). July 1948. 39 pp. (Also as *Journal of Clinical Psychology*, Volume 4, Number 3.)

Number 5. Buck, John N. THE H-T-P TECHNIQUE: A QUALITATIVE AND QUANTITATIVE SCORING MANUAL. October 1948. 120 pp. (Also as *Journal of Clinical Psychology*, Volume 4, Number 4.)

Number 6. Karpman, Ben. OBJECTIVE PSYCHOTHERAPY: PRINCIPLES, METHODS, AND RESULTS. July 1948. 154 pp. (Also as *Journal of Clinical Psychology*, Volume 5, Number 3, July 1949.)

Number 7. Zubin, Joseph, ed. SYMPOSIUM ON STATISTICS FOR THE CLINICIAN. January 1950. 76 pp. (Also as *Journal of Clinical Psychology*, Volume 6, Number 1.)

1019. *Journal of Social Issues. Supplement Series.*

TITLE VARIATIONS: None.

DATES OF PUBLICATION: Number 1–4+, December 1948–1950+.

FREQUENCY: Irregular. *See* Contents *below.*

NUMBERING VARIATIONS: None.

PUBLISHER: **New York:** Published by the Association Press for the Society for the Psychological Study of Social Issues, A Division of the American Psychological Association, 1948–1950+.

PRIMARY EDITOR: **Ronald Lippitt,** 1948–1950.

CONTENTS:
Number 1. Chisholm, George Brock. SOCIAL RESPONSIBILITY. December 1948. 34 pp.
Number 2. Hart, Hornell. SOCIAL SCIENCE AND THE ATOMIC CRISIS. April 1949. 30 pp.
Number 3. Tolman, Edward C. THE PSYCHOLOGY OF SOCIAL LEARNING. December 1949. 18 pp.
Number 4. Allport, Gordon W. PREJUDICE: A PROBLEM IN PSYCHOLOGICAL AND SOCIAL CAUSATION. 1950. 26 pp.

1020. *Kölner Zeitschrift für Soziologie. Neue Folge der Kölner Vierteljahrshefte für Soziologie.* [Published by order of the Forschungsinstitut für Sozial- und Verwaltungswissenschaften.]

TITLE VARIATIONS: Continued by *Kölner Zeitschrift für Soziologie und Sozialpsychologie* after 1950.

DATES OF PUBLICATION: Band 1–2 +, 1948–1950 +.

FREQUENCY: Quarterly.

NUMBERING VARIATIONS: None.

PUBLISHER: **Cologne:** Westdeutscher Verlag, 1948–1950 +.

PRIMARY EDITOR: **Leopold von Wiese,** 1948–1950 +.

1021. *Modern Trends in Psychological Medicine.*

TITLE VARIATIONS: None.

DATES OF PUBLICATION: 1948.

FREQUENCY: Annual.

NUMBERING VARIATIONS: Publication is numbered only by date.

PUBLISHER: **New York** and **London:** Paul B. Hoeber, Inc., Medical Book Department of Harper & Brothers, 1948.

PRIMARY EDITOR: **Noel G. Harris,** 1948.

1022. *New York. Josiah Macy, Jr. Foundation. Conference on Problems of Aging. Transactions.*

TITLE VARIATIONS: None.

DATES OF PUBLICATION: 10th/11th–12th +, 1948/1949–1950 +.

FREQUENCY: Annual.

NUMBERING VARIATIONS: Transactions of the 1st–9th conferences were not published.

PUBLISHER: **New York:** Josiah Macy, Jr. Foundation, 1950–1951 +.

PRIMARY EDITOR: **Nathan W. Shock,** 1948–1950 +.

CONTENTS:
10th/11th. CONFERENCE ON PROBLEMS OF AGING. TRANSACTIONS OF THE

TENTH AND ELEVENTH CONFERENCES FEBRUARY 9–10, 1948, AND APRIL 25–26, 1949, NEW YORK. Sponsored by the Josiah Macy, Jr. Foundation. 1950. 258 pp.

12th. CONFERENCE ON PROBLEMS OF AGING. TRANSACTIONS OF THE TWELFTH CONFERENCE FEBRUARY 6–7, 1950, NEW YORK. Sponsored by the Josiah Macy, Jr. Foundation. 1951. 215 pp.

1023. *North Carolina Psychological Association. Bulletin.*

TITLE VARIATIONS: None.

DATES OF PUBLICATION: Volume 1–2+, December 1948–November 1949+. (Volume 3 published March 1951.)

FREQUENCY: Annual.

NUMBERING VARIATIONS: Only one issue per year.

PUBLISHER: **[Raleigh, North Carolina]:** North Carolina Psychological Association, 1948–1949+.

PRIMARY EDITORS: None listed.

1024. *Persona. The Intercollegiate Journal of Psychology.*

TITLE VARIATIONS: None.

DATES OF PUBLICATION: Volume 1–2+, Winter 1948/1949–Fall 1950+.

FREQUENCY: Quarterly.

NUMBERING VARIATIONS: Multinumber issues present.

PUBLISHER: **Cleveland, Ohio:** The Intercollegiate Journal of Psychology, Inc., Psychological Laboratory, Western Reserve University, 1948–1950+.

PRIMARY EDITORS: **Arthur Bachrach,** 1948–1950; **Prudence Burchard,** 1948–1950+; **Marjorie Creelman,** 1948–1950; **Alexander Darbes,** 1948–1950; **Carmen Miller,** 1948–1950.

1025. *Personnel Psychology; A Journal of Applied Research.*

TITLE VARIATIONS: None.

DATES OF PUBLICATION: Volume 1–3+, 1948–1950+.

FREQUENCY: Quarterly.

NUMBERING VARIATIONS: None.

PUBLISHER: **Washington, D.C.:** Personnel Psychology, Inc., 1948–1950+.

PRIMARY EDITORS: **G. Frederic Kuder,** 1948–1950+; **Charles I. Mosier,** 1948–1950+; **Erwin K. Taylor,** 1948–1950+.

EDITORIAL ADVISERS: George K. Bennett, 1948–1950+; Walter van Dyke Bingham, 1948–1950+; M. W. Richardson, 1948–1950+.

EDITORIAL BOARD: John D. Coakley, 1948–1950+; Neal Drought, 1948–1950+; Jack Dunlap, 1948–1950+; Paul M. Fitts, 1948–1950+; John Flanagan, 1948–1950+; Edward N. Hay, 1948–1950+; Carl Hovland, 1948–1950+; Jack Jenkins, 1948; Rensis Likert, 1948; Walter J. McNamara,

1948–1950+; Jay L. Otis, 1948–1950+; Robert C. Rogers, 1948–1950+; E. A. Rundquist, 1948, 1950+; C. L. Shartle, 1948–1950+; Robert J. Wherry, 1948–1950+; Daniel Katz, 1949–1950+; William McGehee, 1949–1950+.

1026. *Physical and Mental Rehabilitation Journal.* [Official publication of the Physical and Mental Rehabilitation Association.]

TITLE VARIATIONS: Continues *Association for Physical and Mental Rehabilitation. Journal.* Continued by *Association for Physical and Mental Rehabilitation. Journal* with Volume 3, Number 6, December 1949.

DATES OF PUBLICATION: Volume 2–3, Number 5, August 1948–October 1949.

FREQUENCY: Bimonthly.

NUMBERING VARIATIONS: Volume 2 contains only 3 issues.

PUBLISHER: **Columbia, South Carolina:** Physical and Mental Rehabilitation Association, 1948–1949.

PRIMARY EDITORS: None listed.

1027. *Psychologia i higiena psychiczna pracy. Kwartalnik poświęcony sprawom poradnictwa zawodowego, psychologii przemysłowej i pokrewnym działom psychologii stosowanej.*

TITLE VARIATIONS: None.

DATES OF PUBLICATION: Rok 1, Numer 1–2, 1948–1949.

FREQUENCY: Irregular.

NUMBERING VARIATIONS: None.

PUBLISHER: **Warsaw:** Państwowy instytut higieny psychicznej, 1948–1949.

PRIMARY EDITORS: None listed.

1028. *Psychological Monographs: General and Applied.*

TITLE VARIATIONS: Continues *Psychological Monographs.* Supersedes *Applied Psychology Monographs;* and *Archives of Psychology.*

DATES OF PUBLICATION: Number 288–317+, 1948–1950+.

FREQUENCY: Irregular. *See* Contents *below.*

NUMBERING VARIATIONS: Issues also numbered as Volume 62–64. *See* Contents *below.*

PUBLISHER: **Washington, D.C.:** The American Psychological Association, 1948–1950+.

PRIMARY EDITOR: **Herbert S. Conrad,** 1948–1950+.

CONSULTING EDITORS: Donald E. Baier, 1948–1950+; Frank A. Beach,

1948–1950+; Robert G. Bernreuter, 1948–1950+; William A. Brownell, 1948–1950+; Harold E. Burtt, 1948–1950+; Jerry W. Carter, Jr., 1948–1950+; Clyde H. Coombs, 1948–1950+; Edith L. Cornell, 1948–1950+; John G. Darley, 1948–1950+; John F. Dashiell, 1948–1950+; Eugenia Hanfmann, 1948–1950+; Edna Heidbreder, 1948–1950+; Harold E. Jones, 1948–1950+; Donald W. MacKinnon, 1948–1950+; Lorrin A. Riggs, 1948–1950+; Carl R. Rogers, 1948–1950+; Saul Rosenzweig, 1948–1950+; E. Donald Sisson, 1948–1950; Kenneth W. Spence, 1948–1950+; Ross Stagner, 1948–1950+; Percival M. Symonds, 1948–1950+; Joseph Tiffin, 1948–1950+; Ledyard R. Tucker, 1948–1950+; Joseph Zubin, 1950+.

CONTENTS:

[Volume 62] Number 288. Ansbacher, H. L. ATTITUDES OF GERMAN PRISONERS OF WAR: A STUDY OF THE DYNAMICS OF NATIONAL-SOCIALISTIC FOLLOWERSHIP. 1948. 42 pp.

[———] Number 289. Andrews, T. G. SOME PSYCHOLOGICAL APPARATUS: A CLASSIFIED BIBLIOGRAPHY. 1948. 38 pp.

[———] Number 290. Kunst, Mary S. A STUDY OF THUMB- AND FINGER SUCKING IN INFANTS. 1948. 71 pp.

[———] Number 291. Waldfogel, Samuel. THE FREQUENCY AND AFFECTIVE CHARACTER OF CHILDHOOD MEMORIES. 1948. 39 pp.

[———] Number 292. Ruesch, Jurgen, Annemarie Jacobson, and Martin B. Loeb. ACCULTURATION AND ILLNESS. 1948. 40 pp.

[———] Number 293. Yarrow, Leon J. THE EFFECT OF ANTECEDENT FRUSTRATION ON PROJECTIVE PLAY. 1948. 42 pp.

[———] Number 294. Keet, Charles Douglas. TWO VERBAL TECHNIQUES IN A MINIATURE COUNSELING SITUATION. 1948. 55 pp.

[———] Number 295. Conrad, Herbert S. CHARACTERISTICS AND USES OF ITEM-ANALYSIS DATA. 1948. 49 pp.

[Volume 63] Number 296. Coleman, James C. FACIAL EXPRESSIONS OF EMOTION. 1949. 36 pp.

[———] Number 297. Grimsley, Glen. A COMPARATIVE STUDY OF THE WHERRY-DOOLITTLE AND A MULTIPLE CUTTING-SCORE METHOD. 1949. 24 pp.

[———] Number 298. Michael, William Burton. FACTOR ANALYSES OF TESTS AND CRITERIA: A COMPARATIVE STUDY OF TWO AAF PILOT POPULATIONS. 1949. 55 pp.

[———] Number 299. Baldwin, Alfred L., Joan Kalhorn, and Fay Huffmann Breese. THE APPRAISAL OF PARENT BEHAVIOR. 1949. 85 pp.

[———] Number 300. Burks, Barbara S., and Anne Roe. STUDIES OF IDENTICAL TWINS REARED APART. Foreword and Introduction by Lewis M. Terman. 1949. 62 pp.

[———] Number 301. Warner, Samuel J. THE COLOR PREFERENCES OF PSYCHIATRIC GROUPS. 1949. 25 pp.

[———] Number 302. Witkin, H. A. PERCEPTION OF BODY POSITION AND OF THE POSITION OF THE VISUAL FIELD. 1949. 46 pp.

[———] Number 303. Hartman, A. A. AN EXPERIMENTAL EXAMINATION OF THE THEMATIC APPERCEPTION TECHNIQUE IN CLINICAL DIAGNOSIS. 1949. 48 pp.

[————] **Number 304.** Kirkpatrick, Clifford. Religion and Humanitarianism: A Study of Institutional Implications. 1949. 23 pp.

[————] **Number 305.** Lundin, Robert W. The Development and Validation of a Set of Musical Ability Tests. 1949. 20 pp.

[————] **Number 306.** Elonen, Anna S. A Comparison of Two Tests of Intelligence Administered to Adults. 1949. 35 pp.

[Volume 64] Number 307. Fisher, Seymour. Patterns of Personality Rigidity and Some of Their Determinants. 1950. 48 pp.

[————] **Number 308.** Wells, Charles A. The Value of an Oral Reading Test for Diagnosis of the Reading Difficulties of College Freshmen of Low Academic Performance. 1950. 35 pp.

[————] **Number 309.** Kates, Solis L. Rorschach Responses Related to Vocational Interests and Job Satisfaction. 1950. 34 pp.

[————] **Number 310.** Krout, Johanna. Symbol Elaboration Test (S.E.T.): The Reliability and Validity of a New Projective Technique. 1950. 67 pp.

[————] **Number 311.** Schofield, William. Changes in Responses to the Minnesota Multiphasic Inventory Following Certain Therapies. 1950. 33 pp.

[————] **Number 312.** Leeds, Carroll H. A Scale for Measuring Teacher-Pupil Attitudes and Teacher-Pupil Rapport. 1950. 24 pp.

[————] **Number 313.** Burack, Benjamin. The Nature and Efficacy of Methods of Attack on Reasoning Problems. 1950. 26 pp.

[————] **Number 314.** Singer, Martin. The Validity of a Multiple-Choice Projective Test in Psychopathological Screening. 1950. 40 pp.

[————] **Number 315.** Eron, Leonard D. A Normative Study of the Thematic Apperception Test. 1950. 48 pp.

[————] **Number 316.** Lord, Edith. Experimentally Induced Variations in Rorschach Performance. 1950. 34 pp.

[————] **Number 317.** Tupes, Ernest C. An Evaluation of Personality-Trait Ratings Obtained by Unstructured Assessment Interviews. 1950. 24 pp.

1029. *Psychologie. Monatsbulletin für praktische Psychologie.*

TITLE VARIATIONS: None.

DATES OF PUBLICATION: Band 1–2 +, January 1948–1950 +.

FREQUENCY: Monthly.

NUMBERING VARIATIONS: None.

PUBLISHER: **Bern:** H. R. Hugi, 1948–1950 +.

PRIMARY EDITOR: **Otto Carl Carter,** 1948–1950 +.

1030. *Psychologische achtergronden.* [Organ of the Psychotechnisch Laboratorium, Amsterdam.]

TITLE VARIATIONS: None.

DATES OF PUBLICATION: Nummer 1/2–12+, April 1948–October 1950+.

FREQUENCY: **Bimonthly,** Nummer 1/2–6, April 1948–February 1949. **Quarterly,** Nummer 7–12+, April 1949–December 1950+.

NUMBERING VARIATIONS: Multinumber issues present.

PUBLISHER: **Groningen:** J. B. Wolters Uitgeversmij, 1948–1950+.

PRIMARY EDITOR: **Ph. M. v. d. Heijden,** 1948–1950+.

1031. *Psychology at Work. Journal of the National Institute of Industrial Psychology.*

TITLE VARIATIONS: None.

DATES OF PUBLICATION: Volume 1–3, Number 5+, March 1948–November 1950+.

FREQUENCY: Bimonthly.

NUMBERING VARIATIONS: None.

PUBLISHER: **London:** National Institute of Industrial Psychology, Aldwych House, 1948–1950+.

PRIMARY EDITORS: **J. Vincent Chapman,** 1948–1949; **Elizabeth Loudon,** 1949–1950+.

1032. *Quarterly Journal of Experimental Psychology.*

TITLE VARIATIONS: None.

DATES OF PUBLICATION: Volume 1–2+, April 1948–November 1950+.

FREQUENCY: Quarterly.

NUMBERING VARIATIONS: None.

PUBLISHER: **Cambridge, England:** Published for the Experimental Psychology Group by W. Heffer & Sons Ltd., 1948–1950+.

PRIMARY EDITOR: **R. C. Oldfield,** 1948–1949.

EDITORIAL BOARD: R. C. Oldfield, 1949–1950+; D. Russell Davis, 1948–1950+; G. C. Drew, 1948–1950+; G. C. Grindley, 1948–1950+; M. D. Vernon, 1948–1950+; J. W. Whitfield, 1948–1950+; O. L. Zangwill, 1948–1950+.

1033. *Rorschach Standardization Studies.*

TITLE VARIATIONS: None.

DATES OF PUBLICATION: Number 1, 1948. (Supplementary monograph issued 1952.)

FREQUENCY: Irregular. *See* Contents *below.*

NUMBERING VARIATIONS: None.

PUBLISHER: **[Los Angeles]:** Published by the Authors, 1948.

PRIMARY EDITORS: None listed.

CONTENTS:
Number 1. Bühler, Charlotte, Karl Bühler, and D. Welty Lefever. DE-
VELOPMENT OF THE BASIC RORSCHACH SCORE WITH MANUAL OF DIRECTIONS.
1948. 189 pp.

1034. United States Public Health Service. National Institute of Mental Health. Mental Health Series.

TITLE VARIATIONS: None.

DATES OF PUBLICATION: Number 1–5+, 1948–1950+.

FREQUENCY: Irregular. See Contents below.

NUMBERING VARIATIONS: Number 4 also issued in revised form with altered
title. Number 5 also issued in parts. Certain issues also numbered as Public
Health Service Publications. See Contents below.

PUBLISHER: Washington, D.C.: United States Government Printing Office,
1949–1950+.

PRIMARY EDITORS: None listed.

CONTENTS:
Number 1. FOR MENTAL HEALTH. LEAFLET ON THE PROVISIONS OF THE
NATIONAL MENTAL HEALTH ACT. 1948. [4 pp.]
Number 2. TRAINING AND RESEARCH OPPORTUNITIES UNDER THE NA-
TIONAL MENTAL HEALTH ACT. 1948. 16 pp. (Also as Public Health Service Pub-
lication. Number 22.)
Number 3. THE NATIONAL MENTAL HEALTH ACT AND YOUR COMMUNITY.
1948. [13 pp.]
Number 4. THE NATIONAL MENTAL HEALTH PROGRAM, UNITED STATES OF
AMERICA. 1948. 7 pp. (Revised as NATIONAL INSTITUTE OF MENTAL HEALTH.
1950. 21 pp. Also as Public Health Service Publication. Number 20.)
Number 5. CAREERS IN MENTAL HEALTH. PSYCHIATRY. PSYCHIATRIC
NURSING. CLINICAL PSYCHOLOGY. PSYCHIATRIC SOCIAL WORK. 1950. 19 pp.
(Also issued as 4 pamphlets. Also as Public Health Service Publication. Number
23.)

1035. Universitaire bibliotheek voor psychologie.

TITLE VARIATIONS: None.

DATES OF PUBLICATION: 1–5+, 1948–1950+.

FREQUENCY: Irregular. See Contents below.

NUMBERING VARIATIONS: None.

PUBLISHER: Utrecht: Het spectrum, 1948. Antwerp: Standaard-Boekhandel,
1948–1950+.

PRIMARY EDITORS: A. Michotte, 1948–1950+; J. Nuttin, 1948–1950+.

CONTENTS:
1. Buytendijk, F.J.J. ALGEMENE THEORIE DER MENSELIJKE HOUDING EN

BEWEGING, ALS VERBINDING EN TEGENSTELLING VAN DE PHYSIOLOGISCHE EN DE PSYCHOLOGISCHE BESCHOUWING. 1948. 570 pp.

2. Snoeck, A. DE PSYCHOLOGIE VAN HET SCHULDBEWUSTZIJN. 1948. 281 pp.

3. Chorus, A. INTELLIGENTIE-ONDERZOEK EN ZIJN KWALITATIEVE VERDIEPING. 1948. 300 pp.

4. Witte, A.J.J. de. DE BETEKENISWERELD VAN HET LICHAAM. TAAL-PSYCHOLOGISCHE, TAALVERGELIJKENDE STUDIE. 1949. 476 pp.

5. Nuttin, J. PSYCHOANALYSE EN SPIRITUALISTISCHE OPVATTING VAN DE MENS. TWEEDE VERMEERDERDE UITGAVE. 1950. 240 pp.

1036. *Zeitschrift für Graphologie und Charakterkunde.* [Organ of the Graphologischer Forschungskreis (Hamburg).]

TITLE VARIATIONS: None.

DATES OF PUBLICATION: Jahrgang 1–2, Heft 3, October 1948–September 1949.

FREQUENCY: Bimonthly.

NUMBERING VARIATIONS: None.

PUBLISHER: **Hamburg:** Graphologischer Forschungskreis, 1948–1949.

PRIMARY EDITORS: None listed.

1949

1037. *American Council on Education. Studies. Series VI: Student Personnel Work. (Special Issue).*

TITLE VARIATIONS: None.

DATES OF PUBLICATION: Number 1, 1949.

FREQUENCY: Irregular. *See* Contents *below.*

NUMBERING VARIATIONS: None.

PUBLISHER: **Washington, D.C.:** American Council on Education, 1949.

PRIMARY EDITOR: **Mary Irwin,** 1949.

CONTENTS:

Number 1. Stuit, Dewey B., Gwendolen S. Dickson, Thomas F. Jordan, and Lester Schloerb. PREDICTING SUCCESS IN PROFESSIONAL SCHOOLS. 1949. 187 pp.

1038. *Analytical Psychology Club of Los Angeles. Papers.*

TITLE VARIATIONS: None.

DATES OF PUBLICATION: Number 1–3 +, 1949–1950 +.

FREQUENCY: Irregular. *See* Contents *below.*

NUMBERING VARIATIONS: None.

PUBLISHER: **Los Angeles:** APC of Los Angeles, 1949–1950+.

PRIMARY EDITORS: None listed.

CONTENTS:
   Number 1. Peticolas, Sherry. EMERSON—APOSTLE OF THE SELF. 1949. 11 pp.
   Number 2. Kirsch, James. STORY OF THE SEVEN BEGGARS; A CONTRIBU-TION TO THE UNDERSTANDING OF JEWISH PSYCHOLOGY. 1949. 25 pp.
   Number 3. Keller, Max. UNCONSCIOUS MATERIAL IN A CONFLICT-SITUA-TION. 1950. 26 pp.

1039. *Arbeiten zur Psychologie, Pädagogik und Heilpädagogik.*

TITLE VARIATIONS: None.

DATES OF PUBLICATION: Band 1–3+, 1949–1950+.

FREQUENCY: Irregular. *See* Contents *below.*

NUMBERING VARIATIONS: None.

PUBLISHER: **Freiburg:** Pädagogisches Institut der Universität Freiburg, 1949–1950+.

PRIMARY EDITORS: **L. Dupraz,** 1949–1950+; **E. Montalta,** 1949–1950+.

CONTENTS:
   Band 1. Deplazes, Gion. GESCHICHTE DER SPRACHLICHEN SCHULBÜCHER IM ROMANISCHEN RHEINGEBIET. 1949. 206 pp.
   Band 2. Kunz, Leo. DAS SCHULDBEWUSSTSEIN DES MÄNNLICHEN JUGEND-LICHEN. 1949. 208 pp.
   Band 3. Walther, Leon. ARBEITSPSYCHOLOGIE. 1950. 244 pp.

1040. *Arquivos brasileiros de psicotécnica.*

TITLE VARIATIONS: None.

DATES OF PUBLICATION: Ano 1–2+, 1949–1950+.

FREQUENCY: Quarterly.

NUMBERING VARIATIONS: Ano 1 has only two issues, September and December 1949.

PUBLISHER: **Rio de Janeiro:** Instituto de seleção e orientação profissional da fundação Getúlio Vargas, 1949–1950+.

PRIMARY EDITORS: **Emilio Mira y Lopez,** 1949–1950+; **Walter de Toledo Piza,** 1949–1950+; **João Carlos Vital,** 1949–1950+.

1041. *Association for Physical and Mental Rehabilitation. Journal.* [2.]

TITLE VARIATIONS: Continues *Physical and Mental Rehabilitation Journal.*

DATES OF PUBLICATION: Volume 3, Number 6–Volume 4, Number 6+, December 1949–December 1950/January 1951+.

FREQUENCY: Bimonthly.

NUMBERING VARIATIONS: None.

PUBLISHER: **Columbia, South Carolina:** Association for Physical and Mental Rehabilitation, 1949–1950+.

PRIMARY EDITORS: **Leo Berner,** 1949–1950+; **Gilbert Guarino,** 1949–1950+; **Edward Friedman,** 1949–1950+; **Lou Montevano,** 1949–1950+; **Arthur D. Tauber,** 1949–1950+.

EDITORIAL BOARD: Arthur S. Abramson, 1949–1950+; Harry Kessler, 1949–1950+; Louis Newman, 1949–1950+; Edward Greenwood, 1949–1950+; Sidney Licht, 1949–1950+; A.B.C. Knudson, 1949–1950+; Donald Covalt, 1949–1950+; John E. Davis, 1949–1950+; Richard Kovacs, 1949–1950+; Peter V. Karpovich, 1949–1950+; Eugene Taylor, 1949–1950+; Edward E. Gordon, 1949–1950+.

1042. *Australian Journal of Psychology.*

TITLE VARIATIONS: None.

DATES OF PUBLICATION: Volume 1–2+, 1949–1950+.

FREQUENCY: Semiannual.

NUMBERING VARIATIONS: None.

PUBLISHER: **Melbourne:** Australian Branch of the British Psychological Society at the Melbourne University Press, 1949–1950+.

PRIMARY EDITOR: **D. W. McElwain,** 1949–1950+.

EDITORIAL BOARD: Ernest Beaglehole, 1949–1950+; John F. Clark, 1949; P. H. Cook, 1949; A. J. Marshall, 1949–1950+; W. M. O'Neil, 1949–1950+; O. A. Oeser, 1949–1950+; C. A. Gibb, 1950; P. Lafitte, 1950+; D. F. Buckle, 1950+; R. N. McCulloch, 1950+.

1043. *Barcelona. Instituto psicotécnico. Monografías, estudios y documentaciones psicotécnicas.*

TITLE VARIATIONS: None.

DATES OF PUBLICATION: Número 1–5+, 1949–1950+.

FREQUENCY: Irregular.

NUMBERING VARIATIONS: None.

PUBLISHER: **Barcelona:** Instituto psicotécnico de la Excma. diputación provincial, 1949–1950+.

PRIMARY EDITORS: None listed.

CONTENTS:

[Tomo 1] **Número 1.** Soler y Dopff, Carlos. EL IX CONGRESO INTERNACIONAL DE MEDICINA INDUSTRIAL. LONDRES 13–17 SEPTIEMBRE 1948. 1949. 24 pp.

[———] **Número 2.** Azoy Castane, Adolfo. FUNCIÓN OLFATIVA Y OLFATOMETRÍA. 1949. 71 pp.

[———] **Número 3.** Buen, Victor de. LA EVALUACIÓN DE LOS PROCESOS PSÍQUICOS. 1949. 19 pp.

[Tomo 2] Número 4. Soler y Dopff, Carlos. PROYECTO DE NORMALIZACIÓN DE LA EXPLORACIÓN MÉDICA EN LA SETECCIÓN PROFESIONAL. 1950. 33 pp.

[———] **Número 5.** Palomar Collado, D. F. VALORACIÓN DE LA EFICIENCIA VISUAL PROFESIONAL Y SUS DÉFICITS MEDIANTE LA OPTOMETRÍA CENTESIMAL. 1950.

1044. *Benjamin Rush Bulletin. Devoted to a Scientific Materialist Analysis of Problems in Psychiatry, Psychology and Social Work.*

TITLE VARIATIONS: None.

DATES OF PUBLICATION: Volume 1, Number 1–4, Fall 1949–Summer 1950.

FREQUENCY: Quarterly.

NUMBERING VARIATIONS: None.

PUBLISHER: **New York:** Benjamin Rush Society, 1949–1950.

PRIMARY EDITORS: None listed.

1045. *British Journal of Medical Hypnotism.*

TITLE VARIATIONS: None.

DATES OF PUBLICATION: Volume 1–2, Number 1+, September 1949–Autumn 1950+.

FREQUENCY: Quarterly.

NUMBERING VARIATIONS: None.

PUBLISHER: **Hove, England:** British Society of Medical Hypnotists, 1949–1950.

PRIMARY EDITORS: **S. J. van Pelt,** 1949–1950; **George Newbold,** 1949–1950.

1046. *California. University. Publications in Child Development.*

TITLE VARIATIONS: None.

DATES OF PUBLICATION: Volume 1, Number 1+, 1949+. (Number 2 published 1954.)

FREQUENCY: Irregular. *See* Contents *below.*

NUMBERING VARIATIONS: None.

PUBLISHER: **Berkeley** and **Los Angeles:** University of California Press, 1949+.

PRIMARY EDITORS: **Harold E. Jones,** 1949+; **Catherine Landreth,** 1949+; **Jean W. Macfarlane,** 1949+.

CONTENTS:

Number 1. Jones, Harold E. MOTOR PERFORMANCE AND GROWTH. 1949, pp. 1–182.

1047. *Case Reports in Clinical Psychology.*

TITLE VARIATIONS: None.

DATES OF PUBLICATION: Volume 1, Number 1–3/4+, August 1949–October 1950+.

FREQUENCY: Quarterly.

NUMBERING VARIATIONS: Multinumber issue present.

PUBLISHER: **Brooklyn, New York:** Department of Psychology, Division of Psychiatry, Kings County Hospital, 1949–1950+.

PRIMARY EDITOR: **Karen Machover,** 1949–1950+.

EDITORIAL BOARD: Hanna F. Faterson, 1949–1950+; Irving Fecher, 1949–1950+; Frank S. Puzzo, 1949–1950+; Dante A. Santora, 1949–1950+; Shirley Adler, 1950+; Leo Chalfen, 1950+; Rochelle M. Wexler, 1950+.

1048. *Clinical Psychology. A Quarterly Journal Devoted to the Scientific Study of Human Personality.*

TITLE VARIATIONS: None.

DATES OF PUBLICATION: Volume 1+, July 1949–1950+.

FREQUENCY: Quarterly.

NUMBERING VARIATIONS: None.

PUBLISHER: **Lahore, India:** Institute of Clinical and Applied Psychology, Ewing Hall, 1949–1950+.

PRIMARY EDITOR: **I. Latif,** 1949–1950+.

1049. *Guatemala City. Universidad de San Carlos. Facultad de humanidades. Anuario.*

TITLE VARIATIONS: Also called *Revista de filosofía, pedagogía, historia, letras y psicología.*

DATES OF PUBLICATION: Tomo 1–2+, 1949–1950+.

FREQUENCY: Annual.

NUMBERING VARIATIONS: None.

PUBLISHER: **Guatemala City:** Universidad, Facultad de humanidades, 1949–1950.

PRIMARY EDITOR: **José Rölz Bennett,** 1949–1950+.

NOTE: Information on this title was found in the *Bibliographie de la Philosophie* published by the International Institute of Philosophical Collaboration, Paris. Paris: Librairie philosophique J. Vrin, 1937–1953.

1050. *Industrial Relations Research Association. Publications.*

TITLE VARIATIONS: None.

DATES OF PUBLICATION: Number 1–5+, 1949–1950+.

FREQUENCY: Irregular. *See* Contents *below.*

NUMBERING VARIATIONS: None.

PUBLISHER: **Champaign, Illinois:** Industrial Relations Research Association, 1949–1950+.

PRIMARY EDITOR: **M. Derber,** 1949–1950+.

EDITORIAL BOARD: J. Douglas Brown, 1950+; Clark Kerr, 1950+; Edwin E. Witte, 1950+.

CONTENTS:

Number 1. INDUSTRIAL RELATIONS RESEARCH ASSOCIATION. PROCEEDINGS OF THE 1ST ANNUAL MEETING, CLEVELAND, OHIO, DECEMBER 29–30, 1948. 1949. 255 pp.

Number 2. INDUSTRIAL RELATIONS RESEARCH ASSOCIATION. MEMBERSHIP DIRECTORY, OCTOBER 1949. 137 pp.

Number 3. Kornhauser, Arthur, ed. DENVER. PSYCHOLOGY OF LABOR-MANAGEMENT RELATIONS MEETING. 1949. (1950.) 122 pp.

Number 4. INDUSTRIAL RELATIONS RESEARCH ASSOCIATION. PROCEEDINGS OF THE 2ND ANNUAL MEETING, NEW YORK CITY, DECEMBER 29–30, 1949. 1950. 299 pp.

Number 5. INDUSTRIAL RELATIONS RESEARCH ASSOCIATION. THE AGED AND SOCIETY. 1950. 237 pp.

1051. *Intercollegiate Psychology Association. Journal.*

TITLE VARIATIONS: None.

DATES OF PUBLICATION: Volume 1+, May 1949–1950+.

FREQUENCY: **Semiannual,** Volume 1, 1949–1950. **Triannual,** Volume 2+, 1950+.

NUMBERING VARIATIONS: None.

PUBLISHER: **New York:** Intercollegiate Psychology Association, City College, 1949–1950+.

PRIMARY EDITORS: **Richard R. Korn,** 1949–1950+; **Herbert S. Rabinowitz,** 1949–1950+; **Gerd H. Fenchel,** 1949–1950+; **Hortense Leight,** 1949–1950+; **Gerald Manus,** 1949–1950+; **Daniel Miller,** 1949; **Dorothy Sandman,** 1949; **Bart L. Stafford III,** 1949–1950+.

1052. *Kyoiku Shinrigaku.* [Educational Psychology.]

TITLE VARIATIONS: None.

DATES OF PUBLICATION: Volume 1–2+, 1949–1950+.

FREQUENCY: Unknown.

NUMBERING VARIATIONS: None.

PUBLISHER: **Tokyo:** Tōkyō Kyoiku Daigaku. Shinrigaku Kenkyūshitsu [Tokyo University of Education. Psychological Research Laboratory], 1949–1950.

PRIMARY EDITORS: None listed.

NOTE: Information for this entry was obtained from *Gakujutsu Zasshi Sōgō Mokuroku. Jimbun Kagaku Wabun Hen* [Union List of Scholarly Journals. Japanese Language Section. Humanities Part]. Tokyo, 1973.

1053. *Kyoto. University. Faculty of Letters. Psychological Research Laboratory. Psychology. Abstracts.*

TITLE VARIATIONS: Also cited as *Kyoto. Kyōto Daigaku. Bungakubu. Shinrigaku kenkyūshitsu. Shinri. Gaikatsu* [University of Kyoto. Faculty of Letters. Psychological Research Laboratory. Psychology. Abstracts]; and as *Shinri. Gaikatsu* [Psychology. Abstracts]; and in English as *University of Kyoto. Studies in Psychology. Abstracts.*

DATES OF PUBLICATION: Number 1+, 1949+.

FREQUENCY: Irregular. *See* Contents *below.*

NUMBERING VARIATIONS: None.

PUBLISHER: **Kyoto:** Kyōto Daigaku, Bungakubu, Shinrigaku kenkyūshitsu. [University of Kyoto, Faculty of Letters, Psychological Research Laboratory], 1949+.

PRIMARY EDITOR: **Tatsuro Yatabe,** 1949+.

CONTENTS:
> **Number 1.** Yatabe, Tatsuro. UNIVERSITY OF KYOTO. STUDIES IN PSYCHOLOGY. I. ABSTRACTS. 1949. 26 pp.

NOTE: Publication consists of English language abstracts of articles published in *Kyoto. Kyōto Daigaku. Bungakubu. Shinrigaku kenkyūshitsu. Shinri* [University of Kyoto. Faculty of Letters. Psychological Research Laboratory. Psychology]. Main entry is therefore in English.

1054. *Modern Practice in Psychological Medicine.*

TITLE VARIATIONS: None.

DATES OF PUBLICATION: 1949.

FREQUENCY: Annual.

NUMBERING VARIATIONS: Publication is numbered only by date.

PUBLISHER: **New York:** Paul B. Hoeber, Inc., Medical Book Department of Harper & Brothers, 1949.

PRIMARY EDITOR: **J. R. Rees,** 1949.

1055. *Motor Skills Research Exchange.*

TITLE VARIATIONS: None.

DATES OF PUBLICATION: Volume 1–2+, 1949–1950+.

FREQUENCY: Quarterly.

NUMBERING VARIATIONS: Some issues called "Monograph Supplement" or "Special Issue" form a regular part of the annual volume and continue its volume numbering.

PUBLISHER: **Louisville, Kentucky:** University of Louisville, Department of Psychology, 1949–1950+.

PRIMARY EDITORS: **Robert B. Ammons,** 1949–1950+; **C. H. Ammons,** 1949–1950+.

1056. *New York. Josiah Macy, Jr. Foundation. Conference on Cybernetics. Transactions.*

TITLE VARIATIONS: None.

DATES OF PUBLICATION: 6th–7th+, 1949–1950+.

FREQUENCY: Annual.

NUMBERING VARIATIONS: Transactions of the 1st–5th Conferences were not published.

PUBLISHER: **New York:** Josiah Macy, Jr. Foundation, 1950–1951+.

PRIMARY EDITORS: See Contents *below.*

CONTENTS:

6th. CYBERNETICS. CIRCULAR, CAUSAL, AND FEEDBACK MECHANISMS IN BIOLOGICAL AND SOCIAL SYSTEMS. TRANSACTIONS OF THE SIXTH CONFERENCE MARCH 24–25, 1949, NEW YORK. Edited by Heinz von Foerster. 1950. 209 pp.

7th. CYBERNETICS. CIRCULAR, CAUSAL, AND FEEDBACK MECHANISMS IN BIOLOGICAL AND SOCIAL SYSTEMS. TRANSACTIONS OF THE SEVENTH CONFERENCE MARCH 23–24, 1950, NEW YORK. Edited by Heinz von Foerster, Margaret Mead, and Hans Lukas Teuber. 1951. 251 pp.

1057. *Nordisk Psykologi.* [Official organ of the Dansk Psykologforening, the Suomen Psykologinen Seyra, Norsk Psykologforening, and the Svenska Psykologsamfundet.]

TITLE VARIATIONS: None.

DATES OF PUBLICATION: Volume 1–2+, 1949–1950+.

FREQUENCY: Quarterly.

NUMBERING VARIATIONS: Joint issue present.

PUBLISHER: **Copenhagen:** Ejnar Munksgaards Forlag, 1949–1950+.

PRIMARY EDITORS: **Poul W. Perch,** 1949–1950+; **Irja Piisinen,** 1949; **Emil Østlyngen,** 1949–1950+; **Gösta Ekman,** 1949–1950+; **Kaarlo Helasvuo,** 1950+.

1058. *Progrès de la psychotechnique.* [Publication of the Internationale Vereinigung für Psychotechnik.]

TITLE VARIATIONS: Also called *Progress of Psychotechnics;* and *Fortschritte der Psychotechnik.*

DATES OF PUBLICATION: Numéro 1+, 1949+.

FREQUENCY: Irregular. *See* Contents *below.*

NUMBERING VARIATIONS: None.

PUBLISHER: **Bern:** A. Francke, 1949+.

PRIMARY EDITOR: **Franziska Baumgarten-Tramer,** 1949+.

CONTENTS:

    Number 1. Baumgarten-Tramer, Franziska. FORTSCHRITTE DER PSYCHO-TECHNIK, 1939–1945. 1949. 315 pp.

1059. *Psyche; Eine Zeitschrift für Tiefenpsychologie und Menschenkunde in Forschung und Praxis. Beihefte.*

TITLE VARIATIONS: None.

DATES OF PUBLICATION: Stück 1–2+, 1949+. (Stück 3 published 1953.)

FREQUENCY: Irregular. *See* Contents *below.*

NUMBERING VARIATIONS: None.

PUBLISHER: **Heidelberg:** Verlag L. Schneider, 1949+.

PRIMARY EDITORS: **Hans Kunz,** 1949+; **Alexdr. Mitscherlich,** 1949+; **Fel. Schottlaender,** 1949+.

CONTENTS:

    Stück 1. Kemper, Wern. ENURESIS (BETTNÄSSERLEIDEN). 1949. 77 pp.

    Stück 2. Laiblin, Wilh. EIN KRANKENBERICHT ALS TIEFENPSYCHOLOGIE. BEITRAG ZUM PROBLEM EINER GEISTIG-POLITISCHEN NEUORIENTIERUNG. 1949. 112 pp.

1060. *Psychiatrie, Neurologie und medizinische Psychologie; Zeitschrift für Forschung und Praxis.*

TITLE VARIATIONS: None.

DATES OF PUBLICATION: Band 1–2+, 1949–1950+.

FREQUENCY: Monthly.

NUMBERING VARIATIONS: First issue is a double number.

PUBLISHER: **Leipzig:** Verlag S. Hirzel, 1949–1950+.

PRIMARY EDITOR: **A. Mette,** 1949–1950+.

1061. *Psychologe. Berater für gesunde und praktische Lebensgestaltung. Psychologische Monatsschrift.*

TITLE VARIATIONS: None.

DATES OF PUBLICATION: Band 1–2+, February 1949–1950+.

FREQUENCY: Monthly.

NUMBERING VARIATIONS: None.

PUBLISHER: **Schwarzenburg, Switzerland:** GBS-Verlag, 1949–1950+.

PRIMARY EDITOR: **Gustav Hans Graber,** 1949–1950+.

1062. *Psychological Newsletter.*

TITLE VARIATIONS: None.

DATES OF PUBLICATION: Volume 1–2+, January 1949–December 1950+.

FREQUENCY: Monthly.

NUMBERING VARIATIONS: Issues are also assigned whole numbers, Number 1–24+.

PUBLISHER: **New York:** New York University, Department of Psychology, 1949–1950+.

PRIMARY EDITOR: **Donald S. Leeds,** 1949–1950+.

1063. *Psychological Service Center Bulletin.*

TITLE VARIATIONS: Continued by *Psychological Service Center Journal* with Volume 1, Number 3, September 1949.

DATES OF PUBLICATION: Volume 1, Number 1–2, January 1949–March 1949.

FREQUENCY: Bimonthly.

NUMBERING VARIATIONS: None.

PUBLISHER: **Washington, D.C.:** International Psychological Service Center, 1949.

PRIMARY EDITOR: **Russell Graydon Leiter,** 1949.

1064. *Psychological Service Center Journal.*

TITLE VARIATIONS: Continues *Psychological Service Center Bulletin.*

DATES OF PUBLICATION: Volume 1, Number 3–Volume 2, Number 4+, September 1949–December 1950+.

FREQUENCY: Quarterly.

NUMBERING VARIATIONS: None.

PUBLISHER: **Washington, D.C.:** International Psychological Service Center, 1949–1950+.

PRIMARY EDITORS: **Russell Graydon Leiter,** 1949–1950+; **Joan H. Criswell,** 1949; **Edward Joseph Shoben, Jr.,** 1949–1950+; **W. Grant Dahlstrom,** 1949–1950+.

1065. *Psychologische Hefte der Siemens-Studien-Gesellschaft für praktische Psychologie e. V.*

TITLE VARIATIONS: None.

DATES OF PUBLICATION: Jahrgang 1–2+, January 1949–1950+.

FREQUENCY: Monthly (Irregular).

NUMBERING VARIATIONS: Jahrgang 1 contains 8 Hefte, Jahrgang 2 contains 10 Hefte. Jahrgang 1, Heft 4 incorrectly numbered Jahrgang 3, Heft 4.

PUBLISHER: **Hannover and Bad Homburg:** Siemens-Studien-Gesellschaft, 1949–1950 + .

PRIMARY EDITOR: **Adolf Zeddies,** 1949–1950 + .

1066. *Psychologische reeks.* [2.]

TITLE VARIATIONS: Continues *Psychologische bibliotheek (Amsterdam).* [2.]

PERIOD OF ISSUE: Deel 6 + , 1949 + .

FREQUENCY: Irregular. *See* Contents *below.*

NUMBERING VARIATIONS: Two separate issues were numbered Deel 6. One is listed with this series and the other is listed with *Psychologische bibliotheek. See* Contents *below.*

PUBLISHER: **Amsterdam:** N.V. noord-hollandsche uitgevers maatschappij, 1949 + .

PRIMARY EDITOR: **G. Révész,** 1949 + .

CONTENTS:
Deel 6. Groot, A. D. de. SINT NICOLAAS PATROON VAN LIEFDE. EEN PSYCHOLOGISCHE STUDIE OVER DE NICOLAUS-FIGUUR EN ZIJN VERERING IN VROEGER EEUWEN EN NU. 1949. 228 pp.

1067. *Psychologische Rundschau.*

TITLE VARIATIONS: None.

DATES OF PUBLICATION: Band 1 + , October 1949/October 1950 + .

FREQUENCY: Annual.

NUMBERING VARIATIONS: None.

PUBLISHER: **Amsterdam:** Swets & Zeitlinger N.V., 1949–1950 + .

PRIMARY EDITOR: **Johannes von Allesch,** 1949–1950 + .

1068. *Quarterly Journal of Child Behavior.*

TITLE VARIATIONS: None.

DATES OF PUBLICATION: Volume 1–2 + , January 1949–October 1950 + .

FREQUENCY: Quarterly.

NUMBERING VARIATIONS: None.

PUBLISHER: **New York:** Quarterly Journal of Child Behavior, 1949–1950 + .

PRIMARY EDITORS: **Nolan D. C. Lewis,** 1949–1950 + ; **William S. Langford,** 1949–1950 + .

1069. *Research Conference on Psychosurgery. Proceedings.*

TITLE VARIATIONS: None.

DATES OF PUBLICATION: 1st–2nd + , 1949–1950 + .

FREQUENCY: Annual.

NUMBERING VARIATIONS: 1st–2nd Conference numbered as *U. S. Public Health Service. Publication,* Number 16 and 156, respectively.

PUBLISHER: **Washington, D.C.:** Federal Security Agency, Public Health Service, National Institutes of Health, 1949–1950+.

PRIMARY EDITORS: None listed.

1070. *Soviet Psychology Information Bulletin.*

TITLE VARIATIONS: Above title lacking, Volume 1, Number 4–7. Heading on these issues is *Society for Cultural Relations with the U.S.S.R.*

DATES OF PUBLICATION: Volume 1+, 1949–1950+.

FREQUENCY: Irregular.

NUMBERING VARIATIONS: Number 4 lacks numbering.

PUBLISHER: **London:** Society for Cultural Relations with the U.S.S.R., 14 Kensington Square, 1949–1950+.

PRIMARY EDITORS: None listed.

1071. *Studies in Social Psychology in World War II.*

TITLE VARIATIONS: Volumes are individually titled. *See* Contents *below.*

DATES OF PUBLICATION: Volume 1–4, 1949–1950.

FREQUENCY: Irregular. *See* Contents *below.*

NUMBERING VARIATIONS: None.

PUBLISHER: **Princeton, New Jersey:** Princeton University Press, 1949–1950.

PRIMARY EDITORS: Special Committee of the Social Science Research Council: **Frederick Osborn** (Chairman), 1949–1950; **Leonard S. Cottrell, Jr.,** 1949–1950; **Leland C. DeVinney,** 1949–1950; **Carl I. Hovland,** 1949–1950; **John M. Russell,** 1949–1950; **Samuel A. Stouffer,** 1949–1950; **Donald Young** (ex officio), 1949–1950.

CONTENTS:

Volume 1. Stouffer, Samuel A., Edward A. Suchman, Leland C. De Vinney, Shirley A. Star, and Robin M. Williams, Jr. THE AMERICAN SOLDIER: ADJUSTMENT DURING ARMY LIFE. 1949. 599 pp.

Volume 2. Stouffer, Samuel A., Arthur A. Lumsdaine, Marion Harper Lumsdaine, Robin M. Williams, Jr., M. Brewster Smith, Irving L. Janis, Shirley A. Star, and Leonard S. Cottrell, Jr. THE AMERICAN SOLDIER: COMBAT AND ITS AFTERMATH. 1949. 675 pp.

Volume 3. Hovland, Carl I., Arthur A. Lumsdaine, and Fred D. Sheffield. EXPERIMENTS ON MASS COMMUNICATION. 1949. 345 pp.

Volume 4. Stouffer, Samuel A., Louis Guttman, Edward A. Suchman, Paul F. Lazarsfeld, Shirley A. Star, and John A. Clausen. MEASUREMENT AND PREDICTION. 1950. 756 pp.

1072. *Tokyo Gakugei Daigaku. Kenkyu Hokoku. Dai-8-bunsatsu. Kyoikugaku. Kyoikushinrigaku. Kyoka-kyoiku.*
[Tokyo Gakugei University. Bulletin. Series 8. Education. Educational Psychology. Curriculum.]

TITLE VARIATIONS: None.

DATES OF PUBLICATION: Number 1–2, 1949–1950 + .

FREQUENCY: Annual.

NUMBERING VARIATIONS: None.

PUBLISHER: **Tokyo:** Tōkyō Gakugei Daigaku [Tokyo Gakugei University], 1949–1950 + .

PRIMARY EDITORS: None listed.

NOTE: This entry was compiled from information obtained in *Japan. Higher Education and Science Bureau. Bibliographical List of Japanese Learned Journals. Number 2. Humanities and Social Sciences. 1959.*

1073. *Toronto. University. Institute of Child Study. Bulletin.*

TITLE VARIATIONS: Continues *Toronto. University. Institute of Child Study. Parent Education Bulletin.*

DATES OF PUBLICATION: Number 45–49 + , Fall 1949–Fall 1950 + .

FREQUENCY: Quarterly.

NUMBERING VARIATIONS: None.

PUBLISHER: **Toronto:** University of Toronto, Institute of Child Study, 1949–1950 + .

PRIMARY EDITOR: **Karl S. Bernhardt,** 1949–1950 + .

1074. *Training School Bulletin. Monograph Supplement Series.*

TITLE VARIATIONS: None.

DATES OF PUBLICATION: Number 1–2 + , 1949–1950 + .

FREQUENCY: Irregular. *See* Contents *below.*

NUMBERING VARIATIONS: Also numbered as *Training School Bulletin. Supplement. See* Contents *below.*

PUBLISHER: **Vineland, New Jersey:** Training School, 1949–1950 + .

PRIMARY EDITORS: **Helen F. Hill,** 1949; **Walter Jacob,** 1950 + ; **Alice Morrison Nash,** 1950 + ; **George W. Gens,** 1950 + ; **Robert H. Cassel,** 1950 + ; **Marie Roberts,** 1950 + .

CONTENTS:
Number 1. Cassel, Robert H. THE VINELAND ADAPTATION OF THE OSERETSKY TESTS. 1949. 32 pp. (Also as *Training School Bulletin. Supplement* to Volume 46, Number 3–4, May–June 1949.)

Number 2. French, Edward L., Robert H. Cassel, Herman D. Arbitman, Lila Weissenberg, and Francis W. Irwin. A SYSTEM FOR CLASSIFYING THE MENTALLY DEFICIENT ON THE BASIS OF ANAMNESIS. 1950. 40 pp. (Also as *Training School Bulletin. Supplement* to Volume 47, 1950.)

1075. *Weg zur Seele. Monatsschrift für Seelsorge, Psychotherapie und Erziehung.*

TITLE VARIATIONS: None.

DATES OF PUBLICATION: Jahrgang 1–2+, September 1949–1950+.

FREQUENCY: Monthly.

NUMBERING VARIATIONS: None.

PUBLISHER: **Giessen:** Brunnen Verlag, 1949–1950. **Göttingen:** Vandenhoeck & Ruprecht, 1950+.

PRIMARY EDITOR: **Klaus Thomas,** 1949–1950+.

1076. *Wiener Zeitschrift für praktische Psychologie.*

TITLE VARIATIONS: None.

DATES OF PUBLICATION: Band 1–2, 1949–1950.

FREQUENCY: Quarterly.

NUMBERING VARIATIONS: Issues also assigned whole numbers, Heft 1–8.

PUBLISHER: **Vienna:** Brüder Hollinek (for the Österreichische Gesellschaft für praktische Psychologie), 1949–1950.

PRIMARY EDITOR: **Rob. Schneider,** 1949–1950.

1077. *Zeitschrift für Psycho-Analyse.*

TITLE VARIATIONS: None.

DATES OF PUBLICATION: Band 1, Heft 1/2, 1949/1950.

FREQUENCY: Irregular.

NUMBERING VARIATIONS: None.

PUBLISHER: **Berlin:** Walter de Gruyter, 1949–1950.

PRIMARY EDITOR: **Carl Müller-Braunschweig,** 1949–1950.

1078. *Zurich. C. G. Jung Institut. Studien.*

TITLE VARIATIONS: None.

DATES OF PUBLICATION: Heft 1–2, 1949–1950+. (Heft 3 published 1952.)

FREQUENCY: Irregular. *See* Contents *below.*

NUMBERING VARIATIONS: None.

PUBLISHER: **Zurich:** Rascher, 1949–1950+.

PRIMARY EDITORS: None listed.

CONTENTS:

Heft 1. Meier, C. A. ANTIKE INKUBATION UND MODERNE PSYCHOTHERA-PIE. 1949. 137 pp.

Heft 2. Schaer, Hans. ERLÖSUNGSVORSTELLUNGEN UND IHRE PSYCHOLO-GISCHEN ASPEKTE. 1950. 702 pp.

1950

1079. *Annual Review of Hypnosis Literature.*

TITLE VARIATIONS: None.

DATES OF PUBLICATION: Volume 1/2 +, 1950/1951 +.

FREQUENCY: Annual.

NUMBERING VARIATIONS: Volume 1/2, covering the period 1950–1951, published in 1953.

PUBLISHER: **New York:** The Woodrow Press, Inc., 1950/1951 +.

PRIMARY EDITORS: **Milton V. Kline,** 1950/1951 +; **Arthur D. Haggerty,** 1950/1951 +; **Bernard E. Gorton,** 1950/1951 +; **Henry Guze,** 1950/1951 +.

1080. *Annual Review of Psychology.*

TITLE VARIATIONS: None.

DATES OF PUBLICATION: Volume 1 +, 1950 +.

FREQUENCY: Annual.

NUMBERING VARIATIONS: None.

PUBLISHER: **Stanford, California:** Annual Reviews, Inc., 1950 +.

PRIMARY EDITORS: **Calvin P. Stone,** 1950 +; **Donald W. Taylor,** 1950 +.

EDITORIAL BOARD: J. G. Darley, 1950 +; C. I. Hovland, 1950 +; J. E. Anderson, 1950 +; C. H. Graham, 1950 +; J. G. Miller, 1950 +.

1081. *Annual Survey of Psychoanalysis.*

TITLE VARIATIONS: None.

DATES OF PUBLICATION: Volume 1 +, 1950 +.

FREQUENCY: Annual.

NUMBERING VARIATIONS: None.

PUBLISHER: **New York:** International Universities Press, 1950 +.

PRIMARY EDITOR: **J. French,** 1950 +.

1082. *Behaviour. An International Journal of Comparative Ethology. Supplement.*

TITLE VARIATIONS: None.

DATES OF PUBLICATION: Number 1+, 1950+.

FREQUENCY: Irregular. *See* Contents *below.*

NUMBERING VARIATIONS: None.

PUBLISHER: **Leiden, Netherlands:** E. J. Brill, 1950+.

PRIMARY EDITORS: **G. P. Baerends,** 1950+; **F. A. Beach,** 1950+; **C. R. Carpenter,** 1950+; **H. Hediger,** 1950+; **O. Koehler,** 1950+; **P. Palmgren,** 1950+; **W. H. Thorpe,** 1950+; **N. Tinbergen,** 1950+.

CONTENTS:
Number 1. Baerends, G. P., and J. M. Baerends-Van Roon. AN INTRODUCTION TO THE STUDY OF THE ETHOLOGY OF CICHLID FISHES. 1950. 242 pp.

1083. *Biel. Institut für Psycho-Hygiene. Arbeiten zur Psycho-Hygiene.*

TITLE VARIATIONS: None.

DATES OF PUBLICATION: Heft 1+, 1950+.

FREQUENCY: Irregular. *See* Contents *below.*

NUMBERING VARIATIONS: None.

PUBLISHER: **Biel, Switzerland:** Institut für Psycho-Hygiene, 1950.

PRIMARY EDITOR: **Hans Zulliger,** 1950+.

CONTENTS:
Heft 1. Zulliger, Hans. ÜBER SYMBOLISCHE DIEBSTÄHLE VON KINDERN UND JUGENDLICHEN. 1950. 15 pp. (Second edition issued 1953. 16 pp.)

1084. *Buenos Aires. Universidad nacional. Instituto de filosofía. Seccion de psicología. Monografías psicológicas.*

TITLE VARIATIONS: None.

DATES OF PUBLICATION: Número 1–4+, 1950+.

FREQUENCY: Irregular. *See* Contents *below.*

NUMBERING VARIATIONS: None.

PUBLISHER: **Buenos Aires:** Universidad de Buenos Aires, Facultad de filosofía y letras, 1950+.

PRIMARY EDITORS: None listed.

CONTENTS:
Número 1. Delgado, Honorio. INTRODUCIÓN A LA PSICOPATALOGÍA. 1950. 43 pp.
Número 2. Riekel, August. EIDÉTICA; LA MEMORIA SENSORIAL Y SU INVESTIGACIÓN. Translated by J. Rovira Armengol. 1950. 54 pp.
Número 3. Keller, Wilhelm. EL CONCEPTO POSITIVO DE EXISTENCIA Y LA PSICOLOGÍA. Translated by Angelo Molnos. 1950. 27 pp.
Número 4. Utitz, Emil. CARACTEROLOGÍA. Translated by J. Rovira Armengol. 1950. 44 pp.

1085. *Cahiers de l'enfance inadaptée.*

TITLE VARIATIONS: None.

DATES OF PUBLICATION: Année 1, Numéro 1–3+, July 1950+.

FREQUENCY: Bimonthly (7 times a year).

NUMBERING VARIATIONS: None.

PUBLISHER: **Paris:** Sudel, 1950+.

PRIMARY EDITORS: None listed.

1086. *Canadian Psychologist.*

TITLE VARIATIONS: None.

DATES OF PUBLICATION: Volume 1, Number 1+, November 1950+.

FREQUENCY: Irregular.

NUMBERING VARIATIONS: None.

PUBLISHER: **Toronto:** Canadian Psychological Association, 1950+.

PRIMARY EDITOR: **D. L. Sampson,** 1950+.

1087. *Complex; The Magazine of Psychoanalysis and Society.*

TITLE VARIATIONS: Subtitle varies slightly.

DATES OF PUBLICATION: Number 1–3+, Spring–Fall 1950+.

FREQUENCY: Quarterly (Irregular).

NUMBERING VARIATIONS: None.

PUBLISHER: **New York:** Arts and Science Press, 1950+.

PRIMARY EDITOR: **Kilton Stewart,** 1950+.

1088. *Congreso latinoamericano de psicología. Relatorío.*

TITLE VARIATIONS: None.

DATES OF PUBLICATION: 1°+, 1950+.

FREQUENCY: Irregular. *See* Contents *below.*

NUMBERING VARIATIONS: None.

PUBLISHER: **Montevideo:** Editorial "Cepui," 1950 | .

PRIMARY EDITORS: *See* Contents *below.*

CONTENTS:

    1°. Relatorio del primer congreso latinoamericano de psicologia. Publicado por: W. Radecki (Presidente), C. A. Tuboras (Secretario General) y M. D. Nieto (Secretaria de communicaciones). 1950. 422 pp.

1089. *Encéphale; journal de neurologie, de psychiatrie et de médecine psycho-somatique.*

TITLE VARIATIONS: Continues in part *Encéphale; journal de neurologie et de psychiatrie et l'hygiène mentale,* which was also continued by *Hygiène mentale. Organe de la ligue française d'hygiène mentale.*

DATES OF PUBLICATION: Année 39+, 1950+.

FREQUENCY: Bimonthly.

NUMBERING VARIATIONS: None.

PUBLISHER: **Paris:** G. Doin et Cie, éditeurs, 1950+.

PRIMARY EDITORS: **Jean Lhermitte,** 1950+; **Jean Delay,** 1950+; **H. Baruk,** 1950+; **J. de Ajuriaguerra,** 1950+; **P. Pichot,** 1950+.

1090. *Group Psychotherapy; Journal of Sociopsychopathology and Sociatry.*

TITLE VARIATIONS: Continues *Sociaty. Journal of Group and Intergroup Therapy.*

DATES OF PUBLICATION: Volume 3+, 1950/1951+.

FREQUENCY: Quarterly.

NUMBERING VARIATIONS: None.

PUBLISHER: **New York:** Beacon House, Inc., 1950+.

PRIMARY EDITORS: **J. L. Moreno,** 1950+; **James M. Enneis,** 1950+; **Jane Shannon,** 1950; **Zerka Moreno,** 1950+.

1091. *Hokuriku shinri.* [Hokuriku Psychology Journal.]

TITLE VARIATIONS: None.

DATES OF PUBLICATION: Volume 1, Number 1+, December 1950+.

FREQUENCY: Quarterly.

NUMBERING VARIATIONS: None.

PUBLISHER: **Ishikawa:** Kanazawa Daigaku. Hokuriku Shinrigakkai [Kanazawa University. Hokuriku Psychological Association], 1950+.

PRIMARY EDITOR: None listed.

NOTE: Information on this title was found in *Japan. Higher Education and Science Bureau. Bibliographical List of Japanese Learned Journals. Number 2. Humanities and Social Sciences.* 1959.

1092. *Hygiène mentale. Organe de la ligue française d'hygiène mentale.*

TITLE VARIATIONS: Continues in part *Encéphale; journal de neurologie et de psychiatrie et l'hygiène mentale,* which was also continued by *Encéphale; journal de neurologie, de psychiatrie et de médecine psycho-somatique.*

DATES OF PUBLICATION: Année 39+, March–November 1950+.

FREQUENCY: Triannual.

NUMBERING VARIATIONS: None.

PUBLISHER: **Paris:** G. Doin et Cie, éditeurs, 1950+.

PRIMARY EDITORS: **Jean Lhermitte**, 1950+; **Jean Delay**, 1950+; **H. Baruk**, 1950+; **J. de Ajuriaguerra**, 1950+; **P. Pichot**, 1950+.

1093. *Journal of Projective Techniques.*

TITLE VARIATIONS: Continues *Rorschach Research Exchange and Journal of Projective Techniques.*

DATES OF PUBLICATION: Volume 14+, March 1950+.

FREQUENCY: Quarterly.

NUMBERING VARIATIONS: None.

PUBLISHER: **Glendale, California:** Society for Projective Techniques and Rorschach Institute, Inc., 1950+.

PRIMARY EDITORS: **Bruno Klopfer**, 1950+; **Mortimer M. Meyer**, 1950+; **Winafred B. Lucas**, 1950+; **Jeanne M. Reitzel**, 1950+; **Theodora M. Abel**, 1950+; **Bertram R. Forer**, 1950+; **Marguerite R. Hertz**, 1950+; **Walther Joel**, 1950+; **Edwin S. Shneidman**, 1950+; **Miriam G. Siegel**, 1950; **Evelyn Troup**, 1950+; **Florence Diamond**, 1950+.

EDITORIAL BOARD: Elizabeth Anderson, 1950+; Susan Deri, 1950+; Lawrence K. Frank, 1950+; Robert R. Holt, 1950+; Max L. Hutt, 1950+; Karen Machover, 1950+; Lois B. Murphy, 1950+; L. Joseph Stone, 1950+; Frederick Wyatt, 1950+.

1094. *Menninger Quarterly.*

TITLE VARIATIONS: Continues *Menninger Foundation. News Letter.*

DATES OF PUBLICATION: Volume 4+, 1950+.

FREQUENCY: Quarterly.

NUMBERING VARIATIONS: None.

PUBLISHER: **Topeka, Kansas:** Menninger Foundation, 1950+.

PRIMARY EDITORS: None listed.

1095. *Mental Health Progress.*

TITLE VARIATIONS: None.

DATES OF PUBLICATION: Volume 1, Number 1–8+, March–December 1950+.

FREQUENCY: Monthly (except July and August).

NUMBERING VARIATIONS: None.

PUBLISHER: **Minneapolis:** Minnesota Department of Health, 1950+.

PRIMARY EDITORS: None listed.

1096. *New York. Josiah Macy, Jr. Foundation. Conference on Problems of Consciousness. Transactions.*

TITLE VARIATIONS: None.

DATES OF PUBLICATION: 1st +, 1950 +.

FREQUENCY: Annual.

NUMBERING VARIATIONS: None.

PUBLISHER: **New York:** Josiah Macy, Jr. Foundation, 1951.

PRIMARY EDITOR: **Harold A. Abramson, 1950** +.

CONTENTS:
    1st. PROBLEMS OF CONSCIOUSNESS. TRANSACTIONS OF THE FIRST CONFER-ENCE MARCH 20–21, 1950, NEW YORK. 1951. 200 pp.

1097. *New York. National Psychological Association for Psychoanalysis. Bulletin.*

TITLE VARIATIONS: None.

DATES OF PUBLICATION: Number 1 +, 1950 +.

FREQUENCY: Annual.

NUMBERING VARIATIONS: None.

PUBLISHER: **New York:** National Psychological Association for Psychoanalysis, Inc., 1950 +.

PRIMARY EDITORS: None listed.

1098. *Pastoral Psychology.*

TITLE VARIATIONS: None.

DATES OF PUBLICATION: Volume 1 +, 1950 +.

FREQUENCY: Monthly (except July and August).

NUMBERING VARIATIONS: None.

PUBLISHER: **Great Neck, New York:** Pulpit Digest Publishing Company, Lester L. Doniger, Publisher, 1950 +.

PRIMARY EDITORS: **Simon Doniger, 1950** +; **Muriel Nordsiek, 1950.**

EDITORIAL BOARD: Oren H. Baker, 1950 +; David D. Eitzen, 1950 +; Daniel Blain, 1950 +; W. B. Blakemore, 1950 +; John Sutherland Bonnell, 1950 +; Russell L. Dicks, 1950 +; Rollin J. Fairbanks, 1950 +; Lawrence K. Frank, 1950 +; Seward Hiltner, 1950 +; Molly Harrower, 1950 +; Paul E. Johnson, 1950 +; C. E. Krumbholz, 1950 +; Lawson G. Lowrey, 1950 +; Halford E. Luccock, 1950 +; Rollo May, 1950 +; William C. Menninger, 1950 +; Wayne E. Oates, 1950 +; Carl R. Rogers, 1950 +; Luther E. Woodward, 1950 +; Ernest E. Bruder, 1950 +; Roy A. Burkhart, 1950 +.

1099. *Personality. Symposia on Topical Issues.*

TITLE VARIATIONS: Continued by *Personality Monographs* with Volume 3, 1952.

DATES OF PUBLICATION: [Volume 1/2+, 1950/1951+.] *See* Numbering Variations *below.*

FREQUENCY: **Irregular,** Symposium 1–2, 1950. **Quarterly,** Volume 1, 1951. *See* Numbering Variations *below.*

NUMBERING VARIATIONS: 1950 issues numbered Symposium 1 and Symposium 2. Volume numbering begins with Volume 1, 1951. Volume 1, Numbers 3–4 published together. Volume 2 omitted in numbering, hence from the publisher's point of view, 1950–1951 issues constitute Volumes 1–2.

PUBLISHER: **New York:** Grune and Stratton, 1950+.

PRIMARY EDITOR: **Werner Wolff,** 1950+.

ASSISTANT EDITOR: Joseph Precker, 1950+.

EDITORIAL BOARD: Harold H. Anderson, 1950+; Samuel J. Beck, 1950+; Leonard W. Doob, 1950+; Flanders Dunbar, 1950+; Lawrence K. Frank, 1950+; Erich Fromm, 1950+; Gustave M. Gilbert, 1950+; Kurt Goldstein, 1950+; Edna Heidbreder, 1950+; Abram Kardiner, 1950+; Otto Klineberg, 1950+; Clyde Kluckhohn, 1950+; David Krech, 1950+; Ernst Kris, 1950+; Mark May, 1950+; Abraham Maslow, 1950+; Margaret Mead, 1950+; Karl Menninger, 1950+; O. Hobart Mowrer, 1950+; Gardner Murphy, 1950+; Watson O'D. Pierce, 1950; David Rapaport, 1950+; Saul Rosenzweig, 1950+; Robert R. Sears, 1950+; Laurance F. Shaffer, 1950+; David Shakow, 1950+; Ross Stagner, 1950+; L. Joseph Stone, 1950+; Percival M. Symonds, 1950+; Silvan S. Tomkins, 1950+.

1100. *Personnel Psychology Monographs.*

TITLE VARIATIONS: None.

DATES OF PUBLICATION: Number 1, 1950.

FREQUENCY: Irregular. *See* Contents *below.*

NUMBERING VARIATIONS: *See* Contents *below.*

PUBLISHER: **Washington, D.C.:** Personnel Psychology, 1950.

PRIMARY EDITORS: **G. Frederic Kuder,** 1950; **Charles I. Mosier,** 1950; **Erwin K. Taylor,** 1950.

CONTENTS:
Number 1. Evans, Chester E., and LaVerne N. Laseau. MY JOB CONTEST. 1950. (Also as *Personnel Psychology; A Journal of Applied Research,* Volume 2, 1949, pp. 1–16, 185–227, 461–474, and 475–490.)

1101. *Psychological Book Previews.*

TITLE VARIATIONS: None.

DATES OF PUBLICATION: Specimen Issue, September 1950. (First regular issue 1951.)

FREQUENCY: Quarterly.

NUMBERING VARIATIONS: None.

PUBLISHER: **Princeton, New Jersey:** Psychological Book Previews, 1950.

PRIMARY EDITOR: **John W. French,** 1950.

1102. *Revista de psicología y pedagogía aplicadas.*

TITLE VARIATIONS: None.

DATES OF PUBLICATION: Año 1 +, 1950 +.

FREQUENCY: Semiannual.

NUMBERING VARIATIONS: None.

PUBLISHER: **Valencia:** Escuela especial de orientación aprovechamiento del ercmo. Ayuntamiento, 1950 +.

PRIMARY EDITORS: None listed.

1103. *Revue belge de psychologie et de pédagogie.*

TITLE VARIATIONS: Continues *Revue des sciences pédagogiques.*

DATES OF PUBLICATION: Tome 12 +, 1950 +.

FREQUENCY: Quarterly.

NUMBERING VARIATIONS: Issues also assigned whole numbers, Numéro 49–52 +.

PUBLISHER: **Brussels:** Publiée avec le concours de la fondation universitaire de belgique, 1950 +.

PRIMARY EDITORS: **Sylvain de Coster** (Director), 1950 +; **Gérard Goosens** (Secretary), 1950 +.

1104. *Revue de psychologie appliquée.* [2.]

TITLE VARIATIONS: None.

DATES OF PUBLICATION: Tome 1, Numéro 1 +, October 1950 +.

FREQUENCY: Quarterly.

NUMBERING VARIATIONS: None.

PUBLISHER: **Paris:** Éditions du Centre de psychologie appliquée, 1950 +.

PRIMARY EDITORS: **J.-M. Faverge,** 1950 +; **P. Pichot,** 1950 +; **P. Rennes,** 1950 +.

1105. *South African Psychological Association. Proceedings.*

TITLE VARIATIONS: Also titled *Suid-Afrikaanse sielkundige Vereniging. Verrigtings.*

DATES OF PUBLICATION: Number 1 +, 1950 +.

FREQUENCY: Annual.

NUMBERING VARIATIONS: None.

PUBLISHER: None listed.

PRIMARY EDITORS: None listed.

1106. *Southern California. University. Psychological Laboratory. Reports.*

TITLE VARIATIONS: None.

DATES OF PUBLICATION: Number 1–2+, June 1950–October 1950+.

FREQUENCY: Irregular. *See* Contents *below.*

NUMBERING VARIATIONS: None.

PUBLISHER: **Los Angeles, California:** University of Southern California, 1950+.

PRIMARY EDITORS: None listed.

CONTENTS:

Number 1. Guilford, J. P., A. L. Comrey, R. F. Green, and P. R. Christensen. A FACTOR-ANALYTIC STUDY OF REASONING ABILITIES. I. HYPOTHESES AND DESCRIPTION OF TESTS. June, 1950. 23 pp.

Number 2. Warren, N. D., R. C. Wilson, G. A. Green, G. L. Bryan, and N. E. Willmorth. AN INVESTIGATION OF CERTAIN AFTEREFFECTS OF INTERMITTENT RADIAL ACCELERATION. October, 1950. 19 pp.

1107. *United States. Air Force. Air Training Command. Training Analysis and Development. Informational Bulletin.*

TITLE VARIATIONS: None.

DATES OF PUBLICATION: Volume 1+, 1950+.

FREQUENCY: Quarterly.

NUMBERING VARIATIONS: None.

PUBLISHER: **Scott Air Force Base, Illinois:** Training Analysis and Development Directorate, Deputy Chief of Staff Operations, Headquarters, Air Training Command, 1950+.

PRIMARY EDITOR: **Russell N. Cassel,** 1950+.

Appendix

This section includes titles of serial publications which are not primarily psychological but which contain material relevant to psychology or written by psychologists. Years of publication follow each title. For title variations and continuations, numbering and numbering variations, consult relevant entries in the *National Union List of Serials*.

Anthropology/Social Science/Sociology

1108. *Académie des sciences morales et publiques (Paris). Revue des travaux et comptes-rendus.* (1842–1950+).

1109. *American Academy of Political and Social Science. Annals.* (1890–1950+).

1110. *American Anthropologist.* (1888–1950+).

1111. *American Journal of Physical Anthropology.* (1918–1942).

1112. *American Journal of Sociology.* (1895–1950+).

1113 *American Sociological Association. Papers.* (1906–1935).

1114. *American Sociological Review.* (1936–1950+).

1115. *Annales de sociologie et mouvement sociologique international.* (1900–1910).

1116. *Annales sociologiques. Série A. Sociologie générale.* (1934–1941).

1117. *Année sociologiques.* (1896–1912, 1923/24–1924/25).

1118. *Anthropologie.* (1890–1950+).

1119. *Archiv für angewandte Soziologie.* (1928–1933).

1120. *Archiv für Kriminologie.* (1898–1946+).

1121. *Bibliothek für praktische Menschenkenntnis.* (1921–1926).

1122. *British Journal of Delinquency.* (1950/1951+).

1123. *British Journal of Sociology.* (1950+).

1124. *Geisteswissenschaften.* (1913–1914).

1125. *Homo. Zeitschrift für die vergleichende Forschung am Menschen.* (1949–1950+).

1126. *International Social Science Bulletin.* (1949–1950+).

1127. *Joint Committee on Methods of Preventing Delinquency. Publication.* (1923–1925).

1128. *Journal of Criminal Law and Criminology and Police Science.* (1910–1950+).

1129. *Journal of Educational Sociology.* (1927–1950+).

1130. *Journal of Social Hygiene.* (1914–1950+).

1131. *Journal of Social Science.* (1869–1909).

1132. *Journal of the Anthropological Institute of New York.* (1871/1872).

1133. *Mens en maatschappij.* (1925–1950+).

1134. *National Opinion Research Center. Report.* (1941–1950+).

1135. *Public Affairs Pamphlets.* (1936–1950+).

1136. *Revue internationale de sociologie.* (1893–1939).

1137. *Rivista di sociologia.* (1927–1938).

1138. *Rivista italiana di sociologia.* (1897–1921).

1139. *Smith College. Studies in Social Work.* (1930–1950+).

1140. *Social Forces.* (1922–1950+).

1141. *Social Research. An International Quarterly of Political and Social Science.* (1934–1950+).

1142. *Social Science Abstracts.* (1929–1933).

1143. *Social Science Monographs.* (1925–1928).

1144. *Social Science Research Council. Bulletin.* (1930–1950+).

1145. *Social Service Review.* (1927–1950+).

1146. *Société d'anthropologie de Paris. Bulletins et mémoires.* (1860–1950+).

1147. *Sociological Papers.* (1904–1906).

1148. *Sociological Review.* (1908–1950+).

1149. *Sociology and Social Research.* (1916–1950+).

1150. *Survey.* (1897–1950+).

1151. *Zeitschrift für Criminal-Anthropologie.* (1897).

Child Study/Child Welfare/Education

1152. *Akademiia kommunisticheskogo vospitaniia imeni N. K. Krupskoi. Biulletin.* (1928–1930).

1153. *American Annals of the Deaf.* (1847–1950+).

1154. *American Childhood.* (1916–1950+).

1155. *American Educational Research Association. Official Report.* (1935–1950+).

1156. *American Physical Education Review.* (1896–1929).

1157. *Annales de l'enfance.* (1926–1934).

1158. *Archiv für Pädagogik.* (1912–1916).

1159. *Beiträge zur Kinderforschung und Heilerziehung.* (1898–1923).

1160. *Bureau of Educational Experiments. Bulletin.* (1917–1922).

1161. *California. University. Publications in Education.* (1893–1950+).

1162. *Catholic Educational Review.* (1911–1950+).

1163. *Catholic University of America. Educational Research Monographs.* (1932–1950+).

1164. *Character.* (1932–1935).

1165. *Chiao yü tsa chih* [Chinese Educational Review]. (1909–1950+).

1166. *Chicago. University. Committee on Education, Training and Research in Race Relations. Inventory of Research.* (1948–1950+).

1167. *Chicago. University. Contributions to Education.* (1901–1902).

1168. *Child Conference for Research and Welfare. Proceedings.* (1909–1910).

1169. *Child Study. A Journal of Parent Education.* (1923–1950+).

1170. *Child Welfare League of America. Bulletin.* (1922–1948).

1171. *Child Welfare League of America. Case Studies.* (1922–1925).

1172. *Childhood Education.* (1924–1950+).

1173. *Columbia University. Teachers College. Bulletin on Higher Education.* (1930–1932).

1174. *Columbia University. Teachers College. Contributions to Education.* (1905–1950+).

1175. *Columbia University. Teachers College. Studies in the Nature of Character.* (1928–1930).

1176. *Crippled Child.* (1923–1950+).

1177. *Duke University. Research Studies in Education.* (1931–1939).

1178. *Education.* (1880–1950+).

1179. *Educational Administration and Supervision.* (1915–1950+).

1180. *Educational Method.* (1921–1943).

1181. *Educational Record.* (1920–1950+).

1182. *Educational Records Bulletin.* (1928–1950+).

1183. *Educational Research Bulletin.* (1922–1950+).

1184. *Educational Review.* (1891–1928).

1185. *Elementary School Journal.* (1900–1950+).

1186. *Elementary School Record.* (1900).

1187. *Exceptional Children.* (1934–1950+).

1188. *Forschungen und Werke zur Erziehungswissenschaft.* (1925–1936).

1189. *Friedrich Manns pädagogisches Magazin.* (1898–1950+).

1190. *George Peabody College for Teachers. Bulletin.* (1931–1950+).

1191. *George Peabody College for Teachers. Contributions to Education.* (1920–1950+).

1192. *Gyermek.* (1908?–1937).

1193. *Harvard Educational Review.* (1931–1950+).

1194. *Harvard Studies in Education.* (1914–1943).

1195. *Heilpädagogische Umschau.* (1906–1907).

1196. *Heilpädagogische Werkblätter.* (1932–1950+).

1197. *Illinois Society for Child Study. Transactions.* (1894–1902).

1198. *Indiana. University. Division of University Extension. Bulletin.* (1946–1950+).

1199. *Indiana. University. Extension Division. Bulletin.* (1915–1940).

1200. *Infanzia anormale.* (1905–1925).

1201. *Inland Educator.* (1895–1900).

1202. *International Education Series.* (1886–1904).

1203. *International Labour Office (Geneva). Studies and Reports. Series J. Education.* (1922–1935).

1204. *Iowa. University. College of Education. Monographs in Education.* (1926–1932).

1205. *Jahrbuch der Erziehungswissenschaft und Jugendkunde.* (1925–1928).

1206. *Johns Hopkins University. Studies in Education.* (1917–1947).

1207. *Journal of Childhood and Adolescence.* (1901–1903).

1208. *Journal of Education.* (1875–1950+).

1209. *Journal of Higher Education.* (1930–1950+).

1210. *Journal of Pedagogy.* (1887–1910).

1211. *Kindergarten.* (1885–1895).

1212. *Marriage and Family Living.* (1939–1950+).

1213. *Maternity and Child Welfare.* (1917–1934).

1214. *Minnesota. University. Studies in Predicting Scholastic Achievement.* (1942).

1215. *National Association for the Study and Education of Exceptional Children. Bulletin.* (1919–1920).

1216. *National Association for the Study and Education of Exceptional Children. Proceedings.* (1910–1911).

1217. *National Education Association. Addresses and Proceedings.* (1858–1950+).

1218. *National Education Association. Journal.* (1916–1919).

1219. *National Society for the Study of Education. Yearbook.* (1895–1899, 1902–1950+).

1220. *National Society of College Teachers of Education. Studies in Education. Monograph.* (1947–1948).

1221. *National Society of College Teachers of Education. Yearbook.* (1911–1939).

1222. *NEA Research Bulletin.* (1923–1950+).

1223. *New Era in Home and School.* (1920–1950+).

1224. *New York Society for the Experimental Study of Education. Bulletin.* (1918–1936).

1225. *New York Society for the Experimental Study of Education. Contributions to Education.* (1924–1928).

1226. *New York Society for the Experimental Study of Education. Yearbook.* (1937–1950+).

1227. *Pädagogisches Zentralblatt.* (1919–1933).

1228. *Pädagogium. Eine Methoden-Sammlung für Erziehung und Unterricht.* (1913–1932).

1229. *Pädagogium. Monatsschrift für Erziehung und Unterricht.* (1878–1896).

1230. *Paidologist.* (1899–1907).

1231. *Paidology; the Science of the Child.* (1900–1901).

1232. *Parents' Magazine.* (1926–1950+).

1233. *Peabody Journal of Education.* (1923–1950+).

1234. *Pedagogické rozhledy.* (1888–1914).

1235. *Progressive Education.* (1924–1950+).

1236. *Purdue University. Division of Educational Reference. Studies in Higher Education.* (1926–1950+).

1237. *Religious Education.* (1906–1950+).

1238. *Research Quarterly.* (1930–1950+).

1239. *Research Relating to Children.* (1948–1950+).

1240. *Review of Educational Research.* (1931–1950+).

1241. *Revue internationale de l'enfant.* (1926–1931).

1242. *Rivista di pedagogia correttiva.* (1907–1939).

1243. *School.* (1912–1936).

1244. *School and Society.* (1915–1950+).

1245. *School Review.* (1893–1950+).

1246. *School Science and Mathematics.* (1901–1950+).

1247. *Scottish Council for Research in Education. Publications.* (1930–1950+).

1248. *Social Casework.* (1920–1950+).

1249. *Sovetskaia pedagogika.* (1937–1950+).

1250. *State Normal Monthly.* (1889–1901).

1251. *Studies in Education . . . Devoted to Child Study and the History of Education.* (1896/1897–1902).

1252. *Teachers College Journal.* (1929–1950+).

1253. *Teachers College Record.* (1900–1950+).

1254. *Tijdschrift voor zielkunde en opvoedingsleer.* (1918–1950+).

1255. *Toronto. University. Ontario College of Education. Department of Educational Research. Bulletin.* (1934–1950+).

1256. *Ungraded.* (1915–1926).

1257. *United States. Office of Education. Bulletin.* (1906–1950+).

1258. *Verein für wissenschaftliche Pädagogik (Dresden). Jahrbuch.* (1869–1917).

1259. *Vierteljahrsschrift für wissenschaftliche Pädagogik.* (1925–1950+).

1260. *Vlaamsch opvoedkundig tijdschrift.* (1921–1950+).

1261. *Volta Review.* (1899–1950+).

1262. *Voprosy defektologii.* (1928–1931).

1263. *Vor ungdom; Tidsskrift for opdragelse og undervisning.* (1879–1928).

1264. *Young Children.* (1948–1949).

1265. *Youth's Companion.* (1827–1929).

1266. *Zeitschrift für die Erforschung und Behandlung des jugendlichen Schwachsinns auf wissenschaftlicher Grundlage.* (1907–1922).

1267. *Zeitschrift für jugendkunde.* (1931–1935).

1268. *Zeitschrift für Kinderforschung.* (1896–1944).

Eugenics

1269. *American Eugenics Society. Proceedings.* (1936–1937).

1270. *American Eugenics Society. Report.* (1925/1926–1935).

1271. *Annals of Eugenics; A Journal for the Scientific Study of Racial Problems.* (1925–1950+).

1272. *Carnegie Institution (Washington). Department of Genetics. Bulletin.* (1911–1933).

1273. *Carnegie Institution (Washington). Department of Genetics. Memoir.* (1912).

1274. *Eugenical News.* (1916–1950+).

1275. *Eugenics; A Journal of Race Betterment.* (1928–1931).

1276. *Eugenics and Social Welfare Bulletin.* (1912–1918).

1277. *Eugenics Research Association. Handbook Series.* (1927).

1278. *Eugenics Research Association. Monograph Series.* (1929–1935).

1279. *Eugenics Review.* (1909–1950+).

1280. *Eugénique.* (1913–1922).

1281. *London. University. Francis Galton Laboratory for National Eugenics. Eugenics Laboratory Lecture Series.* (1909–1927).

1282. *London. University. Francis Galton Laboratory for National Eugenics. Eugenics Laboratory Memoirs.* (1907–1935).

General

1283. *American Magazine.* (1876–1950+).

1284. *American Review.* (1923–1926).

1285. *Andover Review.* (1884–1893).

1286. *Appleton's Journal; A Magazine of General Literature.* (1869–1881).

1287. *Appleton's Magazine.* (1903–1909).

1288. *Arena.* (1889–1909).

1289. *Atlantic Monthly.* (1857–1950+).

1290. *Bibliotheca Sacra.* (1844–1950+).

1291. *Blackwood's Magazine.* (1817–1950+).

1292. *Century Magazine.* (1870–1930).

1293. *Clark University. Library. Publications.* (1903–1945).

1294. *Contemporary Review.* (1866–1950+).

1295. *Deutsche Rundschau.* (1874–1950+).

1296. *Eclectic Magazine of Foreign Literature.* (1844–1907).

1297. *Fortnightly Review.* (1865–1950+).

1298. *Forum and Century.* (1886–1940).

1299. *Harpers Magazine.* (1850–1950+).

1300. *Hibbert Journal.* (1902–1950+).

1301. *Independent.* (1848–1928).

1302. *International Monthly Magazine of Literature, Science & Art.* (1850–1852).

1303. *Macmillan's Magazine.* (1859–1907).

1304. *Nation.* (1865–1950+).

1305. *National Review.* (1855–1864).

1306. *New Englander and Yale Review.* (1843–1892).
1307. *New Republic.* (1914–1950+).
1308. *New World.* (1892–1900).
1309. *Nineteenth Century.* (1879–1895).
1310. *North American Review.* (1815–1939/1940).
1311. *Northwestern Monthly.* (1890–1900).
1312. *Presbyterian Review.* (1880–1889).
1313. *Princeton Review.* (1825–1884, 1886–1888).
1314. *Revue des deux mondes.* (1831–1944).
1315. *Revue mondiale.* (1890–1936).
1316. *Saturday Review of Literature.* (1924–1950+).
1317. *Scribner's Magazine.* (1887–1939).
1318. *Tilskueren.* (1884–1939).
1319. *Umschau.* (1897–1950+).
1320. *Westminster Review.* (1824–1914).

Language

1321. *Archives néerlandaises de phonétique expérimentale.* (1927–1947).
1322. *International Journal of American Linguistics.* (1917–1950+).
1323. *Language.* (1925–1950+).
1324. *Language Monographs.* (1925–1950+).
1325. *Speech Monographs.* (1934–1950+).
1326. *Word.* (1945–1950+).

Medicine/Science

1327. *Abhandlungen zur Physiologie der Sinne.* (1897–1925).
1328. *Académie des sciences (Paris). Comptes-rendus.* (1835–1950+).
1329. *Acoustical Society of America. Journal.* (1929–1950+).
1330. *Acta Biologiae Experimentalis.* (1928–1950+).
1331. *Acta Ophthalmologica.* (1923–1950+).
1332. *Acta Oto-laryngolica.* (1918–1950+).
1333. *Akademie der Wissenschaften (Berlin). Monatsberichte.* (1856–1881).
1334. *Akademie der Wissenschaften (Berlin). Physikalisch-mathematische Klasse. Sitzungsberichte.* (1922–1949).
1335. *Akademie der Wissenschaften (Leipzig). Mathematisch-naturwissenschaftliche Klasse. Berichte.* (1849–1950+).

1336. *Akademie der Wissenschaften (Munich). Philosophisch-historische Abteilung. Sitzungsberichte.* (1871–1944).

1337. *Akademie der Wissenschaften (Vienna). Mathematisch-naturwissenschaftliche Klasse. Sitzungsberichte.* (1848–1950+).

1338. *Akademiia nauk SSSR (Leningrad). Biulletin.* (1860–1888, 1890–1945).

1339. *Akademiia nauk SSSR (Moscow). Fiziologicheskii institut imeni I.P. Pavlova. Problemy fiziologicheskoi akustiki.* (1949–1950+).

1340. *Akademiia nauk SSSR (Moscow). Fiziologicheskii institut imeni I.P. Pavlova. Problemy fiziologicheskoi optiki.* (1941–1950+).

1341. *American Academy of Ophthalmology and Otolaryngology. Transactions.* (1896–1950+).

1342. *American Association for the Advancement of Science. Proceedings.* (1848–1940).

1343. *American Journal of Ophthalmology.* (1884–1950+).

1344. *American Journal of Optometry and Archives of the American Academy of Optometry.* (1924–1950+).

1345. *American Journal of Physical Medicine.* (1922–1950+).

1346. *American Journal of Physiological Optics.* (1920–1926).

1347. *American Journal of Physiology.* (1898–1950+).

1348. *American Journal of the Medical Sciences.* (1827–1950+).

1349. *American Medical Association. Journal.* (1883–1950+).

1350. *American Men of Science.* (1906–1950+).

1351. *American Naturalist.* (1867–1950+).

1352. *American Ophthalmological Society. Transactions.* (1864–1950+).

1353. *American Philosophical Society. Proceedings.* (1838–1950+).

1354. *American Statistical Association. Journal.* (1888/1889–1950+).

1355. *Anatomical Record.* (1906–1950+).

1356. *Annali di ottalmologia e clinica oculistica.* (1871–1950+).

1357. *Annals of Mathematical Statistics.* (1930–1950+).

1358. *Annals of Ophthalmology.* (1897–1917).

1359. *Annals of Ophthalmology and Otology.* (1892–1896).

1360. *Annals of Otology, Rhinology and Laryngology.* (1897–1950+).

1361. *Année biologique.* (1895–1950+).

1362. *Archiv für Anatomie und Physiologie. Physiologische Abteilung.* (1877–1919).

1363. *Archiv für Augenheilkunde.* (1869–1937).

1364. *Archiv für Frauenkunde und Konstitutionsforschung.* (1914–1933).

1365. *Archiv für Laryngologie und Rhinologie.* (1893–1921).

1366. *Archiv für Ohren-, Nasen- und Kehlkopfheilkunde.* (1864–1944).

1367. *Archiv für Ohrenheilkunde.* (1864–1915).

1368. *Archiv für Ophthalmologie.* (1854–1870).

1369. *Archives de physiologie normale et pathologique.* (1868–1898).

1370. *Archives de zoologie expérimentale et générale.* (1872–1950+).

1371. *Archives d'ophthalmologie.* (1880–1936).

1372. *Archives internationales de laryngologie, d'otologie, de rhinologie et de broncho-oesophagoscopie.* (1887–1914, 1922–1930).

1373. *Archives italiennes de biologie.* (1882–1950+).

1374. *Archives néerlandaises de physiologie de l'homme et des animaux.* (1916–1947).

1375. *Archives of Ophthalmology.* (1869–1950).

1376. *Archives of Otolaryngology.* (1925–1950+).

1377. *Archives of Otology.* (1869–1908).

1378. *Association française pour l'avancement des sciences. Comptes rendus.* (1872–1922).

1379. *Beiträge zur Akustik und Musikwissenschaft.* (1898–1924).

1380. *Beobachtungen über den Cretinismus.* (1850–1852).

1381. *Berliner klinische Wochenschrift.* (1864–1921).

1382. *Bibliothèque universelle. Archives des sciences physiques et naturelles.* (1846–1947).

1383. *Biological Bulletin.* (1898–1950+).

1384. *Biologisches Zentralblatt.* (1881–1950+).

1385. *Biometric Bulletin.* (1936–1938).

1386. *Biometrics.* (1945–1950+).

1387. *Biometrika.* (1901–1950+).

1388. *Biotypologie.* (1932–1950+).

1389. *British Association for the Advancement of Science. Reports.* (1831–1938).

1390. *British Journal of Ophthalmology.* (1917–1950+).

1391. *British Journal of Ophthalmology. Monograph Supplement.* (1924–1950).

1392. *Bulletin biologique de la France et de la Belgique.* (1869–1950+).

1393. *Bulletin médical.* (1887–1950+).

1394. *Canadian Medical Association. Journal.* (1911–1950+).

1395. *Carnegie Institution (Washington). Publications.* (1901–1950+).

1396. *Clinique ophthalmologique.* (1895–1928).

1397. *Conference on Nerve Impulse. Transactions.* (1950+).

1398. *Dartmouth College. Medical School. Eye Institute. Publications.* (1921–1922).

1399. *Deutsche medizinische Wochenschrift.* (1875–1950 +).

1400. *Electroencephalography and Clinical Neurophysiology.* (1949–1950 +).

1401. *Ergebnisse der Physiologie.* (1902–1950 +).

1402. *Fiziologicheskii zhurnal SSSR imeni I. M. Sechenova.* (1917–1950 +).

1403. *Folia Neuro-biologica.* (1907–1922).

1404. *Franklin Institute. Journal.* (1826–1950 +).

1405. *Geriatrics.* (1946–1950 +).

1406. *Great Britain. Medical Research Council. Special Reports.* (1915–1920).

1407. *Harvard University. Museum of Comparative Zoology. Bulletin.* (1863–1950 +).

1408. *Harvard University. Museum of Comparative Zoology. Zoological Laboratory Contributions.* (1861–1921).

1409. *Hearing News.* (1933–1950 +).

1410. *Hearing Survey Quarterly.* (1944–1950 +).

1411. *Human Biology.* (1929–1950 +).

1412. *Illinois. State Academy of Science. Transactions.* (1907/1908–1950 +).

1413. *Illuminating Engineering, Including Transactions of the Illuminating Engineering Society.* (1906–1940).

1414. *Indiana. University. Publications. Science Series.* (1935–1950 +).

1415. *Intermédiaire des biologistes et des médecins.* (1897–1899).

1416. *International Clinics.* (1891–1942).

1417. *International Congress of Ophthalmology. Proceedings.* (1857–1950 +).

1418. *International Journal of Sexology.* (1934–1937, 1947–1950 +).

1419. *International Record of Medicine.* (1865–1950 +).

1420. *Internationale Zeitschrift für angewandte Physiologie einschliesslich Arbeitsphysiologie.* (1928–1950 +).

1421. *Iowa Academy of Sciences. Proceedings.* (1887/1893–1950 +).

1422. *Iowa. University. Studies. Series on Aims and Progress of Research.* (1916–1950 +).

1423. *Journal de l'anatomie et de la physiologie normales et pathologiques de l'homme et des animaux.* (1864–1914/1919).

1424. *Journal de la physiologie de l'homme et des animaux.* (1858–1863).

1425. *Journal of Anatomy.* (1866–1950 +).

1426. *Journal of Experimental Biology.* (1923–1950 +).

1427. *Journal of Experimental Zoology.* (1904–1950 +).

1428. *Journal of General Physiology.* (1918–1950 +).

1429. *Journal of Gerontology.* (1946–1950 +).

1430. *Journal of Gerontology. Non-technical Supplement.* (1946).

1431. *Journal of Heredity (Chicago).* (1885–1891).

1432. *Journal of Heredity (Washington, D.C.).* (1910–1950 +).

1433. *Journal of Industrial Hygiene and Toxicology.* (1919–1949).

1434. *Journal of Laryngology and Otology.* (1887–1950 +).

1435. *Journal of Mammology.* (1919–1950 +).

1436. *Journal of Neurophysiology.* (1938–1950 +).

1437. *Journal of Neurosurgery.* (1944–1950 +).

1438. *Journal of Ophthalmology, Otology and Laryngology.* (1889–1929).

1439. *Journal of Physiology.* (1878–1950 +).

1440. *Journal of Rehabilitation.* (1935–1950 +).

1441. *Journal of Speech and Hearing Disorders.* (1936–1950 +).

1442. *Journal of Speech and Hearing Disorders. Monograph Supplement.* (1950 +).

1443. *Klinische Monatsblätter für Augenheilkunde.* (1863–1950 +).

1444. *Klinische Wochenschrift.* (1922–1950 +).

1445. *Lancet.* (1823–1950 +).

1446. *Laryngoscope.* (1896–1950 +).

1447. *Medical Record.* (1866–1922).

1448. *Medical Review of Reviews.* (1895–1937).

1449. *Medico-Legal Journal.* (1933–1950 +).

1450. *Medizinische Klinik.* (1904–1950 +).

1451. *Michigan Academy of Science, Arts and Letters. Papers.* (1921–1950 +).

1452. *Monatsschrift für Ohrenheilkunde und Laryngo-Rhinologie.* (1867–1950 +).

1453. *Monographien zur Frauenkunde und Konstitutionsforschung.* (1921–1933).

1454. *Münchener medizinische Wochenschrift.* (1854–1950 +).

1455. *National Academy of Science. Biographical Memoirs.* (1877–1950 +).

1456. *National Academy of Science. Proceedings.* (1915–1950 +).

1457. *National Research Council (Washington, D.C.). Bulletin.* (1919–1950 +).

1458. *National Research Council (Washington, D.C.). Reprint and Circular Series.* (1919–1950 +).

1459. *Natural Science.* (1892–1899).

1460. *Nature.* (1869–1950 +).

1461. *Naturwissenschaften.* (1913–1950 +).

1462. *Nederlandsch tijdschrift voor geneeskunde.* (1857–1950 +).

1463. *New England Journal of Medicine.* (1828–1950 +).

1464. *New York Academy of Science. Annals.* (1877–1950 +).

1465. *New York Academy of Science. Transactions.* (1881–1897, 1938–1950+).

1466. *Ophthalmologica.* (1899–1950+).

1467. *Optical Journal and Review of Optometry.* (1895–1950+).

1468. *Optical Society of America. Journal.* (1917–1950+).

1469. *Optometric Weekly.* (1910–1950+).

1470. *Orvosi hétilap.* (1857–1940).

1471. *Paris. Société de biologie. Comptes rendus.* (1849–1950+).

1472. *Pediatriia (Moscow).* (1934–1950+).

1473. *Pediatriia (Petersburg).* (1910–1930).

1474. *Pflüger's Archiv für die gesamte Physiologie des Menschen und der Tiere.* (1868–1950+).

1475. *Physiological Reviews.* (1921–1950+).

1476. *Physiological Zoology.* (1928–1950+).

1477. *Physiologie expérimentale.* (1875–1879).

1478. *Popular Science Monthly.* (1872–1950+).

1479. *Presse médicale.* (1893–1950+).

1480. *Progrès médical.* (1873–1950+).

1481. *Public Health Reports.* (1878–1950+).

1482. *Quarterly Journal of Experimental Physiology.* (1908–1950+).

1483. *Quarterly Journal of Speech.* (1915–1950+).

1484. *Quarterly Journal of Studies on Alcohol.* (1940/1941–1950+).

1485. *Quarterly Review of Biology.* (1926–1950+).

1486. *Review of Scientific Instruments.* (1930–1950+).

1487. *Revue des questions scientifiques.* (1877–1950+).

1488. *Revue générale des sciences pure et appliquées.* (1890–1968).

1489. *Revue générale d'ophthalmologie.* (1882–1936).

1490. *Revue scientifique.* (1863–1950+).

1491. *Royal Society (Edinburgh). Proceedings.* (1832–1940).

1492. *Royal Society (London) Philosophical Transactions.* (1665–1950+).

1493. *Royal Society (London). Proceedings.* (1800–1905).

1494. *Sammlung physiologischer Abhandlungen.* (1876–1880).

1495. *Schweizerische medizinische Wochenschrift.* (1870–1950+).

1496. *Science.* (1883–1950+).

1497. *"Scientia," rivista di scienza.* (1907–1950+).

1498. *Scientific American.* (1845–1950+).

1499. *Scientific Monthly.* (1915–1950+).

1500. *Société française d'ophthalmologie. Bulletin et mémoires.* (1883–1950+).

1501. *Society for Experimental Biology and Medicine. Proceedings.* (1903/ 1904–1950+).

1502. *Spain. Consejo superior de investigaciónes científicas. Instituto Santiago Ramón y Cajal. Trabajos.* (1901–1950+).

1503. *Suomalainen Tiedeakatemia. Toimituksia. Annales. Series B.* (1909– 1950+).

1504. *United Kingdom. Ophthalmological Societies. Transactions.* (1880– 1950+).

1505. *Vestnik oftal'mologii (Kiev).* (1884–1917, 1926–1932).

1506. *Vestnik oftal'mologii (Moscow).* (1932–1950+).

1507. *Vestnik oto-rino-laringologii.* (1908–1937).

1508. *Virchows Archiv für pathologische Anatomie und Physiologie und klinische Medizin.* (1847–1950+).

1509. *Wiener klinische Wochenschrift.* (1888–1950+).

1510. *Wiener medizinische Wochenschrift.* (1851–1950+).

1511. *Wissenschaft und Bildung.* (1907–1936).

1512. *Woods Hole, Massachusetts. Marine Biological Laboratory. Biological Lectures.* (1890–1899).

1513. *Yale Journal of Biology and Medicine.* (1928–1950+).

1514. *Yale University. School of Medicine. Laboratory of Applied Physiology. Section on Alcohol Studies. Memoirs.* (1944–1950+).

1515. *Zeitschrift für allgemeine Physiologie.* (1902–1923).

1516. *Zeitschrift für Biologie.* (1865–1950+).

1517. *Zeitschrift für menschliche Vererbungs- und Konstitutionslehre.* (1913– 1950+).

1518. *Zeitschrift für Naturforschung.* (1946).

1519. *Zentralblatt für Gewerbehygiene und Unfallverhütung.* 1913–1922, 1924–1943).

1520. *Zentralblatt für Physiologie.* (1887–1921).

Personnel/Management/Vocational Guidance

1521. *American Job Series. Occupational Monographs.* (1938–1943).

1522. *American Management Association. Manufacturing Series.* (1924–1950+).

1523. *American Management Association. Office Management Series.* (1924– 1950+).

1524. *American Management Association. Personnel Series.* (1930–1950+).

1525. *California. University. School of Education. Vocational Guidance Series.* (1930).

1526. *Guide to Guidance.* (1938–1950 +).

1527. *Human Organization.* (1941–1950 +).

1528. *Minnesota. University. Industrial Relations Center. Bulletin.* (1945–1950 +).

1529. *National Industrial Conference Board. Studies in Personnel Policy.* (1937–1950 +).

1530. *Personnel.* (1919–1950 +).

1531. *Personnel Administration.* (1938–1950 +).

1532. *Personnel Management.* (1920–1950 +).

1533. *Personnel Research Foundation. Reprint and Circular Series.* (1925–1931).

1534. *Public Personnel Quarterly.* (1939–1942).

1535. *Public Personnel Review.* (1940–1950 +).

1536. *Texas Personnel Review.* (1942 1950 +).

1537. *Travail humain.* (1933–1950 +).

1538. *Zentralblatt für Arbeitswissenschaft und soziale Betriebspraxis.* (1947–1950 +).

Philosophy

1539. *Aberdeen Philosophical Society. Transactions.* (1840/1884–1900/1910).

1540. *Abhandlungen der Fries'schen Schule.* (1847–1849, 1904–1930).

1541. *Abhandlungen zur Philosophie und ihrer Geschichte (Erdmann).* (1893–1920).

1542. *Abhandlungen zur Philosophie und ihrer Geschichte (Falckenberg).* (1907–1916).

1543. *Abhandlungen zur Philosophie und Pädagogik.* (1924–1925).

1544. *American Philosophical Association. Proceedings and Addresses . . . of the Various Sections.* (1902–1950 +).

1545. *Annalen der Naturphilosophie.* (1901–1921).

1546. *Annalen der Naturphilosophie. Beihefte.* (1910–1913).

1547. *Annalen der Philosophie und philosophischen Kritik.* (1919–1930).

1548. *Annales de philosophie chrétienne.* (1830–1913).

1549. *Année philosophique.* (1867–1868).

1550. *Année philosophique (Pillon).* (1890–1913).

1551. *Annuaire philosophique.* (1864–1870).

1552. *Archiv für Geschichte der Philosophie.* (1888–1932).

1553. *Archiv für systematische Philosophie und Soziologie.* (1868–1931).

1554. *Archives of Philosophy.* (1907–1922).

1555. *Aristotelian Society for the Systematic Study of Philosophy (London). Proceedings.* (1887–1896, 1900–1950 +).

1556. *Bibliography of Philosophy. A Quarterly Bulletin.* (1933–1936).

1557. *Bibliothek für Philosophie.* (1911–1930).

1558. *Blätter für deutsche Philosophie.* (1927–1944).

1559. *British Journal for the Philosophy of Science.* (1950 +).

1560. *California. University. Publications in Philosophy.* (1904–1950 +).

1561. *Česka mýšl.* (1900–1950 +).

1562. *Chicago. University. Contributions to Philosophy.* (1896–1903).

1563. *Chicago. University. Philosophic Studies.* (1907–1923).

1564. *Columbia University. Department of Philosophy. Studies in the History of Ideas.* (1918–1935).

1565. *Conference on Science, Philosophy and Religion in Their Relation to the Democratic Way of Life. Symposium.* (1940–1950 +).

1566. *Cornell University. Studies in Philosophy.* (1900–1925).

1567. *Critique philosophique.* (1872–1889).

1568. *Divus Thomas; Jahrbuch für Philosophie und speculative Theologie.* (1887–1950 +).

1569. *Einheitswissenschaft.* (1933–1940).

1570. *Etc.* (1943–1950 +).

1571. *Ethical Record.* (1888–1890).

1572. *Ethics.* (1890–1950 +).

1573. *Ethisch-socialwissenschaftliche Vorträgskurse.* (1896–1897).

1574. *Études philosophiques.* (1926–1950 +).

1575. *Experientia.* (1945–1950 +).

1576. *Filosofia delle scuole italiane, rivista bimestrale.* (1870–1885).

1577. *Filosofski pregled'.* (1929–1938).

1578. *Frommanns Klassiker der Philosophie.* (1896–1950 +).

1579. *Grundwissenschaft; Philosophische Zeitschrift der Johannes-Rehmke-Gesellschaft.* (1919–1937).

1580. *International Congress of Philosophy. Acts.* (1900–1950 +).

1581. *Jahrbuch für Philosophie und phänomenologische Forschungen.* (1913–1930).

1582. *Jahrbuch für Philosophie und phänomenologische Forschungen. Ergänzungsband.* (1913–1930).

1583. *Journal of Aesthetics and Art Criticism.* (1941–1950 +).

1584. *Journal of Social Philosophy and Jurisprudence.* (1935–1942).

1585. *Journal of the History of Ideas.* (1940–1950+).

1586. *Journal of Unified Science.* (1930–1940).

1587. *Kant-Studien.* (1897–1950+).

1588. *Kant-Studien. Ergänzungshefte.* (1906–1950+).

1589. *Leitfäden der Philosophie.* (1925–1927).

1590. *Los Angeles. University of Southern California. Studies. Philosophy Series.* (1930–1937).

1591. *Louvain. Université catholique. Institut supérieur de philosophie. Annales.* (1912–1924).

1592. *Monist.* (1890–1936).

1593. *New Scholasticism.* (1927–1950+).

1594. *Open Court.* (1887–1936).

1595. *Personalist. A Quarterly Journal of Philosophy, Theology and Literature.* (1920–1950+).

1596. *Philosophical Quarterly.* (1925–1950+).

1597. *Philosophical Review.* (1892–1950+).

1598. *Philosophical Studies.* (1950+).

1599. *Philosophie positive.* (1867–1883).

1600. *Philosophie und Geisteswissenschaft.* (1923–1937).

1601. *Philosophie und Leben.* (1925–1933).

1602. *Philosophische Arbeiten.* (1906–1915).

1603. *Philosophische Bibliothek.* (1788–1791).

1604. *Philosophische Forschungsberichte.* (1930–1933).

1605. *Philosophische Hefte.* (1928–1936).

1606. *Philosophische Vorträge.* (1875–1899).

1607. *Philosophische Vorträge (Kantgesellschaft).* (1912–1934).

1608. *Philosophischer Anzeiger.* (1925/1926–1930).

1609. *Philosophisches Jahrbuch der Görresgesellschaft.* (1888–1950+).

1610. *Philosophy.* (1926–1950+).

1611. *Philosophy and Phenomenological Research.* (1940–1950+).

1612. *Philosophy of Science.* (1934–1950+).

1613. *Positivismo, revista de philosophia.* (1878–1882).

1614. *Recherches philosophiques.* (1931–1936/1937).

1615. *Revue de métaphysique et de morale.* (1893–1950+).

1616. *Revue de philosophie.* (1900–1939).

1617. *Revue philosophique de la France et de l'étranger.* (1876–1950+).

1618. *Revue philosophique de Louvain.* (1894–1950+).

1619. *Rivista di filosofia e scienze affini.* (1899–1908).

1620. *Rivista filosofica.* (1899–1908).

1621. *Rivista italiana di filosofia.* (1886–1898).

1622. *Rivista speciale di opere di filosofia scientifica.* (1881–1900).

1623. *Société française de philosophie (Paris). Bulletin.* (1901–1950+).

1624. *Studies in Philosophy and Social Science.* (1932–1942).

1625. *Symposion; Philosophische Zeitschrift für Forschung und Aussprache.* (1925/1927).

1626. *Synthesis. Sammlung historischer Monographien philosophischer Begriffe.* (1908–1932).

1627. *Tetsugaku kenkyu* [Philosophical Studies]. (1916–1950+).

1628. *Tijdschrift voor Philosophie.* (1939–1950+).

1629. *Vienna. Verein Ernst Mach. Veröffentlichungen.* (1929).

1630. *Vierteljahrsschrift für wissenschaftliche Philosophie und Soziologie.* (1876–1916).

1631. *Zeitschrift für Aesthetik und allgemeine Kunstwissenschaft.* (1905/1906–1943).

1632. *Zeitschrift für exacte Philosophie im Sinne des neueren philosophischen Realismus.* (1861–1896).

1633. *Zeitschrift für philosophische Forschung.* (1946–1950+).

Phrenology

1634. *Annals of Phrenology.* (1833–1835).

1635. *Cincinnati. Phreno-magnetic Society. Journal.* (1842).

1636. *Phreno-magnet and Mirror of Nature.* (1843).

1637. *Phrenological Journal and Magazine of Moral Science.* (1823–1847).

1638. *Phrenological Journal and Science of Health.* (1838–1911).

1639. *Phrenological Magazine.* (1880–1896).

1640. *Phrenological Magazine and New York Literary Review.* (1835).

1641. *Phrenological Society (Edinburgh). Transactions.* (1820/1823).

1642. *Phrenological Society (Washington). Proceedings.* (1826–1828).

1643. *Société phrénologique de Paris. Journal.* (1832–1834; 1841–1842).

1644. *Tidsskrift for phrenologien.* (1827–1828).

1645. *Tidsskrift for phrenologien. Supplement.* (1829).

1646. *Zeitschrift für Phrenologie.* (1843–1845).

Psychiatry/Neurology

1647. *Abhandlungen zur personellen Sexualökonomie.* (1935–1937).

1648. *Acta Paedopsychiatrica.* (1934–1950 +).

1649. *Acta Psychiatrica et Neurologica Scandinavica.* (1926–1950 +).

1650. *Acta Psychiatrica et Neurologica Scandinavica. Supplementum.* (1932–1950 +).

1651. *Actas luso-españolas de neurología y psiquiatría.* (1940–1950 +).

1652. *Alienist and Neurologist.* (1880–1920).

1653. *Alienists and Neurologists of America under Auspices of Chicago Medical Society. Proceedings.* (1912–1917).

1654. *Allgemeine Zeitschrift für Psychiatrie und ihre Grenzgebiete.* (1844–1949).

1655. *AMA Archives of Neurology and Psychiatry.* (1919–1950 +).

1656. *American Association of Psychiatric Social Workers. Quarterly Newsletter.* (1926–1927).

1657. *American Journal of Neurology and Psychiatry.* (1882–1885).

1658. *American Journal of Psychiatry.* (1844–1950 +).

1659. *American Medical Association. Section on Nervous and Mental Diseases. Transactions.* (1906–1927).

1660. *American Neurological Association. Transactions.* (1875–1950 +).

1661. *American Psychiatric Association. Committee on Relations with the Social Sciences. Proceedings . . . Colloquium on Personality Investigation.* (1928–1929).

1662. *American Psychiatric Association. Proceedings.* (1844–1920).

1663. *Anales de medicina legal, psiquiatría y anatomia patologica.* (1933).

1664. *Annali di freniatria e scienze affini.* (1888–1913).

1665. *Annali di neurologia.* (1883–1931).

1666. *Anomalo. Rivista di antropologia criminale e psichiatria.* (1889–1922).

1667. *Arbeiten aus dem Gesammt-gebiet der Psychiatrie und Neuropathologie von R. Krafft-Ebing.* (1897–1899).

1668. *Arbeiten zur angewandten Psychiatrie.* (1921–1922).

1669. *Archiv für Psychiatrie und Nervenkrankheiten.* (1868–1950 +).

1670. *Archives internationales de neurologie.* (1880–1950 +).

1671. *Archives of Neurology and Psychiatry.* (1899–1939).

1672. *Archivio di antropologia criminale, psichiatria, medicina legale e scienze affini.* (1880–1950 +).

1673. *Archivio italiano per le malattie nervose.* (1864–1907).

1674. *Archivos brasileiros de psychiatria, neurologia e sciencias affines.* (1905–1908).

1675. *Arquivos brasileiros de neuriatria e psichiatria.* (1919–1938).

1676. *Association for Research in Nervous and Mental Disease. Research Publications.* (1920–1950 +).

1677. *Beacon.* (1942).

1678. *Beiträge zur psychiatrischen Klinik.* (1902–1903).

1679. *Boston. Psychopathic Hospital. Collected Contributions.* (1913–1915).

1680. *Brain; A Journal of Neurology.* (1878–1950 +).

1681. *Breslau. Universität. Psychiatrische und Nervenklinik. Arbeiten.* (1892–1895).

1682. *British Journal of Psychiatric Social Work.* (1947–1950 +).

1683. *California. Department of Institutions. Psychiatric Monographs.* (1941).

1684. *Conferencia latino-americana de neurología, psiquiatría y medicina legal. Actas.* (1929).

1685. *Confinia Neurologica.* (1938–1950 +).

1686. *Congrès des médecins aliénistes et neurologistes de France et des pays de langue française. Compte rendu.* (1890–1950 +).

1687. *Connecticut Society for Mental Hygiene. Annual Report.* (1908/ 1912–1920/1922).

1688. *Connecticut Society for Mental Hygiene. Publications.* (1909–1921).

1689. *Connecticut's Mental Health News.* (1922–1950 +).

1690. *Dementia Praecox Studies. A Journal of Psychiatry of Adolescence.* (1918–1922).

1691. *Deutsche Tagung für psychische Hygiene. Bericht.* (1929–1932).

1692. *Deutsche Zeitschrift für Nervenheilkunde.* (1891–1950 +).

1693. *Digest of Neurology and Psychiatry.* (1932–1950 +).

1694. *Diseases of the Nervous System.* (1940–1950 +).

1695. *Ergebnisse der Neurologie und Psychiatrie.* (1912–1917).

1696. *Excerpta Medica. Section 8B: Psychiatry.* (1948–1950 +).

1697. *Folia Psychiatrica et Neurologica Japonica.* (1933–1950 +).

1698. *Folia Psychiatrica, Neurologica et Neurochirurgica Neerlandica.* (1883– 1950 +).

1699. *Fortschritte der Neurologie, Psychiatrie und ihrer Grenzgebiete.* (1929–1950 +).

1700. *Genesis.* (1921–1932).

1701. *Giornale di psichiatria e neuropatologia.* (1874–1950 +).

1702. *Igiene mentale.* (1920–1935).

1703. *Illinois Society for Mental Hygiene. Bulletin.* (1916).

1704. *Illinois Society for Mental Hygiene. Mental Health Bulletin.* (1923–1950 +).

1705. *Illinois Society for Mental Hygiene. Newsletter.* (1945–1950 +).

1706. *Indiana Society for Mental Hygiene. Bulletin.* (1916–1919).

1707. *Intermédiaire des neurologistes et des aliénistes.* (1898–1899).

1708. *International Conference on Child Psychiatry.* (1937–1948).

1709. *International Conference on Psychosurgery.* (1948).

1710. *International Congress for Sex Research. Proceedings.* (1926–1930).

1711. *Jahrbücher für Psychiatrie und Neurologie.* (1879–1937).

1712. *Jahresbericht Neurologie und Psychiatrie.* (1910–1931).

1713. *Jornal brasileiro de psiquiatria.* (1948–1950 +).

1714. *Journal de médecine légale psychiatrique et d'anthropologie criminelle.* (1906).

1715. *Journal of Clinical Pastoral Work.* (1947–1949).

1716. *Journal of Neuropathology and Experimental Neurology.* (1942–1950 +).

1717. *Journal of Pastoral Care.* (1947–1950 +).

1718. *Juristisch-psychiatrische Grenzfragen.* (1903–1919).

1719. *Kansas Mental Hygiene Society. Bulletin.* (1924–1939).

1720. *Klinik für psychische und nervöse Krankheiten.* (1906–1919).

1721. *Ligue d'hygiène mentale. Bulletin mensuel.* (1921–1923).

1722. *Los Angeles Neurological Society. Bulletin.* (1936–1950 +).

1723. *Manicomio.* (1885–1926).

1724. *Maryland Psychiatric Quarterly.* (1911–1923).

1725. *Massachusetts. Department of Mental Health. Bulletin.* (1917–1936).

1726. *Massachusetts Society for Mental Hygiene. Monthly Bulletin.* (1921–1940).

1727. *Massachusetts Society for Mental Hygiene. Publication.* (1914–1931).

1728. *Massachusetts. State Hospital (Boston). Psychopathic Department. Report.* (1910–1920).

1729. *Mental Health and Our Community.* (1948–1950 +).

1730. *Mental Health (Beloit).* (1934–1950 +).

1731. *Mental Health (London).* (1940–1950 +).

1732. *Mental Health (Montreal).* (1930–1935).

1733. *Mental Health (Salt Lake City).* (1934).

1734. *Mental Health (Toronto).* (1920–1936).

1735. *Mental Health Bulletin.* (1921–1950 +).

1736. *Mental Health News.* (1940–1950 +).

1737. *Mental Health Observer.* (1932–1938).

1738. *Mental Health Sentinel.* (1940–1942).

1739. *Mental Health Society of Greater Miami. Monthly Bulletin.* (1948–1950 +).

1740. *Mental Hospital Institute. Proceedings.* (1949–1950 +).

1741. *Mental Hygiene Bulletin (Baltimore).* (1923–1933).

1742. *Mental Hygiene Bulletin (Detroit).* (1938).

1743. *Mental Hygiene Bulletin (Los Angeles).* (1924–1929).

1744. *Mental Hygiene (London).* (1929–1939).

1745. *Mental Hygiene News.* (1930–1943).

1746. *Mental Hygiene Newsletter.* (1947–1950 +).

1747. *Mental Hygiene Review.* (1940–1943).

1748. *Mental Hygiene Survey.* (1938–1948).

1749. *Mentalhygiejne.* (1948–1950 +).

1750. *Monographien aus dem Gesamtgebiete der Neurologie und Psychiatrie.* (1911–1950 +).

1751. *Moscow. Nauchno-issledovatel'skii nevro-psikhiatricheskii institut imeni P. B. Ganuskina. Trudy.* (1936–1940).

1752. *Moscow. Universitet. Clinique psychiatrique. Travaux.* (1914).

1753. *Moscow. Universitet. Obshchestvo nevropatalogov i psikhiatrov. Protokoly.* (1890–1898).

1754. *Munich. Deutsche Forschungsanstalt für Psychiatrie. Arbeiten.* (1920–1940).

1755. *Munich. Universität. K. psychiatrische Klinik. Jahresbericht.* (1904/1905–1908/1909).

1756. *National Committee for Mental Hygiene. Annual Report.* (1940–1948/1949).

1757. *Neopsichiatria; rassegna di psichiatria, neurologia, endocrinologia.* (1935–1939).

1758. *Nervenarzt.* (1928–1950 +).

1759. *Neurologica. Rivista italiana di neuropatologia e psichiatria.* (1924–1926).

1760. *Neurologisches Zentralblatt.* (1882–1921).

1761. *Nevrologicheskii vestnik.* (1893–1913).

1762. *Nevropatalogiia i psikhiatriia.* (1932–1950 +).

1763. *New York. Institute for Child Guidance. Report of the Director.* (1927/1928).

1764. *New York. Neurological Institute. Annual Report.* (1910–1930).

1765. *New York. Neurological Institute. Bulletin.* (1931–1938).

1766. *New York. State Department of Mental Hygiene. Annual Report.* (1928–1950 +).

1767. *New York. State Hospitals. Psychiatric Bulletin.* (1896–1897, 1908–1917).

1768. *Nordisk psykiatrisk Tidsskrift.* (1947–1950 +).

1769. *Note e riviste de psichiatria.* (1912–1950 +).

1770. *Nouvelle iconographie de la Salpêtriére.* (1888–1918).

1771. *Nowiny psychjatryczne.* (1924–1934).

1772. *Obshchestvo psikhiatrov v S-Peterburgie. Protokoly.* (1880–1898).

1773. *Ontario Journal of Neuro-Psychiatry.* (1921–1937).

1774. *Perugia. Ospedale psichiatrico provinciale. Annali.* (1907–1939).

1775. *Problemy sudebnoi psikhiatrii.* (1938–?).

1776. *Progress in Neurology and Psychiatry.* (1944/1945–1950 +).

1777. *Prophylaxie mentale.* (1925–1938).

1778. *Psikhiatricheskaia gazeta.* (1914).

1779. *Psychiatria et Neurologia Japonica.* (1902–1940).

1780. *Psychiatria et Neurologica.* (1897–1950 +).

1781. *Psychiatric Aid.* (1944–1950 +).

1782. *Psychiatric Quarterly.* (1927–1950 +).

1783. *Psychiatric Quarterly. Supplement.* (1927–1950 +).

1784. *Psychiatrisch-neurologische Wochenschrift.* (1899–1945).

1785. *Psychiatry.* (1938–1950 +).

1786. *Quaderni di psichiatria.* (1911–1930).

1787. *Quarterly Review of Psychiatry and Neurology.* (1946–1950 +).

1788. *Rassegna di studi psichiatrici.* (1911–1939).

1789. *Review of Neurology and Psychiatry.* (1903–1919).

1790. *Revista argentina de neurología, psiquiatría y medicina legal.* (1927–1931).

1791. *Revista de criminología, psiquiatría y medicina legal.* (1914–1935).

1792. *Revista de medicina legal, criminología y psiquiatría forense.* (1932).

1793. *Revista de neuro-psiquiatria.* (1938–1950 +).

1794. *Revista de neurologia e psiquiatria de São Paulo.* (1934–1941).

1795. *Revista de psiquiatría.* (1935–1950 +).

1796. *Revista de psiquiatría del Uruguay.* (1936–1950 +).

1797. *Revista de psiquiatría y criminología.* (1936–1939).

1798. *Revista de psiquiatría y disciplinas conexas.* (1918–1924).

1799. *Revista de psiquiatría y neurología.* (1929–1931).

1800. *Revista mexicana de psiquiatría, neurología y medicina legal.* (1934–1947).

1801. *Revue neurologique.* (1893–1950 +).

1802. *Rio de Janeiro. Universidade do Brasil. Instituto de psiquiatria. Anais.* (1942–1946/1947).

1803. *Rivista di neurologia.* (1928–1938).

1804. *Rivista italiana di neuropatologia, psichiatria ed elettroterapia.* (1907–1923).

1805. *Rivista mensile di psichiatria forense, antropologia criminale e scienze affini.* (1898–1904).

1806. *Rivista sperimentale di freniatria e medicina legale delle alienazioni mentali.* (1875–1938).

1807. *Rocznik psychjatryczny.* (1923–1950 +).

1808. *Rome. Università. Istituto psichiatrico. Annali.* (1901–1910).

1809. *Rosario (Argentina). Universidad nacional del Litoral. Instituto psiquiatrico. Boletin.* (1929–1933, 1937–1940).

1810. *Royal Society of Medicine (London). Proceedings. Psychiatric Section.* (1907–1950 +).

1811. *São Paulo. Serviço de assistencia a psicopatas do estado de São Paulo. Arquivos.* (1937–1950 +).

1812. *Schweizer Archiv für Neurologie und Psychiatrie.* (1917–1950 +).

1813. *Sendai. Tohoku Teikoku Daigaku. Psychiatrische Klinik. Arbeiten.* (1932–1939).

1814. *Sexual-probleme; Zeitschrift für Sexualwissenschaft und Sexualpolitik.* (1908–1915).

1815. *Società italiana di psichiatria. Atti.* (1880–1939).

1816. *Société de psychiatrie de Bucarest. Bulletin.* (1936–1939).

1817. *Sovetskaia nevropsikhiatriia; Sbornik trudov.* (1936–1948).

1818. *Sovetskoe meditsinskoe obozrenie: nevropatologiia i psikhiatriia.* (1949–1950 +).

1819. *Sovremennaia psikhiatriia.* (1907–1917).

1820. *Tidsskrift for nordisk retsmedicin og psykiatri.* (1901–1913).

1821. *Toronto. Ontario Hospitals for the Insane. Bulletin.* (1907–1915/1916).

1822. *Utrecht. Rijksuniversiteit. Psychiatrisch-neurologische Kliniek. Onderzoekingen.* (1920–1934).

1823. *Vestnik klinicheskoi i sudebnoi psikhiatrii i nevropatalogii.* (1883–1899).

1824. *Vienna. Universität. Neurologisches Institut. Österreichisches interakademisches Zentralinstitut für Hirnforschung. Arbeiten.* (1892–1934/1935).

1825. *Voprosy psikhiatrii i nevrologii.* (1912–1914).

1826. *Washington, D.C. St. Elizabeth's Hospital. Medical Research Bulletin.* (1909–1932).

1827. *Wiener Zeitschrift für Nervenheilkunde und deren Grenzgebiete.* (1947–1950 +).

1828. *World Mental Health.* (1949–1950 +).

1829. *Yearbook of Neurology, Psychiatry and Endocrinology.* (1933–1950 +).

1830. *Zeitschrift für psychische Hygiene.* (1928–1944).

1831. *Zhurnal nevropatalogiia i psikhiatrii.* (1901–1931).

Psychical Research

1832. *American Psychical Institute. Bulletin.* (1933–1938).

1833. *American Society for Psychical Research. Section "B" of American Institute for Scientific Research. Journal.* (1907–1938).

1834. *American Society for Psychical Research. Section "B" of American Institute for Scientific Research. Proceedings.* (1884/1889, 1907–1933).

1835. *Annales des sciences psychiques. Recueil d'observations et d'expériences.* (1891–1919).

1836. *Annales du spiritisme.* (1922–1928).

1837. *Annali dello spiritismo in Italia; rivista psicologica.* (1864–1898).

1838. *Annals of Psychical Science; A Monthly Journal Devoted to Critical and Experimental Research.* (1905–1910).

1839. *Année occultiste et psychique; ou, exposé annuel des observations scientifiques et des travaux publiés en France et à l'étranger dans les sciences mystérieuses.* (1907–1908).

1840. *International Congress for Psychical Research.* (1921–1923).

1841. *Journal of Psychosophy.* (1899).

1842. *London. University. Council for Psychical Investigations. Bulletin.* (1931–1933, 1935–1936).

1843. *London. University. Council for Psychical Investigations. Proceedings.* (1927–1929).

1844. *Psyche.* (1913–1927).

1845. *Revue métaphysique.* (1920–1931).

1846. *Zeitschrift für kritische Okkultismus und Grenzfragen des Seelenlebens.* (1925–1928).

Indexes

Title Index

This index lists the titles of all serial publications that appear in the Bibliography, including those that appear in the Appendix. The titles are arranged alphabetically; variant titles are also provided, followed by a cross-reference to the main entry title. All citations refer to entry numbers.

A.A.M.D. News, 1001
Aarskrift for psykisk Forskning, 323
Aberdeen Philosophical Society. Transactions, 1539
Abhandlungen aus dem Gebiete der Psychologie, Jugendkunde und Pädagogik, 485
Abhandlungen aus dem Gebiete der Psychotherapie und medizinischen Psychologie, 486
Abhandlungen aus dem Gebiete der Sexualforschung, 369
Abhandlungen aus dem Gesamtgebiete der Kriminalpsychologie, 294
Abhandlungen aus der Neurologie, Psychiatrie, Psychologie und ihren Grenzgebieten, 357
Abhandlungen der Fries'schen Schule, 1540
Abhandlungen und Monographien zur Philosophie des Wirklichen, 650
Abhandlungen zur personellen Sexualökonomie, 1647
Abhandlungen zur Philosophie, Psychologie und Soziologie der Religion. *See* Abhandlungen zur Philosophie und Psychologie der Religion, 433
Abhandlungen zur Philosophie und ihrer Geschichte (Erdmann), 1541
Abhandlungen zur Philosophie und ihrer Geschichte (Falckenberg), 1542
Abhandlungen zur Philosophie und Pädagogik, 1543
Abhandlungen zur Philosophie und Psychologie der Religion, 433
Abhandlungen zur Physiologie der Sinne, 1327
Abhandlungen zur Wehrpsychologie. *See* Zeitschrift für angewandte Psychologie und Charakterkunde. Beihefte, 767
Academia Sinica. National Research Institute of Psychology. Contributions, 668
Academia Sinica. National Research Institute of Psychology. Monographs, 669
Académie des sciences morales et publiques (Paris). Revue des travaux et comptes-rendus, 1108
Académie des sciences (Paris). Comptes-rendus, 1328
Acoustical Society of America. Journal, 1329
Acta Biologiae Experimentalis, 1330
Acta neurologica et psychiatrica belgica, 1002
Acta Ophthalmologica, 1331
Acta Oto-laryngolica, 1332
Acta Paedopsychiatrica, 1648

Title Index

Acta Psychiatrica et Neurologica Scandinavica, 1649
Acta Psychiatrica et Neurologica Scandinavica. Supplementum, 1650
Acta Psychologica, 746
Acta Psychologica Keijo, 630
Actas luso-españolas de neurología y psiquiatría, 1651
Action et pensée, 487
After-Care Conference Report. *See* London. National Association for the Feeble-Minded. Conference Report, 220
Air Force (United States). *See* United States. Air Force. Air Training Command. Training Analysis and Development. Informational Bulletin, 1107
Akademie der Wissenschaften (Berlin). Monatsberichte, 1333
Akademie der Wissenschaften (Berlin). Physikalisch-mathematische Klasse. Sitzungsberichte, 1334
Akademie der Wissenschaften (Leipzig). Mathematisch-naturwissenschaftliche Klasse. Berichte, 1335
Akademie der Wissenschaften (Munich). Philosophisch-historische Abteilung. Sitzungsberichte, 1336
Akademie der Wissenschaften (Vienna). Mathematisch-naturwissenschaftliche Klasse. Sitzungsberichte, 1337
Akademiia kommunisticheskogo vospitaniia imeni N. K. Krupskoi. Biulletin, 1152
Akademiia kommunisticheskogo vospitaniia (Moscow). Psikhologicheskaia laboratoriia. *See* Moscow. Akademiia kommunisticheskogo vospitaniia. Psikhologicheskaia laboratoriia. Raboty, 590; *and* Moscow. Akademiia kommunisticheskogo vospitaniia. Psikhologicheskaia laboratoriia. Trudy, 565
Akademiia nauk Gruzinskoi SSR (Tiflis). Institut psikhologii. Trudy, 882
Akademiia nauk SSSR. Fiziologicheskii institut imeni I. P. Pavlova. Trudy, 902
Akademiia nauk SSSR (Leningrad). Biulletin, 1338
Akademiia nauk SSSR (Leningrad). Fiziologicheskii institut. Fiziologicheskii laboratorii akademika I. P. Pavlova. Trudy, 488
Akademiia nauk SSSR (Moscow). Fiziologicheskii institut imeni I. P. Pavlova. Problemy fiziologicheskoi akustiki, 1339
Akademiia nauk SSSR (Moscow). Fiziologicheskii institut imeni I. P. Pavlova. Problemy fiziologicheskoi optiki, 1340
Akademiia pedagogicheskikh nauk RSFSR (Moscow). Izvestiia. Otdelenie psikhologii, 913
Akademiia sotsial'nogo vospitaniia (Moscow). Psikhologicheskaia laboratoriia. Zapiski. *See* Moscow. Akademiia sotsial'nogo vospitaniia. Psikhologicheskaia laboratoriia. Zapiski, 464
Akademiya navuk BSSR (Minsk). Instytut psykhaneuralogii. Zbornik prats, 686
Albany Journal of Neurology; Devoted to Physiology, Phrenology, Medicine, and the Philosophy of Mesmerism, 31
Algemeen nederlands tijdschrift voor Wijsbegeerte en psychologie, 721
Alienist and Neurologist, 1652
Alienists and Neurologists of America under Auspices of Chicago Medical Society, Proceedings, 1653
Allgemeine ärztliche Gesellschaft für Psychotherapie. *See* Allgemeine ärztliche Zeitschrift für Psychotherapie und psychische Hygiene einschliesslich der klinischen und sozialen Grenzgebiete, 572; *and* Allgemeiner ärztlicher Kongress für Psychotherapie. Bericht, 521; *and* Zentralblatt für Psychotherapie und ihre Grenzgebiete einschliesslich der medizinischen Psychologie und psychischen Hygiene, 649
Allgemeine ärztliche Zeitschrift für Psychotherapie und psychische Hygiene einschliesslich der Klinischen und sozialen Grenzgebiete, 572
Allgemeine Zeitschrift für Psychiatrie und ihre Grenzgebiete, 1654
Allgemeiner ärztlicher Kongress für Psychotherapie. Bericht, 521
Allgemeiner deutscher Lehrerinnenverein. Pädagogisch-psychologische Schriftenreihe, 489
Allgemeines Repertorium für empirische Psychologie und verwandte Wissenschaften, 5
Almanach, 522
Almanach der Psychoanalyse, 631
Almanach magnétique, 47
Almanach populaire du magnétiseur practicien, 39

Title Index

Title Index

Analele de psihologie. *See* Societatea română de cercetări psihologice (Bucharest). Analele de psihologie, 741

Anales de medicina legal, psiquiatría y anatomia patologica, 1663

Anales de psicología, 255

Anales de psicotecnia, 874

Analytical Psychology Club of Los Angeles. Papers, 1038

Analytical Psychology Club of New York. Annual. *See* Spring, 881

Analytical Psychology Club of New York. Bulletin, 830

Analytical Psychology Club of New York. Newsletter, 814

Analytical Psychology Club of New York. Papers, 769

Anatomical Record, 1355

Andover Review, 1285

Angewandte Psychologie in Industrie. *See* Industrielle Psychotechnik; Angewandte Psychologie in Industrie. Handel. Verkehr. Verwaltung, 473

[Animal Psychology]. *See* Dobutsu Shinri [Animal Psychology]. [1], 726; *and* Dobutsu Shinri [Animal Psychology]. [2], 966

Annalen der Naturphilosophie, 1545

Annalen der Naturphilosophie. Beihefte, 1546

Annalen der Philosophie und philosophischen Kritik, 1547

Annales de la psychologie zoologique, 168

Annales de l'enfance, 1157

Annales de philosophie chrétienne, 1548

Annales de psychiatrie et d'hypnologie dans leurs rapports avec la psychologie et la médecine légale, 106

Annales de sociologie et mouvement sociologique international, 1115

Annales des sciences psychiques. Recueil d'observations et d'experiences, 1835

Annales du magnétisme animal, 11

Annales du spiritisme, 1836

Annales médico-psychologiques. Journal de l'aliénation mentale et de la médicine légale des aliénés, 32

Annales sociologiques. Série A. Sociologie générale, 1116

Annali dello spiritismo in Italia; rivista psicologica, 1837

Annali di freniatria e scienze affini, 1664

Annali di neurologia, 1665

Annali di ottalmologia e clinica oculistica, 1356

Annals of Animal Magnetism. *See* Magnetiser's Magazine, and Annals of Animal Magnetism, 13

Annals of Eugenics; A Journal for the Scientific Study of Racial Problems, 1271

Annals of Mathematical Statistics, 1357

Annals of Mesmerism and Mesmero-Phrenology, 33

Annals of Ophthalmology, 1358

Annals of Ophthalmology and Otology, 1359

Annals of Otology, Rhinology and Laryngology, 1360

Annals of Phrenology, 1634

Annals of Psychical Science; A Monthly Journal Devoted to Critical and Experimental Research, 1838

Année biologique, 1361

Année occultiste et psychique; ou, exposé annuel des observations scientifiques et des travaux publiés en France et à l'étranger dans les sciences mystérieuses, 1839

Année philosophique, 1549

Année philosophique (Pillon), 1550

Année psychologique, 119

Année psychologique polonaise. *See* Prace z psychologii doświadczalnej, 312

Année sociologiques, 1117

Annuaire philosophique, 1551

[Annual of Animal Psychology]. *See* Dobutsu Shinri Nenpo [Annual of Animal Psychology], 967; *and* Dobutsu Shinrigaku Nenpo [Annual of Animal Psychology], 905

Annual of General and Linguistic Psychology. *See* Psyche; An Annual of General and Linguistic Psychology, 705

673

Title Index

Title Index

Title Index

Title Index

Title Index

Berlin. Psychologische Gesellschaft zu Berlin. *See* Psychologie und Medizin. Vierteljahrsschrift für Forschung und Anwendung auf ihren Grenzgebieten, 510
Berlin. Universität. Kaiser Wilhelm Institut für Hirnforschung. *See* Journal für Psychologie und Neurologie, 177
Berlin. Universität. Neuro-biologisches Institut. *See* Journal für Psychologie und Neurologie, 177
Berlin. Universität. Psychologisches Institut. *See* Psychologische Studien (Berlin). Abteilung I. Beiträge zur Analyse der Gesichtswahrnehmungen, 197; *and* Psychologische Studien (Berlin). Abteilung II. Beiträge zur Psychologie der Zeitwahrnehmungen, 198
Berlin. Universität. Sexualpsychologisches Seminar. Arbeiten, 470
Berlin. Verein für Kinderpsychologie. Veröffentlichungen. *See* Zeitschrift für pädagogische Psychologie, Pathologie und Hygiene, 180
Berlin. Verein für Schulgesundheitspflege. Veröffentlichungen. *See* Zeitschrift für pädagogische Psychologie, Pathologie und Hygiene, 180
Berliner Gesellschaft für Psychologie und Charakterologie. *See* Psychologie und Medizin. Vierteljahrsschrift für Forschung und Anwendung auf ihren Grenzgebieten, 510
Berliner klinische Wochenschrift, 1381
Berner Abhandlungen zur Psychologie und Pädagogik. *See* Mensch und Welt. Berner Abhandlungen zur Psychologie und Pädagogik, 755
Bibliographie der Philosophie und Psychologie, 393
Bibliography of Philosophy. A Quarterly Bulletin, 1556
Bibliography of the Literature of Psychology and Cognate Subjects. *See* Psychological Index, 121
Bibliography on War-Problem, War-Psychology, War-Psychiatry. *See* Nederlandsche maatschappij tot bevordering der geneeskunst. Commissie inzake oorlagsprophylaxis. Bibliography on War-Problem, War-Psychology, War-Psychiatry, 757
Bibliotheca Psychiatrica et Neurologica, 1004
Bibliotheca Sacra, 1290
Bibliothek des Seelen- und Sexuallebens, 187
Bibliothek für Philosophie, 1557
Bibliothek für praktische Menschenkenntnis, 1121
Bibliothèque de pédagogie et de psychologie, 149
Bibliothèque de psychologie de l'enfant et de pédagogie. [1], 490
Bibliothèque de psychologie de l'enfant et de pédagogie. [2], 555
Bibliothèque de psychologie expérimentale et de métapsychie, 240
Bibliothèque des archives de philosophie. (Nouvelle série). Deuxième section: Logique et psychologie, 1005
Bibliothèque du magnétisme animal, 15
Bibliothèque universelle. Archives des sciences physiques et naturelles, 1382
Biel. Institut für Psycho-Hygiene. Arbeiten zur Psycho-Hygiene, 1083
Bildung und Erziehung. Monatsschrift für Pädagogik mit besonderer Betonung der pädagogischen Psychologie, der vergleichenden Erziehungswissenschaft und der pädagogischen Bibliographie, 1006
Bio-Psychology, 471
Biological Bulletin, 1383
Biologisches Zentralblatt, 1384
Biometric Bulletin, 1385
Biometrics, 1386
Biometrika, 1387
Biotypologie, 1388
Blackwood's Magazine, 1291
Blätter für Charakterologie und angewandte Psychologie. *See* Zeitschrift für Menschenkunde. Blätter für Charakterologie und angewandte Psychologie, 518
Blätter für Charakterologie und Zentralblatt für Graphologie. *See* Zeitschrift für Menschenkunde. Blätter für Charakterologie und Zentralblatt für Graphologie, 768
Blätter für deutsche Philosophie, 1558
Blätter für Psychiatrie, 26
Bloomington (Indiana). Bureau of Co-operative Research (and Field Service). *See* Conference on Educational Measurements. Proceedings, 327

Title Index

Boston. Psychopathic Hospital. *See* Massachusetts. State Hospital (Boston). Psychopathic Department. Monograph(s), 345; *and* Massachusetts. State Hospital (Boston). Psychopathic Department. Report, 1728

Boston. Psychopathic Hospital. Collected Contributions, 1679

Brain; A Journal of Neurology, 1680

Brazil. Universidade. Instituto de psicología (Rio de Janeiro). Monografías psicológicas, 1007

Bratislava. Slovenska akademia vied a umeni. *See* Psychologický sborník. Časopis psychologického ústavu SAVU, 950

Breslau. Psychologische Gesellschaft. Vortrags-Cyklus über die Entwicklung der Psychologie und verwandter Gebiete des Wissens und des Lebens im neunzehnten Jahrhundert, 159

Breslau. Universität. Psychiatrische und Nervenklinik. Arbeiten, 1681

Brief Psychotherapy Council. Proceedings, 885

British Association for the Advancement of Science. Reports, 1389

British Journal for the Philosophy of Science, 1559

British Journal of Delinquency, 1122

British Journal of Educational Psychology, 653

British Journal of Medical Hypnotism, 1045

British Journal of Medical Psychology; Being the Medical Section of the British Journal of Psychology, 456

British Journal of Ophthalmology, 1390

British Journal of Ophthalmology. Monograph Supplement, 1391

British Journal of Psychiatric Social Work, 1682

British Journal of Psychiatry. *See* Journal of Mental Science, 50

British Journal of Psychology, 188

British Journal of Psychology. General Section, 394

British Journal of Psychology. Medical Section, 395

British Journal of Psychology. Monograph Supplements, 285

British Journal of Psychology. Statistical Section, 963

British Journal of Sociology, 1123

British Medical Association. *See* Journal of Neurology and Psychiatry, 817; *and* Journal of Neurology and Psychopathology, 401; *and* Journal of Neurology, Neurosurgery and Psychiatry, 907

British Psychological Society. Bulletin, 1008

British Psychological Society. Proceedings. *See* British Journal of Psychology, 188; *and* British Journal of Psychology. General Section, 394

British Society for the Study of Sex Psychology. Publications, 326

British Society of Medical Hypnotists. *See* British Journal of Medical Hypnotism, 1045

British Union of Practical Psychologists. *See* Practical Psychology, 803; *and* Practical Psychology Magazine, 781; *and* You, 826

Brush Foundation. Study of Child Growth and Development. *See* Society for Research in Child Development. Monographs, 762

Brussels. Cercle de pédagogie. *See* Revue du cercle de pédagogie, 740

Bryn Mawr College. Monographs. Reprint Series. Contributions from the Psychological Laboratory, 347

Bucharest. Societatea romana de cercetări psihologice. Analele de psihologice. *See* Societatea română de cercetări psihologice (Bucharest). Analele de psihologie, 741

Bucharest. Université. Laboratoire de psychologie expérimentale. *See* Jurnal de psihologie militara, 838; *and* Jurnal de psihotehnica, 798

Budapest. Magyar Psychológiai Táraság. *See* Magyar Psychologiai Szemle, 588

Buen deseo; Periodico mensual de estudios psicologicos, 83

Buenos Aires. Asociación psicoanalítica Argentina. *See* Revista de psicoanálisis, 900; *and* Revista de psicoanálisis. Monografías, 931

Buenos Aires. Instituto psicopedagógico para niños nerviosos. *See* Clínica psicopedagógica. Revista de neuropsiquiatría infantil, 457

Buenos Aires, Sociedad de psicología. *See* Anales de psicología, 255

Buenos Aires. Sociedad de psicología. Anales, 692

Buenos Aires. Sociedad de psicología. Boletín, 633

Title Index

Buenos Aires. Universidad nacional. Facultad de filosofía y letras. Archivos del laboratorio de facultad de filosofía y letras psicológicas, 654

Buenos Aires. Universidad nacional. Instituto de filosofía. Seccion de psicología. Monografías psicológicas, 1084

Buenos Aires. Universidad nacional. Instituto de psicología. Anales, 747

Bulletin analytique; Philosophie. *See* France. Centre national de la recherche scientifique. Bulletin analytique: Philosophie, 968

Bulletin bibliographique mensuel de psychiatrie et de psychologie expérimentale. *See* Revue de psychiatrie et de psychologie expérimentale, 179

Bulletin biologique de la France et de la Belgique, 1392

Bulletin de psychologie. *See* Paris. Université. Groupe d'études de psychologie. Bulletin, 987

Bulletin médical, 1393

Bulletin of Animal Behaviour, 815

Bulletin of Bio-Psychology. *See* Bio-Psychology, 471

Bulletin of Industrial Psychology and Personnel Practice, 914

Bulletin of Military Clinical Psychologists, 935

Bulletin signalétique. *See* France. Centre national de la recherche scientifique. Bulletin analytique: Philosophie, 968

Bureau of Educational Experiments. Bulletin, 1160

Bureau of Educational Research. *See* Illinois. University. Bureau of Educational Research. Bulletin, 373; *and* Illinois. University. Bureau of Educational Research. Educational Research Circular, 441; *and* Journal of Educational Research, 400

Bureau of Public Personnel Administration (Washington, D.C.) Institute of Government Research. *See* Public Personnel Studies, 466

C.A.M.D. Report. *See* Central Association for the Care of the Mentally Defective. Report, 307

C.C.I. Reports. *See* American Jewish Congress. Commission on Community Interrelations. Reports, 933

C. G. Jung Institut (Zurich). Studien. *See* Zurich. C.G. Jung Institut. Studien, 1078

Cahiers de l'enfance inadaptée, 1085

Cahiers de pédagogie expérimentale et de psychologie de l'enfant. (Nouvelle série), 936

Cahiers de pédagogie expérimentale et de psychologie de l'enfant. (Première série), 723

Cahiers de psychologie clinique et de psychopathologie générale. *See* Évolution psychiatrique. Cahiers de psychologie clinique et de psychopathologie générale, 607

Cairo. Society of Integrative Psychology. *See* Egyptian Journal of Psychology, 915

California Bureau of Juvenile Research. Whittier State School. *See* Journal of Delinquency, 349; *and* Journal of Delinquency. Monograph, 385; *and* Journal of Juvenile Research, 586

California. Department of Institutions. Psychiatric Monographs, 1683

California Educational Research Association, Southern Section. *See* Educational Measurement Review, 492

California Society for Mental Hygiene. *See* Martin Mental Hygiene Publications, 374

California Society for Mental Hygiene. Publications, 371

California. University. Applications of Psychology to Education. *See* California. University. School of Education. Bureau of Research in Education. Studies. (Sub-Series). Applications of Psychology to Education, 437

California. University. Institute of Child Welfare. Bulletin, 575

California. University of California at Los Angeles. Publications in Education, Philosophy and Psychology, 693

California. University. Publications in Child Development, 1046

California. University. Publications in Education, 1161

California. University. Publications in Philosophy, 1560

California. University. Publications in Psychology, 267

California. University. School of Education. Bureau of Research in Education. Studies. (Sub-Series). Applications of Psychology to Education, 437

California. University. School of Education. Vocational Guidance Series, 1525

Title Index

Cambridge. Orthological Institute. *See* Psyche; An Annual of General and Linguistic Psychology, 705; *and* Psyche Miniatures; General Series, 543; *and* Psyche Miniatures; Medical Series, 544

Canadian Journal of Mental Hygiene, 381

Canadian Journal of Psychology, 964

Canadian Medical Association. Journal, 1394

Canadian National Committee for Mental Hygiene. *See* Canadian Journal of Mental Hygiene, 381

Canadian Psychological Association. *See* Canadian Psychologist, 1086

Canadian Psychological Association. Bulletin, 853

Canadian Psychological Association. Journal. *See* Canadian Journal of Psychology, 964

Canadian Psychologist, 1086

Canton [National Sun Yat-sen University]. *See* Chiao yü yen Chiu [Studies in Education], 576

Canton. Sun Yat-sen University. Institute of Educational Research. Psychological Laboratory. Studies. Series A, 670

Carnegie Institution (Washington). Department of Genetics. Bulletin, 1272

Carnegie Institution (Washington). Department of Genetics. Memoir, 1273

Carnegie Institution (Washington). Publications, 1395

Cartesian Research Society (Philadelphia). Bulletin. *See* Bio-Psychology, 471

Case Reports in Clinical Psychology, 1047

Časopis psychologického ústavu SAVU (Slovenska akademia vied a umeni, Bratislava). *See* Psychologický sbornik. Časopis psychologického ústavu SAVU, 950

Catholic Educational Review, 1162

Catholic University of America. Educational Research Monographs, 1163

Catholic University of America. Psychological Studies, 204

Catholic University of America. Studies in Psychology and Psychiatry, 524

[Catholic University. Peking] *See* Chiao yü yü hsin li [Education and Psychology]. [2], 725; *and* Peking. Catholic University. College of Education. Publications, 866

Central Association for Mental Welfare (London). *See* Studies in Mental Inefficiency, 409; *and* Mental Welfare, 502

Central Association for Mental Welfare. Report, 414

Central Association for the Care of the Mentally Defective (London). *See* Studies in Mental Inefficiency, 409

Central Association for the Care of the Mentally Defective. Report, 307

[Central Research Institute. Research Institute of Psychology. China]. *See* Academia Sinica. National Research Institute of Psychology. Contributions, 668; *and* Academia Sinica. National Research Institute of Psychology. Monographs, 669

[Central University. Chungking]. *See* Chiao yü hsin li yen Chiu. [Studies in Educational Psychology], 854; *and* Chinese Journal of Educational Psychology, 855

Centralblatt . . . *See as if* Zentralblatt . . .

Centre de psychologie appliquée (Paris). *See* Revue de psychologie appliquée. [2], 1104

Centre national de la recherche scientifique. Bulletin analytique: Philosophie. *See* France. Centre national de la recherche scientifique. Bulletin analytique: Philosophie, 968

Centro de estudios psicopedagógicos del Uruguay. Publicaciones, 770

Century Magazine, 1292

Cercle de pédagogie (Brussels). *See* Revue de pédagogie, 760

Česka myśl, 1561

Chaine magnétique, 77

Character, 1164

Character and Personality; An International Psychological Quarterly, 724

Character and Personality; An International Quarterly of Psychodiagnostics and Allied Subjects, 671

Charakter; Eine Vierteljahrsschrift für psychodiagnostische Studien und verwandte Gebiete, 672

Charakter und Persönlichkeit. *See* Neue psychologische Studien, 538

Charakterologische Jahrbücher, 491

Chiao yü hsin li yen Chiu [Studies in Educational Psychology], 854

Chiao yü tsa chih [Chinese Educational Review], 1165

Title Index

[Chinese Psychological Society]. *See* Hsin li [Psychology], 440

Ch'ing-hua hsüeh hsi'ao [Ching-hua College. Peking].*See* Chiao yü yü hsin li [Education and Psychology]. [1], 577; *and* Chung-hua hsin li hsüeh pao [Chinese Journal of Psychology], 771; *and* Peking. National Tsing Hua University. Science Reports. Series B: Biological and Psychological Sciences, 661

Ch'ing-hua ta hsüeh [Ching-hua University. Peking]. *See* Chiao yü yü hsin li [Education and Psychology]. [1], 577; *and* Chung-hua hsin li hsüeh pao [Chinese Journal of Psychology], 771; *and* Peking. National Tsing Hua University. Science Reports. Series B: Biological and Psychological Sciences, 661

Chung-hua hsin li hsüeh hui [Chinese Psychological Society]. *See* Hsin li. [Psychology], 440

Chung-hua hsin li hsüeh pao [Chinese Journal of Psychology], 771

Chung-hua p'ing Min Chiao yü Ts'u Chin Hui (Peking). *See* Chinese National Association of the Mass Education Movement. Research Committee in Educational Psychology. Report, 748

Chung-kuo hsin li hsüeh hsieh hui [Chinese Psychological Association. Peking]. *See* Chung-hua hsin li hsüeh pao [Chinese Journal of Psychology], 771

Chung-shan ta hsüeh [Sun Yat-sen University. Canton]. *See* Chiao yü yen Chiu [Studies in Education], 576; *and* Canton. Sun Yat-sen University. Institute of Educational Research. Psychological Laboratory. Studies. Series A, 670

Chung-yang ta hsüeh [Central University. Chungking]. *See* Chiao yü hsin li yen Chiu. [Studies in Educational Psychology], 854; *and* Chinese Journal of Educational Psychology, 855

Chung-yang yen chiu yüan. Hsin li hsüeh yen chiu so [Central Research Institute. Research Institute of Psychology]. *See* Academia Sinica. National Research Institute of Psychology. Contributions, 668; *and* Academia Sinica. National Research Institute of Psychology. Monographs, 669

Chungking. Chung-yang ta hsüeh [Central University]. *See* Chiao yü hsin li yen Chiu [Studies in Educational Psychology], 854; *and* Chinese Journal of Educational Psychology, 855

Chungking. Kuo li Chung-yang ta hsüeh [National Central University]. *See* Chiao yü hsin li yen Chiu [Studies in Educational Psychology], 854; *and* Chinese Journal of Educational Psychology, 855

Cincinnati. Phreno-magnetic Society. Journal, 1635

Ciudad Trujillo. Instituto de investigaciones psicopedagógicas. Boletín, 937

Clark University. Library. Publications, 1293

Clark University. Psychological Laboratory. Minor Studies. *See* American Journal of Psychology, 90

Clínica psicopedagógica. Revista de neuropsiquiatría infantil, 457

Clinical Psychology. A Quarterly Journal Devoted to the Scientific Study of Human Personality, 1048

Clinical Psychology Monographs. *See* Journal of Clinical Psychology. Monograph Supplement, 1018

Clinique hypnotherapique de la charité (Paris). Bulletin mensuel. *See* Paris. Clinique hypnotherapique de la charité. Bulletin mensuel, 100

Clinique ophthalmologique, 1396

Cluj (Rumania). Universitatea. Institutul de psihologie. *See* Revista de psihologie. Teoretică şi aplicată, 824

Cluj (Rumania). Universitatea. Institutul de psihologie experimentală, comparată şi aplicată. Studii şi cercetări psihologice, 604

Cocodès, journal des imbéciles, 58

Collection de psychologie expérimentale et de métapsychie, 268

Collection de psychologie scientifique, 1009

College Entrance Examination Board. Commission on Scholastic Aptitude. Annual Reports, 525

Cologne. Forschungs institut für Sozial- und Verwaltungswissenschaften. *See* Kölner Zeitschrift für Soziologie. Neue Folge der Kölner Vierteljahrshefte für Soziologie, 1020

Colorado College. Department of Psychology and Education. Studies in Education and Psychology, 358

Colorado College. Publications. Education and Psychology Series, 382

Colorado. University. Department of Psychology and Education. Investigations, 175

Columbia University. Contributions to Philosophy and Psychology, 205

Columbia University. Contributions to Philosophy, Psychology and Education, 120

683

Title Index

Congrès international de médecine mentale. Comptes rendus, 75
Congrès international de neurologie, de psychiatrie, d'électricité médicale et d'hypnologie. Compte rendu. *See* Congrès international de neurologie, de psychiatrie et de psychologie. Compte rendu, 139
Congrès international de neurologie, de psychiatrie et de psychologie. Compte rendu, 139
Congrès international de psychiatrie, de neurologie, de psychologie et de l'assistance des aliénés. Compte rendu, 224
Congrès international de psychologie et physiologie sportives. Compte rendu, 308
Congrès international de psychologie expérimentale. Compte rendu, 269
Congrès international de psychologie physiologique. *See* International Congress of Psychology. Proceedings and Papers, 96
Congrès international de psychologie religieuse. Travaux, 1010
Congreso latinoamericano de psicología. Relatorio, 1088
Congresso internazionale di psicologia. *See* International Congress of Psychology. Proceedings and Papers, 96
Congresso psicoanalitico internazionale. *See* International Psycho-Analytical Congress, 242
Connecticut Psychologist, 1011
Connecticut Society for Mental Hygiene. Annual Report, 1687
Connecticut Society for Mental Hygiene. Publications, 1688
Connecticut State Psychological Society. *See* Connecticut Psychologist, 1011
Connecticut's Mental Health News, 1689
Constitutional Psychology Series, 856
Consulting Psychologist, 749
Contemporary Review, 1294
Contributions à l'étude de la morphologie des mouvements humains. *See* Études de psychologie, 295
Contributions in Principles of Education. *See* Ohio. State University. Contributions in Principles of Education, 540
Contributions to Philosophy and Psychology. *See* Columbia University. Contributions to Philosophy and Psychology, 205
Contributions to Philosophy, Psychology and Education. *See* Columbia University. Contributions to Philosophy, Psychology and Education, 120
Contributions to Philosophy, Psychology and the Science of Education by Northern Scientists. *See* Scandinavian Scientific Review; Contributions to Philosophy, Psychology and the Science of Education by Northern Scientists, 452
Contributions to Psychological Theory. *See* Duke University. Contributions to Psychological Theory, 727
Contributions to Psychology. *See* Journal of Abnormal Psychology, 219
Convegno di psicologia sperimentale e psicotecnia. *See* Società italiana di psicologia. Atti di Convegno, 290
Copenhagen. Psykoteknisk Institut. *See* Psykologien og Erhvervslivet; Tidsskrift for anvendt Psykologi, 888
Cornell University. Psychological Laboratory. Minor Studies. *See* American Journal of Psychology, 90
Cornell University. Studies in Philosophy, 1566
Correspondenzblatt der deutschen Gesellschaft für Psychiatrie und gerichtliche Psychologie. *See* Deutsche Gesellschaft für Psychiatrie und gerichtliche Psychologie. Correspondenzblatt, 48
Cracovie. Université. Laboratoire de psychologie expérimentale. Travaux. *See* Krakow. Uniwersytet Jagielloński. Zakład psychológii doświadczalnej. Praca, 530
Criminal Science Monographs, 344
Crippled Child, 1176
Critique philosophique, 1567
Current Trends in Psychology, 965
Cuyo. Universidad nacional. Instituto de psicología experimental. Publicaciones. *See* Mendoza (Argentina). Universidad nacional de Cuyo. Instituto de psicología experimental. Publicaciones, 895
Cybernetics. Conference. Transactions. *See* New York. Josiah Macy, Jr. Foundation. Conference on Cybernetics. Transactions, 1056

685

Title Index

Danmarks Social-pædagogisk Forening. *See* Pædagogisk-psykologisk Tidsskrift, 865

Dansk Psykologforening. *See* Nordisk Psykologi, 1057

Dartmouth College. Medical School. Eye Institute. Publications, 1398

Darvinskii muzei (Moscow). Zoopsikhologicheskaia laboratoriia. *See* Moscow. Gosudarstvennyi Darvinskii muzei. Zoopsikhologicheskaia laboratoriia. Otchet, 331; *and* Moscow. Gosudarstvennyi Darvinskii muzei. Zoopsikhologicheskaia laboratoriia. Trudy, 465

Debrecen (Hungary). Tudomány-egyetem. Pedagógiai Szemináriumából és Pszihológiai Intézét. Közlemények, 606

Dementia Praecox Studies. A Journal of Psychiatry of Adolescence, 1690

Denison University. *See* Journal of Comparative Neurology [1], 108; *and* Journal of Comparative Neurology and Psychology, 191

Deutsche Gesellschaft für Psychiatrie und gerichtliche Psychologie. Archiv, 52

Deutsche Gesellschaft für Psychiatrie und gerichtliche Psychologie. Correspondenzblatt, 48

Deutsche Gesellschaft für Psychiatrie und gerichtliche Psychologie. Verhandlungen, 49

Deutsche Gesellschaft für Psychologie. *See* Archiv für die gesamte Psychologie, 181; *and* Zeitschrift für Psychologie, 869; *and* Zeitschrift für Psychologie und Physiologie der Sinnesorgane. Abteilung I. Zeitschrift für Psychologie, 223; *and* Zeitschrift für Psychologie und Physiologie der Sinnesorgane. Abteilung I. Zeitschrift für Psychologie. Ergänzungsband, 236; *and* Zeitschrift für Psychologie und Physiologie der Sinnesorgane. Abteilung II. Zeitschrift für Sinnesphysiologie, 237

Deutsche Gesellschaft für Psychologie. Kongress. Bericht, 655

Deutsche Gesellschaft für Tierpsychologie. *See* Zeitschrift für Tierpsychologie, 812

Deutsche medizinische Wochenschrift, 1399

Deutsche Psychologie. Arbeitenreihe, 396

Deutsche Psychologie. Arbeitenreihe zur Kulturpsychologie und Psychologie der Praxis. Psychotechnik, 578

Deutsche Psychologie. Zeitschrift für reine und angewandte Seelenkunde, 348

Deutsche Rundschau, 1295

Deutsche Tagung für psychische Hygiene. Bericht, 1691

Deutsche Zeitschrift für Nervenheilkunde, 1692

Digest of Neurology and Psychiatry, 1693

Diseases of the Nervous System, 1694

Divus Thomas; Jahrbuch für Philosophie und speculative Theologie, 1568

Dobutsu Shinri [Animal Psychology]. [1], 726

Dobutsu Shinri [Animal Psychology]. [2], 966

Dobutsu Shinri Nenpo [Annual of Animal Psychology], 967

Dobutsu Shinrigaku Nenpo [Annual of Animal Psychology], 905

Dokumente zur Geschichte der Sexualität. *See* Sexualpsychologie; Dokumente zur Geschichte der Sexualität, 548

Dominican Republic. Instituto de investigaciones psicopedagógicas. Boletín. *See* Ciudad Trujillo. Instituto de investigaciones psicopedagógicas. Boletín, 937

Duke University. Contributions to Psychological Theory, 727

Duke University. Psychological Monographs, 656

Duke University. Research Studies in Education, 1177

Eastman School of Music. Studies in Psychology. *See* Rochester (New York). University. Eastman School of Music. Studies in Psychology, 591

Eclectic Magazine of Foreign Literature, 1296

École de psychologie (Paris). *See* Revue de psychothérapie et de psychologie appliquée [1], 276; *and* Paris. École de psychologie. Bulletin, 758

École pratique des hautes études (Paris). Laboratoire de psychologie physiologique. Travaux. *See* Paris. Sorbonne. Laboratoire de psychologie physiologique. Travaux, 118

Education, 1178

[Education and Psychology]. *See* Chiao yü yü hsin li [Education and Psychology]. [1], 577; *and* Chiao yü hsin li [Education and Psychology]. [2], 725

Educational Administration and Supervision, 1179

Title Index

Educational American Journal of Psychoanalysis Devoted to an Understanding and Education of Human Behavior. *See* Psychoanalytic Review. An Educational American Journal of Psychoanalysis Devoted to an Understanding and Education of Human Behavior, 867

Educational and Psychological Measurement, 875

Educational Journal of Neuropsychiatry. *See* Journal of Nervous and Mental Disease; An Educational Journal of Neuropsychiatry, 73

Educational Measurement Review, 492

Educational Method, 1180

Educational Problem Series, 458

Educational, Psychological, and Personality Tests, 750

[Educational Psychological Research]. *See* Kyoiku Shinri Kenkyū [Educational Psychological Research], 560

[Educational Psychological Research Record]. *See* Kyoiku Shinri Kenkyū Kijō [Educational Psychological Research Record], 877

[Educational Psychology]. *See* Kyoiku Shinri [Educational Psychology], 735; *and* Kyoiku Shinrigaku [Educational Psychology], 1052

Educational Psychology Monographs, 270

Educational Psychology Series. *See* Iowa. University. Educational Psychology Series, 698

Educational Record, 1181

Educational Records Bulletin, 1182

Educational Research Association. *See* Journal of Educational Research, 400

Educational Research Bulletin, 1183

Educational Research Monographs, 557

Educational Review, 1184

Educational Testing Service (Princeton). *See* Invitational Conference on Testing Problems. Proceedings, 776

Egyptian Journal of Psychology, 915

Einheitswissenschaft, 1569

Electroencephalography and Clinical Neurophysiology, 1400

Elementary School Journal, 1185

Elementary School Record, 1186

Encéphale; journal de neurologie, de psychiatrie, de biologie et de physiologie pathologique du système nerveux, 493

Encéphale; journal de neurologie, de psychiatrie et de médecine psycho-somatique, 1089

Encéphale; journal de neurologie et de psychiatrie [1], 415

Encéphale; journal de neurologie et de psychiatrie [2], 558

Encéphale; journal de neurologie et de psychiatrie et l'hygiene mentale, 1012

Encéphale; journal de psychiatrie, 216

Encéphale; journal des maladies mentales et nerveuses, 78

Encéphale; journal des maladies mentales et nerveuses et de physiologie cérébrale, 95

Encéphale; journal mensuel de neurologie et de psychiatrie, 225

Encéphale. Supplement mensuel. *See* Informateur des aliénistes et des neurologistes. Journal d'information, d'intérêts professionnels et d'assistance, 218

Enfance; psychologie, pédagogie, neuro-psychiatrie, sociologie, 1013

Eranos Jahrbuch, 695

Ergebnisse der Neurologie und Psychiatrie, 1695

Ergebnisse der Physiologie, 1401

Estudios de patología nerviosa y mental, 189

Etc., 1570

Ethical Record, 1571

Ethics, 1572

Ethisch-socialwissenschaftliche Vorträgskurse, 1573

Études carmélitaines. *See* Congrès international de psychologie religieuse. Travaux, 1010

Études de psychologie, 295

Études de psychologie et de philosophie, 834

Études de psychologie pédagogique, 1014

Études et recherches de pédagogie expérimentale, 1015

Title Index

Études philosophiques, 1574
Eugenical News, 1274
Eugenics: A Journal of Race Betterment, 1275
Eugenics and Social Welfare Bulletin, 1276
Eugenics (Education) Society. *See* Occasional Papers on Eugenics, 925
Eugenics Research Association. *See* Studies in Social Eugenics, 716
Eugenics Research Association. Handbook Series, 1277
Eugenics Research Association. Monograph Series, 1278
Eugenics Review, 1279
Eugénique, 1280
Évolution psychiatrique. Cahiers de psychologie clinique et de psychopathologie générale, 607
Évolution psychiatrique. Psychanalyse. Psychologie clinique, 494
Exceptional Children, 1187
Excerpta Medica. Section 8B: Psychiatry, 1696
Experientia, 1575
[Experimental Psychological Research]. *See* Jikken Shinrigaku Kenkyū [Experimental Psychological Research], 734
Experimental Psychology Group. *See* Quarterly Journal of Experimental Psychology, 1032
Experimental Studies in Psychology and Pedagogy, 176
Experimentelle Pädagogik, 206
Exposés sur la psycho-biologie de l'enfant, 772

Federation of Practical Psychology Clubs of Great Britain. *See* Practical Psychologist, 507
Fels Monograph Series. *See* Society for Research in Child Development. Monographs, 762
Filosofia delle scuole italiane, rivista bimestrale, 1576
Filosofski pregled', 1577
Fiziologicheskii institut imeni I.P. Pavlova. Trudy. *See* Akademiia nauk SSSR. Fiziologicheskii institut imeni I.P. Pavlova. Trudy, 902
Fiziologicheskii zhurnal SSSR imeni I. M. Sechenova, 1402
Florence. Università. Istituto di psicologia. Studi e ricerche di psicologia, 816
Florence. Università. Laboratorio di psicologia sperimentale. Ricerche di psicologia, 207
Folia Neuro-biologica, 1403
Folia Psychiatrica et Neurologica Japonica, 1697
Folia Psychiatrica, Neurologica et Neurochirurgica Neerlandica, 1698
Forschungen und Werke zur Erziehungswissenschaft, 1188
Forschungen zur Völkerpsychologie und Soziologie, 495
Forschungsinstitut für Psychologie. *See* Leipzig. Sächsische staatliche Forschungsinstitute. Forschungsinstitut für Psychologie. Abhandlungen, 423; *and* Leipzig. Sächsische staatliche Forschungsinstitute. Forschungsinstitut für Psychologie. Veröffentlichungen, 352
Forschungsinstitut für Sozial- und Verwaltungswissenschaft (Köln). *See* Kölner Zeitschrift für Soziologie. Neue Folge der Kölner Vierteljahrshefte für Soziologie, 1020
Fort Hays Kansas State College. Studies. *See* Kansas. Fort Hays Kansas State College. Studies. Psychology Series, 864
Fortnightly Review, 1297
Fortschritte der Neurologie, Psychiatrie und ihre Grenzgebiete, 1699
Fortschritte der Psychologie und ihrer Anwendungen, 296
Fortschritte der Psychotechnik. *See* Progrès de la psychotechnique, 1058
Forum and Century, 1298
Forum of Education, 459
Foster Parents' Plan for War Children. Report, 857
France. Centre national de la recherche scientifique. Bulletin analytique: Philosophie, 968
Franklin Institute. Journal, 1404
Freiburg (Switzerland). Universität. Heilpädagogischen Seminar. Arbeiten, 773
Freiburg. Universität. Pädagogisches Institut. *See* Arbeiten zur Psychologie, Pädagogik und Heilpädagogik, 1039

Title Index

Friedrich Manns pädagogisches Magazin, 1189; *Also see* Arbeiten zur Pädagogik und psychologischen Anthropologie, 831; *and* Beiträge zur Pädagogik und Psychologie, 413; *and* Philosophische und psychologische Arbeiten, 425; *and* Sprachpsychologische Untersuchungen, 744; *and* Studien zur psychologischen Ästhetik und Kunstpsychologie mit pädagogischen Anwendungen, 621

Friends Conference on Religion and Psychology. *See* Inward Light, 795

Frommanns Klassiker der Philosophie, 1578

Fujen ta hsüeh [Fujen University, Peking]. *See* Chiao yü yü hsin li [Education and Psychology]. [2], 725; *and* Peking. Catholic University. College of Education. Publications, 866

Fukushima. Fukushima Daigaku. Gakugeigakubu. Ronshu. III. Kyoiku. Shinrigaku [Fukushima University. Faculty of Arts and Sciences. Bulletin. III. Education. Psychology], 858

Galton Lecture. *See* Occasional Papers on Eugenics, 925

Geisteswissenschaften, 1124

Genesis, 1700

Genetic Psychology Monographs, 526

Geneva. Institut de psychologie. *See* Action et pensée, 487

Geneva. Université. Institut des sciences de l'éducation. Cahiers de pédagogie expérimentale et de psychologie de l'enfant. *See* Cahiers de pédagogie expérimentale et de psychologie de l'enfant. (Nouvelle série, 936; *and* Cahiers de pédagogie expérimentale et de psychologie de l'enfant. (Première série), 723

George Peabody College for Teachers. Bulletin, 1190

George Peabody College for Teachers. Contributions to Education, 1191

Georgia Psychological Association. Bulletin, 938

Georgia Psychologist. *See* Georgia Psychological Association. Bulletin, 938

Geriatrics, 1405

Germany. Hauptstelle der Wehrmacht für Psychologie und Rassenkunde. *See* Soldatentum. Zeitschrift für Wehrpsychologie, Wehrerziehung, Menschenauslese, 743

Germany. Reichskriegsministerium. Psychologisches Laboratorium. *See* Soldatentum. Zeitschrift für Wehrpsychologie, Wehrerziehung, Menschenauslese, 743; *and* Zeitschrift für angewandte Psychologie und Charakterkunde. Beihefte, 767

Gesellschaft für Experimental-Psychologie (Berlin). Schriften. *See* Berlin. Gesellschaft für Experimental-Psychologie. Schriften, 92

Gesellschaft für experimentelle Psychologie. *See* Archiv für die gesamte Psychologie, 181; *and* Kongress für experimentelle Psychologie. Bericht, 193; *and* Zeitschrift für Psychologie und Physiologie der Sinnesorgane. Abteilung I. Zeitschrift für Psychologie, 223; *and* Zeitschrift für Psychologie und Physiologie der Sinnesorgane. Abteilung I. Zeitschrift für Psychologie. Ergänzungsband, 236

Gesellschaft für psychologische Forschung. Schriften, 107

Gesellschaft für Religionspsychologie. *See* Archiv für Religionspsychologie, 325; *and* Archiv für Religionspsychologie und Seelenführung, 603

Gesellschaft für Tierpsychologie. Kurzmitteilungen, 579

Gesellschaft für Tierpsychologie. Mitteilungen, 309

Gesellschaft; Sammlung sozialpsychologischer Monographien, 217

Giornale del magnetismo ed ipnotismo, 99

Giornale di psichiatria e neuropatologia, 1701

Gnothi Sauton. Magazin zur Erfahrungsseelenkunde als ein Lesebuch für Gelehrte und Ungelehrte, 1

Gosudarstvennyi Darvinskii muzei (Moscow). Zoopsikhologicheskaia laboratoriia. Otchet. *See* Moscow. Gosudarstvennyi Darvinskii muzei. Zoopsikhologicheskaia laboratoriia. Otchet, 331

Gosudarstvennyi Darvinskii muzei (Moscow). Zoopsikhologicheskaia laboratoriia. Trudy. *See* Moscow. Gosudarstvennyi Darvinskii muzei. Zoopsikhologicheskaia laboratoriia. Trudy, 465

Gosudarstvennyi institut muzykal'noi nauki (Moscow). Fiziologo-psikhologicheskaia sektsiia. Sbornik rabot. *See* Moscow. Gosudarstvennyi institut muzykal'noi nauki. Fiziologo-psikhologicheskaia sektsiia. Sbornik rabot, 504

Title Index

Gosudarstvennyi institut po izucheniiu mozga. *See* Leningrad. Gosudarstvennyi institut po izucheniiu mozga. Novoe v refleksologii i fiziologii nervnoi sistemy, 531

Gosudarstvennyi institut psikhologii (Moscow). *See* Moscow. Gosudarstvennyi institut psikhologii. Psikhologicheskie issledovaniia, 756

Gosudarstvennyi refleksologicheskii institut po izucheniiu mozga (Leningrad). *See* Leningrad. Gosudarstvennyi refleksologicheskii institut po izucheniiu mozga. Novoe v refleksologii i fiziologii nervnoi sistemy, 500; *and* Obozrenie psikhiatrii, nevrologii i eksperimental'noi psikhologii, 133; *and* Obozrenie psikhiatrii, nevrologii i refleksologii imeni V. M. Bekhtereva, 539; *and* Voprosy izucheniia i vospitaniia lichnosti; Pedologiia i defektologiia, 410

Gothenburg. University. Institute of Psychotechnics. *See* International Association of Applied Psychology. Congress. Proceedings, 416

Graphologia. *See* Schweizerische Zeitschrift für Psychologie und ihre Anwendungen. Beiheft, 901

Graphologischer Forschungskreis (Hamburg). *See* Hamburg. Graphologischer Forschungskreis. Rundbrief für der Mitarbeiter und Mitglieder, 939; *and* Zeitschrift für Graphologie und Charakterkunde, 1036

Great Britain. British Union of Practical Psychologists. *See* Practical Psychology, 803; *and* Practical Psychology Magazine, 781

Great Britain. Federation of Practical Psychology Clubs. *See* Practical Psychologist, 507

Great Britain. Home and School Council. *See* London. University. Institute of Education. Concerning Children. Pamphlet Series, 800

Great Britain. Industrial Fatigue Research Board. Annual Report, 372

Great Britain. Industrial Health Research Board. Annual Report, 580

Great Britain. Industrial Health Research Board. Reports, 383

Great Britain. Industrial Health Research Board. (War) Emergency Reports, 859

Great Britain. Medical Research Council. Special Reports, 1406

Great Britain. Medico-Psychological Association. *See* Journal of Mental Science, 50

Great Britain. Psychological Society. Proceedings. *See* Psychological Society of Great Britain. Proceedings, 71

Grenzfragen des Nerven- und Seelenlebens, 160

Group for the Advancement of Psychiatry. Report, 969

Group Psychotherapy; Journal of Sociopsychopathology and Sociatry, 1090

Groupement belge d'études oto-ophthalmologiques et neuro-chirurgicales. *See* Journal belge de neurologie et de psychiatrie, 699; *and* Journal de neurologie et de psychiatrie [1], 461

Groupes d'études de psychologie (Paris). Bulletin. *See* Paris. Université. Groupes d'études de psychologie. Bulletin, 987

Grundwissenschaft; Philosophische Zeitschrift der Johannes-Rehmke-Gesellschaft, 1579

Guatemala City. Universidad de San Carlos. Facultad de humanidades. Anuario, 1049

Guide to Guidance, 1526

Guild of Pastoral Psychology. Lectures, 835

Gyermek, 1192

ha-Hinuch. Yarhon Pedagog' la-Morim ve-la-horim, 496

Hamburg. Graphologischer Forschungskreis. Rundbrief für der Mitarbeiter und Mitglieder, 939

Hamburger Arbeiten zur Begabungsforschung. *See* Zeitschrift für angewandte Psychologie. Beihefte, 356

Hamburger Untersuchungen zur Jugend- und Sozialpsychologie. *See* Zeitschrift für angewandte Psychologie. Beihefte, 356

Handbooks of Moral and Religious Education, 310

Harpers Magazine, 1299

Harvard Educational Review, 1193

Harvard Monographs in Education. Studies in Educational Psychology and Educational Measurement, 439

Harvard Psychological Studies, 184

Harvard Studies in Education, 1194

Harvard University. Graduate School of Education. Bureau of Vocational Guidance. *See* National Vocational Guidance Association. Bulletin, 424; *and* Vocational Guidance Magazine, 483

Harvard University. Graduate School of Education. Harvard Education Papers, 860

Title Index

Harvard University. Museum of Comparative Zoology. Bulletin, 1407
Harvard University. Museum of Comparative Zoology. Zoological Laboratory Contributions, 1408
Harvard University. Psycho-acoustic Laboratory. Reports, 916
Harvard University. Psychological Laboratory. Minor Studies. *See* American Journal of Psychology, 90
Harvard University. School of Public Health. Center for Research in Child Health and Development. Studies. *See* Society for Research in Child Development. Monographs, 762
Hauptstelle der Wehrmacht für Psychologie und Rassenkunde (Germany). *See* Soldatentum. Zeitschrift für Wehrpsychologie, Wehrerziehung, Menschenauslese, 743
Havre (Le). Institut havrais de sociologie économique et de psychologie des peuple. *See* Revue de psychologie des peuples, 953
Health Record, 226
Hearing News, 1409
Hearing Survey Quarterly, 1410
Heath's Pedagogical Library, 85
Heidelberger Abhandlungen. *See* Abhandlungen aus dem Gesamtgebiete der Kriminalpsychologie, 294
Heilpädagogische Umschau, 1195
Heilpädagogische Werkblätter, 1196
Henderson Trust. Lectures, 472
Henderson Trust. Reports, 208
Hermès. Journal du magnétisme animal, 21
Hibbert Journal, 1300
Hoja de psicología, 970
Hokuriku Shinri [Hokuriku Psychology Journal], 1091
Homo. Zeitschrift für die vergleichende Forschung am Menschen, 1125
Hospice de la Salpêtrière (Paris). Laboratoire de psychologie. Travaux. *See* Paris. Hospice de la Salpêtrière. Laboratoire de psychologie. Travaux, 151
Hsin li [Psychology], 440
Hsin li chi Kan [Psychology Quarterly], 774
Hsin li Chiao yu Shih yen Chuan pien [Monograph of Psychology and Education]. *See* Nanking. Kuo li Chung-yang ta hsüeh. Chiao yü hsüeh yüan. Chiao yü Shih yen so. Hsin li Chiao yu Shih yen Chuan pien [National Central University. School of Education. Institute for Educational Experimentation. Monograph of Psychology and Education], 736
Hsin li hsüeh pan nien Kan [Psychology Semi-Annual], 728
Hsin li hsüeh pan nien Kan. Hsin li fu Kan [Psychology Semi-Annual. Supplement], 729
Human Biology, 1411
Human Engineering for Executives. *See* Industrial Psychology Monthly; The Magazine of Manpower, 528
Human Factor, 674
Human Organization, 1527
Human Relations. A Quarterly Journal of Studies towards the Integration of the Social Sciences, 971
Hungarian Psychological Review. *See* Magyar Psychológiai Szemle, 588
Ilverdagens Psykologi, 917
Hygiène mentale. Journal d'assistance psychiatrique, d'anthropologie criminelle et d'interêts professionnels, 497
Hygiène mentale. Journal d'assistance psychiatrique et de psychiatrie appliquée, 581
Hygiène mentale. Journal de psychiatrie appliquée, 608
Hygiène mentale. Organe de la Ligue française d'hygiène mentale, 1092

Igiene mentale, 1702
Illinois Society for Child Study. Transactions, 1197
Illinois Society for Mental Hygiene. Bulletin, 1703
Illinois Society for Mental Hygiene. Mental Health Bulletin, 1704
Illinois Society for Mental Hygiene. Newsletter, 1705
Illinois. State Academy of Science. Transactions, 1412

Title Index

Institut für angewandte Psychologie (Leipzig). See Zeitschrift für angewandte Psychologie [1], 355; and Zeitschrift für angewandte Psychologie. Beihefte, 356; and Zeitschrift für angewandte Psychologie und Charakterkunde, 766; and Zeitschrift für angewandte Psychologie und Charakterkunde. Beihefte, 767; and Zeitschrift für angewandte Psychologie und psychologische Sammelforschung, 254; and Zeitschrift für angewandte Psychologie und psychologische Sammelforschung. Beihefte, 291

Institut für experimentelle Pädagogik und Psychologie des Leipziger Lehrervereins. See Leipzig. Institut für experimentelle Pädagogik und Psychologie des Leipziger Lehrervereins. Veröffentlichungen. Pädagogisch-psychologische Arbeiten, 272

Institut für Psycho-Hygiene (Biel, Switzerland). Arbeiten zur Psycho-Hygiene. See Biel. Institut für Psycho-Hygiene. Arbeiten zur Psycho-Hygiene, 1083

Institut für Sozialpsychologie (Karlsruhe). See Karlsruhe. Technische Hochschule. Institut für Sozialpsychologie. Sozialpsychologische Forschungen, 443

Institut général psychologique (Paris). See Paris. Institut général psychologique. Bulletin, 163; and Paris. Institut général psychologique. Mémoires, 210

Institut havrais de sociologie économique et de psychologie des peuples (Le Havre). See Revue de psychologie des peuples, 953

Institut pédagogique Saint-Georges. Université de Montréal. Bulletin. See Montreal. Université. Institut pédagogique Saint-Georges. Bulletin, 841

Institut po izucheniiu mozga i psikhicheskoi deiatelnosti (Leningrad). See Voprosy izucheniia i vospitaniia i lichnosti; Pedologiia i defektologiia, 410

Institut psychique international (Paris). Bulletin. See Paris. Institut général psychologique. Bulletin, 163

Institut psychologique international (Paris). Bulletin. See Paris. Institut général psychologique. Bulletin, 163

Institut psychoneurologique ukrainien (Kharkov). See Kharkov. Ukrainskii psikhonevrologicheskii institut. Trudy, 529

Institut sotsial'noi psikhonevrologii psikhogigieny (Kharkov). See Psikhogigienu v massy, 704

Institut superieur de philosophie (Louvain). See Louvain. Université catholique. Laboratoire de psychologie expérimentale. Travaux, 209

Institute for Psychoanalysis (Chicago). See Brief Psychotherapy Council. Proceedings, 885; and Chicago. Institute for Psychoanalysis. Leaflet, 673; and Chicago. Institute for Psychoanalysis. Report, 694

Institute for Studies in Social Psychology and Public Opinion (Mexico City). See Mexico City. Instituto científico de la opinión pública mexicana. Boletín, 909; and Mexico City. Instituto científico de la opinión pública mexicana. Problemas y resultados de las investigaciones de la opinión pública. Monografías, 923

Institute for the Study of Animal Behaviour. See Bulletin of Animal Behaviour, 815

Institute of Clinical and Applied Psychology (Lahore, India). See Clinical Psychology. A Quarterly Journal Devoted to the Scientific Study of Human Personality, 1048

Institute of Psycho-Analysis (London). See Psycho-Analytical Epitomes, 804; and International Psycho-Analytical Library, 417

Institutet för psykologisk Forskning. Meddelanden. See Uppsala. Institutet för psykologisk Forskning. Meddelanden, 278

Instituto científico de la opinión pública mexicana (Mexico City). See Mexico City. Instituto científico de la opinión pública mexicana. Boletín, 909; and Mexico City. Instituto científico de la opinión pública mexicana. Problemas y resultados de las investigaciones de la opinión pública. Monografías, 923

Instituto cultural "Joaquin V. Gonzalez" filial Rosario. Comisión de información y estudios psicotécnicos. See Anales de psicotecnia, 874

Instituto de estudios de psicología social y opinión pública (Mexico City). See Mexico City. Instituto científico de la opinión pública mexicana. Boletín, 909; and Mexico City. Instituto científico de la opinión pública mexicana. Problemas y resultados de las investigaciones de la opinión pública. Monografías, 923

Instituto de investigaciones psicopedagógicas. Boletín. See Ciudad Trujillo. Instituto de investigaciones psicopedagógicas. Boletín, 937

Instituto de seleção e orientação profissional da fundação Getúlio Vargas (Rio de Janeiro). *See* Arquivos brasileiros de psicotécnica, 1040

Instituto nacional de psicotecnia (Madrid). *See* Psicotecnia, 842; *and* Revista de psicología general y aplicada, 951

Instituto psicopedagógico nacional. *See* Lima. Instituto psicopedagógico nacional. Boletín, 887; *and* Lima. Instituto psicopedagógico nacional. Boletín. Supplemento, 943

Instituto psicopedagógico para niños nerviosos (Buenos Aires). *See* Clínica psicopedagógica. Revista de neuropsiquiatría infantil, 457

Instituto psicotécnico (Barcelona). *See* Barcelona. Instituto psicotécnico. Anales, 961; *and* Barcelona. Instituto psicotécnico. Monografías, estudios y documentaciones psicotécnicas, 1043

Institutul de psihologie experimentală, comparată şi aplicată. Studii şi cercetări psihologice. *See* Cluj (Rumania). Universitatea. Institutul de psihologie experimentală, comparată şi aplicată. Studii şi cercetări psihologice, 604

Instituut voor preventieve geneeskunde. *See* Mens en onderneming, 981

Intelligenz und Arbeitsschule. *See* Untersuchungen zur Psychologie, Philosophie und Pädagogik, 481

Intercollegiate Journal of Psychology. *See* Persona. The Intercollegiate Journal of Psychology, 1024

Intercollegiate Psychology Association. Journal, 1051

Intermédiaire des neurologistes et des aliénistes, 1707

Intermédiaires des biologistes et des médecins, 1415

International Association of Applied Psychology. Congress. Proceedings, 416

International Association of Psychotechnics. Publications. *See* Progrès de la psychotechnique, 1058

International Bi-monthly Journal of Psychoanalysis, Applied Psychology and Psychotherapeutics. *See* Psyche and Eros. An International Bi-monthly Journal of Psychoanalysis, Applied Psychology and Psychotherapeutics, 405

International Clinics, 1416

International Conference on Child Psychiatry, 1708

International Conference on Psychosurgery, 1709

International Congress for Psychical Research, 1840

International Congress for Sex Research. Proceedings, 1710

International Congress of Criminal Anthropology and Psychiatry. Proceedings, 775

International Congress of Experimental Psychology. *See* International Congress of Psychology. Proceedings and Papers, 96

International Congress of Ophthalmology. Proceedings, 1417

International Congress of Philosophy. Acts, 1580

International Congress of Psychology. Proceedings and Papers, 96

International Congress on Mental Hygiene. Proceedings, 635

International Education Series, 1202

International Journal of American Linguistics, 1322

International Journal of Comparative Ethology. *See* Behaviour: An International Journal of Comparative Ethology, 962; *and* Behaviour: An International Journal of Comparative Ethology. Supplement, 1082

International Journal of Individual Psychology, 751

International Journal of Opinion and Attitude Research, 973

International Journal of Psycho-Analysis, 397

International Journal of Psycho-Analysis. Research Supplement, 862

International Journal of Psycho-Analysis. Supplements, 583

International Journal of Sexology, 1418

International Labour Office (Geneva). Studies and Reports. Series J. Education, 1203

International Monthly Magazine of Literature, Science & Art, 1302

International Psycho-Analytical Congress, 242

International Psycho-Analytical Library, 417

International Psycho-Analytical Association. *See* International Journal of Psycho-Analysis, 397

International Psychological Quarterly. *See* Character and Personality; An International Psychological Quarterly, 724

International Psychological Service Center (Washington, D.C.). *See* Psychological Service Center Bulletin, 1063; *and* Psychological Service Center Journal, 1064

Title Index

International Quarterly of Psychodiagnostics and Allied Subjects. *See* Character and Personality; An International Quarterly of Psychodiagnostics and Allied Subjects, 671

International Record of Educational Literature, Institutions and Progress. *See* Pedagogical Seminary. An International Record of Educational Literature, Institutions and Progress, 110

International Record of Medicine, 1419

International Social Science Bulletin, 1126

International University Series in Psychology. *See* Psychological Register, 617

Internationale Bibliothek für Psychologie und Soziologie, 940

Internationale Gesellschaft für medizinische Psychologie und Psychotherapie. Verhandlungen, 286

Internationale Gesellschaft für Religionspsychologie. *See* Archiv für Religionspsychologie und Seelenführung, 603

Internationale Gesellschaft für Sexualforschung. *See* Abhandlungen aus dem Gebiete der Sexualforschung, 369; *and* Zeitschrift für Sexualwissenschaft und Sexualpolitik, 553

Internationale Monatsschrift für die gesamte Neurologie in Wissenschaft und Praxis mit besonderer Berücksichtigung der Degenerations-Anthropologie. *See* Zentralblatt für Nervenheilkunde und Psychiatrie. Internationale Monatsschrift für die gesamte Neurologie in Wissenschaft und Praxis mit besonderer Berücksichtigung der Degenerations-Anthropologie, 105

Internationale psychoanalytische Bibliothek, 384

Internationale psychoanalytische Vereinigung. *See* Internationale Zeitschrift für ärztliche Psychoanalyse, 311, *and* Internationale Zeitschrift für Psychoanalyse, 398; *and* Internationale Zeitschrift für Psychoanalyse. Beiheft, 328, *and* Internationale Zeitschrift für Psychoanalyse und "Imago," 836; *and* Internationale Zeitschrift für Psychoanalyse und "Imago." Beiheft, 732; *and* Zentralblatt für Psychoanalyse. Medizinische Monatsschrift für Seelenkunde, 283; *and* Zentralblatt für Psychoanalyse und Psychotherapie. Medizinische Monatsschrift für Seelenkunde, 322

Internationale religionspsychologische Gesellschaft. *See* Zeitschrift für Religionspsychologie. Beiträge zur religiösen Seelenforschung und Seelenführung, 598; *and* Zeitschrift für Religionspsychologie. Sonderhefte, 628

Internationale Tagung für angewandte Psychopathologie und Psychologie. Referate und Vorträge. *See* Abhandlungen aus der Neurologie, Psychiatrie, Psychologie und ihren Grenzgebieten, 357

Internationale Vereinigung für Psychotechnik. Veröffentlichungen. *See* Progrès de la psychotechnique, 1058

Internationaler Verein für Medizin, Psychologie und Psychotherapie. Offizieller Bericht der Verhandlungen. *See* Zeitschrift für Pathopsychologie. Ergänzungsband, 338

Internationale Zeitschrift für angewandte Physiologie einschliesslich Arbeitsphysiologie, 1420

Internationale Zeitschrift für Arbeitspädagogik, Arbeitspsychologie, Arbeitstechnik und Betriebswirtschaft. *See* Mensch und Arbeit. Internationale Zeitschrift für Arbeitspädagogik, Arbeitspsychologie, Arbeitstechnik und Betriebswirtschaft 982; *and* Mensch und Arbeit. Internationale Zeitschrift für Arbeitspädagogik, Arbeitspsychologie, Arbeitstechnik und Betriebswirtschaft. Beihefte, 983

Internationale Zeitschrift für ärztliche Psychoanalyse, 311

Internationale Zeitschrift für Individualpsychologie. Arbeiten aus dem Gebiete der Psychotherapie, Psychologie und Pädagogik, 460

Internationale Zeitschrift für Individualpsychologie. Beihefte, 636

Internationale Zeitschrift für Psychoanalyse, 398

Internationale Zeitschrift für Psychoanalyse. Beihefte, 328

Internationale Zeitschrift für Psychoanalyse und "Imago," 836

Internationale Zeitschrift für Psychoanalyse und "Imago." Beihefte, 732

Internationaler psychoanalytischer Kongress. *See* International Psycho-Analytical Congress, 242

Internationaler Kongress für Psychologie. *See* International Congress of Psychology. Proceedings and Papers, 96

Internationales Zentralblatt für die Biologie, Psychologie, Pathologie und Soziologie der Sexuallebens. *See* Zeitschrift für Sexualwissenschaft. Internationales Zentralblatt für die Biologie, Psychologie, Pathologie und Soziologie der Sexuallebens, 339

Invitational Conference on Testing Problems. Proceedings, 776

Inward Light, 795

Title Index

Iowa Academy of Sciences. Proceedings, 1421
Iowa. University. Child Welfare Pamphlets, 676
Iowa. University. Child Welfare Pamphlets. Narrative Supplements, 752
Iowa. University. Child Welfare Research Station. See Iowa. University. Studies in Child Welfare, 399
Iowa. University. Child Welfare Research Station. Report, 609
Iowa. University. College of Education. Monographs in Education, 1204
Iowa. University. Educational Psychology Series, 698
Iowa. University. Institute of Character Research. See Iowa. University. Studies in Character, 559
Iowa. University. Research Studies in Educational Measurements, 733
Iowa. University. Studies in Character, 559
Iowa. University. Studies in Child Welfare, 399
Iowa. University. Studies in Clinical Psychology. See Iowa. University. Studies in Psychology, 140; and Psychological Monographs, 275
Iowa. University. Studies in General Psychology. See Iowa. University. Studies in Psychology, 140; and Psychological Monographs, 275
Iowa. University. Studies in Psychology, 140
Iowa. University. Studies in Psychology of Reading. See Iowa. University. Studies in Psychology, 140; and Psychological Monographs, 275
Iowa. University. Studies in the Psychology of Art. See Iowa. University. Studies in Psychology, 140; and Psychological Monographs, 275
Iowa. University. Studies in the Psychology of Music, 677
Iowa. University. Studies. Series on Aims and Progress of Research, 1422
Ipnotismo, 117
Ireland. Medico-Psychological Association. See Journal of Mental Science, 50
Ishikawa. Kanazawa Daigaku [Kanazawa University]. See Hokuriku Shinri [Hokuriku Psychology Journal], 1091
Istanbul. Üniversite. Pedagoji enstitüsü. Psikoloji ve pedagoji çalişmalari, 863
Istituto di psicologia sperimentale (Rome). See Rivista di psicologia [1], 302; and Rivista di psicologia [2], 450; and Rivista di psicologia applicata, 262; and Rivista di psicologia applicata alla pedagogia ed alla psicopatologia, 212; and Rivista di psicologia e rassegna di studi pedagogici e filosofici, 429; and Rivista di psicologia normale e patologica, 709; and Rome. Università. Istituto di psicologia sperimentale. Contributi psicologici, 451
Istituto di psicologia sperimentale (Turin). See Archivio italiano di psicologia, 392; and Rivista di psicologia [1], 302; and Rivista di psicologia [2], 450; and Rivista di psicologia applicata, 262; and Rivista di psicologia applicata alla pedagogia ed alla psicopathologia, 212; and Rivista di psicologia e rassegna di studi pedagogici e filosofici, 429; and Rivista di psicologia normale e patologica, 709

Jagielloński Uniwersytet (Krakow). Zakład psychológii doświadczalnej. Praca. See Krakow. Uniwersytet Jagielloński. Zakład psychológii doświadczalnej. Praca, 530
Jahrbuch der Charakterologie, 474
Jahrbuch der Erziehungswissenschaft und Jugendkunde, 1205
Jahrbuch der Psychoanalyse, 329
Jahrbuch für Philosophie und phänomenologische Forschungen, 1581
Jahrbuch für Philosophie und phänomenologische Forschungen. Ergänzungsband, 1582
Jahrbücher für Psychiatrie und Neurologie, 1711
Jahrbuch für psychoanalytischen und psychopathologischen Forschungen, 256
Jahresbericht Neurologie und Psychiatrie, 1712
James Millikin University. Bulletin. Linguistic Psychology Series. See Studies in Linguistic Psychology, 303
[Japanese Journal of Experimental Psychology]. See Jikken Shinrigaku Kenkyū. [Experimental Psychological Research], 734
[Japanese Journal of Psychology]. See Nihon Shinrigaku Zasshi [Japanese Journal of Psychology]. [1], 403; and Nihon Shinrigaku Zasshi [Japanese Journal of Psychology]. [2], 477; and Shinrigaku Kenkyū [Psychological Research], 467
[Japanese Journal of Psychology. New Series]. See Shinrigaku Kenkyū. Shin Shirīzu [Psychological Research. New Series], 549

Title Index

[Japanese Psychological Society. Congress. Reports]. *See* Shinrigaku Kenkyū. Shin Shirīzu [Psychological Research. New Series], 549

[Japanese Society for Animal Psychology. Tokyo]. *See* Dobutsu Shinrigaku Nenpo [Annual of Animal Psychology], 905

Jaunatnes un Arodu Piemērotibas Pētišanas Institūta (Riga). *See* Riga. Jaunatnes un Arodu Piemērotibas Pētišanas Institūta. Zinojumi A, 643; *and* Riga. Jaunatnes un Arodu Piemērotibas Pētišanas Institūta. Zinojumi B, 644

Jen shih hsin li yen chiu she ts'ung shu. [Personnel Psychology Research Society. Collectanea], 893

Jenaer Beiträge zur Jugend- und Erziehungs-Psychologie, 498

Jeugd en beroep. Tijdschrift voor jeugdpsychologie, voorlichting bij beroepskeuze en beroepsvorming, 584

Jido Shinri [Child Psychology], 974

Jikken Shinrigaku Kenkyū [Experimental Psychological Research], 734

Johannesburg. Psychological Society. *See* South African Psychological Review, 955

Johannesburg. South African Council for Scientific and Industrial Research. National Institute for Personnel Research. Bulletin, 1017

Johns Hopkins University. Psychological Laboratory. Studies. *See* Johns Hopkins University. Studies in Philosophy and Psychology, 243; *and* Psychological Review. Monograph Supplements, 126

Johns Hopkins University. Studies in Education, 1206

Johns Hopkins University. Studies in Philosophy and Psychology, 243

Joint Committee on Methods of Preventing Delinquency. Publication, 1127

Jornal brasileiro de psiquiatria, 1713

Josiah Macy, Jr. Foundation (New York). *See* New York. Josiah Macy, Jr. Foundation. Conference on Cybernetics. Transactions, 1056; *and* New York. Josiah Macy, Jr. Foundation. Conference on Problems of Aging. Transactions, 1022; *and* New York. Josiah Macy, Jr. Foundation. Conference on Problems of Consciousness. Transactions, 1096; *and* New York. Josiah Macy, Jr. Foundation. Conference on Training in Clinical Psychology. Transactions, 985

Journal belge de neurologie et de psychiatrie, 699

Journal d'assistance psychiatrique, d'anthropologie criminelle et d'intérêts professionnels. *See* Hygiène mentale. Journal d'assistance psychiatrique, d'anthropologie criminelle et d'intérêts professionnels, 497

Journal d'assistance psychiatrique et de psychiatrie appliquée. *See* Hygiène mentale. Journal d'assistance psychiatrique et de psychiatrie appliquée, 581

Journal de l'afrique du sud de philosophie et de psychologie. *See* Koers; maanblad vir Calvinistiere denke, 700

Journal de l'anatomie et de la physiologie normales et pathologiques de l'homme et des animaux, 1423

Journal de la physiologie de l'homme et des animaux, 1424

Journal de magnétisme animal. *See* Journal du magnétisme animal [1], 28; *and* Révélateur. Journal de magnétisme animal, 27

Journal de médecine légale psychiatrique et d'anthropologie criminelle, 1714

Journal de médecine mentale, 55

Journal de neurologie, de psychiatrie, de biologie et de physiologie pathologique du système nerveux. *See* Encéphale; journal de neurologie, de psychiatrie, de biologie et de physiologie pathologique du système nerveux, 493

Journal de neurologie, de psychiatrie et de médecine psycho-somatique. *See* Encéphale; journal de neurologie, de psychiatrie et de médecine psycho-somatique, 1089

Journal de neurologie et de psychiatrie [1], 461

Journal de neurologie et de psychiatrie [2]. *See* Encéphale; journal de neurologie et de psychiatrie [1], 415; *and* Encéphale; journal de neurologie et de psychiatrie [2], 558

Journal de neurologie et de psychiatrie et l'hygiène mentale. *See* Encéphale; journal de neurologie et de psychiatrie et l'hygiène mentale, 1012

Journal de neurologie & d'hypnologie. Neurologie, hypnologie, psychiatrie, psychologie, 124

Journal of Clinical Psychopathology, 941

Journal of Clinical Psychopathology and Psychotherapy, 906

Journal of Clinical Psychopathology. Monograph Series, 919

Journal of College Student Personnel. *See* Personnel-O-Gram, 988

Title Index

Journal des maladies mentales et nerveuses et de physiologie cérébrale. *See* Encéphale; journal des maladies mentales et nerveuses et de physiologie cérébrale, 95

Journal des sciences magnétiques, hypnotiques et occultes. *See* Magnétisme. Journal des sciences magnétiques, hypnotiques et occultes, 57

Journal Devoted to the Development of Psychology as a Quantitative Rational Science. *See* Psychometrika; A Journal Devoted to the Development of Psychology as a Quantitative Rational Science, 785

Journal d'information, d'intérêts professionnels et d'assistance. *See* Informateur des aliénistes et des neurologistes. Journal d'information, d'intérêts professionnels et d'assistance, 218

Journal du magnétisme, 38

Journal du magnétisme animal [1], 28

Journal du magnétisme animal [2]. *See* Hermès. Journal du magnétisme animal, 21

Journal för Animal Magnetism, 12

Journal for the Study and Treatment of Mental Retardation and Deviation. *See* Psychological Clinic. A Journal for the Study and Treatment of Mental Retardation and Deviation, 231

Journal für Psychologie und Neurologie, 177

Journal mensuel de neurologie et de psychiatrie. *See* Encéphale; journal mensuel de neurologie et de psychiatrie, 225

Journal of Aesthetics and Art Criticism, 1583

Journal of Abnormal and Social Psychology, 499

Journal of Abnormal Psychology, 219

Journal of Abnormal Psychology and Social Psychology, 418

Journal of Anatomy, 1425

Journal of Animal Behavior, 287

Journal of Animal Magnetism. *See* Mesmeric Magazine; or, Journal of Animal Magnetism, 30

Journal of Applied Psychology, 359

Journal of Cerebral Physiology and Mesmerism, and Their Applications to Human Welfare. *See* Zoist; A Journal of Cerebral Physiology and Mesmerism, and Their Applications to Human Welfare, 35

Journal of Child Psychiatry. Neurology and Clinical Psychology of the Child, 975

Journal of Childhood and Adolescence, 1207

Journal of Clinical and Experimental Psychopathology. *See* Journal of Clinical Psychopathology, 941

Journal of Clinical Pastoral Work, 1715

Journal of Clinical Psychology, 918

Journal of Clinical Psychology. Monograph Supplement, 1018

Journal of Neurology and Psychiatry, 817

Journal of Neurology and Psychopathology, 401

Journal of Neurology, Neurosurgery and Psychiatry, 907

Journal of Neuropathology and Experimental Neurology, 1716

Journal of Neurophysiology, 1436

Journal of Neurosurgery, 1437

Journal of Ophthalmology, Otology and Laryngology, 1438

Journal of Orthogenics for the Normal Development of Every Child. *See* Psychological Clinic. A Journal of Orthogenics for the Normal Development of Every Child, 333

Journal of Orthogenics for the Study and Treatment of Retardation and Deviation. *See* Psychological Clinic. A Journal of Orthogenics for the Study and Treatment of Retardation and Deviation, 247

Journal of Parapsychology, 797

Journal of Parapsychology; A Scientific Quarterly Dealing with Extra-Sensory Perception and Related Topics, 886

Journal of Parapsychology; A Scientific Quarterly Dealing with Extra-Sensory Perception, the Psychokinetic Effect, and Related Topics, 908

Journal of Pastoral Care, 1717

Journal of Pedagogy, 1210

Journal of Personality, 920

Journal of Personnel Research, 442

Journal of Philosophy, 422

Title Index

Journal of Philosophy, Psychology and Scientific Methods, 192
Journal of Physiology, 1439
Journal of Projective Techniques, 1093
Journal of Psycho-Asthenics; Devoted to the Care, Training and Treatment of the Feeble-Minded and of the Epileptic, 131
Journal of Psycho-Asthenics. Monograph Supplements, 298
Journal of Psychological Medicine; A Quarterly Review of Diseases of the Nervous System, Medical Jurisprudence, and Anthropology, 63
Journal of Psychological Medicine and Mental Pathology, 40
Journal of Psychological Medicine and Mental Pathology. New Series, 70
Journal of Psychological Studies. See Psychological Newsletter, 1062
Journal of Psychology; The General Field of Psychology, 753
Journal of Psychosophy, 1841
Journal of Rehabilitation, 1440
Journal of Religious Psychology, Including Its Anthropological and Sociological Aspects, 299
Journal of Sexology and Psychoanalysis, 462
Journal of Social Hygiene, 1130
Journal of Social Issues, 921
Journal of Social Issues. Supplement Series, 1019
Journal of Social Philosophy and Jurisprudence, 1584
Journal of Social Psychology; Political, Racial, and Differential Psychology, 637
Journal of Social Science, 1131
Journal of Speculative Philosophy, 59
Journal of Speech and Hearing Disorders, 1441
Journal of Speech and Hearing Disorders. Monograph Supplement, 1442
Journal of the Anthropological Institute of New York, 1132
Journal of the History of Ideas, 1585
Journal of The Proceedings of the London Psycho-therapeutic Society. See Psycho-therapeutic Journal. A Journal of the Proceedings of the London Psycho-therapeutic Society, 171
Journal of Unified Science, 1586
Journal of Vital Magnetism. See Mesmerist; A Journal of Vital Magnetism, 34
Journal roumain pour la psychologie pratique. See Jurnal de psihotehnica, 798
Jugendanthropologie und Neuformung des Menschentums. See Zeitschrift für angewandte Psychologie und Charakterkunde. Beihefte, 767
Jung Institut (Zurich). Studien. See Zurich. C. G. Jung Institut. Studien, 1078
Juristisch-psychiatrische Grenzfragen, 1718
Jurnal de psihologie militara, 838
Jurnal de psihotehnica, 798

Kaiser Wilhelm Institut für Hirnforschung der Universität Berlin. See Journal für Psychologie und Neurologie, 177
Kanazawa Daigaku [Kanazawa University]. See Hokuriku Shinri [Hokuriku Psychology Journal], 1091
Kansas. Fort Hays Kansas State College. Studies. Psychology Series, 864
Kansas Mental Hygiene Society. Bulletin, 1719
Kansas. University. Journal of Psychology, 942
Kansas. University. Studies in Psychology. See Psychological Monographs, 275
Kant-Studien, 1587
Kant-Studien. Ergänzungshefte, 1588
Karlsruhe. Technische Hochschule. Institut für Sozialpsychologie. Sozialpsychologische Forschungen, 443
Kazan. Kazanskii institut nauchnoi organizatsii truda. See Voprosy psikhofiziologii, refleksologii i gigieny truda, 468
Keijo. Keijo Teikoku Daigaku [Keijo Imperial University]. See Acta Psychologica Keijo, 630
Kharkov. Institut sotsial'noi psikhonevrologii i psikhogigieny. See Psikhogigienu v massy, 704
Kharkov. Ukrainskii nauchno-issledovatel'skii institut pedagogiki. See Ukrains'kyi visnyk ekspery-

Title Index

mental'noi pedagogiky ta refleksologii, 570; *and* Ukrains'kyi visnyk refleksologii ta eksperymental'noi pedagogiky, 515; *and* Za Markso-Lenins'ku pedagogiku, 667

Kharkov. Ukrainskii psikhonevrologicheskii institut. Trudy, 529

Kharkov. Vseukrainskaia psikhonevrologicheskaia akademiia. Trudy, 754

Kiev. Narodnyi komitet zdravookhraneniia Ukrainskoi SSR. *See* Sovremennaia psikhonevrologiia, 514

Kindergarten, 1211

Kinderstudie, Paedologische bladen, 351

Kinderstudie. Paedologische en psychologische bladen, 475

Kings County Hospital (Brooklyn). Division of Psychiatry. Department of Psychology. *See* Case Reports in Clinical Psychology, 1047

Kleine Schriften zur Seelenforschung, 444

Klinik für psychische und nervöse Krankheiten, 1720

Klinische Monatsblätter für Augenheilkunde, 1443

Klinische Wochenschrift, 1444

Koers; maanblad vir Calvinistiere denke, 700

Kölner Zeitschrift für Soziologie. Neue Folge der Kölner Vierteljahrshefte für Soziologie, 1020

Komisja filozoficzna (Poznan). Prace. *See* Poznan. Poznańskie towarzystwo przyjaciół nauk. Komisja filozoficzna. Prace, 426

Komisja pedagogiczna (Warsaw). Wydawnictwa. *See* Warsaw. Komisja pedagogiczna. Wydawnictwa, 453

Kongress für experimentelle Psychologie. Bericht, 193

Königliche sächsische Forschungsinstitute zu Leipzig. Forschungsinstitut für Psychologie. *See* Leipzig. Sächsische staatliche Forschungsinstitute. Forschungsinstitut für Psychologie. Veröffentlichungen, 352; *and* Psychologische Studien. Neue Folge der philosophischen Studien, 221

Kosmos. A Monthly Magazine Devoted to Cultural Ideals, the Psychology of Education, and the Educational Values of Citizenship, 141

Krakow. Naukowe towarzystwo pedagogiczne. Psychologja niewidomych, 610

Krakow. Uniwersytet Jagiellonski. Zakład psychologii doświadczalnej. Praca, 530

Kriminalbiologische Gesellschaft. *See* Monatsschrift für Kriminalbiologie und Strafrechtsreform, 801

Kuo li Ch'ing-hua ta hsüeh [National Ch'ing-hua University. Peking]. *See* Chiao yü yü hsin li [Education and Psychology]. [1], 577; *and* Chung-hua hsin li hsüeh pao [Chinese Journal of Psychology], 771; *and* Peking. National Tsing Hua University. Science Reports. Series B: Biological and Psychological Sciences, 661

Kuo li Chung-shan ta hsüeh [National Sun Yat-sen University. Canton]. *See* Chiao yü yen Chiu [Studies in Education], 576; *and* Canton. Sun Yat-sen University. Institute of Educational Research. Psychological Laboratory. Studies. Series A, 670

Kuo li Chung-yang ta hsüeh [National Central University. Chungking]. *See* Chiao yü hsin li yen Chiu [Studies in Educational Psychology], 854; *and* Chinese Journal of Educational Psychology, 855

Kuo li Chung-yang ta hsüeh [National Central University. Nanking]. *See* Hsin li hsüeh pan nien Kan [Psychology Semi-Annual], 728; *and* Hsin li hsüeh pan nien Kan. Hsin li fu Kan [Psychology Semi-Annual. Supplement], 729; *and* Nanking. Kuo li Chung yang ta hsüeh. Chiao yü hsüeh yüan. Chiao yü Shih yen so. Hsin li Chiao yu Shih yen Chuan pien [National Central University. School of Education. Institute for Educational Experimentation. Monograph of Psychology and Education], 736

Kuo li Shih-fan ta hsüeh (Peking). *See* Hsin li [Psychology], 440

Kwartalnik póświęcony sprawom poradnictwa zawodowego, psychologii przemysłowej i pokrewnym działom psychologii stosowanej. *See* Psychologia i hygiena psychiczna pracy. Kwartalnik póświęcony sprawom poradnictwa zawodowego, psychologii przemysłowej i pokrewnym działom psychologii stosowanej, 1027

Kwartalnik póświęcony zagadnieniom psychologji teoretycznej i stosowanej wydawany przez związek polskiego nauczycielstwa szkól powszechnych. *See* Polskie archiwum psychologji. Kwartalnik póświęcony zagadnieniom psychologji teoretycznej i stosowanej wydawany przez związek polskiego nauczycielstwa szkól powszechnych, 541

Title Index

Leningrad. Fiziologicheskii institut. Fiziologicheskii laboratorii Akademika I.P. Pavlova. Trudy. *See* Akademiia nauk S.S.S.R., Leningrad. Fiziologicheskii institut. Fiziologicheskii laboratorii Akadmika I.P. Pavlova. Trudy, 488

Leningrad. Gosudarstvennyi institut po izucheniiu mozga. Novoe v refleksologii i fiziologii nervnoi sistemy, 531

Leningrad. Gosudarstvennyi refleksologicheskii institut po izucheniiu mozga. *See* Obozrenie psikhiatrii, nevrologii i eksperimental'noi psikhologii, 133; *and* Obozrenie psikhiatrii, nevrologii i refleksologii imeni V.M. Bekhtereva, 539; *and* Voprosy izucheniia i vospitaniia lichnosti; Pedologiia i defektologiia, 410

Leningrad. Gosudarstvennyi refleksologicheskii institut po izucheniiu mozga. Novoe v refleksologii i fiziologii nervnoi sistemy, 500

Leningrad. Institut po izucheniiu mozga i psikhicheskoi deiatelnosti. *See* Voprosy izucheniia i vospitaniia lichnosti; Pedologiia i defektologiia, 410

Library of Genetic Science and Philosophy, 257

Liga mexicana de higiene mental. *See* Revista mexicana de higiene mental, 952

Liga mexicana de salud mental. *See* Psiquis; revista mexicana de higiene mental, 990

Ligue d'hygiène mentale. Bulletin. *See* Psyché. Revue internationale de psychanalyse et des sciences de l'homme, 948

Ligue d'hygiène mentale. Bulletin mensuel, 1721

Ligue française d'hygiène mentale. *See* Hygiène mentale. Organe de la ligue française d'hygiène mentale, 1092

Lima. Instituto psicopedagógico nacional. Boletín, 887

Lima. Instituto psicopedagógico nacional. Boletín. Supplemento, 943

London. Central Association for Mental Welfare. *See* Studies in Mental Inefficiency, 409; *and* Mental Welfare, 502

London. Central Association for the Care of the Mentally Defective. *See* Studies in Mental Inefficiency, 409

London. Institute for the Study of Animal Behaviour. *See* Bulletin of Animal Behaviour, 815

London. Institute of Psycho-Analysis. *See* Psycho-Analytical Epitomes, 804; *and* International Psycho-Analytical Library, 417

London. Medical Society of Individual Psychology. *See* Individual Psychology Medical Pamphlets, 730; *and* Individual Psychology Pamphlets, 697; *and* Individual Psychology Publications. Medical Pamphlets, 657

London. National Association for the Feeble-Minded. Conference Report, 220

London. National Institute of Industrial Psychology. (Annual) Report, 561

London. National Institute of Industrial Psychology. Institute Report, 532

London. National Institute of Industrial Psychology. Journal, 445

London. National Institute of Industrial Psychology. News, 799

London. National Institute of Industrial Psychology. Report, 533

London. National Laboratory of Psychical Research. Proceedings, 562

London. Psycho-therapeutic Society. Proceedings. *See* Psycho-therapeutic Journal. A Journal of the Proceedings of the London Psycho-therapeutic Society, 171

London. Society for Cultural Relations with the U.S.S.R. *See* Soviet Psychology Information Bulletin, 1070

London. Tavistock Institute of Human Relations. *See* Human Relations. A Quarterly Journal of Studies towards the Integration of the Social Sciences, 971

London. University. Bedford College for Women. Psychological Laboratory. Psychological Studies, 330

London. University. Council for Psychical Investigations. Bulletin, 1842

London. University. Council for Psychical Investigations. Proceedings, 1843

London. University. Francis Galton Laboratory for National Eugenics. Eugenics Laboratory Lecture Series, 1281

London. University. Francis Galton Laboratory for National Eugenics. Eugenics Laboratory Memoirs, 1282

London. University. Institute of Education. Concerning Children. Pamphlet Series, 800

London. University. University College. Psychological Laboratory. Collected Papers, 300

Title Index

Los Angeles City School District. Department of Psychology and Educational Research. Yearbook, 563
Los Angeles City School District. Division of Educational Research. Yearbook, 360
Los Angeles Neurological Society. Bulletin, 1722
Los Angeles. University of Southern California. Psychological Laboratory. Reports. *See* Southern California. University. Psychological Laboratory. Reports, 1106
Los Angeles. University of Southern California. Studies. Philosophy Series, 1590
Louisville. University. Department of Psychology. *See* Motor Skills Research Exchange, 1055
Louvain. Université catholique. Institut de psychologie appliquée et de pédagogie. Extraits de dissertations, 840
Louvain. Université catholique. Institut de psychologie appliquée et de pédagogie. Extraits de dissertations. Série A, 978
Louvain. Université catholique. Institut de psychologie appliquée et de pédagogie. Extraits de dissertations. Série B, 979
Louvain. Université catholique. Institut supérieur de philosophie. Annales, 1591
Louvain. Université catholique. Laboratoire de psychologie expérimentale. Travaux, 209
Louvain. Université. Institut de philosophie. *See* Études de psychologie, 295
Louvain. Université. Laboratoire de psychologie expérimentale. Travaux, 944
Loyola Educational Index; A Readers' Guide to Education and Psychology, 587
Luzern. Institut für Heilpädagogik. *See* Arbeiten zur Psychologie, Erziehungswissenschaft und Sondererziehungswissenschaft, 883

Macmillan's Magazine, 1303
Macy Conference. *See* New York. Josiah Macy, Jr. Foundation. Conference on Cybernetics. Transactions, 1056; *and* New York. Josiah Macy, Jr. Foundation. Conference on Problems of Aging. Transactions, 1022; *and* New York. Josiah Macy, Jr. Foundation. Conference on Problems of Consciousness. Transactions, 1096; *and* New York. Josiah Macy, Jr. Foundation. Conference on Training in Clinical Psychology. Transactions, 985
Madrid. Instituto nacional de psicotecnia. *See* Psicotecnia, 842; *and* Revista de psicología general y aplicada, 951
Magazin für die psychische Heilkunde, 10
Magazin für philosophische, medicinische und gerichtliche Seelenkunde, 23
Magazin zur Erfahrungsseelenkunde als ein Lesebuch für Gelehrte und Ungelehrte. *See* Gnothi Sauton. Magazin zur Erfahrungsseelenkunde als ein Lesebuch für Gelehrte und Ungelehrte, 1
Magazine of Labor Relations and Personnel Practices. *See* Personnel Journal, 566
Magazine of Manpower. *See* Industrial Psychology Monthly; The Magazine of Manpower, 528
Magazine of Psychoanalysis and Society. *See* Complex; The Magazine of Psychoanalysis and Society, 1087
Magnetisches Magazin für Niederdeutschland, 4
Magnetiser's Magazine, and Annals of Animal Magnetism, 13
Magnétiseur spiritualiste, 41
Magnétisme. Journal des sciences magnétiques, hypnotiques et occultes, 57
Magnétisme. Revue générale des sciences physio-psychologiques, 88
Magnetismo ed ipnotismo, 109
Magyar Psychológiai Szemle, 588
Manchester (England) Literary and Philosophical Society. Memoirs and Proceedings. *See* Auserlesene Abhandlungen für Ärzte, Naturforscher und Psychologen, aus den Schriften der literarisch-philosophischen Gesellschaft zu Manchester, 6
Manicomio, 1723
Manns pädagogisches Magazin. *See* Friedrich Manns pädagogisches Magazin, 1189. *Also see* Arbeiten zur Pädagogik und psychologischen Anthropologie, 831; *and* Beiträge zur Pädagogik und Psychologie, 413; *and* Philosophische und psychologische Arbeiten, 425; *and* Sprachpsychologische Untersuchungen, 744; *and* Studien zur psychologischen Ästhetik und Kunstpsychologie mit pädagogischen Anwendungen, 621
Maravilloso. Revista de psicología y dinamismo inexplicados, 258

Title Index

Title Index

Monatliche Zeitschrift vorzüglich der Untersuchung der wenig bekannten Phänomene des Seelenlebens gewidmet. *See* Psychische Studien. Monatliche Zeïtschrift vorzüglich der Untersuchung der wenig bekannten Phänomene des Seelenlebens gewidmet, 67

Monatsschrift für die gesamte angewandte Psychologie, für Berufsberatung und industrielle Psychotechnik. *See* Praktische Psychologie. Monatsschrift für die gesamte angewandte Psychologie, für Berufsberatung und industrielle Psychotechnik, 387

Monatsschrift für Kriminalbiologie und Strafrechtsreform, 801

Monatsschrift für Kriminalpsychologie und Strafrechtsreform, 194

Monatsschrift für Kriminalpsychologie und Strafrechtsreform. Beiheft, 536

Monatsschrift für Ohrenheilkunde und Laryngo-Rhinologie, 1452

Monatsschrift für Pädagogik mit besonderer Betonung der pädagogischen Psychologie, der vergleichenden Erziehungswissenschaft und der pädagogischen Bibliographie. *See* Bildung und Erziehung. Monatsschrift für Pädagogik mit besonderer Betonung der pädagogischen Psychologie, der vergleichenden Erziehungswissenschaft und der pädagogischen Bibliographie, 1006

Monatsschrift für Seelsorge, Psychotherapie und Erziehung. *See* Weg zur Seele. Monatsschrift für Seelsorge, Psychotherapie und Erziehung, 1075

Monist, 1592

Monografías de psicología normal y patológica, 924

Monografías, estudios y documentaciones psicotécnicas. *See* Barcelona. Instituto psicotécnico. Monografías, estudios y documentaciones psicotécnicas, 1043

Monografías psicológicas de la universidad nacional (Buenos Aires). *See* Buenos Aires. Universidad nacional. Instituto de filosofía. Seccion de psicología. Monografías psicológicas, 1084

[Monograph of Psychology and Education]. *See* Nanking. Kuo li Chung-yang ta hsüeh. Chiao yü hsüeh yüan. Chiao yü Shih yen so. Hsin li Chiao yu Shih yen Chuan pien. [National Central University. School of Education. Institute for Educational Experimentation. Monograph of Psychology and Education], 736

Monographien aus dem Gesamtgebiete der Neurologie und Psychiatrie, 1750

Monographien über die seelische Entwicklung des Kindes, 228

Monographien zur Ethno-Psychologie, 658

Monographien zur Frauenkunde und Konstitutionsforschung, 1453

Monographien zur Grundlegung der philosophischen Anthropologie und Wirklichkeitsphilosophie, 611

Montana. University. Publications in Psychology, 245

Montevideo. Centro de estudios psicológicos de Montevideo. *See* Hoja de psicología, 970

Montevideo. Centro de estudios psicopedagógicos del Uruguay. Publicaciones. *See* Centro de estudios psicopedagógicos del Uruguay. Publicaciones, 770

Montevideo. Laboratorio de psicopedagogía Sebastian Morey Otero. Boletín, 896

Montreal. Université. Institut de psychologie. *See* Revue de psychologie. Revue trimestrielle, 954

Montreal. Université. Institut pédagogique Saint-Georges. Bulletin, 841

Moscow. Akademiia kommunisticheskogo vospitaniia. Psikhologicheskaia laboratoriia. Raboty, 590

Moscow. Akademiia kommunisticheskogo vospitaniia. Psikhologicheskaia laboratoriia. Trudy, 565

Moscow. Akademiia sotsial'nogo vospitaniia. Psikhologicheskaia laboratoriia. Zapiski, 464

Moscow. Gosudarstvennyi Darvinskii muzei. Zoopsikhologicheskaia laboratoriia. Otchet, 331

Moscow. Gosudarstvennyi Darvinskii muzei. Zoopsikhologicheskaia laboratoriia. Trudy, 465

Moscow. Gosudarstvennyi institut muzykal'noi nauki. Fiziologo-psikhologicheskaia sektsiia. Sbornik rabot, 504

Moscow. Gosudarstvennyi institut psikhologii. Psikhologicheskie issledovaniia, 756

Moscow. Moskovskoe psikhologicheskoe obshchestvo. *See* Voprosy filosofii i psikhologii, 98

Moscow. Nauchno-issledovatel'skii nevro-psikhiatricheskii institut imeni P. B. Ganuskina. Trudy, 1751

Moscow. Universitet. Clinique psychiatrique. Travaux, 1752

Moscow. Universitet. Obshchestvo nevropatalogov i psikhiatrov. Protokoly, 1753

Moscow. Universitet. Psikhiatricheskaia klinika. *See* Psikho-nevrologicheskii vestnik'; Zhurnal' psikhiatrii, nevrologii, eksperimentalnoi psikhologii, obshchestvennoi i kriminalnoi psikhopatologii, 363

Title Index

[National Ch'ing-hua University. Peking]. *See* Chiao yü yü hsin li [Education and Psychology].
[1], 577; *and* Chung-hua hsin li hsüeh pao [Chinese Journal of Psychology], 771; *and* Peking.
National Tsing Hua University. Science Reports. Series B: Biological and Psychological Sciences, 661

National Committee for Mental Hygiene. *See* Mental Hygiene, 361; *and* Mental Hygiene Bulletin,
463; *and* Understanding the Child. A Magazine for Teachers, 666

National Committee for Mental Hygiene. Annual Report, 1756

National Education Association. Addresses and Proceedings, 1217

National Education Association. Journal, 1218

National Industrial Conference Board. Studies in Personnel Policy, 1529

National Institute for Personnel Research (Johannesburg, South Africa). *See* Johannesburg. South
African Council for Scientific and Industrial Research. National Institute for Personnel Research. Bulletin, 1017

National Institute of Industrial Psychology. *See* London. National Institute of Industrial Psychol-
ogy. (Annual) Report, 561; *and* London. National Institute of Industrial Psychology. Institute
Report, 532; *and* London. National Institute of Industrial Psychology. Journal, 445; *and*
London. National Institute of Industrial Psychology. News, 799; *and* London. National In-
stitute of Industrial Psychology. Report, 533; *and* Human Factor, 674; *and* Occupational
Psychology, 819; *and* Psychology at Work. Journal of the National Institute of Industrial
Psychology, 1031

National Institute of Mental Health (United States. Public Health Service). *See* United States.
Public Health Service. National Institute of Mental Health. Mental Health Series, 1034

National Laboratory of Psychical Research (London). Proceedings. *See* London. National Laboratory of Psychical Research. Proceedings, 562

[National Normal University, Peking]. *See* Hsin li [Psychology], 440

National Occupational Conference. *See* Occupations: The Vocational Guidance Journal, 702

National Opinion Research Center. Report, 1134

National Psychological Association for Psychoanalysis (New York). Bulletin. *See* New York. National Psychological Association for Psychoanalysis. Bulletin, 1097

National Research Council (Washington, D.C.). Activities of Divisions and Divisional Committees.
Reports. *See* Washington, D.C. National Research Council. Activities of Divisions and Divisional Committees. Reports, 354

National Research Council (Washington, D.C.). Bulletin, 1457

National Research Council (Washington, D.C.). Committee on Aviation Psychology. Annual Meeting. *See* Washington, D.C. National Research Council. Activities of Divisions and Divisional
Committees. Reports, 354

National Research Council (Washington, D.C.). Division of Anthropology and Psychology. Committee on Child Development. *See* Child Development, 634; *and* Child Development Abstracts and Bibliography, 556; *and* Society for Research in Child Development. Monographs,
762; *and* Society for Research in Child Development. Proceedings, 742; *and* Washington,
D.C. National Research Council. Committee on Child Development. Conference on Research
in Child Development. Proceedings, 516

National Research Council (Washington, D.C.). Division of Anthropology and Psychology. Committee on Problems of Neurotic Behavior. *See* Psychosomatic Medicine. Experimental and
Clinical Studies, 845; *and* Psychosomatic Medicine Monographs, 846

National Research Council (Washington, D.C.). Division of Anthropology and Psychology. Committee on Selection and Training of Aircraft Pilots. Annual Meeting. *See* Washington, D.C.
National Research Council. Activities of Divisions and Divisional Committees. Reports, 354

National Research Council (Washington, D.C.). Division of Anthropology and Psychology. Report.
See Washington, D.C. National Research Council. Activities of Divisions and Divisional Committees. Reports, 354

National Research Council (Washington, D.C.). Reprint and Circular Series, 1458

National Research Council (Washington, D.C.). Society for Research in Child Development. *See*
Child Development, 634; *and* Child Development Abstracts and Bibliography, 556; *and*
Society for Research in Child Development. Monographs, 762; *and* Society for Research in
Child Development. Proceedings, 742

Title Index

Pädagogisch-psychologische Arbeiten. *See* Leipzig. Institut des Leipziger Lehrervereins.
Pädagogisch-psychologische Arbeiten, 402; *and* Leipzig. Institut für experimentelle Pädagogik und Psychologie des Leipziger Lehrervereins. Veröffentlichungen. Pädagogisch-psychologische Arbeiten, 272 .
Pädagogisch-psychologische Schriftenreihe. *See* Allgemeiner deutscher Lehrerinnenverein. Pädagogisch-psychologische Schriftenreihe, 489
Pädagogisch-psychologische Studien, 162
Pädagogische Monographien, 230
Pädagogisches Zentralblatt, 1227
Pädagogium. Eine Methoden-Sammlung für Erziehung und Unterricht, 1228
Pädagogium. Monatsschrift für Erziehung und Unterricht, 1229
Paedagogisk-psykologisk Tidsskrift, 865
Paidologist, 1230
Paidology; the Science of the Child, 1231
Państwowy instytut higieny psychicznej (Warsaw). *See* Psychologia i higiena psychiczna pracy. Kwartalnik poświęcony sprawom poradnictwa zawodowego, psychologii przemysłowej i pokrewnym działom psychologii stosowanej, 1027
Parapsychology Bulletin, 946
Parent Education Bulletin, 820
Parents' Magazine, 1232
Paris. Centre de psychologie appliquée. *See* Revue de psychologie appliquée [2], 1104
Paris. Clinique hypnotherapique de la charité. Bulletin mensuel, 100
Paris. École de psychologie. *See* Revue de psychothérapie et de psychologie appliquée [1], 276
Paris. École de psychologie. Bulletin, 758
Paris. École pratique des hautes études. Laboratoire de psychologie physiologique. Travaux. *See* Paris. Sorbonne. Laboratoire de psychologie physiologique. Travaux, 118
Paris. Hospice de la Salpêtrière. Laboratoire de psychologie. Travaux, 151
Paris. Institut général psychologique. Bulletin, 163
Paris. Institut général psychologique. Mémoires, 210
Paris. Laboratoire de psychobiologie de l'enfant. *See* Enfance; psychologie, pédagogie, neuropsychiatrie, sociologie, 1013
Paris. Société clinique de médecine mentale. Bulletin. *See* Société clinique de médecine mentale (Paris). Bulletin, 251
Paris. Société de biologie. Comptes rendus, 1471
Paris. Société de psychothérapie. *See* Revue de psychothérapie et de psychologie appliquée [1], 276
Paris. Société de psychothérapie, d'hypnologie et de psychologie. *See* Revue de psychothérapie et de psychologie appliquée [2], 620
Paris. Société des magnétiseurs spiritualistes. *See* Magnétiseur spiritualiste, 41
Paris. Société psychanalytique de Paris. *See* Revue française de psychanalyse, 569
Paris. Sorbonne. Laboratoire de psychologie physiologique. *See* Année psychologique, 119
Paris. Sorbonne. Laboratoire de psychologie physiologique. Travaux, 118
Paris. Université. Groupe d'études de psychologie. Bulletin, 987
Pastoral Psychology, 1098
Peabody Journal of Education, 1233
Pedagogical Seminary. An International Record of Educational Literature, Institutions and Progress, 110
Pedagogical Seminary and Journal of Genetic Psychology, 505
Pedagogické rozhledy, 1234
Pedagogy-Psychology Quarterly. *See* ha-Hinuch. Yarhon Pedagog' la-Morim ve-la-horim, 496
Pediatriia (Moscow), 1472
Pediatriia (Petersburg), 1473
Pedologiia, 613
Pedologiia i defektologiia. *See* Voprosy izucheniia i vospitaniia lichnosti; Pedologiia i defektologiia, 410
Peking. [Catholic University]. *See* Chiao yü yü hsin li [Education and Psychology]. [2], 725
Peking. Catholic University. College of Education. Publications, 866

Title Index

Peking. Ch'ing-hua hsüeh hsi'ao [Ching-hua College]. *See* Chiao yü yü hsin li [Education and Psychology]. [1], 577; *and* Chung-hua hsin li hsüeh pao [Chinese Journal of Psychology], 771; *and* Peking. National Tsing Hua University. Science Reports. Series B: Biological and Psychological Sciences, 661

Peking. Ch'ing-hua ta hsüeh [Ch'ing-hua University]. *See* Chiao yü yü hsin li [Education and Psychology]. [1], 577; *and* Chung-hua hsin li hsüeh pao. [Chinese Journal of Psychology], 771; *and* Peking. National Tsing Hua University. Science Reports. Series B: Biological and Psychological Sciences, 661

Peking. Chung-hua p'ing Min Chiao yü Ts'u Chin Hui [Chinese National Association of the Mass Education Movement]. *See* Chinese National Association of the Mass Education Movement. Research Committee in Educational Psychology. Report, 748

Peking. Chung-kuo hsin li hsüeh hsieh hui [Chinese Psychological Association]. *See* Chung-hua hsin li hsüeh pao. [Chinese Journal of Psychology], 771

Peking. Chung-yang yen chiu yüan. Hsin li hsüeh yen chiu so [Central Research Institute. Research Institute of Psychology]. *See* Academia Sinica. National Research Institute of Psychology. Contributions, 668; *and* Academia Sinica. National Research Institute of Psychology. Monographs, 669

Peking. Fujen ta hsüeh [Fujen University]. *See* Chiao yü yü hsin li [Education and Psychology]. [2], 725; *and* Peking. Catholic University. College of Education. Publications, 866

Peking. Kuo li Ch'ing-hua ta hsüeh [National Ch'ing-hua University]. *See* Chiao yü yü hsin li [Education and Psychology]. [1], 577; *and* Chung-hua hsin li hsüeh pao [Chinese Journal of Psychology], 771; *and* Peking. National Tsing Hua University. Science Reports. Series B: Biological and Psychological Sciences, 661

Peking. Kuo li Shih-fan ta hsüeh [National Normal University]. *See* Hsin li [Psychology], 440

Peking [National Tsing-hua University]. *See* Chiao yü yü hsin li [Education and Psychology]. [1], 577; *and* Chung-hua hsin li hsüeh pao [Chinese Journal of Psychology], 771; *and* Peking. National Tsing Hua University. Science Reports. Series B: Biological and Psychological Sciences, 661

Peking. National Tsing Hua University. Science Reports. Series B: Biological and Psychological Sciences, 661

Peking. Yenching ta hsüeh. Hsin li hsüeh hsi [Yenching University. Department of Psychology]. *See* Chung-hua hsin li hsüeh pao [Chinese Journal of Psychology], 771

Pennsylvania. State College. Audio-Visual Aids Library. *See* Psychological Cinema Register, 843

Pennsylvania. University. Publications. Experimental Studies in Psychology and Pedagogy. *See* Experimental Studies in Psychology and Pedagogy, 176

Pennsylvania. University. Publications. Series in Philosophy, 101

Perceptual and Motor Skills (Research Exchange). *See* Motor Skills Research Exchange, 1055

Periódico de estudios psicológicos. *See* Revista espiritista. Periódico de estudios psicológicos, 62

Periodico mensile dedicato alle ricerche sperimentali e critiche sui fenomeni di telepatia, telestesia, premonizione, medianità, ecc. *See* Rivista di studi psichici; Periodico mensile dedicato alle ricerche sperimentali e critiche sui fenomeni di telepatia, telestesia, premonizione, medianità, ecc., 128

Perm. Ural'skaia oblastnaia psikhiatricheskaia lechebnitsa. Trudy, 641

Perm. Ural'skii nauchno-issledovatel'skii psikhonevrologicheskii institut. Trudy, 737

Persona. The Intercollegiate Journal of Psychology, 1024

Personalist. A Quarterly Journal of Philosophy, Theology and Literature, 1595

Personality Monographs. *See* Personality. Symposia on Topical Issues, 1099

Personality. Symposia on Topical Issues, 1099

Personnel, 1530

Personnel Administration, 1531

Personnel and Guidance Journal. *See* Occupations; The Vocational Guidance Journal, 702

Personnel Journal, 566

Personnel Management, 1532

Personnel-O-Gram, 988

Personnel Practice Bulletin. *See* Bulletin of Industrial Psychology and Personnel Practice, 914

Personnel Psychology; A Journal of Applied Research, 1025

Personnel Psychology Monographs, 1100

Title Index

Title Index

Title Index

Psiquis; revista mexicana de higiene mental, 990

Psychanalyse. Psychologie clinique. *See* Évolution psychiatrique. Psychanalyse. Psychologie clinique, 494

Psyche, 1844

Psyche. A Quarterly Review of Psychology, 427

Psyche; An Annual of General and Linguistic Psychology, 705

Psyche and Eros. An International Bi-monthly Journal of Psychoanalysis, Applied Psychology and Psychotherapeutics, 405

Psyche; Eine Zeitschrift für Tiefenpsychologie und Menschenkunde in Forschung und Praxis, 991

Psyche; Eine Zeitschrift für Tiefenpsychologie und Menschenkunde in Forschung und Praxis. Beihefte, 1059

Psyche Miniatures; General Series, 543

Psyche Miniatures; Medical Series, 544

Psyche Monographs, 567

Psyché. Revue internationale de psychanalyse et des sciences de l'homme, 948

Psyche. Zeitschrift für die Kenntniss des menschlichen Seelen- und Geisteslebens, 51

Psychiatria et Neurologia Japonica, 1779

Psychiatria et Neurologica, 1780

Psychiatric Aid, 1781

Psychiatric Quarterly, 1782

Psychiatric Quarterly. Supplement, 1783

Psychiatrie, Neurologie und medizinische Psychologie; Zeitschrift für Forschung und Praxis, 1060

Psychiatrisch-juridisch gezelschap. Verslagen, 662

Psychiatrisch-neurologische Wochenschrift, 1784

Psychiatrische Klinik (Berlin). Beiträge. *See* Berlin. Psychiatrische Klinik. Beiträge, 173

Psychiatrisches Centralblatt, 64

Psychiatry, 1785

Psychic Research Quarterly, 406

Psychical Research Monographs. *See* Stanford University. Publications. Psychical Research Monographs, 367

Psychical Review. A Quarterly Journal of Psychical Science and Organ of the American Psychical Society, 113

Psychische Studien. Monatliche Zeitschrift vorzüglich der Untersuchung der wenig bekannten Phänomene des Seelenlebens gewidmet, 67

Psycho-acoustic Laboratory. Reports. *See* Harvard. University. Psycho-acoustic Laboratory. Reports, 916

Psycho-Analytical Epitomes, 804

Psycho-biologie de l'enfant, 821

Psycho-medical Society. Transactions, 274

Psycho-physiologische Arbeiten. *See* Riga. Jaunatnes un Arodu Piemērotibas Pētišanas Institūta. Zinojumi. A, 643

Psycho-therapeutic Journal. A Journal of the Proceedings of the London Psycho-therapeutic Society, 171

Psycho-therapeutic Society (London). Proceedings. *See* Psycho-therapeutic Journal. A Journal of the Proceedings of the London Psycho-therapeutic Society, 171

Psychoanalysis and the Social Sciences, 992

Psychoanalytic Institute (Stamford, Connecticut). *See* Archives of Psychoanalysis; A Quarterly Devoted to the Theory and Treatment of the Neuroses and Psychoses, 523

Psychoanalytic Quarterly, 680

Psychoanalytic Review. A Journal Devoted to an Understanding of Human Conduct, 313

Psychoanalytic Review. An American Journal of Psychoanalysis Devoted to an Understanding of Human Conduct, 681

Psychoanalytic Review. An Educational American Journal of Psychoanalysis Devoted to an Understanding and Education of Human Behavior, 867

Psychoanalytic Study of the Child, 927

Psychoanalytische Bewegung, 616

Psychoanalytische Praxis. Vierteljahrsschrift für die aktive Methode der Psychoanalyse, 663

Psychobiology, 364

Title Index

Title Index

Psychotechnisches Institut (Arbeitsgemeinschaft für Psychotechnik in Österreich, Vienna). *See* Mensch und Arbeit. Internationale Zeitschrift für Arbeitspädagogik, Arbeitspsychologie, Arbeitstechnik und Betriebswirtschaft, 982; *and* Mensch und Arbeit. Internationale Zeitschrift für Arbeitspädagogik, Arbeitspsychologie, Arbeitstechnik und Betriebswirtschaft. Beihefte, 983

Psychotherapeutische Praxis. Vierteljahresschrift für praktische ärztliche Psychotherapie, 739

Psychotherapy. A Course of Reading in Sound Psychology, Sound Medicine and Sound Religion, 248

Psyke. Tidskrift för psykologisk Forskning, 222

Psyke. Tidskrift för psykologisk Forskning. Bilaga. *See* Uppsala. Institutet för psykologisk Forskning. Meddelanden, 278

Psyke. Tidskrift. Tidskriften Psykes Monografiserie, 261

Psykhaneuralagichny instytut. Akademiya navuk BSSR (Minsk). Zbornik prats. *See* Akademiya navuk BSSR (Minsk). Instytut psykhaneuralogii. Zbornik prats, 686

Psykologien og Erhvervslivet; Tidsskrift for anvendt Psykologi, 888

Public Affairs Pamphlets, 1135

Public Health Reports, 1481

Public Health Service (United States). *See* United States. Public Health Service. National Institute of Mental Health. Mental Health Series, 1034

Public Personnel Quarterly, 1534

Public Personnel Review, 1535

Public Personnel Studies, 466

Publication internationale pour recherches de psychologie positive. *See* Revue de psychologie concrète. Publication internationale pour recherches de psychologie positive, 619

Publications in Child Development. *See* California. University. Publications in Child Development, 1046

Purdue University. Division of Educational Reference. Studies in Higher Education, 1236

Quaderni di psichiatria, 1786

Quarterly Journal in Yiddish for Research into the Normal and Abnormal Psychical Life. *See* Mentsch vissenschaft, 639

Quarterly Journal of Child Behavior, 1068

Quarterly Journal of Experimental Physiology, 1482

Quarterly Journal of Experimental Psychology, 1032

Quarterly Journal of Medicine, Surgery, Magnetism, Mesmerism and the Collateral Sciences. *See* New-York Dissector; A Quarterly Journal of Medicine, Surgery, Magnetism, Mesmerism, and the Collateral Sciences, 36

Quarterly Journal of Psychical Science. *See* Psychical Review. A Quarterly Journal of Psychical Science and Organ of the American Psychical Society, 113

Quarterly Journal of Psychological Medicine and Medical Jurisprudence, 60

Quarterly Journal of Psychopathology, Psychotherapy, Mental Hygiene and Guidance of the Child. *See* Nervous Child; Quarterly Journal of Psychopathology, Psychotherapy, Mental Hygiene and Guidance of the Child, 878

Quarterly Journal of Speech, 1483

Quarterly Journal of Studies on Alcohol, 1484

Quarterly Journal of Studies towards the Integration of the Social Sciences. *See* Human Relations. A Quarterly Journal of Studies towards the Integration of the Social Sciences, 971

Quarterly Review of Biology, 1485

Quarterly Review of Diseases of the Nervous System, Medical Jurisprudence, and Anthropology. *See* Journal of Psychological Medicine; A Quarterly Review of Diseases of the Nervous System, Medical Jurisprudence, and Anthropology, 63

Quarterly Review of Psychiatry and Neurology, 1787

Quarterly Review of Psychology. *See* Psyche. A Quarterly Review of Psychology, 427

Quarterly Review of Psychology and Philosophy. *See* Mind. A Quarterly Review of Psychology and Philosophy, 74

Quellen und Studien zur Jugendkunde, 513

Quellenschriften zur seelischen Entwicklung, 388

Title Index

Radovi psihologijskog instituta univerziteta u zagrebu. *See* Zagreb. Univerzitet. Psihologijski institut. Acta, 685
Rassegna di studi psichiatrici, 1788
Rassenkunde und psychologische Anthropologie. *See* Zeitschrift für angewandte Psychologie und Charakterkunde. Beihefte, 767
Readers Guide to Education and Psychology. *See* Loyola Educational Index; A Readers' Guide to Education and Psychology, 587
Recent Progress in Psychiatry, 911
Recherches philosophiques, 1614
Refleksy, instinkty i navyki. *See* Moscow. Gosudarstvennyi institut psikhologii. Psikhologicheskie issledovaniia, 756
Reich der Seele: Arbeiten aus dem Münchener psychologischen Arbeitskreis, 807
Reichskriegsministerium (Germany). Psychologisches Laboratorium. *See* Soldatentum. Zeitschrift für Wehrpsychologie, Wehrerziehung, Menschenauslese, 743; and Zeitschrift für angewandte Psychologie und Charakterkunde. Beihefte, 767
Religionspsychologie, 546
Religionspsychologie. Beihefte. *See* Zeitschrift für Religionspsychologie. Sonderhefte, 628
Religionspsychologische Reihe; Studien über Aufbau und Führung des Charakters und des religiösen Lebens, 642
Religious Education, 1237
Repertorium der Psychologie und Physiologie nach ihrem Umfange und ihrer Verbindung. *See* Repertorium für Physiologie und Psychologie nach ihrem Umfange und ihrer Verbindung, 2
Repertorium für Physiologie und Psychologie nach ihrem Umfange und ihrer Verbindung, 2
Repertorium und Bibliothek für empirische Psychologie. *See* Allgemeines Repertorium für empirische Psychologie und verwandte Wissenschaften, 5
Research and Statistical Methodology. Books and Reviews. *See* Statistical Methodology Reviews, 715
Research Bulletin of the University of California Institute of Child Welfare. *See* California. University. Institute of Child Welfare. Bulletin, 575
Research Conference on Psychosurgery. Proceedings, 1069
Research Group on Psychosurgery. Proceedings. *See* Research Conference on Psychosurgery. Proceedings, 1069
Research Quarterly, 1238
Research Relating to Children, 1239
Researches in Parent Education. *See* Iowa. University. Studies in Child Welfare, 399
Révélateur. Journal de magnétisme animal, 27
Review of Educational Research, 1240
Review of Neurology and Psychiatry, 1789
Review of Scientific Instruments, 1486
Revista argentina de neurología, psiquiatría y medicina legal, 1790
Revista de criminología, psiquiatría y medicina legal, 1791
Revista de estudios psicológicos. *See* Plus Ultra. Revista de estudios psicológicos, 506
Revista de filosofía, pedagogía, historia, letras y psicología. *See* Guatemala City. Universidad de San Carlos. Facultad de humanidades. Anuario, 1049
Revista de medicina legal, criminología y psiquiatría forense, 1792
Revista de neuro-psiquiatria, 1793
Revista de neurologia e psiquiatria de São Paulo, 1794
Revista de neuropsiquiatría infantil. *See* Clínica psicopedagógica. Revista de neuropsiquiatría infantil, 457
Revista de psicoanálisis, 900
Revista de psicoanálisis. Monografías, 931
Revista de psicología general y aplicada, 951
Revista de psicología i pedagogía, 708
Revista de psicología y dinamismo inexplicados. *See* Maravilloso. Revista de psicología y dinamismo inexplicados, 258
Revista de psicología y pedagogía aplicadas, 1102
Revista de psihologie. Teoretică şi aplicată, 824
Revista de psiquiatría, 1795

Title Index

Revue psychiatrique. *See* Annales médico-psychologiques. Journal de l'aliénation mentale et de la médicine légale des aliénés, 32

Revue psycho-neurologique. *See* Psikho-nevrologicheskii vestnik'; Zhurnal' psikhiatrii, nevrologii, eksperimentalnoi psikhologii, obshchestvennoi i kriminalnoi psikhopatologii, 363

Revue psychologie hongroise. *See* Magyar Psychológiai Szemle, 588

Revue psychologique, 250

Revue scientifique, 1490

Revue suisse de psychologie et de psychologie appliquée. *See* Schweizerische Zeitschrift für Psychologie und ihre Anwendungen, 889

Ricerche di psicologia. *See* Florence. Università. Laboratorio di psicologia sperimentale. Ricerche di psicologia, 207

Riga. Jaunatnes un Arodu Piemērotibas Pētišanas Institūta. Zinojumi. A, 643

Riga. Jaunatnes un Arodu Piemērotibas Pētišanas Institūta. Zinojumi. B, 644

Rio de Janeiro. Instituto de seleção e orientação profissional da fundação Getúlio Vargas. *See* Arquivos brasileiros de psicotécnica, 1040

Rio de Janeiro. Universidade do Brasil. Instituto de psicologia. Monografias psicológicas. *See* Brazil. Universidade. Instituto de psicologia (Rio de Janeiro). Monografias psicológicas, 1007

Rio de Janeiro. Universidade do Brasil. Instituto de psiquiatria. Anais, 1802

Rivista di filosofia e scienze affini, 1619

Rivista di neurologia, 1803

Rivista di patologia nervosa e mentale, 135

Rivista di pedagogia correttiva, 1242

Rivista di psicologia [1], 302

Rivista di psicologia [2], 450

Rivista di psicologia applicata, 262

Rivista di psicologia applicata alla pedagogia ed alla psicopatologia, 212

Rivista di psicologia e rassegna di studi pedagogici e filosofici, 429

Rivista di psicologia normale e patologica, 709

Rivista di sociologia, 1137

Rivista di studi psichici; Periodico mensile dedicato alle ricerche sperimentali e critiche sui fenomeni di telepatia, telestesia, premonizione, medianità, ecc., 128

Rivista di studi psicologici. *See* Psiche. Rivista di studi psicologici, 301

Rivista filosofica, 1620

Rivista italiana di filosofia, 1621

Rivista italiana di neuropatologia, psichiatria ed elettroterapia, 1804

Rivista italiana di sociologia, 1138

Rivista mensile di neuropatologia e psichiatria, 165

Rivista mensile di psichiatria forense, antropologia criminale e scienze affini, 1805

Rivista quindicinale di psicologia, psichiatria, neuropatologia ad uso dei medici e dei giuristi, 145

Rivista quindicinale di psicologia, psicopatologia umana e comparata, di medicina legale e di psichiatria forense ad uso dei medici, magistrati ed avvocati. *See* Archivio delle psicopatie sessuali. Rivista quindicinale di psicologia, psicopatologia umana e comparata, di medicina legale e di psichiatria forense ad uso dei medici, magistrati ed avvocati, 129

Rivista speciale di opere di filosofia scientifica, 1622

Rivista sperimentale di freniatria e medicina legale delle alienazioni mentali, 1806

Rivista ungherese di psicologia. *See* Magyar Psychológiai Szemle, 588

Rochester (New York). University. Eastman School of Music. Studies in Psychology, 591

Rocznik psychjatryczny, 1807

Rome. Istituto di biopsicoterapia. *See* Archivio generale di biopsicologia, biopsicopatologia e biopsicoterapia. Periodico internazionale di scienza medica esatta, 652

Rome. Università. Istituto di psicologia sperimentale. *See* Rivista di psicologia [1], 302; *and* Rivista di psicologia [2], 450; *and* Rivista di psicologia applicata, 262; *and* Rivista di psicologia applicata alla pedagogia e alla psicopatologia, 212; *and* Rivista di psicologia e rassegna di studi pedagogici e filosofici, 429; *and* Rivista di psicologia normale e patologica, 709

Rome. Università. Istituto di psicologia sperimentale. Contributi psicologici, 451

Rome. Università. Istituto psichiatrico. Annali, 1808

Rome. Università. Laboratorio di psicologia sperimentale. Contributi psicologici, 263

Title Index

Rorschach Institute. *See* Journal of Projective Techniques, 1093; *and* Rorschach Research Exchange, 786; *and* Rorschach Research Exchange and Journal of Projective Techniques, 995

Rorschach Research Exchange, 786

Rorschach Research Exchange and Journal of Projective Techniques, 995

Rorschach Standardization Studies, 1033

Rorschachiana. *See* Schweizerische Zeitschrift für Psychologie und ihre Anwendungen. Beiheft, 901

Rosario (Argentina). Instituto cultural "Joaquin V. Gonzalez" filial Rosario. Comisión de información y estudios psicotécnicos. *See* Anales de psicotecnia, 874

Rosario (Argentina). Universidad nacional del Litoral. Instituto psiquiatrico. Boletin, 1809

Royal Medico-psychological Association. *See* Recent Progress in Psychiatry, 911

Royal Society (Edinburgh). Proceedings, 1491

Royal Society (London). Philosophical Transactions, 1492

Royal Society (London). Proceedings, 1493

Royal Society of Medicine (London). Proceedings. Psychiatric Section, 1810

RSFSR. Narodnyi komissariat prosveshcheniia (Moscow). Sektor nauki. *See* Pedologiia, 613

Russian Psychoanalytic Society. Report. *See* Internationale Zeitschrift für Psychoanalyse, 398

Rutgers University. School of Education. Mental Measurements Yearbook. *See* Mental Measurements Yearbook, 818

Rutgers University. Studies in Psychology, 848

S.-A. tydskrif vir sielkunde en opvoedkunde, 710

Sächsische staatliche Forschungsinstitute. Forschungsinstitut für Psychologie (Leipzig). *See* Leipzig. Sächsische staatliche Forschungsinstitute. Forschungsinstitut für Psychologie. Abhandlungen, 423; *and* Leipzig. Sächsische staatliche Forschungsinstitute. Forschungsinstitut für Psychologie. Veröffentlichungen, 352

Sacro Cuore. Università Cattolica (Milan). Istituto di psicologia sperimentale. Contributi. *See* Milan. Università Cattolica del Sacro Cuore. Istituto di psicologia sperimentale. Contributi, 503

Saint-Georges. Institut pédagogique. Université de Montréal. Bulletin. *See* Montreal. Université. Institut pédagogique Saint-Georges. Bulletin, 841

Salpêtrière (Paris). Laboratoire de psychologie. Travaux. *See* Paris. Hospice de la Salpêtrière. Laboratoire de psychologie. Travaux, 151

Samiksa. Journal of the Indian Psychoanalytic Society, 996

Sammlung physiologischer Abhandlungen, 1494

Sammlung sozialpsychologischer Monographien. *See* Gesellschaft; Sammlung sozialpsychologischer Monographien, 217

Sammlung von Abhandlungen aus dem Gebiete der pädagogischen Psychologie und Physiologie, 146

Sammlung von Abhandlungen zur psychologischen Pädagogik, aus dem Archiv für die gesamte Psychologie, 199

Sammlung zwangloser Abhandlungen zur Neuro- und Psychopathologie des Kindesalters, 315

San Francisco. Old Age Counseling Center. Publications, 711

Santiago. Universidad de Chile. Instituto de psicología. Archivos. *See* Chile. Universidad. Instituto de psicología. Archivos, 904

São Paulo. Serviço de assistencia a psicopatas do estado de São Paulo. Arquivos, 1811

Saturday Review of Literature, 1316

Scandinavian Scientific Review; Contributions to Philosophy, Psychology and the Science of Education by Northern Scientists, 452

School, 1243

School and Society, 1244

School Review, 1245

School Science and Mathematics, 1246

Schriften für angewandte Individualpsychologie, 365

Schriften zur angewandten Seelenkunde, 233

Schriften zur landwirtschaftlichen Arbeitsforschung auf psychologischer Grundlage, 592

Schriften zur Psychologie der Berufe und der Arbeitswissenschaft, 808

Title Index

Schriften zur Psychologie der Berufseignung und des Wirtschaftslebens, 377
Schriften zur Psychologie der Strafrechtspflege, 593
Schriften zur Psychologie und Soziologie von Sexualität und Verbrechen, 594
Schriften zur Seelenforschung, 595
Schriften zur Seelenkunde und Erziehungskunst, 430
Schriften zur Wirtschaftspsychologie und zur Arbeitswissenschaft, 712
Schriftenreihe der psychologischen Rundschau, 645
Schriftenreihe für Erziehung und Jugendpflege. *See* Psychologische Praxis; Schriftenreihe für Erziehung und Jugendpflege, 899
Schriftenreihe zur Völkerpsychologie, 912
Schulreifetest, 664
Schweizer Archiv für Neurologie und Psychiatrie, 1812
Schweizerische Gesellschaft für Psychologie und ihre Anwendungen. *See* Schweizerische Zeitschrift für Psychologie und ihre Anwendungen, 889; *and* Schweizerische Zeitschrift für Psychologie und ihre Anwendungen. Beiheft, 901
Schweizerische medizinische Wochenschrift, 1495
Schweizerische Monatsschrift für das Gesamtgebiet der modernen Psychologie. *See* Psychologische Rundschau; Schweizerische Monatsschrift für das Gesamtgebiet der modernen Psychologie, 618
Schweizerische pädagogische Schriften. Reihe: Psychologie, 809
Schweizerische Vereinigung der Freunde Coués. *See* Schweizerische Zeitschrift für angewandte Psychologie, 547; *and* Zeitschrift für angewandte Psychologie [2], 517
Schweizerische Zeitschrift für angewandte Psychologie, 547
Schweizerische Zeitschrift für Psychologie und ihre Anwendungen, 889
Schweizerische Zeitschrift für Psychologie und ihre Anwendungen. Beiheft, 901
Science, 1496
"Scientia," rivista di scienza, 1497
Scientific American, 1498
Scientific Monthly, 1499
Scientific Quarterly Dealing with Extra-Sensory Perception and Related Topics. *See* Journal of Parapsychology; A Scientific Quarterly Dealing with Extra-Sensory Perception and Related Topics, 886
Scientific Quarterly Dealing with Extra-Sensory Perception, the Psychokinetic Effect, and Related Topics. *See* Journal of Parapsychology; A Scientific Quarterly Dealing with Extra-Sensory Perception, the Psychokinetic Effect, and Related Topics, 908
Scottish Council for Research in Education. Publications, 1247
Scribner's Magazine, 1317
Sebastian Morey Otero. Laboratorio de psicopedagogía (Montevideo). Boletín. *See* Montevideo. Laboratorio de psicopedagogía Sebastian Morey Otero. Boletín, 896
Section de psychologie artistique. Mémoire. *See* Paris. Institut général psychologique. Mémoires, 210
Section de psychologie zoologique. Mémoire. *See* Paris. Institut général psychologique. Mémoires, 210
Sektor nauki narodnogo komissariata prosveschcheniia RSFSR (Moscow). *See* Pedologiia, 613
Selected Child Development Abstracts. *See* Child Development Abstracts and Bibliography, 556
Selskabet for psykisk Forskning. *See* Aarsskrift for psykisk Forskning, 323
Sendai. Tohoku Daigaku. [Tohoku University]. *See* Tohoku Psychologica Folia, 717
Sendai. Tohoku Teikoku Daigaku. Psychiatrische Klinik. Arbeiten, 1813
Sexual-probleme; Zeitschrift für Sexualwissenschaft und Sexualpolitik, 1814
Sexualpsychologie; Dokumente zur Geschichte der Sexualität, 548
Sexuelle Aufklärung der Jugend. *See* Zeitschrift für pädagogische Psychologie, Pathologie und Hygiene, 180
Shanghai. Chung-yang yen chiu yüan. Hsin li hsüeh yen chiu so [Central Research Institute. Research Institute of Psychology]. *See* Academia Sinica. National Research Institute of Psychology. Contributions, 668; *and* Academia Sinica. National Research Institute of Psychology. Monographs, 669
Shanghai. Ta-hsia ta hsüeh [Ta-hsia University]. *See* Hsin li chi Kan [Psychology Quarterly], 774

Title Index

Shinri [Psychology]. *See* Kyoto. Kyōto Daigaku. Bungakubu. Shinrigaku Kenkyūshitsu. Shinri [University of Kyoto. Faculty of Letters. Psychological Research Laboratory. Psychology], 977; *and* Kyoto. University. Faculty of Letters. Psychological Research Laboratory. Psychology. Abstracts, 1053

Shinri. Gaikatsu [Psychology. Abstracts]. *See* Kyoto. University. Faculty of Letters. Psychological Research Laboratory. Psychology. Abstracts, 1053

Shinri Kenkyū [Psychological Research], 316

Shinrigaku Kenkyū [Psychological Research], 467

Shinrigaku Kenkyū. Shin Shirīzu [Psychological Research. New Series], 549

Shriftn far Psichologye un Pedagogik. *See* Yidischer wisnaschaftlicher Institut. Psichologish-pedagogishe Sekzye. Shriftn far Psichologye un Pedagogik, 719

Sibiu (Rumania). Universitatea. Institutul de psihologie. *See* Revista de psihologie. Teoretică şi aplicată, 824

Siemens-Studien-Gesellschaft für praktische Psychologie. *See* Praktische Psychologie, 989; *and* Psychologische Hefte der Siemens-Studien Gesellschaft für praktische Psychologie e. V., 1065

Slovenska akademia vied a umeni (Bratislava). *See* Psychologický sborník. Casopis psychologickêho ũstavu SAVU, 950

Smith College. Studies in Social Work, 1139

Smith College. William Allan Neilson Research Laboratory. Studies in Psychology, 646

Social Casework, 1248

Social Forces, 1140

Social-Paedagogisk Forening for Ny Opdragelse. *See* Paedagogisk-psykologisk Tidsskrift, 865

Social Research. An International Quarterly of Political and Social Science, 1141

Social Science Abstracts, 1142

Social Science Monographs, 1143

Social Science Research Council. *See* Studies in Social Psychology in World War II, 1071

Social Science Research Council. Bulletin, 1144

Social Service Review, 1145

Sociatry. Journal of Group and Intergroup Therapy, 997

Sociedad de psicología de Buenos Aires. *See* Anales de psicología, 255; *and* Buenos Aires. Sociedad de psicología. Anales, 692; *and* Buenos Aires. Sociedad de psicología. Boletín, 633

Sociedad mexicana de psicología. *See* Psiquis; revista mexicana de higiene mental, 990

Società italiana di psichiatria. Atti, 1815

Società italiana di psicologia. *See* Rivista di psicologia [1], 302; *and* Rivista di psicologia [2], 450; *and* Rivista di psicologia applicata, 262; *and* Rivista di psicologia applicata alla pedagogia ed alla psicopatologia, 212; *and* Rivista di psicologia e rassegna di studi pedagogici e filosofici, 429; *and* Rivista di psicologia normale e patologica, 709

Società italiana di psicologia. Atti di Convegno, 290

Società medico-psicologica italiana. *See* Giornale del magnetismo ed ipnotismo, 99; *and* Ipnotismo, 117; *and* Magnetismo ed ipnotismo, 109

Societatea română de cercetări psihologice (Bucharest). Analele de psihologie, 741

Societatea română de neurologie, psichiatrie, psichologie şi endocrinologie. Bulletin. *See* Association des psychiatres roumaines. Bulletin, 435; *and* Société de neurologie, psychiatrie et psychologie de Jassy. Bulletin, 389; *and* Société roumaine de neurologie, psychiatrie, psychologie et endocrinologie. Bulletin, 479; *and* Société roumaine de neurologie, psychiatrie, psychologie et endocrinologie. Section d'endocrinologie. Bulletins et mémoires, 761

Société Alfred Binet. Psychologie de l'enfant et pédagogie expérimentale. Bulletin, 366

Société belge de neurologie. *See* Journal belge de neurologie et de psychiatrie, 699; *and* Journal de neurologie et de psychiatrie [1], 461

Société belge de psychologie. Annales. *See* Psychologica belgica. Annales de la société belge de psychologie, 949

Société clinique de médecine mentale (Paris). Bulletin, 251

Société d'anthropologie de Paris. Bulletins et mémoires, 1146

Société de médecine mentale de belgique. *See* Journal belge de neurologie et de psychiatrie, 699; *and* Journal de neurologie et de psychiatrie [1], 461

Société de médecine mentale de Belgique. Bulletin, 65

Société de neurologie, psychiatrie et psychologie de Jassy. Bulletin, 389

Title Index

Société de psychiatrie. *See* Encéphale; Journal mensuel de neurologie et de psychiatrie, 225
Société de psychiatrie de Bucarest. Bulletin, 1816
Société de psychologie physiologique. Bulletins, 86
Société de psychotherapie, d'hypnologie et de psychologie (Paris). *See* Revue de psychothérapie et de psychologie appliquée [2], 620
Société de psychothérapie (Paris). *See* Paris. École de psychologie. Bulletin, 758; *and* Revue de psychothérapie et de psychologie appliquée [1], 276
Société des magnétiseurs spiritualistes (Paris). *See* Magnétiseur spiritualiste, 41
Société du magnétisme animal. Journal, 16
Société française de philosophie (Paris). Bulletin, 1623
Société française de psychosociologie. *See* Psychosociologie, 993
Société française d'ophthalmologie. Bulletin et mémoires, 1500
Société internationale de psychagogie (et de psychothérapie). Bulletin. *See* Action et pensée, 487
Société libre pour l'étude psychologique de l'enfant. Bulletin, 155
Société lorraine de psychologie appliquée. Bulletin, 317
Société médico-psychologique. Bulletin. *See* Annales médico-psychologiques. Journal de l'aliénation mentale et de la médicine légale des aliénés, 32
Société phrénologique de Paris. Journal, 1643
Société psychanalytique de Paris. *See* Revue française de psychanalyse, 569
Société roumaine de neurologie, psychiatrie, psychologie et endocrinologie. Bulletin, 479
Société roumaine de neurologie, psychiatrie, psychologie et endocrinologie. Section d'endocrinologie. Bulletins et mémoires, 761
Société suisse de psychologie et de psychologie appliquée. *See* Schweizerische Zeitschrift für Psychologie und ihre Anwendungen, 889; *and* Schweizerische Zeitschrift für Psychologie und ihre Anwendungen. Beiheft, 901
Sociétés magnétiques de France et de l'étranger. *See* Chaine magnétique, 77
[Society for Animal Psychology. Kyoto]. *See* Dobutsu Shinri [Animal Psychology]. [2], 966
[Society for Animal Psychology. Tokyo]. *See* Dobutsu Shinri [Animal Psychology]. [1], 726; *and* Dobutsu Shinri Nenpo [Annual of Animal Psychology], 967
Society for Cultural Relations with the U.S.S.R. (London). *See* Soviet Psychology Information Bulletin, 1070
Society for Experimental Biology and Medicine. Proceedings, 1501
Society for Personnel Administration. Pamphlet Series, 849
Society for Projective Techniques and Rorschach Institute. *See* Journal of Projective Techniques, 1093; *and* Rorschach Research Exchange and Journal of Projective Techniques, 995, *and* TAT Newsletter, 956
Society for Psychical Research. Journal, 84
Society for Psychical Research. Proceedings, 79
[Society for Psychological Research. Tokyo]. *See* Shinri Kenkyū. [Psychological Research], 316
Society for Research in Child Development. *See* Child Development, 634; *and* Child Development Abstracts and Bibliography, 556
Society for Research in Child Development. Monographs, 762
Society for Research in Child Development. Proceedings, 742
[Society for Research in Educational Psychology]. *See* Kyoiku Shinri [Educational Psychology], 735
Society for the Psychological Study of Social Issues. Bulletin, 787
Society for the Psychological Study of Social Issues. Yearbook, 850
Society of Integrative Psychology (Cairo, Egypt). *See* Egyptian Journal of Psychology, 915
Sociological Papers, 1147
Sociological Review, 1148
Sociologus. Zeitschrift für Völkerpsychologie und Soziologie, 683
Sociologus. Zeitschrift für Völkerpsychologie und Soziologie. Beiheft, 713
Sociology and Social Research, 1149
Sociometric Review, 788
Sociometry: A Journal of Inter-personal Relations, 810
Sociometry Monographs, 880
Soldatentum. Zeitschrift für Wehrpsychologie, Wehrerziehung, Menschenauslese, 743

Title Index

Sorbonne (Paris). Laboratoire de psychologie physiologique. *See* Année psychologique, 119; *and* Paris. Sorbonne. Laboratoire de psychologie physiologique. Travaux, 118

South African Council for Scientific and Industrial Research. National Institute for Personnel Research. Bulletin. *See* Johannesburg. South African Council for Scientific and Industrial Research. National Institute for Personnel Research. Bulletin, 1017

South African Journal of Psychology and Education. *See* S.-A. tydskrif vir sielkunde en opvoedkunde, 710

South African Psychological Association. Proceedings, 1105

South African Psychological Review, 955

Southern California Educational Research Association. *See* Educational Measurement Review, 492

Southern California. University. Psychological Laboratory. Reports, 1106

Sovetskaia nevropsikhiatriia; Sbornik trudov, 1817

Sovetskaia pedagogika, 1249

Sovetskaia psikhonevrologiia, 665

Sovetskaia psikhotekhnika, 684

Sovetskoe meditsinskoe obozrenie: nevropatologiia i psikhiatriia, 1818

Soviet Psychology Information Bulletin, 1070

Sovremennaia psikhiatriia, 1819

Sovremennaia psikhonevrologiia, 514

Sozialpsychologische Forschungen [1], 431

Sozialpsychologische Forschungen [2]. *See* Karlsruhe. Technische Hochschule. Institut für Sozialpsychologie. Sozialpsychologische Forschungen, 443

Spain. Consejo superior de investigaciónes científícas. Instituto Santiago Ramón y Cajal. Trabajos, 1502

Speech Monographs, 1325

Sphinx. Neues Archiv für den thierischen Magnetismus, 20

Sprachpsychologische Untersuchungen, 744

Spring, 881

Sredne-aziatskii gosudarstvennyi universitet (Tashkent). *See* Tashkent. Universitet. Trudy. Seriia lc. Psikhologiia, 622

SSSR. Tsentral'naia mezhduvedomstvennaia komissia (Moscow). *See* Pedologiia, 613

St. Petersburg. Obshchestvo psikhiatrov i nevropatologov. *See* Psikhiatriia, nevrologiia i eksperimental'naia psikhologiia, 448

St. Petersburg. Psikhonevrologicheskii institut. *See* Vestnik psikhologii, kriminal'noi antropologii i gipnotizma, 202; *and* Vestnik psikhologii, kriminal'noi antropologii i pedologii, 305

St. Petersburg. S.-Peterburgskoe filosofskoe obshchestvo. *See* Voprosy filosofii i psikhologii, 98

Staatliches Forschungsinstitut für Psychologie. *See* Leipzig. Sächsische staatliche Forschungsinstitute. Forschungsinstitut für Psychologie. Abhandlungen, 423; *and* Leipzig. Sächsische staatliche Forschungsinstitute. Forschungsinstitut für Psychologie. Veröffentlichungen, 352

Stanford University. Psychological Laboratory. Minor Studies. *See* American Journal of Psychology, 90

Stanford University. Publications. Psychical Research Monographs, 367

Stanford University. Publications. University Series. Education and Psychology, 714

State Normal Monthly, 1250

Statistical Methodology Reviews, 715

Stockholm. Högskola. Psykotekniska Institutet. *See* Praktisk Psykologi, 947

Student Personnel Work. *See* American Council on Education. Studies. Series VI: Student Personnel Work, 828

Studi e ricerche di psicologia. *See* Florence. Università. Istituto di psicologia. Studi e ricerche di psicologia, 816

Studia Psychologica et Paedagogica. Series Altera. Investigationes, 998

Studii și cercetări psihologice. *See* Cluj (Rumania). Universitătea. Institutul de psihologie experimentală, comparată și aplicată. Studii și cercetări psihologice, 604

Studien aus dem Gebiete der Psychotherapie, Psychologie und Pädagogik. *See* Zeitschrift für Individualpsychologie. Studien aus dem Gebiete der Psychotherapie, Psychologie und Pädagogik, 337

Studien aus den C. G. Jung Institut (Zurich). *See* Zurich. C. G. Jung Institut. Studien, 1078

Title Index

Studien über Aufbau und Führung des Charakters und des religiösen Lebens. *See* Religionspsychologische Reihe; Studien über Aufbau und Führung des Charakters und des religiösen Lebens, 642

Studien über Spielgaben und Lernspiele. *See* Zeitschrift für pädagogische Psychologie, experimentelle Pädagogik und jugendkundliche Forschung, 519

Studien zur psychologischen Ästhetik und Kunstpsychologie mit pädagogischen Anwendungen, 621

Studies in Abnormal Psychology. *See* Journal of Abnormal Psychology, 219

Studies in Cerebral Function. *See* California. University of California at Los Angeles. Publications in Education, Philosophy and Psychology, 693

Studies in Character. *See* Iowa. University. Studies in Character, 559

Studies in Child Welfare. *See* Iowa. University. Studies in Child Welfare, 399

Studies in Clinical Psychology. *See* Iowa. University. Studies in Psychology, 140; *and* Psychological Monographs, 275

[Studies in Education]. *See* Chiao yü yen Chiu [Studies in Education], 576

Studies in Education . . . Devoted to Child Study and the History of Education, 1251

[Studies in Educational Psychology]. *See* Chiao yü hsin li yen Chiu [Studies in Educational Psychology], 854

Studies in Educational Psychology and Educational Measurement. *See* Harvard Monographs in Education. Studies in Educational Psychology and Educational Measurement, 439

Studies in Emotional Adjustment. *See* Iowa. University. Studies in Child Welfare, 399

Studies in Experimental and Theoretical Psychology. *See* Iowa. University. Studies in Psychology, 140

Studies in General Psychology. *See* Iowa. University. Studies in Psychology, 140; *and* Psychological Monographs, 275

Studies in Infant Behavior. *See* Iowa. University. Studies in Child Welfare, 399

Studies in Language Behavior. *See* Iowa. University. Studies in Psychology, 140

Studies in Linguistic Psychology, 303

Studies in Mental Inefficiency, 409

Studies in Philosophy and Psychology. *See* Johns Hopkins University. Studies in Philosophy and Psychology, 243

Studies in Philosophy and Social Science, 1624

Studies in Preschool Education. *See* Iowa. University. Studies in Child Welfare, 399

Studies in Psychology and Psychiatry. *See* Catholic University of America. Studies in Psychology and Psychiatry, 524

Studies in Psychology of Reading. *See* Iowa. University. Studies in Psychology, 140; *and* Psychological Monographs, 275

Studies in Social Eugenics, 716

Studies in Social Psychology in World War II, 1071

Studies in the Psychology of Art. *See* Iowa. University. Studies in Psychology, 140; *and* Psychological Monographs, 275

Studies in the Psychology of Learning. *See* Iowa. University. Educational Psychology Series, 698

Studies in the Psychology of Music. *See* Iowa. University. Studies in the Psychology of Music, 677

Studies in the Psychology of the Deaf. *See* Psychological Monographs, 275

Studies in Topological and Vector Psychology. *See* Iowa. University. Studies in Child Welfare, 399

Studies towards the Integration of the Social Sciences. *See* Human Relations. A Quarterly Journal of Studies towards the Integration of the Social Sciences, 971

Studievereniging voor "psychical research." *See* Tijdschrift voor parapsychologie. Gewijd aan de studie van het occultisme in zijn vollen omvang, 596

Suid-Afrikaanse sielkundige vereniging. Verrigtings. *See* South African Psychological Association. Proceedings, 1105

Suid-Afrikaanse tydskrif vir sielkunde en opvoedkunde. *See* S.-A. tydskrif vir sielkunde en opvoedkunde, 710

[Sun Yat-sen University. Canton]. *See* Chiao yü yen Chiu. [Studies in Education], 576; *and* Canton. Sun Yat-sen University. Institute of Educational Research. Psychological Laboratory Studies. Series A, 670

Title Index

Suomalainen Tiedeakatemia. Toimituksia. Annales. Series B, 1503
Suomen Psykologinen Seyra. *See* Nordisk Psykologi, 1057
Supplementary Educational Monographs, 368
Survey, 1150
Svenska Psykologsamfundet. *See* Nordisk Psykologi, 1057
Svenskt Arkiv för Pedagogik, 318
Swedish Journal of Philosophy and Psychology. *See* Theoria; A Swedish Journal of Philosophy and Psychology, 763
Sydney. University. Reprints of Papers Contributed to Scientific Journals, 123
Sydney. University. University Reprints. Series 12. Social Science. Economics, Education, History, Philosophy and Psychology, 480
Symposion; Philosophische Zeitschrift für Forschung und Aussprache, 1625
Synthesis. Sammlung historischer Monographien philosophischer Begriffe, 1626

Ta-hsia ta hsüeh [Ta-hsia University, Shanghai]. *See* Hsin li chi Kan [Psychology Quarterly], 774
Tashkent. Universitet. Trudy. Seriia lc. Psikhologiia, 622
TAT Newsletter, 956
Tavistock Institute of Human Relations. *See* Human Relations. A Quarterly Journal of Studies towards the Integration of the Social Sciences, 971
Teachers Association of Palestine. *See* ha-Hinuch. Yarhon Pedagog' la-Morim ve-la-horim, 496
Teachers College. Child Development Institute. Child Development Monographs. *See* Columbia University. Teachers College. Child Development Institute. Child Development Monographs, 605
Teachers College Journal, 1252
Teachers College Record, 1253
Tel-Aviv. Histadrut ha-Morim be-Erets Yisrael. *See* ha-Hinuch. Yarhon Pedagog' la-Morim ve-la-horim, 496
Test Method Help. *See* World Book Company. Department of Research and Test Service. Test Method Help, 648
Test Service Bulletin [1], 647
Test Service Bulletin [2]. *See* World Book Company. Division of Test Research and Service. Test Service Bulletin, 626
Test Service Notebook. *See* World Book Company. Division of Test Research and Service. Test Service Notebook, 626
Tetsugaku kenkyu [Philosophical Studies], 1627
Texas Personnel Review, 1536
Thematic Apperception Test. *See* TAT. Newsletter, 956
Theoria: A Swedish Journal of Philosophy and Psychology, 763
Tidskrift för filosofi och psykologi. *See* Theoria; A Swedish Journal of Philosophy and Psychology, 763
Tidskrift för psykologi och pedagogik, 890
Tidskrift för psykologisk Forskning. *See* Psyke. Tidskrift för psykologisk Forskning, 222
Tidskrift för psykologisk och pedagogisk forskning, 623
Tidskriften Psykes Monografiserie. *See* Psyke. Tidskrift. Tidskriften Psykes Monografiserie, 261
Tidsskrift for anvendt Psykologi. *See* Psykologien og Erhvervslivet; Tidsskrift for anvendt Psykologi, 888
Tidsskrift for nordisk retsmedicin og psykiatri, 1820
Tidsskrift for phrenologien, 1644
Tidsskrift for phrenologien. Supplement, 1645
Tidsskrift for Racebiologi, Racepsykologi og Racehygiene. *See* Nordiske Race. Tidsskrift for Racebiologi, Racepsykologi og Racehygiene, 404
Tierseele. Zeitschrift für vergleichende Seelenkunde, 319
Tiflis. Institut psikhologii. Trudy. *See* Akademiia nauk Gruzinskoe SSR (Tiflis). Institut psikhologii. Trudy, 882
Tijdschrift voor jeugdpsychoïogie, voorlichting bij beroepskeuze en beroepsvorming. *See* Jeugd en beroep. Tijdschrift voor jeugdpsychologie, voorlichting bij beroepskeuze en beroepsvorming, 584

Title Index

Turin. Università. Istituto di psicologia sperimentale. *See* Archivio italiano di psicologia, 392; *and* Rivista di psicologia [1], 302; *and* Rivista di psicologia [2], 450; *and* Rivista di psicologia applicata, 262; *and* Rivista di psicologia applicata alla pedagogia ed alla psicopatologia, 212; *and* Rivista di psicologia e rassegna di studi pedagogici e filosofici, 429; *and* Rivista di psicologia normale e patologica, 709

Turkestanskii gosudarstvennyi universitet (Tashkent). *See* Tashkent. Universitet. Trudy. Seriia 1c. Psikhologiia, 622

Ukrainskaia psikhonevrologicheskaia akademiia (Kharkov). Trudy. *See* Kharkov. Vseukrainskaia psikhonevrologicheskaia akademiia. Trudy, 754

Ukrainskii nauchno-issledovatel'skii institut pedagogiki (Kharkov). *See* Ukrains'kyi visnyk eksperymental'noi pedagogiky ta refleksologii, 570; *and* Ukrains'kyi visnyk refleksologii ta eksperymental'noi pedagogiky, 515; *and* Za Markso-Lenins'ku pedagogiku, 667

Ukrainskii psikhonevrologicheskii institut (Kharkov). Trudy. *See* Kharkov. Ukrainskii psikhonevrologicheskii institut. Trudy, 529

Ukrainskii SSR. Narodnyi komitet zdravookhraneniia (Kiev). *See* Sovetskaia psikhonevrologiia, 665; *and* Sovremennaia psikhonevrologiia, 514

Ukrains'kyi visnyk eksperymental'noi pedagogiky ta refleksologii, 570

Ukrains'kyi visnyk refleksologii ta eksperymental'noi pedagogiky, 515

Umschau, 1319

Understanding the Child. A Magazine for Teachers, 666

Ungarische Zeitschrift für Psychologie. *See* Magyar Psychológiai Szemle, 588

Ungraded, 1256

United Kingdom. Ophthalmological Societies. Transactions, 1504

United States. Air Force. Air Training Command. Training Analysis and Development. Informational Bulletin, 1107

United States. Army Air Forces. Aviation Psychology Program. Research Reports, 999

United States. Army Air Forces. Office of the Air Surgeon. Medical Research Division. Psychology Section. *See* Aviation Psychology Abstract Series, 884

United States. Office of Education. Bulletin, 1257

United States. Public Health Service. National Institute of Mental Health. Mental Health Series, 1034

United States. Public Health Service. (Washington, D.C.). Publication. *See* Research Conference on Psychosurgery. Proceedings, 1069

United States. Surgeon General's Office. Neuropsychiatry Consultant's Division. Clinical Psychology Branch. Bulletin. *See* Bulletin of Military Clinical Psychologists, 935

Universitaire bibliotheek voor psychologie, 1035

Untersuchungen zur Handlungs- und Affekt-Psychologie. *See* Psychologische Forschung; Zeitschrift für Psychologie und ihre Grenzwissenschaften, 428

Untersuchungen zur Lehre von der Gestalt. *See* Psychologische Forschung; Zeitschrift für Psychologie und ihre Grenzwissenschaften, 428

Untersuchungen zur Psychologie, Philosophie und Pädagogik, 481

Untersuchungen zur Psychologie und Philosophie, 277

Uppsala. Institutet för psykologisk Forskning. Meddelanden, 278

Ural'skaia oblastnaia psikhiatricheskaia lechebnitsa (Perm). Trudy. *See* Perm. Ural'skaia oblastnaia psikhiatricheskaia lechebnitsa. Trudy, 641

Ural'skii nauchno-issledovatel'skii psikhonevrologicheskii institut (Perm). Trudy. *See* Perm. Ural'skii nauchno-iddledovatel'skii psikhonevrologicheskii institut. Trudy, 737

Utrecht. Rijksuniversiteit. Psychiatrisch-neurolgische Kliniek. Onderzoekingen, 1822

Utrecht. Rijksuniversiteit. Psychologisch laboratorium. Mededeelingen, 482

Valencia. Escuela especial de orientación aprovechamiento del ercmo. Ayuntamiento. *See* Revista de psicología y pedagogía aplicadas, 1102

Vassar College. Psychological Laboratory. Studies. *See* American Journal of Psychology, 90

Verein für freie psychoanalytische Forschung. Schriften, 304

Verein für Individualpsychologie. Schriften, 335

Title Index

Title Index

Title Index

Title Index

Title Index

Zentralblatt für Graphologie. *See* Zeitschrift für Menschenkunde. Blätter für Charakterologie und Zentralblatt für Graphologie, 768; *and* Zeitschrift für Menschenkunde und Zentralblatt für Graphologie, 790

Zentralblatt für Naturwissenschaften und Anthropologie, 46

Zentralblatt für Nervenheilkunde, Psychiatrie und gerichtliche Psychopathologie, 76

Zentralblatt für Nervenheilkunde und Psychiatrie. Internationale Monatsschrift für die gesamte Neurologie in Wissenschaft und Praxis mit besonderer Berücksichtigung der Degenerations-Anthropologie, 105

Zentralblatt für Physiologie, 1520

Zentralblatt für Psychoanalyse. Medizinische Monatsschrift für Seelenkunde, 283

Zentralblatt für Psychoanalyse und Psychotherapie. Medizinische Monatsschrift für Seelenkunde, 322

Zentralblatt für Psychologie und psychologische Pädagogik, 340

Zentralblatt für Psychotherapie und ihre Grenzgebiete einschliesslich der medizinischen Psychologie und psychischen Hygiene, 649

Zentralblatt für Psychotherapie und ihre Grenzgebiete einschliesslich der medizinischen Psychologie und psychischen Hygiene. Beihefte, 791

Zentralblatt für Psychotherapie und ihre Grenzgebiete einschliesslich der medizinischen Psychologie und psychischen Hygiene. Sonderheft, 872

Zhurnal nevropatalogiia i psikhiatrii, 1831

Zhurnal posviashchennyi voprosam' psikhiatrii, nervnoi patologii, fiziologicheskoi psikhologii, nervno-psikhicheskoi gigieny i pr. *See* Voprosy nervno-psikhicheskoi meditsiny. Zhurnal posviashchennyi voprosam' psikhiatrii, nervnoi patologii, fiziologicheskoi psikhologii, nervno-psikhicheskoi gigieny i pr, 136

Zhurnal psikho-grafologii, 185

Zhurnal psikhologii, nevrologii i psikhiatrii, 454

Zhurnal psikhologii, pedologii i psikhotekhniki. Seriia A. Psikhologiia, 599

Zhurnal psikhologii, pedologii i psikhotekhniki. Seriia B. Pedologii, 600

Zhurnal psikhologii, pedologii i psikhotekhniki. Seriia V. Psikhofiziologiia truda i psikhotekhnika, 601

Zoist; A Journal of Cerebral Physiology and Mesmerism, and Their Applications to Human Welfare, 35

Zoopsikhologicheskaia laboratoriia. Gosudarstvennyi Darvinskii muzei (Moscow). *See* Moscow. Gosudarstvennyi Darvinskii muzei. Zoopsikhologicheskaia laboratoriia. Otchet, 331; *and* Moscow. Gosudarstvennyi Darvinskii muzei. Zoopsikhologicheskaia laboratoriia. Trudy, 465

Zurich. C. G. Jung Institut. Studien, 1078

Zurich. Psychologischer Club. Jahrbuch. *See* Aus dem Jahresbericht, 690

Zurich. Universität. Psychologisches Institut. Veröffentlichungen, 411

Związek nauczycielstwa polskiego (Warsaw). *See* Psychologia wychowawcza, 822

Zydowski instytut naukowy (Vila). *See* Yidischer wisnaschaftlicher Institut. Psichologish-pedagogishe Sekzye. Shriftn far Psichologye un Pedagogik, 719

Name Index

This index provides entry numbers for the monograph authors and series editors associated with the publications included in the main body of the Bibliography. Names of monograph authors are followed immediately by the relevant entry numbers. Names of editors are followed by an editorial designation and relevant entry numbers with an indication as to whether editorship was primary or associate.

Name Index

Anderson, John Edward, ed., *primary:* 196, 346, 501, 516, 564, 634, 762; *assoc.:* 438, 505, 526, 556, 796, 1080
Anderson, L. Dewey, 215
Anderson, Lewis O., 438
Anderson, Margaret M., 270
Anderson, Meta, ed., *assoc.:* 851
Anderson, Oscar Daniel, 438, 846
Anderson, R. L., ed., *assoc.:* 785
Anderson, Rose G., 215
André-Thomas, A., 229
André-Thomas, A., ed., *assoc.:* 225, 415, 493, 558
Andreas Salome, Lou, 217
Andress, James Mace, ed., *primary:* 666
Andress, Judith, ed., *primary:* 666
Andrew, Gwen, 438
Andrews, Elizabeth Gordon, 559
Andrews, Tom Gaylord, 1028
Anfimov, Ia. A., ed., *primary:* 363
Angell, Frank, ed., *assoc.:* 90, 585
Angell, James Rowland, 126, 275, 660
Angell, James Rowland, ed., *primary:* 126, 246, 270, 275; *assoc.:* 122
Angell, Robert, ed., *assoc.:* 921
Angier, Roswell P., 275
Angier, Roswell P., ed., *primary:* 213; *assoc.:* 122
Anglade, D., ed., *assoc.:* 32, 493, 558
Angyal, Andreas, 423, 538
Ansbacher, Heinz L., 215, 1028
Ansbacher, Heinz L., ed., *primary:* 568
Anschütz, Georg, 199, 578
Antheaume, André, ed., *primary:* 216, 218, 225, 415, 493, 497, 558
Antona, Emilio, ed., *assoc.:* 900
Antonelli, Carlos, ed., *assoc.:* 970
Antonini, Giuseppe, ed., *primary:* 412; *assoc.:* 391
Antonius, Otto, ed., *primary:* 812
Antonov, Aleksandr Nikolaevich, 762
Anwander, Anton, 433
Appel, Elsbeth, 324
Appell, P., ed., *assoc.:* 163
Appley, Lawrence Asa, 849
Arantigui, Malaquias Gil. *See* Gil Arantigui, Malaquias
Arbitman, Herman D., 1074
Archer, R. L. [Richard Lawrence?], ed., *assoc.:* 459, 653
Archevêque, Paul L', 841
Archibald, O. W., ed., *primary:* 72
Arco, George, Graf von, 444
Arensberg, Conrad M., 526
Argelander, Annelies, 498, 513
Argelander, Annelies, ed., *primary:* 498
Arias Belarmino Rodriguez. *See* Rodriguez Arias, Belarmino

Arlitt, Ada Hart, 275
Arluck, Edward Wiltcher, 215
Armitage, Stewart G., 275
Armstrong, Andrew Campbell, ed., *assoc.:* 122
Armstrong, J. T., ed., *primary:* 72
Armstrong-Jones, Robert, 472
Arnold, Felix, 203, 205
Arnold, J. W. S., ed., *primary:* 69
Arnold, Richard, 377
Arps, George F., 275
Arrington, Marion Graves, 438
Arrington, Ruth E., 275, 605
Arroyo C., Enriqueta, 943
Arsonval, Arsène [?] d', ed., *assoc.:* 163, 210
Artemov, Vladimir Alekseevich, ed., *primary:* 599; *assoc.:* 614
Ås, Arvid, ed., *primary:* 972
Asatian, M. M., ed., *assoc.:* 273
Asch, Solomon E., 215, 526
Asch, Solomon E., *assoc.:* 802
Aschaffenburg, Gustav, ed., *primary:* 194, 536
Ascham, Roger, 85
Ash, Isaac Emery, 215
Ashbaugh, Ernest J., 421
Ashbaugh, Ernest J., *primary:* 400
Asher, Ollie, 373
Asmus, Karl, 425
Asnaourow, Felix, 304
Asnaourow, Felix, ed., *assoc.:* 751
Aspelin, Gunnar, ed., *primary:* 763
Assagioli, Roberto G., ed., *primary:* 283, 301; *assoc.:* 273
Astell, Louis A., 373
Aster, Ernst von, 211
Astor, Frank, 745
Astvatsaturov, M. I., ed., *primary:* 539
Ataka, K., ed., *primary:* 734
Atchley, Dana W., ed., *assoc.:* 845, 846
Atkins, Ruth Ellen, 564
Aub, Joseph C., 762
Aubert, Hermann, ed., *assoc.:* 104
Augustinus, Aurelius, *Sanktus*, 548
Aveling, Francis, 300
Aveling, Francis, ed., *assoc.:* 394, 724
Avery, George T., 526
Axel, Robert, 215
Ayres, Leonard Porter, ed., *primary:* 400
Aznaurov', F. M., ed., *assoc.:* 273
Azoy Castane, Adolfo, 1043

Baade, Walter, 230
Baar, Edeltrud, 513
Babcock, Harriet, 215
Babinski, Joseph, ed., *assoc.:* 163, 276
Bach, George R., 275

Name Index

Name Index

Dearborn, George Van Ness, 120, 126, 270, 275

Dearborn, Walter Fenno, 203, 205, 215, 439, 660, 762

Dearborn, Walter Fenno, ed., *primary:* 439, 666

DeCamp, J. Edgar, 275

DeCillis, Olga Elena, 215

Decroly, Ovid, 490

Decsi, Emerich, 444

Deemer, Walter L., Jr., 999

Defoe, Daniel, 543

Defrenne, Louise, 979

Degan, James W., 892

Degardin, E., 978

Dejerine, (Mme.) ———, ed., *assoc.:* 225, 415, 493, 558

Dejerine, Joseph Jules, ed., *primary:* 225; *assoc.:* 225

Del Torto, John, 910

Del Torto, Olinto, ed., *primary:* 99, 109, 117

Delage, Yves, ed., *assoc.:* 163, 210

Delahaye, Karl, 433

Delasiauve, Louis J. F., ed., *primary:* 55

Delay, Jean, ed., *primary:* 190, 558, 1012, 1089, 1092; *assoc.:* 32

Delboeuf, Joseph Remi Leopold, ed., *assoc.:* 90

Delgado, Honorio, 1084

Delgado, Honorio, ed., *assoc.:* 499

Dell, Floyd, 676

Delmas, François Achille. *See* Achille-Delmas, François

Delmas-Marsalet, P., ed., *assoc.:* 32, 558

Demay, ———, ed., *assoc.:* 32

Dembo, Tamara, 399

Dembo, Tamara, ed., *assoc.:* 921

DeMonchy, S. J. R., ed., *assoc.:* 397

Dempf, A., ed., *primary:* 1000

Dennis, Wayne, 526, 965

Dennis, Wayne, ed., *primary:* 965

Denny-Brown, D., ed., *primary:* 817, 907; *assoc.:* 907

Deny, G., ed., *assoc.:* 225, 415

Deplazes, Gion., 1039

Derber, M., ed., *primary:* 1016, 1050

Dercum, F. X., ed., *primary:* 73; *assoc.:* 73

Deri, Susan, ed., *assoc.:* 995, 1093

Desai, Maheshchandra Maneklal, 285

Despert, J. Louise, 526

Despert, J. Louise, ed., *assoc.:* 878, 975

Dessoir, Max, 92, 260

Dessoir, Max, ed., *assoc.:* 671, 672, 724

Deuchler, Gustav, ed., *primary:* 180, 230, 321

Deuss, B., ed., *primary:* 547

Deutsch, Helene, 417, 476

Deutsch, Helene, ed., *primary:* 680; *assoc.:* 397, 836

Deutschberger, Paul, 880

Deutschberger, Paul, ed., *assoc.:* 810

Deutsche, Jean Marquis, 564

Deuzing, Hans, 498

Deventer, Ch. M. van, ed., *primary:* 105, 234

Devereux, George, 778

Devereux, George, ed., *assoc.:* 837, 906, 941

Devine, Henry, ed., *primary:* 50; *assoc.:* 401

DeVinney, Leland C., 1071

DeVinney, Leland C., ed., *primary:* 1071

Devlin, William J. (S.J.), 524

Dewey, Doris M., 526

Dewey, John, ed., *primary:* 637; *assoc.:* 122, 637, 810

Dexter, Edwin Grant, 120, 126

Diamond, Florence, ed., *primary:* 1093

Diamond, Solomon, 215

Diaz Molano, Elias, ed., *primary:* 874

Diaz Valdepares, Julian, ed., *primary:* 937

Dick, Lillian, ed., *assoc.:* 797

Dicks, Henry Victor, 730

Dicks, Russell L., ed., *assoc.:* 1098

Dickson, Gwendolen S., 1037

Dieck, Herman, 377

Dieffenbacher, Julius, 291

Dienel, H. F., 916

Diepenhorst, Isaac Arend, 662

Dietrich, Werner, 538

Dillingham, Louise Bulkley, 275

DiMattia, A. L., 916

Dimock, Hedley S., 676

Dimpfel, Rudolf A., ed., *primary:* 393

Dingwall, Eric John, 543

Disher, Dorothy Rose, 447

Dixon, Edward T., 567

Dixon, R. F., ed., *assoc.:* 528

Dobrzyńska-Rybicka, Ludwika, 426

Dockeray, Floyd Carlton, 447

Dodd, Stuart C., ed., *assoc.:* 810

Dodge, Arthur F., ed., *assoc.:* 702

Dodge, Clayton T. J., ed., *assoc.:* 556

Dodge, Raymond, 126, 275

Dodge, Raymond, ed., *primary:* 275; *assoc.:* 90, 122, 585

Does, J. C. van der, 706

Does, L. P. van der, Jr., 706

Doevenspeck, Heinrich, 377

Döhl, Ilse, 791

Doležal, Jan, 423, 538

Doll, Edgar A., 275, 336, 447

Doll, Edgar A., ed., *assoc.:* 796, 891

Dollard, John, ed., *assoc.:* 499, 992

Name Index

Durkin, Helen E., 215
Durost, Walter N., 526, 648
Durost, Walter N., ed., *primary*: 626, 627, 648
Dürr, Ernst, 260
Durville, Henri, ed., *primary*: 269
Duszyńska, Boleslawa, 426
Dybowski, Mieczyslaw, 426
Dyer, Clara A., 368
Dyke, Charles Bartlett, 120
Dyroff, Adolf, ed., *assoc.*: 325, 603
Dzendolet, E., 916
Dziembowska, Anna, 426

Eagleson, Helen E., 438
Earle, Frank Maynard, 383, 533
East, W. Norwood, 472, 662
Eaton, Amerette G., 693
Eaton, Merrill T., ed., *primary*: 327
Ebaugh, Franklin G., ed., *assoc.*: 995
Ebbe, Thorleif Schjelderup. *See* Schjelderup-Ebbe, Thorleif
Ebbinghaus, Hermann, 375
Ebbinghaus, Hermann, ed., *primary*: 104, 167, 223, 236, 260
Ebeltoft, Arne, ed., *primary*: 972
Eberhardt, Margarete, 306
Ebert, Elizabeth, 762
Ebert, Ernst Hermann, 199
Eby, Kermit, ed., *assoc.*: 921
Eccles, W. McAdam, 697
Eckle, Christian, 767
Eckoff, William J., 120
Ecob, Katherine G., ed., *assoc.*: 796
Edelston, Harry, 526
Eder, Montague David, 274
Edgell, Beatrice, ed., *primary*: 330; *assoc.*: 188, 394
Edgerton, Harold Asahel, 270
Edlund, Sven, 998
Edmonson, James B., 458
Edson, Newell W., 676
Edwards, Allen L., ed., *assoc.*: 499
Edwards, Austin S., ed., *primary*: 938
Edwards, Florence Marjory, 697, 730
Edwards, Isaac Newton, ed., *primary*: 368
Edwards, Lyford, ed., *assoc.*: 788
Edwards, Violet, ed., *assoc.*: 787, 921
Egan, J. P., 916
Eggert, Bruno, 146
Ehrenfels, Christian von, 160
Ehrhardt, Adolf, 423, 538
Ehrler, Fritz, 423, 538
Eichler, Oskar, 470
Eidelberg, Ludwig, 229
Eisenberg, Philip, 215
Eisenberg, Philip, ed., *assoc.*: 802

Eisenhardt, Louise, ed., *primary*: 378
Eisenson, Jon, 215
Eiserer, Paul E., 526
Eisler, Edwin R., ed., *assoc.*: 397
Eissler, Ruth S., ed., *primary*: 927
Eitingon, Max, ed., *primary*: 398; *assoc.*: 397, 398, 836
Eitzen, David D., ed., *assoc.*: 1098
Ekdahl, Adolph Gustavus, 526
Ekman, Gösta, ed., *primary*: 1057
Ekstein, Rudolf, ed., *assoc.*: 777
El Koussy, Abdel Aziz Hamid. *See* Koussy, Abdel Aziz Hamid El
Elder, James H., 438
Elder, James H., ed., *assoc.*: 921
Eliasberg, Wladimir, 356, 377
Eliasberg, Wladimir, ed., *primary*: 521, 572; *assoc.*: 941
Eliot, Abigail A., 526
Eliot, Martha M., ed., *assoc.*: 556
Eliot, Ruth M., ed., *primary*: 516
Elkind, Henry B., ed., *primary*: 666
Elkisch, Paula, 275
Elkus, Savilla Alice, 205
Elliott, A. Marshall, 85
Elliott, Frank R., 215
Elliott, Merle Hugh, 267
Ellis, Albert, 275, 526
Ellis, Havelock, 326
Ellis, Havelock, ed., *assoc.*: 637, 671, 672, 724
Ellis, William J., ed., *assoc.*: 851
Elmgren, John, ed., *primary*: 763
Elonen, Anna S., 1028
Elster, Günter, ed., *primary*: 939
Elton, P. M., 383
Emden, Jan Egbert Gustaaf van, ed., *assoc.*: 397, 398
Emerson, Lynn A., ed., *primary*: 702
Emmert, Beverly, ed., *primary*: 879
Emmett, W. G., ed., *assoc.*: 963
Endara, Julio, ed., *assoc.*: 617
Endicott, Frank S., ed., *assoc.*: 702
Eng, Helga, 291, 356
Engelhart, Max D., 373
Engelhart, Max D., ed., *assoc.*: 785
Englert, Othmar, 773
Englhauser, Johann, 433
English, Horace B., ed., *assoc.*: 753, 787
English, O. Spurgeon, 745
English, O. Spurgeon, ed., *assoc.*: 397
Enke, Elizabeth, ed., *assoc.*: 671, 672, 724
Enke, Willi, ed., *assoc.*: 671, 672
Enneis, James M., 910
Enneis, James M., ed., *primary*: 1090
Eppelbaum, Vera (Strasser). *See* Strasser-Eppelbaum, Vera

Name Index

Hebb, Donald O., ed., *primary*: 853; *assoc.*:
920, 964
Heberer, Gerhard, 495
Heckel, Richard, 571
Hecker, Walther, 538
Hector, Heinz, 901
Hediger, H., ed., *primary*: 962, 1082
Hedlun, J. M., 916
Hedrick, Blanche E., 399
Hefferline, Ralph Franklin, 526
Hegge, Thorleif G., 236
Hegge, Thorleif G., ed., *assoc.*: 617, 851
Heidbreder, Edna, 215
Heidbreder, Edna, ed., *assoc.*: 499, 1028,
1099
Heidenhain, Adolf, 160
Heider, Fritz, 275, 646
Heider, Grace Moore, 275, 306, 646
Heider, Werner, 835
Heijden, Ph. M. van der, 994
Heijden, Ph. M. van der, ed., *primary*: 994,
1030
Heilbronner, Karl, 160
Heiliger, Louise, 399
Heilman, Jacob Daniel, 176
Heindl, Robert, ed., *assoc.*: 671, 672, 724
Heiney, Adelia Boynton, 526
Heinitz, Wilhelm, 377
Heinlein, Julia Heil, 438
Heinrich, Richard, 481
Heinrich, Władysław, ed., *primary*: 530
Heise, G. A., 916
Heiser, Florien, 215
Heiss, Alfred, 423, 538
Heitsch, Lenore, 356
Helasvuo, Kaarlo, ed., *primary*: 1057
Held, Omar C., 270
Helfenberger, Alfons, 578
Heller, Walter S., 267
Hellmuth, Hermine von Hug. *See* Hug-
Hellmuth, Hermine von
Hellpach, Willy Hugo, 160, 217, 443, 912
Hellpach, Willy Hugo, ed., *primary*: 443, 912
Hellwald, Friedrich von, 92
Helmholtz, Hermann von, ed., *assoc.*: 104
Helson, Harry, ed., *assoc.*: 90
Hemm, Ludwig, 767
Henderson, Ernest Norton, 120, 126
Henderson, W. R., ed., *assoc.*: 907
Hendrick, Ives, ed., *assoc.*: 397
Hendrix, S. Gertrude, 373
Hendry, Charles E., 910
Hénin de Cuvillers, Étienne Félix, *Baron* d',
ed., *primary*: 18
Henle, Mary, 727
Henley, Eugene M., 215
Henmon, Vivian Allen Charles, 203, 205, 215,
660

Henmon, Vivian Allen Charles, ed., *assoc.*:
420
Henneman, Richard Hubbard, 215
Hennig, Richard, 107
Henning, Hans, 377
Henning, Hans, ed., *assoc.*: 223
Henri, Victor, 149
Henri, Victor, ed., *primary*: 119; *assoc.*: 90
Henriquez, Guillermina Kunz. *See* Kunz-
Henriquez, Guillermina
Henriquez, S. Colombino. *See* Colombino
Henriquez, S.
Henry, Charles, 210
Henry, Charles Eric, 762
Henry, Jules, 792
Henry, Jules, ed., *primary*: 632; *assoc.*: 632
Henry, Lyle K., 698
Henry, William E., 526
Henry, Zunia, 792
Henshaw, E. M., 383
Hensley, R. M., ed., *assoc.*: 174
Hentig, Hans von, 160
Hentig, Hans von, ed., *primary*: 194, 536
Hentze, Rudolf, 767
Herbart, Johann Friedrich, 85
Herbette, Louis, ed., *assoc.*: 163, 210
Herderschee, D., ed., *primary*: 475
Hering, Ewald, ed., *assoc.*: 104
Hermaden, Viktor Winkler. *See* Winkler-
Hermaden, Viktor
Herman, Samuel S., ed., *primary*: 556
Hermann, Erich, 767
Hermann, Imre, 732
Hermann, Imre, ed., *assoc.*: 992
Hermsmeier, Friedrich, 356
Hernandez, V., ed., *assoc.*: 276
Herold, J.L.M., ed., *primary*: 981
Heron, William T., 438
Herrick, Charles Judson, 543
Herrick, Charles Judson, ed., *primary*: 108,
191, 288; *assoc.*: 191, 288
Herrick, Clarence Luther, ed., *primary*: 108,
191
Herrick, Colin J., 215
Herrick, Virgil E., 368
Herriott, Francis, 910
Herriott, Marion Eugene, 373, 441
Herrlin, Axel, ed., *primary*: 434
Herrmann, Georg, 357
Herrmann, Gertrud, 356
Herrmann, Johannes, 423, 538
Herskovits, Melville J., ed., *assoc.*: 762
Hertz, Joseph H., 120
Hertz, Marguerite R., ed., *primary*: 995,
1093
Hertzman, Max, 215
Hertzman, Max, ed., *assoc.*: 802
Hervat, ———, 657

Name Index

Hutton, Laura, 657
Huxtable, Zelma Langdon, 275
Hylan, John Perham, 126
Hylla, Erich, ed., *primary:* 1006
Hyman, Herbert Hiram, 215
Hymes, James L., Jr., ed., *primary:* 666
Hyslop, James H., 120
Hyslop, Theophilus Bulkeley, 274

Ibrahim, Jusuff, ed., *assoc.:* 315
Ibukiyama, T., ed., *primary:* 734
Ichheiser, Gustav, 495, 880
Ide, Gladys, ed., *primary:* 722, 749
Iglesias, Gregorio B. Palacin. *See* Palacin Iglesias, Gregorio B.
Iinuma, Rynon, ed., *assoc.:* 549
Imada, M., ed., *assoc.:* 549
Infield, Henrik F., 880
Ingebritsen, Otis Clarence, 526
Ingegnieros, José, 189
Ingegnieros, José, ed., *primary:* 189, 255
Ingelrans, [Pierre?], ed., *assoc.:* 225
Ingersoll, Hazel L., 526
Inhelder, Bärbel, 723, 936
Ioteyko, I., ed., *primary:* 250
Iozefovich, A. B., ed., *assoc.:* 665
Ipsen, Gunther, 423, 538
Ipsen, Gunther, ed., *primary:* 629
Irving, J. A., ed., *primary:* 853
Irving, Washington, 543
Irwin, Francis W., 1074
Irwin, Francis W., ed., *primary:* 350
Irwin, Mary, ed., *primary:* 813, 828, 1037
Irwin, Orvis C., 399, 526, 676
Isaacs, Susan S. (Brierley) 800
Isaacs, Susan S. (Brierley), ed., *primary:* 456, 800; *assoc.:* 394, 653
Ishii, Toshitada, ed., *assoc.:* 549
Isotoff, Andrei, 703
Isreali, Nathan, 215
Isserlin, M., ed., *primary:* 340
Ito, Sangoro, 267
Iudin, T. I., ed., *assoc.:* 665
Iushchenko, A. I., ed., *assoc.:* 665
Ivanovskii, V. N., ed., *assoc.:* 98
Ivantsov, N. A., ed., *assoc.:* 98
Ivimey, Muriel, ed., *primary:* 873; *assoc.:* 873
Iwai, Katsujiro, 538

Jack, Lois M., 399
Jackson, Edith B., ed., *assoc.:* 927
Jackson, Theodore A., 526
Jacob, Joseph Simeon, 526
Jacob, M., ed., *primary:* 496

Jacob, Walter, ed., *primary:* 320, 1074
Jacobi, Jolande, 924
Jacobi, Walter, 160, 357
Jacobsen, Carlyle F., 438, 965
Jacobsohn-Lask, Louis, 356, 357
Jacobson, Annemarie, 1028
Jacoby, Hans J., 835
Jaeck, Lena, ed., *assoc.:* 973
Jaederholm, Gustav A., ed., *primary:* 520; *assoc.:* 452, 617
Jaehner, Doris, 356
Jaensch, Erich Rudolf, 233, 377, 390, 611, 650, 767, 831
Jaensch, Erich Rudolf, ed., *primary:* 223, 236, 390, 611, 621, 650, 720, 831; *assoc.:* 223
Jahn, Ulrich, ed., *primary:* 54
Jahoda, Marie. *See* Lazarsfeld-Jahoda, Marie
James, A. Lloyd, 543
James, William, 449
James, William, ed., *assoc.:* 122
James, William Thomas, 438
Jamin, J. Crepieux. *See* Crepieux-Jamin, J.
Janer, Albert Christ. *See* Christ-Janer, Albert
Janet, Pierre, 151
Janet, Pierre, ed., *primary:* 96, 163, 190; *assoc.:* 32, 122, 143, 585, 671, 672, 724
Janeway, E. G., ed., *primary:* 69
Janis, Irving L., 1071
Janota, Otakar, 357
Japha, Käthe, 425
Jaques, Elliott, ed., *assoc.:* 971
Jaspers, Ludger, 433
Jastrow, Joseph, ed., *assoc.:* 122
Jauguaribe, ———, ed., *assoc.:* 276
Jay, L., ed., *primary:* 134
Jefferson, G., ed., *primary:* 817, 907
Jeffreys, Harold, 543
Jelgersma, Gerbrandus, 328
Jelliffe, Smith Ely, 229
Jelliffe, Smith Ely, ed., *primary:* 73, 229, 313, 681, 867
Jenkins, Jack, ed., *assoc.:* 1025
Jenkins, John Gamewell, ed., *assoc.:* 90
Jenkins, Marion, 526
Jenkins, Richard L., ed., *primary:* 632; *assoc.:* 632
Jenkins, Thomas N., 215
Jenkins, William Leroy, 839
Jenness, Arthur, ed., *assoc.:* 499
Jennings, Helen Hall, 880
Jennings, Helen Hall, ed., *primary:* 810; *assoc.:* 788, 810
Jennings, Herbert S., ed., *primary:* 191; *assoc.:* 191, 287
Jennings, O., ed., *assoc.:* 276
Jensen, Jan, ed., *assoc.:* 288

Name Index

Koch, Helen Lois, 275, 526
Koch, Helen Lois, ed., *primary:* 805
Koch, Julius Ludwig August, 160
Koeber, Raphael Gustav von, 107
Koekebakker, J., ed., *primary:* 981
Koester, Theodore, 215
Koffka, Kurt, 306, 646
Koffka, Kurt, ed., *primary:* 306, 428, 646;
    assoc.: 325
Koga, Yukiyoshi, ed., *assoc.:* 549
Kogan, Tatiana Lvovna, ed., *assoc.:* 614
Köhler, Elsa, 489, 545
Kohler, Josef, 217
Köhler, Otto, ed., *primary:* 812, 962, 1082
Köhler, Wolfgang, ed., *primary:* 428
Kohlhagen, Franz, 602
Kohlrausch, A., ed., *assoc.:* 237, 871
Kohnstamm, Philipp, 706
Kohnstamm, Philipp, ed., *primary:* 234, 706
Kohs, Samuel C., 341
Kohs, Samuel C., ed., *primary:* 341
Kolb, Eduard, 230
Kolbanovskii, V. N., ed., *primary:* 614, 756
Kollarits, Jeno, 396
Kölle, Hermann, 578
Kolnai, Aurel, 384
Komora, Paul O., ed., *primary:* 463
König, Arthur, ed., *primary:* 104, 167
Koort, Juan G. Zela. *See* Zela Koort, Juan G.
Koos, Leonard V., 368
Korn, Richard R., ed., *primary:* 1051
Kornhauser, Arthur William, 783, 1050
Kornhauser, Arthur William, ed., *assoc.:* 787,
    796, 891, 921
Kornilov, A. A., ed., *primary:* 363
Kornilov, Konstantin Nikolaevich, ed.,
    primary: 599, 614; *assoc.:* 614, 637
Korsakov, S. S., ed., *assoc.:* 98
Korte, Adolf, 306
Koshuk, Ruth Pearson, 762
Koskoff, Yale David, 965
Koslowsky, F., ed., *primary:* 187
Kostir, Wencel J., 526
Kotik, Naum, 160
Kots, Nadezhda Nikolaevna, 465
Kots, Nadezhda Nikolaevna, ed., *primary:*
    331, 465
Kötscher, Louis Max, 160
Koty, John, 495
Kounin, Jacob, ed., *assoc.:* 921
Koussy, Abdel Aziz Hamid El, 285
Kovacs, Richard, ed., *assoc.:* 1041
Kovalevskii, P. I., ed., *primary:* 81
Kowalewski, Arnold, 160
Kraemer, William P., 835
Kraeplin, Emil, 229
Kraeplin, Emil, ed., *primary:* 127

Krafft, Elsie, 371, 374
Krais, Dora, 377
Krall, Karl, ed., *primary:* 309, 319
Kramer, Bernard M., 933
Kramer, Franz, ed., *assoc.:* 315
Krämer, H., ed., *primary:* 309
Kramer, Josefine, 773
Kranenburg, R., ed., *primary:* 234
Krapf, E. Eduardo, ed., *assoc.:* 900
Krause, Lawrence J., 524
Krauss, Reinhard, 356
Krausz, Erwin O., ed., *primary:* 751; *assoc.:*
    751
Krautter, Otto, 356
Krech, David, 267
Krech, David, ed., *assoc.:* 787, 920, 921, 973,
    1099
Krechevsky, Isadore. *See* Krech, David
Kreezer, George L., ed., *assoc.:* 90
Kremer, Alphonse H., 524
Kretschmer, Ernst, 229
Kretschmer, Ernst, ed., *primary:* 160, 521,
    649; *assoc.:* 671, 724, 920
Kreusch, Max von, ed., *primary:* 491
Kreuser, Heinrich, 160
Krevelen, D. A. van, 901
Kriedjung, J. K., 279
Kries, Johannes von, ed., *assoc.:* 104, 223,
    237
Kris, W. Ernst, ed., *primary:* 696, 836, 927;
    assoc.: 499, 992, 1099
Krisch, Hans, 357
Krische, Paul, 495
Krogman, Wilton Marion, 762
Krogman, Wilton Marion, ed., *assoc.:* 556
Kroh, Oswald, 236
Kroh, Oswald, ed., *primary:* 223, 236, 356,
    519, 571, 720, 869; *assoc.:* 223
Kronacher, Carl, ed., *primary:* 812
Kronfeld, Arthur, 199, 377, 444
Kronfeld, Arthur, ed., *primary:* 444, 595,
    649, 663, 739
Krout, Johanna, 1028
Krout, Maurice H., 275
Krueger, Felix Emil, 324, 423, 538, 901
Krueger, Felix Emil, ed., *primary:* 324, 352,
    423, 538; *assoc.:* 223, 538, 585, 603
Krueger, Louise, 215
Krueger, William C. F., 215
Krug, C. A., ed., *primary:* 853
Krugman, Morris, ed., *assoc.:* 796
Krumbholz, C. E., ed., *assoc.:* 1098
Kruse, Paul J., 526
Kryter, K. D., 916
Kubie, Lawrence S., 985
Kubie, Lawrence S., ed., *primary:* 680, 793;
    assoc.: 845, 846, 927

Langton, H. H., ed., *primary:* 153
Lanier, Lyle H., 275, 501
Lanier, Lyle H., ed., *primary:* 196
Lannois, [Maurice?], ed., *assoc.:* 225
Lantz, Beatrice, 275
Lanzenauer, Reiner Haehling von. *See* Haehling von Lanzenauer, Reiner
Laquer, Benno H., 160
Largueze, ———, ed., *primary:* 134
Larguier des Bancels, Jean, ed., *primary:* 119, 169
Larsell, Olof, ed., *assoc.:* 288
Larsen, Karl, ed., *primary:* 404
Laseau, LaVerne N., 1100
Lashley, Karl S., 438, 526
Lashley, Karl S., ed., *assoc.:* 438, 505, 526, 753
Lask, Louis Jacobsohn. *See* Jacobsohn-Lask, Louis
Lasurski, Aleksandr Fedorovich, 230
Latham, Darrell E., 762
Lathers, Eleanor, 215
Latif, I., ed., *primary:* 1048; *assoc.:* 527
Lau, Ernst, 356
Lauer, Alvhh R., 447
Laurent-Lucas-Championniere, O., ed., *assoc.:* 607
Laurier, Blaise, ed., *assoc.:* 954
Lausanne, A. de (pseudonym). *See* Montferrier, Alexandre André Victor Sarrazin de
Lauzier, Jean, ed., *assoc.:* 32
Lavastine, Maxime Paul Marie Laignel. *See* Laignel-Lavastine, Maxime Paul Marie
Lavrand, Hubert, 240
Lawley, D. N., ed., *assoc.:* 963
Lawlor, Gerald W., 215
Lawrence, Evelyn M., 285
Lawrence, S., ed., *assoc.:* 836
Laws, Frederick, ed., *primary:* 1008
Lay, Wilfrid, 120, 126
Lay, Wilhelm August, ed., *primary:* 206
Layard, John, 835
Laycock, Samuel R., 270
Laycock, Samuel R., ed., *primary:* 666, 853
Layman, John D., 438, 693
Layton, F. G., 697
Layton, Warren K., ed., *assoc.:* 702
Lazarev, V. G., ed., *assoc.:* 665
Lazarsfeld, Paul F., 513, 965, 1071
Lazarsfeld-Jahoda, Marie, 545
Lazarus, Moritz, ed., *primary:* 54
Lazzeroni, V., ed., *primary:* 709
Le Guillant, L., 901
Leahy, Alice M., 526, 564
Learned, Janet, 399
Leatherman, Zoe Emily, 447

Lebrun, M., ed., *assoc.:* 1013
Leburn, D., ed., *primary:* 409
Leclainche, E., ed., *assoc.:* 163
Lederer, Ruth Klein, 399
Lee, Alfred McClung, ed., *assoc.:* 921, 973
Lee, Ang Lanfen, 275
Lee, Douglas, ed., *assoc.:* 777
Lee, Edwin A., ed., *assoc.:* 702
Lee, Harry B., ed., *assoc.:* 397
Lee, Imogen, 383
Lee, Kwanyong, 413
Lee, Porter, R., ed., *primary:* 632
Leeds, Carroll H., 1028
Leeds, Donald S., ed., *primary:* 1062
Leemann, Lydia, 413
Leeper, Robert, 526, 898
Leeper, Robert, ed., *assoc.:* 921
Leeuw, G. van der, 706
Leeuw, P. J. van der, ed., *assoc.:* 397
Lefever, D. Welty, 1033
Lefevre, Arthur, 85
Lefevre, Ch., ed., *primary:* 103, 106
Legewie, H., 495
Legrain, Maurice Paul, 268
Legrain, Maurice Paul, ed., *assoc.:* 143, 276
Legros, Lucien Alphonse, 383
Lehman, Harvey C., 368
Lehmann, Alfred Georg Ludwig, 199
Lehmann, Rudolph, 146
Lehner, George F. J., ed., *assoc.:* 920
Lehoczky, Tibor, ed., *primary:* 588
Lehrer, L., ed., *primary:* 719
Lehrer, Ruth, ed., *primary:* 802
Lehrman, Philip R., ed., *assoc.:* 397
Leib, Karl A., 676
Leibniz, Gottfried Wilhelm, *freiherr* von, 93
Leibold, Rudolf, 324, 423
Leidesdorf, Max, ed., *primary:* 61, 64
Leight, Hortense, ed., *primary:* 1051
Leighton, Alexander E., ed., *assoc.:* 843
Leinweber, Berthold, 621
Leiper, Margaret A., 383
Leiter, Russell Graydon, ed., *primary:* 1063, 1064
Leitner, Hans, 324, 423
Lemay, Edmour, ed., *primary:* 954
Lemesle, ———, ed., *assoc.:* 276
Lemmon, Vernon W., 215
Lenard, Ferenc, ed., *primary:* 588
Lenk, Erhard, 423, 538
Lennelongue, O. M., ed., *assoc.:* 210
Lennon, Roger T., ed., *primary:* 626, 627
Lenz, Joseph, 433
Lenzen, Victor Fritz, 693
Leo, M., *Frère (S.É.C.)*. *See* Macarius, Leo *Frère (S.E.C.)*
Léon, Paul, ed., *assoc.:* 163

Name Index

Leonard, Eugenie Andruss, 605
Leonard, J. Paul, ed., *assoc.:* 678
Lépine, J., ed., *assoc.:* 32, 225, 415, 493, 558
Lepley, William M., 275, 999
Lerchenthal, Erich Menninger. *See* Menninger-Lerchenthal, Erich
Lerebours, Ch., ed., *primary:* 95
Lerner, Eugene, 723, 762
Lerner, Eugene, ed., *assoc.:* 787
Leroy, Raoul Pierre Achille, ed., *primary:* 251, 461, 699
Lersch, Philipp, ed., *primary:* 355, 356, 766, 767
Lessing, Theodor, 160, 396
Leuba, James H., 160
Leuba, James H., ed., *assoc.:* 186
Leuba, John, ed., *assoc.:* 397
Leubuscher, Georg, 146
Leuzinger-Schuler, Amélie, 901
Levi-Bianchini, Marco, ed., *primary:* 391, 412
Lévi-Valensi, J., ed., *assoc.:* 32, 415, 493, 558
Levin, D., ed., *primary:* 496
Levin, Max, 438
Levine, Estelle M., 275
Levine, Israel, 384
Levine, Kate Natalie, 215
Levkovsky, A. M., ed., *primary:* 363
Levy, D., ed., *primary:* 496
Levy, David M., 792
Levy, David M., *assoc.:* 397, 836, 845, 846
Levy, Jack Morris, 267
Levy, John, 745
Lévy-Bruhl, Lucien, ed., *assoc.:* 603, 637, 671, 724
Levy-Suhl, Max, 486
Lewandowsky, Max, ed., *primary:* 281, 282
Lewin, Bertram D., ed., *primary:* 680; *assoc.:* 397, 398, 836, 927, 932
Lewin, D., *See* Levin, D.
Lewin, F., ed., *primary:* 496
Lewin, Kurt, 399, 727, 880, 922
Lewin, Kurt, ed., *assoc.:* 617, 787, 878, 971
Lewis, Aubrey, ed., *primary:* 817, 907
Lewis, Claudia, 526
Lewis, Ervin E., 458
Lewis, Nolan D. C., 229
Lewis, Nolan D. C., ed., *primary:* 73, 867, 1068; *assoc.:* 995
Lewis, Virginia W., 215
Lewy, Ernst, ed., *assoc.:* 397
Ley, Auguste, ed., *primary:* 740, 760
Ley, Rodolphe, ed., *primary:* 461, 699
Leysens, Bl., ed., *primary:* 760
Leyser, Edgar, 357
Lezin', Boris Andreevich, ed., *primary:* 264
Lhermitte, Jean, ed., *primary:* 558, 581, 608, 1012, 1089, 1092; *assoc.:* 32, 225, 415, 493, 558

Lhota, Brian, 524
Liard, L., ed., *assoc.:* 163, 210
Licht, Hans, 369
Licht, Sidney, ed., *assoc.:* 1041
Lichten, William, 916
Lichtenberger, Marguérite, ed., *primary:* 119
Lichtensteiger, Albert, 773
Lichtenstein, Arthur, ed., *assoc.:* 556
Licklider, J.C.R., 916
Liddell, Howard S., 438
Liddell, Howard S., ed., *assoc.:* 845, 846
Liddy, R. B., ed., *primary:* 853
Liebmann, Albert, 146
Liedloff, Werner, 498
Liefmann, Else, 356, 901
Liepmann, Hugo, ed., *primary:* 281
Liepmann, Wilhelm, ed., *primary:* 470
Lifschitz, Samuel, 486
Liggett, John Riley, 526
Ligon, Ernest Mayfield, 438
Likert, Rensis, 215, 965
Likert, Rensis, ed., *assoc.:* 1025
Likhnitski, V. N., ed., *assoc.:* 273
Lilienthal, Karl von, ed., *primary:* 194, 294, 536
Liljencrants, Johan, 275
Lincoln, Edward A., 439
Lincoln, Mildred E., ed., *primary:* 702
Lind, Melva, 526
Lindemann, Erich, 306
Lindemann, Erich, ed., *assoc.:* 397
Lindner, Gustav Adolf, 85
Lindner, Robert M., ed., *assoc.:* 906, 941
Lindstaedt, Willi, 481
Lindworsky, Johannes, 375
Lindworsky, Johannes, ed., *assoc.:* 603
Line, William, 285
Line, William, ed., *primary:* 666; *assoc.:* 724, 920
Linfert, Hariette-Elise, 524
Ling, Bing-Chung, 438
Link, Henry C., ed., *primary:* 359; *assoc.:* 796
Linke, Heinz, 187
Linton, Ralph, ed., *assoc.:* 787, 837
Lipmann, Otto, 291, 356, 377, 712
Lipmann, Otto, ed., *primary:* 254, 291, 355, 356, 377, 712; *assoc.:* 671
Lippert, Elisabeth O., 423, 538
Lippitt, Ronald, 910, 922, 933, 965
Lippitt, Ronald, ed., *primary:* 787, 921, 1019; *assoc.:* 787, 921, 971
Lippitt, Rosemary, 910
Lipps, Gottlob Friedrich, ed., *primary:* 411, 413
Lipps, Theodor, 107, 160, 211, 449
Lipps, Theodor, ed., *primary:* 211; *assoc.:* 104, 223, 237

Name Index

Name Index

Name Index

Name Index

Name Index

Racker, Enrique, ed., *assoc.*: 900
Rada, Margarete, 664
Radbruch, G., ed., *primary*: 294
Radcliffe-Browne, Alfred Reginald, ed., *assoc.*: 751
Radecki, Waclaw, ed., *primary*: 970, 1088
Radestock, Paul, 85
Radke, Marian J., 526, 564, 922, 933
Radke, Marian J., ed., *assoc.*: 971
Rado, Sandor, ed., *primary*: 297, 398, 582, 680, 867; *assoc.*: 793
Radossawljewitsch, Paul R., 230
Rădulescu-Motru, Constantin, ed., *primary*: 741, 798, 838; *assoc.*: 617
Radvanyi, Laszlo, 923
Radvanyi, Laszlo, ed., *primary*: 923, 973
Raecke, Julius, 160
Raeder, O. J., ed., *primary*: 378
Raffegeau, ———, ed., *assoc.*: 276
Rahn, Carl, 275
Rakić, Vićentiji, 199
Ramirez, Emiliano Pisculich. *See* Pisculich Ramirez, Emiliano
Ramirez, Santiago, ed., *primary*: 990; *assoc.*: 952
Ramon y Cajal, D. Santiago, ed., *assoc.*: 380
Ramsay, H. H., ed., *assoc.*: 851
Ramsay, J., 533
Ramsey, Lettice, 383
Ramul, Konstantin, ed., *assoc.*: 617
Rand, Gertrude, 275, 347
Randall, John H., Jr., ed., *primary*: 422
Rank, Otto, 160, 229, 233, 279, 384, 476
Rank, Otto, ed., *primary*: 297, 311, 398; *assoc.*: 397
Ranschburg, Paul, ed., *assoc.*: 617, 671, 724
Ransy, C., 295
Rantz, J., 543
Rapaies, Raymond, 495
Rapaport, David, 778
Rapaport, David, ed., *assoc.*: 1099
Rascovsky, Arnaldo, ed., *primary*: 900; *assoc.*: 900
Rascovsky, Luis, ed., *assoc.*: 397, 900
Rascovsky, Matilde Wencelblat de. *See* Wencelblat de Rascovsky, Matilde
Rashevsky, Nicholas, ed., *assoc.*: 785
Rath, Carl, 332
Rau, Hans, 187
Raubenheimer, Albert Sydney, 275
Rauth, John William, 524
Rauth, John William, ed., *assoc.*: 524
Rauzier, G., ed., *assoc.*: 225
Ravenhill, A., ed., *assoc.*: 174
Raviart, G., ed., *assoc.*: 32, 225, 415, 493, 558
Rawson, R. E., 533

Ray, Matthew Burrow, 544, 657
Ray, Wilbert S., ed., *primary*: 1011
Raymond, Fulgence, 151
Raymond, Fulgence, ed., *primary*: 225; *assoc.*: 143, 170, 276
Rayner, Doris, 657
Rayner, Henry, ed., *primary*: 50
Raynier, Julien, ed., *assoc.*: 32
Razran, Gregory H. S., 215
Read, Carveth, 300
Read, Carveth, ed., *assoc.*: 188, 394
Read, Charles Stanford, ed., *assoc.*: 401
Read, Katherine H., 526
Reagan, George W., 441
Reamer, Jeanette Chase, 275
Reaney, Mabel Jane, 285
Reavis, William Clause, 368, 676
Reavis, William Clause, ed., *primary*: 368
Redfield, Janet, 399
Redl, Fritz, ed., *assoc.*: 921
Reed, Homer B., 275
Reed, Mary Frances, 891
Reeder, Edwin Hewett, 441
Reeder, Rudolph Rex, 120
Rees, John Rawlings, ed., *primary*: 1054
Reese, Thomas Whelan, 275
Reeves, Cora D., 284
Reeves, Joan Wynn, ed., *primary*: 674, 799, 819; *assoc.*: 394
Regensburg, Jeanette, 215
Régis, E., ed., *assoc.*: 143, 170, 225
Regnault, ———, ed., *assoc.*: 276
Régnier, L. R., ed., *primary*: 106
Rehm, Otto, 357
Rehwoldt, Friedrich, 221
Reich, Eduard, 52
Reich, Wilhelm, 476
Reichard, Suzanne, 215
Reichmann, Frieda Fromm. *See* Fromm-Reichmann, Frieda
Reiff, Paul, 230
Reik, Theodor, 384, 417, 931
Reil, Johann Christian, ed., *primary*: 10
Reiman, M. Gertrude, 524
Reinhart, Miriam, *Sister*, 524
Reininger, Karl, 484
Reiser, Oliver Leslie, 543
Reisner, Edward Hartman, 205
Reiter, Hans, ed., *primary*: 801
Reitler, Rudolph, 279
Reitts, G. V., ed., *primary*: 539
Reitzel, Jeanne M., ed., *primary*: 995, 1093
Reiwald, Paul, 940
Reiwald, Paul, ed., *primary*: 940
Remer, Laura L., 399
Remmelts, R., ed., *primary*: 981
Remmers, Hermann H., ed., *assoc.*: 420, 678

787

Name Index

Rube, P., ed., *assoc.*: 607
Rubenstein, Boris B., 846
Rubenstein, Lawrence, 215
Rubin, Edgar J., ed., *primary*: 746; *assoc.*:
  223, 617
Rubin-Rabson, Grace, 215
Ruch, Floyd Leon, ed., *assoc.*: 891
Ruch, Giles Murrel, 275, 386, 698
Ruckmick, Christian A., 275
Ruckmick, Christian A., ed., *primary*: 121,
  140; *assoc.*: 90
Rudert, Johannes, 423, 538
Rudert, Johannes, ed., *assoc.*: 538
Rudin, Josef, 883
Rudmose, H. W., 916
Ruediger, William Carl, 205, 215
Ruelius, Alwin, 498
Ruesch, Jurgen, 846, 1028
Ruger, Henry Alford, 205, 215
Rugg, Bertha Miller, 368
Rugg, Harold Ordway, 270, 368
Rugg, Harold Ordway, ed., *primary*: 420;
  assoc.: 420
Rühle-Gerstel, Alice, ed., *primary*: 460
Ruin, Hans W., ed., *assoc.*: 617
Ruland, Michael, 230
Rulon, Phillip Justin, ed., *assoc.*: 785
Rümke, Henricus Cornelius, 706
Rümke, Henricus Cornelius, ed., *primary*:
  945
Ruml, Beardsley, 275
Ruml, Beardsley, ed., *assoc.*: 420
Rundquist, Edward A., 564
Rundquist, Edward A., ed., *assoc.*: 1025
Runes, Augusta, ed., *assoc.*: 878
Runes, Dagobert D., ed., *primary*: 679
Runge, Werner, 357
Runze, Georg, ed., *primary*: 238
Rupp, Hans, ed., *primary*: 512, 827
Ruppert, Hans, 236
Rush, Grace Preyer, 215
Rüssel, Arnulf, 377, 396, 423, 511, 538
Rüssel, Arnulf, ed., *assoc.*: 538
Russell, Bertrand, ed., *assoc.*: 637
Russell, Dorothy, ed., *assoc.*: 907
Russell, Elias Harlow, 85
Russell, G. E., 698
Russell, John M., ed., *primary*: 1071
Russell, W. Ritchie, ed., *primary*: 907; *assoc.*:
  907
Rust, Hans, 160
Rust, Metta Maund, 605
Rusu, Liviu, 604
Rusu, Liviu, ed., *assoc.*: 824
Rutgers, V. H., 662
Rutishauser, Eugen, 901
Rux, Curt, 277

Ryan, W. Carson, ed., *primary*: 666
Rybakov, Th. E., ed., *primary*: 363
Rybicka, Ludwika Dobrzyńska. *See*
  Dobrzyńska-Rybicka, Ludwika
Rybnikov, N. A., ed., *assoc.*: 614
Ryle, Gilbert, ed., *primary*: 74
Rymarkiewicz, Maria, 426

Sachs, Bernard, 229
Sachs, Bernard, ed., *primary*: 73; *assoc.*: 73
Sachs, Hanns, 160, 229, 279
Sachs, Hanns, ed., *primary*: 297, 582, 829
Sachs, Heinrich, 159, 160
Sachs, Hildegard. *See* Grünbaum-Sachs,
  Hildegard
Sackett, Leroy Walter, 284
Sacristan, José M., ed., *primary*: 380, 924;
  assoc.: 380
Sadée, Leopold, 160
Sadger, Isidor, 160, 229, 233, 279
Sadger, J. *See* Sadger, Isidor
Sadowsky, Florence, ed., *primary*: 802;
  assoc.: 802
Sagara, M., ed., *primary*: 549
Sainton, P., ed., *assoc.*: 225, 415, 493, 558
Sait, Una Bernard, 205
Sakel, Manfred, 229
Sakuma, Kanae, ed., *assoc.*: 549, 585
Sallwürk, Ernst von, 146, 230
Salmon, Thomas W., ed., *assoc.*: 361
Salome, Lou Andreas. *See* Andreas-Salome,
  Lou
Salter, Helen de Gaudrion (Verrall), ed.,
  primary: 79, 84
Salter, Mary Dinsmore. *See* Ainsworth, Mary
  Dinsmore (Salter)
Salter, W. H., ed., *primary*: 84
Saltzman, Eleanor, 752
Salzedo, S. L., 543
Salzy, Pierre, ed., *assoc.*: 948
Sampson, D. L., ed., *primary*: 1086
San Martín, Raquel de, 895
Sanchez, Modesto, ed., *assoc.*: 952
Sanchiz Banus, J., ed., *primary*: 380; *assoc.*:
  380
Sanctis, Sante de, ed., *primary*: 96, 145, 263,
  301, 412, 451; *assoc.*: 170, 391, 505, 526,
  617, 709
Sand, Margaret Cole, 215
Sander, Friedrich, 377, 423, 538
Sander, Friedrich, ed., *primary*: 181, 744,
  833; *assoc.*: 538, 617
Sander, Julie, 425
Sanders, Jack H., 215
Sandiford, Peter, 368
Sandig, Hans, 538

Name Index

Name Index

Name Index

Name Index

Name Index

Name Index